Ellicott's COMMENTARY ON THE WHOLE BIBLE

A VERSE BY VERSE EXPLANATION

EDITED BY
CHARLES JOHN ELLICOTT

VOLUME V

Jeremiah — Malachi

WIPF & STOCK · Eugene, Oregon

Wipf and Stock Publishers
199 W 8th Ave, Suite 3
Eugene, OR 97401

Ellicott's Commentary on the Whole Bible Volume V
Jeremiah - Malachi
By Ellicott, Charles J.
ISBN 13: 978-1-4982-0140-7
Publication date 3/31/2015
Previously published by Cassell, 1897

This is a reprint of the 1959 Zondervan edition. Originally
published in 1897 by Cassell as A Bible Commentary for English Readers.

Jeremiah

BY

THE VERY REV. E H. PLUMPTRE, D.D.

Late Dean of Wells.

Lamentations

BY

THE VERY REV. E. H. PLUMPTRE, D.D.

Ezekiel

BY

THE REV. F. GARDINER, D.D.

Professor of Divinity, Middletown, Connecticut, U.S.A.

Daniel

BY

THE REV. H. DEANE, B.D.

Fellow of St. John's College, Oxford

Hosea

BY

THE REV. H. R. REYNOLDS, D.D.

AND

THE REV. PROFESSOR WHITEHOUSE

Joel

BY

THE REV. S. L. WARREN, M.A.

Late Fellow of Wadham College, Oxford.

Amos

BY

THE REV. H. R. REYNOLDS, D.D.

AND

THE REV. PROFESSOR WHITEHOUSE

Obadiah

BY

THE REV. ARCHDEACON AGLEN, M.A.

Jonah

BY

THE REV. ARCHDEACON AGLEN, M.A.

Micah

BY

THE REV. S. L. WARREN.

Nahum

BY

THE REV. A. C. JENNINGS, M.A.

Habakkuk

BY

THE REV. A. C. JENNINGS, M.A.

Zephaniah

BY

THE REV. A. C. JENNINGS, M.A.

Haggai

BY

THE REV. A. C. JENNINGS, M A.

Zechariah

BY

THE REV. W. H. LOWE, M.A.

Malachi

BY

THE REV. W. H. LOWE, M.A.

CONTENTS

CONTENTS

THE BOOK OF THE PROPHET
JEREMIAH

INTRODUCTION

TO

THE BOOK OF THE PROPHET JEREMIAH

I. **Life.**—The materials for a biography of Jeremiah are supplied in his collected writings with unusual fulness. We know more of his personal history than we do of that of Isaiah or Ezekiel, much more than of that of the minor prophets, who have left for the most part only a few chapters as the record of their work. With the help of inferences from acknowledged facts, and of a few fairly authenticated traditions, we are able to enter into the circumstances in the midst of which he worked, and into the joys and sorrows, the hopes and fears, of which they were the occasion. Of him it may be said, more than of any other of the goodly fellowship of the prophets, that his whole life lies before us as in an open scroll.

It will be convenient to arrange the main facts of the history thus laid open to us under the reigns of the several kings with whom he was a contemporary.

1. Under Josiah (B.C. 638—608).—In the thirteenth year of this king the prophet speaks of himself as still "a child." That word is, however, somewhat vague in its significance, extending from infancy, as in Exod. ii. 6; 1 Sam. iv. 21, to adult manhood, as in 1 Sam. xxx. 17; 1 Kings iii. 7. All that it can be held to imply is that the prophet felt himself to be relatively young for the work to which he had been called, that he had not attained the average age of a prophet; and this, it may be inferred, was not far distant from that at which the Levites entered on their work, which varied, at different periods, from twenty to thirty (Num. iv. 3, viii. 24; 1 Chron. xxiii. 3, 24). We may reasonably infer, then, from the way in which the prophet speaks of himself, that he was, at the time when he felt himself called to his high and perilous work, somewhere between twenty and twenty-five, *i.e.*, that the first seven, or, it may be, the first twelve years of his life, were passed in the reigns of Manasseh and his son Amon.

He is described, further, as "being the son of Hilkiah, of the priests that were in Anathoth" (Jer. i. 1). That name, it will be remembered, was borne by the high priest who played so prominent a part in Josiah's reformation. (2 Kings xxii. 8.) There are, however, no sufficient grounds for identifying that Hilkiah with the father of the prophet. The manner in which the latter is named, without any mention of special dignity, is against it. The priests of Anathoth were of the line of Ithamar (1 Kings ii. 26; 1 Chron. xxiv. 3), while the high priests, from Zadok downwards, were of the line of Eleazar. The identity of name may, however, be regarded as probably indicating some close connection of affinity or friendship. Other coincidences point in the same direction. The uncle of Jeremiah, Shallum (Jer. xxxii. 7), bore the same name as the husband of Huldah the prophetess (2 Kings xxii. 14). Ahikam, the son of Shaphan, the great supporter of Hilkiah the high priest and Huldah in their work (2 Chron. xxxiv. 20), was also throughout the protector of the prophet (Jer. xxvi. 24). The strange Rabbinic tradition that eight of the persons most conspicuous in the history of this period (Jeremiah, Baruch, Seraiah, Maaseiah, Hilkiah, Hananeel, Huldah, Shallum) were all descended from the harlot Rahab (Carpzov, *Introd. in lib. V.T. Jerem.*) may possibly have been a distortion of the fact that the persons so named were united together, as by community of feeling, so also by affinity or friendship. With regard to two others of the number, we know that both Baruch and Seraiah, who appear as disciples of the prophet (chap. xxxvi. 4, li. 59), were sons of Neriah, the son of Maaseiah, and that Maaseiah (2 Chron. xxxiv. 8) was governor of Jerusalem, acting with Hilkiah, Huldah, and Shaphan in the reforms of Josiah.

With these facts we can picture to ourselves some of the influences which entered into Jeremiah's education, and prepared the way for his prophetic mission. The name given to him by his father, with its significance as "Jehovah exalts," or "is exalted," or "Jehovah throws down" (the latter meaning resting on the more accurate etymology), may fairly be looked on as embodying what was contemplated and prayed for as the ideal of his life. It may be noted that the name was common at that time, *e.g.*, in the case of the father of the wife of Josiah (2 Kings xxiii. 31), and of one of the Rechabites (chap. xxxv. 3). That name may be thought of, accordingly, as not without its influence on the prophet's early years. As he grew to boyhood he would hear of the cruelties and the apostasy of Manasseh and of Amon. For him, as for Isaiah, there would be a training in the law and literature of Israel, in whatever form it then existed, in Job, and Proverbs, and such of the Psalms and the writings of the earlier prophets as were then extant. The so-called Alphabetic Psalms (ix., xxv., xxxiv., xxxvii., cxi., cxii., cxix., cxlv.) may have helped to form the taste and style which afterwards displayed themselves in the alphabetic structure of the *Lamentations*. The writings of the greatest of his predecessors, Isaiah, at least, as far as chaps. i.—xxxix. are concerned, could scarcely have been otherwise than familiar to him. His early manhood must have coincided with the earlier reforms of Josiah, whose life would seem to have run parallel with his own, each being apparently about the same age when the prophet received his call, Josiah having ascended the throne at the age of eight (2 Kings xxii. 1). The reverence with which he looks on the Rechabites, the fact that one of those Rechabites bears the same name (chap. xxxv. 3), the probability that one trained in the household of a devout priest would not be unmindful of the teaching of Isaiah (xxviii. 7) and Amos (ii. 11, 12), as to the perils of wine and strong drink, make it probable that he too was one of the Nazarites to whom the latter prophet looked as the strength of Israel, and whom Jeremiah himself names with reverence and admiration (Lam. iv. 7). To such an outward consecration to an ascetic life, the words which speak of him as having been "sanctified from his mother's womb" (chap. i. 5) naturally seem to point. The child was to be the father of the man, the priestly Nazarite boy was already half-way on the road to a prophet's work, was already, by God's calling and election, "ordained a prophet unto the nations" (chap. i. 5).

In such a character, reminding us, in many of its features, of the young Timotheus, we find, as might be expected, the notes of the ascetic temperament. He is devout, sensitive, easily depressed and made self-distrustful, kindling all too easily into a bitter and angry indignation, gifted, in a special measure, with the gift of tears. The circumstances of his call imply a previous preparation, as did those of Isaiah's. He had mourned over his people's sins, and yearned to bear his witness against them; but then there came the question, which has been asked a thousand times by men of like character, Who is sufficient for these things? The burden of the task of being a prophet of the Lord seemed too heavy to be borne. The answer to this feeling came in the special call, neither to be ignored nor resisted, for the circumstances of which the reader is referred to the Notes on chap. i. His weakness was to be fortified with a strength higher than his own. As in the case of Isaiah, so also here, it would seem that the call was not followed by immediate prophetic action. Jeremiah is not named in the history of Josiah's reformation, which he must have watched, however, with intense interest, not, perhaps, without some misgivings, like those which Isaiah had felt during the like work of Hezekiah, as to its reality and inward thoroughness. The prophet's keen eye, in this as in other things, saw below the surface, and discerned that something more was wanted than the breaking down of idol sanctuaries, or the abolition of the worship of the high places. He looked in vain for the righteousness without which national restoration was impossible. It can scarcely be doubted, too, that he must have seen with some disquietude the foreign policy which led statesmen and people to seek safety, as their fathers had done, in an alliance with Egypt (chap. ii. 36). For Josiah personally, who, acting on a different policy, opposed that alliance, and fell in battle against Pharaoh Necho at Megiddo (2 Kings xxiii. 29), he would naturally feel a warm and admiring affection, and it is probable that his first appearance as a writer was in the lamentations which he composed on that king's death, but which are not now extant, their fame having apparently been overshadowed by the greater elegies that now bear that name. Possibly we may also refer to this period some of the earlier chapters of the prophet's writings, which have the character of a general survey of the moral and religious condition of the people, and to which no specific date is assigned, as in the case of most of the later chapters.

2. Under Jehoahaz (or Shallum).—The short reign of this king, who was chosen by the people on hearing of Josiah's death, and deposed after three months by Pharaoh Necho, gave little scope for direct prophetic action. As representing an anti-Egyptian policy, and thus continuing in the line of action which Josiah had adopted, the prophet probably sympathised with and supported him, and the tone of respectful sorrow with which he speaks of him in his exile (chap. xxii. 10), contrasts strikingly with the stern rebuke which he addresses to his successor (chap. xxii. 13—19). It lies in the nature of the case, that most of those who were Jeremiah's protectors in the reigns that followed —Shaphan, Ahikam, Maaseiah, and others—were supporters of his policy at this crisis.

3. Under Jehoiakim (b.c. 607—597).—The eleven years of this king's reign were for the prophet a time of conspicuous activity. He found little ground for hope in the Egyptian alliance of which the king was the representative, still less in the self-indulgent and luxurious character of the king himself (chap. xxii. 13—16), or in the priests and prophets, the Pashurs, Hananiahs, and the rest, who were dominant in his council and his court. For him the rising power of the Chaldæans under Nabopolassar and Nebuchadnezzar was to be accepted, not only as inevitable, but as appointed for the punishment, and therefore for the education, of his people. The King of Babylon was God's servant doing His work (chaps. xxv. 9, xxvii. 6). To resist him was to resist the ordinance of God. As he had foretold (chap. xlvi.), the short-lived triumph of Pharaoh Necho in the capture of Carchemish was followed by a crushing defeat, which placed Jehoiakim at the mercy of the Chaldæan king, and compelled him to renounce his dependence on the "broken reed" of Egypt, and to accept the position of a vassal king under Nebuchadnezzar. Some of the more striking incidents of this time of conflict call for a special notice. At the opening of Jehoiakim's reign, the prophet foretells the desolation of the Temple. It should be laid waste, even as Shiloh had been (chap. xxvi. 6). Priests, prophets, people are enraged, and threaten him with death (chap. xxvi. 8), but are foiled by the influence of his lay protectors, who urge the precedent of a like prediction uttered by Micah in the days of Hezekiah, as an argument in his defence (chap. xxvi. 10—18). The fate of a contemporary prophet, Urijah, is recorded by him at this juncture, apparently as showing how narrow his own escape had been (chap. xxvi. 23). The catastrophe of Carchemish naturally led to a fuller utterance. He foretells the seventy years of the captivity (chap. xxv. 11), and symbolically gives the cup of Jehovah's wrath to all the nations which, one after another, were to fall under the Babylonian yoke, ending in predicting, under the cypher form of Sheshach, the fate of Babylon itself (chap. xxv. 17—26). To this period, when the armies of the Chaldæans were driving those who lived in tents or villages to take refuge in Jerusalem, or other fortified cities, we must refer the interesting episode of the Rechabites in chap. xxxv.

In the same year we have the first indication of the prophet's work as the editor of his own prophecies. His secretary and disciple Baruch writes, as he dictates, a collection of his more striking prophecies, probably corresponding roughly with the earlier chapters of our present book. Jeremiah himself was hindered, we know not how, whether by illness or by prudence, from appearing in public, but Baruch solemnly read what he had written in the crowded courts of the Temple. Once again priests and prophets were stirred to wrath. The matter came to the ears of the king, who, in his impotent anger, burnt the parchment roll, in spite of the protest of Jeremiah's friends. Orders were given to arrest the prophet and the scribe; but they again escaped, and re-wrote all that had been destroyed with many like words (chap. xxxvi.). The contrasted characters of the two friends—one seeking great things for himself, eager to play a prominent part in the history of the time, the other content, and wishing to make his disciple content, if his life was "given him for a prey"—come out in the interesting episode of chap. xlv., which belongs probably to this period.

To this reign we may also probably refer the symbolic teaching which was presented in a somewhat startling form, when Jeremiah, having first been directed to learn the lesson of the potter's work as a parable of God's teaching with the nations of the world (chap. xviii.), was afterwards told to go to the valley of Ben-Hinnom, and to warn king and people of the destruction that was coming upon them by breaking in their presence the potter's vessel, which was condemned as worthless (chap. xix.). This was followed by another outburst of malignant rage on the part of Pashur the priest, from which this time the prophet did not escape. The painful and ignominious punishment of the stocks entered into his soul, and called forth a burst at once of denunciation and passionate despair which, except in Pss. lxix. and cix., has scarcely a parallel in the literature of the Old Testament (chap. xx).

If we accept the received text and the literal interpretation of chap. xiii. 1—11, we have to assign to this period of Jeremiah's life the two journeys to Euphrates which are there narrated. Such journeys were not in the nature of the case improbable. Jonah, and probably Nahum, had already found their way to Nineveh (Jonah iii. 3). Manasseh and other members of his royal household had been taken to Babylon (2 Chron. xxxiii. 11). Over and above the symbolism of the narrative there may have been a personal motive connected with such a journey, the desire to do what he could for his country's welfare by becoming acquainted with its destined conquerors. Possibly we may trace the special orders which were given by Nebuchadnezzar for his protection (chap. xxxix. 11) to the acquaintance thus begun. If we might assign the visits to a period after the first deportation of Jewish captives to Babylon in the third year of Jehoiakim (Dan. i. 1), we might connect them with the desire to watch over the fortunes of the exiles, and to renew his intercourse with the prophet who was settled with his companions on the banks of Chebar (Ezek. i. 1), or with Daniel and his friends in the court at Babylon. The fact that the former prophet was with him at Jerusalem during great part of the reign of Jehoiakim, and that his teaching shows many traces of Jeremiah's influence (comp. in particular Ezek. xviii. 2 and Jer. xxxi. 29), may, at all events, be noted as throwing light upon the surroundings of the latter's life, and on the influence which he exercised over his contemporaries.

4. Under Jehoiachin (B.C. 597).—The short three months' reign of this king witnessed the fulfilment of Jeremiah's predictions, in the captivity first of his predecessor, and then of Jehoiachin himself, together with all the officers of their courts and the wealthier part of the population. We may infer, from the fact of his being deposed by Nebuchadnezzar, that he was led by his counsellors (he himself was a mere boy) to enter into intrigues against the Chaldæan sovereignty; and the tone in which Jeremiah speaks of him (chap. xxii. 24—30) implies that he and the queen-mother—probably the master-mind of the policy of the court (2 Kings xxiv. 15)—were disposed to reject his counsels. In him and in his childless age the prophet saw the close of the dynasty, in the direct line of succession, of the house of David. It is noticeable that Jeremiah, though a priest, escaped the doom of exile which probably fell on his friend and disciple Ezekiel, and the difference in their fortunes may be traced without much risk of error to the prominent part which the former had taken from first to last as counselling subjection, possibly to the personal favour with which he was already regarded by the Chaldæan rulers. The effect of the separation must, however, have added to his sense of loneliness. Not a few of his friends and protectors must have shared in the captivity. He had to fight the battle of his life during his remaining years more single-handed than before.

5. Under Zedekiah (B.C. 597—586).—As might be expected from the fact that he had been appointed by Nebuchadnezzar, as likely to be a more submissive vassal than his predecessors, appointed possibly with Jeremiah's approval, the prophet receives at the hands of this prince, on the whole, a better treatment than at those of his predecessors. The king respects him, keeps his counsel, endeavours to protect him (chap. xxxvii. 3—17, xxxviii. 16). The very name which he adopted on his accession to the throne, "Righteous is Jah," or "Jehovah" (2 Kings xxiv. 18), seems to have been intended to identify him with the acceptance of the prophet's teaching that in "the Lord our Righteousness" (chap. xxiii. 6) was to be found the archetype and the source of all righteous government. The king, however, was weak and vacillating. The prophet felt keenly that only the most worthless remnant of the people, the "vile figs" of the crop, were left in Judah (chap. xxiv. 5—8). It was to the other remnant in the exile of Babylon that he turned with words of counsel in the letter, which more than any other Old Testament document seems to foreshadow the epistles of the New (chap. xxix.). Even there also, however, there were false prophets, among whom Zedekiah, Ahab, and Shemaiah were conspicuous, who spoke of him as a "madman" (chap. xxix. 26), and urged the priests at Jerusalem to more active measures of persecution, not knowing that they were thus drawing upon themselves a quick and terrible retribution.

Soon matters came to a crisis. The apparent revival of the power of Egypt under Apries (the Pharaoh-hophra of chap. xliv. 30) raised false hopes in the minds of Zedekiah and his advisers, and drew Judah and the neighbouring nations into projects of revolt (chap. xxxvii. 5). The clearness with which Jeremiah foresaw the ultimate destruction of Babylon, made him all the more certain that it was not to come at once or through the intervention of Egypt. He appeared in the streets of Jerusalem with bonds and yokes upon his neck, announcing that they were meant for Judah and its cities (chap. xxvii. 2). The false prophet Hananiah, who broke the offensive symbols, and predicted the destruction of the power of Babylon within two years, learnt that a yoke of iron was upon the neck of all the nations, and died himself while it was still pressing heavily on Judah (chap. xxviii. 3—17). The approach of an Egyptian army, however, and the consequent departure of the Chaldæans, made the position of Jeremiah full of danger, and he sought to effect his escape from a city in which he seemed powerless for good, and to take refuge in his own town of Anathoth (chap. xxxvii. 12), the men of that city who had sought his life (chap. xi. 21) having probably been taken into exile after the first Chaldæan invasion. The discovery of this plan led not unnaturally to the charge of desertion. He was arrested, as "falling away to the Chaldæans," as others were doing (chap. xxxvii. 14), and, in spite of his denial, was thrown into a dungeon (chap. xxxvii. 16). The interposition of the king, who still respected and consulted him, led to some mitigation of the rigours of his confinement (chap. xxxvii. 21); but as this milder treatment left him able to speak to the people, the princes of Judah, bent on the Egyptian alliance, and counting on the king's being unable to resist them, threw him into the prison-pit, and would have left him to die there in its foulness (chap. xxxviii. 6). From this horrible fate he was delivered by the kindness of the Ethiopian eunuch, Ebed-Melech, and the king's lingering regard for him, and was restored to the milder custody in the king's house where Baruch and other friends could visit him (chap. xxxii. 16). The king himself sent Pashur (not the one already named) and Zephaniah, both, it would appear, friendly to the prophet (chap. xxix. 29), to consult him. The prophet, as if touched by this humility, speaks to the king in gentler terms. Exile is inevitable, but he shall at least "die in peace," and receive, in marked contrast with Jehoiakim, an honourable burial (chap. xxxiv. 3—5). At no period of his life is the prophet truer to his calling. He had before to fight against false hopes of liberation. He has now to contend against the despair which made men lose all faith in the promises of God and in their own future. That danger the prophet was taught to meet in the most effectual way. With a confidence in that future which has been compared to that of the Roman who bought at its full value the very ground on which the forces of Hannibal were encamped (Livy xxvi. 11), he too bought, with all requisite formalities, the field at Anathoth, which his kinsman Hanameel wished to get rid of (chap. xxxii. 6—9), and proclaimed not only that "fields and vineyards should again be possessed in the lands," but that the "voice of gladness" should once more be heard there, and that under "the Lord our Righteousness" the house of David and the priests the Levites should never be without representatives (chap. xxxiii. 21—26). To this period also we may assign the prophecy of a New Covenant (chap. xxxi. 31), which was destined to have so marvellous a fulfilment, and which has fashioned, under the teaching of Him who came to be the Mediator of that covenant, the faith and the terminology of Christendom. His influence may also be traced in the renewal of the national covenant with Jehovah (chap. xxxiv. 18, 19), princes, priests, and people walking in procession between the two parts of the sacrifice (chap. xxxiv. 19), and in the proclamation of liberty to the Hebrew servants and handmaids whom the oppression of the rich had brought into bondage (chap. xxxiv. 9—14). The reformation thus effected was, however, only on the surface. Covenant and proclamation were alike disregarded. The law of the Sabbatic year was set at nought as that of the Sabbath day had been before (chap. xvii. 21—27). The cup of iniquity was full, and the judgment came. The armies of Nebuchadnezzar besieged Jerusalem, and it was exposed to all the horrors of famine (Lam. ii. 12, 20, iv. 9). At last the city was taken, and the Temple burnt. The king and his princes endeavoured to escape, but were taken prisoners in the plains of Jericho. Zedekiah had to see his children slain before his eyes, and, as if that were to be the last sight he was to look upon, was afterwards blinded, and taken, as Jehoiachin had been, to pass the remainder of his days as a prisoner at Babylon (chap. lii. 10, 11).

6. After the Capture of Jerusalem (B.C. 586—?)—The prophet and his protectors, who had all along counselled submission to the king of Babylon, had now the prospect of better treatment than their fellows. A special charge was given to Nebuzar-adan to protect the person of Jeremiah (chap. xxxix. 11), and after being carried to Ramah with the crowd of prisoners, he was set free, and offered his choice whether he would go to Babylon with the prospect of rising, as Daniel and his friends had risen, to an honourable position in the king's court, or remain under the protection of Gedaliah, the son of his steadfast friend Ahikam, who had been appointed governor over the cities of Judah (chap xl. 1—5). The prophet's love for his people led him to choose the latter alternative, and the Chaldæan commander "gave him a reward," and set him free. Then followed a short interval of peace, soon broken, however, by the murder of Gedaliah by Ishmael and his confederates. We are left to conjecture how the prophet himself escaped with life, but the fulness of his narrative of these events leads to the conclusion that he was among the captives whom Ishmael carried off to the Ammonites, and who were released by the intervention of Johanan (chap. xli.). Jeremiah was thus deprived of one of his most valued friends, but Baruch was still with him, and it is significant that the people turned to him for counsel. They wanted, it would seem, his sanction to the foregone conclusion that their only chance of escaping the punishment, likely enough to be indiscriminate, which the Chaldæans would exact for the murder of Gedaliah, was in an immediate flight to Egypt (chap. xlii. 14). That sanction he refused, at the risk of bringing on himself and Baruch the old charge of treachery (chap. xliii. 3), but the people, bent on following their own plans, forced him and his disciple to accompany them to Tahpanhes. There we have the last recorded scene of the prophet's life. He once more rebukes the people vehemently for their multiplied idolatries, among which the worship of the Queen of Heaven had been the most conspicuous (chap. xliv.), does not shrink from again speaking of Nebuchadnezzar as "the servant of Jehovah" (chap. xliii. 10), and foretells that he will conquer Egypt as he had conquered Judah. After all this all is uncertain. If we were to accept chap. lii. as the work of the prophet, we should have to think of him as living for twenty-six years after the destruction of Jerusalem. Probabilities are, however, against this conclusion, and there is greater likelihood on the side of the tradition, reported by Tertullian (*adv. Gnost.* c. 8), Jerome (*adv. Jovin.* ii. 37), and others, that he was stoned to death at Tahpanhes by the Jews whom he had provoked by his rebukes. Most commentators on the New Testament see a reference to this in Heb. xi. 37, just as they refer the words "were sawn asunder" to the martyrdom of Isaiah. An Alexandrian tradition reported that his bones were brought to that city by Alexander the Great (*Chron. Pasch*, p. 156, ed. Dindorf), and up to the eighteenth century travellers were told that he was buried near the pyramid of Ghizeh (Lucas, *Travels in the Levant*, p. 28). On the other hand, there is the Jewish statement (quoted in Smith's *Dictionary of the Bible*), that he and Baruch escaped to Babylon or Judæa, and died there in peace. Josephus is silent as to his fate. Other traditions have, at least, the interest of showing the impression which Jeremiah's work and life left on later generations. His prophecy of the seventy years' exile, which had at first been full of terror, came to be a ground of hope (chap. xxv. 11; Dan. ix. 2; 2 Chron. xxxvi. 21). The fulfilment of that prophecy probably impressed itself on the mind of Cyrus. On the return from Babylon his writings were received, probably under Ezra or the scribes of the Great Synagogue, among the sacred

books of Israel, and in the Babylonian recension they, and not those of Isaiah, took the foremost place in the company of the prophets, Ezekiel coming between the two. The Jewish saying "that the Spirit of Jeremiah dwelt in Zechariah" bears witness to the influence which the one prophet was believed to have exercised on the mind of the other. The fulfilment of his prediction of the return of the exiles from the Babylonian captivity led to his being regarded, so to speak, as the patron saint of his country. It was believed that he had taken the tabernacle and the ark and the altar of incense, and had concealed them in a cave on Mount Nebo till the time when God should gather His people together once again (2 Macc. ii. 1—8). He appeared to Judas Maccabeus as "a man with gray hairs and exceeding glorious," as one who "prayed much for the holy city," and gave the hero a "golden sword" with which to "fight the battles of the Lord" (2 Macc. xv. 13—16). He is recognised as having a chief place among the prophets of Israel, sanctified from his mother's womb (Ecclus. xlix. 6, 7). His authority is claimed for an apocryphal letter to the captives of Babylon, containing a long polemic against the follies of idolatry (Bar. vi.). At a later period his name was attached, as in Matt. xxvii. 9, to prophecies from another book in the sacred canon, either as having been their original author, or in the belief that he was the representative of all the prophets of the captivity. In the time of our Lord's ministry, his re-appearance was expected, like that of Elijah, to prepare the way for the Christ. Some said of Jesus of Nazareth that He was "Jeremiah, or one of the prophets" (Matt. xvi. 14). Probably he was "*that* prophet" referred to in John i. 21. The belief that he was the prophet of Deut. xviii. 18, has been held by later Jewish commentators (Abarbanel, in Carpzov, *Introd. in V. T. Jerem.*). The traditions as to his re-appearance lingered even in the Christian Church, and appeared in the belief that he was one of the "two witnesses" of Rev. xi. 3 (Victorinus, *in loc.*). Yet wilder forms of legends were found in Egypt. It was he who had foretold that the idols of that country should one day fall to the ground, at the presence of the Virgin and her child. He had played the part of a St. Patrick, and had delivered the region of the Delta of the Nile, where he dwelt, from serpents (Epiphan. *de Vit., proph.* op. ii. p. 239). He had returned from Egypt to Jerusalem, and had lived there for three hundred years (D'Herbelot, *Bibl. Orient.*, p. 499). The narrative of his sufferings was expanded into a history like that of a Christian martyrdom (Eusebius, *Praep. Evang.* ix. 39).

II. **Character and Style.**—In the popular description of Jeremiah as the "weeping prophet," in the form in which Michael Angelo has portrayed him in the Sistine Chapel, as brooding, with downcast eyes, in sorrowful meditation, we have a true conception of the prophet's character and life. Of all the prophets of the Old Testament, he would seem to have had the hardest lot of suffering. He was pre-eminently "the man who had seen affliction:" "no sorrow was like unto his sorrow" (Lam. i. 12, iii. 1). His whole life was spent in what seemed a fruitless strife with the evils of his time. Cassandra-like, he had to utter warnings which were disregarded. Like Phocion, in the history of Athens, he had to counsel submission to an alien conqueror, and to incur the reproach of being treacherous and faint-hearted. Had the horizon of his hopes been that of his own times only, his heart must have shrunk back into despair. That which sustained him was the inextinguishable hope, which he had inherited from Isaiah, of the kingdom of God, the restoration of the true Israel of God, the new and better Covenant, the faith in "the Lord our Righteousness." In his loneliness and his sorrows, in his susceptibility to intensest suffering and keenest indignation, his nearest parallel in the history of literature may, perhaps, be found in Dante. In him, at all events, the great Florentine found one of the founts of his inspiration, quotes him again and again, both in his poetry and his prose writings, and borrows from him the opening symbolism of the *Divina Commedia.* (Comp. Jer. v. 6 with Dante's *Inferno*, c. i.)

To associate the name of Jeremiah with other portions of the Old Testament than those which bear his name, is to pass from the region of history into that of conjecture; but the fact that some commentators (*e.g.*, Hitzig) assign not less than thirty Psalms to his authorship (*sc.*, Pss. v., vi., xiv., xxii.—xli., lii.—lv., lxix.—lxxi.), indicates at least what were the hymns in his national literature with which he had most affinity, and which exercised most influence on his thoughts and language. The hypothesis of some later critics (*e.g.*, Bunsen, *God in History*, b. ii. c. 2), who assign the second part of Isaiah to the time of the exile, and to the authorship of Baruch, that Jeremiah was the Servant of the Lord, who is there conspicuous, has a like suggestiveness. Reference to others of the earlier books of the Old Testament canon show parallelisms with the Law, a special prominence being given to Deuteronomy, as, *e.g.*—

Comp. Jer. xi. 3—5 with Deut. iv. 20, vii. 12, xxvii. 26.
„ „ xxxiv. 14 „ „ xv. 12
„ „ xxxii. 18 „ Exod. xx. 6
„ „ xxxii. 21 „ „ vi. 6,

with Job (comp. Job iii. with Jer. xv. 10, xx. 14), with both parts of Isaiah.

Comp. Isaiah iv. 2, xi. 1 with Jer. xxxiii. 15
„ „ xl. 19, 20 „ „ x. 3—5
„ „ xlii. 16 „ „ xxxi. 9
„ „ xiii., xlvii. „ „ l., li.

and with the earlier prophets.

The style of Jeremiah, if less conspicuous for its loftiness and majesty than that of Job or Isaiah, has yet a passionate intensity, a vividness of imagery, a capacity for invective or for pathos, which are not surpassed and scarcely equalled elsewhere, in this also reminding us of Dante. It was characteristic both of the man and of the time that this passionate temperament welcomed, when it uttered itself in the Lamentations, the artificial restraints of the alphabetic arrangement which had appeared before in some of the Psalms, and seems to have been a fashion of the times. (See *Introduction to Lamentations.*) Connected, perhaps, with this, as concentrating attention upon the alphabet and its possible uses, is Jeremiah's use of a peculiar cypher writing, the use of an inverted alphabet, known among the later Jews as the Atbash (A standing for T, and B for SH), by which the Sheshach of Jer. xxv. 26 became for the initiated the symbol of Babylon; and the Hebrew letters of "in the midst of those who rise up against me" of Jer. li. 1, was equivalent to "the Chaldæans," which accordingly takes its place in the LXX. version.

III. **Arrangement.**—It is a noticeable fact, as throwing light upon the chances to which even the writings of a prophet may be subject, that the order of the

LXX. version of the greater part of Jeremiah is altogether different from that of the Hebrew. Up to chap. xxv. 13 they agree. From that point onward to the end of chap. li. the divergency may be presented as follows :—

LXX.	Hebrew.
xxv. 14—18.	xlix. 34—39.
xxv.	xlvi.
xxvii., xxviii.	l., li.
xxix. 1—7.	xlvii. 1—7.
„ 8—22.	xlix. 7—24.
xxx. 1—5.	xlix. 1—6.
„ 6—11.	„ 28—33.
„ 12—16.	„ 23—27.
xxxi.	xlviii.
xxxiii.—li.	xxv. 13—39.
lii.	xxvi.—xlv.

It is obvious that the Alexandrian translators must have had before them a MS., or, more probably, a mass of MSS., arranged by them, or for them, in a different order from that adopted by the scribes of Judæa, to whom we owe our present Hebrew recension. It is a natural inference from this (1) that the prophet's writings were left by him in a scattered, unarranged state, in the hands of his disciples, Baruch and others, and that two of these, or some later scribes, thought fit to arrange them in a different order. It was, so to speak, as if the sermons of an eminent preacher in later times had come to us as they were found in his drawers, unsorted. (2) That the large sections in which the order is the same in chaps. i.—xxv. 13 (Heb.), and xxvi—xlv. (Heb.) represent two collections, which contained the chief prophecies that were connected with the prophet's work in relation to Judah, while the others, bearing chiefly on the heathen nations, were left in a less continuous form, and were arranged by the two editors at their discretion.

It is to be noted that in neither case is the arrangement chronological. To read the prophet's writings in the order of time, either as regards the facts to which they refer, or the date of their composition, we must adopt an arrangement different from both of those which are now before us. In regard to some of the sections where we have a definite note of time, specifying, if not the exact year, at least the reign to which they of right belong, the task is comparatively easy. In regard to the others, we are in the wider, and therefore more difficult, field of conjecture. Taking the dates given in the Authorised version as approximately right, the following gives the order in which Jeremiah's prophecies ought to be read in connection with his life, and which has been practically followed in the preceding biography :—

B.C. 629	... Chap.	i. ii. iii. (probably *written* later).
„ 612	„	iii.—vi.
„ 610	„	xxii, xxvi.
„ 608	„	xi., xii.
„ 607	„	xxxv., xlv.
„ 606	„	xxv., xxx., xxxi.
„ 605	„	xviii., xix., xx.
„ 602	„	xiii.
„ 601	„	xiv., xv., xvi., xvii.
„ 600	„	vii., viii., ix., x., xlvii., xlviiii.
„ 599	„	xxiii., xxix.
„ 598	„	xxiv., xxvi. xxvii. (Jehoiakim in chap. xxvii. 1 is clearly an error of transcription for Zedekiah).
„ 596	„	xxviii.
„ 595	„	l., li.
B.C. 591	„	xxxiv.
„ 590	„	xxxii., xxxiii.
„ 590—588	„	xxxix., xl., xli., xlii., xliii., xliv.
„ 589	„	xxi., xxxvii, xxxviii.
„ 587	„	xliv.
„ 598—562	„	lii. Appendix and historical summary.

The wide divergency of this order from that of either of the two recensions that have come down is not without its teaching (1) as showing that during the length of time over which the prophet's work was spread but little care was taken by him to provide for their transmission in any definite order. Like a true prophet, he did his work for his own generation, thinking little of himself and his after-fame. Like the Sibyl of classical antiquity, he gave his writings, as it were, to the winds, careless of their fate, and left it to others, through his long career, to collect, copy, and arrange them as they could. (2) As suggesting the probability that what happened in his case may have befallen the writings of other prophets also, such as Isaiah, Ezekiel, Hosea, Amos, whose labours were spread over a considerable period of time; and, consequently, as leaving it open to us to deal freely with the order in which we find them, so as to connect them, as we best can, with the successive stages of the prophet's life.

It need not be inferred, however, from this chronological dislocation, that the order of the chapters in the Hebrew, and, therefore, in the English version, is altogether without a plan. The following scheme gives, it is believed, an adequate explanation of the principles on which the Palestine editor may have acted :—

1. Chaps. i.—xxi.—Containing probably the substance of the book of chap. xxxvi. 32, and including prophecies from the thirteenth year of Josiah (with a long interval of silence) to the fourth year of Jehoiakim. Chap. i. 3, however, indicates a later revision, and the whole of chap. i. may have been added as the prophet's retrospect of his whole work from this its first beginning. Chap. xxi. belongs to a later period, but may have been placed here, as connected by the recurrence of the name of Pashur with chap. xx.

2. Chaps. xxii.—xxv.—Short prophecies against the kings of Judah and the false prophets. Chap. xxv. 13, 14, evidently marks the conclusion of a series, and that which follows (chap. xxv. 15—38), the germ of the fuller predictions of chaps. xlvi.—xlix., has apparently been placed here, as a completion to that of the seventy years of exile.

3. Chaps. xxvi.—xxviii.—The two great prophecies of the fall of Jerusalem. Chap. xxvi. belongs to the earlier, chaps. xxvii. and xxviii. to the later portion of the prophet's work.

4. Chaps. xxix.—xxxi.—The message of comfort to exiles in Babylon.

5. Chaps. xxxii.—xliv.—The history of Jeremiah's work immediately before and after the capture of Jerusalem. Chaps. xxxv. and xxxvi. are remarkable as interrupting the chronological order, which would otherwise have been followed here more closely than elsewhere. The position of chap. xlv. as an isolated fragment, suggests that it may have been added by Baruch at the close of his narrative of his master's life.

6. Chaps. xlvi.—li.—The prophecies against foreign nations, ending with the great utterance against Babylon.

7. Chap. lii.—Historical appendix.

IV. Text and Authenticity.—Over and above the variations in order, the LXX. presents some noticeable variations and omissions, which have led some critics to reject some portions of the present Hebrew text as being probably interpolations. Other passages have been questioned on grounds more or less subjective as prophecies after the event, or for other reasons. The limits of this *Introduction* will not admit of a full description of each portion, but a statement of the objections will, in the one case, direct attention to some striking variations, and in the other, in some instances at least, to parallelisms of some interest. To the present writer, who holds (1) that there are antecedent probabilities in favour of the Hebrew text as compared with the Greek, and (2) that the inspiration of the prophet implies, at least the possibility of a prediction before the event, neither ground of objection seems conclusive.

(*a*) Questioned, as omitted in the LXX.

(1) chap. x. 6, 7, 8, 10.
(2) „ xxvii. 7.
(3) „ xxvii. 16—21 (not omitted, but with many variations).
(4) „ xxxiii. 14—26.
(5) „ xxxix. 4—13.

(*b*) Questioned on other grounds.

(1) Chap. x. 1—16.—On being the work of a later writer, probably the so-called Deutero-Isaiah. The Aramaic of verse 11 is urged in favour of this view.
(2) „ xxvii. 14.
(3) „ xxvii. 7.
(4) „ xxxiii. 14—26.
(5) „ xxxix. 1, 2, 4—13.
} as having the character of prophecies after the event.
(6) „ xxvii.—xxix.—As showing, in the shortened form of the name (Jeremiah instead of Jeremiahu), and in the epithet "the prophet," the work of a later writer.
(7) „ xxx.—xxxiii.—As showing the influence of the Deutero-Isaiah.
(8) „ xlviii., for the same reason as (7).
(9) „ l. li.—As being a prophecy after the event, foreign in style and thought to Jeremiah's writings.
(10) „ lii.—As an historical summary compiled from 2 Kings xxv. and other sources by the editor of the collection.

In the notes that follow I have been mainly indebted to Ewald, Hitzig, and Keil, and to the notes on Jeremiah by Dr. Payne Smith in the *Speaker's Commentary*, and those by Nägelsbach in Lange's *Commentary*, edited by Dr. Philip Schaff. The *Introduction* is mainly based upon an article on Jeremiah which I contributed to Dr. Smith's *Dictionary of the Bible*, and on the very able dissertation by Nägelsbach in the Commentary just named.

THE BOOK OF THE PROPHET

JEREMIAH

CHAPTER I.—(1) The words of Jere-
miah the son of Hilkiah, of the priests
that *were* in Anathoth in the land of
Benjamin: (2) to whom the word of the
LORD came in the days of Josiah the
son of Amon king of Judah, in the
thirteenth year of his reign. (3) It came
also in the days of Jehoiakim the son of
Josiah king of Judah, unto the end of
the eleventh year of Zedekiah the son
of Josiah king of Judah, unto the carry-
ing away of Jerusalem captive in the
fifth month.

(4) Then the word of the LORD came
unto me, saying, (5) Before I [a]formed
thee in the belly I knew thee; and
before thou camest forth out of the
womb I [b]sanctified thee, *and* I [1]or-

B.C. cir. 629.

a Isa. 49. 1, 5.

b Gal. 1. 15, 16.

1 Heb., *gave*.

(1–3) The first three verses contain the title prefixed to the collection of prophecies by some later editor. This title would seem, from its unusual fulness, to have received one or more additions—verse 1 giving the general title, verse 2 the commencement of Jeremiah's prophetic work, verse 3 the period of his chief activity and its conclusion. Strictly speaking, indeed, we see from the book itself that his work continued after the beginning of the captivity.

The words of Jeremiah.—The more usual title of prophetic books is "the word of the Lord by the prophet," but the title of Amos (i. 1) is in the same form as this. The Hebrew for "words" has a somewhat wider connotation than the English, and is translated "acts" in 1 Kings xi. 41; 2 Chron. xxxiii. 18.

Hilkiah.—Possibly the high priest of that name (2 Kings xxii. 4, xxiii. 4). See *Introduction.*

Anathoth.—In the tribe of Benjamin, one of the cities assigned to the priests, apparently to the house of Ithamar, to which Abiathar belonged (1 Kings ii. 26; Josh. xxi. 18; 1 Chron. vi. 60).

That were in Anathoth.—There is no verb in the Hebrew, and the description belongs to Jeremiah individually, not to the priests.

(2) **In the thirteenth year of his reign.**—If we take the *data* of 2 Kings xxii., Josiah was at that time in his twentieth or twenty-first year, having grown up under the training of Hilkiah. His active work of reformation began five years later. The images of Baal and Asherah (the groves) were thrown down, and the high places desecrated. The near coincidence of the commencement of Jeremiah's work as prophet with that of the king must not be forgotten. As Josiah reigned for thirty-one years, we have to place eighteen years of the prophet's ministry as under his rule.

(3) **It came also . . .**—The short reigns of Jehoahaz (three months) and Jehoiachin or Jeconiah (three months also) are passed over, and mention made of the more conspicuous reigns of Jehoiakim (eleven years) and Zedekiah (also eleven). Assuming Jeremiah to have been about twenty when the prophetic call came to him, he was sixty or sixty-one at the time of the captivity.

(4) **The word of the Lord came unto me.**—The words imply obviously a revelation, the introduction of a new element into the human consciousness. In many cases such a revelation implied also the spiritual tension of an ecstatic or trance-like state, a dream, or an open vision. It almost presupposed a previous training, outward or inward, a mind vexed by hot thoughts and mourning over the sins of the people. Here there is no mention of dream or vision, and we must assume, therefore, a distinct consciousness that the voice which he heard in his inmost soul was from Jehovah. For the thought of pre-natal calling, see Isa. xlix. 1.

(5) **I knew thee.**—With the force which the word often has in Hebrew, as implying, not foreknowledge only, but choice and approval (Ps. i. 6, xxxvii. 18, Amos iii. 2).

I sanctified thee.—*i.e., consecrated thee, set thee apart as hallowed for this special use.*

Ordained.—Better, *I have appointed,* without the conjunction, this verb referring to the manifestation in time of the eternal purpose.

Unto the nations.—*i.e., to the outlying Gentile nations.* This was the distinguishing characteristic of Jeremiah's work. Other prophets were sent to Israel and Judah, with occasional parentheses of prophecies that affected the Gentiles. The horizon of Jeremiah was to extend more widely. In part his work was to make them drink of the cup of the Lord's fury (chap. xxv. 15—17); but in part also he was a witness to them of a brighter future (chap. xlviii. 47, xlix. 39). It is as though he had drunk in the Spirit of Isaiah, and thought of the true prophet as one who was to be a light of the Gentiles (Isa. xlix. 6).

In this way, seemingly abrupt, yet probably following on a long process of divine education, was the youthful Jeremiah taught that he was to act a part specially appointed for him in the drama of his nation's history. He could not see a chance in the guidance that had led him thus far. The call that now came to him so clearly was not the echo of his own thoughts. All his life from infancy had been as that of one consecrated to a special work. Could he stop there? Must he not, like St. Paul, think of the divine pur-

dained thee a prophet unto the nations.
(6) Then said I, Ah, [a]Lord GOD! behold,
I cannot speak: for I *am* a child.
(7) But the LORD said unto me, Say not,
I *am* a child: for thou shalt go to
all that I shall send thee, and whatso-
ever I command thee thou shalt speak.
(8) [b]Be not afraid of their faces: for [c]I
am with thee to deliver thee, saith the
LORD. (9) Then the LORD put forth his
hand, and [d]touched my mouth. And
the LORD said unto me, Behold, I have
[e]put my words in thy mouth. (10) See,
I have this day set thee over the nations
and over the kingdoms, to [f]root out, and
to pull down, and to destroy, and to
throw down, to build, and to plant.
(11) Moreover the word of the LORD
came unto me, saying, Jeremiah, what
seest thou? And I said, I see a rod of
an almond tree. (12) Then said the LORD
unto me, Thou hast well seen: for I
will hasten my word to perform it.
(13) And the word of the LORD came
unto me the second time, saying, What
seest thou? And I said, I see a seething

a Exod. 4. 10.
b Ezek. 3. 9.
c Exod. 3. 12; Deut. 31. 6, 8; Josh. 1. 5; Heb. 13. 6.
d Isa. 6. 7.
e ch. 5. 14.
f ch. 18. 7; 2 Cor. 10. 4, 5.

---

pose as prior to the very germ of his existence? (Gal. i. 15.)

(6) **Ah, Lord God!**—Better, *Alas, O Lord Jehovah!* as answering to the Hebrew Adonai Jehovah.

I cannot speak.—In the same sense as the "I am not eloquent" of Moses (Exod. iv. 10), literally, "a man of words," *i.e.*, have no gifts of utterance.

I am a child.—Later Jewish writers fix the age of fourteen as that up to which the term rendered "child" might be used. With Jeremiah it was probably more indefinite, and in the intense consciousness of his own weakness he would naturally use a word below the actual standard of his age; and there is accordingly nothing against assuming any age within the third hebdomad of life. In Gen. xxxiv. 19 it is used of a young man old enough for marriage. The words are memorable as striking a note common to the lives of many prophets; common, also, we may add, to most men as they feel themselves called to any great work. So Moses draws back: "I am slow of speech, and of a slow tongue" (Exod. iv. 10). So Isaiah cries, "Woe is me! for . . . I am a man of unclean lips" (Isa. vi. 5); and Peter, "Depart from me; for I am a sinful man, O Lord" (Luke v. 8). Something of the same shrinking is implied in St. Paul's command to Timothy (1 Tim. iv. 12). In tracing the whole course of Jeremiah's work, we must never forget the divine constraint by which he entered on them. A necessity was laid upon him, as afterwards on St. Paul (1 Cor. ix. 16).

(7) **The Lord said unto me.**—The misgiving, which was not reluctance, is met by words of encouragement. God gave the work; He would also give the power.

(8) **Be not afraid.**—The words imply, as in those spoken to Ezekiel (ii. 6), to St. Peter (Luke v. 10), and St. Paul (Acts xviii. 9), the fear that sprang from the sense of personal weakness and unfitness to cope with the dangers to which his work exposed him. The "faces" of his adversaries would be a source of terror to him. The consciousness that Jehovah was with him was to raise him from that timidity.

(9) **The Lord put forth his hand . . .**—The symbolic act seems to imply something like a waking vision, like that of Isaiah (vi. 6), and the act itself reminds us of the "live coal" laid upon the prophet's mouth, as there recorded. The "hand of the Lord," as in Ezek. iii. 14, viii. 1., and elsewhere, was the received symbol of the special influence of the Spirit of the Lord; and here, as in the case of Isaiah, the act implied the gift of new powers of thought and utterance. The words which a prophet speaks, like those which were to be spoken by the Apostles of Christ (Matt. x. 20), are not his own words, but those put into his heart by the Spirit of the Father. So "the finger of God" in Luke xi. 20 answers to "the Spirit of God" in Matt. xii. 28.

(10) **I have this day set thee . . .**—With the gift, and therefore the consciousness, of a new power, there comes what would at first have been too much for the mortal vessel of the truth to bear—a prospective view of the greatness of the work before him. He is at once set (literally, made the "deputy," or representative, of God, as in Judges ix. 28 and 2 Chron. xxiv. 11, the "officer," or in chap. xx. 1, "chief governor") over the nations, *i.e.*, as before, the nations external to Israel, and the "kingdoms" including it. The work at first seems one simply of destruction—to *root out and ruin* (so we may represent the alliterative assonance of the Hebrew), *to destroy and rend asunder.* But beyond that there is the hope of a work of construction. He is to "build up" the fallen ruins of Israel, to "plant" in the land that had been made desolate. The whole sequel of the book is a comment on these words. It passes through terror and darkness to the glory and the blessing of the New Covenant (chap. xxxi. 31).

(11) **The word of the Lord . . .**—As before, we have the element of ecstasy and vision, symbols not selected by the prophet, and yet, we may believe, adapted to his previous training, and to the bent and, as it were, genius of his character.

The poetry of the symbols is of exquisite beauty. In contrast to the words of terror, in harmony with the words of hope, he sees the almond-bough, with its bright pink blossoms and its pale green leaves, the token of an early spring rising out of the dreariness of winter. The name of the almond-tree (here the poetical, not the common, name) made the symbol yet more expressive. It was the *watcher,* the tree that "hastens to awake" (*shâkêd*) out of its wintry sleep, and thus expresses the divine haste which would not without cause delay the fulfilment of its gracious promise, but would, as it were, make it bud and blossom, and bear fruit.

(12) **I will hasten.**—The Hebrew, by using a participle formed from the same root (*shôkêd*), presents a play upon the name of the "almond," as the *watcher,* which it is impossible to reproduce; literally, *I, too, am watching over my word to perform it.*

(13) **A seething pot; and the face thereof is toward the north.**—More correctly, *from the north.* The next symbol was one that set forth the darker side of the prophet's work: a large cauldron (probably of

pot; and the face thereof *is* [1]toward the
north. (14) Then the LORD said unto
me, Out of the [a]north an evil [2]shall
break forth upon all the inhabitants
of the land. (15) For, lo, I will [b]call all
the families of the kingdoms of the
north, saith the LORD; and they shall
come, and they shall set every one his
throne at the entering of the gates of
Jerusalem, and against all the walls
thereof round about, and against all the
cities of Judah. (16) And I will utter
my judgments against them touching
all their wickedness, who have forsaken
me, and have burned incense unto other
gods, and worshipped the works of their
own hands. (17) Thou therefore gird up
thy loins, and arise, and speak unto
them all that I command thee: be not
dismayed at their faces, lest I [3]confound
thee before them. (18) For, behold, I
have made thee this day [c]a defenced
city, and an iron pillar, and brasen
walls against the whole land, against
the kings of Judah, against the princes
thereof, against the priests thereof, and
against the people of the land. (19) And
they shall fight against thee; but they
shall not prevail against thee; for I *am*
with thee, saith the LORD, to deliver
thee.

CHAPTER II. — (1) Moreover the
word of the LORD came to me, saying,

1 Heb., *from the face of the north.*

a ch. 4. 6.

2 Heb., *shall be opened.*

b ch. 5. 15, & 6. 22, & 10. 22.

3 Or, *break to pieces.*

c Isa. 50. 7; ch. 6. 27, & 15. 20.

---

metal) placed (as in Ezekiel's vision, xxiv. 3—11) on a great pile of burning wood, boiling and steaming, with its face turned *from the north,* and so on the point of emptying out its scalding contents towards the south. This was as strong a contrast as possible to the vernal beauty of the almond-bough, and told too plainly the terrors which were to be expected from the regions that lay to the north of the land of Israel, Assyria and Chaldæa. The flood of water at the boiling point went beyond the "waters of the great river" of Israel's symbolism (Isa. viii. 7).

(14) **Out of the north an evil.**—Literally, *the evil,* long foretold, as in Micah iii. 12, and elsewhere, and long expected.

(15) **I will call.**—Literally, *I am calling.* The evil is not merely future, but is actually begun.

All the families of the kingdoms of the north.—In the Hebrew the words are in apposition, *all the families, even the kingdoms of the north.* The words point chiefly to the Chaldæans and other inhabitants of Babylonia, but may probably include also the Scythians, who about this time spread like a deluge over Asia Minor and Syria, and penetrated as far as Ascalon (Herod. i. 105).

They shall set every one his throne.—*i.e.,* shall usurp the administration of justice, and set up their thrones of judgment in the space near the gates in which kings usually sat to hear complaints and decide causes (2 Sam. xv. 2; Ps. cxxvii. 5). In chap. xxxix. 3 we have a literal fulfilment of the prediction.

Against all the walls.—As the previous words speak of a formal usurpation of power, so do these of invasion and attack, the storming of the lesser cities of Judah, while Jerusalem became the centre of the foreign government.

(16) **I will utter my judgments against them.**—Here, again, we get a literal correspondence in the words of chap. xxxix. 5, "he gave [or uttered] judgment upon him," of Nebuchadnezzar's sentence on Zedekiah. And yet the invaders in their sentence are to be but the ministers of a higher judgment than their own. In the words "*my* judgments" He recognises their work.

Who have forsaken.—The remainder of the verse gives, as it were, the formal enumeration of the crimes for which Judah was condemned: (1) Apostacy from the true God; (2) the transfer of adoration to other Gods, such as Baal, Ashtaroth, and the Queen of Heaven; sins against the First Commandment; (3) the worship of graven images; a sin against the Second. The sins were of long standing, but the words point specially to the proportions they had assumed in the reign of Manasseh (2 Chron. xxxiii. 1—7).

(17) **Gird up thy loins.**—Be as the messenger who prepares to be swift on his errand, and to go whithersoever he is sent (1 Kings xviii. 46; 2 Kings iv. 29, ix. 1). The vivid image of intense activity re-appears in the New Testament (Luke xii. 35; 1 Pet. i. 13), and has become proverbial in the speech of Christendom.

Be not dismayed.—The repeated calls to courage appear to indicate—like St. Paul's exhortations to Timothy (1 Tim. iv. 12, vi. 13; 2 Tim. ii. 3)—a constitutional timidity. We must remember, as some excuse for this, that the reign of Manasseh had shown that the work of the prophet might easily lead to the fate of the martyr (2 Kings xxi. 16). Even Ezekiel, among the remnant of exiles on the banks of Chebar, needed a like encouragement (Ezek. ii. 6).

Lest I confound thee.—The Hebrew emphasises the command by repeating the same words: *Be not dismayed, lest I dismay thee.*

(18) **I have made thee . . . a defenced city . . .**—Images of strength are heaped one upon another. The prophet is represented as attacked by kings, princes, priests, and people, as the cities of Judah are by the invading armies. But the issue is different. They fall: he will hold out. The iron pillar is that which, rising in the centre of an Eastern house or temple (as, *e.g.,* in Judges xvi. 25; 1 Kings vii. 21), supports the flat roof, and enables it to be used as a terrace or platform on which men may meet. The "brasen walls" probably refer to the practice of fastening plates of copper over the brick or stonework of a fortification.

(19) **I am with thee.**—That thought was in itself enough. The presence, and therefore the protection, of the All-wise and the Almighty was the one condition of safety. Even in its lower sense, "Immanuel," God with us (Isa. vii. 14), was the watchword of every true combatant in God's great army.

II.

(1) The first chapter had given the narrative of the call which had impressed itself indelibly on the prophet's mind. The next five run on as one continuous whole, and, looking to the fact that the

(2) Go and cry in the ears of Jerusa-
lem, saying, Thus saith the LORD; I
remember [1]thee, the kindness of thy
[a]youth, the love of thine espousals,
when thou wentest after me in the
wilderness, in a land *that was* not
sown. (3) Israel *was* holiness unto
the LORD, *and* the firstfruits of his
increase: [b]all that devour him shall
offend; evil shall come upon them,
saith the LORD.
(4) Hear ye the word of the LORD,
O house of Jacob, and all the families
of the house of Israel: (5) Thus saith
the LORD, What iniquity have your
fathers found in me, that they are
gone far from me, and have walked
after vanity, and are become vain?
(6) Neither said they, Where *is* the
LORD that [c]brought us up out of the
land of Egypt, that led us through the
wilderness, through a land of deserts
and of pits, through a land of drought,
and of the shadow of death, through a
land that no man passed through, and
where no man dwelt? (7) And I brought
you into a plentiful country, to eat the
fruit thereof and the goodness thereof;
but when ye entered, ye [d]defiled my
land, and made mine heritage an
abomination. (8) The priests said not,
Where *is* the LORD? and they that

1 Or, *for thy sake.*

a Ezek. 16. 8.

b ch. 12. 14.

c Isa. 63. 9, 11, 13; Hos. 13. 4.

d Ps. 78. 58, & 106. 38.

original record of his prophetic work during the reign of Josiah had been destroyed by Jehoiakim (chap. xxxvi. 23), and was afterwards re-written from memory, it is probable that we have a kind of *précis* of what was then destroyed, with some additions (chap. xxxvi. 32), and possibly some omissions. In chap. iii. 6 we have the name of Josiah definitely mentioned.

(2) **Go and cry . . .**—The scene of the call, was, we may believe, in his home at Anathoth. Now the prophet is sent to begin his work in Jerusalem.

I remember thee.—Literally, *I have remembered for thee.*

The love of thine espousals.—The imagery was one derived, as we find so often in Jeremiah's writings, from the older prophets. It was implied in the "jealous God" of Exod. xx. 5, illustrated by an actual history, which was also a parable, in Hosea i.—iii., and after its use by Jeremiah, expanded more fully by Ezekiel (chap. xvi.). The "espousals" are thought of as coinciding with the great covenant of Exod. xxiv. 8, when the people solemnly entered into the relation to which God called them. Then the bride was ready to follow her lord and husband even in an "unsown land"—the "waste howling wilderness" of Deut. xxxii. 10. The faithfulness of the past is contrasted with the unfaithfulness of the present.

When thou wentest after me.—Literally, *thy going after me.*

(3) **Holiness unto the Lord.**—The thought was that expressed in the inscription on the gold plate worn on the high priest's forehead (Exod. xxviii. 36), and in the term "holy thing" (Lev. xxii. 10; Matt. vii. 6), applied to the consecrated gifts which were the portion of the priests. The prophet was taught that Israel, as a nation, had a priestly character, and was consecrated to the Lord as the "firstfruits" of the great harvest of the world. Compare the use of the same figure in James i. 18; Rom. xi. 16.

All that devour him shall offend.—The imagery of the firstfruits is continued. The Hebrew for the word "offend" is used for transgressions against the ceremonial law in Lev. v. 5, 19; Num. v. 7. Here, however, it is probably better rendered, *shall be condemned,* or *shall be made to suffer,* as in Ps. xxxiv. 21, 22, where the Authorised version has "shall be desolate." Those who devour Israel—the enemies and invaders, the tyrants and oppressors—are guilty as of a sacrilege that will not remain unpunished.

(5) **Vanity.**—In the special sense, as a synonym for idol-worship (Deut. xxxii. 21; 1 Kings xvi. 13). As in the character of a husband wronged by his wife's desertion Jehovah pleads with His people, and asks whether He has failed in anything.

(6) **Neither said they.**—In somewhat of the same tone as in Deut. viii. 15, xxxii. 10, the horrors of the wilderness are painted in vivid colours, to heighten the contrast with the land into which they had been brought. The picture was true of part, but not of the whole, of the region of the wanderings. But the people had forgotten this. There was no seeking for the Lord who had then been so gracious. The question, Where is He? never crossed their thoughts.

(7) **A plentiful country.**—Literally, *a land of Carmel,* that word, as meaning a vine-clad hill, having become a type of plenty. So "the forest of his Carmel," in Isa. xxxvii. 24; elsewhere, as in Isa. x. 18, xxxii. 15, "fruitful." The LXX. treats the word as a proper name, "I brought you unto Carmel."

When ye entered.—The words point to the rapid degeneracy of Israel after the settlement in Canaan, as seen in the false worship and foul crimes of Judges xvii.—xxi. So in Ps. lxxviii. 56—58. Instead of being the pattern nation, the firstfruits of mankind, they sank to the level, or below the level, of the heathen.

(8) **The priests said not . . .**—As throughout the work of Jeremiah and most of the prophets of the Old Testament, that which weighed most heavily on their souls was that those who were called to be guides of the people were themselves the chief agents in the evil. The salt had lost its savour. The light had become darkness. The rebuke, we must remember, came from the lips of one who was himself a priest.

The priests said not, Where is the Lord?—The same failure to seek as that condemned in verse 6. To them, too, all was a routine. Jehovah was absent from their thoughts even in the very act of worship.

They that handle the law.—These, probably, were also of the priestly order, to whom this function was assigned in Deut. xxxiii. 10. The order of non-priestly scribes, in the sense of interpreters of the law, does not appear till after the captivity. Their sin was that they "dealt with the law" as interpreters and judges, and forgot Jehovah who had given it.

The pastors.—Better, *shepherds,* the English "pastors" having gained a too definitely religious connotation. The Hebrew word was general in its

handle the [a]law knew me not: the
pastors also transgressed against me,
and the prophets prophesied by Baal, and
walked after *things that* do not profit.
(9) Wherefore I will yet plead with
you, saith the LORD, and with your
children's children will I plead. (10) For
pass [1]over the isles of Chittim, and
see; and send unto Kedar, and consider
diligently, and see if there be such a
thing. (11) Hath a nation changed *their*
gods, which *are* [b]yet no gods? but my
people have changed their glory for *that
which* doth not profit. (12) Be astonished,
O ye heavens, at this, and be horribly
afraid, be ye very desolate, saith the
LORD. (13) For my people have com-
mitted two evils; they have forsaken
me the [c]fountain of living waters, *and*
hewed them out cisterns, broken cis-
terns, that can hold no water.
(14) *Is* Israel a servant? *is* he a home-
born *slave?* why is he [2]spoiled? (15) The
young lions roared upon him, *and* [3]yelled,
and they made his land waste: his cities
are burned without inhabitant. (16) Also
the children of Noph and Tahapanes
[4]have broken the crown of thy head.
(17) Hast thou not procured this unto
thyself, in that thou hast forsaken the

a Rom. 2. 20.

1 Or, *over to.*

b ch. 16. 20.

c Ps. 36. 9; ch. 17. 13, & 18. 14.

2 Heb., become a *spoil?*

3 Heb., *gave out their voice.*

4 Or, *feed on thy crown,* Deut. 33. 12; Isa. 8. 8.

---

significance, but in its Old Testament use was applied chiefly to civil rulers, as in Ps. lxxviii. 71; 1 Kings xxii. 17. Even in Ezek. xxxiv., where the spiritual aspect of rule is most prominent, the contrast between the false shepherds and the one true shepherd of the house of David (verse 23) shows that the kingly, not the priestly, office was in the prophet's mind.

The prophets prophesied by Baal.—The precise form of the sin described was probably connected with the oracular power ascribed to Baal-zebub, as in 2 Kings i. 2. The evil was of long standing. It was one of the sins of the people in Isaiah's time that they were "soothsayers like the Philistines" (Isa. ii. 6). When Ahab first introduced the Phœnician worship, it was by the prophets rather than the priests of Baal that the new *cultus* was propagated (1 Kings xviii. 19, xxii. 6).

Things that do not profit.—The word had acquired an almost proverbial force as applied to idols (1 Sam. xii. 21; Isa. xliv. 9). So the phrase is repeated in verse 11.

(9) **I will yet plead with you.**—We hear, as it were, the echo of the words of Hosea ii. 2. The injured lord and husband will appear as the accuser of the faithless bride, and set forth her guilt as in an indictment.

(10) **Pass over the isles . . .**—Chittim is named as being, from the prophet's point of view, the furthest country in the west (Gen. x. 4; Num. xxiv. 24), Kedar (Gen. xxv. 13; Ps. cxx. 5) in the east. The whole earth might be searched without finding a parallel to the guilt of Israel.

(11) **Hath a nation . . .**—Emphatically a heathen "nation," as contrasted with the "people" of Jehovah. They were faithful to their false gods; Israel was unfaithful to the true. The words "changed their glory" find an echo in Rom. i. 23, though here they express the thought that the worship of Jehovah was the true glory of Israel as a people, and that they had wilfully abandoned it.

(12) **Be astonished, O ye heavens.**—The adjuration had been made familiar by a like utterance in Isa. i. 2; Deut. xxxii. i. "Astonished"—in the old sense, "thunder-stricken," stupefied. The whole universe is thought of as shocked and startled at the offence against its Creator.

(13) **The fountain of living waters.**—The word rendered "well," as in Prov. x. 11, xviii. 4; "fountain," as in Ps. xxxvi. 9, is used of water flowing from the rock. The "cistern," on the other hand, was a tank for surface water. A word identical in sound and meaning, though differently spelt, is variously rendered by "pit," "well," or "cistern."

(14) **Is Israel a servant?**—The word "servant," we must remember, had become, through its frequent use in Isaiah (xx. 3, xli. 8, *et al.*), a word not of shame, but honour; and of all servants, he who was born in the house—as in the case of Eleazar (Gen. xv. 3)—occupied the most honourable place, nearest to a son. The point of the question is accordingly not "Is Israel become a slave," kidnapped, as it were, and spoiled, but rather this: "Is Israel the servant of Jehovah, as one born in His house? Why, then, is he treated as one with no master to protect him?"

(15) **The young lions roared . . .**—The real answer to the question, that Israel had forsaken its true master, is given in verse 17. Here it is implied in the description of what the runaway slave had suffered. Lions had attacked him; not figuratively only, as symbolising invaders, but in the most literal sense, they had made his land waste (2 Kings xvii. 25).

Are burned.—Better, *levelled with the ground.*

(16) **Also the children of Noph . . .**—We pass from the language of poetry to that of history, and the actual enemies of Israel appear on the scene, not as the threatening danger in the north, but in the far south. The words indicate that the prophet set himself from the first, as Isaiah had done (Isa. xxxi. 1), against the policy of an Egyptian alliance. The LXX. translators, following, we must believe, an Egyptian tradition, identify the Hebrew Noph with Memphis in northern Egypt; later critics, with Napata in the south. Its conjunction with Tahapanes, the Daphnæ of the Greeks, which was on the Pelusiac mouth of the Nile, and on the frontier, seems in favour of the former view.

Have broken.—More accurately, *shall feed on, lay waste, depasture,* so as to produce baldness. Baldness among the Jews, as with other Eastern nations, was a shame and reproach (Isa. iii. 24, xv. 2, xxii. 12; 2 Kings ii. 23), and was therefore a natural symbol of the ignominy and ruin of a people.

(17) **Hast thou not procured this . . . ?**—The secret cause of the calamities is brought to light. Jehovah was leading Israel, but Israel has chosen another path, and so has procured sorrow upon sorrow to himself. The "way" here is scarcely the literal path through the wilderness, but much rather the true way of life.

LORD thy God, when he led thee by
the way? (18) And now what hast thou
to do in the way of Egypt, to drink the
waters of Sihor? or what hast thou to
do in the way of Assyria, to drink the
waters of the river? (19) Thine own
[a]wickedness shall correct thee, and thy
backslidings shall reprove thee: know
therefore and see that *it is* an evil *thing*
and bitter, that thou hast forsaken the
LORD thy God, and that my fear *is* not
in thee, saith the Lord GOD of hosts.
(20) For of old time I have broken thy
yoke, *and* burst thy bands; and thou
saidst, I will not [1]transgress; when
[b]upon every high hill and under every
green tree thou wanderest, playing the
harlot. (21) Yet I had [c]planted thee a
noble vine, wholly a right seed: how
then art thou turned into the degener-
ate plant of a strange vine unto me?
(22) For though thou [d]wash thee with
nitre, and take thee much sope, *yet*
thine iniquity is marked before me,
saith the Lord GOD. (23) How canst
thou say, I am not polluted, I have not
gone after Baalim? see thy way in the
valley, know what thou hast done: [2]*thou*

a Isa. 3. 9; Hos. 5. 5.

1 Or, *serve.*

b Isa. 57. 5, 7; ch. 3. 6.

c Ex. 15. 17; Ps. 44. 2, & 80. 8; Isa. 5. 1, &c.; Matt. 21. 33; Mark 12. 1; Luke 20. 9.

d Job 9. 30.

2 Or, *O swift dromedary.*

---

(18) **In the way of Egypt . . .?**—The rebuke becomes more and more specific. Great rivers were, in the poetry of the prophets, the natural symbols of the kingdoms through which they flowed. Sihor (= the turbid or muddy river) here, and in Isa. xxiii. 3 the Nile (though in Josh. xiii. 3 it stands for the border stream between Palestine and Egypt), represented Egypt. The "river," or "flood," needing no other name as pre-eminent in its greatness (comp. Josh. xxiv. 14, 15), the Euphrates, stood for Assyria (comp. Isa. viii. 7). The words point to the tendency to court the alliance now of one, now of the other of the great kingdoms of the world. The policy was no new one. Menahem in Israel, Ahaz in Judah, had courted Assyria (2 Kings xv. 19, xvi. 7, 8); Hezekiah, Babylon (Isa. xxxix.); Hoshea had sought help from Egypt (2 Kings xvii. 4). The prophet Hosea had rebuked both policies (v. 13, vii. 11, viii. 9). Even under Hezekiah there was a party seeking the Egyptian alliance (Isa. xviii., xix., xxxi. Under Manasseh and Amon that party was in power, and the very name of the latter probably bears witness to its influence. Josiah kept as far as possible the position of a neutral, but, when forced into action, and probably guided by the counsels of Hilkiah, resisted the advance of Pharaoh-nechoh (2 Kings xxiii. 29). On his death the Egyptian party again gained ground under Jehoiakim, while Jeremiah, opposing its strength, urged the wisdom of accepting the guidance of events, and submitting to the Chaldæans (so far continuing the line of action adopted by Hezekiah), and ultimately was accused of deserting his own people and "falling away" to their oppressors (chap. xxxvii. 13).

(19) **Thine own wickedness.**—The strain is now of a higher mood, and rises from what is local and temporary to the eternal law of retribution. Punishment comes as the natural consequence of sins. Our "pleasant vices" become "whips to scourge us." The "backslidings" of Israel, in courting the favour of foreign states by adopting their creed and worship, shall involve her in ever fresh calamities.

(20) **I have broken thy yoke.**—Better, with the LXX. and Vulg., *thou hast broken thy yoke—i.e.*, cast off all allegiance and restraint. The Authorised Version, which follows the received Hebrew reading, may, however, be understood as referring to the deliverance of Israel from their Egyptian bondage.

Thou saidst, I will not transgress.—Perhaps, following a various reading adopted by the LXX., Vulg., and Luther, *I will not serve.* The words so taken paint vividly the wilful defiance of the rebellious nation. It threw off its allegiance. If we retain the Authorised version rendering, it would be better to take the verb in the present, *I transgress not,* as expressing a like defiance.

When.—Better, *for,* as giving an illustration of the rebellious temper. The "high hill" and the "green tree" point to the localities of idol-worship—the "high places" that meet us so frequently in 1 and 2 Kings, the "tops of the mountains," and the "oaks and poplars and elms" of Hosea iv. 13. Tree-worship in Judæa, as elsewhere, appears to have exercised a wonderful power of fascination, and though the word translated "grove" (*Asherah*) has not that meaning, it was probably connected with the same *cultus.*

Playing the harlot.—Literally, *laying thyself down.* The idolatrous prostration was as an act of spiritual prostitution, often, as in the orgiastic worship of Baal and Ashtaroth, united with actual impurity.

(21) **A noble vine.**—Literally, *a Sorek vine.* Elsewhere rendered *choice* or *choicest* (Gen. xlix. 11; Isa. v. 2). The word "Sorek" points primarily to the dark purple of the grape, and then to the valley of Sorek, between Ascalon and Gaza (Judges xvi. 4).

Wholly a right seed.—Literally, *a seed of truth,* parallel with the "good seed" in the Parable of the Tares. Here, however, as in Isa. v. 1—7, which Jeremiah seems to have in his mind, stress is laid not on the mingling of the evil with the good, but on the degeneration which had changed the character of that which God had planted.

Art thou turned . . .?—Better, *hast thou changed thyself . . .?*

Plant.—Better, *branches.*

(22) **Nitre.**—The mineral alkali found in the natron lakes of Egypt that took their name from it. The Hebrew word *nether* is the origin of the Greek and English words. (Comp. Prov. xxv. 20.)

Sope.—Not the compounds of alkali and oil or fat now known by the name, but the potash or alkali, obtained from the ashes of plants, which was used by itself as a powerful detergent. The thought is the same as that of Job ix. 30, and, we may add, as that of *Macbeth,* Act ii., sc. 2:—

> "Will all great Neptune's ocean wash this blood
> Clean from my hand? No; this my hand will rather
> The multitudinous seas incarnadine,
> Making the green one red."

The guilt was too strongly "marked," too "deep-dyed in grain" to be removed by any outward palliatives.

(23) **How canst thou say . . .?**—The prophet hears, as it were, the voice of the accused criminal, with its plea of "not guilty." Had not the worship

art a swift dromedary traversing her
ways; (24) [1]a wild ass [2]used to the
wilderness, *that* snuffeth up the wind
at [3]her pleasure; in her occasion who
can [4]turn her away? all they that seek
her will not weary themselves; in her
month they shall find her. (25) With-
hold thy foot from being unshod, and
thy throat from thirst: but thou saidst,
[5]There is no hope: no; for I have loved
strangers, and after them will I go.

(26) As the thief is ashamed when he is
found, so is the house of Israel ashamed;
they, their kings, their princes, and their
priests, and their prophets, (27) saying
to a stock, Thou *art* my father; and to
a stone, Thou hast [6]brought me forth:
for they have turned [7]*their* back unto
me, and not *their* face: but in the time
of their [a]trouble they will say, Arise,
and save us. (28) But where *are* thy
gods that thou hast made thee? let
them arise, if they [b]can save thee in
the time of thy [8]trouble: for [c]*according
to* the number of thy cities are thy
gods, O Judah. (29) Wherefore will
ye plead with me? ye all have trans-
gressed against me, saith the LORD.

1 Or, *O wild ass, &c.*
2 Heb., *taught.*
3 Heb., *the desire of her heart.*
4 Or, *reverse it?*
5 Or, *Is the case desperate?*
6 Or, *begotten me.*
7 Heb., *the hinder part of the neck.*
a Isa. 26. 16.
b Isa. 45. 20.
8 Heb., *evil.*
c ch. 11 13.

---

of Jehovah been restored by Josiah? Had he not, acting on Hilkiah's counsels, suppressed Baal-worship (2 Kings xxiii. 4, 5; 2 Chron. xxxiv. 4)? The answer to such pleas is to point to the rites that were still practised openly or in secret. In the "valley" of Ben-Hinnom, which Josiah had defiled (2 Kings xxiii. 10), the horrid ritual of Molech (Lev. xviii. 21, xx. 2) was still in use (chap. vii. 31), reviving, we may believe, on the death of Josiah; and this, though not actually the worship of Baal, was at least as evil, and probably, in the confluence of many forms of worship which marked the last days of the monarchy of Judah, was closely associated and practically identified with it, both by the prophet and the people (chaps. xix. 5, xxxii. 35).

A swift dromedary.—Better, *she-camel,* the Hebrew word not pointing to any specific difference. The words paint with an almost terrible vividness the eager, restless state of the daughter of Zion in its harlot-like lust for the false gods of the heathen. The female camel, in the uncontrollable violence of its brute passion, moving to and fro with panting eagerness—that was now the fit image for her who had once been the betrothed of Jehovah.

(24) **A wild ass . . .**—One image of animal desire suggests another, and the "wild ass" appears (as in the Hebrew of Gen. xvi. 12; Job xi. 12, xxxix. 5) as even a stronger type of passion that defies control. The description is startling in its boldness, but has a parallel in that of Virgil (*Georg.* iii. 250).

That snuffeth up the wind at her pleasure.—Better, *in the desire of her heart,* as it bears to her the scent that draws her on. The "occasion" and the "month" are, of course, the season when the stimulus of animal desire is strongest. There is no need for the stallion to seek her with a weary search, she presents herself and pursues him. So there was in Israel what we should describe as a mania for the hateful worship of the heathen.

(25) **Withhold thy foot.**—From the brute types of passion the prophet passes to the human. Here he has Hosea as giving a prototype (ii. 5, 7), perhaps also Isaiah (xxiii. 15, 16). The picture may probably enough have been drawn from the life, but that sketched in Prov. vii. 10—23 may well have supplied the outline. Jehovah, as her true husband, bids the apostate wife to refrain for very shame from acting as the harlot, rushing barefoot into the streets, panting, as with a thirst that craves to be quenched, for the gratification of her desires. The "unshod" may possibly refer to one feature of the worship of Baal or Ashtaroth, men and women taking off their shoes when they entered into their temples, as being holy ground (Exod. iii. 5), and joining in orgiastic dances.

Thou saidst, There is no hope: no.—Here also we find a parallel to the thought and language of Hosea. There the one effectual remedy for the evil into which the apostate wife had fallen was to speak to her heart, and to open the door of hope (Hosea ii. 14, 15). Now the malignity of the evil is shown by the loss of all hope of recovery in returning to Jehovah:—

> "Small sins the heart first desecrate,
> At last despair persuades to great."

Like Gomer, she will go after her "lovers," though they are "strangers," as if they were her only protectors. It would seem, from the recurrence of the phrase in chap. xviii. 12, as if it were the formula of a despairing fatalism, like the proverb of the fathers eating sour grapes (chap. xxxi. 29, 30; Ezek. xviii. 2).

(26) **As the thief . . .**—The words point to the sense of shame as already felt, and as therefore bringing with it the possibility of repentance. Once they gloried in their false worship; now they feel as if detected in a crime. Conscience had once again been roused into activity.

(27) **Saying to a stock . . .**—The "stock" and the "stone" represent respectively the images of wood and marble. In Hebrew the latter word is feminine, and thus determines the parts assigned to them in the figurative parentage.

To a stock, Thou art my father.—Literally, *to a tree.* The words seem as if they were an actual quotation from the hymns of the idolatrous ritual.

In the time of their trouble.—So in Hosea (ii., iii.) it is the discipline of suffering that leads the adulterous wife to repentance. In times of trouble and dismay those who had before turned their backs on Jehovah shall seek Him with outstretched hands, and the cry for help. The prophet half implies that then it may be too late till chastisement has done its perfect work.

(28) **Where are thy gods . . . ?**—The question is asked in indignant scorn. "Thou madest the gods, and yet they cannot profit thee." Though every city had its tutelary deity, there was none found to deliver. The LXX. adds, as in chap. xi. 13, the words "according to the number of the streets in Jerusalem they sacrificed to Baal."

(29) **Wherefore will ye plead with me?**—The reply of the accuser to the false pleas of the accused. The transgression was too open to be glossed over. No plea was available but that of a full confession of the guilt into which Israel had fallen.

(30) In vain have I [a]smitten your chil-
dren; they received no correction:
your own sword hath [b]devoured your
prophets, like a destroying lion.
(31) O generation, see ye the word of
the LORD. [c]Have I been a wilderness
unto Israel? a land of darkness? where-
fore say my people, [1]We are lords; we
will come no more unto thee? (32) Can
a maid forget her ornaments, *or* a
bride her attire? yet my people have
forgotten me days without number.
(33) Why trimmest thou thy way to seek
love? therefore hast thou also taught
the wicked ones thy ways. (34) Also in
thy skirts is found the blood of the
souls of the poor innocents: I have
not found it by [2]secret search, but upon
all these. (35) Yet thou sayest, Because
I am innocent, surely his anger shall
turn from me. Behold, I will plead
with thee, because thou sayest, I have
not sinned. (36) Why gaddest thou
about so much to change thy way?
thou also shalt be ashamed of Egypt,
as thou wast ashamed of Assyria.
(37) Yea, thou shalt go forth from him,
and thine hands upon thine head: for
the LORD hath rejected thy confidences,
and thou shalt not prosper in them.

CHAPTER III.—(1) [3]They say, If a
man put away his wife, and she go from
him, and become another man's, [d]shall

a Isa. 9. 13; ch. 5. 3.

b Matt. 23. 29, &c.

c ver. 5.

1 Heb., *We have dominion.*

2 Heb., *digging.*

3 Heb., *Saying.*

d Deut. 24. 4.

---

(30) **Your own sword hath devoured your prophets.**—So in the long reign of Manasseh, the prophets who rebuked him had to do so at the risk of their lives. Isaiah, as the tradition ran, had been foremost among the sufferers. Much innocent blood had been shed from one end to another of Jerusalem (2 Kings xxi. 11—16).

(31) **O generation, see ye.**—The pronoun occupies a different position in the Hebrew, "*O generation, you, I mean, see ye.*" The prophet speaks to the men who are actually his contemporaries. *They* are to look to the word of the Lord. Has He been to them as a waste land, a land of thick darkness (literally, according to one interpretation, *darkness of Jah*, in the sense of intensity), that they are thus unmindful of Him? So in Song of Sol. viii. 6 we have "flame of Jah," as representing the Hebrew, in the margin, and "very vehement flame" in the text, of the Authorised version.

We are lords.—Better, *We rove at will*, as in Gen. xxvii. 40, where, however, the Authorised version gives "when thou shalt have the dominion." The sense is practically the same. Israel claims the power to do as she likes.

(32) **Or a bride her attire.**—The word is rendered "headbands" in Isa. iii. 20, but here it probably means the "girdle" which formed the special distinction of the wife as contrasted with the maiden. Such a girdle, like the marriage ring with us, would be treasured by the bride all her life long. Even the outward memorial of her union with her husband would be dear to her. But Israel had forgotten her lord and husband Himself.

(33) **Why trimmest thou thy way . . . ?**—The verb is the same as that rendered "amend" in chap. vii. 3, 5, and was probably often on the lips of those who made a show of reformation. Here it is used with a scornful irony, "What means this reform, this show of amendment of thy ways, which leads only to a further indulgence in adulterous love?"

Hast thou also taught the wicked ones thy ways.—Better, *hast thou also taught thy ways wickednesses.* The professed change for the better was really for the worse.

(34) **Also in thy skirts . . .**—The general meaning is clear, and points to the guilt of Israel in offering her children—the "poor innocents"—in horrid sacrifice to Molech; perhaps, also, to her maltreatment of the prophets. Their "blood" is on the "skirts" of her raiment; perhaps, if we take another reading, on the "palms" of her hands. The last clause is, however, obscure enough. We have to choose, according to variations of reading and construction, between (1) *I have not found it as by secret search* (literally, *by digging*, as men dig through the wall of a house in search of plunder), *but under every oak* or *terebinth*, or, more probably, as in the Authorised version, *upon all these—i.e.*, the sin was patent, flagrant, everywhere; and (2) *Thou didst not find them* (those who had been put to death) *in the place of breaking through—i.e., in the act of the robber that would have deserved death* (Exod. xxii. 2; Job xxiv. 16); *but because of all this—i.e.*, thou didst slay them through thy passion for idolatry. Of these (1) commends itself most.

(35) **Yet thou sayest . . .**—Once again we have the equivocating plea of the accused. She takes up the word that had been used by the accuser: "You speak of the innocents; *I, too, am innocent. His anger has turned away from me.* Here, as in verse 33, there is an implied reference to the partial reformation under Josiah. The accuser retorts, and renews his pleadings against her. Confession might have led to forgiveness, but this denial of guilt excluded it, and was the token of a fatal blindness (comp. 1 John i. 8).

(36) **Why gaddest thou . . . ?**—The vigorous English expresses well, perhaps even with some added force, the frequentative force of the Hebrew. What meant this perpetual change of policy, this shifting of alliances? Shame and confusion should follow from the alliance with Nechoh, as it had followed from that with Tiglath-pileser (2 Kings xvi. 10; 2 Chron. xxviii. 20).

(37) **From him.**—Better, *from it, sc.*, from Egypt as a people.

Thine hands upon thine head.—The outward sign of depression and despair (2 Sam. xiii. 19).

Thy confidences.—*i.e.*, the grounds or objects of thy confidence.

III.

(1) The parable of the guilty wife who is condemned in spite of all her denials is carried out to its logical results.

They say.—Better, *So to speak*, as introducing a new application of the figure. The direct reference

he return unto her again? shall not
that land be greatly polluted? but thou
hast played the harlot with many lovers;
yet return again to me, saith the LORD.
(2) Lift up thine eyes unto the high
places, and see where thou hast not
been lien with. In the ways hast thou
sat for them, as the Arabian in the
wilderness; and thou hast polluted the
land with thy whoredoms and with thy
wickedness. (3) Therefore the [a]showers
have been withholden, and there hath
been no latter rain; and thou hadst a
[b]whore's forehead, thou refusedst to be
ashamed. (4) Wilt thou not from this
time cry unto me, My father, thou *art*
the guide of my youth? (5) Will he
reserve *his anger* for ever? will he keep
it to the end? Behold, thou hast
spoken and done evil things as thou
couldest.

(6) The LORD said also unto me in
the days of Josiah the king, Hast thou
seen *that* which backsliding Israel hath
done? she is [c]gone up upon every
high mountain and under every green

a Deut. 28. 24; ch. 9. 12.
b ch. 6. 15.
B. C. cir. 612.
c ch. 2. 20.

---

is to Deut. xxiv. 4, which forbade the return to the past husband as an abomination, a law which the recent discovery of the Book of the Law (2 Kings xxii. 10, 11) had probably brought into prominence. But there is also an obvious allusion to the like imagery in Hosea. There the prophet had done, literally or in parable, what the law had forbidden (Hos. ii. 16, iii. 3), and so had held out the possibility of return and the hope of pardon. Jeremiah has to play a sterner part, and to make the apostate adulteress at least feel that she had sinned too deeply to have any claims to forgiveness. It might seem as if Jehovah could not now return to the love of His espousals, and make her what she once had been.

Yet return again to me, saith the Lord.—The words sound in the English like a gracious invitation, and—in spite of the authority of many interpreters who take it as an indignant exclamation, *and return to me!* an invitation given in irony, and so equivalent to rejection, as though that return were out of the question—it must, I think, be so taken. The prophet has, as we have seen, the history of Hosea in his mind, where there had been such a call to return (Hos. ii. 19, iii. 3), and actually refers to it and repeats it in verses 7, 12, 14. It surely implies a want of insight into the character of Jeremiah to suppose that he ever came before men as proclaiming an irrevocable condemnation, excluding the possibility of repentance.

(2) **Lift up thine eyes.**—The consciousness of guilt was, however, the only foundation of repentance, and the prophet's work, therefore, in very tenderness, is to paint that guilt in the darkest colours possible. Still keeping to the parable of the faithless wife, he bids Israel, as such, to look to the "high places" that have witnessed her adulteries with those other lords for whom she had forsaken Jehovah. Like the harlots of the east, she had sat by the wayside, as Tamar had done (Gen. xxxviii. 14; comp. also Prov. vii. 12; Ezek. xvi. 31), not so much courted by her paramours as courting them.

As the Arabian in the wilderness.—The Arabian is chosen as the representative of the lawless predatory tribes of the desert. As they, like the modern Bedouins, lay in ambush, waiting eagerly for their victims, so had the harlot Israel laid wait for her lovers, and so the land had been polluted.

(3) **Therefore the showers . . .**—Outward calamities were looked upon as chastisements for these sins. There had apparently been a severe drought in the reign of Josiah (chap. ix. 12, xxv. 1—6). There had been no showers in spring, no "latter rain" in autumn. So like calamities are described in Amos iv. 7; Haggai i. 11; Joel i. 18—20. The influence of the newly-discovered book of Deuteronomy (2 Chron. xxxiv. 14; 2 Kings xxii. 8) had doubtless given a fresh emphasis to this view of natural disasters.

(4) **Wilt thou not from this time cry unto me . . . ?**—Better, *Hast thou not from this time cried unto me . . . ?* The prophet paints with a stern irony the parade of the surface repentance of Josiah's reign. There had been a pathetic appeal to God as the forgiving husband of the faithless wife, but not the less had the wife returned to her wickedness.

Guide.—The same word as in Prov. ii. 17; the "chief friend," as applied to the husband.

(5) **Will he reserve his anger for ever . . . ?**—The questions were such as might well be asked in the first burst of sorrowing though superficial repentance. The implied answer was in the negative, "No, He will not keep His anger to the end." Yet, so far, facts were against that yearning hope. It will be noted that the word "anger" is not in the Hebrew. It is, however, rightly inserted, after the precedent of Nah. i. 2; Ps. ciii. 9. The words seem, indeed, almost a quotation from the latter, and verses 4 and 5 may probably be looked on as cited from the penitential litanies in which the people had joined, and which were too soon followed by a return to the old evils (chap. ii. 1—13).

Thou hast spoken and done evil things as thou couldest.—*i.e.*, resolutely and obstinately. That pathetic appeal to the mercy and love of Jehovah was followed by no amendment, but by a return to evil. Here the first prophecy, as reproduced from memory, ends, and the next verse begins a separate discourse.

(6) **The Lord said also unto me . . .**—The main point of the second prophecy (we might almost call it sermon), delivered, like the former, under Josiah, is the comparison of the guilt of the two kingdoms of Israel and Judah. The latter had been looking on the former with contemptuous scorn. She is now taught—the same imagery being continued that had begun in the first discourse—that her guilt is by far the greater of the two.

Backsliding Israel.—The epithet strikes the keynote of all that follows, and is, as it were, the text of the sermon. The force of the Hebrew is stronger than that of the English, and implies actual "apostasy," being, indeed, a substantive rather than an adjective. Apostasy is, as it were, personified in Israel; she is the *renegade* sister.

She is gone up.—Better, *she goes, i.e.*, is going continually.

tree, and there hath played the harlot.
(7) And I said after she had done all
these *things*, Turn thou unto me. But
she returned not. And her treacherous
sister Judah saw *it*. (8) And I saw,
when for all the causes whereby back-
sliding Israel committed adultery I had
put her away, and given her a bill
of divorce; yet her treacherous sister
Judah feared not, but went and played
the harlot also. (9) And it came to pass
through the [1]lightness of her whoredom,
that she defiled the land, and committed
adultery with stones and with stocks.
(10) And yet for all this her treacherous
sister Judah hath not turned unto me
with her whole heart, but [2]feignedly,
saith the LORD.
(11) And the LORD said unto me, The
backsliding Israel hath justified her-
self more than treacherous Judah.
(12) Go and proclaim these words to-
ward the north, and say, Return, thou
backsliding Israel, saith the LORD; *and*
I will not cause mine anger to fall upon
you: for I *am* [a]merciful, saith the LORD,
and I will not keep *anger* for ever.
(13) Only acknowledge thine iniquity,
that thou hast transgressed against the
LORD thy God, and hast scattered thy
ways to the strangers under every
green tree, and ye have not obeyed
my voice, saith the LORD. (14) Turn, O
backsliding children, saith the LORD;
for I am married unto you: and I will
take you one of a city, and two of a
family, and I will bring you to Zion:
(15) and I will give you [b]pastors ac-
cording to mine heart, which shall
feed you with knowledge and under-

1 Or, *fame*.

2 Heb., *in falsehood*.

a Ps. 86. 15; & 103. 8, 9.

b ch. 23. 4.

---

(7) **And I said . . .**—The call to Israel to return had been slighted, and Judah, the *traitress* or faithless, "one with falsehood," had not taken warning from the sin or its punishment.

Turn thou unto me.—The verb may be either the second or third person, *I said, thou shalt return;* or, *I said, she will return,* as expressing a hope rather than a direct return. The latter seems, on the whole, the preferable rendering.

(8) **And I saw, when for all the causes.**—Better, perhaps (following a conjectural emendation, which gives a much better sense), *And she saw that for all the causes.* The technical fulness of the words suggests the thought that they were actually the customary formula with which every writing of divorcement began, recapitulating the offences which were alleged by the husband against the wife. The actual repudiation consisted, of course, in the bitter exile and loss of national life, which Hosea (ii. 1—13) had predicted under a like figure. Judah had witnessed the sin and the punishment, and yet was following in the same path.

(9) **The lightness of her whoredom.**—Lightness in the ethical sense of "levity." Apostasy was treated once more as if it had been a light thing (1 Kings xvi. 31). The word is, however, very variously interpreted, and the meaning of "voice," or "cry," in the sense in which the "cry" of Sodom and Gomorrah was great (Gen. xviii. 20), seems more satisfactory. On "stones" and "stocks," see Note on chap. ii. 27.

(10) **And yet for all this . . .**—Judah was so far worse than Israel that there had been a simulated repentance, as in the reformations under Hezekiah and Josiah, but it was not with the whole heart and soul, but "feignedly," or, more literally, *with a lie.*

(11) **Hath justified herself.**—Literally, *hath justified her soul,* has put in a better plea in her defence. The *renegade* was better than the *traitress.* Even open rebellion was better than hypocrisy, as the publicans and sinners in the Gospel story were better than the Pharisees (Matt. xxi. 31).

(12) **Toward the north.**—The prophet utters his message as towards the far land of Assyria and the cities of the Medes to which the ten tribes of Israel had been carried away captive (2 Kings xvii. 6, 23). He had a word of glad tidings for the far-off exiles.

Return, thou backsliding Israel.—It is hard to reproduce the pathetic assonance of the original, "*Shubah, mashubah,*"—*turn back, thou that hast turned away; return, thou renegade.*

I will not cause mine anger to fall upon you.—Literally, *my face;* the face so awful in its wrath.

I will not keep anger for ever.—With perhaps a latent reference to the hope held out in Hosea iii. 5, and to the words which Judah had uttered in her hypocrisy (verse 5), but which were truer of Israel.

(13) **Only acknowledge . . .**—This was the one sufficient, indispensable condition of pardon—the confession that kept nothing back, and made no vain excuses.

Hast scattered thy ways.—The phrase is a strong one, *thou hast left traces of thy way everywhere, i.e.,* hast gone this way and that in search of new and alien forms of worship. The "green tree" as before (chap. ii. 20) was the familiar scene of the hateful worship.

(14) **Turn, O backsliding children.**—In his desire to individualise his call to repentance, the prophet drops his parable, or rather combines the sign and the thing signified, with the same assonance as before—*turn back, ye children who have turned away.*

I am married unto you.—The tender pity of Jehovah leads Him to offer pardon even to the adulterous wife. Jeremiah had learned, in all their fulness, the lessons of Hosea i.—iii.

One of a city, and two of a family.—The latter word is the wider in its range of the two—a clan, or tribe, that might embrace many cities. The limitation to the "one" and the "two" is after the manner of Isaiah's reference (i. 9) to the "remnant" that should be saved, and reminds of the "ten righteous men" who might have saved the cities of the plain (Gen. xviii. 32).

(15) **Pastors.**—As in chap. ii. 8, of kings and rulers, not of priests. Compare chap. xxiii. 1—5. The phrase "according to mine heart" brings David to our thoughts (1 Sam. xiii. 14). There should be a return to the true pattern of the ideal ruler. In the "knowledge and understanding" we have an echo from Isa. xi. 1—4.

standing. (16) And it shall come to pass,
when ye be multiplied and increased in
the land, in those days, saith the LORD,
they shall say no more, The ark of the
covenant of the LORD: neither shall it
[1]come to mind: neither shall they re-
member it; neither shall they visit *it;*
neither shall [2]*that* be done any more.
(17) At that time they shall call Jeru-
salem the throne of the LORD; and all
the nations shall be gathered unto it,
to the name of the LORD, to Jerusalem:
neither shall they walk any more after
the [3]imagination of their evil heart.
(18) In those days the house of Judah
shall walk [4]with the house of Israel,
and they shall come together out of
the land of the north to the land that
I have [5]given for an inheritance unto
your fathers. (19) But I said, How shall
I put thee among the children, and give
thee a [6]pleasant land, [7]a goodly heritage
of the hosts of nations? and I said,
Thou shalt call me, My father; and
shalt not turn away [8]from me.
(20) Surely *as* a wife treacherously de-

1 Heb., *come upon the heart.*
2 Or, *it be magnified.*
3 Or, *stubbornness.*
4 Or, *to.*
5 Or, *caused your fathers to possess.*
6 Heb., *land of desire.*
7 Heb., *an heritage of glory,* or, *beauty.*
8 Heb., *from after me.*

---

(16) **In those days.**—No time had been named, but the phrase had become familiar for the far-off better time of the true king of the Messianic kingdom.

They shall say no more, The ark of the covenant of the Lord.—Noteworthy both for its exceeding boldness and as containing the germ, or more than the germ, of the great thought of the New Covenant developed in chap. xxxi. 31. The ark, the very centre of the worship of Israel, the symbol and, it might seem, more than the symbol, of the Divine presence, that, too, should pass away, as the brasen serpent had become Nehushtan (2 Kings xviii. 4), and take its place as belonging only to the past. Foremost among the prophets was Jeremiah to perceive and proclaim that

"God fulfils Himself in many ways."

The legend of 2 Macc. ii. 4, 5, that Jeremiah had hidden the tabernacle and the ark in a cave that they might be restored in the latter days, presents a singular contrast to the higher thoughts of the prophet.

Neither shall it come to mind.—Literally, *come upon the heart,* which throughout the Old Testament implies the intellect rather than the affections.

Neither shall they visit it.—Better, *shall they miss it,* as men miss what they value. The words probably refer to the feelings with which the ark had been restored to its place by Josiah (2 Chron. xxxv. 3) after its displacement by Manasseh (2 Chron. xxxiii. 7).

Neither shall that be done any more.—Better, *neither shall it* [*the ark*] *be made any more.* It shall be left to decay and perish, and none shall care to reconstruct it. The words had, of course, a fulfilment in the ritual of the second Temple, where there was no ark in the Holy of Holies, and that loss was probably what Jeremiah foresaw most clearly, and for which he sought to prepare his people, as the writer of the Epistle to the Hebrews (viii. 13) did to prepare those of his time for the more entire destruction of the Temple and its worship. But even within this horizon the thought was bold in itself and pregnant with yet greater truths.

(17) **They shall call Jerusalem the throne of the Lord.**—Up to Jeremiah's time that title, "the throne of God," though the language of the Old Testament had referred it to the "heavens" (Ps. xi. 4, ciii. 19), had probably been applied, in popular language, to the ark where the Lord "dwelt between the cherubim" (1 Sam. iv. 4; 2 Kings xix. 15). The prophet extends it to the whole city, in that future of which he was doubtless thinking. To him, as to Micah (iv. 1, 2) and Isaiah (ii. 1—3), there came a vision of the holy city as the centre of the divine Kingdom. It was not given to him to see what even the Apostles were slow to understand, that there is no holy city upon earth, and that his hopes would only be fulfilled in the heavenly Jerusalem which is the Church or family of God.

The imagination.—Better, *stubbornness,* as in the margin.

(18) **In those days . . .**—As with Isaiah (xi. 13), so with Jeremiah, the hope, however distant, of national reformation was bound up with that of a restoration of national unity. The healing of the long-standing breach between Israel and Judah, coeval almost with the commencement of Israel as a people, was to be the glory of the Messiah's kingdom.

Out of the land of the north.—The thoughts of the prophet turn chiefly to the land of the exile of the ten tribes; but his words imply that he foresees a like exile also in the north for Judah. In that far-off land the house of Judah shall walk *to* (rather than *with*) the house of Israel, seeking its alliance, asking for reconciliation, and both should once again dwell in the land of their inheritance.

(19) **But I said.**—Better, *And I said.* There is no contrast with what precedes. The speaker is, of course, Jehovah. The *How shall I put thee!* is an exclamation rather than a question, the utterance of a promise as with an intensity of affirmation. Special stress is laid on the pronoun "I." The words have been rendered by some commentators, following the Targum, *How shall I clothe thee with children?*

A pleasant land.—Literally, as in the margin, *a land of desire, i.e.,* desirable.

A goodly heritage of the hosts of nations.—More accurately, *a heritage of the beauty of beauties* (Hebrew for "chief beauty") *of the nations.* The English version rests on the assumption that the word translated "beauties" is the same as that elsewhere rendered "Sabaoth," or "hosts," which it closely resembles.

And I said.—Not, as in the English, the answer to a question, but the continuance of the same thought. God will treat repentant Israel as His child: He will lead Israel to trust Him as a father. The days of apostasy ("turning away") will then be over. The original Hebrew seems, to judge from the LXX. version, to have had the plural "*ye* shall call," "*ye* shall not turn away," the prophet passing from the collective unity to the individuals that composed it.

(20) **Surely as a wife . . .**—In the midst of the bright vision of the future there comes unbidden the thought of the dark present: the faithless wife is not yet restored to her true friend and husband. Her

parteth from her [1]husband, so have ye
dealt treacherously with me, O house of
Israel, saith the LORD.
(21) A voice was heard upon the high
places, weeping *and* supplications of
the children of Israel: for they have
perverted their way, *and* they have for-
gotten the LORD their God.
(22) [a]Return, ye backsliding children,
and I will heal your backslidings.
Behold, we come unto thee; for thou
art the LORD our God. (23) Truly in vain
is salvation hoped for from the hills, *and*
from the multitude of mountains: truly
in the LORD our God *is* the salvation of
Israel. (24) For shame hath devoured
the labour of our fathers from our
youth; their flocks and their herds,
their sons and their daughters. (25) We
lie down in our shame, and our confusion
covereth us: for we have sinned against
the LORD our God, we and our fathers,
from our youth even unto this day, and
have not obeyed the voice of the LORD
our God.

1 Heb., *friend.*

a Hos. 14. 1.

b Joel 2. 12.

c 2 Cor. 10. 17.

CHAPTER IV.—(1) If thou wilt re-
turn, O Israel, saith the LORD, [b]return
unto me: and if thou wilt put away
thine abominations out of my sight,
then shalt thou not remove. (2) And
thou shalt swear, The LORD liveth, in
truth, in judgment, and in righteous-
ness; and the nations shall bless them-
selves in him, and in him shall they
[c]glory. (3) For thus saith the LORD to
the men of Judah and Jerusalem, Break
up your fallow ground, and sow not
among thorns. (4) Circumcise your-
selves to the LORD, and take away the

---

guilt must be again pressed home upon her, so as to lead her to repentance.

(21) **A voice was heard.**—Yes, the guilty wife was there, but she was also penitent. The "high places" which had been the scene of the guilt of the sons of Israel, where the cries of their orgiastic worship had been heard, now echoed with their weeping and supplication (or, more literally, *the weeping of suppliant prayers*), as they called to mind the hateful sins of the past.

(22) **Return, ye backsliding children . . .**—We lose, as before, the force of the Hebrew repetition of the same root, *Turn, ye children that have turned, I will heal your turnings.* As so often in Hebrew poetry, we have the answer to the invitation given in dramatic form, and hear the cry—we might almost call it the litany—of the suppliants, "Behold, we come unto thee." They at last own Jehovah as their one true God.

(23) **Truly in vain . . .**—The italics show the difficulty of the verse, and represent an attempt to get over it. According to the senses given to the word translated "multitude" we get, *in vain* (literally, *as a lie*) *from the hills is the revelry* (as in Amos v. 23), or *the wealth*, or *the multitude, of the mountains.* The first gives the best meaning, and expresses the confession of the repentant Israelites that their wild ritual on the high places had brought them loss and not gain.

(24) **Shame.**—The Hebrew noun has the article, "*the* shame," and is the word constantly used as the interchangeable synonym for Baal, as in Jerubbaal and Jerubbesheth (Judges vi. 32; 2 Sam xi. 21), Mephibosheth and Merib-baal (2 Sam. iv. 4; 1 Chron. viii. 34). The words point accordingly to the prodigal waste of victims, possibly of human life also, in the worship of Baal and that of Molech, which in the prophet's mind was identified with it, and which had brought with it nothing but a lasting shame. This also forms part of the confession of the repentant people (comp. chap. xi. 13).

(25) **We lie down.**—Better, *We will lie down—Our confusion shall cover us.* The words are those of penitents accepting their punishment: "We chose the shameful thing, therefore let us bear our shame."

IV.

(1) **If thou wilt return.**—The "if" implies a return from the hopes with which chap. iii. ended to the language of misgiving, and so, inferentially, of earnest exhortation.

Abominations.—Literally, *things of shame*, as in chap. iii. 24; the idols which Israel had worshipped.

Then shalt thou not remove.—Better, as continuing the conditions of forgiveness, *if thou wilt not wander.*

(2) **And thou shalt swear.**—The conditions are continued: *If thou wilt swear by the living Jehovah* ["the Lord liveth" being the received formula of adjuration], in truth, in judgment, and in righteousness.

And the nations shall bless themselves in him.—This forms the completion of the sentence. If the conditions of a true repentance are fulfilled by Israel, then the outlying heathen nations shall bless themselves in Jehovah—*i.e.*, shall own Him and adore Him, be blessed by Him.

(3) **For thus saith the Lord . . .**—The words seem the close of one discourse, the opening of another. The parable of Israel is left behind, and the appeal to Judah and Jerusalem is more direct.

To the men of Judah.—Literally, *to each man* individually.

Break up your fallow ground.—The Hebrew has the force which comes from the verb and noun being from the same root, *Break up for you a broken ground* or *fallow a fallow field.* The metaphor had been used before by Hosea (x. 12). What the spiritual field needed was to be exposed to God's sun and God's free air, to the influences of spiritual light and warmth, and the dew and soft showers of His grace.

Sow not among thorns.—Not without a special interest as, perhaps, containing the germ of the Parable of the Sower in Matt. xiii. 7. Here, as there, the seed is the "word of God," spoken by the prophet, and taking root in the heart, and the thorns are the "cares of this world," the selfish desires which choke the good seed and render it unfruitful.

(4) **Circumcise yourselves to the Lord.**—The

foreskins of your heart, ye men of Judah
and inhabitants of Jerusalem: lest my
fury come forth like fire, and burn that
none can quench *it*, because of the evil
of your doings.
(5) Declare ye in Judah, and publish
in Jerusalem; and say, Blow ye the
trumpet in the land: cry, gather to-
gether, and say, Assemble yourselves,
and let us go into the defenced cities.
(6) Set up the standard toward Zion:
[1]retire, stay not: for I will bring evil
from the [a]north, and a great [2]destruc-
tion. (7) The lion is come up from his
thicket, and the destroyer of the Gen-
tiles is on his way; he is gone forth
from his place to make thy land deso-
late; *and* thy cities shall be laid waste,
without an inhabitant. (8) For this [b]gird
you with sackcloth, lament and howl:
for the fierce anger of the LORD is not
turned back from us. (9) And it shall
come to pass at that day, saith the
LORD, *that* the heart of the king shall
perish, and the heart of the princes;
and the priests shall be astonished, and
the prophets shall wonder.
(10) Then said I, Ah, Lord GOD! surely
thou hast greatly deceived this people
and Jerusalem, saying, Ye shall have
peace; whereas the sword reacheth unto
the soul.
(11) At that time shall it be said to this
people and to Jerusalem, A dry wind of
the high places in the wilderness toward
the daughter of my people, not to fan,
nor to cleanse. (12) *Even* [3]a full wind
from those *places* shall come unto me:

1 Or, *strengthen.*

a ch. 1. 13, 14, 15; & 6. 1, 22.

2 Heb., *breaking.*

b ch. 6. 26.

3 Or, *a fuller wind than those.*

---

words show that the prophet had grasped the meaning of the symbol which to so many Jews was merely an outward sign. He saw that the "foreskin of the heart" was the fleshly, unrenewed nature, the "flesh" as contrasted with the "spirit," the "old man" which St. Paul contrasts with the new (Rom. vi. 6, viii. 7). The verbal coincidence with Deut. x. 16, xxx. 6 shows the influence of that book, of which we find so many traces in Jeremiah's teaching.

Lest my fury come forth like fire . . .—The words, which describe the righteousness of Jehovah as a consuming fire, have their parallel in chap. vii. 20, Amos v. 6, and form the transition to the picture of terror which opens in the next verse.

(5) **Declare.**—*i.e.*, proclaim as a herald proclaims. The cry is that of an alarm of war. The prophet sees, as it were, the invading army, and calls the people to leave their villages and to take refuge in the fortified cities.

(6) **Set up the standard toward Zion.**—Still the language of alarm. The words are as a command, "Raise the signal which shall point to Zion as a place of refuge from the foe, by whom the rest of the country is laid waste."

Retire.—*Withdraw*, in the transitive sense, "gather, with a view to removing" (as in Exod. ix. 19), and this is followed by "stay not," *linger not*, be quick. The call to retreat was urgent.

I will bring.—Literally, *I am bringing.*

From the north.—The Chaldæan, and possibly the Scythian, invasion, as in chap. i. 14.

(7) **The lion is come up . . .**—The "lion" is, of course, the Chaldæan invader, the destroyer, not of men only, but of nations. So in Dan. vii. 4 the lion is the symbol of the Assyrian monarchy. The winged lions that are seen in the palaces of Mosul and Nimroud gave a special character to what was in any case a natural metaphor. The word "Gentiles" answers to the meaning, but there is no special reason why it should be used here, rather than *nations.*

Is on his way.—Literally, *has broken up his encampment*, *i.e.*, has started on his march.

Without an inhabitant.—The language, like that of Isaiah (vi. 11), was probably in some measure hyperbolical but the depopulation caused by the Chaldæan invasion (as seen in chap. xxxix. 9) must have been extreme.

(8) **Gird you with sackcloth.**—From the earliest times the outward sign of mourning, and therefore of repentance (Joel i. 8; Isa. xxii. 12).

(9) **The heart of the king shall perish.**—The heart, as representing the mind generally. Judgment and wisdom were to give way to panic and fear.

(10) **Ah, Lord God!** (literally, *my Lord Jehovah!*) **surely thou hast greatly deceived this people.**—The words are startling, but are eminently characteristic. Jeremiah had been led to utter words that told of desolation and destruction. But if these were true, what was he to think of the words of the other prophets, who, speaking in the name of the Lord, had promised peace through the reign of Josiah, and even under Jehoiakim? Had not Jehovah apparently sanctioned those prophets also? and, if so, had He not deceived the people? (Comp. chap. xx. 7.) This seems, on the whole, preferable to the interpretations which see in it a dramatic irony representing the prophet as having shared in the hopes of the people and awakening to a terrible disappointment, or refer the words to the contrast between the glorious visions of the future in Isaiah and his own terrible predictions, or to the bolder course of an alteration of the text, so that the words would run "it is said," the complaint being represented as coming from the people.

(11) **At that time.**—*i.e.*, when the lion and destroyer of verse 7 should begin his work of destruction.

A dry wind.—Literally, *a clear wind*, the simoom, the scorching blast from the desert, coming clear and without clouds. Other winds might be utilised for the threshing-floor, but this made all such work impossible, and was simply devastating, and was therefore a fit symbol of the terrible invader.

(12) **A full wind from those places.**—Better, *a wind fuller than those*, or, *fuller than for this . . . i.e.*, more tempestuous than those which serve for the work of the thresher, and blowing away both grain and chaff together.

Shall come unto me.—Better, *for me, as doing my pleasure.*

Give sentence against them.—*sc.*, against the sinful people of Judah and Jerusalem.

now also will I [1]give sentence against
them. (13) Behold, he shall come up as
clouds, and his chariots *shall be* as a
whirlwind: his horses are swifter than
eagles. Woe unto us! for we are spoiled.
(14) O Jerusalem, [a]wash thine heart from
wickedness, that thou mayest be saved.
How long shall thy vain thoughts lodge
within thee? (15) For a voice declareth
[b]from Dan, and publisheth affliction from
mount Ephraim. (16) Make ye mention
to the nations; behold, publish against
Jerusalem, *that* watchers come from a
far country, and give out their voice
against the cities of Judah. (17) As
keepers of a field, are they against her
round about; because she hath been
rebellious against me, saith the LORD.
(18) [c]Thy way and thy doings have pro-
cured these *things* unto thee; this *is*
thy wickedness, because it is bitter, be-
cause it reacheth unto thine heart.
(19) My [d]bowels, my bowels! I am pained
at [2]my very heart; my heart maketh a
noise in me; I cannot hold my peace,
because thou hast heard, O my soul, the
sound of the trumpet, the alarm of war.
(20) Destruction upon destruction is cried;
for the whole land is spoiled: suddenly
are my tents spoiled, *and* my curtains
in a moment. (21) How long shall I see
the standard, *and* hear the sound of the

1 Heb., *utter judgments.*

a Isa. 1. 16.

b ch. 8. 16.

c Ps. 107. 17; Isa. 50. 1.

d Isa. 22. 4; ch. 9. 1.

2 Heb., *the walls of my heart.*

---

(13) **He shall come up as clouds.**—He, the destroyer of nations, with armies that sweep like storm-clouds over the land they are going to destroy. (Comp. Ezek. xxxviii. 16.)

Swifter than eagles.—A possible quotation from David's lament over Saul and Jonathan (2 Sam. i. 23). The fact that another phrase is quoted in verse 30 ("clothest thyself with crimson," where the Hebrew is the same as the "scarlet" of 2 Sam. i. 24), makes the possibility something like a certainty. It was natural that one who himself wrote two sets of lamentations, one early (2 Chron. xxxv. 25), the other late, in life, should have been a student of earlier elegies. For the flight of the eagle as representing the swift march of the invader, comp. Lam. iv. 19; Hos. viii. 1; Hab. i. 8.

Woe unto us! for we are spoiled.—Probably the cry of the terrified crowds of Jerusalem, with which the prophet, with dramatic vividness, as in chap. ix. 18, 19, interrupts his description.

(14) **O Jerusalem.**—The prophet's answer to the cry that comes from the city. In that "washing of the heart" which had seemed impossible before (chap. ii. 22), but is thought of now as "possible with God," is the one hope of salvation. (Comp. Isa. i. 16.)

Vain thoughts.—The Hebrew has a force which the English does not reproduce, *thoughts of vanity, thoughts of aven, i.e.,* of the word which had been specially applied, as in Beth-aven for Beth-el (the "house of vanity" for the "house of God") to the idols which Israel and Judah worshipped (Hosea iv. 15, x. 5; Amos v. 5).

(15) **Dan . . . Mount Ephraim.**—The two places are chosen, not like Dan and Beer-sheba, as extreme limits, but as stages in the march of the invader: first Dan (as in chap. viii. 16), the northernmost point (Deut. xxxiv. 1; Judg. xx. 1) of the whole land of Israel, then Mount Ephraim, as the northern boundary of Judæa. The verbs grow in strength with the imagined nearness, first *announce,* as of a rumour from a distance, then *proclaim,* as of a danger more imminent.

Affliction.—In the Hebrew the same word (*aven*) as in the "thoughts of vanity." Playing on the two aspects of the word, the prophet says that *aven* comes as the penalty of *aven*—the "nothingness" of destruction as that of the "nothingness" of the idol.

(16) **Make ye mention.**—Better, *Proclaim ye to the nations; behold.* Call them to gaze on the ruin of Jerusalem, then, *Cry aloud as for Jerusalem, that watchers* (*i.e.,* the besieging armies) *are coming from a far country, and that they will give out their voice* (*i.e.,* raise the cry of war) *against the cities of Judah.*

(17) **Field.**—With the meaning, as in all early English, of "open," not "enclosed," country (Lev. xiv. 7, xvii. 5). The image is that of a nomadic tribe encamped in the open country, or of men watching their flocks (Luke ii. 8) or crops (Job xxvii. 18). So shall be the tents of the invaders round Jerusalem—keeping, or (as in 2 Sam. xi. 16) "observing," *i.e.,* "blockading" the city.

(18) **This is thy wickedness.**—Better, *this is thy evil.* She was reaping the fruit of her own doing, and this gave her sorrows a fresh bitterness. The Hebrew word, like the English "evil," includes both guilt and its punishment.

(19) **My bowels, my bowels!**—As with verse 13, the words may be Jeremiah's own cry of anguish, or that of the despairing people with whom he identifies himself. The latter gives more dramatic vividness, as we thus have the utterances of three of the great actors in the tragedy: here of the people, in verse 22 of Jehovah, in verse 23 of the prophet. The "bowels" were with the Hebrews thought of as the seat of all the strongest emotions, whether of sorrow, fear, or sympathy (Job xxx. 27; Isa. xvi. 11).

At my very heart.—Literally (reproducing the physical fact of palpitation), *I writhe in pain; the walls of my heart! my heart moans for me.* The verb for "I am pained" is often used for the "travail" or agony of childbirth (Isa. xxiii. 4, xxvi. 18).

Thou hast heard, O my soul . . .—Silence at such a time was impossible. The prophet, as in the language of strong emotion, addresses his own soul, his very self (Comp. Ps. xvi. 2, xlii. 5, 11).

(20) **Destruction upon destruction is cried.**—Literally, *Breaking upon breaking,* or *crash upon crash, is reported.*

Suddenly are my tents spoiled.—The tent dwelling retained its position even amid the cities and villages of Israel (2 Sam. xviii. 17; 1 Kings viii. 66). The "curtains" are, of course, those of the tent (Isa. liv. 2). Conspicuous among such survivals of the nomad form of life we find the Rechabites of chap. xxxv.

(21) **How long shall I see . . .**—The "standard," as in verse 6, is the alarm signal given to the fugitives. The "trumpet" sounds to give the alarm, and quicken

trumpet? (22) For my people *is* foolish,
they have not known me; they *are* sot-
tish children, and they have none under-
standing: they *are* wise to do evil, but
to do good they have no knowledge.
(23) I beheld the earth, and, lo, *it was*
without form, and void; and the heavens,
and they *had* no light. (24) I beheld the
mountains, and, lo, they trembled, and
all the hills moved lightly. (25) I beheld,
and, lo, *there was* no man, and all the
birds of the heavens were fled. (26) I
beheld, and, lo, the fruitful place *was*
a wilderness, and all the cities thereof
were broken down at the presence of the
LORD, *and* by his fierce anger.
(27) For thus hath the LORD said, The
whole land shall be desolate; [a] yet will I
not make a full end. (28) For this shall the
earth mourn, and the heavens above be
black: because I have spoken *it*, I have
purposed *it*, and will not repent, neither
will I turn back from it. (29) The whole
city shall flee for the noise of the horse-
men and bowmen; they shall go into
thickets, and climb up upon the rocks:
every city *shall be* forsaken, and not
a man dwell therein. (30) And *when*
thou *art* spoiled, what wilt thou do?
Though thou clothest thyself with crim-
son, though thou deckest thee with or-
naments of gold, though thou rentest
thy [1] face with painting, in vain shalt
thou make thyself fair; *thy* lovers will
despise thee, they will seek thy life.
(31) For I have heard a voice as of a
woman in travail, *and* the anguish as
of her that bringeth forth her first child,
the voice of the daughter of Zion, *that*
bewaileth herself, *that* spreadeth her
hands, *saying*, Woe *is* me now! for my
soul is wearied because of murderers.

a ch. 5. 18.

1 Heb., *eyes*.

---

their flight to the defenced city. The prophet sees no end to the miseries of the coming war.

(22) **For my people is foolish.**—Jehovah answers the prophet's question. The misery comes to punish the folly and sottishness of the people. It shall last as long as they last, or till it has accomplished its work of chastisement.

(23) **I beheld the earth.**—In words of terrible grandeur the prophet speaks, as if he had already seen the consummated destruction; and repeating the words "I beheld," as if he had passed through four distinct visions, describes its completeness.

Without form, and void.—An obvious quotation from the *tohu va-bohu* of Gen. i. 2. The goodly land of Israel was thrown back, as it were, into a formless chaos, before the words "Let there be light" had brought it into order.

(24) **The mountains, and, lo, they trembled.**—The great earthquake in the days of Uzziah (Amos i. 1), of which we find traces in Isaiah (xxiv. 19, 20), had probably made imagery of this kind familiar.

(25) **There was no man.**—To chaos and darkness and the earthquake was added the horrible sense of solitude. Not man only, but the creatures that seemed least open to man's attack, were fled. (Comp. chap. ii. 6.) The same thought re-appears in chap. ix. 10.

(26) **The fruitful place.**—The Carmel, or vine-land, became as "*the* wilderness." The Hebrew article points probably to the well-known desert of the wanderings.

At the presence of the Lord.—Literally, *from before Jehovah, from before the heat of his anger.* The original has the emphasis of repeating the preposition.

(27) **Yet will I not make a full end.**—The thought is echoed from Amos ix. 8; Isa. vi. 13, x. 21, and repeated in chap. v. 18. There was then hope in the distance. The destruction, terrible as it seemed, was not final. The penalty was a discipline. (Comp. Lev. xxvi. 44.)

(28) **For this shall the earth mourn . . .**—As with all true poets, the face of nature seems to the prophet to sympathise with human suffering. (Comp. Amos viii. 9; Matt. xxiv. 29.)

(29) **The horsemen and bowmen.**—A specially characteristic picture, as we see from the Nineveh sculptures, of Assyrian and Chaldæan armies.

Thickets . . . rocks.—Both words are Aramaic in the original. The former, elsewhere rendered "clouds," is here used for the dark shadowy coverts in which men sought for shelter; the latter is the root of the name Cephas (= Peter). On the caves of Palestine as places of refuge in time of war, see Isa. ii. 19; 1 Sam. xiii. 6.

(30) **And when thou art spoiled . . .**—The sentence is clearer without the insertion of the words in italics: *Thou spoiled one, what dost thou work, that thou clothest . . . that thou deckest . . . that thou rentest . . .? In vain dost thou beautify thyself.* The "clothing with crimson" and "ornaments of gold" are, as before noticed (Note on verse 13), an echo from 2 Sam. i. 24. The "rending the face" is, literally, *enlarging the eyes* with *kohl*, or antimony, still used for this purpose in the east, the black powder being laid on horizontally with a small *stylus*, or pencil, drawn between the eyelashes. The daughter of Zion is represented as a woman who puts on her costliest attire, as Jezebel had done (2 Kings ix. 30), in the vain hope of fascinating her lovers. The imagery points to the foreign alliances in which the statesmen and people of Jerusalem were trusting, and they are told that they shall be in vain. The lovers, *i.e.*, the allies, shall become her foes.

(31) **A woman in travail.**—Literally, *writhing in pain*, as in verse 19.

Bewaileth herself.—Literally, *pants for breath.* The prophet draws his pictures with a terrible intensity. On the one side is Zion as the harlot, in her gold and crimson and cosmetics; on the other we see the forlorn and desperate castaway, in the hour of a woman's utter helplessness, outraged and abandoned, stretching out her hands to implore mercy from the assassins who attack her, and imploring it in vain.

CHAPTER V.—(1) Run ye to and fro
through the streets of Jerusalem, and
see now, and know, and seek in the
broad places thereof, if ye can find a
man, if there be *any* that executeth
judgment, that seeketh the truth; and
I will pardon it. (2) And though they
say, The LORD liveth; surely they swear
falsely. (3) O LORD, *are* not thine eyes
upon the truth? thou hast [a] stricken
them, but they have not grieved; thou
hast consumed them, *but* they have re-
fused to receive correction: they have
made their faces harder than a rock;
they have refused to return. (4) There-
fore I said, Surely these *are* poor; they
are foolish: for they know not the way
of the LORD, *nor* the judgment of their
God. (5) I will get me unto the great
men, and will speak unto them; for
they have known the way of the LORD,
and the judgment of their God: but
these have altogether broken the yoke,
and burst the bonds. (6) Wherefore a
lion out of the forest shall slay them,
and a wolf of the [1] evenings shall spoil
them, a leopard shall watch over their
cities: every one that goeth out thence
shall be torn in pieces: because their
transgressions are many, *and* their back-
slidings [2] are increased.
(7) How shall I pardon thee for this?
thy children have forsaken me, and
sworn by *them that are* no gods: when

a Isa. 9. 13; ch. 2. 30.

1 Or, *deserts.*

2 Heb., *are strong.*

V.

(1) **Run ye to and fro.**—The dark shades of the picture seem at first hardly to belong to the reign of Josiah, which is brought before us in 2 Kings xxii., xxiii.; 2 Chron. xxxiv., xxxv., as one of thorough reformation. It is, of course, possible that parts of the picture may have been worked up when the prophecies were re-written under Jehoiakim (chap. xxxvi. 32); but, on the other hand, it is equally possible that the prophet may have seen even at the time how hollow and in-complete that reformation was. The form in which he utters his conviction reminds one of the old story of the Greek sage, Diogenes, appearing in the streets of Athens with a lantern, searching for an honest man. In the thought that the pardon of the city depended on its containing some elements of good which might make reformation possible, we find an echo of Gen. xviii. 25; but the picture is of a state more utterly hopeless. There were not ten righteous men found in Sodom (Gen. xviii. 32); in Jerusalem there was not one.

(2) **The Lord liveth.**—The words imply that a distinction between the binding powers of different formulæ of adjuration, like that of the later scribes (Matt. xxiii. 16), was already in some degree prevalent. The guilt of the men of Jerusalem was that they took the most solemn formula of all, "Jehovah liveth," and yet were guilty of perjury. In verse 7 we find traces of the practice of swearing by other gods, with which this "oath of Jehovah" is apparently contrasted.

Falsely.—Literally, *upon falsehood.*

(3) **Upon the truth.**—The Hebrew word, which has no article, implies truth in the inward parts, *faithfulness,* as well as truth in words. The "eyes" of God looked for this, and He found the temper that hardens itself against discipline, and refuses to repent.

(4) **Therefore.**—Literally, *And.* The prophet makes for the poor the half-pitying plea of ignorance. Looking upon the masses that toil for bread, those whom the Scribes afterwards called the "people of earth," it was not strange that they who had been left untaught should have learnt so little. The thought finds a parallel in our Lord's compassion for the multitude who were as "sheep having no shepherd" (Matt. ix. 36), for the servant who "knew not his Lord's will" (Luke xii. 48).

The way of the Lord.—That which He approves, that which leads to Him, as in Gen. xviii. 19; Deut. xxxi. 29.

(5) **I will get me.**—The prophet turns from the masses to the few, from the poor to the great, repeating, as with a grave, indignant irony, the words that describe the true wisdom which he has not found in the former, but hopes to find in the latter.

But these.—Better, as less ambiguous, *Surely they too.* The clause begins with the same word as that in verse 4. What is meant is that the great as well as the poor, the learned as well as the ignorant, are altogether evil, the former even more defiant in breaking through all conventional constraints than the latter.

(6) **A lion out of the forest.**—The imagery is vivid in itself. The three forms of animal ferocity, lion, wolf, leopard—representing, perhaps, the three phases of simple fierceness, ravenousness, and cunning; possibly even three oppressors in whom those attributes were to be impersonated—are brought together to embody the cruelty of the invader. The three animals were all common in Palestine, but it seems a weak rendering of the prophet's words to take them literally as simply predicting that the land would be ravaged by the beasts of prey.

A wolf of the evenings.—Better, as in the margin, *of the deserts;* but the term "evening," as applied to the habits of the beast of prey prowling in the darkness, is supported by Hab. i. 8; Zeph. iii. 3. The same three animals appear in the symbolism of the first canto of Dante's *Inferno,* and the coincidence can hardly be thought of as accidental.

A leopard shall watch . . .—There is no adequate reason for substituting "panther." The leopard finds its place in the *Fauna* of Syria (Hosea xiii. 7; Hab. i. 8). The "watching" is that of the crouching beast making ready for its spring.

(7) **When I had fed them to the full.**—The reading of the Hebrew text gives, *though I had bound them by oath, &c.,* by the covenant, as of marriage; and this, as heightening the enormity of the sin that follows, gives a better sense than the English version, which follows the marginal reading of the Hebrew. The latter finds its parallel in Deut. xxxii. 15; Hos. xiii. 6. There is probably an implied reference to the covenant to which the people had sworn in the time of Josiah.

Houses.—Literally, *house.* The singular is, perhaps, used because the prophet thinks primarily of

I had fed them to the full, they then
committed adultery, and assembled
themselves by troops in the harlots'
houses. (8) [a] They were *as* fed horses in
the morning: every one neighed after
his neighbour's wife. (9) Shall I not
visit for these *things?* saith the LORD:
and shall not my soul be avenged on
such a nation as this?

(10) Go ye up upon her walls, and de-
stroy; but make not a full end: take
away her battlements; for they *are* not
the LORD'S. (11) For the house of Israel
and the house of Judah have dealt very
treacherously against me, saith the
LORD. (12) They have belied the LORD,
and said, [b] *It is* not he; neither shall
evil come upon us; neither shall we see
sword nor famine: (13) and the pro-
phets shall become wind, and the word
is not in them: thus shall it be done
unto them. (14) Wherefore thus saith
the LORD God of hosts, Because ye
speak this word, [c] behold, I will make
my words in thy mouth fire, and this
people wood, and it shall devour them.
(15) Lo, I will bring a [d] nation upon you
from far, O house of Israel, saith the
LORD: it *is* a mighty nation, it *is* an
ancient nation, a nation whose lan-
guage thou knowest not, neither un-
derstandest what they say. (16) Their
quiver *is* as an open sepulchre, they *are*
all mighty men. (17) And they shall eat
up thine [e] harvest, and thy bread, *which*
thy sons and thy daughters should eat:
they shall eat up thy flocks and thine
herds: they shall eat up thy vines and
thy fig trees: they shall impoverish thy
fenced cities, wherein thou trustedst,
with the sword. (18) Nevertheless in
those days, saith the LORD, I [f] will not
make a full end with you.

(19) And it shall come to pass, when
ye shall say, [g] Wherefore doeth the LORD
our God all these *things* unto us? then
shalt thou answer them, Like as ye
have forsaken me, and served strange

a Ezek. 22. 11.
b Isa. 28. 15.
c ch. 1. 9.
d Deut. 28. 49; ch. 1. 15; & 6. 22.
e Lev. 26. 16; Deut. 28. 31, 33.
f ch. 4. 27.
g ch. 13. 22; & 16. 10.

---

the idol's temple as the scene of the adulteress's guilt, which here, as elsewhere, is the symbol of national apostasy.

(8) **They were as fed horses in the morning.**—Better, *As fed stallion horses they rove about.* The animal passion is taken, as in Ezek. xxiii. 20, (1) as answering to the same passion in man; (2) as symbolical of the lust for idolatrous ritual. (Comp. chap. ii. 24.)

(10) **Walls.**—Better, *her palm-trees.* The Hebrew word is found in Ezek. xxvii. 25, though not in the English Version, in the sense of "mast," and here, apparently, means the tall, stately trunk of the palm-tree. So, for "battlements" it is better to read *branches* (as in Isa. xviii. 5), as carrying on the same imagery, and indicating the limits of the destruction, that is not to make a "full end." The rendering "walls," still adopted by some commentators, may refer to the "walls" of a vineyard, but the second word would in that case be the *tendrils* of the vine. Both the palm-tree and the vine appear on Maccabean coins as symbols of Judah, and the latter had been treated as such in Isa. v. 1—7; Ps. lxxx. 8—16.

(12) **It is not he.**—*i.e.,* It is not Jehovah who speaks. They listened to the prophet's warnings as if they came from himself only, and brought with them no certainty of the "sword" or "famine" which they foretold. Perhaps, however, the words refer also to the denial that Jehovah was working in the sufferings that fell upon the people, or even to a more entire denial, like that of the fool in Ps. xiv. 1.

(13) **The word.**—Literally, *He who speaketh, i.e.,* Jehovah, as the speaker.

Thus shall it be done unto them.—Better, as a wish, *may it so happen to them;* may the evils the prophets foretell fall on their own heads. The speech comes from the lips of the unbelieving mockers.

(14) **The Lord God of hosts.**—The solemn name (*Jehovah Elohim Zebaoth*) used for the second time in Jeremiah's teaching (chap. ii. 19). The message is partly to the people—"Because *ye* speak this word," partly to the prophet who was sent to bear his witness against them—"I will make my words in *thy* mouth."

(15) **O house of Israel.**—Apparently, as there is no contrast with Judah, in its wider sense, as including the whole body of the twelve tribes.

A mighty nation.—The strict force of the adjective is that of "lasting, enduring," as of mountains (Micah vi. 2) and rivers (Amos v. 24; Ps. lxxiv. 15).

Whose language thou knowest not.—To the Jew, as to the Greek, the thought of being subject to a people of alien speech, a "barbarian," added a new element of bitterness. Compare Isa. xxviii. 11; Deut. xxviii. 49.

(16) **An open sepulchre.**—Every arrow in the quivers of the Chaldæan bowmen was to be as a messenger of death, a blast or pestilence from the grave.

(17) **Which thy sons and thy daughters should eat.**—There is no relative pronoun in the Hebrew, and the clause stands parallel with the others, *they shall eat* (*i.e.,* destroy) *thy sons and thy daughters,* and is so translated in all the older versions. In the other clauses the verb is in the singular, "*it* (*i.e.,* the invading army) shall eat."

Impoverish.—Better, *break down,* or *shatter.* The "sword" is used, as in Ezek. xxvi. 9, for "battle-axes" and other weapons used in attacking cities.

(18) **I will not make a full end.**—As before, in chap. iv. 27, and in this chapter, verse 10, what seems the extremest sentence is tempered by the assurance that it is not absolutely final. It is intended to be reformatory, and not merely penal.

(19) **When ye shall say.**—The implied promise in verse 18 is explained. Then there shall come the backward glance at the past, which brings with it questionings and repentance.

Strange gods.—Stronger than the "*other* gods" of chap. i. 16, "gods of an alien race." The threats that they should "serve strangers" in a "land" that

gods in your land, so shall ye serve
strangers in a land *that is* not your's.
(20) Declare this in the house of
Jacob, and publish it in Judah, saying,
(21) Hear now this, O [a] foolish people,
and without [1] understanding; which have
eyes, and see not; which have ears, and
hear not: (22) fear ye not me? saith
the LORD: will ye not tremble at my
presence, which have placed the sand
for the [b] bound of the sea by a perpetual
decree, that it cannot pass it: and
though the waves thereof toss them-
selves, yet can they not prevail; though
they roar, yet can they not pass over it?
(23) But this people hath a revolting
and a rebellious heart; they are re-
volted and gone. (24) Neither say they
in their heart, Let us now fear the
LORD our God, that giveth rain, both
the [c] former and the latter, in his season:
he reserveth unto us the appointed
weeks of the harvest. (25) Your ini-
quities have turned away these *things*,
and your sins have withholden good
things from you. (26) For among my
people are found wicked *men*: [2] they lay
wait, as he that setteth snares; they
set a trap, they catch men. (27) As a
[3] cage is full of birds, so *are* their houses
full of deceit: therefore they are be-
come great, and waxen rich. (28) They
are waxen [d] fat, they shine: yea, they
overpass the deeds of the wicked: they
judge not the [e] cause, the cause of the
fatherless, yet they prosper; and the
right of the needy do they not judge.
(29) Shall I not visit for these *things?*
saith the LORD: shall not my soul be
avenged on such a nation as this?
(30) [4] A wonderful and horrible thing is
committed in the land; (31) the prophets
prophesy [f] falsely, and the priests [5] bear
rule by their means; and my people

a Isa. 6. 9; Matt. 13. 14; John 12. 40; Acts 28, 26; Rom. 11. 8.

1 Heb., *heart.*

b Job 38. 10, 11; Ps. 104. 9.

c Deut. 11. 14.

2 Or, *they pry as fowlers lie in wait.*

3 Or, *coop.*

d Deut. 32. 15.

e Isa. 1. 23; Zech. 7. 10.

4 Or, *Astonishment and filthiness.*

f ch. 14. 14; & 23. 25, 26; Ezek. 13. 6.

5 Or, *take into their hands.*

---

was not theirs points to the Chaldæan rather than to the Scythian invasion. With this ends the section which began in verse 14.

(20) **Declare—publish.**—The words indicate, as in chap. iv. 5, 16, the beginning of a fresh section of the prophecy, though no definitely new topic is introduced. The command is given by Jehovah, not to the prophet only, but to his disciples.

(21) **Which have eyes, and see not.**—An almost verbal reproduction from Isa. vi. 10.

(22) **Which have placed the sand . . .**—The greatness of Jehovah is shown by the majesty of His work in nature. As in Job xxxviii. 8—11, so, probably, here also there is something of the wonder of one to whom, as dwelling in an inland village, the billows breaking on the shore was an unfamiliar sight. Here was the token that even the forces which seem wildest and least restrained are subject to an overruling law. Even the sand which seems so shifting keeps in the surging waters.

(23) **But this people . . .**—The contrast seems to lie in the fact that the elements are subject to God's will, but that man's rebellious will, with its fatal gift of freedom, has the power to resist it. The two adjectives "revolting" and "rebellious" (the negative and positive aspects of apostasy) are joined together, as in Deut. xxi. 18, 20.

(24) **The Lord our God, that giveth rain . . .**—In the climate of Palestine, as it is now, there are not two distinct rainy seasons. The whole period from October to March has that character. The "early" rains are those that come in autumn, the latter those which close the season in spring. The former argument in what we may call the prophet's natural theology had been drawn from the presence of law in the midst of what seemed the lawless elements of nature. Now he urges that drawn from regularity of succession. Compare Gen. viii. 22; Ps. cxlviii. 8; Acts xiv. 17.

Rain, both the former and the latter.—Again a Deuteronomic phrase (Deut. xi. 14). Compare also James v. 7; Prov. xvi. 15.

The appointed weeks of the harvest.—Literally, *the weeks, the statutes,* or *ordinances, of the harvest,* the seven weeks included between the beginning of the barley harvest at the Passover and the completion of the wheat harvest at Pentecost.

(25) **These things.**—*i.e.,* the rain and the harvest which, from the prophet's point of view, had been withheld in consequence of the sins of the people.

(26) **They lay wait.**—Literally, *he lieth in wait* (used of the leopard in Hosea xiii. 7), *as in the crouching down of fowlers: they have set the snare.* The indefinite singular in the first clause brings before us the picture of isolated guilt, the plural that of confederate evil.

(27) **A cage.**—The large wicker basket (Amos viii. 1, 2) in which the fowler kept the birds he had caught, or, possibly, used for decoy-birds.

(28) **They overpass the deeds of the wicked.**—Better (the English being ambiguous), *they exceed in deeds* (literally, *words* or *things*) *of wickedness.* The prophet dwells not only on the prosperity of the wicked, but on their callous indifference to the well-being of the poor.

Yet they prosper.—Better, *so that they* (the fatherless) *may prosper.* They do not judge with a view to that result. The words admit, however, in Hebrew as in English, of the sense *that they* (the wicked themselves) *may prosper.* That was all they aimed at or cared for.

(30) **Wonderful.**—Better, *terrible.*

Is committed.—Better, *has come to pass.*

(31) **Prophesy falsely.**—Literally, *with a lie,* so in chap. xx. 6, xxix. 9.

Bear rule by their means.—Better, *move at their hands, i.e.,* according to their direction (as in 1 Chron. xxv. 2; 2 Chron. xxiii. 18. The Vulg. and LXX. translate *The priests applauded with their hands.* So taken, the words of Jeremiah make the priests follow the prophets, not the prophets the instruments of the priests. In Isa. ix. 15 the prophets are as "the tail," the basest element in the nation.

My people love to have it . . .—The words imply more than an acquiescence in evil, and describe

love *to have it* so: and what will ye do in the end thereof?

CHAPTER VI.—(1) O ye children of Benjamin, gather yourselves to flee out of the midst of Jerusalem, and blow the trumpet in Tekoa, and set up a sign of fire in Beth-haccerem: for evil appeareth out of the north, and great destruction. (2) I have likened the daughter of Zion to a [1] comely and delicate *woman.* (3) The shepherds with their flocks shall come unto her; they shall pitch *their* tents against her round about; they shall feed every one in his place. (4) Prepare ye war against her; arise, and let us go up at noon. Woe unto us! for the day goeth away, for the shadows of the evening are stretched out. (5) Arise, and let us go by night, and let us destroy her palaces. (6) For thus hath the LORD of hosts said, Hew ye down trees, and [2] cast a mount against Jerusalem: this *is* the city to be visited; she *is* wholly oppression in the midst of her. (7) [a] As a fountain casteth out her waters, so she casteth out her wickedness: violence and spoil

1 Or, *dwelling at home.*

2 Or, *pour out the engine of shot.*

a Isa. 57. 20.

---

an ethical condition like that of Rom. i. 32. The final question implies that the people were running into a destruction which they would have no power to avert.

VI.

(1) The new discourse, or section of a discourse, deals more locally with the coming desolation of Jerusalem.

O ye children of Benjamin.—The city, though claimed as belonging to Judah, was actually on the border of the two tribes, the boundary running through the valley of Ben-Hinnom (Josh. xv. 8; xviii. 16), and its northern walls were in that of Benjamin. It was natural that the prophet of Anathoth should think and speak of it as connected with his own people.

Blow the trumpet in Tekoa.—*i.e.,* "give the signal for the fugitives to halt, but not till they have reached the southernmost boundary of Judah." Tekoa was about twelve miles south of Jerusalem (2 Chron. xi. 6). The Hebrew presents a play upon the name Tekoa, as nearly identical with its sound is the verb "blow," and the town is probably mentioned for that reason. The play upon the name is analogous to those that meet us in Micah i. 10—16.

Sign of fire.—Better, *signal.* The word, though applied to a fire or smoke signal in Judges xx. 38, 40, does not necessarily imply it. Such signals were, however, in common use in all ancient warfare.

Beth-haccerem.—*i.e., the house of the vineyard,* halfway on the road from Jerusalem to Tekoa. There, too, the signal was to be raised that the fugitives might gather round it. Jerome states (Comm. on Jer. vi.) that it was on a mountain, and was known in his time as Bethacharma. It has been identified with the modern *Jebel Fureidis,* or "Hill of the Franks."

Evil appeareth out of the north.—Literally, *is bending over us,* as looking down on its prey. The word is that used of "righteousness *looking down* from heaven" in Ps. lxxxv. 11.

(2) **To a comely and delicate woman.**—"Woman" is not in the Hebrew, and the word translated "comely" is elsewhere (Isa. lxv. 10; Jer. xxiii. 3; Exod. xv. 13) rendered "fold" or "habitation;" and the passage should probably stand thus, *I have likened the daughter of Zion to a fair pasturage,* thus suggesting the imagery which is developed in the next verse. The clause is, however, rendered by some scholars as *the fair and delicate one* (or, *the fair pasturage*), *the daughter of Zion, I have destroyed.*

(3) **Shall come unto her.**—Better, *Unto it* (*sc.,* the pasture) *shall come shepherds with their flocks*—*i.e.,* the leaders and the armies of the invaders. The other verbs are in the past tense, the future being seen, as it were, realised, *They have pitched, they have pastured.*

Every one in his place.—Literally, *each on his hand,* or perhaps, "they shall feed, *each his hand,*" *i.e.,* shall let it rove in plunder at will by the side of his own tent. The work of plunder was to go on everywhere. The imagery is drawn from the attack of a nomadic tribe on a richly-cultivated plain.

(4) **Prepare ye war.**—Literally, *Sanctify.* The opening of the battle was accompanied by sacrifices, divinations, and prayers. Compare Deut. xx. 1—3 for the practice of the Israelites, and Ezek. xxi. 20—22 for that of the Chaldæans, which was, of course, present to Jeremiah's mind. The cry thus given with dramatic force comes from the soldiers of the invading army impatient for the fight. They are so eager that, instead of resting at noon, as usual, for their mid-day meal, they would fain press on for the assault. Their orders are against this, and, as the shadows lengthen, they raise their cry of complaint, "Alas for us, the day declines . . ." Then, impatient still, unwilling to wait, as their commanders bid them, for an attack at day-break, they shout, "Let us go by night."

(6) **Hew ye down trees, and cast a mount.**—The words describe graphically the process of an Eastern siege as seen in the Assyrian bas-reliefs (Layard, *Mon. of Nineveh,* i. 73—76). Compare 2 Sam. xx. 15; Job xix. 12; Isa. xxix. 3; Ezek. iv. 2. First the neighbouring country is cleared by cutting down the trees; next, either by piling earth on these as a timber framework, or using the earth alone, a "mount" (or, in later English, a *mound*) was raised till it reached the level of the wall of the besieged city; and then the assault was made. The law of Israel forbade, it may be noted, this destruction, but apparently only in the case of fruit-trees (Deut. xx. 19, 20). There is no adequate ground for the marginal rendering, "pour out the engine of shot."

Is . . . to be visited.—Literally, *is visited,* in the sense of "punished," but Hebrew usage gives to the verb so employed a gerundive force. The words admit, however, of the rendering, *this is the city; it is proved that wholly oppression is in the midst of her.*

(7) **As a fountain casteth out her waters.**—The English is plain enough, but the Hebrew presents two difficulties: (1) The word rendered "fountain" (better, *cistern*) is not spelt with the usual vowels, and the etymology of the verb is quite uncertain. It has

is heard in her; before me continually
is grief and wounds. (8) Be thou in-
structed, O Jerusalem, lest my soul
[1]depart from thee; lest I make thee
desolate, a land not inhabited.
(9) Thus saith the LORD of hosts, They
shall throughly glean the remnant of
Israel as a vine: turn back thine hand
as a grape-gatherer into the baskets.
(10) To whom shall I speak, and give
warning, that they may hear? behold,
their [a]ear *is* uncircumcised, and they
cannot hearken: behold, the word
of the LORD is unto them a re-
proach; they have no delight in it.
(11) Therefore I am full of the fury of
the LORD; I am weary with holding in:
I will pour it out upon the children
abroad, and upon the assembly of young
men together: for even the husband
with the wife shall be taken, the aged
with *him that is* full of days. (12) And
their houses shall be turned unto others,
with their fields and wives together:
for I will stretch out my hand upon the
inhabitants of the land, saith the LORD.
(13) For from the least of them even
unto the greatest of them every one *is*
given to [b]covetousness; and from the
prophet even unto the priest every one
dealeth falsely. (14) They have [c]healed
also the [2]hurt *of the daughter* of my
people slightly, saying, Peace, peace;
when *there is* no peace. (15) Were they
[d]ashamed when they had committed
abomination? nay, they were not at
all ashamed, neither could they blush:
therefore they shall fall among them
that fall: at the time *that* I visit them
they shall be cast down, saith the LORD.

1 Heb., *be loosed*, or, *disjointed*.

a ch. 7. 26.

b Isa. 56. 11; ch. 8. 10.

c ch. 8. 11; Ezek. 13. 10.

2 Heb., *bruise*, or, *breach*.

d ch. 3. 3; & 8. 12.

---

been rendered, *As a cistern "gathers,"* or *"keeps in,"* or *"keeps its waters cool,"* or *"lets them flow."* The general meaning is probably given by the Authorised Version. Jerusalem was literally "overflowing" with wickedness.

Grief.—Better, *sickness*. The word and the imagery are the same as in Isa. i. 5.

(8) **Be thou instructed.**—Better, *Be thou corrected*, or, *chastened*. Comp. Ps. ii. 10; Lev. xxvi. 23 (where we have "reformed"); and Prov. xxix. 19.

Lest my soul.—As in chap. iv. 19, the Hebrew formula for emphasised personality. The word for "depart" may be better rendered *tear itself away*.

(9) **Turn back thine hand.**—The image of the grape-gatherer carrying on his work to the last grape or tendril was a natural parable of unsparing desolation. The command is addressed to the minister of destruction, Nebuchadnezzar, or, it may be, to the angel of death.

Into the baskets.—The noun is found here only, and probably means, like a kindred word in Isa. xviii. 5, *the tendrils of the vine* upon which the hand of the gatherer was to be turned.

(10) **To whom shall I speak . . . ?**—The prophet, who now speaks in his own name, has heard the message from the Lord of Hosts; but what avails it? who will listen? As elsewhere the lips (Exod. vi. 30) and the heart (Lev. xxvi. 41; Ezek. xliv. 7), so here the ear of Israel was uncircumcised, as though it had never been brought into covenant with Jehovah or consecrated to His service.

A reproach.—*i.e.*, the object of their scorn.

(11) **I am full of the fury . . .**—The prophet feels himself filled, frail vessel as he is, with the righteous wrath of Jehovah. It will not be controlled.

I will pour it out.—Better, as the command coming from the mouth of Jehovah, *Pour it out*. The words that follow describe the several stages of man's life, upon all of which that torrent of wrath is to flow forth—the children abroad, *i.e.*, playing in the streets (as in Zech. viii. 5); the assembly, or gathering of young men, whether in their natural mirth (chap. xv. 17) or for secret plans (Prov. xv. 22); the husband and wife in full maturity; the "aged," *i.e.*, the elder, still active as well as venerable; lastly, the man "full of days," whose time is nearly over and his sand run out.

(13) **Is given to covetousness.**—Literally, *gained gain*. The Hebrew word (as in Gen. xxxvii. 26; Job xxii. 2) does not necessarily involve the idea of dishonest gain, though this (as in Prov. i. 19; Hab. ii. 9) is often implied. What the prophet condemns is the universal desire of gain (*rem . . . rem . . . quocunque modo rem*), sure to lead, as in the second clause, to a gratification of it by fair means or foul.

From the prophet even unto the priest . . .—The two orders that ought to have checked the evil are noted as having been foremost in promoting it. (Comp. Note on chap. v. 31.)

Dealeth falsely.—Literally, *worketh a lie*, in the sense of "dishonesty."

(14) **They have healed . . . slightly.**—Literally, *as a thing of nought, a light matter*. The words "of the daughter" are in italics, as indicating that the marginal reading of the Hebrew omits them. They are found, however, in the present text.

Peace, peace.—The word is taken almost in the sense of "health," as in Gen. xliii. 27, 28, and elsewhere. The false prophets were as physicians who told the man suffering from a fatal disease that he was in full health. As the previous words show, the prophet has in his mind the false encouragements given by those who should have been the true guides of the people. Looking at Josiah's reformation as sufficient to win the favour of Jehovah, they met Jeremiah's warnings of coming evil by the assurance that all was well, and that invasion and conquest were far-off dangers.

(15) **Were they ashamed . . . ?**—The Hebrew gives an assertion, not a question—*They are brought to shame* (as in chap. ii. 26), *because they have committed abominations*. And yet, the prophet adds, "they were not ashamed" (the verb is in a different voice). There was no inward feeling of shame even when they were covered with ignominy and confusion. They had lost the power to blush, and were callous and insensible. This was then, as always, the most hopeless of all states. To "fall among them that fall" was its inevitable sequel.

(16) Thus saith the LORD, Stand ye in
the ways, and see, and ask for the [a]old
paths, where *is* the good way, and walk
therein, and ye shall find [b]rest for your
souls. But they said, We will not walk
therein. (17) Also I set watchmen over
you, *saying*, Hearken to the sound of
the trumpet. But they said, We will
not hearken. (18) Therefore hear, ye
nations, and know, O congregation,
what *is* among them. (19) Hear, O earth:
behold, I will bring evil upon this people,
even the fruit of their thoughts, be-
cause they have not hearkened unto my
words, nor to my law, but rejected it.
(20) [c]To what purpose cometh there to
me incense from Sheba, and the sweet
cane from a far country? your burnt
offerings *are* not acceptable, nor your
sacrifices sweet unto me. (21) Therefore
thus saith the LORD, Behold, I will lay
stumblingblocks before this people, and
the fathers and the sons together shall
fall upon them; the neighbour and his
friend shall perish.
(22) Thus saith the LORD, Behold, a
people cometh from the [d]north country,
and a great nation shall be raised from
the sides of the earth. (23) They shall
lay hold on bow and spear; they *are*
cruel, and have no mercy; their voice
roareth like the sea; and they ride
upon horses, set in array as men for
war against thee, O daughter of Zion.
(24) We have heard the fame thereof:
our hands wax feeble: anguish hath
taken hold of us, *and* pain, as of a
woman in travail. (25) Go not forth

a Isa. 8. 20; Mal. 4. 4; Luke 16. 29.

b Matt. 11. 29.

c Isa. 1. 11; & 66. 3; Amos 5. 21; Mic. 6. 6, &c.

d ch. 1. 15; & 5. 15; & 10. 22.

---

(16) **Stand ye in the ways.**—In the prophet's mind the people were as a traveller who has taken a self-chosen path, and finds that it leads him to a place of peril. Is it not well that they should stop and ask where the old paths (literally, *the eternal paths;* the words going, as in chap. xviii. 15, beyond the mere antiquity of the nation's life) were, on which their fathers had travelled safely. Of these old paths they were to choose that which was most distinctly "the good way," the way of righteousness, and therefore of peace and health also. The call, however, was in vain. The people chose to travel still in the broad way that led them to destruction.

(17) **Watchmen.**—*i.e.*, the sentinels of the army, as in 1 Sam. xiv. 16, giving the signal in this case, not for advance but for retreat (comp. verse 1, and Amos iii. 6). The watchmen are, of course (as in Isa. lii. 8, lvi. 10; Ezek. iii. 17; Hab. ii. 1), the prophets blowing the trumpet of alarm, proclaiming, as in verse 1, the nearness of the invader, and calling on them to flee from the wrath of Jehovah. They call, however, in vain. The people refuse to hearken.

(18) **Therefore hear, ye nations . . .**—The obstinate refusal with which the people met the summons of the prophet leads him once more to a solemn appeal (1) to the heathen nations, then (2) to the "congregation" of Israel (as in Exodus and Numbers *passim*), or, possibly, of mankind collectively, (3) to earth as the witness of the judgments of Jehovah.

What is among them.—Better, *what comes to pass for them, i.e.*, for the sinful people.

(20) **Incense from Sheba.**—The land that had a proverbial fame both for gold and frankincense (Isa. lx. 6; Ezek. xxvii. 22), the *thus Sabæum of* Virg., *Æn.* i. 416, 417. So Milton, *Par. Lost*, iv.—

> "Sabæan odours from the spicy shores
> Of Araby the blest."

So the Queen of Sheba brought spices and gold (1 Kings x. 10).

The sweet cane.—Literally, *the good cane*, or, as in Exod. xxx. 23, *sweet calamus* (comp. Isa. xliii. 24; Song Sol. iv. 14), numbered among the ingredients of the Temple incense. The LXX. renders it by "cinnamon." It came from the "far country" of India The whole passage is a reproduction of the thought of Isa. i. 11—13.

(21) **And the fathers and the sons together . . .**—Better, *I give unto this people stumblingblocks, and they shall stumble over them: fathers and sons together, neighbour and his friend, shall perish.*

(22) **From the north country . . .**—The words point, as in chap. i. 13—15, to the Chaldæan, perhaps, also, to the Scythian, invasion. So the "north quarters" are used in Ezek. xxxviii. 6, 15, xxxix. 2 of the home of Gog as the representative of the Scythian tribes.

Shall be raised.—Literally, *shall be roused,* or *awakened.*

The sides of the earth.—*sc.*, its ends, *or* far-off regions.

(23) **Bow and spear.**—As before (chap. v. 16), the special weapons of the Chaldæans. The "spear" was a javelin, shot or hurled against the enemy.

Cruel.—The ferocity of the Chaldæans seems to have been exceptional. Prisoners impaled, or flayed alive, or burnt in the furnace (chap. xxix. 22; Dan. iii. 11), were among the common incidents of their wars and sieges.

They ride upon horses.—This appears to have been a novelty to the Israelites, accustomed to the war-chariots of Egypt and their own kings rather than to actual cavalry. (Comp. chap. viii. 16; Job xxxix. 21—25; Hab. i. 8; Isa. xxx. 16.) Both archers and horsemen appear as prominent in the armies of Gog and Magog, *i.e.*, of the Scythians, in Ezek. xxxviii. 4, xxxix. 3.

Set in array . . .—The Hebrew is singular, and implies a new clause. *It* (the army of bowmen and riders) *is set in array as a warrior, for war against thee.*

(24) **We have heard the fame.**—Another dramatic impersonation of the cry of terror from the dwellers in Jerusalem, when they shall hear of the approach of the army. The imagery of the woman in travail is reproduced from chap. iv. 31.

(25) **The field.**—*i.e., the open country.* To pass beyond the walls of the beleaguered city would be full of danger. The warning has its parallel in Matt. xxiv. 17, 18. In the same chapter we find also an echo of the prophet's reference to the pangs of childbirth (Matt. xxiv. 8).

Fear is on every side.—The words are more

into the field, nor walk by the way; for
the sword of the enemy *and* fear *is* on
every side. (26) O daughter of my people,
gird *thee* with [a] sackcloth, and wallow
thyself in ashes: make thee mourning,
as for an only son, most bitter lamenta-
tion: for the spoiler shall suddenly come
upon us.

(27) I have set thee *for* a tower *and*
[b] a fortress among my people, that
thou mayest know and try their way.
(28) They *are* all grievous revolters, walk-
ing with slanders: *they are* [c] brass and
iron; they *are* all corrupters. (29) The
bellows are burned, the lead is con-
sumed of the fire; the founder melteth
in vain: for the wicked are not plucked
away. (30) [d] [1] Reprobate silver shall *men*
call them, because the LORD hath re-
jected them.

a ch. 4. 8; & 25. 34.

B. C. cir. 600.

b ch. 1. 18; & 15. 20.

c Ezek. 22. 18.

d Isa. 1. 22.

1 Or, *Refuse silver.*

e ch. 18. 11; & 26. 13.

CHAPTER VII.—(1) The word that
came to Jeremiah from the LORD, say-
ing, (2) Stand in the gate of the LORD'S
house, and proclaim there this word,
and say,

Hear the word of the LORD, all *ye of*
Judah, that enter in at these gates to
worship the LORD. (3) Thus saith the
LORD of hosts, the God of Israel,
[e] Amend your ways and your doings,
and I will cause you to dwell in
this place. (4) Trust ye not in lying
words, saying, The temple of the LORD,

---

notable than they seem. They impressed themselves on the prophet's mind, and became to him as a watchword. So, in chap. xx. 3, he gives them as a name (*Magor-missabib*) to Pashur, and apparently (as in chap. xx. 10) it was used as a cry of derision against himself.

(26) **Wallow thyself in ashes.**—So in chap. xxv. 34; Ezek. xxvii. 30. The ordinary sign of mourning was to sprinkle dust or ashes on the head (2 Sam. i. 2, xiii. 19; Josh. vii. 6). This, as in chap. xxv. 34; Micah i. 10; Job ii. 8, indicated more utter wretchedness and prostration. The English verb belongs to the class of those which were once used reflexively, and have now come to be intransitive. "Endeavour" supplies another example.

(27) **I have set thee . . .**—The verse is difficult, as containing words in the Hebrew which are not found elsewhere, and have therefore to be guessed at. The following rendering is given on the authority of the most recent commentators, and has the merit of being in harmony with the metallurgic imagery of the following verses. *As a prover of ore I have set thee among my people, and thou shalt know and try their way.* The words are spoken by Jehovah to the prophet, and describe his work. By others, the first part of the sentence is rendered as follows: *As a prover of ore I have set thee like a fortress,* as if with a reference to chap. i. 18, where the same word is used.

(28) **Grievous revolters . . .**—Literally, *rebels of rebels,* as a Hebraism for the worst type of rebellion.

Walking with slanders.—The phrase was a common one (Lev. xix. 16; Prov. xi. 13, xx. 19), and pointed to the restless eagerness of the tale-bearer to spread his falsehoods. (Comp. 1 Tim. v. 13, "wandering about . . . idle tattlers.")

Brass and iron.—Base metals serving for vile uses, no gold or silver in them. The imagery, which carries on the thought of the previous verse, had been made familiar by Isaiah (i. 22, 25), and was reproduced afterwards by Ezekiel (xxii. 18—22) and Malachi (iii. 3).

Corrupters.—Better, *workers of destruction.*

(29) **The bellows are burned.**—Better, *burn,* or *glow.* In the interpretation of the parable the "bellows" answer to the life of the prophet as filled with the breath or spirit of Jehovah. He is, as it were, consumed with that fiery blast, and yet his work is faulty.

The lead is consumed . . .—Better, *from their fire is lead only.* A different punctuation gives, *The bellows burn with fire; yet lead is the only outcome.* The point lies in the fact that lead was used as a flux in smelting silver ore. The founder in the case supposed went on with his work till the lead was melted, but he found no silver after all.

Plucked away.—Better, *separated* or *purified,* as in keeping with the metaphor.

(30) **Reprobate silver.**—Better, as in the margin, *refuse silver;* the dross and not the metal; so worthless that even Jehovah, as the great refiner, rejects it utterly, as yielding nothing. The adjective and the verb have in the Hebrew the emphasis of being formed from the same root, *Refuse silver . . . because Jehovah had refused them.*

VII.

(1) This chapter and the three that follow form again another great prophetic sermon, delivered to the crowds that flocked to the Temple. There is nothing in the discourse which absolutely fixes its date, but the description of idolatry, as prevalent, and, possibly, the reference to the presence of the Chaldæan invader in chaps. viii. 16, x. 22, fit in rather with the reign of Jehoiakim than with that of Josiah; and from the special reference to Shiloh in chap. xxvi. 6, 9, as occurring in a prophecy delivered at the beginning of that reign, it was probably this discourse, or one like it, and delivered about the same time, that drew down that king's displeasure (see verse 14).

(2) **The gate of the Lord's house.**—As a priest, Jeremiah would have access to all parts of the Temple. On some day when the courts were thronged with worshippers (verse 10), probably a fast-day specially appointed, he stands at the inner gate of one of the courts, possibly, as in chap. xvii. 19, that by which the king entered in ceremonial state, and looking about on the multitudes that thronged it, speaks to them "the word of the Lord," the message which he had been specially commissioned to deliver.

(3) **Your ways and your doings.**—"Ways," as in Zech. i. 6, of general habits, "doings" of separate acts.

I will cause you to dwell.—The English suggests the thoughts of something new, but what Jeremiah promises is simply the continuance of the blessings they had hitherto enjoyed. *I will let you dwell.*

(4) **Trust ye not in lying words . . .**—The emphatic threefold repetition of the words thus condemned

The temple of the LORD, The temple
of the LORD, *are* these. (5) For if ye
throughly amend your ways and your
doings; if ye throughly execute judg-
ment between a man and his neighbour;
(6) *if* ye oppress not the stranger, the
fatherless, and the widow, and shed not
innocent blood in this place, neither
walk after other gods to your hurt:
(7) then will I cause you to dwell in
this place, in the land that I gave to
your fathers, for ever and ever.

(8) Behold, ye trust in lying words,
that cannot profit. (9) Will ye steal,
murder, and commit adultery, and swear
falsely, and burn incense unto Baal, and
walk after other gods whom ye know
not; (10) and come and stand before me
in this house, [1] which is called by my
name, and say, We are delivered to do
all these abominations? (11) Is [a] this
house, which is called by my name,
become a [b] den of robbers in your eyes?
Behold, even I have seen *it*, saith the
LORD. (12) But go ye now unto my place
which *was* in Shiloh, where I set my
name at the first, and see [c] what I did
to it for the wickedness of my people

1 Heb., *whereupon my name is called.*

a Isa. 56, 7.

b Matt. 21. 13; Mark 11. 17; Luke 19. 46.

c 1 Sam. 4. 10, 11; Ps. 78. 60; ch. 26. 6.

"The temple of the Lord," points to its having been the burden of the discourses of the false prophets, possibly to the solemn iteration of the words in the litanies of the supplicants. With no thought of the Divine Presence of which it was the symbol, they were ever harping on its greatness, identifying themselves and the people with that greatness, and predicting its perpetuity. So in Matt. xxiv. 1 the disciples of our Lord point, as with a national pride, to the buildings of the later Temple. The plural "these" is used rather than the singular, as representing the whole complete fabric of courts and porticoes. The higher truth that the "congregation" of Israel was the living Temple (1 Cor. iii. 16; 1 Pet. ii. 5), was not likely to be in the thoughts of those whom Jeremiah rebuked.

(5) **A man and his neighbour.**—The Jewish idiom for the English "one man and another."

(6) **The stranger, the fatherless, and the widow.**—Grouped together, as in Deut. xiv. 29, xxiv. 19—21, as the three great representatives of the poor and helpless, standing most in need therefore of man's justice and of the divine protection.

(7) **For ever and ever.**—Literally, *from eternity to eternity*, or, perhaps, *from age to age*. The English punctuation connects these words with "I will cause you to dwell," but the accentuation of the Hebrew with "I gave to your fathers;" the gift was to have been in perpetuity (Gen. xvii. 8), but the guilt of the people had brought about its forfeiture.

(8) **Lying words.**—With special reference to those already cited in verse 4.

(9) **Will ye steal.**—The English obscures the emphasis of the Hebrew idiom which gives the verbs as a series of infinitives, *What! to steal, to murder, to burn incense to Baal . . . and then have ye come before me . . .!*

(10) **And come and stand.**—Better, *and then have ye come, and stood before me.*

We are delivered.—Taking the word as it stands (a different punctuation adopted by some commentators and versions gives *Deliver us*, as though reproducing, with indignant scorn, the very prayer of the people), the sense seems to be this. The people tried to combine the worship of Baal and Jehovah, and passed from the one temple to the other. They went away from the fast or feast in the house of the Lord with the feeling that they were "saved," or "delivered." They had gone through their religious duties, and might claim their reward. The prophet seems to repeat their words in a tone of irony, They were "delivered," not *from* their abominations, but as if set free to do them.

(11) **A den of robbers.**—The words had a special force in a country like Palestine, where the limestone rocks presented many caves, which, like that of Adullam (1 Sam. xxii. 1, 2), were the refuge of outlaws and robbers. Those who now flocked to the courts of the Temple, including even priests and prophets, were as such robbers, finding shelter there, and soothing their consciences by their worship, as the brigands of Italy do by their devotions at the shrine of some favourite Madonna. It had for them no higher sanctity than "a den of robbers." The word for "robber" implies the more violent form of lawless plunder. The words are memorable, as having re-appeared in our Lord's rebuke of the money-changers and traffickers in the Temple (Matt. xxi. 13; Mark xi. 17; Luke xix. 46); and, taken together with the reference at the last Supper to the New Covenant of chap. xxxi. 31, suggest the thought that our Lord was leading His disciples to see in the prophet's work a foreshadowing of His own relation to the evils of His time, and more than a foreshadowing of the great remedy which He was to work out for them.

(12) **My place which was in Shiloh.**—The history of the past showed that a Temple dedicated to Jehovah could not be desecrated with impunity. Shiloh had been chosen for the centre of the worship of Israel after the conquest of Canaan (Josh. xviii. 1), and was reverenced as such through the whole period of the Judges. It had not, however, been a centre of light and purity. It had been defiled by wild dances of a half-idolatrous character; by deeds of shameless violence (Judges xxi. 19—21), and by the sins of the sons of Eli (1 Sam. ii. 22). And so the judgment came. It lost the presence of the ark (1 Sam. iv. 17; Ps. lxxviii. 58—64); its people were slaughtered by the Philistines; it fell into decay. It is possible, as the words "temple" (1 Sam. i. 9, iii. 3) and "house" (1 Sam. iii. 15; Judges xviii. 31) applied to it suggest, that substantial buildings may have gathered round the original tabernacle, and that those wasted ruins may have given a special force to Jeremiah's allusion. It will be seen from chap. xxvi. 6, 9, 11, that it was this reference that more than anything else provoked the wrath of priest and people. They thought with a half-concealed exultation of the fate of the earlier sanctuary in Ephraim, which had given way to that of Judah. They forgot that like sins bring about like punishments, and were startled when they heard that as terrible a doom was impending over the Temple of which they boasted. It would appear from chap. xli. 5 that the ruin was not total, perhaps that it was still visited by pilgrims. Jerome describes

Israel. (13) And now, because ye have
done all these works, saith the LORD,
and I spake unto you, rising up early
and speaking, but ye heard not; and
I [a]called you, but ye answered not;
(14) therefore will I do unto *this* house,
which is called by my name, wherein ye
trust, and unto the place which I gave
to you and to your fathers, as I have
done to [b]Shiloh. (15) And I will cast
you out of my sight, as I have cast out
all your brethren, *even* the whole seed
of Ephraim.

(16) Therefore [c]pray not thou for this
people, neither lift up cry nor prayer
for them, neither make intercession to
me: for I will not hear thee. (17) Seest
thou not what they do in the cities of
Judah and in the streets of Jerusalem?
(18) [d]The children gather wood, and the
fathers kindle the fire, and the women
knead *their* dough, to make cakes to the
[1]queen of heaven, and to pour out drink
offerings unto other gods, that they
may provoke me to anger. (19) Do
they provoke me to anger? saith the
LORD: *do they* not *provoke* themselves
to the confusion of their own faces?
(20) Therefore thus saith the Lord GOD;
Behold, mine anger and my fury shall
be poured out upon this place, upon
man, and upon beast, and upon the
trees of the field, and upon the fruit
of the ground; and it shall burn, and
shall not be quenched.

(21) Thus saith the LORD of hosts, the
God of Israel; [e]Put your burnt offer-
ings unto your sacrifices, and eat flesh.
(22) For I spake not unto your fathers,
nor commanded them in the day that I

a Prov. 1. 24; Isa. 65. 12; & 66. 4.

b 1 Sam. 4. 10, 11; Ps. 78. 60; & 132. 6; ch. 26. 6.

c Exod. 32. 10; ch. 11. 14; & 14. 11.

d ch. 44. 19.

1 Or, *frame*, or, *workmanship of heaven.*

e Isa. 1. 11; ch. 6. 20; Amos 5. 21.

---

it as a heap of ruins. It has been identified by modern travellers with the village of *Seilun.*

(13) **Rising up early and speaking.**—A characteristic phrase of Jeremiah's, and used by him only (verse 25, chap. xxv. 4, xxvi. 5, xxix. 19). In its bold anthropomorphism it takes the highest form of human activity, waking from sleep and beginning at the dawn of day, to represent the like activity in God.

I called you, but ye answered not.—An echo of earlier complaints from prophets and wise men (Prov. i. 24; Isa. lxv. 12, lxvi. 4), destined itself to be used again by One greater than the prophets (Matt. xxiii. 37).

(15) **The whole seed of Ephraim.**—The fate of the tribes of the Northern kingdom, among which Ephraim had always held the leading position, was already familiar to the people. They were dwelling far off by Habor or Gozan, and the cities of the Medes (2 Kings xv. 29, xvii. 6, xviii. 11). A like exile was, they were now told, to be their own portion.

(16) **Pray not thou.**—The words imply that a prayer of intercession, like that which Moses had offered of old (Exod. xxxii. 10), was rising up in the heart of the prophet. He is told that he must check it. Judgment must have its way. The discipline must be left to do its work. A like impulse met by a like repression is found in chaps. xi. 14, and xiv. 11. It is obvious that the utterance of the conflict between his human affections and the Divine will made the sentence which he pronounced more terrible than ever.

(17) **Seest thou not . . . ?**—We enter on one of the darker regions of Jewish idolatry, such as Ezekiel (chap. viii.) saw in vision. A foreign worship of the basest kind was practised, not only in secret, but in the open places.

(18) **The queen of heaven.**—The goddess thus described was a kind of Assyrian Artemis, identified with the moon, and connected with the symbolic worship of the reproductive powers of Nature. Its ritual probably resembled that of the Babylonian Aphrodite, Mylitta, the mother-goddess, in its impurities (Herod. i. 199; Baruch vi. 43), and thus provoked the burning indignation of the prophet here and in chap. xliv. 19, 25. The word rendered "cakes," and found only in connection with this worship, was clearly a technical term, and probably of foreign origin. Cakes of a like kind, made of flour and honey, round like the full moon, and known, therefore, as *selenæ* or "moons," were offered, like the *Minchah* or meat-offerings in the Mosaic ritual, the *Neideh* in the Egyptian worship of the goddess *Neith*, at Athens to Artemis, and in Sicily to Hecate (Theocr., *Idylls*, ii. 33). The worship of Ashtoreth (Milton speaks of her as "Astarte, Queen of Heaven, with crescent horn"), though of kindred nature, was not identical with that of the Queen of Heaven, that name signifying a star, and being identified with the planet Venus. A various reading gives, as in the margin, "the frame of heaven."

(19) **Do they not provoke themselves . . . ?**—The interpolated words, though they complete the sense, mar the abrupt force of the Hebrew. *Is it not themselves, to the confusion of their own faces?*

(20) **Shall be poured out.**—The word is used in Exod. ix. 33 of the plague of rain; here, of the great shower of the fire of the wrath of Jehovah (comp. Nah. i. 6). It is significant that it had been used by Josiah on hearing of the judgments denounced in the new-found copy of the Law (2 Chron. xxxiv. 21).

(21) **Put your burnt offerings.**—*i.e.,* "Add one kind of sacrifice to another. Offer the victim, and then partake of the sacrificial feast. All is fruitless, unless there be the true conditions of acceptance, repentance, and holiness."

(22) **I spake not . . . concerning burnt offerings or sacrifices.**—"Concerning" is, literally, *for,* or *with a view to, the matter of sacrifices.* The words seem at first hard to reconcile with the multiplied rules as to sacrifices both in Exodus and Leviticus. They are, however, rightly understood, strictly in harmony with the facts. They were not the end contemplated. The first promulgation of the Law, the basis of the covenant with Israel, contemplated a spiritual, ethical religion, of which the basis was found in the ten great Words, or commandments, of Exod. xx. The ritual in connection with sacrifice was prescribed partly as a concession to the feeling which showed itself, in its evil form, in the worship of the golden calf, partly as an education. The book of Deuteronomy, representing the

brought them out of the land of Egypt,
[1]concerning burnt offerings or sacrifices:
(23) but this thing commanded I them,
saying, [a]Obey my voice, and [b]I will be
your God, and ye shall be my people:
and walk ye in all the ways that I have
commanded you, that it may be well
unto you. (24) But they hearkened not,
nor inclined their ear, but walked in
the counsels *and* in the [2]imagination of
their evil heart, and [3]went backward,
and not forward. (25) Since the day
that your fathers came forth out of the
land of Egypt unto this day I have
even [c]sent unto you all my servants the
prophets, daily rising up early and
sending *them:* (26) yet they hearkened
not unto me, nor inclined their ear, but
[d]hardened their neck: they did worse
than their fathers. (27) Therefore thou
shalt speak all these words unto them;
but they will not hearken to thee:
thou shalt also call unto them; but
they will not answer thee. (28) But
thou shalt say unto them, This *is* a
nation that obeyeth not the voice of
the LORD their God, nor receiveth [4]cor-
rection: truth is perished, and is cut
off from their mouth.
(29) Cut off thine hair, *O Jerusalem,*
and cast *it* away, and take up a lamen-
tation on high places; for the LORD

1 Heb., *concerning the matter of.*
a Deut. 6. 3.
b Exod. 19. 5; Lev. 26. 12.
2 Or, *stubbornness.*
3 Heb., *were.*
c 2 Chron. 36. 15.
d ch. 16. 12.
4 Or, *instruction.*

higher truth from which Moses started (Exod. xix. 5), and upon which he at last fell back, bore its witness to the original purport of the Law (Deut. vi. 3; x. 12). Its re-discovery under Josiah left, here as elsewhere, its impress on the mind of Jeremiah; but prophets, as in 1 Sam. xv. 22; Hosea vi. 6, viii. 11—13; Amos v. 21—27; Micah vi. 6—8; Pss. l., li., had all along borne a like witness, even while recognising to the full the fact and the importance of a sacrificial ritual.

(23) **But this thing commanded I them.**—The words that follow are a composite quotation, partly from the lately re-found Deuteronomy (v. 33), partly from the words that were strictly true of the "day" when Israel came out of Egypt (Exod. xix. 5), partly from the very book which seemed to be most characterised by sacrificial ritual, Leviticus (xxvi. 12). The influence of Jeremiah's teaching on later Jewish thought is shown by the fact that this very section of Jeremiah (vii. 21—28) appears in the Synagogue ritual as the *Haphtara*, or second lesson from the prophets, after Lev. vi.—viii., as the *Parashah*, or first lesson from the Law. The Synagogue worship, indeed, was, in the nature of the case, the result of the teaching of scribes and prophets rather than of priests, and therefore a witness for the spiritual truth symbolised in sacrifice, and not for the perpetuation of the symbol.

(24) **Imagination.**—Better, *stubbornness*, as in chap. iii. 17.

Went backward and not forward.—The whole sacrificial system, even at its best, to say nothing of its idolatrous corruptions, was accordingly, from Jeremiah's point of view, a retrograde movement. The apostasy of the people in the worship of the golden calf involved a like deflection, necessary and inevitable though it might be as a process of education, from the first ideal polity, based upon the covenant made with Abraham, *i.e.*, upon a pure and spiritual theism, the emblems and ordinances of which, though "shadows of good things to come," were in themselves "weak and beggarly elements" (Heb. x. 1; Gal. iv. 9).

(25) **Daily rising up.**—Stress is laid on the continual succession of prophets as witnesses of the Truth from the beginning. The prophet was not tied to the actual letter of his statement, and the prominence given to Samuel, as the first who bore the name of prophet (1 Sam. ix. 9), seems at first against him. On the other hand, the gift of prophecy (as seen in Num. xi. 25—29) was bestowed freely even during the wilderness wanderings, and the mention of prophets (Judges iv. 4, vi. 8) and men of God (Judges xiii. 6), perhaps, also, that of the "angel" or messenger of God, in Judges v. 23, as well as the honour paid to seers before the time of Samuel (1 Sam. ix. 8), show that, great as he was, it was that name and the organisation, rather than the gift, that were new in his ministry.

(26) **Worse than their fathers.**—The rapid survey of the past makes it doubtful whether the comparison is made between the generations that came out of Egypt and their immediate followers, or between those followers and their successors. Probably the general thought was that the whole history of Israel had been one of progressive deterioration, reaching its climax in the generation in which Jeremiah lived. His words find a striking parallel in the complaint of the Roman historian (Livy, *Præf.*), or of the poet:—

"Ætas parentum, pejor avis, tulit
Nos nequiores."—Hor., *Od.* iii. 6.

"Our fathers' age, more stained with crime
Than were their sires in older time,
Has brought us forth a later race
Yet more iniquitous and base."

(27) **Therefore . . . also.**—Better, in both cases, *though thou shalt speak, yet they will not hearken; though thou shalt call unto them, yet they will not answer thee.*

(28) **But thou shalt say.**—Better, *And thou shalt say*, with an implied "therefore."

This is a nation.—Better, *This is the nation*, as pre-eminent in its sin.

Truth.—Better, as in verse 2, *faithfulness.*

(29) **Cut off thine hair.**—Literally, as in 2 Sam. i. 10; 2 Kings xi. 12, *thy crown* or *diadem;* but the verb determines the meaning. The word *Netzer* ("consecration" in the Authorised version) is applied to the unshorn locks of the Nazarite (Num. vi. 7), and from it he took his name. As the Nazarite was to shave his head if he came in contact with a corpse, as cutting the hair close was generally among Semitic races the sign of extremest sorrow (Job i. 20; Micah i. 16), so Jerusalem was to sit as a woman rejected by her husband, bereaved of her children. (Comp. the picture in Lam. i. 1—3.) The word is applied also to the "crown" of the high priest in Exod. xxix. 6, the "crown" of the anointing oil in Lev. xxi. 12.

O Jerusalem.—The italics show that the words are not in the Hebrew, but the insertion of some such words was rendered necessary by the fact that the verb "cut off" is in the feminine. Those who heard or read

hath rejected and forsaken the genera-
tion of his wrath. (30) For the children
of Judah have done evil in my sight,
saith the LORD: they have set their
abominations in the house which is
called by my name, to pollute it.
(31) And they have built the [a]high places
of Tophet, which *is* in the valley of the
son of Hinnom, to burn their sons and
their daughters in the fire; which I
commanded *them* not, neither [1]came it
into my heart. (32) Therefore, behold,
the days [b]come, saith the LORD, that it
shall no more be called Tophet, nor the
valley of the son of Hinnom, but the
valley of slaughter: for they shall bury
in Tophet, till there be no place.
(33) And the [c]carcases of this people shall
be meat for the fowls of the heaven,
and for the beasts of the earth; and
none shall fray *them* away. (34) Then
will I cause to [d]cease from the cities
of Judah, and from the streets of
Jerusalem, the voice of mirth, and
the voice of gladness, the voice of the
bridegroom, and the voice of the bride:
for the land shall be desolate.

CHAPTER VIII.—(1) At that time,
saith the LORD, they shall bring out
the bones of the kings of Judah, and
the bones of his princes, and the bones

[a] 2 Kings 23. 10; ch. 19. 5.

[1] Heb., *came it upon my heart.*

[b] ch. 19. 6.

[c] Ps. 79. 2; ch. 16. 4; & 34. 20.

[d] Isa. 24. 7; ch. 16. 9; & 25. 10; & 33. 11; Ezek. 26. 13; Hosea 2. 11.

---

the words of the prophet, who so often spoke of "the daughter of Zion" (chap. vi. 2), of "the daughter of his people" (chaps. vi. 14, viii. 11), of "the betrothed of Jehovah" (chaps. ii., iii.), would be at no loss to understand his meaning.

(30) **In the house which is called by my name.**—This had been done by Ahaz (2 Chron. xxviii. 2), and after the Temple had been cleansed by Hezekiah (2 Chron. xxix. 5) had been repeated by Manasseh (2 Kings xxi. 4—7; 2 Chron. xxxiii. 3—7). Josiah's reformation again checked the tendency to idolatry (2 Kings xxiii. 4; 2 Chron. xxxiv. 3); but it is quite possible that the pendulum swung back again when his death left the idolatrous party in Judah free to act, and that this special aggravation of the evil, the desecration of the Temple of Jehovah by "abominations" of idol-worship, re-appeared together with the worship of the Queen of Heaven and the sacrifices to Molech.

(31) **High places.**—Not the same word as in verse 29, but *bamoth,* as in the "high places" of Baal, in Num. xxii. 41, xxiii. 3, the Bamoth-baal of Josh. xiii. 17. The word had become almost technical for the mounds, natural or (as in this passage) artificial, on which altars to Jehovah or to other gods were erected, and appears in 1 Sam. ix. 12; 1 Kings iii. 4; Ezek. xx. 29; Amos vii. 9.

Tophet.—This appears to have been originally, not a local name, but a descriptive epithet. The word appears in Job xvii. 6 ("by-word" in the Authorised version) as a thing spat upon and loathed. Its use is probably therefore analogous to the scorn with which the prophets substituted *bosheth,* the "shameful thing," for Baal (*e.g.,* chap. iii. 24, xi. 13). When the prediction is repeated in chaps. xix. 5, xxxii. 35, we have the "high places of Baal," and "Tophet" here is obviously substituted for that name in indignant contempt. The word in Isa. xxx. 33, though not identical in form (*Tophteh,* not *Tophet*), had probably the same meaning. Other etymologies give as the meaning of the word "a garden," "a place of burning," or "a place of drums," *i.e.,* a music grove, and so connect it more closely with the Molech ritual. Possibly the last was the original meaning of the name, for which, as said above, the prophets used the term of opprobrium.

The son of Hinnom.—Possibly the first recorded owner, or a local hero. The name is perpetuated in later Jewish language in Ge-henna = Ge-Hinnom = the vale of Hinnom. It was older than the Molech worship with which it became identified, and appears in the "Doomsday Book" of Israel (Josh. xv. 8, xviii. 16).

To burn their sons and their daughters.—The words are important as determining the character of the act more vaguely described in chap. xxxii. 35, as "making to pass through the fire." The children were, in some cases at least, actually burnt, though often, perhaps (see Ezek. xvi. 21), slain first. Horrible as the practice seems to us, it was part of the Canaanite or Phœnician worship of Molech or Malcom (Lev. xviii. 21, xx. 2—5), and had been practised by Ahaz (2 Kings xvi. 3; 2 Chron. xxviii. 3) and Manasseh (2 Kings xxi. 6; 2 Chron. xxxiii. 6).

(32) **Till there be no place.**—Better, *because there is no room*—*i.e.,* for want of space the dead should be buried even in the spot which the worshippers of Molech looked on as sacred, and the worshippers of Jehovah as accursed, and which both therefore would willingly avoid using as a place of sepulture.

(33) **None shall fray them away.**—No picture could be more appalling in its horrors—streets and valleys filled with the bodies of the slain, vultures and jackals feeding on them, and not one hand raised, like that of Rizpah (2 Sam. xxi. 10), to protect the dead from that extremest desecration. Here, again, we have an almost literal quotation from Deut. (xxviii. 26).

(34) **Then will I cause to cease . . . the voice of mirth.**—The special imagery of the picture of desolation is characteristic of Jeremiah (xvi. 9, xxv. 10, xxxiii. 11). No words could paint the utter break-up of the life of the nation more forcibly. Nothing is heard but wailing and lamentation, or, more terrible even than that, there is the utter silence of solitude. The capacity for joy and the occasions for rejoicing (comp. 1 Macc. ix. 39 for the bridal rejoicings of Israel) belong alike to the past.

Shall be desolate.—The same word as in the "waste places" of Isa. li. 3, lviii. 12; it is used in Ezek. xiii. 4 for the haunts of the "foxes," or rather the "jackals" of the "deserts," but always of places that, having been once inhabited, have fallen into ruins (Lev. xxvi. 31).

VIII.

(1) **At that time.**—There is, it is obvious, no break in the discourse, and the time is therefore that of the destruction of Jerusalem by the Chaldæans, and of the burial of the slain. Not even the dead should sleep in peace. With an awful re-iteration of the word, so as to give the emphasis as of the toll of a funeral bell, the prophet heaps clause upon clause, "the *bones* of the

of the priests, and the bones of the
prophets, and the bones of the in-
habitants of Jerusalem, out of their
graves: (2) and they shall spread them
before the sun, and the moon, and all
the host of heaven, whom they have
loved, and whom they have served, and
after whom they have walked, and
whom they have sought, and whom
they have worshipped: they shall not
be gathered, nor be buried; they shall
be for dung upon the face of the earth.
(3) And death shall be chosen rather
than life by all the residue of them that
remain of this evil family, which remain
in all the places whither I have driven
them, saith the LORD of hosts.
(4) Moreover thou shalt say unto them,

a Isa. i. 3.

Thus saith the LORD; Shall they fall,
and not arise? shall he turn away, and
not return? (5) Why *then* is this people
of Jerusalem slidden back by a per-
petual backsliding? they hold fast
deceit, they refuse to return. (6) I
hearkened and heard, *but* they spake
not aright: no man repented him of
his wickedness, saying, What have I
done? every one turned to his course,
as the horse rusheth into the battle.
(7) Yea, *a* the stork in the heaven knoweth
her appointed times; and the turtle
and the crane and the swallow observe
the time of their coming; but my
people know not the judgment of the
LORD. (8) How do ye say, We *are* wise,
and the law of the LORD *is* with us?

---

kings," "the *bones* of the princes," and so on. The motives of this desecration of the sepulchres might be either the wanton ferocity of barbarian conquerors, bent, after the manner of savage warfare, on the mutilation of the dead, or the greed of gain and the expectation of finding concealed treasures. So Hyrcanus, to the great scandal of the Jews, broke open the sepulchre of David (Joseph., *Ant.* vii. 15).

(2) **Whom they have loved . . .**—Here, again, there is a peculiar characteristic emphasis in the piling up, one upon another, of verbs more or less synonymous. So far as there is a traceable order, it is from the first inward impulse prompting to idolatry to the full development of that feeling in ritual. The sun, moon, and stars shall look, not on crowds of adoring worshippers, but on the carcases of those whose love and worship, transferred from Jehovah to the host of heaven, have brought on them that terrible doom.

(3) **The residue of them that remain.**—Once more the emphasis of re-iteration, "the remnant of a remnant." The "evil family" is the whole house of Israel, but the words contemplate specially the exile of Judah and Benjamin, rather than that of the ten tribes.

(4) **Shall he turn.**—Better, as both clauses are indefinite, *Shall men fall and not arise? Shall one turn away and not return?* The appeal is made to the common practice of men. Those who fall struggle to their feet again. One who finds that he has lost his way retraces his steps. In its spiritual aspect the words assert the possibility of repentance in all but every case, however desperate it may seem. St. Paul's question, "Have they stumbled that they should fall?" (Rom. xi. 11), expresses something of the same belief in the ultimate triumph of the Divine purpose of good. As yet, that purpose, as the next verse shows, seemed to be thwarted.

(5) **Slidden back . . . backsliding.**—The English fails to give the full emphasis of the re-iteration of the same word as in the previous verse. *Why doth this people of Jerusalem turn away with a perpetual turning?* Here, so far, there was no retracing the evil path which they had chosen.

(6) **I hearkened and heard.**—Jehovah himself is introduced here, as probably in the question of the previous verse, as speaking, listening for cries of penitence, and hearing only the words of the evil-doers.

Rusheth.—The word is primarily used of the rushing of a torrent (Isa. viii. 8, x. 22, xxviii. 17), and is applied to the frantic impetuosity with which Israel was rushing into evil, and therefore into the misery that followed it.

(7) **The stork in the heaven.**—The eye of the prophet looked on nature at once with the quick observation of one who is alive to all her changes, and with the profound thought of a poet finding inner meanings in all phenomena. The birds of the air obey their instincts as the law of their nature. Israel, with its fatal gift of freedom, resists that which is its law of life. The stork arrives in Palestine in March, and leaves for the north of Europe in April or May. The Hebrew name, *chasideh* (literally, *the pious bird*), indicating its care for its young, is suggestive, as also is the phrase "in the heavens," as applied to its characteristic mode of flight. The turtle-dove appears at the approach of spring (Song Sol. ii. 12).

The crane and the swallow.—In the judgment of Tristram and other modern naturalists, the words should change places, and perhaps "swift" take the place of swallow. The word for "swallow" in Ps. lxxxiv. 3 is different. The same combination meets us in Isa. xxxviii. 14.

Judgment.—Better, perhaps, *ordinance*, the appointed rule of life which brute creatures obey and man transgresses.

(8) **How do ye say . . . ?**—The question is put to priests and prophets, who were the recognised expounders of the Law, but not to them only. The order of scribes, which became so dominant during the exile, was already rising into notice. Shaphan, to whom Hilkiah gave the re-found Book of the Law, belonged to it (2 Chron. xxxiv. 15), and the discovery of that book would naturally give a fresh impetus to their work. They were boasting of their position as the recognised instructors of the people.

Lo, certainly . . .—Better, *Verily, lo! the lying pen of the scribes hath made it* (*i.e., the Law*) *as a lie.* The *pen* was the iron *stylus* made for engraving on stone or metal. The meaning of the clause is clear. The sophistry of men was turning the truth of God into a lie, and emptying it of its noblest meaning.

Lo, certainly [1]in vain made he *it;* the
pen of the scribes *is* in vain. (9) [a][2]The
wise *men* are ashamed, they are dis-
mayed and taken: lo, they have
rejected the word of the LORD; and
[3]what wisdom *is* in them? (10) There-
fore will I give their wives unto others,
and their fields to them that shall in-
herit *them:* for every one from the least
even unto the greatest is given to [b]covet-
ousness, from the prophet even unto
the priest every one dealeth falsely.
(11) For they have [c]healed the hurt of
the daughter of my people slightly,
saying, [d]Peace, peace; when *there is* no
peace. (12) Were they [e]ashamed when
they had committed abomination? nay,
they were not at all ashamed, neither
could they blush: therefore shall they
fall among them that fall: in the time
of their visitation they shall be cast
down, saith the LORD. (13) [4]I will surely
consume them, saith the LORD: *there
shall be* no grapes [f]on the vine, nor figs
on the [g]fig tree, and the leaf shall fade;
and *the things that* I have given them
shall pass away from them.
(14) Why do we sit still? assemble
yourselves, and let us enter into the
defenced cities, and let us be silent
there: for the LORD our God hath put
us to silence, and given us [h]water of
[5]gall to drink, because we have sinned
against the LORD. (15) We [i]looked for
peace, but no good *came; and* for a
time of health, and behold trouble!
(16) The snorting of his horses was heard
from [k]Dan: the whole land trembled at
the sound of the neighing of his strong
ones; for they are come, and have de-
voured the land, and [6]all that is in it;
the city, and those that dwell therein.
(17) For, behold, I will send serpents,
cockatrices, among you, which *will* not

1 Or, *the false pen of the scribes worketh for falsehood.*
a ch. 6. 15.
2 Or, *Have they been ashamed,* &c.
3 Heb., *the wisdom of what thing.*
b Isa. 56. 11; ch. 6. 13.
c ch. 6. 14.
d Ezek. 13. 10.
e ch. 3. 3; & 6. 15.
4 Or, *In gathering I will consume.*
f Isa. 5. 1, &c.
g Matt. 21. 19; Luke 13. 6, &c.
h ch. 9. 15; & 23. 15.
5 Or, *poison.*
i ch. 14. 19.
k ch. 4. 15.
6 Heb., *the fulness thereof.*

Already, as in other things, so here, in his protest against the teaching of the scribes, with their traditional and misleading casuistry, Jeremiah appears as foreshadowing the prophet of Nazareth (Matt. v. 20—48, xxiii. 2—26).

(9) **They have rejected the word of the Lord.**—The "wise men" are apparently distinguished from the scribes, probably as students of the ethical or sapiential books of Israel, such as the Proverbs of Solomon, as distinct from the Law. The reign of Hezekiah, it will be remembered, had been memorable for such studies (Prov. xxv. 1). They, too, kept within the range of traditional maxims and precepts, perhaps with stress on ceremonial rather than moral obligations; and when the word of Jehovah came to them straight from the lips of the prophets, they refused to listen to it, and with that refusal, what wisdom could they claim?

(10—12) **Every one from the least . . .**—The prophet reproduces, though not verbally, what he had already said in chap. vi. 12—15. (Comp. Notes there.) It is as though that emphatic condemnation of the sins of the false teachers were burnt into his soul, and could not but find utterance whenever he addressed the people.

(13) **I will surely consume.**—Literally, *Gathering, I will sweep away—i.e.,* I will gather and sweep away, the two verbs being all but identical in sound and spelling, so that the construction has almost the force of the emphatic Hebrew reduplication.

There shall be.—These words are not in the Hebrew, and the verse describes, not the judgment of Jehovah on the state of Israel, but that state itself. *There are no grapes on the vine, no figs on the fig-tree, the leaf fadeth.* The words are figurative rather than literal, after the manner of chap. ii. 21; Isa. v. 2. Israel is a degenerate vine, a barren fig-tree. Here, again, we find an echo of the teaching of Jeremiah in that of Jesus (Matt. xxi. 19; Luke xiii. 6—9). In Micah vii. 1 we have another example of the same figurative language.

The things that I have given them . . .—The words have been differently rendered, (1) *I gave them that which they transgress—i.e.,* the divine law of righteousness; and (2) *therefore I will appoint those that shall pass over them—i.e.,* the invaders who shall overrun their country. The former seems on the whole best suited to the context.

(14) **Why do we sit still? . . .**—The cry of the people in answer to the threatening of Jehovah is brought in by the prophet with a startling dramatic vividness. They are ready to flee into the defenced cities, as the prophet had told them in chap. iv. 5, but it is without hope. They are going into the silence as of death, for to that silence Jehovah himself has brought them.

Water of gall.—The idea implied is that of poison as well as bitterness. It is uncertain what the "gall-plant" was; possibly, from its connection with "grapes" or "clusters," as in Deut. xxxii. 32, belladonna or colocynth is meant. Others have suggested the poppy, and this is in part confirmed by the narcotic properties implied in Matt. xxvii. 34. In Deut. xxix. 18 it is joined with "wormwood."

(15) **A time of health . . .**—Better, *healing,* or, following another etymology, *a time of quietness, and behold alarm.* "Peace," in the first clause, is used in its wider sense as including all forms of good.

(16) **Heard from Dan.**—As in chap. iv. 13, the invasion by an army of which cavalry and war chariots formed the most terrible contingent was a special terror to Israelites. Even at Dan, the northern boundary of Palestine (see Note on chap. iv. 15), there was a sound of terror in the very snortings of the horses. The patristic interpretation that the prophet indicates the coming of Antichrist from the tribe deserves a passing notice as one of the eccentricities of exegesis.

(17) **Serpents, cockatrices.**—There is a sudden change of figure, one new image of terror starting from the history of the fiery serpents of Num. xxi. 6, or, possibly, from the connection of Dan with the "serpent"

be [a]charmed, and they shall bite you,
saith the LORD.
(18) *When* I would comfort myself
against sorrow, my heart *is* faint[1] in
me. (19) Behold the voice of the cry of
the daughter of my people [2]because of
them that dwell in a far country: *Is*
not the LORD in Zion? *is* not her king
in her? Why have they provoked me
to anger with their graven images, *and*
with strange vanities? (20) The harvest
is past, the summer is ended, and we
are not saved. (21) For the hurt of the
daughter of my people am I hurt; I
am black; astonishment hath taken
hold on me. (22) *Is there* no [b]balm in
Gilead; *is there* no physician there?
why then is not the health of the
daughter of my people [3]recovered?

CHAPTER IX.—(1) Oh [4c]that my
head were waters, and mine eyes a foun-
tain of tears, that I might weep day and
night for the slain of the daughter of
my people! (2) Oh that I had in the
wilderness a lodging place of wayfaring
men; that I might leave my people, and
go from them! for they *be* all adulterers,

a Ps. 58. 4, 5.
1 Heb., *upon.*
2 Heb., *because of the country of them that are far off.*
b ch. 46. 11.
3 Heb., *gone up?*
4 Heb., *Who will give my head, &c.*
c Isa. 22. 4; ch. 4. 19.

---

and "adder" in Gen. xlix. 17. It is not easy to identify the genus and species of the serpents of the Bible. Here the two words are in apposition. "Cockatrice," however, cannot be right, that name belonging, as an English word, to legendary zoology. The Vulg. gives "basilisk." In Prov. xxiii. 32 it is translated by "adder." In any case it implies a hissing venomous snake (probably the *cerastes* or *serpens regulus*), and the symbolism which identified it with the Assyrian or Chaldæan power had already appeared in Isa. xiv. 29.

Which will not be charmed.—The figure is that of Ps. lviii. 4, 5. The "deaf adder" that "refuseth to hear the voice of the charmer" represents an implacable enemy waging a pitiless war. Serpent-charming, as in the case of the Egyptian sorcerers (Exod. vii. 11), seems to have been from a very early time, as it is now, both in Egypt and India, one of the most prominent features of the natural magic of the East.

(18) **When I would comfort myself . . .**—The word translated *comfort* is not found elsewhere, and has been very differently understood. Taking the words as spoken after a pause, they come as a cry of sorrow following the proclamation of the judgment of Jehovah, *Ah, my comfort against sorrow!* (mourning for it as dead and gone); *my heart is sick within me.* The latter phrase is the same as in Isa. i. 5.

(19) **Because of them that dwell . . .**—The verse should read thus: *Behold, the voice of the cry for help of the daughter of my people from the land of those that are far off.* The prophet, dramatising the future, as before, in verse 14, hears the cry of the exiles in a far-off land, and that which they ask is this—"Is not Jehovah in Zion? Is not her king in her?" That question is asked half in despair, and half in murmuring complaint. But Jehovah himself returns the answer, and it comes in the form of another question, "Why have they provoked me to anger . . ?" They had forsaken Him before. He forsook them now and left them, for a time, to their own ways.

(20) **The harvest is past . . .**—The question of Jehovah, admitting of no answer but a confession of guilt, is met by another cry of despair from the sufferers of the future. They are as men in a year of famine—"The harvest is past," and there has been no crop for men to reap.

Summer.—In Isa. xvi. 9; Jer. xl. 10, and elsewhere, the word is rendered by "summer fruits." "The summer" (better, *the fruit-gathering*) is ended, and yet they are not saved from misery and death. All has failed alike. The whole formula had probably become proverbial for extremest misery. It is well to remember that the barley-harvest coincided with the Passover, the wheat-harvest with Pentecost, the fruit-gathering with the autumn Feast of Tabernacles.

(21) **For the hurt . . .**—Now the prophet again speaks in his own person. He is *crushed* in that *crushing* of his people. His face is *darkened*, as one that mourns. (Comp. Ps. xxxviii. 6; Josh. v. 11.)

(22) **Is there no balm in Gilead . . . ?**—The resinous gums of Gilead, identified by some naturalists with those of the terebinth, by others with mastich, the gum of the *Pistaccia lentiscus*, were prominent in the pharmacopœia of Israel, and were exported to Egypt for the embalmment of the dead (Gen. xxxvii. 25, xliii. 11; Jer. xlvi. 11, li. 8). A plaister of such gums was the received prescription for healing a wound. The question of the prophet is therefore a parable. "Are there no means of healing, no healer to apply them, for the spiritual wounds of Israel? The prophets were her physicians, repentance and righteousness were her balm of Gilead. *Why has no balsam-plaister been laid on the daughter of my people?* Why so little result from the means which Jehovah has provided?" The imagery re-appears in chap. xlvi. 11, li. 8. The balm which was grown at Jericho under the Roman Empire (Tac., *Hist.* v. 6; Plin., *Nat. Hist.* xii. 25), and was traditionally reported to have been brought by the Queen of Sheba, was probably the *Amyris Opobalsamum*, now cultivated at Mecca, which requires a more tropical climate than that of Gilead. Wyclif's version, "Is there no *triacle* in Gilead?" may be noted as illustrating the history of a word now obsolete. "Triacle" was the English form of *theriacum*, the mediæval panacea for all wounds, and specially for the bites of serpents and venomous beasts.

IX.

(1) **Oh, that my head were waters . . . !**—Literally, *Who will give my head waters . . . ?* The form of a question was, in Hebrew idiom as in Latin, the natural utterance of desire. In the Hebrew text this verse comes as the last in chap. viii. It is, of course, very closely connected with what precedes; but, on the other hand, it is even more closely connected with what follows. Strictly speaking, there ought to be no break at all, and the discourse should flow on continuously.

A fountain.—Here, as in chap. ii. 13, xvii. 13, and elsewhere, the Hebrew word *makor* is a tank or *réservoir* rather than a spring.

(2) **Oh, that I had . . . !**—Literally, as before, *Who will give . . . ?*

an assembly of treacherous men. (3) And
they bend their tongues *like* their bow
for lies: but they are not valiant for
the truth upon the earth; for they
proceed from evil to evil, and they know
not me, saith the LORD.
(4) [a]Take ye heed every one of his
[1]neighbour, and trust ye not in any
brother: for every brother will utterly
supplant, and every neighbour will walk
with slanders. (5) And they will [2]deceive
every one his neighbour, and will not
speak the truth: they have taught
their tongue to speak lies, *and* weary
themselves to commit iniquity. (6) Thine
habitation *is* in the midst of deceit;
through deceit they refuse to know me,
saith the LORD.
(7) Therefore thus saith the LORD of
hosts, Behold, I will melt them, and
try them; for how shall I do for the
daughter of my people? (8) Their
tongue *is as* an arrow shot out; it
speaketh [b]deceit: *one* speaketh [c]peace-
ably to his neighbour with his mouth,
but [3]in heart he layeth [4]his wait.
(9) [d]Shall I not visit them for these
things? saith the LORD: shall not my
soul be avenged on such a nation as
this?
(10) For the mountains will I take up
a weeping and wailing, and for the
[5]habitations of the wilderness a lamen-
tation, because they are [6]burned up,
so that none can pass through *them;*
neither can *men* hear the voice of the
cattle; [7]both the fowl of the heavens
and the beast are fled; they are gone.

a ch. 12. 6; Micah 7. 5, 6.
1 Or, *friend.*
2 Or, *mock.*
b Ps. 12. 2; & 120. 3.
c Ps. 28. 3.
3 Heb., *in the midst of him.*
4 Or, *wait for him.*
d ch. 5. 9, 29
5 Or, *pastures.*
6 Or, *desolate.*
7 Heb., *from the fowl even to, &c.*

A lodging place of wayfaring men.—*i.e.*, a place of shelter, a *khan* or *caravanserai*, such as were built for travellers, such, *e.g.*, as the "inn" of Gen. xlii. 27, the "habitation" of Chimham (chap. xli. 17), which the son of Barzillai had erected near Bethlehem, as an act of munificent gratitude to his adopted country (2 Sam. xix. 40). In some such shelter, far from the cities of Judah, the prophet, with a feeling like that of the Psalmist (Ps. lv. 6—8) would fain find refuge from his treacherous enemies—"adulterers," alike spiritually and literally (chap v. 8).

(3) **Like their bow for lies.**—The inserted words turn the boldness of the metaphor into a comparatively tame simile. *They bend their tongue to be their bow of lies.* The same figure meets us in Pss. lvii. 4, lviii. 7, lxiv. 3.

They are not valiant for the truth upon the earth.—Better, *they are not mighty for truth,* i.e., *faithfulness, in the land*—*i.e.*, they do not rule faithfully. It is not without some regret that we part with a phrase which has gained something of a proverbial character as applied to the champions of speculative truth or abstract right, but the above gives the true meaning of the Hebrew.

They know not me.—"Know" in the sense of acknowledging and obeying (1 Sam. ii. 12; Job xviii. 21). This was the root evil from which all other evils issued.

(4) **Take ye heed . . .**—The extreme bitterness of the prophet's words is explained in part by what we read afterwards of his personal history (chap. xii. 6, xviii. 18). Then, as at other times, a man's foes were those of his own household (Matt. x. 36).

Every brother will utterly supplant.—The word is that which gave the patriarch his significant name of Jacob, the supplanter (Gen. xxv. 26, xxvii. 36). Jeremiah seems to say that the people have forfeited their claims to the name of the true Israel. Every brother Israelite is found to be a thorough-paced Jacob. The adverb "utterly" expresses the force of the Hebrew reduplication of the verb.

Will walk with slanders.—Better, *walketh a slanderer.*

(5) **Deceive.**—The word is commonly translated, as in the margin, *mock.* (So in 1 Kings xviii. 27; Judges xvi. 10, 13, 15.) The context here shows, however, that the kind of mockery is that which at once deludes and derides; and as the former meaning is predominant, the text of the English version had better stand as it is.

To commit iniquity.—Literally, *to go crookedly,* or, in the strict sense of the word, *to do wrong.*

(6) **Thine habitation . . .**—The words may be an individualised, and therefore more emphatic, reproduction of the general warning of verse 4. It is, however, better to take them as spoken by Jehovah to the prophet individually. The LXX., following a different reading and punctuation, translates "usury upon usury, deceit upon deceit; they refuse to know Me, saith the Lord." And this has been adopted by Ewald, among recent commentators.

(7) **I will melt them, and try them.**—The prophet, speaking in the name of Jehovah, falls back upon the imagery of chap. vi. 28—30; Isa. xlviii. 10. The evil has come to such a pass that nothing is left but the melting of the fiery furnace of affliction. How else could He act for the daughter of His people? The phrase throws us back upon chap. viii. 21, 22. The balm of Gilead had proved ineffectual. The disease required a severer remedy.

(8) **An arrow shot out.**—Better, *an arrow that pierceth,* or *slayeth.*

In heart.—More literally, *inwardly.*

(9) **Shall I not visit . . . ?**—The previous use of the same warning in chap. v. 9, 29 gives these words also the emphasis of iteration.

(10) **For the mountains . . .**—The Hebrew preposition means both "upon" and "on account of," and probably both meanings were implied. The prophet sees himself *upon* the mountains, taking up the lamentation *for* them because they are "burned up."

The habitations.—Better, as in the margin, *pastures.* The wilderness is simply the wild open country.

So that none can pass . . . neither can men hear.—Better, *with none to pass through them . . . neither do men hear.*

Both the fowl . . .—The Hebrew is more emphatic; *from the fowl of the heavens to the beast . . . they are fled.*

(11) And I will make Jerusalem heaps,
and [a]a den of dragons; and I will make
the cities of Judah [1]desolate, without
an inhabitant.
(12) Who *is* the wise man, that may
understand this? and *who is he* to whom
the mouth of the LORD hath spoken,
that he may declare it, for what the
land perisheth *and* is burned up like a
wilderness, that none passeth through?
(13) And the LORD saith, Because they
have forsaken my law which I set before
them, and have not obeyed my voice,
neither walked therein; (14) but have
walked after the [2]imagination of their
own heart, and after Baalim, which
their fathers taught them: (15) there-
fore thus saith the LORD of hosts, the
God of Israel; Behold, I will feed
them, *even* this people, [b]with wormwood,
and give them water of gall to drink.
(16) I will [c]scatter them also among the
heathen, whom neither they nor their
fathers have known: and I will send a
sword after them, till I have consumed
them.
(17) Thus saith the LORD of hosts,
Consider ye, and call for the mourning
women, that they may come; and send
for cunning *women*, that they may
come: (18) and let them make haste,
and take up a wailing for us, that our
eyes may run down with tears, and our
eyelids gush out with waters. (19) For
a voice of wailing is heard out of Zion,
How are we spoiled! we are greatly
confounded, because we have forsaken
the land, because our dwellings have
cast *us* out. (20) Yet hear the word of
the LORD, O ye women, and let your
ear receive the word of his mouth, and
teach your daughters wailing, and every
one her neighbour lamentation. (21) For
death is come up into our windows, *and*
is entered into our palaces, to cut off
the children from without, *and* the
young men from the streets. (22) Speak,
Thus saith the LORD, Even the carcases

a ch. 10. 22.
1 Heb., *desolation*.
2 Or, *stubbornness*.
b ch. 8. 14; & 23. 15.
c Lev. 26. 33.

---

(11) **A den of dragons.**—Better, here and in chap. x. 22; Isa. xiii. 22, *jackals*. The word means, literally, *a howler*. The English version follows the LXX. and Vulgate versions; but even taking "dragons" in its non-mythical sense as applied to some species of serpent, there is nothing in the word to lead us to assign this meaning. The mistake has probably arisen from the likeness of the word to those translated "serpent" in Exod. vii. 9, 10, 12, "whale" in Gen. i. 21 and Job vii. 12, and "dragons" in Pss. lxxiv. 13, xci. 13.

(12) **Who is the wise man . . .?**—Sage (comp. chap. viii. 9) and prophet are alike called on to state why the misery of which Jeremiah speaks is to come upon the people. But they are asked in vain, and Jehovah, through the prophet, makes answer to Himself.

That none passeth through.—The English is ambiguous. "That" stands either for a relative with "wilderness" as its antecedent, or as a conjunction equivalent to "so that." Better, *and none there is that passeth through.*

(14) **Imagination.**—*Stubbornness*, as in chap. iii. 17.

Baalim.—The generic name for false gods of all kinds, and therefore used in the plural. (Comp. chap. ii. 8, 23.)

(15) **Wormwood.**—As a plant, probably a species of *Artemisia*, four species of which are found in Palestine. In Deut. xxix. 18 it appears as the symbol of moral evil, here of the bitterness of calamity.

Water of gall.—See Note on chap. viii. 14.

(17) **Mourning women . . . cunning women.**—Eastern funerals were, and are, attended by mourners, chiefly women, hired for the purpose. Wailing was reduced to an art, and they who practised it were cunning. There are the "mourners" that "go about the streets" (Eccles. xii. 5), those that "are skilful of lamentation" (Amos v. 16), those that mourned for Jehoiakim (Jer. xxii. 18), those that "wept and wailed greatly" in the house of Jairus (Mark v. 38). They are summoned as to the funeral, not of a friend or neighbour, but of the nation.

(18) **Take up a wailing for us.**—There is in all such figures of speech an inevitable blending of metaphors. The mourners wail for the dead nation, and yet the members of the nation are sharers in the obsequies, and their eyes run down with tears.

(19) **We have forsaken.**—Better, *we have left.* The English version suggests a voluntary abandonment, which is not involved in the Hebrew.

(20) **Teach your daughters wailing.**—The thought of verse 9 is continued. The words rest upon the idea that wailing was an art, its cries and tones skilfully adapted to the special sorrows of which it was in theory the expression. They perhaps imply also that death would do its work so terribly that the demand for mourners would be greater than the supply, and that supernumeraries must be trained to meet it. Looking to the many other coincidences between our Lord's teaching and that of Jeremiah, it is not too much to see in His words to the daughter of Jerusalem, "Weep for yourselves and for your children" (Luke xxiii. 27, 28), a parallel to what we read here.

(21) **Death is come up into our windows.**—"Death" stands here, as in chap. xv. 2, specifically for the pestilence, which is to add its horrors to those of the famine and the sword, and which creeps in with its fatal taint at the windows, even though the invader is for a time kept at bay, and cuts off the children who else would play "without," *sc.*, in the court-yard of the house, and the "young men" who else would gather, as were their wont, in the streets or the *open places* of the city. The Hebrew word *rehoboth* (comp. Gen. xxvi. 22) answers to "piazza," "square," "market-place," rather than to our street.

(22) **Speak, Thus saith the Lord.**—The abrupt opening indicates a new prediction, coming to him un-

of men shall fall as dung upon the
open field, and as the handful after
the harvestman, and none shall gather
them.
(23) Thus saith the LORD, Let not the
wise *man* glory in his wisdom, neither
let the mighty *man* glory in his might,
let not the rich *man* glory in his
riches: (24) but [a] let him that glorieth
glory in this, that he understandeth
and knoweth me, that I *am* the LORD
which exercise loving-kindness, judg-
ment, and righteousness, in the earth:
for in these *things* I delight, saith the
LORD.

(25) Behold, the days come, saith the
LORD, that I will [1] punish all *them which
are* circumcised with the uncircumcised;
(26) Egypt, and Judah, and Edom, and
the children of Ammon, and Moab, and
all *that are* [2] in the [b] utmost corners,
that dwell in the wilderness: for all
these nations *are* uncircumcised, and all
the house of Israel *are* [c] uncircumcised
in the heart.

CHAPTER X.—(1) Hear ye the word
which the LORD speaketh unto you,
O house of Israel: (2) Thus saith the
LORD, Learn not the way of the heathen,

a 1 Cor. 1. 31; 2 Cor. 10. 17.

1 Heb., *visit upon.*

2 Heb., *cut off into corners,* or, *having the corners of their hair polled.*

b ch. 25. 23.
c Rom. 2. 28, 29.

---

bidden, which he is constrained to utter as a message from Jehovah.

As the handful.—The reaper gathered into swathes, or small sheaves, what he could hold in his left hand, as he went on cutting with his sickle. These he threw down as they became too big to hold, and they were left strewn on the field till he returned to gather them up into larger sheaves. So should the bodies of the dead be strewn, the prophet says, on the open field, but there should be none to take them up and bury them.

(23) **Let not the wise man glory in his wisdom.**—The long prophecy of judgment had reached its climax. Now there comes the conclusion of the whole matter—that the one way of salvation is to renounce all reliance on the wisdom, greatness, wealth of the world, and to glory only in knowing Jehovah. The "wise man" is, as before in chap. viii. 9, and verse 12, the scribe, or recognised teacher of the people

(24) **Let him that glorieth glory in this . . .**—The passage is interesting as having clearly been present to the mind of St. Paul in writing 1 Cor. i. 31; 2 Cor. x. 17. He had learnt from it to estimate the wisdom and the greatness on which the Corinthians prided themselves at their true value. We may find a parallel even in the higher words which teach us that "eternal life is to know God" (John xvii. 3), to understand those attributes, love, judgment, righteousness, which we associate with our thoughts of Him, as indeed they are in their infinite perfection, and which when we know them as we ought to know, we must needs strive to reproduce.

(25) **I will punish all them which are circumcised with the uncircumcised.**—The passage is difficult, but the English verse is misleading. Better, *I will punish all those that are circumcised in uncircumcision*—all, *i.e.*, who have the outward sign, but not the inward purity of which it was the symbol. In the day of God's judgments (this being the connecting link with the preceding verse) there would be no difference between the Jew and other races who like him practised circumcision on the one hand, and the outlying heathen world on the other. Here, again, Jeremiah anticipated St. Paul, "To the Jew first, and also to the Gentile; for there is no respect of persons with God" (Rom. ii. 9). The true circumcision is that which is "in the spirit, not in the letter" (Rom. ii. 29).

(26) **Egypt, and Judah . . .**—The nations enumerated were all alike, the Egyptians certainly (Herod. ii. 36, 37), and the others, as belonging to the same race as Judah, probably, in the fact of circumcision, and are apparently brought together not without some touch of scornful humour. How could Israel pride itself in that which it had in common with some of the nations that it most abhorred. The later Idumæans seem to have abandoned the practice till it was forced upon them by John Hyrcanus (Joseph., *Ant.* xi. 9, xv. 7). Jerome (*in loc.*) affirms that the nations named practised circumcision in his time, and its adoption by Islam indicates its prevalence among the Arabs in that of Mahomet.

All that are in the utmost corners.—Better, *all that have the corners* (*of their temples*) *shorn.* The epithet, like our "cross-eared" or "round-head," was obviously one of scorn, and was applied (as again in chaps. xxv. 23, xlix. 32) to a wild Arabian tribe who, as described by Herodotus (iii. 8), shaved their temples and let their hair grow long behind. The "wilderness" is the Arabian desert to the east of Palestine, inhabited by the Ishmaelites and other kindred races. As if to complete the contempt which he pours on circumcision, the prophet speaks of the barbarous people, whose customs were specially forbidden to Israel (Lev. xix. 27), as in this respect standing on the same level with Israel. If circumcision by itself were enough to secure immunity from judgment, they too, as practising a rite analogous though not identical, might claim it.

All these nations are uncircumcised.—The English Version makes the prophet say exactly the opposite of what he really said. *All the heathen* (not "these nations") are in God's sight as uncircumcised, whether they practise the outward rite or not—and the state of Israel was not a whit better than theirs, for she too was uncircumcised in heart. Once again Jeremiah is the forerunner of St. Paul's Rom. ii. 25—29. It may be noted that the same nations are enumerated afterwards as coming under Nebuchadnezzar's conquests (chap. xxv. 23).

X.

(1) **House of Israel.**—This forms the link that connects what follows with what precedes. The "house of Israel" had been told that it was "uncircumcised in heart," on a level with the heathen; now the special sin of the heathen, which it was disposed to follow, is set forth in words of scorn and indignation.

(2) **Be not dismayed at the signs of heaven.**—The special reference is to the "astrologers, the stargazers, the monthly prognosticators" of the Chaldæans (Isa. xlvii. 13), finding portents either in the conjuncture of planets and constellations, or in eclipses, comets, and other like phenomena. In singular contrast with

and be not dismayed at the signs of
heaven; for the heathen are dismayed
at them. (3) For the [1]customs of the
people *are* vain: for *one* cutteth a tree
out of the forest, the work of the hands
of the workman, with the ax. (4) They
deck it with silver and with gold; they
fasten it with nails and with hammers,
that it move not. (5) They *are* upright
as the palm tree, [a]but speak not: they
must needs be [b]borne, because they
cannot go. Be not afraid of them; for
[c]they cannot do evil, neither also *is it*
in them to do good.

(6) Forasmuch as *there is* none [d]like
unto thee, O LORD; thou *art* great, and
thy name *is* great in might. (7) [e]Who
would not fear thee, O King of na-
tions? for [2]to thee doth it appertain:
forasmuch as among all the wise *men* of
the nations, and in all their kingdoms,
there is none like unto thee. (8) But they
are [3]altogether [f]brutish and foolish: the
stock *is* a doctrine of vanities. (9) Silver
spread into plates is brought from Tar-
shish, and gold from Uphaz, the work
of the workman, and of the hands of
the founder: blue and purple *is* their

1 Heb., *statutes*, or, *ordinances are vanity*.
a Ps. 115. 5.
b Isa. 46. 1, 7.
c Isa. 41. 23.
d Ps. 86. 8, 10.
e Rev. 15. 4.
2 Or, *it liketh thee*.
3 Heb., *in one*, or, *at once*.
f Isa. 41. 29; Hab. 2. 18; Zech. 10. 2.

---

the abject attitude of mind thus produced, the prophet shows that what has been called in scorn an anthropomorphic theology, was then the one effectual safeguard against the superstition that bows in fear before anything that is unusual and unexplained.

(3) **The customs of the people.**—Better, *ordinances of the peoples.* The prophet is speaking, not of common customs, but of religious institutions, and of these as belonging, not to "the people," *i.e.,* Israel, but to the nations round them. The verses that follow are so closely parallel to Isa. xli. 7, xliv. 9—17, xlvi. 5—7 (where see Notes), that the natural conclusion is that one writer had seen the work of the other. The grandeur and fulness of Isaiah's language, and the unlikeness of what we find here to Jeremiah's usual style, makes it more probable that he was the copyist, and so far adds to the argument for the authorship of the chapter ascribed to Isaiah. It is, however, possible, as some critics have thought, that these verses are an interpolation, and in that case they supply no evidence either way. The fact that they are found in the LXX. as well as in the Hebrew is, however, in favour of their genuineness. It may be noted that the substance of what follows has a parallel in the Epistle ascribed to Jeremiah in the apocryphal book of Baruch.

(5) **Upright as the palm tree.**—Better, perhaps, *A pillar in a garden of gourds are they.* The Hebrew word translated "upright" has two very different, though not entirely unconnected, meanings—(1) "twisted, rounded, carved," and in this sense it is translated commonly as "beaten work" (Exod. xxv. 18, 31, 36), and is here applied (if we accept this meaning) to the twisted palm-like columns of a temple, to which the stiff, formal figure of the idol, with arms pressed close to the side, and none of the action which we find in Greek statues, is compared; (2) the other meaning adopted by many commentators is that of "a garden of gourds or cucumbers," and the word is so rendered in Isa. i. 8. The comparison, in the so-called "Epistle of Jeremy" in the apocryphal book of Baruch (verse 70), of an idol to "a scarecrow in a garden of cucumbers" shows that the latter meaning was the accepted one when that Epistle was written. The thought, on this view, is that the idol which the men of Judah were worshipping was like one of the "pillars" (so the word for "palm tree" is translated in Song of Sol. iii. 6; Joel ii. 30), the Hermes, or Priapus-figures which were placed by Greeks and Romans in gardens and orchards as scarecrows. Like figures appear to have been used by the Phœnicians for the same purpose, and the practice, like the kindred worship of the *Asherah*, would seem to have been gaining ground even in Judah.

(6) **Forasmuch as.**—A somewhat flat addition to the Hebrew text, which opens with a vigorous abruptness, *None is there like unto thee . . .*

Great in might.—The latter is an almost technical word (as in Isa. xxxiii. 13; Ps. xxi. 13, cxlv. 11) for the Divine Omnipotence. (Compare "the Mighty God" of Isa. ix. 6.)

(7) **King of nations.**—Emphatically, "King of *the heathen*," expressing the universal sovereignty of Jehovah in contrast with the thought that He was the God of the Jews only. (Compare Rom. iii. 29.)

To thee doth it appertain.—Better, *for it is thine, i.e.,* the kingdom over the heathen implied in the title just given.

The wise men.—The word "men" is better omitted. Jehovah is not compared with the sages of the heathen only, but with all to whom they looked as sources and givers of wisdom.

In all their kingdoms.—Better, *in all their sovereignty.*

(8) **Altogether.**—Literally, *in one,* probably in the sense *in one word, in one fact, sc.,* that which follows in the next clause.

The stock is a doctrine of vanities.—Better, inverting the subject and predicate, *the teaching of vanities* (*i.e.,* of idols) *is a word,* or *is a log.* That is all it comes to; that one word is its condemnation.

(9) **Tarshish.**—As elsewhere in the Old Testament, Spain, the Tartessus of the Greeks (Gen. x. 4; Jonah i. 3; Ezek. xxvii. 12), from whence Palestine, through the Phœnicians, was chiefly supplied with silver, tin, and other metals.

Uphaz.—Possibly an error of transcription, or dialectical variation, for Ophir, giving the meaning "gold-coast." The word is found only here and in Dan. x. 5. Some interpreters, however, connect it with the name of Hyphasis, one of the tributaries of the Indus. We cannot attain to greater certainty. (See Note on 1 Kings ix. 28.)

Blue and purple.—Both were colours obtained from the *murex,* a Mediterranean shell-fish, and were used both for the curtains of the Tabernacle (Exod. xxv. 4) and for the gorgeous apparel of the idols of the heathen. "Purple," as elsewhere in the English of the Bible, must be understood of a deep crimson or scarlet. (Comp. Matt. xxvii. 28; Mark xv. 17.)

clothing: they *are* all the work of cun-
ning *men.* (10) But the LORD *is* the [1] true
God, he *is* the living God, and an [2] ever-
lasting king: at his wrath the earth
shall tremble, and the nations shall not
be able to abide his indignation.
(11) Thus shall ye say unto them, The
gods that have not made the heavens
and the earth, *even* they shall perish
from the earth, and from under these
heavens. (12) He [a] hath made the earth
by his power, he hath established the
world by his wisdom, and hath stretched
out the heavens by his discretion.
(13) When he uttereth his voice, *there is*
a [3] multitude of waters in the heavens,
and he causeth the vapours to ascend
from the ends of the earth; he maketh
lightnings [4] with rain, and bringeth
forth the wind out of his treasures.
(14) Every man [5] is [b] brutish in *his* know-
ledge: every founder is confounded by
the graven image: for his molten image
is falsehood, and *there is* no breath in
them. (15) They *are* vanity, *and* the
work of errors: in the time of their
visitation they shall perish. (16) [c] The
portion of Jacob *is* not like them: for
he *is* the former of all *things;* and Israel
is the rod of his inheritance: The LORD
of hosts *is* his name.
(17) Gather up thy wares out of the

1 Heb., *God of truth.*
2 Heb., *king of eternity.*
a Gen. 1. 6; ch. 51. 15.
3 Or, *noise.*
4 Or, *for rain.*
5 Or, *is more brutish than to know.*
b ch. 51. 17, 18.
c ch. 51. 19.

---

(10) **The Lord is the true God.**—Literally, *Jehovah is the God that is Truth.* The thought expressed is that for which St. John, as indeed the LXX. does here, uses the word *alēthinos* (John xvii. 3; 1 John v. 20), Truth in its highest and most perfect form. So "I am the way, the truth, and the life" (John xiv. 6).

An everlasting king.—Here, as in other like passages, the English Version is not wrong, but the Hebrew idiom "King of Eternity" is far grander.

(11) **Thus shall ye say unto them.**—The verse presents an almost unique phenomenon. It is not, like the rest of the book, in Hebrew, but in Chaldee or Aramaic, the language of the enemies of Israel. Two explanations have been offered—(1) that a marginal note, added by one of the exiles in Babylon, found its way at a later period into the text; (2) a far more probable view, viz., that the prophet, whose intercourse with the Chaldeans had made him familiar with their language, put into the mouths of his own countrymen the answer they were to give when they were invited to join in the worship of their conquerors. Little as they might know of the strange language, they might learn enough to give this answer. The words have the ring of a kind of popular proverb, and in the original there is a play of sound which can only be faintly reproduced in English—*The gods that have not made . . . they shall be made away with.* The apocryphal Epistle of Jeremiah, already referred to, may, perhaps, be regarded as a rhetorical sermon on this text.

(12) **He hath made . . . he hath established.**—The words are participial in form, *making . . . establishing,* and complete the list of divine attributes in verse 10, contrasting the creative might of Jehovah with the impotence of the gods of the heathen.

The world.—As contrasted with the material earth, the inhabited world, the world considered in its relation to man, as in Prov. viii. 31.

Discretion.—Better, *skill.*

(13) **A multitude of waters.**—Better, *a rush of waters,* following on the thunder, which is thought of as the voice of God (comp. Ps. xxix. 3). The prophet finds the tokens of Almighty Power alike in the fixed order of the Cosmos and its most catastrophic perturbations. The strict construction of the Hebrew gives, *At the voice of His giving the roar of waters.*

He maketh lightnings.—The last half of the verse agrees verbally with Ps. cxxxv. 7 (where see Note), and one is obviously a quotation from the other, or both from some common source. We have no data, however, for saying which is the older of the two. The idea of the "treasure chambers" from which the winds are brought appears in Job xxxviii. 22.

(14) **Brutish in his knowledge.**—Literally, *from knowing,* i.e., *too brutish to know,* or, as some take it, *brutish without knowledge,* overwhelmed and astounded, so that the power of knowing fails.

Every founder.—The smelter, or worker in molten metal.

(15) **The work of errors.**—Better, *a work of mockery,* i.e., *worthy of that and of that only,* the word being apparently substituted, after Jeremiah's manner, for the technical word, not unlike in sound, which is translated "image work" in 2 Chron. iii. 10.

In the time of their visitation.—*i.e.,* in the time when they are visited with punishment, as in 1 Pet. ii. 12; Isa. x. 3, and Luke xix. 44.

(16) **The portion of Jacob.**—As in Ps. xvi. 5, cxix. 57, God is described as the "portion," *i.e.,* as the treasure and inheritance of His people. He is no powerless idol, but the former, *i.e.,* the creator, of all things, or more literally *of the all, i.e.,* of the universe.

The rod of his inheritance.—The phrase was familiar in the poetry of Israel (Ps. lxxiv. 2; Isa. lxiii. 17—Heb.), but its exact meaning is not clear. The word may be "rod" in the sense of "sceptre," as in Gen. xlix. 10; Micah vii. 14. Israel is that over which, or by means of which, God rules. But the other meaning in which it stands for "stem," "division," "tribe" (as in Isa. xix. 13; Exod. xxviii. 21), is equally tenable.

The Lord of hosts is his name.—The time-honoured and awful name is obviously brought in as in emphatic contrast to all the names of the gods of the heathen. Among them all there was no name like "Jehovah Sabaoth," the Lord of the armies of heaven, of the stars in their courses, of the angels in their ordered ranks, and of the armies of Israel upon earth.

(17) **Gather up thy wares.**—The section from verses 1—16 inclusive had been as a long parenthesis, reproving Israel for the sin which placed it among the "uncircumcised in the heart" (chap. ix. 26). Now the prophet returns to his main theme, the devastation of the land of Israel as the penalty of that sin. He begins with a vivid touch in the picture of utter misery. The daughter of Israel (the word "inhabitant" is feminine), sitting as in a besieged fortress, is to gather up her goods and chattels into one small

land, O [1]inhabitant of the fortress.
(18) For thus saith the LORD, Behold, I
will sling out the inhabitants of the
land at this once, and will distress them,
that they may find *it so.* (19) Woe is me
for my hurt! my wound is grievous:
but I said, Truly this *is* a grief, and
I must bear it. (20) My tabernacle is
spoiled, and all my cords are broken:
my children are gone forth of me, and
they *are* not: *there is* none to stretch
forth my tent any more, and to set up
my curtains. (21) For the pastors are
become brutish, and have not sought
the LORD: therefore they shall not
prosper, and all their flocks shall be
scattered. (22) Behold, the noise of the
bruit is come, and a great commotion
out of the [a]north country, to make the
cities of Judah desolate, *and* a [b]den of
dragons.
(23) O LORD, I know that the [c]way of
man *is* not in himself: *it is* not in
man that walketh to direct his steps.
(24) O LORD, [d]correct me, but with judg-
ment; not in thine anger, lest thou [2]bring
me to nothing. (25) [e]Pour out thy fury
upon the heathen that know thee not,
and upon the families that call not
on thy name: for they have eaten up

1 Heb., *inhabitress.*

a ch. 1. 15; & 5 15; & 6. 22.

b ch. 9. 11.

c Prov. 16. 1; & 20. 24.

d Ps. 6. 1; & 38. 1; ch. 30. 11.

2 Heb., *diminish me.*

e Ps. 79. 6.

---

bundle (the English "wares" suggests the idea of trade, which is foreign to the context), and with that as the sole remnant of her possessions, to go forth into exile. Probably, indeed, the word may mean simply the *travelling carpet* or mantle which the exile was to take with him. The whole phrase has something of a proverbial type, like our "bag and baggage" or the *collige sarcinulas et exi* ("take up your packages and begone") of Juven. *Sat.* vi. 146.

(18) **I will sling out.**—The same bold metaphor, though not the same word, for violent expulsion, is found in the prophecy of the fate of Shebna (Isa. xxii. 18).

That they may find it so.—In the Hebrew, the verb, though transitive, stands by itself, without an object. The ellipsis has been filled up either by "it," as in the English Version, *i.e.*, may feel it in all its bitterness; or by "me," as in the Syriac version, *i.e.*, may be led through their misery to seek and find Jehovah. The parallelism of Deut. iv. 29; chap. xxix. 13, makes the latter meaning probable (see also Acts xvii. 27); but it may be suggested that the very omission of an object was intended to be suggestive in its abruptness. "They would *find* . . . ;" what they found would depend upon themselves. A possible construction is *that they* (the enemy) *may find them* (the people besieged), but this is hardly the natural sequel of the exile of which the previous words speak.

(19) **Woe is me . . .**—From this verse to the end of the chapter we have, with the prophet's characteristic dramatic vividness, the lamentation of the daughter of Israel in her captivity, bewailing the transgressions that had led to it. That this follows immediately on verse 18 gives some support to the view above given as to the force of the words "that they may find." Israel is represented as having "found" in both aspects of the word.

Grievous.—In the sense of all but incurable.

This is a grief . . .—Better, *this is my grief* or *plague*, that which I have brought upon myself and must therefore bear. To accept the punishment was in this, as in all cases, the first step to reformation.

(20) **My tabernacle . . .**—The tent which had been the home of Israel is destroyed, the cords that fastened it to the ground are broken, the children that used to help their mother in arranging the tent and its curtains "are not," *i.e.* (as in Gen. xlii. 36; chap. xxxi. 15; Matt. ii. 18), they are either dead or in exile. There is something significant in the fact that the destruction of the city is represented under the imagery of that of a tent. The daughter of Zion has, as it were, been brought back to her nomadic state.

(21) **The pastors.**—The "shepherds," used, as in chaps. ii. 8, iii. 15, and elsewhere, of rulers generally, rather than of priests as such.

Therefore they shall not prosper.—Better, *therefore they have not done wisely.* This is the primary meaning of the word (that of prosperity, as the result of prudence, the secondary), and is adopted by the LXX., Vulg., and most other versions.

All their flocks.—Literally, *all their pasture*, the place, or the act, of pasturing, taken practically for the sheep that fed on it.

(22) **Behold, the noise of the bruit is come.**—Better, *A cry is heard, Behold, it cometh.* The cry of terror is heard and it utters the tidings, terrible in their brevity, that the army of the invader is come, and with it the "great commotion," the stir and rush of the army, coming from the north country of the Chaldeans. (Comp. chap. i. 13.) In Matt. xxv. 6, "There was a cry made, Behold, the bridegroom cometh," we have a striking parallel. The word "bruit" (here and in Nah. iii. 19) may be noted as one of those which have become obsolete since the date of the Authorised Version.

A den of dragons.—*i.e., jackals*, as in chap. ix. 11.

(23) **O Lord, I know . . .**—The confession is made not by the prophet for himself, but as by and for Israel.

The way of man.—The path which a man takes for good or evil, for failure or success. His conduct in life depends, the prophet says, on something more than his own choice:—

> "There's a divinity that shapes our ends,
> Rough-hew them how we will."

Compare Prov xvi. 9, xx. 24, as expressing the same thought of the necessity of divine guidance. The two Hebrew words for "man" are used in the two clauses, the first expressing the weakness, the latter the strength of men. Even the strong man has to confess that he needs a hand other than his own to direct his steps.

(24) **With judgment.**—The rendering is accurate, but the idea is, perhaps, better expressed by the translation of the same word in chaps. xxx. 11, xlvi. 28 as "in measure." In either case the discipline that comes from God as the righteous Judge, at once retributive and reformative, is contrasted with the punishment which is simply vindictive.

Lest thou bring me to nothing.—Literally, *lest*

Jacob, and devoured him, and consumed
him, and have made his habitation
desolate.

CHAPTER XI.—(1) The word that
came to Jeremiah from the LORD,
saying,
(2) Hear ye the words of this covenant,
and speak unto the men of Judah,
and to the inhabitants of Jerusalem;
(3) and say thou unto them, Thus saith
the LORD God of Israel; [a]Cursed *be*
the man that obeyeth not the words
of this covenant, (4) which I com-
manded your fathers in the day *that*
I brought them forth out of the land
of Egypt, from the iron furnace, say-
ing, [b]Obey my voice, and do them,
according to all which I command
you: so shall ye be my people, and
I will be your God: (5) that I may
perform the [c]oath which I have sworn
unto your fathers, to give them a land
flowing with milk and honey, as *it is*
this day. Then answered I, and said,
[1]So be it, O LORD. (6) Then the LORD
said unto me, Proclaim all these words
in the cities of Judah, and in the streets
of Jerusalem, saying, Hear ye the words
of this covenant, and do them. (7) For
I earnestly protested unto your fathers
in the day *that* I brought them up out
of the land of Egypt, *even* unto this
day, rising early and protesting, saying,
Obey my voice. (8) Yet they obeyed
not, nor inclined their ear, but walked
every one in the [2]imagination of their
evil heart: therefore I will bring upon
them all the words of this covenant,
which I commanded *them* to do; but
they did *them* not.
(9) And the LORD said unto me, A
conspiracy is found among the men of
Judah, and among the inhabitants of

a Deut. 27. 26; Gal. 3. 10.

B. C. cir. 608.

b Lev. 26. 3, 12.

c Deut. 7. 12.

1 Heb., *Amen.*

2 Or, *stubbornness.*

---

thou make me small; but the English Version is an adequate expression of the meaning.

(25) **Pour out thy fury.**—The words are identical with those of Ps. lxxix. 6, 7, but it is more probable that the Psalmist borrowed from the Prophet. By many critics the Psalm is referred to the time of the Maccabees, and it would seem, from the language of verses 1—3, that it must at any rate have been after the destruction of the Temple by the Chaldeans. On the last supposition the two writers may have been contemporaries.

XI.

(1) **The word that came to Jeremiah.**—The words indicate that we are entering on a distinct message or discourse, which goes on probably to the end of chap. xii. No date is given, and we are driven to infer it from the internal evidence of the message itself. This points to an early period of Jeremiah's work, probably in the reign of Josiah. The invasion of the Chaldeans is not so near, as in the preceding chapter. Jeremiah is still residing at Anathoth (chap. xi. 21). By some critics, however, it is referred to the reign of Jehoiachin.

(2) **The words of this covenant.**—The phrase had obviously acquired a definite and special sense in consequence of the discovery of the lost book of the Law under Josiah, and the covenant into which the people had then entered (comp. 2 Kings xxiii. 3). The "curse" under which the people had fallen was practically identical with that in Deut. xxvii. 26, the word "obeyeth" being substituted for "confirmeth."

(3) **Cursed be the man . . .**—The verse is, as it were, a mosaic, so to speak, of phrases, with slight verbal changes, from the recently discovered book of Deuteronomy—the "iron furnace" from Deut. iv. 20; 1 Kings viii. 51, "Hear my voice and do them" from Deut. xxviii. 1, "Ye shall be my people" from Deut. xxix. 13. The "iron furnace" was, of course, Egypt, the "furnace of affliction," as in Isa. xlviii. 10, in which the people had endured sufferings of which that was the only adequate symbol. The word used denoted the "furnace" of the smelter, but the actual form of bondage through which the Israelites had passed, working in the brick-kiln furnaces (Exod. i. 14), had probably given a special force to the phrase.

(5) **A land flowing with milk and honey.**—The description appears for the first time in Exod. iii. 8, 17. It rapidly became proverbial, and is prominent in Deut. vi. 3 and Josh. v. 6. It points primarily, it may be noticed, to the plenty of a pastoral rather than an agricultural people (see Note on Isa. vii. 22), and so far to the earlier rather than the later stages of the life of Israel.

So be it, O Lord.—The *Amen* of the liturgies and litanies of Israel, brought probably into fresh prominence by Deut. xxvii. 15—26, and uttered by princes and people in the solemn ceremonial of 2 Kings xxiii. 3.

(6) **In the cities of Judah . . .**—It is, at least, probable that the words are to be taken literally, and that the prophet went from city to city, doing his work as a preacher of repentance, and taking the new-found book of Deuteronomy as his text. The narrative of 2 Kings xxiii. 13—20 indicates an iconoclastic journey throughout the kingdom as made by Josiah; and the prophetic discourse now before us, enforcing the observance of the covenant just made, would have been a fit accompaniment for such a mission.

(7) **Rising early.**—The phrase in its spiritual meaning, as applied to Jehovah, is almost peculiar to Jeremiah, and is used by him twelve times. In its literal sense, or as denoting only ordinary activity, it is found often, *e.g.*, Gen. xx. 8; Prov. xxvii. 14. (See Note on chap. vii. 13.)

(8) **Imagination.**—Better, as before (chap. iii. 17), *stubbornness.*

Therefore I will bring upon them.—Better, *I have brought upon them.* The words contain not a direct prediction, but an appeal to the experience of the past as in itself foreshadowing the future.

(9) **A conspiracy.**—The words explain the rapid apostasy that followed on the death of Josiah. There

Jerusalem. (10) They are turned back
to the iniquities of their forefathers,
which refused to hear my words; and
they went after other gods to serve
them: the house of Israel and the
house of Judah have broken my cove-
nant which I made with their fathers.
(11) Therefore thus saith the LORD, Be-
hold, I will bring evil upon them, which
they shall not be able [1]to escape; and
[a]though they shall cry unto me, I will
not hearken unto them. (12) Then shall
the cities of Judah and inhabitants of
Jerusalem go, and cry unto the gods
unto whom they offer incense: but they
shall not save them at all in the time of
their [2]trouble. (13) For *according to* the
number of thy [b]cities were thy gods, O
Judah; and *according to* the number of
the streets of Jerusalem have ye set up
altars to *that* [3]shameful thing, *even* altars
to burn incense unto Baal. (14) There-
fore [c]pray not thou for this people,
neither lift up a cry or prayer for them:
for I will not hear *them* in the time that
they cry unto me for their [4]trouble.
(15) [d5]What hath my beloved to do in
mine house, *seeing* she hath wrought
lewdness with many, and the holy flesh
is passed from thee? [6]when thou doest
evil, then thou rejoicest. (16) The LORD
called thy name, A green olive tree,
fair, *and* of goodly fruit: with the noise
of a great tumult he hath kindled fire
upon it, and the branches of it are
broken. (17) For the LORD of hosts,
that planted thee, hath pronounced evil
against thee, for the evil of the house
of Israel and of the house of Judah,
which they have done against them-

1 Heb., *to go forth of.*

a Prov. 1. 28; Isa. 1. 15; ch. 14. 12; Ezek. 8. 18; Micah 3. 4.

2 Heb., *evil.*

b ch. 2. 28.

3 Heb., *shame.*

c ch. 7. 16; & 14. 11.

4 Heb., *evil.*

d Isa. 1. 11, &c.

5 Heb., *What is to my beloved in my house?*

6 Or, *when thy evil is.*

---

had been all along, even while he was urging his reforms, an organised though secret resistance to the policy of which he was the representative.

(10) **Their forefathers.**—The Hebrew is more specific—*their first fathers* (as in Isa. xliii. 27), with special reference to the idolatries of the forty years' wandering and the first settlement in Canaan.

They went after other gods.—The Hebrew pronoun is emphatically repeated, as pointing back to the subject of the first clause of the verse, the men of Jeremiah's own time—"they have gone after other gods."

(11) **I will bring evil.**—The Hebrew expresses immediate action, *I am bringing.*

(13) **According to the number of thy cities . . .**—This and verse 12 reproduce what we have heard already in chaps. ii. 27, 28 and vii. 17. The "shameful thing" is, as in chap. iii. 24, the image of Baal, which would seem to have been set up openly in some prominent place in every city of Judah, every street of Jerusalem. The reference is probably made, as before, to the formal recognition of Baal-worship in the days of Manasseh (2 Kings xxi. 3; 2 Chron. xxxiii. 3), but the sin may have been repeated as soon as the restraint of Josiah's reign had been removed.

(14) **Therefore pray not.**—The words imply, as in chap. vii. 16, that the prophet's human feelings had led him to pour his soul in passionate intercession that the penalty might be averted. He is told that it is at once too early and too late for that prayer. The people have not yet been moved to repentance, and their cry is simply the wail of suffering. The discipline must do its work, and the judgment they have brought down on themselves can be stayed no longer.

(15) **My beloved.**—*sc.*, Judah—or, perhaps, Israel collectively—as the betrothed of Jehovah. What has she to do, what part or lot has she in that house of Jehovah which she pollutes?

Seeing she hath wrought lewdness with many.—The Hebrew is difficult, and probably corrupt. The most probable rendering is *What hath my beloved to do in my house, to work it even evil devices? Thy many, i.e.* (probably, as in chap. iii. 1), thy many lovers, *and the holy flesh* (*i.e.*, her sacrifices), *will they make it* (the guilt of her devices) *to pass away from thee?* Keeping the present text of the Hebrew the latter clause would run, *they shall pass away from thee, i.e.*, shall leave thee, as thou wert, unreconciled and unforgiven. A conjectural emendation, following the LXX., gives, *will thy vows and the holy flesh remove thy evil from thee* . . . The general sense is, however, clear. A religion of mere ritual-sacrifices and the like will not avail to save. The Hebrew for "lewdness" does not convey the idea which we now attach to the English word, but means primarily a plan of any kind, and then a "device" or "scheme" in a bad sense, as in Ps. x. 2, xxi. 11; Prov. xiv. 17. Probably the translators, here, as in Acts xvii. 5, xviii. 14, used the word in this more general sense. Primarily, indeed, "lewd" in Old English was simply the opposite of "learned."

When thou doest evil, then thou rejoicest.—The clause is involved in the same difficulty as the rest of the verse. The English version is tenable, and gives an adequate meaning. By some commentators, however, the passage is rendered, referring evil to the previous sentence, *Will they* (*vows, &c.*) remove evil from thee? Then mightest thou rejoice.

(16) **A green olive tree.**—The parable is essentially the same, though a different symbol is chosen, as that of the vine of Isa. v. 1; Jerem. ii. 21, or the fig-tree of Luke xiii. 6. The olive also was naturally a symbol of fertility and goodness, as in Ps. lii. 8; Hos. xiv. 6; Zech. iv. 3, 11. In the words "the Lord called thy name" we have the expression of the Divine purpose in the "calling and election" of Israel. This was what she was meant to be.

Fair, and of goodly fruit.—The words point, as before, to the ideal state of Israel. She had made no effort to attain that ideal, and therefore the thunder-storm of God's wrath fell on it. The word for "tumult" is used in Ezek. i. 24 for the sound of an army on its march, and is probably used as combining the literal or figurative meaning.

(17) **The Lord of hosts, that planted thee.**—As in chap. ii. 21, stress is laid on the fact that Jehovah had planted the tree and bestowed on it all the conditions of fruitfulness, and that it was He who now passed the sentence of condemnation.

selves to provoke me to anger in offering
incense unto Baal.
(18) And the LORD hath given me
knowledge *of it*, and I know *it*: then
thou shewedst me their doings. (19) But
I *was* like a lamb *or* an ox *that* is
brought to the slaughter; and I knew
not that they had devised devices
against me, *saying*, Let us destroy [1]the
tree with the fruit thereof, and let us
cut him off from the land of the living,
that his name may be no more re-
membered. (20) But, O LORD of hosts,
that judgest righteously, that [a]triest
the reins and the heart, let me see thy
vengeance on them: for unto thee have
I revealed my cause.
(21) Therefore thus saith the LORD of
the men of Anathoth, that seek thy
life, saying, Prophesy not in the name
of the LORD, that thou die not by our
hand: (22) therefore thus saith the LORD
of hosts, Behold, I will [2]punish them:
the young men shall die by the sword;
their sons and their daughters shall die
by famine: (23) and there shall be no
remnant of them: for I will bring evil
upon the men of Anathoth, *even* the
year of their visitation.

CHAPTER XII.—(1) Righteous *art*
thou, O LORD, when I plead with thee:
yet [3]let me talk with thee of *thy* judg-
ments: [b]Wherefore doth the way of the

1 Heb., *the stalk with his bread.*

a 1 Sam. 16. 7; 1 Chron. 28. 9; Ps. 7. 9; ch. 17. 10; & 20. 12; Rev. 2. 23.

2 Heb., *visit upon.*

3 Or, *let me reason the case with thee.*

b Job 21. 7; Ps. 37. 1; & 73. 3; Hab. 1. 4.

---

(18) **And the Lord hath given me knowledge.**—A new section opens abruptly, and the prophet speaks no longer of the sins of Israel and Judah at large, but of the "doings" of his own townsmen, of their plots against his life. Unless this is altogether a distinct fragment, connected, possibly, with chap. ix. 8, the abruptness suggests the inference that the plots of the men of Anathoth against him had suddenly been brought under his notice.

(19) **Like a lamb or an ox.**—Better, *as a tame lamb, i.e.*, one, like the ewe-lamb of Nathan's parable (2 Sam. xii. 3), brought up in the home of its master. There is no "or" in the Hebrew, and the translators seem to have mistaken the adjective (tame) for a noun. The LXX., Vulg., and Luther agree in the rendering now given. Assuming the earlier date of Isa. liii. 7, the words would seem to have been an allusive reference to the sufferer there described.

The tree with the fruit thereof.—Literally, *the tree with its bread*, here taken for its "fruit." Some scholars, however, render the word "sap," or adopt a reading which gives that meaning. The phrase would seem to be proverbial for total destruction, not of the man only, but of his work. While the prophet's life had been innocent and unsuspecting, his own townsmen were conspiring to crush him, and bury his name and work in oblivion. The sufferings of the prophet present, in this matter, a parallel to those of the Christ (Luke iv. 29).

(20) **Let me see thy vengeance on them.**—The prayer, like that of the so-called vindictive Psalms (lxix., cix.), belongs to the earlier stage of the religious life when righteous indignation against evil is not yet tempered by the higher law of forgiveness. As such it is not to be imitated by Christians, but neither is it to be hastily condemned. The appeal to a higher judge, the desire to leave vengeance in His hands, is in itself a victory over the impulse to take vengeance into our own hands. Through it, in most cases, the sufferer from wrong must pass before he can attain to the higher and more Christ-like temper which utters itself in the prayer, "Father, forgive them, for they know not what they do" (Luke xxiii. 34).

Unto thee have I revealed my cause.—*i.e.*, laid it bare before thee. The thought and the phrase were characteristic of Jeremiah, and meet us again in chap. xx. 12.

(21) **Thus saith the Lord.**—The "men of Anathoth," it would seem, had at first tried to stop the preaching of Jeremiah by threats, as Amaziah, the priest of Bethel, had tried to stop that of Amos (Amos vii. 12, 13). Failing in this, after the manner of the men of Nazareth in their attack on the Christ (Luke iv. 28, 29), and of the later Jews in their dealings with St. Paul, they conspired against his life (Acts ix. 23, 29, xiv. 19, xxiii. 12).

(22) **The young men.**—As the context shows, these are the men of military age who would die fighting, while their children should perish from famine within the walls of the besieged cities.

(23) **There shall be no remnant of them.**—In Ezra ii. 23; Neh. vii. 27 we find that 128 of Anathoth returned from exile. The words must therefore be limited either to the men who had conspired against the prophet, or to the complete deportation of its inhabitants. The situation of Anathoth, about three or four miles north-east of Jerusalem, would expose it to the full fury of the invasion. The words are apparently spoken with reference to the ever-recurring burden of Isaiah's prophecy that "a remnant" should return (Isa. i. 9, vi. 13, x. 21). The conspirators of Anathoth were excluded from that promise.

Even the year of their visitation.—See Notes on chaps. viii. 12, x. 15.

XII.

The sequence of the several sections is not very clear, and possibly we have a series of detailed prophecies put together without system. Verses 1—3 seem to continue the address to the men of Anathoth, verse 4 points to a drought, verse 12 to the invasion of the Chaldeans, verse 14 to the "evil neighbours"—Edomites, Moabites, and others—who exulted in the fall of Judah.

(1) **Yet let me talk with thee.**—The soul of the prophet is vexed, as had been the soul of Job (chap. xxi. 7), of Asaph (Ps. lxxiii.), and others, by the apparent anomalies of the divine government. He owns as a general truth that God is righteous, "yet," he adds, *I will speak* (or *argue*) *my cause* (literally, *causes*) *with Thee.* He will question the divine Judge till his doubt is removed. And the question is the ever-recurring one, Wherefore doth the way of the wicked

wicked prosper? *wherefore* are all they
happy that deal very treacherously?
(2) Thou hast planted them, yea, they
have taken root: [1]they grow, yea, they
bring forth fruit: thou *art* near in their
mouth, and far from their reins. (3) But
thou, O LORD, [a]knowest me: thou hast
seen me, and tried mine heart [2]toward
thee: pull them out like sheep for the
slaughter, and prepare them for the
day of slaughter. (4) How long shall
the land mourn, and the herbs of every
field wither, [b]for the wickedness of them
that dwell therein? the beasts are
consumed, and the birds; because
they said, He shall not see our last
end.

(5) If thou hast run with the footmen,
and they have wearied thee, then how
canst thou contend with horses? and
if in the land of peace, *wherein* thou
trustedst, *they wearied thee*, then how
wilt thou do in the swelling of Jordan?
(6) For even [c]thy brethren, and the
house of thy father, even they have
dealt treacherously with thee; yea, [3]they
have called a multitude after thee:
believe them not, though they speak
[4]fair words unto thee.

(7) I have forsaken mine house, I have

[1] Heb., *they go on.*
[a] Ps. 17. 3.
[2] Heb., *with thee.*
[b] Ps. 107. 34.
[c] ch. 9. 4.
[3] Or, *they cried after thee fully.*
[4] Heb., *good things.*

---

prosper? (Comp. Ps. xxxvii. 1, lxxiii. 3.) The "treacherous dealing" implies a reference to the conspirators of the previous chapter.

Wherefore are all they happy . . .—Better, *at rest*, or *secure*.

(2) **Thou hast planted them.**—The words express, of course, the questioning distrust of the prophet. The wicked flourish, so that one would think God had indeed planted them. Yet all the while they were mocking Him with hypocritical worship (here we have an echo of Isa. xxix. 13), uttering His name with their lips while He was far from that innermost being which the Hebrew symbolised by the "reins."

(3) **Thou, O Lord, knowest me.**—Like all faithful sufferers from evil-doers before and after him, the prophet appeals to the righteous Judge, who knows how falsely he has been accused. In words in which the natural impatience of suffering shows itself as clearly as in the complaints of Pss. lxix., cix., he asks that the judgment may be immediate, open, terrible. As if recalling the very phrase which he had himself but lately used (chap. xi. 19), he prays that they too may be as "sheep for the slaughter," *dragged* or *torn away* from their security to the righteous penalty of their wrong.

Prepare.—Better, *devote*. The Hebrew word, as in chap. vi. 4, involves the idea of consecration.

(4) **How long shall the land mourn . . .**—The Hebrew punctuation gives a different division, *How long shall the land mourn, and the herbs of the whole field* (*i.e.*, all the open country) *wither? For the wickedness of them that dwell therein, cattle and birds perish, for, say they, he* (*i.e.*, the prophet) *will not see our latter end* (*i.e.*, we shall outlive him, though he prophesies our destruction). A slightly different reading, however, adopted by the LXX. and by some modern scholars, would give for the last clause, "He (God) seeth not our *ways*," *i.e.*, will leave us unpunished. The opening words point to a time of distress, probably of drought and famine. But out of this wretchedness, the men who were Jeremiah's enemies—the forestallers, and monopolists, and usurers of the time—continued to enrich themselves, and scornfully defied all his warnings.

(5) **If thou hast run with the footmen.**—The prophet is compelled to make answer to himself, and the voice of Jehovah is heard in his inmost soul rebuking his impatience. What are the petty troubles that fall on him compared with what others suffer, with what might come on himself? The thought is not unlike that with which St. Paul comforts the Corinthians (1 Cor. x. 13), or what we find in Heb. xii. 4. The meaning of the first clause is plain enough. The man who was wearied in a foot-race should not venture (as Elijah, *e.g.*, had done, 1 Kings xviii. 46) to measure his speed against that of horses. The latter ("the swelling of Jordan") suggests the thoughts of the turbid stream of the river overflowing its banks in the time of harvest (Josh. iii. 15; 1 Chron. xii. 15). In Zech. xi. 3, however, the same phrase (there translated "the pride of Jordan") is used apparently in connection with the lions and other beasts of prey that haunted the jungle on its banks (chap. xlix. 19; l. 44), and that may be the thought here. Commentators differ, and there are no *data* for deciding. In any case, there is no need for the interpolated words of the English Version. The sentence should run, "*In a land of peace thou art secure* (*i.e.*, it is easy to be tranquil when danger is not pressing). *What wilt thou in the swelling* (or, *amid the pride*) *of Jordan?*

(6) **Thy brethren.**—It is not certain whether we are to think actually of the sons of the same father, or only of the men of Anathoth (chap. xi. 23), as belonging to the same section of the priesthood. The language of chap. ix. 5 favours the more literal rendering. In any case, it is interesting to note that the proverb which our Lord more than once quotes, "A prophet is not without honour save in his own country and in his own house" (Matt. xiii. 57; Luke iv. 24; John iv. 44), probably had its origin in the sad experience of Jeremiah.

They have called a multitude after thee.—Better, *have shouted a full shout* (in our English phrase, "have raised a hue and cry") *after thee*.

(7) **I have forsaken mine house.**—The speaker is clearly Jehovah, but the connection with what precedes is not clear. Possibly we have, in this chapter, what in the writings of a poet would be called fragmentary pieces, written at intervals, and representing different phases of thought, and afterwards arranged without the devices of headings and titles and spaces with which modern bookmaking has made us familiar. So far as a sequence of thought is traceable, it is this, "Thou complainest of thine own sufferings, but there are worse things yet in store for thee; and what after all are thine, as compared with those that I, Jehovah, have brought upon mine heritage, dear as it is to me?"

I have left.—Better, *I have cast away*.

Into the hand.—Literally, *the palm*, as given over utterly, unable to resist, and not needing the "grasp" of the whole hand.

left mine heritage; I have given [1]the
dearly beloved of my soul into the
hand of her enemies. (8) Mine heritage
is unto me as a lion in the forest; it
[2][3]crieth out against me: therefore have
I hated it. (9) Mine heritage *is* unto
me *as* a [4]speckled bird, the birds
round about *are* against her; come ye,
assemble all the beasts of the field,
[5]come to devour. (10) Many pastors have
destroyed my vineyard, they have trod-
den my portion under foot, they have
made my [6]pleasant portion a desolate
wilderness. (11) They have made it de-
solate, *and being* desolate it mourneth
unto me; the whole land is made de-
solate, because no man layeth *it* to heart.

1 Heb., *the love.*

2 Or, *yelleth.*

3 Heb., *giveth out his voice.*

4 Or, *taloned.*

5 Or, *cause them to come.*

6 Heb., *portion of desire.*

a Lev. 26. 16; Deut. 28. 38; Micah 6. 15; Haggai 1. 6.

b Deut. 30. 3; ch. 32. 37.

(12) The spoilers are come upon all high
places through the wilderness: for the
sword of the LORD shall devour from
the *one* end of the land even to the
other end of the land: no flesh shall
have peace. (13) [a]They have sown wheat,
but shall reap thorns: they have put
themselves to pain, *but* shall not profit:
and they shall be ashamed of your
revenues because of the fierce anger of
the LORD.
(14) Thus saith the LORD against all
mine evil neighbours, that touch the
inheritance which I have caused my
people Israel to inherit; Behold, I will
[b]pluck them out of their land, and pluck
out the house of Judah from among

---

(8) **As a lion in the forest.**—*i.e.,* fierce, wild, untamed, uttering its sharp yells of passion. That mood was utterly unlovable, and therefore, speaking after the manner of men, the love which Jehovah had once felt for it was turned to hatred.

(9) **Mine heritage is unto me as a speckled bird.**—The Hebrew is interrogative, *Is mine heritage . . . ? Are the birds come round about against her?* The word for "bird" in both cases means a "bird of prey" (Isa. xlvi. 11; Gen. xv. 11), and the "speckled bird" is probably, but not certainly, some less common species of vulture. The image was probably suggested by something the prophet had observed, birds of prey of one species collecting and attacking a solitary stranger of another, joined by the "beasts of the field," the wolves and jackals and hyænas, who scent their prey. The word "speckled," perhaps, points to the bird attacked as being of more goodly plumage than the others (one, it may be, of the kingfishers that abound in Palestine), and therefore treated as a stranger and an enemy. The fact is one which strikes every observer of bird life (Tac. *Ann.* vi. 28; Sueton. *Cæs.* c. 81).

(10) **Many pastors have destroyed my vineyard.**—The use of the word "pastors," with all its modern spiritual associations, instead of "shepherds" (Jeremiah is the only book in the Old Testament, it may be noted, in which the word occurs), is peculiarly unhappy in this passage, where the "pastors" are reckless and destructive. Here the image (as in chap. vi. 3) is that of the *shepherds* of a wild, nomadic tribe (who represent the Chaldean and other invaders), breaking down the fence of the vineyard, and taking in their flocks to browse upon the tender shoots of the vine. The thought is the same as that of the "boar out of the wood" of Ps. lxxx. 13, but the "shepherds" are introduced to bring in the thought of the organisation and systematic plan of destruction.

(11) **They have made it desolate.**—The Hebrew is impersonal. "*One has made it . . . ,*" *i.e., it is made desolate.* As in other poetry of strong emotion, the prophet dwells with a strange solemn iteration on the same sound—"desolate," "desolate," "desolate"—thrice in the same breath. The Hebrew word *shemâma,* so uttered, must have sounded like a wail of lamentation.

Because no man layeth it to heart.—Better, *no man laid it . . .* The neglect of the past was bearing fruit in the misery of the present.

(12) **All high places.**—*i.e.,* the bare treeless heights so often chosen as the site of an idolatrous sanctuary.

The sword of the Lord.—As in the cry of "the sword of Jehovah and of Gideon" (Judges vii. 18) all man's work in war is thought of as instrumental in working out a Will mightier than his own. The sword of the Chaldean invader was, after all, His sword. The thought was more or less the common inheritance of Israel, but it had recently received a special prominence from Deut. xxxii. 41.

No flesh shall have peace.—The context limits the prediction to the offenders of the cities of Judah. As peace was for the Israelite the sum and substance of all blessedness, so its absence was the extremest of all maledictions. "Flesh" is used, as in Gen. vi. 3, for man's nature as evil and corrupt.

(13) **But shall reap thorns.**—Better, *have reaped thorns;* and so in the next clause *they have profited nothing.* This which is truer to the Hebrew is also truer to the Prophet's meaning. The sentence of failure is already written on everything. The best plans are marred, the "wheat" turned to "thorns." The words are obviously of the nature of a proverbial saying, of the same type as that of Hagg. i. 6.

They shall be ashamed.—The word is imperative, *be ashamed.*

Revenues.—The word had not acquired, at the time of the translation of 1611, the exclusively financial sense which now attaches to it, and was used as equivalent to *increase* or "produce" generally. By some commentators the words are referred to the conquerors, who are to be ashamed of their scanty spoil; by others to the conquered, who are to find all their hopes of increase disappointed. The latter seems preferable.

(14) **Thus saith the Lord.**—The introduction of a new message from Jehovah, speaking through the prophet, is indicated by the usual formula.

Mine evil neighbours.—These were the neighbouring nations—Edomites, Moabites, Hagarenes—who rejoiced in the fall of Judah, and attacked her in her weakness (2 Kings xxiv. 2; Pss. lxxxiii. 6—9; cxxxvii. 7). In the midst of his burning indignation against the sins of his own people the prophet is still a patriot, and is yet more indignant at those who attack her. For them, too, there shall be a like chastisement

them. (15) And it shall come to pass,
after that I have plucked them out I
will return, and have compassion on
them, and will bring them again, every
man to his heritage, and every man
to his land. (16) And it shall come to
pass, if they will diligently learn the
ways of my people, to swear by my
name, The LORD liveth; as they taught
my people to swear by Baal; then shall
they be built in the midst of my people.
(17) But if they will not [a]obey, I will
utterly pluck up and destroy that nation, saith the LORD.

B. C. cir. 602.

a Isa. 60. 12.

CHAPTER XIII.—(1) Thus saith the
LORD unto me, Go and get thee a linen
girdle, and put it upon thy loins, and
put it not in water. (2) So I got a
girdle according to the word of the
LORD, and put *it* on my loins.
(3) And the word of the LORD came unto
me the second time, saying, (4) Take the
girdle that thou hast got, which *is*

(comp. chap. xxv. 18—26), but not for them so signal a deliverance as that in store for Judah. They should be "plucked out" from their own land, Judah from the land of its exile.

(15) **I will return, and have compassion on them.**—The words refer, as verse 16 shows, not to Judah only, but to the "evil neighbours." For them also there is hope, and that hope is bound up with the return of Judah. Strong as was the prophet's desire for retribution, it is overpowered by the new love shed abroad in his soul, and he sees that it does not exclude, even in their case, the pity and the yearning that look beyond it for an ultimate restoration.

(16) **To swear by my name.**—There is an obvious reference to the hopes expressed in chap. iv. 2. To acknowledge Jehovah in all the most solemn forms of adjuration (comp. chap. v. 2; Ps. lxiii. 11), and to do this, not hypocritically, but in the spirit of reverence and righteousness, was the ideal state of the restored Judah. To be led by her example of faith and holiness, instead of leading her to acknowledge Baal by like forms of speech as they had done, was the ideal state of the nations round about her. In this hope the prophet was echoing that of Isa. ii. 3; Micah iv. 2.

(17) **I will utterly pluck up.**—In this, as in the preceding verse, there is an obvious reference to the prophet's calling as described in chap. i. 10, the self-same word being used as that which is there rendered "root out." The adverb "utterly" answers to the usual Hebrew reduplication of emphasis.

XIII.

The prophecies of Jeremiah are arranged, it must be remembered, in an order which is not chronological, and that which we have now reached belongs to a later date than many that follow. Comparing the notes of time in the writings of the prophet with those in the history, we get the following as the probable sequence of events. In the early years of Jehoiakim the prophet's preaching so provoked the priests and nobles that they sought his life (chap. xxvi. 15). Then came the burning of the roll (chap. xxxvi. 23), which Jeremiah had not ventured to read in person. This was in the fourth year of that king's reign (chap. xxxvi. 1). During the seven years that followed we hear little or nothing of the prophet's work. Then came the short three months' reign of Jehoiachin, and he re-appears on the scene with the prophecy in this chapter. The date is fixed by the reference, in verse 18, to the queen (*i.e.*, as the Hebrew word implies, the queen-mother) Nehushta (2 Kings xxiv. 8), who seems to have exercised sovereign power in conjunction with her son. During this interval, probably towards its close, we must place the journey to the Euphrates now recorded. There are absolutely no grounds whatever for looking upon it as a vision or a parable, any more than there are for so looking on the symbolic use of the "potter's earthen bottle" (chap. xix. 1) or the "bonds and yokes" (chap. xxvii. 2), or on Isaiah's walking "naked and barefoot" (Isa. xx. 2). It may be added that the special command given by Nebuchadnezzar in Jeremiah's favour (chap. xxxix. 11) implies some previous knowledge which may reasonably be connected with this visit.

(1) **A linen girdle.**—The point of comparison is given in verse 11. Of all garments worn by man the girdle was that most identified with the man's activity, nearest to his person. The "linen girdle" was part of Jeremiah's priestly dress (Exod. xxviii. 40; Lev. xvi. 4), and this also was significant in the interpretation of the symbolic act. Israel, represented as the girdle of Jehovah, had been chosen for consecrated uses. The word "get" implies the act of purchasing, and this too was not without its symbolic significance.

Put it not in water.—The work of the priest as a rule necessarily involved frequent washings both of flesh and garments. The command in this case was therefore exceptional. The unwashed girdle was to represent the guilt of the people unpurified by any real contact with the "clean water" of repentance (Ezek. xxxvi. 25). In the "filthy garments" of Joshua, in Zech. iii. 3, we have a like symbolism. This seems a much more natural interpretation than that which starts from the idea that water would spoil the girdle, and sees in the command the symbol of God's care for His people.

(3) **The second time.**—No dates are given, but the implied interval must have been long enough for the girdle to become foul, while the prophet apparently waited for an explanation of the strange command.

(4) **Go to Euphrates.**—The Hebrew word *Phrath* is the same as that which, everywhere else in the O.T., is rendered by the Greek name for the river, Euphrates. It has been suggested (1) that the word means "river" generally, or "rushing water," applied by way of pre-eminence to the "great river." and therefore that it may have been used here in its general sense; and (2) that it may stand here for Ephratah, or Bethlehem, as the scene of Jeremiah's symbolic actions, the place being chosen on account of its suggestive likeness to Euphrates. These conjectures, however, have no other basis than the assumed improbability of a double journey of two hundred and fifty miles, and this, as has been shown, can hardly be weighed as a serious element in the question. In chap. li. there can be no doubt that the writer means Euphrates. It may be noted, too, as a coincidence confirming this view, that Jeremiah appears as personally known to Nebuchadnezzar in chap. xxxix. 11.

upon thy loins, and arise, go to
Euphrates, and hide it there in a hole
of the rock. (5) So I went, and hid it
by Euphrates, as the LORD commanded
me.
(6) And it came to pass after many
days, that the LORD said unto me,
Arise, go to Euphrates, and take the
girdle from thence, which I commanded
thee to hide there. (7) Then I went to
Euphrates, and digged, and took the
girdle from the place where I had hid
it: and, behold, the girdle was marred,
it was profitable for nothing.
(8) Then the word of the LORD came
unto me, saying, (9) Thus saith the
LORD,
After this manner will I mar the
pride of Judah, and the great pride of
Jerusalem. (10) This evil people, which
refuse to hear my words, which walk
in the [1]imagination of their heart, and
walk after other gods, to serve them,
and to worship them, shall even be as
this girdle, which is good for nothing.
(11) For as the girdle cleaveth to the
loins of a man, so have I caused to
cleave unto me the whole house of Israel
and the whole house of Judah, saith the
LORD; that they might be unto me for
a people, and for a name, and for a
praise, and for a glory: but they would
not hear.
(12) Therefore thou shalt speak unto
them this word; Thus saith the LORD
God of Israel,
Every bottle shall be filled with wine:
and they shall say unto thee, Do we not
certainly know that every bottle shall
be filled with wine? (13) Then shalt thou
say unto them, Thus saith the LORD,
Behold, I will fill all the inhabitants of
this land, even the kings that sit upon
David's throne, and the priests, and the

[1] Or, *stubbornness.*

Those who make Ephratah the scene of what is here recorded, point to the caves and clefts in the rocky region between Bethlehem and the Dead Sea as agreeing with the description. On the other hand, the form *Prath* is nowhere found as substituted for the familiar Ephratah.

A hole of the rock.—Better, *cleft.* In the lower part of its course the Euphrates flows through an alluvial plain, and the words point therefore to some part of its upper course above Pylæ, where its course is through a valley more or less rocky.

(6) **After many days.**—Here again the interval is undefined, but it must have been long enough (we may conjecture, perhaps, seventy days) to be an adequate symbol of the seventy years' exile which the act of placing the girdle by Euphrates represented. So in Hosea iii. 3 we have "many days" for the undefined duration of the exile of the Ten Tribes.

(7) **The girdle was marred.**—The symbolism is explained in verse 9. The girdle stained, decayed, worthless, was a parable of the state of Judah after the exile, stripped of all its outward greatness, losing the place which it had once occupied among the nations of the earth.

(9) **The pride of Judah.**—As the girdle was the part of the dress on which most ornamental work was commonly lavished, so that it was a common gift among princes and men of wealth (1 Sam. xviii. 4; 2 Sam. xviii. 11), it was the natural symbol of the outward glory of a kingdom. As Jeremiah was a priest, we may, perhaps, think of the embroidered girdle "for glory and for beauty" of the priestly dress (Exod. xxviii. 40; Ezek. xliv. 17).

(10) **Imagination.**—Better, as before, *stubbornness.*

Shall even be as this girdle.—The same thought is reproduced in the imagery of the potter's vessel in chap. xviii. 4. On the other hand there is a partial reversal of the sentence in chap. xxiv. 5, where the "good figs" represent the exiles who learnt repentance from their sufferings, and the "bad" those who still remained at Jerusalem under Zedekiah.

Which is good for nothing.—Better, *profitable for nothing,* the Hebrew verse being the same as in verse 7.

(11) **The whole house of Israel.**—The acted parable takes in not only, as in verse 9, Judah, to whom the warning was specially addressed, but the other great division of the people. The sense of national unity is still strong in the prophet's mind. Not Judah only, but the whole collective Israel had been as the girdle of Jehovah, consecrated to His service, designed to be, as the girdle was to man, a praise and glory (Deut. xxvi. 19).

(12) **Every bottle shall be filled with wine.**—Another parable follows on that of the girdle. The germ is found in the phrase "drunken, but not with wine" (Isa. xxix. 9), and the thought rising out of that germ that the effect of the wrath of Jehovah is to cause an impotence and confusion like that of drunkenness (Ps. lx. 3; Isa. li. 17). The "bottle" in this case is not the "skin" commonly used for that purpose, but the earthen jar or flagon, the "potter's vessel" of Isa. xxx. 14, the "pitcher" of Lam. iv. 2. So taken we find an anticipation of the imagery of chaps. xix. 1, 10, xxv. 15. The prophet is bidden to go and proclaim to the people a dark saying, which in its literal sense would seem to them the idlest of all truisms. They would not understand that the "wine" of which he spoke was the wrath of Jehovah, and therefore they would simply repeat his words half in astonishment, half in mockery, "Do we not know this? What need to hear it from a prophet's lips?"

(13) **The kings that sit upon David's throne.**—Literally, *that sit for David* (*i.e.*, as his successors and representatives) *on his throne.* The plural is probably used in pointing to the four—Jehoahaz, Jehoiakim, Jehoiachin, and Zedekiah—who were all of them involved in the sufferings that fell on Judah.

With drunkenness.—The intoxication of the "strong drink"—here, probably, palm-wine—rather than that of the juice of the grape, involving more confusion and loss of power.

prophets, and all the inhabitants of
Jerusalem, with drunkenness. (14) And
I will dash them [1]one against another,
even the fathers and the sons together,
saith the LORD: I will not pity, nor
spare, nor have mercy, [2]but destroy
them.
(15) Hear ye, and give ear; be not
proud: for the LORD hath spoken.
(16) Give glory to the LORD your God,
before he cause [a]darkness, and before
your feet stumble upon the dark moun-
tains, and, while ye look for light, he
turn it into the shadow of death, *and*
make *it* gross darkness. (17) But if
ye will not hear it, my soul shall weep
in secret places for *your* pride; and
[b]mine eye shall weep sore, and run down
with tears, because the LORD's flock is
carried away captive.
(18) Say unto the king and to the
queen, Humble yourselves, sit down:
for your [3]principalities shall come down,
even the crown of your glory. (19) The
cities of the south shall be shut up, and
none shall open *them*: Judah shall be
carried away captive all of it, it shall be
wholly carried away captive. (20) Lift
up your eyes, and behold them that
come from the north: where *is* the flock
that was given thee, thy beautiful flock?
(21) What wilt thou say when he shall
[4]punish thee? for thou hast taught them
to be captains, *and* as chief over thee:

1 Heb., *a man against his brother.*
2 Heb., *from destroying them.*
a Isa. 8. 22.
b Lam. 1. 2, 16; & 2. 18.
3 Or, *head tires.*
4 Heb., *visit upon.*

---

(14) **One against another.**—The rendering answers to the Hebrew idiom, but that idiom, as in the margin, *a man against his brother,* has a force which is lacking in the English, and forms a transition from the symbol to the reality. The words point to what we should call the "crash" of a falling kingdom, when all bonds that keep society together are broken.

(15) **Be not proud.**—With special reference to the besetting sin of Judah, as described in verse 9; perhaps also to the character of the symbols applied—the marred girdle and the broken jar—as being in themselves humiliating, and therefore a trial to their pride.

(16) **Give glory to the Lord your God.**—Probably in the same sense as in Josh. vii. 19 and John ix. 24, perhaps also in Mal. ii. 2, "give glory by confessing the truth, even though that truth be a sin that involves punishment." "Confess your guilt ere it be too late for pardon." This fits in better with the context than the more general sense of "ascribing praise to God."

Before your feet stumble upon the dark mountains.—Literally, *the mountains of twilight,* the word used being employed exclusively first of the coolness and then of the gathering gloom of evening twilight, and never of the dawn. (Compare its use in Job iii. 9, xxiv. 15; Prov. vii. 9.) The fact that the shadows are deepening is obviously one of the vivid touches of the figurative language used. The "gloaming" of the dusk is to pass on into the midnight darkness of the "shadow of death." The same thought is found in Isa. lix. 10, and (probably with some reference to this very passage) in our Lord's words, "If a man walk in the night he stumbleth" (John xi. 10, xii. 35).

(17) **My soul shall weep in secret places for your pride.**—The words present no difficulty that requires explanation, but deserve to be noted in their exquisite tenderness as characteristic of the prophet's temperament (comp. Lam. i. 16), reminding us of the tears shed over Jerusalem (Luke xix. 41) and of St. Paul's "great heaviness and continual sorrow" (Rom. ix. 2). Nothing remained for one who found his labours fruitless but silent sorrow and intercession. The "secret places" find a parallel in our Lord's withdrawal for prayer into a "solitary place" (Mark i. 35).

(18) **The queen.**—Not the usual word, the Hebrew feminine of king, but literally "the great lady" ("*dominatrix,*" Vulg.), the title of a queen-mother (in this case, probably, of Nehushta, the mother of Jehoiachin, 2 Kings xxiv. 8), sharing the throne during her son's minority. The same word is used of Maachah, the mother of Asa (1 Kings xv. 13; 2 Kings x. 13; 2 Chron. xv. 16), and meets us again in chap. xxix. 2.

Your principalities.—Literally, as in the margin, *your head-tires, i.e.,* the diadems which were signs of kingly state. The word is used nowhere else, and may have been coined by the prophet or taken from the court vocabulary of the time.

(19) **The cities of the south.**—The term thus rendered (the *Negeb*) is throughout the Old Testament used for a definite district, stretching from Mount Halak northward to a line south of Engedi and Hebron. The strategy of Nebuchadnezzar's attack (as it had been of Sennacherib's, 2 Kings xviii. 13) was to blockade the cities of this region, and then, when they were cut off from sending assistance, to attack Jerusalem.

Shall be shut up . . . shall be carried away.—Both verbs should be in the present tense, *are shut up, is carried away.*

(20) **Lift up your eyes.**—The Hebrew verb is feminine and singular, the possessive pronoun masculine and plural. Assuming the reading to be correct, the irregularity may have been intended to combine the ideal personification of Jerusalem, the daughter of Zion, as the natural protectress of the other cities, with the concrete multitude of her inhabitants. The "beautiful flock" of those cities had been committed to her care, and she is now called to give an account of her stewardship.

Them that come from the north.—These are, of course, as in chap. i. 14 and elsewhere, the invading army of the Chaldeans, and probably also their Scythian allies.

(21) **What wilt thou say?**—The verse is difficult, and requires an entire retranslation. *What wilt thou* (the daughter of Zion) *say? for He* (Jehovah) *shall set over thee as head those whom thou taughtest* (=tried to teach) *to be thy familiar friends.* This was to be the end of the alliance in which Judah had trusted. She had courted the Chaldean nobles as her lover-guides and friends (the word is the same as in Jer. iii. 4; Ps. lv. 13; Prov. ii. 17, xvi. 28). Another possible construction gives, *shall set over thee those whom thou delightest*

shall not sorrows take thee, as a woman
in travail? (22) And if thou say in thine
heart,[a] Wherefore come these things upon
me? For the greatness of thine iniquity
are thy skirts discovered, *and* thy heels
[1]made bare.
(23) Can the Ethiopian change his
skin, or the leopard his spots? *then*
may ye also do good, that are [2]accus-
tomed to do evil. (24) Therefore will I
scatter them as the stubble that passeth
away by the wind of the wilderness.
(25) This *is* thy lot, the portion of thy
measures from me, saith the LORD;
because thou hast forgotten me, and
trusted in falsehood. (26) Therefore
will I discover thy skirts upon thy face,
that thy shame may appear. (27) I
have seen thine adulteries, and thy
neighings, the lewdness of thy whore-
dom, *and* thine abominations on the
hills in the fields. Woe unto thee, O
Jerusalem! wilt thou not be made
clean? [3]when *shall it* once *be?*

CHAPTER XIV.—(1) The word of
the LORD that came to Jeremiah con-
cerning [4]the dearth.
(2) Judah mourneth, and the gates
thereof languish; they are black unto
the ground; and the cry of Jerusalem
is gone up. (3) And their nobles have
sent their little ones to the waters:
they came to the pits, *and* found no
water; they returned with their vessels
empty; they were ashamed and con-

[a] ch. 5. 19; & 16. 10.

[1] Or, *shall be violently taken away.*

B. C. cir. 601.

[2] Heb., *taught.*

[3] Heb., *after when yet?*

[4] Heb., *the words of the dearths,* or, *restraints.*

---

to be thy friends as head over thee, i.e., those whose supremacy Judah had acknowledged in order that she might court their alliance. What could come then but that which was to the Hebrew the type of extremest anguish (Isa. xiii. 8, xxi. 3; Ps. xlviii. 6), the travail-pangs which were followed by no joy that a man was born into the world (John xvi. 21)?

(22) **Are thy skirts discovered.**—The "skirts," or flowing train, worn by women of rank, the removal of which was the sign of extremest degradation (Isa. xx. 4, xlvii. 2; Ezek. xxiii. 29; Hos. ii. 3; Nahum iii. 5).

Thy heels made bare.—Better, *outraged,* or *disgraced,* made to walk barefoot, like menial slaves; possibly, like the outcast harlot. Compare Isaiah's walking "naked and barefoot" as the symbol of the coming degradation of his people (Isa. xx. 2—4).

(23) **Can the Ethiopian . . .?**—Literally, *the Cushite.* The meaning of the question is obvious. The evil of Judah was too deep-ingrained to be capable of spontaneous reformation. There remained nothing but the sharp discipline of the exile. The invasion of Tirhakah and Pharaoh-nechoh, the presence of Ethiopians among the servants of the royal household (chap. xxxviii. 10), the intercourse with the upper valley of the Nile implied in Zeph. iii. 10 and Pss. lxviii. 31, lxxxvii. 4, had made the swarthy forms of Africa familiar objects. Possibly the use of leopard-skins by Ethiopian princes and warriors, as seen on Egyptian monuments and described by Herodotus (vii. 69), had associated the two thoughts together in the prophet's mind. If the king's household were present (as in verse 18), he may have pointed to such an one, Ebed-melech (chap. xxxviii. 10), or another so arrayed, in illustration of his words.

(24) **Stubble.**—Our English word means the "stalks of the corn left in the field by the reaper" (Johnson). The Hebrew word is applied to the broken straw left on the threshing-floor after the oxen had been driven over the corn, which was liable to be carried away by the first gale (Isa. xl. 24, xli. 2).

The wind of the wilderness.—*i.e.,* the *simoom* blowing from the Arabian desert (chap. iv. 11; Job i. 19).

(25) **The portion of thy measures.**—The meaning of the latter word is doubtful, but it is probably used, as in 1 Sam. iv. 12; Lev. vi. 11; 2 Sam. xx. 8; Ruth iii. 15, for the "upper garment" or "lap" of the dress. In this sense the phrase is connected with those which speak of reward or punishment being given men "into their bosom" (chap. xxxii. 18; Ps. lxxix. 12; Prov. xxi. 14).

In falsehood.—Better, perhaps, *in a lie, i.e.,* in the worship of false gods that were no gods.

(26) **Therefore will I discover . . .**—The threat is substantially the same as that in verse 22. The form is verbally identical with that of Nahum iii. 5.

(27) **Thine adulteries.**—The words refer primarily to the spiritual adultery of the idolatries of Judah. The "neighings," as in chap. ii. 24, v. 8, express the unbridled eagerness of animal passion transferred in this passage to the spiritual sin. The "abominations on the hills" are the orgiastic rites of the worship of the high places, which are further described as "in the field" to emphasise their publicity.

Wilt thou not be made clean?—Better, *thou wilt not be cleansed; after how long yet?* Sad as the last words are, they in some measure soften the idea of irretrievable finality, "Will the time ever come, and if so, when?" Like the cry addressed to God, "How long, O Lord . . ." (Rev. vi. 10), it implies a hope, though only just short of despair.

XIV.

(1) **Concerning the dearth.**—Literally, *on the word or tidings of the drought.* This is clearly the opening of a new discourse, which continues to chap. xvii. 18; but as no special calamity of this kind is mentioned in the historical account of Jeremiah's life, its date cannot be fixed with certainty. As chap. xv. 15 implies that he had already suffered scorn or persecution for his prophetic work, we may reasonably assume some period not earlier than the reign of Jehoiakim.

(2) **The gates thereof languish.**—The "gates" of the cities, as the chief places of concourse, like the *agora* of Greek cities, are taken figuratively for the inhabitants, who in the "black" garments of sorrow and with the pallor of the famine, in which all faces gather blackness, are crouching upon the ground in their despair.

(3) **Their little ones.**—Not their children, but their menial servants. The word is peculiar to Jeremiah, and occurs only here and in chap. xlviii. 4. The vivid

founded, and covered their heads.
(4) Because the ground is chapt, for
there was no rain in the earth, the
plowmen were ashamed, they covered
their heads. (5) Yea, the hind also
calved in the field, and forsook *it*, be-
cause there was no grass. (6) And the
wild asses did stand in the high places,
they snuffed up the wind like dragons;
their eyes did fail, because *there was* no
grass.

(7) O LORD, though our iniquities
testify against us, do thou *it* for thy
name's sake: for our backslidings are
many; we have sinned against thee.
(8) O the hope of Israel, the saviour
thereof in time of trouble, why shouldest
thou be as a stranger in the land, and
as a wayfaring man *that* turneth aside
to tarry for a night? (9) Why shouldest
thou be as a man astonied, as a mighty
man *that* cannot save? yet thou, O
LORD, *art* in the midst of us, and [1]we
are called by thy name; leave us not.

(10) Thus saith the LORD unto this
people, Thus have they loved to wander,
they have not refrained their feet, there-
fore the LORD doth not accept them; he
will now remember their iniquity, and
visit their sins.

(11) Then said the LORD unto me,
[a]Pray not for this people for *their* good.
(12) [b]When they fast, I will not hear their
cry; and when they offer burnt offering

1 Heb., *thy name is called upon us.*

a Exod. 32. 10; ch. 7. 16; & 11. 14.

b Prov. 1. 28; Isa. 1. 15; ch. 11. 11; Ezek. 8. 18; Micah 3. 4.

---

picture of the messengers running hither and thither to all wells, and springs, and tanks, reminds us of Ahab's search for wells or springs in the time of the great drought of his reign (1 Kings xviii. 5), of the "two or three cities wandering" to the one city that was yet supplied with water of Amos iv. 8.

The pits.—The tanks or reservoirs where, if anywhere, water might be looked for.

Covered their heads.—The extremest sign of a grief too great to utter itself to others, craving to be alone in its wretchedness (2 Sam. xv. 30, xix. 4). The student will recollect it as occurring also in the account of the painting of Agamemnon at the Sacrifice of Iphigenia, ascribed to Timanthes.

(4) **The ground is chapt.**—The word is so vivid as describing the long fissures of the soil in a time of drought that one admits with reluctance that no such meaning is found in the Hebrew word, which simply means *is struck with terror*. The translators apparently followed Luther, who gives *lechzet*—"languishes for thirst," "gapes open with exhaustion," and so applied to the earth, "is cracked or chapt."

As the "gates" in verse 2 stood for the people of the city, so the "ground" stands here as in visible sympathy with the tillers of the soil, the "plowmen" of the next clause.

They covered their heads.—There is a singular, almost awful, pathos in the iteration of this description. Cities and country alike are plunged into the utter blackness of despair.

(5) **Yea.**—Better, *For*, as the Hebrew is usually translated. What follows gives the reason of the terror which has come upon the people. Each region has its representative instance of misery. The hind of the field (the female of the common stag—the *Cervus elaphus* of zoologists), noted for its tenderness to its young, abandons it, and turns away to seek pasture for itself, and fails to find any.

(6) **The wild asses.**—From the field the prophet's eye turns to the bare hill-tops of the "high places," and sees a scene of like distress. The "wild asses" seem turned to beasts of prey, and stand gaping for thirst, as the *jackals* (not "dragons"—comp. chap. ix. 11) stand panting for their prey. By some scholars the word is taken as meaning, like a kindred word in Ezek. xxix. 3, xxxii. 2, "crocodiles," with their wide gaping jaws.

There was no grass.—The word is not the same as that in verse 5, and implies a larger and ranker herbage than that on which the hind fed.

(7) **O Lord . . .**—From the picture of suffering the prophet turns to a prayer for pardon and a confession of sins. He is sure that the drought has not come without cause, and that it calls men to repentance.

Do thou it.—Better, more generally, *act thou*, not according to the rigour of inexorable justice, but according to the Name which witnesses of mercy and long-suffering (Exod. xxxiv. 6).

(8) **As a wayfaring man . . .**—No image could paint more vividly the sense of abandonment which weighed on the prophet's heart. Israel had looked to Jehovah as its help and stay, its watchful guardian. Now he seemed as indifferent to it as the passing traveller is to the interests of the city in the inn or *khan* of which he lodges for a single night.

(9) **As a man astonied.**—The word so rendered is not found elsewhere, but cognate words in Arabic have the meaning of being startled and perplexed.

Thou, O Lord, art in the midst of us.—After all, then, so the prophet's reviving faith tells him, Jehovah is more than the passing guest. He abides still among His people. He is as a mighty man, strong to save, though as yet He refrains from action.

We are called by thy name.—Literally, as in the margin, *Thy name is called upon us, i.e.* (as in Isa. iv. 1, lxiii. 19, lxv. 1), "we are still recognised as Thine, the people of Jehovah."

(10) **Thus have they loved to wander.**—The prophet has to tell the people that Jehovah's answer to his prayer is one of seeming refusal. The time of pardon has not yet come. The prophet is told that *now* (the adverb is emphasised) is the time for remembering iniquity and visiting sins. The latter half of the verse is a verbal quotation from Hosea viii. 13. The opening word "thus" appears to point back to the "many backslidings" of verse 7.

(11) **Pray not . . .**—As before, in chaps. vii. 16, xi. 14, the saddest, sternest part of the prophet's work is to feel that even prayer—the prayer that punishment may be averted—is unavailing and unaccepted.

(12) **An oblation.**—The *minchah* or meat-offering of Lev. ii. 1. We need not assume that the fast and the sacrifice were necessarily hypocritical, though doubtless much of this mingled itself with the worship of

and an oblation, I will not accept them:
but I will consume them by the sword,
and by the famine, and by the pesti-
lence.
(13) Then said I, Ah, Lord God! be-
hold, the prophets say unto them, Ye
shall not see the sword, neither shall
ye have famine; but I will give you
[1]assured peace in this place.
(14) Then the Lord said unto me, The
prophets prophesy lies in my name: [a]I
sent them not, neither have I com-
manded them, neither spake unto them:
they prophesy unto you a false vision
and divination, and a thing of nought,
and the deceit of their heart. (15) There-
fore thus saith the Lord concerning the
prophets that prophesy in my name, and
I sent them not, yet they say, Sword
and famine shall not be in this land;
By sword and famine shall those pro-
phets be consumed. (16) And the people
to whom they prophesy shall be cast
out in the streets of Jerusalem because
of the famine and the sword; and they
shall have none to bury them, them,
their wives, nor their sons, nor their
daughters: for I will pour their wicked-
ness upon them.
(17) Therefore thou shalt say this word
unto them; [b]Let mine eyes run down
with tears night and day, and let them
not cease: for the virgin daughter of
my people is broken with a great breach,
with a very grievous blow. (18) If I go
forth into the field, then behold the slain
with the sword! and if I enter into the
city, then behold them that are sick
with famine! yea, both the prophet
and the priest [2]go about into a land that
they know not. (19) Hast thou utterly
rejected Judah? hath thy soul lothed
Zion? why hast thou smitten us, and
there is no healing for us? [c]we looked for
peace, and *there is* no good; and for the
time of healing, and behold trouble!

1 Heb., *peace of truth.*

a ch. 23. 21; & 27. 15; & 29. 8, 9.

b ch. 13. 17; Lam. 1. 16; & 2. 18.

2 Or, *make merchandise against a land, and men acknowledge it not,* ch. 5. 31.

c ch. 8. 15.

Israel now as it had done in the days of Isaiah, and met with a like rejection (Isa. i. 15). The lesson here is rather that they came too late to stay the discipline of chastisement.

By the sword, and by the famine, and by the pestilence.—The history of the world shows how constantly the latter plagues have followed in the wake of the former, and the union of the three has become proverbial (Lev. xxvi. 25, 26; Ezek. v. 12). In Ezek. xiv. 21 the "noisome beast" is added to make up the list of the four sore judgments of God.

(13) **Ah, Lord God!**—Literally, as in chap. i. 6, *Alas, my Lord (Adonaï) Jehovah!* We have had in chap. v. 31 a glimpse of the evil influence of the great body of the prophetic order; and now the true prophet feels more bitterly than ever the misery of having to contend against it. The colleges or schools of the prophets had rapidly degenerated from their first ideal, and had become (as the Mendicant Orders did in the history of mediæval Christendom) corrupt, ambitious, seekers after popularity. So Micah (chap. iii. 8—11), whose words were yet fresh in the memories of men (see chap. xxvi. 18), had spoken sharp words of the growing evil. So Ezekiel through one whole chapter (chap. xiii.) inveighs against the guilt of the prophets, male or female, who followed their own spirit, and had seen no true vision.

Ye shall not see . . .—To the eye of Jeremiah the future was clear. The sins of the people must lead to shame, defeat, and exile. Out of that discipline, but only through that, they might return with a better mind to better days. The false prophets took the easier and more popular line of predicting victory and "assured peace" (literally, *peace of truth*, i.e., *true peace*) for the people and their city.

(14) **They prophesy unto you . . .**—The four forms of the evil are carefully enumerated: (1) the false vision, false as being but the dream of a disordered fancy; (2) divination, by signs and auguries, as, *e.g.*, by arrows (Ezek. xxi. 21) or cups (Gen. xliv. 5); (3) by "a thing of nought," or, more accurately, the "idol" or small image of a god, used as the Teraphim were used (Ezek. xxi. 21; Zech. x. 2), as in some way forecasting the future; (4) the deceit of their heart, *i.e.*, an imposture pure and simple, the fraud of a deliberately counterfeit inspiration.

(15) **Therefore thus saith the Lord.**—To the mind of a true prophet, feeling that he was taught of God, nothing could be more hateful than the acts of those who, for selfish ends, were leading the people to their destruction. For them there was therefore the righteous retribution that they should perish in the very calamities which they had asserted would never come.

(17) **Thou shalt say this word.**—Though not in form a prediction, no words could express more emphatically the terrible nature of the judgments implied in the preceding verse. The language (in part a reproduction of chap. xiii. 17) is all but identical with that which recurs again and again in the Lamentations (chap. i. 16, ii. 11, 18), and may be looked upon as the germ of which those elegies of woe were the development.

(18) **Them that are sick with famine.**—Literally, with even a more awful force, as summing all individual sufferings in one collective unity, *the sickness of famine*—the pestilence that follows on starvation.

Go about into a land that they know not.—Literally, *go about* (as in Gen. xxxiv. 10, where the Authorised version has "trade") *in a land and know not, i.e.*, whither they go—are in a land of exile, and know not where to find a home, or where they may be dragged next, or, perhaps, with some commentators, *learn no wisdom* from their bitter experience. There is no adequate ground for the rendering in the margin, which, besides, gives no satisfactory meaning.

(19) **Hast thou utterly rejected Judah?**—The heart of the patriot overpowers even the conviction of the prophet, and, though bidden not to pray, he bursts forth, in spite of the command, with a prayer of passionate intercession.

(20) We acknowledge, O LORD, our
wickedness, *and* the iniquity of our
fathers: for [a]we have sinned against
thee. (21) Do not abhor *us*, for thy
name's sake, do not disgrace the throne
of thy glory: remember, break not thy
covenant with us. (22) Are there *any*
among the vanities of the Gentiles that
can cause rain? or can the heavens give
showers? *art* not thou he, O LORD our
God? therefore we will wait upon thee:
for thou hast made all these *things*.

CHAPTER XV.—(1) Then said the
LORD unto me, [b]Though [c]Moses and
[d]Samuel stood before me, *yet* my mind
could not *be* toward this people: cast
them out of my sight, and let them
go forth. (2) And it shall come to pass,
if they say unto thee, Whither shall we
go forth? then thou shalt tell them,
Thus saith the LORD; [e]Such as *are* for
death, to death; and such as *are* for
the sword, to the sword; and such as
are for the famine, to the famine; and
such as *are* for the captivity, to the cap-
tivity. (3) And I will [f]appoint over
them four [1]kinds, saith the LORD: the
sword to slay, and the dogs to tear, and
the fowls of the heaven, and the beasts
of the earth, to devour and destroy.
(4) And [2]I will cause them to be [g]re-
moved into all kingdoms of the earth,
because of [h]Manasseh the son of Heze-
kiah king of Judah, for *that* which he
did in Jerusalem.
(5) For who shall have pity upon thee,
O Jerusalem? or who shall bemoan
thee? or who shall go aside [3]to ask how
thou doest? (6) Thou hast forsaken
me, saith the LORD, thou art gone back-
ward: therefore will I stretch out my

a Ps. 106. 6; Dan. 9. 8.
b Ezek. 14. 14.
c Exod. 32. 11, 12.
d 1 Sam. 7. 9.
e ch. 43. 11; Zech. 11. 9.
f Lev. 26. 16.
1 Heb., *families*.
2 Heb., *I will give them for a removing*.
g Deut. 28. 25; ch. 24. 9.
h 2 Kings 21. 11.
3 Heb., *to ask of thy peace?*

Hath thy soul lothed Zion?—The Hebrew implies the act of rejection as well as the feeling which leads to it.

(20) **And the iniquity.**—The insertion of the conjunction weakens the force of the original. The wickedness which Israel confesses is the iniquity of its fathers, inherited, accepted, on the way to be perpetuated.

(21) **Do not abhor us . . .**—Even in the English, and yet more in the Hebrew, we seem to hear the broken accents, words and sobs intermingled, of the agony of the prayer. "Abhor us not . . . disgrace not . . . remember, break not." The prophet can make no plea of extenuation, but he can appeal to the character of God, and urge, with a bold anthropomorphism, that mercy is truer to that character than rigorous justice, and that His covenant with Israel pledges Him to that mercy.

The throne of thy glory.—This is, of course, the Temple (see chap. xvii. 12). Shall that become a bye-word of reproach, scorned (so the word means) as a fool is scorned?

(22) **Vanities.**—*sc.*, as in chap. x. 8, the idols of the heathen, powerless and perishable.

Are there any . . . that can cause rain?—The question is asked with a special reference to the drought which had called forth the prophet's utterance (verse 1). Israel remembers at last that it is Jehovah alone who gives the rain from heaven and the fruitful seasons, and turns to Him in patient waiting for His gifts. The words contain an implied appeal to the history of Elijah (1 Kings xviii. 41) and that of Joel ii. 23).

XV.

(1) **Then said the Lord unto me.**—With a bold and terrible anthropomorphism, the prophet again speaks as if he heard the voice of Jehovah rejecting all intercession for the apostate people. The passage reminds us of the mention of Noah, Daniel, and Job, in Ezek. xiv. 14, as "able to deliver their own souls only by their righteousness." Here Moses (Exod. xxxii. 11; Num. xiv. 13—20) and Samuel (1 Sam. vii. 9, xii. 23) are named as having been conspicuous examples of the power of the prayer of intercession.

Cast them out of my sight.—*i.e.*, from my presence, from the courts of the Temple which they profane. That would be the answer of Jehovah, even if Moses and Samuel "stood before Him" (the phrase, as in chap. xxxv. 19, has a distinctly liturgical meaning), ministering in the Courts of the Temple.

(2) **Such as are for death . . .**—The difference between the first two forms of punishment is that the first points possibly to being led out to execution as criminals, as in Deut. xix. 6, but more probably to death from pestilence, as in Job xxvii. 15; the second, to falling in a vain and hopeless conflict.

(3) **Four kinds.**—The sword, as the direct instrument of death, is followed by those that follow up its work, the beasts and birds of prey that feed on the corpses of the slain. The latter feature has naturally been from the earliest stages of human history the crowning horror of defeat. So Homer, *Il.* i. 4:—

> "And many mighty souls of heroes sent
> To Hades, and their bodies made a prey
> To dogs and to all birds."

(4) **Manasseh the son of Hezekiah.**—The horror of that long and evil reign still lingered in the minds of men, and the prophet saw in it the beginning of the evils from which his people were now suffering. The name of Hezekiah may have been inserted as an aggravation of the guilt of his successor.

(5) **To ask how thou doest?**—This is a fair paraphrase of the original, but it wants the Oriental colouring of the more literal *to ask after thy peace.* As "Peace be with thee" was the usual formula of salutation, sc.," Is it peace?" was the equivalent for our more prosaic question, "How do you do?" (Gen. xliii. 27; Judges xviii. 15). The same phrase meets us in Exod. xviii. 7, "They asked each other of their welfare," literally, *of their peace.*

(6) **Thou hast forsaken me.**—The Hebrew word has the stronger sense of rejecting or repudiating as

hand against thee, and destroy thee; I
am weary with repenting. (7) And I
will fan them with a fan in the gates of
the land; I will bereave *them* of [1]chil-
dren, I will destroy my people, *since*
they return not from their ways. (8) Their
widows are increased to me above the
sand of the seas: I have brought upon
them [2]against the mother of the young
men a spoiler at noonday: I have
caused *him* to fall upon it suddenly,
and terrors upon the city. (9) She that
hath borne seven languisheth: she hath
given up the ghost; [a]her sun is gone
down while *it was* yet day: she hath
been ashamed and confounded: and the
residue of them will I deliver to the
sword before their enemies, saith the
LORD.
(10) [b]Woe is me, my mother, that thou
hast borne me a man of strife and a man
of contention to the whole earth! I
have neither lent on usury, nor men
have lent to me on usury; *yet* every one
of them doth curse me. (11) The LORD
said, Verily it shall be well with thy
remnant; verily [3]I will cause the enemy
to entreat thee *well* in the time of evil

1 Or, *whatsoever is dear.*

2 Or, *against the mother city a young man spoiling, &c.*; or, *against the mother and the young men.*

a Amos 8. 9.

b Job 3. 1, &c.; ch. 20. 15.

3 Or, *I will intreat the enemy for thee.*

---

well as simply leaving, and gives the reason for a like rejection on the part of Jehovah.

I am weary with repenting.—The long-suffering of God is described, as before, in anthropomorphic language (comp. 1 Sam. xv. 35). He had "repented," *i.e.*, changed His purpose of punishing, but patience was now exhausted, and justice was weary of the delay, and must take its course. Perhaps, however, *I am weary of pitying* or *of relenting* would be a better rendering.

(7) **I will fan them with a fan.**—The image is, of course, the familiar one of the threshing-floor and the winnowing-fan or shovel (Pss. i. 4, xxxv. 5; Matt. iii. 12). The tenses should be past in both clauses—*I have winnowed . . . I have bereaved . . . I have destroyed.*

In the gates of the land . . .—Possibly the "gates" stand for the fortified cities of Judah, the chief part being taken for the whole, more probably for the "approaches" of the land. So the Greeks spoke of the passes of the Taurus as the Cilician gates, and so we speak of the Khyber and Bolam passes as "the gates of India."

Since they return not.—The insertion of the conjunction, which has nothing corresponding to it in the original, weakens the vigour of the abruptness of the clause, and probably suggests a wrong sequence of thought. Jehovah had chastened them, but it was in vain. They returned not from their ways. *Yet*, as in the Vulgate, rather than "since," is the implied conjunction.

(8) **I have brought . . .**—Better, *I have brought upon them, even upon the mother of the young warrior* (*i.e.*, upon the woman who rejoices most in her son's heroism), *a spoiler at noon-day*, *i.e.*, coming, when least expected, at the hour when most armies rested. (See Note on chap. vi. 4.)

I have caused him to fall upon it suddenly . . .—Better, *I have brought suddenly upon her* (the "mother" of the previous sentence) *travail-pangs* (as in Isa. xiii. 8) *and dismay.* The Aramaic word for the anguish of childbirth is also the Hebrew word for "city," and this has misled translators. The LXX. gives the true meaning.

(9) **She that hath borne seven.**—In the picture of the previous verse the glory of the mother was found in the valour of her son, here in the number of her children. "Seven," as the perfect number, represented, as in 1 Sam. ii. 5, Ruth iv. 15, the typical completeness of the family.

Her sun is gone down while it was yet day.—The image of this eclipse of all joy and brightness may possibly have been suggested by the actual eclipse of the sun (total in Palestine), Sept. 30, B.C. 610, the year of the battle of Megiddo, just as the earthquake in the reign of Uzziah suggested much of the imagery of Isaiah and Amos (Isa. ii. 19; Amos i. 1, 2, iv. 11; Zech. xiv. 5). A like image meets us in Amos viii. 9.

(10) **Woe is me . . .**—The abruptness of the transition suggests the thought that we have a distinct fragment which has been merged in the artificial continuity of the chapter. Possibly, as some have thought, verses 10 and 11 have been misplaced in transcription, and should come after verse 14, where they fit in admirably with the context. The sequence of thought may, however, be that the picture of the sorrowing mother in the previous verses suggests the reflection that there may be other causes for a mother's sorrow than that of which he has spoken, and so he bursts out into the cry, "Woe is me, my mother!" The prophet feels more than ever the awfulness of his calling as a vessel of God's truth. He, too, found that he had come "not to send peace on earth, but a sword" (Matt. x. 34). His days were as full of strife as the life of the usurer, whose quarrels with his debtors had become the proverbial type of endless litigation. As examples of the working of the law of debt, see Exod. xxii. 25; 2 Kings iv. 1; Prov. vi. 1—5; Isa. xxiv. 2; Pss. xv. 5, cix. 11.

We note, as characteristic of the pathetic tenderness of the prophet's character, the address to his mother. We may think of her probably as still living, and the thought of her suffering embitters her son's grief. The sword was piercing through her soul also (Luke ii. 35). There, too, there was a *Mater dolorosa.*

(11) **Verily it shall be well with thy remnant.**—The passage is obscure, and the reading uncertain; (1) *Thy freedom shall be for good*, or (2) *I afflict thee for thy good*, or (3) *I strengthen thee for thy good*, have been proposed as better renderings. The second seems to give the meaning most in harmony with the context. Jehovah comforts the despairing prophet by the promise that in due time there shall be a deliverance from the discords of his life, and that "all things shall work together for his good."

I will cause the enemy to entreat thee well.—The final adverb, which is not found in the Hebrew, obscures the sense, suggesting the English phrase of "treating well." Better, *I will cause the enemy to be a suppliant to thee in time of evil.* Partial fulfilments of the promise are found in chaps. xxi. 1, xxxvii. 3, xlii. 2.

and in the time of affliction. (12) Shall
iron break the northern iron and the
steel? (13) Thy substance and thy
treasures will I give to the [a]spoil with-
out price, and *that* for all thy sins, even
in all thy borders. (14) And I will make
thee to pass with thine enemies into a
land *which* thou knowest not: for a [b]fire
is kindled in mine anger, *which* shall
burn upon you.
(15) O LORD, thou knowest: remember
me, and visit me, and revenge me of my
persecutors; take me not away in thy
longsuffering: know that for thy sake
I have suffered rebuke. (16) Thy words
were found, and I did [c]eat them; and
thy word was unto me the joy and re-
joicing of mine heart: for [1]I am called
by thy name, O LORD God of hosts.
(17) I sat not in the assembly of the
mockers, nor rejoiced; I sat alone be-
cause of thy hand: for thou hast filled
me with indignation. (18) Why is my
[d]pain perpetual, and my wound incur-
able, *which* refuseth to be healed? wilt
thou be altogether unto me as a liar,
and as waters *that* [2]fail?
(19) Therefore thus saith the LORD, If

a ch. 17. 3.

b Deut. 32. 22.

c Ezek. 3. 3; Rev. 10. 9.

1 Heb., *thy name is called upon me.*

d ch. 30. 15.

2 Heb., *be not sure?*

---

(12) **Shall iron break . . .?**—The abruptness of the question and the boldness of the imagery make the interpretation difficult. That which most harmonises with the context (assuming this verse to carry on the thought of verses 1—9, after the interruption, possibly the interpolation, of verses 10 and 11) is, that the prayer of the prophet, strong though it may be, cannot change the inflexible purpose of Jehovah to chastise His people's sins. Some have, however, taken the words as declaring (1) the powerlessness of Judah to resist the titanic strength of the Chaldæans, or (2) the impotence of the prophet's enemies to deter him from his work, or (3) the prophet's want of power against the obdurate evil of the people, or (4) the weakness of Pharaoh-nechoh as compared with Nebuchadnezzar. Of these (3) has a show of plausibility from chaps. i. 18 and xv. 20, but does not harmonise so well with what precedes and follows. The "northern iron" is probably that of the Chalybes of Pontus, mentioned as the "artificers in iron" by Æschylus (*Prom. Bound,* 733), as the coast of the Euxine is called by him the land which is "the mother of iron" (*Ibid.* 309), famous for being harder than all others. For "steel" we should read *bronze.* The word is commonly translated "brass," but that compound, in its modern sense, was unknown to the metallurgy of Israel.

(13) **Thy substance and thy treasures . . .**—Assuming the words to stand in their right place, we must look on them as addressed to Jeremiah as the intercessor, and therefore the representative, of his people. If we admit a dislocation, of which there seem many signs, we may connect them with verses 5 and 6, and then they are spoken to Jerusalem. The recurrence of the words in chap. xvii. 3, 4, as addressed to the mountain of the plain, *i.e.,* Zion, makes this probable.

Without price.—As in Ps. xliv. 12; Isa. lii. 3, this implies the extremest abandonment. The enemies of Israel were to have an easy victory, for which they would not have to pay the usual price of blood; nor did God, on His side, demand from them any payment for the victory He bestowed. He gave away His people as men give that which they count worthless.

(14) **I will make thee to pass with thine enemies . . .**—The Hebrew text is probably corrupt, and a slight variation of the reading of one word brings the verse into harmony with the parallel passage of chap. xvii. 4, and gives a better meaning, *I will make thee serve thine enemies in a land thou dost not know.* As it stands without the pronoun "thee" in the Hebrew we may take it, with some commentators, as meaning, *I will make them* (the "treasures" of verse 13) *pass with thine enemies . . .*

A fire is kindled in mine anger.—Another quotation from Deuteronomy (chap. xxxii. 22).

(15) **O Lord, thou knowest . . .**—The prophet continues in the bitterness of his spirit the complaint that had begun in verse 10. The words remind us of the imprecations of the so-called vindictive psalms (such, *e.g.,* as Pss. lxix. and cix.), and may help us to understand the *genesis* of the emotions which they express. Not even the promise of verse 11 has given rest to his soul. He craves to see the righteous retribution for the sufferings which men have wrongfully inflicted on him.

(16) **Thy words were found . . .**—The words go back to the mission of chap. i., and paint, with a wonderful power, the beginning of a prophet's work, the new-born intensity of joy in the sense of communion with the Eternal. The soul feeds on the words that come to it (see the same figure in a bolder form in Ezek. ii. 8, iii. 1—3; Rev. x. 9). They are "sweeter than honey and the honeycomb" (Ps. xix. 10). They are incorporated with its life, are "the rejoicing of its heart." He is called by the Name of "the Lord God of hosts," or, more literally, that Name *is called upon him.* As the witness of his special consecration, he becomes, like other prophets, "a man of God" (1 Kings xiii. 1; 2 Kings vii. 2; 1 Tim. vi. 11).

(17) **In the assembly of the mockers.**—Rather, *of the mirthful.* The word, which is the same as that found in Isaac (= laughter), does not necessarily imply an evil or cynical mirth, like that of the "scorner" of Ps. i. 1. What is meant is, that from the time of his consecration to his office the prophet's life had not been as the life of other men, but had been marked by a strange loneliness, filled with the consuming wrath of Jehovah against the evils that surrounded him. The "hand" of Jehovah is used here, as in Ezek. i. 3, iii. 22, viii. 1, for the special overpowering consciousness of the fulness of inspiration.

(18) **Wilt thou be altogether unto me as a liar . . .?**—The words express a bitter sense of failure and disappointment. God had not prospered the mission of His servant as He had promised. The Hebrew, however, is not so startlingly bold as the English, and is satisfied by the rendering, *wilt thou be unto me as a winter torrent, i.e.,* as in Job vi. 15, like one which flows only in that season, and is dried up and parched in summer. See the play upon the word *achzib* (= a lie) in Micah i. 14.

(19) **Therefore thus saith the Lord . . .**—The Divine voice within makes answer to the passionate

thou return, then will I bring thee
again, *and* thou shalt stand before me:
and if thou take forth the precious from
the vile, thou shalt be as my mouth:
let them return unto thee; but return
not thou unto them. (20) And I will
make thee unto this people a fenced
brasen [a]wall: and they shall fight
against thee, but [b]they shall not pre-
vail against thee: for I *am* with thee to
save thee and to deliver thee, saith the
LORD. (21) And I will deliver thee out
of the hand of the wicked, and I will
redeem thee out of the hand of the
terrible.

CHAPTER XVI.—(1) The word of
the LORD came also unto me, saying,
(2) Thou shalt not take thee a wife,
neither shalt thou have sons or daugh-
ters in this place. (3) For thus saith
the LORD concerning the sons and con-
cerning the daughters that are born in
this place, and concerning their mothers
that bare them, and concerning their
fathers that begat them in this land;
(4) They shall die of [c]grievous deaths;
they shall not be [d]lamented; neither
shall they be buried; *but* they shall be
as dung upon the face of the earth: and
they shall be consumed by the sword,
and by famine; and their [e]carcases shall
be meat for the fowls of heaven, and for
the beasts of the earth.
(5) For thus saith the LORD, Enter
not into the house of [1]mourning,
neither go to lament nor bemoan them:
for I have taken away my peace from

a ch. 1. 18; & 6. 27.
b ch. 20. 11.
c ch. 15. 2.
d ch. 25. 33.
e Ps. 79. 2; ch. 7. 33; & 34. 20.
1 Or, *mourning feast.*

---

complaint. The prophet also needs, not less than the people, to "return" to his true mind, to repent of his murmurings and distrust. Upon that condition only can he again "stand before" the Lord in the full sense of that word, and minister to Him as a prophet-priest (comp. 1 Kings xvii. 1, xviii. 15; 2 Kings iii. 14). He has to distinguish between "the precious and the vile," between the gold and the dross, between a righteous zeal and the despondent bitterness which is its spurious counterfeit, not in the people only to whom he speaks but in himself. Above all he must beware of being tempted by his sense of failure, to *return* to the people in the temper of one who tunes his voice according to the time. Rather must they "return" to him and rise to his level, both "returning" to Jehovah.

(20) **I will make thee unto this people . . .**—It is significant that the promise reproduced the very words which the prophet had heard when he was first summoned to his work (see Note on chap. i. 18, 19). Jehovah had not been unfaithful to His word, but, like all promises, it depended on implied conditions, and these the faint-hearted, desponding prophet had but imperfectly fulfilled. Let him "return" to the temper of trust, and there should be an abundant deliverance for him.

XVI.

(1) **The word of the Lord came also unto me.**—The formula introduces a new and distinct message, extending to chap. xvii. 18, and it is one even more terrible in its threatenings than any that have preceded it. There is nothing in its contents to fix the date with any certainty, but we may think of it as probably about the close of the reign of Jehoiakim, when that king was trusting in an alliance with Egypt (chap. xvii. 13), and the people taunted the prophet with the non-fulfilment of his predictions (chap. xvii. 15).

(2) **Thou shalt not take thee a wife . . .**—The words came to an Israelite and to a priest with a force which we can hardly understand. With them marriage, and the hopes which it involved, was not only a happiness but a duty, and to be cut off from it was to renounce both, because the evil that was coming on the nation was such as to turn both into a curse. We may compare our Lord's words in Matt. xxiv. 19 and those spoken to the daughters of Jerusalem (Luke xxiii. 29), and what, in part at least, entered into St. Paul's motives for a like abstinence on account of "the present distress" (1 Cor. vii. 26).

(4) **Of grievous deaths.**—Literally, *deaths from diseases,* including, perhaps, famine (as in chap. xiv. 18), as contrasted with the more immediate work of the sword.

They shall not be lamented.—Among a people who attached such importance to the due observance of funeral obsequies as the Jews did, the neglect of those obsequies was, of course, here, as in chap. xxii. 18, a symptom of extremest misery. Like features have presented themselves in the pestilences or sieges of other cities and other times, as in the description in Lucretius (vi. 1278):—

> "Nec mos ille sepulturæ remanebat in urbe,
> Quo pius hic populus semper consuerat humari."

> "No more the customed rites of sepulture
> Were practised in the city, such as wont
> Of old to tend the dead with reverent care."

Compare the account of the plague at Athens in Thucydides (ii. 52).

(5) **The house of mourning.**—Better, *mourning-feast.* The word is found only here and in Amos vi. 7, where it is translated "banquet." So the Vulg. gives here *domus convivii,* and the LXX. the Greek word for a "drinking party." The word literally means a "shout," and is so far applicable to either joy or sorrow. The context seems decisive in favour of the latter meaning, but the idea of the "feast" or "social gathering" should be, at least, recognised. Not to go into the house of mirth would be a light matter as compared with abstaining even from visits of sympathy and condolence. In Eccles. vii. 4 the Hebrew gives a different word.

My peace.—The word is used in its highest power, as including all other blessings. It is Jehovah's peace: that which He once had given, but which He now withholds (comp. John xiv. 27). Men were to accept that withdrawal in silent awe, not with the conventional routine of customary sorrow.

this people, saith the Lord, *even* loving-
kindness and mercies. (6) Both the
great and the small shall die in this
land: they shall not be buried, neither
shall *men* lament for them, nor [a] cut
themselves, nor make themselves bald
for them: (7) neither shall *men* [1] tear
themselves for them in mourning, to
comfort them for the dead; neither
shall *men* give them the cup of consola-
tion to drink for their father or for their
mother.
(8) Thou shalt not also go into the
house of feasting, to sit with them to
eat and to drink. (9) For thus saith the
Lord of hosts, the God of Israel; Be-
hold, [b] I will cause to cease out of this
place in your eyes, and in your days,
the voice of mirth, and the voice of
gladness, the voice of the bridegroom,
and the voice of the bride.
(10) And it shall come to pass, when
thou shalt shew this people all these
words, and they shall say unto thee,
[c] Wherefore hath the Lord pronounced
all this great evil against us? or what
is our iniquity? or what *is* our sin that
we have committed against the Lord
our God? (11) Then shalt thou say unto
them, Because your fathers have for-
saken me, saith the Lord, and have
walked after other gods, and have
served them, and have worshipped
them, and have forsaken me, and have
not kept my law; (12) and ye have done
[d] worse than your fathers; for, behold,
ye walk every one after the [2] imagination
of his evil heart, that they may not
hearken unto me: (13) [e] therefore will I
cast you out of this land into a land
that ye know not, *neither* ye nor your
fathers; and there shall ye serve other
gods day and night; where I will not
shew you favour.
(14) Therefore, behold, the [f] days come,
saith the Lord, that it shall no more be
said, The Lord liveth, that brought up
the children of Israel out of the land

[a] Lev. 19. 28; Deut. 14. 1.
[1] Or, *break bread for them*, as Ezek. 24. 17.
[b] Isa. 24. 7, 8; ch. 7. 34; & 25. 10; Ezek. 26. 13.
[c] ch. 5. 19; & 13. 22.
[d] ch. 7. 26.
[2] Or, *stubbornness.*
[e] Deut. 4. 27; & 28. 64, 65.
[f] ch. 23. 7, 8.

(6) **Nor cut themselves, nor make themselves bald.**—Both practices were forbidden by the Law (Lev. xix. 28, xxi. 5; Deut. xiv. 1), probably in order to draw a line of demarcation between Israel and the nations round, among whom such practices prevailed (1 Kings xviii. 28). Both, however, seem to have been common, and probably had gained in frequency under Ahaz and Manasseh (chaps. vii. 29, xli. 5; Ezek. vii. 18; Amos viii. 10; Micah i. 16). The "baldness" (*i.e.*, shaving the crown of the head) seems to have been the more common of the two.

(7) **Neither shall men tear themselves.**—The marginal reading, "Neither shall men *break bread for them*," as in Isa lviii. 7; Lam. iv. 4, gives the true meaning. We are entering upon another region of funeral customs, reminding us of some of the practices connected with the "wakes" of old English life. After the first burst of sorrow and of fasting, as the sign of sorrow (2 Sam. i. 12, iii. 35, xii. 16, 17), friends came to the mourner to comfort him. A feast was prepared for them, consisting of "the bread of mourners" (Hosea ix. 4; Ezek. xxiv. 17) and the "cup of consolation," as for those of a heavy heart (Prov. xxxi. 6). It is probable that some reference to this practice was implied in our Lord's solemn benediction of the bread and of the cup at the Last Supper. As His body had been "anointed for the burial" (Matt. xxvi. 12), so, in giving the symbols of His death, He was, as it were, keeping with His disciples His own funeral feast. The thought of the dead lying unburied, or buried without honour, is contemplated in all its horrors.

(8) **Into the house of feasting.**—Literally, *the house of drinking, i.e.*, in this case, as interpreted by the next verse, of festive and mirthful gathering. This prohibition follows *à fortiori* from the other. If it was unmeet for the prophet to enter into the house of mourning, much more was he to hold himself aloof from mirth. He was to stand apart, in the awful consciousness of his solitary mission. The words of Eccles. vii. 2 come to our thoughts as teaching that it was better even so.

(9) **The voice of mirth . . .**—The words had been used once before (chap. vii. 34), and will meet us yet again (chaps. xxv. 10, xxxiii. 11), but they gain rather than lose in their solemnity by this verbal iteration.

(10) **What is our iniquity? . . .**—Now, as before (chap. v. 19), the threatenings of judgment are met with words of real or affected wonder. "What have we done to call for all this? In what are we worse than our fathers, or than other nations?" All prophets had more or less to encounter the same hardness. It reaches its highest form in the reiterated questions of the same type in Mal. i., ii.

(12) **Imagination.**—Better, as before, *stubbornness.*

(13) **There shall ye serve other gods day and night.**—The words are spoken in the bitterness of irony: "You have chosen to serve the gods of other nations here in your own land; therefore, by a righteous retribution, you shall serve them in another sense, as being in bondage to their worshippers, and neither night nor day shall give you respite."

Where I will not shew you favour.—Better, *since*, or *for*, I will not shew you favour.

(14, 15) **Behold, the days come . . .**—Judgment and mercy are tempered in the promise. Here the former is predominant. Afterwards, in chap. xxiii. 5—8, where it is connected with the hope of a personal Deliverer, the latter gains the ascendant. As yet the main thought is that the Egyptian bondage shall be as a light thing compared with that which the people will endure in the "land of the north," *i.e.*, in that of the Chaldæans; so that, when they return, their minds will turn to their deliverance from it, rather than to the Exodus from Egypt, as an example of the mercy and might of Jehovah. Then once again, and in a yet higher degree, it should be seen that man's extremity is God's opportunity.

of Egypt; (15) but, The LORD liveth,
that brought up the children of Israel
from the land of the north, and from
all the lands whither he had driven
them: and I will bring them again
into their land that I gave unto their
fathers.

(16) Behold, I will send for many
fishers, saith the LORD, and they shall
fish them; and after will I send for
many hunters, and they shall hunt
them from every mountain, and from
every hill, and out of the holes of the
rocks. (17) For mine [a]eyes *are* upon all
their ways: they are not hid from my
face, neither is their iniquity hid from
mine eyes. (18) And first I will re-
compense their iniquity and their sin
double; because they have defiled my
land, they have filled mine inheritance
with the carcases of their detestable
and abominable things.

(19) O LORD, my strength, and my
fortress, and my refuge in the day of
affliction, the Gentiles shall come unto
thee from the ends of the earth, and
shall say, Surely our fathers have in-
herited lies, vanity, and *things* wherein
there is no profit. (20) Shall a man
make gods unto himself, and [b]they *are*
no gods? (21) Therefore, behold, I will
this once cause them to know, I will
cause them to know mine hand and my
might; and they shall know that my
name *is* The LORD.

CHAPTER XVII.—(1) The sin of
Judah *is* written with a [c]pen of iron,
and with the [1]point of a diamond: *it is*
graven upon the table of their heart,

a Job 34. 21; Prov. 5. 21; ch. 32. 19.

b ch. 2. 11.

c Job 19. 24.

1 Heb., *nail.*

(16) **I will send for many fishers . . .**—The words refer to the threat, not to the promise. The "fishers," as in Amos iv. 2; Hab. i. 15, are the invading nations, surrounding Judah and Jerusalem as with a drag-net, and allowing none to escape. The process is described under this very name of "drag-netting" the country by Herodotus (iii. 149, vi. 31), as applied by the army of Xerxes to Samos, Chios, Tenedos, and other islands. The application of the words either to the gathering of the people after their dispersion or to the later work of the preachers of the Gospel is an after-thought, having its source in our Lord's words, "I will make you fishers of men" (Matt. iv. 19). It is, of course, possible enough that those words may have been suggested by Jeremiah's, the same image being used, as in the parable of Matt. xiii. 47, to describe the blessing which had before presented its darker aspect of punishment.

Hunters.—Another aspect of the same thought, pointing, so far as we can trace the distinction between the two, to the work of the irregular skirmisher as the former image did to that of the main body of the army: men might take refuge, as hunted beasts might do, in the caves of the rocks, but they should be driven forth even from these.

(17) **Mine eyes are upon all their ways.**—The context shows that here also the thought is presented on its severer side. The sins of Israel have not escaped the all-seeing eye of Jehovah.

(18) **I will recompense their iniquity and their sin double.**—A restitution, or fine, to double the amount of the wrong done was almost the normal standard of punishment under the Law of Moses (Exod. xxii. 4, 7). The words threaten accordingly a full punishment according to the utmost rigour. In Isa. xl. 2 the same thought is presented in its brighter aspect. Israel has received "double for all her sins," and therefore, having paid, as it were, "the uttermost farthing" (Matt. v. 26), she may now hope for mercy.

The carcases . . .—The word may be used in scorn of the lifeless form of the dumb idols which the people worshipped, to touch which was to be polluted, as by contact with a corpse (Num. xix. 11); but it more probably points to the dead bodies of the victims that had been sacrificed to them. The phrase occurs also in a like context in Lev. xxvi. 30. It would appear from Isa. lxv. 4 that these often included animals which by the Law were unclean: "swine's flesh and broth of abominable things."

(19) **O Lord, my strength, and my fortress.**—The words speak of a returning confidence in the prophet's mind, and find utterance in what is practically (though the Hebrew words are not the same) an echo of Ps. xviii. 2, or more closely of Pss. xxviii. 1, 8, lix. 17; 2 Sam. xxii. 3.

The Gentiles shall come unto thee.—The sin and folly of Israel are painted in contrast with the prophet's vision of the future. Then, in that far-off time of which other prophets had spoken (Micah iv. 1; Isa. ii. 2), the Gentiles should come to Jerusalem, turning from the "vanities" they had inherited; and yet Israel, who had inherited a truer faith, was now abasing herself even to their level or below it. Israel had answered in the affirmative the question which seemed to admit only of an answer in the negative: "Shall a man make gods unto himself, and they are no gods?"

(21) **I will this once cause them to know . . .**—The warning comes with all the emphasis of iteration, *this once.* As in a way without a parallel, once for all, they should learn that the name of the God they had rejected was Jehovah, the Eternal (Exod. iii. 14), unchangeable in His righteousness. The thought is parallel to that of Ezek. xii. 15.

XVII.

(1) **A pen of iron.**—*i.e.*, a *stylus,* or graving tool, as in Job xix. 24, chiefly used for engraving in stone or metal. In Ps. xlv. 1 it seems to have been used of the instrument with which the scribe wrote on his tablets.

With the point of a diamond.—The word expresses the idea of the hardness rather than the brilliancy of the diamond, and is rendered "adamant" in Ezek. iii. 9; Zech. vii. 12. (For the diamond as a precious stone a different word is used in Exod. xxviii. 18.) Strictly speaking, it was applied only to the diamond-point set in iron used by engravers. Such instruments were known to the Romans (Pliny, *Hist.*

and upon the horns of your altars;
(2) whilst their children remember their
altars and their [a]groves by the green
trees upon the high hills. (3) O my
mountain in the field, [b]I will give thy
substance *and* all thy treasures to the
spoil, *and* thy high places for sin,
throughout all thy borders. (4) And
thou, even [1]thyself, shalt discontinue
from thine heritage that I gave thee;
and I will cause thee to serve thine
enemies in the land which thou know-
est not: for ye have kindled a fire
in mine anger, *which* shall burn for
ever.
(5) Thus saith the LORD; Cursed *be*
the man that trusteth in man, and
maketh flesh his arm, and whose heart
departeth from the LORD. (6) For he
shall be like the heath in the desert,
and shall not see when good cometh;
but shall inhabit the parched places in
the wilderness, *in* a salt land and not
inhabited.
(7) [c]Blessed *is* the man that trusteth
in the LORD, and whose hope the LORD

[a] Judges 3. 7; Isa. 1. 29.
[b] ch. 15. 13.
[1] Heb., *in thyself.*
[c] Ps. 2. 12; & 34. 8; & 125. 1; Prov. 16. 20; Isa. 30. 18.

Nat. xxxvii. 15), and may have been in use in Phœnicia or Palestine. The words describe a note of infamy that could not be erased, and this was stamped in upon the tablets of the heart (comp. 2 Cor. iii. 3), and blazoned upon the "horns of the altars" of their false worship, or of the true worship of Jehovah which they had polluted and rendered false. The plural "altars" points probably to the former.

(2) **Whilst their children remember . . .**—If we take "children" as referring to age, there may be a reference to the way in which the horrors of Molech worship were burnt in upon the minds of boys who were present at such a spectacle, so as never to be forgotten, but the general sense in which we speak of the "children" of Israel or Judah seems sufficient. The thought expressed is that every locality that could be used for idolatrous worship made them "remember" that worship, and set about reproducing it. By some interpreters the clause is rendered, *as they remember their children so do they their altars and their groves; i.e.*, their idols are as dear to them as their offspring. The former construction is, however, the more natural, and is best supported by the versions.

Groves.—*i.e.*, as throughout the Old Testament, when connected with idolatry, the wooden columns that were the symbols of the Phœnician goddess Asherah, possibly the same as Astarte (Exod. xxxiv. 13; Deut. xvi. 21; 1 Kings xiv. 23). The "green trees" suggested the thought of this worship—for the Asherah, though not a grove, was generally connected with one—as the "high hills" did that of the altars. Commonly the worship is described as "*under* every green tree." Here a different preposition is used, "*on* the green trees," connecting them with the verb "remember."

(3) **My mountain in the field.**—As in chap. xxi. 13; Isa. ii. 2; Micah iv. 2, a poetic phrase for Jerusalem or Zion, its greatness consisting not in its material elevation above the "field" or surrounding country, but in being "my mountain," *i.e.*, the mountain of Jehovah. The words predict the plunder of the city, perhaps specially the plunder of the Temple.

Thy high places.—As having been from the time of Samuel onward the chief scene of the false worship of the people. The threat is repeated almost verbally from chap. xv. 13.

(4) **Thou, even thyself.**—Literally, *in* or *by thyself*, an emphatic form for expressing loneliness and abandonment.

Shalt discontinue . . .—The word was a half-technical one, used to describe the act of leaving lands untilled and releasing creditors in the sabbatical year (Exod. xxiii. 11; Deut. xv. 2). The land would have its rest now, would "enjoy its sabbaths" (Lev. xxvi. 34; 2 Chron. xxxvi. 21), though Judah had failed in obedience to the Law which prescribed them. For the rest of the verse, see Note on chap. xv. 14.

(5) **Cursed be the man . . .**—The words are vehement and abrupt, but they burst from the prophet's lips as proclaiming the root evil that had eaten into the life of his people. Their trust in an arm of flesh had led them to Egyptian and Assyrian alliances, and these to "departing from the Lord." The anathema has its counterpart in the beatitude of verse 7. The opening words, *Thus saith the Lord*, indicate, perhaps, a pause, followed as by a new message, which the prophet feels bound to deliver. It is significant that the prophet uses two words for the English "man," the first implying strength, and the second weakness.

(6) **Like the heath in the desert.**—The word rendered heath is, literally, *bare* or *naked*, and as such is translated by "destitute" in Ps. cii. 17. That meaning has accordingly been given to it here by some recent commentators. No picture of desolation could be more complete than that of a man utterly destitute, yet inhabiting the "parched places of the wilderness." All the older versions, however, including the Targum, and some of the best modern (*e.g.* Ewald), take the word as describing the "heath" or other like shrubs standing alone in a barren land. A like word with the same meaning is found in chap. xlviii. 6, and stands in Arabic for the "juniper." Both views are tenable, but the latter, as being a bolder similitude, and balancing the comparison to a "tree planted by the waters" in verse 8, is more after the manner of a poet-prophet. There is something weak in saying "A man shall be like a destitute man." The word rendered "desert" (*arabah*) is applied specially to the Jordan valley (sometimes, indeed, to its more fertile parts), and its connection here with the "salt land" points to the wild, barren land of the Jordan as it flows into the Dead Sea (Deut. xxix. 23).

Shall not see when good cometh.—The words describe the yearning that has been so often disappointed that at last, when the brighter day dawns, it is blind to the signs of its approach. It comes too late, as rain falls too late on the dead or withered heath.

(7) **Blessed is the man . . .**—The words that follow in verse 8 are almost a paraphrase of Ps. i. 3, and, we may well believe, were suggested by them. The prophet has, as it were, his own Ebal and Gerizim: trust in God inheriting the blessing, and distrust the curse.

is. (8) For he shall be [a]as a tree planted
by the waters, and *that* spreadeth out
her roots by the river, and shall not
see when heat cometh, but her leaf shall
be green; and shall not be careful in
the year of [1] drought, neither shall cease
from yielding fruit.
(9) The heart *is* deceitful above all
things, and desperately wicked: who
can know it? (10) I the LORD [b] search
the heart, *I* try the reins, even to give
every man according to his ways, *and*
according to the fruit of his doings.
(11) *As* the partridge [2]sitteth *on eggs*,
and hatcheth *them* not; *so* he that
getteth riches, and not by right, shall
leave them in the midst of his days,
and at his end shall be a fool.
(12) A glorious high throne from the
beginning *is* the place of our sanctuary.
(13) O LORD, the hope of Israel, [c]all that
forsake thee shall be ashamed, *and* they
that depart from me shall be written in
the earth, because they have forsaken
the LORD, the [d]fountain of living waters.
(14) Heal me, O LORD, and I shall be
healed; save me, and I shall be saved:
for thou *art* my praise. (15) Behold,

a Ps. 1. 3.

1 Or, *restraint.*

b 1 Sam. 16. 7; Ps. 7. 9; ch. 11. 20; & 20. 12.

2 Or, *gathereth young which she hath not brought forth.*

c Ps. 73. 27; Isa. 1. 28.

d ch. 2. 13.

---

(8) **Shall not see when heat cometh.**—Another reading, followed by the LXX. and Vulgate, gives *shall not fear;* there is, however, more force in the repetition of the same word as in verse 6. The man who trusts is like the strong tree, clothed with foliage, that "does not see," *i.e.,* does not regard or feel, the presence of the heat. Technically the meaning is the same in both cases, but in the latter case with the emphasised contrast of a parallelism. Fed by the stream that never fails, it "shall not be careful" or anxious about the scorching heat of summer. As the blasted heath sees no good, so the tree, in this case, sees no evil.

(9) **The heart is deceitful . . .**—The sequence of ideas seems as follows: If the blessing and the curse are thus so plainly marked, how is it that man chooses the curse and not the blessing, the portion of the "heath in the desert" rather than that of the "tree planted by the waters"? And the answer is found in the inscrutable self-deceit of his nature blinding his perceptions of good and evil.

Desperately wicked.—Rather, *incurably diseased,* as in chaps. xv. 18, xxx. 12, 15; Isa. xvii. 11, and elsewhere. Wickedness is, of course, implied, but it is regarded rather as a moral taint following on the deliberate choice, than as the choice itself.

(10) **According to his ways.**—The Hebrew word is in the singular, *his way,* and the interpolated conjunction "and" is better omitted, so as to leave the last words as an explanation of what is meant by it. Jehovah, who "searches the heart," answers the question "who can know it?" He does know, and will, in the end, judge with a perfectly righteous judgment. Men should live as in the presence of One to whom all hearts are open.

(11) **As the partridge sitteth on eggs . . .**—Better, following the LXX. and Vulg., and the marginal reading of the Authorised Version, *heaps up eggs and hath not laid them.* The words point to a popular belief among the Jews that the partridge steals the eggs of other birds and adds them to her own, with the result that when the eggs are hatched the broods desert her (see *Bibl. Educ.* iii. p. 73). It thus became a parable of the covetous man, whose avarice leads him to pile up riches which are not rightly his, and which after a while "make to themselves wings" and are seen no more. Modern naturalists have not observed this habit, but it is probable that the belief originated in the practice of the cuckoo laying its eggs in the nest of the partridge, as in that of other birds. The cuckoo (Lev. xi. 16; Deut. xiv. 15) was and is a common bird in Palestine (*Bibl. Educ.* ii. p. 363).

Shall leave them in the midst of his days.—If we retain the rendering of the Authorised Version the words may refer to the practice of hunting the partridge by driving it from its nest and then striking it with a club (see *Bibl. Educ.* iii. p. 73). Many commentators, however, adopt the rendering, *they* (the riches) *shall leave him.* As covetousness was the besetting sin of Jehoiakim (chap. xxii. 17), the prediction may have pointed specially to him.

(12) **A glorious high throne . . .**—The verse is better taken in connection with the following, and not, as the interpolated "is" makes it, as a separate sentence, the nouns being all in the vocative. *Thou throne of glory on high from the beginning, the place of our sanctuary, the hope of Israel, Jehovah . . .* The thoughts of the prophet rise from the visible to the eternal temple, and that temple is one with the presence of Jehovah. The term "throne" is applied to Jerusalem in chap. iii. 17; practically, to the ark of the covenant in Pss. lxxx. 2, xcix. 1; to the throne in heaven in Ezek. i. 26; Dan. vii. 9; Pss. ix. 4, xi. 4.

(13) **They that depart from me.**—The rapid change of person from second to first and first to third is eminently Hebrew.

Written in the earth.—In implied contrast with the name graven on the rock for ever (Job xix. 24) are those written on the dust or sand. The Eastern habit of writing on the ground (of which John viii. 6 supplies one memorable instance, and which was the common practice in Jewish schools) gave a vividness to the similitude which we have almost lost. For "the fountain of living waters," compare Note on chap. ii. 13.

(14) **Heal me.**—The prophet, consciously or unconsciously, contrasts himself with the deserters from Jehovah. He needs "healing" and "salvation," but he knows where to seek for them, and is sure that his Lord will not leave the work incomplete. The prayer of the prophet is like that of the Psalmist (Pss. vi. 2, xxx. 2). In "thou art my praise" we have an echo of Deut. x. 21; Ps. lxxi. 6.

(15) **Behold, they say unto me.**—The speakers are not named or defined, but they are clearly the mockers who questioned Jeremiah's prophetic character, on the ground (comp. Deut. xviii. 22) that his threats had received no fulfilment. Presumably, therefore, the words were written before the death of Jehoiakim and the capture of Jerusalem.

Let it come now.—The last word is the usual formula of request, and implies a mocking tone in the speakers: "Let it come, *if you please.*"

they say unto me, [a]Where *is* the word
of the LORD? let it come now. (16) As
for me, [b]I have not hastened from *being*
a pastor [1]to follow thee: neither have I
desired the woeful day; thou knowest:
that which came out of my lips was
right before thee. (17) Be not a terror
unto me: thou *art* my hope in the day
of evil. (18) [c]Let them be confounded
that persecute me, but let not me be
confounded: let them be dismayed,
but let not me be dismayed: bring upon
them the day of evil, and [2][d]destroy them
with double destruction.
(19) Thus said the LORD unto me; Go
and stand in the gate of the children
of the people, whereby the kings of
Judah come in, and by the which they
go out, and in all the gates of Jerusalem;
(20) and say unto them, Hear
ye the word of the LORD, ye kings
of Judah, and all Judah, and all
the inhabitants of Jerusalem, that
enter in by these gates: (21) Thus
saith the LORD; [e]Take heed to yourselves,
and bear no burden on the
sabbath day, nor bring *it* in by the
gates of Jerusalem; (22) neither carry
forth a burden out of your houses on
the sabbath day, neither do ye any
work, but hallow ye the sabbath day,
as I [f]commanded your fathers. (23) But
they obeyed not, neither inclined their
ear, but made their neck stiff, that they

a Isa. 5. 19.
b ch. 1. 4, &c.
1 Heb., *after thee.*
c Ps. 35. 4; & 40. 14.
2 Heb., *break them with a double breach.*
d ch. 11. 20.
e Neh. 13. 19.
f Exod. 20. 8; & 23. 12; & 31. 13; Ezek. 20. 12.

---

(16) **I have not hastened . . .**—The words of the English Version are somewhat obscure, and a better rendering would perhaps be, *I have not been quick to withdraw from my work in following thee, as a shepherd and guide of the people.* A possible meaning, adopted by some commentators, would be, "I have not hastened from my work as a shepherd (in the literal sense) to follow thee," as presenting a parallel to the words of Amos (vii. 14, 15); and, though we cannot get beyond conjecture, it is quite possible that Jeremiah, in his youth, before the call of chap. i. 4, may have been employed in the pasture grounds that belonged to Anathoth as a city of the priests (Num. xxxv. 4; Josh. xxi. 4, 18; 1 Chron. vi. 60). It is to some extent in favour of this view, that throughout the book the work of the shepherd, when used figuratively, answers to the work of the ruler, and not to that of the prophet. What he means, if we keep the version given above, is that he had not been too slack in his obedience, but neither had he been over eager. He had no desire to see the woful day that would fulfil his predictions. What had come from his lips was just what he had been bidden to say and no more (chap. xv. 16—19), and thus he had spoken as in the sight of God. The interpolated word "right" mars rather than mends the meaning.

(17) **Be not a terror . . .**—*i.e.,* a cause of terror or dismay. The words are explained by what follows. The prophet had put his hope in Jehovah, but if he were left to himself, his message unfulfilled, himself a by-word and a jest, what a contrast would all this be to what he had been led to hope! Would not his work as a prophet be more terrible than ever? The feeling expressed is like that of chap. xv. 10.

(18) **Let them be confounded . . .**—The prayer reminds us of that of the Psalmist (Pss. xxxv. 4, xl. 14).

Double destruction.—Literally, *break them with a two-fold breaking—i.e.,* the "double recompense" of chap. xvi. 18. (See Note there.)

(19) **Thus said the Lord unto me . . .**—We enter here on an entirely fresh series of messages, arranged probably in chronological order, but having no immediate connection with what precedes, and narrated with a much fuller account of the circumstances connected with them. This, which begins the series, would appear from verse 25 to have been delivered before the sins of the people had assumed the hopeless, irremediable character which is implied in the two previous chapters; and the first part of this may probably be referred therefore to the early years of the reign of Jehoiakim. In its circumstances and mode of delivery it is parallel with the discourse of chap. xxii. 1—5.

The gate of the children of the people . . .—No gate so described is mentioned in the great topographical record of Neh. iii. or elsewhere, and we are therefore left to conjecture where it was. The context shows that it was a place of concourse, a gate of the Temple rather than of the city, perhaps the special gate by which the kings and people of Judah entered into the enclosure of the Temple. The name may indicate, as in chap. xxvi. 23, that it was that "of the common people," or "laity," as in 2 Chron. xxxv. 5, as distinguished from that used by the priests and Levites; and it would appear, from the nature of the warning proclaimed there, to have been the scene of some open desecration of the Sabbath—possibly of the sale of sheep or doves for sacrifice, like that of John ii. 14; Matt. xxi. 12, or of the more common articles of the market, as in Neh. xiii. 15. By some writers it has been identified with the "gate of Benjamin" (chaps. xx. 2, xxxviii. 7), but this would seem to have been more conspicuous as a place of judgment than of trade; nor is there any reason why it should be described by a different name here. Some, indeed, have conjectured that we should read "gate of *Benjamin*" instead of "gate of *Beni-am,*" which gives the meaning "children of the people." It is noticeable that the message was to be delivered at the other gates as well, as being a protest against a prevalent sin.

(22) **Neither carry forth a burden.**—Interpreted by the parallel passage in Neh. xiii. 15—22, the *burden* would be the baskets of fruit, vegetables, or fish which were brought in from the country by the villagers who came to the Temple services, and the wares of the city which were taken to the gates to be sold in turn to them. The Sabbath was observed after a fashion, but, as Sunday has been for many centuries and in many parts of Christendom, it was turned into a market-day, and so, though men abstained probably from manual labour, the quiet sanctity which of right belonged to it was lost. Passages like Isa. lvi. 2—6, lviii. 13 show that the evil was one of some standing, and the practice of the time of Jehoiakim was not likely to be more rigorous

might not hear, nor receive instruction.
(24) And it shall come to pass, if ye
diligently hearken unto me, saith the
LORD, to bring in no burden through
the gates of this city on the sabbath
day, but hallow the sabbath day, to do
no work therein; (25) [a]then shall there
enter into the gates of this city kings
and princes sitting upon the throne of
David, riding in chariots and on horses,
they, and their princes, the men of
Judah, and the inhabitants of Jeru-
salem: and this city shall remain for
ever. (26) And they shall come from the
cities of Judah, and from the places
about Jerusalem, and from the land of
Benjamin, and from the plain, and from
the mountains, and from the south,
bringing burnt offerings, and sacrifices,
and meat offerings, and incense, and
bringing sacrifices of praise, unto the
house of the LORD. (27) But if ye will
not hearken unto me to hallow the
sabbath day, and not to bear a burden,
even entering in at the gates of Jeru-
salem on the sabbath day; then will I
kindle a fire in the gates thereof, and it
shall devour the palaces of Jerusalem,
and it shall not be quenched.

a ch. 22. 4.

1 Or, *frames*, or, *seats*.

B. C. cir. 605.

2 Or, *that he made was marred, as clay in the hand of the potter.*

3 Heb., *returned and made.*

CHAPTER XVIII. — (1) The word
which came to Jeremiah from the
LORD, saying,
(2) Arise, and go down to the potter's
house, and there I will cause thee to
hear my words. (3) Then I went down
to the potter's house, and, behold, he
wrought a work on the [1]wheels. (4) And
the vessel [2]that he made of clay was
marred in the hand of the potter: so
he [3]made it again another vessel, as
seemed good to the potter to make *it*.
(5) Then the word of the LORD came
to me, saying,

---

than it had been in the time of Isaiah, or was, at a later period, after the return from the Captivity.

(25) **Kings and princes.**—The plural is obviously used to give greater vividness and grandeur to the picture of revived majesty which would be the reward of faithfulness, perhaps also to express the idea that the majesty would be enduring.

(26) **They shall come . . .**—The verse has a special interest (1) as a topographical description of the country about Jerusalem, and (2) as a summary of the chief forms of sacrifice under the Mosaic Law. (1) The "plain" (*Shephelah*) is the lowland country of Philistia, stretching to the Mediterranean; the "mountain" the hill-country of Judah; the "south" (*Negeb*) the region lying to the south of Hebron, and including Beersheba (comp. Josh. xv. 21, 28). Each name, though descriptive in meaning, was used in almost as definite a sense as that in which we speak of the "Campagna" of Rome or the "Weald" of Kent. (2) The list includes the "burnt offerings," in which the flesh of the victim was consumed entirely on the altar; the "sacrifices," in which the flesh of the victim was eaten partly by the priest and partly by the worshipper; the "meat offerings," which were of meal and salt, not of flesh, and were always accompanied by incense (Lev. ii. 1); and, lastly, *praise*—the word "sacrifice" not being found in the Hebrew—the utterance of prayer and psalm, which the Psalmist had named as more acceptable than the flesh of bulls and goats (Ps. l. 14).

(27) **Then will I kindle a fire . . .**—The fire is figurative rather than literal: the "fierce anger" of the Lord which man cannot quench, and which brings destruction in its train, of which an actual conflagration may have been the instrument (Hos. viii. 14; Amos i. 14). Compare chaps. vii. 20, xxi. 14.

XVIII.

(1) **The word which came to Jeremiah.**—The message that follows comes in close sequence upon that of the preceding chapter, *i.e.*, probably before the fourth year of the reign of Jehoiakim. It has the character of a last warning to king and people, and its rejection is followed in its turn by the more decisive use of the same symbol in chap. xix.

(2) **The potter's house.**—The place was probably identical with the "potter's field" of Zech. xi. 13, the well-known spot where the workers in that art carried on their business. The traditional Aceldama, the "potter's field" of Matt. xxvii. 7, is on the southern face of the valley of Hinnom, south of Jerusalem. The soil is still a kind of clay suitable and employed for the same purpose (Ritter, *Palestine*, iv. 165, Eng. Trans.). The purchase of the field to "bury strangers in" (Matt. xxvii. 7) implies, however, that it was looked upon as a piece of waste ground, and that its use had been exhausted.

(3) **He wrought a work on the wheels.**—Literally, *the two wheels*. The nature of the work is described more graphically in Ecclus. xxxviii. 29, 30. The potter sat moving one horizontal wheel with his feet, while a smaller one was used, as it revolved, to fashion the shape of the vessel he was making with his hands. The image had been already used of God's creative work in Isa. xxix. 16, xlv. 9, lxiv. 8.

(4) **Of clay.**—The reading in the margin, which gives "as clay," must be regarded as a clerical error, originating, probably, in the desire to bring the text into conformity with verse 6, that in the text of the Authorised Version being confirmed by many MSS. and Versions.

He made it again.—Literally, and more vividly, *he returned and made*. As we read, we have to remember that what is narrated in a few words implied a long train of thoughts. The prophet went by the impulse which he knew to be from God to the "field" in the valley of Hinnom; he stood and gazed, and then as he watched he was led to see in the potter's work a parable of the world's history: God as the great artificer, men and nations as the vessels which He makes for honourable or dishonourable uses (2 Tim. ii. 20; Rom. ix. 21).

(6) O house of Israel, [a]cannot I do with
you as this potter? saith the LORD.
Behold, as the clay *is* in the potter's
hand, so *are* ye in mine hand, O house
of Israel. (7) *At what* instant I shall
speak concerning a nation, and con-
cerning a kingdom, to [b]pluck up, and to
pull down, and to destroy *it;* (8) if that
nation, against whom I have pronounced,
turn from their evil, [c]I will repent of
the evil that I thought to do unto them.
(9) And *at what* instant I shall speak
concerning a nation, and concerning a
kingdom, to build and to plant *it;* (10) if
it do evil in my sight, that it obey not
my voice, then I will repent of the good,
wherewith I said I would benefit them.

(11) Now therefore go to, speak to the
men of Judah, and to the inhabitants
of Jerusalem, saying, Thus saith the
LORD;

Behold, I frame evil against you, and
devise a device against you: [d]return ye
now every one from his evil way, and
make your ways and your doings good.
(12) And they said, [e]There is no hope:
but we will walk after our own devices,
and we will every one do the imagina-
tion of his evil heart. (13) Therefore thus
saith the LORD; [f]Ask ye now among the
heathen, who hath heard such things:
the virgin of Israel hath done a very
horrible thing. (14) Will *a man* leave
[1]the snow of Lebanon *which cometh* from

a Isa. 45. 9; Wisd. 15. 7; Rom. 9. 20.

b ch. 1. 10

c Jonah 3. 10.

d 2 Kings 17. 13; ch. 7. 3; & 25. 5; & 35. 15.

e ch. 2. 25.

f ch. 2. 10.

1 Or, *my fields for a rock, or for the snow of Lebanon? shall the running waters be forsaken for the strange cold waters?*

---

(6) **Cannot I do with you as this potter?**—The question implies a theory of the universe, which is neither (as some have thought) one of absolute fatalism, crushing man's freedom, nor, on the other hand, one which merges God's sovereignty in man's power of choice. The clay can resist the potter, or can yield itself willingly to his hands to be shaped as he wills. Its being "marred" is through no fault of the potter, but—in the framework of the parable—through the defect of the material, and, in its application, through the resistance of the human agents whom God is fashioning. And when it is so marred one of two courses is open to the potter. He can again re-mould and fashion it to his purpose, to a new work which may be less honourable than that for which it was originally designed; or, if it be hopelessly marred, can break it and cast it away, and with fresh clay mould a fresh vessel. The history of nations and churches and individual men offers many examples of both processes. They frustrate God's gracious purpose by their self-will, but His long-suffering leads them to repentance, and gives them, to speak after the manner of men, yet another chance of being moulded by His hands. Here the prophet invites the people, as the clay, to accept the former alternative. St. Paul, taking the same analogy, looks forward to the time when the marred vessel of Israel shall be restored to the Master's house and be honoured in His service (Rom. ix. 21, xi. 26). The closing verses of Browning's poem, "Rabbi Ben-Ezra," in *Men and Women,* may be referred to as embodying the same thought:—

"But I need Thee, as then,
Thee, God, who mouldest men;
And since, not even while the whirl was worst,
Did I—to the wheel of life,
With shapes and colours rife,
Bound dizzily—mistake my end, to slake Thy thirst,

"So take and use Thy work!
Amend what flaws may lurk,
What strain o' the stuff, what warpings past the aim!
My times be in Thy hand;
Perfect the cup as planned!
Let age approve of youth, and death comprete the same."

(7–10) **At what instant I shall speak concerning a nation . . .**—The words carry the thoughts of the prophet back to those which had been stamped indelibly on his memory when he was first called to his work (chap. i. 10). He is now taught that that work was throughout conditional. In bold anthropomorphic speech Jehovah represents himself as changing His purpose, even suddenly, "in an instant," if the nation that is affected by it passes from evil to good or from good to evil. The seeming change is but the expression of an unchanged eternal Law of Righteousness, dealing with men according to their works. This, and not the assertion of an arbitrary, irresistibly predestinating will, was the lesson the prophet had been taught by the parable of the potter's wheel.

(11) **I frame evil.**—The verb chosen is that which specially describes the potter's work, and from which the Hebrew word for potter is itself derived. This, so to speak, is the shape of the vessel actually in hand, determining its use, but its form is not unalterably fixed. It is shown *in terrorem,* and the people are invited to accept the warning by repentance.

(12) **And they said.**—Better, *But they say,* as of continued action. This was the ever-recurring answer (see Note on chap. ii. 25) which they made to the prophet's pleas. It was the answer of defiance rather than of despair. "There is no hope, *you* need not hope, that we will do as you bid us. We will go on our way, and walk after our own devices."

Imagination.—Better, as elsewhere, *stubbornness.*

(13) **Ask ye now among the heathen.**—The appeal of chap. ii. 10, 11 is renewed. Judah had not been true, even as heathen nations were true, to its inherited faith and worship. The virgin daughter of Israel (Isa. i. 8; Jer. xiv. 17)—the epithet is emphasised, as contrasted with the shame that follows—had fallen from a greater height to a profounder depth of debasement.

(14) **Will a man leave . . .?**—The interpolated words "a man" pervert the meaning of the verse, which should run thus: *Will the snow of Lebanon fail from the rock of the field? or shall the cold* (or, with some commentators, "rushing") *flowing waters from afar* (literally, *strange,* or, as some take it, *that dash down*) *be dried up?* The questions imply an answer in the negative, and assert in a more vivid form what had been expressed more distinctly, though less poetically, in chap. ii. 13. The strength of Jehovah was like the unfailing snow of Lebanon (the "white" or snow mountain, like Mont Blanc or Snowdon), like the dashing stream that flows from heights so distant that they belong to a strange country, and which along its whole course was never dried up, and yet men forsook that strength for their own devices. The "streams of

the rock of the field? *or* shall the cold
flowing waters that come from another
place be forsaken? (15) Because my
people hath forgotten [a]me, they have
burned incense to vanity, and they have
caused them to stumble in their ways
from the [b]ancient paths, to walk in
paths, *in* a way not cast up; (16) to
make their land [c]desolate, *and* a per-
petual hissing; every one that passeth
thereby shall be astonished, and wag
his head. (17) I will scatter them as
with an east wind before the enemy; I
will shew them the back, and not the
face, in the day of their calamity.
(18) Then said they, Come, and let
us devise devices against Jeremiah;
[d]for the law shall not perish from the
priest, nor counsel from the wise, nor
the word from the prophet. Come, and
let us smite him [1]with the tongue, and
let us not give heed to any of his words.
(19) Give heed to me, O LORD, and
hearken to the voice of them that
contend with me. (20) Shall evil be re-
compensed for good? for they have

a ch. 2. 13; & 17. 13

b ch. 6. 16.

c ch. 19. 8; & 49. 13; & 50. 13.

d Mal. 2. 7.

1 Or, *for the tongue.*

Lebanon" appear as the type of cool refreshing waters in Song of Sol. iv. 15. The term "rock of the field" is applied in chaps. xvii. 3, xxi. 13 to Jerusalem, but there is no reason why it should not be used of Lebanon or any other mountain soaring above the plain. The notion that the prophet spoke of the brook Gihon on Mount Zion, as fed, by an underground channel, from the snows of Lebanon, has not sufficient evidence to commend it, but the "dew of Hermon, *and as the dew* that descended upon the mountains of Zion" (Ps. cxxxiii. 3) presents, to say the least, a suggestive parallel. Possibly the prophet has the Jordan in his mind. Tacitus (*Hist.* v. 6) describes it as fed by the snows of Lebanon, the summit of which is, in his expressive language, faithful to its snows through the heat of summer.

(15) **Vanity.**—The word is not that commonly so translated (as in chaps. ii. 5, x. 8; Eccles. i. 2, *et al.*, *q. v.*), but that which had been used of idols in chaps. ii. 30, iv. 30, vi. 29, rendered "in vain." See also Ezek. xiii. 6, 8, 9.

They have caused.—No persons have been named, but the prophet clearly has in view the prophets and teachers who had led the people astray.

To stumble in their ways from the ancient paths.—The preposition "from" is not in the Hebrew, and does not improve the sense. The words "the ancient paths," literally, *the paths of the age*, or *of eternity*, are in apposition with "their ways," and point to the old immemorial faith of the patriarchs, a faith not of to-day or yesterday. The second "paths" is a different word from the first, and implies rather the "by-ways," as contrasted with the "way cast up," the raised causeway, the "king's highway," on which a man could not well lose his way.

(16) **Desolate . . . astonished.**—Better, *desolate* in both clauses. The Hebrew verb is the same, and there is a manifest emphasis in the repetition which it is better to reproduce in English.

A perpetual hissing.—The Hebrew word is onomatopoetic, and expresses the inarticulate sounds which we utter on seeing anything that makes us shudder, rather than "hissing" in its modern use as an expression of contempt or disapproval.

Wag his head.—Better, *shake his head.* The verb is not the same as that which describes the gesture of scorn in Pss. xxii. 7, cix. 25; Lam. ii. 15; Zeph. ii. 15, and describes pity or bemoaning rather than contempt. Men would not mock the desolation of Israel, but would gaze on it astounded and pitying, themselves also desolate.

(17) **With an east wind.**—MSS. vary, some giving "with" and some "as an east wind." The difference does not much affect the meaning. The east wind blowing from the desert was the wind of storms, tempests, and parching heat (Jon. iv. 8; Ps. xlviii. 7; Isa. xxvii. 8).

I will shew them the back, and not the face.—The figure is boldly anthropomorphic. The light of God's countenance is the fulness of joy (Num. vi. 25). To turn away that light was to leave the people to the darkness of their misery. What was thus done by Jehovah was but a righteous retribution on the people who had "turned their back" and "not their face" to Him (chap. ii. 27).

(18) **Come, and let us devise devices.**—The priests and people thus far appear to have listened to the prophet, but at the threatening words of the preceding verse their anger becomes hatred, and their hatred seeks to kill (verse 23). We are reminded of the oft-recurring statement in the Gospels that priests and elders "took counsel" against our Lord to "put Him to death" (Matt. xii. 14, xxvii. 1; Mark iii. 6; Luke vi. 11; *et al.*).

For the law shall not perish . . .—The words meant apparently (1) that they had enough guidance in the Law, in the priests, and in the prophets who met their wishes, and (2) that they might trust in the continuance of that guidance in spite of the threatenings of destruction that the prophet had just spoken. The words are suggestive as showing the precise nature of the guidance expected from each. The priests interpret the Law, the wise give the counsel of experience, the prophet speaks what claims to be the word, or message, of the Lord. A striking parallel is found in Ezek. vii. 26.

Come, and let us smite him with the tongue.—We probably find the result of the conspiracy in the measures taken by Pashur in chap. xx. 1—3. He had "heard that Jeremiah prophesied these things," and we may well believe that his informants were some of those who thus announced their intentions. There is no sufficient reason for the marginal reading, "for the tongue."

(19) **Give heed to me . . .**—This is the prophet's answer to the resolve of the people, "Let us not give heed." He appeals in the accents of a passionate complaint to One who will heed his words. The opening words are almost as an echo of Ps. xxxv. 1.

(20) **They have digged a pit for my soul.**—The image has become so familiar that we have all but lost its vividness. What it meant here (as in Ps. lvii. 6) was that the man was treated as a beast, the prophet who sought their good as the wolf or the jackal whom they entrapped and slew.

Remember that I stood before thee.—The phrase is used frequently, though not uniformly, of

digged a pit for my soul. Remember
that I stood before thee to speak good
for them, *and* to turn away thy wrath
from them. (21) Therefore [a]deliver up
their children to the famine, and [1]pour
out their *blood* by the force of the
sword; and let their wives be bereaved
of their children, and *be* widows; and
let their men be put to death; *let* their
young men *be* slain by the sword in
battle. (22) Let a cry be heard from
their houses, when thou shalt bring a
troop suddenly upon them: for they
have digged a pit to take me, and hid
snares for my feet. (23) Yet, LORD, thou
knowest all their counsel against me
[2]to slay *me*: forgive not their iniquity,
neither blot out their sin from thy
sight, but let them be overthrown
before thee; deal *thus* with them in
the time of thine anger

CHAPTER XIX.—(1) Thus saith the
LORD,
Go and get a potter's earthen bottle,
and *take* of the ancients of the people,
and of the ancients of the priests;
(2) and go forth unto the valley of the

[a] Ps. 109. 10.

[1] Heb., *pour them out.*

[2] Heb., *for death.*

---

the act of worship, of the communion of the soul with God (comp. chap. vii. 10; Deut. x. 8, xix. 17, xxix. 10; 1 Kings xix. 11), and is clearly used in this sense here. The prophet refers to his repeated though fruitless entreaties for the people in chaps. xiv. and xv. It is interesting to note the description of Jeremiah, in 2 Macc. xv. 14, as "a lover of the brethren who prayeth much for the people and the holy city." Men had come to recognise that the spirit of intercession had been the prophet's dominant characteristic.

(21) **Therefore deliver up their children . . .**—The bitter words that follow startle and pain us, like the imprecations of Pss. xxxv., lxix., and cix. To what extent they were the utterances of a righteous indignation, a true zeal for God, which had not yet learnt the higher lesson of patience and forgiveness, or embodied an element of personal vindictiveness, we are not called on to inquire, and could not, in any case, decide. It is not ours to judge another man's servant. In all like cases we have to remember that the very truthfulness with which the prayer is recorded is at least a proof that the prophet felt, like Jonah, that he did well to be angry (Jon. iv. 9), that a righteous anger is at least one step towards a righteous love, and that we, as disciples of Christ, have passed, or ought to have passed, beyond that earlier stage.

Pour out their blood by the force of the sword.—Literally, with a bolder metaphor, *pour them out into the hands of the sword.*

(22) **Let a cry be heard from their houses.**—*i.e.*, let their city be taken by the enemy and the people suffer all the outrage and cruelty which their heathen invaders can inflict. What these were, the history of all wars, above all of Eastern wars, tells us but too plainly (2 Kings viii. 12; Hos. xiii. 16). Some of them, prisoners impaled or flayed alive, are brought vividly before our eyes by the Assyrian sculptures.

The "snares" are those of the bird-catcher (Pss. cxl. 5, cxlii. 3).

(23) **Yet, Lord, thou knowest all their counsel . . .**—Secret as their plots had been, they were not hidden from Jehovah, nor, indeed, as the words show, from the prophet himself. The words might seem, at first, to refer specially to the conspiracy of the men of Anathoth (chap. xi. 21), but by this time, as verse 18 shows, the hatred provoked by the warnings of the prophet had spread further, and united the priests and false prophets of Jerusalem in a common hostility against him. So afterwards, in the Gospel history, the conspiracies that began at Capernaum (Mark iii. 6) were developed in Jerusalem (Matt. xxvii. 1).

Deal thus with them.—The interpolated word "thus," intended to emphasise the prayer, really weakens it: *in the time of Thine anger deal with them,* as implying that the day of grace was past, that nothing now remained but retribution. The prayer was the utterance of an indignation, not unrighteous in itself, yet showing all too plainly, as has been said above, like the language of the so-called imprecatory Psalms, the contrast between the Jewish and the Christian and Christ-like way of meeting wrong and hatred. For us such prayers are among the things that have passed away, and we have learnt to admire and imitate the nobler temper of the proto-martyr, "Lord, lay not this sin to their charge" (Acts vii. 60). The New Testament utterances of St. Peter against Simon the sorcerer (Acts viii. 20), of St. Paul against Ananias (Acts xxiii. 3), the Judaisers of Galatia (Gal. i. 9), and Alexander the coppersmith (2 Tim. iv. 14), present an apparent parallelism; but the words spoken in these cases have more the character of an authoritative judicial sentence.

XIX.

(1) **And get a potter's earthen bottle.**—The word for "get" involves *buying* as the process. The similitude—one might better call it, the parable dramatised—represents the darker side of the imagery of chap. xviii. 3, 4. There the vessel was still on the potter's wheel, capable of being re-shaped. Now we have the vessel which has been baked and hardened. No change is possible. If it is unfit for the uses for which it was designed, there is nothing left but to break it. As such it became now the fit symbol of the obdurate people of Israel. Their polity, their nationality, their religious system, had to be broken up. The word for "vessel" indicates a large earthen jar with a narrow neck, the "cruse" used for honey in 1 Kings xiv. 3. Its form, *bakbuk,* clearly intended to represent the gurgling sound of the water as it was poured out, is interesting as an example of *onomatopœia* in the history of language.

Take of the ancients of the people, and of the ancients of the priests.—The elders, and therefore the representatives of the civil and ecclesiastical rulers, were to be the witnesses of this acted prophecy of the destruction of all that they held most precious. The word "take" is not in the Hebrew, but either some such verb has to be supplied or the verb "go" has to be carried on, "Let the ancients . . . go with thee."

(2) **Unto the valley of the son of Hinnom.**—The

son of Hinnom, which *is* by the entry
of [1]the east gate, and proclaim there
the words that I shall tell thee, (3) and
say, Hear ye the word of the LORD,
O kings of Judah, and inhabitants of
Jerusalem; Thus saith the LORD of
hosts, the God of Israel; Behold, I
will bring evil upon this place, the
which whosoever heareth, his ears shall
[a]tingle. (4) Because they have forsaken
me, and have estranged this place, and
have burned incense in it unto other
gods, whom neither they nor their fathers
have known, nor the kings of Judah,
and have filled this place with the blood
of innocents; (5) they have built also
the high places of Baal, to burn their
sons with fire *for* burnt offerings unto
Baal, [b]which I commanded not, nor
spake *it*, neither came *it* into my mind:

1 Heb., *the sun gate.*

a 1 Sam. 3. 11; 2 Kings 21. 12.

b ch. 7. 31, 32.

c ch. 7. 33; & 16. 4.

d ch. 18. 16; & 49. 13; & 50. 13.

e Lev. 26. 29; Deut. 28. 53; Lam. 4. 10.

(6) therefore, behold, the days come,
saith the LORD, that this place shall no
more be called Tophet, nor The valley
of the son of Hinnom, but The valley
of slaughter. (7) And I will make void
the counsel of Judah and Jerusalem in
this place; and I will cause them to
fall by the sword before their enemies,
and by the hands of them that seek
their lives: and their [c]carcases will I
give to be meat for the fowls of the
heaven, and for the beasts of the earth.
(8) And I will make this city [d]desolate,
and an hissing; every one that passeth
thereby shall be astonished and hiss
because of all the plagues thereof.
(9) And I will cause them to eat the
[e]flesh of their sons and the flesh of their
daughters, and they shall eat every
one the flesh of his friend in the siege

---

site was chosen as having been the scene of the most hateful form of idolatry to which the people had addicted themselves, perhaps also as connected locally with the potter's field. (See Note on chap. vii. 31; and Matt. xxvii. 7.)

By the entry of the east gate.—The Hebrew word is obscure. The Authorised Version adopts a doubtful etymology, connecting the word with the sun (so "sun gate" in the margin) and therefore with the East. Luther, with the Vulgate and most modern scholars, renders it as "the potter's gate," or more literally, *the gate of pottery*. The LXX. treats it as a proper name, and gives "the gate Kharsith." No such gate appears in the topographical descriptions of Neh. ii., iii.; and the two gates which led into the valley of Hinnom were the Fountain and the Dung gate (Neh. iii. 13—15). Hence it has been inferred that this was a small postern gate leading into the valley just at the point where it was filled with rubbish, possibly with broken fragments like those which were now to be added to it. On this supposition the connection both of the name of the gate and its use with the symbolism of the prophet's act may have determined the command which was thus given him.

(3) **O kings of Judah.**—The plural seems used to include both the reigning king, Jehoiakim, and his heir-apparent or presumptive.

His ears shall tingle.—The phrase, occurring as it does in 1 Sam. iii. 11, in the prophecy of the doom of the earlier sanctuary, seems intentionally used to remind those who heard it of the fate that had fallen on Shiloh. The destruction of the first sanctuary of Israel was to be the type of that of the second (Ps. lxxviii. 60; Jerem. vii. 14). The phrase had, however, been used more recently (2 Kings xxi. 12).

(4) **Have estranged this place.** — *i.e.*, have alienated it from Jehovah its true Lord, and given it to a strange god. The words refer specially to the guilt of Manasseh (2 Chron. xxxiii. 4).

The blood of innocents.—The words seem at first to refer to the Molech sacrifices, which had made the valley of Hinnom infamous. These, however, are mentioned separately in the next verse, and the prophet probably spoke rather here, as in chaps. ii. 34, vii. 6, of the "innocent blood" with which Manasseh had filled Jerusalem (2 Kings xxi. 16, xxiv. 4, where the same word is used).

(5) **The high places of Baal.**—Baal, as in chap. ii. 23, is identified with Molech, and the terms in which the guilt of the people and its punishment are described are all but identical with those of chap. vii. 31, 32. The fact that such sacrifices were offered is indicated in Ps. cvi. 37, 38.

(6) **Tophet.**—See Notes on chap. vii. 31, 32.

(7) **I will make void.**—The Hebrew verb (*bakak*) is onomatopoetic, as representing the gurgling sound of water flowing from the mouth of a jar, and contains, as stated in the note on verse 1, the root of the word rendered "bottle," and was obviously chosen with an allusive reference to it. Such a play upon the sound and sense of words is quite in accordance with the genius of Hebrew prophecy, but it is obviously in most cases impossible to reproduce it in another language. The primary meaning is "to pour out, to spill," and so "to waste, *or* bring to nought." (Comp. Isa. xix. 3.) Some interpreters have supposed that the words were accompanied by corresponding acts, and that the earthen bottle, which the prophet had brought filled with water, was now emptied in the sight of the people, with a symbolism like that of 1 Sam. vii. 6; 2 Sam. xiv. 14.

(8) **Desolate, and an hissing.**—See chap. xviii. 16.

Because of all the plagues thereof.—The word is used in its wider, and yet stricter, sense as including all the *blows* or *smitings* (as in Isa. xiv. 6) that are thought of as coming from the hand of God.

(9) **I will cause them to eat . . .**—Once again an echo, almost a quotation, from Deuteronomy (chap. xxviii. 53). The woes of that memorable chapter had obviously furnished the prophet both with imagery and language. In Lam. ii. 20, iv. 10 we find proof of the fulfilment of the prediction. Thus, by the dread law of retribution, were the people to pay the penalty of their sin in the Molech sacrifices, in which they, sinning at once against natural affection and against the faith of their fathers, had slain their sons and daughters.

and straitness, wherewith their enemies, and they that seek their lives, shall straiten them.
(10) Then shalt thou break the bottle in the sight of the men that go with thee,
(11) and shalt say unto them, Thus saith the LORD of hosts; Even so will I break this people and this city, as *one* breaketh a potter's vessel, that cannot [1]be made whole again: and they shall [a]bury *them* in Tophet, till *there be* no place to bury.
(12) Thus will I do unto this place, saith the LORD, and to the inhabitants thereof, and *even* make this city as Tophet:
(13) and the houses of Jerusalem, and the houses of the kings of Judah, shall be defiled as the place of Tophet, because of all the houses upon whose [b]roofs they have burned incense unto all the host of heaven, and have poured out drink offerings unto other gods.
(14) Then came Jeremiah from Tophet, whither the LORD had sent him to prophesy; and he stood in the court of the LORD's house; and said to all the people,
(15) Thus saith the LORD of hosts, the God of Israel; Behold, I will bring upon this city and upon all her towns all the evil that I have pronounced against it, because they have hardened their necks, that they might not hear my words.

CHAPTER XX.—(1) Now Pashur the son of [c]Immer the priest, who *was* also chief governor in the house of the LORD,

1 Heb., *be healed.*

a ch. 7. 32.

b ch. 32. 29.

c 1 Chron. 24. 14.

---

(10) **Then shalt thou break the bottle . . .**—Those who heard the prophet and saw his act were not unfamiliar with the imagery. The words of Ps. ii. 9 had portrayed the Messianic king as ruling over the nations, even as "breaking them in pieces like a potter's vessel." But it was a new and strange thing to hear these words applied to themselves, to see their own nation treated, not as the potter's clay that could be remodelled, as in chap. xviii. 1—6, either for a nobler, or, at least, for some serviceable use, but as the vessel which once broken could never be restored. Happily for Israel, there was a depth of Divine compassion which the parable failed to represent. The after-history showed that though, as far as that generation went, the punishment was final, and their existing polity could never be made whole again, there was yet hope for the nation. The things that were "impossible with man" were "possible with God." The fragments of the broken vessel might be gathered from the heap of rubbish on which the prophet had flung them, and brought into a new shape, for uses less glorious indeed than that for which it had been originally designed, but far other than those of a mere vessel of dishonour.

(12) **And even make this city as Tophet.**—This is an allusive reference partly to the state of the valley of Hinnom as a heap of ruins and rubbish, partly to the meaning of the name Tophet, as a place spat upon and scorned. (See Note on chap. vii. 31.)

(13) **Defiled as the place of Tophet.** — A difficulty affecting the construction, but not the sense, of the passage, makes the rendering *as the place of Tophet the defiled* preferable.

Upon whose roofs they have burned incense.—The flat roofs of Eastern houses were used, as for exercise (2 Sam. xi. 2) so also, as in Peter's vision at Joppa (Acts x. 9), for prayer and meditation, and seem from Zeph. i. 5 to have been specially chosen, as was natural, for worship addressed to the host of heaven. The two altars "on the top of the upper chamber of Ahaz" (2 Kings xxiii. 12) were probably so situated. Where men had been wont to keep the holy days of the Feast of Tabernacles (Neh. viii. 16) they had celebrated their idolatrous rites. (See chap. xxxii. 29.) So Strabo (xvi. p. 1,131) describes the Nabathœans as worshipping the sun, and offering incense on an altar on the roof of their houses.

(14) **He stood in the court of the Lord's house.**—The acted sermon had been preached in Tophet, in the valley of Ben-Hinnom, in the presence of a few chosen representatives of priests and people. It is followed by one addressed to the whole assembled congregation, announcing the same doom.

(15) **Thus saith the Lord of hosts.**—The address to the people could hardly have been confined to the limits of a single verse, and it is probable, therefore, that we have here but the summary of a discourse, so like in substance to what had been given before that the prophet did not think it necessary to report it at length.

XX.

(1) **Pashur the son of Immer.**—The description must be remembered as distinguishing him from the son of Melchiah of the same name in chap. xxi. 1. We may probably identify him with the father of the Gedaliah named in chap. xxxviii. 1 as among the "princes" that at a later date opposed the prophet's work, and with the section of the priesthood, the sixteenth, named in 1 Chron. xxiv. 14, as headed in the time of David by Immer. The name here (like that of "the sons of Korah") may indicate simply the fact that he belonged to this section; or, possibly, the name of the patriarch (so to speak) who gave its name to it may have re-appeared from time to time in the line of his descendants. The name of Pashur appears again, after the Captivity, in Ezra ii. 37, 38.

Chief governor.—Better, *deputy-governor.* The word for *governor* is *Nâgid,* and this office was assigned to the high priest as the "ruler of the house of God" (1 Chron. ix. 11; 2 Chron. xxxi. 13). In the case of Zephaniah, who appears as *Nâgid* in chap. xxix. 26, it was given to him as the "second priest" (2 Kings xxv. 18; Jer. lii. 14). Next in order to him was the *Pakid,* the deputy, or, perhaps, better, *superintendent.* Here Pashur is described by the combination of the two titles, possibly as implying that he was invested, though a "deputy," with the full powers of the "governor." By some commentators, however, the relation of the two words is inverted, the *Nâgid* being added to the *Pakid,* to imply that Pashur was the chief warden or overseer. As such, on either view, the act and the words of Jeremiah came under his official notice.

heard that Jeremiah prophesied these
things. (2) Then Pashur smote Jere-
miah the prophet, and put him in the
stocks that *were* in the high gate of
Benjamin, which *was* by the house of
the LORD. (3) And it came to pass on
the morrow, that Pashur brought forth
Jeremiah out of the stocks. Then said
Jeremiah unto him, The LORD hath not
called thy name Pashur, but [1]Magor-
missabib. (4) For thus saith the LORD,
Behold, I will make thee a terror to
thyself, and to all thy friends: and they
shall fall by the sword of their enemies,
and thine eyes shall behold *it:* and I
will give all Judah into the hand of the
king of Babylon, and he shall carry them
captive into Babylon, and shall slay them
with the sword. (5) Moreover I [a]will
deliver all the strength of this city,
and all the labours thereof, and all the
precious things thereof, and all the
treasures of the kings of Judah will I
give into the hand of their enemies,
which shall spoil them, and take them,
and carry them to Babylon. (6) And
thou, Pashur, and all that dwell in thine
house shall go into captivity: and thou
shalt come to Babylon, and there thou
shalt die, and shalt be buried there,
thou, and all thy friends, to whom thou
hast prophesied lies.

(7) O LORD, thou hast deceived me,
and I was [2]deceived: thou art stronger

1 That is, *Fear round about.*

a 2 Kings, 20. 17.

2 Or, *enticed.*

That such words should be spoken in the court of the Temple to the multitude assembled there was, we must believe, something new, and Pashur was resolved at any cost to prevent its repetition.

(2) **Then Pashur smote Jeremiah the prophet.**—It is the first time that he has been so described, the office to which he was called being apparently named to emphasise the outrage which had been inflicted on him. Other prophets had, under Ahab or Manasseh, been slain with the sword, but none, so far as we know (with the one exception of Hanani the seer in 2 Chron. xvi. 10), had ever before been subjected to an ignominious punishment such as this. It was so far analogous to the outrage against which St. Paul protested in Acts xxiii. 2, 3. The word "smote" implies a blow struck with the priest's own hands rather than the infliction of the legal punishment of forty stripes save one (Deut. xxv. 3). The English word "stocks" expresses adequately enough the instrument of torture which, like the *nervus* of Roman punishment, kept the body (as in Acts xvi. 24) in a crooked and painful position. The word here used occurs in the Hebrew of 2 Chron. xvi. 10, as above, and in chap. xxix. 26, but the A. V. there renders it as "prison-house." In that humiliating position the prophet was left for the whole night in one of the most conspicuous places of the city, the temple-gate of Benjamin (the *upper* gate) on the northern side of the inner court, probably the higher or northern gate of Ezek. viii. 3, 5; ix. 2.

(3) **Magor-missabib.**—The words are a quotation from Ps. xxxi. 13, and are rightly rendered, "Fear is round about;" they had already been used by the prophet in chap. vi. 25. We may venture to think that the Psalm had been his comfort in those night-watches of suffering, and that he now uttered the words which described the bitterness of the Psalmist's sorrow, as at last feeling sure that they belonged to his persecutor rather than to himself. It is scarcely necessary to seek a special significance in the name of Pashur as contrasted with this new *nomen et omen;* but Hebrew scholars, according to various, and it must be owned, conjectural etymologies, have found in it the ideas of wide-spread joy, "joy round about," or else of freedom and deliverance. The prophet repeats the combination in chaps. xlvi. 5, xlix. 29; Lam. ii. 22, and it had evidently become a kind of "burden" in both senses of the word, weighing on the prophet's thoughts and finding frequent utterance. The word that stands for "fear" is a rare one, and outside the passages now referred to is found only in Isa. xxxi. 9.

(4) **I will make thee a terror to thyself, and to all thy friends.**—We should have looked for a different explanation, indicating that terrors from without should gather round the cruel and relentless persecutor, but the prophet's words go deeper. He should be an object of self-loathing, outer fears intensifying his inward terror and acting through him on others. He is the centre from which terrors radiate as well as that to which they converge.

(5) **All the strength.**—*i.e.,* the treasure or "substance" of the city.

(6) **Thou shalt come to Babylon . . .**—The sons of Immer, the section of priests to which Pashur belonged, were found in large numbers at Babylon (Ezra ii. 37, 38), and it lies in the nature of the case that he, as a high official, would be among the captives when Nebuchadnezzar carried into exile all but the "poorer sort of the people of the land."

To whom thou hast prophesied lies.—The special predictions in question are not recorded, but we may infer that Pashur was one of those who encouraged the people to fight against the Chaldæans, and to despise Jeremiah's warnings by holding out the hope that an alliance with Egypt would avert the threatened danger (chaps. xiv. 13, xxiii. 17).

(7) **O Lord, thou hast deceived me.**—There is an obvious break between verses 6 and 7. The narrative ends, and a psalm of passionate complaint begins. Its position probably indicates that the compiler of the prophecies in their present form looked on the complaints as belonging to this period of the prophet's work, representing the thoughts of that night of shame which was, as it were, the extremest point of apparent failure. This then was the end of his prophetic calling, this the fulfilment of the promise which told him that he was set over the nations, and that his enemies should not prevail against him (chap. i. 8—10). Some touches of this feeling we have heard already in chap. xv. 18. Now it is more dominant and continuous.

Thou art stronger than I, and hast prevailed.—Better, *thou hast laid hold on me.* Jehovah now appears to the prophet as a hard taskmaster who had forced him, against his will (chap. xvii. 16), to

than I, and hast prevailed: I am in
derision daily, every one mocketh me.
(8) For since I spake, I cried out, I cried
violence and spoil; because the word of
the LORD was made a reproach unto me,
and a derision, daily.
(9) Then I said, I will not make mention of him, nor speak any more in his
name. But *his word* was in mine heart
as a [a]burning fire shut up in my bones,
and I was weary with forbearing, and [b]I
could not *stay*. (10) For I heard the
defaming of many, fear on every side.
Report, *say they*, and we will report it.
[1]All my familiars watched for my halting,
saying, Peradventure he will be enticed, and we shall prevail against
him, and we shall take our revenge on
him.
(11) But the LORD *is* with me as a
mighty terrible one: therefore my persecutors shall stumble, and they shall
not [c]prevail: they shall be greatly
ashamed; for they shall not prosper:
their [d]everlasting confusion shall never
be forgotten. (12) But, O LORD of hosts,
that [e]triest the righteous, *and* seest the
reins and the heart, let me see thy vengeance on them: for unto thee have I
opened my cause. (13) Sing unto the
LORD, praise ye the LORD: for he hath
delivered the soul of the poor from the
hand of evildoers.
(14) [f]Cursed *be* the day wherein I was

a Ps. 39. 3.

b Job 32. 18.

1 Heb., *Every man of my peace.*

c ch. 15. 20; & 17. 18.

d ch. 23. 40.

e ch. 11. 20; & 17. 10.

f Job 3. 3; ch. 15. 10.

---

enter on a work from which he shrank, and who gave him scorn and derision as his only wage. He felt, in St. Paul's language, that "a necessity was laid upon" him (1 Cor. ix. 16); or in Isaiah's, that the "strong hand" of the Lord was on him (Isa. viii. 11).

Daily.—Literally, *all the day.*

(8) **I cried out, I cried.**—The two Hebrew words are not, as in the English, alike, the first being the cry of complaint, the second of protest: *When I speak* (the tense implies from the beginning of his work till now), *I complain; I call out* (*against*) *violence and spoil.* They had formed the burden of his discourses, he had borne his witness against them, and yet "the word of Jehovah" so proclaimed by him had exposed him simply to derision. He had been the champion of the people's rights, and yet they mocked and scorned him.

(9) **Then I said . . .**—The sense of a hopeless work, destined to fail, weighed on the prophet's soul, and he would fain have withdrawn from it; but *it* (the words in italics, though they do not spoil the sense, are hardly needed) burnt like fire within him, and would not be restrained.

I could not stay.—Better, *I prevailed not.* Here again the interpolated word is needless, and in part spoils the emphasis. The "I could" is the same word as the "prevailed" of verse 7. God had prevailed against him, compelled him to undertake a work against his will, but he could not prevail against God. Like so much of Jeremiah's language this also came from the hymns of Israel (Ps. xxxix. 3).

(10) **The defaming of many.**—Another quotation from the Psalms (xxxi. 13), where the Authorised Version has "the slander of many."

Fear on every side.—The *Magor-missabib* still rings in the prophet's ears, and, for himself as for others, is the burden of his cry. It may be noted that this also comes from the same verse of the psalm just quoted.

Report, say they, and we will report it.—Better, *do you report.* The words are not spoken as to the prophet, but are those with which his persecutors encouraged each other to inform against him. (Comp. chaps. xi. 19, xviii. 18.)

All my familiars.—Literally, *every man of my peace, i.e.,* the men who used to greet him with the wonted "Peace be with thee." The same phrase is used in the "familiar friends" of Ps. xli. 9, but it does not in itself describe the intimacy of friendship, but rather the courtesy and good-will of acquaintances who thus salute each other.

Watched for my halting.—Comp. Pss. xxxv. 15 (where the same word is rendered "adversity") and xxxviii. 17.

He will be enticed.—The same word as the "deceived" of verse 7. They were on the look-out for some rash and hasty word spoken in prophetic zeal, and the prophet, in the bitterness of his soul, looked on their work and that of Jehovah as tending to the same result. Compare the conduct of the Scribes and Pharisees towards our Lord (Matt. xii. 10, xxii. 15; Mark xii. 13).

(11) **But the Lord is with me.**—As in Ps. xxii. and other like utterances, the prophet, though perplexed, is yet not in despair (2 Cor. iv. 8). He passes through the deep waters, but struggles out of them to the rock of refuge. The word "terrible" was used with a special significance. Jehovah had promised to deliver the prophet from the "terrible" ones (chap. xv. 21). He, the mighty God (Isa. ix. 6) would now show that He was more terrible than the prophet's foes, that it was better to come under their wrath than His (Isa viii. 12, 13).

For they shall not prosper.—Better, *because they have not dealt wisely.* The word is the same as in chap. x. 21, where see Note.

Their everlasting confusion.—Better, as carrying on the structure of the previous clause, *with an everlasting confusion that shall never be forgotten.*

(12) **But, O Lord of hosts . . .**—The verse is almost verbally identical with chap. xi. 20, where see Note.

(13) **Sing unto the Lord . . .**—It was as though heaviness had endured for a night, and joy had come in the morning. As with so many of the Psalms (Ps. xxii. 22 is, perhaps, the most striking parallel), what began in a cry *De profundis* ends in a Hallelujah.

(14) **Cursed be the day wherein I was born . . .**—The apparent strangeness of this relapse from the confidence of the two previous verses into a despair yet deeper than before is best explained by the supposition that it is in no sense part of the same poem or meditation, but a distinct fragment belonging to the same period, and placed in its present position by Jeremiah himself, or by the first editor of his prophecies

born: let not the day wherein my
mother bare me be blessed. (15) Cursed
be the man who brought tidings to my
father, saying, A man child is born unto
thee; making him very glad. (16) And
let that man be as the cities which the
LORD [a]overthrew, and repented not:
and let him hear the cry in the morn-
ing, and the shouting at noontide;
(17) because he slew me not from the
womb; or that my mother might have
been my grave, and her womb *to be*
always great *with me.* (18) [b]Wherefore
came I forth out of the womb to see
labour and sorrow, that my days should
be consumed with shame?

a Gen. 19. 25.

B. C. cir. 589.

b Job 3. 20.

CHAPTER XXI. — (1) The word
which came unto Jeremiah from the
LORD, when king Zedekiah sent unto
him Pashur the son of Melchiah, and
Zephaniah the son of Maaseiah the
priest, saying, (2) Enquire, I pray thee,
of the LORD for us; for Nebuchadrezzar
king of Babylon maketh war against us;
if so be that the LORD will deal with us
according to all his wondrous works,
that he may go up from us.

By some, indeed, it has been thought that we have here an accidental dislocation, and that verses 14—18 should stand before verse 7. The prophet utters a cry of anguish yet keener than that which now precedes it, and borrows the language of that cry from the book of Job (chap. iii. 3). The prophet turned in the depth of his suffering to the words in which the great representative of sufferers had "cursed his day." The question whether we are to blame or to palliate such utterances, how far they harmonise with Christian feeling, is one on which we need not dwell long. It is enough to note (1) that, while we cannot make for them the half-evasive apology which sees in Jeremiah's prayers against his enemies, and in the imprecatory psalms, prophecies rather than prayers, they indicate the same temper as those psalms and prayers indicate when taken in their natural sense, and so help us to understand them; and (2) that in such cases, while we give thanks that we have the blessing of a higher law and the example of a higher life, we are not called upon to apportion praise or blame. It is enough to reverence, to sympathise, to be silent.

(15) **Making him very glad.**—The memory, or rather the thought of that day, the joy of father and mother when their child was born (John xvi. 21) was wanted, as in the irony of destiny, to add the keenest pang to the misery of the present. The "sorrow's crown of sorrow" was found in remembering happier days. We note the same tenderness turned to bitterness as in chap. xv. 10. The day of his birth was to him a day of darkness and not of light.

(16) **The cities which the Lord overthrew.**—The verb is the same as that used in Gen. xix. 29, and the reference is clearly to the "cities of the plain," whose destruction is there described. The reference to them in Deut. xxxii. 32; Isa. i. 9, 10, shows that they had already become familiar to men as the great representative instances both of evil and its punishment.

The cry . . . the shouting.—The former word describes the wail of lamentation, the latter the shout of an invading army.

(17) **Because he slew me not . . .**—The wish that he had never been born is uttered by the prophet in strange, bold language. It would have been better that the messenger that told that he was born had slain him before his birth, that his mother's womb had been his grave, that she had never had strength to bring him forth. Thought, structure, even grammar are, in their abruptness and irregularities, alike significant of intense emotion.

(18) **Wherefore came I forth . . .?**—Like the preceding verse, this is in its tone, almost in its words, an echo of Job iii. 11, 12, 20.

XXI.

(1) **The word which came unto Jeremiah . . .**—There is obviously a great gap at this point in the collection of the prophet's utterances, and we enter on a new body or group of prophecies which extends to the close of chap. xxxiii. Thus far we have had his ministry under Jehoiakim, the roll which was read before that king, and formed the first part of his work. Now we pass to the later stage, which forms what has been called the roll of Zedekiah. The judgment predicted in the previous roll had come nearer. The armies of Nebuchadnezzar were gathering round the city. The prophet was now honoured and consulted, and the king sent his chief minister, Pashur (*not* the priest who had been the prophet's persecutor, as in the preceding chapter, but the head of the family or course of Melchiah), and Zephaniah, the "second priest," or deputy of chap. lii. 24, to ask his intercession. We learn from their later history that they were in their hearts inclined to the policy of resistance, and ready to accuse Jeremiah of being a traitor (chap. xxxviii. 1—4).

(2) **Nebuchadrezzar.**—This form of the name, as might be expected in the writings of one who was personally brought into contact with the king and his officers, is more correct than that of Nebuchad*nezzar*, which we find elsewhere, and even in Jeremiah's own writings (chaps. xxxiv. 1, xxxix. 5).

The name has been variously interpreted by scholars as "Nebo protects against misfortune," "Nebo protects the land-marks," "Nebo protects the crown," or "Fire, the shining God."

If so be that the Lord will deal with us . . .—The messengers come to inquire of the prophet, and yet suggest the answer which he is expected to give. Jehovah is to show His wondrous works in the deliverance of the city. The history of Sennacherib's army (2 Kings xix.; Isa. xxxvii.) was probably present to their minds. It was apparently an attempt on the part of the king and his counsellors, under the show of a devout reverence, to entice Jeremiah to change his tone and side with the policy of resistance to the Chaldæans. In chap. xxxvii. 3 we have another like mission, coming apparently at a somewhat later date in the reign of Zedekiah

That he may go up from us.—*i.e.*, in modern phraseology, that he may "raise the siege."

(3) Then said Jeremiah unto them, Thus shall ye say to Zedekiah: (4) Thus saith the LORD God of Israel; Behold, I will turn back the weapons of war that *are* in your hands, wherewith ye fight against the king of Babylon, and *against* the Chaldeans, which besiege you without the walls, and I will assemble them into the midst of this city. (5) And I myself will fight against you with an [a]outstretched hand and with a strong arm, even in anger, and in fury, and in great wrath. (6) And I will smite the inhabitants of this city, both man and beast: they shall die of a great pestilence. (7) And afterward, saith the LORD, I will deliver Zedekiah king of Judah, and his servants, and the people, and such as are left in this city from the pestilence, from the sword, and from the famine, into the hand of Nebuchadrezzar king of Babylon, and into the hand of their enemies, and into the hand of those that seek their life: and he shall smite them with the edge of the sword; he shall not spare them, neither have pity, nor have mercy.

(8) And unto this people thou shalt say, Thus saith the LORD; Behold, I set before you the way of life, and the way of death. (9) He that [b]abideth in this city shall die by the sword, and by the famine, and by the pestilence: but he that goeth out, and falleth to the Chaldeans that besiege you, he shall live, and [c]his life shall be unto him for a prey. (10) For I have set my face against this city for evil, and not for good, saith the LORD: it shall be given into the hand of the king of Babylon, and he shall burn it with fire.

(11) And touching the house of the king of Judah, *say*, Hear ye the word of the LORD; (12) O house of David, thus saith the LORD; [d] [1]Execute judgment in the morning, and deliver *him that is* spoiled out of the hand of the oppressor, lest my fury go out like fire, and burn

a Exod. 6. 6.
b ch. 38. 2.
c ch. 39. 18; & 45. 5.
d ch. 22. 3.
B. C. Cir. 609.
1 Heb., *Judge.*

---

(4) **Behold, I will turn back . . .**—Jeremiah's answer is far other than they looked for, and had even ventured to suggest. The judgment could no longer be averted. The hand of Jehovah was against them, and would bring the Chaldæans that were now outside the walls nearer and nearer, till they came within them. In the structure of the sentence, however, "without the walls" belongs to "wherewith ye fight." The defenders of the city were to be driven back within its gates from the outer line of fortifications.

(6) **They shall die of a great pestilence.**—This was doubtless, as in other instances (Thuc. ii. 52), the natural consequence of the siege, but it came before the people as another proof that Jehovah had stretched out his arm against them, that they were fighting against that arm as well as against the host of the invaders. The "outstretched hand" may be noted as another Deuteronomic phrase (Deut. iv. 34, v. 15, xxvi. 8).

(7) **He shall smite them with the edge of the sword.**—The words were bold words for the prophet to utter while the king was still on the throne, and urged on by his princes to defy the power of the Chaldæan king. In chap. lii. 10, 24—27 we find their literal fulfilment.

(8) **The way of life, and the way of death.**—The words are not unlike those of Deut. xi. 26, 27, xxx. 15, 19, but there is something like a solemn irony in their application here. They obviously present themselves, not with the wide spiritual application with which they meet us there, but are to be taken in their lowest and most literal sense. The "way of life" is no longer that way of righteousness which the men of Judah had forsaken, leading to the life of eternal blessedness, but simply submission to the Chaldæans, and the life so gained was one of exile and poverty, if not of bondage also.

(9) **And falleth to the Chaldeans.**—The words must have seemed to the messengers to counsel treachery and desertion, and were remembered against the prophet in the taunt of chap. xxxvii. 13. They were, however, acted on by not a few (chaps. xxxix. 9, lii. 15).

His life shall be unto him for a prey.—The phrase is characteristic of Jeremiah, and forcibly illustrates the misery of the time. Life itself was not a secure possession, but as the spoil which a man seizes on the field of battle, and with which he hastens away, lest another should deprive him of it. It occurs again in chaps. xxxix. 18, xlv. 5.

(10) **He shall burn it with fire.**—Another detail of prediction fulfilled literally in chap. lii. 13. Such a destruction was, of course, common enough as an incident of the capture of besieged cities, but it was not universal. Often, indeed, the conquerors sought to preserve the city and to occupy its palaces. The actual answer to Zedekiah's messengers possibly ended with this verse.

(11) **Say, Hear ye the word of the Lord.**—The interpolated "say" is not wanted, and tends to convey the probably wrong impression that we are dealing with a new message rather than a continuation of the former one. The question whether it is such a continuation has been variously answered by different commentators. On the one hand, the conditional threatenings are said to imply an earlier stage of Jeremiah's work than the doom, absolute and unconditional, pronounced in verses 1—10, and so have led men to refer the message to the earlier years of Jehoiakim. On the other, it is urged that the words may have the character of a last promise, and therefore a last warning.

(12) **Execute judgment in the morning.**—The words point to one of the chief duties of the ideal Eastern king. To rise at dawn of day, to sit in the gate and listen to the complaints of those who had been wronged, was the surest way to gain the affection of his people. It was David's neglect of this that gave an opening for the rebellion of Absalom (2 Sam. xv. 2). Solomon's early fame for wisdom rested on his discharge

that none can quench *it*, because of the
evil of your doings. (13) Behold, I *am*
against thee, O [1]inhabitant of the valley,
and rock of the plain, saith the LORD;
which say, Who shall come down against
us? or who shall enter into our habitations?
(14) But I will [2]punish you according
to the [a]fruit of your doings, saith
the LORD: and I will kindle a fire in
the forest thereof, and it shall devour
all things round about it.

CHAPTER XXII.—(1) Thus saith the
LORD; Go down to the house of the
king of Judah, and speak there this
word, (2) and say, Hear the word of the
LORD, O king of Judah, that sittest upon
the throne of David, thou, and thy servants,
and thy people that enter in by
these gates: (3) Thus saith the LORD;
[b]Execute ye judgment and righteousness,
and deliver the spoiled out of the hand
of the oppressor: and do no wrong, do
no violence to the stranger, the fatherless,
nor the widow, neither shed innocent
blood in this place. (4) For if ye
do this thing indeed, [c]then shall there
enter in by the gates of this house kings
sitting [3]upon the throne of David, riding
in chariots and on horses, he, and his
servants, and his people. (5) But if ye
will not hear these words, I swear by
myself, saith the LORD, that this house
shall become a desolation.
(6) For thus saith the LORD unto the
king's house of Judah; Thou *art* Gilead

1 Heb., *inhabitress.*
2 Heb., *visit upon.*
a Prov. 1. 31.
b ch. 21. 12.
c ch. 17. 25.
3 Heb., *for David upon his throne.*

---

of this duty (1 Kings iii. 28). If the king remained slothfully in his palace in those golden hours of morning, the noon-tide heat made it impossible for him to retrieve the lost opportunity. (Comp. 2 Sam. iv. 5.) Still worse was it when, as with luxurious and sensual kings, the morning hours were given to revelry and feasting (Eccl. x. 16, 17).

(13) **O inhabitant of the valley . . .**—The noun, as the marginal "inhabitress" shows, is feminine; and, as in "the daughter of Zion" for Zion itself, describes the lower city of Jerusalem, Isaiah's "valley of vision" (Isa. xxii. 1, 5), the Tyropœon of Josephus. The "rock of the plain" (comp. Notes on chaps. xvii. 3, xviii. 14) is, in like manner, the higher city built on the hill of Zion. The king and his people trusted, as the Jebusites had done of old (2 Sam. v. 8), in what seemed to them the impregnable strength of their natural position. There seems no adequate reason for taking the words as symbolising the kingly house of Judah, but it is probable enough that local associations, palaces on the hill or in the valley, may have given the words a specially pointed application.

(14) **I will kindle a fire in the forest thereof.**—The "forest" thus referred to may be either literally the woods, then covering a larger surface than in later times, at Kirjath-jearim (Ps. cxxxii. 6; 1 Sam. vii. 2), or the wood of the lone wilderness of Ziph (1 Sam. xxiii. 15), or the valley of Rephaim (2 Sam. v. 22), or, figuratively, the royal palace, which, from its cedar columns (1 Kings vii. 2, x. 21), was known as "the house of the forest of Lebanon." (Comp. the comparison of the king's house to "Gilead and the head of Lebanon," in chap. xxii. 6.) The desolation wrought by an invading army such as that of Nebuchadnezzar, cutting down the "choice fir-trees of Lebanon and the forest of Carmel" (2 Kings xix. 23), showed itself in this destruction of forests in its most conspicuous form, and explains the comparative scarcity of trees in modern Palestine. So Assur-nasirpal narrates, in the history of his conquests, how he had cut down the pine, box, cypress, and other trees of the forest (*Records of the Past,* iii. p. 74).

XXII.

(1) **Thus saith the Lord . . .**—The message, delivered in continuation of chap. xxi., and therefore probably as following up the answer to the messengers of Zedekiah (chap. xxi. 1), reviews the history of the three preceding reigns, and apparently reproduces the very words of the warnings which he had uttered in each to the king who then ruled, and which had been but too terribly fulfilled. It was delivered, we are told, in the very palace of the king.

(2) **That sittest upon the throne of David.**—The words obviously imply that the message was delivered to the king as he sat in the gate in the presence of his people.

(3) **Execute ye judgment.**—As the Hebrew verb is not identical with that in chap. xxi. 12, and implies a less formal act, it might be better to render it, *do ye judgment . . .*

Do no wrong . . .—The Hebrew order connects both verbs with the substantives—*to the stranger, the fatherless, and the widow, do no wrong, no violence*—and gives the latter the emphasis of position. The whole verse paints but too vividly a reign which presented the very reverse of all that the prophet describes as belonging to a righteous king.

(4) **Then shall there enter in . . .**—The picture of renewed and continued prosperity gains a fresh force, as reproducing the very terms of chap. xvii. 25. In both the "chariots and horses" are conspicuous as the symbol of kingly pomp (1 Kings iv. 26), just as their absence furnished a topic to the sarcastic taunts of Rabshakeh (Isa. xxxvi. 8), and entered into the picture of the true, peaceful king in Zech. ix. 9, 10.

(5) **I swear by myself.**—The formula is an exceptionally rare one, but meets us in Gen. xxii. 16. In Deut. xxxii. 40 the same thought is embodied in the language of the loftiest poetry. The principle in both cases is that on which the writer of the Epistle to the Hebrews dwells in chap. vi. 13. Men swear by the greater, but God can swear by nothing greater than Himself.

This house.—The context determines the application of the word as meaning the king's palace, not the Temple.

(6) **Thou art Gilead unto me, and the head of Lebanon.**—The conjunction, which is not found in the Hebrew, is better omitted. Even in his utterance of woes the prophet's mind is still that of a poet. The chief point of the comparison in both cases is to be found in the forests that crowned the heights of both

unto me, *and* the head of Lebanon: *yet*
surely I will make thee a wilderness,
and cities *which* are not inhabited.
(7) And I will prepare destroyers against
thee, every one with his weapons: and
they shall cut down thy choice cedars,
and cast *them* into the fire. (8) And
many nations shall pass by this city,
and they shall say every man to his
neighbour, [a] Wherefore hath the LORD
done thus unto this great city? (9) Then
they shall answer, Because they have
forsaken the covenant of the LORD their
God, and worshipped other gods, and
served them.
(10) Weep ye not for the dead, neither
bemoan him: *but* weep sore for him
that goeth away: for he shall return no
more, nor see his native country. (11) For
thus saith the LORD touching Shallum
the son of Josiah king of Judah, which
reigned instead of Josiah his father,
which went forth out of this place; He
shall not return thither any more:
(12) but he shall die in the place whither
they have led him captive, and shall see
this land no more.
(13) Woe unto [b] him that buildeth his
house by unrighteousness, and his
chambers by wrong; *that* useth his
neighbour's service without wages,
and giveth him not for his work;
(14) that saith, I will build me a wide
house and [1] large chambers, and cutteth

[a] Deut. 29. 24; 1 Kings 9. 8.

[b] Lev. 19. 13; Deut. 24. 14, 15; Hab. 2. 9.

[1] Heb., *throughaired.*

ranges of mountains. The "oaks of Bashan," in the Gilead district (Isa. ii. 13; Zech. xi. 2), were as famous as the cedars of Lebanon, and both were alike the fit symbol of the glory of sovereignty (Isa. xxxvii. 24; Ezek. xvii. 3). There may be a reference to the group of cedar-buildings, which of old gave to one of the palaces the name of "the house of the forest of Lebanon" (2 Sam. vii. 2, 7; 1 Kings vii. 2, x. 21).

(7) **I will prepare destroyers.**—The verb, as in chap. vi. 4, implies the idea of a solemn appointment or consecration.

They shall cut down thy choice cedars.—The metaphor of the preceding verse is carried further, and the "choice cedars" are the princes of the royal house of Judah, and the chief counsellors and generals, as well as the actual columns of cedar-wood.

(8, 9) **Wherefore hath the Lord done thus . . .** —The coincidence of thought and language with Deuteronomy (xxix. 24—26) again calls for notice.

(10) **Weep ye not for the dead.**—With this verse begins the detailed review of the three previous reigns, the prophecies being reproduced as they were actually delivered. The "dead" for whom men are not to weep is Josiah, for whom Jeremiah had himself composed a solemn dirge, which seems from 2 Chron. xxxv. 25 to have been repeated on the anniversary of his death.

For him that goeth away.—This is obviously Jehoahaz, the son and successor of Josiah, who was deposed by Pharaoh-nechoh, and carried into Egypt (2 Kings xxiii. 31—34; 2 Chron. xxxvi. 2—4). The latter passage shows that he was younger than his successor, Jehoiakim, by two years. The doom of the exile who was to return no more was a fitter subject for lamentation than the death of the righteous king who died a warrior's death (2 Kings xxiii. 29), and was thus "taken away from the evil to come."

(11) **Shallum.**—Josiah's successor appears in the historical books as Jehoahaz ("Jehovah sustains," meant as a *nomen et omen*), the latter being probably the name assumed on his succession to the throne. Such changes were common at the time, as in the case of Jehoiakim and Zedekiah (2 Kings xxiii. 34, xxiv. 17). Shallum (= retribution) might probably have seemed a name of evil augury. In 1 Chron. iii. 15 a Shallum appears as the fourth son of Josiah, Jehoiakim being the second, and one otherwise unknown, Johanan, the eldest. This may have been the same as the one now referred to (the order of the last two names being in some way inverted), or there may have been two brothers bearing the same name. The short and disastrous reign of Shallum, and the meaning of the word probably account for the prophet's using the private rather than the kingly name. The fact that the name had been borne by one of the later kings of Israel whose reign lasted but for a single month (2 Kings xv. 13) may have given a further point to its use, as being full of disastrous memories that made it ominous of evil. The title "king of Judah" belongs grammatically to Shallum, not to Josiah.

(12) **Shall see this land no more.**—There is no record of the duration of the life of Shallum in his Egyptian exile, but the total absence of his name in the history that follows is presumptive evidence of the fulfilment of the prediction. There is no trace of his being alive when the prophet is dragged by his countrymen to Egypt (chap. xliii. 6, 7).

(13) **Woe unto him that buildeth . . .**—The prophet now turns to Jehoiakim, and apparently reproduces what he had before uttered in denouncing the selfish bearing of that king. The feelings of the people, already suffering from the miseries of foreign invasion, were outraged by the revival of the forced labour of the days of Solomon, pressing in this instance not on the "strangers" of alien blood (1 Kings v. 13—15; 2 Chron. ii. 17, 18), but on the Israelites themselves. We are reminded of the general characteristics of Eastern, and perhaps of all other, despotism. Like the modern rulers of Constantinople, Jehoiakim went on building palaces when his kingdom was on the verge of ruin, and his subjects were groaning under their burdens.

His chambers.—Strictly speaking, the upper storeys of the house. This is dwelt on as aggravating the severity of the work.

Without wages.—The labourers were treated as slaves, and, like the Israelites in their Egyptian bondage (Exod. xvi. 3), received their food, but nothing more.

(14) **Large chambers.**—As before, "upper storeys *or* chambers."

Cutteth him out windows.—The verb is the same as that used in chap. iv. 30 for dilating the eyes by the use of antimony, and implies accordingly the construction of windows of unusual width. These, after

him out [1]windows; and *it is* cieled with
cedar, and painted with vermilion.
(15) Shalt thou reign, because thou clos-
est *thyself* in cedar? did not thy father eat
and drink, and do judgment and justice,
and then *it was* well with him? (16) He
judged the cause of the poor and needy;
then *it was* well *with him*: *was* not this
to know me? saith the LORD. (17) But
thine eyes and thine heart *are* not but for
thy covetousness, and for to shed inno-
cent blood, and for oppression, and for
[2]violence, to do *it*. (18) Therefore thus
saith the LORD concerning Jehoiakim
the son of Josiah king of Judah; They
shall not lament for him, *saying*, Ah my
brother! or, Ah sister! they shall not
lament for him, *saying*, Ah lord! or, Ah
his glory! (19) He shall be buried with
the burial of an ass, drawn and cast
forth beyond the gates of Jerusalem.
(20) Go up to Lebanon, and cry; and
lift up thy voice in Bashan, and cry
from the passages: for all thy lovers are
destroyed. (21) I spake unto thee in thy
[3]prosperity; *but* thou saidst, I will not
hear. This *hath been* thy manner from
thy youth, that thou obeyedst not my

1 Or, *my windows.*

2 Or, *incursion.*

B. C. 599.

3 Heb., *prosperities.*

---

the Eastern fashion, were fitted with lattice-work, or shielded by curtains.

Vermilion.—Probably the red pigment (sulphuret of mercury?) still conspicuous in the buildings of Egypt. The word meets us again in Ezek. xxiii. 14. The king was probably impelled by a vainglorious desire to imitate the magnificence of the Egyptian king (Pharaoh-nechoh) who had placed him on the throne.

(15) **Thou closest thyself in cedar.**—Better, *thine ambition is in cedar.* The verb means strictly, as in chap. xii. 5, "to vie with" or "to contend," and Jehoiakim is reproached for endeavouring to outdo the magnificence even of his greatest predecessors. A various reading, followed by the LXX., gives, "thou viest with Ahaz," or "Ahab," probably, in this latter case, with reference to the ivory palace built by that king (1 Kings xxii. 39).

Did not thy father eat and drink . . .?—The words are obviously those of praise, and paint a healthy, blameless enjoyment like that of Eccles. ii. 24; like those, we may add, which the Son of Man used to describe the outward portion of His own life (Matt. xi. 19). Josiah was not an ascetic, devotee king, but lived his life happily, and did his work—the true kingly work of judgment and justice—well. There was a truer greatness in that than in the stateliness of Jehoiakim's palaces. "Then it was well with him" is repeated with the emphasis of iteration.

(16) **Was not this to know me?**—The prophet, as a true witness of the law of righteousness, proclaims that the religious fame of Josiah rested not on his restoration of the Temple worship, nor on his suppression of idolatry, but much more on his faithfulness in his kingly work to the cause of righteousness and mercy. They only could know Him who, in this respect, strove to be like Him (1 John iii. 2).

(17) **Thy covetousness.**—More literally, *thy gain,* the word used implying (as in chaps. vi. 13, viii. 10) the idea of violence and oppression as the means by which it was obtained. The verb from which the noun is derived is so translated—"violence" (literally, "crushing")—in Deut. xxviii. 33. The marginal reading, "incursion," has nothing to commend it. In "the blood of the innocent" here, as in verse 3, we have an allusive reference to many, for the most part unrelenting, acts of cruelty. One of these, the murder of Urijah, meets us in chap. xxvi. 23.

(18) **They shall not lament for him.**—The words contrast the death as well as the life of Jehoiakim with that of Josiah. For him there should be no lamentation such as was made for the righteous king (2 Chron. xxxv. 25), either from kindred mourning, as over a brother or a sister (perhaps, however, as "sister" would not be appropriate to the king, the words are those of a chorus of mourners, male and female, addressing each other), or from subjects wailing over the death of their "lord" and the departure of his "glory." For the funeral ceremonies of Israel, see 1 Kings xiii. 30; Matt. ix. 23; Mark v. 38.

(19) **He shall be buried with the burial of an ass.**—The same prediction appears in another form in chap. xxxvi. 30. The body of the king was "to be cast out in the day to the heat, and in the night to the frost." We have no direct record of its fulfilment, but its reproduction shows that the prophet's word had not failed. The king was dragged in chains with the other captives, who were being carried off to Babylon (2 Chron. xxxvi. 6), and probably died on the journey, his corpse left behind unburied as the army marched. The phrase "he slept with his fathers" in 2 Kings xxiv. 6 cannot be pressed as meaning more than the mere fact of death. So Ahab, who died in battle, "slept with his fathers" (1 Kings xxii. 40).

(20) **Go up to Lebanon.**—The great mountain-ranges—Lebanon and Bashan (Ps. lxviii. 15)—running from north to south, that overlooked the route of the Babylonians, are invoked by the prophet, as those of Gilboa had been by David (2 Sam. i. 21), as witnesses of the misery that was coming on the land and people. Even here, as in verse 23, there is probably still the same reference as before to the cedar-palaces of Jerusalem. The people are called from the counterfeit "forests of Lebanon" to the height of the real mountains, and bidden to look forth from thence.

Cry from the passages.—It is better to take the word *Abarim* as a proper name. As in Num. xxvii. 12, xxxiii. 47; Deut. xxxii. 49, it was part of the range of Nebo, south of Gilead and Bashan, and coming therefore naturally after the last of those two mountains.

All thy lovers.—The word points, as in the corresponding language of Ezek. xxiii. 5, 9, to the Egyptians and other nations with whom Judah had made alliances. The destruction reached its climax in the overthrow of Pharaoh-nechoh's army by Nebuchadnezzar at Carchemish (chap. xlvi. 2).

(21) **In thy prosperity.**—Literally, *prosperities.* The word is used, as in Prov. i. 32; Ezek. xvi. 49; Ps. xxx. 6, in reference to what in old English was called "security," the careless, reckless temper engendered by outward prosperity. The plural is used to include all the forms of that temper that had been manifested in the course of centuries.

voice. (22) The wind shall eat up all
thy pastors, and thy lovers shall go into
captivity: surely then shalt thou be
ashamed and confounded for all thy
wickedness. (23) O [1]inhabitant of Leba-
non, that makest thy nest in the
cedars, how gracious shalt thou be
when pangs come upon thee, the pain
as of a woman in travail!

(24) *As* I live, saith the LORD, though
Coniah the son of Jehoiakim king of
Judah were the signet upon my right
hand, yet would I pluck thee thence;
(25) and I will give thee into the hand
of them that seek thy life, and into the
hand *of them* whose face thou fearest,
even into the hand of Nebuchadrezzar
king of Babylon, and into the hand of
the Chaldeans. (26) And I will cast thee
out, and thy mother that bare thee, into
another country, where ye were not
born; and there shall ye die. (27) But
to the land whereunto they [2]desire to
return, thither shall they not return.

(28) *Is* this man Coniah a despised
broken idol? *is he* a vessel wherein *is* no
pleasure? wherefore are they cast out,
he and his seed, and are cast into a land
which they know not? (29) O earth,
earth, earth, hear the word of the LORD.
(30) Thus saith the LORD, Write ye
this man childless, a man *that* shall not
prosper in his days: for no man of his
seed shall prosper, sitting upon the
throne of David, and ruling any more
in Judah.

[1] Heb., *inhabitress.*

[2] Heb., *lift up their mind.*

---

(22) **The wind shall eat up all thy pastors.**—The word for "eat up" is the root of the noun rendered "pastors," and the play of sound may be expressed in English by *shall feed on them that feed thee—i.e.,* thy princes and statesmen. The "lovers" are, as before in verse 20, the king's chosen allies.

(23) **O, inhabitant of Lebanon.**—The phrase developes the thought of verse 6. The king, in his cedar-palace, is as one who has made Lebanon his home, literally and figuratively (see Note on verse 7), and is as an eagle nestling in the cedar.

How gracious shalt thou be . . .!—Better, *how wilt thou sigh!* or, *how wilt thou groan!* as connected with the pangs of travail. No pomp or majesty could save the royal house from the inevitable doom.

(24) **Coniah the son of Jehoiakim.**—The grammatical structure of the sentence fixes the original utterance of the message, now reproduced, at a time when Coniah was actually king, during his short three months' reign. The name of this prince appears in three forms:—(1) The abbreviated Coniah, as here and in chap. xxxvii. 1: this was probably the name by which he was known before he was proclaimed as king. (2) Jeconiah, with slight variations, in chaps. xxiv. 1, xxvii. 20, and elsewhere. (3) Jehoiachin, also with varied spelling—probably the regal title assumed on his accession (chap. lii. 31; Ezek. i. 2). The meaning of the name "Jehovah establishes" is constant in all the forms. In 2 Kings xxiv. 8 he is said to have been eighteen years old when he began to reign. In 2 Chron. xxxvi. 9 the age is given as eight. The latter is obviously an error of transcription. His reign lasted for three months only. There is probably a touch of scorn, as in the case of Shallum, in the prophet's use of the earlier name instead of that which he had assumed as king.

The signet upon my right hand.—The seal-ring was, as in Hagg. ii. 23, the symbol of kingly power (Gen. xli. 42; Esth. iii. 10, viii. 2), authenticating every edict, and was therefore the type of all that was most precious. (Comp. Song of Sol. viii. 6.)

(26) **Thy mother that bare thee.**—The youth of Coniah probably led to his mother assuming the authority of a queen-regent. She directed the policy of his brief reign, and shared in his downfall. Her name, Nehushta, is given in 2 Kings xxiv. 8, and in chap. xxix. 2 she is named as the *gebirah,* the "great lady" or "princess-queen."

(27) **Whereunto they desire to return.**—The English expresses the sense, but lacks the poetic force, of the Hebrew, *to which they lift up their souls to return,* yearning thitherward with the longing of unsatisfied desire.

(28) **Is this man Coniah a despised broken idol?**—Better, *a broken piece of handiwork.* The word is not the same as that elsewhere rendered "idol," though connected with it, and the imagery which underlies the words is not that of an idol which men have worshipped and flung away, but of the potter (as in chap. xix. 11) rejecting and breaking what his own hands have made. (Comp. Pss. ii. 9, xxxi. 12.) The question implies an affirmative answer. The prophet speaks as identifying himself with those who gazed with wonder and pity at the doom which fell on one so young, and yet not the less does he pronounce that doom to be inevitable.

(29) **O earth, earth, earth.**—The solemnity of the mystic threefold repetition expresses the certainty of the Divine decree (comp. chap. vii. 4). So in our Lord's most solemn utterances we have the twice-repeated "Simon, Simon" (Luke xxii. 31), and the recurring "Verily, verily" of St. John's Gospel (viii. 51 *et al.*).

(30) **Write ye this man childless.**—The meaning of the prediction, as explained by the latter clause of the verse, was fulfilled in Jeconiah's being the last kingly representative of the house of David, his uncle Zedekiah, who succeeded him, perishing before him (chap. lii. 31). In him the sceptre departed, and not even Zerubbabel sat upon the throne of Judah. Whether he died actually childless is less certain. In 1 Chron. iii. 17 Assir (possibly, however, the name should be translated "Jeconiah the prisoner") appears as his son, and as the father of Salathiel, or Shealtiel; and in Matt. i. 12 we find "Jechonias begat Salathiel." In these genealogies, however, adoption or succession, or a Levirate marriage so constantly takes the place of parentage, that nothing certain can be inferred from these *data,* and St. Luke (iii. 27) places Salathiel among the descendants of Nathan, as though the line of Solomon became extinct in Jeconiah, and was replaced by the collateral branch of the house of David (see Note on Luke iii. 23). The command, "write ye

CHAPTER XXIII.—(1) [a]Woe be unto
the pastors that destroy and scatter the
sheep of my pasture! saith the LORD.
(2) Therefore thus saith the LORD God
of Israel against the pastors that feed
my people; Ye have scattered my flock,
and driven them away, and have not
visited them: behold, I will visit upon
you the evil of your doings, saith the
LORD. (3) And I will gather the rem-
nant of my flock out of all countries
whither I have driven them, and will
bring them again to their folds; and

a Ezek. 34. 2.

b ch. 3. 15; Ezek. 34. 11, 12.

c Isa. 4. 2; & 40. 11; ch. 33. 14, 15; Dan. 9. 24; John 1. 45.

d Deut. 33. 28.

they shall be fruitful and increase.
(4) And I will set up [b]shepherds over
them which shall feed them: and they
shall fear no more, nor be dismayed,
neither shall they be lacking, saith the
LORD.
(5) Behold, [c]the days come, saith the
LORD, that I will raise unto David a
righteous Branch, and a King shall
reign and prosper, and shall execute
judgment and justice in the earth. (6) [d]In
his days Judah shall be saved, and
Israel shall dwell safely: and this *is*

---

this man childless," is apparently addressed to the scribes who kept the register of the royal genealogies (Ezek. xiii. 9; Ps. lxix. 28, 29). They were told how, without waiting for his death, they were to enter Coniah's name in that register.

XXIII.

(1) **Woe be unto the pastors . . .**—The message that follows in verses 1—8 comes as a natural sequel to that of chap. xxii. The unfaithful shepherds who had been there denounced are contrasted with those, more faithful to their trust, whom Jehovah will raise up. As before, in chap. ii. 8 and elsewhere, we have to remember that the "pastors" are (like the "shepherds of the people" in Greek poets) the civil rulers, not the prophets or the priests, of Israel. The parallelism with the prophecy of Ezek. xxxiv., delivered about the same time in the land of exile, is suggestive either of direct communication between the two writers, or of traditional lines of thought common to the two priest-prophets.

The sheep of my pasture.—The words assert the claims of Jehovah to be the true Shepherd of His people. (Comp. Pss. lxxix. 13, c. 3.)

(2) **Ye have scattered my flock.**—The charge was true literally as well as spiritually. The dispersion of the people in Egypt, Assyria, and Chaldæa was the result of the neglect, the tyranny, the feebleness of their rulers. They had been led, not as the Eastern shepherd leads (John x. 4, 5), but "driven"—not to the fold, but "away" into far lands.

Have not visited.—*i.e.*, cared for and regarded. They were negligent, but God was not, and He therefore would "visit" them by reproof and chastisement.

(3) **To their folds.**—Better, *habitations*, or *pastures*. There was hope, as in Isa. i. 9, vi. 13, for the "remnant" of the people, though the sentence on their rulers, as such, was final and irreversible.

(4) **I will set up shepherds . . .**—The words imply, in one sense, a return to the theocracy, the breaking off the hereditary succession of the house of David, and the giving of power to those who, like Ezra and Nehemiah, and, later on in history, the Maccabees, were called to rule because they had the capacity for ruling well. The plural is noticeable, as in chap. iii. 15, as not limiting the prophecy to the Christ who is yet the "chief Shepherd" (1 Pet. v. 4). In the verb for "set up" there is an allusive reference to the names of Jehoiakim and Jehoiachin, into both of which it entered. Jehovah would "raise up" shepherds, but not such as they had proved themselves to be.

Neither shall they be lacking.—*i.e.*, the flock would be so cared for that not one sheep should be lost. Care extending even to every individual member was the true ideal of the Shepherd's work (John x. 3, xvii. 12), and therefore of the ruler's.

(5) **Behold, the days come.**—The words point to an undefined, far-off future, following on the provisional order implied in verse 4, when the kingdom should once more rest in one of the house of David.

A righteous Branch.—The idea is the same, though the word is different (here *Zemach*, and there *Netzer*), as in Isa. xi. 1. In both cases, however, the word means a "sprout" or "scion," springing up from the root even after the tree had been cut down (Isa. vi. 13), and not a branch growing from the trunk. It is probably in reference to this prophecy that we find the name of "the Branch" (*Zemach*) so prominent in Zech. iii. 8, vi. 12. Here, it is obvious, the prophet speaks of the one great Shepherd.

A King shall reign.—Better, *he shall reign as King*, the Branch or Sprout being the subject of the sentence. As with all the Messianic prophecies of this class, the thoughts of the prophet dwell on the acts and attributes of a sovereignty exercised personally on earth. Such a sovereignty, "all power in heaven and on earth" (Matt. xxviii. 18), was indeed given to the Christ, but not after the fashion that men expected.

(6) **Judah shall be saved, and Israel shall dwell safely.**—The true King shall reign over a re-united people. The Ten Tribes of the Northern Kingdom, as well as the two of the Southern, should find in Him deliverance and peace.

Whereby he shall be called.—Literally, *whereby one shall call him*, the indefinite, almost impersonal active having the force of the English passive.

The Lord our Righteousness.—It is significant that in chap. xxxiii. 16 the same name is given to Jerusalem. There it is clearly not, in logical language, the predicate of the city, but that which she takes as her watchword, and blazons, as it were, on her banner; and we cannot consistently press more than that meaning here. So in Ezek. xlviii. 35 the new name of Jerusalem is "Jehovah-shammah" (= the Lord is there). So in Exod. xvii. 15 Moses calls the altar which he builds "Jehovah-nissi" (= the Lord is my banner). The interpretation which sees in the words (1) the identification of the Messianic King with Jehovah, the Eternal, and (2) the doctrine of imputed righteousness, must accordingly be regarded as one of the applications of the words rather than their direct meaning. That meaning would seem to be that the King, the righteous Branch, will look to Jehovah as giving and working righteousness. Some commentators, indeed, refer the pronoun "he" to Israel, and not to the

his name whereby he shall be called,
[1]THE LORD OUR RIGHTEOUS-
NESS. (7) Therefore, behold, [a]the days
come, saith the LORD, that they shall
no more say, The LORD liveth, which
brought up the children of Israel out of
the land of Egypt; (8) but, The LORD
liveth, which brought up and which led
the seed of the house of Israel out of
the north country, and from all coun-
tries whither I had driven them; and
they shall dwell in their own land.

(9) Mine heart within me is broken
because of the prophets; all my bones
shake; I am like a drunken man, and
like a man whom wine hath overcome,
because of the LORD, and because of the
words of his holiness. (10) For the land
is full of adulterers; for because of
[2]swearing the land mourneth; the
pleasant places of the wilderness are
dried up, and their [3]course is evil, and
their force *is* not right. (11) For both
prophet and priest are profane; yea, in
my house have I found their wickedness,
saith the LORD. (12) Wherefore their
way shall be unto them as slippery *ways*
in the darkness: they shall be driven
on, and fall therein: for I will bring
evil upon them, *even* the year of their
visitation, saith the LORD. (13) And
I have seen [4][5]folly in the prophets of
Samaria; they prophesied in Baal,
and caused my people Israel to err.
(14) I have seen also in the prophets of
Jerusalem [6]an horrible thing: they
commit adultery, and walk in lies: they
strengthen also the hands of evildoers,
that none doth return from his wicked-
ness: they are all of them unto me as

1 Heb., *Jehovah-tsidkenu.*
a ch. 16. 14, 15.
2 Or, *cursing.*
3 Or, *violence.*
4 Or, *an absurd thing.*
5 Heb., *unsavoury.*
6 Or, *filthiness.*

---

righteous Branch. We cannot forget that, at the very time when Jeremiah uttered this prophecy, a king was on the throne whose name (Zedekiah = righteous is Jehovah) implied the same thought. His reign had been a miserable failure, and the prophet looks forward to a time when the ideal, which was then far off, should at last be realised. If with many critics we refer the prediction to the reign of Jehoiakim (see Note on verse 1), we might almost see in Mattaniah's adoption of the new name a boast that he was about to fulfil it. The Christ, we may say, answered to the name, not as being Himself one with Jehovah, though He was that, but as doing the Father's will, and so fulfilling all righteousness (comp. Matt. iii. 15).

(7) **The days come, saith the Lord.**—See Notes on chap. xvi. 14, 15, of which the words are almost verbally a reproduction. There, however, stress is laid chiefly on the fact of the exile, here on that of the restoration. The LXX. version omits them here, but inserts them, where they are obviously out of place, at the end of the chapter. It was fitting that they should be repeated here, as connecting the hope that had before been general with the personal reign of the "Branch" of the house of David.

(9) **Mine heart within me is broken . . .**—The abrupt transition shows that we are entering on an entirely new section. In the Hebrew order and punctuation of the words this is shown still more clearly—*Concerning the prophets: My heart is broken within me*—the first words being the superscription and title of what follows. The four clauses describe the varied phenomena of horror and amazement, and then comes the cause of the horror—the contrast between the words of Jehovah and His holiness on the one side, and the wickedness of priests and prophets on the other. The whole section is the complement of that which denounced the wickedness of the pastors—*i.e.*, of the civil rulers—in verses 1—4.

(10) **The land is full of adulterers.**—The context shows that the words must be taken literally, and not of the spiritual adultery of the worship of other Gods. The false prophets and their followers were personally profligates, like those of 2 Pet. ii. 14. (Comp. chaps. v. 7, 8, xxix. 23.)

Because of swearing.—Better, *because of the curse*—*i.e.*, that which comes from Jehovah on account of the wickedness of the people.

The land mourneth.—This, and the "drying up" of the "pleasant places" or "pastures," refers apparently to the drought described in chaps. xii. 4, xiv. 2, or to some similar visitation.

Their course.—Literally, *their running*—*i.e.*, their way or mode of life.

Their force is not right.—Literally, *their might* or *their valour:* that in which they exulted was might, not right.

(11) **In my house have I found their wickedness.**—Prophet and priest are joined, as before (chaps. v. 31, vi. 13, viii. 10), as playing into each other's hands. It seems probable, from chap. xxxii. 34, that the sins of Ahaz and Manasseh had been repeated under Jehoiakim, and that the worship of other gods had been carried on side by side with that of Jehovah. With this, almost as its natural accompaniment, there may have been sins of another kind—shameless greed or yet more shameless profligacy—like those of the sons of Eli (1 Sam. ii. 22).

(12) **Slippery ways . . . darkness . . . driven on.**—The words and the thoughts flow in upon the prophet's mind from Isa. viii. 22; Ps. xxxv. 5, 6.

The year of their visitation.—The prophet returns to his characteristic word for the time appointed by the Divine Judge for chastisement. (Comp. chaps. viii. 12, x. 15, xi. 23.)

(13) **I have seen folly. . .**—Literally, as in Job vi. 6, *that which is unsavoury*—*i.e.*, *insipid*, and so, ethically, *foolish*. The guilt of the prophets of Samaria cannot be passed over, but it is noticed, as in chap. iii. 6—10, only in order to compare it with the darker evils of those of Judah and Jerusalem.

They prophesied in Baal.—*i.e.*, in the name and as if by the power of Baal. Comp. 1 Kings xviii. 19, xxii. 6, 7.

(14) **They commit adultery, and walk in lies . . .**—The union of the claim to prophesy in the name of Jehovah with these flagrant breaches of His law was more hateful in the prophet's eyes even than the open recognition of Baal. In the terrible language of

[a]Sodom, and the inhabitants thereof as
Gomorrah.
(15) Therefore thus saith the LORD of
hosts concerning the prophets; Behold,
I will feed them with [b]wormwood, and
make them drink the water of gall: for
from the prophets of Jerusalem is [1]pro-
faneness gone forth into all the land.
(16) Thus saith the LORD of hosts,
Hearken not unto the words of the
prophets that prophesy unto you: they
make you vain: they speak a vision of
their own heart, *and* not out of the
mouth of the LORD. (17) They say still
unto them that despise me, The LORD
hath said, [c]Ye shall have peace; and
they say unto every one that walketh
after the [2]imagination of his own heart,
No evil shall come upon you. (18) For
who hath stood in the [3]counsel of the
LORD, and hath perceived and heard
his word? who hath marked his word,
and heard *it?* (19) Behold, a [d]whirlwind
of the LORD is gone forth in fury, even
a grievous whirlwind: it shall fall griev-
ously upon the head of the wicked.
(20) The [e]anger of the LORD shall not
return, until he have executed, and
till he have performed the thoughts of
his heart: in the latter days ye shall
consider it perfectly. (21) [f]I have not
sent these prophets, yet they ran: I
have not spoken to them, yet they pro-
phesied. (22) But if they had stood in
my counsel, and had caused my people
to hear my words, then they should
have turned them from their evil way,
and from the evil of their doings.
(23) *Am* I a God at hand, saith the LORD
and not a God afar off? (24) Can any

a Isa. 1. 9.
b ch. 8. 14; & 9. 15.
1 Or, *hypocrisy.*
c ch. 6. 14; & 8. 11; Ezek. 13. 10; Zech. 10. 2.
2 Or, *stubbornness.*
3 Or, *secret.*
d ch. 30. 23.
e ch. 30. 24.
f ch. 14. 14; & 27. 15.

Isaiah (i. 10), prophets and people had become like the dwellers in the cities of the plain. Here, also, the language of Deuteronomy (xxix. 23, xxxii. 32) probably influenced that of the prophet.

(15) **Wormwood . . . water of gall.**—See Notes on chaps. viii. 14, ix. 15.

Profaneness.—The root-meaning of the Hebrew word is that of "veiling," hence that of simulated holiness, or, as in the margin, "hypocrisy;" but the associations of the word attached to it the further sense of the hypocrisy that desecrates, so that "profaneness" is, on the whole, the best rendering. The corresponding concrete noun is rendered in Isa. ix. 17 by "hypocrite;" in Ps. xxxv. 16 by "hypocritical mocker;" above, in verse 11, by "profane."

(16) **They make you vain.**—*i.e., they befool, deceive you.* As the next verse shows, they filled the people with vain hopes of peace. This was then, as always, the crucial test between the true prophet and the false. The one roused the conscience, caused pain and anger by his reproofs; the other soothed and quieted men with a false assurance (chaps. vi. 14, xiv. 13). They invented a vision which did not come to them from the mouth of Jehovah. (Comp. Deut. xiii. 1—5.)

(17) **Imagination.**—As before (chap. iii. 17 and elsewhere), *stubbornness.* The tendency of all that the false prophets uttered was to confirm the people in their sins, not to lead them to repentance. It is noticeable that the Hebrew verb for "hath *said*" is not the same as the received formula of the true prophets, "The Lord hath *spoken.*" The prophet seems to indicate in this way that those whom he condemns placed the Divine message on a level with a man's every-day utterance. They were self-convicted by the very phrase they used.

(18) **The counsel.**—Better, perhaps, *the council,* the "assembly" of chosen friends with whom a man shares his secret plans. So in chaps. vi. 11, xv. 17; Ps. lxxxix. 7, "assembly." Could any of the false prophets say that they had thus been called as into the privy council of Jehovah? (Comp. Amos iii. 7; 1 Kings xxii. 19—23.)

(19) **Behold, a whirlwind . . .**—Better, *Behold, the storm of Jehovah, wrath is gone forth, a whirling storm, upon the heads of the wicked shall it whirl down.* The word translated "whirlwind" is properly more generic in its meaning ("tempest" in Isa. xxix. 6), and gets its specific force here from the associated word rendered in the Authorised Version "grievous," but rightly, as above, *whirling.*

(20) **Shall not return . . .**—*i.e.,* shall not *turn back* from its purpose. Men should look back on it in the "latter days"—literally, *the end of the days* (Gen. xlix. 1; Num. xxiv. 14; Deut. iv. 30, xxxi. 29), *i.e.,* in the then distant future of the exile and the return—and should see that it had done its work both of chastisement and discipline. (Comp. Ezek. xiv. 22, 23.)

(21) **Yet they ran.**—The image is that of messengers who rush eagerly, as from the king's council-chamber, on their self-appointed mission, without waiting for the command of the Master in whose name they profess to come. (Comp. the question, "Who will go for us?" in Isa. vi. 8.)

(22) **If they had stood in my counsel.**—Better, as before, *council.* The test of the true mission is seen in results. Are the people better or worse for the prophet's work? What are the fruits of his teaching? (Comp. Matt. vii. 20.) The question meets us, Is this always a test? Was Jeremiah's own work successful in this sense? Must not the true teacher speak "whether they [men] will hear, or whether they will forbear?" (Ezek. ii. 5.) The answer is found (1) in the fact that true teaching seldom fails altogether of its work; (2) that where it seems to fail it satisfies the other test, and at least stirs and rouses men from lethargy, even if it stirs them to antagonism. It is never satisfied with speaking smooth things and acquiescing in the evil that surrounds it.

(23) **Am I a God at hand . . .?**—This and the two questions that follow are essentially the same in thought. The false prophets acted as if God were far away out of their sight (Pss. x. 11, lxxiii. 11, xciv. 7), not knowing or caring what men did, as if their affairs, as it has been epigrammatically said, came under a "colonial department." The true prophet feels that He is equally near, equally God, in all places alike. Familiar as the word omnipresence is to us—so familiar as almost to have lost its power—the fact, when we realise it, is as awful now as it was when it presented itself to the souls

[a]hide himself in secret places that I shall
not see him? saith the LORD. Do not
I fill heaven and earth? saith the LORD.
(25) I have heard what the prophets
said, that prophesy lies in my name,
saying, I have dreamed, I have dreamed.
(26) How long shall *this* be in the heart
of the prophets that prophesy lies? yea,
they are prophets of the deceit of their
own heart; (27) which think to cause
my people to forget my name by their
dreams which they tell every man to his
neighbour, [b]as their fathers have for-
gotten my name for Baal. (28) The pro-
phet [1]that hath a dream, let him tell a
dream; and he that hath my word, let
him speak my word faithfully. What
is the chaff to the wheat? saith the
LORD. (29) *Is* not my word like as a
fire? saith the LORD; and like a ham-
mer *that* breaketh the rock in pieces?
(30) Therefore, behold, [c]I *am* against the
prophets, saith the LORD, that steal my
words every one from his neighbour.
(31) Behold, I *am* against the prophets,
saith the LORD, [2]that use their tongues,
and say, He saith. (32) Behold, I *am*
against them that prophesy false dreams,
saith the LORD, and do tell them, and
cause my people to err by their lies, and
by their lightness; yet I sent them not,
nor commanded them: therefore they
shall not profit this people at all, saith
the LORD.

[a] Ps. 139. 7, &c.; Amos 9. 2, 3.

[b] Judges 3. 7; & 8. 33.

[1] Heb., *with whom is.*

[c] Deut. 18. 20; ch. 14. 14, 15.

[2] Or, *that smooth their tongues.*

---

of Patriarch, Psalmist, or Prophet. (Gen. xvi. 13; Pss. xxxii. 6, 7, lxxiii. 23—26, cxxxix. 7—12; Amos ix. 2—4; Job xi. 8—9.

(25) **I have dreamed . . .**—The words point to the form of the claim commonly made by the false prophets. Dreams took their place among the recognised channels of divine revelation (Gen. xl. 8, xli. 16; Joel ii. 28; Dan. vii. 1), but their frequent misuse by the false prophets brought them into discredit, and the teaching of Deut. xiii. 1—5 accordingly brought the "dreamer of dreams" no less than the prophet to the test whether what he taught was in accordance with the law of Jehovah. The iteration of "I have dreamed" represents the affected solemnity with which the false prophets proclaimed their visions. Of the disparagement of dreams, consequent on this abuse, we have a striking example in Eccles. v. 3, and later still in Ecclus. xxxiv. 1—7.

(26) **How long shall this be . . . ?**—The Hebrew text gives a double interrogative: *How long? Is it in the heart of the prophets that prophesy lies, prophets of the deceit of their own hearts? Do they think to cause my people . . . ?* A conjectural alteration of the text gives "How long is the fire in the heart of the prophets . . . ?" as if anticipating the thought of verse 29, and reproducing that of chap. xx. 9.

(27) **As their fathers have forgotten . . .**—The two evils of open idolatry and of false claims to prophecy stood, the prophet seems to say, on the same footing. The misuse of the name of Jehovah by the false prophets was as bad as the older worship of Baal and the prophesying in his name. (Comp. verses 13, 14.)

(28) **Let him tell a dream.**—The point of the words lies in the contrast between the real and the counterfeit revelation. Let the dreamer tell his dream as such, let the prophet speak the word of Jehovah truly, and then it will be seen that the one is as the chaff and stubble, and the other as the wheat—one worthless, the other sustaining life. What have they in common? What has one to do with the other?

(29) **Is not my word like as a fire? . . .**—The prophet speaks out of the depths of his own experience. The true prophetic word burns in the heart of a man, and will not be restrained (chaps. v. 14, xx. 9; Ps. xxxix. 3), and when uttered it consumes the evil, and purifies the good. It will burn up the chaff of the utterances of the false prophets. (Comp. 1 Cor. iii. 12, 13.) As the hammer breaks the rock, so it shatters the pride and stubbornness of man, is mighty to the pulling down of strongholds (2 Cor. x. 4), and the heart of him who hears it as it should be heard is broken and contrite. What these words paint in the language of poetry, St. Paul describes without imagery in 1 Cor. xiv. 24, 25. (Comp. also Heb. iv. 12.)

(30) **That steal my words . . .**—Another note of the counterfeit prophet is found in the want of any living personal originality. The oracles of the dreamers were patchworks of plagiarism, and they borrowed, not as men might do legitimately, and as Jeremiah himself did, from the words of the great teachers of the past, but from men of their own time, false and unreal as themselves. What we should call the "clique" of false prophets went on repeating each other's phrases with a wearisome iteration. In "my words" we have, probably, the fact that, in part also, they decked out their teaching with the borrowed plumes of phrases from true prophets.

(31) **That use their tongues, and say, He saith.**—Literally, *that take their tongues.* There is no adequate evidence for the marginal rendering "that smooth their tongues." The scornful phrase indicates the absence of a true inspiration. These false prophets plan their schemes, and take their tongue as an instrument for carrying them into effect. The formula which they used, "He saith," was not the word for common speaking, but that which indicated that the speaker was delivering an oracle from God. (See Note on verse 17.) Elsewhere the word is only used of God, but the prophet, in his stern irony, uses it of the false prophets, *they say oracularly, This is an oracle.*

(32) **False dreams.**—The words may mean either actual dreams, which have nothing answering to them in the world of facts, or dreams which are not really such, but simply, as in verse 31, the form in which the deceiver seeks to work out his plans.

By their lightness.—The Hebrew word is the same in meaning as the "unstable as water" of Gen. xlix. 4, the "light persons" of Judges ix. 4; Zeph. iii. 4, and points primarily to the gushing or spurting forth of water. Here it points to what we may call the "babbling" of the false prophets. We are almost reminded of the words in which an English poet describes a hollow and pretentious eloquence as poured out—

"In one weak, washy, everlasting flood."

(33) And when this people, or the prophet, or a priest, shall ask thee, saying, What *is* the burden of the LORD? thou shalt then say unto them, What burden? I will even forsake you, saith the LORD.
(34) And *as for* the prophet, and the priest, and the people, that shall say, The burden of the LORD, I will even [1]punish that man and his house.
(35) Thus shall ye say every one to his neighbour, and every one to his brother, What hath the LORD answered? and, What hath the LORD spoken?
(36) And the burden of the LORD shall ye mention no more: for every man's word shall be his burden; for ye have perverted the words of the living God, of the LORD of hosts our God.
(37) Thus shalt thou say to the prophet, What hath the LORD answered thee? and, What hath the LORD spoken?
(38) But since ye say, The burden of the LORD; therefore thus saith the LORD; Because ye say this word, The burden of the LORD, and I have sent unto you, saying, Ye shall not say, The burden of the LORD;
(39) therefore, behold, I, even I, will utterly forget you, and I will forsake you, and the city that I gave you and your fathers, *and cast you* out of my presence:
(40) and I will bring [a]an everlasting reproach upon you, and a perpetual shame, which shall not be forgotten.

1 Heb., *visit upon.*

a ch. 20. 11.

B. C. cir. 598.

b 2 Kings 24. 12; 2 Chron. 36. 10.

CHAPTER XXIV. — (1) The LORD shewed me, and, behold, two baskets of figs *were* set before the temple of the LORD, after that Nebuchadrezzar [b]king

---

Therefore . . .—Better, simply, *and they shall not profit.*

(33) **The burden of the Lord.**—The English expresses the literal meaning of the word, "something lifted up, or borne." It passed, however, as the English equivalent has done, through many shades of meaning, and became, in the language of the prophets, one of the received terms for a solemn, emphatic utterance. In 1 Chron. xv. 22, 27 it is applied to the chanted music of the Temple. Isaiah had brought it into use (see Note on Isa. xiii. 1), and employs it twelve times as the title of special prophecies. Jeremiah never uses it of his own messages, probably, as this verse indicates, because it had become a favourite formula with the false prophets. This seems a more rational view than that which assumes that the false prophets applied the words in mockery to his utterances as being "burdens" in the ordinary sense of the word, oppressive and intolerable.

What burden?—The false prophets had come, not without a supercilious scorn, asking, with affected grandeur, what burden, what oracle Jeremiah had from Jehovah. He repeats their question with a deeper scorn, and tells them that for them the "burden" tells of exile and shame. A different division of the words of the prophet's answer (which presents some exceptional grammatical difficulties) gives a rendering adopted by the LXX. and Vulgate, "Ye are the burden"—*i.e.*, it is about you and for you.

I will even forsake you.—Better, *I will cast you off,* with a play upon the literal sense of the word "burden." They have made themselves too grievous to be borne. Jehovah will *disburden* Himself of them.

(34) **That shall say, The burden of the Lord.**—The language thus put into the mouths of the false prophets is not that of derision, but of boastful assumption. It is for that the boaster will, in due time, be punished.

(35) **Thus shall ye say . . .**—The words are a protest against the high-sounding phrase, "This is the burden, the oracle of Jehovah." This, with which the false prophets covered their teachings of lies, the prophet rejects, and he calls men back to the simpler terms, which were less open to abuse. The true prophet's message was to be called an "answer" when men had come to him with questions—a "word of the Lord" when it was spoken to them without any previous inquiry.

(36) **The burden of the Lord shall ye mention no more . . .**—The misused term was no longer to be applied to the messages of Jehovah. If men continued to apply it to the words of their own heart, they would find it a "burden" in another sense (the prophet plays once more on the etymology of the word) too heavy to be borne. This would be the righteous punishment of the reckless levity with which they had treated the sacred Name which Jeremiah reproduces in all the amplitude of its grandeur. They had never realised the awfulness of speaking in the name "of the living God, the Lord of Sabaoth."

(37) **Thus shalt thou say to the prophet . . .**—The verse repeats verse 35, with the one difference that men are to use this, the simpler form of language, when they come to the prophet, as well as when they are speaking one to another. The affectation of big words was equally out of place in either case. In modern phraseology, the whole passage is a protest against the hypocrisy which shows itself in cant—*i.e.*, in the use of solemn words that have become hollow and unmeaning.

(38) **But since ye say.**—Better, *if ye say.*

(39) **I, even I, will utterly forget you . . .**—A very slight alteration in a single letter of the Hebrew verb gives a rendering which was followed by the LXX. and Vulgate, and is adopted by many modern commentators, and connects it with the root of the word translated "burden"—*I will take you up as a burden, and cast you off.* The words in italics, *and cast you,* in the latter clause have nothing corresponding to them in the Hebrew, but show that some at least of the translators felt that this was the true meaning of the words. This "everlasting reproach" was to be the outcome of these big swelling words of vanity in which they claimed prophetic inspiration.

XXIV.

(1) **The Lord shewed me . . .**—The chapter belongs to the same period as the two preceding, *i.e.*, to the reign of Zedekiah, after the first capture of Jerusalem and the captivity of the chief inhabitants. The

of Babylon had carried away captive
Jeconiah the son of Jehoiakim king of
Judah, and the princes of Judah, with
the carpenters and smiths, from Jeru-
salem, and had brought them to Baby-
lon. (2) One basket *had* very good figs,
even like the figs *that are* first ripe: and
the other basket *had* very naughty figs,
which could not be eaten, [1]they were so
bad.
(3) Then said the LORD unto me, What
seest thou, Jeremiah? And I said, Figs;
the good figs, very good; and the evil,
very evil, that cannot be eaten, they are
so evil.
(4) Again the word of the LORD came
unto me, saying, (5) Thus saith the
LORD, the God of Israel; Like these
good figs, so will I acknowledge [2]them
that are carried away captive of Judah,
whom I have sent out of this place into
the land of the Chaldeans for *their* good.
(6) For I will set mine eyes upon them
for good, and I will bring them again to
this land: and I will build them, and
not pull *them* down; and I will plant
them, and not pluck *them* up. (7) And
I will give them [a]an heart to know me,
that I *am* the LORD: and they shall be
[b]my people, and I will be their God: for
they shall return unto me with their
whole heart.

1 Heb., *for badness.*

2 Heb., *the captivity.*

a Deut. 30. 6; ch. 32. 39; Ezek. 11. 19; & 36. 26, 27.

b ch. 30. 22; & 31. 33; & 32. 38.

---

opening words indicate that the symbols on which the prophet looked were seen in vision, as in Amos vii. 1, 4, 7; Zech. i. 8, ii. 1, and the symbols of chap. i. 11, 13; or, if seen with the eyes of the body, were looked on as with the prophet-poet's power of finding parables in all things. The fact that the figs were set before the Temple of the Lord is significant. They were as a votive offering, first-fruits (Exod. xxiii. 19; Deut. xxvi. 2) or tithes brought to the Lord of Israel. A like imagery had been used by Amos (viii. 1, 2) with nearly the same formulæ.

The carpenters and smiths.—See 2 Kings xxiv. 14. The word for "carpenters" includes *craftsmen* of all kinds. The deportation of these classes was partly a matter of policy, making the city more helpless by removing those who might have forged weapons or strengthened its defences, partly, doubtless, of ostentation, that they might help in the construction of the buildings with which Nebuchadnezzar was increasing the splendour of his city. So Esar-haddon records how he made his captives "work in fetters, in making bricks" (*Records of the Past*, iii. p. 120). So, from the former point of view, the Philistines in the time of Samuel either carried off the smiths of Israel or forbade the exercise of their calling (1 Sam. xiii. 19). The word for "smith" is found in Isa. xxiv. 22, xlii. 7 in the sense of "prison," but, as applied to persons, only here and in the parallel passage of 2 Kings xxiv. 14, 16. It has been differently interpreted as meaning "locksmiths," "gatekeepers," "strangers," "hod-carriers," and "day-labourers." Probably the rendering of the E.V. is right.

(2) **Like the figs that are first ripe.**—Figs were usually gathered in August. The "first ripe," the "summer fruits" of Micah vii. 1, the "hasty fruit before the summer" (Isa. xxviii. 4; Hosea ix. 10) were looked upon as a choice delicacy. The "naughty" (*i.e.*, worthless) fruits were those that had been left behind on the tree, bruised and decayed. The word was not confined in the 16th century to the language of the nursery, and was applied freely to things as well as persons. So North's translation of Plutarch speaks of men "fighting on *naughty* ground."

"So shines a good deed in a *naughty* world."
SHAKESPEARE, *Merchant of Venice*, v. 1.

(3) **What seest thou, Jeremiah?**—The question is asked as if to force the symbol as strongly as possible on the prophet's mind, leaving him to wait till another word of the Lord should come and reveal its true interpretation. We are reminded, as he must have been, of the vision and the question which had first called him to his work as a prophet (chap. i. 11).

(4) **Again the word of the Lord came unto me.**—The words seem to imply an interval, during which the prophet was left to ponder over the symbols that he had thus seen. At last "the word of the Lord came" and made their meaning clear.

(5) **So will I acknowledge.**—The expected revelation came. The two baskets represented the two sections of the people. The captives who had been carried to Babylon were, as the list shows, for the most part of higher rank than those who were left behind. The workmen were the skilled labourers of the artisan class. There are many indications that under the teaching of Daniel and his companions, and of Ezekiel, they were improving morally under their discipline of suffering. Their very contact with the monstrous idolatry of Babylon made them more conscious than they had ever been before of the greatness of their own faith. The process which, at the end of the seventy years of exile, made them once more and for ever a purely monotheistic people had already begun.

(6) **I will set mine eyes upon them for good.**—The state of the Jews at Babylon at the time of the return from exile was obviously far above that of slaves or prisoners. They had money (Ezra ii. 69), they cultivated land, they built houses (chap. xxix. 4, 28). Many were reluctant to leave their new home for the land of their fathers, and among these must have been the families represented at a later date by Ezra and the priests and Levites who accompanied him (Ezra viii. 15). They were not subjected, as many conquered nations have been, to the misery of a second emigration to a more distant land. The victory of Cyrus manifestly brought with it every way an improvement in their condition; but even under Nebuchadnezzar they rose, as in the case of Daniel and his companions, to high honour.

(7) **I will give them an heart to know me . . .**—Of this also the history of the return gives at least a partial proof. Whatever other faults might be growing up, they never again fell into the apostasy from the true faith in God, which up to the time of the exile had been their besetting sin.

They shall be my people . . .—The prophet clearly remembers and reproduces the promise of Hosea ii. 23.

(8) And as the evil [a]figs, which cannot
be eaten, they are so evil; surely thus
saith the LORD, So will I give Zedekiah
the king of Judah, and his princes, and
the residue of Jerusalem, that remain in
this land, and them that dwell in the
land of Egypt: (9) and I will deliver
them [1]to [b]be removed into all the king-
doms of the earth for *their* hurt, *to be* a
reproach and a proverb, a taunt and a
curse, in all places whither I shall drive
them. (10) And I will send the sword,
the famine, and the pestilence, among
them, till they be consumed from off the
land that I gave unto them and to their
fathers.

CHAPTER XXV.—(1) The word that
came to Jeremiah concerning all the
people of Judah in the fourth year of
Jehoiakim the son of Josiah king of
Judah, that *was* the first year of Nebu-
chadrezzar king of Babylon; (2) the
which Jeremiah the prophet spake unto
all the people of Judah, and to all the
inhabitants of Jerusalem, saying,

(3) From the thirteenth year of Josiah
the son of Amon king of Judah, even
unto this day, that *is* the three and
twentieth year, the word of the LORD
hath come unto me, and I have spoken
unto you, rising early and speaking;
but ye have not hearkened. (4) And the
LORD hath sent unto you all his servants
the prophets, [c]rising early and sending
them; but ye have not hearkened, nor
inclined your ear to hear. (5) They said,
[d]Turn ye again now every one from his
evil way, and from the evil of your
doings, and dwell in the land that the
LORD hath given unto you and to your
fathers for ever and ever: (6) and go
not after other gods to serve them, and
to worship them, and provoke me not to
anger with the works of your hands;
and I will do you no hurt. (7) Yet ye
have not hearkened unto me, saith the
LORD; that ye might provoke me to
anger with the works of your hands to
your own hurt.

(8) Therefore thus saith the LORD of
hosts; Because ye have not heard my

a ch. 29. 17.

1 Heb., *for removing,* or, *vexation.*

b Deut. 28. 37; ch. 15. 4.

c ch. 29. 19.

B. C. 607 ending. B. C. 606 beginning.

d 2 Kings 17. 13; ch. 18. 11; & 35. 15; Jonah 3. 8.

---

(8) **And them that dwell in the land of Egypt.**—These were, in fact, such as had been carried into captivity with Jehoahaz by Pharaoh-nechoh (see Note on chap. xxii. 11), or had fled thither in order to avoid submission to Nebuchadnezzar, and were settled in Migdol, and Tahpanhes, and Noph. We meet with them later on in chap. xliv. For these there was to be no return, no share in the work of restoration. They formed the nucleus of the Jewish population of Egypt, and in course of time (B.C. 150) set up a rival temple at Leontopolis. (See Note on Isa. xix. 19.)

(9) **To be a reproach and a proverb.**—The language of the verse is coloured by that of Deut. xxviii. 25, 37, from which most of the words are chosen.

(10) **The sword, the famine, and the pestilence.**—The three forms of suffering are grouped together, as in chap. xiv. 12 and Ezek. xiv. 21. The two latter followed almost inevitably in the wake of the first.

XXV.

(1) **In the fourth year of Jehoiakim the son of Josiah.**—We are carried back in the present arrangement of Jeremiah's prophecies to a much earlier period than that of the preceding chapter. It is the fourth (in Dan. i. 1, the third) year of the reign of Jehoiakim, who had been made king by Pharaoh-nechoh after his defeat of Josiah and capture of Jerusalem. Since the prophet had been called to his work, B.C. 629, a great revolution had been brought about in the relations of the colossal monarchies of the East. Nineveh had fallen (B.C. 606) under the attacks of Cyaxares the Mede, and Nabopolassar the Chaldæan. Nebuchadnezzar, the son of the latter, though his father did not die till the following year, was practically clothed with supreme authority, and had defeated Pharaoh-nechoh at Carchemish, on the banks of the Euphrates, in B.C. 605. The form of the name used here, Nebuchadrezzar, corresponds with the Assyrian, *Nabu-kudu-ur-uzur.* (Chap. xlvi. 1; 2 Kings xxiii. 29; 2 Chron. xxxv. 20.) He was now the master of the East, and it was given to Jeremiah to discern the bearings of the new situation on the future destinies of Judah, and to see that the wisdom of its rulers would be to accept the position of tributary rulers under the great conqueror instead of rashly seeking either to assert their independence or to trust to the support of Egypt, crushed as she was by the defeat at Carchemish. The clear vision of the prophet saw in the Chaldæan king the servant of Jehovah—in modern phrase, the instrument of the designs of the Providence which orders the events of history—and he became, from that moment, the unwelcome preacher of the truth—that the independence of Judah had passed away, and that nothing but evil could follow from fanatical attempts, or secret intrigues and alliances, aiming at resistance.

(3) **The three and twentieth year** (B.C. 603—4).—Thus there had been nineteen years of prophetic work under Josiah, and between three and four under Jehoiakim (chap. i. 2). Of the former period we have but scanty record. The year is noticeable as that which apparently witnessed the first collection of Jeremiah's prophetic utterances (chap. xxxvi. 5—8).

Rising early and speaking.—See Note on vii. 13.

(5) **Turn ye again now . . .**—The sum and substance of the work of all true prophets has always been found, it need scarcely be said, in the call to repentance and conversion; but there is, perhaps, a special reference to the substance of their preaching as recorded in 2 Kings xvii. 13. The words are interesting as showing that Jeremiah was probably seconded in his work by other prophets whose names have not come down to us.

(6) **The works of your hands.**—These were, of course, the idols which they had made and worshipped.

words, (9) behold, I will send and take
all the families of the north, saith the
LORD, and Nebuchadrezzar the king of
Babylon, my servant, and will bring
them against this land; and against the
inhabitants thereof, and against all
these nations round about, and will
utterly destroy them, and make them
an astonishment, and an hissing, and
perpetual desolations. (10) Moreover [1]I
will take from them the [a]voice of mirth,
and the voice of gladness, the voice of
the bridegroom, and the voice of the
bride, the sound of the millstones, and
the light of the candle. (11) And this
whole land shall be a desolation, *and* an
astonishment; and these nations shall
serve the king of Babylon seventy years.
(12) And it shall come to pass, [b]when
seventy years are accomplished, *that* I
will [2]punish the king of Babylon, and
that nation, saith the LORD, for their
iniquity, and the land of the Chaldeans,
and will make it perpetual desolations.
(13) And I will bring upon that land all
my words which I have pronounced
against it, *even* all that is written in
this book, which Jeremiah hath pro-
phesied against all the nations. (14) For
many nations and great kings shall
[c]serve themselves of them also: and I
will recompense them according to their
deeds, and according to the works of
their own hands.
(15) For thus saith the LORD God of
Israel unto me; Take the [d]wine cup
of this fury at my hand, and cause
all the nations, to whom I send thee,
to drink it. (16) And they shall drink,
and be moved, and be mad, because of

1 Heb., *I will cause to perish from them.*

a ch. 7. 34; & 16. 9; Ezek. 26. 13; Hosea 2. 11.

b 2 Chron. 36. 21, 22; Ezra 1. 1; ch. 29. 10; Dan. 9. 2.

2 Heb., *visit upon.*

c ch. 27. 7.

d Job 21. 20; Ps. 75. 8; Isa. 51. 17.

---

(9) **The families of the north.**—The phrase reminds us of the vision of "the seething pot *from the face of the north*" in chap. i. 13, and includes all the mingled races, Scythians and others, who owned the sway of the Chaldæan king.

Nebuchadrezzar . . . my servant.—The use of the word which is applied by psalmists and prophets to David (Ps. lxxviii. 70; 2 Sam. vii. 8) and to the future Christ (Isa. xlii. 1, lii. 13) is every way remarkable. It has its parallel, and, in fact, its explanation, in the language in which Isaiah speaks of Cyrus as the shepherd, the anointed, of Jehovah. (Isa. xliv. 28, xlv. i.) Each ruler of the great empires of the world was, in ways he knew not, working out the purposes of God. The phrase "I will utterly destroy" may be noted as specially characteristic of Deuteronomy (ii. 34, iii. 6, *et al.*) and Joshua (ii. 10, vi. 21, viii. 26).

(10) **The voice of mirth, and the voice of gladness.**—The language is mainly an echo of chaps. vii. 34 and xvi. 9, but there are new features in the cessation of "the sound of the millstone," *i.e.*, of the grinding of corn by female slaves for the mid-day meal (Exod. xi. 5; Matt. xxiv. 41), and the lighting of the candle when the day's work was done (Matt. v. 15). No words could paint more terribly the entire breaking up of family life, not only in its occasional festivities, but in its daily routine. The imagery reappears in Rev. xviii. 22, 23.

(11) **Shall serve the king of Babylon seventy years.**—This is the first mention of the duration of the captivity. The seventy years are commonly reckoned from B.C. 606, the date of the deportation of Jehoiakim and his princes, to B.C. 536, when the decree for the return of the exiles was issued by Cyrus. In 2 Chron. xxxvi. 21 the number is connected with the land "enjoying her Sabbaths," as though the long desolation came as a retribution for the people's neglect of the law of the Sabbatical year, and, perhaps, also for their non-observance of the weekly Sabbaths. (Isa. lvi. 4; Jer. xvii. 21, 22.) For the apportionment of the reigns of the Babylonian kings that made up the seventy years, see the *Chronological Table* in the *Introduction*. Symbolically the number, as the multiple of seven and ten, represents the highest measure of completeness (comp. Matt. xviii. 22).

(12) **I will punish the king of Babylon . . .**—The words are omitted in the LXX. version of the chapter, which differs materially from the Hebrew text, and there are some internal grounds for suspecting it to be a later addition, possibly from the hand of the prophet himself, or, more probably, from that of Baruch as collecting and editing his writings, or of some later transcriber. In verse 26, as commonly interpreted, there is a prediction of the destruction of the king of Babylon veiled in enigmatic language. That we can understand well enough, if it was meant only for the initiated, but it is not easy to see why the same prophetic discourse should contain both the veiled and the open prediction. On the relation of the LXX. version to the Hebrew, see *Introduction*.

(13) **Which Jeremiah hath prophesied . . .**—Here again we have the trace of an interpolation. In the LXX. the words appear detached, as a title, and are followed by xlix. 35—39, and the other prophecies against the nations which the Hebrew text places at the end of the book (chaps. xlvi.—li.). The words "all that is written in this book" are manifestly the addition of a scribe. (See *Introduction.*)

(14) **Shall serve themselves of them.**—Better, *shall make them their servants.* The English "serve themselves" (a Gallicism in common use in the seventeenth century), which occurs again in chap. xxvii. 7, is now ambiguous, and hardly conveys the force of the original. What is meant is that the law of retribution will in due time be seen in its action upon those who were now masters of the world. The thought is the same as that expressed in the familiar "*Græcia capta ferum victorem cepit*" of Horace (Ep. II. i., 156).

(15) **For thus saith the Lord God.**—In the LXX. this is preceded by chaps. xlvi.—li., which are in their turn in a different order from that of the Hebrew.

The wine cup of this fury.—Literally, *the cup of wine, even this fury*, or, better, *this wrath.*

(16) **They shall drink . . .**—The words describe what history has often witnessed, the panic-terror of lesser nations before the onward march of a great conqueror—they are as if stricken with a drunken madness, and their despair or their resistance is equally infatuated. The imagery is one familiar in earlier

the sword that I will send among
them.
(17) Then took I the cup at the LORD'S
hand, and made all the nations to drink,
unto whom the LORD had sent me: (18) *to
wit*, Jerusalem, and the cities of Judah,
and the kings thereof, and the princes
thereof, to make them a desolation, an
astonishment, an hissing, and a curse;
as *it is* this day; (19) Pharaoh king of
Egypt, and his servants, and his princes,
and all his people; (20) and all the min-
gled people, and all the kings of the land
of Uz, and all the kings of the land
of the Philistines, and Ashkelon, and
Azzah, and Ekron, and the remnant of
Ashdod, (21) [a]Edom, and [b]Moab, and
the children of [c]Ammon, (22) and all the
kings of [d]Tyrus, and all the kings of
Zidon, and the kings of the [1]isles which
are beyond the [e]sea, (23) [f]Dedan, and
Tema, and Buz, and all [2]*that are* in the
utmost corners, (24) and all the kings of
Arabia, and all the kings of the [g]mingled
people that dwell in the desert, (25) and
all the kings of Zimri, and all the kings

a ch. 49. 7, &c.
b ch. 48. 1.
c ch. 49. 1.
d ch. 47. 4.
1 Or, *region by the sea side.*
e ch. 49. 23.
f ch. 49. 8.
2 Heb., *cut off into corners*, or, *having the corners of the hair polled*: ch. 9. 26.
g ch. 49. 31.

---

prophets. (Isa. li. 17, 22; Hab. ii. 16; Pss. lx. 5, lxxv. 8; Ezek. xxiii. 31.)

(17) **Then took I the cup . . .**—The words describe the act of the prophet as in the ecstasy of vision. One by one the nations are made to drink of that cup of the wrath of Jehovah of which His own country was to have the first and fullest draught. It is a strange example of the literalism of minds incapable of entering into the poetry of a prophet's work, that one commentator (Michaelis) has supposed that the prophet offered an actual goblet of wine to the ambassadors of the states named, who were then, as he imagines, assembled at Jerusalem, as in chap. xxvii. 3.

(18) **As it is this day.**—The words are not in the LXX., and may probably have been added after the prediction had received its fulfilment in the final capture of Jerusalem and the desolation of the country. Here, as before in verse 13, we trace the hand of a transcriber. It will be noted that the prophet begins with the judgment about to fall on his own people, and then passes on from "the house of God" (1 Pet. iv. 17) to those that are without.

(19) **Pharaoh king of Egypt . . .**—The list of the nations begins, it will be seen, from the south and proceeds northwards; those that lay on the east and west being named, as it were, literally, according to their position. The Pharaoh of the time was Nechoh, who had been defeated at Carchemish.

(20) **All the mingled people.**—The word is all but identical with that used in Exod. xii. 38 of the "mixed multitude" that accompanied the Israelites from Egypt, and in Neh. xiii. 3 of the alien population of Jerusalem. It occurs again in verse 24, chap. l. 37, and Ezek. xxx. 5, and is applied to the tribes of mixed races who were, in various degrees tributary to the state in connection with which they are named. Here the word probably refers to the Ionians or Carians whom Psammitichus, the father of Nechoh, had settled at Bubastis, and who served in his army as auxiliaries. (Herod. ii. 152, 154.)

Uz.—A district of Edom, famous as the scene of the great drama of the book of Job. It is commonly identified with the *Arabia Deserta* of classical geography. (See Notes on Job i. 1; Gen. x. 23.)

The land of the Philistines.—The four cities that follow belong to the same region. "Azzah" is the same as Gaza, the translators of the Authorised Version having in this instance, and in Deut. ii. 23; 1 Kings iv. 24, adopted this instead of the more familiar form of the LXX. and Vulgate. "Gath," which appears in the older lists of the five lords of the Philistines (1 Sam. v. 8, vi. 17, vii. 14), has disappeared, having possibly seceded from the confederacy. The "remnant of Ashdod" (the Greek Azotus) is a phrase characteristic of the prophet's time, the Egyptian king Psammitichus having captured it, after a siege of twenty-nine years, in B.C. 630. (Herod. ii. 157.)

(22) **The isles which are beyond the sea.**—Better, *island*. The Hebrew word is in the singular, and is properly, as in the margin, a "region by the sea-side"—a "coast-land," and thus wider in its extent than our "island." Here the position in which it occurs tends to identify it either with Cyprus or the coast of Cilicia, or Phœnician colonies generally in the Mediterranean. Cyprus seems the most probable of these.

(23) **Dedan, and Tema, and Buz.**—From the west we pass again to the east, the first two districts lying to the south-east of Edom, the last probably in the same region. For Dedan see Gen. x. 7, xxv. 3, 2; 1 Chron. i. 9, 32; Isa. xxi. 13; Ezek. xxv. 13. For Tema, on the modern pilgrims' road from Damascus to Mecca, see Isa. xxi. 14; Job vi. 19. For Buz see Gen. xxii. 21. The fact that the "travelling companies of Dedanim" (Isa. xxi. 13) carried on the trade between Tyre and Arabia (Ezek. xxvii. 15) accounts in part for their mention here.

All that are in the utmost corners.—The marginal reading gives the true meaning—*all that have the corners of their temples shorn.* (See Note on chap. ix. 26.) The words point to the nomad tribes of Kedar, who were distinguished by this peculiarity. For "mingled people," see Note on verse 20. The genealogies of Gen. x., xxv. 1—16, and 1 Chron. i. point to a great intermingling of Cushite and Semitic races in these regions.

(24) **All the kings of Arabia.**—The same phrase occurs in 1 Kings x. 15, and is used for the nomadic tribes bordering on Palestine rather than in the wider sense of classical geographers.

(25) **Zimri.**—The name occurs nowhere else in the Bible or out of it as the name of a country. It is possibly connected with Zimran, the eldest son of Abraham by Keturah (Gen. xxv. 2), and points, therefore—as does its position here—to a nomad tribe in Arabia lying between the Red Sea, Arabia, and the Persian Gulf. The name Zabram occurs in Greek geographers as that of a city on the Red Sea west of Mecca, and there was a Zimara on the Upper Euphrates. "Elam," properly applied to the region of which Susa was the capital (Dan. viii. 2), was extended by the Hebrew writers to the whole of Persia. (See Notes on Gen. x. 22, xiv. 1—12; Isa. xxi. 2.) As in the last of these references, it is coupled here with Media.

of [a]Elam, and all the kings of the Medes,
(26) and all the kings of the north, far
and near, one with another, and all the
kingdoms of the world, which *are* upon
the face of the earth: and the king of
Sheshach shall drink after them.
(27) Therefore thou shalt say unto
them, Thus saith the LORD of hosts,
the God of Israel; Drink ye, and be
drunken, and spue, and fall, and rise
no more, because of the sword which I
will send among you. (28) And it shall
be, if they refuse to take the cup at
thine hand to drink, then shalt thou
say unto them, Thus saith the LORD
of hosts; Ye shall certainly drink.
(29) For, lo, I begin to bring evil on the
[b]city [1]which is called by my name, and
should ye be utterly unpunished? Ye
shall not be unpunished: for I will call
for a sword upon all the inhabitants
of the earth, saith the LORD of hosts.
(30) Therefore prophesy thou against
them all these words, and say unto
them,

The LORD shall [c]roar from on high,
and utter his voice from his holy habi-
tation; he shall mightily roar upon his
habitation; he shall give a shout, as
they that tread *the grapes*, against all

[a] ch. 49. 34.
[b] 1 Peter 4. 17.
[1] Heb., *upon which my name is called.*
[c] Joel 3. 16; Amos 1. 2.

---

(26) **The kings of the north.**—The term is used generally (the Jews knowing comparatively little of the detailed geography of that region, the Gog, Magog, Meshech, and Tubal of Ezek. xxxviii. and xxxix.), as in chap. i. 14, for the Scythians and other nations lying between the Caspian Sea and the Tigris. In the corresponding passage of chap. li. 27, Ararat, Minni, and Ashkenaz are specially named.

The kingdoms of the world.—The words are, of course, limited by the horizon of the prophet's vision. As the "world" of the New Testament writers was the Roman Empire, so in the life of Jeremiah it was identical with that of Babylon. (Comp. Dan. ii. 38, iv. 22.)

The king of Sheshach.—The name, which obviously is, from its position, the culminating point of the whole prophecy, is found only here and in chap. li. 41. No city or country bearing this name is mentioned in the Old Testament or in any ancient writer. The traditional Rabbinic explanation is beyond doubt the true one. We have here the earliest known example of the use of a cypher-writing to disguise the meaning of what was written from all but the initiated. The cypher in this instance, known by the significant name of ATBASH (*i.e.*, A taking the place of T, and T of A, B of SH, and SH of B, and so on), consisted in the use of the Hebrew alphabet in an inverted order, thus giving SHeSHaCH as an equivalent for BaBeL. This, then, was the crowning mystery reserved to the last. The Chaldæan kingdom was to do its work as the scourge of God upon the nations; but it was simply an instrument in His hand, as the Assyrians had been in their day (Isa. x. 15); and when the work was done, the law of a righteous retribution would be felt by it and by its rulers. It adds to the point of the enigma that the word Sheshach would suggest to an Hebrew, taking its probable etymology, the idea of "crouching" or "sinking." It may be noted (1) that the use of such a cypher seems to belong to the same mental characteristics as the prominence of the Hebrew alphabet in the acrostic structure of the Lamentations; (2) that the name is omitted by the LXX. both here and in chap. li. 41; and (3) that another instance of the same cypher is found in chap. li. 1. The second fact is presumptive evidence that it was not found in the copy which the Greek translators had before them; and the natural inference from this is that there were two editions of the prophecy even in the prophet's time—one with and the other without the enigmatic word, the latter being probably the earlier of the two, the former adding, for the comfort of Israel, at once the limits of their exile (verse 14), and this intimation (so veiled that the Chaldæans, if they came across it, would not be likely to understand its meaning) of the way in which it would at last be brought to its close. The use of the cypher has, however, been questioned by some writers, who refer the name to *shishaki*, a possible form of the name of the moon-god of the Chaldæans (Rawlinson: Herod. i., p. 616). If the existence of any obscure region bearing the name could be proved, it would still be perfectly compatible with the use of the cypher, as veiling its true significance. Other meanings for the word, such as "the warlike city," "the king's palace," have been suggested by recent scholars.

(27) **Drink ye, and be drunken . . .**—The bold imagery points, like that of verse 16, to the terror and dismay which made joint action impossible, and reduced the nations whom it affected to a helpless impotence. The word most alien to our modern feeling—"spue"—is significant, as implying that the spoilers of Israel should be spoiled. They should be made, to use a word which expresses essentially the same thought, to *disgorge* their prey.

(28) **Ye shall certainly drink.**—Literally, *Drinking, ye shall drink.*

(29) **I begin to bring evil . . .?**—The thought is the same as that of 1 Pet. iv. 17, "If judgment shall begin at the house of God . . .?" If this were His chastisement of those who were His chosen people, it followed *à fortiori* that those who were less favoured and had less claims should not escape. For them, as for Judah, the one wise and safe course was to accept their punishment and submit. (Comp. chap. xlix. 12.)

(30) **He shall mightily roar upon his habitation.**—The use of the same English word for two Hebrew words of very different meaning is here singularly infelicitous. The first "habitation" is the dwelling-place of Jehovah, from which the thunders of His wrath are heard. The second is the "*pasture*" or dwelling-place of the flock and its shepherds, as in chaps. vi. 2, x. 25; Ps. lxxix. 7, upon whom the storm falls. Possibly, under its association with this new word, the roaring becomes to the prophet's mind as that of the lion which attacks the flock. The same bold imagery for the Divine judgments meets us in Joel iii. 16; Amos i. 2, iii. 8.

A shout, as they that tread the grapes.—The image is reproduced from Isa. lxiii. 3. The "shout" of those who tread the wine-press, crushing

the inhabitants of the earth. (31) A
noise shall come *even* to the ends of the
earth; for the LORD hath a controversy
with the nations, he will plead with all
flesh; he will give them *that are* wicked
to the sword, saith the LORD. (32) Thus
saith the LORD of hosts, Behold, evil
shall go forth from nation to nation,
and a great whirlwind shall be raised
up from the coasts of the earth.
(33) And the slain of the LORD shall be
at that day from *one* end of the earth
even unto the *other* end of the earth:
they shall not be [a]lamented, neither
gathered, nor buried; they shall be
dung upon the ground. (34) [b]Howl, ye
shepherds, and cry; and wallow your-
selves *in the ashes*, ye principal of the
flock: for [1]the days of your slaughter
and of your dispersions are accom-
plished; and ye shall fall like [2]a
pleasant vessel. (35) And [3]the shepherds
shall have no way to flee, nor the
principal of the flock to escape. (36) A
voice of the cry of the shepherds, and
an howling of the principal of the flock,
shall be heard: for the LORD hath
spoiled their pasture. (37) And the
peaceable habitations are cut down
because of the fierce anger of the LORD.
(38) He hath forsaken his covert, as the
lion: for their land is [4]desolate because
of the fierceness of the oppressor, and
because of his fierce anger.

a ch. 16. 4.

b ch. 4. 8; & 6. 26.

1 Heb., *your days for slaughter.*

2 Heb., *a vessel of desire.*

3 Heb., *flight shall perish from the shepherds, and escaping from,* &c.

B. C. 610 ending.
B. C. 609 beginning.

4 Heb., *a desolation.*

CHAPTER XXVI.—(1) In the be-
ginning of the reign of Jehoiakim the
son of Josiah king of Judah came this

---

the grapes beneath their feet (Isa. xvi. 10), is as the victorious war-cry of the Lord of Hosts, working through human conquerors, and crushing the nations of the earth in His avenging wrath.

(31) **A noise.**—*i.e.*, the tumult of an advancing army (Isa. xiii. 4, xvii. 12).

A controversy.—The term properly denotes a legal process, like the "pleading" of chap. ii. 9, 35, rather than a debate or discussion, and is therefore rightly followed by the technical term "will plead" or "judge." Jehovah appears, so to speak, as the Accuser in the suit in which He is also the supreme Judge.

(32) **Whirlwind.**—The word, as in chap. xxiii. 19, is more generic, *a tempest*. The storm is seen as it were rising from the "coasts"—*i.e.*, the *sides* or horizon of the earth, as in chap. vi. 22—and spreading over all the nations.

(33) **They shall not be lamented . . .**—As in other pictures of slaughter (chaps. viii. 2, xvi. 4) the omission of the usual rites of sepulture is brought in as an aggravation of the wretchedness. The corpses of the slain are to lie rotting on the ground. The phrase "slain of the Lord" reproduces Isa. lxvi. 16.

(34) **Howl, ye shepherds.**—The idea of the flock suggested in the "habitation" or "pasture" of verse 30 is here expanded. The "shepherds" are, as usual, the rulers of the people (chaps. x. 21, xxii. 22, *et al.*).

Wallow yourselves in the ashes.—The words in italics have probably been added to bring the passage into conformity with chap. vi. 26, but they are not needed, and the interpretation is unauthorised. Better, therefore, *roll on the ground*. By some interpreters the word is rendered "sprinkle yourselves." The "principal of the flock" are the "strong ones," *i.e.*, the best and fattest of the rams, denoting figuratively the princes and captains of the people.

And of your dispersions.—The Hebrew text seems faulty, and a slight alteration, now generally accepted, gives, *and I will scatter you*.

Like a pleasant vessel.—The sudden change of metaphor is somewhat startling, as judged by our rules of rhetoric; but the poets and prophets of Israel wrote without the fear of criticism, and used each image that presented itself, if it was fit for its immediate purpose, without caring much for continuity. The thought of the scattered flock suggested the idea of a dispersion or breaking-up of another kind, even that of the "pleasant vessel" (literally, *the vessel of desire, i.e.*, a vase made as for kingly and honourable uses), falling with a crash and shivered into fragments, which Jeremiah had presented to the people in his acted parable and spoken words in chap. xix. 10, 11, and in chap. xxii. 28. The LXX. translators give *like the chosen rams*, as if anxious to avoid the mixed metaphor, and venturing on a conjectural emendation of the text.

(36) **A voice of the cry . . . shall be heard.**—Here again the insertion of the words in italics is a change for the worse, and reduces the dramatic vividness of the Hebrew to the tamest prose. The prophet speaks as if he actually heard the "cry of the shepherds"—*i.e.*, the princes—and the howling of the "principal of the flocks"—*i.e.*, of the captains under them. The work of spoiling was begun.

(37) **Peaceable habitations.**—Better, as before (verse 30), *peaceful pastures*.

(38) **He hath forsaken his covert . . .**—The image of verse 30 is reproduced. The thunder of Jehovah's wrath is as the roaring of the lion (Amos iii. 8). He is as the lion leaving its hiding-place in the forest, and going forth to do its work of vengeance.

Because of the fierceness of the oppressor.—A slight alteration, adopted by many commentators, gives "because of the *sword* of oppression," as in chaps. xlvi. 16, l. 16. The word for "oppressor" or "oppression" also means "dove," and is so taken by the Vulg., *a facie iræ columbæ*, and it has been stated that this bird was blazoned on the standards of the Babylonians (Diod. Sic. ii. 4), and so had become a symbol of their power. In chaps. xlvi. 16, l. 16 the LXX., which here gives "the great sword," reads "the Greek sword," as though the Hebrew word (*Iona*) meant Javan or Ionia. That meaning is, of course, out of the question here. On the whole there seems no reason for altering the English version, though the precise combination of words is an unusual one.

XXVI.

(1) **In the beginning of the reign of Jehoiakim.**—The section which follows is among the earlier frag-

word from the LORD, saying, (2) Thus
saith the LORD;
Stand in the court of the LORD'S
house, and speak unto all the cities of
Judah, which come to worship in the
LORD'S house, all the words that I
command thee to speak unto them;
[a]diminish not a word: (3) if so be they
will hearken, and turn every man from
his evil way, that I may [b]repent me of
the evil, which I purpose to do unto
them because of the evil of their doings.
(4) And thou shalt say unto them, Thus
saith the LORD; If ye will not hearken
to me, to walk in my law, which I have
set before you, (5) to hearken to the
words of my servants the prophets,
whom I sent unto you, both rising up
early, and sending *them,* but ye have
not hearkened; (6) then will I make
this house like [c]Shiloh, and will make
this city a curse to all the nations of
the earth.
(7) So the priests and the prophets
and all the people heard Jeremiah speak-
ing these words in the house of the
LORD. (8) Now it came to pass, when
Jeremiah had made an end of speaking
all that the LORD had commanded *him*
to speak unto all the people, that the
priests and the prophets and all the
people took him, saying, Thou shalt
surely die. (9) Why hast thou prophe-
sied in the name of the LORD, saying,
This house shall be like Shiloh, and this
city shall be desolate without an in-
habitant? And all the people were
gathered against Jeremiah in the house
of the LORD.
(10) When the princes of Judah heard
these things, then they came up from
the king's house unto the house of the

a Acts 20. 27.

b ch. 18. 8.

c 1 Sam. 4. 12; Ps. 78. 60; ch. 7. 12, 14.

---

ments of the book, some three years before that of the preceding chapter. It will be noted that there is no mention of the Chaldæans, and that Jehoiakim is on friendly terms with Egypt (verse 22). This points to the very earliest period of his reign. The chapter that follows, though referred to the same period in the present Hebrew text, really belongs to the reign of Zedekiah. (See Note on chap. xxvii. 1.) The common element that led the compiler of the book to bring the narratives together is the conflict of Jeremiah with the false prophets.

(2) **Stand in the court of the Lord's house.**—The occasion was probably one of the Feasts, and drew worshippers from all parts of the kingdom. As in chap. vii. 1, the prophet had to stand in the crowded court of the Temple and utter his warning. Some critics have supposed, indeed, that in chap. vii.—xi. we have the full text of the discourse, while here there is only an epitome of the discourse itself, and a narrative of the circumstances connected with it. The command, "diminish not a word," reminds us of Deut. iv. 2, xii. 32; Rev. xxii. 19. There was something in the message that the prophet felt himself called to deliver from which he would naturally have shrunk.

(3) **If so be they will hearken . . .**—The threat that follows in verse 6 is a very terrible one, but it is uttered in order that it may *not* be realised. So in the same spirit St. Paul warns men of his power to inflict a supernatural punishment, yet prays that he may have no occasion to use it (2 Cor. xiii. 3—10).

(4, 5) **To walk in my law, which I have set before you.**—The words present more vividly than in the parallels of chaps. vii. 25 and xxv. 4 the relation of the Law as the groundwork of the teaching of the Prophets, their office being that of preachers and expounders, making men feel that the commandment was "exceeding broad." The "Law and the Prophets" are already coupled together, as in Matt. v. 17, xxii. 40, as making up God's revelation of His will to Israel.

(6) **I will make this house like Shiloh.**—See Notes on chap. vii. 14. The surprise and anger with which the announcement was received indicate that it was now heard for the first time, and so far confirms the view that we have here a summary of the discourse given *in extenso,* and probably edited, as it were, with many additions, in chaps. vii.—x.

(7) **The priests and the prophets.**—The mention of the latter is significant. Jeremiah had to separate himself from both the orders to which he belonged, in the one case, by birth, in the other, by a special vocation. His bitterest foes were found among those who claimed to speak as he did, in the name of the Lord, but who tuned their voice according to the time, and prophesied deceits. See Notes on chap. xxiii. 9—40.

(8) **Thou shalt surely die.**—Better, as expressing the Hebrew emphasis of reduplication, *Thou shalt die the death.* The phrase is the same as in Gen. ii. 17. The threat of the men of Anathoth (chap. xi. 21) is repeated by the priests and prophets of Jerusalem. They look on Jeremiah as one who has incurred the condemnation of Deut. xviii. 20.

(9) **Why hast thou prophesied in the name of the Lord . . . ?**—The threat that the house in which they gloried should be as the old sanctuary of Ephraim, over whose fall they had exulted, was as the last drop that made the cup of wrath and bitterness run over. They had chanted their psalms, which told how that God "forsook the tabernacle of Shiloh, even the tent which He had pitched among men" (Ps. lxxviii. 60). They could not bear to hear that a like fate was impending over them.

(10) **When the princes of Judah heard these things . . .**—The princes appear not to have been present when the words were spoken. The report was carried to them as they sat in council with the king, and they came down to the Temple and took their place, to watch and listen what would come next. They went apparently by what was known as the king's entry into the Temple (2 Kings xvi. 18), the high gate which had been built by Jotham (2 Chron. xxvii. 3), from which they could command a view of the crowds in the Temple court. (See Note on chap. xxii. 2). One of them, in all probability, was Ahikam, the

LORD, and sat down [1]in the entry of the
new gate of the LORD's *house.* (11) Then
spake the priests and the prophets unto
the princes and to all the people, saying,
[2]This man *is* worthy to die; for he
hath prophesied against this city, as ye
have heard with your ears.
(12) Then spake Jeremiah unto all the
princes and to all the people, saying,
The LORD sent me to prophesy against
this house and against this city all the
words that ye have heard. (13) There-
fore now [a]amend your ways and your
doings, and obey the voice of the LORD
your God; and the LORD will [b]repent
him of the evil that he hath pronounced
against you. (14) As for me, behold, I
am in your hand: do with me [3]as
seemeth good and meet unto you.
(15) But know ye for certain, that if ye
put me to death, ye shall surely bring
innocent blood upon yourselves, and
upon this city, and upon the inhabitants
thereof: for of a truth the LORD hath
sent me unto you to speak all these
words in your ears.
(16) Then said the princes and all the
people unto the priests and to the
prophets; This man *is* not worthy to
die: for he hath spoken to us in the
name of the LORD our God.
(17) Then rose up certain of the elders
of the land, and spake to all the as-
sembly of the people, saying, (18) [c]Micah
the Morasthite prophesied in the days
of Hezekiah king of Judah, and spake
to all the people of Judah, saying, Thus
saith the LORD of hosts; [d]Zion shall be
plowed *like* a field, and Jerusalem shall
become heaps, and the mountain of the

1 Or, *at the door.*

2 Heb., *The judgment of death is for this man.*

a ch. 7. 3.

b ver. 19.

3 Heb., *as it is good and right in your eyes.*

B. C. cir. 710.

c Micah 1. 1.

d Micah 3. 12.

---

son of Shaphan (verse 24). As in chap. xxxvi. 19, 25, the princes are less bitterly hostile than the priests.

(11) **This man is worthy to die.**—Literally, *A judgment of death for this man.* The phrase seems to have been in current forensic use. (See Deut. xix. 6, xxi. 22.) Among the accusers we may think of Pashur, the son of Immer (chap. xx. 1). Personal rancour mingles with the class feeling which animates the whole body of the priesthood. They appeal to what, in later language, would be known as the secular arm, to be the instrument of their vindictiveness against the heretic and blasphemer.

(12) **The Lord sent me to prophesy . . .**—The answer of the accused is that of all true prophets and preachers of the word, "The Lord God hath spoken, and he can but prophesy" (Amos iii. 8). He must "obey God rather than man" (Acts v. 29). And in this instance the prophet has nothing in the way of credentials but the message itself. He worked no signs or wonders.

(13) **Therefore now amend your ways . . .**—The prophet's *apologia* consists in repeating the substance of his message. He had not denounced an irreversible doom. He had held out the assurance of pardon on repentance. He had threatened only to bring about repentance. The whole history reminds us of the accusation brought against One greater than Jeremiah. He had foretold a destruction of the Second Temple as complete as that of Shiloh (Luke xix. 44). He, too, was accused of having said that He would destroy the Temple (Matt. xxvi. 61). And He, foreseeing that the people would not repent, had pronounced, though not publicly, a sentence on the Temple which succeeded that against which Jeremiah had prophesied, which was irrevocable (Matt. xxiv. 2; Mark xiii. 2; Luke xix. 44).

(14) **As for me, behold . . .**—Literally, *And I, behold, I am in your hands;* and for "as seemeth good and meet unto you," read *in your eyes.* The prophet feels himself powerless in the presence of his accusers and judges, and can but appeal to the Judge of all.

(15) **But know ye for certain.**—Literally, with the Hebrew emphasis of reduplication, *Knowing, know ye.* The appeal is addressed, it will be remembered, to the lay judges, the princes, and the people, not to the priests and prophets who accused him. He believes that they at least would shrink from shedding innocent blood. And he solemnly protests that he is innocent of any wilful attack upon what his countrymen revered. He has spoken, but it has been by a constraint above his own will. A "necessity has been laid upon him" (1 Cor. ix. 16).

(16) **This man is not worthy to die.**—Literally, as before in verse 11, *There is no judgment of death for this man.* Here again the later parallel comes unbidden to our memory. The lay-rulers are in favour of the true prophet, whom the priests and false prophets would have condemned. Pilate declares, in presence of priests and scribes, and the clamouring multitude, "I find no fault in this man" (Luke xxiii. 4). Here, however, as yet the people are with the true prophet, and against the priests, as they were when they shouted their Hosannas to the prophet's great antitype.

(17) **Certain of the elders of the land.**—The word is probably to be taken rather in the literal than in an official sense—or, if officially, then as including the literal meaning also. The elders speaking in the time of Jehoiakim (cir. B.C. 608) remembered the tradition of what had passed, a century or so before, in the reign of Hezekiah (B.C. 726—698), and could appeal to it as a precedent in favour of the prophet. The word for "assembly" (elsewhere rendered "congregation") corresponds to the *Ecclesia* of a Greek city.

(18) **Micah the Morasthite.**—On the general history and work of this prophet, see *Introduction to Micah.* The Hebrew text gives Micaiah, the two forms being (as in Judges xvii. 1, 4, compared with 5, 12), in the Hebrew interchangeable. The epithet indicated his birth in Moresheth-gath in Philistia (Micah i. 14). As Micah had prophesied under Jotham and Ahaz (Mic. i. 1), the prediction here referred to must have been delivered towards the close of his ministry. The words cited are from Mic. iii. 12, and immediately precede the prediction of an ultimate restoration of Judah in the last days in Mic. iv. 1, 2, which we find in identical terms in Isa. ii. 2, 3. Here, then, was a case, is the implied argument of the elders, in which a threat did its work, and therefore was not fulfilled. It did good, and not evil. The phrase "mountain of

house as the high places of a forest.
(19) Did Hezekiah king of Judah and all
Judah put him at all to death? did he
not fear the LORD, and besought [1]the
LORD, and the LORD repented him of
the evil which he had pronounced
against them? Thus might we procure
great evil against our souls. (20) And
there was also a man that prophesied
in the name of the LORD, Urijah the
son of Shemaiah of Kirjath-jearim, who
prophesied against this city and against
this land according to all the words of
Jeremiah: (21) and when Jehoiakim the
king, with all his mighty men, and all
the princes, heard his words, the king
sought to put him to death: but when
Urijah heard it, he was afraid, and fled,
and went into Egypt; (22) and Jehoiakim
the king sent men into Egypt, *namely*,
Elnathan the son of Achbor, and *certain*
men with him into Egypt. (23) And
they fetched forth Urijah out of Egypt,
and brought him unto Jehoiakim the
king; who slew him with the sword,
and cast his dead body into the graves
of the [2]common people.
(24) Nevertheless the hand of Ahikam

[1] Heb., *the face of the LORD.*

B. C. cir. 609.

[2] Heb., *sons of the people.*

the house" is not found elsewhere in Jeremiah as a description of the Temple.

(19) **Did Hezekiah . . . put him at all to death?**—Literally, *make him die the death*, the same phrase as in verse 8. There is no special record of the repentance thus referred to, but it is quite in accord with Hezekiah's general character, as seen in 2 Chron. xxix. 6—10 (which may be the occasion referred to) and xxxii. 26. The whole tone of the advice of "old experience," approximating to something like "prophetic strain," in this case, reminds us of the counsels of Gamaliel in Acts v. 35—39. The closing words, "Thus might we procure great evil to our souls," present an exact parallel to "lest haply we be found even to fight against God." The result of the counsel thus given is left to be inferred. It obviously left the prophet free to continue his work as a preacher, though probably under a kind of police surveillance, like that implied in chap. xxxvi. 1—5. The favourable result is attributed in verse 24 to the influence of Ahikam.

(20) **And there was also a man that prophesied . . .**—The verses that follow, seeing that they state a fact which tends in the opposite direction, cannot be regarded as part of the argument of the "elders" of verse 17. Nor is there any sufficient reason for supposing, in the absence of any statement to that effect, that the case of Urijah was alleged in a counter-argument by the priests and prophets. Verse 24 shows rather that Jeremiah, or the compiler of the book, wished to record the fact that he did not stand absolutely alone, and that at least one prophet had been, as an Abdiel,—"faithful found among the faithless,"—who had courage to follow his example. He took up the strain of Jeremiah, and reproduced it. Of this Urijah we know nothing beyond what is here recorded. It is, perhaps, worth noting that the history of his native place may in some measure have influenced his thoughts, as presenting, like Shiloh, the history of a sacred place that had lost its sanctity (1 Sam. vii. 1; 2 Sam. vi. 2), and that its position on the border of the tribe of Benjamin may have brought him into contact with the prophet of Anathoth. The distance between the two towns was but a short day's journey.

(21) **And when Jehoiakim the king . . .**—The fact that the princes of Judah, who defended Jeremiah, were against Urijah, suggests the inference either that his words were more vehemently denunciatory, or that he was less fortunate in finding a personal friend and protector like Ahikam. The flight into Egypt presents a parallel to that of Jeroboam (1 Kings xi. 40), Hadad (1 Kings xi. 18), and Joseph and Mary (Matt. ii. 13—15). Egypt was at all times the natural asylum for political refugees from Judæa. The presence of the deposed Jehoahaz and of other Jews in Egypt may possibly have been an attraction (2 Chron. xxxvi. 4; Jer. xxiv. 8, xliv. 1).

(22) **And Jehoiakim the king sent men into Egypt.**—It will be remembered that the king had been appointed by Pharaoh-necho, and rested therefore on his alliance. Elnathan, the envoy employed on this mission, was the king's father-in-law (2 Kings xxiv. 8). His father, Achbor, had taken a prominent part, together with Shaphan, the father of Ahikam, in the work of reformation under Josiah, and was sent by the king to the prophetess Huldah (2 Kings xxii. 12). Elnathan appears again in the list of princes in chap. xxxvi. 12 as favourable to Jeremiah.

(23) **And they fetched forth Urijah out of Egypt.**—The martyr-death of the prophet had its parallels in the earlier history of Judah. So Jezebel had slain the prophets of Jehovah with the edge of the sword (1 Kings xviii. 4, xix. 10, 14), and Zechariah the son of Jehoiada had been stoned to death at the command of Joash (2 Chron. xxiv. 21), and Isaiah, as the Jewish tradition runs, had been sawn asunder (Heb. xi. 37). The fact now recorded was to Jewish feeling an act of brutal outrage. The body of the prophet was not allowed to rest in the sepulchre of his fathers, with the due honour of embalmment, but flung into the loathsome pits of "the sons of the people," in the Kidron valley (2 Kings xxiii. 6). It is not without interest to those who believe in a special as well as righteous retribution, to note the fact that the king who thus added brutality to cruelty was himself afterwards "buried with the burial of an ass," without honours or lamentations (chap. xxii. 18, 19). For the phrase, "children of the people," see Note on chap. xvii. 19. The circumstances are apparently narrated in detail either by the prophet himself or by the compiler of his prophecies, to show how narrow his escape had been.

(24) **Nevertheless the hand of Ahikam . . .**—The family to whom the prophet's protector belonged played a conspicuous part in the history of this period, and may be said to have furnished examples of three generations of Jewish patriotism. Shaphan, the father, was prominent as a scribe in the reformation of Josiah (cir. A.D. 624). He superintended the restoration of the Temple (2 Chron. xxxiv. 8). To him Hilkiah the priest gave the book of the Law which had been found in the house of the Lord, and Shaphan took it to the king. He took his son Ahikam with him when he was sent to consult the prophetess Huldah (2 Kings xxii. 12:

the son of Shaphan was with Jeremiah,
that they should not give him into the
hand of the people to put him to death.

CHAPTER XXVII.—(1) In the be-
ginning of the reign of Jehoiakim the
son of Josiah king of Judah came this
word unto Jeremiah from the LORD,
saying, (2) Thus saith the LORD to me;
Make thee bonds and yokes, and put
them upon thy neck, (3) and send them
to the king of Edom, and to the king of
Moab, and to the king of the Ammon-
ites, and to the king of Tyrus, and to
the king of Zidon, by the hand of the
messengers which come to Jerusalem
unto Zedekiah king of Judah; (4) and
command them [1] to say unto their mas-
ters, Thus saith the LORD of hosts, the
God of Israel; Thus shall ye say unto
your masters; (5) I have made the
earth, the man and the beast that are
upon the ground, by my great power
and by my outstretched arm, and [a] have
given it unto whom it seemed meet
unto me. (6) And now have I given all
these lands into the hand of Nebu-
chadnezzar the king of Babylon, [b] my
servant; and the beasts of the field
have I given him also to serve him.

1 Or, *concerning their masters, saying.*

B. C. cir. 598.

a Dan. 4. 17, 25, 32.

b ch. 25. 9; & 43. 10.

---

2 Chron. xxxiv. 20). Here the son meets us, true to the early lessons of his life, as the protector of the prophet, whose work rested so largely on the impression made by the Book of the Law thus discovered. A brother of Ahikam, Gemariah, appears in a like character in chap. xxxvi. 12, 25. After the conquest of the land by Nebuchadnezzar, Jeremiah finds refuge with Gedaliah, the son of Ahikam (chap. xl. 6), who had been made, apparently through the prophet's influence, satrap, or governor, of the lands under the Chaldæan king; and he, after a fruitless warning, falls a victim to the conspiracy of the princes of the royal house (chap. xli. 1, 2). Here stress is laid on the fact of Ahikam's protection, as showing how it was that Jeremiah escaped the fate which fell on Urijah.

XXVII.

(1) **In the beginning of the reign of Jehoiakim.**—The mention of the name of Zedekiah as king of Judah in verse 3 shows that the Hebrew text has here perpetuated an error, due probably to the transcriber or first editor of the collected prophecies. We have to think, accordingly, of the state of things which followed on the death of Jehoiakim, and the deposition and exile of Jehoiachin. The tone of the prophecy seems to indicate a time about the middle of Zedekiah's reign. His position was that of a tributary sovereign, subject to Nebuchadnezzar. He and the neighbouring kings, who were in a like position, had not quite renounced the hope of throwing off the yoke, and asserting their independence.

(2) **Make thee bonds and yokes.**—This method of vivid symbolic prediction had a precedent in the conduct of Isaiah when he walked "naked and barefoot" (Isa. xx. 2). We have to realise the infinitely more vivid impression which the appearance of the prophet in this strange guise, as though he were at once a captive slave and a beast of burden, would make on the minds of men, as compared with simply warning them of a coming subjugation. The principle on which the prophet acted was that of Horace (*Ep. ad Pis.* 180):—

> "*Segnius irritant animos demissa per aures,*
> *Quam quæ sunt oculis subjecta fidelibus, et quæ*
> *Ipse sibi tradit spectator.*"
>
> "Things that we hear less stir the inmost soul,
> Than what the eye sees dramatised in act."

So Agabus bound himself with Paul's girdle (Acts xxi. 11). So Ezekiel dug through the wall of his house and carried out his stuff (Ezek. xii. 5, 7). We find from chap. xxviii. 10 that the prophet obeyed the command quite literally.

(3) **And send them to the king of Edom.**—The princes that are named had, as the context shows, sent their ambassadors to Zedekiah, proposing an alliance against Nebuchadnezzar. They are named in the same order as in the prophecy of chap. xxv. 21, 22, which had been delivered fifteen years before. The prophecy then delivered had been in part fulfilled, but these princes were still struggling against it, encouraged, apparently, by the difficulties which in Media and elsewhere seemed to delay the complete triumph of the Chaldæan king; and the prophet is commissioned to tell all of them alike that their efforts are in vain, and that the supremacy of Babylon was, for the time, part of God's order, for the chastisement of the nations. In chap. xlix. we have a fuller, and probably later, development of the same strain of prediction.

(4) **Thus saith the Lord of hosts, the God of Israel.**—As addressed to the outlying heathen nations, who were not His worshippers, the proclamation of the message, as coming from Jehovah Sabaoth, the God of Israel, had a special force, which we hardly appreciate as we read the English. They, with their hosts of earth, were setting themselves against the Lord of the hosts alike of heaven and of earth.

(5) **I have made the earth . . .**—The pronoun is emphatic. For "upon the ground" read *on the face of the earth,* and for "it seemed meet unto me" *it seemed meet to my eyes.* The "stretched-out arm" is a phrase specially characteristic of the Book of Deuteronomy (iv. 34, v. 15, vii. 19, xxvi. 8), and may be noted among the many traces of its influence on Jeremiah's language. The whole preface, which rises to a height of rhythmic loftiness not common in Jeremiah's writings, asserts the truth that the Creator of the material world is also the ruler over the kingdoms of the earth. For a like utterance of the same thought, see Amos iv. 13, ix. 6.

(6) **Nebuchadnezzar . . . my servant.**—See Note on chap. xxv. 9 for the title thus given. The special stress laid on "the beasts of the field" is, perhaps, connected with the resistance of the nations to the levies made by the Babylonian officers upon their horses and cattle, or their claim to use the land they had subdued, after the manner which we see depicted on Assyrian sculptures, as a hunting-ground. Compare especially the account of Tiglath-Pileser I.'s hunting expedition in *Records of the Past,* xi., p. 9.

(7) And all nations shall serve him, and
his son, and his son's son, until the very
time of his land come: and then many
nations and great kings shall serve
themselves of him. (8) And it shall
come to pass, *that* the nation and king-
dom which will not serve the same
Nebuchadnezzar the king of Babylon,
and that will not put their neck under
the yoke of the king of Babylon, that
nation will I punish, saith the LORD,
with the sword, and with the famine,
and with the pestilence, until I have
consumed them by his hand. (9) There-
fore hearken not ye to your prophets,
nor to your diviners, nor to your
[1] dreamers, nor to your enchanters, nor
to your sorcerers, which speak unto you,
saying, Ye shall not serve the king of
Babylon: (10) for they prophesy a lie
unto you, to remove you far from your
land; and that I should drive you out,
and ye should perish. (11) But the na-
tions that bring their neck under the
yoke of the king of Babylon, and serve
him, those will I let remain still in their
own land, saith the LORD; and they
shall till it, and dwell therein.
(12) I spake also to Zedekiah king of
Judah according to all these words,
saying, Bring your necks under the yoke
of the king of Babylon, and serve him
and his people, and live. (13) Why will
ye die, thou and thy people, by the
sword, by the famine, and by the pesti-
lence, as the LORD hath spoken against
the nation that will not serve the king
of Babylon? (14) Therefore hearken not
unto the words of the prophets that
speak unto you, saying, Ye shall not
serve the king of Babylon: for they
prophesy [a] a lie unto you. (15) For I
have not sent them, saith the LORD,
yet they prophesy [2] a lie in my name;
that I might drive you out, and that ye
might perish, ye, and the prophets that
prophesy unto you.
(16) Also I spake to the priests and to
all this people, saying, Thus saith the
LORD; Hearken not to the words of

B. C. 598.

1 Heb., *dreams.*

a ch. 14. 14; & 23. 21; & 29. 8.

2 Heb., *in a lie,* or, *lyingly.*

---

(7) **And his son, and his son's son.**—The words may have had the meaning that this was to be the farthest limit of Nebuchadnezzar's dynasty, as defined by the "seventy years" of chap. xxv. 11. The use of the phrase, however, in Exod. xxxiv. 7, Deut. iv. 25, points rather to an undefined prolongation, subject only to the fact that there was an appointed limit. Historically we may note the fact that Nebuchadnezzar was succeeded by his son, Evil-merodach (chap. lii. 31); he by his brother-in-law, Neriglissar, and he by Nabounahid and his son Belshazzar. (See *Introduction.*)

Shall serve themselves of him.—Better, *shall make him to serve.* It lies in the nature of the case that the pronoun refers to the King of Babylon for the time being. The confederacy of nations which shall overthrow the Babylonian monarchy, Medes and others, is described more fully in chap. li. 11, 27, 28. The words were clearly meant to point both ways. They warn the nations not to resist the Chaldæan king then. They warn the king not to think that he is founding a dynasty of long duration. The whole verse is wanting in the LXX., perhaps because they imagined that the "son's son" of verse 7 was inconsistent with the facts of history, as they read them.

(8) **That nation will I punish.**—Better, *I will visit.* The three forms of punishment go naturally together. In Ezek. xiv. 21 they appear, with the addition of the "noisome beast," as the four sore judgments of God.

(9) **Therefore hearken ye not to your prophets.**—The almost exhaustive list of the names given to the men who claimed the power of prevision, may have had its ground in the fact that each of the five names was characteristic of this or that among the five nations to whom the message was sent. Of the names themselves, the prominent idea in "prophet" is that of full-flowing utterance; in "diviners," that of casting lots, as in Ezek. xxi. 21; in "dreamers," what the English word indicates; in enchanters, that of practising "veiled" or "secret" arts (Lev. xix. 26; Deut. xviii. 10); in "sorcerers," that of muttered and whispered spells (Isa. viii. 19, xlvii. 9—13; 2 Kings ix. 22). It is clear that the five nations of the confederacy were sustained in their rebellion against Nebuchadnezzar by a unanimity of prediction from men of all these classes like that which lured Ahab to his destruction (1 Kings xxii. 22). Every oracle was tuned, as it were, in favour of the policy of resistance.

(10) **To remove you far from your land.**—The prophet speaks of what he foresees will be the result of the rebellion to which soothsayers and diviners were urging men, as if it were actually contemplated by them. They are to him like the lying spirit in the mouth of Ahab's prophets persuading him to go up to Ramoth Gilead to battle, in order that he might perish.

(11) **But the nations that bring their neck under the yoke . . .**—The advice thus given to the five nations that were seeking an alliance with Judah before the actual invasion, is specifically addressed to Judah in the next verse, and is repeated more fully after the population of Judæa had been carried into captivity, in chap. xxix. The first warning had been despised, and the exiles were then reaping the fruit of their selfwill, but the principle that obedience was better than resistance remained the same.

(12) **I spake also to Zedekiah . . .**—There was, as we see in chap. xxviii. 13, a party of resistance in Judah also, and they, too, were trusting in delusive prophecies of the overthrow of the Chaldæan monarchy. Sadly and earnestly the prophet pleads with them in the question, "Why will ye die, thou and thy people, by the sword . . .?

(16) **Behold the vessels of the Lord's house . . .**—The importance attached to this specific prediction, on which apparently the false prophets staked their credit, can easily be understood. The vessels referred

your prophets that prophesy unto you,
saying, Behold, the vessels of the LORD's
house shall now shortly be brought
again from Babylon: for they prophesy
a lie unto you. (17) Hearken not unto
them; serve the king of Babylon, and
live: wherefore should this city be laid
waste? (18) But if they *be* prophets,
and if the word of the LORD be with
them, let them now make intercession
to the LORD of hosts, that the vessels
which are left in the house of the
LORD, and *in* the house of the king of
Judah, and at Jerusalem, go not to
Babylon. (19) For thus saith the LORD
of hosts concerning the pillars, and con-
cerning the sea, and concerning the
bases, and concerning the residue of the
vessels that remain in this city, (20) which
Nebuchadnezzar king of Babylon took
not, when he carried away [a]captive Je-
coniah the son of Jehoiakim king of
Judah from Jerusalem to Babylon, and
all the nobles of Judah and Jerusalem;
(21) yea, thus saith the LORD of hosts,
the God of Israel, concerning the vessels
that remain *in* the house of the LORD,
and *in* the house of the king of Judah
and of Jerusalem; (22) they shall be
[b]carried to Babylon, and there shall
they be until the day that I [c]visit them,
saith the LORD; then will I bring them
up, and restore them to this place.

a 2 Kings 24. 14, 15.

b 2 Kings 25. 13; 2 Chron. 36. 18.

B. C. cir. 596.

c 2 Chron. 36. 22; ch. 29. 10.

CHAPTER XXVIII.—(1) And it came
to pass the same year, in the beginning
of the reign of Zedekiah king of Judah,
in the fourth year, *and* in the fifth
month, *that* Hananiah the son of Azur
the prophet, which *was* of Gibeon, spake
unto me in the house of the LORD, in the
presence of the priests and of all the

---

to are those which had been carried off by Nebuchadnezzar in his first invasion, and before the accession of Zedekiah (2 Kings xxiv. 13; 2 Chron. xxxvi. 7). The people mourned over the absence of what they had so prized among the treasures of the Temple, and the prophets accordingly soothed them with predictions that they would before long be brought back. In marked contrast to these prophecies of their restoration "shortly," we find them brought out for use at Belshazzar's feast, towards the close of the Babylonian exile (Dan. i. 2; v. 2), and restored to the Jews by Cyrus, after the capture of Babylon (Ezra i. 7). In the apocryphal book of Baruch (i. 8) we find a tradition that some of them (silver, not gold) were restored in the reign of Zedekiah, but this can hardly be regarded as historical. It is noticeable that the restoration is connected, in that narrative, with the agency of Baruch himself, and it is scarcely probable that he would have brought about a fulfilment of the prediction of the false prophets, who were his Master's enemies.

(17) **Hearken not unto them.**—The prophecy of the restoration of the vessels of the Temple was clearly not a mere prediction. It had been used as an incentive to rebellion. "Make one last effort," the prophets virtually said, "and the spoiler shall be compelled to disgorge his booty." The prophet saw that such an effort would but hasten the utter destruction of the Temple and the city.

(18) **But if they be prophets . . .**—The rivals of Jeremiah had, as has been said, staked their credit upon the return of the vessels that had already been taken. He stakes his on the prediction that what had been spared in the first invasion should be taken on the second. They had better use their gift of the Spirit, if they had any, in interceding for their preservation.

(19) **For thus saith the Lord of hosts concerning the pillars . . .**—The "pillars" referred to were probably the two bronze columns known as Jachin and Boaz, on each side of the porch of the Temple (1 Kings vii. 21). The molten "sea," standing on twelve oxen as its supporters, is described in 1 Kings vii. 23—26. The ten "bases" for the ten lavers, with their engraved work of cherubim, lions, and palm-trees, are described in 1 Kings vii. 27—37. The work of plunder was apparently confined, in the first instance, to the more portable vessels—cups, flagons, and the like. The absence of the specific list of the vessels in the LXX. version has led some critics to the conclusion that it was a later addition to the Hebrew text.

(22) **They shall be carried to Babylon.**—The fulfilment of the prediction is recorded in 2 Kings xxv. 13—17.

Until the day that I visit them.—The date is not given definitely, but seventy years had been already named as the period between the plunder and the restoration (chap. xxv. 12). Here the undefined vagueness of "the day that I will visit them" is contrasted with the equally indefinite but more exciting "shortly" of the false prophets (verse 16).

XXVIII.

(1) **And it came to pass the same year . . .**—The chapter stands in immediate sequence with that which precedes and confirms the conclusion that the name Jehoiakim in chap. xxvii. 1 is simply a transcriber's mistake. Of the Hananiah who appears as the most prominent of the prophet's adversaries, we know nothing beyond what is here recorded. He was clearly one of the leaders of the party of resistance whom we have seen at work trying to form an alliance with the neighbouring nations in chap. xxvii., and whose hopes had been revived by the accession of Pharaoh Hophra (Apries) to the throne of Egypt in B.C. 595. The mention of Gibeon suggests two or three thoughts not without interest:—(1) It was, like Anathoth, within the tribe of Benjamin, about six or seven miles from Jerusalem, and so the antagonism between the true prophet and the false in Jerusalem may have been the revival of older local conflicts. (2) Gibeon, like Anathoth, was one of the cities of priests (Josh. xxi. 17), and Hananiah was probably, therefore, a priest as well as prophet. (3) As still retaining the venerable relics of a worship that had passed away; it had also once been the sanctuary of Jehovah (1 Chron. xvi. 39). There the old tabernacle stood which had been with the people in the wilderness—which had been removed from

people, saying, (2) Thus speaketh the LORD of hosts, the God of Israel, saying, I have broken the yoke of the king of Babylon. (3) Within [1]two full years will I bring again into this place all the vessels of the LORD'S house, that Nebuchadnezzar king of Babylon took away from this place, and carried them to Babylon: (4) and I will bring again to this place Jeconiah the son of Jehoiakim king of Judah, with all the [2]captives of Judah, that went into Babylon, saith the LORD: for I will break the yoke of the king of Babylon.

(5) Then the prophet Jeremiah said unto the prophet Hananiah in the presence of the priests, and in the presence of all the people that stood in the house of the LORD, (6) even the prophet Jeremiah said, Amen: the LORD do so: the LORD perform thy words which thou hast prophesied, to bring again the vessels of the LORD'S house, and all that is carried away captive, from Babylon into this place. (7) Nevertheless hear thou now this word that I speak in thine ears, and in the ears of all the people; (8) the prophets that have been before me and before thee of old prophesied both against many countries, and against great kingdoms, of war, and of evil, and of pestilence. (9) The prophet which prophesieth of peace, when the word of the prophet shall come to pass, *then* shall the prophet be known, that the LORD hath truly sent him.

(10) Then Hananiah the prophet took the [a]yoke from off the prophet Jeremiah's neck, and brake it. (11) And Hananiah spake in the presence of all the people, saying, Thus saith the LORD; Even so will I break the yoke of Nebuchadnezzar king of Babylon from the neck of all nations within the space

1 Heb., *two years of days.*

2 Heb., *captivity.*

a ch. 27. 2.

Shiloh when the sacred ark was taken (2 Chron. i. 3). There Solomon, at the beginning of his reign, offered a stately sacrifice (1 Kings iii. 4). Ought not the prophet who had grown up in the midst of those surroundings to have learnt that no place, however sacred, could count on being safe from the changes and chances of time, all fulfilling the righteous purposes of God? The occasion on which he now appears was probably one of the new moon, Sabbath, or other feast-days on which the courts of the Temple were crowded.

(2) **I have broken the yoke . . .**—The word is obviously used with special reference to the symbol which Jeremiah had made so conspicuous (chap. xxvii. 2). With something, it may be, of ironical repetition, he reproduces the very formula with which the true prophet had begun his message. He, too, can speak in the name of "the Lord of Sabaoth, the God of Israel."

(3) **Within two full years.**—Literally, *two years of days.* Hananiah, not deterred by the previous warnings of Jeremiah, becomes bolder in the definiteness of his prediction. The conspiracy of Judah and the neighbouring states against Nebuchadnezzar was clearly ripening, and he looked on its success as certain. Prediction stood against prediction, and, as there were no signs or wonders wrought, men had to judge from what they knew of the lives of the men who uttered them which of them was most worthy of credit. The contest between the two prophets reminds us of Deut. xviii. 20—22.

(4) **And I will bring again to this place Jeconiah the son of Jehoiakim . . .**—We get here a new glimpse into the nature of the anti-Chaldæan confederacy. Zedekiah was to be deposed as too submissive to Nebuchadnezzar, and the young Jeconiah was to be brought back from his prison at Babylon, and re-established in the kingdom as the representative of the policy of resistance, resting on the support of Pharaoh-Hophra.

(6) **Amen, the Lord do so.**—It is impossible to mistake the tone of keen, incisive irony with which the words were spoken. The speaker could, without falsehood, echo the wish as far as it was a wish, but he knew that it was a wish for the impossible. The whole condition of things would have to be altered before there could be the slightest prospect of its fulfilment. It was not wise to pray for that which was obviously out of the lines of God's normal methods of working in history, and against His purpose, as uttered by His prophets.

(8) **The prophets that have been before me and before thee . . .**—The appeal to the past is of the nature of an inductive argument. The older prophets whose names were held in honour had not spoken smooth things. They had not prophesied of peace; war, pestilence, and famine had been the burden of their predictions. And there was, therefore, an antecedent probability in favour of one who spoke in the same tone now, rather than of those who held out flattering hopes of peace and victory. The *onus probandi* in such a conflict of claims lay with the latter, not the former. Prophecies like those of Elijah (1 Kings xvii. 1, xxi. 21—24), Micaiah (1 Kings xxii. 17), Elisha (2 Kings viii. 1), Joel (i. 1—20), Hosea (ii. 11, 12), Amos (i.—iv.), Micah (iii. 12), Isaiah (ii.—vi.), were probably in Jeremiah's thoughts.

(9) **The prophet which prophesieth of peace.**—"Peace," with its Hebrew associations, includes all forms of national prosperity, and is therefore contrasted with famine and pestilence, not less than with war. The obvious reference to the test of a prophet's work, as described in Deut. xviii. 22, shows, as other like references, the impression which that book had made on the prophet's mind.

(10, 11) **Then Hananiah the prophet took the yoke . . .**—We are reminded of the conduct of Zedekiah, the son of Chenaanah, in 1 Kings xxii. 24. Personal violence, as has been the case in some Christian controversies, takes the place of further debate. The hateful symbols of servitude should not be allowed to outrage the feelings of the people any longer. His success in breaking that was to be the pledge of the destruction of the power which it represented. Jeremiah, it will be noted, does not resist or retaliate, but commits him-

of two full years. And the prophet
Jeremiah went his way.
(12) Then the word of the LORD came
unto Jeremiah *the prophet*, after that
Hananiah the prophet had broken the
yoke from off the neck of the prophet
Jeremiah, saying, (13) Go and tell Hana-
niah, saying, Thus saith the LORD;
Thou hast broken the yokes of wood;
but thou shalt make for them yokes of
iron. (14) For thus saith the LORD of
hosts, the God of Israel; I have put a
yoke of iron upon the neck of all these
nations, that they may serve Nebuchad-
nezzar king of Babylon; and they shall
serve him: and I have given him the
beasts of the field also.
(15) Then said the prophet Jeremiah
unto Hananiah the prophet, Hear now,
Hananiah; the LORD hath not sent thee;
but thou makest this people to trust in
a lie. (16) Therefore thus saith the
LORD; Behold, I will cast thee from off
the face of the earth: this year thou
shalt die, because thou hast taught
[a] [1] rebellion against the LORD.
(17) So Hananiah the prophet died the
same year in the seventh month.

CHAPTER XXIX.—(1) Now these *are*
the words of the letter that Jeremiah
the prophet sent from Jerusalem unto
the residue of the elders which were
carried away captives, and to the
priests, and to the prophets, and to all
the people whom Nebuchadnezzar had
carried away captive from Jerusalem to
Babylon; (2) (after that [b] Jeconiah the
king, and the queen, and the [2] eunuchs,
the princes of Judah and Jerusalem,
and the carpenters, and the smiths,
were departed from Jerusalem;) (3) by

a Deut. 13. 5; ch. 29. 32.

B. C. cir. 595.

B. C. cir. 599.

1 Heb. *revolt.*

b 2 Kings 24. 12, &c.

2 Or, *chamberlains.*

self to Him that judgeth righteously. "He went his way."

(12) **Then the word of the Lord . . .**—The narrative suggests the thought of a time of silent suffering and of prayer, to which the "word of the Lord" came as an answer. And that word declared, keeping to the same symbolism as before, that all attempts at resistance to the power which was for the time the scourge, and therefore the servant, of Jehovah, would only end in a more bitter and aggravated bondage. In the "iron yoke" we have an echo of Deut. xxviii. 48.

(14) **I have given him the beasts of the field also.**—On the significance of this addition see Note on chap. xxvii. 6.

(15) **Hear now, Hananiah . . .**—The narrative leaves the time and place of the interview uncertain, but suggests an interval of some days between it and the scene in the Temple court just narrated. In the strength of the "word of the Lord" which had come to him, the prophet can now tell his rival that he is a pretender, claiming the gift of prophecy for his own purposes and that of his party. There is a strange significance in the fact that the same official title is applied to both the true and the false prophets.

(16) **I will cast thee . . .**—Literally, *I send thee.* The verb is the same as in the preceding verse, and is repeated with an emphatic irony.

This year thou shalt die . . .—The punishment is announced, with time given for repentance. In part, perhaps, the threat may have tended to work out its own fulfilment through the gnawing consciousness of shame and confusion in the detection of the false prophet's assumptions. He knew that the Lord had not sent him. Seven months passed, and then the stroke fell. It is one of the instances of the prophet's work, as "rooting out" and "pulling down" (chap. i. 10), and has its parallels in the punishment of Ananias, in Acts v. 4, 5, and of Elymas, in Acts xiii. 11.

XXIX.

(1) **These are the words.**—The prophecy in this chapter was addressed to those whom we may describe as the first of the Babylonian exiles who had been carried into captivity with Jeconiah (see Note on chap. xxxv. 2). Among these also, probably in connection with the projects which we have traced in the preceding chapter, there was a restless disquietude, fostered by false prophets, who urged the people to rebel against their conquerors. Against that policy Jeremiah, in accordance with the convictions on which he had all along acted, enters an earnest protest. The letter was sent by special messengers, of whom we read in verse 3, and shows that Jeremiah had been kept well informed of all that passed at Babylon. The spelling of the prophet's name, in the Hebrew text, as Jeremiah, instead of the form Jeremia*hu*, which is the more common form throughout the book, is probably an indication that the opening verse which introduces the letter was the work of a later hand. The date of the letter was probably early in the reign of Zedekiah, before the incidents of the previous chapter. It is brought before us as following in almost immediate sequel on the deportation mentioned in verse 2. The term "residue of the elders," in connexion with "priests and prophets," points to the fact that the whole body of counsellors, so named, had not been carried into exile, but only the more prominent members. Such "elders" we find in Ezek. viii. 1, xx. 1. Ezekiel himself may be thought of as among the priests and prophets.

(2) **The queen.**—This was probably the queen-mother, Nehushta, the daughter of Elnathan (2 Kings xxiv. 8). The name probably indicates a connection with the Elnathan the son of Achbor, of chap xxvi. 22, but we cannot assert with any confidence the identity of the one with the other.

The carpenters, and the smiths.—See Note on chap. xxiv. 1. Among the exiles thus referred to as "princes" we have to think of Daniel, and those who are best known to us by their Babylonian names as Shadrach, Meshach, and Abed-nego (Dan. i. 6, 7). The conduct, we may well believe, was in accordance with Jeremiah's teaching.

(3) **By the hand of Elasah . . .**—The names of the messengers are of some interest. Elasah, the son of Shaphan, was the brother of Jeremiah's protector.

the hand of Elasah the son of Shaphan,
and Gemariah the son of Hilkiah,
(whom Zedekiah king of Judah sent
unto Babylon to Nebuchadnezzar king
of Babylon) saying, (4) Thus saith the
Lord of hosts, the God of Israel, unto
all that are carried away captives,
whom I have caused to be carried away
from Jerusalem unto Babylon;
(5) Build ye houses, and dwell *in them;*
and plant gardens, and eat the fruit of
them; (6) take ye wives, and beget sons
and daughters; and take wives for your
sons, and give your daughters to husbands,
that they may bear sons and
daughters; that ye may be increased
there, and not diminished. (7) And
seek the peace of the city whither I
have caused you to be carried away
captives, and pray unto the Lord for
it: for in the peace thereof shall ye
have peace.
(8) For thus saith the Lord of hosts,
the God of Israel; Let not your
prophets and your diviners, that *be* in
the midst of you, [a]deceive you, neither
hearken to your dreams which ye cause
to be dreamed. (9) For they prophesy
[1]falsely unto you in my name: I have
not sent them, saith the Lord. (10) For
thus saith the Lord, That after [b]seventy
years be accomplished at Babylon I will
visit you, and perform my good word
toward you, in causing you to return to
this place. (11) For I know the thoughts
that I think toward you, saith the
Lord, thoughts of peace, and not of
evil, to give you an [2]expected end.

a ch. 14. 14; & 23. 21; & 27. 15.

1 Heb., *in a lie.*

B. C. cir. 606.

b 2 Chron. 36. 21, 22; Ezra 1. 1; ch. 25. 12; & 27. 22; Dan. 9. 2.

2 Heb., *end and expectation.*

Ahikam (chap. xxvi. 24). Gemariah (to be distinguished from his namesake the son of Shaphan in chap. xxxvi. 12) was probably the son of Hilkiah, the high-priest under Josiah who found the lost Book of the Law (2 Kings xxii. 4), and took a prominent part in the work of reformation. Each would therefore naturally take his place among the prophet's friends and supporters. They carried his letter as well as the diplomatic missive of the king. That they had been sent as envoys by Zedekiah indicates that the policy of the weak and vacillating king had been to some extent affected by the counsels of Jeremiah, and that he had at least half abandoned the idea of revolt, and had sent to acknowledge the suzerainty of Nebuchadnezzar. It is hardly likely, at least, that the letter from the prophet, of which they were the bearers, should have been in flagrant antagonism with their mission as envoys from the king. The embassy was probably prior to the personal visit of Zechariah recorded in chap. li. 59.

(4) **Thus saith the Lord of hosts . . .**—We have here the nearest parallel in the Old Testament to the Epistles which make up so large a portion of the New, the very text of a written letter sent to those with whom the teacher was no longer able to hold personal communication. It obviously furnished the type which was followed by the writer of the apocryphal letter from Jeremiah in Baruch vi.

(5) **Build ye houses, and dwell in them.**—The command had a two-fold bearing. It counselled a patient acceptance of the present state of things. It announced, as the next verse does yet more emphatically, that their exile would last for at least two generations. It indicates, also, the comparative leniency with which the exiles were treated. They were allowed to become possessors both of lands and houses. The favour shown to Daniel and his friends would, of course, tend to make their condition more tolerable.

(7) **And seek the peace of the city . . .**—This was, we may believe, the hardest command of all. To refrain from all curses and imprecations, even from such as came from the lips of those who hung their harps on the willows by the waters of Babylon (Ps. cxxxvii.), to pray for the peace and prosperity of the city where they were eating the bread of captivity—this surely required an almost superhuman patience. Yet this was the prophet's counsel. It seems almost to follow—unless we apply Augustine's rule, *Distingue tempora,* and refer the psalm to a time prior to Jeremiah's letter, or nearer the day of vengeance—that those imprecations, natural as they seem, belonged to a lower stage of spiritual progress than that represented by the prophet. He was, to those impatient exiles, as our Lord was to the impatient disciples who sought to call down fire on the village of the Samaritans (Luke ix. 54—56). So, we may remember, Christians living under Nero were told to pray for the Emperor (1 Tim. ii. 2).

(8) **Let not your prophets and your diviners . . .**—The words are significant as showing that the same agencies which were counteracting the prophet's teaching in Jerusalem were at work also in Babylon. There, too, "prophets and diviners," whom the Lord had not sent, were prophesying of a speedy deliverance, and it was necessary to reiterate for those who would listen to the prophet's warnings, that the exile would run its appointed course of seventy years, as Jeremiah had announced to the people of Jerusalem in chap. xxv. 12, xxvii. 22. The "dreams which ye cause to be dreamed" (an altogether exceptional phrase) indicates that the supply was created by a demand for visions of this nature.

(11) **For I know the thoughts . . .**—The word used for "*saith* the Lord" implies that the gracious promise came to the prophet's soul as an oracle from heaven. In the "thoughts" of God there is, perhaps, a reference to what had been said before of the Babylonian exiles in chap. xxiv. 6.

To give you an expected end.—Better, *to give you a future* (that which is to be hereafter) *and a hope.* This is the literal rendering of the words, and it is far more expressive than that of the English version. An "expected end" may be one from which we shrink in fear or dislike. Each word, in the amended translation, has its full meaning. The "future" tells them that their history as a people is not yet over; the "hope" that there is a better time in store for them. To wait for that future, instead of trusting in delusive assurances of immediate release, was the true wisdom of the exiles.

(12) Then shall ye [a] call upon me, and ye
shall go and pray unto me, and I will
hearken unto you. (13) And ye shall
seek me, and find *me*, when ye shall
search for me with all your heart.
(14) And I will be found of you, saith
the LORD: and I will turn away your
captivity, and I will gather you from
all the nations, and from all the places
whither I have driven you, saith the
LORD; and I will bring you again into
the place whence I caused you to be
carried away captive.
(15) Because ye have said, The LORD
hath raised us up prophets in Babylon;
(16) *know* that thus saith the LORD of
the king that sitteth upon the throne
of David, and of all the people that
dwelleth in this city, *and* of your
brethren that are not gone forth with
you into captivity; (17) thus saith the
LORD of hosts; Behold, I will send upon
them the [b]sword, the famine, and the
pestilence, and will make them like
[c]vile figs, that cannot be eaten, they
are so evil. (18) And I will persecute
them with the sword, with the famine,
and with the pestilence, and will deliver
them to be removed to all the kingdoms
of the earth, [1]to be a curse, and an as-
tonishment, and an hissing, and a re-
proach, among all the nations whither
I have driven them: (19) because they
have not hearkened to my words, saith
the LORD, which [d]I sent unto them by
my servants the prophets, rising up
early and sending *them;* but ye would
not hear, saith the LORD.
(20) Hear ye therefore the word of the
LORD, all ye of the captivity, whom I
have sent from Jerusalem to Babylon:
(21) Thus saith the LORD of hosts, the
God of Israel, of Ahab the son of
Kolaiah, and of Zedekiah the son of
Maaseiah, which prophesy a lie unto
you in my name; Behold, I will deliver
them into the hand of Nebuchadrezzar
king of Babylon; and he shall slay
them before your eyes; (22) and of them
shall be taken up a curse by all the cap-
tivity of Judah which *are* in Babylon,
saying, The LORD make thee like Zede-
kiah and like Ahab, whom the king of
Babylon roasted in the fire; (23) because
they have committed villany in Israel,
and have committed adultery with their

a Dan. 9. 3, &c.

b ch. 24. 10.

c ch. 24. 8.

1 Heb., *for a curse.*

d ch. 25. 4; & 32. 33.

(12, 13) **Then shall ye call upon me . . .**—The words need no comment, but they cannot be passed over without dwelling on the infinite tenderness which they manifest in the prophet's soul, the reflex of a like tenderness in the mind of God, from whom he gives the message. It is the anticipation of the like message from the lips of Christ, "He that seeketh findeth, and to him that knocketh it shall be opened" (Matt. vii. 8). As they stand, the words are an echo of Deut. iv. 29, 30, as verse 14 is of Deut. xxx. 3—5.

(14) **I will turn away your captivity . . .**—On the substance and fulfilment of the prediction, see Notes on chap. xxiii. 3—8.

(15) **Because ye have said, The Lord hath raised us up prophets . . .**—The words point to the boast of some of the exiles, that they, too, had the guidance of prophets whom, as in verses 20 and 24, they were inclined to follow in preference to Jeremiah. In answer to that boast, he emphasises the contrast between the exiles in whom the prophet sees the future hope of his nation and the worthless king (Zedekiah) and people who had been left in Jerusalem, and for whom he foretells yet sharper sufferings. The symbolism of the "vile figs" is reproduced in verse 17 from chap. xxiv. 1, 2. The word for "vile" is, however, not the same as in that passage, and has the stronger force of "horrible" or "loathsome."

(21, 22) **Ahab the son of Kolaiah . . .**—We know nothing, beyond what is here recorded, of either of these prophets. They would seem to have been the leaders of the party of revolt, and to have been conspicuous, like their brethren at Jerusalem (chap. xxiii. 14), for base and profligate lives. The record of the prediction of their fate implies its fulfilment. They were punished by the Chaldæan king as traitors and rebels, and were burnt alive. The history of the "three children" in Dan. iii. 6, 20, shows that this was a sufficiently familiar punishment. A strange legend in the Targum of Rabbi Joseph on 2 Chron. xxviii. 3 records that the future high-priest Joshua, the son of Jozedek, was thrown into the furnace with them, and came out uninjured (Smith's *Dict. of the Bible*, Art. "Zedekiah"). We may, perhaps, trace the source of the legend in the figurative language of Zech. iii. 2, "Is not this a brand plucked out of the fire?" The name Kolaiah (which admits of being derived from a verb meaning "roasting") possibly suggested the cruel mockery of a punishment which turned it into an omen of the false prophet's fate.

(22) **Of them shall be taken up a curse . . .**—We note the characteristic tendency of Hebrew thought to fix on individual cases of highest blessedness, as in Ruth iv. 11, or of deepest shame, as here, and to bring them into formulæ of blessing and of cursing.

(23) **Because they have committed villany . . .**—The Hebrew noun is almost always used for sins of impurity. It is more commonly rendered "folly" (comp. Gen. xxxiv. 7; Deut. xxii. 21; Judg. xix. 23, 24). The English word "villainy" is used definitely with this meaning by Bishop Hall (*Sat.* i. 9).

Even I know, and am a witness, saith the Lord.—The words find an echo in Mal. iii. 5. We are left to conjecture whether the prophet refers his own knowledge of the facts to a direct supernatural source, or had received private information from his friends at Babylon. The special stress laid on the Lord's knowledge of their guilt suggests the thought that the false prophets with their restricted

neighbours' wives, and have spoken
lying words in my name, which I have
not commanded them; even I know,
and *am* a witness, saith the LORD.
(24) *Thus* shalt thou also speak to
Shemaiah the [1] Nehelamite, saying,
(25) Thus speaketh the LORD of hosts,
the God of Israel, saying, Because thou
hast sent letters in thy name unto all
the people that *are* at Jerusalem, and
to Zephaniah the son of Maaseiah the
priest, and to all the priests, saying,
(26) The LORD hath made thee priest in
the stead of Jehoiada the priest, that
ye should be officers in the house of the
LORD, for every man *that is* [a] mad, and
maketh himself a prophet, that thou
shouldest put him in prison, and in the
stocks. (27) Now therefore why hast
thou not reproved Jeremiah of Anathoth,
which maketh himself a prophet to you?
(28) For therefore he sent unto us *in*
Babylon, saying, This *captivity is* long:
build ye houses, and dwell *in them*;
and plant gardens, and eat the fruit of
them. (29) And Zephaniah the priest
read this letter in the ears of Jeremiah
the prophet.
(30) Then came the word of the
LORD unto Jeremiah, saying, (31) Send
to all them of the captivity, saying,
Thus saith the LORD concerning
Shemaiah the Nehelamite; Because
that Shemaiah hath prophesied unto
you, and I sent him not, and he caused
you to trust in a lie: (32) therefore thus
saith the LORD; Behold, I will punish
Shemaiah the Nehelamite, and his
seed: he shall not have a man to
dwell among this people; neither shall
he behold the good that I will do for
my people, saith the LORD; [b] because
he hath taught [2] rebellion against the
LORD.

1 Or, *dreamer.*

B. C. 598.

a 2 Kings 9. 11; Acts 26. 24.

b ch. 28. 16.

2 Heb., *revolt.*

---

ideas of God had persuaded themselves that Jehovah the God of Israel hardly exercised his attributes of power in a distant place like Babylon. There they might sin without fear of detection or of punishment. They thought of him as a God not nigh at hand, but far off (chap. xxiii. 23).

(24) **Thus shalt thou also speak to Shemaiah the Nehelamite.**—It is clear that this section (verses 24—32) is of the nature of a fragment attached to the Epistle to Babylon on account of its associations with it, but not forming part of it. It gives, in fact (as verse 28 shows), the sequence of events, and so far stands in the same relation to it as the Second Epistle to the Corinthians does to the First. Jeremiah's letter had naturally roused the indignation of the rival prophets at Babylon, and they organised a movement, of which Shemaiah was the chief instigator, for his destruction. Of Shemaiah himself we know nothing more than is here recorded. The description "Nehelamite" gives us no information, as the name Nehelam does not appear as belonging to any person or place in the Old Testament. It is just possible, as in the marginal reading, that there may be a play upon the Hebrew word (*Halam*) for "dreamer."

(25) **Because thou hast sent letters in thy name . . .**—The letters were probably sent through the envoys named in verse 3 on their return from Babylon. Their object was to urge Zephaniah, who appears in 2 Kings xxv. 18 as the *Sagan*, or second priest, to exercise his authority to restrain Jeremiah from prophesying, and to punish him as a false prophet. It was an attempt to turn the tables on him for the manner in which he had thwarted the plans of the party of revolt at Babylon. The part taken by Zephaniah in acting for the king when he wished to consult Jeremiah (chap. xxi. 1), and imploring his intercession (chap. xxxvii. 3), makes it probable that he endeavoured to maintain a neutral Gamaliel-like position between the two parties, and had seemed so lukewarm and temporising that he was open to the influence of threats. On the capture of Jerusalem by Nebuzaradan he was taken prisoner and slain (chap. lii. 24—27).

(26) **The Lord hath made thee priest in the stead of Jehoiada . . .**—The priest so named had apparently been deposed, as not favouring the stringent policy of the party of revolt. As *Sagan*, it was probably his special duty to maintain order in the Temple, and punish pretenders to the gift of prophecy, and the letter reproaches him for his lukewarm timidity in discharging that duty. In the word "mad," as in 2 Kings ix. 11, Hos. ix. 7, we have the habitual term of scorn applied to such pretenders. On the punishment of the stocks, see Note on chap. xx. 2. The word translated "prison" is probably another form of punishment like that of the stocks.

(28) **This captivity is long . . .**—As the italics show, there is no word corresponding to "captivity" in the Hebrew, and some commentators render the words, *It is far off* . . . as though Jeremiah had counted on the distance of Babylon as enabling him to write the letter with impunity, or possibly in all the emphasis of abruptness. "All is a long way off—the end of your exile, your present distance from your native land, and haste, therefore, is but folly."

(29) **And Zephaniah the priest . . .**—The fact thus related agrees with what has been said as to the character of Zephaniah. He does not act as Shemaiah wished him. At the most he only uses the letters as a threat, possibly to put the prophet on his guard against the machinations of his enemies, possibly also to induce him to moderate his tone. We are reminded of the like conduct of the Pharisees who reported Herod's threats to our Lord, in Luke xiii. 31.

(31) **Send to all them of the captivity.**—The words imply something in the nature of another epistle to the exiles, sent, probably, like the previous one, by the hands of envoys from one government to the other. We have no record of the fulfilment of the prediction but its insertion implies its fulfilment. This frequent intercourse between Jerusalem and Babylon is noticeable (1) as confirming the literal interpretation of the journey to Euphrates in chap. xiii. 4, and (2) as accounting for the special instructions given to Nebuzar-adan by Nebuchadnezzar in chap. xxxix. 11.

CHAPTER XXX.—(1) The word that
came to Jeremiah from the LORD, say-
ing, (2) Thus speaketh the LORD God of
Israel, saying,
Write thee all the words that I have
spoken unto thee in a book. (3) For,
lo, the days come, saith the LORD, that
I will bring again the captivity of
my people Israel and Judah, saith the
LORD: and I will cause them to return
to the land that I gave to their fathers,
and they shall possess it.
(4) And these *are* the words that the
LORD spake concerning Israel and con-
cerning Judah. (5) For thus saith the
LORD;
We have heard a voice of trembling,
[1]of fear, and not of peace. (6) Ask ye
now, and see whether [2]a man doth
travail with child? wherefore do I see
every man with his hands on his loins,
as a woman in travail, and all faces are
turned into paleness? (7) [a]Alas! for
that day *is* great, so that none *is* like
it: it *is* even the time of Jacob's
trouble; but he shall be saved out of
it. (8) For it shall come to pass in that
day, saith the LORD of hosts, *that* I
will break his yoke from off thy neck,
and will burst thy bonds, and strangers
shall no more serve themselves of him:
(9) but they shall serve the LORD their
God, and [b]David their king, whom I
will raise up unto them.
(10) Therefore [c]fear thou not, O my
servant Jacob, saith the LORD; neither
be dismayed, O Israel: for, lo, I will
save thee from afar, and thy seed from
the land of their captivity; and Jacob
shall return, and shall be in rest, and
be quiet, and none shall make *him*
afraid. (11) For I *am* with thee, saith
the LORD, to save thee: though I make
a full end of all nations whither I have

[1] Or, *there is fear, and not peace.*

[2] Heb., *a male.*

[a] Joel 2. 11; Amos 5. 18; Zeph. 1. 14, &c.

[b] Ezek. 34. 23; & 37. 24; Hosea 3. 5.

[c] Isa. 41. 13; & 43. 5; & 44. 1; ch. 46. 28.

XXX.

(2) **Write thee all the words . . .**—The opening words emphasise the fact that what follows was not spoken at first, like chaps. xxvii. and xxviii., in the presence of the people, but was from the first committed to writing. There is no definite point at which we may be certain that the section ends, and there is room for many conjectures as to interpolations here and there, but the opening of chap. xxxii. suggests the conclusion that it takes in the whole of chaps. xxx. and xxxi. The general character of the prophecy, probably in part consequent on the acceptance of the prophet's teaching by the exiles of Babylon, is one of blessing and restoration, and he is thus led on to the great utterance which, from one point of view, makes him more the prophet of the Gospel even than Isaiah. It is here that we find that promise of a New Covenant (chap. xxxi. 31) which both as a word and a fact has been prominent in the history of Christendom.

(3) **I will bring again the captivity of my people Israel and Judah . . .**—The oracle of chap. xxix. 10—14 becomes, as it were, the text of a new utterance, and that with a wider range more distinctly including the ten tribes of Israel as well as the two of Judah and Benjamin. There is no narrow provincialism in the prophet's heart. He yearns for the exiles who are far off on the Euphrates; he yearns also for those who are yet farther in Assyria and the cities of the Medes (2 Kings xvii. 6).

(5, 6) **Thus saith the Lord; We have heard a voice of trembling . . .**—There is a strange mingling of the divine and human elements in these words. The prophet speaks with the sense that the words are not his own, and yet what he utters is, at first, the expression of his own horror and astonishment at the vision of woe that is opening before his eyes. He sees, as it were, the famine-stricken people, their faces gathering blackness, the strong men giving way to a woman's anguish, wailing with their hands on their loins. In horror rather than in scorn, he asks the question, What means all this? Are these men in the pangs of childbirth? (Comp. chaps. iv. 31, vi. 24, xiii. 21.) In Lament. ii. 19—22 we have a fuller picture of a like scene. By some commentators the three verses (5—7) are referred to the alarm caused in Babylon by the advance of Cyrus, and "that day" is the day of his capture of the city, but there seems no sufficient reason for such an interpretation.

(8) **For it shall come to pass in that day . . .**—Better, *And it shall come.* Here there comes in the ground of the hope uttered in the words "he shall be saved out of it," which keeps the prophet from sinking under the burden of his sorrow. The second and third person are strangely mingled. Jehovah speaks to Israel, "thy bonds," "thy yoke," and "his yoke" is that of the oppressor, *i.e.*, of the Babylonian ruler, and then, the person changing, "strangers shall no more get service done for them by *him*," *i.e.*, by Israel. The prophet echoes the words of Isa. x. 27.

(9) **David their king . . .**—The name of the old hero-king appears as that of the new representative of the house who is to restore the kingdom. There is to be a second David for Israel, a true king answering to the ideal which he imperfectly represented. Zerubbabel, in whom some interpreters have seen the fulfilment of Jeremiah's words, was, in his measure, another partial representative of such a king (Hagg. ii. 21—23). The same mode of speech appears in Hos. iii. 5, Isa. lv. 4, and was probably deliberately reproduced by Jeremiah.

(10) **Therefore fear thou not.**—The higher strain of language into which the prophecy has here risen is indicated by the parallelism of the two clauses in each member of the sentence. The whole verse is poetic in its form. The words have in them something of the ring of Isa. xli. 10.

(11) **Though I make a full end of all nations.**—On the phrase, see Notes on chaps. iv. 27, v. 10, 18. It is eminently characteristic of the prophets of Jeremiah's time (Ezek. xi. 13, xx. 17; Nah. i. 8, 9). Here the thought, implied elsewhere, and reproduced in

scattered thee, yet will I not make a
full end of thee: but I will correct thee
[a]in measure, and will not leave thee
altogether unpunished.
(12) For thus saith the LORD, Thy
bruise *is* incurable, *and* thy wound *is*
grievous. (13) *There is* none to plead
thy cause, [1]that thou mayest be bound
up: thou hast no healing medicines.
(14) All thy lovers have forgotten thee;
they seek thee not; for I have wounded
thee with the wound of an enemy, with
the chastisement of a cruel one, for the
multitude of thine iniquity; *because*
thy sins were increased. (15) Why
[b]criest thou for thine affliction? thy
sorrow *is* incurable for the multitude of
thine iniquity: *because* thy sins were
increased, I have done these things
unto thee. (16) Therefore all they that
devour thee [c]shall be devoured; and all
thine adversaries, every one of them,
shall go into captivity; and they that
spoil thee shall be a spoil, and all that
prey upon thee will I give for a prey.
(17) For I will restore health unto thee,
and I will heal thee of thy wounds, saith
the LORD; because they called thee an
Outcast, *saying*, This *is* Zion, whom no
man seeketh after.
(18) Thus saith the LORD; Behold, I
will bring again the captivity of Jacob's
tents, and have mercy on his dwelling-
places; and the city shall be builded
upon her own [2]heap, and the palace
shall remain after the manner thereof.
(19) And out of them shall proceed
thanksgiving and the voice of them that
make merry: and I will multiply them,
and they shall not be few; I will also
glorify them, and they shall not be
small. (20) Their children also shall
be as aforetime, and their congrega-
tion shall be established before me, and

[a] Ps. 6. 1; ch. 10. 24; & 46. 28.

[1] Heb., *for binding up*, or, *pressing*.

B. C. cir. 606.

[b] ch. 15. 18.

[c] Exod. 23. 22; Isa. 41. 11.

[2] Or, *little hill*.

---

chap. xlvi. 28, is expressed more fully than before, that while the destruction of the national life of the heathen nations on whom judgment was to fall should be complete and irreversible, so that Moab, Ammon, Edom, should no more have a place in the history of the world, the punishment of Israel should be remedial as well as retributive, working out, in due time, a complete restitution. In "correcting in measure" we trace an echo of Ps. vi. 1 (see Note on chap. x. 24). That thought sustains the prophet in his contemplation of the captivity and apparent ruin of his people. To be left "altogether unpunished" would be, as in the "let him alone" of Hos. iv. 17, the most terrible of all punishments.

(12) **Thy bruise is incurable . . .**—The mind of the prophet dwells on the seeming hopelessness, in words which sound like an echo from his Lamentations (chap. ii. 13), in order to enhance the blessedness of the reverent utterance of hope which appears in verse 17.

(13) **There is none to plead thy cause . . .**—The words bring before us two images of extremest misery—the criminal who, standing before the dread judgment-seat, has no advocate, the plague-stricken sufferer who has no physician. The word is that used of Josiah in chap. xxii. 16. There, and commonly elsewhere, it is translated "judge." The second part of the sentence is better rendered, with a different punctuation, by *Thou hast no healing medicines for binding up*. It continues the symbolism of verse 12, and reproduces that of Isa. i. 6. There, and in Isa. xxxviii. 21, Hos. v. 13, and probably in Prov. iii. 8, we have indications of the prominence given to external applications such as plasters, bandages, and the like, in the Eastern treatment of disease.

(14) **All thy lovers have forgotten thee . . .**—The lovers of a nation are, of course, as in chap. xxii. 20, its allies and tributaries. Moab, Ammon, Edom, Tyre, had at one time courted the favour of Judah (chap. xxvii. 3). They looked on her now as "smitten of God and afflicted." He had smitten her as an enemy smites. His chastisement had seemed to imply that she was given over to a deserved destruction. In chaps. xl. 14, xlviii. 27, Lam. iv. 21, Ps. cxxxvii. 7, we have traces of this change of feeling.

(15) **Why criest thou . . . ?**—The personification of the previous verse is continued. The prophet looks on Judah—as in Lam. i. 1, 2—as on some forlorn and desperate castaway smitten with pestilence, crying in the agony of her hopelessness; and he reminds her that she is but bearing the righteous punishment of her iniquities. In accepting the law of retribution, as seen in her own sufferings, she might find hope for the future. Her oppressors also would come under that law. The wheel would come full circle, and the devourers would be themselves devoured.

(17) **I will restore health unto thee . . .**—Literally, *I will place a healing plaster on thee.* The image of the plague-stricken sufferer is resumed from verse 13. Men had scorned her. The contemptuous term of outcast had been flung at her. She was like Tyre, as a "harlot that had been forgotten" (Isa. xxiii. 16). There were none who sought her company. No nation courted her alliance. It was as though that extremest misery had touched the heart of Jehovah with pity, even for the adulteress who had forsaken Him. The whole passage brings the history, or the parable, of Gomer very vividly to our memory (Hos. i.—iii.).

(18) **I will bring again the captivity of Jacob's tents . . .**—The promise of restoration takes naturally a material form. The prophet sees the tents of those who still kept up the old nomadic life, pitched once more in the land of Israel (comp. 1 Kings xii. 16; Jer. xxxv. 10), while for those who dwell in towns, city (the Hebrew has no article) and palace shall rise again from their ruins upon their old foundations on the hills of Judah. The verses that follow carry on the picture of restored prosperity—the streets of the city thronged; the joyous procession of triumphant leaders or of bride and bridegroom; the children playing in the market-place (Zech. viii. 5; Matt. xi. 16); the Temple-courts filled with the "congregations" of worshippers; the people ruled by their own councillors and princes, and not by the satraps of their conquerors.

I will punish all that oppress them.
(21) And their nobles shall be of them-
selves, and their governor shall proceed
from the midst of them; and I will
cause him to draw near, and he shall
approach unto me: for who *is* this that
engaged his heart to approach unto me?
saith the LORD. (22) And ye shall be
my people, and I will be your God.
(23) Behold, the [b]whirlwind of the
LORD goeth forth with fury, a [1]con-
tinuing whirlwind: it shall [2]fall with
pain upon the head of the wicked.
(24) The fierce anger of the LORD shall
not return, until he have done *it*, and
until he have performed the intents of
his heart: in the latter days ye shall
consider it.

CHAPTER XXXI.—(1) At the same
time, saith the LORD, will I be the God
of all the families of Israel, and they
shall be my people. (2) Thus saith the
LORD, The people *which were* left of the
sword found grace in the wilderness;
even Israel, when I went to cause him
to rest. (3) The LORD hath appeared
[3]of old unto me, *saying*, Yea, I have
loved thee with an everlasting love:
therefore [4]with lovingkindness have I
drawn thee. (4) Again I will build
thee, and thou shalt be built, O virgin
of Israel: thou shalt again be adorned
with thy [c][5]tabrets, and shalt go forth in
the dances of them that make merry.
(5) Thou shalt yet plant vines upon the
mountains of Samaria: the planters

a ch. 24. 7; & 31. 33; & 32. 38.
b ch. 23. 19, 20.
1 Heb., *cutting*.
2 Or, *remain*.
3 Heb., *from afar*.
4 Or, *have I extended lovingkindness unto thee*.
c Exod. 15. 20; Judges 11. 34.
5 Or, *timbrels*.

---

(21) **Their nobles.**—Literally, *His glorious one*, as pointing to some single ruler. The word is the same as the "excellent" of Ps. viii. 1.

Who is this that engaged his heart to approach unto me?—The question points to the ruler of the house of David whom the prophet sees in visions —in other words, to the far-off Messiah. So in Isaiah we have a like introduction of the figure of the conqueror, "Who is this that cometh from Edom?" (Isa. lxiii. 1). As in Isa. xi. 1—3, xlii. 1—4, the dominant thought is that of one who will not be treacherous or faithless, like the degenerate heirs of the house of David whom Jeremiah had known, but one who would "engage" (literally, *pledge*, or *give as security*) his heart and soul to the service of Jehovah. In the advent of such a king the true relation between God and His people (Hos. i. 10; Jer. xxiv. 7) should yet be re-established. In the words "to approach unto me" we have the germ of the thought that the true King will also be a priest, and will enter, as others could not enter, into the Holy Place (see Note on chap. xxxv. 19, and Num. xvi. 5); a priest, such as Ps. cx. 4 had spoken of, after the order of Melchizedek.

(23, 24) **Behold, the whirlwind of the Lord . . .** —The "wicked" who are thus threatened are the enemies and oppressors of the penitent and rescued people. In the "latter days," the far-off future (Gen. xlix. 1; Num. xxiv. 14; Isa. ii. 2), it should be seen that He was their avenger. (See Notes on chap. xxiii. 19, 20.) A right division of chapters would probably connect this with the great promise of chap. xxxi. 1.

XXXI.

(1) **The God of all the families of Israel.**— The union of the ten tribes of Israel and the two of Judah is again prominent in the prophet's mind. He cannot bear to think of that division, with its deep lines of cleavage in the religious and social life of the people, being perpetuated. Israel should be Israel. This is the crown and consummation of the promise of chap. xxx. 24.

(2) **The people which were left of the sword . . .**—The main thought of this and the next verse is that the past experience of God's love is a pledge or earnest for the future. Israel of old had "found grace in the wilderness" (comp. Hos. xi. 1). But as the prophet has in his thoughts a new manifestation of that love, his language is modified accordingly. He thinks of the captives that had escaped, or should hereafter escape, the sword of the Chaldæans (there had been no such deliverance in the case of the Egyptian exodus), and of their finding grace in the wilderness that lies between Palestine and the Euphrates. The verses that follow show, however, that the prophet is thinking also of the more distant exiles, the ten tribes in the cities of the Medes beyond the Tigris (2 Kings xvii. 6).

Even Israel, when I went to cause him to rest.—The verb that answers to the last five words includes the meaning of "settling" or "establishing," as well as of giving rest; and the whole clause is better translated *Let me go*, or *I will go* (the verb is in the infinitive with the force of an imperative, but this is its meaning) *to set him at rest, even Israel.*

(3) **The Lord hath appeared of old unto me . . .**—The Hebrew adverb more commonly refers to distance than to time. *From afar the Lord appeared unto me.* The thought is that of a deliverer who hears the cry of his people in the distance, and then draws near to help them. Jehovah enthroned in Zion, or in the heaven of heavens, hears the cry of the exiles by the waters of Babylon or Nineveh.

Therefore with lovingkindness have I drawn thee.—Some translators render *I have preserved* (or *respited*) *thee*, others *I have continued my lovingkindness to thee*, as in Ps. xxxvi. 10, cix. 12; but the LXX., Vulg., and Luther agree with the English Version, and it finds sufficient support in the meaning of the Hebrew verb and in the parallel of Hos. xi. 4.

(4) **Thou shalt again be adorned with thy tabrets . . .**—The implied idea is that of a time of rejoicing after triumphant restoration (the "building" of the previous sentence is more than that of material walls and towers), when the daughters of Israel (as in Exod. xv. 20; Judg. xi. 34; 1 Sam. xviii. 6; Ps. lxviii. 11) should again go forth with "timbrels and dances," with tabrets and joy and instruments of music. The "tabret" was a musical instrument of the drum type, somewhat like the Spanish or Italian tambourine, with bells attached to the metal hoop.

(5) **Thou shalt yet plant vines upon the mountains of Samaria . . .**—The mention of

shall plant, and shall [1]eat *them* as
common things. (6) For there shall be
a day, *that* the watchmen upon the
mount Ephraim shall cry, Arise ye, and
let us go up to Zion unto the LORD our
God.

(7) For thus saith the LORD; Sing
with gladness for Jacob, and shout
among the chief of the nations: publish
ye, praise ye, and say, O LORD, save thy
people, the remnant of Israel. (8) Be-
hold, I will bring them from the north
country, and gather them from the
coasts of the earth, *and* with them the
blind and the lame, the woman with
child and her that travaileth with child
together: a great company shall return
thither. (9) They shall come with weep-
ing, and with [2]supplications will I lead
them: I will cause them to walk by
the rivers of waters in a straight way,
wherein they shall not stumble: for I
am a father to Israel, and Ephraim *is*
my [a]firstborn.

1 Heb., *profane them.*

2 Or, *favours.*

a Exod. 4. 22.

Samaria shows that the prophet is thinking of the restoration of the northern kingdom, as well as of Judah, under the rule of the true King. In the Hebrew words "shall eat them as common things" we have a singular train of associations. The primary meaning of the verb is to "profane." The rule of Lev. xix. 23, 24, based partly, perhaps, on grounds of culture, partly with a symbolic meaning, required that a vineyard for three years after it was planted should be treated as "uncircumcised" (*i.e.*, that no use should be made of the fruit), in the fourth year the fruit was to "be holy to praise the Lord with," and in the fifth the planter might take the fruit for himself. So accordingly in Deut. xx. 6 we have, as one of the laws affecting war, that if a man had planted a vineyard and had not made it common—the same word as that used here—*i.e*, had not got beyond the fixed period of consecration, he might be exempted from military service, lest he should die and another eat of it. Compare also Deut. xxviii. 30, where the English "gather" answers, as the marginal reading shows, to the same verb. What is meant here, therefore, is, in contrast with the chances and changes of a time of war, that the planters of the vineyard should not be disturbed in their possession of it. They should not plant, and another eat thereof. (Comp. Isa. lxv. 22; Deut. xxviii. 30.)

(6) **The watchmen upon the mount Ephraim shall cry . . .**—The special fact is given as the ground of the previous prediction. The two kingdoms should be united, and therefore the possession of the vineyards should be undisturbed. The city of Samaria stood on one of the mountains of Ephraim. The "watchmen" may be either the sentinels stationed in the towers of the city, or, more probably, those that were on the look-out for the first appearance of the crescent moon as the signal for the observance either of the Passover or the new-moon festival. What follows is all but decisive in favour of the latter view. What is implied is that the rival worship in Bethel and in Dan, which had so long kept the ten tribes of Israel from the Temple at Jerusalem, should cease, and that from the mountains of Ephraim there should be heard the cry which, with a solitary exception in the reign of Hezekiah (2 Chron. xxx. 11, 18), had not been heard for centuries—"Let us go up to Zion." The long schism which had caused the ruin of the nation would at last be healed. Unity of worship, at once the ground and symbol of national unity, should be restored.

(7) **Shout among the chief of the nations . . .**—Better, *Shout over the head of the nations, i.e.*, over Israel. It would seem from Amos vi 1 as if this was a title specially claimed by the kingdom of the Ten Tribes. (Comp. Exod. xix. 5; Lev. xx. 24, 26; Deut. vii. 6, xxvi. 19.) The prophet, in his vision of the future, calls even on the heathen (see verse 10) to rejoice in the restoration of the remnant of Israel, and pray for their prosperity. In "deliver" we have the same verb as in the "Hosanna" of Ps. cxviii. 25, Matt. xxi. 9. The old bitterness of feeling was to pass away, and heathen and Israelite were to join together in a chorus of praise and prayer. The thought is the same as that of Isa. xlix. 6, lx. 3.

(8) **And with them the blind and the lame . . .**—The vision of restoration continues, and the prophet sees in the spirit the great company of those that return. Even those who are commonly left behind in such an expedition, as incumbrances hindering its march, the blind, the lame, the women with child or in the very pangs of childbirth, will be seen in that company. None shall remain behind. They are to come from the land of the North, the wide range of the term covering the exiles both of Judah in Babylon and of Israel in the cities of the Medes. For "the coasts of the earth" see Note on chap. xxv. 32.

Shall return thither—*i.e.*, to the land of Israel, as the goal of the company of travellers.

(9) **They shall come with weeping . . .**—The present version agrees with the Hebrew punctuation, but a slight change would give, *They shall come with weeping and with supplications; I will lead them; I will cause them to walk . . .* The procession of those whom the prophet sees with his mental eye is that of those who weep tears of sorrow for the past, of joy for the present, and pour out prayers for the future. Of this we have a partial fulfilment in the memorable and touching scene brought before us in Ezra iii. 12, 13. A hand which they do not see shall lead them by the "rivers of waters," both literally and figuratively. (Comp. Isa. xxxv. 7, 8, xliii. 19, xlviii. 21, xlix. 10, 11, for like promises.)

Ephraim is my firstborn.—Ephraim stands here, as often elsewhere (*e.g.*, Hos. xi. 3, 12, xiii. 1, 12) for the whole northern kingdom of the Ten Tribes, of which it was the most conspicuous member. The term "firstborn" is used, as an echo of Exod. iv. 22, as marking out Ephraim as the object of the special favour of Jehovah, the birthright of Reuben having been transferred to the sons of Joseph (1 Chron. v. 1). The prominence of Ephraim over the other tribes is conspicuous throughout the whole history (Judg. xii. 1—3). The prophet apparently recognised it as taking its place once more in the restored unity of the people, when the king should be of the house of David, Jerusalem the centre of worship, Ephraim the leading tribe. (Comp. the contemporary prophecy of Ezek. xxxvii. 19.) It is not without interest to note how the northern prophet looks to Judah as more faithful than Ephraim (Hos. xi. 12), while Jeremiah turns from the sins of the

(10) Hear the word of the LORD, O ye
nations, and declare *it* in the isles afar
off, and say, He that scattered Israel
will gather him, and keep him, as a
shepherd *doth* his flock. (11) For the
LORD hath redeemed Jacob, and ran-
somed him from the hand of *him that*
was stronger than he. (12) Therefore
they shall come and sing in the height
of Zion, and shall flow together to the
goodness of the LORD, for wheat, and
for wine, and for oil, and for the young
of the flock and of the herd: and their
soul shall be as a [a]watered garden; and
they shall not sorrow any more at all.
(13) Then shall the virgin rejoice in the
dance, both young men and old to-
gether: for I will turn their mourning
into joy, and will comfort them, and make
them rejoice from their sorrow. (14) And
I will satiate the soul of the priests with
fatness, and my people shall be satisfied
with my goodness, saith the LORD.

(15) Thus saith the LORD; [b]A voice
was heard in Ramah, lamentation, *and*
bitter weeping; Rahel weeping for her
children refused to be comforted for
her children, because they *were* not.
(16) Thus saith the LORD; Refrain thy
voice from weeping, and thine eyes
from tears: for thy work shall be re-
warded, saith the LORD; and they shall
come again from the land of the enemy.
(17) And there is hope in thine end, saith
the LORD, that thy children shall come
again to their own border.

a Isa. 58. 11.

b Matt. 2. 18.

---

princes and priests of Judah to look with hope on the remnant of Israel.

(10) **Declare it in the isles afar off . . .**—The "isles" appear here, as in Ps. lxxii. 10, Isa. xl. 15, xli. 1, xlix. 1, lxvi. 19, as the vague representative of the distant lands of the west—sometimes (as in Num. xxiv. 24; Jer. ii. 10) with the addition of Chittim. Of the isles so referred to, Cyprus and Crete, so far as any definite localities were thought of, would probably be most conspicuous. Both the "nations" and the "isles" represent the heathen whom the prophet calls to join in the praises offered by Israel.

(11) **For the Lord hath redeemed Jacob . . .**—Of the two verbs "redeem" and "ransom" here used, the first expresses the act of setting free, the other that of acting as the *goel*, or nearest kinsman, who was not only the liberator, but the avenger of those to whom he stood in that relation. (Comp. Num. xxxv. 19; Deut. xix. 6; 2 Sam. xiv. 11; Isa. lix. 20; Ps. xix. 14.) The idea of a "ransom," however—*i.e.*, of a price paid for freedom—does not lie in the Hebrew word.

(12—14) **Therefore they shall come and sing . . .**—The vision of return culminates in a picture of the prosperity of the restored kingdom. The "goodness of the Lord" is, as in Hos. iii. 5, the attribute on which the prophets love to dwell, as shown in all forms of outward abundance. The picture, always among the brightest which an Eastern mind can draw, of a "watered garden" (comp. Isa. li. 3, lviii. 11; Gen. xiii. 10) should be but the symbol of the continuous joy and freshness of their life. The dances of joy, as in the days of Miriam (Exod. xv. 20), and Jephthah (Judg. xi. 34), and David (1 Sam. xviii. 6), should take the place of lamentation. It will be noticed that in all these instances, the dancing company consists of women only. Sacrifices should be offered in the thankfulness of a prosperous people, beyond the utmost expectations of the priests, who had the right of eating of the victims' flesh. Young and old, priests and laity, should rejoice together.

(15) **A voice was heard in Ramah.**—The sharp contrast between this and the exulting joy of the previous verse shows that we are entering on a new section which repeats in altered form the substance of the foregoing, presenting in succession the same pictures of present woe and future gladness. The prophet sees first the desolation of the captivity. Rachel, as the mother of Joseph, and therefore of Ephraim, becomes the ideal representative of the northern kingdom. Her voice is heard in Ramah (possibly, as in 1 Sam. xxii. 6, Ezek. xvi. 24, and in the Vulgate here, not as the name of a locality, but in its general meaning, *from a mountain height*) weeping for the children who have been slain or carried into exile. When used elsewhere as a proper name, the noun always has the article. Here it stands without it. If Ramah be definitely one of the places of that name, known fully as Ramathaim-zophim (1 Sam. i. 1, 19), it is probably that within the borders of Benjamin (Josh. xviii. 25), not far from Rachel's sepulchre (1 Sam. x. 2). She, even in her grave, weeps for her children. The mention of Ramah in Isa. x. 29 seems to indicate that it was the scene of some special massacre in the progress of the Assyrian invader, in the reign of Hezekiah; and Jeremiah may possibly refer to it, as well as to some later atrocity, in connection with that of the Chaldæans (comp. chap. xl. 1), over which Rachel, in her sepulchre near Bethlehem, is supposed to weep. Possibly also the meaning of the name Rachel (= ewe) may have added something to the force of the prophet's description. He hears the cry of the ewe on the hill-top bleating for her lambs. The passage has gained a special significance as being cited by St. Matthew (ii. 18), as fulfilled in Herod's massacre of the infants of Bethlehem. On the nature of this fulfilment see Note on Matt. ii. 18.

(16) **Thy work shall be rewarded, saith the Lord.**—Literally, *there shall be a reward for thy work.* The words are a reproduction of the old prophecy of Azariah, the son of Oded (2 Chron. xv. 7). Rachel, personifying the northern kingdom, perhaps even the collective unity of all Israel, is thought of as labouring in the work of repentance and reformation, as with a mother's care, and is comforted with the thought that her labour shall not be in vain. This seems a more satisfactory interpretation than that which refers the "work" of the weeping Rachel to the travail of child-birth.

(17) **And there is hope in thine end . . .**—Better, *There is hope for thy future.* The words are the same as in chap. xxix. 11, where the English version has "an expected end." The hope here is defined as that of the return of Rachel's children to their own border

(18) I have surely heard Ephraim bemoaning himself *thus;* Thou hast chastised me, and I was chastised, as a bullock unaccustomed *to the yoke:* turn thou me, and I shall be turned; for thou *art* the LORD my God.
(19) Surely [a]after that I was turned, I repented; and after that I was instructed, I smote upon *my* thigh: I was ashamed, yea, even confounded, because I did bear the reproach of my youth.
(20) *Is* Ephraim my dear son? *is he* a pleasant child? for since I spake against him, I do earnestly remember him still: therefore my bowels [1]are troubled for him; I will surely have mercy upon him, saith the LORD.
(21) Set thee up waymarks, make thee high heaps: set thine heart toward the highway, *even* the way *which* thou wentest: turn again, O virgin of Israel, turn again to these thy cities.
(22) How long wilt thou go about, O thou backsliding daughter? for the LORD hath created a new thing in the earth, A woman shall compass a man.

a Deut. 30. 2.

1 Heb., *sound.*

—the return, that is, of the Ten Tribes from their captivity.

(18) **I have surely heard Ephraim bemoaning himself.**—The prophet's thoughts still dwell upon the exiles of the northern kingdom. They have been longer under the sharp discipline of suffering. By this time, he thinks, they must have learnt repentance. He hears—or Jehovah, speaking through him, hears—the moaning of remorse; and in that work, thought of as already accomplished, he finds a new ground for his hope for Judah. Ephraim at last owned that he had deserved the chastisement of the yoke that had been laid on him.

As a bullock unaccustomed to the yoke.—The comparison is the nearest approach in the Old Testament to the Greek proverb about "kicking against the pricks" (Acts ix. 5, xxvi. 14). In Hos. x. 11 ("Ephraim is as an heifer that is taught"), which may well have been in Jeremiah's thoughts, we have a like comparison under a somewhat different aspect. The cry which is heard from the lips of the penitent, "Turn thou me . . . ," is, as it were, echoed from chap. iii. 7, 12, 14, and is reproduced in Lam. v. 21.

(19) **After that I was turned.**—The words have been referred by some commentators (Hitzig) to the previous turning away from God—the apostasy of Ephraim; but the repetition of the word that had been used in the previous verse makes it far more natural to connect it with the first movement of repentance. The "smiting upon the thigh" is, like the Publican's "smiting on his breast" (Luke xviii. 13), an Eastern expression of extremest grief. So in Ezek. xxi. 17 we have the "smiting of the hands together" as a symbol of anger, which is also sorrow. In Homer (*Odyss.* xiii. 193) we have the very gesture here depicted—

> "And then he groaned, and smote on both his thighs
> With headlong hands, and so in sorrow spoke."

The reproach of my youth—*i.e.,* the shame which the sins of his youth had brought upon him.

(20) **Is Ephraim my dear son?**—Literally, *a child of delight—i.e.,* fondled and caressed.

Is he a pleasant child?—We have to ask whether an affirmative or negative answer is implied to these questions. On the former view, the words express the yearning of a father's heart towards the son whom he still loves in spite of all his faults. Jehovah wonders, as it were, at his affection for one who has been so rebellious. On the latter, they give prominence to the faults as having deprived him of all claim to love, even though the father's heart yearned towards the prodigal in pity. The former gives, beyond all doubt, the best meaning. In every word, whether of reproof or invitation, there was implied a loving remembrance.

For since I spake against him.—Better, *As often as I speak to him.* The preposition can hardly have the meaning of "against," for which Jeremiah uses different words, and implies rather (as in the "communed with" of 1 Sam. xxv. 39; "When she shall be spoken for," Song Sol., viii. 8)—speaking with a view to win. By some commentators (Ewald) the word for "speak" is rendered "smite," but the ordinary rendering gives an adequate meaning. The original gives both for "earnestly remember" and "surely have mercy" the Hebrew idiom of reduplication—*Remembering, I remember; pitying, I pity.* The thought expressed is that Jehovah could not bring himself to utter the sentence of rejection. His love turned to the penitent who turned to Him. We have something like a foreshadowing of the love of the father of the prodigal in Luke xv. 20.

(21) **Set thee up waymarks . . .**—It will be noted that the figure is changed, and that instead of "Ephraim, the dear son," we have Israel, the "backsliding daughter." The idea of the return of the exiles is still prominent, and she, as represented by the first group of those who came back, is called on to set up "heaps of stones," after the manner of Eastern travellers, as waymarks for those who followed. (Comp. Ezek. xxxix. 15.) The way which she had trodden when she was led out into captivity was to be re-trodden in the fulness of joy on her return. She was to pass in her joy through the self-same cities that had then seen her in her shame.

(22) **How long wilt thou go about . . ?**—The word describes the restless pacing to and fro of impatient, unsatisfied desire. The backsliding daughter—*i.e.,* the adulterous yet now penitent wife—is described, like Gomer in the parable or history of Hos. ii. 7, as hesitating between her lovers and her husband.

A woman shall compass a man.—The verse is obscure, and has received very different interpretations. It will be well to begin our inquiry with the meaning which the translators attached to it. On this point the following quotation from Shakespeare is decisive:—

> "If I can check my erring love, I will;
> If not, to *compass* her I'll use my skill."
> *Two Gentlemen of Verona,* ii. 1.

To "compass" is to woo and win. And this gives, it is believed, the true meaning. The Hebrew verb (which presents a striking assonance with the word for "backsliding") means literally "to go round about," and this (as in Ps. xxvi. 6, xxxii. 7, 10) as an act of

(23) Thus saith the LORD of hosts, the
God of Israel; As yet they shall use
this speech in the land of Judah and in
the cities thereof, when I shall bring
again their captivity; The LORD bless
thee, O habitation of justice, *and*
mountain of holiness. (24) And there
shall dwell in Judah itself, and in all
the cities thereof together, husbandmen,
and they *that* go forth with flocks.
(25) For I have satiated the weary soul,
and I have replenished every sorrowful
soul. (26) Upon this I awaked, and be-
held; and my sleep was sweet unto me.

a Ezek. 18. 2.

(27) Behold, the days come, saith the
LORD, that I will sow the house of
Israel and the house of Judah with the
seed of man, and with the seed of beast.
(28) And it shall come to pass, *that* like
as I have watched over them, to pluck
up, and to break down, and to throw
down, and to destroy, and to afflict; so
will I watch over them, to build, and to
plant, saith the LORD. (29) [a]In those
days they shall say no more, The
fathers have eaten a sour grape, and the
children's teeth are set on edge. (30) But
every one shall die for his own iniquity:

---

reverential tenderness and love. In the normal order of man's life, the bridegroom woos the bride. In the spiritual relationship which the prophet has in view, this shall be inverted, and Israel, the erring but repentant wife, shall woo her Divine husband. The history of Gomer in Hos. ii. 14—20 again presents a striking parallel. A like inversion of the normal order is indicated, though with a different meaning, in Isa. iv. 1, where the seven women might be said to "compass" the one man. It may be noticed that the words used express the contrast of the two sexes in the strongest possible form. *A female shall compass* (i.e., *woo*) *a male*, possibly as emphasising the fact that what the prophet describes was an exception to the normal order, not of human society only, but of the whole animal society. By some interpreters (Ewald) the words are rendered "a woman shall be turned into a man;" meaning that the weak shall be made strong, as a kind of contrast to the opposite kind of transformation in chap. xxx. 6; but this gives a far less satisfactory meaning, and the same may be said of such translations as "the woman shall protect the man," and "a woman shall put a man to flight." The notion that the words can in even the remotest degree be connected with the mystery of the Incarnation belongs to the region of dreams, and not of realities; and, lacking as it does the support of even any allusive reference to it in the New Testament, can only be regarded, in spite of the authority of the many Fathers and divines who have adopted it, as the outgrowth of a devout but uncritical imagination. The word used for "woman," indeed, absolutely excludes the idea of the virgin-birth.

(23) **As yet they shall use this speech in the land of Judah . . .**—Better, *Once more*, or *yet again*. The phrase is the same as in verse 5. The eye of the prophet turns from the northern kingdom to that of Judah, and sees it also as a sharer in the restoration. Jerusalem should be blest, and be worthy of blessing—once more a faithful city, a holy mountain, righteousness dwelling in it (Isa. i. 21). The "holy mountain" is used with a special reference to Moriah and the Temple.

(24) **Husbandmen, and they that go forth with flocks.**—The prophet's ideal of the restored life of Israel is that it should combine the best features of the patriarchal and the kingly life. A people pastoral, yet not nomadic—agricultural, yet sharing in the culture and safety of cities—this was the picture that rose up in Jeremiah's thoughts, in sharp contrast to the facts that actually surrounded him in the shape of devastated fields and pastures, with no flocks and herds (chap. iv. 26—29).

(25) **I have satiated the weary soul . . .**—Here again we note an instance of an anticipation of the thought, almost of the very language, of the Gospel, "The hungry and the thirsty" shall be "filled" (Matt. v. 6), the weary shall be refreshed (Matt. xi. 28, 29).

(26) **Upon this I awaked . . .**—The words that follow have been very differently interpreted. By some writers (Rosenmüller) they have been referred to Jehovah under the figure of the husband who has dreamt of his wife's return. Others (Ewald) have seen in them a quotation from some well-known psalm or hymn, like Ps. xvii. 15, indicating that in the golden days to which Jeremiah looked forward there should be freedom even from the evil and dark dreams of a time of peril, so that every man should be able to give thanks for the "sweet" gift of sleep (Ps. cxxvii. 2). It is, however, far more natural to take them as the prophet's own words. The vision of a restored Israel, such as he paints it in the preceding verses, had come to him in his sleep. (See chap. xxiii. 28; Joel ii. 28, as to this mode of revelation.) And when he woke up there was no sense of bitter disappointment like that of the dreamer described in Isa. xxix. 8. The promise that came to him when he woke was as distinct and blessed as the dream had been. The "sweet sleep" has its parallel in Prov. iii. 24.

(27) **I will sow the house of Israel . . .**—The same image of a fertile and happy population appears in Hos. ii. 23; Zech. x. 9; Ezek. xxxvi. 9, 10, 11. It will be noted that it embraces both Israel and Judah, which had once been rivals, each watching the increase of the other with jealousy and suspicion.

(28) **Like as I have watched over them . . .**—Some twenty-three years had passed since the prophet's call to his office, but the words that called him to it are living still. The very symbolism of the "almond," with the play upon its meaning, as the "wakeful" or "watching" tree (see Notes on chap. i. 10, 11), the very terms in which his two-fold work was painted, are present to his thoughts, yet are seen under a new and brighter aspect. Up to this time his task had been mainly that of a prophet of evil, "rooting out" and "pulling down." Now he sees before him the happier work of "building up" and "planting."

(29, 30) **The fathers have eaten a sour grape . . .**—The proverb was one which, as we find from Ezek. xviii. 2, 3, had at this time come into common use. Men found in it an explanation of their sufferings which relieved their consciences. They were suffering, they said, for the sins of their fathers, not for their own.

every man that eateth the sour grape,
his teeth shall be set on edge.
(31) Behold, the [a]days come, saith
the LORD, that I will make a new
covenant with the house of Israel,
and with the house of Judah: (32) not
according to the covenant that I
made with their fathers in the day
that I took them by the hand to
bring them out of the land of Egypt;
which my covenant they brake, [1]al-
though I was an husband unto them,
saith the LORD: (33) but this *shall be*
the covenant that I will make with
the house of Israel; After those days,
saith the LORD, I will put my law in
their inward parts, and write it in their
hearts; [b]and will be their God, and
they shall be my people. (34) And they
shall teach no more every man his
neighbour, and every man his brother,
saying, Know the LORD: for [c]they shall

a Heb. 8. 8.

1 Or, *should I have continued an husband unto them.*

b ch. 24. 7; & 30. 22.

c Isa. 54. 13; John 6. 45.

They distorted the words which, as asserting the continuity of national life, were attached to the second Commandment (Exod. xx. 5), and instead of finding in them a warning restraining them from evil by the fear of transmitting evil to another generation, they found in them a plea for their own recklessness. Both Ezekiel and Jeremiah felt that the time was come when, even at the risk of a seeming contradiction to words clothed with a Divine authority, the other aspect of God's government had to be asserted in all its fulness: and therefore they lay stress on the truth that each man is responsible for his own acts, and for those alone, and that the law of the inheritance of evil (what we have learnt to call the law of *hérédité*) leaves untouched the freedom of man's will. The "eater of the sour grape, his teeth shall be set on edge," is, as it were, an emendation of the proverbial saying. The words of the Latin poet, "Delicta majorum immeritus lues," "Thou, for no guilt of thine, shalt pay the forfeit of thy fathers' sins" (Hor. *Od.* iii. 6, 1), show how ready men have been at all times to make a like excuse. How the two truths are to be reconciled, the law of hereditary tendencies, and punishments that fall not on the original offenders, but on their children, and the law of individual responsibility, is a question to which we can give no formal answer. We must be content to accept both laws, and rest in the belief that the Judge of all the earth will assuredly do right.

(31) **I will make a new covenant . . .**—Both in itself, and as the germ of the future of the spiritual history of mankind, the words are of immense significance. It was to this that the Lord Jesus directed the thoughts of His disciples, as the prophecy which, above all other prophecies, He had come to fulfil by the sacrifice of Himself. In that "New Covenant" in His blood, which He solemnly proclaimed at the Last Supper (Matt. xxvi. 28), and which was commemorated whenever men met to partake of the Supper of the Lord (1 Cor. xi. 25), there was latent the whole argument of the writer of the Epistle to the Hebrews (chaps. viii.—x.), the whole Gospel of justification by faith as proclaimed by St. Paul (Gal. iii. 15—17). From it the Church took the title of the New Covenant, the New Testament, which it gave to the collected writings of the Apostolic age. This title in its turn gave the name of the Old Testament to the collected writings which recorded how "in sundry times and divers manners" God had spoken in time past to Israel.

The promise is too commonly dealt with as standing by itself, without reference to the sequence of thought in which we find it placed. That sequence, however, is not hard to trace. The common proverb about the sour grapes had set the prophet thinking on the laws of God's dealings with men. He felt that something more was needed to restrain men from evil than the thought that they might be transmitting evil to their children's children—something more even than the thought of direct personal responsibility, and of a perfectly righteous retribution. And that something was to be found in the idea of a law—not written on tablets of stone, not threatening and condemning from without, and denouncing punishment on the transgressors and their descendants, but written on heart and spirit (2 Cor. iii. 3—6). It is noticeable, as showing how like thoughts were working in the minds of the two prophets, that in Ezekiel also the promise of a "new heart and new spirit" comes in close sequence upon the protest against the adage about the "children's teeth being set on edge" (Ezek. xviii. 31). In the words for "saith the Lord" we have the more solemn word which carries with it the announcement as of an oracle from God.

(32) **Not according to the covenant . . .**—Our familiarity with the words hinders us, for the most part, from recognising what must have seemed their exceeding boldness. That the Covenant with Israel, given with all conceivable sanctions as coming directly from Jehovah (Exod. xxiv. 7, 8), should thus be set aside, as man repeals an earthly law;—the man who could say this without trembling must indeed have been confident that he too was taught of God, and that the new teaching was higher than the old.

Although I was an husband unto them.—The words declare the ground on which Jehovah might well have looked for the allegiance of Israel. (See Notes on chaps. ii. 2, iii. 20.)

(33) **This shall be the covenant . . .**—The prophet felt that nothing less than this would meet the wants of the time, or, indeed, of any time. The experiment, so to speak, of a law requiring righteousness had been tried and had failed. There remained the hope—now, by the Divine word that came to him, turned into an assurance—of a Power imparting righteousness, writing the "law in the inward parts," the centre of consciousness and will, in which God required truth (Ps. li. 6), in the heart as the region at once of thoughts and of affections. In 2 Cor. iii. 3—6 we have a manifest reference not only to the idea, but to the very words of Jeremiah's prophecy.

(34) **They shall teach no more every man his neighbour . . .**—We trace in that hope for the future the profound sense of failure which oppressed the mind of the prophet, as it has oppressed the minds of many true teachers since. What good had come of all the machinery of ritual and of teaching which the Law of Israel had provided so abundantly? Those repeated exhortations on the part of preachers and prophets that men should "know the Lord," what did they present but the dreary monotony as of an "old worm-eaten homily"? To know Him, as indeed He is,

all know me, from the least of them
unto the greatest of them, saith the
LORD: for [a]I will forgive their iniquity,
and I will remember their sin no
more.
(35) Thus saith the LORD, [b]which giveth
the sun for a light by day, *and* the
ordinances of the moon and of the stars
for a light by night, which divideth
[c]the sea when the waves thereof roar;
The LORD of hosts *is* his name: (36) [d]if
those ordinances depart from before me,
saith the LORD, *then* the seed of Israel
also shall cease from being a nation
before me for ever. (37) Thus saith the
LORD; If [e]heaven above can be mea-
sured, and the foundations of the earth
searched out beneath, I will also cast
off all the seed of Israel for all that
they have done, saith the LORD.
(38) Behold, the days come, saith the
LORD, that the city shall be built to
the LORD from the tower of Hananeel
unto the gate of the corner. (39) And
the measuring line shall yet go forth
over against it upon the hill Gareb, and
shall compass about to Goath. (40) And
the whole valley of the dead bodies, and

a ch. 33. 8; Micah 7. 18; Acts 10. 43.
b Gen. 1. 16.
c Isa. 51. 15.
d Isa. 54. 9; ch. 33. 20.
e ch. 33. 22.

required nothing less than a special revelation of His presence to each man's heart and spirit, and that revelation was now, for his comfort, promised for all who were willing to receive it as the special gift of the near or distant future which opened to his view in his vision of a restored Israel. Here also the words of Jeremiah echo those of an older prophet (Isa. liv. 13), and find their fulfilment in those of Christ (John vi. 45).

I will forgive their iniquity . . .—The second clause repeats the promise of the first, in a form which is, perhaps, from the necessity of the case, after the manner of men. Our thoughts of God as the All-knowing preclude the idea of any limitation of His knowledge, such as the words "I will remember no more" imply. What is meant is that He will be to him who repents and knows Him as indeed He is, in His essential righteousness and love, as men are to men when they "forget and forgive." He will treat the past offences, even though their inevitable consequences may continue, as though they had never been, so far as they affect the communion of the soul with God. He will, in the language of another prophet, "blot out" the sins which yet belong to the indelible and irrevocable past (Isa. xliii. 25, xliv. 22).

(35, 36) **Which giveth the sun for a light by day . . .**—The leading thought in the lofty language of this passage is that the reign of law which we recognise in God's creative work has its counterpart in His spiritual kingdom. The stability and permanence of natural order is a pledge and earnest of the fulfilment of His promises to Israel as a people. The new Covenant of pardon and illumination is to be, what the first Covenant was not, eternal in its duration. We have learnt, through the teaching of St. Paul, while not excluding Israel according to the flesh from its share in that fulfilment, to extend its range to the children of the faith of Abraham, the true Israel of God (Rom. ii. 28, 29, iv. 11, 12).

(37) **If heaven above can be measured . . .**—The thought of the preceding verse is reproduced with a slight modification of meaning. Over and above the idea, as stated above, that the stability of nature is a parable of the steadfastness of God's laws and purposes in the spiritual world, there is implied a feeling, like that of Rom. xi. 33, that man's finite intellect cannot fathom His modes of working out that purpose any more than it can measure what to the prophet's mind were the illimitable heaven and the unfathomable earth.

(38) **From the tower of Hananeel unto the gate of the corner.**—There seems to us something almost like an anti-climax in this sudden transition from the loftiest Gospel promises to the obscure localities of the ancient Jerusalem. With Jeremiah, however, as before with Isaiah (chap. lxv. 17—25), and on a much larger scale with Ezekiel (chaps. xl.—xlviii.), this was the natural outgrowth of the vividness with which the restored city came before his mental vision. He saw a goodly city rise as from the ruins of the old, truly and not in name only consecrated to Jehovah, and describes, as best he can, how it differed from them. The tower of Hananeel appears from Neh. iii. 1, xii. 39, to have been identical, or connected, with the tower of Meah, and to have been between the fish-gate and the sheep-gate, at the north-east corner of the city walls. It is named again, as one of the conspicuous landmarks of the city, in Zech. xiv. 10. The "corner-gate" at the north-west corner, and near the present Jaffa-gate, appears in 2 Kings xiv. 13; 2 Chron. xxvi. 9; Zech. xiv. 10; Neh. iii. 24, 32. The wall in this quarter had apparently been battered during the siege of Jerusalem, and the prophet naturally sees the rebuilding of the wall as among the first-fruits of the restoration.

(39) **The hill Gareb . . .**—Neither of the two localities named is mentioned elsewhere, and their position is accordingly simply matter for conjecture. The name of the first, as signifying "the leper's hill" (the term being one that includes leprosy as well as other skin-diseases, Lev. xxi. 20, xxii. 22), indicates probably a position outside the walls assigned as a dwelling to persons suffering from that disease, corresponding, as some think, with the hill on the north side of Jerusalem which Josephus describes as Bezetha (*Wars*, v. 4, § 2). Others, however, assign its position to the south-west corner of the walls. The name Gareb appears in 2 Sam. xxiii. 38 as belonging to one of David's thirty heroes, but there is nothing to connect him with the locality. Goath is a word of doubtful etymology. Some scholars (Hitzig) interpret it as "high-towering," and refer it to the height overlooking Kidron, afterwards surmounted by the tower Antonia. The Targum, however, paraphrases it as "the pool of the heifers," and connects the name with the verb for the lowing of that animal. By some writers it has been identified with Golgotha, but both topography and etymology are against this view.

(40) **The whole valley of the dead bodies . . .**—We have to think of this city as Jeremiah saw it

of the ashes, and all the fields unto the brook of Kidron, unto the corner of the horse gate toward the east, *shall be* holy unto the LORD; it shall not be plucked up, nor thrown down any more for ever.

CHAPTER XXXII.—(1) The word that came to Jeremiah from the LORD in the tenth year of Zedekiah king of Judah, which *was* the eighteenth year of Nebuchadrezzar. (2) For then the king of Babylon's army besieged Jerusalem: and Jeremiah the prophet was shut up in the court of the prison, which *was* in the king of Judah's house. (3) For Zedekiah king of Judah had shut him up, saying, Wherefore dost thou prophesy, and say, Thus saith the LORD, [a]Behold, I will give this city into the hand of the king of Babylon, and he shall take it; (4) and Zedekiah king of Judah shall not escape out of the hand of the Chaldeans, but shall surely [b]be delivered into the hand of the king of Babylon, and shall speak with him mouth to mouth, and his eyes shall behold his eyes; (5) and he shall lead Zedekiah to Babylon, and there shall he be until I visit him, saith the LORD: though ye fight with the Chaldeans, ye shall not prosper.

(6) And Jeremiah said, The word of the LORD came unto me, saying, (7) Behold, Hanameel the son of Shallum thine uncle shall come unto thee, saying,

a ch. 34. 2.

B. C. cir. 590.

b ch. 34. 3.

---

during the horrors of the siege—the lower part, the "plain" or "valley" of the city, the valley of Hinnom (comp. chap. xix. 11), filled with corpses lying unburied in the streets (Lam. ii. 21, iv. 9), the "ashes" of burnt and shattered houses encumbering the streets with their *débris,* the fields or open spaces that stretched to the Kidron valley, and the "horse-gate" by the king's palace (2 Kings xi. 16; 2 Chron. xxiii. 15; Neh. iii. 28)—all this now lay before him as a scene of unspeakable desolation; but in his vision of the restored city he sees it all cleansed from whatever was defiling, consecrated to Jehovah, and holy as the precincts of the Temple. It is, perhaps, not without significance in connection with this passage, that when the city was restored, the region above the "horse-gate" was repaired by the priests, who seem to have had their houses in that quarter (Neh. iii. 28, 29). They appear to have been anxious to restore the sanctity of that over which Jeremiah had lamented as desecrated and defiled. The word for "ashes" was a technical one (Lev. vi. 10, 11) for the refuse which remained on the altar after a burnt-offering, and which was to be carried without the camp (Lev. iv. 12, vi. 11). Probably this and the sweepings of the Temple were thrown into the valley of Hinnom.

XXXII.

(1) **In the tenth year of Zedekiah . . .**—We are carried over a period of six years from the prophecy of chap. xxviii. 1 to B.C. 589, when the treacherous and intriguing policy of Zedekiah had provoked Nebuchadnezzar to besiege Jerusalem in the ninth year of the king of Judah's reign, and the king, irritated by Jeremiah's continued predictions of defeat, had imprisoned him in the dungeon for state-prisoners attached to the palace (Neh. iii. 25). It would appear from chaps. xxxvii. 15, xxxviii. 26, both of an earlier date than this chapter, that he had previously been confined in the house of Jonathan the scribe as a private prison, and that the king had removed him thence with a view to consulting him on the probable issue of the siege. He was not allowed to leave his prison, but friends were permitted to have access to him.

(3, 4) **Behold, I will give this city into the hand of the king of Babylon . . .**—A comparison of these verses with chaps. xxxiv. 2, 3, xxxviii. 23, shows that Jeremiah never for a moment varied in his tone. To see the king of Babylon face to face, to stand before him in shame and confusion—that was to be the end of the king's frantic resistance to the Divine purpose. The prophecy of Ezekiel (xii. 13), and the fact that Nebuchadnezzar put out the eyes of the captive king (chap. xxxix. 7), give a special force to Jeremiah's word. The face of the great king, in all the terror of his wrath, was to be the last object Zedekiah was to behold on earth (2 Kings xxv. 6, 7; Jer. xxxix. 6, lii. 10, 11).

(5) **There shall he be until I visit him . . .**—The word for "visit" is ambiguous, being used elsewhere both for "punishing" and "delivering." Its use in chap. xxix. 10 is in favour of the latter meaning here. The prophet looks forward to a general deliverance, or at least mitigation of suffering, for the exiles in Babylon, and, though he does not in distinct terms predict that Zedekiah will share in it, seems to cherish the hope that he will not be altogether excluded. Of his fate after he arrived in Babylon we know nothing, but the absence of his name when Jehoiachin was released from his imprisonment (chap. lii. 31) by Evil-merodach suggests the conclusion that he was then dead.

(7) **Behold, Hanameel the son of Shallum . . .**—The teaching of the narrative that follows lies almost on the surface, and is brought out distinctly in verse 44. With all the certainty of desolation, misery, exile in the immediate future, the prophet was to give a practical proof that he was as certain of the ultimate restoration. It was worth while to buy a field even for what might seem the contingency of that remote reversion. Roman history records a parallel act of patriotic faith in the purchase of land at Rome at its full market value, at the very time when the armies of Hannibal were marching to the gate of the city (Livy, xxvi. 11). Nothing more is known of the Hanameel who is here mentioned than that he was the first cousin of the prophet (verses 8, 9). The word "uncle" in this verse therefore applies strictly to Shallum. As the lands belonging to the priests and Levites as such could not be alienated (Lev. xxv. 34), we must assume either that the land in question had come into the family by marriage and was private property, or that the law had been so far relaxed as to allow of the transfer of

Buy thee my field that *is* in Anathoth:
for the [a]right of redemption *is* thine to
buy *it*. (8) So Hanameel mine uncle's son
came to me in the court of the prison
according to the word of the LORD, and
said unto me, Buy my field, I pray thee,
that *is* in Anathoth, which *is* in the
country of Benjamin: for the right of
inheritance *is* thine, and the redemp-
tion *is* thine; buy *it* for thyself. Then
I knew that this *was* the word of the
LORD. (9) And I bought the field of
Hanameel my uncle's son, that *was* in
Anathoth, and weighed him the money,
even [1]seventeen shekels of silver. (10) And
I [2]subscribed the evidence, and sealed
it, and took witnesses, and weighed *him*
the money in the balances. (11) So I
took the evidence of the purchase, *both*
that which was sealed *according* to the

a Lev. 25. 24; Ruth 4. 4.

1 Or, *seven shekels and ten pieces of silver.*

2 Heb., *wrote in the book.*

---

land within the limits of the family, and up to the date of the next year of jubilee. In such a case, as in Ruth iii. 12, iv. 4, the option of purchase was offered in the first instance to the next of kin (the *Goël*, or "redeemer," of the family), so that it might still be kept in the line of succession (Lev. xxv. 24, 32). The prophet naturally lays stress on the fact that he was warned beforehand of the visit of Hanameel and of its object. The coincidence was to him what the arrival of the messenger of Cornelius was to Peter (Acts x. 19—21).

(8) **Buy my field, I pray thee, that is in Anathoth . . .**—We are not told what led Hanameel to make the offer of sale. Probably, as in the Assyrian invasion (Isa. x. 30), Anathoth was occupied and ravaged by the army of the Chaldæans, and the field seemed to its possessor little more than a *damnosa hæreditas* ("an inheritance of ruin"), which he was glad to get rid of at any price. Perhaps, too, looking to the part that Jeremiah had taken in urging submission to Nebuchadnezzar, it seemed prudent to transfer the ownership of the field to one whom the Chaldæans were disposed to protect, while, as Jeremiah was in prison, Hanameel might well expect to remain in occupation as his representative. The words "the right of inheritance is thine" indicate that Hanameel had no children. The description "Anathoth, which is in the country of Benjamin," hardly natural in the lips of cousin speaking to cousin, is wanting in the LXX. version, and is traceable probably to the Jewish habit of writing in the text what with us would be notes in the margin.

(9) **Weighed him the money, even seventeen shekels of silver.**—The Hebrew presents the singular combination, *seven shekels and ten [pieces of] silver*, and is followed by the LXX. and Vulg. There is no ground for thinking that there is any difference between the coins or bullion so described, and the formula was probably one of the technicalities of Jewish conveyancing. As regards the price it is not easy, in the absence of any measurement of the field, to form an estimate of its value; but, speaking roughly, as compared with the four hundred shekels paid by Abraham for the field of Ephron (Gen. xxiii. 16), or the fifty paid by David for the threshing-floor and oxen of Araunah (2 Sam. xxiv. 24; in 1 Chron. xxi. 25 the price is fixed at six hundred shekels of gold), or to the thirty shekels paid for the potter's field in Matt. xxvii. 9, or to the market price of a slave varying from fifteen (Hos. iii. 2) to thirty shekels (Zech. xi. 12), the price, under £2 sterling, would seem to have been far below its average market value, and in this respect the story falls short of the dignity of its Roman parallel (see Note on verse 7). Hanameel, as said above, was probably glad to part with it at any price. It is possible, however, that the smallness of the sum was owing to the fact that the sale, as above suggested, conveyed possession only for the unexpired term of a tenancy which was to end with the next year of Jubilee. On that assumption the prophet's motive in purchasing may have been to keep it in the family instead of letting it pass to a stranger who might be unwilling to surrender it when the year of Jubilee arrived. As the prophet was unmarried he had no son to inherit it. The precise sum fixed, perhaps even the form in which the sum is stated, may have originated in Jeremiah's wish to connect in this way the two numbers, ten and seven, which when multiplied together produced the number which he had fixed for the years of captivity, and therefore for the term of restoration. Such an elaborate artifice of symbolism would, at least, be quite in character in a prophet who adopts the acrostic form in his Lamentations and the cypher of an inverted alphabet known as the *Athbash*. (See Note on chap. xxv. 26.)

(10) **And I subscribed the evidence . . .**—Literally, as in the margin, *I wrote in the book*—the last word being used for any kind of document, as for an indictment in Job xxxi. 35, and here for a deed of conveyance. The minuteness with which the transaction is recorded is every way remarkable, partly as showing that the prophet was careful that no legal formality should be lacking to give validity to the purchase; partly, as the next verse shows, because there was a secret, unattested, unsealed (and in that sense "open") document, which the witnesses did not subscribe, and with the contents of which they were probably not acquainted. The sealed document was one closed up as a safeguard against fraudulent alterations (comp. Isa. xxix. 11). In the weighing of the money we see an indication of the old practice—probably consequent on the practice of "clipping" coined money—of dealing even with the current coin as if it were bullion, just as bankers weigh a parcel of sovereigns now before giving credit for the amount. (Comp. Gen. xxiii. 16; Zech. xi. 12.)

(11) **Both that which was sealed . . . and that which was open.**—We are left to conjecture why there were two documents, and why one was sealed and the other open. Possibly, as in modern transactions, one was simply a duplicate copy of the other, the sealed document being the formal evidence of purchase kept by the buyer, and the other left with the vendor for reference. The more probable explanation, however, is that the unsealed document, which the witnesses did not subscribe or see, contained details which did not concern the witnesses, the price paid (though the mention of the witnesses before the weighing of the money militates against this view), the conditions of resumption by the vendor, possibly some reference to the period of seventy years, at the end of which, and not before, the heirs of Jeremiah might expect to enter on possession.

According to the law and custom.—Better, *to wit, the agreement and the conditions.* The

law and custom, and that which was
open: (12) and I gave the evidence of
the purchase unto Baruch the son of
Neriah, the son of Maaseiah, in the
sight of Hanameel mine uncle's *son*,
and in the presence of the witnesses
that subscribed the book of the pur-
chase, before all the Jews that sat in
the court of the prison. (13) And I
charged Baruch before them, saying,
(14) Thus saith the LORD of hosts, the
God of Israel; Take these evidences,
this evidence of the purchase, both
which is sealed, and this evidence which
is open; and put them in an earthen
vessel, that they may continue many
days. (15) For thus saith the LORD of
hosts, the God of Israel; Houses and
fields and vineyards shall be possessed
again in this land.
(16) Now when I had delivered the
evidence of the purchase unto Baruch
the son of Neriah, I prayed unto the
LORD, saying,
(17) Ah Lord GOD! behold, thou hast
made the heaven and the earth by thy
great power and stretched out arm,
and there is nothing [1]too hard for thee:
(18) thou shewest [a]lovingkindness unto
thousands, and recompensest the ini-
quity of the fathers into the bosom of
their children after them: the Great,
the Mighty God, the LORD of hosts,
is his name, (19) great in counsel, and
mighty in [2]work: for thine [b]eyes *are*
open upon all the ways of the sons of

1 Or, *hid from thee.*

a Exod. 34. 7; Deut. 5. 9.

2 Heb., *doing.*

b Job 34. 21; Prov. 5. 21; ch. 16. 17.

---

whole transaction may be compared, as an example of ancient conveyancing, with the transfer of the field and cave of Machpelah in Gen. xxiii.

(12) **Baruch the son of Neriah, the son of Maaseiah.**—This is the first mention of a man who played a more or less prominent part in connection with Jeremiah's later work. Nothing is known of his father or grandfather, but the fact that both are named indicates that he belonged to the nobler families of Judah; and this is confirmed, partly by the fact that his brother Seraiah (chap. li. 59, where see Note) held a high position in the court of Zedekiah, partly by Josephus, who describes him as of "a very illustrious house," and "highly educated" (*Ant.* x. 6, § 12). The mention of Chelcias (the Greek form for Hilkiah) among his ancestors, in the apocryphal book that bears his name (Bar. i. 1), may indicate a connection with the family of the high-priest in the reign of Josiah (2 Kings xxii. 4—14), and we may find in this fact an explanation of his regard for Jeremiah. In relation to the prophet, he appears in chap. xxxvi. 4 as acting as his secretary, as accused of instigating Jeremiah to preach submission to the Chaldæans (chap. xliii. 3), as sharing his sufferings and dangers (chap. xxxvi. 26), and, according to Josephus (as above), as thrown into prison with him. He was probably an influential member of the Chaldæan party in the court of Judah, protesting against the policy which courted an alliance with Egypt and entered into intrigues and schemes of rebellion against the power of Babylon. The book that bears his name is probably pseudonymous, but it bears witness, in the very fact of its being ascribed to him, to the importance of the position which he occupied in the politics of the time. Here he is present as at least visiting the prophet in prison, even if he did not share his imprisonment, and Jeremiah hands over the deeds of conveyance to his custody.

Before all the Jews that sat in the court of the prison.—The incidental mention of these is interesting, as showing the freedom of access which was permitted to the prisoner. Looking to the freedom and fulness of the prayer that follows (verses 17—25), it is a legitimate inference that they formed, as it were, a congregation of disciples, on whom the prophet sought to impress, by the transaction of the purchase, his own sure and certain hope of the restoration of his people.

(14) **Put them in an earthen vessel . . .**—We are reminded of the "earthen vessels" in which men kept their most precious treasures (2 Cor. iv. 7). Such a vessel was obviously a better protection against damp or decay than one of wood, and was, as it were, the "safe" of a Jewish household. (See Note on chap. xli. 8.) In the "many days" we have an implied warning to the listeners that they were not to expect a speedy deliverance or restoration, however certain might be their assurance that it would come at last.

(15) **Houses and fields and vineyards . . .**—It is a natural, though, of course, not a certain inference, that the land which Jeremiah had purchased included the three items that are thus specified.

(16) **I prayed unto the Lord.**—The prophet, it is obvious, records his own prayer. Nowhere, perhaps—the prayer of Ezra (Ezra ix. 5—15), of Hezekiah (Isa. xxxvii. 16—20), of Daniel (Dan. ix. 4—19), being the nearest parallels—do the writings of the Old Testament present us with so striking an example of the manner in which a devout Israelite poured out his heart to God, dwelling on the greatness of His attributes—praying for himself, interceding for his people.

(17) **There is nothing too hard for thee.**—The thought of the omnipotence of God was here, as always, the ground of prayer. The occurrence of the self-same phrase in Gen. xviii. 14 shows that it had been, even from patriarchal times, one of the axioms of the faith of Israel. We note its repetition in verse 27.

(18) **Thou showest lovingkindness unto thousands . . .**—The words are, in part, an echo from Exod. xx. 6, yet more from the revelation of the Divine glory in Exod. xxxiv. 7. They recognise the laws of a righteous retribution, working even through the seeming injustice of that visiting the sins of the fathers upon the children which is inseparable from the continuity of family or national life, and which had been caricatured in the "sour grapes" proverb of chap. xxxi. 29. They recognise also a mercy which is wider than that retribution, and at last triumphant. In the "Mighty God" we have the reproduction of the name used by Isaiah in his great Messianic prediction (Isa. ix. 6).

(19) **Great in counsel . . .**—So far as this is more than the continuance of the adoring ecstasy of the previous verse, it gives a fresh prominence to the law of direct, equitable, individual retribution. No law

men: to give every one according to his ways, and according to the fruit of his doings: (20) which hast set signs and wonders in the land of Egypt, *even* unto this day, and in Israel, and among *other* men; and hast made thee a name, as at this day; (21) and hast brought forth thy people Israel [a]out of the land of Egypt with signs, and with wonders, and with a strong hand, and with a stretched out arm, and with great terror; (22) and hast given them this land, which thou didst swear to their fathers to give them, a land flowing with milk and honey; (23) and they came in, and possessed it; but they obeyed not thy voice, neither walked in thy law; they have done nothing of all that thou commandedst them to do: therefore thou hast caused all this evil to come upon them: (24) behold the [1]mounts, they are come unto the city to take it; and the city is given into the hand of the Chaldeans, that fight against it, because of the sword, and of the famine, and of the pestilence: and what thou hast spoken is come to pass; and, behold, thou seest *it*. (25) And thou hast said unto me, O Lord God, Buy thee the field for money, and take witnesses; for the city is given into the hand of the Chaldeans.

(26) Then came the word of the Lord unto Jeremiah, saying,

(27) Behold, I *am* the Lord, the [b]God of all flesh: is there any thing too hard for me? (28) Therefore thus saith the Lord; Behold, I will give this city into the hand of the Chaldeans, and into the hand of Nebuchadrezzar king of Babylon, and he shall take it: (29) and the Chaldeans, that fight against this city, shall come and set fire on this city, and burn it with the houses, [c]upon whose roofs they have offered incense unto Baal, and poured out drink offerings unto other gods, to provoke me to anger. (30) For the children of Israel and the children of Judah have only done evil before me from their youth: for the children of Israel have only provoked me to anger with the work of their hands, saith the Lord. (31) For this city hath been to me *as* [2]a provocation of mine anger and of my fury from the day that they built it even unto

a Ex. 6. 6; 2 Sam. 7. 23; 1 Chron. 17. 21.

1 Or, *engines of shot.*

b Num. 16. 22.

c ch. 19. 13.

2 Heb., *for my anger.*

---

of the transmission of the inheritance of good or evil will be found, in the long-run, to clash with that.

(20) **Even unto this day . . .**—The reference to the signs and wonders in Egypt seems natural enough, but in what sense, we ask, could those wonders have been said to have been wrought "unto this day"? It is conceivable that what he had heard of the frogs, and the lice, and the boils of Egypt might seem to Jeremiah the perpetuation, in part, of the old plagues; but we get, perhaps, an adequate meaning by seeing in the words the assertion that the old signs and wonders continued in their effect and in their memory. The "name" continued, though the signs themselves had passed away.

Among other men.—Better, *among men.* There is no word for "other" in the Hebrew, and the words have their full force of declaring God's universal government over mankind at large.

(21–23) **And hast brought forth thy people Israel . . .**—The verses travel over ground so familiar as to require no comment, but the parallelism with Deut. xxvi. 8, with the other prophetic prayers above referred to, and with Ps. cxxxvi. 11, 12, is significant. The thoughts of all true worshippers moved more or less in the same groove, and clothed themselves in the same language, when they meditated on the past history of their people.

(24) **Behold the mounts . . .**—The mounts (better, *mounds*) are (as in chap. vi. 6, where see Note) the banks or towers of wood which formed the chief part of ancient siege operations. What the prophet had then predicted had now come to pass, and Jerusalem was now exposed to the sword, the famine, and the pestilence, which were its inevitable accompaniments. And it was at such a time as this, when the darkness was thickest, that a ray of hope for the future was given by the command to buy the field at Anathoth. And yet the command was so strange, and the hope so apparently against all probabilities, that the prophet ends his prayer by leaving the whole matter in the hands of Jehovah.

(27) **Is there any thing too hard for me?**—The answer to the prayer is an echo of the prayer itself (verse 17). The prophet is assured that he was not wrong when he cast himself, in the full confidence of faith, on the loving omnipotence of God. The words which he had used were more than a liturgical formula to one who had that confidence.

(29) **Upon whose roofs they have offered incense unto Baal . . .**—On the mode of worship to which the words refer, see Note on chap. xix. 13. Here the leading thought is that of the righteous judgment which is to fall on the very spots that had thus been turned from the worship of Jehovah to that of the false gods whom men had worshipped in His stead. The incense-smoke of their false worship had, as its end, the smoke of burning roof and timbers.

(30) **The children of Israel have only provoked me to anger . . .**—The words "the children of Israel" are apparently taken with a different range of extension in the two clauses—(1) for the northern kingdom, as contrasted with Judah; and (2) for the collective unity of Israel before, and perhaps also after, the division of the monarchy. The latter words of the verse reproduce Deut. xxxi. 29.

(31) **From the day that they built it . . .**—The words confirm the inference already drawn in the preceding note, that the thoughts of the prophet turn to the time when Israel was yet one people under David

this day; that I should remove it from
before my face, (32) because of all the
evil of the children of Israel and of the
children of Judah, which they have
done to provoke me to anger, they, their
kings, their princes, their priests, and
their prophets, and the men of Judah,
and the inhabitants of Jerusalem.
(33) And they have turned unto me the
[1][a]back, and not the face: though I
taught them, rising up early and teach-
ing *them*, yet they have not hearkened
to receive instruction. (34) But they
[b]set their abominations in the house,
which is called by my name, to defile
it. (35) And they built the high places
of Baal, which *are* in the valley of the
son of Hinnom, to [c]cause their sons and
their daughters to pass through *the
fire* unto [d]Molech; which I commanded
them not, neither came it into my mind,
that they should do this abomination,
to cause Judah to sin.
(36) And now therefore thus saith
the LORD, the God of Israel, concerning
this city, whereof ye say, It shall be
delivered into the hand of the king of
Babylon by the sword, and by the
famine, and by the pestilence; (37) Be-
hold, I will [e]gather them out of all
countries, whither I have driven them
in mine anger, and in my fury, and in
great wrath; and I will bring them
again unto this place, and I will cause
them to dwell safely: (38) and they shall
be [f]my people, and I will be their God:
(39) and I will [g]give them one heart, and
one way, that they may fear me [2]for
ever, for the good of them, and of their
children after them: (40) and I will
make an everlasting covenant with
them, that I will not turn away [3]from
them, to do them good; but I will put
my fear in their hearts, that they shall
not depart from me. (41) Yea, I will
rejoice over them to do them good, and
I will plant them in this land [4]assuredly
with my whole heart and with my whole
soul. (42) For thus saith the LORD;
Like as I have brought all this great
evil upon this people, so will I bring
upon them all the good that I have
promised them. (43) And fields shall be
bought in this land, whereof ye say,
It is desolate without man or beast; it
is given into the hand of the Chaldeans.
(44) Men shall buy fields for money, and
subscribe evidences, and seal *them*, and

1 Heb., *neck*.
a ch. 2. 27.
b ch. 23. 11.
c ch. 7. 31; & 19. 5.
d Lev. 18. 21.
e Deut. 30. 3.
f ch. 24. 7; & 30. 22; & 31. 33.
g Ezek. 11. 19.
2 Heb., *all days*.
3 Heb., *from after them*.
4 Heb., *in truth*, or, *stability*.

---

and Solomon. Even then, he seems to say, the city had fallen far short of the holiness which it ought to have attained, and which David sought for it (Ps. xv.—xxiv.), and had only been *for anger* and *for fury* to the Lord. There is no Hebrew word answering to "provocation." It is noticeable that the prophet, as if forgetting that Jerusalem had been a Jebusite city before David took possession (2 Sam. v. 6—10), speaks as if it had been built by Israel. It is obvious, however, that it was so much enlarged and altered after this capture, that the words which so describe it may have been not only practically, but almost literally, true.

(33) **They have turned unto me the back . . .**—It will be remembered that this image was more or less a favourite one with the prophet. (See Notes on chaps. ii. 27; vii. 24.) The same holds good of the "rising up early." (See Notes on chap. vii. 13, 25.)

(34, 35) **They set their abominations in my house . . .**—On the sins thus referred to, see Notes on chap. vii. 30, 31, which are here almost verbally reproduced.

(39) **I will give them one heart, and one way.**—The previous verse has described the restoration of Israel in the old familiar all-inclusive terms—"They shall be my people, and I will be their God" (Exod. vi. 7; Deut. xiv. 2; Hos. ii. 23). Here a new feature is added. The prophet, in his vision of the future, in place of the discords of the present—some serving Jehovah, and some Baal and Molech; some urging submission to Babylon, and some intriguing with Egypt—sees a unity in faith showing itself in unity of action. The hope of Jeremiah has never yet been realised, but it has appeared as with a transfigured glory in the prayer of the Christ for His people that they "all may be one," even as He and the Father are one (John xvii. 21—23), in the prayer of the Apostle, that all might be joined together "in the unity of the faith" (Eph. iv. 13). And that prayer also waits for its fulfilment, and receives only partial and (to use Bacon's phrase) "germinant" accomplishments. "For ever" represents the Hebrew *all the days*.

(40) **I will make an everlasting covenant . . .**—The "covenant" thus promised is, it must be remembered, identical with that of chap. xxxi. 31—the "new covenant," which shall never wax old and decay, but shall abide for ever. "My fear" is identical with "the fear of the Lord," which is "the beginning of wisdom." The curse of Israel had been that they had been without that fear to restrain them from evil, and that the mere dread of punishment had proved powerless to supply its place.

(41) **I will plant them in this land assuredly.**—Literally, *in truth*, as in 1 Sam. xii. 24, and elsewhere. By some interpreters the words have been referred to the stability of possession implied in the promise, but it is better to see in them an attestation of the faithfulness of the Promiser. In meaning, as in form, the word corresponds closely with the frequent "Amen," "Verily, verily," in our Lord's teaching.

(43, 44) **And fields shall be bought in this land . . .**—The significance of the whole transaction of the purchase of the field in Anathoth is again solemnly confirmed. Men were desponding, as though the land were to belong to the Chaldæans for ever. They are told that the very region which was now covered with

take witnesses in the land of Benjamin, and in the places about Jerusalem, and in the cities of Judah, and in the cities of the mountains, and in the cities of the valley, and in the cities of the south: for I will cause their captivity to return, saith the LORD.

CHAPTER XXXIII.—(1) Moreover the word of the LORD came unto Jeremiah the second time, while he was yet [a]shut up in the court of the prison, saying,

(2) Thus saith the LORD [b]the maker thereof, the LORD that formed it, to establish it; the LORD *is* his name; (3) Call unto me, and I will answer thee, and shew thee great and [1]mighty things, which thou knowest not. (4) For thus saith the LORD, the God of Israel, concerning the houses of this city, and concerning the houses of the kings of Judah, which are thrown down by the mounts, and by the sword; (5) They come to fight with the Chaldeans, but *it is* to fill them with the dead bodies of men, whom I have slain in mine anger and in my fury, and for all whose wickedness I have hid my face from this city. (6) Behold, I will bring it health and cure, and I will cure them, and will reveal unto them the abundance of peace and truth. (7) And I will cause the captivity of Judah and the captivity of Israel to return, and will build them, as at the first. (8) And I will cleanse them from all their iniquity, whereby they have sinned against me; and I will [c]pardon all their iniquities, whereby they have sinned, and whereby they have transgressed against me. (9) And it shall be to me a name of joy, a praise and an honour before all the nations of the earth, which shall hear all the good that I do unto them: and they shall fear and tremble for all the goodness and for all the prosperity that I procure unto it.

(10) Thus saith the LORD; Again there shall be heard in this place, which ye say *shall be* desolate without man and without beast, *even* in the cities of Judah, and in the streets of Jerusalem,

a ch. 32. 2, 3.

b Isa. 37. 26.

B. C. cir. 590.

1 Or, *hidden*

c ch. 31. 34; Mic. 7. 18.

---

their encampments should once again be possessed freely by its own people. In the "mountains," the "valleys," and the south, or *negeb* district, stretching towards the country of the Philistines, we have, as before in chap. xvii. 26, the familiar division of the land of Judah, which had been transmitted from what has well been called the Domesday Book of Israel (Josh. xv. 21, 33, 48).

XXXIII.

(1–3) **The second time, while he was yet shut up.**—The discourse that follows belongs to the same period as the preceding chapter, and presents the same general characteristics. Its connexion with the operations of the siege to which Jerusalem was exposed will be traced in verse 4. As with other prophecies, its starting-point is found in the thought of the majesty of the attributes of God.

Great and mighty things.—The two adjectives occur in the same combination in Deut. i. 28, ix. 1, and this fact is in favour of the rendering "mighty" rather than "hidden," as in the margin of the A.V.

(4) **Concerning the houses of this city . . .**—The words point to the incident which was the occasion of the prophecy. The houses referred to had either been destroyed by the invaders, or, more probably, by the besieged, in order to erect a counter-work against the "mounts" which the Chaldæans had set against it. The "swords" (the word is translated by "axes" in Ezek. xxvi. 9) include tools used for breaking down walls.

(5) **They come to fight with the Chaldeans . . .**—The Hebrew construction is participial, and has the force expressed in English by "they" used indefinitely. The prophet sees, as it were, a *sortie* of the besieged, but it is doomed to failure, and the houses of the city are filled with those who were slain by the sword, as well as by the "famine and pestilence" (chap. xxxii. 24).

(6) **Health and cure . . .**—The first word is, as in chap. viii. 22, xxx. 17, the bandage, or "plaister," which was prominent in the therapeutics of the East. It is possible that both words may have been spoken in direct contrast with the pestilence which was ravaging the city (chaps. xxi. 9; xxvii. 13; xxxviii. 2). In any case, however, the words have a higher and figurative meaning. It was true of the city and its people that the "whole head was sick, and the whole heart faint" (Isa. i. 5); and Jehovah promises to manifest Himself as the healer of that spiritual disease which was worse than any pestilence.

(7, 8) **I . . . will build . . . I will cleanse . . . I will pardon . . .**—The vision of the return of the exiles and of a restored city, prominent in chap. xxxi. 38—40, is not allowed to overshadow the yet more glorious vision of spiritual blessings of purity and pardon.

(9) **It shall be to me a name of joy . . .**—The thought presents two aspects in its bearing on the outlying nations. On the one hand, they shall sing the praises of the restored city; on the other, they shall fear and tremble before its greatness, as showing that it was under the protection of the Lord of Israel. The word for "fear" is used in Isa. lx. 5; Hos. iii. 5, for the quivering, trembling emotion that accompanies great joy, and is, perhaps, used here to convey the thought that the fear would not be a mere slavish terror.

(10) **Again there shall be heard in this place.**—The promise of restoration is repeated with a more local distinctness. "This place" is probably, as in chap. xlii. 18, Jerusalem. The "streets" are, more strictly, the "open places," the "bazaars," or even the "outskirts" of the city, which were deserted during the progress of the siege. Now they were waste and silent.

that are desolate, without man, and
without inhabitant, and without beast,
(11) the [a]voice of joy, and the voice of
gladness, the voice of the bridegroom,
and the voice of the bride, the voice of
them that shall say, Praise the LORD of
hosts: for the LORD *is* good; for his
mercy *endureth* for ever: *and* of them
that shall bring the sacrifice of praise
into the house of the LORD. For I will
cause to return the captivity of the
land, as at the first, saith the LORD.
(12) Thus saith the LORD of hosts;
Again in this place, which is desolate
without man and without beast, and in
all the cities thereof, shall be an habi-
tation of shepherds causing *their* flocks
to lie down. (13) In the cities of the
mountains, in the cities of the vale, and
in the cities of the south, and in the
land of Benjamin, and in the places
about Jerusalem, and in the cities of
Judah, shall the flocks pass again under
the hands of him that telleth *them*, saith
the LORD.
(14) Behold, the days come, saith the
LORD, that I will perform that good
thing which I have promised unto the
house of Israel and to the house of
Judah. (15) In those days, and at that
time, will I cause the [b]Branch of
righteousness to grow up unto David;
and he shall execute judgment and
righteousness in the land. (16) In those
days shall Judah be saved, and Jeru-
salem shall dwell safely: and this *is the
name* wherewith she shall be called,
[1]The LORD our righteousness. (17) For
thus saith the LORD; [2]David shall never
[c]want a man to sit upon the throne of

a ch. 7. 34; & 16. 9.

b Isa. 4. 2; & 11. 1; ch. 23. 5.

1 Heb., *Jehovah-tsidkenu.*

2 Heb., *There shall not be cut off from David.*

c 2 Sam. 7. 16; 1 Kings 2. 4.

The time would come when they would once again re-echo with the sounds of jubilant exultation.

(11) **The voice of joy, and the voice of gladness . . .**—The words gain greater emphasis as being those which the prophet had himself used (chaps. vii. 34; xvi. 9; xxv. 10) in foretelling the desolation of the city. He points, as it were, by implication to the fulfilment of the one prediction, as a guarantee that the other also will, in due season, have its fulfilment.

Praise the Lord of hosts . . .—The words were used as the ever-recurring doxology of the Temple-services (Ezra iii. 11; 2 Chron. vii. 6; xx. 21; Ps. cxxxvi. 2, 3; 1 Macc. iv. 24). The Courts of the Temple, now hushed in silence, should once again re-echo with the Hallelujahs of the Priests and Levites. The "sacrifice of praise" (the same phrase as in chap. xvii. 26; Ps. lvi. 12) may be either "the sacrifice which consists in praise," or the "sacrifices of thanksgiving" of Lev. vii. 12, which were offered in acknowledgment of special blessings. The ground of the thanksgiving in either case would be that the Lord had "turned again the captivity" of Jacob. The phrase was a familiar one, as in Ps. xiv. 7; liii. 6; Deut. xxx. 3. The words "as at the first" (literally, *as at the beginning*) do not refer to any previous restoration, like that of the Exodus from Egypt, but to the state before the exile.

(12, 13) **Again in this place.**—The "place" includes, as in verse 10, "the cities of Judah and the streets of Jerusalem." The "habitation" for shepherds is translated sometimes by "sheepcote" (1 Chron. xvii. 7; 2 Sam. vii. 8), sometimes by "fold" (Isa. lxv. 10; Ezek. xxxiv. 14), sometimes by "dwelling" or "habitation." It would seem here to answer to the "towns" of our old English speech, as meaning enclosed spaces, with the tower of the watchman (2 Kings xvii. 9; Isa. i. 8), in which, in times of average tranquillity, shepherds and their flocks found shelter, but which were abandoned when the land was overrun by an invading army. In verse 13 the eye of the prophet travels over such districts within the kingdom of Judah to the north and south of Jerusalem, and adds to the picture the vivid touch that the "sheep shall pass under the hands of him that telleth them," the shepherd whose work it was to count the flock—in older English, "to tell his tale"—as it went out in the morning and returned at nightfall, should find that he had lost none of them.

(14, 15) **Behold, the days come, saith the Lord . . .**—The words are manifestly a conscious reproduction of chap. xxiii. 5, 6. In "I have promised" we may indeed trace a distinct reference to that passage. Once more "the Branch of righteousness" (Isa. iv. 2; xi. 1)—the coming heir of the throne of David, the true King who is to execute judgment—is put forward, as seen in the vision of the prophet's hopes.

(16) **This is the name wherewith she shall be called, The Lord our righteousness.**—It will be noticed that, while this reproduces the language of chap. xxiii. 6, it does so with a remarkable difference. There the title, "The Lord our Righteousness," is given to the future King, and the passage has accordingly been used as a proof of the full divinity of the Christ, who is that King. Here it is given to the city, and, so given, can only mean that that name will be, as it were, the motto and watchword of her being. She will be a city marked by a righteousness which will be the gift of Jehovah; He will inscribe that name on her banners, and grave it on her portals. It is obvious that this throws light on the meaning of the title as applied to the King.

(17) **David shall never want a man . . .**—The words are hardly more than a repetition of promises like those of 2 Sam. vii. 16; 1 Kings ii. 4; Ps. lxxxix. 29, 36, but it is here repeated under very different circumstances. Then it had been given when the line of David was in all the freshness of its strength. Now it is uttered when that line seemed on the very point of dying out. The hope of the prophet is, however, inextinguishable. He is certain that the true King will always be of the house of David. It lay almost in the nature of the case that the words of the prophet should find a fulfilment other than that which was present to his thoughts; and that, while he pictured to himself an unbroken succession of sovereigns of David's line, there was in fact a higher fulfilment in the continuous sovereignty of the Christ as the true Son of David. We have something like an echo of the words in the words of the Angel at the Annuncia-

the house of Israel; (18) neither shall the
priests the Levites want a man before
me to offer burnt offerings, and to
kindle meat offerings, and to do sacri-
fice continually.
(19) And the word of the LORD came
unto Jeremiah, saying, (20) Thus saith
the LORD; [a]If ye can break my cove-
nant of the day, and my covenant of
the night, and that there should not
be day and night in their season;
(21) *then* may also my covenant be broken
with David my servant, that he should
not have a son to reign upon his throne;
and with the Levites the priests, my
ministers. (22) As [b]the host of heaven
cannot be numbered, neither the sand
of the sea measured: so will I multiply
the seed of David my servant, and the
Levites that minister unto me.

a Isa. 54. 9; ch. 31. 36.

b ch. 31. 37.

(23) Moreover the word of the LORD
came to Jeremiah, saying, (24) Con-
siderest thou not what this people
have spoken, saying, The two families
which the LORD hath chosen, he
hath even cast them off? thus they
have despised my people, that they
should be no more a nation before
them.
(25) Thus saith the LORD; If my
covenant *be* not with day and night,
and if I have not appointed the ordi-
nances of heaven and earth; (26) then
will I cast away the seed of Jacob,
and David my servant, *so* that I
will not take *any* of his seed *to be*
rulers over the seed of Abraham,
Isaac, and Jacob: for I will cause
their captivity to return, and have
mercy on them.

---

tion (Luke i. 32, 33), and it is an echo that interprets them.

(18) **Neither shall the priests the Levites want a man . . .**—Here again we have a promise which received a fulfilment other than that which the words appeared to imply, and which doubtless was in the prophet's thoughts. The Levitical priesthood passed away (Heb. vii. 11), but Christ was made a Priest after the order of Melchizedek; and by virtue of their union with Him, His people became a holy priesthood (Heb. x. 19—22), offering, not the burnt-offerings and meat-offerings which were figures of the true, but the spiritual sacrifices of praise and thanksgiving (1 Pet. ii. 5), the sacrifice of body, soul, and spirit, which alone was acceptable to God (Rom. xii. 1).

The special combination, "the priests the Levites," is not found elsewhere in Jeremiah, but appears in Deut. xvii. 9; xviii. 1; Josh. iii. 3; 2 Chron. xxx. 27; Ezek. xliii. 19; xliv. 15; Isa. lxvi. 21. As far as it has any special significance, it may indicate either that the priestly character, though not the specific priestly functions, extended to the whole tribe of Levi, or, more probably, that Jeremiah speaks of the Levite-priests of Judah as contrasted with the priests of the "high places," or such as Jeroboam had made of the lowest of the people.

To kindle meat offerings.—The meat-offering, or *minchah*, it will be remembered, was of meal and frankincense, not of flesh (Lev. ii. 1—15). It was burnt with fire on the altar, and the fragrant smoke was a "sweet savour unto the Lord."

(19—22) **And the word of the Lord came unto Jeremiah, saying . . .**—The new introduction here and in verse 23 indicates a fresh message borne in on the prophet's mind after an interval of time. In substance it repeats the promise of verses 17, 18, but it reproduces them with yet greater solemnity. The covenant of Jehovah with David and with the Levites the priests is placed on the same level of permanence as the ordered succession of day and night. If the old order ultimately gave way to the new, it was only because the new was the transfigured and glorified reproduction of the old. Whatever may have been the thoughts of the prophet, we are authorised in looking for the seed of David and of the Levites in those who, by virtue of their union with Christ, are made both kings and priests unto the Father (Rev. i. 6). Just as the promise to the seed of Abraham is fulfilled in those who are spiritually the children of the faith of Abraham (Rom. ix. 7, 8), so in this sense only can it be true that the seed of David and the Levites shall outnumber the host of the heaven and the sand of the sea.

(24—26) **Considerest thou not what this people have spoken . . .**—The words that follow have been regarded by many commentators as the taunt of the heathen nations—Chaldæans, Egyptians, Edomites, and others—as they beheld what seemed to them the entire downfall of the kingly and the priestly orders, such as we find put into the lips of the heathen in Ezek. xxxv. 10; xxxvi. 20. The words "this people," however, used as they are invariably of that to which the prophet himself belonged (chap. iv. 10; v. 14, 23; vi. 19, and elsewhere), and indeed in the hundred or more passages in which the phrase occurs in the Old Testament, lead to a different conclusion. The prophet's declaration of the steadfastness of God's covenant was made in answer, not to the taunts of the heathen, but to the despair of Israel, such as had found utterance in the words recorded in verse 10 and chap. xxxii. 43. If the words "thus they have despised my people" seem to favour the former interpretation, it must be remembered that the subject of the verb is not necessarily the same as that of the previous clause, and that the scorn of other nations would be the natural outcome of the despondency into which Israel had fallen; or they might emphasise the fact that the despondency was itself, as it were, suicidal. Those who despised their own nation were despising the people of Jehovah. In contrast with this despondency, the prophet renews his assurance of the permanence of the kingly and priestly lines, and strengthens it by reference to the three great patriarchs of the race, with whom the truth of Jehovah's promises was identified (Exod. iii. 15), and by connecting it with the promise of a return from the captivity. When that return came, it would be the pledge and earnest of the yet greater blessings which were involved in the new and everlasting covenant.

CHAPTER XXXIV.—(1) The word
which came unto Jeremiah from the
LORD, [a]when Nebuchadnezzar king of
Babylon, and all his army, and all the
kingdoms of the earth [1]of his dominion,
and all the people, fought against Je-
rusalem, and against all the cities
thereof, saying, (2) Thus saith the LORD,
the God of Israel;

Go and speak to Zedekiah king of
Judah, and tell him, Thus saith the
LORD; Behold, I will give this city into
the hand of the king of Babylon, and he
shall burn it with fire: (3) and thou shalt
not escape out of his hand, but shalt
surely be [b]taken, and delivered into his
hand; and thine eyes shall behold the
eyes of the king of Babylon, and [2]he
shall speak with thee mouth to mouth,
and thou shalt go to Babylon. (4) Yet
hear the word of the LORD, O Zedekiah
king of Judah; Thus saith the LORD of
thee, Thou shalt not die by the sword:
(5) *but* thou shalt die in peace: and
with the burnings of thy fathers, the
former kings which were before thee,
so shall they burn *odours* for thee; and
they will lament thee, *saying,* Ah lord!
for I have pronounced the word, saith
the LORD.

(6) Then Jeremiah the prophet spake
all these words unto Zedekiah king of
Judah in Jerusalem, (7) when the king
of Babylon's army fought against Je-
rusalem, and against all the cities of
Judah that were left, against Lachish,
and against Azekah: for these defenced
cities remained of the cities of Judah.

(8) *This is* the word that came unto
Jeremiah from the LORD, after that the
king Zedekiah had made a covenant
with all the people which *were* at Jeru-

a 2 Kings 25. 1, &c.; ch. 52. 4.

1 Heb., *the dominion of his hand.*

b ch. 32. 4.

B. C. cir. 591.

2 Heb., *his mouth shall speak to thy mouth.*

XXXIV.

(1) **When Nebuchadnezzar king of Babylon . . .**—The prophecy that follows is probably a fuller statement of that in chap. xxxii. 3, 4, and delivered shortly before it, being referred to there as the cause of his imprisonment. In the form of the name Nebuchad*n*ezzar (*n* instead of *r*, as in chap. xxiv. 1; xxv. 1), we may probably trace the hand of a later transcriber. The same hand is, perhaps, traceable in the accumulation of substantives after the manner of Dan. iii. 7; v. 19.

(2, 3) **Go and speak to Zedekiah . . .**—See Notes on chap. xxxii. 3, 4.

(4) **Thou shalt not die by the sword.**—The tone is one of comparative mildness, the motive apparently being the wish to persuade the king to abandon his useless resistance, and to court the favour of the conqueror. His going to Babylon would not necessarily shut him out from a life of comparative ease and an honourable burial. Jeconiah, it is true, had been thrown into prison (chap. li. 31), and remained there during the whole reign of Nebuchadnezzar, but that was the result of his obstinate resistance, and Zedekiah might avert that doom by a timely submission.

(5) **And with the burnings of thy fathers . . .**—Spices and perfumes were burnt as a mark of honour at the burial of kings and persons of high rank, and this is the burning here referred to (2 Chron. xvi. 14; xxi. 19). The Hebrews never adopted the practice of burial by cremation, and for the most part embalmed their dead after the manner of Egypt (comp. Gen. l. 2; John xix. 39, 40).

They will lament thee, saying, Ah lord! . . .—The words derive their full effect from their contrast with the prediction which the prophet had uttered (chap. xxii. 18) as to the burial of Jehoiakim without any of the usual honours of the funeral dirges of the mourners. Here he comforts Zedekiah with the thought that no such shameful end was in store for him, leaving the place where he was to die uncertain.

(7) **Against Lachish, and against Azekah . . .**—The two cities are named in this book for the first time. Lachish was one of the strongest towns of the Amorites in the time of Joshua (Josh. x. 3, 5), and was situated in the *Shephelah*, or lowland district (Josh. xv. 39). It was restored or fortified by Rehoboam, as a defence against the northern kingdom (2 Chron. xi. 9). Amaziah took refuge there on his flight from the conspiracy at Jerusalem (2 Chron. xiv. 19; 2 Chron. xxv. 27). It was taken by Sennacherib on his way from Assyria to Egypt, and made the monarch's head-quarters (2 Chron. xxxii. 9; 2 Kings xviii. 17). A slab at Kouyunjik (Layard's *Nineveh and Babylon*, 149—152; *Monuments of Nineveh*, 2nd Series, Plates 21, 24) represents the siege of *Lakhisha* by the armies of Sennacherib, and gives something like a ground-plan of the city. Its site has not been identified with certainty, but ruins still known as *Um-lakis* are found between Gaza and Eleutheropolis. It is mentioned here as being, next to Jerusalem, one of the strongest fortresses of the kingdom of Judah, which as yet had resisted the attack of Nebuchadnezzar's armies. Azekah, less conspicuous in history, was also in the *Shephelah* region, and is named with other cities in Josh. x. 10, 11, xv. 35. The Philistines were encamped between it and Shochoh in the days of Saul (1 Sam. xvii. 1). It also was fortified by Rehoboam (2 Chron. xi. 9). Its site has not been ascertained, but Eusebius and Jerome speak of it as lying between Eleutheropolis and Jerusalem.

(8) **After that the king Zedekiah had made a covenant . . .**—The remainder of the chapter brings before us an historical episode of considerable interest. The law of Moses did not allow in the case of a free-born Hebrew more than a temporary bondage of seven years (Exod. xxi. 2; Deut. xv. 12—18), extended (but under the form of serfage rather than slavery) in the later regulations of Lev. xxv. 39, 40 to the time that might intervene between the date of purchase and the commencement of the next year of jubilee. In 2 Kings iv. 1 we have an instance of the working of the law, as bringing even the sons of a prophet into this modified slavery. Only if the man preferred his state as a slave to the risks of freedom could his master retain him after the appointed limit (Exod. xxi. 5, 6). The law had appa-

salem, to proclaim [a]liberty unto them;
(9) that every man should let his man-
servant, and every man his maidservant,
being an Hebrew or an Hebrewess, go
free; that none should serve himself of
them, *to wit*, of a Jew his brother.
(10) Now when all the princes, and all
the people, which had entered into the
covenant, heard that every one should let
his manservant, and every one his maid-
servant, go free, that none should serve
themselves of them any more, then they
obeyed, and let *them* go. (11) But after-
ward they turned, and caused the ser-
vants and the handmaids, whom they
had let go free, to return, and brought
them into subjection for servants and
for handmaids.

(12) Therefore the word of the LORD
came to Jeremiah from the LORD,
saying, (13) Thus saith the LORD, the
God of Israel; I made a covenant with
your fathers in the day that I brought

a Ex. 21. 2.

b Ex. 21. 2; Deut. 15. 12.

1 Or, *hath sold himself.*

B. C. cir. 590.

2 Heb., *to day.*

3 Heb., *whereupon my name is called.*

them forth out of the land of Egypt,
out of the house of bondmen, saying,
(14) At the end of [b]seven years let ye go
every man his brother an Hebrew,
which [1]hath been sold unto thee; and
when he hath served thee six years,
thou shalt let him go free from thee:
but your fathers hearkened not unto
me, neither inclined their ear. (15) And
ye were [2]now turned, and had done
right in my sight, in proclaiming liberty
every man to his neighbour; and ye
had made a covenant before me in the
house [3]which is called by my name:
(16) but ye turned and polluted my name,
and caused every man his servant, and
every man his handmaid, whom he had
set at liberty at their pleasure, to re-
turn, and brought them into subjection,
to be unto you for servants and for
handmaids.

(17) Therefore thus saith the LORD;
Ye have not hearkened unto me, in

---

rently fallen into disuse, and the nobles of Judah, like those of Athens before Solon, and Rome before the institution of the Tribunate, had used the law of debt to bring a large number of their fellow citizens into slavery, just as their successors did after the return from Babylon (Neh. v. 5). Under the pressure of the danger from the Chaldæan invasion, and that he might have the ready service of freemen instead of the forced work of slaves, perhaps also in consequence of the revival of the law, that followed on its discovery, probably in the form of the Book of Deuteronomy, in the days of Josiah (2 Kings xxii. 8), Zedekiah had been led to promise freedom to all the slave population of this class that were within the walls of Jerusalem, either as a celebration of a Sabbatic year, or jubilee, or, irrespective of any such observance, as a reparation for past neglect. The step was probably not without its influence in giving fresh energy to the defenders of the city. The Chaldæans, threatened by the approach of an Egyptian army (chap. xxxvii. 5), raised the siege (verse 21). When the danger was past, however, the princes who had agreed to the emancipation returned to their old policy of oppression (verse 11), and those who had been liberated were brought under a bondage all the more bitter for the temporary taste of freedom. Against this perfidious tyranny the prophet, stirred by "the word of the Lord," bears his protests. His sympathies, like those of true prophets at all times, were with the poor and the oppressed. The phrase "proclaim liberty" was closely connected with the year of jubilee, as in Lev. xxv. 10, Isa. lxi. 1.

(13) **Thus saith the Lord . . .**—The prophet takes as his text the law which had been so flagrantly broken (Exod. xxi. 2), reminding them under what circumstances that law had been given. Their fathers had then been delivered from the house of bondage, and this was part of the covenant which God had made with them—freedom and blessing being given by Him, obedience promised by them. They were never to forget the bitterness of the bondage they had known (comp. the form of the fourth commandment in Deut. v. 15), and were to make it one of the fundamental laws of their national polity that no Israelite should ever pass, except by his own free choice, into a condition of hopeless life-long slavery.

(14) **At the end of seven years . . .**—The immediate context, "when he hath served thee six years," shows that the liberation was intended to take place at the beginning of the seventh year. The Sabbath-year was to bring its rest to the slave as well as to the land.

Your fathers hearkened not unto me . . .—The words imply the fact already stated, that there had been a long-continued violation of the law to which the prophet refers. In Isa. lviii. 6, lxi. 1 (assuming the earlier date of those prophecies) we may trace a protest against that violation.

(15) **Ye had made a covenant before me in the house which is called by my name.**—The words point to the solemnity with which the new engagements had been contracted. It was not merely that the king had issued an edict, or that judges had given their decisions in accordance with the old law, but princes and people had met together in the courts of the Temple, and there, in the presence of Jehovah, had entered into this covenant, as did their descendants afterwards in the days of Nehemiah (Neh. v. 12, 13), with Him and with each other. Their sin in breaking their covenant was therefore a sin against Him as well as against their brethren.

(16) **But ye turned and polluted my name . . .**—The second verb is the same as that translated "*profane* the name of the Lord" in Lev. xix. 12, in close connexion with the sin of swearing falsely. The sin of which the princes and rich men had been guilty was not merely an act of injustice. They had broken the third commandment as well as the eighth, and were accordingly guilty of sacrilege.

(17) **Behold, I proclaim a liberty for you . . .** The phrase "proclaim liberty," prominent in connexion with the law which had been broken (Lev. xxv.

proclaiming liberty, every one to his
brother, and every man to his neigh-
bour: behold, I proclaim a liberty for
you, saith the LORD, to the sword, to
the pestilence, and to the famine;
and I will make you [1]to be [a]removed
into all the kingdoms of the earth.
(18) And I will give the men that have
transgressed my covenant, which have
not performed the words of the cove-
nant which they had made before
me, when they cut the calf in twain,
and passed between the parts thereof,
(19) the princes of Judah, and the
princes of Jerusalem, the eunuchs, and
the priests, and all the people of the
land, which passed between the parts
of the calf; (20) I will even give them
into the hand of their enemies, and into
the hand of them that seek their life:
and their [b]dead bodies shall be for
meat unto the fowls of the heaven, and
to the beasts of the earth. (21) And
Zedekiah king of Judah and his princes
will I give into the hand of their
enemies, and into the hand of them that
seek their life, and into the hand of the
king of Babylon's army, which are gone
up from you. (22) Behold, I will com-
mand, saith the LORD, and cause them
to return to this city; and they shall
fight against it, and take it, and burn
it with fire: and I will make the cities
of Judah a desolation without an in-
habitant.

1 Heb., *for a removing.*

a Deut. 28. 64; ch. 29. 18.

b ch. 7. 33; & 16. 4.

B.C. cir. 607.

CHAPTER XXXV.—(1) The word
which came unto Jeremiah from the
LORD in the days of Jehoiakim the son
of Josiah king of Judah, saying,

10; Isa. lxi. 1), is emphasised with an indignant irony. They had refused to act "as the servants of Jehovah" (Lev. xxv. 55) under His protection, finding in that service their perfect freedom; and He, therefore, in His righteous wrath, would punish them by giving them the emancipation which they denied to others. He would set them free from His service, and therefore from His protection, and leave them to their fate—to the sword, to the famine, to exile. They had refused the obedience which was freedom: they should have the freedom which would be bondage.

(18) **When they cut the calf in twain . . .**—The passage is interesting, as showing the survival of one of the oldest rites of Patriarchal times. So, when Jehovah made a covenant with Abraham, the victims that had been slain were cut up and arranged opposite each other, and when the "burning lamp" passed between the pieces it was the token that Jehovah had completed the covenant, even as men complete it (Gen. xv. 10—17). The implied thought thus symbolised was that the parties to the contract prayed, as in the analogous case of 1 Sam. xi. 7, that they might be torn limb from limb like the victims if they broke the covenant. The antiquity and wide extent of the symbolism is shown by its appearing in the ritual of Greece, as in the phrase ὅρκια τέμνειν—to ratify (literally, to *cut*) oaths, in Homer (*Iliad*, ii. 124, *Od.* xxiv. 483, and elsewhere), and the Latin *fœdus ferire.* In Livy (i. 24) we have both the phrase, the act which it implied, and the prayer which accompanied it, that if the Roman people proved unfaithful to their covenant Jupiter would slay them as the priest slew the victim. "*Tu illo die, Jupiter, populum Romanum sic ferito, ut ego hunc porcum hic hodie feriam, tantoque magis ferito, quanto magis potes pollesque.*" ("Do thou, Jupiter, on that day so smite the Roman people [if they break the covenant] as I this day smite this swine —yea, so much the more smite them as thou art mightier and more prevailing.")

(19) **The eunuchs.**—See Note on chap. xxix. 2. They were for the most part, if not always, of alien birth (comp. Isa. lvi. 3), as in the case of Ebed-melech (chap. xxxviii. 7), who had become proselytes on entering the king's service. The prominence given to them indicates that in Judah as in Assyria, and we may add, in all Oriental monarchies, they held high position in the king's court, and had probably, like the princes of Judah and Jerusalem, enriched themselves by lending money to the poorer Israelites, and then bringing them into bondage. It is significant that here they take precedence of the priests, as in chap. xxix. 2 of the princes.

(20) **Their dead bodies shall be for meat . . .**—As in chaps. vii. 33, xvi. 4, xix. 7, this takes its place as the extremest penalty of transgression. The sentence on Zedekiah and his princes—*i.e.*, those who were more immediately connected with his policy—is as before (verse 5) somewhat milder, probably because he, though too weak and vacillating to stop the evil which the prophet condemned, had not been actively prominent in the transgression of the covenant, and showed more disposition, as in chap. xxxvii. 17, to listen to his counsels.

(21) **The king of Babylon's army, which are gone up from you . . .**—The words are important, as showing, as before stated, that the siege had actually been raised, and that the nobles of Judah were flattering themselves that the danger which had led them to a simulated, or, at best, transient repentance, had passed away altogether. They were reckoning once again on the help that they trusted was to come from Egypt (chap. xxxvii. 7). They are warned, however, in the next verse that the Babylonian army shall return, as executing the judgment of Jehovah, and that then there will be no escape for them.

XXXV.

(1) **In the days of Jehoiakim.**—The prophecy that follows carries us back over a period of about seventeen years to the earlier period of the prophet's life and work. Jerusalem was not yet besieged. Jehoiakim had not filled up the measure of his iniquities. The armies of the Chaldæans were, however, in the meantime moving on the outskirts of the kingdom of Judah (verse 11) or were driving the nomad inhabitants, who had hitherto dwelt in tents, to take refuge in the cities. The first capture of the city by Nebuchadnezzar was in B.C. 607.

(2) Go unto the house of the Rechabites, and speak unto them, and bring them into the house of the LORD, into one of the chambers, and give them wine to drink.
(3) Then I took Jaazaniah the son of Jeremiah, the son of Habaziniah, and his brethren, and all his sons, and the whole house of the Rechabites; (4) and I brought them into the house of the LORD, into the chamber of the sons of Hanan, the son of Igdaliah, a man of God, which *was* by the chamber of the princes, which *was* above the chamber

---

(2) **Go unto the house of the Rechabites . . .**—The word "house" is used throughout the chapter in the sense of "family." Among those who had thus taken refuge were the tribe, or sect, or even fraternity known by this name. Their founder was the Jonadab, or Jehonadab, who appears as the ally of Jehu in the overthrow of the house of Ahab (2 Kings x. 15). It is clear from that history that he exercised an influence over the people which Jehu was glad to secure, and that he welcomed "the zeal for the Lord" which led Jehu to the massacre of the worshippers of Baal. He is described as the "son of Rechab," but seeing that that name, which means "chariot," was applied to the great Tishbite prophet, as in "the chariot of Israel, and the horsemen thereof" (2 Kings ii. 12), it has been thought, with some probability, that the name "son of Rechab" means "Son of the chariot" (so in later Jewish history we have Bar-cochba = son of the star), *i.e.*, "disciple of the great prophet." Anyhow, the life which Jonadab enforced on his followers presented all the characteristic features of that of Elijah. It was a protest against the Baal-worship that had flowed into Israel from Phœnicia, against the corruption of the life of cities, against the intemperance which was tainting the life of Israel (Amos vi. 4—6). It reminds us in this respect of the more ascetic sects, such as the Wahabees of Arabia in the eighteenth century (see Burckhardt's *Bedouins and Wahabys*, p. 283; Palgrave's *Arabia*), that have at times arisen among the followers of Mahomet. It has some points of resemblance to the Mendicant Orders of mediæval Christendom. From 1 Chron. ii. 55 it appears that "the house of Rechab" belonged to the Kenites who had joined the Israelites on their exodus from Egypt, and had settled in their lands, retaining their old habits (Judg. i. 16; iv. 11; Num. x. 29—32; 1 Sam. xv. 6; xxvii. 10). Such a people naturally retained many of the habits of patriarchal life, and it is not improbable that Elijah himself issued from their tents.

(3) **Then I took Jaazaniah the son of Jeremiah . . .**—The names (Jaazaniah = Jehovah hears, Jeremiah = Jehovah exalts, Habaziniah = Jehovah gathers) are not without significance, as showing that the Rechabites were sharers in the faith of Israel, perhaps, as an order, conspicuous witnesses for that faith. The name Jeremiah may possibly indicate that there was some previous connexion between the Rechabites and the prophet's family.

His brethren, and all his sons . . .—The words may be taken in their literal sense, but on the assumption that the Rechabites were a religious order rather than a family, the terms may indicate different stages or degrees of membership, the "brethren" being those who were fully incorporated, the "sons," those who like "the sons of the prophets" (2 Kings iv. 38; vi. 1; ix. 1; Amos vii. 14) were still in training as probationers. Such a use of the word "brethren" would grow naturally out of that of "sons," and is found in this wider sense of priests and Levites (1 Chron. xv. 5—18; xxvi. 7—32 and elsewhere) and of prophets (Rev. xxii. 9).

(4) **I brought them into the house of the Lord . . .**—The Temple of Solomon appears from 1 Kings vi. 5 to have had, like a cathedral, apartments constructed in its precincts which were assigned, by special favour, for the residence of conspicuous priests or prophets. Huldah the prophetess seems to have dwelt in some such apartments known as "the college" (see 2 Kings xxii. 14). In this case the chamber was occupied by the sons of Hanan. He, or Igdaliah (the Hebrew punctuation is decisive in favour of Hanan), is described as "a man of God—*i.e.*, as a prophet—and therefore sympathising, we may believe, with Jeremiah's work (Deut. xxxiii. 1; 1 Sam. ii. 27; 1 Kings xiii. 1; xx. 28; 2 Kings iv. 7, 9; 1 Chron. xxiii. 14; 2 Chron. xi. 2). It would seem, from the narrative, that Jeremiah had no chamber of his own. Here also "the sons of Hanan" are probably a company of scholars under the training of the prophet, Jeremiah introducing as it were the two religious orders to each other. The "princes," as in chaps. xxvi. 10, xxxvi. 12, were probably official persons who, though not priests, were entitled to residence in the precincts, as we see in the case of Gemariah in chap. xxxvi. 10. The "keeper of the door," as in chap. lii. 24, was probably one of the higher section of the priesthood. The stress laid on all these details was probably intended to show that the memorable dramatic scene that followed, daring as it seemed, was acted in the presence of representatives of the priestly, prophetic, and official orders. The name of Maaseiah has, however, a special interest attached to it. Shallum, the name of his father, is found in 2 Kings xxii. 14 as that of the husband of Huldah the prophetess of the reign of Josiah, and he is described as the "keeper of the wardrobe," *i.e.*, probably of the vestments of the priests, and as dwelling in the "college" (literally, the "second" part, or *annexe* of some other building). It is hardly possible to resist the inference that in the Maaseiah who now appears as receiving Jeremiah and the Rechabites, we have the son of the prophetess who had taken so active a part in the work of reformation in the reign of Josiah, whose influence had coloured the whole of the prophet's life, who had brought up her son within the precincts of the Temple. We are brought as it were into the innermost circle of the prophetic company of Jerusalem, and are reminded of Simeon and Anna, and those who waited for the consolation, for the redemption of Israel (Luke ii. 25, 38). The influence of Shallum may, perhaps, be traced in the fact that the king who appears in history as Jehoahaz had probably been named by Josiah after him (2 Kings xxiii. 30; 1 Chron. iii. 15), as David named one of his sons after Nathan (2 Sam. v. 14). It is, perhaps, from this point of view, characteristic of Jeremiah that he adheres in chap. xxii. 1 to the old name given on his birth, and not to that which he had apparently adopted upon his accession to the throne. The name Shallum, it may

of Maaseiah the son of Shallum, the
keeper of the [1]door: (5) and I set
before the sons of the house of the
Rechabites pots full of wine, and cups,
and I said unto them, Drink ye wine.
(6) But they said, We will drink no
wine: for Jonadab the son of Rechab
our father commanded us, saying,
Ye shall drink no wine, *neither* ye,
nor your sons for ever: (7) neither
shall ye build house, nor sow seed,
nor plant vineyard, nor have *any*:
but all your days ye shall dwell in
tents; that ye may live many days
in the land where ye *be* strangers.
(8) Thus have we obeyed the voice of
Jonadab the son of Rechab our father
in all that he hath charged us, to drink
no wine all our days, we, our wives, our
sons, nor our daughters; (9) nor to build
houses for us to dwell in: neither have
we vineyard, nor field, nor seed: (10) but
we have dwelt in tents, and have
obeyed, and done according to all that
Jonadab our father commanded us.
(11) But it came to pass, when Nebu-
chadrezzar king of Babylon came up
into the land, that we said, Come, and
let us go to Jerusalem for fear of the
army of the Chaldeans, and for fear of
the army of the Syrians: so we dwell at
Jerusalem.
(12) Then came the word of the
LORD unto Jeremiah, saying, (13) Thus
saith the LORD of hosts, the God of
Israel; Go and tell the men of Judah
and the inhabitants of Jerusalem, Will
ye not receive instruction to hearken to
my words? saith the LORD. (14) The
words of Jonadab the son of Rechab,
that he commanded his sons not to
drink wine, are performed; for unto this
day they drink none, but obey their
father's commandment: notwithstand-
ing I have spoken unto you, rising early
and speaking; but ye hearkened not
unto me. (15) I have sent also unto
you all my servants the prophets, rising
up early and sending *them*, saying,
[a]Return ye now every man from his
evil way, and amend your doings, and
go not after other gods to serve them,
and ye shall dwell in the land which I
have given to you and to your fathers:
but ye have not inclined your ear, nor
hearkened unto me. (16) Because the
sons of Jonadab the son of Rechab have
performed the commandment of their
father, which he commanded them; but
this people hath not hearkened unto

1 Heb., *threshold*, or, *vessel*.

a ch. 18. 11; & 25. 5.

---

be noted, means "retribution," whether for good or for evil.

(6—8) **We will drink no wine . . .**—We have here, as it were, the rule of the tribe or order which looked to Jonadab as its founder. Like Samson (Judg. xiii. 4, 5), Samuel (inferentially from 1 Sam. i. 11, 15), and the Baptist (Luke i. 15), they were life-long Nazarites (Num. vi. 1—6). Jonadab's intention was obviously to keep them as a separate people, retaining their nomadic form of life, free from the contamination of cities, or the temptations of acquired property, or the risks of attack which such property brought with it. They are now invited, and it must have seemed to them a strange invitation to come from a prophet's lips, to break that rule, and they answer almost in the tone of a calm but indignant protest. They have been faithful hitherto, and they will continue faithful still. In the words "that your days may be long in the land" we may, perhaps, trace an echo of the fifth commandment (Exod. xx. 12), viewed as extending to the relations which connect the members of an order with its head. The rule has descended to the followers of Islam, and the law of abstinence has been extended by Abd-ul-Wahab to tobacco. Diodorus Siculus (xix. 94) relates that the Nabathæans adopted the Rechabite rule in its completeness. Possibly they were Rechabites.

(11) **When Nebuchadrezzar king of Babylon came up into the land . . .**—The statement has the character of an apologetic explanation. They had been driven, as the peasants of Judæa had been (chaps. iv. 6; viii. 14), to take refuge from the invading armies, probably in the invasion of Nebuchadnezzar in the eighth year of Jehoiakim (2 Kings xxiv. 1, 2), bringing their flocks and their herds, as far as they could, with them, but this was only a temporary casualty, and they intended, when the danger was over, to return to their former mode of life. The Syrians are joined with the Chaldees in the invasion, as in 2 Kings xxiv. 2.

(12) **Then came the word of the Lord unto Jeremiah.**—Up to this time the prophet had acted on the thought which came into his mind as an inspiration, without apparently more than a partial insight into its meaning. Now, as the words indicate, he passes at once into the prophetic state and speaks the prophetic words. It follows from verse 18 that it was uttered in the presence of the Rechabites and formed, we may believe, the conclusion of this strange dramatic scene.

(13) **Will ye not receive instruction . . .**—The argument of the prophet is naturally an *à fortiori* one. The words of Jonadab had been kept faithfully as a rule of life for 300 years by his descendants or his order. The words of Jehovah, "rising early and speaking" through His prophets (we note the repetition of the characteristic phrase of chaps. vii. 13 and xxv. 3), were neglected by the people whom He had adopted as His children. They, too, had the same promise that by obeying they should dwell in the land which He had given them, but they had turned a deaf ear both to the promise and the warning which it implied.

(15) **Return ye now every man from his evil way.**—The words are more than a general summary of the teaching of earlier prophets, and we find in them an almost verbal reproduction of the burden of Jere-

me: (17) therefore thus saith the LORD
God of hosts, the God of Israel; Behold, I will bring upon Judah and upon all the inhabitants of Jerusalem all the evil that I have pronounced against them: because I have spoken unto them, but they have not heard; and I have called unto them, but they have not answered.

(18) And Jeremiah said unto the house of the Rechabites, Thus saith the LORD of hosts, the God of Israel; Because ye have obeyed the commandment of Jonadab your father, and kept all his precepts, and done according unto all that
he hath commanded you: (19) therefore
thus saith the LORD of hosts, the God of Israel; [1]Jonadab the son of Rechab shall not want a man to stand before me for ever.

1 Heb., *There shall not a man be cut off from Jonadab the son of Rechab to stand, &c.*

CHAPTER XXXVI.—(1) And it came to pass in the fourth year of Jehoiakim the son of Josiah king of Judah, *that* this word came unto Jeremiah from the LORD, saying, (2) Take
thee a roll of a book, and write therein all the words that I have spoken unto

---

miah's own preaching, in chap. xxv. 5, 6, in the fourth year of Jehoiakim, *i.e.*, before the incident here recorded.

(17) **Because I have spoken unto them, but they have not heard.**—The prophet in part reproduces his own earlier complaint from chaps. vii. 13, xxv. 7, a complaint which has been the ever-recurring burden of all teachers of wisdom (Prov. i. 24) and of all true prophets (Isa. lxv. 12, lxvi. 4).

(18) **Because ye have obeyed the commandment of Jonadab your father.**—The words decide nothing as to the obligation of the commandment referred to upon others. The law which Jeremiah received as given by God laid down no such rule of life. A righteous life was possible without it (chap. xxii. 15; Matt. xi. 19). What he was taught to praise was the steadfastness and loyalty with which they adhered to a merely human precept, not at variance with the letter of any divine law, and designed, like the Nazarite vow, to carry the spirit of that law—the idea of a life-long consecration—to its highest point. The temper of faithfulness to any rule of life sanctioned by prescription, whether it be that of a school, a college, a guild, or a religious order, is in itself praiseworthy as compared with that of individual self-assertion and self-will.

(19) **Jonadab the son of Rechab shall not want a man to stand before me for ever.**—Taking the words in their simplest literal sense, they find a fulfilment in the strange unlooked-for way in which the name and customs of the Rechabites have cropped up from time to time. The Jewish historian Hegesippus (see Euseb. *Hist. Eccl.* ii. 23), in his account of the martyrdom of James the Just, names the sons of the Rechabites as looking on in reverential sympathy with one whose life, like their own, carried the Nazarite type to its highest perfection. In the account which Diodorus Siculus (xix. 94) gives of the Nabathæans as neither sowing seed, nor planting fruit-trees, nor building houses, and enforcing this rule of life under pain of death, we can scarcely fail to recognise the Rechabite type. Benjamin of Tudela, in the twelfth century, reports that he found 100,000 Jews who were named Rechabites, and who lived after their fashion near *El Jubar*, and that they were governed by a prince of the house of David. More recent travellers, Dr. Wolff (*Journal*, 1829, ii. 334; 1839, *p.* 389) and Signor Pierotti (*Transactions of British Association*, 1862), report that they have met tribes near Mecca, on the Dead Sea, or in Yemen and Senaar, who observed the rule of Jonadab, claimed to be his descendants, referred to Jerem. xxxv. 19 as fulfilled in them, and led the life of devout Jews. It is probable, however, that in these later instances we may trace the effect of the Wahabee ascetic movement among the Mahomedan Arabs, identifying its rule with the old practice of the son of Rechab (Burckhardt: *Bedouins and Wahabys*, p. 283).

The words "stand before" have, however, in Hebrew a distinct secondary meaning. It was a definitely liturgical expression for the ministrations of the Levites who were chosen to "stand before" the Lord (Deut. x. 8, xviii. 5, 7), and a like meaning is prominent in chap. vii. 10, xv. 19; Gen. xviii. 22; Judges xx. 28; Ps. cxxxiv. 1. The Targum of this passage, indeed, actually gives "ministering before me" as its paraphrase. The natural inference would be that the Rechabites were by these words admitted, in virtue of their Nazarite character, to serve as Levites in the Temple—to be, in fact, a higher class of Nethinim (see Notes on 1 Chron. ix. 2; Ezra ii. 43)—and this view is confirmed (1) by the fact that the LXX. ascribes Ps. lxxi. to "the sons of Jonadab, the first that were led captive;" (2) that a son of Rechab is associated in Neh. iii. 14 with priests and Levites and nobles in repairing the walls of Jerusalem; (3) in 1 Chron. ii. 55 the Rechabites have become scribes, and in the Vulgate (evidence of a Jewish tradition as to the meaning of the words), the proper names of the English version, "Tirathites, Shimeathites, and Sucathites," which add nothing to our knowledge, are represented by "*canentes et resonantes et in tabernaculis commorantes*" ("singing, and playing instruments, and dwelling in tents"), which unite the functions of Levites with the mode of life of the Rechabites. So Hegesippus (as above) speaks of priests who were of the sons of Rechab in the Apostolic age.

XXXVI.

(1) **The fourth year of Jehoiakim . . .**—The prophetic message that follows is brought by the date thus given into close contact with chap. xxv., and it is a reasonable inference that we have in that chapter the substance of part, at least, of what was written by Baruch from the prophet's dictation in verse 4. The contents exactly agree with the description of the prophecy given here in verse 2.

(2) **Take thee a roll of a book.**—The same phrase meets us in Ps. xl. 7 (ascribed by some critics to Jeremiah), but does not occur in any earlier prophet or historical book. It is found in later prophets (Ezek. ii. 9, iii. 1; Zech. v. 1, 2). It probably followed on the introduction of parchment as a material for writing

thee against Israel, and against Judah,
and against all the nations, from the
day I spake unto thee, from the days
of [a]Josiah, even unto this day. (3) It
may be that the house of Judah will
hear all the evil which I purpose to do
unto them; that they may return every
man from his evil way; that I may
forgive their iniquity and their sin.
(4) Then Jeremiah called Baruch the
son of Neriah: and Baruch wrote from
the mouth of Jeremiah all the words of
the LORD, which he had spoken unto
him, upon a roll of a book. (5) And
Jeremiah commanded Baruch, saying,
I *am* shut up; I cannot go into the
house of the LORD: (6) therefore go
thou, and read in the roll, which thou
hast written from my mouth, the words
of the LORD in the ears of the people
in the LORD's house upon the fasting
day: and also thou shalt read them in
the ears of all Judah that come out of
their cities. (7) It may be [1]they will
present their supplication before the
LORD, and will return every one from
his evil way: for great *is* the anger and
the fury that the LORD hath pronounced
against this people. (8) And Baruch
the son of Neriah did according to all
that Jeremiah the prophet commanded
him, reading in the book the words of
the LORD in the LORD's house.
(9) And it came to pass in the fifth
year of Jehoiakim the son of Josiah king
of Judah, in the ninth month, *that* they
proclaimed a fast before the LORD to
all the people in Jerusalem, and to all
the people that came from the cities of
Judah unto Jerusalem. (10) Then read
Baruch in the book the words of Jere-
miah in the house of the LORD, in the
chamber of Gemariah the son of
Shaphan the scribe, in the higher court,

a ch. 25. 3.

B. C. cir. 606.

1 Heb., *their supplication shall fall.*

---

on, and the consequent substitution of the roll for the papyrus books, for which, from their fragile fabric, a different form was necessary. The command thus given to Baruch is interesting as letting us, so to speak, into the "workshop" of the prophet. He speaks probably without premeditation, as the word of the Lord comes to him (Matt. x. 19). A disciple acts as reporter, and preserves the utterance in writing. It is interesting in this respect to note the parallelism between Jeremiah's *modus operandi* and St. Paul's (Rom. xvi. 22; Gal. vi. 11; 2 Thess. iii. 17). From time to time the prophet collects, repeats, revises, and, in modern phrase, edits what he has uttered. We have here accordingly what may be described as the history of the first volume of his discourses—a volume which perished, as the chapter records, but of which the earlier chapters of the present book are substantially a reproduction.

(3) **It may be that the house of Judah will hear . . .**—Better, *hearken to*, as implying more than the physical act of listening. Here again, in the expression of the hope that Israel would "return every man from his evil way," we have a distinct echo from chap. xxv. 5.

(4) **Then Jeremiah called Baruch the son of Neriah.**—See Note on chap. xxxii. 12. The prophet was, as the next verse shows, in some way hindered, though apparently not by imprisonment, as he and Baruch could hide themselves (verse 19): Baruch therefore had to act not only as the prophet's amanuensis, but as the preacher of his sermon. It will be noted that an interval of some months elapsed between the dictation and the public utterance.

(6) **In the Lord's house upon the fasting day.**—Literally, *a fast day*. We learn from verse 9 that this was one of the special fasts "proclaimed" in times of national distress (comp. Joel ii. 1; 2 Chron. xx. 3, 4; 1 Kings xxi. 10), and it was accordingly a time when the courts of the Temple would be more than usually thronged, and when, it might be hoped, the people gathered in them would be more than usually disposed to listen to warnings and exhortations to repentance. Probably, however, the king had proclaimed the fast by the advice of the priests and false prophets, to rouse the people to the "holy war" of an enthusiastic religious resistance to the Chaldeans, and this may account for the eagerness of Jeremiah to counteract the scheme by the unlooked-for sermon. The addition, "and also thou shalt read them in the ears of all Judah," implies that Baruch was, if opportunity offered, to read the words of the prophecy on other occasions and to other gatherings of the people. The ordinary fast of the Day of Atonement was, it will be remembered, in the seventh month—*i.e.*, October; this accordingly was in November or December. This agrees, it may be noted, with the charcoal fire which was burning in the king's chamber (verse 22).

(9) **It came to pass in the fifth year of Jehoiakim.**—The LXX. gives "the *eighth* year," but the Hebrew text gives much the more probable date. What follows refers apparently to the same occasion as verse 8, and is of the nature of a note explaining the circumstances under which the prophetic discourse was read. An interval of some months thus passed between the writing of the book and its delivery in the Temple, during which its substance was, perhaps, made known to the inner circle of the prophet's disciples. The fast was probably proclaimed on the king's hearing of the approach of Nebuchadnezzar's army, as described by the Rechabites in chap. xxxv. 11.

(10) **In the chamber of Gemariah the son of Shaphan.**—The man thus named belonged to a family which, through three successive generations, presented conspicuous examples of devout patriotism. His father Shaphan was energetic in the work of re-building the Temple under Josiah (2 Kings xxii. 3), in conjunction with the high priest Hilkiah, and had taken an active part in publishing the contents of the newly-discovered book of the Law of the Lord (2 Kings xxiii. 12). As a scribe, he must have taken part in the king's edicts for the restoration of the true worship, and probably also in ordering copies of the new-found treasure—the

at the [1][a]entry of the new gate of the
LORD's house, in the ears of all the
people.
(11) When Michaiah the son of Gema-
riah, the son of Shaphan, had heard out
of the book all the words of the LORD,
(12) then he went down into the king's
house, into the scribe's chamber: and,
lo, all the princes sat there, *even*
Elishama the scribe, and Delaiah the
son of Shemaiah, and Elnathan the
son of Achbor, and Gemariah the son
of Shaphan, and Zedekiah the son of
Hananiah, and all the princes. (13) Then
Michaiah declared unto them all the
words that he had heard, when Baruch
read the book in the ears of the people.
(14) Therefore all the princes sent Jehudi
the son of Nethaniah, the son of Shele-
miah, the son of Cushi, unto Baruch,
saying, Take in thine hand the roll
wherein thou hast read in the ears of
the people, and come. So Baruch the
son of Neriah took the roll in his hand,
and came unto them. (15) And they said
unto him, Sit down now, and read it in
our ears. So Baruch read *it* in their
ears.
(16) Now it came to pass, when they
had heard all the words, they were
afraid both one and other, and said
unto Baruch, We will surely tell the
king of all these words. (17) And they
asked Baruch, saying, Tell us now, How
didst thou write all these words at his
mouth? (18) Then Baruch answered

1 Or, *door*.

a ch. 26. 10.

---

whole Law, or, more probably, the book of Deuteronomy—to be made by the scribes who worked under him. We have seen one of his sons, Ahikam, protecting the prophet Jeremiah in chap. xxvi. 24. Here Gemariah places his chamber in the Temple court at the service of the prophet's delegate. The "new gate" may well have been a prominent part of the work effected by Shaphan and Hilkiah (2 Kings xxii. 5, 6), and this may have led to a chamber over it being assigned to his son. (See Note on chap. xxxv. 4.) The people addressed may have been either in the outer court of the Temple, or gathered outside the gate. A chamber over the gateway would naturally have an opening on either side. The general use of the word for "entry" is in favour of the latter hypothesis.

(11) **When Michaiah the son of Gemariah . . .**—Gemariah himself was, as we find in the next verse, not one of the listeners, but took his place with the other princes, in the "scribe's chamber," probably used as a council-room, in the king's palace. It seems obvious from Michaiah's relation to him that his purpose in reporting Baruch's discourse was not unfriendly. Probably it was part of a preconcerted plan, arranged between the prophet and his friends, that he should report it, and so give an opening for bringing Baruch into the presence of the king and his counsellors, as they sat in what we may call their council-chamber.

(12) **And, lo, all the princes sat there.**—The following particulars may be noted as to the princes thus named. Elishama may have been identical with the prince of that name in 2 Kings xxv. 25, and, if so, was the grandfather of a man who afterwards plays a conspicuous part in the history of the prophet's life (chap. xli.) He appears to have taken a purely official line, as scribe, standing neutral between the prophet and his opponents. Delaiah (the name signifies "the Lord delivers," and is found as that of a priest in the time of David, 1 Chron. xxiv. 18) joins Elnathan and Gemariah in pleading against the king's destruction of the prophetic roll. The name Shemaiah, which appears here as that of his father, is found in Neh. vi. 10 as belonging to a son of Delaiah, and this probably indicates relationship. On Elnathan, the son of Achbor, see Note on chap. xxvi. 22. On Gemariah, see Note on verse 10. Of Zedekiah nothing more is known, unless his father Hananiah be the prophet who opposes Jeremiah in chap. xxviii. 1—17.

(14) **Therefore all the princes sent Jehudi the son of Nethaniah. . . .**—There must obviously have been some reason for the exceptionally long genealogy thus given. It is probably indicated by the first and last names on the list. Cushi (= Ethiopian)—the name appears, probably with this sense, as that of a courier of Joab's in 2 Sam. xviii. 21—was an alien by birth, who, like Ebed-melech the Ethiopian (chap. xxxviii. 7), had gained the favour of one of Jehoiakim's predecessors, and had become a proselyte. The rule of Deut. xxiii. 8 did not admit of the full incorporation of the descendants of such proselytes—Edomite or Egyptian, the latter term being taken probably as including Ethiopian—till the third generation, and the name Jehudi (= Jew) was naturally enough given to the child who first became entitled to that privilege. The part he takes in the proceedings, though not more than ministerial, indicates sympathy with the prophet, and we may perhaps connect this with the like sympathy shown by Ebed-melech in chap. xxxviii. 7. In Ps. lxxxvii. 4 (probably belonging to the reign of Hezekiah) we have, it may be noted, a record of the admission of such Ethiopian proselytes. The purpose of his mission was to bring Baruch to the council of princes, that they might judge, on hearing the contents of the roll, how far it corresponded with Michaiah's report. He comes, the princes listen, and the impression made on them is given in verse 16. We note a tone of respect in the request that Baruch would "sit down"—*i.e.*, take the attitude of a teacher (Luke iv. 20).

(16) **They were afraid both one and other . . .**—The words indicate a conflict of feelings. They were alarmed for themselves and their country as they heard, with at least a partial faith, the woes that were threatened as impending. They were alarmed also for the safety of the prophet and the scribe who had the boldness to utter those woes. They have no hostile purpose in communicating what they had heard to the king, but the matter had come to their official knowledge, and they had no alternative but to report it (Lev. v. 1; Prov. xxix. 24).

(17—19) **Tell us now, How didst thou write . . .?**—The question was clearly put as a judicial interrogatory. The princes were anxious to ascertain how far

them, He pronounced all these words
unto me with his mouth, and I wrote
them with ink in the book. (19) Then
said the princes unto Baruch, Go, hide
thee, thou and Jeremiah; and let no man
know where ye be.
(20) And they went in to the king into
the court, but they laid up the roll in
the chamber of Elishama the scribe, and
told all the words in the ears of the king.
(21) So the king sent Jehudi to fetch the
roll: and he took it out of Elishama
the scribe's chamber. And Jehudi read
it in the ears of the king, and in the
ears of all the princes which stood be-
side the king. (22) Now the king sat in
the winterhouse in the ninth month:
and *there was a fire* on the hearth burn-
ing before him. (23) And it came to pass,
that when Jehudi had read three or four
leaves, he cut it with the penknife, and
cast *it* into the fire that *was* on the
hearth, until all the roll was con-
sumed in the fire that *was* on the
hearth. (24) Yet they were not afraid,
nor rent their garments, *neither* the
king, nor any of his servants that
heard all these words. (25) Nevertheless
Elnathan and Delaiah and Gemariah
had made intercession to the king that
he would not burn the roll: but he
would not hear them. (26) But the king

---

each of the parties concerned was responsible. Had Baruch exercised any discretion in writing so that the words were his, though the substance was Jeremiah's? or had he, on his own responsibility, and without the prophet's will, published what had been written privately? or had every syllable as it was read come from the prophet's lips? The scribe's answer showed that the last hypothesis answered to the facts of the case. On hearing this they, obviously with a friendly regard, advise him and the prophet to hide themselves till they should see what effect the report would have on the king's mind. It would appear from verse 19 that Jeremiah, though "shut up" and unable to go into the house of the Lord (verse 5), was not actually so imprisoned as to hinder him from concealing himself. Either, therefore, we must assume that he was in a "*libera custodia*," that gave him facilities for an escape, which the princes connived at, or that by "shut up" he meant only hindered by some cause or other. The latter seems the more probable hypothesis. In the concealment of the prophet we find a parallel to that of Elijah and the other prophets under Ahab (1 Kings xvii. 3, xviii. 4), of Polycarp (*Mart. Polyc.* c. 5), perhaps also of Luther in the Wartburg.

(20) **They laid up the roll in the chamber of Elishama . . .**—The step was a material one, from the official standpoint. If either the prophet or the disciple were to be prosecuted for what had been spoken, it was important that the *corpus delicti* should itself be ready for reference, whether on behalf of the accusers or accused. The precaution taken by the princes of lodging it with Elishama, as the scribe or keeper of the archives, indicates an apprehension that the king, in his passionate waywardness, might act as he actually did. They accordingly content themselves with reporting from memory the substance of what they had heard.

(21) **So the king sent Jehudi . . .**—The prudence of the counsellors was foiled by the king's impatience. He was not satisfied with hearing a general report. He would have the words themselves.

(22) **Now the king sat in the winterhouse in the ninth month.**—The "winterhouse" (the palaces of kings seem to have been commonly provided with such a special apartment; comp. Amos iii. 15) was probably the southern wing of the palace. It was in November or December, and, as glass windows were unknown, a charcoal fire, placed after the Eastern fashion in a brazier, or earthen pot, in the middle of the room, was a necessity. So we find a fire in the court of the high priest's palace in the raw early morning of a Passover in March or April (John xviii. 18).

(23) **Three or four leaves . . .**—The English words suggest the idea of a papyrus book rather than a parchment roll (see Note on verse 4), but the Hebrew word (literally = a door) may indicate the column of writing on such a roll, as well as a leaf. The act, in its childish impatience, betrayed the anger of the king. He could not bear to hear of the seventy years of exile which were in store for his people, and which, if we assume the roll to have included the substance of chap. xxv., would have come into one of the earlier columns. The word for "pen-knife" is used generally for any sharp instrument of iron—for a razor (Ezek. v. 1), and for a sword (Isa. vii. 20). Here it is the knife which was used to shape the reed, or *calamus*, used in writing. It should, perhaps, be noted that the Hebrew, like the English, leaves it uncertain whether the king himself cut and burnt the roll, or Jehudi with his approval. Verse 25 is in favour of the former view. We are reminded, as we read the words, of like orders given by Antiochus Epiphanes for the destruction of the Law (1 Macc. i. 56), by Diocletian for that of the sacred books of the Christians, perhaps also of those of the Court of Rome for the destruction of the writings of Wyclif and Luther.

(24—25) **Yet they were not afraid, nor rent their garments . . .**—If we suppose that the "servants" are identical with the princes, these were the very men who, when they first heard the words, had been afraid, "both one and other." Now the king's presence restrains them, and they dare not show their alarm at the contents of the scroll, nor "rend their clothes" (comp. Matt. xxvi. 65; Acts xiv. 14) at what must have seemed to them the sacrilege of burning a scroll that contained a message from Jehovah. Three only had the courage, though they did not show their abhorrence, to entreat the king to refrain from his impiety. (See Note on verse 12.) Possibly, however, the "servants" or "courtiers" are distinguished from the princes, and are specially named in the next verse.

(26) **But the king commanded Jerahmeel . . .**—Instead of "the son of Hammelech," we have to read, if we take the usual meaning of the words, "the king's son," as, indeed, the LXX. rightly renders it. The term would not imply more than that he belonged

commanded Jerahmeel the son [1]of Hammelech, and Seraiah the son of Azriel, and Shelemiah the son of Abdeel, to take Baruch the scribe and Jeremiah the prophet: but the LORD hid them.

(27) Then the word of the LORD came to Jeremiah, after that the king had burned the roll, and the words which Baruch wrote at the mouth of Jeremiah, saying, (28) Take thee again another roll, and write in it all the former words that were in the first roll, which Jehoiakim the king of Judah hath burned. (29) And thou shalt say to Jehoiakim king of Judah, Thus saith the LORD; Thou hast burned this roll, saying, Why hast thou written therein, saying, The king of Babylon shall certainly come and destroy this land, and shall cause to cease from thence man and beast? (30) Therefore thus saith the LORD of Jehoiakim king of Judah; He shall have none to sit upon the throne of David: and his dead body shall be [a]cast out in the day to the heat, and in the night to the frost. (31) And I will [2]punish him and his seed and his servants for their iniquity; and I will bring upon them, and upon the inhabitants of Jerusalem, and upon the men of Judah, all the evil that I have pronounced against them; but they hearkened not.

(32) Then took Jeremiah another roll, and gave it to Baruch the scribe, the son of Neriah; who wrote therein from the mouth of Jeremiah all the words of the book which Jehoiakim king of Judah had burned in the fire: and there were added besides unto them many [3]like words.

CHAPTER XXXVII.—(1) And king [b]Zedekiah the son of Josiah reigned instead of Coniah the son of Jehoiakim, whom Nebuchadrezzar king of Babylon made king in the land of Judah. (2) But neither he, nor his servants, nor the people of the land, did hearken unto the words of the LORD, which he spake [4]by the prophet Jeremiah. (3) And Zedekiah the king sent Jehucal the son of Shelemiah and Zephaniah the son of Maaseiah the priest to the prophet Jeremiah, saying, Pray now unto the LORD

1 Or, *of the king.*

B. C. cir. 605.

a ch. 22. 19.

2 Heb., *visit upon.*

B. C. cir. 599.

3 Heb., *as they.*

b 2 Kings 24. 17; 2 Chron. 36. 10; ch. [illegible]. 24.

B. C. 590.

4 Heb., *by the hand of the prophet.*

---

to the "royal house." Jehoiakim was only twenty-five when he came to the throne, and could not have had a son old enough to execute the orders given to Jerahmeel. Of Seraiah nothing more is known. He is clearly not identical with the "quiet prince," the son of Neriah, in chap. li. 59. The name of Shelemiah appears in chap. xxxvii. 3, as the father of Jehucal, who is first sent by Zedekiah to consult the prophet, and who afterwards arrested him (chap. xxxviii. 1). It is probable in the nature of the case that they belonged to the party of the prophet's enemies. The counsel of verse 19 had fortunately been given in time, and the attempt to seize the prophet and his scribe was, as we say, providentially frustrated.

(27) **Then the word of the Lord came to Jeremiah.**—This was probably during the concealment of the two friends, and to the command thus given we probably owe the present form of chap. xxv.—perhaps, also, of the earlier chapters of the book. But, in addition to the reproduction of the judgment denounced upon the nation at large, there was now a special prediction as to Jehoiakim himself. (1) He was to have "none to sit upon the throne of David." As a matter of fact, he was succeeded by his son Jehoiachin, or Jeconiah, but the reign of the boy-prince as a tributary king lasted for three months only, and Zedekiah, who succeeded him, was the brother and not the son of Jehoiakim (comp. chap. xxii. 30). (2) His dead body was to be "cast out in the day to the heat, and in the night to the frost." The same prediction is found in chap. xxii. 18, 19, written probably after the incident thus recorded. See Note there as to its fulfilment.

(32) **And there were added besides unto them many like words.**—The passage is interesting as showing, as it were, the *genesis* of the present volume of the prophet's writings. The discourse delivered in the Temple court was, in modern phrase, revised and enlarged, dictated to Baruch as before, and in this shape has probably come down to us in chap. xxv.

XXXVII.

(1) **And king Zedekiah the son of Josiah . .** —The eight chapters that follow form a continuous narrative of the later work and fortunes of the prophet. They open with recording the accession of Zedekiah, following on the deposition of Coniah or Jeconiah. Here, as in chap. xxii. 24, we have the shortened form of the name of the latter. The relative pronoun "whom Nebuchadrezzar . . . made king" refers to Zedekiah.

(2) **But neither he, nor his servants . . .**— The verse gives a general survey of the character of Zedekiah's reign preparatory to the actual history that follows, which falls towards its close, probably in the seventh or eighth year of his reign. It will be noted that the "servants" here, as in chap. xxxvi. 24, are the personal attendants of the king, his courtiers, as distinct from the "princes" of Judah and the "people of the land," that is, the great body of unofficial laymen.

(3) **And Zedekiah the king sent Jehucal . . .** —The time and, probably, occasion of the mission is given in verse 5. The Chaldæans had raised the siege of Jerusalem on hearing of the approach of the Egyptian army under Pharaoh-Hophra, the Apries of Herodotus (Herod. ii. 161—169. Ezek. xvii. 15, xxix. 1—16, xxx.—xxxii.), and the king seems to have thought that an opportunity presented itself for asserting his independence, and wished to gain the sanction and the prayers of the prophet for this policy. Of the two officers who are here named, Jehucal appears as accusing the prophet

our God for us. (4) Now Jeremiah came
in and went out among the people: for
they had not put him into prison.
(5) Then Pharaoh's army was come forth
out of Egypt: and when the Chaldeans
that besieged Jerusalem heard tidings
of them, they departed from Jerusalem.
(6) Then came the word of the LORD
unto the prophet Jeremiah, saying,
(7) Thus saith the LORD, the God of
Israel; Thus shall ye say to the king
of Judah, that sent you unto me to
enquire of me; Behold, Pharaoh's army,
which is come forth to help you, shall
return to Egypt into their own land.
(8) And the Chaldeans shall come again,
and fight against this city, and take it,
and burn it with fire. (9) Thus saith the
LORD; Deceive not [1]yourselves, saying,
The Chaldeans shall surely depart from
us: for they shall not depart. (10) For
though ye had smitten the whole army
of the Chaldeans that fight against you,
and there remained *but* [2]wounded men
among them, *yet* should they rise up
every man in his tent, and burn this
city with fire.
(11) And it came to pass, that when the
army of the Chaldeans was [3]broken up
from Jerusalem for fear of Pharaoh's
army, (12) then Jeremiah went forth
out of Jerusalem to go into the land of
Benjamin, [4]to separate himself thence
in the midst of the people. (13) And
when he was in the gate of Benjamin,
a captain of the ward *was* there, whose
name *was* Irijah, the son of Shelemiah,
the son of Hananiah; and he took Jere-

1 Heb., *souls.*

2 Heb., *thrust through.*

3 Heb., *made to ascend.*

4 Or, *to slip away from thence in the midst of the people.*

---

in chap. xxxviii. 1, Zephaniah in chaps. xxi. 1, xxix. 25. They clearly belonged to the anti-Chaldæan party, and were therefore, for the most part, openly hostile to the prophet. Their application to him was either simply an official act in obedience to the king's commands, or sprang from the hope, as before in chap. xxi. 1, that they might, by a show of religious zeal for Jehovah, win him over to their cause. The stress which they lay on his praying to "the Lord our God" indicates the latter alternative as probable.

(4) **Jeremiah came in and went out among the people.**—The statement is made in reference to the event narrated in verse 15. He was free when the king's message came to him: it was his answer to that message that led to his imprisonment.

(5) **Then Pharaoh's army was come forth out of Egypt.**—The despatch of the Egyptian army was the result of negotiations which Zedekiah had opened with Pharaoh-Hophra, with a view to resisting the power of Nebuchadnezzar (Ezek. xvii. 15). Like the Egyptian armies in general, it was strong in chariots and horses (Ezek. xvii. 15; Isa. xxxi. 1, xxxvi. 9), and able to carry out the operations of a siege (Ezek. xvii. 17). In chap. xliv. 30 we have the full name of the Egyptian king.

(7) **Behold, Pharaoh's army, which is come forth to help you, shall return to Egypt.**—A like prediction as to the fate of the Egyptian army is found in Ezek. xvii. 17, and is there connected with the fact that Zedekiah's application to Egypt was a distinct breach of the compact which he had made with the Chaldæans. Their arrival, like that of Tirhakah in the Assyrian invasion (2 Kings xix. 9; Isa. xxxvii. 9), caused only a temporary suspension of hostilities, and led finally to the conquest and subjugation of Egypt by Nebuchadnezzar.

(9, 10) **Deceive not yourselves . . .**—Literally, *Deceive not your souls.* The words indicate that the king and his counsellors had buoyed themselves up with expectations of deliverance. The chariots and horses of Egypt were, they thought, certain to defeat the Chaldæans in a pitched battle. The prophet tells them, in the language of a bold hyperbole, reminding us of Isa. xxx. 17, that even the wounded remnant of the Chaldæan army should be strong enough to accomplish the purpose of Jehovah in the destruction of Jerusalem.

(12) **Then Jeremiah went forth out of Jerusalem . . .**—The prophet's motive in leaving the city may well have been his apprehension that the answer he had sent would move the king's anger, and lead, as it actually led, to an order for his arrest. The fact that the Chaldæans had raised the siege gave him free egress.

To separate himself thence in the midst of the people.—More accurately, *to take a share from thence in the midst of the people.* This gives probably the ostensible reason of his journey. As a priest belonging to Anathoth, he had property (like that which he afterwards bought of his uncle, chap. xxxii.) in the land of Benjamin, and he now went to look after it, either in the way of ploughing and sowing, or to receive his share of its produce during his sojourn in Jerusalem. If, as seems probable from chap. xxxiv. 8—16, this was a Sabbatical year, the former, assuming the siege to have been raised when the year was over, would be the more probable alternative, and would better explain, as in Ruth iv. 2, 9, the addition of the clause "in the midst of the people," as showing that there was nothing clandestine in his proceedings. Other meanings that have been given to the words, "to buy bread," "to till a field," "to separate a field," "to conciliate," "to divide the spoil," are less satisfactory. At such a time all the owners of land would be eager to take advantage of the opportunity presented by the departure of the Chaldæan army to transact any business connected with it.

(13) **And when he was in the gate of Benjamin . . .**—The prophet's fears were not groundless. He had to leave the city by the entrance known as the gate of Benjamin (chap. xxxviii. 7), on the north side (Zech. xiv. 10). The officer in command, Irijah, the son of Shelemiah (probably, therefore, the brother of Jehucal, who is named in verse 3, and so probably acquainted with Jeremiah's last prophetic utterance), charged him with treachery. He was "falling away to the Chaldæans." It was assumed that, though the Chaldæans had gone, the prophet was about to make his way to their encampment to incite them to return, and so work out the fulfilment of his own prediction. The very phrase "thou fallest away" may have been

miah the prophet, saying, Thou fallest
away to the Chaldeans. (14) Then said
Jeremiah, *It is* [1]false; I fall not away
to the Chaldeans. But he hearkened
not to him: so Irijah took Jeremiah,
and brought him to the princes.
(15) Wherefore the princes were wroth
with Jeremiah, and smote him, and put
him in prison in the house of Jonathan
the scribe: for they had made that the
prison.
(16) When Jeremiah was entered into
the dungeon, and into the [2]cabins, and
Jeremiah had remained there many days;
(17) then Zedekiah the king sent, and took
him out: and the king asked him secretly
in his house, and said, Is there *any*
word from the LORD? And Jeremiah
said, There is: for, said he, thou shalt
be delivered into the hand of the king
of Babylon. (18) Moreover Jeremiah said
unto king Zedekiah, What have I offended
against thee, or against thy servants, or
against this people, that ye have put
me in prison? (19) Where *are* now your
prophets which prophesied unto you,
saying, The king of Babylon shall not
come against you, nor against this land?
(20) Therefore hear now, I pray thee, O
my lord the king: [3]let my supplication,
I pray thee, be accepted before thee;
that thou cause me not to return to
the house of Jonathan the scribe, lest
I die there. (21) Then Zedekiah the king
commanded that they should commit
Jeremiah into the court of the prison,
and that they should give him daily a
piece of bread out of the bakers' street,

1 Heb., *falsehood, or, a lie.*

2 Or, *cells.*

B. C. 589.

3 Heb., *let my supplication fall.*

---

an allusive reference to Jeremiah's own words in chap. xxi. 9, if, with the best critics, we refer those words to an earlier date than the raising of the siege.

(14) **Irijah took Jeremiah, and brought him to the princes.**—These were probably, as a body, identical with those named in chap. xxxvi. 12, but the party opposed to the prophet were now apparently stronger than they had been. Neither they nor Irijah would listen to the prophet's denial of the accusation. The fact that the siege had been raised by the Chaldæans may have given fresh strength to the party of resistance. Possibly also many of the prophet's friends had shared the captivity of Jehoiakim.

(15) **The princes . . . put him in prison in the house of Jonathan the scribe.**—The house was probably chosen as being under the direct control of one who, as scribe, exercised functions like those of a minister of police. It had not only the subterranean dungeon and pit common to all Eastern prisons, but separate "cabins" or cells (the Hebrew word does not occur elsewhere) for the confinement of individual prisoners (verse 16). Of the severity with which the prophet was treated there, we may judge from his entreaty not to be taken back there after his release (chap. xxxviii. 26). We have fairly adequate data for measuring the duration of the "many days" of his imprisonment. It began before the second siege of Jerusalem, which lasted for nearly two years (2 Kings xxv. 1—3), and when the city was taken he was still in the court of the prison. The incidents of chap. xxxii.—xxxiv. belong to this period.

(17) **Then Zedekiah the king sent, and took him out . . .**—The king seems to have been at once better than his counsellors, and afraid of them. He regrets the severity of the prophet's treatment, and hopes that there may yet be "a word of the Lord" less harsh than before, and with this view summons him to his palace, as before he had sent asking for his intercession. The prophet is, however, true to his calling, and not even the hope of gaining protection against his persecutors will lead him to change one jot or tittle of his message. He answers with a stern abruptness, and adds the new prediction, that the king himself shall be taken prisoner,—what is now reported being earlier than chap. xxxii. 4—5.

(18) **What have I offended against thee . . .?**—The cruelty of his treatment draws from the prophet an indignant protest. Of what crime had he been guilty, but that of speaking the word which the Lord had given him to speak, and was this a crime in the eyes of any true Israelite? No act of treachery or desertion could be proved against him.

(19) **Where are now your prophets . . .?**—The failure of the past predictions of the false prophets is urged on the king as a reason why he should not trust them in the present crisis. They had assured him (chap. xxviii. 3) that within two years the city should be delivered, and the result had been that it had been besieged. The temporary departure of the Chaldæans had again raised their hopes, and they were now tempting the king with the assurance that the Egyptian army would make short work of them.

(20) **That thou cause me not to return to the house of Jonathan the scribe . . .**—The petition shows the cruelty with which the prophet had been treated. Half-starved, and thrust into a foul and fœtid dungeon, he felt that to return to it would be death.

(21) **Into the court of the prison . . .**—This was obviously a concession to Jeremiah's request, and here he remained (see chaps. xxxii. 2, xxxiii. 1), with one brief exception (chap. xxxviii. 6), till the capture of the city. It was "in the king's house," above ground, with free access for light and air, and it was therefore in his power to see that the prophet was treated with respect, and not left to starve.

A piece of bread out of the bakers' street.—The locality is not mentioned elsewhere, but Jerusalem, like other Eastern cities, seems to have had distinct localities assigned as bazaars to special trades. Thus, one of the broad streets running through the city was known, in New Testament times, as the valley of Tyropœon (= cheesemakers). Merchants and goldsmiths appear in Neh. iii. 32 as having their separate quarters, and apothecaries in Neh. iii. 8. The "street of the bakers" was probably connected with "the tower of the furnaces" in Neh. iii. 11. The order given by the king indicates that the city was already blockaded, and that the supply of provisions was falling short.

until all the bread in the city were spent.
Thus Jeremiah remained in the court of
the prison.

CHAPTER XXXVIII.—(1) Then
Shephatiah the son of Mattan, and
Gedaliah the son of Pashur, and Jucal
the son of Shelemiah, and Pashur the
son of Malchiah, heard the words that
Jeremiah had spoken unto all the people,
saying, (2) Thus saith the LORD, [a]He that
remaineth in this city shall die by the
sword, by the famine, and by the pesti-
lence: but he that goeth forth to the
Chaldeans shall live; for he shall have
his life for a prey, and shall live.
(3) Thus saith the LORD, This city shall
surely be given into the hand of the
king of Babylon's army, which shall
take it. (4) Therefore the princes said
unto the king, We beseech thee, let
this man be put to death: for thus
he weakeneth the hands of the men of
war that remain in this city, and the
hands of all the people, in speaking such
words unto them: for this man seeketh
not the [1]welfare of this people, but the
hurt. (5) Then Zedekiah the king said,
Behold, he *is* in your hand: for the
king *is* not *he that* can do *any* thing
against you. (6) Then took they Jere-
miah, and cast him into the dungeon of
Malchiah the son [2]of Hammelech, that
was in the court of the prison: and
they let down Jeremiah with cords.
And in the dungeon *there was* no
water, but mire: so Jeremiah sunk in
the mire.

(7) Now when Ebed-melech the Ethio-
pian, one of the eunuchs which was in
the king's house, heard that they had
put Jeremiah in the dungeon; the king

a ch. 21. 9.

1 Heb., *peace.*

2 Or, *of the kin*.

XXXVIII.

(1) **Then Shephatiah the son of Mattan . . .**—Of the four princes of Judah who are named here, Jucal or Jehucal has been mentioned in chap. xxxvii. 3, and would appear, from the frequent occurrence of the name Shelemiah in 1 Chron. xxvi. 1, 2, 9, 14, to have been a Levite; Pashur is named in chap. xxi. 1. Of the other two nothing is known, but the name Shephatiah appears in three or four instances in the royal house of Judah, beginning with a son of David (2 Sam. iii. 4; 2 Chron. xxi. 2; Ezra ii. 4; Neh. vii. 9), and may, perhaps, indicate a connexion with it, like that of Jerahmeel in chap. xxxvi. 26. Gedaliah, the son of Pashur (possibly of the man of that name who is mentioned last in the list), must be distinguished from Jeremiah's protector, the son of Ahikam (chaps. xxvi. 24, xl. 5). They all belonged obviously to the party of the prophet's enemies.

(2) **Thus saith the Lord.**—The words carry us back to chap. xxi. 9, and in any chronological arrangement of the book the one chapter would follow the other. It is obvious that to all who did not recognise the divine mission of the prophet, words like those which he had then spoken would seem to come from the lips of a traitor. Desertion to the enemy was represented as the only way of safety, and this was the counsel given to those who were defending the city of their fathers against an alien invader. What made it appear worse was that the prophet himself had been caught in an act which, though he denied the charge, might not unnaturally seem like an act of treacherous desertion.

(4) **Let this man be put to death.**—The hatred of the princes of Judah becomes more bitter than ever, and they seek to overcome the king's lingering reverence for the prophet. In the reign of Jehoiakim they had said that he was worthy of death (chap. xxvi. 11). Within the last few weeks he had been thrown into a loathsome dungeon, from which the king had but just delivered him. Now they press for a yet severer sentence. The weak king, conscious of his want of power to resist, yields a reluctant consent. The whole history reminds us of Pilate's conduct in circumstances more or less analogous.

(6) **The dungeon of Malchiah the son of Hammelech.**—Literally, *the pit*, or *cistern*. The LXX. agrees with the marginal reading in describing him as "a son of the king." The same phrase is so translated in 1 Kings xxii. 26; 2 Chron. xxviii. 7, and would seem to have been an official or court title, applied to one of the royal house, as distinguished from others. (See Note on Jerahmeel in chap. xxxvi. 26.) We have no data for judging whether this Malchiah is identical with the father of Pashur in verse 1; but it is not unlikely. In Lam. iii. 53—55 we have probably a reminiscence of these days of horrible suffering. The cistern had been partly dried up (possibly through the supply of water having been cut off during the protracted siege), but there remained a thick deposit, three or four feet deep, of black fœtid mud, and there, it is obvious from verse 9 of this chapter, his enemies meant to leave him to die of hunger. They probably shrank from the odium of a public execution, or thought, with the strange superstition of the Eastern mind, that in this way they could escape the guilt of shedding the prophet's blood. The death by starvation might easily be represented, even to themselves, as a death by disease.

(7) **Ebed-melech the Ethiopian.**—The name signifies "servant of the king," but the absence of the article in the Hebrew makes it probable that it had come to be used as a proper name, and so both the LXX. and Vulgate take it. The use of Ethiopian or Cushite slaves in the king's household, probably as keeping guard over the harem, had been of some standing; perhaps even as early as the time of David, as in the case of Cushi (or *the Cushite*), in 2 Sam. xviii. 21. Then, as in other countries and times (Terent., *Eunuch.* i. 2), there was a fashion which led princes and men of wealth to think that eunuchs were part of their magnificence. The law of Moses, it may be noted, forbade such mutilation in the case of Israelites (Deut. xxiii. 1). In Ps. lxxxvii. 4, we find probably a record of the admission of such persons on the register of the citizens of Zion. Of the previous history of the Eunuch thus named we know nothing.

then sitting in the gate of Benjamin;
(8) Ebed-melech went forth out of the
king's house, and spake to the king,
saying, (9) My lord the king, these men
have done evil in all that they have
done to Jeremiah the prophet, whom
they have cast into the dungeon; and
[1]he is like to die for hunger in the
place where he is: for *there is* no more
bread in the city. (10) Then the king
commanded Ebed-melech the Ethiopian,
saying, Take from hence thirty men
[2]with thee, and take up Jeremiah the
prophet out of the dungeon, before he
die. (11) So Ebed-melech took the men
with him, and went into the house of
the king under the treasury, and took
thence old cast clouts and old rotten
rags, and let them down by cords into
the dungeon to Jeremiah. (12) And Ebed-
melech the Ethiopian said unto Jere-
miah, Put now *these* old cast clouts and
rotten rags under thine armholes under
the cords. And Jeremiah did so. (13) So
they drew up Jeremiah with cords, and
took him up out of the dungeon: and
Jeremiah remained in the court of the
prison.
(14) Then Zedekiah the king sent, and
took Jeremiah the prophet unto him
into the [3]third entry that *is* in the
house of the LORD: and the king said
unto Jeremiah, I will ask thee a thing;
hide nothing from me. (15) Then Jere-
miah said unto Zedekiah, If I declare *it*
unto thee, wilt thou not surely put me
to death? and if I give thee counsel,
wilt thou not hearken unto me? (16) So
Zedekiah the king sware secretly unto
Jeremiah, saying, *As* the LORD liveth,

1 Heb., *he will die.*

2 Heb., *in thine hand.*

3 Or, *principal.*

---

but he appears here as the favourite of the king, using his influence to protect the prophet. The Ethiopian descent of Jehudi (chap. xxxvi. 21) may probably have brought him into contact with an officer of the king's household of the same race, and Ebed-melech's feelings may have been drawn to the prophet by what he thus heard.

In the gate of Benjamin.—This was on the northern wall of the city, the most exposed to the attack of the invading army, and the king apparently had gone there either to direct the operations of the defence, or, perhaps, to prevent others from following, as they might think, Jeremiah's example, and either deserting to the enemy or abandoning the defence of the city (chap. xxxvii. 13). Ebed-melech had accordingly to leave the palace, and went to seek the king at his post, in order to obtain an order of release in time to save the prophet's life. He alone, as if inheriting the blessing of Isa. lvi. 3—6, has the courage to appear as the friend of the persecuted.

(9) **These men have done evil. . . .**—It is noticeable that some MSS. of the LXX., following apparently a different text, represent the Eunuch as assuming that the king himself had given the order, "Thou hast done evil in all that thou hast done."

He is like to die for hunger.—Literally, *and he dies . . .* painting vividly what would be the certain issue if no help were sent. It lies in the nature of the case that those who had thrown the prophet into the pit were not likely to continue the supply of his daily rations (chap. xxxvii. 21), and the scarcity that prevailed in the besieged city made it all but impossible that his friends, even if they could gain access to him, should help him out of their own resources. Ebed-melech had obviously no power to help him without the king's sanction.

(10) **Take from hence thirty men.**—The number seems a large one for the purpose, especially when we consider that the men were sent from a post from which they could ill be spared, but the king may have wished to guard against resistance on the part of the princes. Hitzig, however, conjectures that "three men" was the original reading of the Hebrew text.

(11) **Under the treasury . . .**—This was obviously what we should call the "lumber-room" of the palace. Nothing could show the acuteness of the prophet's sufferings more vividly than the precautions which the thoughtful kindness of the Eunuch thus suggested. The pit was so deep that ropes were needed to draw him up, as they had been to let him down, and lest they should cut into the flesh of Jeremiah's emaciated form, improvised cushions had to be fastened to the ropes, that he might rest his arm-pits on them. He was, however, at last rescued, and re-instated in his former position, as a prisoner under the king's protection.

"Clout" in old English was used for a patch of cloth as distinct from the "rags," which were of linen. So Spenser, "His garments nought but many ragged clouts."

(14) **The third entry that is in the house of the Lord.**—In 2 Kings xvi. 18 we read of "the king's entry without," an outside entrance, and of "a covert," or covered gallery, both leading from the palace to the Temple. The passage now mentioned (the name does not occur elsewhere) was probably distinct from both these, leading from the lower city, and may therefore have been chosen by Zedekiah as a more suitable place for a private interview with the prophet. It seems probable from 2 Kings xxiii. 11, that there was a chamber for the chief Eunuch, or chamberlain of the king's household, and if so, it may have been arranged by Ebed-melech that the meeting should take place there. As in chap. xxxvii. 17, the king has still a secret respect for Jeremiah's mission, and, it may be, guided now by the Eunuch's better counsels, hankers after a word of the Lord from him. Will the prophet, after what has passed, tell him the whole truth?

(15) **Wilt thou not surely put me to death?**—The prophet obviously speaks as if he believed the king to have sanctioned the severe measures that had been taken against him, and having no other "word of the Lord" to speak than that which he had spoken before, fears to provoke his wrath. The latter part of the sentence is better taken with the LXX., Vulg., and Luther, "*thou wilt not hearken unto me*"; or the form of the question altered so as to imply that answer.

(16) **As the Lord liveth, that made us this soul.**—The formula of the oath was obviously intended

that made us this soul, I will not put
thee to death, neither will I give thee
into the hand of these men that seek
thy life. (17) Then said Jeremiah unto
Zedekiah, Thus saith the LORD, the God
of hosts, the God of Israel; If thou wilt
assuredly go forth unto the king of
Babylon's princes, then thy soul shall
live, and this city shall not be burned
with fire; and thou shalt live, and thine
house: (18) but if thou wilt not go forth
to the king of Babylon's princes, then
shall this city be given into the hand of
the Chaldeans, and they shall burn it
with fire, and thou shalt not escape
out of their hand. (19) And Zedekiah
the king said unto Jeremiah, I am
afraid of the Jews that are fallen to
the Chaldeans, lest they deliver me into
their hand, and they mock me. (20) But
Jeremiah said, They shall not deliver
thee. Obey, I beseech thee, the voice of
the LORD, which I speak unto thee: so
it shall be well unto thee, and thy soul
shall live. (21) But if thou refuse to go
forth, this *is* the word that the LORD
hath shewed me: (22) and, behold, all
the women that are left in the king of
Judah's house *shall be* brought forth to
the king of Babylon's princes, and those
women shall say, [1]Thy friends have set
thee on, and have prevailed against
thee: thy feet are sunk in the mire,
and they are turned away back. (23) So
they shall bring out all thy wives and
thy children to the Chaldeans: and
thou shalt not escape out of their
hand, but shalt be taken by the hand
of the king of Babylon: and [2]thou shalt
cause this city to be burned with fire.

(24) Then said Zedekiah unto Jeremiah,
Let no man know of these words, and
thou shalt not die. (25) But if the
princes hear that I have talked with
thee, and they come unto thee, and say
unto thee, Declare unto us now what
thou hast said unto the king, hide it
not from us, and we will not put thee
to death; also what the king said unto
thee: (26) then thou shalt say unto them,

1 Heb., *Men of thy peace.*

2 Heb., *thou shalt burn, &c.*

---

to be one of unusual solemnity; more so even than the simpler form of "The Lord liveth" (chap. xvi. 14, 15). The king swears by Jehovah as the living God, author and giver of his own life. The two-fold promise shows that the king felt the implied reproof of Jeremiah's question. He separates himself from those who sought the prophet's life, and declares that for the future he will not give them even the sanction of acquiescence. It is characteristic of his weakness that even now the oath is given secretly.

(17) **If thou wilt assuredly go forth.**—Literally, *If going thou wilt go*, the Hebrew idiom of emphasis. The prophet places before the king the alternative of surrender and safety, resistance and destruction, and leaves him to make his choice. The princes of the king of Babylon were those in command of the army by which Jerusalem was invested. The king himself was at Riblah, on the Orontes, in Northern Syria (chap. xxxix. 5).

(19) **I am afraid of the Jews . . .**—The special form of fear was characteristic of the weak and vacillating king. It was not enough to know that his life would be safe. Would he also be saved from the insults of his own subjects, who had already deserted to the enemy? These were, in the nature of the case, friends and followers of the prophet, and had acted on his advice (chap. xxi. 9). The king, who had shrunk from Jeremiah's taunts (chap. xxxvii. 19), could not, for very shame, expose himself to the derision of others. Perhaps even he feared more than mere derision—outrage, death, mutilation, such as Saul feared at the hands of the Philistines (1 Sam. xxxi. 4).

(20—22) **Obey, I beseech thee. . . .**—The king's misgiving is met in part by an earnest entreaty to obey the voice of the Lord, in part by the assurance that thus it "shall be well with him" (literally, *there shall be peace to thee*); in part also by bringing before him the mockery which is certain to await him if he persists in his defiance. The women of the harem, the surviving wives and concubines of former kings, as well as his own, should become the spoil of the Chaldæan princes, and should take up their taunting proverbs against him. "Thy friends" (literally, *the men of thy peace*, as in chap. xx. 10; the men who promised peace and safety), "they set thee on, and having dragged thee into the mire of shame, have left thee there." The imagery of the taunt seems drawn from the prophet's recent experience (verse 6). The king was plunging into a worse "slough of despond" than that into which Jeremiah had sunk in the dungeon of Malchiah.

(23) **So they shall bring out . . .**—The picture of defeat and destruction is once more repeated from verse 18. Probably, the last clause should be read with a different punctuation of the Hebrew, "This city shall be burnt with fire." As the text now stands, the marginal rendering, *Thou shalt burn*, gives the true force of the word. The king himself would have that destruction to answer for. It would be his own act and deed.

(24—26) **Let no man know . . .**—The weak king vacillated to the last moment. He feared the prophet, he feared the princes yet more. To hush up all that had passed in the interview, to urge the prophet to baffle the eager suspicions of the princes by a prevaricating statement, as if it had been he who had sought the meeting, and had petitioned the king, as before (chap. xxxvii. 20), to protect him from the cruelties which he had suffered in the house of Jonathan: this was the only course he could bring himself to follow. The plan so far succeeded that the prophet returned and gave the evasive answer which the king suggested. The nature of the interview was concealed, and events took their course; and Jeremiah remained in the court of the prison till the city was taken. The king's suggestion as to the house of Jonathan implies either that he believed that the princes would urge that Jeremiah

I presented my supplication before the
king, that he would not cause me to
return to Jonathan's house, to die there.
(27) Then came all the princes unto
Jeremiah, and asked him: and he told
them according to all these words that
the king had commanded. So [1] they
left off speaking with him; for the
matter was not perceived.
(28) So Jeremiah abode in the court of
the prison until the day that Jerusalem
was taken: and he was *there* when Jeru-
salem was taken.

CHAPTER XXXIX.—(1) In the
[a] ninth year of Zedekiah king of Judah,
in the tenth month, came Nebuchad-
rezzar king of Babylon and all his army
against Jerusalem, and they besieged it.

B. C. 588.

1 Heb., *they were silent from him.*

a 2 Kings 25. 1; ch. 52. 4.

B. C. 590.

(2) *And* in the eleventh year of Zedekiah,
in the fourth month, the ninth *day* of
the month, the city was broken up.
(3) And all the princes of the king of
Babylon came in, and sat in the middle
gate, *even* Nergal-sharezer, Samgar-nebo,
Sarsechim, Rab-saris, Nergal-sharezer,
Rab-mag, with all the residue of the
princes of the king of Babylon.
(4) And it came to pass, *that* when
Zedekiah the king of Judah saw them,
and all the men of war, then they fled,
and went forth out of the city by night,
by the way of the king's garden, by the
gate betwixt the two walls: and he went
out the way of the plain. (5) But the
Chaldeans' army pursued after them,
and overtook Zedekiah in the plains
of Jericho: and when they had taken

---

should be sent there after his rescue from the dungeon of Malchiah, or else a wish to slur over that transaction altogether.

XXXIX.

(1) **In the ninth year of Zedekiah . . .**—The great crisis came at last, as Jeremiah had long ago predicted. A fuller narrative of the siege and capture is given in chap. lii. The two verses which open the chapter seem to have been inserted here by the editor of the prophecies in their present form, as explaining the fact with which chap. xxxviii. had closed. The siege had lasted eighteen months, beginning in B.C. 590 and ending B.C. 588. It came to an end, as we learn from chap. lii. 6, through the pressure of the famine, of which we have seen traces in chap. xxxvii. 21.

(3) **In the middle gate.**—The term indicates a position in the line of walls between the citadel of Zion—the "upper city" of Josephus (*Ant.* v. 20. 2), which as yet was not surrendered (verse 4)—and the lower city, in the walls of which a breach had been effected. Here an open space, originally used as a *forum*, or place of judgment, now gave the Chaldæan generals a central encampment, from which they could command both quarters of the city, and by taking their place in the heart of its life, formally assert their mastery. Each of the names that follow has a meaning and history of its own.

Nergal-sharezer.—The first half of the name appears in 2 Kings xvii. 30 as that of a Cuthite, or Assyrian deity, and means the "great hero." It occurs frequently in the inscriptions of Tiglath-pileser and Assur-banipal (*e.g., Records of the Past*, i. 77, 103). The whole name appears in Assyrian monuments as Nergal-shar-uzur. Two of the generals mentioned here bore the same name, and each apparently was distinguished by a special title.

Samgar-nebo.—Here the second half is the name of a Babylonian deity (Isa. xlvi. 1; Jer. xlviii. 1), possibly connected with the Hebrew *Nabi* (= prophet), and so answering to the Egyptian Thoth and the Greek Hermes. The great temple at Borsippa, known as *Birs Nimroud*, was dedicated to him (*Records of the Past*, vii. 77). The first half has been explained by some scholars as meaning "warrior," by others as "cup-bearer," and so equivalent to Rabshakeh (Isa. xxxvi. 2), and as such is attached to the foregoing name of Nergal-sharezer. As a rule, the name of Nebo appears always in the beginning of compound words, as in Nebuchadnezzar, Nebuzar-adan, &c.; and probably we should connect it here with the name that follows.

Sarsechim, Rab-saris.—Probably, as indicated in the previous Note, the name should stand as Nebo-sarsechim. The two names go together, the first as a proper name, the second as a title, meaning "the chief eunuch." In verse 13, Nebushasban appears as bearing the same title. In 2 Kings xviii. 17 it appears simply as a title, as in Rab-shakeh we have "the chief cup-bearer."

Nergal-sharezer, Rab-mag. — Here also the second name is the title of office, meaning probably "chief of the Magi," or "chief of the priests." The man thus named, who appears on the Assyrian monuments as *Nergal-shar-uzur Rubu-emga*, played a prominent part afterwards as murdering Evil-merodach, the son of Nebuchadnezzar, whose sister he had married. He reigned for three or four years, and appears in Berosus (Joseph. *c. Apion*, i. 20) under the name of Neriglissar. The older name is found on the bricks of a palace at Babylon, on the right bank of the Euphrates (Smith's *Dict. of Bible.* Art. *Nergal-sharezer*).

(4) **When Zedekiah the king of Judah saw them. . .**—The hasty flight is narrated again in chap. lii. 7. The gate between the two walls was one apparently that opened from the park-like garden of the palace, near the pool of Siloah (Neh. iii. 15); probably identical with the garden of Uzza, which was used as a burial-place for Manasseh and Amon (2 Kings xxi. 18—26); and led to the *Arabah*, the plain (always known by this distinctive name) of the valley of the Jordan (Deut. i. 1; iii. 17; iv. 49; Josh. xii. 1, and elsewhere). The "two walls" appear as part of the defence of the city in Isa. xxii. 11, and connected Zion with the fortress known as Ophel (2 Chron. xxvii. 3; xxxiii. 14).

(5) **In the plains of Jericho.**—Here again we have the distinctive word, the *Araboth* of the Jordan, the enlargement of the Jordan valley, three miles wide, near Jericho. The intention of the king was apparently to make his way to the ford near Jericho, cross the river, and escape to the open country of Gilead.

him, they brought him up to Nebuchad-
nezzar king of Babylon to Riblah in the
land of Hamath, where he [1]gave judg-
ment upon him. (6) Then the king of
Babylon slew the sons of Zedekiah in
Riblah before his eyes: also the king of
Babylon slew all the nobles of Judah.
(7) Moreover he put out Zedekiah's eyes,
and bound him [2]with chains, to carry
him to Babylon. (8) And the Chaldeans
burned the king's house, and the houses
of the people, with fire, and brake down
the walls of Jerusalem.
(9) Then Nebuzar-adan the [3][4]captain
of the guard carried away captive into
Babylon the remnant of the people that
remained in the city, and those that
fell away, that fell to him, with the
rest of the people that remained. (10) But
Nebuzar-adan the captain of the guard
left of the poor of the people, which had
nothing, in the land of Judah, and gave
them vineyards and fields [5]at the same
time.
(11) Now Nebuchadrezzar king of
Babylon gave charge concerning Jere-
miah [6]to Nebuzar-adan the captain of
the guard, saying, (12) Take him, and
[7]look well to him, and do him no harm;
but do unto him even as he shall say
unto thee. (13) So Nebuzar-adan the
captain of the guard sent, and Nebu-

1 Heb., *spake with him judgments.*

2 Heb., *with two brasen chains*, or, *fetters.*

3 Or, *chief marshal.*

4 Heb., *chief of the executioners*, or, *slaughtermen*: and so ver. 10, 11, &c.

5 Heb., *in that day.*

6 Heb., *by the hand of.*

7 Heb., *set thine eyes upon him.*

Riblah in the land of Hamath.—The city of Hamath stood on the Orontes, about half-way from its source, near *Baalbek*, to the bend which it makes at *Jisr-hadid*, and commanded the whole valley of the river to the defile of Daphne, below Antioch. It was a well-known city at the time of the Exodus (Num. xiii. 21; xxxiv. 8), and in that of David was the capital of a kingdom, which became tributary to him and Solomon (2 Sam. viii. 10; 1 Kings iv. 21—24). Riblah (still retaining its name, *Ribleh*), also on the Orontes, and near its source, was a centre from which the great lines of traffic led by the Euphrates to Nineveh, by Palmyra to Babylon, by Lebanon and the coast to Palestine and Egypt, and through the Jordan valley to the Holy Land. It was, therefore, a natural post of observation for the Chaldæan king while his generals were carrying on the sieges of Tyre and Jerusalem. So when Pharaoh-necho was for a time, before the battle of Carchemish, master of the Assyrian territory, it was to Riblah that he summoned Jehoahaz, and there imprisoned him (2 Kings xxiii. 33). In this instance Zedekiah was brought before Nebuchadnezzar as a vassal prince who, having received his authority from the Chaldæan king (2 Kings xxiv. 17), had rebelled, and met with scant mercy.

(6) **The sons of Zedekiah.**—The history of Eastern monarchies presents us with many examples of this refinement of cruelty, notably in the case of Œobazus under Darius (Herod. iv. 84), and Pythius under Xerxes (Herod. vii. 39). The slaughter of the "nobles" probably included most of those whom we have seen in chap. xxxvi. 12, and elsewhere.

(7) **Moreover he put out Zedekiah's eyes.**—The special form of punishment is noticeable as fulfilling the two prophecies—(1) that Zedekiah should see the king of Babylon and be taken to that city (chap. xxxii. 4); and (2) that though he was to die in Babylon, he should never see it (Ezek. xii. 13). Beyond this, the fate of the last king of Judah is buried in darkness. His brother Jehoiachin was already a prisoner in Babylon (2 Kings xxiv. 15), but we do not know whether the two were allowed to meet. Twenty-six years later Jehoiachin was released by Evil-merodach (2 Kings xxv. 27); but there is no mention of Zedekiah, and it is a natural inference that his sufferings had ended previously.

Bound him with chains.—Literally, as in the margin, with two brazen chains.

(8) **And the Chaldeans burned the king's house.**—In the fuller account of chap. lii. 12, we find that this was the work of Nebuzar-adan, who had been sent by Nebuchadnezzar, on hearing of the capture of the city, and that it included the destruction of the Temple as well as the palace.

(9) **Then Nebuzar-adan the captain of the guard.**—Here again the title in the Hebrew—*Rab-tab-bachim*—takes a form like that of Rab-saris and Rab-shakeh, and means literally, "chief of the slaughterers." The title is given to Potiphar in Gen. xxxvii. 36, and probably answered to our "commander of the king's body-guard." The name has been interpreted as "the prince-lord, or the worshipper, of Nebo," but the etymology of the last three syllables is uncertain. He does not appear as taking part with the other generals in the siege of Jerusalem, but comes on the capture of the city, arriving a month afterwards (chap. lii. 12) to direct, even in its minute details, the work of destruction (2 Kings xxv. 9). The defenders and deserters were involved in the same doom of exile. It need scarcely be said that, as in the case of the conquests of Tiglath-pileser (2 Kings xv. 29), Shalmaneser (2 Kings xvii. 6), Esar-haddon (2 Kings xvii. 24), and Sennacherib (2 Kings xviii. 32), this wholesale deportation was part of the systematic policy of the great Assyrian and Babylonian monarchs. So Darius carried off the Pæonians from Thrace (Herod. v. 14). To distribute the lands of the exiles thus dispossessed among "the poor of the people," was, it was thought, likely to enlist their interests on the side of the conqueror; and, by keeping up the cultivation of the soil secured the payment of tribute.

(11) **Nebuchadrezzar king of Babylon. . . .**—It is clear that Nebuchadrezzar had been well informed of the part which Jeremiah had taken from first to last in counselling submission. This he may have heard from the deserters named in verse 9, or even from the lips of Zedekiah. Possibly the journey to Euphrates, of which we read in chap. xiii. 5, may, at even an earlier period, have brought the king and the prophet into contact. From the time of Nebuzar-adan's arrival, the position of Jeremiah was obviously changed for the better, and he became an honoured and trusted counsellor. It appears from chap. xl. 1 that the prophet had at first been taken in chains to Ramah, with the other captives. Probably he had been sent back to Jerusalem when the others were carried off to Riblah, or Babylon (verses 6—9).

(13) **Nebushasban.**—The name, which occurs in the *Annals* of Assur-banipal (*Records of the Past*, **i.**

shasban, Rab-saris, and Nergal-sharezer, Rab-mag, and all the king of Babylon's princes; (14) even they sent, and took Jeremiah out of the court of the prison, and committed him unto Gedaliah the son of Ahikam the son of Shaphan, that he should carry him home: so he dwelt among the people.

(15) Now the word of the LORD came unto Jeremiah, while he was shut up in the court of the prison, saying, (16) Go and speak to Ebed-melech the Ethiopian, saying, Thus saith the LORD of hosts, the God of Israel; Behold, I will bring my words upon this city for evil, and not for good; and they shall be *accomplished* in that day before thee. (17) But I will deliver thee in that day, saith the LORD: and thou shalt not be given into the hand of the men of whom thou *art* afraid. (18) For I will surely deliver thee, and thou shalt not fall by the sword, but thy life shall be for a prey unto thee: because thou hast put thy trust in me, saith the LORD.

CHAPTER XL.—(1) The word that came to Jeremiah from the LORD, after that Nebuzar-adan the captain of the guard had let him go from Ramah, when he had taken him being bound in [1]chains among all that were carried away captive of Jerusalem and Judah, which were carried away captive unto Babylon.

(2) And the captain of the guard took Jeremiah, and said unto him, The LORD thy God hath pronounced this evil upon this place. (3) Now the LORD hath brought *it*, and done according as he hath said: because ye have sinned against the LORD, and have not obeyed his voice, therefore this thing is come upon you. (4) And now, behold, I loose thee this day from the chains which *were* upon thine hand. If it seem good unto thee to come with me into Babylon, come; and [2]I will look well unto thee: but if it seem ill unto thee to come with me into Babylon, forbear: behold, all the land *is* before thee: whither it

1 Or, *manicles.*

2 Heb., *I will set mine eye upon thee.*

64), is possibly another form of the Nebo-sarsechim of verse 3. Rab-saris (= chief eunuch, or chamberlain) is, as before, his title. Ashpenaz appears as holding the same position, possibly, as Nebushasban's predecessor, in Dan. i. 3.

(14) **Out of the court of the prison.**—There is a slight apparent discrepancy between this statement and that in chap. xl. 1, that the prophet was set free at Ramah. It seems likely that, at first, he was sent back to the prison where he had been found, till he could be placed under the protection of Gedaliah.

Gedaliah the son of Ahikam the son of Shaphan.—The reason of the choice lies almost on the surface. Gedaliah was the representative of a house which for three generations had been true to the prophets who spoke in the name of the Lord. Shaphan had been the king's scribe in the early years of Josiah, and had taken an active part in the restoration of the Temple (2 Kings xxii. 3—7). He was the first to read the newly-found lost copy of the Law, which we identify with the Book of Deuteronomy (2 Kings xxii. 8—14), and his son Ahikam acted with him. The latter protected Jeremiah in the reign of Jehoiakim (chap. xxvi. 24). His brother Gemariah gave the prophet the use of his chamber in the Temple (chap. xxxvi. 10), and tried to turn aside the king's wrath (chap. xxxvi. 25). And now the son of Ahikam appears as the prophet's friend and protector.

(16) **Go and speak to Ebed-melech.**—It lies in the nature of the case that the prophet, when he put this prediction, given during the progress of the siege, on record, knew that it had been fulfilled. We hear nothing more of the faithful Ethiopian, but we may believe that he was spared by the Chaldæans, probably at the prophet's intercession. It is not without significance that the promise is given in the same terms as that to Baruch in chap. xlv. 5. The "men" of whom he was afraid were obviously the princes whom he had irritated by his interference on behalf of Jeremiah.

XL.

(1) **The word that came to Jeremiah from the Lord.**—It is noticeable that this introduction is not followed by any specific utterance of prophecy until we come to chap. xlii. 7. It is a natural conclusion that it stands as a kind of heading to the section of the collected prophecies subsequent to the capture of the city.

Had let him go from Ramah.—The town so named was in the tribe of Benjamin (Josh. xviii. 25), about six miles from Jerusalem, and retains its old name in the form *Er-Ram.* It was used on this occasion as a depôt for the prisoners who were brought to it from Jerusalem, to await the orders of Nebuzar-adan as to their ultimate disposal. The captain of the guard and the prophet had apparently not met before, and the latter had been brought in chains (literally, *manacles,* chains fastened to the wrists, verse 4), like the other captives.

(2—4) **The Lord thy God . . .**—It is significant that the Chaldæan general speaks as if recognising Jehovah as the God of Israel, and the prophet's mission from Him. Such a recognition did not, however, imply more than the belief of the polytheist, that each nation had its own guardian deity. We find language of a like kind, though spoken with a tone of sarcasm, coming even from the lips of Rab-shakeh (2 Kings xviii. 25). As a prophet, however, Jeremiah is treated with marked respect—in part, perhaps, due to the policy he had advocated; in part, possibly, to the influence of men like Daniel and his friends at Babylon—and offered the option of going, with the promise of honourable treatment, to that city, from which, however, it is assumed, that he would not return, or remaining in Judæa, to go where he will. The prophet obviously chooses the

seemeth good and convenient for thee to go, thither go. (5) Now while he was not yet gone back, *he said*, Go back also to Gedaliah the son of Ahikam the son of Shaphan, whom the king of Babylon hath made governor over the cities of Judah, and dwell with him among the people: or go wheresoever it seemeth convenient unto thee to go. So the captain of the guard gave him victuals and a reward, and let him go. (6) Then went Jeremiah unto Gedaliah the son of Ahikam to Mizpah; and dwelt with him among the people that were left in the land.

(7) Now when all the captains of the forces which *were* in the fields, *even* they and their men, heard that the king of Babylon had made Gedaliah the son of Ahikam governor in the land, and had committed unto him men, and women, and children, and of the poor of the land, of them that were not carried away captive to Babylon; (8) then they came to Gedaliah to Mizpah, even Ishmael the son of Nethaniah, and Johanan and Jonathan the sons of Kareah, and Seraiah the son of Tanhumeth, and the sons of Ephai the Netophathite, and Jezaniah the son of a Maachathite, they and their men. (9) And Gedaliah the son of Ahikam the son of Shaphan sware unto them and to their men, saying, Fear not [1] to serve the Chaldeans: dwell in the land, and serve the king of Babylon, and it shall be well with you. (10) As for me, behold, I will dwell at Mizpah, to serve the Chaldeans, which will come unto us: but ye, gather ye wine, and

1 Heb., *to stand before:* and so ver. 10.

---

second alternative, but before he acts on it another plan occurs to Nebuzar-adan.

(5) **Go back also to Gedaliah the son of Ahikam.**—The captain of the guard seems to have felt, on second thoughts, possibly after hearing the prophet's unrecorded answer, that he had not taken sufficient precaution for Jeremiah's safety, and therefore consigns him once more to the care of his friend and protector. On parting with him he treats him as an honoured guest, sends him a portion of food from his own table (comp. chap. lii. 34)—a welcome gift, doubtless, after the privations of the siege—and an *honorarium* in money as a compensation for the sufferings he had undergone as a preacher of submission to the conqueror.

Governor over the cities of Judah.—The official title is significant. Jerusalem is treated as if it had been blotted from the face of the earth, and required no superintendence. Gedaliah, the prophet's friend, had obviously acted on his counsels, and accepted the sovereignty of Nebuchadnezzar as being for the time the ordinance of God. A true patriot might well hold it to be his duty at such a time to accept office under the conqueror, in the hope of being able to do something for the remnant of the nation that was left under his charge.

(6) **To Mizpah.**—The name, which signifies "watchtower" (Gen. xxxi. 49), was naturally not uncommon. Of the six or seven cities that were so called, that which comes before us here was Mizpah of Benjamin (Josh. xviii. 25, 26), prominent in the history of Samuel and Saul (1 Sam. vii. 5—13, x. 17—25), not far from Gibeah of Saul (Isa. x. 29; Judg. xix. 13). It has been identified by Dr. Robinson (*Bibl. Res.* i. 460) with *Neby-Samwil*, about six miles north of Jerusalem. Dean Stanley, Mr. Grove, and Dr. Bonar, however, find it in the ridge which forms a continuation of the Mount of Olives on the north, and which Josephus (*Wars*, v. 2), apparently giving the Greek equivalent of the old Hebrew name, calls *Skopos*, or "the watchtower." Mizpah, it may be noted, is twice translated *Skopia* in the LXX. version (Hos. v. 1; 1 Sam. xxii. 3). It will be seen that the latter identification fits in better with the narrative than the former.

(7) **Now when all the captains of the forces.**—A new section of the history begins, ending with the murder of Gedaliah and its sequel, in chap. xli. 18. The commanders of the armies that had fought against the invader in the open country found it hopeless to continue the struggle after the capture of Jerusalem. What were they to do? The king of Babylon had, by appointing Gedaliah, himself a prince of Judah, shown a disposition to treat the conquered people leniently. Could they do better than apply to him for protection?

(8) **Then they came to Gedaliah.**—Of the captains thus named, Ishmael, "of the seed royal" (we have no date for determining his precise position in the line of successors) (chap. xli. 1), is prominent in the history of the next chapter, Johanan (the Hebrew form of Joannes or John) in that of chap. xlii., Seraiah and Jaazaniah are named in the parallel passage of 2 Kings xxv. 23, but nothing more is known of them. Netophah, to which the sons of Ephai belonged, was a town of Benjamin not far from Bethlehem (1 Chron. ii. 54, ix. 16; Ezr. ii. 22; Neh. vii. 26). The Maachathite, whose father is not named, was probably a naturalised alien from the small kingdom of Maachah, on the east side of the Jordan, near Argob (Deut. iii. 14; 2 Sam. x. 6, 8) and Bashan (Josh. xii. 5), not far from the modern *Lejah*.

(9) **Fear not to serve the Chaldeans . . .**—Gedaliah, acting as Satrap of the province, assures them that, though they had fought against the conquerors, there would be a full amnesty, and that they might therefore banish all fears of being maltreated. He will remain at his post, and they may return to their own homes.

(10) **Gather ye wine, and summer fruits.**—The words show that the application took place in the autumn. The captains and their followers were invited to help themselves freely from the fields and vineyards and olive-yards, the owners of which had been carried off to Babylon, so as to relieve their immediate wants and provide for the coming winter. The "summer fruits" would probably include figs, apples, and the like.

summer fruits, and oil, and put *them* in your vessels, and dwell in your cities that ye have taken.

(11) Likewise when all the Jews that *were* in Moab, and among the Ammonites, and in Edom, and that *were* in all the countries, heard that the king of Babylon had left a remnant of Judah, and that he had set over them Gedaliah the son of Ahikam the son of Shaphan; (12) even all the Jews returned out of all places whither they were driven, and came to the land of Judah, to Gedaliah, unto Mizpah, and gathered wine and summer fruits very much.

(13) Moreover Johanan the son of Kareah, and all the captains of the forces that *were* in the fields, came to Gedaliah to Mizpah, (14) and said unto him, Dost thou certainly know that Baalis the king of the Ammonites hath sent Ishmael the son of Nethaniah [1] to slay thee? But Gedaliah the son of Ahikam believed them not. (15) Then Johanan the son of Kareah spake to Gedaliah in Mizpah secretly, saying, Let me go, I pray thee, and I will slay Ishmael the son of Nethaniah, and no man shall know *it:* wherefore should he slay thee, that all the Jews which are gathered unto thee should be scattered, and the remnant in Judah perish? (16) But Gedaliah the son of Ahikam said unto Johanan the son of Kareah, Thou shalt not do this thing: for thou speakest falsely of Ishmael.

[1] Heb., *to strike thee in soul?*

CHAPTER XLI.—(1) Now it came to pass in the seventh month, *that* Ishmael the son of Nethaniah the son of Elishama, of the seed royal, and the princes of the king, even ten men with him, came unto Gedaliah the son of Ahikam to Mizpah; and there they did eat bread together in Mizpah. (2) Then arose Ishmael the son of Nethaniah, and the ten men that were with him, and smote Gedaliah the son of Ahikam the son of Shaphan with the sword, and slew him, whom the king of Babylon had made governor over the land. (3) Ishmael also slew all the Jews that were with him, *even* with Gedaliah, at Mizpah, and the Chaldeans that were found there, *and* the men of war.

(4) And it came to pass the second day after he had slain Gedaliah, and no man knew *it,* (5) that there came certain from Shechem, from Shiloh, and from

---

(11, 12) **When all the Jews that were in Moab . . .**—It lay in the nature of things that many of the dwellers in Judæa fled before the march of the Chaldæan armies, and took refuge in the neighbouring regions. In Ruth i. 2, 1 Sam. xxii. 3, Isa. xvi. 4, we find analogous instances of fugitives from Judah finding shelter in the Moabite country. These, on hearing of the generous policy adopted by Gedaliah, took courage and returned in time to profit by his permission to gather the produce which otherwise would have been left to perish on the soil.

(14) **Dost thou certainly know that Baalis . . .**—The king of the Ammonites so named appears from chap. xxvii. 3 to have been in alliance with Zedekiah; and Ishmael, as belonging to the royal house of Judah, seems to have been still plotting with him against the authority of the Chaldæans. Open resistance being now impossible, they have recourse to assassination. The plot becomes known, and Johanan, faithful to his new protector, warns him against it, but, as the sequel shows, in vain. Gedaliah, in the guileless trustfulness of his character, does not believe that Ishmael is capable of such a crime, and will not sanction another crime by way of precaution.

XLI.

(1) **It came to pass in the seventh month.**—It lies in the nature of the case that the visit purported to be one of courtesy and recognition. The remaining representatives of the house of David (chap. xl. 8) would show that they were ready to welcome the new Satrap. As the seventh month included the Feast of Tabernacles, it is not unlikely that they came as if to share in its festivities. Three months had passed since the capture of the city (chap. xxxix. 2).

(2) **Then arose Ishmael.**—The narrative suggests the thought that, as in the massacre of Glencoe, the guests murdered their host at the very time when he was receiving them with open arms.

(3) **Ishmael also slew all the Jews. . . .**—We wonder at first that ten men were able to effect so much. It does not follow, however, that the massacre went beyond the Jews and Chaldæan officers who were sharing Gedaliah's hospitality, and they may easily have been surprised, like Gedaliah, unarmed, and in the act of feasting. Possibly, too, the ten princes may each have brought their retinue of attendants. Greek history presents two analogous massacres—that of the Persian generals by Alexander, the son of Amyntas (Herod. v. 19, 20); and that of Archias and Leontiades, the tyrants of Thebes, by Pelopidas and his associates. The massacre in this case was so complete that none escaped to tell the tale (verse 4). The italics in the last clause of the verse indicate that the conjunction "and" is not in the Hebrew, and that the words, "the men of war," are in apposition with the previous clause, and limit their extent.

(5) **There came certain from Shechem, from Shiloh, and from Samaria.**—The LXX. gives Salem instead of Shiloh, and this agrees better with the order of the names, Salem being a tower or fortress near Shechem (Gen. xxxiii. 18), while Shiloh lay further off. The eighty travellers were coming apparently on a pilgrimage of mourning to the ruins of the Temple,

Samaria, *even* fourscore men, having
their beards shaven, and their clothes
rent, and having cut themselves, with
offerings and incense in their hand, to
bring *them* to the house of the LORD.
(6) And Ishmael the son of Nethaniah
went forth from Mizpah to meet them,
[1]weeping all along as he went: and it
came to pass, as he met them, he said
unto them, Come to Gedaliah the son
of Ahikam. (7) And it was *so*, when
they came into the midst of the city,
that Ishmael the son of Nethaniah slew
them, *and cast them* into the midst of
the pit, he, and the men that *were* with
him. (8) But ten men were found
among them that said unto Ishmael,
Slay us not: for we have treasures in
the field, of wheat, and of barley, and
of oil, and of honey. So he forbare, and
slew them not among their brethren.
(9) Now the pit wherein Ishmael had
cast all the dead bodies of the men,
whom he had slain [2] [3]because of Ge-
daliah, *was* it which Asa the king had
made for fear of Baasha king of Israel:
and Ishmael the son of Nethaniah filled
it with *them that were* slain. (10) Then
Ishmael carried away captive all the
residue of the people that *were* in
Mizpah, *even* the king's daughters, and
all the people that remained in Mizpah,
whom Nebuzar-adan the captain of
the guard had committed to Gedaliah
the son of Ahikam: and Ishmael the
son of Nethaniah carried them away
captive, and departed to go over to
the Ammonites.

(11) But when Johanan the son of
Kareah, and all the captains of the
forces that *were* with him, heard of all
the evil that Ishmael the son of Ne-
thaniah had done, (12) then they took all
the men, and went to fight with Ishmael

1 Heb., *in going and weeping.*

2 Or, *near Gedaliah.*

3 Heb., *by the hand*, or, *by the side of Gedaliah.*

---

perhaps to keep the Feast of Tabernacles, in the hope of finding at least an altar there on which they might present their oblations. Mizpah lay directly on their road from all three places. It is significant that they bring with them not burnt offerings but the *mincha*, or meat offering, the cakes of flour with incense. The outward signs of mourning were, perhaps, connected either with the approaching Day of Atonement, which fell in the seventh month; or with some special fast day belonging to the same season (Zech. vii. 5); or in token of their sorrow for the destruction of the Temple. In the signs themselves we note a relapse into a half-heathen custom which the Law had forbidden (Lev. xix. 27; Deut. xiv. 1; Jer. xlviii. 37).

(6) **Weeping all along as he went.**—The treacherous prince met them as sharing in their grief. He does not tell them of the murder; but assuming that they have heard of Gedaliah's appointment as Satrap, invites them to come and see him, as being now within the bounds of his jurisdiction. The LXX., it may be noted, represents the pilgrims, and not Ishmael, as weeping.

(7) **Ishmael the son of Nethaniah slew them.**—The purpose of the new murder does not appear at first sight. The very presence of the devout mourners may have roused him to bitterness. Their recognition of Gedaliah may have seemed the act of traitors to their country. Possibly also the act may have been one of vindictive retaliation for the murder of his kinsmen (chap. lii. 10), or have been perpetrated for the sake of plunder.

(8) **But ten men were found among them.**—The stores which formed the purchase-money by which the ten saved their lives represented probably the produce of the previous year, which, after the manner of the East, had been concealed in pits, far from the habitations of men, while the land was occupied by the Chaldæan armies.

(9) **Because of Gedaliah.**—Literally, *by the hand of Gedaliah; i.e.*, by using his name to entrap the unsuspecting pilgrims.

Which Asa the king had made for fear of Baasha . . .—See 1 Kings xv. 22; 2 Chron. xvi. 6. Baasha had tried to fortify Ramah as an outpost of his kingdom. Asa called in the help of Benhadad, king of Syria, and compelled him to desist, and then carried off the stones and timber to strengthen Mizpah as a position of defence. The "pit" was probably a trench with a drawbridge over it, so constructed as to stop all approach from the neighbouring kingdom; or else one of the tanks or reservoirs constructed to supply the fortress with water. A various reading gives "the pit of Gedaliah," instead of "because of Gedaliah."

(10) **Even the king's daughters.**—We find in chap. xxxix. 6 that the sons of Zedekiah were slain at Riblah. The daughters (the word was probably used generally for all the princesses of the royal house) were spared, and consigned to the protection of Gedaliah. In taking possession of them, Ishmael was asserting, after the fashion of the East, his claim as the representative of the royal house. The Ammonites had been in alliance with Zedekiah (chap. xxvii. 3), and Ishmael reckoned on finding a safe refuge with them. It would seem, indeed, from chap. xl. 14, that he had been sent, or was believed to have been sent, by the king of the Ammonites for the very purpose of the murder of Gedaliah.

(12) **By the great waters that are in Gibeon.**—Johanan and his friends had been unable to prevent the slaughter of which they had warned Gedaliah (chap. xli. 15), but they were not too late to avenge it. Gibeon, retaining its name with little alteration in the modern *El-jibe*, lay about two miles from Mizpah; so that Ishmael must have halted on thinking himself safe against attack. On the east side of the hill on which it stands there are the remains of a large tank, about 120 feet by 100. It appears as the "pool of Gibeon" in 2 Sam. ii. 13, as the scene of a conflict between Joab and Abner. Josephus (*Ant.* x. 9—15) places the attack on Ishmael at "the pool in Hebron," which is mentioned in 2 Sam. iv. 12. This, however, would hardly

the son of Nethaniah, and found him by
the great waters that *are* in Gibeon.
(13) Now it came to pass, *that* when all
the people which *were* with Ishmael
saw Johanan the son of Kareah, and all
the captains of the forces that *were*
with him, then they were glad. (14) So
all the people that Ishmael had carried
away captive from Mizpah cast about
and returned, and went unto Johanan
the son of Kareah. (15) But Ishmael the
son of Nethaniah escaped from Jo-
hanan with eight men, and went to the
Ammonites. (16) Then took Johanan the
son of Kareah, and all the captains of
the forces that *were* with him, all the
remnant of the people whom he had
recovered from Ishmael the son of Ne-
thaniah, from Mizpah, after *that* he had
slain Gedaliah the son of Ahikam, *even*
mighty men of war, and the women,
and the children, and the eunuchs, whom
he had brought again from Gibeon:
(17) and they departed, and dwelt in the
habitation of Chimham, which is by
Bethlehem, to go to enter into Egypt,
(18) because of the Chaldeans: for they
were afraid of them, because Ishmael
the son of Nethaniah had slain Gedaliah
the son of Ahikam, whom the king of
Babylon made governor in the land.

CHAPTER XLII.—(1) Then all the
captains of the forces, and Johanan the
son of Kareah, and Jezaniah the son of
Hoshaiah, and all the people from the
least even unto the greatest, came near,
(2) and said unto Jeremiah the prophet,
[1] Let, we beseech thee, our supplication
be accepted before thee, and pray for
us unto the LORD thy God, *even* for all
this remnant; (for we are left *but* a
few of many, as thine eyes do behold
us:) (3) that the LORD thy God may
shew us the way wherein we may walk,
and the thing that we may do.
(4) Then Jeremiah the prophet said
unto them, I have heard *you;* behold, I
will pray unto the LORD your God
according to your words; and it shall
come to pass, *that* whatsoever thing the
LORD shall answer you, I will declare *it*
unto you; I will keep nothing back
from you. (5) Then they said to Jeremiah,
The LORD be a true and faithful witness
between us, if we do not even according

1 Or, *Let our supplication fall before thee.*

---

have been in Ishmael's route to the country of the Ammonites.

(13) **They were glad.**—The words are significant as implying the popularity of Gedaliah, and the joy of those who had been under him at seeing the prospect of his murder being avenged. They at once took refuge with the leader of the avenging party.

(15) **With eight men.**—He had come with ten (verse 1), and it is a natural inference that two had perished in one or other of the conflicts of verses 2, 12.

(16) **Mighty men of war . . .**—These were apparently such as had escaped the massacre of verse 2. In the women, the children, and the eunuchs we find the survivors of the king's harem. Ebed-melech may well have been among the latter.

(17) **They departed, and dwelt in the habitation of Chimham.**—The word translated "habitation" is not found elsewhere, but it is connected with one which means "stranger," "foreigner," and means probably a *caravanserai*, or *hospitium* for travellers. The name of Chimham throws us back on the history of Barzillai in 2 Sam. xix. 37. When the Gileadite chief pleaded his age as a ground for not accepting David's invitation to live at his court, the offer was transferred to his son Chimham. On the king's death-bed he was specially commended to the care of Solomon (1 Kings ii. 7). It seems probable that some part of David's personal patrimony, as distinct from his royal domains, had been bestowed on him, and that he had perpetuated his gratitude by erecting a resting-place for travellers, probably enough identical with the "inn" of the Nativity (Luke ii. 7). The plan of the fugitives under Johanan took them to Bethlehem, as lying on the road to Egypt, where they hoped to find a refuge both from the anarchy in which the land had been left by the death of Gedaliah, and from the severe punishment which the Chaldæans were likely to inflict, without too careful an inquiry into the question who had been guilty of it, for the murder of the ruler whom they had appointed. The mere fact of their having remained with Ishmael might be construed into circumstantial evidence of complicity. There they halt, and take counsel.

XLII.

(1) **Jezaniah the son of Hoshaiah.**—Possibly identical with "Jezaniah the son of a Maachathite" (chap. xl. 8). In Azariah the son of Hoshaiah (chap. xliii. 2) we may recognise his brother. The LXX., indeed, reads Azariah here, and it is possibly the true reading.

(2) **Pray for us unto the Lord thy God.**—The prophet had gone to Gedaliah at Mizpah (chap. xl. 6), and would seem to have been among the captives whom Ishmael was carrying off when they were rescued by Johanan at Gibeon (chap. xli. 13, 14). The people now turn to him, acknowledging him as a true prophet, and, trusting to his patriotism, ask for his guidance. Their position was difficult and dangerous. Would he not pray to Jehovah for wisdom, that they might see their way—the way to escape from the threatening peril—clearly? He complies with their wishes, and they, on their side, promise to follow the guidance for which they ask.

(5, 6) **The Lord be a true and faithful witness . . .**—The emphatic adjuration implies that they are ready to accept the punishment which the righteous Judge will inflict in the event of their proving unfaithful

to all things for the which the LORD thy God shall send thee to us. (6) Whether *it be* good, or whether *it be* evil, we will obey the voice of the LORD our God, to whom we send thee; that it may be well with us, when we obey the voice of the LORD our God.

(7) And it came to pass after ten days, that the word of the LORD came unto Jeremiah. (8) Then called he Johanan the son of Kareah, and all the captains of the forces which *were* with him, and all the people from the least even to the greatest, (9) and said unto them, Thus saith the LORD, the God of Israel, unto whom ye sent me to present your supplication before him;

(10) If ye will still abide in this land, then will I build you, and not pull *you* down, and I will plant you, and not pluck *you* up: for I repent me of the evil that I have done unto you. (11) Be not afraid of the king of Babylon, of whom ye are afraid; be not afraid of him, saith the LORD: for I *am* with you to save you, and to deliver you from his hand. (12) And I will shew mercies unto you, that he may have mercy upon you, and cause you to return to your own land.

(13) But if ye say, We will not dwell in this land, neither obey the voice of the LORD your God, (14) saying, No; but we will go into the land of Egypt, where we shall see no war, nor hear the sound of the trumpet, nor have hunger of bread; and there will we dwell: (15) and now therefore hear the word of the LORD, ye remnant of Judah; Thus saith the LORD of hosts, the God of Israel; If ye wholly set your faces to enter into Egypt, and go to sojourn there; (16) then it shall come to pass, *that* the sword, which ye feared, shall overtake you there in the land of Egypt, and the famine, whereof ye were afraid, [1] shall follow close after you there in Egypt; and there ye shall die. (17) [2] So shall it be with all the men that set their faces to go into Egypt to sojourn there; they shall die by the sword, by the famine, and by the pestilence: and none of them shall remain or escape from the evil that I will bring upon them. (18) For thus saith the LORD of hosts, the God of Israel; As mine anger and my fury hath

1 Heb., *shall cleave after you.*

2 Heb., *So shall all the men be.*

---

to their promise. The name of the place where they had lately been staying may have reminded them of the history of Gen. xxxi. 49 (though that refers to another Mizpah), in which we find the same formula.

(7) **After ten days.**—The interval is significant, as indicating that the prophet would not give an answer of his own on the spur of the moment, but waited in prayer and meditation until there came into his mind that which he could utter as an oracle of God. So Ezekiel waited for seven days among the exiles that dwelt by the river of Chebar, till the word of the Lord came to him (Ezek. iii. 16). When the hour came, the prophet preached to a multitude whose eagerness to hear him had been intensified by the suspense.

(10) **Then will I build you, and not pull you down . . .**—We note the characteristic recurrence of the formulæ with which Jeremiah's work as a prophet had begun (chap. i. 10). The word for "repent" does not imply regret for the past, as men repent of their sin, but, as in chaps. xviii. 8, xxvi. 3, a change of purpose from what had been the mind of judgment to one of mercy. The prophet's counsel is, as it had been all along, that the people should accept the punishment which God had inflicted on them, that they should stay where they were and as they were, and not in terror or suspicion seek safety in plans of their own devising.

(12) **And cause you to return to your own land.**—The words admit of two interpretations—(1) that they should be carried away to Babylon, as others had been, and should afterwards return to their own country; (2) that they (the remnant who had been allowed by Nebuzaradan to remain to till the soil) should at once be allowed to return each man to his own field and vineyard. The latter is clearly more in harmony with the prophet's aim and temper, and it was probably in his purpose to intercede with their conquerors to this effect. The thought of a far-off exile as impending over them in the nearer future would hardly have induced them to remain where they were.

(14) **No; but we will go into the land of Egypt.**—The thoughts that were in the hearts of the applicants are stated with dramatic vividness. Egypt, then under Apries (the Pharaoh-hophra of chap. xliv. 30), seemed to them so safe and peaceful. As of old, it was still the granary of the East, and its plenteous harvests formed a bright contrast to the famine which they had experienced during the invasion of the Chaldæans. Jeremiah, however, has simply to reject the plan, as from first to last he had resisted altogether the thought of an Egyptian alliance (chaps. ii. 36, xxxvii. 7): there would be no safety nor peace nor plenty found in acting on it. Ezekiel's prophecies as to Egypt and her king were in this respect in harmony with Jeremiah's (Ezek. xvii. 11—18, xxix.—xxxii.), and were, as nearly as possible, contemporary with them.

(17) **So shall it be with all the men . . .**—The words possibly imply that others were taking the same course as those who had applied to Jeremiah. There was something like a "rush" from many nations—Moab, Edom, and others (chap. xxvii. 3)—of fugitives, looking to Egypt as their one hope of safety against the Chaldæans, and joining with the Jews that had sought shelter in their respective territories (chap. xl. 11). We note in the prophet's warning the recurrence of the old familiar phrases, "by the sword, by the famine, by the pestilence" (chap. xxiv. 10; Ezek. vi. 11), of an "execration and an astonishment and a curse and a reproach" (chaps. xxiv. 9, xxvi. 6, xxix. 18). They

been poured forth upon the inhabitants of Jerusalem; so shall my fury be poured forth upon you, when ye shall enter into Egypt: and ye shall be an execration, and an astonishment, and a curse, and a reproach; and ye shall see this place no more.

(19) The LORD hath said concerning you, O ye remnant of Judah; Go ye not into Egypt: know certainly that I have [1] admonished you this day. (20) For [2] ye dissembled in your hearts, when ye sent me unto the LORD your God, saying, Pray for us unto the LORD our God; and according unto all that the LORD our God shall say, so declare unto us, and we will do *it*. (21) And *now* I have this day declared *it* to you; but ye have not obeyed the voice of the LORD your God, nor any *thing* for the which he hath sent me unto you. (22) Now therefore know certainly that ye shall die by the sword, by the famine, and by the pestilence, in the place whither ye desire to go *and* to sojourn.

CHAPTER XLIII.—(1) And it came to pass, *that* when Jeremiah had made an end of speaking unto all the people all the words of the LORD their God, for which the LORD their God had sent him to them, *even* all these words, (2) then spake Azariah the son of Hoshaiah, and Johanan the son of Kareah, and all the proud men, saying unto Jeremiah, Thou speakest falsely: the LORD our God hath not sent thee to say, Go not into Egypt to sojourn there: (3) but Baruch the son of Neriah setteth thee on against us, for to deliver us into the hand of the Chaldeans, that they might put us to death, and carry us away captives into Babylon.

(4) So Johanan the son of Kareah, and all the captains of the forces, and all the people, obeyed not the voice of the LORD, to dwell in the land of Judah. (5) But Johanan the son of Kareah, and all the captains of the forces, took all the remnant of Judah, that were returned from all nations, whither they had been driven, to dwell in the land of Judah; (6) *even* men, and women, and children, and the king's daughters, and every person that Nebuzar-adan the captain of the guard had left with Gedaliah the son of Ahikam the son of Shaphan, and Jeremiah the prophet, and

[1] Heb., *testified against you.*

[2] Or, *ye have used deceit against your souls.*

---

would involve themselves by rejecting his counsels in all the worst evils that he had prophesied before. What had been addressed to the mixed multitude is emphatically repeated in verse 19 to the "remnant of Judah."

(20) **For ye dissembled in your hearts . . .**—Looks and whispers betrayed, we may believe, the feelings of the prophet's hearers. He saw by such outward signs, or he read, as by the intuition of inspiration, the secret counsels of their hearts (1 Cor. xiv. 24, 25), that they had made a false profession of their readiness to obey, and really meant all along to act as they liked, with the prophet's approval, if they could get it; if not, without. Hypocrisy such as this could not fail to draw down a righteous punishment.

XLIII.

(2) **Azariah the son of Hoshaiah.**—The LXX., it will be remembered, gives this name in chap. xlii. 1, where the Hebrew has Jezaniah. Possibly, however, as suggested above, the two names represent brothers who were both prominent as leaders of the people. Here, we may note, he takes precedence of Johanan, probably as the chief spokesman of the prevailing discontent. The special mention of "all the proud men" suggests the thought that there were some who, left to themselves, would have been willing to follow the prophet's counsel. Those who join in the protest content themselves with a flat denial of his inspiration, and charge him, as he had been charged before (chap. xxxvii. 13), with sinister intentions. It is suggestive, in connexion with the view taken in the Note on chap. xlii. 17, that the LXX., following apparently a different reading of the Hebrew, gives "all the aliens" instead of "all the proud."

(3) **Baruch the son of Neriah setteth thee on against us.**—This was the solution which presented itself to the suspicions of the murmurers. The prophet's amanuensis had become his leader, and was making use of him as a tool for the furtherance of his own designs, and those designs were to court the favour of the conqueror by delivering the remnant of the people into his hands. The warning of chap. xlv. 5 may perhaps be taken as an indication that there was a certain ambition and love of eminence in Baruch's character which gave a colour to the suspicion. Baruch himself has not appeared on the scene since the days of Jehoiakim (chap. xxxvi. 32), but it lies in the nature of the case that he would be known as advocating, like Jeremiah, the policy of submission to Nebuchadnezzar. The apocryphal Book of Baruch (i. 1) represents him as being actually at Babylon at the time of the capture of Jerusalem, and this was in itself probable enough. On this assumption Jeremiah was perhaps suspected of actually receiving instructions from the Babylonian Court through Baruch, who in verse 6 suddenly re-appears as the prophet's companion. Prophet and scribe were apparently seized and carried off by force, to prevent their carrying out the schemes of which they were suspected. The "remnant of Judah returned from all nations" refers to the fugitives from Moab, Ammon, or Edom, mentioned in chap. xl. 11. As the emigration included all who had gathered together under the protection of Gedaliah, it must have left the lands of Judah almost entirely depopulated, and the fear of this

Baruch the son of Neriah. (7) So they
came into the land of Egypt: for they
obeyed not the voice of the LORD: thus
came they *even* to Tahpanhes.
(8) Then came the word of the LORD
unto Jeremiah in Tahpanhes, saying,
(9) Take great stones in thine hand, and
hide them in the clay in the brickkiln,
which *is* at the entry of Pharaoh's
house in Tahpanhes, in the sight of the
men of Judah; (10) and say unto them,
Thus saith the LORD of hosts, the
God of Israel; Behold, I will send and
take Nebuchadrezzar the king of Babylon,
my servant, and will set his throne
upon these stones that I have hid; and
he shall spread his royal pavilion over
them. (11) And when he cometh, he
shall smite the land of Egypt, *and deliver*
[a] such *as are* for death to death;
and such *as are* for captivity to captivity;
and such *as are* for the sword to the
sword. (12) And I will kindle a fire in
the houses of the gods of Egypt; and
he shall burn them, and carry them
away captives: and he shall array
himself with the land of Egypt, as
a shepherd putteth on his garment;
and he shall go forth from thence
in peace. (13) He shall break also the
[1] images of [2] Bethshemesh, that *is* in
the land of Egypt; and the houses
of the gods of the Egyptians shall
he burn with fire.

a ch. 15. 2; Zech. 11. 9.

B. C. 588. ending.

1 Heb., *statues*, or, *standing images*.

2 Or, *the house of the sun*.

---

result may well have been among the reasons that determined Jeremiah's counsels.

(7) **Thus came they even to Tahpanhes.**—The town was obviously on the north-eastern frontier of Egypt. In Judith i. 9 it appears between the river of Egypt (the Rhinocolura, which divided Egypt from Palestine) and Ramesse (the Raamses of Exod. i. 11, or Rameses of Num. xxxiii. 3, 5) and all the land of Gesen, or Goshen. In Ezek. xxx. 16—18 it is named, in conjunction with No (= Thebes) and Noph (= Memphis), among the chief cities of Egypt. In Greek historians it appears as *Daphnæ* and as near Pelusium (Herod. ii. 30), and in the *Itinerary* of Antoninus is placed, under the name of Dafno, at a distance of sixteen Roman miles from the latter city. Its name may be connected with that of the Egyptian Queen Tahpenes, mentioned in 1 Kings xi. 19. Here apparently the emigrants determined to settle and found a new home for themselves.

(9) **Take great stones in thine hand, and hide them in the clay in the brickkiln.**—Better, *in the mortar on the platform*. There seems something incongruous in the idea of a brickkiln, or a place for baking bricks, at the entrance of a royal palace; nor is it easy to see why Nebuchadrezzar should have chosen it as a place for his throne. It seems better, with Hitzig, Furst, and others, to take the Hebrew word, which occurs only here and in 2 Sam. xii. 31 and Nah. iii. 14, as meaning a structure of brick, a *dais* or raised *pavement*, like the Gabbatha or Pavement on which Pilate sat (John xix. 13), in front of the entrance of the palace, on which the king naturally placed his throne when he sat in judgment or received petitions. Assyrian and Babylonian monuments present many instances of kings thus seated. As making his prediction more vivid, the prophet places stones in the *mortar* or *cement* (not "clay") with which the mass was covered, and conceals them apparently with a fresh coat of mortar. There they were to remain till his prediction should be fulfilled. The symbolic act was of the same type as the breaking of the potter's vessel in chap. xix. 10, and the yoke worn on the prophet's shoulders (chap. xxvii. 2), and Ezekiel's digging through the wall (Ezek. xii. 7). It may be noted that our version follows Luther in translating "brickkiln." The LXX. evades the difficulty by taking refuge in vague terms "in the vestibule (πρόθυρα), in the gate of the house," and the Vulgate gives "in the crypt which is under the brick walls."

(10) **He shall spread his royal pavilion over them.**—Here, again, the meaning of the Hebrew word is doubtful. The English Version, as before, follows Luther in taking it for the awning or canopy which was stretched over the throne when the king sat in state as judge. Others (*e.g.*, Hitzig) find in it the leather covering which was placed over the pavement on which the throne was set, upon which the criminal knelt as on a scaffold to receive the death-stroke of the executioner. So taken, the prediction assumes a more definite and terrible aspect. The king was to sit upon the stones which Jeremiah had hidden, not merely in his regal pomp, but in the character of an avenger executing the wrath of Jehovah against the rebellious.

(11) **Such as are for death to death.**—Again we note the re-appearance of a characteristic formula (chap. xi. 2).

(12) **I will kindle a fire.**—The change of person is full of significance. Jehovah Himself kindles the fire which is to destroy the temples of the gods of Egypt, and the Chaldæan king is but His instrument.

As a shepherd putteth on his garment.—The words may point simply to the easiness of the conquest. To take possession of the whole country will be as quick and light a matter as when the shepherd takes up his garment at night and wraps it round him. Possibly (as Hitzig suggests) there may be a reference to the fact that when the shepherd so wraps himself he turns the fleecy coat which he wears inside out (the "*pellibus inversis*" of Juvenal, *Sat.* xiv. 136). So, the prophet may suggest, shall the conqueror turn the whole land upside down. (Comp. 2 Kings xxi. 13).

(13) **He shall break also the images of Bethshemesh.**—This name, which means "Home of the Sun" (so the Vulgate renders it here by *domus solis*), was naturally not an uncommon one where sun-worship had prevailed, and we find it accordingly in Judah (Josh. xv. 10; 1 Sam. vi. 9, 12), in Issachar (Joshua xix. 22), and in Naphtali (Joshua xix. 38; Judges i. 33). Here the context shows that it was the name of an Egyptian city. The LXX. renders the words "he shall break the pillars of Heliopolis, which are in On," and so identifies it with the city of that name on the Pelusiac branch of the Nile, just below the point of the Delta,

CHAPTER XLIV.—(1) The word that
came to Jeremiah concerning all the
Jews which dwell in the land of Egypt,
which dwell at Migdol, and at Tahpanhes,
and at Noph, and in the country of
Pathros, saying,
(2) Thus saith the LORD of hosts, the
God of Israel; Ye have seen all the
evil that I have brought upon Jerusalem,
and upon all the cities of Judah; and,
behold, this day they *are* a desolation,
and no man dwelleth therein, (3) because
of their wickedness which they have
committed to provoke me to anger, in
that they went to burn incense, *and* to
serve other gods, whom they knew not,
neither they, ye, nor your fathers.
(4) Howbeit I sent unto you all my ser-
vants the prophets, rising early and
sending *them*, saying, Oh, do not this
abominable thing that I hate. (5) But
they hearkened not, nor inclined their
ear to turn from their wickedness, to
burn no incense unto other gods.
(6) Wherefore my fury and mine anger
was poured forth, and was kindled in
the cities of Judah and in the streets of
Jerusalem; and they are wasted *and* deso-
late, as at this day. (7) Therefore now thus
saith the LORD, the God of hosts, the God
of Israel; Wherefore commit ye *this* great
evil against your souls, to cut off from
you man and woman, child and suckling,
[1] out of Judah, to leave you none to
remain; (8) in that ye provoke me unto
wrath with the works of your hands,
burning incense unto other gods in the
land of Egypt, whither ye be gone to
dwell, that ye might cut yourselves off,
and that ye might be a curse and a
reproach among all the nations of the
earth? (9) Have ye forgotten the [2] wicked-
ness of your fathers, and the wickedness
of the kings of Judah, and the wicked-
ness of their wives, and your own
wickedness, and the wickedness of your
wives, which they have committed in
the land of Judah, and in the streets of

B. C. 587.

1 Heb., *out of the midst of Judah.*

2 Heb., *wickednesses,* or, *punishments,* &c.

---

and about twenty miles north-east of Memphis. Under the name of On it appears in Gen. xli. 45. The "images" or "pillars" are now represented by a solitary obelisk of red granite, sixty-eight feet high, its companion having been brought to Rome and erected in the Vatican Circus in front of St. Peter's (Herod. II., III.; Plin. *Hist. Nat.* xxxvi. 11). There were at one time many others, besides colossal statues. The fulfilment of the prediction, as far as it referred to the defeat and death of Pharaoh-hophra, is related by Josephus (*Ant.* x. 9, § 7).

XLIV.

(1) **At Migdol, and at Tahpanhes . . .**—We find from verse 15 that the discourse that follows was delivered at a large gathering of the Jews at Pathros. The number of places named (the three appear in the same combination in chap. xlvi. 14) indicates the extent of the emigration. Migdol (here, as elsewhere, meaning a "tower" or "fortress") is named in Exod. xiv. 2 as on the route of the Israelites before they crossed the Red Sea, between Pi-hahiroth and Baal-zephon, and again in Ezek. xxix. 10, xxx. 6. It appears in the *Itinerary* of Antoninus, under the name *Magdolo*, as twelve miles south of Pelusium. The latter is thought by Lepsius to be different from the former, and to answer to the *Stratopeda* or "camp" which Herodotus mentions as having been founded by Psammetichus I. as a settlement for his Ionian or Carian mercenaries (Smith's *Dict. of the Bible*, Art. *Migdol*). Noph was identical with Memphis, and appears in Isa. xix. 13; Jer. ii. 16; Ezek. xxx. 13, 16: and as Moph in the Hebrew of Hos. ix. 6. The position of Pathros is less certain, but it may be inferred from the mention of the other cities with it that it was in Lower Egypt, and possibly, from verse 15, that it was the name of the region in which it was situated. So in Isa. xi. 11, it appears in conjunction with Mizraim (= Egypt) and Cush (= Ethiopia), both of which are names of regions and not of cities. By Brugsch (*Egypt*, I. 242) it has been identified with Upper Egypt, the region of the Thebaid. There is no certain note of the interval between the arrival of the Jews in Egypt and the delivery of the discourse, but it would appear that there had been time for the Jews to disperse and settle in the three or four cities here named, and to adopt the worship of the Egyptians. It is, however, implied throughout that the prophet is speaking to the emigrants themselves, and not to their descendants (verses 17, 21).

(2) **Ye have seen . . .**—The prophet begins, naturally enough, with an appeal to the personal experience of his hearers. Was not that enough to show them that the source of all their evils had been their falling away from the faith or worship of their fathers?

(4) **Rising early and sending them . . .**—The prophet uses the same anthropomorphic language as of old (chaps. vii. 25, xxv. 4, xxvi. 5, xxix. 19). The term "abominable thing," or "abomination," though common in many of the books of the Old Testament, as in the Proverbs, where it is applied to moral enormities (*e.g.*, Prov. iii. 32, vi. 16), is specially characteristic, as applied to idolatry, of Deuteronomy (xxvii. 15, xxxii. 16), Jeremiah (here and chaps. vii. 10, viii. 12, xxxii. 35), and Ezek. (v. 11, and some forty other passages).

(8) **Burning incense unto other gods in the land of Egypt.**—The words imply that the exiles were not only carrying on the old idolatrous practices with which they had been familiar in their own lands, but had adopted those of the Egyptians. This was the evil which the prophet had all along dreaded, and which had made him from the first, like his predecessor, Isaiah (xxx. 2, xxxi. 1), hostile to every plan of an alliance with Egypt.

(9) **The wickedness of their wives.**—As in the first introduction of idolatry under Solomon (1 Kings xi. 4) so in the reigns of his successors, as in the case of Asa (1 Kings xv. 13) and Ahaziah (2 Chron. xxii. 2),

Jerusalem? (10) They are not [1] humbled
even unto this day, neither have they
feared, nor walked in my law, nor in my
statutes, that I set before you and before
your fathers.
(11) Therefore thus saith the LORD of
hosts, the God of Israel; Behold, [a] I
will set my face against you for evil, and
to cut off all Judah. (12) And I will
take the remnant of Judah, that have
set their faces to go into the land of
Egypt to sojourn there, and they shall
all be consumed, *and* fall in the land of
Egypt; they shall *even* be consumed by
the sword *and* by the famine: they shall
die, from the least even unto the greatest,
by the sword and by the famine: and
they shall be an execration, *and* an
astonishment, and a curse, and a re-
proach. (13) For I will punish them that
dwell in the land of Egypt, as I have
punished Jerusalem, by the sword, by
the famine, and by the pestilence:
(14) so that none of the remnant of Judah,
which are gone into the land of Egypt
to sojourn there, shall escape or remain,
that they should return into the land of
Judah, to the which they [2] have a desire
to return to dwell there: for none shall
return but such as shall escape.
(15) Then all the men which knew that
their wives had burned incense unto
other gods and all the women that
stood by, a great multitude, even all
the people that dwelt in the land of
Egypt, in Pathros, answered Jeremiah,
saying,
(16) *As for* the word that thou hast
spoken unto us in the name of the
LORD, we will not hearken unto thee.
(17) But we will certainly do whatsoever
thing goeth forth out of our own mouth,
to burn incense unto the [3] [b] queen of hea-
ven, and to pour out drink offerings unto
her, as we have done, we, and our fathers,
our kings, and our princes, in the cities
of Judah, and in the streets of Jerusalem:
for *then* had we plenty of [4] victuals, and
were well, and saw no evil. (18) But since
we left off to burn incense to the queen
of heaven, and to pour out drink offer-
ings unto her, we have wanted all *things*,
and have been consumed by the sword
and by the famine. (19) [c] And when we
burned incense to the queen of heaven,
and poured out drink offerings unto
her, did we make her cakes to worship
her, and pour out drink offerings unto
her, without our [5] men?
(20) Then Jeremiah said unto all the
people, to the men, and to the women,
and to all the people which had given
him *that* answer, saying, (21) The incense
that ye burned in the cities of Judah,

1 Heb., *contrite.*

a Amos 9. 4

2 Heb., *lift up their soul.*

3 Or, *frame of heaven.*

b ch. 7. 18.

4 Heb., *bread.*

c ch. 7. 18.

5 Or, *husbands?*

---

the queens for the time being, often of alien birth, seem to have been the chief patrons of foreign and idolatrous worship, and their example was naturally followed by the wives of the nobles and other citizens.

(13) **I will punish them that dwell in the land of Egypt.**—The words point, like those of chap. xliii. 11, to a punishment which should fall on the whole of Egypt, and from which the Jews who dwelt in it should find no exemption.

(14) **To the which they have a desire to return.**—Literally, *unto which they lift up their souls to return.* The words are significant as showing that the exiles still cherished the hope of getting back to the land of their fathers.

None shall return but such as shall escape.—The words seem at first a truism, but they imply that the escape would be difficult. The formula seems to have been not uncommon (Ezek. vii. 16). In verse 28 we have the fact more definitely stated: there should be, as in previous chastisements, a remnant, and a remnant only (Isa. i. 9, vi. 13). By some critics the limiting clause has been looked on as an interpolation, inserted to bring the verse into agreement with verse 28.

(15) **All the men which knew that their wives had burned incense.**—The fact thus mentioned incidentally shows that the prophet's words in verse 9 had not missed their mark. As of old—as, we may add, in the Rome of the Empire (Juvenal, *Sat.* vi. 526—534)—the women practised a *cultus* in which their husbands acquiesced, even though they did not join in it.

(18) **To burn incense to the queen of heaven.**—This form of worship, characterised specially by its offerings of crescent-shaped cakes, would seem to have been the dominant fashion of the idolatry of the time. (See Note on chap. vii. 18.) The men who felt themselves condemned by the prophet's words vindicate their line of action. They had practised this worship of old, and would practise it still, and they set their experience of the prosperity of those past days against the prophet's picture of the evil that had followed. Might they not argue, as the Romans did in the calamities that fell on the Empire (Tertull. *Apol.* c. 40; August. *De Civ. Dei*, I. c. 36), that they suffered because they had left off the worship under the influence of a different teaching?

(19) **Without our men.**—Better, as in the margin, *without our husbands.* We have here, it is obvious, the very words of the women who were stung by what they looked on as Jeremiah's intimation that the chief guilt lay on them. They disclaim any special responsibility. Their husbands had joined in the worship, or had, at least, sanctioned it.

(20—23) **Then Jeremiah said . . .**—The prophet makes an effective rejoinder to the assertion that the prosperity of past years had coincided with the idolatrous worship which he condemned. That prosperity had not been lasting, and though the long-suffering

and in the streets of Jerusalem, ye, and
your fathers, your kings, and your
princes, and the people of the land, did
not the LORD remember them, and came
it *not* into his mind? (22) So that the
LORD could no longer bear, because of
the evil of your doings, *and* because of
the abominations which ye have com-
mitted; therefore is your land a desola-
tion, and an astonishment, and a curse,
without an inhabitant, as at this day.
(23) Because ye have burned incense, and
because ye have sinned against the
LORD, and have not obeyed the voice of
the LORD, nor walked in his law, nor in
his statutes, nor in his testimonies;
therefore this evil is happened unto you,
as at this day.

(24) Moreover Jeremiah said unto all
the people, and to all the women, Hear
the word of the LORD, all Judah that
are in the land of Egypt: (25) Thus saith
the LORD of hosts, the God of Israel,
saying; Ye and your wives have both
spoken with your mouths, and fulfilled
with your hand, saying, We will surely
perform our vows that we have vowed,
to burn incense to the queen of heaven,
and to pour out drink offerings unto
her: ye will surely accomplish your
vows, and surely perform your vows.
(26) Therefore hear ye the word of the
LORD, all Judah that dwell in the land
of Egypt; Behold, I have sworn by my
great name, saith the LORD, that my
name shall no more be named in the
mouth of any man of Judah in all the
land of Egypt, saying, The Lord GOD
liveth. (27) Behold, I will watch over
them for evil, and not for good: and all
the men of Judah that *are* in the land
of Egypt shall be consumed by the
sword and by the famine, until there be
an end of them. (28) Yet a small number
that escape the sword shall return out
of the land of Egypt into the land of
Judah, and all the remnant of Judah,
that are gone into the land of Egypt to
sojourn there, shall know whose words
shall stand, [1] mine, or their's.

(29) And this *shall be* a sign unto you,
saith the LORD, that I will punish you
in this place, that ye may know that
my words shall surely stand against
you for evil: (30) Thus saith the LORD;
Behold, I will give Pharaoh-hophra king
of Egypt into the hand of his enemies,
and into the hand of them that seek his
life; as I gave Zedekiah king of Judah
into the hand of Nebuchadrezzar king
of Babylon, his enemy, and that sought
his life.

1 Heb., *from me, or from them.*

B. C. 589.

B. C. cir. 607.

CHAPTER XLV.—(1) The word that
Jeremiah the prophet spake unto Baruch
the son of Neriah, when he had written

---

of God had borne with them, the judgments had at last come. The tenor of his argument was that which Augustine adopts in his treatise *De Civitate Dei*. See Note on verse 16.

(24–28) **Hear the word of the Lord . . .**—The appeal to the experience of the past is followed by a prediction of the future, addressed to the wives as well as to the husbands. The new sin would lead to a new punishment. A tone of irony is perceptible in the words, "Ye will surely accomplish your vows." That, at all events, was a promise they were likely to keep, however faithless they might have shown themselves in keeping their vows to the God of their fathers. But the Lord of Israel meets that vow by another. By that "great name" (Gen. xxii. 16) of the Lord God (*Jehovah Adonai*), which they had slighted and profaned, He declares that it shall be profaned no more by the Egyptian exiles, not because they, of their own accord, would cease to use it, but because none of them should be left there. The small remnant that survived the sword and the famine should return to Judah as a witness of the judgment that had fallen on them, and of the truth of the prophet's warning. The words of Jehovah should stand, while those of men should fail.

(30) **Behold, I will give Pharaoh-hophra . . .**—The fate of the Egyptian king is announced, coming, as it did, before that of the fugitives, as a "sign" that the prediction of their doom also would in due course be accomplished. The king thus named—the Apries of Herod. II., 161, 163, 169—was the son of Psammis, and reigned for twenty-five years. He attacked Sidon by land and Tyre by sea, presumably before Nebuchadnezzar's invasion of Phœnicia, and then sent his armies against Cyrene. The issue of that campaign was disastrous, and his subjects revolted. His general, Amasis, who was sent to pacify the rebels, put himself at their head. Apries was deposed, kept in honourable imprisonment at Sais for a time, and afterwards strangled. His reign extended from B.C. 594 to 569. Jeremiah probably delivered his prediction *circ.* B.C. 580, and it is the last recorded event in his life. A late Christian tradition, resting probably on a Jewish one, states that then, or shortly afterwards, the Egyptian Jews, irritated by his reproaches, rose up against him and stoned him to death. (Tertull. *Adv. Gnost*, c. 8; Hieron. *Adv. Jovin*, ii. 37.) In Heb. xi. 37 ("they were stoned") we may probably find a reference to his fate as one of the "noble army of martyrs."

XLV.

(1) **The word that Jeremiah the prophet spake unto Baruch . . .**—The chapter is obviously misplaced as far as chronological order is concerned, and ought to follow on chaps. xxxv. and xxxvi. It gives us a glimpse of singular interest into the

these words in a book at the mouth of
Jeremiah, in the fourth year of Jehoia-
kim the son of Josiah king of Judah,
saying,
(2) Thus saith the LORD, the God of
Israel, unto thee, O Baruch; (3) Thou
didst say, Woe is me now! for the LORD
hath added grief to my sorrow; I fainted
in my sighing, and I find no rest.
(4) Thus shalt thou say unto him, The
LORD saith thus; Behold, *that* which I
have built will I break down, and that
which I have planted I will pluck up,
even this whole land. (5) And seekest
thou great things for thyself? seek *them*
not: for, behold, I will bring evil upon
all flesh, saith the LORD: but thy life
will I give unto thee [a] for a prey in all
places whither thou goest.

a ch. 39. 18.

CHAPTER XLVI.—(1) The word of
the LORD which came to Jeremiah the
prophet against the Gentiles;
(2) Against Egypt, against the army
of Pharaoh-necho king of Egypt, which
was by the river Euphrates in Carche-
mish, which Nebuchadrezzar king of
Babylon smote in the fourth year of
Jehoiakim the son of Josiah king of
Judah.
(3) Order ye the buckler and shield,
and draw near to battle. (4) Harness

---

character of the prophet's helper. He was discouraged and desponding, and yet the very despondency was that of an ambitious temperament eager to take the lead. His master was in prison. Neither king nor nobles listened to him. He had, it may be, drawn for himself an ideal picture of a successful work, in which he himself should be a chief agent. (See Note on chap. xliii. 3.) "Grief was added to his sighing, and he found no rest." And now all seemed failure. The prophet had passed through such moods himself (chaps. xv. 10—21, xx. 7—18), and knew, when they found utterance in words that were the very echo of his own, how to deal with them. The scribe must accept the doom that fell on him as on others. He must not hope to pass unscathed, still less to attain the "great things" which he had imagined for himself. It was enough that his life was given him "as a prey" (chaps. xxi. 9, xxxix. 18), as spoil rescued from the spoiler. What his future was to be was not revealed unto him, but the closing words pointed to a life of wandering and exile; and Baruch was, we know, among those who went down to Egypt (chap. xliii. 6), and had probably been for some years at Babylon (Bar. i. 1). According to one tradition he died in Egypt (Jerome, *Comm. in Isa.* xxx.); another represents him as having returned to Babylon after his master's death, and ending his life there. The apocryphal book that bears his name testifies to the reverence felt for him by a later generation. It is not without interest to note the general parallelism of the words in which Elisha rebuked the covetousness of Gehazi (2 Kings v. 26) and those with which our Lord met the ambitious request of the sons of Zebedee (Matt. xx. 20—23).

XLVI.

(1) **The word of the Lord . . .**—We come here upon something like the traces of a plan in the arrangement of Jeremiah's prophecies. Those that were concerned exclusively with the outside nations of the heathen were collected together, and attached as an appendix to those which were addressed directly to his own people. Most of those that follow were connected historically with chap. xxv. 15—26, and may be regarded as the development of what is there given in outline, and belong accordingly to the reign of Jehoiakim (*circ.* B.C. 607).

(2) **Against Egypt, against the army of Pharaoh-necho.**—The king of Egypt thus named was the last of its great native sovereigns. He was the sixth king of the twenty-sixth dynasty of Manetho, and succeeded his father Psammetichus in B.C. 610, and reigned for sixteen years. Herodotus (ii. 158, 159) relates as his chief achievements that he anticipated the Suez Canal by endeavouring to connect the Nile with the Red Sea, but was stopped by an oracle, and sent a fleet of Phœnician ships to circumnavigate Africa. One hundred and twenty thousand lives were said to have been sacrificed in the former enterprise. On desisting from it, he turned his attention to other plans of conquest, defeated the Syrians at Magdolus, near Pelusium, and took Cadytis, a great city of Syria, which Herodotus describes as not much less than Sardis. By some writers this has been identified with the capture of Jerusalem in 2 Chron. xxxvi. 3, the name Cadytis being looked on as equivalent to *Kadusha* (=the holy city), and so anticipating the modern Arabic name of *El-Khuds*. Herodotus, however (iii. 5), describes it as being near the coast, and this has led to its being identified with Gaza, or Kedesh-Naphtali, or a Hittite city—Ketesh—on the Orontes, near which the great commercial and military road turned off for Damascus and the Euphrates. In any case, it was in the course of this invasion, directed against the Babylonian Empire, then ruled by Nabopolassar, the father of Nebuchadnezzar, that he defeated and slew Josiah at Megiddo (2 Chron. xxxv. 20—24), deposed Jehoahaz, and appointed Jehoiakim (2 Chron. xxxvi. 4). By some writers, accordingly (R. S. Poole, in Smith's *Dict. Bible*, Art. *Pharaoh-necho*), Megiddo is identified with the Magdolus of Herodotus. His army advanced, and took the city of Carchemish, by some (Hitzig) identified with Circesium, an island formed by the confluence of the Chaboras and the Euphrates; by others (Rawlinson) with a Hittite city, now *Jerablus*, a corruption of the Greek Hierapolis, much higher up the Euphrates. (See Note on Isa. x. 9). After the capture Necho appears to have returned to Egypt. Three years later (B.C. 606) Carchemish was taken by Nebuchadnezzar with the almost total defeat of Necho's army, he himself having returned to Egypt, and it is this defeat of which Jeremiah now proceeds to speak as in a song of anticipated triumph at the downfall of the Egyptian oppressor.

(3, 4) **Order ye the buckler and shield . . .** The poem opens with a summons to the hosts of Nebuchadnezzar to prepare for their victory. First the foot-soldiers are called, then the horse, lastly the light-armed troops.

the horses; and get up, ye horsemen,
and stand forth with *your* helmets;
furbish the spears, *and* put on the
brigandines. (5) Wherefore have I seen
them dismayed *and* turned away back?
and their mighty ones are [1] beaten down,
and are [2] fled apace, and look not back:
for fear *was* round about, saith the
LORD. (6) Let not the swift flee away,
nor the mighty man escape; they shall
stumble, and fall toward the north by
the river Euphrates. (7) Who *is* this *that*
cometh up as a flood, whose waters are
moved as the rivers? (8) Egypt riseth
up like a flood, and *his* waters are moved
like the rivers; and he saith, I will go
up, *and* will cover the earth; I will
destroy the city and the inhabitants
thereof. (9) Come up, ye horses; and
rage, ye chariots; and let the mighty
men come forth; [3] the Ethiopians and
[4] the Libyans, that handle the shield;
and the Lydians, that handle *and* bend
the bow. (10) For this *is* the day of the
Lord GOD of hosts, a day of vengeance,
that he may avenge him of his adver-
saries: and the sword shall devour, and
it shall be satiate and made drunk with
their blood: for the Lord GOD of hosts
hath a sacrifice in the north country by
the river Euphrates. (11) Go up into
Gilead, and take balm, O virgin, the
daughter of Egypt: in vain shalt thou
use many medicines; *for* [5] thou shalt

1 Heb., *broken in pieces.*
2 Heb., *fled a flight.*
3 Heb., *Cush.*
4 Heb., *Put.*
5 Heb., *no cure shall be unto thee.*

Put on the brigandines.—The history of the word is not without interest. Light-armed skirmishers were known in Italian as "brigands" (*briganti*—literally, "quarrellers"); the light coat of mail worn by them was accordingly known as a "brigandine." When the Italian word became synonymous with robbers by land or sea, the ship used by them was called a *brigantino*, and from this is derived our English "brig" (W. A. Wright: *Bible Word Book*). The word "brigandine" is accordingly used by writers of the sixteenth century in both senses: by Spenser, for a ship—

> "Like as a warlike brigandine applied
> To fight;"

and by Milton—

> "Then put on all thy gorgeous arms, thy helmet
> And brigandine of brass"

(*Sams. Agonist.*, 1120)—in the same sense as here and in chap. li. 3.

(5) **Wherefore have I seen them dismayed . . .?**—The prophet speaks as seeing already in his mind's eye the confusion of the defeated army, with no way to escape, driven back on the Euphrates. In the "fear round about" (*Magor-missabib*) we have one of his characteristic formulæ (chaps. vi. 25, xx. 3, 10, xlix. 29).

(7, 8) **Who is this that cometh up as a flood? . . .**—The Hebrew word for "flood" is used as a proper name almost exclusively (Dan. xii. 5, 6 being the only exception) for the Nile (*e.g.*, Gen. xli. 1—3; Exod. ii. 3, iv. 9; Amos viii. 8, ix. 5), and thus the very form of the question points to the answer that follows. The prophet goes back, as an English poet might have done after the destruction of the Spanish Armada, to the time when all the strength of Egypt had been poured forth in the exultation of anticipated victory, as the great river of Egypt poured its waters. The word for "rivers," though more general, has a like allusive reference, being used in Exod. vii. 19, viii. 5 and Ezek. xxxii. 2, 14 for the arms or canals of the Nile.

(9) **The Ethiopians and the Libyans.**—In the Hebrew, *Cush* and *Put*. The verse describes the prominent elements in the composition of the Egyptian army. The "chariots and horses" had long been proverbial (1 Kings x. 28, 29; 2 Chron. i. 16; Exod. xv. 19). The Cushites were the Ethiopians of the Upper Valley of the Nile, sometimes, as under Zerah (2 Chron. xiv. 9) and Tirhakah (2 Kings xix. 9), asserting their independence, but at this time subject to Necho. The name Phut meets us, with Cush and Mizraim, in the list of the sons of Ham in Gen. x. 6; and presumably, therefore, belongs to an African people. Wherever it is mentioned by the prophets it is as an ally or tributary of Egypt (Nahum iii. 9; Ezek. xxvii. 10, xxx. 5, xxxviii. 5). The LXX. version renders it by Libyan, and is followed by the Vulgate and the English. In Nahum iii. 9, however, Phut is distinguished from the Libyans (=Lubim); and the LXX. has but one word for both. The word PET is found on Egyptian inscriptions, both as meaning a "bow" and as the name of a people, and this may correspond to the *Put* of the Hebrew text. The Lydians, or *Ludim*, are named in the list of Hamite nations as descended from Mizraim (Gen. x. 13); the name is joined with Phut in Ezek. xxvii. 10, with Cush and Phut in Ezek. xxx. 4, 5. This would seem to point to an African rather than an Asiatic people like the Lydians. On the other hand, we learn from Herodotus (ii. 153) that, some thirty or forty years before the time of Jeremiah and Ezekiel, Psammetichus I. had settled a large colony of Ionian and Carian emigrants on both banks of the Nile, between Bubastis and the Pelusiac mouth of that river, and that Amasis afterwards formed them into a body-guard at Memphis. It is obvious that the fame of the monarchy which had its capital at Sardis might easily lead to these Greeks being classed as Lydians, and that thus the name (without entering into its earlier ethnological significance) would acquire a new prominence at the time when the prophets wrote in connexion with Egypt.

(10) **This is the day of the Lord God of hosts.**—The prophet contemplates the issue of all these great preparations, and sees that they will end in a disastrous overthrow, the righteous retribution for long years of cruelty and outrage. In doing so he falls back upon the language of earlier prophets (Isa. xxxiv. 8; Zeph. i. 7), in part also upon that of Deut. xxxii. 42. There is to be a "great sacrifice," and the army of Egypt is the destined victim; and the banks of the Euphrates (*i.e.*, Carchemish) are to be as the altar.

(11) **Go up into Gilead, and take balm . . .**—The words have the tone of a triumphant irony. The "balm of Gilead" was looked on as a cure for all

not be cured. (12) The nations have
heard of thy shame, and thy cry hath
filled the land: for the mighty man
hath stumbled against the mighty, *and*
they are fallen both together.
(13) The word that the LORD spake
to Jeremiah the prophet, how Nebuchad-
rezzar king of Babylon should come *and*
smite the land of Egypt.
(14) Declare ye in Egypt, and publish
in Migdol, and publish in Noph and in
Tahpanhes: say ye, Stand fast, and
prepare thee; for the sword shall devour
round about thee. (15) Why are thy
valiant *men* swept away? they stood
not, because the LORD did drive them.
(16) He [1] made many to fall, yea, one fell
upon another: and they said, Arise, and
let us go again to our own people, and
to the land of our nativity, from the
oppressing sword. (17) They did cry
there, Pharaoh king of Egypt *is but* a
noise; he hath passed the time ap-
pointed. (18) *As* I live, saith the King,
whose name *is* the LORD of hosts, Surely
as Tabor *is* among the mountains, and
as Carmel by the sea, *so* shall he come.
(19) O thou daughter dwelling in Egypt,
[2] furnish thyself to go into captivity:
for Noph shall be waste and desolate

1 Heb., *multiplied the faller.*

2 Heb., *make thee instruments of captivity.*

---

wounds (chaps. viii. 22, li. 8), but the wounds which Egypt received at Carchemish would be found incurable. It proved, in fact, to be a blow from which the old Egyptian monarchy never recovered. In the "virgin, the daughter of Egypt"—virgin, as being till then, as it boasted, unconquered (Isa. xxiii. 12)—we have a like touch of sarcasm. The report of the defeat and the utter rout and confused flight that followed (verse 12) would spread far and wide among the nations.

(13) **The word that the Lord spake . . .**—The opening words clearly point to this as a distinct prophecy from the preceding, pointing to subsequent events, and it was probably delivered much later, possibly in connexion with chap. xliii. 10, and placed where it is as belonging to the series of predictions which had Egypt as their subject.

(14) **Declare ye in Egypt.**—The general proclamation is afterwards defined by the names of the cities which were the more immediate objects of Nebuchadrezzar's attack. For the three cities named see Note on chap. xliv. 1.

(15) **Why are thy valiant men swept away?**—Better, *Why is thy strong bull dragged away?* The Hebrew verbs are in the singular, and the adjective is given in the same number both in the LXX. and Vulgate. The former gives the rendering "Why did Apis flee from thee, and thy chosen calf abode not" as if referring to the bull Apis as the representative of Osiris, the chief deity of Egypt; and this version receives some support from the use of the Hebrew words for "oxen," "bulls," "beasts," in Isa. xxxiv. 7 and Pss. xxii. 12, lxviii. 30, and from the fact that the same word is used in Isa. i. 24, xlix. 26 as a Divine name "the mighty one of Israel." So understood, the prophet's words contemplate the triumph of the God of Israel over the theriomorphic deity of Egypt. We may find a literal fulfilment of the words in the slaughter of the sacred bull by Cambyses (Herod. iii. 29).

(16) **Arise, and let us go again to our own people.**—The case contemplated is that of the settlers in Egypt, the Lydians, Ionians, and Carians (see Note on verse 9) whom Psammetichus had encouraged, or the fugitives from Judæa of chap. xliii. 5—7. These should find that it was no longer a safe home for them. The "oppressing sword" is beyond question the right rendering, but it is curious that both the LXX. and Vulgate have taken the adjective in different senses: the former giving "from the Greek sword," as if the word for oppressing (*Ionah*) meant Ionian; and the latter, the apparently strange version, *a facie gladii columbæ* ("from before the sword of the dove"). See, however, as giving a possible explanation of the words as referring to the dove as a symbol of the Chaldæan power, the Note on chap. xxv. 38.

(17) **They did cry there . . .**—Better, *There they cry . . .* The difficulty of the verse has led to very various renderings. The meaning of the English version is that the exiles returning to their own land would say that Pharaoh with all his haughty boasts was but an empty noise, that he had passed the limit of God's long-suffering, and that the day of retribution had come. A slight change in the Hebrew words, however, gives, *They have called the name of Pharaoh king of Egypt, A Noise; he hath passed* (*or lost*) *the appointed season*—*i.e.*, the time allowed by the long-suffering of God. This is supported by some of the ancient versions, and may be accepted as the best rendering. The LXX. and Vulg. agree in taking the opening words as an imperative, "Call ye the name of Pharaoh . . . ;" but the former, as if despairing of the meaning, simply reproduces the Hebrew words that follow in Greek letters, while the latter translates, *Tumultum adduxit tempus* ("Time, the appointed time, has brought the noise"—*i.e.*, of war and destruction), as if it were, like *Magor-missabib*, a new *nomen et omen* given to the Egyptian king. Luther, giving another meaning to the words translated "appointed time," renders "Pharaoh king of Egypt lies prostrate, he has left his tent." Ewald, following the line of the Vulgate, renders the name by which Pharaoh is spoken of as "tumult, which a sign or 'moment' disperses," the "tumult" being his boastful clamour, the "sign" the token of Jehovah's will. Hitzig agrees more closely with the English version in the latter clause, and it may be accepted as having on the whole most in its favour.

(18) **Surely as Tabor is among the mountains . . .**—Nebuchadnezzar in his high-towering greatness is compared to two of the most conspicuous mountains of Palestine, Tabor rising in solitary greatness 1,350 feet above the plain, Carmel 1,805 feet above the sea. So, in chap. xxii. 6, the king of Judah is compared to "Gilead and the head of Lebanon."

(19) **O thou daughter dwelling in Egypt.**—As in verse 11, the daughter is Egypt itself personified. She is to prepare herself (literally, *with the instruments of captivity*), as with "bag and baggage" for a long journey. (Comp. Ezek. xii. 3.) Noph (= Memphis) is to be left as a depopulated city.

without an inhabitant. (20) Egypt *is like*
a very fair heifer, *but* destruction cometh;
it cometh out of the north. (21) Also
her hired men *are* in the midst of her
like [1] fatted bullocks; for they also are
turned back, *and* are fled away together:
they did not stand, because the day of
their calamity was come upon them, *and*
the time of their visitation. (22) The
voice thereof shall go like a serpent;
for they shall march with an army, and
come against her with axes, as hewers
of wood. (23) They shall cut down her
forest, saith the LORD, though it cannot
be searched; because they are more
than the grasshoppers, and *are* innumer-
able. (24) The daughter of Egypt shall
be confounded: she shall be delivered
into the hand of the people of the
north. (25) The LORD of hosts, the
God of Israel, saith; Behold, I will
punish the [2][3] multitude of No, and
Pharaoh, and Egypt, with their gods,
and their kings; even Pharaoh, and *all*
them that trust in him: (26) and I will
deliver them into the hand of those
that seek their lives, and into the
hand of Nebuchadrezzar king of
Babylon, and into the hand of his
servants: and afterward it shall be
inhabited, as in the days of old, saith
the LORD.

(27) [a] But fear not thou, O my servant
Jacob, and be not dismayed, O Israel:
for, behold, I will save thee from afar
off, and thy seed from the land of their
captivity; and Jacob shall return, and
be in rest and at ease, and none shall
make *him* afraid. (28) Fear thou not, O
Jacob my servant, saith the LORD: for
I *am* with thee; for I will make a full
end of all the nations whither I have
driven thee: but I will not make [b] a full
end of thee, but correct thee in measure;
yet will I [4] not leave thee wholly un-
punished.

1 Heb., *bullocks of the stall.*

2 Or, *nourisher.*

3 Heb., *Amon.*

a Isa. 41. 13; & 43. 5; & 44. 2; ch. 30. 10.

b ch. 10. 24; & 30. 11.

4 Or, *not utterly cut thee off*

---

(20) **Egypt is like a very fair heifer.**—The similitude points, like the "strong one" of verse 15, to the Apis worship of Egypt. The nation is like its god. The figure is continued in the words that follow. There comes from the north (from the land of the Chaldees, as in chap. i. 1), not "destruction," but a *gadfly* that shall sting the heifer into the madness of agony. So, in Isa. vii. 18, the "fly" of Egypt and the "bee" of Assyria are invited to work evil on Judah. The words find a striking parallel in the Greek legend of Io (probably to be identified with the Egyptian Isis) transformed into a heifer, and her gadfly tormentor, this also connected with the Apis or Mnevis deities of Egypt (Æschyl. *Prom.* v. 569). The word for "destruction" is not found elsewhere, but the etymology suggests the idea of "pinching" or "stinging," and the meaning "gadfly" is accepted by many recent scholars.

(21) **Her hired men are in the midst of her like fatted bullocks.**—Literally, *bullocks of the stall.* The prophet harps, as it were, on the same image. The mercenaries—Ionians, Carians, and others —in the army of Pharaoh-Hophra, who had their camp at Bubastis (Herod. ii. 152, 163), should be like a drove of terrified cattle, fed to the full, driven to the slaughter-house.

(22) **The voice thereof shall go like a serpent.** —Better, *her voice*—*i.e.*, the voice of Egypt. In early prophecies Egypt had been compared to a "dragon" or "serpent" (Isa. xxvii. 1, li. 9; Ps. lxxiv. 13). Here the serpent is represented as hissing in its rage and terror in the forest against which the enemies are advancing. The sign then gives way to the thing signified, and the latter clause of the verse brings before us the hosts of the Chaldæan allies, barbarous tribes like the Scythians, Massagetæ, and Sacæ, armed with axes instead of swords or spears (Herod. i. 275, iv. 5). They come, but it is to cut down the trees of the forest, *i.e.*, the symbols of the power of Egypt, and there is no power to resist them (Isa. x. 33). The forest is so dense that the trees cannot be counted, but the fellers of the trees are as numerous, and the forest is destined to destruction at the hands of "the people of the north."

(25) **The multitude of No.**—More accurately, *I will punish Amon No.* The first word is the Egyptian Ammon or Hammon, but is probably used also, with a natural paronomasia on the name of the city, in its Hebrew sense of "multitude." "No" here, and as No Amon in Nah. iii. 8, stands for Thebes, the capital of Upper Egypt. The name appears in the form NIA in Assyrian inscriptions. Compare also Ezek. xxx. 14—16.

(26) **Afterward it shall be inhabited, as in the days . . .**—As in the earlier utterance of Isaiah (xix. 21—25) and the contemporary prophecies of Ezekiel (xxix. 11—16) there is a gleam of hope at the end of the vision of judgment. Egypt was to revive, though not again to take its place among the conquerors and tyrants of the world. (Comp. chaps. xlviii. 47, xlix. 39.)

(27, 28) **Fear not thou, O my servant Jacob . . .** —The words that follow are found also in chap. xxx. 10, 11, and have been commented on there, and were either inserted here by the prophet himself, or by some later editor of his writings, as an appropriate conclusion, contrasting the care of Jehovah for His people with the sentence upon the power in which they were trusting for protection. Why should they insist, as in chap. xliii. 7, on placing themselves in a position which would involve them in the destruction which the prophet thus foretells? The words, it may be noticed, are a manifest echo of the words of Isaiah (xli. 13, xliii. 5). Such a consolation was, we may well believe, needed by the people when they saw the armies of Nebuchadnezzar laying waste the country in whose protection they had trusted, and where they had hoped to find a home. Better things, they are told, were in store for them, even a return to the land of their fathers.

CHAPTER XLVII.—(1) The word of
the LORD that came to Jeremiah the
prophet against the Philistines, before
that Pharaoh smote [1] Gaza.
(2) Thus saith the LORD;
Behold, [a] waters rise up out of the
north, and shall be an overflowing flood,
and shall overflow the land, and [2] all
that is therein; the city, and them that
dwell therein: then the men shall cry,
and all the inhabitants of the land shall
howl. (3) At the noise of the stamping
of the hoofs of his strong *horses*, at the
rushing of his chariots, *and at* the
rumbling of his wheels, the fathers shall
not look back to *their* children for feeble-
ness of hands; (4) because of the day
that cometh to spoil all the Philistines,
and to cut off from Tyrus and Zidon
every helper that remaineth: for the
LORD will spoil the Philistines, the
remnant of [3] the country of Caphtor.
(5) Baldness is come upon Gaza; Ash-
kelon is cut off *with* the remnant of
their valley: how long wilt thou cut
thyself? (6) O thou sword of the LORD,
how long *will it be* ere thou be quiet?
[4] put up thyself into thy scabbard, rest,
and be still. (7) [5] How can it be quiet,
seeing the LORD hath given it a charge
against Ashkelon, and against the sea
shore? there hath he appointed it.

CHAPTER XLVIII. — (1) Against
Moab thus saith the LORD of hosts, the
God of Israel;
Woe unto Nebo! for it is spoiled:
Kiriathaim is confounded *and* taken:

B. C. cir. 600.

1 Heb., *Azzah.*

a Isa. 8. 7

2 Heb., *the fulness thereof.*

3 Heb., *the isle.*

4 Heb., *gather thyself.*

5 Heb., *How canst thou?*

XLVII.

(1) **Against the Philistines.**—Here also we have, as in the preceding chapter, a message connected with chap. xxv. 20. The Gaza of this verse is the Azzah of that, and the date is fixed at a time prior to Necho's attack on that city. Writers who, like Hitzig, identify the Cadytis of Herod. ii. 159, iii. 5, with Gaza, suppose his attack to have been made on his return from his victory at Carchemish. The date of the prophecy is thus fixed in the interval between the two events. Ezek. xxv. 15 should be compared as a contemporary and parallel prediction.

(2) **Behold, waters rise up out of the north.**—The reference to the north indicates that the invasion which the prophet contemplates is that of Nebuchadnezzar, not of Pharaoh-necho. For the metaphor of the overflowing river see chap. xlvi. 7; Isa. viii. 7. For "the land and all that is therein" read, as in the margin, "the land and the fulness thereof."

(3) **The fathers shall not look back to their children.**—The selfishness of panic was to reach its highest point, and to crush out the instincts of natural affection. Even fathers would be content to save themselves, regardless of their children's lives.

(4) **To cut off from Tyrus and Zidon.**—The two Phœnician cities are coupled with Philistia. Both, as occupying the sea-board of Palestine, were to suffer from Nebuchadnezzar's invasion. Ps. lxxxiii. 7 indicates that they were not unfrequently in alliance. In the "helper that remaineth" we have probably a reference to the foreign mercenaries, especially the Philistines, employed by the two great commercial cities. "Caphtor" has been identified with Crete, Cyprus, Caria, Cappadocia, and the delta of the Nile. On the latter view the name is held to be connected with *Coptic.* Amos ix. 7 points to a migration of the people known as Philistines from that region, and there is accordingly a touch of scorn in the way in which Jeremiah speaks of them as the mere "remnant of Caphtor." In agreement with the first view we find among David's mercenaries the Cherethim and Pelethim (2 Sam. viii. 18), the two names being probably modifications of Cretans and Philistines. The ethnological table of Gen. x. 14 connects both the Philistines and the Caphtorim with Mizraim or Egypt, and is, so far as it goes, in favour of the Egyptian identification.

(5) **Baldness is come upon Gaza.**—The baldness is the outward sign of extremest mourning (chap. xlviii. 37; Isa. xv. 2, 3), perhaps, also, of extremest desolation (Isa. vii. 20).

Ashkelon is cut off . . .—Better, perhaps, *Ashkelon is speechless.* The LXX. apparently followed a different text, and gives "the remnant of the Anakim" instead of "the remnant of their valley." Hitzig adopts this rendering, and connects it with the known fact that a remnant of the old gigantic non-Semitic race had taken refuge among the Philistines (1 Sam. xvii. 4; 2 Sam. xxi. 22; 1 Chron. xx. 5—8) after they had been driven from Hebron (Josh. xiv. 12—15, xv. 13, 14). Others, without adopting the LXX. reading, interpret the word rendered "their valley" as meaning, as in Isa. xxxiii. 19, those that speak an unintelligible language, barbarians (*Amakim*), and suppose this form to have passed in the LXX. into the more familiar form of Anakim. The English version, however, is accepted by many critics, and may refer to Ashkelon and Gaza as the "remnant," the last resource of the valley (*Emek*) or low-country of the Philistines, more commonly known as the *Shephelah.*

How long wilt thou cut thyself?—The words point to a ritual of supplication, like that of the priests of Baal in 1 Kings xviii. 28, as prevailing among the Philistines.

(6) **O thou sword of the Lord . . .**—This is the question and entreaty of the Philistines, "When will there be an end of war?" And the prophet has but one answer: the sword must do its work till it has done what Jehovah had appointed it to do.

(7) **Against the sea shore.**—In the "sea shore," as in Ezek. xxv. 16, we have the term specially appropriate to the territory of the Philistines.

XLVIII.

(1) **Against Moab thus saith the Lord of hosts . . .**—Better, with a different punctuation, *Concerning Moab* (this being the title of the section), *Thus saith the Lord of hosts.* In the long prophecy that follows Jeremiah in part follows in the wake of "the

[1] Misgab is confounded and dismayed.
(2) *There shall be* no more praise of Moab:
in Heshbon they have devised evil against
it; come, and let us cut it off from *being*
a nation. Also thou shalt [2] be cut down,
O Madmen; the sword shall [3] pursue
thee. (3) A voice of crying *shall be* from
Horonaim, spoiling and great destruc-
tion. (4) Moab is destroyed; her little
ones have caused a cry to be heard.
(5) For in the going up of Luhith [4] [a] con-
tinual weeping shall go up; for in the
going down of Horonaim the enemies
have heard a cry of destruction.
(6) Flee, save your lives, and be like
[5] the [b] heath in the wilderness. (7) For
because thou hast trusted in thy works
and in thy treasures, thou shalt also be
taken: and Chemosh shall go forth into
captivity *with* his [c] priests and his princes
together. (8) And the spoiler shall come
upon every city, and no city shall escape:

1 Or, *the high place.*
2 Or, *be brought to silence.*
3 Heb., *go after thee.*
4 Heb., *weeping with weeping.*
a Isa. 15. 5.
5 Or, *a naked tree.*
b ch. 17. 6.
c ch. 49. 3.

---

burden of Moab" in Isa. xv., xvi., entering even more fully into geographical details. (See Notes there.) The relations between Moab and Israel had for a long period been more or less uneasy. The former had been tributary to the latter under Ahab, but on his death Mesha revolted, and a war ensued, which ended in the defeat of the Moabites by the allied forces of Israel, Judah, and Edom (2 Kings iii.). They repeated their attack, however (2 Kings xiii. 20), and appear to have occupied the territory of the Trans-jordanic tribes on their deportation by Tiglath-pileser. Of the three places named, Nebo, memorable as the summit of Pisgah, from which Moses looked upon the land of promise, and forming part of the range of the mountains of Abarim (Deut. xxxii. 49, xxxiv. 1), has been identified conjecturally with *Djebel-el-Attarus*, or *Djebel-el-Jel'ad*. Hitzig derives the name from the Sanscrit *Nabho* (=the cloud-heaven). Kiriathaim (=the double city) is named in Gen. xiv. 5 and Num. xxxii. 37, in the latter passage in conjunction with Elealeh, Heshbon, and Nebo. Jerome places it at a distance of ten miles west of Medaba, as one of the cities rebuilt by the Reubenites, but it has not been identified. Misgab, the "high fort" or "citadel" of Isa. xxv. 12, has shared the same fate, but has been referred by some writers to Kir-Moab, or Kir-heres, as the chief fortified city of the country (see verses 31, 36; Isa. xv. 1, xvi. 7). The article which is prefixed to it in the Hebrew has led Fürst (Lexicon) to take it in a wider sense, as meaning the plateau or highland country of Moab generally.

(2) **There shall be no more praise of Moab.**—The self-glorifying boasts of Moab (of which the Moabite Inscription discovered at Dibân in 1868 is a conspicuous instance, see Ginsburg's *Moabite Stone* and *Records of the Past*, xi. p. 163) seem to have been almost proverbial (verse 29; Isa. xvi. 6). Heshbon (the city is perhaps chosen on account of the similarity of sound with the word for "devise") was on the Ammonite or northern frontier of Moab (chap. xlix. 3), and is represented therefore as the scene of the plans and hopes of the invading Chaldæans. The site of Madmen is unknown, but the cognate form Madmenah is translated "dunghill" in Isa. xxv. 10, and may have been chosen by each prophet on account of its ignominious meaning. The name appears as belonging to a town in Benjamin (Isa. x. 31) and in Judah (Josh. xv. 31). Here again there is an obvious assonance or paronomasia, the verb "thou shalt be cut down," or better, *thou shalt be brought to silence*, reproducing the chief consonants of the noun. The LXX., Vulgate, and Syriac, indeed, take the words with this meaning, "In silence thou shalt be made silent," but are probably wrong in doing so. If we take the word in somewhat of the same sense as in Isaiah, the words may point to the place being filled with the mouldering carcases of the silent dead.

(3) **Horonaim**—literally, *the two caverns*, or the two Horons—may imply, like other dual names of towns, that there was an upper and a lower city. It is mentioned in Isa. xv. 5, but has not been identified.

(4) **Her little ones.**—The Hebrew adjective is the same as the Zoar, the little one, of Gen. xix. 20, and that city may probably have been, as in Isa. xv. 5, in the prophet's mind. In any case the "little ones" are cities, and not children.

(5) **In the going up of Luhith.**—Here again we have an echo from Isa. xv. 5. Jerome (*Onomast. s.v. Luith*) describes it as between Zoar and Areopolis (=Rabbath-Moab). The ascent was probably to a local sanctuary. A various reading, *Laboth*, followed by the LXX., gives the meaning "the ascent of planks," as though it were a wooden staircase. Alike in that and in the descent from Horonaim (possibly the fugitives who came down from the heights of the one city are represented as going up with wailing to the other) the enemies of Moab would hear the cry that proclaimed its downfall.

(6) **Be like the heath in the wilderness.**—Here, as in chap. xvii. 6, the stunted solitary shrub in the desert is taken as the type of desolation. The LXX., which adopts the meaning in xvii. 6, here strangely enough gives "as a wild ass in the wilderness." Ps. xi. 1 gives us an example of a like comparison. Here probably there is, as before, a paronomasia on the name of the Moabite city Aroer, which closely resembles the Hebrew word for "heath." In thus finding an ominous significance in the names of cities, Jeremiah follows in the wake of Mic. i.

(7) **Chemosh shall go forth into captivity.**—The name appears as that of the national deity of Moab in Num. xxi. 29, as worshipped also by the Ammonites in Judg. xi. 24. Solomon introduced and Josiah abolished his worship at Jerusalem (1 Kings xi. 7; 2 Kings xxiii. 13). He is identified by Jerome (*Comm.* on Isa. xv. 2) with the Baal-peor of Num. xxv. 3. The name is prominent in the Moabite Inscription as that of the national deity, who subdues the people of his rival, Jehovah. The captivity of the idol implies, of course, that of the people. The "works" in which Moab is said to have trusted are represented in the LXX. and Vulgate as "fortresses," but the word is not used in this sense elsewhere, and it is more probable that the prophet represents Moab as relying on its past achievements and deeds of prowess. The last words of the verse are an echo of Amos i. 15.

(8) **The valley also shall perish . . .**—The cities of "the plain" are enumerated in verses 21—24. They belonged to the Arabah, the sunken valley of the

the valley also shall perish, and the
plain shall be destroyed, as the LORD
hath spoken. (9) Give wings unto Moab,
that it may flee and get away: for the
cities thereof shall be desolate, without
any to dwell therein. (10) Cursed *be* he
that doeth the work of the LORD [1] deceit-
fully, and cursed *be* he that keepeth back
his sword from blood.
(11) Moab hath been at ease from his
youth, and he hath settled on his lees,
and hath not been emptied from vessel
to vessel, neither hath he gone into
captivity: therefore his taste [2] remained
in him, and his scent is not changed.
(12) Therefore, behold, the days come,
saith the LORD, that I will send unto
him wanderers, that shall cause him to
wander, and shall empty his vessels, and
break their bottles. (13) And Moab shall
be ashamed of Chemosh, as the house
of Israel was ashamed of [a] Beth-el their
confidence.
(14) How say ye, We *are* mighty and
strong men for the war? (15) Moab is
spoiled, and gone up *out of* her cities,
and [3] his chosen young men are gone
down to the slaughter, saith the King,
whose name *is* the LORD of hosts.
(16) The calamity of Moab *is* near to
come, and his affliction hasteth fast.
(17) All ye that are about him, bemoan
him; and all ye that know his name,
say, How is the strong staff broken, *and*
the beautiful rod!
(18) Thou daughter that dost inhabit
Dibon, come down from *thy* glory, and
sit in thirst; for the spoiler of Moab
shall come upon thee, *and* he shall de-
stroy thy strongholds. (19) O [4] inhabitant
of Aroer, stand by the way, and espy;
ask him that fleeth, and her that

[1] Or, *negligently.*

[2] Heb., *stood.*

[a] 1 Kings 12. 29.

[3] Heb., *the choice of.*

[4] Heb., *inhabitress.*

Jordan, the "plains of Moab" of Num. xxii. 1; Deut. iii. 10, iv. 43. The "valley" here is not connected with anything that helps us to identify it, but it may have been that of the Arnon, or the words may be used generically for "every valley" and "every plain."

(9) **Give wings unto Moab . . .**—"No other prayer," the prophet seems to say, in grave, stern irony, "is left but this. Resistance is hopeless. There is nothing left but to wish for the wings of a bird that safety may be found in flight." (Comp. Ps. lv. 6.)

(10) **Cursed be he . . .**—To the prophet the destruction of the tyrannous haughtiness was a righteous retribution in which he saw the work of Jehovah, and he could not wish that it should be done otherwise than effectually. The thought rests on the belief in the Divine government that works through war as well as through pestilence and famine (chaps. xxv. 31, xlvi. 10). (Comp. like utterances in Judg. v. 23; 1 Sam. xv. 3, 18; 1 Kings xx. 42.) Even Christian nations fighting against slave-traders or pirates might legitimately echo the same prayer. It has been used, with less justification, in the religious wars of our own and other countries.

(11) **He hath settled on his lees.**—The image, found also in Zeph. i. 12, is drawn from the practice of pouring wine from one vessel into another to clarify it and improve its flavour. Wine not so treated retained its first crude bitterness. So, the prophet says, it is with nations. It is not good for them to remain too long in a prosperity which does but strengthen their natural arrogance. There is a wholesome discipline in defeat, even in exile. In verse 47 we have the hope of the prophet that the discipline will do its work. The "vessels" and "bottles" of verse 12 are, of course, the cities and villages of Moab. (Comp. the imagery of chap. xix. 10.)

(13) **Beth-el their confidence.**—The name of the sanctuary stands for the golden calf that was worshipped there as the symbol of Jehovah (1 Kings xii. 29; Amos vii. 10). That worship had been put to shame in the captivity of the Ten Tribes. So also should it be with the Chemosh-worship of Moab.

(14—17) **How say ye . . .**—In the boast that follows we trace the characteristic pride of Moab. The prophet points to the fact that the pride is brought low. She, too, is subject, like other nations, to invasion and defeat. He summons her people to wail for her overthrow. The "staff" is the sceptre of the ruler, as in Ps. cx. 2. The "rod" is the stick with which a man walks (Gen. xxxii. 10; Exod. xii. 11), but which may also be used as a weapon. The epithet "beautiful" perhaps points to the splendour of a royal staff or wand of ivory and gold.

(18) **Thou daughter that dost inhabit Dibon.**—Dibon is mentioned among the cities of Moab in Num. xxi. 30; Isa. xv. 2, and as rebuilt by the Gadites in Num. xxxiii. 45. It is prominent in the Moabite Stone inscription as a royal city. In the distribution of the conquered territory it fell to the lot of Reuben (Josh. xiii. 7, 9), but must afterwards have been retaken by Moab. The "strongholds" indicate a fortress. In Isa. xv. 9 it appears under the form of Dimon, and is there described as abounding in water, the site being probably on the north bank of the Arnon. This last feature gives point to the words of the prophet here. Its waters will not save its inhabitants from the thirst which falls on those who are dragged as captives into exile.

(19) **O inhabitant of Aroer.**—There seems to have been two cities of this name: one which had belonged first to the territory of Sihon, then to Reuben, then to Moab, on the north side of the Arnon (Deut. ii. 36, iii. 12, iv. 48; Josh. xii. 2); another in the Ammonite territory belonging to Gad, near Rabbath-Ammon, in the valley of the Jabbok (Num. xxxii. 34; Josh. xiii. 25; Judges xi. 33). Both are probably comprised under the "cities of Aroer" in Isa. xvii. 2. The name exists in the modern *Arair*. As lying on the frontier, the inhabitants of the Northern Aroer are represented as seeing the fugitives, male and female, from Dibon, and asking what had happened to drive them from their city. Milton's lines (*Par. Lost*, I. 407) may be quoted as illustrating the topography:

> "From Aroer to Nebo, and the wild
> Of Southmost Abarim; in Hesebon
> And Horonaim, Seon's realm . . ."

escapeth, *and* say, What is done?
(20)Moab is confounded; for it is broken
down: [a]howl and cry; tell ye it in
Arnon, that Moab is spoiled, (21) and
judgment is come upon the plain country;
upon Holon, and upon Jahazah, and
upon Mephaath, (22) and upon Dibon, and
upon Nebo, and upon Beth-diblathaim,
(23) and upon Kiriathaim, and upon
Beth-gamul, and upon Beth-meon, (24) and
upon Kerioth, and upon Bozrah, and
upon all the cities of the land of Moab,
far or near. (25) The horn of Moab is
cut off, and his arm is broken, saith the
LORD.
(26) Make ye him drunken: for he
magnified *himself* against the LORD:
Moab also shall wallow in his vomit, and
he also shall be in derision. (27) For was
not Israel a derision unto thee? was he
found among thieves? for since thou
spakest of him, thou [1] skippedst for joy.

a Isa. 16. 7.

1 Or, *movedst thyself.*

---

(20) **Tell ye it in Arnon.**—The name, which means a rushing stream, belonged to the chief river of Moab, now the *Mugab*, which rises in the Arabian mountains and flows into the Dead Sea. It appears in the war-song quoted, in Num. xxi. 14, from the "Book of the Wars of the Lord," and the "high places" on either side its course were crowned with the castles of the lords of Moab (Num. xxi. 28). The verse contains the answer to the question that precedes it—"This is what has come to pass, Moab is confounded and spoiled." For the "plain country" see Note on verse 8.

(21) **And judgment is come upon the plain country . . .**—We enter here upon a list of less known names, of which Jahaz, Beth-diblathaim, Beth-Baal-meon are found on the Moabite Stone inscription (*Records of the Past*, xi. 165—168). Holon does not appear elsewhere. Jahazah (under the form Jahaz) appears in Num. xxi. 23; Deut. ii. 32; Judges xi. 20, as the scene of a famous battle between Sihon and the Israelites, and in Isa. xv. 4 in connexion with Heshbon and Elealeh. Mephaath was assigned to the Reubenites (Josh. xiii. 18), and afterwards to the Levites (Josh. xxi. 37; 1 Chron. vi. 79), but it had clearly fallen afterwards into the hands of the Moabites. Like the other cities named, it was in the *Mishor*, or "plain," on the north of the Arnon.

(22) **Beth-diblathaim.**—The name signifies "the house of the double cake of figs," and was, probably, applied to one of the more fertile districts of the Moabite country. In Num. xxxiii. 46, 47, the name Almon-diblathaim appears as one of the stations of the Israelites between Dibon and "the mountains of Abarim before Nebo," and the conjunction of the names implies its identity with the place here mentioned. For Dibon and Nebo, see Notes on verses 1, 18.

(23) **Kiriathaim.**—See verse 1.

Beth-gamul.—The place is not named in the earlier lists of Num. xxxii. 34—38 and Josh. xiii. 16—20. The name (=house of the camel) has a parallel in Gamala, and appears in the modern *Um-el-Jemal*, south of Buzrah, in the Haûran. This, however, lies out of the range of the *Mishor*, or "plain country," to which the cities here enumerated belonged.

Beth-meon.—The name appears in its full form as Beth-baal-meon in Josh. xiii. 17, as Baal-meon in Num. xxxii. 38; 1 Chron. v. 8; Ezek. xxv. 8. The name *Meon* (=citadel of heaven) survives in the modern *Mi'un*. Its combination with Baal makes it probable that it was famous as a sanctuary where the Moabite Baal was worshipped.

(24) **Kerioth.**—The name, plural in form (= cities), has been identified by Mr. Porter (*Five Years, &c.*, ii. 191—198) with *Kureiyeh*, a ruined town lying not far from *Buzrah*, identified with the Bozrah that is coupled with it here, in the Haûran. These are, however, some sixty miles north of Heshbon, and this has been thought adverse to the identification. On the other hand, the expression "far and near" indicates that Jeremiah takes in the more distant cities to which the power of Moab may have extended. From the mention of "the palaces of Kirioth" in Amos ii. 2, it appears to have been a place of importance. Mr. Grove (art. *Kerioth* in Smith's *Dict. Bible*) suggests its possible identity with *Kureiyat*, not far from Dibon and Beth-meon.

Bozrah.—The name (= fortification) is familiar as belonging to the more famous city of Edom (chap. xlix. 13). The Moabite town, identified as above with the *Buzrah* of the Haûran, appears in 1 Macc. v. 26 as Bosora, one of the towns of Galaad or Gilead, and in Roman history as Bostra, the birthplace of the Emperor Philip, known as the Arabian.

(25) **The horn of Moab.**—The horn of animals was naturally the symbol of their strength, and it was as natural that the symbolism should be extended to men and nations. (Comp. 1 Sam. ii. 1; Ps. xcii. 10; Lam. ii. 3; Dan. vii. 7, 8; Luke i. 69.) The figure of the broken arm, powerless to grasp sword or sceptre, meets us again in Ezek. xxx. 21.

(26) **Make ye him drunken . . .**—The image is suggested by the wine-cup of Jehovah's fury in chap. xxv. 15, and was familiar in the symbolic language of the prophets (Isa. li. 17; Job xxi. 20; Ezek. xxiii. 32; Rev. xiv. 10). The words that follow paint the image in its strongest colours. As men looked with scorn on the drunkard wallowing in his shame, so should they look on Moab, that had been so boastful in its pride, when it was brought low.

(27) **Was not Israel a derision unto thee?**—The "derision" had been shown at an earlier stage in the history of Judah (Zeph. ii. 8; comp. Ezek. xxv. 6), but was, we may well believe, reproduced when the Moabites heard of the disasters that fell on Israel in the days of Josiah and his successors. The question that follows "Was he found among thieves?" implies an answer in the negative. Israel had not been among the lawless, aggressive nations, the robbers of the earth. Compare 2 Sam. iii. 33, where the question, "Died Abner as a fool dieth?" implies that he had not deserved his death as guilty of any crime. By some critics, however, the Hebrew interrogative is taken as meaning "when," and so involving the admission that Israel had been guilty of unjust invasion, and been led to that guilt by her alliance with the robber nations of the heathen.

Thou skippedst for joy.—The gesture described, like the wagging of the head of chap. xviii. 16, or the shrugging of the shoulders, is one of triumphant malice. The symbolism of Oriental gesture is, it may be noted, specially rich in expressions of this form of evil. (Comp. Isa. lvii. 4; Ps. xxii. 7.)

(28) O ye that dwell in Moab, leave the
cities, and dwell in the rock, and be like
the dove *that* maketh her nest in the
sides of the hole's mouth. (29) We have
heard the [a] pride of Moab, (he is exceed-
ing proud) his loftiness, and his arro-
gancy, and his pride, and the haughtiness
of his heart. (30) I know his wrath, saith
the LORD; but *it shall* not *be* so; [1] his
lies shall not so effect *it*.
(31) Therefore will I howl for Moab,
and I will cry out for all Moab; *mine
heart* shall mourn for the men of Kir-
heres. (32) O vine of Sibmah, I will
weep for thee with the weeping of Jazer:
thy plants are gone over the sea,
they reach *even* to the sea of Jazer:
the spoiler is fallen upon thy summer
fruits and upon thy vintage. (33) And
[b] joy and gladness is taken from the
plentiful field, and from the land of
Moab; and I have caused wine to fail
from the winepresses: none shall tread
with shouting; *their* shouting *shall be*
no shouting. (34) From the cry of Hesh-
bon *even* unto Elealeh, *and even* unto
Jahaz, have they uttered their voice,
[c] from Zoar *even* unto Horonaim, *as* an
heifer of three years old: for the waters
also of Nimrim shall be [2] desolate.

a Isa. 16. 6, &c.

1 Or, *those on whom he stayeth* (Heb., *his bars*) *do not right.*

b Isa. 16. 10.

c Isa. 15. 5, 6.

2 Heb., *desolations.*

---

(28) **O ye that dwell in Moab . . .**—The general thought is the same as in verses 6 and 9, but is more vivid as being more specific. The Moabites are to leave their cities and take refuge in the caves, always in Palestine the asylum of fugitives (1 Sam. xiii. 6; 2 Sam. xvii. 9), as the wild dove flies to "the clefts of the rock" (Song Sol. ii. 14).

(29) **We have heard the pride of Moab . . .**—It will be seen that here and in the next verse the very words of Isaiah (xvi. 6) are reproduced. The prophet seems to find a pleasure in going back to the old words as showing that the fault of which he spoke was inveterate, and had shown itself incurable. It is, however, a free reproduction, and Jeremiah, instead of making the whole utterance that of the Jews, inserts the words, "I know his wrath, saith the Lord," which come as an oracle from God, affirming the judgment of the people.

(30) **His lies shall not so effect it.**—The Hebrew for "lies" has also, as in the margin, the meaning of "bars" or "staves" or "branches" as the symbol of defence (Hos. xi. 6), but the version in the text is preferable. The emphasis of the original lies in the iteration. "Not so," the sentence of frustration, is written alike on the wrath which leads to passionate outrage, and on the lies in which it seeks to find safety.

(31) **Therefore will I howl for Moab.**—The changes of person are remarkable. The "I" that speaks is neither Jehovah nor the prophet, but the unnamed mourner, who in the next clause appears in the third person ("she shall mourn," the English "mine heart" having no equivalent in the Hebrew) as the representative of those who mourn for Moab. In verse 33, "I have caused wine to fail" appears as the utterance of Jehovah. In Isa. xvi. 7, of which the whole passage is a free reproduction, Moab is named as the mourner. Possibly, however, Jeremiah in his sympathy may speak here in his own person.

For the men of Kir-heres.—The name appears in Isa. xvi. 7 as Kirhareseth, and is probably identical with the "Kir of Moab" of Isa. xv. 1. The place was obviously an important stronghold. The Targum on Isaiah and Jeremiah renders it by *Crac*, and this has led to its being identified with the modern *Kerak*, occupying a strong position on one of the Moabite mountains to the south-east of the Dead Sea. The name, which signifies "City of the Sun," may indicate its connection with that form of nature-worship.

(32) **O vine of Sibmah.**—Here again we have an echo of Isa. xvi. 9. Sibmah appears in Josh. xiii. 19 as assigned to the Reubenites, in the region east of Jordan. After that date it does not appear again till we find it in these prophetic notices. Jerome (*Comm. in Isa.* chap. v.) names it as a strong city about half a mile from Heshbon, but its site has not been identified by modern travellers. It would appear from these notices to have been famous for vineyards that extended to Jazer. The city so named, identified with the modern *Es Szir*, had belonged to the Amorites (Num. xxi. 32, there spelt *Jaazer*), and lay between Heshbon and Bashan, about fifteen miles north of the former city. It passed afterwards into the possession of the Gadites (Josh. xiii. 25; 2 Sam. xxiv. 5), and was evidently, when the two prophets wrote, in that of the Moabites. The phrase "weeping of Jazer" implies that it was to share in the desolation of Sibmah. The "sea of Jazer" (if the text is right, the LXX. giving "city") must have been some inland lake or pond, which has not since been identified. The "sea" of the parallel passage of Isa. xvi. 8 is commonly interpreted of the Dead Sea. The "summer fruits" were the figs and pomegranates which were commonly cultivated together with the vine.

(33) **None shall tread with shouting.**—The words bring before us the vintage-song of those who trod out the grapes (chap. xxv. 30; Isa. xvi. 10). Of this the prophet says, in a form which reminds us of the δῶρα ἄδωρα ("gifts that are no gifts") of Soph. Aias. 674, that it shall be "no shouting," *i.e.*, that it shall be turned to wailing and lamentation, or the shout and tumult of battle shall have taken its place.

(34) **From the cry of Heshbon . . .**—Elealeh (now *El-Al*) and Heshbon (now *Hesbân*) were about two miles apart. The panic-cry of the one city was echoed in the other; it reached even to Jahaz (see Note on verse 21), to the south-west of Heshbon.

From Zoar even unto Horonaim . . .—Both names represent the south district of Moab. In the "heifer of three years old" (see Isa. xv. 5) many critics find simply a proper name, "the third Eglath," and conjecture that it was either one of three towns having the same name, or part of a *tripolis* or tripartite city, the other two members of which were Zoar and Horonaim. Nothing is known, however, of any town so constituted, and the epithet of the "third-year heifer," *i.e.*, a heifer not brought under the yoke, would be a suitable name enough for either Zoar or Horonaim, as a virgin fortress, as yet untaken by the foe. (Comp. Hos. iv. 16, x. 11.)

(35) Moreover I will cause to cease in
Moab, saith the LORD, him that offereth
in the high places, and him that burneth
incense to his gods. (36) Therefore mine
heart shall sound for Moab like pipes,
and mine heart shall sound like pipes
for the men of Kir-heres: because the
riches *that* he hath gotten are perished.
(37) For [a] every head *shall be* bald, and
every beard [1] clipped: upon all the hands
shall be cuttings, and upon the loins
sackcloth. (38) *There shall be* lamenta-
tion generally upon all the housetops of
Moab, and in the streets thereof: for I
have broken Moab like a vessel wherein
is no pleasure, saith the LORD. (39) They
shall howl, *saying,* How is it broken
down! how hath Moab turned the [2] back
with shame! so shall Moab be a derision
and a dismaying to all them about him.
(40) For thus saith the LORD; Behold,
he shall fly as an eagle, and shall spread
his wings over Moab. (41) [3] Kerioth is
taken, and the strong holds are sur-
prised, and the mighty men's hearts in
Moab at that day shall be as the heart
of a woman in her pangs. (42) And
Moab shall be destroyed from *being* a
people, because he hath magnified *him-
self* against the LORD. (43) [b] Fear, and
the pit, and the snare, *shall be* upon
thee, O inhabitant of Moab, saith the
LORD. (44) He that fleeth from the fear
shall fall into the pit; and he that
getteth up out of the pit shall be taken
in the snare: for I will bring upon it,
even upon Moab, the year of their
visitation, saith the LORD. (45) They
that fled stood under the shadow of
Heshbon because of the force: but [c] a
fire shall come forth out of Heshbon,
and a flame from the midst of Sihon,
and shall devour the corner of Moab,
and the crown of the head of the

a Isa. 15. 2. 3.

1 Heb., *diminished.*

2 Heb., *neck.*

3 Or, *The cities.*

b Isa. 24. 17, 18.

c Num. 21. 28.

The waters also of Nimrim shall be desolate.—Recent travellers, Seetzen and De Saulcy, have found a brook Nimrah, with a mass of ruins near it, near the southern extremity of the Dead Sea. The Nimrah of Num. xxxii. 3, 36; Josh. xiv. 27, is probably too far to the north. Tristram (*Land of Israel,* p. 54) identifies it with the *Wady-Shaib* near the fords of the Jordan, and possibly with the Bethabara of John i. 28.

(35) **I will cause to cease in Moab . . .**—The words indicate that the pilgrimages to the sanctuary of Chemosh, on the mountains of Moab, were a prominent feature in the nation's life. One result of the Chaldæan conquest would be that they should be brought to an end.

(36) **Mine heart shall sound for Moab like pipes . . .**—The words reproduce Isa. xvi. 11. His heart becomes, as it were, musical in its groans and sighs. He cannot look on the panic-stricken and mourning city without sharing in its misery. In the baldness (chaps. vii. 29, xvi. 6), the clipped beard, the cuttings (chaps. xvi. 6, xli. 5), the sackcloth (chaps. iv. 8, vi. 26; Joel i. 8) we have the wonted signs of mourning for the dead. The "pipe" is chosen rather than the harp, as in Isa. xvi. 11, because it had come to be the recognised music for funerals (so in Matt. ix. 23).

(38) **Upon all the housetops of Moab.**—The flat roof of Eastern houses was the natural gathering-place of men in a time of panic and distress, as it was, in a time of peace, for prayer or meditation, or even for festive meetings. So in Isa. xxii. 1, the city described as "the valley of vision" (Samaria or Jerusalem) is represented as "gone up to the housetops."

I have broken Moab like a vessel wherein is no pleasure.—The image is one with which the prophet had made men familiar by his symbolic act in chap. xix. 10. So Coniah was "a vessel wherein is no pleasure" (chap. xxii. 28).

(39) **They shall howl, saying, How is it broken down!**—Better, taking the words in the Hebrew order, *How is she broken down! How do they howl!* In the word "derision" we have the emphatic iteration of the term that had been pointedly used in verses 26, 27. At this stage the parallelism with Isa. xv., xvi. ceases, and the prediction has a more independent character.

(40) **He shall fly as an eagle . . .**—The image, as in Deut. xxviii. 49; Isa. xlvi. 11; Ezek. xvii. 3, was the natural symbol of a fierce invader, probably, in this case, of Nebuchadnezzar. Here it receives a fresh vividness from the previous comparison of Moab to the dove that had its nest in the clefts of the rock. The verse is reproduced in chap. xlix. 22, in reference to Edom.

(41) **Kerioth.**—(See Note on verse 24.) Here the word is used with the article, and should probably be translated, as in the margin, *the cities,* as painting the wide-spread devastation that was to come on all the fortresses.

As the heart of a woman in her pangs.—See Notes on chap. xxx. 6; Isa. xiii. 8, xxi. 3. The precise phrase, however, occurs only here and in chap. xlix. 22.

(42) **Moab shall be destroyed . . .**—What is predicted is not annihilation (see verse 47), but the loss of national independence. And the cause of this punishment is once more asserted. With Moab, as with other nations, it was her self-exalting pride that called for chastisement.

(43) **Fear, and the pit, and the snare.**—The words are a reproduction of Isa. xxiv. 17, which had probably passed into something like proverbial use. The sequence in each case shows that each word plays a distinct part in the imagery. First there is the terror of the animal pursued by huntsmen, then the pit dug in the earth that it may fall into it (Ps. vii. 15; Prov. xxvi. 27; Eccles. x. 8); then, if it scrambles out of the pit, the snare or trap which finally secures it.

(45) **Because of the force.**—Better, *without strength.* What is meant is that the fugitives of Moab seek shelter in Heshbon, the capital of the Ammonites (chap. xlix. 3), and find no protection there.

[1] tumultuous ones. (46) Woe be unto
thee, O Moab! the people of Chemosh
perisheth: for thy sons are taken [2] cap-
tives, and thy daughters captives. (47) Yet
will I bring again the captivity of
Moab in the latter days, saith the LORD.
Thus far *is* the judgment of Moab.

CHAPTER XLIX.—(1) [3] Concerning
the Ammonites,
Thus saith the LORD;
Hath Israel no sons? hath he no
heir? why *then* doth [4] their king inherit
[a] Gad, and his people dwell in his cities?
(2) Therefore, behold, the days come,
saith the LORD, that I will cause an
alarm of war to be heard in [b] Rabbah of
the Ammonites; and it shall be a desolate
heap, and her daughters shall be burned
with fire: then shall Israel be heir unto
them that were his heirs, saith the
LORD. (3) Howl, O Heshbon, for Ai is
spoiled: cry, ye daughters of Rabbah,
gird you with sackcloth; lament, and
run to and fro by the hedges; for [5] their
king shall go into captivity, *and* his
[c] priests and his princes together.
(4) Wherefore gloriest thou in the valleys,
[6] thy flowing valley, O backsliding
daughter? that trusted in her treasures,

1 Heb., *children of noise.*
2 Heb., *in captivity.*
3 Or, *Against.*
4 Or, *Melcom.*
a Amos i. 13.
b Amos i. 14.
5 Or, *Melcom.*
c ch. 48. 7.
6 Or, *thy valley floweth away.*

A fire shall come forth out of Heshbon . . .—The words are interesting as being a quotation from a fragment of an old poem, probably from the "Book of the Wars of the Lord," which is also to be found in Num. xxi. 28. Heshbon, at the time of the Exodus the capital of the Amorites, is here identified with Sihon as their king. In the prophet's application of the words, the Moabites are represented as taking refuge under the walls of Heshbon, but, instead of finding shelter, fire bursts out from walls and gates. They have come to look on its conflagration. The flames spread far and near. They devour the "corner" as of the beard, the hair on the crown of the head. The symbolism of destruction is the same as in Isa. vii. 20. In the "tumultuous ones" (literally, *children of tumult*) we have the panic-stricken clamorous crowds of the Moabite fugitives. The phrase in the Hebrew is nearly the same as "the children of Seth" in Num. xxiv. 17.

(47) **Yet will I bring again . . .**—This intermingling of the hope of a far-off return is specially characteristic of these later chapters, as in the case of the Ammonites (chap. xlix. 6) and Elam (chap. xlix. 39).

Thus far is the judgment of Moab.—This is very probably originally a note made by editor or transcriber to indicate the close of one section and the beginning of another. A like conclusion meets us in chap. li. 64.

XLIX.

(1) **Concerning the Ammonites.**—The history of this people was, to a great extent, parallel with that of the Moabites. They had been conquered by Sihon, the great Amorite king, and when that monarch was, in his turn, conquered by the Israelites (Num. xxi. 21—31) their territory was assigned to the tribes of Gad and Reuben (Num. xxxii. 34—38). In Judges xi. 12—33 we have the record of an unsuccessful attempt to recover their lost territory, and like attempts appear to have been made by Nahash (1 Sam. xi. 1—11), and Hanun (2 Sam. x. 6—14, xii. 26—31). On the deportation of the Trans-jordanic tribes by Tiglath-pileser (2 Kings xv. 29; 1 Chron. v. 6, 26), they made a more successful effort, and their king Baalis appears as prompting the conspiracy of Ishmael, the son of Nethaniah (chap. xl. 14). The prophecy on which we now enter was probably delivered before that time, in or about the fourth year of Jehoiakim (chap. xxv. 21). Its opening words recall the long-standing territorial controversy. "Had Israel no heir?" Was the land he had occupied so long to pass into the possession of a stranger?

Why then doth their king inherit Gad . . .?—Better, with the margin and all the older versions, *Melcom.* The name, all but identical with the "Malcham" of Zeph. i. 5, and connected with Moloch, was that of the god of the Ammonites, as Chemosh was that of the Moabite deity. He, as his very name implied, was their true king; and the complaint of the prophet is that he inherits Gad, which had been in the possession of Israel.

(2) **Rabbah of the Ammonites.**—More fully, *of the children of Ammon.*—Rabbah, or Rabbath, the "city of waters" (the word signifies "Great," and the city was, as it were, the Megalopolis of Ammon), was the capital, and this was its full and formal title (Deut. iii. 11; 2 Sam. xi. 1, xii. 26). It had been captured by Joab after the siege made memorable by the death of Uriah the Hittite. Jeremiah now predicts its destruction as Amos (i. 14) had done before him. Israel shall then re-enter on its occupation. Its site is now marked by ruins of a stately temple and theatres of the Syrian period (Tristram, *Land of Israel*, p. 540).

(3) **Howl, O Heshbon, for Ai is spoiled.**—Heshbon has appeared in chap. xlviii. 2, 45, as connected with the fortunes of Moab, but it was strictly an Ammonite city. The "Ai" here is obviously not the city near Jericho of Josh. viii. 28, and unless we assume an error in the text ("Ai" for "Ar"=city), we must infer the existence of a Trans-jordanic city of the same name.

Run to and fro by the hedges.—Hedges, in the English sense of the word, have never been common in the East, and the word here denotes either the palings round the sheep-folds, or the walls round the vineyards of the villages that are described as the "daughters of Rabbah." The word is never used for the walls of a city, but appears in Num. xxii. 24, xxxii. 16, 24, 36 in the sense of "sheep-folds."

Their king shall go into captivity.—Better, as before, *Melcom.* As in chap. xlviii. 7, the captivity of the national deity with his priests (the fact that they are named is decisive as to the meaning) involves the captivity of the people.

(4) **In the valleys.**—The word exactly describes the conformation of the Ammonite country, as a high plateau intersected by streams which make their way to the Jordan. For "thy flowing valley" read "thy valley" (this is, of course, the valley in which Rabbah

saying, Who shall come unto me?
(5) Behold, I will bring a fear upon thee,
saith the Lord GOD of hosts, from all
those that be about thee; and ye shall
be driven out every man right forth;
and none shall gather up him that
wandereth. (6) And afterward I will
bring again the captivity of the children
of Ammon, saith the LORD.
(7) Concerning Edom,
Thus saith the LORD of hosts;
[a] *Is* wisdom no more in Teman? is
counsel perished from the prudent? is
their wisdom vanished? (8) Flee ye,
[1] turn back, dwell deep, O inhabitants
of Dedan; for I will bring the calamity
of Esau upon him, the time *that* I will
visit him. (9) If [b] grapegatherers come
to thee, would they not leave *some*
gleaning grapes? if thieves by night,
they will destroy [2] till they have enough.
(10) But I have made Esau bare, I have
uncovered his secret places, and he shall
not be able to hide himself: his seed is
spoiled, and his brethren, and his neigh-
bours, and he *is* not. (11) Leave thy
fatherless children, I will preserve *them*
alive; and let thy widows trust in me.
(12) For thus saith the LORD; Behold,
they whose judgment *was* not to drink
of the cup have assuredly drunken; and
art thou he *that* shall altogether go un-
punished? thou shalt not go unpunished,
but thou shalt surely drink *of it*. (13) For
I have sworn by myself, saith the LORD,
that Bozrah shall become a desolation,

a Obad. 8.

1 Or, *they are turned back.*

b Obad. 5.

2 Heb., *their sufficiency.*

---

was situated) "that floweth with plenty." The words admit, however, of being rendered, "Thy valley floweth away," *i.e.*, is wasted and emptied.

O backsliding daughter.—There is something suggestive in the fact that the prophet applies to Ammon the epithet which he had applied before to the kingdom of the Ten Tribes (chap. iii. 6, 8, 11, 14). Ammon also had the opportunity of worshipping the God of Israel, and had probably, as long as the Israelites were her rulers, adopted that worship wholly or in part, and so she also was an *apostate*. The question which follows, as in chap. xxi. 13, implies that the people of Rabbah looked on their city as impregnable.

(5, 6) **I will bring a fear upon thee . . .**—As in the case of Moab, there is the doom of exile for Ammon also, but the sentence of punishment is tempered with mercy, and there is to be a return from the seemingly hopeless captivity.

(7) **Concerning Edom.**—A short survey of the past history is necessary that we may enter into the force of the prophet's words. On the journey of the Israelites to Canaan the Edomites were left unmolested (Num. xiv. 21; Deut. ii. 4). Conquered by Saul (1 Sam. xiv. 47), and yet more completely by David (2 Sam. viii. 14), they made an unsuccessful attempt to throw off the yoke in the time of Solomon (1 Kings xi. 14—22), but finally revolted with success in that of Joram (2 Kings viii. 20—22; 2 Chron. xxi. 8). Amaziah and Uzziah endeavoured to reassert dominion over them (2 Kings xiv. 7, 22), but under Ahaz they invaded Judah (2 Chron. xxviii. 17), and in the reign of Zedekiah appear as an independent power seeking to ally themselves with that king against their common enemy Nebuchadnezzar (chap. xxvii. 3). Soon, however, they allied themselves with the Chaldæans, and were conspicuous for their triumphant exultation in the destruction of Jerusalem (Ps. cxxxvii. 7; Lam. iv. 21; Ezek. xxxv. 15, xxxvi. 5). Obadiah had prophesied against them, probably shortly before Jeremiah's utterance, and what we find here stands in the same relation to his language as the prophecy against Moab in chap. xlviii. does to Isa. xv., xvi. Possibly, however, as Obad. verse 11 seems to indicate, Obadiah was the later of the two. (See *Introduction* to Obadiah.)

Is wisdom no more in Teman . . .?—The exact locality of Teman has not been determined, but it is always closely connected with Edom, and, as the word means "south," may describe that region of the Edomite country. Its fame for wisdom seems to have been proverbial. So Eliphaz the Temanite appears as the chief speaker among Job's three friends (Job ii. 11, iv. 1). So Obadiah (verse 8) speaks of the "wise men" of Edom. So Solomon's wisdom excelled that of "the children of the East" (1 Kings iv. 30). The form of the questions implies that all three are to be answered in the affirmative.

(8) **O inhabitants of Dedan.**—See Note on chap. xxv. 23. In Ezek. xxv. 13 Dedan appears, as here, in company with Edom and Teman. In Isa. xxi. 13 the "travelling companies of Dedanim" appear as carrying on the traffic of Edom with other countries. The words "dwell deep" are as a warning, bidding them retire as far as possible, so as to escape from the Chaldæan invaders.

(9) **If grapegatherers come to thee . . .**—The words are reproduced in Obad. verse 5. Vine-gatherers leave some bunches for the gleaner; robbers are at last satiated with plunder; but the destroyers of Edom would be insatiable (comp. Isa. xvii. 6). Esau (the name stands for Edom) should be laid bare, and perish utterly. It is significant that there is no promise to Edom that her captivity should be brought back.

(11) **Leave thy fatherless children . . .**—Were the words uttered in the stern irony of one who veils a threat in the form of a promise, as some have thought, or was there even in the case of Edom a mingling of pity for the helpless? The latter view seems truer to the prophet's character (chap. xlviii. 36). If the sentence was passed which left the wives of Edom widows, and their children orphans, yet God had not forgotten that He was the God of the widow and the fatherless.

(12) **Behold, they whose judgment . . .**—The imagery is taken up from chap. xxv. 15. Even those of whom it might have seemed that they were exempted, by God's decree, from drinking of the cup of His wrath, had drunk. Could Esau hope for immunity? The thought is parallel to that of 1 Pet. iv. 17.

(13) **Bozrah.**—This, as in Isa. xxxiv. 6, lxiii. 1, was one of the chief cities of Edom, probably identical with the modern *El-Busaireh*, half-way between Petra and the Dead Sea.

a reproach, a waste, and a curse; and
all the cities thereof shall be perpetual
wastes.
(14) I have heard a [a] rumour from the
LORD, and an ambassador is sent unto
the heathen, *saying*, Gather ye together,
and come against her, and rise up to
the battle. (15) For, lo, I will make thee
small among the heathen, *and* despised
among men. (16) Thy terribleness hath
deceived thee, *and* the pride of thine
heart, O thou that dwellest in the clefts
of the rock, that holdest the height of
the hill: though thou shouldest make
thy [b] nest as high as the eagle, I will
bring thee down from thence, saith the
LORD. (17) Also Edom shall be a desola-
tion: [c] every one that goeth by it shall
be astonished, and shall hiss at all the
plagues thereof. (18) [d] As in the over-
throw of Sodom and Gomorrah and the
neighbour *cities* thereof, saith the LORD,
no man shall abide there, neither shall
a son of man dwell in it.
(19) Behold, he shall come up like a
lion from the swelling of Jordan against
the habitation of the strong: but I will
suddenly make him run away from her:
and who *is* a chosen *man*, *that* I may
appoint over her? for who *is* like me?
and who will [1] [e] appoint me the time?
and who *is* that shepherd that will stand

a Obad. 1.
b Obad. 4.
c ch. 50. 13.
d Gen. 19. 25: ch. 50. 40.
1 Or, *convent me in judgment.*
e Job 41. 10; ch. 50. 44, 45.

---

(14) **I have heard a rumour from the Lord . . .**—The thought is that of Jehovah, as the great King, sending forth His herald or envoy to call the nations to the attack on Edom. (Comp. chap. xlvi. 3, 4.)

(15) **Among the heathen.**—Better here, as no marked contrast with Israel is intended, *among the nations.*

(16) **Thy terribleness hath deceived thee.**—The substantive does not occur elsewhere. Etymologically it may mean "terror of," or "object of terror;" but a cognate word is found in 1 Kings xv. 13; 2 Chron. xv. 16 in the sense of an "idol," probably of the Phallic or Priapus type, and that is probably the meaning. Such an idol is called scornfully the *horror* of Edom, just as the God of Israel was "the fear of Isaac" (Gen. xxxi. 42). So Milton speaks of Chemosh as the "obscene *dread* of Moab's sons" (*Par. Lost,* I. 406.)

O thou that dwellest in the clefts of the rock.—Better, perhaps, *in the fortresses of Sela.* The words describe with a wonderful vividness the aspect of the rock-fortresses of Edom, the cities built into a ravine. The remains of Petra (the Sela of 2 Kings xiv. 7; Isa. xvi. 1), commonly referred to as illustrating this description, are, it must be remembered, of Roman origin; but there can be little doubt that it occupied the site of an earlier city, and that there were other fortresses, even more like the eagle's nest, perched upon the summit of the crags. In Job xxxix. 27—30 we have a picture of the eagle's nest drawn by a writer who was probably familiar with these rock fortresses.

(17) **Edom shall be a desolation.**—The words did not receive an immediate or even a rapid fulfilment. Idumæa was a populous and powerful country in the time of John Hyrcanus. Petra, as we have seen, was rebuilt by the Romans as a centre of trade and government, and had its baths, and theatres, and temples. But the end came at last, and there are few lands, once the seat of a thriving nation, more utterly desolate than that of Edom. From the ninth century of the Christian era it disappears from history (Robinson's *Researches*, ii. 575).

(18) **Sodom and Gomorrah and the neighbour cities thereof.**—The destruction of the two cities named had become proverbial, as in Isa. i. 9; Jer. xiii. 19; Amos iv. 11. What is noticeable here is the mention of the "neighbour cities." We may connect it with the fact that they are named as Admah and Zeboim in Deut. xxix. 23.

(19) **Like a lion from the swelling of Jordan.**—Better, as in chap. xii. 5, *the pride of Jordan—i.e.,* the thick jungle-forests which were the glory of its banks.

Against the habitation of the strong.—Better, *against the evergreen pasturage.* The word for "habitation" is that used in chap. vi. 2 for the place where shepherds encamp, the other substantive conveys the idea of permanence rather than strength, and the image by which the prophet paints the Chaldæan invasion is that of a lion (comp. chap. v. 6) making its way through the jungle, and rushing upon the flocks and herds in one of the meadow tracts along the course of the Jordan.

But I will suddenly make him run away from her.—Literally, *I will wink, I will make him* . . . The pronouns are obscure in the Hebrew as in the English, but the meaning seems to be, "I will, as in the twinkling of an eye, drive him (Edom) away from it" (his pasturage, or habitation).

And who is a chosen man, that I may appoint over her?—Better, *who is a chosen one, and I will appoint him . . .?* The word translated "chosen one" is commonly associated with the idea of youth, the flower of a nation's strength, its chosen champions. Commentators for the most part apply it to Nebuchadnezzar as being, in the full vigour of his strength, the chosen ruler whom Jehovah would appoint over Edom. The interrogative form, however, and the implied negative answer to the questions that follow suggest a different interpretation. "Who," the prophet asks in a tone of scorn, as though Jehovah spoke by him, "is a chosen champion of Edom? and I will appoint him." The implied answer is that Edom has no such champion. Compare the taunting words uttered by Jehu (2 Kings x. 2, 3)—"Look even out the best and meetest of your master's sons"—and Rabshakeh (2 Kings xviii. 23).

Who is like me? and who will appoint me the time?—The questions follow rapidly one on another in the same tone. To "appoint a time" was the technical phrase, as in Job ix. 19, for the notice by which a prosecutor summoned the accused to trial. "Who," Jehovah asks, "will thus summon Me, and before what tribunal?" "What shepherd (*i.e.,* what ruler) will stand before Me to defend his flock against My power?"

before me? (20) Therefore hear the
counsel of the LORD, that he hath taken
against Edom; and his purposes, that
he hath purposed against the inhabitants
of Teman: Surely the least of the flock
shall draw them out: surely he shall
make their habitations desolate with
them. (21) The earth is moved at the
noise of their fall, at the cry the noise
thereof was heard in the [1] Red sea.
(22) Behold, he shall come up and fly as
the eagle, and spread his wings over
Bozrah: and at that day shall the heart
of the mighty men of Edom be as the
heart of a woman in her pangs.
(23) Concerning Damascus.
Hamath is confounded, and Arpad:
for they have heard evil tidings: they
are [2] fainthearted; *there is* sorrow [3] on
the sea; it cannot be quiet. (24) Damas-
cus is waxed feeble, *and* turneth herself
to flee, and fear hath seized on *her*:
anguish and sorrows have taken her, as
a woman in travail. (25) How is the city
of praise not left, the city of my joy!
(26) Therefore her young men shall fall
in her streets, and all the men of war
shall be cut off in that day, saith the
LORD of hosts. (27) And I will kindle a
[a] fire in the wall of Damascus, and it
shall consume the palaces of Ben-hadad.
(28) Concerning Kedar, and concerning
the kingdoms of Hazor, which Nebu-
chadrezzar king of Babylon shall smite,
Thus saith the LORD;
Arise ye, go up to Kedar, and spoil

1 Heb., *Weedy sea.*
2 Heb., *melted.*
3 Or, *as on the sea.*
a Amos 1. 4.

---

(20) **Surely.**—Literally, *If not . . .*"—the strongest Hebrew idiom of asseveration.

The least of the flock shall draw them out . . .—The English is obscure, probably because the object of the verb has been taken as its subject. Better, *Surely they* (*i.e.*, the Chaldæan invaders) *will vex them, the feeble ones of the flock; surely he will make their pasturage terror-stricken at them.* The thought expressed is that the very fields of Edom would, as it were, shudder at the cruelty of their conquerors. It is noticeable that the whole passage is repeated in chap. l. 44, 45, and is there applied to Babylon.

(21) **The noise thereof was heard in the Red sea.**—Literally, as in the margin, *the Weedy, or Reed sea.* The crash of the fall of Edom, the cries of the slaughtered people, were to be heard far off on the waters of the sea that washed its shores. Elath, on the Gulf of Akaba, was the sea-port of Edom (2 Chron. xxvi. 2).

(22) **He shall come up and fly as the eagle.**—The prophet passes from one symbol of sovereignty to another, and instead of the lion we have (see Note on chap. xlviii. 40) the eagle. What Kerioth was to Moab, Bozrah was to Edom, and its capture is painted in the same terms.

(23) **Concerning Damascus.**—Damascus is named as the capital of Aram, or Syria. The kingdom first became powerful under Rezon after David's death (1 Kings xi. 23, 24). In the history of 1 and 2 Kings we find it engaged in constant wars against Israel and Judah (1 Kings xxii. 1; 2 Kings vi. 8) or in alliance with Israel against Judah (1 Kings xv. 19; 2 Kings xvi. 5, 6). The last of these alliances was the memorable confederacy of Isa. vii. 2, between Rezin and Pekah. That ended, as Isaiah foretold, in the subjugation of Damascus by the Assyrians (2 Kings xvi. 9). And so the Syrians continued subject till the downfall of the Assyrian Empire, when they naturally fell before the power of Nebuchadnezzar. The language of the prophet is vague, but probably points to his attack.

Hamath is confounded, and Arpad.—The former town was originally pointed out as the northern limit of the territory of Israel (Num. xxxiv. 8), and this was attained under Solomon (2 Chron. viii. 4). It lies in a strong position in the valley of the Orontes, and under the name of *Hamah* is still a flourishing city with 30,000 inhabitants, Arpad, always joined with Hamath (Isa. x. 9, xxxvi. 19, xxxvii. 13), must at the time have been nearly as important. The name *Arpaddu* has been found in cuneiform inscriptions, and its site has been placed at about fourteen miles north of Aleppo. For further details see Notes on Isa. x. 9.

There is sorrow on the sea; it cannot be quiet.—The mention of the sea in connexion with Damascus presents some difficulty. The most simple solution is probably the truest. The terror that prevails at Damascus is thought of as extending to the sea (*i.e.*, to the Mediterranean), possibly with special reference to its commerce with Tyre (Ezek. xxvii. 18). All is restless and unquiet as the sea itself. The last clause seems like a reminiscence of Isa. lvii. 20. Many MSS. give the various reading "*like* the sea," which would make the parallelism more complete.

(25) **How is the city of praise not left . . . !**—The exclamation, half scornful, half ironical, points to the fact that the inhabitants of Damascus had tried in vain to flee (verse 24). The city so fair and glorious, with its rivers Abana and Pharphar (2 Kings v. 12), had not been "left," would not be empty when it was taken. The people would perish with it. Her young warriors and her veterans should be cut off within the walls.

(27) **It shall consume the palaces of Ben-hadad.**—Three kings of the name appear in Old Testament history; one as warring against Omri (1 Kings xx. 34), another as a contemporary of Elisha (2 Kings viii. 7), a third as the son of Hazael, and therefore belonging to a different dynasty (2 Kings xiii. 3). It is possible, as the name was thus associated with the greatness of the kingdom, that it may have been borne also by later kings. It appears in the form Ben-hidri in Assyrian inscriptions. The prophet's words are, at any rate, a proof that the palaces of Damascus were either built by one of them, probably the first, or at any rate bore their name.

(28) **Concerning Kedar . . .**—The name belonged to a tribe of the Bedouin type, descended from Ishmael (Gen. xxv. 13), and at this time conspicuous as supplying the markets of Tyre with sheep and goats (Ezek. xxvii. 21). In Ps. cxx. 5 it appears as the representative of the fierce nomadic life of the Arabians. Hazor appears

the men of the east. (29) Their tents
and their flocks shall they take away:
they shall take to themselves their
curtains, and all their vessels, and their
camels; and they shall cry unto them,
Fear *is* on every side. (30) [a] Flee, [1] get
you far off, dwell deep, O ye inhabitants
of Hazor, saith the LORD; for Nebu-
chadrezzar king of Babylon hath taken
counsel against you, and hath conceived
a purpose against you. (31) Arise, get
you up unto the [2] wealthy nation, that
dwelleth without care, saith the LORD,
which have neither gates nor bars, *which*
dwell alone. (32) And their camels shall
be a booty, and the multitude of their
cattle a spoil: and I will scatter into
all winds them *that are* [3] in the utmost
corners; and I will bring their calamity
from all sides thereof, saith the LORD.
(33) And Hazor shall be a dwelling for
dragons, *and* a desolation for ever: there
shall no man abide there, nor *any* son
of man dwell in it.
(34) The word of the LORD that came
to Jeremiah the prophet against Elam
in the beginning of the reign of Zede-
kiah king of Judah, saying,
(35) Thus saith the LORD of hosts;
Behold, I will break the bow of Elam,
the chief of their might. (36) And upon
Elam will I bring the four winds from the
four quarters of heaven, and will scatter
them toward all those winds; and there

a ver. 8

1 Heb., *flit greatly.*

B.C. 598.

2 Or, *that is at ease.*

3 Heb., *cut off into corners,* or, *that have the corners of their hair polled.*

---

as the name of many cities in Palestine (Josh. xi. 1, xv. 23, xix. 36), but the combination with Kedar points to quite a different region. The probable explanation is that Jeremiah uses the term (as a like word, *hazērein*, is used in Isa. xlii. 11 for the "villages" of Kedar) for the region in which the Kedar Arabs had ceased to be nomadic, and had made a permanent settlement. According to Niebuhr (*Assur u. Bab.*, p. 210) it answers to the modern *Hadschar* in the angle formed by the southern course of the Euphrates and the Persian Gulf.

Spoil the men of the east.—Literally, the *B'eni-Kedem*, or children of the East. The term appears in the Old Testament history from a very early date (Gen. xxix. 1; Judges vi. 3, 33, vii. 12; 1 Kings iv. 30; Job i. 3), and has, as might be expected, though obviously indicating a nomadic form of life, like that of the Midianites, a somewhat wide and undefined connotation. The picture of the attack on them presents a marked contrast to that of the attack on Damascus: not palaces and treasures, but tents and flocks, the curtains or hangings of the tent, their implements (weapons, kneading troughs, and the like), their very camels, seized by the conquerors.

(29) **Fear is on every side.**—There is a striking individuality in this reproduction of the *Magor-missabib* cry which had been so prominent in the prophet's own life and preaching (chaps. vi. 25, xx. 3, 10, xlvi. 5).

(30) **Dwell deep.**—See Note on verse 8. The dwellers in the villages of Hazor are told, as those of Dedan had been, to flee into the furthest recesses of the wilderness. The words probably point to the time after the battle of Carchemish, when Nebuchadnezzar established his sovereignty over the lower Euphrates, Northern Arabia, and the Syrian desert.

(31—33) **Arise, get you up . . .**—The command of Jehovah goes forth to the invaders. Their work will be an easy one, for they are sent against a people that dwell defenceless in the open country, with no walls or gates, dwelling alone, without allies, their camels and their flocks offering an easy prey. Compare the description of Laish in Judges xviii. 7. The prophet repeats the characteristic term of scorn which we have found in chaps. ix. 26, xxv. 23, "them that dwell in the utmost corners," or more accurately, *those with cropped-hair temples*, as descriptive of the wild tribes that are thus doomed to destruction. Their land shall be a dwelling-place for *jackals* (not "dragons"; see Note on chap. ix. 11), desolate for ever.

(34) **The word of the Lord that came to Jeremiah the prophet against Elam . . .**—It is noticeable that this is the only prophecy in chaps. xlviii., xlix. with a date attached to it. Assuming the date to be rightly given, it indicates a time later than that of those that precede it, which belong probably to the group of predictions connected with chap. xxv. It has been maintained, however, by many critics that the absence of the name of Nebuchadnezzar, so prominent in Jeremiah's predictions after the deportation of Jehoiachin, indicates an earlier rather than a later date, and that the compiler of the prophecies was mistaken in thus fixing the time of its delivery. The inference is, however, somewhat precarious, as the fact is common to the prophecies against the Philistines, Moabites, Ammonites, &c., that precede this. Elam, though commonly identified with Persia, as in Isa. xi. 11, xxi. 2, xxii. 6, appears to be used with a somewhat wider connotation for the tribes beyond the Tigris (chap. xxv. 25). The tone of the prophecy seems to imply that Elam had been prominent among the enemies of the people of Jehovah (as in Isa. xxii. 6), and this has led to the inference that they had taken part in the attack on Judah, as auxiliaries in the army of Nebuchadnezzar. It is significant that the thought that Elam is to be the instrument of Jehovah for the destruction of Babylon (Isa. xxi. 2), and that out of it was to come the appointed deliverer of Israel, does not seem to have been present to the prophet's mind. His horizon is, as it were, bounded for the time by the more immediate future.

(35) **I will break the bow of Elam.**—As in Isa. xxii. 6; Herod. vii. 61, Elam was conspicuous for its archers. We are reminded of the account which Herodotus gives (ii. 136) of the three things taught to the youth of Persia—to ride, to draw the bow, and to speak the truth. This weapon was "the chief of their might."

(36) **Upon Elam will I bring the four winds . . .**—The words reproduce those of verse 32 as to the extent of the dispersion, but there is an added circumstance of terror in the picture of destruction. The "four winds" whirling round as in a *cyclone* are to be the instruments of destruction. The imagery of the threshing-floor seems once more brought before us, and

shall be no nation whither the outcasts
of Elam shall not come. (37) For I will
cause Elam to be dismayed before their
enemies, and before them that seek their
life: and I will bring evil upon them,
even my fierce anger, saith the LORD;
and I will send the sword after them,
till I have consumed them: (38) and I
will set my throne in Elam, and will
destroy from thence the king and the
princes, saith the LORD. (39) But it
shall come to pass in the latter days,
that [a] I will bring again the captivity
of Elam, saith the LORD.

a ch. 48. 47; ver. 6.

B. C. 595.

CHAPTER L.—(1) The word that the
LORD spake against Babylon *and* against
the land of the Chaldeans [1] by Jeremiah
the prophet.

(2) Declare ye among the nations, and
publish, and [2] set up a standard; publish,
and conceal not: say, Babylon is taken,

1 Heb., *by the hand of Jeremiah.*

2 Heb., *lift up.*

---

the Elamites are as the chaff which the winds, in such a tempest, carry off in all directions.

(38) **I will set my throne in Elam.**—The throne of Jehovah is, it is clear, the throne of the king who is, for the time, His chosen instrument and servant, in this case therefore the throne of Nebuchadnezzar (chap. xliii. 10), against whom Elam, like the other nations in chap. xxv. 13—25, and in chaps. xlviii., xlix., had apparently risen in rebellion. Of this we have, perhaps, a trace in the statement of Judith i. 1—13, that Nebuchadnezzar defeated Arphaxad, a king of Media, in the seventeenth year of his reign. The words find an historical fulfilment in the fact that Shushan, "in the province of Elam," became one of the royal residences of the Chaldæan kings (Dan. viii. 2), and continued to be so under those of Persia, who, as regards the population of Elam proper, were as conquerors (Neh. i. 1; Esth. i. 2). A like prediction of the fall of Elam, among other nations, before the attack of the King of Babylon is found in Ezek. xxxii. 24.

(39) **I will bring again the captivity of Elam.**—Of the special history of Elam, as distinct from the other provinces of the Persian Empire, history records but little. The mention of Elamites among those who were present at Jerusalem on the day of Pentecost (Acts ii. 9) shows that they were a recognised province under the Parthian monarchy, and that Jews had settled among them in large numbers, and so supplies a partial fulfilment of their return from their captivity.

L.

The long continuous prophecy which occupies the place of a great finale in the collection of Jeremiah's writings (chaps. l. and li.) is in many ways the most important of the whole book. It presents an aspect of the prophet's mind and character which elsewhere is almost or altogether latent. For the most part, he appears as the supporter of the Chaldæans, opposing the policy of the kings and rulers who were bent on resistance, bidding the exiles to pray for the peace of Babylon (chap. xxix. 7). Only once before, as in a germinal hint afterwards to be developed, and veiled beneath the cypher of the mysterious Sheshach (chap. xxv. 26), had he given any intimation that it came within the horizon of his vision that she, too, was to drink of "the wine-cup of the Lord's fury" (chap. xxv. 15). It can scarcely be imagined, however, that the predictions of Isaiah against the Chaldæan city in chaps. xiii.—xiv. 22, or (if we acknowledge the later chapters of that book as authentic) those in chaps. xlvi., xlvii., were unknown to him; and we may well believe that when the great catastrophe had come upon Jerusalem, and the people were in exile by the waters of Babylon, he desired to comfort them with the thought that the righteous law of retribution under which they were suffering would in due time bring down the pride of their oppressor. When he had told them that their captivity would last for seventy years (chap. xxix. 10), that lands should once again be bought and sold, and ploughed and planted in Judah (chap. xxxii. 15), there was an implied fore-knowledge of the doom of the golden city; and at last, probably as the closing vision of his life, the last case in which he was to "root out, and to pull down, and to destroy," it was given to him to see how that destruction would be accomplished.

The authenticity of the chapter has, it is true, been questioned by some critics, partly on the assumption that prophecy cannot be prediction, and that the fulness of detail with which the apparent prediction is given implies a prophecy after the event, partly on the ground that the style differs from that of the other writings ascribed to Jeremiah's name, and that it presents so many traces of acquaintance with Babylon and its customs that it must have been written by one who had been resident in that city. On this hypothesis Baruch has been named as its possible author.

The first ground of objection opens a wide question which cannot well be discussed on every occurrence of the principle which it involves. Here it will be enough to say that the assumption in question is at variance with the whole idea of their office which the prophets themselves recognised, and that it is not that on which the lines of interpretation followed in this Commentary have been based. Judgments based upon variations and differences in style are always more or less precarious. For my own part I do not see any such differences as to clash with the belief that these chapters were written by Jeremiah, and I find many parallelisms and coincidences, which will be noticed as we proceed, falling in with that belief. The third difficulty is sufficiently met by the thought that one who was in frequent intercourse both with the captive Jews at Babylon and with the Chaldæans as Jeremiah was (chap. xxix. 1—32), to say nothing of his personal journeys to the Euphrates (chap. xiii. 1—7), might well have acquired such a knowledge of the country as is indicated in these chapters.

(1) **By Jeremiah the prophet.**—Literally, *by the hand of Jeremiah.* The phrase is not found elsewhere in Jeremiah's writings, with the one exception of chap. xxxvii. 2. It probably indicates that the prophecy that follows was written with his own hand, and not dictated. (See chap. li. 60.)

(2) **Set up a standard.**—Better, *lift up a signal.* The noun is the same as in chap. iv. 6, 21. Here, however, its use is not that of furnishing a rallying-point for an army, but that of a means of rapid communication, like the succession of beacon-fires in the opening of the *Agamemnon* of Æschylus (*Agam.*, 272

Bel is confounded, Merodach is broken
in pieces; her idols are confounded, her
images are broken in pieces. (3) For
out of the north there cometh up a
nation against her, which shall make
her land desolate, and none shall dwell
therein: they shall remove, they shall
depart, both man and beast.

(4) In those days, and in that time,
saith the LORD, the children of Israel
shall come, they and the children of
Judah together, going and weeping:
they shall go, and seek the LORD their
God. (5) They shall ask the way to Zion
with their faces thitherward, *saying,*
Come, and let us join ourselves to the
LORD in a perpetual covenant *that* shall
not be forgotten.

(6) My people hath been lost sheep:
their shepherds have caused them to go
astray, they have turned them away *on*
the mountains: they have gone from
mountain to hill, they have forgotten
their [1] restingplace. (7) All that found
them have devoured them: and their
adversaries said, We offend not, because
they have sinned against the LORD, the
habitation of justice, even the LORD, the
hope of their fathers. (8) [a] Remove out
of the midst of Babylon, and go forth
out of the land of the Chaldeans, and
be as the he goats before the flocks.

[1] Heb., *place to lie down in.*

[a] Isa. 48. 20; ch. 51. 6; Rev. 18. 4.

—307). The tidings of the fall of Babylon are to be proclaimed as quickly as may be throughout the world.

Bel is confounded, Merodach is broken in pieces.—Strictly speaking these, as found in the inscriptions, were names of the same deity (see Note on Isa. xlvi. 1). The name of Bel appears in the names of the two great walls of Babylon, Imgur-Bel and Nimetti-Bel (*Records of the Past*, v. 125). The latter name, sometimes in the form of Marduk, appears as lord of heaven and earth, and Nebo is subordinate to him. Nebuchadnezzar's devotion to him is indicated by the name he gave his son, Evil-merodach (chap. lii. 31), and by describing himself in his inscriptions as "worshipper of Marduk" (*Records of the Past*, v. 113). So we have among Chaldæan names Merodach-baladan (2 Kings xx. 12; Isa. xxxix. 1), Kurdur-Marduk, and others. The inscriptions at Borsippa speak of him as "the great lord, the most ancient of the gods, the lord of the gates of heaven," and so on (Rawlinson's *Herodotus*, i. 627—631).

Idols . . . images.—The words had better be inverted. The former word denotes sculptured pillars, the latter blocks or columns. (See Note on Lev. xxvi. 30.)

(3) **Out of the north there cometh up a nation.**—It is significant that the very phrase which had described the danger that threatened Judah from Babylon (chap. i. 10) is now used for the danger that threatened Babylon itself from Media. It is as though the prophet watched that northern quarter of the heavens, and saw storm after storm, torrent after torrent, bursting out upon the south. The nations are named in chap. li. 27, 28. We are almost irresistibly reminded of the language in which the historians of the fourth and fifth centuries speak of the Gothic and Teutonic tribes that poured down upon the Roman Empire.

(4) **The children of Israel shall come . . .**—The union of the divided sections of the people is significant as being that which the prophet had all along hoped for (chap. iii. 14—16). And the united people are to return with tears of mingled joy and penitence (comp. Ezra iii. 13, viii. 21—23), no longer worshipping Baal and the queen of heaven (chaps. vii. 18, xliv. 17), but "seeking Jehovah their God."

(5) **They shall ask the way to Zion with their faces thitherward.**—Literally, *hitherward.* The correction is not without significance, as showing that the prophecy was written in Judah, and therefore as far as that fact goes, as being in favour of Jeremiah's authorship.

A perpetual covenant.—The prophet may have had the promise of the new covenant of chap. xxxi. 31 in his thoughts, as being about to receive at least a partial fulfilment. In Ezra viii. 21—23, x. 3 we find what we may look on as an effort of the people to enter into such a covenant.

(6) **My people hath been lost sheep . . .**—We note as interesting the dominance of this imagery here as in Isa. liii. 6; Ezek. xxxiv. 5. The "shepherds" are, as ever, the kings and civil rulers of the people. In the "mountains" and "hills" we see partly the natural surroundings of the imagery, partly a special reference to the idolatrous worship of the high places (chap. iii. 2, 6). The Hebrew text as it stands gives, *they have led them on seducing mountains, i.e.,* the "high places" which had so strange a fascination for them. The Authorised version follows the marginal reading of the Hebrew. The "forgotten restingplace," or, perhaps, the *fold,* is, as in verse 7, the "habitation of justice," the *true pasturage,* the righteousness which is found in fellowship with Jehovah Himself.

(7) **Their adversaries said, We offend not . . .**—The words are suggestive as indicating a special aspect of the thoughts of the prophet as to the idolatry of Judah. What was to him its extremest humiliation was that it put a taunt into the mouths of the enemies of her people. They were able to say, "We are acting rightly: we are but instruments in the hands of God." The words that follow can scarcely be thought of as those of the enemies of Israel, but as added by the prophet to emphasise the guilt of his own people.

(8) **Remove out of the midst of Babylon . . .**—The prophet re-echoes almost the very words of Isa. xlviii. 20, lii. 11. It is obviously in marked contrast with the counsels in chap. xxix. 5—7 that the exiles should build houses and plant gardens, and seek the peace of the city of their conquerors. That was a wise and right counsel for the time, but it was for a time only; and when the hour of the fall of Babylon came they were to be as the he-goats (better, *rams*) of the flock, leading the captives of other nations in the work of liberation and of flight. That was their only way of escape from being involved in the destruction of the doomed city.

(9) For, lo, I will raise and cause to come
up against Babylon an assembly of great
nations from the north country: and
they shall set themselves in array
against her; from thence she shall be
taken: their arrows *shall be* as of a
mighty [1] expert man; none shall return
in vain. (10) And Chaldea shall be a
spoil: all that spoil her shall be satisfied,
saith the LORD. (11) Because ye were
glad, because ye rejoiced, O ye de-
stroyers of mine heritage, because ye are
grown [2] fat as the heifer at grass, and
bellow as bulls; (12) your mother shall
be sore confounded; she that bare you
shall be ashamed: behold, the hinder-
most of the nations *shall be* a wilderness,
a dry land, and a desert. (13) Because
of the wrath of the LORD it shall not
be inhabited, but it shall be wholly
desolate: [a] every one that goeth by
Babylon shall be astonished, and hiss at
all her plagues.
(14) Put yourselves in array against
Babylon round about: all ye that bend
the bow, shoot at her, spare no arrows:
for she hath sinned against the LORD.
(15) Shout against her round about: she
hath given her hand: her foundations
are fallen, her walls are thrown down:
for it *is* the vengeance of the LORD:
take vengeance upon her; as she hath
done, do unto her. (16) Cut off the
sower from Babylon, and him that
handleth the [3] sickle in the time of har-
vest: for fear of the oppressing sword

1 Or, *destroyer.*

2 Heb., *big,* or, *corpulent.*

a ch. 49. 17.

3 Or, *scythe.*

---

(9) **An assembly of great nations from the north country.**—Like all the great monarchies of the East, the Medo-Persian kingdom, which was to be the destroyer of Babylon, was made up of a congeries of many different races. Herodotus (vii. 61—69), in his account of the army of Xerxes, names twenty-two, from the Medes and Persians at the head of the list to the Arabians and Ethiopians at its close.

From thence she shall be taken.—The Hebrew adverb may be taken either of time or place. The latter, as referring to the region from which the assailants come, gives the better sense.

As of a mighty expert man.—The marginal rendering, "destroyer," follows the Vulgate and the Targum, and represents a various reading. There is no sufficient reason for rejecting the Authorised Version, which has the support of the LXX. and the Syriac versions.

None shall return in vain.—Grammatically the words may refer either to the warrior or the arrow. The use of the same phrase in 2 Sam. i. 22; Isa. lv. 11 is perhaps in favour of the latter.

(10) **Chaldea.**—The same word is used as for Chaldæans, but it is treated as the name of the country, and is therefore joined with a verb in the feminine singular.

(11) **Destroyers of mine heritage.**—Better, *plunderers* or *robbers.*

Ye are grown fat as the heifer at grass.—Better, the Hebrew text being in the singular, *thou leapedst as the heifer while threshing.* The rule of Deut. xxv. 4 ("Thou shalt not muzzle the ox that treadeth out the corn") made the image significant enough. The English version has, however, the support of the LXX. and Vulg.

And bellow as bulls.—Better, *thou didst neigh as strong steeds.* The verb is the same as in chap. v. 8, the noun the same as in chap. viii. 16.

(12) **Your mother shall be sore confounded . . .**—The prophet speaks to the people of Babylon, and the city is therefore described as their mother.

The hindermost of the nations shall be a wilderness . . .—The interpolated words mar the force of the sentence. Better, *behold the hindermost of the nations, a wilderness, a waste, and a desert.* This was to be the state to which Babylon should be reduced.

(13) **Every one that goeth . . .**—We note the reproduction of the formula of chaps. xix. 8, xlix. 17.

(14) **All ye that bend the bow.**—The words are descriptive of the light-armed troops that formed the strength of the Medo-Persian army (see chaps. xlix. 35, l. 14). The words belong properly to the previous clause, and the colon should come after them. Stress is laid in the latter clause on the fact that Babylon has sinned in her cruelty and luxury and tyranny against the righteous government of Jehovah.

(15) **She hath given her hand.**—The words paint the attitude of one who submits and stretches forth his hand, as a sign that he gives himself into the power of the conqueror. (Comp. Ezr. x. 19; 2 Chron. xxx. 8; Lam. v. 6.) So in Latin "*dare manum*" was a synonym for submission (Cic. *de Amic.* 26).

Her foundations are fallen.—Better, with the LXX., *bastions* or *bulwarks.*

As she hath done, do unto her.—We note an identity of thought and almost of language with Ps. cxxxvii. 8. Had the Psalmist heard the prophecy, or the prophet the psalm? The former seems the more probable alternative.

(16) **Cut off the sower . . .**—The rich alluvial plains of Babylon, so plentiful that they yielded an increase of two hundred-fold (Herod. iii. 8), were to be laid waste. There may, possibly, be a special reference to the fields within the walls of the city, upon which the population largely depended, and which were now to be devastated. (Diod. Sic. ii. 9; Pliny, *Hist. Nat.* xi. 111.)

For fear of the oppressing sword.—The versions present the same noticeable variations, as in chap. xlvi. 16, the LXX. giving "from the Greek sword," possibly with reference to the belief that Cyrus had subdued the Æolians and Ionians before the conquest of Babylon, and that they were fighting in his army, or to Alexander's capture of the city, and the Vulg. "from the sword of the dove," the latter rendering being supposed to refer to the dove on the Babylonian standard, as the emblem of Semiramis. Here, however, as Babylon is the object of attack, the latter allusion is scarcely applicable, and there is no sufficient reason for altering the English version. (See Note on chaps. xxv. 38, xlvi. 16.)

They shall flee every one to his own land.—The words are significant as showing that the Jews

they shall turn every one to his people,
and they shall flee every one to his own
land.
(17) Israel *is* a scattered sheep; the
lions have driven *him* away: first the
king of Assyria hath devoured him;
and last this Nebuchadrezzar king of
Babylon hath broken his bones. (18) There-
fore thus saith the LORD of hosts, the
God of Israel; Behold, I will punish
the king of Babylon and his land, as I
have punished the king of Assyria.
(19) And I will bring Israel again to his
habitation, and he shall feed on Carmel
and Bashan, and his soul shall be satis-
fied upon mount Ephraim and Gilead.
(20) In those days, and in that time, saith
the LORD, the iniquity of Israel shall be
sought for, and *there shall be* none; and
the sins of Judah, and they shall not be
found: for I will pardon them whom I
reserve.
(21) Go up against the land [1] of Mera-
thaim, *even* against it, and against the
inhabitants of [2] Pekod: waste and utterly
destroy after them, saith the LORD, and
do according to all that I have com-
manded thee. (22) A sound of battle *is*
in the land, and of great destruction.
(23) How is the hammer of the whole
earth cut asunder and broken! how is
Babylon become a desolation among the
nations! (24) I have laid a snare for thee,
and thou art also taken, O Babylon,

1 Or, *of the rebels.*

2 Or, *visitation.*

were not the only people for whom the fall of Babylon was the signal of a return from exile. The policy of Nebuchadnezzar, like that of Assyria, had been to people his own territory with the captive populations of other countries, and Israel (as in verse 8) was to lead the way in the return.

(17) **Israel is a scattered sheep . . .**—The words paint vividly the two blows that had fallen on Israel, as a sheep driven from the fold: first from the Assyrian conquest of the northern kingdom by Salmaneser, and then, when, as it were, the carcase was half devoured and only the bones left, from that of Judah by Nebuchadnezzar. The "lion" appears here, as in Dan. vii. 4, as the symbol of the great Eastern monarchies. The fact that the sculptured winged lion appears so constantly in the remains both of Assyria and Babylon gives the imagery a special force.

(18) **As I have punished the king of Assyria.**—Nineveh had fallen before Cyaxares and Nabopolassar, and Babylon was in like manner to fall before Cyrus. The one judgment was the pledge and earnest of the other.

(19) **I will bring Israel again to his habitation.**—Better, *to his pasturage* (as in chaps. x. 25, xxiii. 3), as keeping up the figure of verse 17. The "scattered sheep" was to be brought back and to find pasture. The regions named are the representatives of the most fertile districts of Palestine, Carmel and Mount Ephraim on the west (Ezek. xxxiv. 13), Bashan and Gilead on the east, of Jordan (Num. xxxii. 1; Mic. vii. 14).

(20) **In those days, and in that time . . .**—The formula is that which in prophetic language points to the far-off times of the Christ. Their restoration to their earthly homes was but a small thing. That which was to the prophet the great blessing of the future was that it would bring with it the New Covenant of chap. xxxi. 31, pardon and peace, iniquity and sin remembered no more.

I will pardon them whom I reserve.—The latter verb contains the root of the "remnant" which is so prominent in Isaiah (i. 9, vii. 3), and expresses the same thought. "The remnant," the reserved ones, shall be pardoned.

(21) **Go up against the land of Merathaim.**—No such name is found in Babylonian inscriptions or is mentioned by historians. The most probable explanation of its use is that the prophet coined it as a descriptive word (= land of two rebellions), and then substituted it, after his manner (as with Sheshach, chap. xxv. 6; Magor-missabib, chap. xx. 3), for the name Aram-Naharaim (= land of the two rivers = Mesopotamia), which was, as in Gen. xxiv. 10; Deut. xxiii. 4; Judges iii. 8, 10, the recognised name of the country between the Tigris and Euphrates. It was, he seems to say, the country, not of rivers, but of rebellions, choosing the dual form, partly for the sake of assonance, partly to express the fact that Babylon having rebelled against Assyria, as, *e.g.*, Merodach-baladan (Isa. xxxix. 1) and Nabopolassar had done, had also rebelled against Jehovah. Possibly, however, the dual may simply express intensity. Such changes of names were quite after the manner of Old Testament usage. So Beth-aven was substituted for Bethel (Hos. x. 5), Mephibosheth for Meribbaal (2 Sam. iv. 4; 1 Chron. viii. 34). Micah i. is full of such paronomasiæ.

Against the inhabitants of Pekod.—Here we have a name which is found in Ezek. xxiii. 23 and in inscriptions as that of a Babylonian town, as in a list of rebels, and in the form *Bukudu*, as in the Cylinder of Sennacherib (*Records of the Past*, i. 26), and is the name of a city, *Nahar-Pekod*, mentioned in the Talmud (Fürst, *Lex. s.v.*, and Neubauer, *Géog. du Talm.*, p. 363). We can scarcely doubt, however, that the prophet chose this name for the sake of its meaning, "visitation." It was necessary to find a word to be at once *nomen et omen* for the guilt of Babylon. There was one ready at hand applicable to its punishment.

Waste and utterly destroy.—Better, *slay and devote to destruction.* The latter verb is connected with the Hebrew *Cherem*, which expressed, as in Deut. vii. 26; Josh. vii. 13, the idea of a solemn anathema.

(23) **How is the hammer of the whole earth cut asunder . . .!**—The image had been used before (chap. xxiii. 29) of the might of right as seen in the words of Jehovah. Here it describes the right of might as seen in the despotism of Babylon. The name of Charles Martel and, according to one etymology, that of Judas Maccabæus, present interesting parallelisms. And now the hammer itself, which had been as an instrument in the hand of Jehovah (chap. li. 20), is to be, in its turn, crushed by a power mightier than its own.

(24) **I have laid a snare for thee.**—The two captures of Babylon by Cyrus and Darius both

and thou wast not aware: thou art
found, and also caught, because thou
hast striven against the LORD. (25) The
LORD hath opened his armoury, and
hath brought forth the weapons of his
indignation: for this *is* the work of the
Lord GOD of hosts in the land of the
Chaldeans. (26) Come against her [1] from
the utmost border, open her storehouses:
[2] cast her up as heaps, and destroy her
utterly: let nothing of her be left.
(27) Slay all her bullocks; let them go
down to the slaughter: woe unto them!
for their day is come, the time of their
visitation. (28) The voice of them that
flee and escape out of the land of Baby-
lon, to declare in Zion the vengeance of
the LORD our God, the vengeance of his
temple. (29) Call together the archers
against Babylon: all ye that bend the
bow, camp against it round about; let
none thereof escape: recompense her
according to her work; according to all
that she hath done, do unto her: for
she hath been proud against the LORD,
against the Holy One of Israel. (30) There-
fore shall her young men fall in the
streets, and all her men of war shall be
cut off in that day, saith the LORD.
(31) Behold, I *am* against thee, *O thou*
[3] most proud, saith the Lord GOD of
hosts: for thy day is come, the time
that I will visit thee. (32) And [4] the
most proud shall stumble and fall, and
none shall raise him up: and I will
kindle a fire in his cities, and it shall
devour all round about him.

(33) Thus saith the LORD of hosts;
The children of Israel and the children
of Judah *were* oppressed together: and
all that took them captives held them
fast; they refused to let them go.
(34) Their Redeemer *is* strong; the LORD
of hosts *is* his name: he shall throughly

1 Heb., *from the end.*

2 Or, *tread her.*

3 Heb., *pride.*

4 Heb., *pride.*

---

answered to this description. Cyrus turned aside the waters of the Euphrates into another channel, and entered by the river-bed, so that the city was taken before those who lived in the middle of the city knew that it was attacked (Herod. i. 191). In the latter case the gates were opened to Darius by the treachery of the Babylonian general Zopyrus (Herod. iii. 158). (Comp. Dan. v. 30; Isa. xlv. 1.) In chap. li. 31, 32 we have the same fact more vividly described.

(25) **The Lord hath opened his armoury.**—The word is the same as that for "treasures" in chaps. x. 13, li. 16, the choice of the appropriate English word being determined, in each case, by the context. Here the figure is that of a mighty king going to his arsenal and equipping himself with the weapons which will insure his victory. An expansion of the same imagery is found in Wisd. v. 17—23, xviii. 15, 16.

This is the work of the Lord God of hosts.—Better, *the Lord God of hosts hath a work . . .*

(26) **Open her storehouses.**—The noun is not found elsewhere. Probably *granaries* would be a better rendering. The word for "heaps" is used in Song Sol. vii. 2; Ruth iii. 7 for "heaps of corn," and this is probably its meaning here. In Neh. iv. 2, however, it is used of heaps of rubbish. The stored-up provisions of the captured city are to be piled up in its open places, as men pile the sheaves of corn after harvest, and burnt (for "destroy" read *devote to destruction*), as had been done, *e.g.*, in the capture of Jericho and other cities (Josh. vi. 24, xi. 12, 13).

Let nothing of her be left.—Literally. *let there be no remnant*, as in marked contrast with the "remnant" of Israel (verse 20).

(27) **Slay all her bullocks.**—The words are probably to be taken figuratively of the captains and men of war of Babylon, as in Ps. xxii. 12; Isa. xxxiv. 7; Jer. xlviii. 15 (see Note), and li. 40.

(28) **The voice of them that flee . . .**—The abruptness of the opening words, as if the prophet heard the cry of the escaping exiles, would be perhaps best represented by *Hark, the voice . . .* The words that follow define the cry as coming chiefly from the captive Jews, who see in the destruction of Babylon the vengeance of Jehovah for the destruction of His Temple.

(29) **Recompense her according to her work . . .**—As before, in verse 15, the prophet sees in the fall of Babylon the working of the Divine law of retribution. In "the Holy One of Israel" we note the occurrence, for the first time in Jeremiah, of the characteristic name which is so prominent in Isaiah, and is seldom found elsewhere. It occurs again in chap. li. 5.

(30) **Therefore shall her young men fall . . .**—The verse is reproduced almost *literatim* from the prophecy against Damascus in chap. xlix. 26.

(31) **O thou most proud.**—Literally, *O Pride*, the prophet using the word (*Zadon*) as a proper name for Babylon, as he had before used Merathaim and Pekod (verse 21). It is analogous in its meaning to the Rahab of Isa. li. 9; Pss. lxxxvii. 4, lxxxix. 10, as the name of Egypt. The word points, perhaps, to the self-exaltation of Nebuchadnezzar as embodying that of his people (Dan. iv. 30).

(32) **And the most proud shall stumble . . .**—As before, *Pride*. The gender of the pronoun in "none shall raise *him* up" is determined by that of the Hebrew noun. The words furnish a striking illustration of the teaching of Prov. xvi. 18.

(33) **Were oppressed.**—Better, *are oppressed*, and so on through the verse. The English tense is misleading. The prophet, having described the doom that lies in the future, now returns to the present, and finds in the actual state of Israel that which made the destruction of Babylon a necessary condition of its liberation. All appeals to the mercy of their conquerors, Assyrian or Chaldæan, had been made in vain.

(34) **Their Redeemer is strong.**—The word for "Redeemer" (*Goël*) includes, as elsewhere (Num. xxxv. 12; Ruth iv. 1, 8; Job xix. 25), the thought of "the next of kin," with whom the right of redemption (in

plead their cause, that he may give rest
to the land, and disquiet the inhabitants
of Babylon. (35) A sword *is* upon the
Chaldeans, saith the LORD, and upon
the inhabitants of Babylon, and upon
her princes, and upon her wise *men.*
(36) A sword *is* upon the [1] [2] liars; and
they shall dote: a sword *is* upon her
mighty men; and they shall be dis-
mayed. (37) A sword *is* upon their horses,
and upon their chariots, and upon all
the mingled people that *are* in the midst
of her; and they shall become as women:
a sword *is* upon her treasures; and they
shall be robbed. (38) A drought *is* upon
her waters; and they shall be dried up:
for it *is* the land of graven images, and
they are mad upon *their* idols. (39) There-
fore the wild beasts of the desert with
the wild beasts of the islands shall dwell
there, and the owls shall dwell therein:
and it shall be no more inhabited for
ever; neither shall it be dwelt in from
generation to generation. (40) [a] As God
overthrew Sodom and Gomorrah and the
neighbour *cities* thereof, saith the LORD:
so shall no man abide there, neither
shall any son of man dwell therein.

(41) Behold, a people shall come from
the north, and a great nation, and many
kings shall be raised up from the coasts
of the earth. (42) They shall hold the
bow and the lance: they *are* cruel, and
will not shew mercy: their voice shall
roar like the sea, and they shall ride
upon horses, *every one* put in array, like
a man to the battle, against thee, O
daughter of Babylon. (43) The king of
Babylon hath heard the report of them,
and his hands waxed feeble: anguish

a Or, *chief stays.*

1 Heb., *bars.*

2 Gen. 19. 25; ch. 49. 18.

---

the technical sense) rested, and to whom belonged the duty of pleading for and avenging his kinsman when oppressed. It is interesting to note, in connection with the obvious allusion to Prov. xvi. 18, that here, with the exception of the name of "the Lord of hosts is his name," we have an actual citation from Prov. xxiii. 11.

That he may give rest to the land.—Better, *to the earth*, in its widest extent, as implying that the whole earth had groaned under the oppression of Babylon. "The land," if we retain that rendering, would be, of course, "the land of Israel." Some versions, however (*e.g.*, the Vulg.), and some commentators (*e.g.*, Ewald), give the verbs the sense of "set in motion," *i.e.*, "trouble," and so make the parallelism of the two clauses one of resemblance and not of contrast.

(35) **A sword is upon the Chaldeans.**—Better, *A sword upon the Chaldeans.* Here, and in the verses that follow, the interpolated verb weakens the force of the passage. Jehovah is represented as calling the "sword" and the "drought" to do their work of destruction.

Upon her wise men.—The term points especially to the "wise men" in the technical sense of the term, the soothsayers and astrologers who were prominent among Nebuchadnezzar's counsellors (Dan. ii. 2, 13).

(36) **A sword is upon the liars; and they shall dote.**—The Hebrew word for "liars"—literally, *boastings*—implies the falsehood of folly rather than of purpose. Better, perhaps, *the prating fools.* The marginal readings "chief stays" and "bars" rest on no adequate authority. Here the word applies to the diviners and magicians (comp. Isa. xliv. 25).

(37) **And upon all the mingled people . . .**—The phrase is the same as in chap. xxv. 20. Here it is used of the auxiliaries of Babylon, which were probably as numerous, and to a large extent the same, as those of Persia. (See Note on verse 9.) The "treasures" point to the wealth in which Babylon exulted, and which gave to her the epithet of the "Golden City" (Isa. xiv. 4). Even under the Persian monarchy Æschylus uses "gold-abounding" as a normal epithet for it. (*Persæ*, 53.)

(38) **A drought is upon her waters.**—Better, *A sword.* The Hebrew word for "drought" has the same consonants as that for "sword," with different vowel-points. In the original text the form of the two words must have been identical, as the vowel-points were of later introduction. The editors of the present text were probably guided by the thought that the context in this case determined the meaning of the word as meaning "drought," and not a "sword." So in Deut. xxviii. 22 the text of the Authorised version gives "sword," and the margin "drought." There is, however, a certain loss of rhetorical emphasis in the change of the word with which the three previous verses had begun. The "waters" include the canals of Babylon as well as the Euphrates.

They are mad upon their idols.—The word for "idols" means literally "terrors," or "objects of terror," as in Ps. lxxxviii. 16; Job xx. 25, and this is the only place in which it is used of the objects of worship. In Gen. xiv. 5; Deut. ii. 10, 11 it appears as the name of the Emim, probably as meaning "the terrible, *or* gigantic ones." Here it seems used for the colossal figures—winged bulls, human-headed lions, and the like—which were the objects of Babylonian worship. (See note on chap. xlix. 16.)

(39) **Wild beasts of the desert . . .**—The combination of the two forms of animal life seems taken from Isa. xiii. 21, 22. In the original the two words *tziyyim* and *iiyyim* have a kind of emphatic assonance. The English word in the first case answers to the etymology, but the animal referred to has been identified by some naturalists with the wild cats, which appear from Baruch vi. 22 to have abounded in Babylon. In the second word the Authorised version follows a wrong etymology. Strictly the word means "howlers," and should be translated "jackals." For "owls" read "ostriches," as in Isa. xiii. 21.

(40) **As God overthrew Sodom . . .**—The whole verse is reproduced from chap. xlix. 18. We enter here, indeed, upon a mosaic of quotations, or at least recollections of other prophecies. Thus verses 41—43 are taken from chap. vi. 22—24, "Babylon" being substituted for "Zion," and "the king of Babylon" for "we;" verses 44—46 from chap. xlix. 19—21, with the

took hold of him, *and* pangs as of a woman in travail. (44) Behold, he shall come up [a] like a lion from the swelling of Jordan unto the habitation of the strong: but I will make them suddenly run away from her: and who *is* a chosen *man, that* I may appoint over her? for who *is* like me? and [b] who will [1] appoint me the time? and who *is* that shepherd that will stand before me? (45) Therefore hear ye the counsel of the LORD, that he hath taken against Babylon; and his purposes, that he hath purposed against the land of the Chaldeans: Surely the least of the flock shall draw them out: surely he shall make *their* habitation desolate with them. (46) At the noise of the taking of Babylon the earth is moved, and the cry is heard among the nations.

CHAPTER LI.—(1) Thus saith the LORD; Behold, I will raise up against Babylon, and against them that dwell in the [2] midst of them that rise up against me, a destroying wind; (2) and will send unto Babylon fanners, that shall fan her, and shall empty her land: for in the day of trouble they shall be against her round about. (3) Against *him that* bendeth let the archer bend his bow, and against *him that* lifteth himself up in his brigandine: and spare ye not her young men; destroy ye utterly all her host. (4) Thus the slain shall fall in the land of the Chaldeans, and *they that are* thrust through in her streets. (5) For Israel *hath* not *been* forsaken, nor Judah of his God, of the LORD of hosts; though their land was filled with sin against the Holy One of Israel. (6) [c] Flee out of the midst of Babylon, and deliver every man his soul: be not cut off in her iniquity; for this *is* the time of the LORD's vengeance; he will render unto her a recompence.

a ch. 49. 19.

b Job 41. 10; ch. 49. 19.

1 Or, *convent me to plead?*

2 Heb., *heart.*

c ch. 50. 8; Rev. 18. 4.

---

necessary substitutions of "Babylon" for "Edom," "the Chaldeans" for "Teman," "among the nations" for "in the Red sea." The reader is referred accordingly to the Notes on those passages. The reproduction in identical terms is probably connected with the thoughts of the retribution, on which the prophet dwells in verse 15. All that she had done Babylon was now to suffer.

LI.

(1) **I will raise up . . . a destroying wind.**—Literally, *the wind of a destroyer.* In Hagg. i. 14; Ezra i. 1, 5; 1 Chron. v. 26 the phrase is used for "stirring up the spirit" of a man, and that may be its meaning here. The context, however, suggests, in the "fanners" of the next verse, the literal meaning of "wind," and it is quite possible that the phrase may have been used by Jeremiah in this sense, and afterwards acquired a figurative meaning. It does not appear in any earlier book of the Old Testament.

Against them that dwell in the midst of them that rise up against me.—Literally, *in the heart of my adversaries.* In the judgment of most commentators the Hebrew words *Leb-kamai,* which answer to the last ten words of the English, furnish another example of the *Atbash* or cypher-writing of which we have seen an instance in the *Sheshach* of chap. xxv. 26. Interpreted by that cypher *Leb-kamai* becomes *Chasdim* or Chaldæans. Obviously the significance of the cypher-words gives force to its employment here, and presents a parallel to the use of the names Merathaim and Pekod in chap. l. 21. Some commentators, indeed, rest in that significance without recognising the hidden meaning of the Atbash. The LXX. and Syriac versions translate "against the Chaldæans," as recognising the use of the cypher. Both this and Sheshach had probably become familiar in the correspondence between the exiles and those of their countrymen who remained in Judæa, and so both would understand them when used by Jeremiah.

(2) **Fanners, that shall fan her.**—The Hebrew word as it stands means "strangers," but a change of the vowel-points would give etymologically "winnowers" or "fanners," though the word is not found elsewhere. On the whole it would seem best to accept the meaning of "strangers," the prophet connecting it with the verb for "fan," which contains the same consonants, for the sake of a rhythmical assonance. The imagery in either case is that of the familiar picture of the "threshing-floor," where the "strong wind" scatters the chaff in all directions (Pss. i. 4, xxxv. 5; Isa. xvii. 13, xxix. 5). The word for "empty" is the same as that used with an emphatic significance in chap. xix. 7.

(3) **Let the archer bend his bow.**—The words represent the sense of the original, but the Hebrew word for "archer" is literally *bender,* and so the iteration of the verb gains its full rhetorical force. On "brigandine," as meaning the "coat of mail" of heavy-armed troops, see Note on chap. xlvi. 4. The two classes of soldiers describe collectively the garrison that defended Babylon.

(5) **Israel hath not been forsaken.**—Better, *widowed.* The participle is from the word that commonly represents the idea of widowhood. Judah and Israel, the prophet declares, were not, as men thought, abandoned by their husband Jehovah. He was still their protector. The prophet has in his thoughts at once the image of apparent widowhood, as in Isa. l. 1, liv. 4—6; Lam. i. 1, and the thought that Jehovah is, after all, as the husband ready to forgive (chaps. iii. 4, 14, 20, iv. 1). The assurance of this returning love does not rest on any plea in extenuation of the nation's guilt, which the words that follow admit without reserve. For "his" it would be better to read *her* or *their,* as keeping up the metaphor.

Against the Holy One of Israel.—On Jeremiah's use of the name, see Note on chap. l. 29.

(6) **Flee out of the midst of Babylon.**—The words reproduce the call of chap. l. 8 with a fresh

(7) Babylon *hath been* a golden cup in
the LORD's hand, that made all the
earth drunken: the nations have drunken
of her wine; therefore the nations are
mad. (8) Babylon is suddenly [a] fallen
and destroyed: howl for her; take balm
for her pain, if so be she may be healed.
(9) We would have healed Babylon, but
she is not healed: forsake her, and let
us go every one into his own country:
for her judgment reacheth unto heaven,
and is lifted up *even* to the skies.
(10) The LORD hath brought forth our
righteousness: come, and let us declare
in Zion the work of the LORD our God.

(11) Make [1] bright the arrows; gather
the shields: the LORD hath raised up
the spirit of the kings of the Medes:
for his device *is* against Babylon, to
destroy it; because it *is* the vengeance
of the LORD, the vengeance of his
temple. (12) Set up the standard upon
the walls of Babylon, make the watch
strong, set up the watchmen, prepare
the [2] ambushes: for the LORD hath both
devised and done that which he spake
against the inhabitants of Babylon.
(13) O thou that dwellest upon many
waters, abundant in treasures, thine
end is come, *and* the measure of thy

a Isa. 21. 9; Rev. 14. 8; & 18. 2.

1 Heb., *pure.*

2 Heb., *liers in wait.*

---

motive. The city was doomed. It was ill done for those who had not been guilty of her sins to involve themselves in her destruction. The call is reproduced, as referring to the mystical Babylon, in Rev. xviii. 4.

(7) **Babylon hath been a golden cup . . .**—The "golden cup" points to the splendour of Babylon, outwardly, as a vessel made to honour (see Notes on chap. l. 37). But the "wine" in that cup was poisoned, intoxicating men with wild ambitions and dark idolatries. The same image re-appears in Rev. xiv. 8, xvii. 4, save that there the "golden cup" is in the hand of the harlot, "whose name is MYSTERY, BABYLON THE GREAT."

(8) **Babylon is suddenly fallen . . .**—The form of announcement seems taken in part from Isa. xxi. 9.

Take balm for her pain . . .—The words are significant. The captive people are not invited simply to raise a shout of triumph at the fall of their oppressor: they are to "take balm" (comp. the use of the same image in chaps. viii. 22, xlvi. 11), and try to heal her. They are still to "seek the peace of the city" (chap. xxix. 7), to render kindly service, to pour balm into the bleeding wounds.

(9) **We would have healed Babylon . . .**—This is the dramatic answer of the Israelite exiles to the prophet's appeal. They have done what they could, but all was in vain. The guilt could not be washed away, the punishment could not be averted. The "judgment" is measureless as is the distance from heaven to earth. This is also reproduced in Rev. xviii. 5. For the phrase, as applied to Nebuchadnezzar, see Dan. iv. 20. Possibly there may be an allusive reference to the tower of Babel, "reaching unto heaven," as the type of Babylonian greatness (Gen. xi. 4).

(10) **The Lord hath brought forth our righteousness . . .**—The Hebrew noun is plural—the many *righteous acts* or forms of righteousness. The thought is parallel to that of Isa. lxii. 1. The exile in Babylon had been a time of reformation and growth in righteousness. The day of vengeance on the oppressing city was also a day of acquittal for Israel. It was seen that she had not forfeited the favour of Jehovah. She could still sing, as of old (Judges v. 11), the righteous acts of the Lord, and would sing them, as of old, in the restored sanctuary of Zion.

(11) **Make bright the arrows.**—Better, *Sharpen*, the "polishing" or "making bright" being as the means to that end.

Gather the shields.—Literally, *fill the shields*, *i.e.*, arm yourselves with them. The large shields of the Persian soldiers covered the whole body, and the man literally filled them. The LXX. and Vulgate agree in rendering the noun "quivers" instead of "shields," but this would seem to have been a conjecture rising out of a wish to connect the two clauses. The rendering of the Authorised version agrees with the use of the word in Song Sol. iv. 4; Ezek. xxvii. 11; 2 Kings xi. 10. Some critics interpret the words as meaning "fill the shields with oil," as parallel to "sharpen the arrows," and agreeing with "anoint the shield" in Isa. xxi. 5.

Of the kings of the Medes.—As with the Greeks in their use of the terms Medise and Medism, so with the Hebrews the Medes are more prominent than the Persians in the work of destruction (comp. Isa. xiii. 17). The "kings" are the chieftains of tribes more or less independent, but owning the suzerainty of the Persian king. It is noticeable that the ruler of Babylon, after its capture by Cyrus, in Dan. v. 31, is "Darius the Median," and that he is called a "king."

(12) **Set up the standard upon the walls of Babylon.**—The Authorised version, following the LXX. and the Vulgate, takes the words as an ironical summons to a defence which will prove fruitless. The preposition for "upon" may, however, mean *against*, and this agrees better with the context. The "standards" are the banners or signals that direct an attack on a given point of the walls. The "watch" and "watchmen" are the scouts and sentinels placed to give notice of any attempt at a sally on the part of the besieged. The "ambush" may indicate generally any sudden attack, or, more specifically, the stratagem of a feigned flight, like that employed by Joshua in the attack on Ai (Josh. viii. 14—16; comp. Judges xx. 33—35).

(13) **O thou that dwellest upon many waters.**—The words find an illustration of singular interest in an inscription of Nebuchadnezzar's given by Oppert (*Expéd. en Mésop.* i. p. 231): "I made water to flow all around in this immense dyke of earth. I carried an aqueduct across these great waters that are like unto the depths of the sea." See also *Records of the Past*, v. 128. The channels which were cut for the waters of the Euphrates seemed at once intended for a line of defence against attack, and for irrigation and navigation. To some extent Babylon, though an inland city, must have presented an appearance like that of Venice or Amsterdam.

The measure of thy covetousness.—The measure is literally "an ell," and for "covetousness" many

covetousness. (14) [a] The LORD of hosts
hath sworn [1] by himself, *saying*, Surely
I will fill thee with men, as with cater-
pillers and they shall [2] lift up a shout
against thee.
(15) [b] He hath made the earth by his
power, he hath established the world by
his wisdom, and hath stretched out the
heaven by his understanding. (16) When
he uttereth *his* voice, *there is* a [3] multi-
tude of waters in the heavens; and he
causeth the vapours to ascend from the
ends of the earth: he maketh lightnings
with rain, and bringeth forth the wind
out of his treasures. (17) [c] Every man
[4] is brutish by *his* knowledge; every
founder is confounded by the graven
image: for his molten image *is* falsehood,
and *there is* no breath in them. (18) They
are vanity, the work of errors: in the
time of their visitation they shall perish.
(19) [d] The portion of Jacob *is* not like
them; for he *is* the former of all things:
and *Israel is* the rod of his inheritance:
the LORD of hosts *is* his name.

(20) Thou *art* my battle ax *and* weapons
of war: for [5] with thee will I break in
pieces the nations, and with thee will I
destroy kingdoms; (21) and with thee
will I break in pieces the horse and his
rider; and with thee will I break in
pieces the chariot and his rider; (22) with
thee also will I break in pieces man and
woman; and with thee will I break in
pieces old and young; and with thee
will I break in pieces the young man
and the maid; (23) I will also break in
pieces with thee the shepherd and his
flock; and with thee will I break in
pieces the husbandman and his yoke of
oxen; and with thee will I break in
pieces captains and rulers. (24) And I
will render unto Babylon and to all the
inhabitants of Chaldea all their evil
that they have done in Zion in your
sight, saith the LORD.
(25) Behold, I *am* against thee, O de-
stroying mountain, saith the LORD, which
destroyest all the earth: and I will
stretch out mine hand upon thee, and

a Amos 6. 8.

1 Heb., *by his soul.*

2 Heb., *utter*

b Gen. 1. 1, 6; ch. 10. 12, &c.

3 Or, *noise.*

c ch. 10. 1

4 Or, *is more brutish than to know.*

d ch. 10. 16.

5 Or, *in thee*, or, *by thee.*

---

commentators give the meaning of "that which is cut off," a "piece" or "section." So taken, we may translate *the ell-measure of thy portion*, the allotted time of prosperity decreed in the Divine counsels. Others, following the Vulgate, "*pedalis precisionis tuæ*," give "the ell-measure of thy cutting off," *i.e.*, the appointed time of destruction.

(14) **The Lord of hosts hath sworn by himself.**—This is, as in chap. xlix. 13; Amos vi. 8, the most solemn form of affirmation. Compare Heb. vi. 13, and Note on chap. xlix. 13.

Surely I will fill thee with men, as with caterpillers.—Better, *with grasshoppers* or *locusts*, the fullest type of the swarms of the destroyer (Nah. iii. 15). The "Surely" answers to the Hebrew "For if," as giving the condition on which the shouting depends.

They shall lift up a shout against thee.—The thought is the same as in chap. xxv. 30. The "shout" is that of those who tread the grapes in the wine-press, and that, as in Isa. lxiii. 2, 3, is the received symbol of conquest and destruction.

(15–19) **He hath made the earth by his power . . .**—The five verses are a reproduction of chap. x. 12—16, fitted in here to enhance the majesty of Him Who decrees the destruction of Babylon, and appoints Israel to be the instrument of that destruction. The word "Israel," as the italics show, is wanting in the Hebrew, and we have a sufficient sense without it. "He is the former of all things, and *of the rod* (*i.e.*, the tribe) of his inheritance." The English version follows the Vulgate and the Targum in treating the omission as an error of transcription. (See Notes on chap. x. 12—16.)

(20) **Thou art my battle ax . . .**—Better, *my mace.* The axe is not found on Assyrian monuments as a weapon of war till a comparatively late period. It is a question who is thus addressed—Babylon, or Cyrus as the destroyer of Babylon, or Israel. On the whole, the second seems the more probable answer. The "hammer of the whole earth" is broken by a mightier weapon than itself. (See Note on chap. l. 23.)

With thee will I break in pieces . . .—The tense, in this and in the following, should be the present. The force of the verb is multiplied by the emphatic iteration. All obstacles are to be crushed in the victorious march of the conqueror.

(23) **With thee will I break in pieces captains and rulers.**—The exhausting of all sorts and conditions of men culminates in the ruling caste. The Hebrew word for "captain" (*Pekha*) is interesting as connected with the Arabic, with which we are now familiar in the form *Pacha* (Fürst, *Lex.*).

(25) **O destroying mountain.**—Singularly enough the phrase is the same as that which is applied in 2 Kings xxiii. 13 to the Mount of Olives, and is there rendered by the Authorised version as "the Mount of Corruption." It adds to the interest that this name so given appears in the reign of Josiah, and must therefore have been familiar to Jeremiah. There it is applied to the Mount of Olives as having been the centre of the worship of Ashtoreth and Chemosh and Milcom, destroying the faith and life of Israel. Here, not without the thought that the false worship of Babylon was the root of all its evils, the prophet applies it to that city. The use of the term "mountain," literally quite inapplicable, was symbolical of its sovereignty. The latter clause of the verse suggests the idea that the prophet had before him the picture of a volcano.

And will make thee a burnt mountain.—Literally, *a mountain of burning*—either actively, as rolling down its lava and stones to the destruction of all below; or passively, as spent and burnt out. As the sentence describes the doom of Babylon, the latter meaning seems preferable. It is interesting to note the fact that there is an extinct volcano known

roll thee down from the rocks, and will
make thee a burnt mountain. (26) And
they shall not take of thee a stone for a
corner, nor a stone for foundations ; but
thou shalt be [1] desolate for ever, saith
the LORD.

(27) Set ye up a standard in the land,
blow the trumpet among the nations,
prepare the nations against her, call
together against her the kingdoms of
Ararat, Minni, and Ashchenaz; appoint
a captain against her; cause the horses
to come up as the rough caterpillers.
(28) Prepare against her the nations with
the kings of the Medes, the captains
thereof, and all the rulers thereof, and
all the land of his dominion. (29) And
the land shall tremble and sorrow: for
every purpose of the LORD shall be per-
formed against Babylon, to make the
land of Babylon a desolation without an
inhabitant. (30) The mighty men of
Babylon have forborn to fight, they have
remained in *their* holds: their might
hath failed; they became as women:
they have burned her dwelling-places;
her bars are broken. (31) One post shall
run to meet another, and one messenger
to meet another, to shew the king of
Babylon that his city is taken at *one*
end, (32) and that the passages are stopped,
and the reeds they have burned with
fire, and the men of war are affrighted.
(33) For thus saith the LORD of hosts, the

[1] Heb., *everlasting desolations.*

---

as *Koukal* (= fire), which rises to a height of 300 feet above the river *Khabour*, in Western Assyria (the Chebar of Ezek. i. 3), consisting of loose lava, scoriæ, and ashes. (Rawlinson's *Ancient Monarchies*, i. 189.) Possibly the prophet, who had journeyed to the Euphrates, had seen in this the symbol of the "destroying mountain" that destroyed itself. Babylon was for him an extinct volcano.

(26) **They shall not take of thee a stone for a corner.**—The prophet uses general language applicable to any city destroyed by fire, without noting the special fact that Babylon was built of bricks.

(27) **Prepare the nations.**—The word here and in verse 29 conveys, as in chap. xxii. 7, the idea of consecration.

Call together against her the kingdoms of Ararat, Minni, and Ashchenaz.—The first of these names was unknown to Greek and Roman geographers, and though here rendered *Arareth* by the LXX., is elsewhere translated by Armenia, as in the English version of Isa. xxxvii. 38. The name Ararat is Sanscrit, and means "the holy land." The site of Minni has not been identified, and the name does not occur elsewhere, unless, with some scholars, we find it in Ps. xlv. 9, and translate "out of the ivory palaces of Minni." The name "Minyes" is found in Josephus (*Antt.* i. 3, p. 6), and Minnai in the Assyrian inscriptions. Rawlinson (Herod. i. p. 464) places them above *Lake Urumiyeh*. It is clear from the context that their country formed part of Armenia. Ashchenaz appears in Gen. x. 3 as connected with Gomer, *i.e.*, with the Scythians. The first syllable has been supposed to contain the root of the name *Asia*, which has been gradually extended to the continent. The modern Jews apply the name *Ashkenazim* to those of their race that are settled in Germany and Eastern Europe, the name *Sephardim* being applied to those of Spain and the West.

Appoint a captain against her.—The word for "captain" is found only here and in Nah. iii. 17. It was probably an Assyrian word, meaning either "captain" or "host."

Cause the horses to come up as the rough caterpillers.—Better, *as the bristly locusts.* The word describes the insect in its third stage of growth, when the wings are not yet unfolded from their cases, and when they are most destructive in their ravages.

(28) **All the land of his dominion.**—The use of the singular pronoun indicates that the prophet recognises the fact that the kings, captains, and rulers (see Note on verse 23) are all under one sovereign leader—*i.e.*, under the king of the Medes and Persians.

(29) **And the land shall tremble and sorrow.**—The verbs in the Hebrew are in the past tense, the prophet seeing, as it were, the very event which he portrays passing before him in his vision.

(30) **The mighty men of Babylon have forborn to fight.**—The verses that follow paint the capture of the city by the stratagem related in the Note on chap. l. 24. Those who "have burned" are, of course, the invaders. They here begin by setting the houses of the city on fire and breaking open the gates that led from the river into the streets of the city, while the panic-stricken people fled to their citadel in despair.

(31) **One post shall run to meet another.**—The words exactly answer to the account of the capture of Babylon given in Herod. i. (see Note on chap. li. 24). The history of Belshazzar's feast (Dan. v. 1—30) must obviously have ended in a like result. No words could paint more vividly the panic of the surprised city.

(32) **That the passages are stopped.**—These were probably the ferries across the Euphrates, by which one part of the city was in communication with the other. These were at the ends of the streets that ran at right angles to the river, and gates—left open in the panic of surprise—led down to them. Besides these there was one bridge over the Euphrates in the middle and a tunnel under it (Herod. i. 186). The word is elsewhere used for fords, as in Gen. xxxii. 22; Judges iii. 28, but cannot have that meaning here, as the Euphrates was not fordable at Babylon.

The reeds they have burned with fire.—The word for "reeds" is elsewhere (Isa. xiv. 23, xli. 18; Exod. vii. 19, viii. 5) translated "pool." Here it probably refers to the great pool constructed by Nitocris as a reservoir or dock. This was probably left dry by the diversion of the river into another channel, and the reeds which grew in it, perhaps also the flood-gates of the canals, and the ships that were in dock, were burnt by the Persians. The very pools were the scene of a conflagration.

(33) **The daughter of Babylon . . .**—More literally, *The daughter of Babylon is like a threshing-floor, in the time when it is trodden* (*i.e.*, when it is

God of Israel; The daughter of Babylon
is like a threshingfloor, [1]*it is* time to
thresh her: yet a little while, and the
time of her harvest shall come.
(34) Nebuchadrezzar the king of Baby-
lon hath devoured me, he hath crushed
me, he hath made me an empty vessel,
he hath swallowed me up like a dragon,
he hath filled his belly with my delicates,
he hath cast me out. (35) [2]The violence
done to me and to my [3]flesh *be* upon
Babylon, shall the [4]inhabitant of Zion
say; and my blood upon the inhabitants
of Chaldea, shall Jerusalem say. (36) There-
fore thus saith the LORD; Behold, I will
plead thy cause, and take vengeance for
thee; and I will dry up her sea, and
make her springs dry. (37) And Babylon
shall become heaps, a dwellingplace for
dragons, an astonishment, and an hiss-
ing, without an inhabitant. (38) They
shall roar together like lions: they shall
[5]yell as lions' whelps. (39) In their heat
I will make their feasts, and I will make
them drunken, that they may rejoice,
and sleep a perpetual sleep, and not
wake, saith the LORD. (40) I will bring
them down like lambs to the slaughter,
like rams with he goats.
(41) How is Sheshach taken! and how
is the praise of the whole earth sur-
prised! how is Babylon become an
astonishment among the nations! (42) The
sea is come up upon Babylon: she is

1 Or, *in the time that he thresheth her.*

2 Heb., *My violence.*

3 Or, *remainder.*

4 Heb., *inhabitress.*

5 Or, *shake themselves.*

---

being prepared for the actual process), *yet a little while, and the time of harvest shall come to her.* The imagery is so familiar that it hardly needs an illustration (see Ps. i. 4; Isa. xxi. 10, xxviii. 27, 28; Micah iv. 13). The time of "her harvest" of the Authorised version is ambiguous. What is meant is that the heaped-up treasures of Babylon are but as the harvest which shall be reaped by her conquerors, and the city itself as the threshing-floor on which men shall trample on the plunder.

(34) **He hath made me an empty vessel.**—The pronouns in one form of the Hebrew text are most of them in the plural, "devoured *us*, crushed *us*, made *us*." The prophet speaks of himself and Israel as having suffered wrong and outrage at the hands of Nebuchadnezzar. The land had been spoiled till it was as an "empty vessel."

He hath swallowed me up like a dragon.—The Hebrew noun probably stands for a "crocodile" (as in Isa. xxvii. 1, li. 9; Ezek. xxix. 3), or is used generally for any sea-monster. The "delicates" ("dainties" in Gen. xlix. 20) are the corn and wine and oil and fruits of Palestine with which the Chaldæan armies had enriched themselves.

(35) **The violence done to me and to my flesh . . .**—The imagery of the "dragon" or "crocodile" is continued. The "*inhabitress of Zion*" pleads that her "flesh" and "blood" have been devoured by the Babylonian conqueror, and asks for the application of the law of retribution.

(36) **I will dry up her sea . . .**—The nouns have been variously interpreted, some commentators referring it to the "sea" of confluent nations, and finding the wealth of Babylon in the "springs" that fed its greatness; others to the Euphrates, or to the sea-like alluvial plain, intersected by canals and streams in which the city stood, often flooded by the river, so that it became as an actual sea (Herod. i. 184), or specially to the large lake described in the Note on verse 32. So in Isa. xxi. 1 Babylon is described as "the desert of the sea." The Hebrew word for "springs" is in the singular, her *reservoir*. Probably the literal and figurative meanings run into one another, and the "drying up" describes the exhaustion of the power of which the "sea" was the symbol. In Rev. xvi. 12 we have apparently an allusive reference to the language of this prediction.

(37) **Babylon shall become heaps . . .**—It is significant, as emphasising the law of retribution, that the terms are the same as those used of Jerusalem in chaps. ix. 11, xix. 8, xxv. 9, 18. Nothing is more characteristic of the present aspect of Babylon than the "heaps" or mounds of brickwork, fragments of pottery and earth, that are now scattered over the plain, and are slowly yielding up their records of the past to explorers. The "dragons" here (not the same word as in verse 34) are the "jackals" that howl in the ruins. (See Note on chap. x. 22.)

(38) **They shall roar together like lions . . .**—The words are not a continuation of the picture of the preceding verse, but carry us to the scene of revelry that preceded the capture of the city. The princes of Babylon were as "young lions" (Amos iii. 4) roaring over their prey. The first clause as well as the second conveys this meaning, and there is probably a reference to the youth of rulers like Belshazzar.

(39) **In their heat I will make their feasts . . .**—The words are stern and bitter in their irony. When the revellers are hot with wine and lust (comp. Hos. vii. 4—7) Jehovah would call them to a banquet of another kind. The wine cup which He would give them would be that of His wrath (chap. xxv. 16, 17), and their drunken joy should end in an eternal sleep. So Herodotus (i. 191) narrates that when Cyrus took the city by his stratagem the inhabitants were keeping a feast with their wonted revelry and license. (Compare Xenoph. *Cyropœd.* vii. 23.)

(40) **I will bring them down like lambs to the slaughter . . .**—The figure is changed, and the revellers appear as themselves destined to be the victims of the slaughter-house (chaps. xlviii. 15, l. 27). As the "bullocks" of chap. l. 27 are the chosen warriors, so the lambs, sheep, he-goats represent the different classes of the population of Babylon (Isa. xxxiv. 6; Ezek. xxxix. 18). All alike are given over to the sword.

(41) **How is Sheshach taken!**—"Sheshach," it will be remembered, is the cypher which, as explained in the Note on chap. xxv. 26, stands for Babylon. Here, in the parallelism of Hebrew poetry, it balances the actual name of the city in the second clause of the verse. The word "surprised" is the same as that rendered "stopped" in verse 32.

(42) **The sea is come up upon Babylon . . .**—The literal explanation of the words as referring to the

covered with the multitude of the waves
thereof. (43) Her cities are a desolation,
a dry land, and a wilderness, a land
wherein no man dwelleth, neither doth
any son of man pass thereby. (44) And
I will punish Bel in Babylon, and I will
bring forth out of his mouth that which
he hath swallowed up: and the nations
shall not flow together any more unto
him: yea, the wall of Babylon shall
fall.

(45) My people, go ye out of the midst
of her, and deliver ye every man his
soul from the fierce anger of the LORD.
(46) And lest your heart faint, and ye
fear for the rumour that shall be heard
in the land; a rumour shall both come
one year, and after that in *another* year
shall come a rumour, and violence in the
land, ruler against ruler.

(47) Therefore, behold, the days come,
that I will [1] do judgment upon the graven
images of Babylon: and her whole land
shall be confounded, and all her slain
shall fall in the midst of her. (48) Then
the heaven and the earth, and all that
is therein, shall sing for Babylon: for
the spoilers shall come unto her from
the north, saith the LORD. (49) [2] As
Babylon *hath caused* the slain of Israel
to fall, so at Babylon shall fall the slain
of all [3] the earth. (50) Ye that have
escaped the sword, go away, stand not
still: remember the LORD afar off, and

1 Heb., *visit upon.*

2 Or, *Both Babylon is to fall, O ye slain of Israel, and with Babylon, &c.*

3 Or, *the country.*

---

inundation of the Euphrates adopted by some commentators is clearly inadmissible, and is at variance with the next verse. The prophet falls back on an image which he had used before (chap. xlvi. 7), and which had become familiar through Isaiah (viii. 7, 8, xvii. 12), and speaks of Babylon as covered with the great sea of nations that were sweeping over her.

(43) **Her cities are a desolation . . .**—The word for "wilderness" is *Arabah,* commonly used of the sandy desert south of the Dead Sea. The prophet seems to dwell with a stern delight on the seeming paradox that the sea with which Babylon is to be overflowed, the floods of invaders and destroyers, shall leave her cities and her plains drier and more sandy than before.

(44) **And I will punish Bel in Babylon.**—See Note on chap. l. 2. The god whom Babylon worshipped is, as before, thought of as sharing her downfall. He is made to disgorge his spoil, the vessels of the Temple of Jehovah that had been placed in his temple (Dan. v. 2; Ezra i. 7).

The wall of Babylon shall fall.—The words, though they repeat the statement of chap. l. 15, have here a special significance. The two great walls of the city bore, as has been stated above, the names of Imgur-Bel (= Bel protects) and Nimetti-Bel (= the dwelling of Bel), and were thus specially consecrated to him as their tutelary deity (Oppert, *Expédit. en Mésop.*, i. p. 227; *Records of the Past*, v. 124). The name of the last king of Babylon, Belshazzar, is a further indication of the reverence felt for him as the supreme object of worship.

(45) **Go ye out of the midst of her . . .**—The prophet repeats, with all the emphasis of iteration, the summons of chaps. l. 8, li. 6. The "fierce anger of the Lord" is that which was directed primarily against Babylon, but which would also fall on those who chose to remain and become "partakers in her plagues." (Compare Rev. xviii. 4.)

(46) **And lest your heart faint . . .**—Better, *Let not your heart faint; fear ye not. . .*

For the rumour that shall be heard in the land.—It lies in the nature of the case that the final catastrophe of the city would be preceded by a period of uncertainty and suspense. Men would hear of the union of the Medes and Persians under Cyrus, of the murder of Evil-Merodach by Neriglissar, of the death of Neriglissar in fighting against the enemy (B.C. 555). The child-king, whom Berosus calls Laborosoarchod, was dethroned by his nobles after a few months, and was succeeded by the father of the Belshazzar of Dan. v. 1, the Labynetus of Herodotus, whose true name was Nabo-nahid. The whole empire was in the throes of dissolution. The words present a singular parallel to those which speak of "wars and rumours of wars" in Matt. xxiv. 6, 7; Luke xxi. 9.

(47) **Therefore, behold, the days come . . .**—The first word has its full force. The Israelite exiles were to infer from the rumours and disorders of the preceding verse, that the day of vengeance was at hand. The formula, "behold, the days come," was Jeremiah's customary manner of announcing a prediction (comp. chaps. vii. 32, xvi. 14, *et al.*). For "slain" some commentators read "wounded" or "smitten," as the word is rendered in Ps. lxix. 26; Job xxiv. 12, the words that follow indicating that the wounded shall have no power to escape, but shall fill the city with their corpses.

(48) **Then the heaven and the earth . . .**—The prophet, following in the track of Isaiah (xliv. 23), thinks of the whole creation as rejoicing in the righteous judgment of Jehovah on the guilty city, and in the liberation of His people. They sing, as it were, their *Te Deum* over the fall of Babylon under the attack of the Medo-Persian armies "from the North."

(49) **As Babylon hath caused . . .**—The interpolated words and the marginal reading indicate that the construction is obscure, but the Authorised version probably comes close to the meaning of the original. The punishment that falls on Babylon comes on account of her slaughter of the Israelites, but in that punishment other nations from all parts of the earth who are mingled with her people should be involved. Perhaps, however, we should read *the slain of all the land*, as giving more emphatically the law of retribution. The rendering of the margin, "Both Babylon is to fall, O ye slain of Israel, and with Babylon . . ," is adopted by some recent commentators, but gives a less satisfactory meaning.

(50) **Ye that have escaped the sword . . .**—The words call on the people to fulfil the prediction of chap. l. 4, 5. Even in that distant land, "afar off" from the Temple of Jehovah, they are to remember that they are Israelites, and to think of Jerusalem as

let Jerusalem come into your mind.
(51) We are confounded, because we have
heard reproach: shame hath covered
our faces: for strangers are come into
the sanctuaries of the LORD's house.
(52) Wherefore, behold, the days come,
saith the LORD, that I will do judgment
upon her graven images: and through
all her land the wounded shall groan.
(53) Though Babylon should mount up
to heaven, and though she should fortify
the height of her strength, *yet* from me
shall spoilers come unto her, saith the
LORD.
(54) A sound of a cry *cometh* from
Babylon, and great destruction from
the land of the Chaldeans: (55) because
the LORD hath spoiled Babylon, and
destroyed out of her the great voice;
when her waves do roar like great
waters, a noise of their voice is uttered:
(56) because the spoiler is come upon
her, *even* upon Babylon, and her mighty
men are taken, every one of their bows
is broken: for the LORD God of recom-
pences shall surely requite. (57) And I
will make drunk her princes, and her
wise *men*, her captains, and her rulers,
and her mighty men: and they shall
sleep a perpetual sleep, and not wake,
saith the King, whose name *is* the LORD
of hosts.
(58) Thus saith the LORD of hosts;
[1] The broad walls of Babylon shall be
utterly [2] broken, and her high gates
shall be burned with fire; and the people
shall labour in vain, and the folk in the
fire, and they shall be weary.
(59) The word which Jeremiah the pro-
phet commanded Seraiah the son of
Neriah, the son of Maaseiah, when he
went [3] with Zedekiah the king of Judah

1 Or, *The walls of broad Babylon.*
2 Or, *made naked.*
3 Or, *on the behalf of.*

their home. In Ps. cxxxvii. 5, 6 we have, as it were, by anticipation, the answer of the exiles. They had not forgotten Jerusalem in the revelry of their conquerors. They were not likely to forget her when their conquerors were, in their turn, conquered.

(51) **We are confounded, because we have heard reproach . . .**—The answer which the prophet seems to hear from the lips of the exiles, is, however, for the present, of a different character. They are cast down and oppressed by the disgrace that has fallen on them and on the Holy City. Aliens in blood and faith have profaned their sanctuaries. Can anything wipe off the stain of that disgrace? The prophet had known the bitterness of that thought himself (Lam. i. 10, ii. 7, iv. 12), and had learnt how to deal with it. "Yes," he answers in the next verse, "there is comfort in the thought of retribution. The idol-temples which had been enriched with the spoils of their Temple shall be despoiled; the plunderers shall fall by the sword of the destroyer."

(53) **Though Babylon should mount up to heaven . . .**—The special form of the phrase recalls the language of the builders of the Tower which made the name of Babylon conspicuous (Gen. xi. 4). Even though that boastful attempt should be realised, Jeremiah says, it should prove a vain defence. As it was, the walls of Babylon which Nebuchadnezzar had built were of enormous height. Greek writers, possibly speaking of different walls (as there were two lines of fortifications), give from 75 to 335 feet. Nebuchadnezzar, in one of his inscriptions, records their greatness in words that remind us of Dan. iv. 30. "To make more difficult the attack of an enemy against Imgur Bel, the indestructible wall of Babylon, I constructed a bulwark like a mountain" (Oppert, *Expéd. en Mésop.*, i. p. 230; *Records of the Past*, v. p. 131).

(55) **Because the Lord hath spoiled Babylon . . .**—In verse 54 the prophet hears the cry of the captured city. The "great voice" which Jehovah "destroys" or "makes to cease" is the stir and tumult of life that surged, as it were, through the city (Isa. xviii. 12, 13). The "waves" are those of the "sea" of the legions of her conqueror (see verse 42), and they "roar" while the voices that were heard before are hushed in the silence of death.

(56) **The Lord God of recompences . . .**—The prophet clothes the law of retribution which he has been asserting throughout the chapter with a new majesty by connecting it with a new Divine Name (comp. chap. xxiii. 6). Jehovah delights, as it were, to manifest Himself in that aspect. He is *a God of retribution, Jehovah*, and will be true to that title.

(57) **I will make drunk her princes.**—The imagery is repeated from verse 39, and carries out the thought of chap. xxv. 15, 16, 27. On the list of officers see Note on verse 23.

(58) **Her high gates shall be burned with fire.**—These were part of the works on which Nebuchadnezzar prided himself as the restorer of the city. The inscription already quoted refers to these as well as to the walls: "Babylon is the refuge of the god Merodach. I have finished *Imgur Bel*, his great enclosure. In the threshold of the great gates I have adjusted folding-doors in brass." (Oppert, *ut supra*; Comp. also *Records of the Past*, v. pp. 125, 127).

The people shall labour in vain.—The words are all but verbally identical, in some MSS. absolutely so, with those of Hab. ii. 13. In both the thought is that the stately edifices which had been raised with so much toil by the slave-labour of Nebuchadnezzar's subjects and captives should all be fruitless. The walls of Babylon are described by Herod. (i., 173), possibly with some exaggeration, as 50 cubits (= 75 feet) thick and 200 high.

(59) **Seraiah the son of Neriah.**—The great prophecy has reached its close, and the remainder of the chapter is of the nature of an historical appendix. The mention of both father and grandfather leaves no doubt that Seraiah was the brother of Jeremiah's friend and secretary, Baruch (chap. xxxii. 13). It was, therefore, natural that the prophet should select him as the depository of the great prediction. The term "quiet prince," which the Authorised version adopts from Luther, means really *prince of the resting-place*, and describes an office like that of our quartermaster-general.

into Babylon in the fourth year of his
reign. And *this* Seraiah *was* a [1] quiet
prince. (60) So Jeremiah wrote in a
book all the evil that should come
upon Babylon, *even* all these words that
are written against Babylon.
(61) And Jeremiah said to Seraiah,
When thou comest to Babylon, and
shalt see, and shalt read all these words;
(62) then shalt thou say, O LORD, thou
hast spoken against this place, to cut it
off, that none shall remain in it, neither
man nor beast, but that it shall be
[2] desolate for ever. (63) And it shall be,
when thou hast made an end of reading
this book, *that* thou shalt bind a stone
to it, and cast it into the midst of
Euphrates: (64) and thou shalt say, Thus
shall Babylon sink, and shall not rise
from the evil that I will bring upon her:
and they shall be weary.
Thus far *are* the words of Jeremiah.

CHAPTER LII.—(1) Zedekiah *was*
[a] one and twenty years old when he
[3] began to reign, and he reigned eleven
years in Jerusalem. And his mother's
name *was* Hamutal the daughter of
Jeremiah of Libnah. (2) And he did
that which was evil in the eyes of the
LORD, according to all that Jehoiakim
had done. (3) For through the anger of
the LORD it came to pass in Jerusalem
and Judah, till he had cast them out

1 Or, *prince of Menucha*, or, *chief chamberlain.*

B.C. 599.

2 Heb., *desolations.*

a 2 Kings 24. 18.

3 Heb., *reigned.*

He would seem to have been attendant on Zedekiah, probably appointed by Nebuchadnezzar to regulate the details of the journey to Babylon, and arrange the resting-places at its several stages. The versions seem to have been perplexed by the unusual title, the LXX. giving "ruler of the gifts," and the Vulgate "prince of prophecy." The prediction would seem to have been of the nature of a parting gift to him.

In the fourth year of his reign.—The date is significant as giving a missing link in the history. The beginning of Zedekiah's reign was memorable for the gathering at Jerusalem of ambassadors from the kings of Edom, Moab, Ammon, Tyre, and Zidon, obviously for the purpose of forming a confederacy against Nebuchadnezzar, and Jeremiah had condemned all such schemes as contrary to the will of Jehovah (chap. xxvii. 1—13). It is probable that Nebuchadnezzar summoned the king of Judah to Babylon to question him as to this scheme, and to demand an act of renewed homage. On this journey he was accompanied by the brother of the prophet's friend and fellow-worker, and Jeremiah takes the opportunity of committing to his charge what we may call an esoteric prophecy, lifting up the veil of the future. He counselled submission for the present, because resistance was premature, and would prove futile. He looked forward to the time when the law of retribution would be fulfilled in Babylon as it had been fulfilled in Jerusalem. The whole proceeding was in perfect harmony with the prediction of chap. xxvii. 7, that all nations should serve Nebuchadnezzar and his son and his son's son till the "very time of his land" should come. It lies in the nature of the case that a duplicate copy was kept by Baruch or Jeremiah, of which the present text of chaps. l. and li. is a transcript.

(60) **So Jeremiah wrote in a book.**—The "book" is, as elsewhere, a parchment roll. Stress is laid on the fact that the long prophecy was all written on one roll, so that it might be a fitter symbol of the city that was its subject.

(61) **When thou comest to Babylon, and shalt see, and shalt read . . .**—The meaning of the Hebrew would be better expressed by, *thou shalt see to it and read*, or *see to it and read*. The English version, as it is, leaves it doubtful who or what is to be seen. The verb for "read" implies reading aloud. Seraiah was to read the prophecy to those whom it concerned, probably to a chosen few among his own countrymen. The idea that it was to be read to the Babylonians is in the highest degree improbable.

(62) **Then shalt thou say, O Lord . . .**—The words which recite the predictions of chap. l. 3, 39 are of the nature of an implied prayer, reminding Jehovah of that which He had promised, and entreating him to fulfil it. "Thou hast said" was to be the ground of the suppliant's prayer for the fulfilment.

(63) **Thou shalt bind a stone to it.**—The meaning of the symbolic act, which has its parallel in the girdle of chap. xiii. 1—7, in the potter's vessel of chap. xix. 10, and in the yokes of chap. xxvii. 2, is explained in the following verse. The parchment roll by itself might have floated, and been picked up and read, and so the stone was tied to it that it might sink at once, and thus prefigure the destruction of the city. (Compare the reappearance of the symbols in Rev. xviii. 21, in connection with the destruction of the mystical Babylon.)

(64) **They shall be weary.**—The words are identical with those that had closed the great prophecy in verse 58. What was meant was probably that Seraiah was to repeat the last words of the prediction, and, as they passed his lips, was to fling the roll into the river. That submersion was typical of the end of the futile labour and weariness of the men of the doomed city.

Thus far are the words of Jeremiah.—The words are clearly of the nature of what we should call an editorial note by the compiler of Jeremiah's prophecies, Baruch or another. He is careful to inform his readers that the narrative that follows in chap. lii. was not written by Jeremiah.

LII.

The narrative that follows is of the nature of an historical appendix, and is, to a great extent, identical with 2 Kings xxiv. 18—xxv. 30. For the most part, accordingly, the reader is referred to the Notes on those chapters. Whether the compiler of 2 Kings copied from the editor of Jeremiah, or conversely; whether the prophet was his own editor, or whether that office was undertaken by a contemporary, Baruch or another, or at a much later date; whether it was written at Babylon or Jerusalem, are questions which must remain unsettled. The last fact mentioned in each case, the release of Jehoiachin by Evil-Merodach,

from his presence, that Zedekiah rebelled
against the king of Babylon.
(4) And it came to pass in the [a] ninth
year of his reign, in the tenth month, in
the tenth *day* of the month, *that* Nebu-
chadrezzar king of Babylon came, he
and all his army, against Jerusalem, and
pitched against it, and built forts against
it round about. (5) So the city was be-
sieged unto the eleventh year of king
Zedekiah. (6) And in the fourth month,
in the ninth *day* of the month, the
famine was sore in the city, so that
there was no bread for the people of the
land. (7) Then the city was broken up,
and all the men of war fled, and went
forth out of the city by night by the
way of the gate between the two walls,
which *was* by the king's garden; (now
the Chaldeans *were* by the city round
about:) and they went by the way of
the plain. (8) But the army of the
Chaldeans pursued after the king, and
overtook Zedekiah in the plains of
Jericho; and all his army was scattered
from him. (9) Then they took the king,
and carried him up unto the king of
Babylon to Riblah in the land of Hamath;
where he gave judgment upon him.
(10) And the king of Babylon slew the
sons of Zedekiah before his eyes: he
slew also all the princes of Judah in
Riblah. (11) Then he [1] put out the eyes
of Zedekiah; and the king of Babylon
bound him in [2] chains, and carried him
to Babylon, and put him in [3] prison till
the day of his death.
(12) Now in the fifth month, in the
tenth *day* of the month, which *was* the
nineteenth year of Nebuchadrezzar king
of Babylon, came Nebuzar-adan, [4] [5] cap-
tain of the guard, *which* [6] served the
king of Babylon, into Jerusalem, (13) and
burned the house of the LORD, and the
king's house; and all the houses of
Jerusalem, and all the houses of the
great *men*, burned he with fire: (14) and
all the army of the Chaldeans, that *were*
with the captain of the guard, brake down
all the walls of Jerusalem round about.
(15) Then Nebuzar-adan the captain of
the guard carried away captive *certain*
of the poor of the people, and the
residue of the people that remained in
the city, and those that fell away, that
fell to the king of Babylon, and the rest

a 2 Kings 25. 1; ch. 39. 1.

B.C. 590.

1 Heb., *blinded.*

2 Or, *fetters.*

B.C. 588.

3 Heb., *house of the wards.*

4 Or, *chief marshal.*

5 Heb., *chief of the executioners*, or, *slaughtermen.* And so ver. 14, &c.

6 Heb., *stood before.*

---

indicates a date circ. B.C. 562. It may be noted, as indicating that the copyist, in either case, exercised an independent judgment, that while 2 Kings xxv. presents the form Nebuchad*n*ezzar, Jer. lii. has Nebuchad*r*ezzar, the latter being the more accurate form.

(6) **And in the fourth month.**—Omitted in the Hebrew of 2 Kings xxv. 3, but supplied in the English version.

(7) **Went forth out of the city.**—Omitted in 2 Kings xxv. 4.

They went by the way of the plain.—In 2 Kings xxv. 4 "*the king* (not in the Hebrew) went (verb in the singular) the way toward the plain."

(9) **To Riblah in the land of Hamath.**—The descriptive words are omitted in 2 Kings xxv. 6. (See Note on chap. xxxix. 5.)

He gave judgment upon him.—In 2 Kings xxv. 6, *they gave judgment.* So in the next verse "the king of Babylon slew" takes the place of "they slew" in 2 Kings xxv. 7.

(10) **He slew also all the princes of Judah in Riblah.**—The fact is not stated in 2 Kings xxv., but is found in chap. xxxix. 6.

(11) **And put him in prison till the day of his death.**—This also is an additional detail not mentioned in 2 Kings xxv., and its absence is probably due to the fact that that was the earlier narrative of the two. The word for "prison" is a peculiar one, and differs from that in verse 31. Literally it means "house of visitation," and this may imply either stricter custody, or more severe punishment in addition to imprisonment. The LXX. renders it by "house of the mill," as though Zedekiah, after he had been blinded, had been made to do slave-work like that of Samson. Possibly this was merely an inference from Lam. v. 13. Such treatment of captive kings was, however, quite in keeping with the character of Assyrian and Chaldæan rulers. Thus Assur-bani-pal boasts that he placed a king of Arabia in chains, and bound him with the dogs, and caused him to be kept in one of the great gates of Nineveh (*Records of the Past*, i. p. 93). So Darius, in the *Behistun* inscription, boasts of having taken a rebel king of Sagartia, cut off his nose and ears, and kept him chained at his door (*Records of the Past*, i. p. 119).

(12) **In the tenth day of the month.**—2 Kings xxv. 8 gives the "*seventh* day." We have no means of ascertaining which of the two statements is the more accurate. The Jews have always kept the *ninth* day as a commemorative fast. And this date is given in the Syriac version of 2 Kings.

Which served the king of Babylon.—Better, *which stand before the king.* The Hebrew word is one used continually of honourable service (chap. xxxv. 19; Num. xxvii. 2, 21; Deut. i. 30). In 2 Kings xxv. 8 we have the less accurate term of "servant" or "slave," or "captain of the guard." (See Note on chap. xxxix. 9.)

(13) **All the houses of the great men.**—More accurately, *all the great houses.*

(15) **Certain of the poor of the people.**—Omitted in 2 Kings xxv. 11, and probably inserted here by an error of transcription, as the next verse states that the "poor of the land" were left in their own country.

The rest of the multitude.—Better, perhaps, *the remnant of the work-people*, as in Prov. viii. 30, where many commentators so render the word, "I was with him as a *worker*," and Song Sol. vii. 1. The versions, however, agree in giving "multitude."

of the multitude. (16) But Nebuzar-
adan the captain of the guard left *certain*
of the poor of the land for vinedressers
and for husbandmen. (17) Also the
[a] pillars of brass that *were* in the house
of the LORD, and the bases, and the
brasen sea that *was* in the house of the
LORD, the Chaldeans brake, and carried
all the brass of them to Babylon.
(18) The caldrons also, and the [1] shovels,
and the snuffers, and the [2] bowls, and
the spoons, and all the vessels of brass
wherewith they ministered, took they
away. (19) And the basons, and the
[3] firepans, and the bowls, and the cal-
drons, and the candlesticks, and the
spoons, and the cups; *that* which *was*
of gold *in* gold, and *that* which *was*
of silver *in* silver, took the captain of
the guard away. (20) The two pillars,
one sea, and twelve brasen bulls that
were under the bases, which king Solomon
had made in the house of the LORD:
[4] the brass of all these vessels was
without weight. (21) And *concerning* the
[b] pillars, the height of one pillar *was*
eighteen cubits; and a [5] fillet of twelve
cubits did compass it; and the thickness
thereof *was* four fingers: *it was* hollow.
(22) And a chapiter of brass *was* upon it;
and the height of one chapiter *was* five
cubits, with network and pomegranates
upon the chapiters round about, all *of*
brass. The second pillar also and the
pomegranates *were* like unto these.
(23) And there were ninety and six pome-
granates on a side; *and* all the pome-
granates upon the network *were* an
hundred round about.
(24) And the captain of the guard took
Seraiah the chief priest, and Zephaniah
the second priest, and the three keepers
of the [6] door: (25) he took also out of
the city an eunuch, which had the
charge of the men of war; and seven
men of them that [7] were near the king's
person, which were found in the city;
and the [8] principal scribe of the host,
who mustered the people of the land;
and threescore men of the people of
the land, that were found in the midst
of the city. (26) So Nebuzar-adan the
captain of the guard took them, and
brought them to the king of Babylon
to Riblah. (27) And the king of Babylon
smote them, and put them to death in
Riblah in the land of Hamath. Thus
Judah was carried away captive out of
his own land.
(28) This *is* the people whom Nebu-
chadrezzar carried away captive: in the
seventh year three thousand Jews and

a ch. 27. 19.
1 Or, *instruments to remove the ashes.*
2 Or, *basons.*
3 Or, *censers.*
4 Heb., *their brass.*
b 1 Kings 7. 15; 2 Kings 25. 17; 2 Chron. 3. 15.
5 Heb., *thread.*
6 Heb., *threshold.*
7 Heb., *saw the face of the king.*
8 Or, *scribe of the captain of the host.*

(18—20) **The caldrons also, and the shovels . . .**—The list in 2 Kings xxv. 14—16 omits the basons, the caldrons, the candlesticks, and the cups; in verse 15 it gives the definite article in the Hebrew "*the* one sea," and omits the "twelve brasen bulls. Strictly speaking, the bases (1 Kings vii. 27) were under the ten lavers which were used for washing the meat for the sacrifices, and the twelve bulls (1 Kings vii. 25) supported the molten sea, or bigger laver, for the priests' ablutions; 2 Kings xvi. 17 suggests the thought that the bulk of the bronze had been removed by Ahaz and given to Tiglath Pileser, though possibly not taken away by him.

(21—23) **And concerning the pillars . . .**—In 2 Kings xxv. 16, 17 we have a list abbreviated by the omission of some of the measurements and of the number and arrangement of the pomegranates. "Chapiter" is the old English word for the "capital" of a column.

On a side.—The exact meaning of the Hebrew is *towards a* (=each) *wind—i.e.*, there were twenty-four pomegranates on each side of the square pillars, with one at each corner, making, as in verse 23, one hundred in all.

(25) **An eunuch, which had the charge of the men of war.**—Omit the article before "charge." The Hebrew term (*Pakid*) conveys the meaning of "deputy," a superintendent under a chief commander. The officer in question had probably, together with the persons named in verse 24, been more conspicuous than his fellows in resisting the Chaldæans.

Seven men.—2 Kings xxv. 19 gives "five" as the number. Here also we have to think of the exile as the punishment of prominence in the defence of the city. The chief scribe of the army, the "secretary of war," would naturally occupy such a position. The description of the men as those "that were near the king's person" (literally, *saw the king's face*) implies a high official rank.

(28) **This is the people . . .**—Here the parallelism with 2 Kings xxv., which goes on to give a brief summary of the history of Gedaliah and Ishmael, as narrated in chaps. xl.—xliii., ceases, and the writer of the appendix goes on to give particulars as to the various stages of the deportation of the captives. It presents some difficulties in detail. (1) The date given here, the "seventh year" of Nebuchadnezzar, does not agree with 2 Kings xxiv. 12, which gives the "eighth year" as the time of the first deportation after the defeat of Jehoiachin. (2) The number of the captives then carried into exile, given in 2 Kings xxiv. 14 at 10,000, besides the craftsmen and the smiths, is given here as 3,023. The precision of the number seems to imply reference to a register or record of some kind, and so far bears *primâ facie* evidence of accuracy. Probably the word "ten" has dropped out before "seven," and we have here the record of a second deportation in the *seventeenth* year of Nebuchadnezzar, while the siege of Jerusalem was going on, and made up in part of prisoners taken in skirmishes, and partly of the numerous Jews who "fell away to the Chaldæans" (chap. xxxvii. 13).

three and twenty: (29) in the eighteenth
year of Nebuchadrezzar he carried away
captive from Jerusalem eight hundred
thirty and two [1] persons: (30) in the
three and twentieth year of Nebuchad-
rezzar Nebuzar-adan the captain of the
guard carried away captive of the Jews
seven hundred forty and five persons:
all the persons *were* four thousand and
six hundred.
(31) And it came to pass in the seven
and thirtieth year of the captivity of
Jehoiachin king of Judah, in the twelfth
month, in the five and twentieth *day* of
the month, *that* Evil-merodach king of
Babylon in the *first* year of his reign
lifted up the head of Jehoiachin king of
Judah, and brought him forth out of
prison, (32) and spake [2] kindly unto
him, and set his throne above the throne
of the kings that *were* with him in
Babylon, (33) and changed his prison gar-
ments: and he did continually eat bread
before him all the days of his life.
(34) And *for* his diet, there was a con-
tinual diet given him of the king of
Babylon, [3] every day a portion until the
day of his death, all the days of his life.

B.C. 600.

1 Heb., *souls.*

B.C. 590.

B.C. 585.

2 Heb., *good things with him.*

B.C. 562.

3 Heb., *the matter of the day in his day.*

---

(29) **Eight hundred thirty and two persons.**—The comparatively small number indicates the ravages of the sword, the pestilence, and the famine to which Jeremiah so often refers. The captives were probably the scanty remnant of the defenders of the city, and the deportation that by Nebuzar-adan narrated in verse 15.

(30) **In the three and twentieth year of Nebuchadrezzar . . .**—There is no record of this final deportation, five years after the capture of the city, in the historical books. It probably followed on the conquest of Egypt predicted in chap. xliv. 11, 28, and included some of those who had emigrated to that country; perhaps also on that of the Moabites and Edomites, among whom many Jews had probably taken refuge. The total number, including the 10,000 who are not mentioned here (see Note on verse 28), mounts up to 14,600. In Ezra ii. 64, 65 the number of those who returned from Babylon is given at 42,360, besides 7,337 male and female slaves, and this, as many remained behind in Babylon, is more than can be accounted for by the natural increase of population. Assuming the correctness of the numbers, we are led to the conclusion that after the exiles were settled in Babylon, and found themselves in a more favourable position than was at first anticipated (chap. xxix. 5, 6), they were joined by friends and kindred, who hoped to be better off there than in the desolation and disorders of their own country.

(31) **In the seven and thirtieth year of the captivity of Jehoiachin . . .**—The closing narrative is almost identical with that of 2 Kings xxv. 27, the only differences being (1) that "five and twentieth" stands for "seven and twentieth," (2) that in verse 34 we have "the king of Babylon" instead of "the king," and (3) that the pleonastic words "until the day of his death" are inserted before "all the days of his life." The reader is referred to the notes on that section. The variations between the two chapters, the most important of which have been noticed in the Notes, are not without importance, though insignificant in themselves, as implying that a consistent belief in the substantial truthfulness of the historical records of the Old Testament is independent of mere verbal accordance in matters of minute detail.

THE LAMENTATIONS OF JEREMIAH

INTRODUCTION

TO

THE LAMENTATIONS OF JEREMIAH

I.—**Title.**—We are so familiar with the title which implies Jeremiah's authorship of this book that it would surprise most readers of the English Bible to learn that, as the book stands in the Hebrew text, it is absolutely anonymous. Its only title there is, as with Genesis (*B'reshith*) and Exodus (*V'elle Shemoth*), the opening word of the book (*Echah*). For this the LXX. translators substituted, after their manner, as in Genesis, Exodus, Numbers, and the like, a title descriptive of the character and contents of the book, and found it in *Threnoi*, the equivalent of the Hebrew word rendered *Lamentations* in Jer. vii. 29, ix. 10, 20; 2 Chron. xxiv. 25. The Vulgate simply reproduced the LXX. in *Threni*, Luther translated it by *Klag-lieder*, and the English versions followed in his footsteps in the rendering *Lamentations*.

II.—**Authorship.**—The LXX., however, did something more than give a new and descriptive title to the book. They prefixed a short note by way of introduction: "And it came to pass after Israel had been led into captivity and Jerusalem had been laid waste, Jeremiah sat weeping, and he lamented with this lamentation over Jerusalem, and said—How doth the city," &c.

It would, in the nature of the case, have been natural to recognise in such a note a tradition entitled to respect. Josephus (*Ant.* x. 5, § 1) repeats the statement, but apparently identifies the book now extant with the "lamentations" which the prophet wrote for the funeral of Josiah (2 Chron. xxxv. 25); and the authorship has been received by most critics and commentators without question. A consensus so striking rests, as might be expected, on strong internal evidence. The very fact that Jeremiah began his career as a writer with a work of this kind makes it probable that he would not leave the downfall and the miseries of his people without the same kind of tribute that he had paid to the memory of the reforming king; and there is absolutely no other writer living at the time (and the fact of the book being contemporaneous with the sufferings it describes is transparently evident) to whom it can be ascribed with the slightest shadow of probability. The character of the book shows the same emotional temperament, the same sensitiveness to sorrow, the same glowing and consuming patriotism that are conspicuous in the prophecies that bear Jeremiah's name. A closer comparison brings out striking coincidences in detail. In both we have the picture of the "Virgin daughter of Zion" sitting on the ground in her shame and misery (Lam. i. 15, ii. 13; Jer. xiv. 17. In both the prophet's eyes flow down with tears (Lam. i. 16, ii. 11, iii. 48, 49; Jer. ix. 1, xiii. 17, xiv. 17). There is the same haunting dread as of a man encompassed with "fear round about" on every side (Lam. ii. 22, iii. 48, 49; Jer. vi. 25, xlvi. 5). In both, the worst of all the evils of the nation is represented as being the wickedness of the priests and of the false prophets (Lam. ii. 14, iv. 13; Jer. v. 30, 31, xiv. 13, 14). The sufferer appeals for vengeance to the righteous Judge (Lam. iii. 64—68; Jer. xi. 20). The rival nations, Edom and the rest, which exulted in the fall of Jerusalem, are bidden in each case to prepare for a like judgment (Lam. iv. 21; Jer. xlix. 12). Even in the absence of any external testimony from tradition or otherwise, it would have been perfectly natural for the compilers of the Old Testament, at or after the Return from Babylon, or for any later critic, to assign it to Jeremiah as its author. For the most part, as stated above, this conclusion has been adopted by recent critics. Some, however, among whom we may name Ewald, Bunsen, and Nägelsbach, have been led by real or supposed differences of vocabulary and style to assign it to some other writer of the same period, the first two fixing on Jeremiah's disciple, Baruch, as the probable author. The most exhaustive discussion of the question is to be found in the *Introduction to Lamentations*, in Dr. Schaff's edition of Lange's *Commentary*, the case against the authorship being stated by Nägelsbach, and that in favour of it by Dr. W. H. Hornblower.

III.—**Date and Purpose.**—Assuming authorship, there can be little doubt that the prefatory note of the LXX. gives a true account of the origin of the Lamentations. Josephus, it is true, says that the elegiac lamentations on the death of Josiah were extant in his time, and as there is no trace of any other book bearing that title besides that which now remains to us, he apparently thought that the latter "lamentations," at least, included the former. In this view he has been followed by Jerome, and by some modern critics. The internal evidence is, however, altogether on the other side. From first to last the picture that meets us is not of foreseen but of completed desolation. Famine has done its work (Lam. ii. 19, 20, iv. 3, 4). Judah is gone into captivity (Lam. i. 3). The strongholds and palaces are destroyed (Lam. ii. 5). The anointed of the Lord has been taken in the pits (Lam. iv. 20). The daughter of Edom rejoices in the overthrow of her hereditary enemy (Lam. iv. 21). It can scarcely therefore be questioned that Josephus was in this instance, as in many others, inaccurate and superficial, and that the book belongs to the latest period of Jeremiah's life, that it was written either in Palestine, before the migration to Egypt, or more probably, at Tahpanhes, after that migration. Attempts to connect each chapter with some definite event in the prophet's life are, for the most part, simply a fruitless waste of ingenuity.*

It has to be remembered, however, that the five chapters are distinct and separate poems, each complete in itself, with no link binding them to each other, except the unity of subject and of feeling.† They are the outpourings of a man's heart, full to overflowing with bitter sorrows, as he contemplates now the miseries of his people, and now, as in chap iii., those that concern himself. The language throughout is that of a sufferer rather than a teacher, guided by the Spirit that gave him the power to express thoughts that would otherwise have been unable to clothe themselves in words, but with no direct "Word of Jehovah" to be delivered to the people. It was, one may believe, in consequence of this characteristic feature that the book was placed by the compiler of the Hebrew of the Old Testament among the Hagiographa, the poetical and sapiential writings, and not among the prophets; and that Rabbinic writers (*e.g.*, Kimchi, *Præf. in Psalm.*) spoke of them, and of the other books of that group, as written indeed by the help of the Holy Spirit, but not with the special gift of prophecy.

Other differences between the two books that bear Jeremiah's name grew naturally out of this. The *Lamentations* are more distinctly a work of art than the prophecies. The rhythm is more elaborate and uniform. The whole book, with the exception of the last chapter, which has apparently reached us in an unfinished state, is characterised by the alphabetic arrangement,‡ of which Ps. cxix. is the most familiar example, but which is found also in more or less completeness in Pss. xxv., xxxiv., xxxvii., cxi., cxii., cxlv., and in the singularly beautiful poem on the excellence of an ideal womanhood, which finds a place in Prov. xxxi. 10—31. Traces of it, as if the work had been left half-finished, appear also in Pss. ix. and x. In the *Lamentations* it is found with some noticeable peculiarities. Chaps. i., ii., and iv. contain twenty-two verses each in alphabetic order, each verse falling into three evenly balanced clauses (Ewald, *Introd. to Lam.*). Chap. ii. 19 forms an exception, as having a fourth clause, as if the writer had for the moment, impulsively or deliberately, shaken off the restrictions of his own self-imposed law. In chaps. ii., iii., and iv. the two letters *Ayin* and *Pi* appear in the inverted order of that in which they are found in chap. i., and in the received Hebrew alphabet. The variation has been explained (as, *e.g.*, by Grotius) on the assumption that Jeremiah followed here the order of the Chaldæan alphabet; but there is no evidence that that order was different from that of the Hebrew, and the exception may be regarded as one of those variations which resulted either from oversight or from the inevitable difficulties of the task which had been undertaken. Similar variations meet us, we may note, in the alphabetic order of Ps. xxxvii.

Chap. iii. contains three short verses under each letter of the alphabet, the initial letter being three times repeated.

Chap. v. contains the same number of verses as the first two and the fourth chapters, but with no alphabetical arrangement. The thought suggests itself, either that the writer found himself too overwhelmed by emotion to keep within the limits of the artificial plan he had before prescribed to himself, or that it was his plan to write his thoughts freely at first and then to reduce them into the alphabetic structure.

Our estimate of the excellence of the poems thus written will depend on our insight into the working of strong emotions on the poetic temperament, on our power of throwing ourselves into mental sympathy with such a one as Jeremiah. A superficial and pedantic criticism finds it easy to look down on the alphabetic structure as indicating a genius of an inferior order, and the taste of a degenerate (so De Wette, *Comment. über die Psalm.*, p. 56, and even Ewald, *Poet. Buch.* i. p. 140), or to allow condescendingly that they are "not without a certain degree of merit in their way" (De Wette, as above). A wider induction from the literature of all nations and ages leads, however, to a different conclusion. The man in whom the poetic gift is found fears, it would seem, to trust himself to an unregulated freedom. He accepts the discipline of a self-imposed law just in proportion to the vehemence of his emotions. The metrical systems of Greek and Latin poetry with all their endless complications, hexameters, elegiacs, lyrics, the alliterative verse of Anglo-Saxon writers, the rhymes of mediæval Latin and of modern European poetry in general, the rigid structure of the sonnet, as seen in the great Italian poets and their imitators, the *terza rima* of the "Divina Commedia," and the yet more artificial structure of the *canzoni* and *ballate* of Dante, the stanzas of the "Faërie Queen," are all instances of the working of the same general law of which we find a representative example in the *Lamentations.**

---

* Thus we have a classification given by De Wette :—

Chap.	I.	During the siege of Jerusalem (Jer. xxxvii. 5).
	II.	After the destruction of the Temple.
	III.	At the time of Jeremiah's imprisonment.
	IV.	After the capture of Zedekiah.
	V.	After the destruction of the city.

† The following passage from Lowth's Prælections *de Sacra Poesi Hebræorum* is worth giving in his own exquisite Latinity (*Præl.* xxii.):—

"Qui itaque artificiosam totius argumenti dispositionem, aptam partium collocationem, rerum juncturam et seriem, et in his omnibus singularem aliquam elegantiam requirit, id postulat a vate quod erat a proposito ejus alienum. Patriæ perditæ et extinctæ luctuoso carmine quodammodo parentans, et veluti in exequiis ejus lugentis personam gerens, quicquid ejus animo in tot tantisque miseriis primum obversatur, quicquid maxime calamitosum videtur et miserabile, quicquid ei præcipit instans dolor, id subito quasi in re præsenti exprimit et effundit. In iisdem rebus hæret plerumque et immoratur diutius; eadem novis vocibus, imaginibus, figuris, variat et amplificat; ita ut fiat potius rerum prope similium coacervatio quædam ac cumulus quam plurium et diversarum subtilis aliqua connexio atque per gradus ordinate facta deductio."

I subjoin a translation for those who are not scholars :—

"He who looks for an elaborate arrangement of the whole subject, with a due arrangement of parts, a connected order of events, and a certain peculiar refinement in dealing with each of them, expects that which is altogether foreign to the poet's nature. As if he were, in a manner, attending the funeral obsequies of his ruined and fallen country and sustaining in his mournful dirge the character of chief mourner, he expresses and pours forth at once, as if the thing passed before his eyes, whatever in its many and great miseries first meets his mental vision, whatever seems most calamitous and wretched, whatever the urgency of his grief suggests to him. He dwells, with lingering iteration, on the self-same themes; varies and expands the same facts in ever-fresh words and images and metaphors, so that we have rather an accumulation, heaped up high, of things all but identical, than a subtly arranged series of many different things, and an orderly treatment of them according to the rules of art."

‡ Ewald (*Poet. Buch.* i. p. 140) looks on the tendency to the alphabetic structure as first showing itself in the seventh century B.C. It may be noticed that this writer has succeeded with singular skill in maintaining the alphabetic arrangement in his German version of the *Lamentations*, even in the triple complications of chap. iii.

* A singular example of the extreme application of this straining after the freedom which moves easily in fetters is found in the Latin poetry of Aldhelm, Abbot of Malmesbury, one of whose poems is a double acrostic, the first and last letters of every line forming the hexameter, "*Aldhelmus cecinit millenis versibus odas.*" (Behnsch, *Englische Sprache*, p. 34.)

There are, of course, instances enough in all literature of the form without the spirit, but enough has been said to show that the choice of an artificial method of versification such as this does not necessarily imply anything weak or artificial in the genius of the writer. In the absence of rhyme and of definite metrical laws in Hebrew poetry it was natural that it should be chosen as supplying at once the restraint and the support which the prophet needed. The alphabetic structure had also another advantage as a guide to memory. If, as seems probable, the *Lamentations* were intended to be sung, as in fact they were sung by those who mourned then, or in later times, for the destruction of Jerusalem, then it is obvious that the task of the learner would be much easier with this mnemonic help than without it.

The words of Zechariah at the close of the Captivity give a striking illustration of the way in which the *Lamentations* had impressed themselves on the minds of the exiles. He appeals to the words of the prophets who had gone before him as having taken hold of their fathers, "and they returned and said, Like as the Lord of hosts thought to do unto us, according to our ways and according to our doings, so hath He done with us "(Zech. i. 6), thus putting into their lips the very words which we find in Lam. i. 13, ii. 17. When the exiles returned to Jerusalem this was their book of remembrance. At a later period, probably not till after the destruction of the second Temple, it was read on the ninth day of the month *Ab* in every year with fasting and prayer, as commemorating the destruction of the Temple, and the day and the practice still retain their place in the ritual of the Jewish calendar. It is said to be used often by the pilgrims who still gather at "the place of wailing" in Jerusalem. It enters largely into the order of the services of the Latin Church in Holy Week,* and at the last revision of the Lectionary was admitted to a like position in that of the Church of England. Men have felt that the words of the suffering poet, flowing from the deep fountain of the heart, met the wants of other sufferers, however unlike in their outward conditions, and that therefore they found their fulfilment in *the* Sufferer who gathered up into His own experience the infinite sorrows of humanity.

A few facts in the external history of the book remain to be stated. It has not always occupied the same position in the arrangement of the Old Testament Canon. In the received Hebrew order it is placed, as stated above, among the *Kethûbîm* or Hagiographa, between Ruth and *Koheleth* (Ecclesiastes). In that adopted for synagogue use, and reproduced in some printed editions and in the Bomberg Hebrew Bible of A.D. 1521, it stands among the five *Megilloth* or *Rolls* (see *General Introduction* in Vol. I. of this *Commentary*), after the Books of Moses. The LXX. groups the writings connected with the name of Jeremiah together; but the Book of Baruch comes between the prophecies and the Lamentations.

* Three lessons are assigned to each of the three last days of the week, each ending with the versicle, *Jerusalem, Jerusalem Convertere ad Dominum Deum tuum*.

THE LAMENTATIONS OF JEREMIAH

CHAPTER I.—(1) How doth the city sit solitary, *that was* full of people! *how* is she become as a widow! she *that was* great among the nations, *and* princess among the provinces, *how* is she become tributary! (2) She [a]weepeth sore in the [b]night, and her tears *are* on her cheeks: among all her lovers she hath none to comfort *her:* all her friends have dealt treacherously with her, they are become her enemies. (3) Judah is gone into captivity because of affliction, and [1]because of great servitude: she dwelleth among the heathen, she findeth no rest: all her persecutors overtook her between the straits. (4) The ways of Zion do mourn, because none come to the solemn feasts: all her gates are desolate: her priests sigh, her virgins are afflicted, and she *is* in bitterness. (5) Her adversaries [c]are the chief, her enemies prosper; for the LORD hath afflicted her for the multitude of her transgressions: her [d]children are gone into captivity before the enemy. (6) And from the daughter of Zion all her beauty is departed: her princes are become like harts *that* find no pasture, and they are gone without strength before the pursuer. (7) Jerusalem remembered in the days of her affliction and of her miseries all her [2]pleasant things that she had in the days of old, when her people fell into the hand of the enemy, and none did

B.C. cir. 588.

a Jer. 13. 17.

b Job. 7. 3.

1 Heb., *for the greatness of servitude.*

c Deut. 28. 13, 43, 44.

d Jer. 52. 28.

2 Or, *desirable.*

---

(1) **How doth the city . . .**—The poem of twenty-two verses divides itself into two symmetrical halves, (1) verses 1—11, in which the prophet laments over Jerusalem; and (2) verses 12—22, more dramatic in its form, in which the daughter of Zion bewails her own miseries. Each verse is divided into three lines, each line beginning, in the Hebrew, with the same letter. The opening picture reminds us of the well-known *Judæa capta,* a woman sitting under a palm-tree, on the Roman medals struck after the destruction of Jerusalem.

How is she become.—Better, making one sentence instead of two, *She is become a widow that was great among the nations,* and so with the clause that follows.

Provinces.—The word, used in Esther i. 1, 22, and elsewhere, of the countries subject to Persia and Assyria, and so in Ezra ii. 1; Neh. vii. 6, of Judah itself, here indicates the neighbouring countries that had once, as in the reign of Hezekiah, been subject to Judah. "Tributary," as used here, implies, as in Josh. xvi. 10, personal servitude, rather than the money payment, for which, at a later period, as in Esther x. 1, it was commuted.

(2) **She weepeth sore in the night.**—The intensity of the sorrow is emphasised by the fact that the tears do not cease even in the time which commonly brings rest and repose to mourners. The "lovers" and the "friends" are the nations, Egypt (Jer. ii. 36), Edomites, Moabites, and others, with which Judah had been in alliance, and which now turned against her. (Comp. Ps. cxxxvii. 7; Ezek. xxv. 3—6; Jer. xl. 14, for instances of their hostility, and specially Lam. iv. 21.)

(3) **Because of affliction.**—The Authorised version suggests the thought that the words refer to the voluntary emigration of those who went to Egypt and other countries (Jer. xlii. 14), to avoid the oppression to which they were subject in their own land. The Hebrew admits, however, of the rendering "from affliction," and so the words speak of the forcible deportation of the people from misery at home to a yet worse misery in Babylon as the land of their exile. Even there they found no "rest" (Deut. xxviii. 65). Their persecutors hunted them down to the "straits" from which no escape was possible.

(4) **The ways of Zion do mourn.**—The words paint what we may call the religious desolation of Jerusalem. The roads leading to it, the "gates" by which it was entered, were no longer thronged with pilgrims and worshippers. "Virgins" are joined with "priests" as taking part in the hymns and rejoicing processions of the great festivals (Exod. xv. 20; Ps. lxviii. 25; Judg. xxi. 19—21; Jer. xxxi. 13).

(5) **Her adversaries are the chief.**—Literally, *have become the head* (Deut. xxviii. 13).

Her enemies prosper.—Better, *are at ease,* secure from every resistance on her part. "Before the enemy," driven, *i.e.,* as slaves are driven.

(6) **Her princes are become like harts . .**—Probably a reference to the flight and capture of Zedekiah (2 Kings xxv. 5; Jer. xxxix. 5), who, with his sons and princes, fell into the hands of the Chaldæans, like fainting and stricken deer.

(7) **Jerusalem remembered.**—Better, *remembereth.* The present is contrasted with the past. Still, the "sorrow's crown of sorrow is remembering happier things."

That she had in the days of old.—Better, *which have been since the days of old.*

Did mock at her sabbaths.—The noun is not found elsewhere, but is connected with that commonly rendered "sabbath." It seems coined as a word of pregnant meaning to express at once the enforced sabbaths of the untilled land (Lev. xxvi. 34, 35), and the sabbaths, no longer festivals, but conspicuous for

help her: the adversaries saw her, *and*
did mock at her sabbaths. (8) Jerusalem
hath grievously sinned; therefore she
[1]is removed: all that honoured her de-
spise her, because they have seen her
nakedness: yea, she sigheth, and turneth
backward. (9) Her filthiness *is* in her
skirts; she remembereth not her last
end; therefore she came down wonder-
fully: she had no comforter. O LORD,
behold my affliction: for the enemy
hath magnified *himself*. (10) The adver-
sary hath spread out his hand upon all
her [2]pleasant things: for she hath seen
that the heathen entered into her
sanctuary, whom thou didst command
that [a]they should not enter into thy
congregation. (11) All her people sigh,
they seek bread; they have given their
pleasant things for meat [3]to relieve the
soul: see, O LORD, and consider; for I
am become vile.
(12) [4]*Is it* nothing to you, all ye that
[5]pass by? behold, and see if there be
any sorrow like unto my sorrow, which
is done unto me, wherewith the LORD
hath afflicted *me* in the day of his fierce
anger. (13) From above hath he sent
fire into my bones, and it prevaileth
against them: he hath spread a net for
my feet, he hath turned me back: he
hath made me desolate *and* faint all the
day. (14) The yoke of my transgressions
is bound by his hand: they are wreathed,
and come up upon my neck: he hath
made my strength to fall, the Lord hath
delivered me into *their* hands, *from
whom* I am not able to rise up. (15) The
Lord hath trodden under foot all my
mighty *men* in the midst of me: he

1 Heb., *is become a removing*, or, *wandering*.
2 Or, *desirable*.
a Deut. 23. 3.
3 Or, *to make the soul to come again*.
4 Or, It is *nothing*.
5 Heb., *pass by the way?*

---

the absence of any religious rites, which had followed on the destruction of the Temple.

(8) **Therefore she is removed.**—The verb is used technically for the separation of a woman under ceremonial defilement; and the daughter of Zion in her sin and shame is compared (as in verse 17) to such a woman. The figure is continued with a startling boldness. Like a woman exposed to the gaze of scorners, Jerusalem would fain turn her back upon those who exult in the twofold nakedness of her sin and of its punishment.

(9) **Her filthiness.**—The picture of pollution is pushed to its most loathsome extreme. The very skirts of the garment are defiled.

She remembereth not . .—Better, *she remembered not.* It was her recklessness as to the future (comp. Deut. xxxii. 29, for the phrase) which brought her down to this "wonderful" and extreme prostration.

O Lord, behold my affliction.—The words are not those of the prophet, but of Zion, anticipating the dramatic personation which begins systematically at verse 12.

(10) **Upon all her pleasant things . . .**—The use of a like phrase in 2 Chron. xxxvi. 10, 19, of the vessels of the Temple, leads us to think primarily of them; but the word itself has a wider range, and includes all works of art and ornamentation.

Whom thou didst command.—Stress is laid on the profanation rather than the plunder of the sanctuary. Ammonites and Moabites were excluded from the congregation in Deut. xxiii. 3, and yet they and other heathen nations now rushed even into the Holy of holies, which none but the High Priest might enter.

(11) **All her people sigh . . . .**—The words which describe the famine at Jerusalem are in the present tense, either as painting the sufferings of the past with the vividness of the historic present, or because the sufferings still continued even after the capture of the city. The remnant that was left had to bring out their treasures, jewels, and the like, and offer them for bread.

To relieve the soul. — Better, *to revive*, literally, *to bring back.*

(12) **Is it nothing to you . . .**—Literally, *Not to you, ye passers by,* which the Authorised version takes as a question. The LXX. and Vulg., however, seem to have taken the adverb as an interjection: "*O all ye that pass by . .*" And some interpreters have taken the negative but not the question, "*Nor to you . . . (do I say this).*" The Authorised version, however, has most to commend it. What the mourning city felt most keenly was that her unparalleled sufferings were met with an unparalleled indifference.

(13) **From above . . .**—The words are probably figurative. The judgments that had fallen on Jerusalem were as a fire from heaven, piercing even to "the joints and marrow," the innermost recesses of life.

He hath turned me back . . .—The phrase points not to the defeat and flight of battle, but, completing the figure of the net, paints the failure of every effort to escape. The word for "desolate" implies, as in the case of Tamar (2 Sam. xiii. 20), an utter, hopeless misery.

(14) **Is bound by his hand . .**—The verb is not found elsewhere, but was probably a technical term for the twisting of the thongs by which the yoke was fastened, the "yoke" in this case being the transgressions of Judah, which were as a sore burden too heavy to be borne.

He hath made.—Better, *it hath made; i.e.,* the yoke which was above her strength to bear.

The Lord.—It is noticeable that here, and in thirteen other passages in this book, the word *Adonai* is used instead of the more usual Jehovah, as though the latter, the covenant Name of the God of Israel, was less appropriate in the lips of one who was under His condemnation.

(15) **Trodden under foot.**—Better, *hath made contemptible,* as those who are weighed in the balance and found wanting.

All my mighty men . . .—The adjective is used elsewhere of bulls (Pss. xxii. 12; Isa. xxxiv. 7), but stands here for the heroes of Judah, who fell, not in open battle, but ignominiously "in the midst" of the captured city.

He hath called an assembly.—The point of the phrase lies in its being that commonly used for proclaim-

hath called an assembly against me to
crush my young men: the Lord hath
trodden [1]the virgin, the daughter of
Judah, *as* in a winepress. (16) For these
things I weep; [a]mine eye, mine eye
runneth down with water, because the
comforter that should [2]relieve my soul
is far from me: my children are deso-
late, because the enemy prevailed.
(17) Zion spreadeth forth her hands, *and*
there is none to comfort her: the LORD
hath commanded concerning Jacob, *that*
his adversaries *should be* round about
him: Jerusalem is as a menstruous
woman among them.

(18) The LORD is [b]righteous; for I
have rebelled against his [3]command-
ment: hear, I pray you, all people, and
behold my sorrow: my virgins and my
young men are gone into captivity.
(19) I called for my lovers, *but* they de-
ceived me: my priests and mine elders
gave up the ghost in the city, while
they sought their meat to relieve their
souls. (20) Behold, O LORD; for I *am* in
distress: my [c]bowels are troubled; mine
heart is turned within me; for I have
grievously rebelled: abroad the sword
bereaveth, at home *there is* as death.
(21) They have heard that I sigh: *there*
is none to comfort me: all mine enemies
have heard of my trouble; they are
glad that thou hast done *it*: thou wilt
bring the day *that* thou hast [4]called,
and they shall be like unto me. (22) Let
all their wickedness come before thee;
and do unto them, as thou hast done
unto me for all my transgressions:
for my sighs *are* many, and my heart *is*
faint.

CHAPTER II.—(1) How hath the
Lord covered the daughter of Zion with
a cloud in his anger, *and* cast down

1 Or, *the winepress of the virgin, &c.*

a Jer. 13. 17 & 14. 17; ch. 2. 18.

2 Heb., *bring back.*

b Dan. 9. 7.

3 Heb., *mouth.*

c Isa. 16. 11; Jer. 48. 36.

4 Or, *proclaimed.*

---

ing a religious festival (Lev. xxiii. 4). Here the festival is proclaimed, not for Jerusalem, but against her, and is to be kept by those who exult in the slaughter of her youthful warriors.

The Lord hath trodden the virgin . . . —Better, *hath trodden the winepress for the virgin . . .* For the winepress as the symbol of judgment and slaughter, see Isa. lxiii. 2; Rev. xiv. 19, xix. 15.

(16) **For these things . . .**—The unparalleled misery finds vent in a flood of bitterest tears. We note the emphasis of iteration in "mine eye, mine eye." On "relieve," see Note on verse 11; and on "desolate," see Note on verse 13.

(17) **Zion spreadeth forth her hands . . .** —The normal attitude of Eastern prayer, or, perhaps, of lamentation and despair.

That his adversaries . . .—Better, *that those round about him should be his adversaries*, the nearest neighbours being the bitterest foes.

Jerusalem is as . . .—The image is the same as in verse 8, and might be rendered *as one polluted*, or *as an abomination.*

(18) **The Lord is righteous . . .**—An echo from Jer. xii. 1; 2 Chron. xii. 6. Misery does its work, and issues in repentance. The suffering comes from the all-righteous Judge. It is, perhaps, significant that with this beginning of conversion the name "Jehovah" reappears.

All people . . .—Better, *all peoples.* Those addressed are the heathen nations, who are summoned to gaze on the desolate mourners.

(19) **I called for.**—Better, *to.* The "lovers," as in verse 2, are the former allies of Judah.

My priests and mine elders.—The pressure of the famine of the besieged city is emphasised by the fact that even these, the honoured guides of the people, had died of hunger. On the phrase that follows, see verse 11. A conjectural addition, at the end of the verse, "and found not," is supplied in the LXX and Syriac versions; but rhetorically there is more force in the *aposiopesis*, the suggestive silence, of the Hebrew.

(20) **Behold, O Lord . . .**—Deserted by men, the mourner appeals to Jehovah. "Bowels" and "heart" are used almost as synonymous for the deepest emotions of the soul. The word for "troubled," elsewhere (Ps. lxxv. 8) used of colour, might, perhaps, be better rendered *inflamed.*

At home there is as death.—The "as" seems inserted to give the emphasis of the undefined. It is not death pure and simple that makes each home tremble, but the "*plurima mortis imago*" (Virg. *Aen.* ii. 369), the starvation, disease, exhaustion, which all were deadly, *i.e.* deathlike, in their working.

(21) **They are glad that thou hast done it . . .** —Historically the words refer to the conduct of nations like the Edomites, as described in Ps. cxxxvii. 7.

Thou wilt bring the day that thou hast called.—Better, *proclaimed.* By some commentators the first verb is taken as a perfect, "Thou hast brought," and the "day" is that of vengeance upon Judah. With the rendering of the Authorised version the clause coheres better with that which follows, and the "day" is that of the punishment of the exulting foes.

(22) **Let all their wickedness . . .**—The prayer for a righteous retribution, the first natural prayer of the outraged, reminds us of Pss. lxix., cix., cxxxvii., yet more strongly of the language of the prophet himself in Jer. xviii. 21—23. It is something more than a prayer for revenge, and rests on the underlying thought that righteousness requires the punishment. By some critics, it may be noted, Pss. lxix. and cix. have, on the strength of this parallelism, been ascribed to Jeremiah

II.

(1) **How hath the Lord . . .**—The second dirge follows the pattern of the first, opening with a description of the sufferings of Jerusalem, (verses 1—10), and closing with a dramatic soliloquy spoken as by the daughter of Zion (verses 11—22).

from heaven unto the earth the beauty
of Israel, and remembered not his foot-
stool in the day of his anger! (2) The
Lord hath swallowed up all the habita-
tions of Jacob, and hath not pitied: he
hath thrown down in his wrath the
strong holds of the daughter of Judah;
he hath [1]brought *them* down to the
ground: he hath polluted the kingdom
and the princes thereof. (3) He hath cut
off in *his* fierce anger all the horn of
Israel: he hath drawn back his right
hand from before the enemy, and he
burned against Jacob like a flaming
fire, *which* devoureth round about.
(4) He hath bent his bow like an enemy:
he stood with his right hand as an ad-
versary, and slew [2]all *that were* pleasant
to the eye in the tabernacle of the
daughter of Zion: he poured out his
fury like fire. (5) The Lord was as an
enemy: he hath swallowed up Israel,
he hath swallowed up all her palaces:
he hath destroyed his strong holds, and
hath increased in the daughter of Judah
mourning and lamentation. (6) And he
hath violently [a]taken away his [3]taber-
nacle, as *if it were of* a garden: he hath
destroyed his places of the assembly:
the LORD hath caused the solemn feasts
and sabbaths to be forgotten in Zion,
and hath despised in the indignation
of his anger the king and the priest.
(7) The Lord hath cast off his altar, he
hath abhorred his sanctuary, he hath
[4]given up into the hand of the enemy
the walls of her palaces; they have
made a noise in the house of the LORD,
as in the day of a solemn feast. (8) The
LORD hath purposed to destroy the wall
of the daughter of Zion: he hath
stretched out a line, he hath not with-
drawn his hand from [5]destroying: there-
fore he made the rampart and the wall
to lament; they languished together.
(9) Her gates are sunk into the ground;

1 Heb., *made to touch.*

2 Heb., *all the desirable of the eye.*

a Ps. 80. 12 & 89. 40; Isa. 5. 5.

3 Or, *hedge.*

4 Heb., *shut up.*

5 Heb., *swallowing up.*

The image that floats before the poet's mind is that of a dark thunder-cloud breaking into a tempest, which overthrows the "beauty of Israel," *sc.* the Temple (Is. lxiv. 11), or, as in 2 Sam. i. 19, the heroes who defended it. The footstool is, as in 1 Chron. xxviii. 2; Ps. xcix. 5, the ark of the covenant, which was involved in the destruction of the Temple. The "Lord" is, as before, *Adonai*, not Jehovah.

(2) **The habitations of Jacob . . .**—The term is used primarily for the dwellings of shepherds, and it accordingly stands here for the open unwalled villages as contrasted with the fortified towns that are here mentioned.

He hath polluted the kingdom.—See Ps. lxxxix. 39. The term involves the thought that it had been a consecrated thing. It had become unclean, first through the sins, and then through the defeat and degradation, of its rulers.

(3) **All the horn of Israel . . .**—The horn, as elsewhere (1 Sam. ii. 1; Pss. xcii. 10, cxii. 9), is the symbol of strength, aggressive or defensive, and may therefore stand here for every element of strength, warriors, rulers, fortresses.

He burned against Jacob.—Better, *And He kindled a burning; i.e.,* was as one who applies the torch.

(4) **He stood with his right hand . . .**—The point of the phrase is that the "right hand," the natural symbol of divine power, which had been of old stretched forth to protect, was now seen shooting the arrows and wielding the sword of vengeance.

Slew all that were pleasant . . .—Better, "*Destroyed* all that *was* pleasant," the destruction including not only warriors and youths, but everything dear and precious.

The tabernacle . . .—Not the Temple, but the city itself as the habitation of the people, who are collectively represented as "the daughter of Zion."

(5) **Her palaces: . . . his strong holds . . .**—The change of gender is remarkable, probably rising from the fact that the writer thought of the "palaces" in connection with the "daughters of Zion," and of the "strong holds" in connection with the land or people. A like combination is found in Hosea viii. 14.

Mourning and lamentation.—The two Hebrew nouns are formed from the same root, and have an assonance like "the sorrow and sighing" of Is. xxxv. 10.

(6) **He hath violently taken away his tabernacle . . .**—The noun represents a "booth" or "shed," like those erected in the Feast of Tabernacles. Jehovah is represented as laying waste that "tabernacle," *i.e.,* His own temple, as a man might remove a temporary shed from an orchard or garden.

His places of the assembly.—The noun is the same as that rendered "solemn feasts" in the next clause. The destruction involved the non-observance of all such feasts, as well as of the sabbath. "King and priest," the two representatives of the nation's life (Jer. xxxiii. 21), were alike, as it seemed, rejected.

(7) **Hath cast off . . . hath abhorred.**—The two verbs are used in a like context in Ps. lxxxix. 38.

His sanctuary.—The word points to the Holy of Holies, and "the walls of her palaces" are therefore those of the Temple rather than of the city.

They have made a noise.—The shouts of the enemies in their triumph, perhaps even the shouts of their worship, had taken the place of the hallelujahs of the "solemn feast."

(8) **He hath stretched out a line.**—The phrase implies (See Notes on 2 Kings xxi. 13; Isa. xxxiv. 11; Amos vii. 7) the systematic thoroughness of the work of destruction.

He made the rampart.—Even the very stones of the walls of Zion are thought of as "crying out" and wailing over their own downfall. (Comp. Hab. ii. 11; Luke xix. 40.)

(9) **Her gates . . .**—The picture of ruin is completed. The gates are broken, and hidden by heaps of

he hath destroyed and broken her bars: her king and her princes *are* among the Gentiles: the law *is* no *more;* her [a]prophets also find no vision from the LORD. (10) The elders of the daughter of Zion sit upon the ground, *and* keep silence: they have cast up dust upon their heads; they have girded themselves with sackcloth: the virgins of Jerusalem hang down their heads to the ground. (11) Mine eyes do fail with tears, my bowels are troubled, my liver is poured upon the earth, for the destruction of the daughter of my people; because the children and the sucklings [1]swoon in the streets of the city. (12) They say to their mothers, Where *is* corn and wine? when they swooned as the wounded in the streets of the city, when their soul was poured out into their mothers' bosom. (13) What thing shall I take to witness for thee? what thing shall I liken to thee, O daughter of Jerusalem? what shall I equal to thee, that I may comfort thee, O virgin daughter of Zion? for thy breach *is* great like the sea: who can heal thee? (14) Thy [b]prophets have seen vain and foolish things for thee: and they have not discovered thine iniquity, to turn away thy captivity; but have seen for thee false burdens and causes of banishment. (15) All that pass [2]by clap *their* hands at thee; they hiss and wag their head at the daughter of Jerusalem, *saying, Is* this the city that *men* call [c]The perfection of beauty, The joy of the whole earth? (16) All thine enemies have opened their mouth against thee: they hiss and gnash the teeth: they say, We have swallowed *her* up: certainly this *is* the day that we looked for; we have found, we have seen *it.* (17) The LORD hath done *that* which he had [d]devised; he hath fulfilled his word that he had commanded in the days of old: he hath thrown down, and hath not pitied: and he hath caused *thine* enemy to rejoice

a Ps. 74. 9.

1 Or, *faint.*

b Jer. 2. 8 & 5. 31 & 14. 14 & 23. 16.

2 Heb., *by the way.*

c Ps. 48. 2.

d Lev. 26. 16; Deut. 28. 15.

---

rubbish as if they had been buried in the earth; they cannot be closed, for the bars are gone. King and princes are captives to the Chaldæans. The Law was practically repealed, for the conditions of its observance were absent, and prophecy had become a thing of the past. The outward desolation was but the shadow of that of the nation's spiritual life.

(10) **The elders of the daughter of Zion . .**—The despondency of the people is indicated by the outward signs of woe. Instead of taking counsel for the emergency, the elders sit, like Job's friends (Job ii. 11—13), as if the evil were inevitable. The maidens, who had once joined with timbrels and dances in festive processions, walk to and fro with downcast eyes.

(11) **My liver is poured upon the earth . . .**—The phrase is not found elsewhere, but admits of an easy explanation. The "liver," like the "heart" and the "bowels," is thought of as the centre of all intense emotions, both of joy or sorrow (Prov. vii. 23). As such it is represented as giving way without restraint (comp. verse 19), under the pressure of the horror caused by the calamities which the next words paint, by the starving children who fainted for hunger in the streets of the city.

(12) **They say . . .**—The words seem to paint what was actually passing before the writer's eye, but may be the vivid present which represents the past. The children cried for food, and their mothers had none to give them. They were like wounded men at their last gasp, and breathed out their life as they clung in their despair to their mothers' breasts.

(13) **What thing shall I take to witness . .**—Practically the question is the same as that which follows, and implies that there was no parallel to the sufferings of Zion in the history of the past. Had there been, and had it been surmounted, it might have been cited in evidence, and some consolation might have been derived from it. As it was there was no such parallel, no such witness. Her "breach," *i.e.,* her ruin, was illimitable as the ocean, and therefore irremediable.

(14) **Thy prophets have seen vain and foolish things.**—The words are eminently characteristic of Jeremiah, whose whole life had been spent in conflict with the false prophets (Jer. ii. 8, v. 13, vi. 13, viii. 10, xiv. 14, xxviii. 9, and elsewhere), who spoke smooth things, and prophesied deceit. They did not call men to repent of their iniquity.

False burdens.—The noun is used, as in Jer. xxiii. 33, with a touch of irony, as being that in which the false prophets delighted. What they uttered, however, as a vision of God, did not tend to restoration, but was itself a "cause of banishment," and tended to perpetuate and aggravate the miseries of exile.

(15) **All that pass by.**—The triumphant exultation of the enemies of Zion came to add bitterness to her sorrows. They reminded her of what she had been in the past, and contrasted it with her present desolation.

The perfection of beauty . . .—Like phrases are used of Zion in Pss. xlviii. 2, l. 2; of Tyre in Ezek. xxvii. 3. Now that beauty was turned into squalor and desolation.

(16) **All thine enemies.**—The exultation of the enemies is expressed by every feature in the physiognomy of malignant hate, the wide mouth, the hissing, the gnashing of the teeth. They exult, as in half-broken utterances, in the thought that they have brought about the misery at which they mock. It is what they had long looked for; they had at last seen it.

(17) **The Lord hath done . . .**—The writer points, in opposition to the boasts of the enemies, to the true author of the misery of the people. In that thought, terrible as it might at first seem, there was an element of hope. It was better to fall into the hands of God than into those of men (2 Sam. xxiv. 14). The suffering came as a chastisement for past transgressions,

over thee, he hath set up the horn of
thine adversaries. (18) Their heart cried
unto the Lord, O wall of the daughter
of Zion, [a] let tears run down like a river
day and night: give thyself no rest;
let not the apple of thine eye cease.
(19) Arise, cry out in the night: in the
beginning of the watches pour out thine
heart like water before the face of the
Lord: lift up thy hands toward him for
the life of thy young children, that faint
for hunger in the top of every street.

(20) Behold, O LORD, and consider to
whom thou hast done this. Shall the
women eat their fruit, *and* children [1] of
a span long? shall the priest and the
prophet be slain in the sanctuary of the
Lord? (21) The young and the old lie on
the ground in the streets: my virgins
and my young men are fallen by the
sword; thou hast slain *them* in the day
of thine anger; thou hast killed, *and*
not pitied. (22) Thou hast called as in a
solemn day my terrors round about, so
that in the day of the LORD's anger
none escaped nor remained: those that
I have swaddled and brought up hath
mine enemy consumed.

a Jer. 14. 17; ch. 1. 16.

1 Or, *swaddled with their hands?*

CHAPTER III.— (1) I *am* the man
that hath seen affliction by the rod of
his wrath. (2) He hath led me, and
brought *me into* darkness, but not *into*
light. (3) Surely against me is he
turned; he turneth his hand *against me*
all the day. (4) My flesh and my skin
hath he made old; he hath broken my
bones. (5) He hath builded against me,
and compassed *me* with gall and travel.
(6) He hath set me in dark places, as

---

and might therefore be mitigated by repentance. The Destroyer was also the Healer, and would answer the prayers of those who called on Him.

(18) **Their heart.**—The possessive pronoun does not refer to any immediate antecedent, but points, with a wild abruptness, to the mourners of Zion. Yet more boldly their cry is an appeal to the "wall" of Zion (comp. verse 8, and Isa. xiv. 31), to take up its lamentation, as though it were a human mourner.

Like a river.—Better, *like a torrent.*

The apple of thine eye. — Literally, "the *daughter*," as in the English phrase, the "pupil" of the eye.

(19) **In the beginning of the watches**—*i.e.*, of each watch, so that the lamentation was continued throughout the night.

Lift up thy hands.—The wall is still addressed in its character as a mourner, beholding the children dying of hunger and lifting up her hands as in despairing supplication for them.

(20) **To whom thou hast done this**—*i.e.*, not to a heathen nation, but to the people whom Jehovah Himself had chosen.

Shall the women eat their fruit.—Atrocities of this nature had been predicted in Lev. xxvi. 26; Deut. xxviii. 57; Jer. xix. 9. They were, indeed, the natural incidents of a besieged city reduced to starvation, as in the case of Samaria (2 Kings vi. 28), and the siege of Jerusalem by the Romans (Jos., *B. J.* v. 12), and had been witnessed, as the words show, in that by the Chaldæans. (Comp., as to the famine, Ezek. iv. 16, 17, v. 16.)

Shall the priest . . .—Stress is laid on this as being the next element of horror. The very Holy of Holies was profaned with the blood of the priests and prophets of Jehovah.

(21) **The young and the old . .**—The thoughts of the mourner turn from the massacre in the sanctuary to the slaughter which did its dread work in every corner of the city.

(22) **Thou hast called . . .**—Better, *Thou hast summoned, as for a solemn feast-day.* (Comp. chap. i. 15.) In "terrors round about" we have a characteristic phrase of Jeremiah's (Jer. vi. 25, xx. 3, 10). The LXX., followed by some commentators, gives the rendering, "*Thou hast summoned. . . my villages,*" but on no sufficient grounds.

III.

The elegy which is contained in this chapter is alphabetic in its structure, like the two that precede it, but it is of a more complicated character, three consecutive verses beginning with the same letter of the alphabet.

(1) **I am the man.**—The lamentation is one of more intense personality. For that very reason it has been the true inheritance of all mourners, however widely different in time, country, circumstance, whose sorrows have approximated to that intensity.

The rod of his wrath.—The "wrath" is obviously that of Jehovah (comp. Prov. xxii. 8; Isa. x. 5), but there is something significant in the fact that He is not named.

(2) **Into darkness.**—The moral darkness of perplexity as well as misery. The cry of the mourner was like that of Ajax (Hom. *Il.* xvii. 647), "Slay me if thou wilt, but slay me in the light."

(3) **Against me is he turned.**—Better, *against me He turneth His hand again and again,* the first verb being one of frequentative action, and giving that significance to the second.

(4) **Hath he made old.**—Better, *He hath wasted,* the verb describing the wear and tear of life rather than the effects of age. "Flesh," "skin," "bones," are grouped together as representing the whole being of the mourner.

(5) **He hath builded.**—The attack of sorrow is presented under the figure of a siege. In the next clause the figure is dropped. "Gall" stands, as in Jer. viii. 14, for bitterest sorrow. "Travel" is the old English form of "travail," the two forms, originally identical, being now used with different meanings.

(6) **He hath set me in dark places.**—A verbal reproduction of Ps. cxliii. 3. The "dark places" are those of hell or Hades. For *dead of old* read *dead eternally* or *dead for ever,* the adverb looking forward rather than back.

they that be dead of old. (7) He hath
hedged me about, that I cannot get out:
he hath made my chain heavy. (8) Also
when I cry and shout, he shutteth out
my prayer. (9) He hath inclosed my
ways with hewn stone, he hath made
my paths crooked. (10) He *was* unto me
as a bear lying in wait, *and as* a lion in
secret places. (11) He hath turned aside
my ways, and pulled me in pieces: he
hath made me desolate. (12) He hath
bent his bow, and set me as a mark for
the arrow. (13) He hath caused the
[1]arrows of his quiver to enter into my
reins. (14) I was a [a]derision to all my
people; *and* their song all the day.
(15) He hath filled me with [2]bitterness,
he hath made me drunken with worm-
wood. (16) He hath also broken my teeth
with gravel stones, he hath [3]covered me
with ashes. (17) And thou hast removed
my soul far off from peace: I forgat
[4]prosperity. (18) And I said, My strength
and my hope is perished from the LORD:
(19) [5]remembering mine affliction and
my misery, the wormwood and the gall.
(20) My soul hath *them* still in remem-
brance, and is [6]humbled in me. (21) This
I [7]recall to my mind, therefore have I
hope.
(22) *It is of* the LORD's mercies that we
are not consumed, because his compas-
sions fail not. (23) *They are* new every
morning: great *is* thy faithfulness.
(24) The LORD *is* my [b]portion, saith my
soul; therefore will I hope in him.

1 Heb., *sons.*

a Jer. 20. 7.

2 Heb., *bitternesses.*

3 Or, *rolled me in the ashes.*

4 Heb., *good.*

5 Or, *Remember.*

6 Heb., *bowed.*

7 Heb., *make to return to my heart.*

b Ps. 16. 5 & 73. 26 & 119. 57; Jer. 10. 16.

(7) **He hath hedged.**—From the darkness of Hades we pass to that of the prison-house, in which the mourner is "hedged" or confined, bound with a heavy chain (literally, *brass*).

(8) **He shutteth out my prayer**—*i.e.*, stops it so that it does not reach the ear of Jehovah; and it is Jehovah himself who does this.

(9) **He hath inclosed.**—Yet another figure of resourceless misery follows. A massive wall of stone runs across the mourner's way. When he turns aside into by-paths, they are turned and twisted in labyrinthine confusion, and lead nowhither.

(10) **As a bear . . . as a lion.**—The figure found in Hos. xiii. 8; Amos v. 19, is specially characteristic of Jeremiah (Jer. iv. 7, v. 6, xlix. 19, l. 44). We are reminded of Dante (*Inferno*, i. 31—51).

(11) **He hath turned aside.**—The terror caused by the lion turns the traveller from his path, and there is no other; and then comes the attack by which he is torn in pieces.

He hath made me desolate.—Better, *made me astonied*, as in Ezra ix. 3. The verb (which occurs forty times in Jeremiah's prophecies and three times in Lam.), paints the stupefaction of terror.

(12) **He hath bent his bow.**—(Comp. Job xvi. 12.) The figure is changed, but there is a natural sequence of thought. The lion suggests the huntsman, but he appears on the scene not to save the victim, but to complete the work of destruction.

(13) **The arrows of his quiver.**—Literally, *children.* The other side of the analogy appears in Ps. cxxvii. 5.

(14) **I was a derision.**—The personal experience of the prophet breaks through the succession of imagery. The arrows that pierced to the quick were the taunts of the mockers who derided him (Jer. xx. 7). "Their song." (Comp. Job xxx. 9.)

(15) **Bitterness.**—The Hebrew gives the plural, *bitternesses.* With these, the sorrows which are as the bitter herbs of life (the same word meets us in Exod. xii. 8, and Num. ix. 11), the mourner had been filled even to satiety, even as he had been made drunk with wormwood.

(16) **He hath also broken my teeth.**—The metaphor of food is continued. The mourner eats bread that is gritty, as if made of sand instead of flour. (Comp. Prov. xx. 17.) Here, again, we are reminded of Dante (*Parad.* xvii. 58), when he speaks of the bitterness of the bread which comes as the grudging gift of strangers.

(17) **Thou hast removed my soul far off from peace.**—The verb is found in this sense in Ps. lxxxviii. 14. By some critics it is taken as passive, and in the 3rd person feminine. *My soul loathes peace, i.e.*, has lost even the desire of better things; or, *My soul is despised of peace, i.e.*, is shut out from it. But the Authorised version is preferable.

(18) **I said, My strength.**—The sorrow of the mourner comes to the very verge of despair. There was "no help for him from his God;" even that hope had left him. But, as the sequel shows, this despair was the beginning of a reaction. The very name of Jehovah (no longer Adonai) reminded him of the everlasting mercies.

(19) **Remembering.**—The verb, which is rendered by the Authorised version as a gerundial infinitive, is better taken as an imperative, *Remember mine affliction;* the prayer being addressed to Jehovah. The two terms of the first clause are taken from chap. i. 7. The mourner begins his prayer, as it were, by a recapitulation of his sufferings. (Comp. Ps. lxix. 21.)

(20) **My soul hath . . .**—The verb, as in verse 17, may be either in the second person or the third; the former gives, *Thou wilt surely remember that my soul is humbled.* Ps. xlii. 4 supports the Authorised version.

(21) **This I recall to my mind.**—Better, *This will I recall.* The first gleam of hope breaks through the darkness. The sorrow has not been in vain; it has brought humility, and out of humility springs hope.

(22) **It is of the Lord's mercies.**—It is, perhaps, part of the elaborate art of this poem that verses 22—42, which form its centre, and that of the whole book, represent the highest point of trust to which the mourner attains, being both preceded and followed by words of lamentation.

(23) **They are new.**—The subject of the sentence is found in the "compassions" of the preceding verse. With the dawn of every day there dawn also the mercies of Jehovah.

(24) **The Lord.**—An inversion of the sentence gives a closer and more emphatic rendering: *My portion is*

(25) The LORD *is* good unto them that
wait for him, to the soul *that* seeketh
him. (26) *It is* good that *a man* should
both hope and quietly wait for the
salvation of the LORD. (27) *It is* good
for a man that he bear the yoke in his
youth. (28) He sitteth alone and keepeth
silence, because he hath borne *it* upon
him. (29) He putteth his mouth in the
dust; if so be there may be hope.
(30) He giveth *his* cheek to him that
smiteth him: he is filled full with re-
proach. (31) For the Lord will not cast
off for ever: (32) but though he cause
grief, yet will he have compassion ac-
cording to the multitude of his mercies.
(33) For he doth not afflict [1]willingly nor
grieve the children of men. (34) To crush
under his feet all the prisoners of the
earth, (35) to turn aside the right of a
man before the face of [2]the most High,
(36) to subvert a man in his cause, the
Lord [3]approveth not.

(37) Who *is* he [a]*that* saith, and it
cometh to pass, *when* the Lord com-
mandeth *it* not? (38) Out of the mouth
of the most High proceedeth not [b]evil
and good? (39) Wherefore doth a living
man [4]complain, a man for the punish-
ment of his sins? (40) Let us search and
try our ways, and turn again to the
LORD. (41) Let us lift up our heart with
our hands unto God in the heavens.
(42) We have transgressed and have re-
belled: thou hast not pardoned. (43) Thou
hast covered with anger, and persecuted

1 Heb., *from his heart.*

2 Or, *a superior.*

3 Or, *seeth not.*

a Ps. 33. 9.

b Amos 3. 6.

4 Or, *murmur.*

Jehovah. The phrase is a reminiscence from Pss. xvi. 5, lxxiii. 26, cxlii. 5, cxix. 57, the thought resting primarily on Num. xviii. 20.

(25) **The Lord is good.**—The alliterative form of the Hebrew makes "good" the first word of this and the two following verses, the adjective being predicated, first of the essential character of Jehovah, and then of the conditions in man on which the manifestation of that character depends.

(26) **Quietly wait.**—Literally, *wait in silence: i.e.* abstain from murmurs and complaints.

(27) **Bear the yoke in his youth.**—The words have been pressed "with a strange literalism" in favour of the view that the Lamentations were written in the youth of Jeremiah and on the death of Josiah. It may fairly be contended, on the other hand, that the tone of the maxim is that of one who looks back from the experience of age on the passionate complaints of his earlier years (Jer. xv. 10, xx. 7—18).

(28) **He sitteth alone . . .**—Better, *Let him sit alone, and keep silence when He* (Jehovah) *hath laid it* (the yoke) *upon him;* and so in the next verses, *Let him put his mouth . . Let him give his cheek.*

(29) **He putteth his mouth in the dust . .**—The outward image is that of the prostration of an Eastern subject before a king: his very face laid in the dust, so that he cannot speak.

(30) **He giveth his cheek . . .**—The submission enjoined reaches its highest point—a patience like that of Job xvi. 10; we may add, like that of the Sermon on the Mount (Matt. v. 39.) It was harder to accept the Divine chastisement when it came through human agents. Not so had Jeremiah once taught and acted (Jer. xx. 1—6, xxviii. 15). (Comp. Isa. l. 6.)

(31) **For the Lord . . .**—The counsels of submission are followed by the grounds of hope. The first, a quotation from Ps. lxxvii. 7, had been of old a favourite thought of the writer's (Jer. iii. 5, 12). The second (verse 32) rests on the fact that compassion underlies chastisement (Ps. xxx. 5; Job v. 18; Isa. liv. 8); the third (verse 33) on the truth that the primary eternal will of God is on the side of love, and that punishment is, as it were, against that will.

(33) **Not . . willingly.**—Literally, *not from the heart,* as being the centre of volition as well as emotion

(34—36) **To crush . . .**—The triplet of verses forms one sentence dependent upon the final clause, "The Lord approveth not," literally, *doth not look on.* By some critics the literal meaning is kept in the form of a question: *Doth not the Lord look on this?* The fact that the righteous judgment of God is against those who, unlike Him, cause wilful and needless suffering is another ground of hope to the sufferer. The three forms of evil specified are (1) the cruel treatment of prisoners of war, such as Jeremiah had witnessed daily at the hands of the Chaldeans; (2) the perversion of justice in a public tribunal acting in the name of God (Exod. xxiii. 6); (3) every form even of private injustice.

(37—39) New grounds of patient faith are given: (1) In an echo from Ps. xxxiii. 9, affirming the sovereignty of God. The evil which He permits is under the control of this loving purpose; and (2) as far as it is not absolute evil, may be said to come from Him.

(39) **Wherefore doth a living man . .**—Better, *Why doth a man who lives? i.e.,* whose life is spared him (comp. Jer. xlv. 5), with all its possibilities of good, complain of sufferings which, however unjust as far as those who cause them are concerned, are, in relation to the sufferer, the just punishment of his own sins?

(40) **Let us search . . .**—Warnings against murmurs are followed by counsels which point to a more excellent way. Suffering calls a man to self-scrutiny. We should seek to know the sins which it is meant to punish and correct.

To the Lord.—The preposition is an emphatic one: *even to the Lord.* There is to be no halting half-way in the work of conversion.

(41) **With our hands.**—Literally, *to our hands.* There is, as it were, a psychological analysis of prayer. Men can by an act of will, lift up the heart as the centre of affection: this, in its turn, prompts the outward act of the uplifted hands of supplication; God is the final object to whom the prayer is addressed.

(42) **We have transgressed . . .**—The verses that follow (42—47) give the prayer which answers to the call of verse 41. Both pronouns are emphatic. The suppliant has sinned and God has not yet pardoned, in the sense of ceasing to punish.

(43) **Thou hast covered with anger.**—Better, as in the next verse, *Thou hast covered thyself.* Wrath is

us: thou hast slain, thou hast not
pitied. (44) Thou hast covered thyself
with a cloud, that *our* prayer should not
pass through. (45) Thou hast made us
as the [a]offscouring and refuse in the
midst of the people. (46) All our enemies
have opened their mouths against us.
(47) [b]Fear and a snare is come upon us,
desolation and destruction. (48) Mine
eye runneth down with rivers of water
for the destruction of the daughter of
my people. (49) Mine eye trickleth down,
and ceaseth not, without any intermis-
sion, (50) till the LORD look down, and
behold from heaven. (51) Mine eye affect-
eth [1]mine heart [2]because of all the
daughters of my city. (52) Mine enemies
chased me sore, like a bird, without
cause. (53) They have cut off my life in
the dungeon, and cast a stone upon me.
(54) Waters flowed over mine head; *then*
I said, I am cut off.

(55) I called upon thy name, O LORD,
out of the low dungeon. (56) Thou hast
heard my voice: hide not thine ear at
my breathing, at my cry. (57) Thou
drewest near in the day *that* I called
upon thee: thou saidst, Fear not. (58) O
Lord, thou hast pleaded the causes of
my soul; thou hast redeemed my life.
(59) O LORD, thou hast seen my wrong:
judge thou my cause. (60) Thou hast
seen all their vengeance *and* all their
imaginations against me. (61) Thou hast
heard their reproach, O LORD, *and* all
their imaginations against me; (62) the
lips of those that rose up against
me, and their device against me all
the day. (63) Behold their sitting down,
and their rising up; I *am* their
musick.

(64) Render unto them a recompence,
O LORD, according to the work of their
hands. (65) Give them [3]sorrow of heart,

[a] 1 Cor. 4. 13.

[b] Isa. 24. 17.

[1] Heb., *my soul.*

[2] Or, *more than all.*

[3] Or, *obstinacy of heart.*

---

as the garment in which God wraps Himself to execute His righteous judgments. In verse 44 the wrath is represented more definitely as a cloud through which the prayers of the afflicted cannot pass.

(45) **In the midst of the people.**—Literally, *peoples: i.e.,* the heathen nations of the world. A like phrase meets us in 1 Cor. iv. 13.

(47) **Fear and a snare.**—A quotation from Jer. xlviii. 43, and Isa. xxiv. 17.

Desolation.—Better, *devastation.* The Hebrew noun is not found elsewhere, but the cognate verb in Isa. xxxvii. 26 is rendered "to lay waste."

(48) **Mine eye . . .**—A stronger utterance of the thought of chaps. i. 16, ii. 18; Ps. cxix. 136.

(49) **Trickleth down.**—Better, *poureth down.*

(51) **Affecteth.**—Better, *harmeth,* or *causeth grief to.*

The daughters of my city.—The words have been understood (1) of the maidens of Jerusalem (comp. chaps. i. 4, 18, ii. 20, 21); and (2) of the daughter-towns which looked to it as their metropolis. Of these (1) is preferable.

(52) **Without cause . . .**—The words connect themselves in the Hebrew with "mine enemies" (comp. Pss. xxxv. 7, 19, lxix. 4), and it has been inferred from this that Jeremiah speaks not of the Chaldeans as enemies of his nation, but of those who were individually his persecutors. The hypothesis receives some confirmation from the apparent reference in the "dungeon" and the "waters" to the narrative of Jer. xxxviii. It has been urged, on the other hand, that those expressions may be figurative here, as they are in Pss. xlii. 7, lxxxviii. 7, cxxiv. 4.

(53) **Cast a stone upon me.**—The words admit of two meanings: (1) that they cast stones at him; (2) that they placed a stone over the opening of his dungeon so as to prevent escape.

(55) **Out of the low dungeon.**—Here, again, we have to choose between a literal reference to Jeremiah's sufferings or a figurative interpretation. The phrase is the same as that of Ps. lxxxviii. 6.

(56) **Thou hast heard . . hide not thine . . .**—There is something eminently suggestive in the sequence of the two clauses. The recollection that prayer was answered in the past, prompts its utterance in the present. Historically, the words may point to the intervention of Ebed-melech in Jer. xxxviii. 7.

At my breathing—*i.e.,* the "sighs" or "sobs" of the mourner.

(58) **Thou hast pleaded the causes of my soul**—*i.e.,* Jehovah had appeared as the advocate, or next-of-kin protector, of the prophet in the persecutions which were aimed against his life. Another personal reference to the prophet's sufferings. (Comp. Jer. xxvi. 8—17, xxxvii. 14, xxxviii. 4.)

(60) **All their imaginations . .**—Same word as the "devices" of Jer. xi. 19, xviii. 18, to which the writer obviously refers.

(61) **Thou hast heard.**—The verb governs the "lips" of the next verse as well as the "reproaches" of this. In the last clause we note the emphasis of iteration, the natural dwelling on what was prominent in the prophet's thoughts.

(62) **The lips . . .** The organs of speech are used boldly for the words which they uttered, and so stand parallel with "reproaches" in verse 61.

(63) **Their sitting down, and their rising up . . .**—The two words, as in Deut. vi. 7, xi. 19; Ps. cxxxix. 2; include the whole daily and hourly conduct of those spoken of.

I am their musick.—The noun, though not identical, is cognate with that of Ps. lxix. 12, of which the complaint is, as it were, an echo.

(64) **Render unto them . .**—The words are noticeable as being taken from Ps. xxviii. 4, and reproduced by St. Paul in 2 Tim. iv. 14.

(65) **Sorrow of heart**—Literally, *covering,* with a sense like that of the "veil upon the heart" of 2 Cor. iii. 15, and so signifying the blindness of obstinacy. The imperatives in both verses 65 and 66 are better rendered as futures—*Thou shalt give; Thou shalt persecute.*

thy curse unto them. (66) Persecute and destroy them in anger from under the [a]heavens of the LORD.

CHAPTER IV.—(1) How is the gold become dim! *how* is the most fine gold changed! the stones of the sanctuary are poured out in the top of every street. (2) The precious sons of Zion, comparable to fine gold, how are they esteemed as earthen pitchers, the work of the hands of the potter! (3) Even the [1]sea monsters draw out the breast, they give suck to their young ones: the daughter of my people *is become* cruel, like the ostriches in the wilderness. (4) The tongue of the sucking child cleaveth to the roof of his mouth for thirst: the young children ask bread, *and* no man breaketh *it* unto them. (5) They that did feed delicately are desolate in the streets: they that were brought up in scarlet embrace dunghills. (6) For the [2]punishment of the iniquity of the daughter of my people is greater than the punishment of the sin of Sodom, that was [b]overthrown as in a moment, and no hands stayed on her. (7) Her Nazarites were purer than snow, they were whiter than milk, they were more ruddy in body than rubies, their polishing *was* of sapphire: (8) their visage is [3]blacker than a coal; they are not known in the streets: their skin cleaveth to their bones; it is withered, it is become like a stick. (9) *They that be* slain with the sword are better than *they that be* slain with hunger: for these [4]pine

a Ps. 8. 3.

1 Or, *sea calves.*

2 Or, *iniquity.*

b Gen. 19. 25.

3 Heb., *darker than blackness.*

4 Heb., *flow out.*

---

(66) **From under the heavens of the Lord.**—The phrase is exceptional, but it is obviously equivalent to the whole world, considered as God's kingdom.

IV.

(1) **How is the gold . . .**—The chapter, considered as a distinct poem, reproduces in its general character that of chaps. i. and ii., differing from them, however, in tracing more fully the connection between the sufferings and the sins of Judah. The "gold" and the *stones of holiness* are none other than the material treasures of palace or temple, and the repetition of the phrase "in the top of every street," used in chap. ii. 19 of children, seems intended to indicate that the words include all that was most precious among the possessions of Jerusalem.

(2) **The precious sons of Zion . . .**—The adjective is applied not to a special class, priests, nobles, or the like, but to all the "sons of Zion" in their ideal character as a "kingdom of priests" (Exod. xix. 6). They had been "comparable to" (literally, *weighed with*), *i.e.*, equal to their weight in, fine gold, the work of God. Now they had became as "earthen pitchers," the work of the potter. We note the comparison as characteristic of the writer (Jer. xviii. 1—6, xix. 1—10).

(3) **Even the sea monsters . . .**—Better, *jackals.* The Authorised Version is intended apparently to apply to cetaceous mammals; elsewhere (Jer. xiv. 6) the word is rendered "dragons." "Jackals," it may be noted, are combined with "owls" or "ostriches," as they are here, in Job xxx. 29; Isa. xiii. 21. A like reference to the seeming want of maternal instinct in the ostrich is found in Job xxxix. 16. The comparison was obviously suggested by facts like those referred to in chap. ii. 20.

(5) **They that were brought up . . .**—Literally, *that were carried* (as children are carried). "Scarlet" as in 2 Sam. i. 24, stands for the shawls or garments of the rich, dyed, as they were, in the Tyrian purple or crimson. Those that had been once wrapped in such shawls now threw themselves, "embracing" them as their only refuge, on dunghills.

(6) **The punishment of the iniquity.**—Better, *The iniquity of the daughter of my people was greater than the sin of Sodom.* The words in both cases point to guilt rather than its penalty, though, as the context shows, the greatness of the former is inferred from that of the latter. The point of comparison was that Sodom was not doomed to a protracted misery, like that which had been the lot of Jerusalem.

No hands stayed on her . . .—Literally, *no hands went round about her: i.e.*, her destruction was the direct work of God, and not of human agents, with their more merciless tortures. (Comp. 2 Sam. xxiv. 14.) The main thought may be noticed as reproduced in Matt. x. 15, xi. 24.

(7) **Her Nazarites . . .**—The word has been rendered "princes" by some commentators, on the ground that it means literally those who are "separated" from their brethren (Gen. xlix. 26; Deut. xxxiii. 16), whether by rank or by the vows of consecration. There is no reason, however, for abandoning the rendering of the Authorised version. The reference to the Nazarites in Amos. ii. 11, 12 shows that they were prominent as a body during the history of the monarchy, and the drift of Jeremiah's mind, as seen in his admiration of the Rechabites (chap. xxxv.), shows that he was likely to think of them with reverence. The temperance, purity, cleanliness of such a body seem to have made them conspicuous among their fellows for an almost angelic beauty. (Comp. the interesting parallel of Dan. i. 15.) They had the red and white complexion which was in the East the ideal of comeliness (1 Sam. xvii. 42; Song Sol. v. 10). Their "polishing" (better, *their form*) was faultless, like that of a well-cut sapphire. For "rubies" read *coral.*

(8) **Their visage is blacker . . .**—We look, as it were, on the two pictures: the bloom and beauty of health, the wan, worn, spectral looks of starvation.

(9) **For want of . . .**—The italics indicate the difficulty of the sentence. Literally the clause stands, *from the fruits of the field,* and it has been explained by some as referring to those that died in battle, *stricken through while yet there were fruits, i.e.*, not doomed to perish slowly from hunger. The construction of Ps. cix. 24, however, "faileth of fatness"—*i.e.*, for want of fatness—gives a sufficient support to the Authorised version.

away, stricken through for *want of* the
fruits of the field. (10) The hands of
the pitiful women have [a] sodden their
own children: they were their meat in
the destruction of the daughter of my
people. (11) The LORD hath accomplished
his fury; he hath poured out his fierce
anger, and hath kindled a fire in Zion,
and it hath devoured the foundations
thereof. (12) The kings of the earth, and
all the inhabitants of the world, would
not have believed that the adversary
and the enemy should have entered into
the gates of Jerusalem.
(13) [b] For the sins of her prophets, *and*
the iniquities of her priests, that have
shed the blood of the just in the midst
of her, (14) they have wandered *as* blind
men in the streets, they have polluted
themselves with blood, [1] so that men
could not touch their garments. (15) They
cried unto them, Depart ye; [2] *it is* un-
clean; depart, depart, touch not: when
they fled away and wandered, they said
among the heathen, They shall no more
sojourn *there.* (16) The [3] anger of the
LORD hath divided them; he will no
more regard them: they respected not
the persons of the priests, they favoured
not the elders. (17) As for us, our eyes
as yet failed for our vain help: in our
watching we have watched for a nation
that could not save *us.* (18) They hunt
our steps, that we cannot go in our
streets: our end is near, our days are
fulfilled; for our end is come. (19) Our
persecutors are swifter than the eagles
of the heaven: they pursued us upon
the mountains, they laid wait for us in
the wilderness. (20) The [c] breath of our
nostrils, the anointed of the LORD, was
taken in their pits, of whom we said,
Under his shadow we shall live among
the heathen. (21) Rejoice and be glad,
O daughter of Edom, that dwellest in
the land of Uz; the cup also shall pass

a Deut. 28. 57; 2 Kings 6. 29.

b Jer. 5. 31 & 23. 21.

1 Or, *in that they could not but touch.*

2 Or, *ye polluted.*

3 Or, *face.*

c Gen. 2. 7.

---

(10) **The hands of the pitiful women.**—See Note on chap. ii. 20.

(11) **And hath kindled a fire . . .**—The phrase is partly literal (2 Chron. xxxvi. 19), partly figurative, for the complete destruction of Jerusalem by the wrath of Jehovah.

(12) **Would not have believed.**—In looking to the fact that Jerusalem had been taken by Shishak (1 Kings xiv. 26), Joash (2 Kings xiv. 13), the statement seems at first hyperbolical. It has to be remembered, however, that since the latter of these two the city had been strongly fortified by Uzziah, Hezekiah, and Manasseh, and the failure of Sennacherib's attempt had probably led to the impression that it was impregnable.

(13) **That have shed the blood of the just . . .**—The words point to incidents like the death of Zechariah the son of Jehoiada (2 Chron. xxiv. 21); the "innocent blood" shed by Manasseh (2 Kings xxi. 16); the attempts on Jeremiah's own life (Jer. xxvi. 7); possibly to some unrecorded atrocities during the siege on the part of the priests and false prophets, who looked on the true prophets as traitors (Jer. xxvi. 23).

(14) **They have wandered . . .**—Literally, *reeled.* The blindness, *i.e.*, either that of the insatiable lust of blood, or of hopeless despair, or both. (Comp. Deut. xxviii. 28; Jer. xxiii. 12; Isa. xxix. 10.) The horror of the picture is heightened by the fact that the very garments of the priests were so dripping with blood that men shrank from touching them.

(15) **They cried unto them**—*i.e.*, these, as they passed, cried to the blood-stained priests. The cry "unclean" was that uttered by the leper as a warning to those he met (Lev. xiii. 45). Here it comes from those whom they meet, and who start back in their fear of defilement.

When they fled away.—The words seem to refer to some lost facts, like those suggested by verse 14: the murderers fleeing from their own countrymen, and finding themselves equally abhorred among the heathen.

(16) **The anger of the Lord.**—Literally, *the face,* as the symbol of wrath.

They respected not.—The subject of the verbs has to be supplied. The enemies, or the heathen, or men in general, ceased to feel any reverence for the fugitive priests and elders.

(17) **As for us. . .**—Better, *Still do our eyes waste away, looking for our vain help.*

In our watching.—Better, *upon our watch-tower.* (Comp. Hab. ii. 1.) The people of Judah are represented as looking out for the approach of an ally, probably Egypt (Jer. xxxvii. 7), and looking in vain.

(18) **They hunt our steps.**—Better, *They lie in wait.* The words probably point to the posts occupied here and there near the wide places of the city, which led people to avoid them through fear of being attacked. The only cry possible at such a time was that "all was over."

(19) **Our persecutors.**— Better, *Our pursuers,* the words referring to the Chaldæan enemies rather than to persecutors in the modern sense of the word. The comparison with eagles has a parallel in Deut. xxviii. 49. If we take the second clause as referring to the flight of Zedekiah, mentioned in the next verse, the mountains would be the heights east of Jerusalem, beginning with the Mount of Olives, and the wilderness that of the *Ghor,* or Jordan Valley (Jer. xxxix. 5).

(20) **The breath of our nostrils.**—The "breath of life" of Gen. ii. 7. The phrase emphasises the ideal character of the king as the centre of the nation's life. So Seneca (*Clement.* i. 4) speaks of a ruler as the *spiritus vitalis* of his people.

Of whom we said.—The words that follow point to the scheme which was rendered abortive by Zedekiah's capture. Those who followed him had hoped to find a refuge among some friendly neighbouring nation, where they might at least have maintained the continuity of their national existence, and waited for better days.

(21) **O daughter of Edom.**—The triumph of Edom in the downfall of Zion was, as in Ps. cxxxvii., the crown-

through unto thee: thou shalt be
drunken, and shalt make thyself naked.
(22) [1]The punishment of thine iniquity
is accomplished, O daughter of Zion;
he will no more carry thee away into
captivity: he will visit thine iniquity,
O daughter of Edom; he will [2]discover
thy sins.

CHAPTER V.— (1) Remember, O
LORD, what is come upon us: consider,
and behold our reproach. (2) Our in-
heritance is turned to strangers, our
houses to aliens. (3) We are orphans
and fatherless, our mothers *are* as
widows. (4) We have drunken our water
for money; our wood [3]is sold unto us.
(5) [4]Our necks *are* under persecution:
we labour, *and* have no rest. (6) We
have given the hand *to* the Egyptians,
and to the Assyrians, to be satisfied with
bread. (7) [a]Our fathers have sinned,
and are not; and we have borne their
iniquities. (8) Servants have ruled over
us: *there is* none that doth deliver *us*
out of their hand. (9) We gat our bread
with *the peril of* our lives because of the
sword of the wilderness. (10) Our [b]skin
was black like an oven because of the
[5]terrible famine. (11) They ravished the
women in Zion, *and* the maids in the
cities of Judah. (12) Princes are hanged

1 Or, *Thine iniquity.*

2 Or, *carry thee captive for thy sins.*

3 Heb., *cometh for price.*

4 Heb., *On our necks are we persecuted.*

a Jer. 31. 29; Ezek. 18. 2.

b Ps. 119. 83.

5 Or, *terrors*, or, *storms.*

---

ing sorrow of the mourner. But with this sorrow there is a vision of judgment, which is also a vision of hope; the prophet returning to his favourite image of the wine-cup (Jer. xxv. 17). On the "Land of Uz" see Notes on Job. i. 1, Jer. xxv. 20.

Shalt make thyself naked.—See Note on chap. i. 8, and comp. Nahum iii. 5 for a bolder form of the same image.

(22) **Is accomplished.**—The mourner shares in the Messianic hopes of Isa. xl. 2, and expresses it nearly in the same words.

He will no more carry thee away.—Interpreted by later history, the words take their place in the list of unfulfilled prophecies, for, like all promises, they were dependent upon implied conditions, and in the rejection of the Christ by the Jews of His time there was a sin which involved a forfeiture of the blessing, and made the chastisement of a prolonged guilt necessary. For five centuries, however, the prophet's words held good, and there was no thorough "dispersion" of the Jews till after the Roman conquest.

He will discover thy sins.—To cover sins is to forgive them (Pss. xxxii. 1, 5, lxxxv. 2; so to *dis-* or *un-*cover sins is, therefore, to punish them.

V.

(1) **Remember, O Lord.**—The fact that the number of verses is, as in chaps. i., ii., and iv., the same as that of the Hebrew alphabet suggests the inference that this chapter also, though not actually alphabetic, was intended to have been so, and that we have the last of the five elegies in a half-finished state. It would seem as if Jeremiah first wrote freely what was in his mind, and then set to work as an artist to bring it under the alphabetic scheme. This chapter, it may be stated, has more the character of a prayer than any other, and the prayer begins with recapitulating the woes of Judah as a ground for the compassion of Jehovah.

(2) **Turned.**—Used here as in the sense of *transferred.*

Houses.—In Jer. lii. 13, the Chaldæans are said to have burnt the houses of Jerusalem, and those of the great men elsewhere; here, therefore, the "houses" spoken of are those of the farmers and peasants in the country.

(3) **Our mothers are as widows**—*i.e.*, their husbands, though living, were carried into exile, and they were as destitute as though they had been deprived of them by death. The Chaldee paraphrase gives the same meaning to the last clause also, "We are like orphans."

(4) **Our water . . . our wood.**—The point of the complaint lies in the possessive pronoun. The Chaldæan conquerors were in possession of the country, and the very necessaries of life, which had been looked on as the common property of all, were only to be had for money. In the Hebrew of the first clause the fact appears yet more emphatically: *Our water comes to us for money.* The words have been referred by some commentators to the sufferings of the exiles in Egypt, but the context fits in better with the idea of the hardships of those who were left in Judah.

(5) **Our necks are under persecution.**—Better, *were under pursuit: i.e.*, the enemies were pressing close on them, always, as in our English phrase, at their very heels.

(6) **We have given the hand.**—The recognised phrase for submission (Jer. l. 15). "Assyria," as in Jer. ii. 18; Ezra vi. 22, stands for "Babylon." The people had been forced by sheer pressure of hunger to submit to one or other of these princes. "Egypt" refers, probably, to the fugitives who had sought a home in that country (Jer. xlii. 14).

(7) **We have borne their iniquities.**—The words seem at first parallel to the proverb of the "sour grapes" in Jer. xxxi. 29; Ezek. xviii. 2. Here, however, it is followed in verse 16 by a confession of personal guilt, and the complaint is simply that the former generation of offenders had passed away without the punishment which now fell upon their descendants, who thus had to bear, as it were, a double penalty.

(8) **Servants have ruled over us.**—The Chaldæans, it would seem, added insult to injury, sending as rulers those who had filled menial offices in the courts of their kings. (Comp. Jer. xxxix. 3.)

(9) **The sword of the wilderness.**—Another element of suffering is hinted at. Those who were left in the land were attacked, as they gathered in their scanty harvest, by the nomad tribes of the wilderness, Amalekites, Midianites, and others. (Comp. Jer. xl. 14.)

(10) **Our skin was black . . .**—Better, *fiery red*, and for "terrible famine," *the fever-blast of famine.* The words paint the hot fever of hunger rather than the livid paleness of exhaustion.

(12) **Princes are hanged . .**—The words point to the shameless exposure of the bodies of the dead. (Comp. the treatment of Saul and his sons in 1 Sam. xxxi. 10—12.) This was the common practice of the Assyrian kings (*Records of the Past*, i. 38). Neither age nor dignity (both are implied in the word "elders")

up by their hand: the faces of elders
were not honoured. (13) They took the
young men to grind, and the children
fell under the wood. (14) The elders
have ceased from the gate, the young
men from their musick. (15) The joy of
our heart is ceased; our dance is turned
into mourning. (16) [1]The crown is fallen
from our head: woe unto us, that we
have sinned! (17) For this our heart is
faint; for these *things* our eyes are dim.

(18) Because of the mountain of Zion,
which is desolate, the foxes walk upon
it. (19) Thou, O LORD, [a]remainest for
ever; thy throne from generation to
generation. (20) Wherefore dost thou
forget us for ever, *and* forsake us [2]so
long time? (21) [b]Turn thou us unto
thee, O LORD, and we shall be turned;
renew our days as of old. (22) [3]But thou
hast utterly rejected us; thou art very
wroth against us.

1 Heb., *The crown of our head is fallen.*

a Ps. 9. 7 & 29. 10 & 102. 12 & 145. 13.

2 Heb., *for length of days?*

b Jer. 31. 18.

3 Or, *For wilt thou utterly reject us?*

---

was any safeguard against atrocities, either in life or death.

(13) **They took . . .**—Better, *Young men bear the mill: i.e.,* were not only set to grind the handmill, which was itself the work of a menial slave, commonly of women, but were made to carry the mill itself, probably as they marched along with the Chaldæan armies on their way to Babylon. (Comp. Isa. xlvii. 2.) So in like manner the next clause describes the sufferings of the striplings, who were made to carry the wood which was used as fuel or other purposes, and who literally "fell" (or *staggered*) under their burdens.

(14) **Have ceased from the gate.**—The gate in an Eastern city was the natural place of meeting for the elder citizens as for counsel and judgment (Ruth iv. 1; Josh. xx. 4), and also for social converse (Job. xxix. 7; Prov. xxxi. 23). The "music" of this verse and the "dancing" of the next point to a like interruption of the social joys of the young.

(16) **The crown is fallen.**—The phrase is naturally symbolic of degradation, and need not be restricted to the destruction of the Temple or the devastation of Jerusalem.

We have sinned!—The confession of personal sinfulness produced by the contemplation of the miseries of the people contrasts, as has been already noticed, with the half-complaining tone of verse 7.

(17) **For this . . for these things.**—The first clause refers to the loss of national honour indicated in verse 16; the latter, to all the horrors named in verses 8—15.

(18) **Foxes.**—Better, *jackals,* who are thought of as haunting the ruins of Jerusalem. (Comp. Ps. lxiii. 10.)

(19) **Thou, O Lord, remainest.** — Literally, *Thou sittest: i.e.,* as the next clause shows, upon a throne. The lamentation is drawing to its close, and the mourner finds comfort in the thought of the eternity of God (Ps. cii. 12), and therefore the unchangeableness of His purpose of love towards His people.

(20) **Wherefore dost thou forget . . .**—This was the problem of the mystery of suffering then, as it has been at all times. Jehovah had seemed forgetful of His people, indifferent to their miseries.

(21) **Turn thou us . . O Lord . .**—The answer to the problem was found in man's submission and in prayer. He could not turn himself, and so re-establish the old filial relation. He could ask God to turn him, and he felt that the prayer would not be asked in vain.

(22) **But thou hast . . .**—The Authorised version represents the mourner as falling back from the hopeful prayer into the depths of despair. For "but" we should, however, read *unless.* The hypothesis of utter rejection is just stated as the only thing that could prevent renewal and restoration, and it is stated as *per impossibile;* God has not rejected, and therefore He will renew.

It may be noted that in Synagogue use, and in many MSS., verse 21 is repeated after verse 22, so that the book may not end with words of so terrible a significance. The same practice obtained in the case of the last verse of Isaiah, Ecclesiastes, and Malachi.

THE BOOK OF THE PROPHET
EZEKIEL

INTRODUCTION

TO

THE BOOK OF THE PROPHET

EZEKIEL

THIS book is placed in the Authorised Version, as well as in the order of the Hebrew canon, third among the writings of the four greater prophets. This is certainly its true chronological place; for although Jeremiah and Daniel were both contemporary with Ezekiel, yet the former began his prophecies long before, and the latter continued his visions long afterwards. Of its authenticity and canonicity there is no question.

I. **The personal history of Ezekiel.**—Nothing is known of this beyond what may be gathered from the book itself, and from the circumstances of the times in which the author lived. He is never mentioned in any other book of the Old Testament, and his writings are never directly quoted in the New, although some of the imagery in the Apocalypse is undoubtedly founded upon the visions of Ezekiel. Fortunately, however, everything which it is important to know may be learned from the sources mentioned.

His name, *God will strengthen*, like the names of so many others of the saints of old, was singularly appropriate to his life and work. In the opening of his book (chap. i. 3) he speaks of himself as a "priest, the son of Buzi." Of Buzi nothing whatever is known; but the fact that Ezekiel himself was of the Aaronic family is a most important one in the interpretation of his writings; for he was evidently "every inch a churchman," and his strong ecclesiastical character pervades and gives tone to his prophecies. Whether he actually entered upon the exercise of priestly functions at Jerusalem cannot be known without a previous determination of the uncertain question of the age at which he was carried into captivity; but he was certainly well instructed in what seemed likely to be his future duties. These facts, taken in connection with the disordered condition of the country and the tendency to concentrate the priests in and around the holy city, make it probable that he lived in Jerusalem or its immediate vicinity.

The prophet was carried captive to Babylon with the king Jehoiachin (chap. i. 2; comp. with chap. xxxiii. 21) in the eighth year of the reign of Nebuchadnezzar (B.C. 596), ten thousand of the more important part of the people being transplanted to Babylonia at the same time (2 Kings xxiv. 14), eleven years before the destruction of Jerusalem and the Temple. According to Josephus (Antt. x. 6, 3), he was then a young man. This statement has been called in question, but seems likely to be true, from the fact that one of his prophecies is dated twenty-seven years later (chap. xxix. 17), and that he apparently exercised his office for some time longer. However this may be, it is certain that he entered on his prophetic activity "by the river Chebar" (chap. i. 3), where the mass of the captives had been planted. This river was formerly supposed to be the Chaboras, or *Khabour*, a stream emptying itself into the Euphrates about two hundred miles above Babylon; but this cannot be the river intended, since it is said to be "in the land of the Chaldæans," and the name of Chaldæa was never extended so far north. Recent authorities generally identify it with the *Nahr Malcha*, or royal canal of Nebuchadnezzar, on the excavation of which it is supposed that the Jewish captives were employed for a time. These were doubtless "the rivers of Babylon" by whose side the Jewish exiles wept when they "remembered Zion" (Ps. cxxxvii. 1). Here Ezekiel lived in his own house (chap. viii. 1), to which the elders of Judah resorted to receive his counsels. He was married, and when his wife died suddenly he was forbidden to mourn for her (chap. xxiv. 16, 17). This occurred near the close of the ninth year of his captivity (chap. xxiv. 1), and left the exiled prophet to bear in solitude the great trials of his prophetic life.

There is no record of the time of the close of his prophetic activity or of his life, and the few traditions that remain about him are of little value. Of great interest, however, are—

II. **His relations with contemporary prophets.**—The great prophet of Judæa during Ezekiel's youth, and for a long time after he was carried into captivity, was Jeremiah. Jeremiah was himself a priest who occupied a large share of public attention, and exercised a powerful influence upon the destinies of the nation during the most susceptible years of Ezekiel's life. Neither of them ever mentions the other's name, yet it is scarcely possible that the young priest Ezekiel should not have personally known the older priest and great prophet at Jerusalem. After he had gone into captivity, and in the year before he was called to the prophetic office, Jeremiah sent a prophecy to Babylon, predicting its overthrow (Jer. li. 59); and on another occasion, whether earlier or later is unknown, he sent by another messenger to rebuke the false prophets who had risen up among the captives (Jer. xxix. 21—28). These false prophets had undertaken to thwart Jeremiah and to put a stop to his prophesying, and his denunciation of them must have removed a great obstacle from the way of Ezekiel; while, on the other hand, Ezekiel's own prophecies among the captives must have helped to sustain Jeremiah's authority among the remnant at Jerusalem.

Meantime, while these relations appear to have existed between the prophet of Judæa and the captive by the river Chebar, the "royal prophet" Daniel had also begun his series of wonderful revelations at the court of Babylon. He makes no mention of Ezekiel, as indeed he scarcely speaks of anything outside the immediate scope of his own prophecies; but Ezekiel speaks of him by name three times: twice for his eminent holiness (chap. xiv. 14, 20), and once for his great wisdom (chap. xxviii. 3); but as Daniel was early raised to high office in the internal administration of the kingdom, and must have been intimately acquainted with the affairs of his own captive people, it is hardly possible that he should not have known personally one so eminent among them as Ezekiel. Daniel was of noble, if not of royal, birth (Dan. i. 3), and hence could not have failed to know Jeremiah before he was himself carried from Jerusalem. Thus there seems to have been a very interesting personal connection between these three great prophets, all engaged in their Divine mission at the same time, but under strikingly different circumstances, and each with his own strongly-marked individuality. God was thus pleased to vouchsafe to His Church in the time of its utmost distress and need a fulness of prophetic counsel such as marked no other period of the old dispensation. The only time at all comparable to it was that other critical period, more than a century before, when the northern kingdom had been carried into captivity — a period which was distinguished by the prophecies of Isaiah, Hosea, Amos, and Micah.

The prophecies of Daniel are of so peculiar a character, and, for the most part, embrace such a far-reaching sweep of time, that they throw comparatively little light upon those of Ezekiel. Jeremiah, on the other hand, prophesying at the same time and about the same events, is constantly parallel to Ezekiel, and both his prophecies and his interwoven historical narrative should be read in connection with Ezekiel. The two will be found of great value in mutually illustrating each other.

III. **The character of the captivity.**—Judæa had been made tributary to Babylon some years before Nebuchadnezzar's accession to the throne, and while he was still acting as the general of his aged father. Jehoiakim, in the third year of his reign (2 Kings xxiv. 1), had rebelled against him, and had been conquered and carried captive to Babylon (2 Chron. xxxvi. 6) eight years before the captivity of Ezekiel. It is not known how many other captives were taken at the same time, the only mention of them being in Dan. i. 3, when certain "of the king's seed and of the princes" (among whom were Daniel and his three companions) were selected from the general company of "the children of Israel" to be trained in the learning and tongue of the Chaldæans. It is generally supposed that but few of them were kept in the city of Babylon itself, and that the others were placed in the same region with the subsequent captives "by the river Chebar." They would thus have had time to make homes for themselves, to become familiar with the language and the country, and hence to be of no small service to their brethren when the 10,000 fresh captives arrived. Especially must the learning, the wisdom, the high station of Daniel, together with his familiarity with affairs, have been of great importance to them. It was still eleven years later than this great captivity of Nebuchadnezzar's eighth year (which was also the captivity of Ezekiel) that Zedekiah's rebellion forced Nebuchadnezzar to a fresh capture of Jerusalem and the destruction of the Temple (2 Kings xxv. 1—12). The "rest of the people of the city, and the fugitives," and "the multitude" were carried off at this time, which was "in the nineteenth year of King Nebuchadnezzar" (*ib.*, verse 8). By observing that the first year of Nebuchadnezzar was the fourth of Jehoiakim (Jer. xxv. 1), this and the following dates may be synchronised with those of the Jewish history. Meantime, several minor deportations, amounting in all to 4,600 people, are mentioned by Jeremiah (chap. lii. 28—30) as occurring in the seventh and the eighteenth year of Nebuchadnezzar, and a subsequent one in the twenty-third year. These later captives lived in and around Jerusalem under wicked and idolatrous kings, going down from one wickedness to another, while the captives of Ezekiel's time had been for years under the elevating influences of affliction and of the prophet's counsels. There was, therefore, a marked difference in the character of the people whom he addressed before and after the destruction of Jerusalem. The following table of the several recorded deportations may be useful:—

1. Dan. i. 1.	Jehoiakim	III.*	Jehoiakim, Daniel, and others.
2. Jer. lii. 28.	Nebuchadnezzar	VII.	3,023.
3. 2 Kings xxiv. 14.	"	VIII.	10,000, with Jehoiachin and Ezekiel.
4. Jer. lii. 29.	"	XVIII.	832.
5. 2 Kings xxv. 11.	"	XIX.	"Rest of the city," and "remnant of the multitude."
6. Jer. lii. 30.	"	XXIII.	745.

It thus appears that the progress of the captivity, from first to last, covered twenty-four years, from B.C. 605 to 581, or from thirteen years before to eleven years after the beginning of Ezekiel's prophecies. It is probable that the comparatively small deportations of the seventh and eighteenth years of Nebuchadnezzar took place in the early part of the same campaigns which terminated with the great deportations of the eighth and nineteenth. The numbers mentioned amount in all to 14,600, but in two instances the number is not given, and the latter of these probably included many more captives than all the others together. There were still left behind "of the poor of the land to be vine-dressers and husbandmen" (2 Kings xxv. 12), which implies a certain degree of sifting of the people, the captives being those in better social position, and hence, on the whole, likely to be more intelligent, and more easily brought under the prophet's influence in their affliction.

In regard to the condition of the people in their captivity, it is not improbable that they may at first have been treated with some rigour. Nebuchadnezzar was evidently annoyed and irritated by their repeated rebellions, and showed himself capable of no little harshness towards them. (See Jer. lii. 24—27; 2 Kings xxv. 7.) He was also engaged in the construction of magnificent public works, and on the accession of so large a body of captives, would naturally have employed them for this purpose, and especially for making his royal canal. At the same time, he was a man of too much breadth of view to indulge in national animosity, and from the first he placed Daniel and his Jewish companions in offices of high honour and trust, while the condition of the captives generally appears to have rapidly ameliorated. It has already appeared that in the sixth year of his captivity Ezekiel was living in his own house (chap. viii. 1). It was but little more than thirty years from the last date of his prophecy to the decree of Cyrus for their return. At that time only a portion of the exiles cared to exchange the comforts of the land of their exile for the difficulties of removal to the home of their fathers, and they who remained behind

* The Roman numerals refer to the years of the reign. Nebuchadnezzar is here spoken of as "king" before the formal beginning of his reign, which occurred in the following year. The third year afterwards is called in Dan. ii. 1 the *second* year of Nebuchadnezzar. (Comp. also Jer. xxv. 1).

were able to help those who went "with vessels of silver, with gold, with goods, and with beasts, and with precious things" (Ezra i. 6); and at a little later period the Book of Esther represents them as numerous, with powerful friends at the court, and of sufficient wealth to tempt the cupidity of their enemies. The impression obtained, on the whole, is that they speedily rose, and were encouraged to rise, from a servile condition to one of comfort, and in many cases of opulence.

IV. The date of Ezekiel's prophecies.—A large part of the prophecies are carefully and minutely dated, the era being always that of the captivity of Jehoiachin, which was also that of Ezekiel himself. One other era is mentioned in the first verse: "it came to pass in the thirtieth year," and has been the subject of much discussion. The only thing certain about it is that it coincided (verse 3) with the fifth year of Jehoiachin's captivity. Some writers have supposed it to refer to the thirtieth year from the last jubilee, but this is never elsewhere used for the purpose of date, probably because it began at a special and inconvenient time, on the tenth day of the seventh month (Lev. xxv. 9), and it would have been particularly unlikely to be used under the existing circumstances. Others consider that it dates from the era of the accession of Nebuchadnezzar's father and the commencement of the Chaldean dynasty (Michaelis, Rosenmüller, Ewald, and others); but there is no evidence that this era had then come into use, and the most recent investigations tend to show a discrepancy between this and the date here given. A very common ancient view—(Chaldee, Jerome, Theodoret) also adopted by some moderns (Hävernick and others)—is that the era was that of the finding of the Book of the Law and of the beginning of a great reformation in the eighteenth year of Josiah's reign. This would certainly exactly accord with the time indicated; but if this had been meant we should expect that it would have been indicated. The most probable supposition is that of Origen, that it refers to Ezekiel's own age, particularly impressive to him, because it was the age at which the Levites by the law (Num. iv. 23, 30, 39, 43) entered upon their duties.

Although, as already said, a large part of Ezekiel's prophecies are carefully dated, many also are without date. Are these to be considered as belonging to the time between the preceding and the succeeding dates? If the dates given were all arranged in chronological order this would be the natural and highly probable supposition; and as a matter of fact, they are thus arranged, with the exception of a few prophecies, where the change of order admits of easy explanation. These prophecies are the two parts of chap. xxix., the first part of which is dated nearly three months before the prophecy in chap. xxvi., and the last part is sixteen years later than the prophecy following it; the remaining instances are the two parts of chap. xxxii., dated nearly two months after the prophecy of chap. xxxiii. 21. The reason of these anomalies is that chaps. xxv.—xxxii. form a special section of the book, relating to various heathen nations, and including nearly all the prophecies of this character. The general arrangement in this section also is chronological, but gives way to the extent of placing together all prophecies against the same nation whenever uttered. There being thus an obvious reason for the arrangement of this special section, and the dates of the rest of the book being strictly consecutive, the whole may be considered, with a high degree of probability, as arranged in chronological order, the internal character of the undated prophecies for the most part assimilating them closely to those just before them. This probability is increased by the fact that there remain two other undated prophecies against the heathen (chaps. xxxv., xxxviii., xxxix.), which are so much of the nature of promises to Israel through the destruction of their enemies that they are allowed to stand in connection with those promises, and doubtless in their proper chronological position.

V. The reception of the prophecies by the captives.—During the period of the captivity the Jews were greatly changed. Notwithstanding various sins which lingered among them, they learned generally to repudiate the idolatry which had been hitherto their characteristic sin, and they showed also a disposition to observe the law of Moses more closely than they had ever done before, and with so much zeal that this remained ever after their distinguishing national characteristic. The chief human instrument of this change was the teaching of the prophet Ezekiel. He was, indeed, often called upon to rebuke them (chaps. xiv. 1, 3, xviii., &c.), and was made to understand that while they seemed to listen, they still refused to take his words to heart (chap. xxxiii. 30—33); yet they regarded him as a true prophet, and resorted to him for counsel, and to ask through him the mind of God (chaps. viii. 1, xiv. 1, &c.). Doubtless, as time went on, the people became more and more purified. Jeremiah xxiv. shows distinctly the great moral difference at that time between the people who had gone into captivity and those who still remained behind. Various allusions in the book (see chap. iii. 9, &c.) show that Ezekiel's life, especially in the earlier part of his work, was one of much trial, and that he had to contend against great difficulties in the midst of abounding evil. He himself passed away, as is usually the lot of man, before he was able to see the full result of his labours. Hengstenberg, in his *Christology*, describes him as "a spiritual Samson, who, with a strong arm, seized the pillars of the temple of the idols, and dashed it to the ground: an energetic, gigantic nature, who was thereby suited effectually to counteract the Babylonish spirit of the times, which loved to manifest itself in violent, gigantic, grotesque forms: one who stood alone, but was yet equal to a hundred scholars of the prophets."*

VI. The divisions of the book may be given differently, according to the point of view from which it is regarded. It is quite common to make an arithmetically equal division into two parts, of twenty-four chapters each; and this plan is to a certain extent just, as there occurs a manifest change of subject at the close of chap. xxiv. But it is far better to divide the book in connection with the great historic event of the overthrow of Jerusalem and the destruction of the Temple, the tidings of which reached Ezekiel in the twelfth year of his captivity, at chap. xxxiii. 21. At this point the general tone of the prophecies changes. Up to this time they have been chiefly occupied with sin and consequent judgment; from this time onward, as the great manifestation of the Divine wrath had taken place, they are mainly concerned with promises and consolations. Each great division has an introductory portion: chaps. i.—iii. containing the call of the prophet, with the instructions to him and his installation in his office, and chap. xxxiii., more briefly, as was fitting, a renewal of the charge to

* *Christology of the Old Testament*. By E. W. Hengstenberg. Translated by R. Keith. "Ezek. Introd.," Vol. III., p. 460.

him in relation to that office. Each division closes, too, with a special section: the first with a series of prophecies against heathen nations, the enemies of Israel (chaps. xxv.—xxxii.), and the second with the future glory of the Temple and the Holy Land and city (chaps. xl.—xlviii.). Minor sub-divisions will be treated as they occur.

VII. **The style of Ezekiel** is more varied than that of any other prophet. All forms of prophetic writing are laid under contribution to further the great work he was set to accomplish. Hence different writers, looking at his book from different points of view, have formed very different, and often exaggerated, estimates, on one side or the other, of its literary merits. Ewald justly says of him (*Propheten*, p. 212):—"Considered simply as a writer, this prophet exhibits great excellences, especially as living in so dismal a period. His mode of representation, indeed, like that of most of the later writers, has a tendency to length and expansion, with sentences often very much involved, and rhetorical breadth and copiousness. . . His language has scattered through it several Aramaic and foreign expressions, in which one may perceive the influence of his exiled condition; though for the most part it is formed after the older and better models." Lowth (*Lect. on Sacred Poetry*, 21, p. 294) says:—"His diction is sufficiently perspicuous; all his obscurity consists in the nature of the subject." In regard to this matter of obscurity, which has been so much objected to, Fairbairn * well says, "that the darkness inseparably connected with our prophet's delight in the use of parable and symbol was, when rightly contemplated, by no means at variance with his great design as a prophet. His primary object was impression—to rouse and stimulate, to awaken spiritual thoughts and feelings in the depths of the soul, and bring it back to a living confidence and faith in God. And for this, while great plainness and force of speech were necessary, mysterious symbols and striking parabolical delineations were also fitted to be of service.

Accordingly, while Ezekiel often addresses the people in the simplest language of admonition or of promise, he also abounds in the most elaborate visions (as chaps. i., viii.—x., xxxvii., xl.—xlviiii.) and symbolical actions (chaps. iv., v., and xii.); and has also similitudes (chaps. xv., xxxiii., xxxv.) and parables (chap. xvii.) and prolonged allegories (chap. xxiii.); while in his denunciations, as of Egypt (chaps. xxix.—xxxii.), he sometimes rises to the height of most bold and effective poetry. "He has remarkable power in grouping a mass of somewhat minute details in a way to heighten the effect exceedingly. Witness his portrayal of the horrible impurities of idolatry in Jerusalem and Samaria (chap. xxiii.), or his description of the commerce, the splendour, and the fall of ancient Tyre (chaps. xxvii., xxviii.)." † In such varied ways did inspiration manifest itself in this remarkable prophet that he might accomplish his work under the extraordinary circumstances in which he was placed.

Underlying all this varied form, the personal characteristics of the prophet are always to be kept in mind that we may understand his writings. He was eminently realistic, always striving after a concrete representation of abstract thoughts; and moreover, intensely energetic, always having before his mind the accomplishment of a definite practical result. With all this, he had a rich fancy, and was possessed of deep emotions; he was an earnest priest, and deeply imbued with the symbolism and imagery of the Jewish temple and worship, and was also a captive in Babylonia, where the symbolism of the great Chaldæan works of art had produced a strong impression on his mind. It is sometimes difficult, therefore, to distinguish in his utterances between the *form* in which he so vividly sets forth the truth and the truth itself which he wishes to convey to the mind. But in this great help may be derived from observing the progressive character of his prophecies, and making ourselves thoroughly familiar with the earlier before we attempt to grapple with the difficulties of the later. In no other prophet is it of so great importance to study his writings in the order in which he was inspired to deliver them, and also the personal characteristics of the writer. The main clue to guide us through the difficulties of the interpretation of his book is the appreciation of his tendency to express every thought and every Divine communication in concrete form. This tendency is so intense in Ezekiel, and is so carried into detail, that there has always been a disposition to mistake his ideal descriptions of the future for prophecies of coming realities. It will be seen on examining them that they contain particulars which, if literally interpreted, would be self-contradictory, and that they cannot therefore have been intended to be so understood. Nevertheless, the descriptions are so vivid, and the idea to be conveyed is so concretely expressed, that it is only by following his prophecies in their order, and coming gradually to enter into his spirit, that we can appreciate their truly ideal character.

It is quite in accordance with these general characteristics of Ezekiel's writings that much of them should be on the border-land between poetry and prose. Parts, indeed, are plainly in simple prose, and in other parts the complete poetic form corresponds to the thought; but there are many passages thoroughly poetic in their matter which yet defy the attempt to reduce them to the parallelism which characterises Hebrew poetry, and much that, while it must on the whole be classed as poetry, is yet very irregular in form. The earnestness and impetuosity of the thought continually overrides artificial rules of diction.

VIII. **Literature.**—The principal commentators upon this book are:—Among the ancients, Origen, Jerome, and Theodoret; among the Jews, the Rabbis D. Kimchi and Abarbanel; of the period of the Reformation, Œcolampadius and Calvin, whose work was terminated by his illness and death at chap. xxi.; and of the Romanists, Pradus and Villalpandus, a huge work in three volumes, fol. 1596—1604; more modern commentaries are those of Starck, 1731; Venema, 1790 (this does not include the last nine chapters); Newcome, 1788; W. Greenhill (London, 1645—62, five volumes, 4to reprinted), 1829; Rosenmüller, *Scholia*, second edition, 1826; Ewald, 1841; Umbreit, 1843; Hävernick, 1843; Hitzig, 1847; Henderson, 1855; Fairbairn, third edition, Edinburgh, 1863, a work of exceptional value, from which considerable extracts are made in the translation of Ezekiel in Lange's *Bibelwerk;* Cowles, New York, 1867; G. R. Noyes, *New Trans. of the Heb. Prophets, with notes,* third edition, Boston, 1866, Vol. II.; Hengstenberg, 1867-68, subsequently translated into English; Kleifoth, 1864-65; Dr. G. Currey, in the collection known as *The Speaker's Commentary*, 1876; and the Commentary of Keil, translated and published in *Clark's Foreign Theolog. Library*, 1876.

* Fairbairn: *On Ezekiel*, 2nd Ed., Introd., p. 12.
† *Ezekiel.* By Rev. H. Cowles, D.D. Introd. p. 11.

THE BOOK OF THE PROPHET

EZEKIEL

B.C. 595.

CHAPTER I.—(1) Now it came to
pass in the thirtieth year, in the fourth
month, in the fifth *day* of the month, as
I *was* among the [1]captives by the river
of Chebar, *that* the heavens were opened,
and I saw visions of God. (2) In the fifth
day of the month, which *was* the fifth
year of king Jehoiachin's captivity,
(3) The word of the LORD came expressly
unto [2]Ezekiel the priest, the son of Buzi,
in the land of the Chaldeans by the river
Chebar; and the hand of the LORD was
there upon him.

(4) And I looked, and, behold, a whirl-
wind came out of the north, a great cloud,
and a fire [3]infolding itself, and a bright-
ness *was* about it, and out of the midst
thereof as the colour of amber, out of

1 Heb., *captivity.*

2 Heb., *Jehezkel.*

3 Heb., *catching itself.*

The first three chapters, describing the circumstances and character of Ezekiel's call to the prophetic office, form the introduction to the whole book, and the three first verses, giving the time, the person, and the place, are the introduction to this introduction. (Comp. the similar arrangement of Rev. i., which forms the introduction to that book, and of verses 1—3, which are the introduction to that chapter.)

(1) **The thirtieth year.**—On this date see Introduction, § iv. It may be added here that the concurrence of the "fifth day of the month" in connection with this epoch, and with that of Jehoiachin's captivity in verse 2, shows that the years of the two epochs began at the same time.

Among the captives.—*i.e.,* in the midst of the region where they were settled. The vision which follows was seen by Ezekiel only, and was probably vouchsafed to him in solitude. "The captives," or rather, *the captivity,* as it is in the original, is the same word as is used of Jehoiachin in the next verse, and yet must be somewhat differently understood in the two cases. Jehoiachin was actually in prison for many years; his people, within certain limits, were free. They were more than *exiles,* but less than prisoners. (On "the heavens were opened," comp. Matt. iii. 16; Acts vii. 56.)

Visions of God.—Not merely *great visions,* as the Divine name is often added in Scripture to express greatness or intensity (see Gen. x. 9; Pss. xxxvi. 6, *marg.,* lxxx. 10, *marg.;* Jonah iii. 3, *marg.;* Acts vii. 20, *marg.*), but Divine visions, visions sent from God, as in chaps. viii. 3, xl. 2.

(3) **Came expressly.**—Or, *came certainly,* with the fullest proof of reality. In the original there is simply the ordinary form of the repetition of the verb for the sake of emphasis. The prophet mentions his own name only here and in chap. xxiv. 24.

The hand of the Lord was there upon him.—A form of expression to indicate that special power and influence which the Spirit exercised over the prophets at times when they were called to become the means of the Divine communications. (Comp. 1 Kings xviii. 46, and chap. iii. 22, xxxvii. 1; see also Dan. viii. 18, x. 10; Rev. i. 17.) It is noticeable that Ezekiel here speaks of himself in the third person, while in verse 1, and always after this, he uses the first person. It has been suggested that this, together with the mention of his own name, may indicate the insertion of these two verses on a revision of his work by the prophet.

In entering upon the vision of the glory of the Lord, which fills the rest of this chapter, it is to be remembered that Ezekiel is struggling to portray that which necessarily exceeds the power of human language; it is not therefore surprising that there should be something of repetition and of obscurity in the detail. All similar descriptions of Divine manifestations are marked more or less strongly by the same characteristics. (See Exod. xxiv. 9, 10; Isa. vi. 1—4; Dan. vii. 9, 10; Rev. i. 12—20, iv. 2—6, &c.) It is also to be borne in mind that what the prophet saw was not the eternal Father in His own absolute essence, who dwells in unapproachable light, and whom "no man hath seen, nor can see" (1 Tim. vi. 16); and had it been possible that Ezekiel should have been so transported out of the body as to behold this, it would then have been impossible for him to describe it. But what he saw in vision was such manifestation as man could bear, in which God hides His face, and allows to be seen only His uttermost parts (Exod. xxxiii. 22, 23). In the description that follows may be recognised a mingling of the symbols of the Divine manifestation at Sinai with the "patterns of heavenly things" in the most holy place of the Temple, the whole modified to suit the present occasion, and possibly somewhat coloured by the now familiar symbolic art of Babylonia.

(4) **A whirlwind came out of the north.**—The *north* is seen as the quarter from which the vision proceeded, not because the Babylonians conceived that there was the seat of Divine power (Isa. xiv. 13, 14), but because it was common with the prophets to represent the Divine judgments upon Judæa as coming from the north (see Jer. i. 14, 15, iv. 6, vi. 1), and it was from that direction that the Assyrian and the Chaldæan conquerors were accustomed to descend upon the Holy Land. The vision is actually seen in Chaldæa, but it has reference to Jerusalem, and is described as if viewed from that standpoint.

the midst of the fire. (5) Also out of the midst thereof *came* the likeness of four living creatures. And this *was* their appearance; they had the likeness of a man. (6) And every one had four faces, and every one had four wings. (7) And their feet *were* [1]straight feet; and the sole of their feet *was* like the sole of a

[1] Heb., *a straight foot.*

A great cloud.—As in the Divine manifestation on Sinai (Exod. xix. 9—16). The cloud serves at once as the groundwork for all the other details of the manifestation—a place in, and by means of which, all are located, and also as a hiding-place of the Divine majesty, so that all may be seen which human eye can bear, and that which it cannot bear may yet be known to be there, shrouded in the cloud. The transposition of a single letter from the end of one word in the Hebrew to the beginning of the next will change the reading to "a whirlwind out of the north brought on a great cloud."

A fire infolding itself.—More literally translated in the margin, *catching itself.* The idea intended to be conveyed is that of flames round and round the cloud, the flashes succeeding one another so rapidly that each seemed to lay hold on the one that had gone before; there were tongues of flame, where each one reached to another. The same word occurs in Exod. ix. 24, in connection with "fire," and is there translated *mingled.* The vision thus far seems moulded on the natural appearance of a terrific thunderstorm seen at a distance, in which the great black cloud appears illuminated by the unceasing and coalescing flashes of lightning. So, with all its impressive darkness, "there was a brightness about it."

As the colour of amber.—Colour is, literally, *eye.* The word rendered "amber" (*chasmal*) occurs only in this book (here, and verse 27 and chap. viii. 2), and is now generally recognised as meaning some form of bright metal, either glowing in its molten state, or as the "fine brass" of verse 7 and Rev. i. 15, burnished and glowing in the light of the "infolding flame." There is therefore now superadded to the first appearance of the natural phenomenon, a glowing eye or centre to the cloud, shining out even from the midst of the fire.

(5) **The likeness of four living creatures** next appeared from this centre of the fiery cloud. The word "likeness" is not without significance. The prophet would make it plain that this was a vision, that these were symbolic, not actually existing creatures. Their prominent characteristic is that they were "living." This word is used over and over again in connection with them (see verses 13, 14, 15, 19, 21, &c.); and in fact, in Ezekiel and Revelation (chap. iv. 6, &c., where it is mis-translated *beasts*) it occurs nearly thirty times. The same characteristic is further emphasized in verse 14 by the speed, "as of a flash of lightning," with which they "ran and returned," by the multiplicity of eyes in the wheels connected with them (verse 18), and by their going instantly "whithersoever the spirit was to go" (verse 20); while in Rev. iv. 8 it is said that "they rest not day and night." Their life is represented as most closely connected with the source of all life, the "living God," whose throne is seen in the vision (verse 26) as above the heads of these "living creatures."

Ezekiel does not here say what these living creatures were, but in a subsequent vision, when he saw them again in connection with the Temple, he recognised them as the cherubim (chap. x. 15, 20). Cherubim, whether here, or in the Temple overshadowing the mercy-seat, or in the garden of Eden keeping the way of the tree of life, always indicate the immediate presence of the God of holiness. The prophet again mentions these composite symbolic figures in connection with the vision of the Temple in chap. xli. 18—20. The origin of such ideal figures has been variously ascribed to the Egyptians, the Assyrians, the Phœnicians, and the Arabs; but this symbolism was, in fact, almost universal throughout the East. Dr. Currey (*Speaker's Com.*, note on Ezek. i.) points out the striking difference between this symbolism and that of the Greeks. They tried to delineate the Divine attributes with the utmost beauty of form and harmony of detail under some human figure in which those attributes were conspicuous. In consequence, the mind of the worshipper lost sight of the ideal, and became absorbed in the sensuous imagery by which it was represented; while here, by the very strangeness, and sometimes grotesqueness, of the imagery, its purely symbolic character was kept constantly in view. Cherubim are associated in the Old Testament with that tree of life of which man might not partake save through Him who is "the life," and with that typical holy of holies which man might not enter until the true Holy of Holies was entered once for all by Christ through His own blood (Heb. ix. 8, 12).

They had the likeness of a man.—With all the strange variety of details to be described immediately, they had yet a general human form, and are to be understood as like man in whatever is not specified.

(6) **Four faces.**—The cherubim, being merely symbolical figures, are variously represented. Those placed in the Tabernacle and in the Temple of Solomon appear to have had only a single face; those described in Ezekiel's vision of the Temple (chap. xli. 18, 19) had two; the four living creatures of Rev. iv. 7 were each different from the other: one like a man, one like a lion, one like an ox, and one like an eagle, and these four are combined here in each one of the cherubim (verse 10). Man is the head of the whole animal creation, the lion of wild beasts, the ox of the domestic animals, and the eagle of the birds.

Four wings.—In Rev. iv. 8, six wings are mentioned, as also with the seraphim of Isa. vi. 2. The cherubim in Solomon's Temple had two (1 Kings vi. 27). In chap. x. 21, as here, they have four. The number is plainly not important, though doubtless assigned to them with reference to the number of creatures, and of their faces, and of the wheels; but that they should have more than the normal number of two is here appropriate, partly to concur with the other indications of the fulness of their life and activity, and partly because (verse 11) two of them were used to express their reverence, as were four of those of the seraphim in Isaiah.

(7) **Their feet were straight feet.**—Rather, *each of their legs was a straight leg, i.e.*, without any bend in it, as at the knee, but was equally fitted for motion in any direction. So also "the sole of their feet," the part which rested on the ground, was not, like the human foot, formed to move forward only, but was round and solid, something "like the sole of a calf's foot."

They sparkled.—This refers only to "the sole of the feet," the hoof. The "burnished brass" is a dif-

calf's foot: and they sparkled like the
colour of burnished brass. (8) And *they*
had the hands of a man under their
wings on their four sides; and they four
had their faces and their wings. (9) Their
wings *were* joined one to another; they
turned not when they went; they went
every one straight forward. (10) As for
the likeness of their faces, they four had
the face of a man, and the face of a lion,
on the right side: and they four had the
face of an ox on the left side; they four
also had the face of an eagle. (11) Thus
were their faces: and their wings *were*
[1]stretched upward; two *wings* of every
one *were* joined one to another, and two
covered their bodies. (12) And they went
every one straight forward: whither the
spirit was to go, they went; *and* they
turned not when they went. (13) As for
the likeness of the living creatures, their
appearance *was* like burning coals of
fire, *and* like the appearance of lamps:
it went up and down among the living
creatures; and the fire was bright, and
out of the fire went forth lightning.
(14) And the living creatures ran and returned as the appearance of a flash of
lightning.

(15) Now as I beheld the living creatures, behold one wheel upon the earth
by the living creatures, with his four

1 Or, *divided above.*

---

ferent word from that used in verse 4, and gives another feature to the general brilliancy and magnificence of the vision.

(8) **The hands of a man.**—Implying, of course, also human arms. This particular adds to the generally human appearance of the cherubim, yet we must understand (see verse 11) that there were four hands corresponding to the wings for each cherub. These hands were "under their wings on their four sides." Hence the wings must have been attached at the shoulder. The repetition, "they four had their faces and their wings," is for the sake of emphasis and distinctness.

(9) **Their wings were joined one to another.**—*i.e.*, the outstretched right wing of one cherub was joined at its tip to the left wing of another, so that although four, they yet constituted in some sense but one creature, all moving in harmony and by a common impulse. This applies to the cherubim only when in motion; when they stood, the wings were let down (verse 24). The joining of the extremities of the outstretched wings of the cherubim recalls the arrangement in Solomon's Temple (1 Kings vi. 27), in which the wings of the larger cherubim touched one another above the mercy-seat.

They turned not when they went.—Whichever way they wished to go, they could still go "straight forward," *i.e.*, in the direction towards which they looked, since they looked in all directions, and their round feet made it equally easy to move in any way. It would at first seem that as two of the wings of each cherub were used to cover their bodies (verse 11), the wings would have required their turning when they changed their course; but if we conceive of the four cherubim as arranged to form a square, and with their wings moving as one creature, this difficulty disappears.

(10) **On the right side . . . on the left side.**—The apparent obscurity of this description is due only to the punctuation in the English Bible. "They four had the face of a man" (viz., in front, as Ezekiel viewed them), "and the face of a lion on the right side; and they four had the face of an ox on the left side; they four also had the face of an eagle" (viz., on the back, or side opposite to Ezekiel). These faces are the same as those given to the living creatures in Rev. iv. 7, except that there each creature had but one of them.

(11) **Thus were their faces: and their wings were stretched upward.**—Rather, *and their wings and their faces were separated above.* The word never has the sense of stretched, but always that of separated or divided, as given in the margin. Each cherub was essentially one creature, and yet (not Janus-like, with four faces upon one head) their heads and their wings were separated above, and when they were in flight the two lifted wings touched on either side the wing of the next cherub, while two were used to veil their bodies. There is much of emphatic repetition throughout the description.

(12) **Whither the spirit was to go.**—The one informing spirit which animated all the living creatures alike, and in accordance with which all their movements were ordered.

(13) **Like the appearance of lamps.**—The word "and" before this phrase is not in the original, and should be omitted. The words are merely a further explanation. The cherubim were like burning coals of fire, like torches or lightnings. The word "lamps" does not refer to the material, but to the light, and whether in the Hebrew or in its Greek equivalent, is translated by *torches* (Nahum ii. 4; John xviii. 3), *firebrands* (Judges xv. 4), or *lightnings* (Exod. xx. 18). Ezekiel could find no single word to express his meaning, and has therefore given two, that between them the idea of the fiery brilliancy may be better conveyed.

It went up and down.—"It" refers to the fire. This indescribable fiery appearance went up and down among the living creatures, "bright" in itself, and throwing out coruscations of "lightning."

(14) **A flash of lightning.**—Not only was the appearance of the cherubim thus glittering, but also their speed as they "ran and returned" was that of the lightning.

The vision up to this point, so far as we may venture to interpret its object, seems designed to show forth the power and activity, the irresistible energy of the agencies employed for the fulfilment of the Divine purposes, and at the same time their perfectly harmonious action, controlled by one supreme will. We now enter upon a fresh phase of the vision, in which the same things are represented still further by an additional and peculiar symbolism.

(15) **Behold one wheel upon the earth by the living creatures.**—The prophet sees this while still looking intently upon the cherubim—"as I beheld the living creatures"—showing that it was still a part of one and the same vision. The wheel was *one* in the

faces. (16) The appearance of the wheels
and their work *was* like unto the colour
of a beryl: and they four had one like-
ness: and their appearance and their
work *was* as it were a wheel in the middle
of a wheel. (17) When they went, they went
upon their four sides: *and* they turned
not when they went. (18) As for their
rings, they were so high that they were
dreadful; and their [1] rings *were* full of
eyes round about them four. (19) And
when the living creatures went, the
wheels went by them: and when the
living creatures were lifted up from
the earth, the wheels were lifted up.
(20) Whithersoever the spirit was to go,
they went, thither *was their* spirit to go;
and the wheels were lifted up over against
them: for the spirit [2] of the living crea-
ture *was* in the wheels. (21) When those
went, *these* went; and when those stood,
these stood; and when those were lifted
up from the earth, the wheels were lifted
up over against them: for the spirit [3] of
the living creature *was* in the wheels.
(22) And the likeness of the firmament
upon the heads of the living creature *was*
as the colour of the terrible crystal,

1 Or, *strakes.*

2 Or, *of life.*

3 Or, *of life.*

---

same sense in which the living creatures were one, yet actually four, as appears from the following verse and the whole subsequent description. In the corresponding vision (chap. x. 9), they are at once described as four. The cherubim had been seen in the cloud (verses 4, 5); now they need to be connected below with the earth, and presently (verse 26) above, with the throne of God. Therefore the wheel is "upon the earth," but of a great height (verse 18). There was a wheel in front of each of the cherubim, again forming a square, yet so that, as already said, they might in a sense be all considered as one wheel. Reference has been made for the origin of this imagery to the wheels under the *ten bases* of Solomon's Temple (1 Kings vii. 32, 33); but there seems to be nothing either in size or form to correspond, and, so far as we know, the imagery here is purely original.

(16) **Their work was like unto the colour of a beryl.**—"Work" is used in the sense of workmanship or construction; and "beryl" here, and in chap. x. 9, is not the precious stone of a green colour which we know by that name, but the "chrysolite" of the ancients, the modern topaz, having the lustre of gold, and in harmony with the frequent mention throughout the vision of fire and brilliant light.

A wheel in the middle of a wheel.—We are to conceive of the wheels as double, and one part at right angles to the other, like the equator and a meridian circle upon the globe, so that they could go, without being turned, equally well in any direction. Of course, such a wheel would be impossible of mechanical construction; it is only seen in vision and as a symbol; it was never intended to be actually made.

(17) **Upon their four sides**—*i.e.*, forwards or backwards upon the one wheel, and to the right or the left upon the other. *Four* directions are considered throughout the vision as representing all directions, just as elsewhere the four winds represent all winds, and the four corners of the earth the whole earth.

(18) **Their rings.**—The same word is used twice in this verse, and means what we call the *felloes*. "They were both high and terrible," *i.e.*, they had both these characteristics, but not, as seems to be implied in our translation, that one was the cause of the other. The height might be inferred from the fact that the wheel was "upon the earth," and yet was "by the living creatures" (verse 15) who were seen in the cloud (verse 5). The terribleness was in keeping with all other parts of the vision, and its reason is explained in the circumstances which follow.

Full of eyes.—In chap. x. 12 it is said of the living creatures, "their whole body, and their backs, and their hands, and their wings, and the wheels were full of eyes round about." It was the same vision in either case (chap. x. 20—22), only in the effort to describe it, which the prophet evidently feels it impossible to do adequately, he mentions now one particular and now another. In the corresponding vision in the Apocalypse the four living creatures are represented as "full of eyes within" (Rev. iv. 8). In both places alike the symbolism sets forth God's perfect knowledge of all His works: here as showing the absolute wisdom of all His doings (comp. 2 Chron. xvi. 9), there as resulting in perfect and harmonious praise from all His works. The Hebrew seers ever looked through all secondary causes directly to the ultimate force which originates and controls all nature, and which they represent as intelligent and self-conscious. To do this the more effectively, they often use in their visions such concrete imagery as this before us.

(20, 21) **The spirit of the living creature.**—Not, as in the margin, "the spirit of life." The object of verses 19—21 is by every repetition and variety of expression to represent "the living creatures" and "the wheels" as one, animated by one spirit, and moved by one impulse. The word is the same throughout, and there was no "spirit of life" in the wheels independent of that of the living creatures. All formed together one strange, symbolic whole.

The mention in verses 19—21 of the wheels being "lifted up from the earth" simultaneously with the living creatures is not in opposition to the symbolism already explained, of the wheels resting upon the earth. That was to show that God's purposes are carried out as He wills in this world. This brings out, in addition, the perfect harmony of these purposes, whether relating to earth or to heaven.

(22) **The likeness of the firmament.**—The word rendered "firmament" has undoubtedly originated, etymologically, from a verb originally signifying *to beat out*, as in the case of metals; but the derivative word, in its use in connection with the heavens, had wholly lost this reference, and had come to mean simply an *expanse*. The Hebrews do not appear to have ever entertained the classical idea of the sky as a metallic vault, the only passage seeming to indicate such a notion (Job xxxvii. 18) being capable of quite a different explanation. We are here to conceive, therefore, of that which was "stretched forth over their heads above" as a simple expanse, like the sky, as if he had said, "And above their heads was stretched forth the sky." This expanse is not represented as supported by the cherubim, or resting upon them, and it remained undisturbed when

stretched forth over their heads above.
(23) And under the firmament *were* their
wings straight, the one toward the
other: every one had two, which covered
on this side, and every one had two,
which covered on that side, their bodies.
(24) And when they went, I heard the
noise of their wings, like the noise of
great waters, as the voice of the Almighty,
the voice of speech, as the noise of an
host: when they stood, they let down
their wings. (25) And there was a voice
from the firmament that *was* over their
heads, when they stood, *and* had let down
their wings. (26) And above the firma-
ment that *was* over their heads *was* the
likeness of a throne, as the appearance
of a sapphire stone: and upon the like-
ness of the throne *was* the likeness as
the appearance of a man above upon it.
(27) And I saw as the colour of amber, as
the appearance of fire round about within
it, from the appearance of his loins even
upward, and from the appearance of his
loins even downward, I saw as it were
the appearance of fire, and it had bright-
ness round about. (28) As the appearance
of the bow that is in the cloud in the

---

they let down their wings (verse 25). It was simply "stretched forth over their heads," at once separating them from, and yet uniting them with, the throne above. It fulfils, therefore, the complementary part to the wheels. They connected the vision with the earth; this connects it with God.

The colour of the terrible crystal.—The expression "crystal" is doubtless derived from Exod. xxiv. 10, as in turn it became the foundation for Rev. iv. 6. Yet it is not here any particular crystal; the word is merely used to convey some idea of the appearance of the expanse beneath the throne, clear as crystal, terrible in its dazzling brightness.

(23) **Two, which covered on this side.**—The excessive literalness of this translation obscures the sense, for it seems to imply that each cherub used four wings to cover his body; whereas the true meaning is that "each had two wings covering his body on either side." The other two wings of each cherub were "straight," extended when they were in motion, but let down when at rest (verse 25).

(24) **The noise of their wings.**—The same word translated "noise" three times in this verse is also translated "voice" twice here, and once in the next verse. It is better to keep *voice* throughout. "I heard the voice of their wings, like the voice of many waters." The same comparison is used to describe the voice of God in chap. xliii. 2; Rev. i. 15. Further attempts to convey an impression of the effect are:—"As the voice of the Almighty," by which thunder is often described in Scripture (Job xxxvii. 4, 5; Ps. xxix. 3, 4); "the voice of speech," by which is not to be understood articulate language. The word occurs elsewhere only in Jer. xi. 16, and is there translated *a tumult.* The idea conveyed by the word is probably that of the confused sound from a great multitude, and, finally, "as the voice of an host." All these comparisons concur in representing a vast and terrible sound, but inarticulate.

(25) **A voice from the firmament.**—Rather, *from above the firmament,* not as proceeding from the firmament itself. This is a new feature in the vision: the voice is quite different from the sounds mentioned before, and although not here expressly said to have been articulate, yet it is probably to be identified with the Divine voice spoken of in verse 28, chap. iii. 12, and elsewhere. The latter part of the verse, literally translated, is simply, *In,* or *at, their standing they let down their wings,* and may be simply a repetition of the last clause of the preceding verse. In its connection, however, it seems rather to convey the idea of a fresh act of reverence towards the majesty above. When the voice was heard the cherubim stood still, the mighty sounds of their going were hushed, and their wings fell motionless, all in the attitude of reverential attention.

The vision now advances to another and final stage. We have had the whirlwind from the north, with its great cloud and infolding fire, as the background on which the whole is portrayed; then the cherubim, with all their marvellous symbolism; the wondrous and terrible wheels, connecting them with the earth below, the glowing firmament, connecting them with the throne above; and now we come to the throne itself, and to Him that sat upon it.

(26) **As the appearance of a sapphire stone.**—Comp. Exod. xxiv. 10, where the same description is applied to "the pavement under His feet" as here and in chap. x. 1 to his throne, in either case indicating the intense clearness of the heavenly blue. The constant repetition of the words "likeness" and "appearance" is very striking throughout this vision. They occur five times in this verse, and four times in each of the two following. The prophet thus labours to make it plain that what he saw was not the realities of existing things, but certain symbolic representations given for the purpose of producing their fitting impression upon the mind. It is especially important to remember this in connection with "the *likeness* as the *appearance* of a man" "upon the *likeness* of the throne." It was not the Divine Being Himself whom Ezekiel saw, but certain appearances to impress upon him the character and attributes of Him whom "no man hath seen, nor can see."

The appearance of a man.—As in the case of the cherubim the form of a man, as the highest known in nature, was made the groundwork to which all their peculiarities were attached, so here, in rising to something still higher, the same basis must be retained in the impossibility of anything better; only that which is added is more vague, as being incapable of any definite description. Yet possibly there may be even here a hint at the great truth of the incarnation. (Comp. Dan. vii. 13; Rev. i. 13.)

(27) **As the colour of amber.**—See on the same expression verse 4. Literally, *as an eye of bright metal.* The rest of the verse is simply an attempt, by various repetitions, to convey an idea of the exceeding brightness and glory of the vision, yet also with the notions of purity and holiness, of power and activity always associated with fire. (Comp. Exod. xxiv. 17; Dan. vii. 9; Rev. i. 14, 15, iv. 5.)

(28) **As the appearance of the bow that is in the cloud.**—Comp. Rev. iv. 3, x. 1. The addition,

day of rain, so *was* the appearance of the brightness round about.

This *was* the appearance of the likeness of the glory of the LORD. And when I saw *it*, I fell upon my face, and I heard a voice of one that spake.

CHAPTER II.—(1) And he said unto me, Son of man, stand upon thy feet, and I will speak unto thee.

(2) And the spirit entered into me when he spake unto me, and set me upon my feet, that I heard him that spake unto me. (3) And he said unto me, Son of man, I send thee to the children of Israel, to a rebellious [1]nation

[1] Heb., *nations.*

"in the day of rain," is not merely a reference to the ordinary natural phenomenon, but distinctly connects this vision with the gracious promise in Genesis, and shows that God, who has in this vision presented His attributes of terrible majesty, will add to them also those of mercy and loving-kindness. It was in both alike that He was to be made known to His people through the prophet who is now receiving his commission. This was the merciful "appearance of the brightness round about."

I fell upon my face.—The immediate manifestation of the Divine has always proved overpowering to man. (Comp. chap. iii. 23; Isa. vi. 5; Dan. viii. 17; Acts ix. 4; Rev. i. 17. Comp. also Luke v. 8, viii. 37.)

In considering the general significance of this vision, it is to be remembered that it was seen four times by Ezekiel in various connections in his life-work. First, at this time, when he is called to the exercise of the prophetic office; a second time when, shortly afterwards, he is sent to denounce judgments upon the sinful people, and to foretell the destruction of Jerusalem and the Temple (chap. iii. 23, &c.); again, a year and a half later (chaps. viii. 4, x. 15), he sees the same vision, while he is made to understand the evils and abominations wrought in the Temple (which is still standing), until the "glory of the Lord" forsakes His house and departs from the city (chap. xi. 23), in token that God had given them over to punishment; finally, in the prophecy of future restoration and blessing, he again sees the presence of the Lord, by means of the same vision, re-enter and fill the house (chap. xliii. 3—5). Its meaning, therefore, clearly relates to the whole prophecies of Ezekiel, whether of judgment or mercy; and, without attempting an explanation of the symbolism in detail, we cannot be wrong in assuming that it represents the resistless Divine activity, controlling alike the agencies of judgment and of mercy, directed to every corner of the earth, and requiring of all profoundest homage and veneration. The perfect unity of purpose in all God's doings is made especially prominent, and the consistency of His wrath with His love, of His judgments with His mercy; while over all seems to be written, as on the plate of the mitre which He had of old commanded the high priest to wear in His temple, "Holiness unto the Lord."

II.

Chaps. ii. and iii. record the call of the prophet to his office and the instructions given him for his work. As far as chap. iii. 13, this seems to have been still in the presence of the vision of chap. i.; then he was directed to go to another place, where he remains silent among the captives for seven days (chap. iii. 14, 15). At the end of that time he receives fresh instructions (chap. iii. 16—21), and then he is told to go forth into the plain (chap. iii. 22), where the same vision reappears to him (chap. iii. 23), producing upon him again the same overpowering effect; he is again made to stand up, and further instructed.

The full time occupied by these things is not expressly mentioned, but it was apparently just eight days from the first to the second appearance of the vision—from the beginning to the completion of his prophetic consecration. This period, corresponding to the period of the consecration of Aaron and his sons (Lev. viii. 33—ix. 4), must have been peculiarly impressive to the priestly Ezekiel, and have added its own power of association to the other solemnities of his call. Since the time of Moses there had been no other prophet whose call had been accompanied by such manifestations of the Divine glory, and perhaps no time in which the condition of the Church had made them so important.

(1) **Son of man.**—The voice that now came to Ezekiel was articulate, and spoke to him in words which he could understand. It is not said who it was that spoke, but the "He" in connection with the vision before him could be none other than the Most High, whose glory that vision was given to reveal. The phrase "son of man" is common enough throughout the Scriptures, as meaning simply *man*, but is never used in an address to a prophet, except to Ezekiel and Daniel. To Daniel it is used only once (Dan. viii. 17), while to Ezekiel it is used above ninety times. The reason is, doubtless, that since he was the prophet of the captivity he was addressed in the common terms of the language where he lived. "Son of man" for "man" is so common in the Aramaic languages that it is even used of Adam himself in the Syriac version of 1 Cor. xv. 45—47. The address to Ezekiel here as "man," just as under similar circumstances to Daniel when he had fallen upon his face through awe of the supernatural presence (Dan. viii. 17), is doubtless in compassion to his weakness. And then comes the strengthening command, "Stand upon thy feet," that he may be able to receive the communication God is about to make to him.

(2) **And the spirit entered into me.**—Always Divine strength is vouchsafed to the prophets when thus overcome by the glory of their visions. (Comp. Isa. vi. 5, 6, 7; Dan. viii. 18, x. 15—19; Rev. i. 17.) There can be no doubt, therefore, that *the spirit* is here the Spirit of God, and not merely the prophet's own human vigour and courage; and this is made still more plain in chap. iii. 24. It was this which "set him upon his feet," and enabled him amid such surroundings of awe to receive the word spoken to him; for while the revelation by vision still remained before him (see chap. iii. 12, 13), he was now to be instructed also by the clearer revelation of the direct voice from heaven. We are not to think of any physical force exerted upon the prophet, but of all these things as still taking place in vision.

(3) **I send thee to the children of Israel.**—Here properly begins the distinct commission of the

that hath rebelled against me: they and
their fathers have transgressed against
me, *even* unto this very day. (4) For *they*
are [1]impudent children and stiffhearted.
I do send thee unto them; and thou shalt
say unto them, Thus saith the Lord GOD.
(5) And they, whether they will hear, or
whether they will forbear, (for they *are*
a rebellious house,) yet shall know that
there hath been a prophet among them.
(6) And thou, son of man, be not afraid of
them, neither be afraid of their words,
though [2]briers and thorns *be* with thee,
and thou dost dwell among scorpions:
be not afraid of their words, nor be dismayed at their looks, though they *be*
a rebellious house. (7) And thou shalt
speak my words unto them, whether
they will hear, or whether they will forbear: for they *are* [3]most rebellious.
(8) But thou, son of man, hear what I
say unto thee; Be not thou rebellious
like that rebellious house: open thy
mouth, and [a]eat that I give thee. (9) And
when I looked, behold, an hand *was* sent
unto me; and, lo, a roll of a book *was*

1 Heb., *hard of face.*
2 Or, *rebels.*
3 Heb., *rebellion.*
a Rev. 10. 9.

prophet. After the captivity of the ten tribes, the two forming the kingdom of Judah, with such remnants of the others as had been induced by Hezekiah and others to cast in their lot with them, are constantly spoken of as "Israel." (See Ezra ii. 2.) The continuity of the whole nation was considered as preserved in the remnant, and hence this same mode of expression passed into the New Testament. (See Acts xxvi. 7.) It is only when there is especial occasion to distinguish between the two parts of the nation, as in chap. iv. 5, 6, that the name of Israel is used in contrast with that of Judah.

A rebellious nation.—Literally, as in the margin, *rebellious nations*, the word being the same as that commonly used distinctively for the heathen, so that the children of Israel are here spoken of as "rebellious heathen." There could be no epithet which would carry home more forcibly to the mind of an Israelite the state of antagonism in which he had placed himself against his God. (Comp. the "Lo-ammi" of Hosea i. 9, and also the discourse of our Lord in John viii. 39.) Yet still, the God from whom they had turned aside was even now sending to them His prophet, and seeking to win them back to His love and obedience, in true correspondence to the vision of the bow in the cloud about the majesty on high.

The following verses enlarge, with a variety of epithets and repetitions, upon the hard-heartedness and perverseness of the people. This had always been the character of the Israelites from the time of Moses (see Exod. xxxii. 9, xxxiii. 3, 5, &c.), and continued to be to the end (see Acts vii. 51); so entirely without ground is the allegation that they were chosen as a people peculiarly inclined to the right. It is to such a people that Ezekiel is to be sent, and he needed to be prepared and encouraged for his work.

(4) **Impudent children.**—Literally, as in margin, *hard of face.* The epithet is repeated in chap. iii. 7, and it is with reference to this that in chap. iii. 7, 8 the prophet's face is to be made strong, and his forehead "harder than flint." "The Lord God" is in the original "the Lord Jehovah," the second name taking the pointing of, and being translated "God," because of the word "Lord" preceding.

(5) **Whether they will hear, or whether they will forbear.**—Comp. chap. iii. 11. God's word remains the same whatever reception man may accord to it; it cannot return unto Him void, but must accomplish that which He pleases (Isa. lv. 11); just as the Apostles remained "unto God a sweet savour of Christ" alike "in them that are saved and in them that perish" (2 Cor. ii. 15, 16). But while the mighty power of the Divine word must thus produce its effect, the character of the effect depends upon those to whom it comes; "to the one we are a savour of death unto death, and to the other the savour of life unto life." So it would be among the captives by the Chebar: some would be brought back to their allegiance to their God, and would constitute the remnant through whom He would bless His people and the world; and some, resisting the offered grace, would be thus made more obdurate than ever. In either case, they could not remain as before. Whether for gain or for loss, they should "know that there hath been a prophet among them," by the change his ministrations should produce among them. The offer of grace, imposing the responsibility of accepting or rejecting it, ever becomes thus "a great and terrible day of the Lord." (See Joel ii. 31; Mal. iv. 5, compared with Matt. xvii. 12; Acts ii. 16—22.)

A rebellious house.—Literally, *a house of rebellion.* This phrase, used in Ezekiel about eleven times, seems to be more than a simple epithet; it is a significant substitute for the name in which they gloried. Instead of "house of Israel, the prince of God," they had come to be the "house of rebellion."

(6) **Briers and thorns.**—These words occur only here, but their meaning is sufficiently plain. *Briers*, indeed, might admit of the marginal translation, *rebels*, but both words should be taken together, either as adjectives or nouns, and the latter is more in accordance with the following "scorpions," and with the general strongly figurative style of Ezekiel.

(8) **Eat that I give thee.**—This is to be understood, like all that has gone before, as done in vision, as in the case of the book eaten by St. John in Rev. x. 9, 10. The figure of eating for receiving into the heart, so as to be thoroughly possessed by what is communicated, is not an uncommon one. (Comp. Jer. xv. 16; John vi. 53—58.)

(9) **Was sent unto me.**—Better, *was put forth*, as the same word is translated in Gen. iii. 22, xix. 10; chap. viii. 3. In chap. x. 7 it is rendered *stretched forth*, with the marginal *sent forth*, and the corresponding Chaldee word in Dan. v. 24 is translated "sent." It is not that a hand by itself containing the roll was sent to the prophet, but a hand, either of one of the cherubim, or from the throne above, was stretched forth to him. In the corresponding vision in Rev. x. 8, 9, it is handed to the seer by the angel.

A roll of a book.—Books were anciently written upon skins sewed together, or upon papyrus in long strips, which were rolled up, one hand unrolling and the other rolling up from the other end as the contents were

therein; (10) and he spread it before me;
and it *was* written within and without:
and *there was* written therein lamenta-
tions, and mourning, and woe.

CHAPTER III.—(1) Moreover he said
unto me, Son of man, eat that thou
findest; eat this roll, and go speak unto
the house of Israel. (2) So I opened my
mouth, and he caused me to eat that
roll. (3) And he said unto me, Son of
man, cause thy belly to eat, and fill thy
bowels with this roll that I give thee.
Then did I [a]eat *it;* and it was in my
mouth as honey for sweetness.
(4) And he said unto me, Son of man,
go, get thee unto the house of Israel,
and speak with my words unto them.
(5) For thou *art* not sent to a people [1]of
a strange speech and of an hard lan-
guage, *but* to the house of Israel; (6) not
to many people [2]of a strange speech and
of an hard language, whose words thou
canst not understand. [3]Surely, had I
sent thee to them, they would have
hearkened unto thee. (7) But the house
of Israel will not hearken unto thee;
for they will not hearken unto me: for
all the house of Israel *are* [4]impudent and
hardhearted. (8) Behold, I have made
thy face strong against their faces, and
thy forehead strong against their fore-
heads. (9) As an adamant harder than
flint have I made thy forehead: [b]fear
them not, neither be dismayed at their
looks, though they *be* a rebellious house.
(10) Moreover he said unto me, Son of
man, all my words that I shall speak

a Rev. 10. 9.

1 Heb., *deep of lip, and heavy of tongue:* and so *ver. 6.*

2 Heb., *deep of lip, and heavy of language.*

3 Or, *If I had sent thee, &c., would they not have hearkened unto thee?*

4 Heb., *stiff of forehead and hard of heart.*

b Jer. 1. 8.

---

read. These were ordinarily written on one side only, as it would have been inconvenient to read the other; but in this case it was written on both sides, "within and without," to denote the fulness of the message.

(10) **He spread it before me.**—The roll was given to the prophet open, as the book in Rev. x. 8, that he might first see it all as a whole, before becoming thoroughly possessed with it in detail. What he saw was "lamentations, and mourning, and woe;" in other words, this was the whole character of the message he was commissioned to bear until the great judgment in the destruction of Jerusalem and the Temple should be fulfilled, when, after chap. xxxiii., his prophecies assume a consolatory character. (See Introduction, VI.)

III.

The division between this and the preceding chapter is unfortunate; both should be read as one continuous passage. What is symbolically described in the last verses of chap. ii. and the first of chap. iii. is expressed plainly in verses 10, 11.

(3) **It was in my mouth as honey for sweetness.**—That is, the first impression made upon him by his prophetic call was one of delight. Such it must always be to those whose high privilege it is to bear God's message to their fellows. He does not expressly add, as St. John does (Rev. x. 10) after a similar first sensation, "as soon as I had eaten it my belly was bitter;" but it may easily be inferred from verse 14 that such was his experience also, when he went with his heavy message to a people indisposed to give ear. (Comp. Jer. xv. 16 and xx. 7—18.)

(5) **To a people of a strange speech.**—In verses 4—7 it is emphasised that Ezekiel's immediate mission is to be, like that of his great Antitype, to "the lost sheep of the house of Israel;" and yet that they would not give the heed to him which men far below them in spiritual privilege would have gladly yielded. Similar facts are continually encountered in the Scriptures, whether in its histories, as in those of Naaman the Syrian, of the faith of the Syro-Phœnician woman (Matt. xv. 21—28), and of the Roman centurion (Matt. viii. 10—12), or in the express declarations of our Lord that the teaching and signs given to Chorazin, Bethsaida, and Capernaum in vain would have been more than sufficient for the conversion of Tyre, or Sidon, or even of Sodom (Matt. xi. 21, 23, xii. 41, 42). If it be asked, Why then should so much of the Divine compassion be expended upon a nation which so generally refused to avail itself of its blessings? the answer must be that only thus could even a few be raised at all above the very lowest spiritual plane, and that the raising of these few leads ultimately to the elevation of many. As an accountable being, man must be left free to neglect the proffered grace; and, as in the case of the Israelites to whom Ezekiel was sent, there would always be many who choose to do so. The consequence of this neglect must be such a hardening of the heart as was now shown by these people, and every man is warned by their example of the responsibility attached to the enjoyment of religious privilege. But the same thing would have happened with any other nation; and that God's faithfulness should not fail, and that His purposes for man's salvation should be accomplished, more grace must yet be given and His people must still be pleaded with, that at least a remnant of them might be led to repentance and be saved from the impending ruin. Theodoret calls attention to the contrast between the restriction of the grace of the Old Dispensation to a single people, and the universal diffusion of the preaching of the Gospel.

(7) **All the house of Israel**—Means, of course, the people generally, as the word *all* is often used in Scripture and elsewhere. There were even then among them such saints as Jeremiah and Daniel.

(8) **Thy face strong against their faces.**—The word *strong* is the same here as that rendered *impudent* (marg. *stiff*) in verse 7. Of course it must have a different shade of meaning in its application to the rebellious people and to the prophet; but the main thought is taken from the figure of horned animals in their contests, and God promises Ezekiel to make him in the struggle stronger than those who oppose him. The same thing is expressed by another figure in verse 9.

(9) **An adamant harder than flint.**—*Adamant* is the diamond, as it is translated (Jer. xvii. 1). The people were as hard as flint, but as the diamond cuts flint, so Ezekiel's words should be made by the Divine

unto thee receive in thine heart, and
hear with thine ears. (11) And go, get
thee to them of the captivity, unto the
children of thy people, and speak unto
them, and tell them, Thus saith the Lord
God; whether they will hear, or whether
they will forbear. (12) Then the spirit
took me up, and I heard behind me a
voice of a great rushing, *saying*, Blessed
be the glory of the Lord from his place.
(13) *I heard* also the noise of the wings of
the living creatures that [1]touched one
another, and the noise of the wheels over
against them, and a noise of a great rush-
ing. (14) So the spirit lifted me up, and
took me away, and I went in [2]bitterness,
in the [3]heat of my spirit; but the hand
of the Lord was strong upon me.
(15) Then I came to them of the capti-
vity at Tel-abib, that dwelt by the river
of Chebar, and I sat where they sat, and
remained there astonished among them
seven days. (16) And it came to pass at
the end of seven days, that the word

1 Heb., *kissed.*
2 Heb., *bitter.*
3 Heb., *hot anger.*

---

power to cut through all their resistance. Armed with this strength, he need not fear their obduracy, however great.

(11) **Get thee to them of the captivity.**—Ezekiel's mission is now made more definite. In verse 10 he has been told in plain terms what had already been symbolically conveyed under the figure of the roll, and now he is further informed that his immediate mission to the house of Israel is limited to that part of it which, like himself, was already in captivity. At this time, and for several years to come, this was a comparatively small part of the whole nation; but before Ezekiel's ministrations were finished it embraced the mass of them. (See Introd., III.) It is noticeable that God directs him to go, not to *My*, but to *thy* people; just as in chap. ii. 3 He speaks of them as heathen, so here He refuses to recognise them in their present state as really His people. (Comp. Exod. xxxii. 7; chap. xxxiii. 2, 12, 17; Dan. ix. 24, x. 14.) At the same time, there is thus indirectly suggested to the prophet a reminder that he is himself one of the same people, and needs therefore to be on his guard against the sin and obduracy which characterise them.

(12) **Then the spirit took me up.**—This also is to be understood as done in vision, as in chaps. viii. 3, xi. 1, 24. (Comp. Acts viii. 39.) In the last case the "taking up" is expressly said to have been in vision. This closes one act, so to speak, of the prophet's consecration, and now the vision which he has been seeing all along leaves him for a time. He hears the great voice of ascription of praise, without definite mention of its source, but doubtless, as in Isa. vi. and Rev. iv., from all that surround the throne; and he hears the noise of the moving wings of the cherubim, and of the wheels. He has seen the representation of the glory of Him who sends him, and has heard the character of his message. He must now, in the light of this knowledge, see those to whom he is sent. The Hebrew for "wings that touched one another" is beautifully figurative: "wings that kissed each one its sister."

(14) **I went in bitterness, in the heat of my spirit.**—The prophet now begins to realise the sorrow and the trial of the task laid upon him. The command of the Lord was sweet (verse 3), its performance is bitter. "But the hand of the Lord was strong" upon him, and he could not forbear. Compare the similar experience of Jeremiah (Jer. xx. 8, 9; see also Amos iii. 8), when in his discouragement he had almost resolved to refuse to declare God's message, but the word of the Lord was as a burning fire within, and he could not refrain—an experience which every faithful teacher in God's name is obliged, more or less fully, to pass through.

(15) **I came to them of the captivity at Tel-abib.**—Ezekiel now leaves the place where he had been, and comes to Tel-abib, which is described as still by the same "river of Chebar," and which signifies the "mound of ears (of grain)," and was probably a place of especial fruitfulness, but which cannot be further identified. It appears to have been the central place of the captivity.

I sat where they sat is an expression of so much difficulty in the Hebrew, that it has given rise to various readings in the manuscripts, and to a marginal correction which has been followed by the English. Probably the vowel-pointing of the first word should be changed, and it will then read, "and I saw where they sat."

Remained there astonished among them seven days. — Comp. Dan. iv. 19; Ezra ix. 3, 4. The word implies a fixed and determined silence. "*To be silent* was the characteristic of mourners (Lam. iii. 28); *to sit*, their proper attitude (Isa. iii. 26; Lam. i. 1); *seven days*, the set time of mourning (Job ii. 13)." By this act the prophet shows his deep sympathy with his people in their affliction. This week of silent meditation among those to whom he was commissioned to speak corresponds, as already said, to the week of the consecration of his fathers to their priestly office (Lev. viii.). Such a season of retirement and thought has been given to other great religious leaders—to Moses, in his forty years of exile; to Elijah, in his forty days in Mount Horeb (1 Kings xix. 4—8); to St. Paul, in his journey to Arabia (Gal. i. 17); and to our Lord Himself, when He went into the wilderness after His baptism.

(16) **At the end of seven days.**—A fresh Divine communication comes to the prophet, designed especially to impress upon him the responsibility of his office (verses 16—21). In chap. xxxiii. 1—20 the same charge is repeated with some amplification, and there verses 2—6 are taken up with describing the duties of the military sentinel, upon which both these figurative addresses are founded. The language is there arranged in the parallelism of Hebrew poetry, to which there is indeed an approach here, but too imperfect to be easily represented in English. What is said there, moreover, is expressly required to be spoken to the people (verse 1), while this seems to have been immediately for the prophet's own ear.

The substance of the communication in either place is this: man must in all cases live or die according to his own personal righteousness or sinfulness; but such a responsibility rests upon the watchman, that if he die unwarned his blood will be required at the watchman's hand. The responsibility extends only, however, to the giving of the warning, not to its results: when the warning is given the watchman has "delivered his soul," whether it is heeded or not. The word *soul* in verses 19, 21, as also in chap. xxxiii. 5, 9, is not to be under-

of the Lord came unto me, saying,
(17) [a]Son of man, I have made thee a
watchman unto the house of Israel:
therefore hear the word at my mouth,
and give them warning from me. (18)
When I say unto the wicked, Thou
shalt surely die; and thou givest him
not warning, nor speakest to warn the
wicked from his wicked way, to save his
life; the same wicked *man* shall die in
his iniquity; but his blood will I require
at thine hand. (19) Yet if thou warn the
wicked, and he turn not from his wicked-
ness, nor from his wicked way, he shall
die in his iniquity; but thou hast deli-
vered thy soul. (20) Again, When a
[b]righteous *man* doth turn from his
[1]righteousness, and commit iniquity,
and I lay a stumblingblock before him,
he shall die: because thou hast not
given him warning, he shall die in his
sin, and his righteousness which he hath
done shall not be remembered; but his
blood will I require at thine hand.
(21) Nevertheless if thou warn the righ-
teous *man*, that the righteous sin not,
and he doth not sin, he shall surely live,
because he is warned; also thou hast
delivered thy soul.
(22) And the hand of the Lord was there
upon me; and he said unto me, Arise,
go forth into the plain, and I will there
talk with thee. (23) Then I arose, and
went forth into the plain: and, behold,
the glory of the Lord stood there, as
the glory which I [c]saw by the river of
Chebar: and I fell on my face. (24) Then
the spirit entered into me, and set me
upon my feet, and spake with me, and
said unto me, Go, shut thyself within
thine house. (25) But thou, O son of man,
behold, they shall put bands upon thee,

a ch. 33. 7.
b ch. 18. 24.
1 Heb., *righteousnesses.*
c ch. 1. 28.

---

stood distinctively of the immortal part of man, but is equivalent to life, and forms here, as often in Hebrew, little more than a form of the reflective, thy soul = thyself.

In this charge the individual and personal relation in which every Israelite stood to God is strongly emphasised, that they may neither feel themselves lost because their nation is undergoing punishment, nor, on the other hand, think that no repentance is required of them individually because they "had Abraham to their father." The gradual bringing out more and more fully the individual relation of man to God, at the expense of the comparative sinking of the federal relation, is one of the most strongly marked features of the progress of revelation, and at no other time was this progress so great as under the stern discipline of the captivity. In Ezekiel's office of "watchman," there is even an approach to the pastoral "cure of souls" under the Christian dispensation. Such an office had almost no place under the Old Testament, and Ezekiel is the only one of the prophets who is charged to exercise this office distinctly towards individuals. Habakkuk, indeed, speaks of standing upon his watch on the tower (Hab. ii. 1); Jeremiah, of the watchmen whom the people would not hear (Jer. vi. 17); and Isaiah, of the "blind watchmen" (Isa. lvi. 10); but the duty of all these was far more collective and national.

(20) **When a righteous man doth turn from his righteousness.**—Quite independently of any theological question, it is undeniable that the Scripture here, as often elsewhere, represents the upright man as exposed to temptation, and in danger of falling into sin. The duty of the prophet, therefore, is not only to seek to turn the wicked from his evil way, but also to warn the righteous against falling into the same path. Both terms must necessarily be taken as comparative; but they show that there was even now a considerable difference in character among the captives.

I lay a stumblingblock before him.—A "stumbling-block" is anything at which people actually stumble, whether intended for that purpose or, on the contrary, designed for their highest good. Thus Christ is foretold as a stumbling-block to both the houses of Israel (Isa. viii. 14), and is several times spoken of as such by the apostles (1 Cor. i. 23; Rom. ix. 32, 33; 1 Pet. ii. 8). The word is used oftener by Ezekiel than by all the other Old Testament writers together; in chap. vii. 19 the riches of the people are spoken of as their stumbling-block, and in chap. xliv. 12 (marg.) the sinful Levites are described as a stumbling-block. The meaning here is plainly, "when a man perverts any of God's gifts or providences into an occasion of sin."

(22) **The hand of the Lord was there upon me.**—The prophet's week of silent meditation being past, and the charge of responsibility given, the constraining power of God again comes upon him, and sends him forth to the final act of preparation for his work.

(23) **Went forth into the plain.**—As he was now again to see the same vision as at the first, it was fitting that he should leave the thickly-peopled Tel-abib and seek a place of solitude, and in that solitude God promises him, "I will there talk with thee." The vision reappeared; again the prophet fell on his face, and again the Spirit set him upon his feet, and talked with him.

(24) **Go, shut thyself within thine house.**—The prophet's consecration being now complete, he is to enter upon his actual work; yet, in view of the disposition of the people, he is to begin his prophecies in a private way, shut up in his house. Or it may be that this should be understood of a period of absolute silence and meditation preparatory to entering upon his work. Moreover, fresh warning is given of the reception he must be prepared to meet.

(25) **They shall put bands upon thee.**—Ezekiel's contemporary prophet, Jeremiah, was actually thrown into prison in Judæa, and even into a foul dungeon (Jer. xxxvii. 21, xxxviii. 6); but nothing of this kind is to be understood here. There is no trace of such treatment throughout the book, nor is it likely that it would have been suffered by Nebuchadnezzar among his captives, or possible under the administration of Daniel. Besides, a similar laying of bands upon him (although for a different purpose) is mentioned in chap. iv. 8, which must necessarily be understood

and shall bind thee with them, and thou
shalt not go out among them: (26) and I
will make thy tongue cleave to the roof
of thy mouth, that thou shalt be dumb,
and shalt not be to them [1]a reprover:
for they *are* a rebellious house. (27) But
when I speak with thee, I will open
thy mouth, and thou shalt say unto
them, Thus saith the Lord GOD; He
that heareth, let him hear; and he that
forbeareth, let him forbear: for they *are*
a rebellious house.

CHAPTER IV.—(1) Thou also, son of
man, take thee a tile, and lay it before
thee, and pourtray upon it the city, *even*
Jerusalem: (2) and lay siege against it,
and build a fort against it, and cast
a mount against it; set the camp
also against it, and set [2]*battering* rams
against it round about. (3) Moreover
take thou unto thee [3]an iron pan, and
set it *for* a wall of iron between thee and
the city: and set thy face against it, and
it shall be besieged, and thou shalt lay

1 Heb., *a man reproving.*

2 Or, *chief leaders.*

3 Or, *a flat plate,* or, *slice.*

---

figuratively. The compulsion described in this and the following verse was a moral one. Ezekiel's countrymen, especially during the period of his warnings until the destruction of Jerusalem, should so absolutely refuse to hear him, that it would become practically impossible for him to declare his prophecies; he would be as if he were bound.

(26) **I will make thy tongue cleave to the roof of thy mouth.**—Here, under another figure, this enforced silence is attributed, not to "the rebellious house," by whom it was immediately brought about, but to God Himself, whose providence was the ultimate cause by which the prophet was placed in such circumstances. It is a way of expressing strongly the difficulties under which he was to exercise his ministry.

(27) **When I speak with thee, I will open thy mouth.**—To this Ezekiel evidently refers in chaps. xxiv. 27, xxxiii. 22, when, after the destruction of Jerusalem, his mouth should no longer be shut. But until then, although he should be greatly restrained in his ordinary utterances by the opposition of the people, yet there would be times when God would give him a message with such power that he would be constrained to declare it, whether the people would hear or whether they would forbear. Such messages are those contained in this book, which at this point begin to be recorded. By all this the difficulties and trials under which the prophet must exercise his office are clearly and strongly set before him. (See Excursus I., "On the Figurative and Symbolical Language of Ezekiel.")

IV.

(1) **Take thee a tile.**—The use of tiles for such purposes as that here indicated was common both in Babylonia and in Nineveh. When intended for preservation the writing or drawing was made upon the soft and plastic clay, which was afterwards baked. It is from the remains of great libraries prepared in this way that most of our modern knowledge of Nineveh and Babylon has been derived. It is, of course, quite possible that Ezekiel may have drawn in this way upon a soft clay tile; but from the whole account in this and the following chapters it is more likely that he simply described, rather than actually performed, these symbolical acts.

(2) **Lay siege against it.**—It must have seemed at this time unlikely that Jerusalem would soon become the subject of another siege. The only power by whom such a siege could be undertaken was Babylon, Egypt having been so thoroughly defeated as to be for a long time out of the question; and Nebuchadnezzar had now, within a few years, thrice completely conquered Judæa, had carried two of its kings, one after the other, captive in chains, and had also taken into captivity 10,000 of the chief of the people, setting up as king over the remnant a creature of his own, who was yet of the royal house of Judah. A fresh siege could only be the result of a fresh rebellion, an act, under the circumstances, of simple infatuation. Yet of this infatuation Zedekiah, through the "anger of the LORD" (2 Kings xxiv. 20), was guilty, and thus the prophecy was fulfilled. The prophecy itself is undated, but must have been between the call of Ezekiel in the fifth month of the fifth year (chap. i. 2) and the next date given (chap. viii. 1), the sixth month of the sixth year. The siege began, according to Jer. lii. 4, in the tenth month of the ninth year, so that the prophecy preceded its fulfilment by only about four years.

Build a fort against it.—Rather, *a tower.* The several acts of a siege are graphically described. First the city is invested; then a tower is built, as was customary, of sufficient height to overlook the walls and thus obtain information of the doings of the besieged. Instruments for throwing stones or darts were also sometimes placed in such towers; next is "cast a mound against it," a common operation of the ancient siege (comp. Isa. xxxvii. 33; Jer. xxxii. 24), in which a sort of artificial hill was built to give the besiegers an advantage; then the camps (not merely camp) are set round the city to prevent ingress and egress; and finally "the battering rams" are brought against the walls. These last were heavy beams, headed with iron, and slung in towers, so that they could be swung against the walls with great force. They are frequently to be noticed in the representations of sieges found in the ruins of Nineveh. The practice of forming the end of the beam like a ram's head belongs to the Greeks and Romans; but the instrument itself was much older.

(3) **An iron pan.**—The margin gives the sense more accurately, *a flat plate.* It was used for baking cakes (see Lev. ii. 5, marg.). This was to be set for a wall of iron between the prophet (representing the besiegers) and the city, doubtless as symbolical of the strength of the besiegers' lines, and of the impossibility there would be of an escape from the city by a sally. Their foes should be made too strong for them defensively as well as offensively.

A sign to the house of Israel.—As already said, the tribe of Judah, with the associated remnants of the other tribes, is considered as representing the whole nation after the Assyrian captivity, and is spoken of as "the house of Israel" except when there is occasion to distinguish especially between the two parts of the nation. (See chaps. iii. 7, 17, v. 4, viii. 6; 2 Chron. xxi. 2, xxviii. 27, &c.) The prophecy would have been equally effective whether seen as a symbolic act or only related.

siege against it. This *shall be* a sign to
the house of Israel.
(4) Lie thou also upon thy left side, and
lay the iniquity of the house of Israel
upon it: *according* to the number of the
days that thou shalt lie upon it thou
shalt bear their iniquity. (5) For I have
laid upon thee the years of their iniquity,
according to the number of the days,
three hundred and ninety days: [a]so shalt
thou bear the iniquity of the house of
Israel. (6) And when thou hast accom-
plished them, lie again on thy right
side, and thou shalt bear the iniquity of
the house of Judah forty days: I have
appointed thee [1]each day for a year.
(7) Therefore thou shalt set thy face to-
ward the siege of Jerusalem, and thine
arm *shall be* uncovered, and thou shalt
prophesy against it. (8) And, behold, I
will lay bands upon thee, and thou shalt
not turn thee [2]from one side to another,
till thou hast ended the days of thy
siege.
(9) Take thou also unto thee wheat,
and barley, and beans, and lentiles, and
millet, and [3]fitches, and put them in one
vessel, and make thee bread thereof,
according to the number of the days
that thou shalt lie upon thy side, three
hundred and ninety days shalt thou eat
thereof. (10) And thy meat which thou
shalt eat *shall be* by weight, twenty she-
kels a day: from time to time shalt thou

a Num. 14. 34.

1 Heb., *a day for a year, a day for a year.*

2 Heb., *from thy side to thy side.*

3 Or, *spelt.*

---

(4) **Lie thou also upon thy left side.**—Here a fresh feature of this symbolical prophecy begins, while the former siege is still continued (verse 7).

Lay the iniquity of the house of Israel upon it.—The expression, *to bear the iniquity of any one*, is common in Scripture to denote the suffering of the punishment due to sin. (See, among many other passages, chaps. xviii. 19, 20, xxiii. 35; Lev. xix. 8; Num. xiv. 34; Isa. liii. 12.) It is clear, therefore, that Ezekiel is here to represent the people as enduring the Divine judgment upon their sins. This may seem inconsistent with his representing at the same time the besiegers of Jerusalem, the instruments in the Divine hand for inflicting that punishment; but such inconsistencies are common enough in all symbolic representations, and neither offend nor in any way mar the effect of the representation. "The house of Israel" is here expressly distinguished from "the house of Judah," and means the ten tribes. They are symbolised by the prophet's lying on his *left* side, because it was the Oriental habit to look to the east when describing the points of the compass, and the northern kingdom was therefore on the left.

(5) **The years of their iniquity, according to the number of the days.**—Comp. Num. xiv. 34. In regard to the number of the years, see Excursus II. at the end of this book.

(6) **The iniquity of the house of Judah forty days.**—This forty days is clearly subsequent and additional to the 390 days, making in all a period of 430 days. (On these numbers see Excursus II. at the end of this book.) The great disproportion between the two is in accordance with the difference in the two parts of the nation, and the consequent Divine dealings with them. Judah had remained faithful to its appointed rulers of the house of David, several of whose kings had been eminently devout men; through whatever mixture with idolatry it had yet always retained the worship of Jehovah, and had kept up the Aaronic priesthood, and preserved with more or less respect the law of Moses. It was now entering upon the period of the Babylonish captivity, from which, after seventy years, a remnant was to be again restored to keep up the people of the Messiah. Israel, on the other hand, had set up a succession of dynasties, and not one of all their kings had been a God-fearing man; they had made Baal their national god, and had made priests at their pleasure of the lowest of the people, and in consequence of their sins had been carried into a captivity from which they never returned.

(7) **Set thy face** is a common Scriptural expression for any steadfast purpose. (See Lev. xvii. 10, xx. 3, 5, 6, xxvi. 17; 2 Chron. xx. 3, marg., &c.) It is a particularly favourite phrase with Ezekiel (chap. xv. 7, xx. 46, &c.). Here this steadfastness of purpose was to be exercised "toward the siege of Jerusalem;" there would be no relenting in this matter—God's purpose of judgment should surely be fulfilled. Further symbolism to the same effect is added, "Thine arm shall be uncovered," withdrawn from the loose sleeve of the Oriental robe, and made ready for battle. (Comp. Isa. lii. 10.) Withal he is to "prophesy against it," doubtless by words suited to his actions.

(8) **I will lay bands upon thee.**—See on chap. iii. 25. This is a fresh feature of the unrelenting character of the judgment foretold: God's power should interpose to keep the prophet to his work. Not only pity, but even human weakness and weariness, should be excluded from interfering. The prophet is spoken of as besieging the city, because he is doing so in figure.

(9) **Take thou also unto thee wheat.**—The grains enumerated are of all kinds from the best to the worst, indicating that every sort of food would be sought after in the straitness of the siege. If the mixing of these in one vessel and making bread of them all together was not against the exact letter of the law, it was, at least, a plain violation of its spirit (Lev. xix. 19; Deut. xxii. 9), thus again indicating the stern necessity which should be laid upon the people.

Three hundred and ninety days.—No mention is here made of the additional forty days. (See Excursus.)

(10) **By weight, twenty shekels a day.**—The weight of the shekel is somewhat differently estimated by different authorities. The best computations fix it at about 220 grains, and this would make the allowance of twenty shekels equal to something less than eleven ounces, scarcely enough to sustain life. "Meat" is here used, as often in Scripture, of any kind of food. The extreme scarcity of food is also denoted by its being weighed rather than measured. "From time to time" means at set intervals of time (see 1 Chron. ix. 25), here doubtless once a day. Only the longer period of 390 days is here mentioned, but the same command doubtless applied to both periods.

eat it. (11) Thou shalt drink also water
by measure, the sixth part of an hin:
from time to time shalt thou drink.
(12) And thou shalt eat it *as* barley cakes,
and thou shalt bake it with dung that
cometh out of man, in their sight.
(13) And the LORD said, Even thus shall
the children of Israel eat their defiled
bread among the Gentiles, whither I
will drive them.

(14) Then said I, Ah Lord GOD! behold,
my soul hath not been polluted: for from
my youth up even till now have I not
eaten of that which dieth of itself, or
is torn in pieces; neither came there
abominable flesh into my mouth. (15) Then
he said unto me, Lo, I have given thee
cow's dung for man's dung, and thou
shalt prepare thy bread therewith.

(16) Moreover he said unto me, Son of
man, behold, I will break the [a] staff of
bread in Jerusalem: and they shall eat
bread by weight, and with care; and
they shall drink water by measure, and
with astonishment: (17) that they may
want bread and water, and be astonied
one with another, and consume away for
their iniquity.

[a] Lev. 26. 26; ch. 5. 16; & 14. 13.

CHAPTER V.—(1) And thou, son of
man, take thee a sharp knife, take thee
a barber's razor, and cause *it* to pass
upon thine head and upon thy beard:
then take thee balances to weigh, and
divide the *hair*. (2) Thou shalt burn
with fire a third part in the midst of
the city, when the days of the siege are
fulfilled: and thou shalt take a third

---

(11) **The sixth part of an hin.**—There is also a difference among the authorities as to the measures of capacity for liquids. These would make the sixth part of an hin from six-tenths to nine-tenths of a pint. This also was to be drunk once a day.

(12) **As barley cakes.**—These were commonly cooked in the hot ashes, hence the especial defilement caused by the fuel required to be used. Against this the prophet pleads, not merely as revolting in itself, but as ceremonially polluting (verse 14; see Lev. v. 3, vii. 21), and a mitigation of the requirement is granted to him (verse 15).

In their sight.—This is still a part of the vision. The words have been thought to determine that the whole transaction was an actual symbolic act and not a vision; but this does not follow. It need only have been a part of the vision that what was done was done publicly.

(13) **Eat their defiled bread among the Gentiles.**—The Mosaic law purposely so hedged the people about with detailed precepts in regard to their food and its preparation, that it was impossible for them to share the food of the Gentiles without contracting ceremonial defilement; and the declared object of this symbolism is to teach that the Israelites should thus be forced to contract defilement. Their sins had brought them to that pass, which is so often the result of continued and obdurate sin, that it should be impossible for them to avoid further transgression. Ezekiel shows by his reply, in verse 14, that like St. Peter, in Acts x. 14, he had ever been a scrupulous observer of the law. To St. Peter, however, it was made known that in the breadth of the Christian dispensation this ceremonial law was now done away, while to Ezekiel it still remained in full force.

(15) **Cow's dung.**—In the scarcity of fuel in the East, cow's dung and especially camel's dung, is dried, and becomes the common fuel.

(16) **I will break the staff of bread in Jerusalem.**—In verses 16, 17, the meaning of the foregoing symbolism is declared in plain language. Bread, as the chief article of food is put for all food, the specific for the general. There shall be extreme suffering and distress, as a part of the punishment for their long-continued sins.

V.

This chapter is closely connected with the preceding, forming part of the same denunciation of judgment upon the Jews, although this is here set forth in verses 1—4 by a fresh symbolism, and in the rest of the chapter by plain declarations.

(1) **Take thee a sharp knife, take thee a barber's razor.**—Rather, *take thee a sharp sword, as a barber's razor shalt thou take it to thee.* The word *knife* is the same as that used twice in verse 2, and translated once by *knife* and once by *sword.* It is occasionally used for any sharp-cutting instrument, but is most commonly taken, as here, for a sword. The English version also neglects to notice the pronoun in the second clause. The thought is plainly that the prophet is to take a sword, on account of its symbolism, and use it instead of a razor.

Upon thine head, and upon thy beard.—The cutting off the hair was a common mark of mourning (see Job i. 20; Isa. xxii. 12; Jer. vii. 29); but the allusion here seems to be rather to Isa. vii. 20, in which God describes his coming judgments upon Israel as a shaving, "with a razor that is hired . . . by the king of Assyria," of the head and the beard. The symbolism was the more marked because Ezekiel was a priest, and the priests were expressly forbidden in the law to shave either the head or the beard (Lev. xxi. 5). The shaving, therefore, of a priest's head and beard with a sword betokened a most desolating judgment.

Then take thee balances to weigh is not a mere detail introduced to give vividness to the symbolism, but seems designed to show the absolute certainty of the impending judgment.

(2) **Burn with fire a third part in the midst of the city.**—It is better to suppose this done only in description than to imagine that the prophet carried it out in act upon the tile on which the city (Jerusalem) was portrayed. The meaning of this verse is explained in verse 12, and is made plainer by translating the same word uniformly "sword," instead of changing to "knife." The third, which is scattered, plainly signifies the small part of the people who, escaping destruction, shall be scattered among the heathen. A similar prophecy, referring however to a later time, may be

part, *and* smite about it with a knife:
and a third part thou shalt scatter in
the wind; and I will draw out a sword
after them. (3) Thou shalt also take
thereof a few in number, and bind them
in thy [1]skirts. (4) Then take of them
again, and cast them into the midst of
the fire, and burn them in the fire; *for*
thereof shall a fire come forth into all
the house of Israel.

(5) Thus saith the Lord God; This *is*
Jerusalem: I have set it in the midst of
the nations and countries *that are* round
about her. (6) And she hath changed
my judgments into wickedness more
than the nations, and my statutes more
than the countries that *are* round about
her: for they have refused my judg-
ments and my statutes, they have not
walked in them. (7) Therefore thus saith
the Lord God; Because ye multiplied
more than the nations that *are* round
about you, *and* have not walked in my
statutes, neither have kept my judg-
ments, neither have done according to
the judgments of the nations that *are*

1 Heb., *wings.*

---

found in Zech. xiii. 8, 9. The expression, "when the days of the siege are fulfilled," of course refers to the symbolic siege of the prophet. The words, "I will draw out a sword after them," are taken from Lev. xxvi. 33, and are repeated in verse 12, and again in chap. xii. 14. The suffering from the Divine judgments should still follow them in their exile. Plain prophecy is here mixed with the symbolism.

(3) **A few in number, and bind them in thy skirts.**—A small remnant of the people was still left in the land after the great captivity (2 Kings xxv. 22); but even of these some were to perish by violence ("cast them into the midst of the fire") in the disorders which arose, and from this "shall a fire come forth into all the house of Israel." (See Jer. xl., xli.) The ultimate result was the expatriation of all that remained in Judæa, and the entire emptying of the land of the chosen people.

At this point the use of symbolism ceases for a while, and the prophet now, for the first time, begins to utter his prophecies in plain language. Accordingly, he changes his style from prose to the more ordinary form of prophetic utterance in parallelisms, which constitute the distinctive feature of Hebrew poetry, and this continues until another vision begins with chap. viii.

(5) **I have set it in the midst of the nations.**—This was eminently true of Jerusalem, and of Israel as represented by Jerusalem, in all the ages of its history. It constituted one of the great opportunities of Israel had they been faithful to their calling, while it became a chief source of their disasters when they went astray from God. On the south were Egypt and Ethiopia; on the north, at first the great nation of the Hittites, and later the Syrians, and also Assyrians (who must reach Palestine from the north); on the coast were the Philistines, at the southern end, and on the northern the Phœnicians, the great maritime nation having intercourse with all "the isles of the sea;" while on the deserts of the east and immediate south were the Ishmaelites, the chief inland traders, who kept up an intercourse by land with all these nations. Even with the great but little-known nations of India, commerce was established by Solomon. Thus centrally situated among the chief kingdoms of antiquity, Israel had the opportunity of presenting to the world the spectacle of a people strong and prosperous in the worship, and under the guardianship, of the one true God, and of becoming the great missionary of monotheism in the ancient world. At the same time they were separated from most of these nations by natural barriers, the deserts on the east and south, the sea on the west, the mountains on the north, which were sufficient to isolate them as a nation, and allow of their free development, without interference, as a God-fearing people. But when, by the unfaithfulness of the Israelites to their religion, the one bond of national unity was weakened, they became a ready prey to the nations around them. During the period of the Judges they fell under the power of one and another of the petty tribes on their confines; and later, when the great empire of Solomon was broken up in consequence of their sins, they were easily overcome by the powerful nations on either side. In all their later history the Israelites were a football between Egypt and Chaldæa, alternately spoiled by tribute as friends or devastated as enemies by each of them. So, in the Divine ordering of the world, responsibility must always be proportioned to privilege; and the failure to fulfil the responsibility leads, as in this case, not only to a withdrawal of the privilege, but to corresponding condemnation.

(6) **Changed my judgments into wickedness.**—Better, ***hath wickedly resisted my judgments,*** the sense adopted by most modern expositors.

More than the nations.—Not, of course, absolutely, but in proportion to the knowledge and the privileges given them. It would be an exaggeration to say that the Israelites were actually more evil in their life than the surrounding heathen; for they were, no doubt, far better. Even of those cities which our Lord, at a later day, so strongly upbraided, it would be absurd to suppose that they equalled Sodom and Gomorrah in their iniquity. God's judgments are always relative and proportioned to the opportunities He has granted to men. The point is that the Israelites had *resisted His judgments* more than the heathen; they had sinned against greater light. The pronoun *they* in the last clause refers, of course, to the Israelites, not to the heathen.

(7) **Because ye multiplied.**—Rather, *Because ye have raged,* as the same word is translated in Ps. ii. 1, and as its meaning is given in the lexicons. The meaning is, because they had shown more self-will and opposition to God.

Neither have done according to the judgments of the nations.—These words admit of either of two senses: "neither have kept those natural laws observed by the heathen," and in this case the Israelites would have been represented as worse in their actual conduct than the surrounding heathen; or, "neither have kept your Divine laws as the heathen have observed those laws which they know by the light of

round about you; (8) therefore thus
saith the Lord God; Behold, I, even I,
am against thee, and will execute judg-
ments in the midst of thee in the sight
of the nations. (9) And I will do in
thee that which I have not done, and
whereunto I will not do any more the
like, because of all thine abominations.
(10) Therefore the fathers [a]shall eat the
sons in the midst of thee, and the sons
shall eat their fathers; and I will exe-
cute judgments in thee, and the whole
remnant of thee will I scatter into all
the winds. (11) Wherefore, *as* I live, saith
the Lord God; Surely, because thou hast
defiled my sanctuary with all thy detest-
able things, and with all thine abomi-
nations, therefore will I also diminish
thee; [b]neither shall mine eye spare, nei-
ther will I have any pity. (12) A third
part of thee shall die with the pestilence,
and with famine shall they be consumed
in the midst of thee: and a third part
shall fall by the sword round about thee;
and I will scatter a third part into all
the winds, and I will draw out a sword
after them. (13) Thus shall mine anger
be accomplished, and I will cause my
fury to rest upon them, and I will be
comforted: and they shall know that
I the Lord have spoken *it* in my zeal,
when I have accomplished my fury in
them. (14) Moreover I will make thee
waste, and a reproach among the nations
that *are* round about thee, in the sight
of all that pass by. (15) So it shall be a
[c]reproach and a taunt, an instruction
and an astonishment unto the nations
that *are* round about thee, when I shall
execute judgments in thee in anger and
in fury and in furious rebukes. I the
Lord have spoken *it*. (16) When I shall
send upon them the evil arrows of famine,
which shall be for *their* destruction, *and*
which I will send to destroy you: and I
will increase the famine upon you, and
will break your [d]staff of bread: (17) so
will I send upon you famine and [e]evil
beasts, and they shall bereave thee; and
pestilence and blood shall pass through
thee; and I will bring the sword upon
thee. I the Lord have spoken *it*.

a Lev. 26. 29; Deut. 28. 53; 2 Kings 6. 29; Lam. 4. 10; Baruch 2. 3.

b ch. 7. 4, 9.

c Deut. 28. 37.

d Lev. 26. 26; ch. 4. 16; & 14. 13.

e Lev. 26. 22.

---

nature and tradition." The latter we conceive to be the true sense here. If Israel did precisely what the heathen did, they would be far more unfaithful. (See chap. xi. 12.) In chap. xvi. 47, also, they are distinctly charged with being even more corrupt than the heathen; and there, too, the thought is plainly that they had sinned against more grace. (See Excursus III.)

(8) **In the sight of the nations.**—The conspicuousness of Israel's position (see under verse 5) made it necessary that the punishment for their failure to keep God's law should be as public as their sin. All had seen their unfaithfulness; all must see the consequent judgment.

(9) **That which I have not done, and whereunto I will not do any more the like.**—Our Lord uses similar language (Matt. xxiv. 21) in foretelling the final destruction of Jerusalem by the Romans. But all question whether Ezekiel here looks forward to that calamity, and all comparison between that and the destruction under Nebuchadnezzar, are out of place. What the prophet here intends is not a comparison between different judgments upon the Jews, but between God's treatment of them and of others. As they had received at His hand higher opportunities and privileges than He had before given or would afterwards give to any other nation, so must the punishment for their sin be more severe and more conspicuous than He had inflicted or would inflict on any other. All the Divine judgments upon them through all time may therefore be considered as here coming into view. The present captivity and the impending destruction of the temple were but single features of a long series of judgments, in the course of which the terrible particulars mentioned in verse 10 should have place, ending with what is the present condition of the people before our eyes, scattered "into all the winds." Such evils had been foretold by their prophets all through their history as the consequence of disobedience (see Lev. xxvi. 29; Deut. xxviii. 53—the sons eating their fathers is a fearful addition here; Jer. xix. 9), and from time to time had in some degree come to pass (2 Kings vi. 28, 29; Lam. ii. 20), although the culmination of the punishment, like the culmination of the sin, was still future.

(11) **Because thou . . . therefore will I.**—The parallel between Israel's conduct and God's judgments is here, as everywhere, brought into strong light. God would inflict no evil upon them which they had not themselves called down by their obdurate and infatuated persistence in rebellion against Him.

Also diminish thee.—The word *diminish* is hardly an adequate translation of the original, and the pronoun *thee* is not in the Hebrew. The word properly means to *withdraw*, and is to be taken either as reflective, "withdraw myself," or as having for its object "mine eye" of the following clause, the sense being the same in either case: the Lord will withdraw from them His presence and His compassion.

Verses 12—17 follow in plain language the symbolical prophecies of verses 1—4, and give the inspired interpretation of their meaning. They bring out very distinctly the fact that the judgments should not end with the destruction of Jerusalem.

(13) **I will be comforted.**—The word employed here is used in two different senses: either that of feeling compassion, and so of repenting of one's anger, as in Isa. xii. 1, xlix. 13, li. 3, 12, lii. 9, &c.; or of consoling oneself by taking vengeance, as in Gen. xxvii. 42, Isa. i. 24 (Authorised Version, *ease myself*). (Comp. also chaps. xxxi. 16, xxxii. 31.) The latter is evidently the meaning here; the Divine honour, wounded by the sins of the chosen people and dishonoured before the

CHAPTER VI.—(1) And the word of
the LORD came unto me, saying, (2) Son
of man. set thy face toward the [a]moun-
tains of Israel, and prophesy against
them, (3) and say,
Ye mountains of Israel, hear the word
of the Lord GOD; Thus saith the Lord
GOD to the mountains, and to the hills,
to the rivers, and to the valleys; Behold,
I, *even* I, will bring a sword upon you,
and I will destroy your high places.
(4) And your altars shall be desolate, and
your [1]images shall be broken: and I will
cast down your slain *men* before your
idols. (5) And I will [2]lay the dead car-
cases of the children of Israel before
their idols; and I will scatter your
bones round about your altars. (6) In
all your dwellingplaces the cities shall
be laid waste, and the high places shall
be desolate; that your altars may be
laid waste and made desolate, and your
idols may be broken and cease, and your
images may be cut down, and your works
may be abolished. (7) And the slain shall
fall in the midst of you, and ye shall
know that I *am* the LORD.
(8) Yet will I leave a remnant, that
ye may have *some* that shall escape the
sword among the nations, when ye shall

B.C. 594.

a ch. 36. 1.

1 Or, *sun images*: and so ver. 6.

2 Heb., *give*.

---

heathen, should be vindicated by their punishment in the sight of all the world.

VI.

The two prophecies contained in chaps. vi. and vii. are distinct, although both closely connected with the explanation of the symbolism in chap. v. They were probably uttered at sufficient intervals of time from chap. v. and from each other to allow of a distinct impression being made by each of them; yet the interval could not have been long, since chap. viii. is dated in the sixth month of the sixth year. There must therefore have been such a following up of one blow after another of prophetic denunciation as was calculated to produce the most profound effect. In the present chapter judgment is denounced upon the idolatrous places and people, although a remnant are to be saved who shall recognise the hand of the Lord, and then the terribleness of the judgment of desolation is enlarged upon. In chap. vii. the quickness and inevitableness of this judgment is the chief thought. In both the judgment is no longer denounced merely against Jerusalem, as representing the people, but is expressly extended to the whole land.

(2) **Toward the mountains of Israel.**—It is not uncommon to address prophetic utterances to inanimate objects as a poetic way of representing the people. (Comp. chap. xxxvi. 1; Micah vi. 2, &c.) The mountains are especially mentioned as being the chosen places of idolatrous worship. (See Deut. xii. 2; 2 Kings xvii. 10, 11; Jer. ii. 20, iii. 6; Hosea iv. 13.) Baal, the sun-god, was the idol especially worshipped upon the hills.

(3) **To the rivers, and to the valleys.**—These words stand to each other in the same relation as "mountains and hills," that is, they are specifications of the same general character. The word frequently occurring, and uniformly translated in Ezekiel *rivers*, would be better rendered *ravines*. It is a deep sort of valley, along which, at times, a stream might run. Such places were also favourite places for idolatrous rites (see 2 Kings xxiii. 10; Isa. lvii. 5, 6; Jer. vii. 31, xxxii. 35), especially for the worship of the Phœnician Astaroth, the female divinity worshipped in conjunction with Baal. The same putting together of mountains and hills, valleys and ravines, occurs again in chaps. xxxv. 8, xxxvi. 4, 6. By the expression, "I, even I," strong emphasis is placed on the fact that these judgments are from God. Inasmuch as, like most other events in the world, they were to be wrought out by human instrumentality, the attention might easily be taken up with the secondary causes; but by thus declaring them beforehand, and claiming them as His own work, God would make it evident that all was from Him.

(4) **Your images.**—The original word indicates, as is shown in the margin, that these were images used in connection with the worship of the sun. The whole verse is taken from Lev. xxvi. 30. The same woes were there foretold by Moses in the contingency of the people's disobedience; that contingency had now come to pass, the promised judgments had already begun, and Ezekiel declares that the fulfilment of them was close at hand.

Your slain men before your idols.—Their idols should be worshipped no longer by the living, but by the prostrate bodies of their dead worshippers. In this and the following verse a kind of poetic justice is described. There was nothing so utterly defiling under the Mosaic law as the touch of a dead body. (See Num. ix. 6—10; 2 Kings xxiii. 14, 16.) The Israelites had defiled the land with idols, now the idols themselves should be defiled with their dead bodies.

(6) **May be abolished.**—The word *abolished* is a strong one, meaning utterly obliterated, wiped out. This was what Israel should have done to the nations who inhabited Canaan before them; they and their works should have been so utterly blotted out that no temptations from them should have remained. But Israel had failed to observe the Divine command, and now in turn their works, done in imitation of the guilty nations they had supplanted, must be blotted out.

(7) **And ye shall know.**—As this prophecy began in verse 2 with an address to the mountains, many consider that, by a strong poetic figure, they are still referred to by the pronoun *ye*. It is better, however, to consider that as the discourse has gone on, the figure has gradually been dropped, and the people are spoken to directly. In the same way, the change of the pronoun from the third to the second person, as in verse 5, is very frequent in Ezekiel.

(8) **Yet will I leave a remnant.**—In verses 8—10 the general gloom of this prophecy of judgment is lightened for a moment by the mention of the remnant who shall be brought by their afflictions "to know that I am the Lord" in a far higher and better sense than those mentioned in verse 7. This Divine plan pursued from the beginning, as is shown by St. Paul in Rom. ix. 6—13, of purifying the people by setting aside the mass, and showing mercy to a

be scattered through the countries.
(9) And they that escape of you shall re-
member me among the nations whither
they shall be carried captives, because
I am broken with their whorish heart,
which hath departed from me, and with
their eyes, which go a whoring after
their idols: and they shall lothe them-
selves for the evils which they have
committed in all their abominations.
(10) And they shall know that I *am* the
LORD, *and that* I have not said in vain
that I would do this evil unto them.
(11) Thus saith the Lord GOD; Smite
[a]with thine hand, and stamp with thy
foot, and say, Alas for all the evil abo-
minations of the house of Israel! for
they shall fall by the sword, by the
famine, and by the pestilence. (12) He
that is far off shall die of the pestilence;
and he that is near shall fall by the
sword; and he that remaineth and is
besieged shall die by the famine: thus
will I accomplish my fury upon them.
(13) Then shall ye know that I *am* the
LORD, when their slain *men* shall be
among their idols round about their
altars, upon every high hill, in all the
tops of the mountains, and under every
green tree, and under every thick oak,
the place where they did offer sweet
savour to all their idols. (14) So will I
stretch out my hand upon them, and
make the land desolate, yea, [1]more deso-
late than the wilderness toward Diblath,
in all their habitations: and they shall
know that I *am* the LORD.

CHAPTER VII.—(1) Moreover the
word of the LORD came unto me, say-
ing, (2) Also, thou son of man, thus saith
the Lord GOD unto the land of Israel;
An end, the end is come upon the four
corners of the land. (3) Now *is* the end
come upon thee, and I will send mine
anger upon thee, and will judge thee

a ch. 21. 14.

1 Or, *desolate from the wilderness.*

---

remnant, looks far beyond the Babylonish captivity, as is shown by the parallel prophecy of Zechariah, uttered after the return from that captivity, "They shall remember me in far countries; and they shall live with their children, and turn again" (Zech. x. 9). Beyond this brief glimpse at the remnant, however, the cloud settles down again upon the prophecy; for the period until the destruction of Jerusalem, now but a few years off, must be almost exclusively a period of the denunciation of judgment.

(9) **Because I am broken.**—The verb in the Hebrew is passive in form, but it is better to take it, with most modern commentators, as a middle, in a transitive sense, "Because I have broken their whorish heart . . . and their eyes," the eyes being mentioned as the means by which their hearts had been enticed to evil. Here, as constantly in all parts of Scripture, apostacy from God is described under the figure of unfaithfulness in the marriage relation. "They shall loathe themselves" indicates a true repentance; they shall loathe the sin and themselves for having committed it. Thus their sin has drawn down punishment; punishment has destroyed many, but brought a "remnant" to repentance; and repentance leads to a true knowledge of God, and communion with Him. The Divine word and act has not been "in vain."

(11) **Smite with thine hand, and stamp with thy foot.**—The prophecy returns again to its heavy tidings of woe. To clap the hands and stamp the feet, either singly (Num. xxiv. 10; chaps. xxi. 14, 17, xxii. 13) or together (chap. xxv. 6), is a gesture of strong emotion or earnestness of purpose. The prophet is here directed to use it as indicating God's unchangeable determination united to a sense of grievous wrong.

(12) **That is far off . . . that is near.**—That is, all, wherever they may be, shall be reached and overwhelmed by the coming judgments; yet not in such wise that we are to think of one kind of judgment as especially reserved for one class, and another kind for another. The different forms of punishment shall all fall upon the people; and they that escape one shall fall by another.

(13) **Upon every high hill.**—The various localities especially selected for idolatrous rites are enumerated one after another, to give more vividness and graphic character to the whole judgment. The words "sweet savour" are constantly applied to the commanded sacrifices to the Lord, and are here used ironically of the idol sacrifices.

(14) **More desolate than the wilderness toward Diblath.**—The name *Diblath* does not occur elsewhere; but *Diblathaim*, the dual form, is mentioned in Num. xxxiii. 46, 47, Jer. xlviii. 22, as a double city on the eastern border of Moab, beyond which lay the great desert which stretches thence eastward, nearly to the Euphrates. It was customary to call any wilderness by the name of the nearest town. (See 1 Sam. xxiii. 14, 15, 24, 25, xxv. 2, &c.) That wilderness appears from this passage to have been proverbial for its desolation.

VII.

The prophecy of this chapter is occupied with the nearness and the completeness of the judgment already foretold. It takes the form, to some extent, of a song of lamentation; and is more thoroughly poetic in its structure than anything which has gone before.

(2) **The four corners.** — A frequent Scriptural phrase for every part. (Comp. Isa. xi. 12; Rev. vii. 1.) The origin of the expression is to be sought, not in any supposed popular belief that the earth was square, but in the fact that so many common things had just four sides or four corners (see Exod. xxv. 12, xxvii. 2; Job i. 19; Acts x. 11, &c.), that the phrase came naturally to be a common expression of universality. "An end, the end," is a repetition for the sake of emphasis. It occurs again in verse 6, and, in varied words, also in verses 10, 12, and 26.

Verses 3 and 4 are repeated almost exactly in verses

according to thy ways, and will [1]recom-
pense upon thee all thine abominations.
(4) And mine eye shall not spare thee,
neither will I have pity: but I will
recompense thy ways upon thee, and
thine abominations shall be in the midst
of thee: and ye shall know that I *am*
the LORD.
(5) Thus saith the Lord GOD; An evil,
an only evil, behold, is come. (6) An end
is come, the end is come: it [2]watcheth
for thee; behold, it is come. (7) The
morning is come unto thee, O thou that
dwellest in the land: the time is come,
the day of trouble *is* near, and not
the [3]sounding again of the mountains.
(8) Now will I shortly pour out my fury
upon thee, and accomplish mine anger
upon thee: and I will judge thee accord-
ing to thy ways, and will recompense
thee for all thine abominations. (9) And
mine eye shall not spare, neither will I
have pity: I will recompense [4]thee ac-
cording to thy ways and thine abomina-
tions *that* are in the midst of thee; and
ye shall know that I *am* the LORD that
smiteth.
(10) Behold the day, behold, it is come:
the morning is gone forth; the rod hath
blossomed, pride hath budded. (11) Vio-
lence is risen up into a rod of wicked-
ness: none of them *shall remain*, nor of
their [5]multitude, nor of any of [6]their's:
neither *shall there be* wailing for them.
(12) The time is come, the day draweth
near: let not the buyer rejoice, nor the
seller mourn: for wrath *is* upon all the
multitude thereof. (13) For the seller
shall not return to that which is sold,
[7]although they were yet alive: for the
vision *is* touching the whole multitude
thereof, *which* shall not return; neither
shall any strengthen himself [8]in [9]the
iniquity of his life. (14) They have blown
the trumpet, even to make all ready;
but none goeth to the battle: for

1 Heb., *give.*

2 Heb., *awaketh against thee.*

3 Or, *echo.*

4 Heb., *upon thee.*

5 Or, *tumult.*

6 Or, *their tumultuous persons.*

7 Heb., *though their life were yet among the living.*

8 Or, *whose life is in his iniquity.*

9 Heb., *his iniquity.*

---

8 and 9. The frequent repetitions of this chapter are designed, and give great force to the denunciation of woe. "Thine abominations are in the midst of thee," in the sense of calling down punishment upon them, as appears from the parallel in verse 9.

(5) **An only evil.**—That is, an evil so all-embracing as to be complete in itself, and need no repetition. Compare the same thought in Nahum i. 9, "affliction shall not rise up the second time." Some MSS., and the Chaldee, by the alteration of one letter, read "evil after evil," as in verse 26.

(7) **The morning is come unto thee.**—The word here used is not the usual one for *morning.* This word occurs elsewhere only in verse 10 and Isa. xxviii. 5, where it is translated *crown.* There is much difference of opinion both as to its derivation and its meaning. The most probable sense is *circuit*—"the circuit of thy sins is finished, and the end is come upon thee."

The sounding again of the mountains.—This is again a peculiar word, occurring only here; but it is nearly like and probably has the same meaning as the word in Isa. xvi. 10, Jer. xxv. 10, denoting the joyous sounds of the people, especially at harvest-time, filling the land and echoing back from the mountains. Instead of this shall be the tumult (rather the trouble) of the day of war. (See the opposite contrast in Exod. xxxii. 17, 18.)

(9) **The Lord that smiteth.**—In verse 4 it is only said, "Ye shall know that I am the LORD," without saying in what respect; here this is specified—they shall know that God is a God of judgment, and that these calamities are from Him.

(10) **The morning is gone forth.**—The same word as in verse 7, and in the same sense—the circle is complete, the end is reached, sin hath brought forth death. "The rod" is commonly understood of the Chaldæan conqueror; but as the word is the same for *rod* and for *tribe,* and is very often used in the latter sense, it will be more in accordance with the connection to understand here a play upon the word. There will be then an allusion to the rods of the tribes in Num. xvii. 8. There the rod of Aaron was made to bud and blossom by Divine power in evidence of his having been chosen of God; here the rod representing the tribe at Jerusalem in its self-will and pride has budded and blossomed to its destruction. So the description continues in the next verse, "Violence is risen up into a rod of wickedness." Not a rod for the punishment of wickedness; but into a wicked people.

(11) **Neither shall there be wailing for them.**—The word for *wailing* is another of those words occurring only in this passage which have been variously understood. It is now generally taken for that which is glorious or beautiful. Israel has run its circle; prosperity has developed pride, and pride has culminated in all wickedness; now the end has come, they and their tumult (marg., *for multitude*) disappear together, and of their glory there shall be nothing left.

(13) **The seller shall not return.**—The previous verse described the general cessation of all the business of life in the utter desolation of the land. Among the Israelites the most important buying and selling was that of land, and it was provided in the law (Lev. xxv 14—16) that this should in no case extend beyond the year of jubilee, when all land must revert to its possessor by inheritance. The seller in that year should return to his possession. Now it is foretold that the desolation shall continue so long that, even if the seller lived, he should be unable to avail himself of the jubilee year. "It is a natural thing to rejoice in the purchase of property, and to mourn over its sale, but when slavery and captivity stare you in the face, rejoicing and mourning are equally absurd" (S. Jerome). The idea of the latter part of the verse is, that no one shall grow strong since his life is passed in iniquity.

(14) **None goeth to the battle.**—The last thought is followed up here. The people are so enfeebled by their sins as to have no power against the enemy.

my wrath *is* upon all the multitude
thereof.
(15) The sword *is* without, and the
pestilence and the famine within: he
that *is* in the field shall die with the
sword; and he that *is* in the city, famine
and pestilence shall devour him. (16) But
they that escape of them shall escape,
and shall be on the mountains like doves
of the valleys, all of them mourning,
every one for his iniquity. (17) All [a]hands
shall be feeble, and all knees shall [1]be
weak *as* water. (18) They shall also [b]gird
themselves with sackcloth, and horror
shall cover them; and shame *shall be*
upon all faces, and baldness upon all
their heads. (19) They shall cast their
silver in the streets, and their gold shall
be [2]removed: their [c]silver and their gold
shall not be able to deliver them in the
day of the wrath of the LORD: they
shall not satisfy their souls, neither fill
their bowels: [3]because it is the stum-
blingblock of their iniquity. (20) As for
the beauty of his ornament, he set it in
majesty: but they made the images of
their abominations *and* of their detest-
able things therein: therefore have I
[4]set it far from them. (21) And I will
give it into the hands of the strangers
for a prey, and to the wicked of the
earth for a spoil; and they shall pollute
it. (22) My face will I turn also from
them, and they shall pollute my secret
place: for the [5]robbers shall enter into
it, and defile it.
(23) Make a chain: for the land is full
of bloody crimes, and the city is full of
violence. (24) Wherefore I will bring the
worst of the heathen, and they shall pos-
sess their houses: I will also make the
pomp of the strong to cease; and [6]their
holy places shall be defiled. (25) [7]Destruc-
tion cometh; and they shall seek peace,
and *there shall be* none. (26) Mischief
shall come upon mischief, and rumour
shall be upon rumour; then shall they
seek a vision of the prophet; but the

a Isa. 13. 7; Jer. 6. 24

1 Heb., *go into water.*

b Isa. 15. 2, 3; Jer. 48. 37.

2 Heb., *for a separation,* or, *uncleanness.*

c Prov. 11. 4; Zeph. 1. 18; Ecclus. 5. 8.

3 Or, *because their iniquity is their stumblingblock.*

4 Or, *made it unto them an unclean thing.*

5 Or, *burglers.*

6 Or, *they shall inherit their holy places.*

7 Heb., *Cutting off.*

Consequently (verse 15) they shall all perish, directly or indirectly, at the hands of their foes.

(16) **Like doves of the valleys.**—To this general destruction there will be exceptions, as generally in war there are fugitives and captives; but these, like doves whose home is in the valleys driven by fear to the mountains, shall mourn in their exile. In the mourning "every one for his iniquity," iniquity is to be understood in the sense of the punishment for iniquity; the thought of repentance is not here brought forward. Their utter discouragement and feebleness and grief are further described in verses 17, 18.

(19) **Cast their silver in the streets.**—As in the rout of an army the soldier throws away everything, even his most valuable things, as impediments to his flight and temptations to the pursuing enemy, so the Israelites in their terror should abandon everything. Their riches will be utterly unavailing. The expression in the original is even stronger: their gold shall be to them "an unclean thing," "filth," because they shall perceive that it has been to them an occasion of sin.

(20) **In majesty.**—Rather, *for pride.* That which had been given them "for the beauty of ornament," viz., their silver and gold (verse 19), they had perverted to purposes of pride. Nay, further, they had even made their idols of it; therefore God "set it far from them." The same strong word is used here as in verse 19 = made it filth unto them. The singular and plural pronouns, "he," "his," "they," "their," "them," all alike refer to the people.

(22) **My secret place.**—The holy of holies, sacredly guarded from all intrusion, and representing the very culmination both of the religion and of the national life of Israel, shall be polluted. If the pronoun "they" represents any one in particular, it must be the Chaldæans; but it is better to take the verb, as often in the third person plural, impersonally, *i.e.,* "shall be polluted." The agents in this pollution are immediately mentioned as "the robbers," *i.e.,* the Chaldæan armies.

(23) **Make a chain.**—In the midst of this plain prophecy the strong tendency of the prophet's mind still runs to the symbolic act; but this can be thought of here only as done in word. The chain is to bind captive the guilty people.

(24) **Worst of the heathen.**—*Worst* refers to the power and thoroughness of their work against the Israelites. (Comp. Deut. xxviii. 49, 50; also Lev. xxvi. 19, where the word here rendered "pomp of the strong" is translated "pride of power.") Both passages are the warnings, long ages ago, of the judgments now declared to be close at hand. "*Their* holy places;" no longer God's, since He has abandoned them for the sin of the people. (See chap. xi. 23.)

(25) **Destruction cometh.**—This is another of the peculiar words occurring only in this chapter. It is generally explained of the dismay and horror accompanying great judgments, and vividly described by our Lord as "men's hearts failing them for fear" (Luke xxi. 26).

(26) **Then shall they seek a vision.**—Comp. chap. xx. 1—3. The three chief sources of counsel, the prophets, the priests, and the elders, are all represented as applied to in vain. God had forsaken the people who had rejected Him. (Comp. Prov. i. 28, and the story of Saul's despair at his abandonment by God, 1 Sam. xxviii. 15.) In the following verse the trouble is described as affecting all classes alike, the king, the prince, and the people of the land, and, further, as being the fitting consequence and retribution of their own chosen way.

Here closes the first series of Ezekiel's prophecies, extending from the beginning of the fourth to the end of the seventh chapter. They were all uttered within the period of a year and two months. Like the following series (chaps. viii.—xix), they begin with a remarkable series of symbolic acts, or rather of descriptions of such acts, and are continued by plain prophecies. Ezekiel and his fellow-captives had now been between five

law shall perish from the priest, and
counsel from the ancients. (27) The king
shall mourn, and the prince shall be
clothed with desolation, and the hands of
the people of the land shall be troubled:
I will do unto them after their way, and
[1] according to their deserts will I judge
them; and they shall know that I *am*
the LORD.

CHAPTER VIII.—(1) And it came to
pass in the sixth year, in the sixth *month*,
in the fifth *day* of the month, *as* I sat in
mine house, and the elders of Judah sat
before me, that the hand of the Lord
GOD fell there upon me. (2) Then I
beheld, and lo a likeness as the appear-
ance of fire: from the appearance of his
loins even downward, fire; and from his
loins even upward, as the appearance
of brightness, as the colour of amber.
(3) And he [a] put forth the form of an

1 Heb., *with their judgments.*

a Dan. 5. 5.

B.C. 594.

---

and six years in exile, and they still looked to Jerusalem and the Temple as their pride and the strength of their nation, and doubtless many of them hoped to be able to return there to lead again their former lives. There could be no hope of affecting a thorough and lasting reformation among the people except by utterly dashing these hopes to the ground, and showing that the people must be led to repentance through a thorough humiliation and heavy punishment. Such is the purpose of these prophecies, and it is carried out with extraordinary vigour and power of language.

VIII.

Here begins a fresh series of prophecies, extending through chap. xix. This is introduced as before, by a remarkable vision which, with its accompanying messages, occupies chaps viii.—xi. The date (chap. viii. 1) shows that this series began just a year and two months after Ezekiel's call to the prophetic office (chap. i. 1, 2), while the next date (chap. xx. 1) allows eleven months and five days for its completion. As in the former case, it is probable that its several prophecies, twelve or thirteen in all, were uttered at short intervals, allowing time for each to produce its impression upon the people. The previous series of prophecies was directed against the whole nation, including alike those already in captivity, and those who remained behind in Jerusalem; but that the exiles might understand the reason, and therefore the certainty of the impending judgment upon Jerusalem, it was necessary that the extreme sinfulness of the people remaining there should be especially set forth. Accordingly, the vision of chaps. viii.—xi., and the following prophecies of chap. xii., are directed to Jerusalem exclusively. Afterwards they again become more general, and there are some especially relating to the exiles; but still this whole section, to chap. xix. inclusive, is mainly occupied with the people still remaining in their own land.

The prophet is transported in vision to Jerusalem, and to the Temple itself (chap. viii. 1—4), where he is first made to see the various idolatries of Israel (chap. viii. 5—18), and then the consequent judgment whereby all who have not received the mark of God upon their foreheads are to be destroyed (chap. ix.); he sees the city itself given over to fire, and the glory of the Lord depart from the Temple (chap. x.); after this he is charged to pronounce judgment, especially upon certain leaders of the people (chap. xi. 1—13), with God's mercy and blessing upon a repenting remnant (chap. xi. 14—21); then the glory of the Lord leaves the city altogether (verses 22, 23), and the prophet is brought back in vision to declare what he has seen to his fellow-captives (verses 24, 25). This closes the vision, after which he is directed to set forth the impending captivity by a symbolical action interpreted to the people by a plain prophecy, and this is followed by two short further prophecies, meeting the objection that there is no reason to fear the judgment because its coming is delayed (chap. xii.). Chap. xiii. is directed against false prophets. The first half of chap. xiv. is called out by an inquiry from the elders, but is made general against any attempt to combine asking counsel of the Lord with alienation of the heart from Him, recurring again (verses 9, 10) to the case of the false prophets; the latter half of the chapter is another prophecy, showing the certainty and terribleness of the judgment upon Jerusalem. In chap. xv. the same thing is set forth under the parable of the vine; and in chap. xvi. still the same is declared with a recounting of Israel's strange history, under the figure of matrimonial unfaithfulness. Still another parable is employed in chap. xvii. for the purpose of showing that Zedekiah and his court shall utterly fail to deliver them, and shall themselves be carried captive, while there shall again be prosperity under his descendant. Chap. xviii. is occupied with showing that God's punishments come upon the people for their own sins, and not for those of their fathers; while chap. xix. closes this whole series of prophecies with a lament over the captivity and the desolated country.

(1) **The elders of Judah sat before me.**—It is plain from this that Ezekiel, as a priest, and now already known as a prophet, was held in consideration among the captives. It also appears that he lived in his own house. Judah is not used in contradistinction to Israel; but as the captives were chiefly of the tribe of Judah, so their elders were known as "the elders of Judah."

(2) **A likeness as the appearance of fire.**—This is not, as often supposed, a reappearance of the vision of chap. i. That vision bursts again on the prophet after he has been carried in the spirit to the Temple at Jerusalem (verse 4). This is not expressly described as a human form, but from the mention of the loins, and of "the form of an hand," in verse 3 it is implied that it was so. No further description is given, except that it was something bright and glorious like fire; and by the repetition of the words "likeness," "appearance," and "form of an hand," the prophet here, as in chap. i., takes pains to show that it was only a vision, not an outward reality. It is also to be remembered that this and the subsequent vision occurred while the elders were sitting before the prophet. They saw nothing themselves, but must have witnessed his ecstasy, and thus have been prepared for his telling them at its close (chap. xi. 25) "all the things that the Lord had showed" him. "The colour of amber" is the same as in chap. i. 4, where see Note.

(3) **Took me by a lock of mine head.**—Not, of course, literally, in the body, but in vision. Ezekiel

hand, and took me by a lock of mine
head; and the spirit lifted me up be-
tween the earth and the heaven, and
brought me in the visions of God to
Jerusalem, to the door of the inner gate
that looketh toward the north; where
was the seat of the image of jealousy,
which provoketh to jealousy. (4) And,
behold, the glory of the God of Israel
was there, according to the vision that I
[a] saw in the plain.

(5) Then said he unto me, Son of man,
lift up thine eyes now the way toward
the north. So I lifted up mine eyes the
way toward the north, and behold north-
ward at the gate of the altar this image
of jealousy in the entry. (6) He said
furthermore unto me, Son of man, seest
thou what they do? *even* the great abo-
minations that the house of Israel com-
mitteth here, that I should go far off
from my sanctuary? but turn thee yet
again, *and* thou shalt see greater abomi-
nations.

(7) And he brought me to the door of
the court; and when I looked, behold a

a ch. i. 28.

---

did not actually leave Chaldæa at all, as is shown by chap. xi. 24.

The door of the inner gate.—This is one of the gates which led from the court of the people to the court of the priests which was on a higher level. In the account of the building of the temple there is no mention of gates leading from the one to the other, but they would naturally have been placed there, as we know they were in the later temple of Herod. The particular gate was the one "which looketh toward the north," as the one by which the priests went directly to the great altar.

The image of jealousy is explained in the following clause, "which provoketh to jealousy." It is not necessary to consider "jealousy" as a proper name—the name of any particular heathen divinity—but rather as a descriptive name, an image which aroused the Divine indignation. It has even been thought that it is not meant to indicate any particular idol, but is only a picture to set forth the prevailing idolatry. It is, however, altogether probable that at this time there actually were heathen idols set up in the temple, and nothing could give a more vivid picture of the corruption of priests and people alike than the mention of their presence. Idolatry had been growing more general and more bold from the time of Solomon. He built places of worship for the various idols of his wives "in the hill that is before Jerusalem" (1 Kings xi. 7); but Ahaz, under the influence of the Assyrian king, had placed an idolatrous altar in the temple itself, removing the brazen altar to make room (2 Kings xvi. 10—16), and Manasseh afterwards did the same (2 Kings xxi. 4). All the subsequent kings of Judah, except Josiah, were wicked men, and although this particular sin is not distinctly recorded of Zedekiah, yet it seems altogether likely that he too made use of the temple for idolatrous worship, and that Ezekiel in vision now saw his idols standing in the court.

(4) **The glory of the God of Israel was there.**—Not the glory of the Lord filling the temple as in the days of old, but the glory "according to the vision that I saw in the plain"—*i.e.*, the same vision which had before appeared to the prophet now in his vision—a vision within a vision—appeared to him again in the temple. The identity of the vision is again particularly mentioned in chap. x. 15, 22, and even without this would be plain from the description given of it in chap. x. At the same time, various particulars are mentioned (as in chap. x. 12) which were omitted in chap. i., and others are mentioned there which are omitted here, as the cloud and the firmament (chap. i. 4, 22); and there are also some entirely new features introduced, as the "six men" and "the man clothed in linen" (chap. ix. 2), for which there was no occasion in the former vision. "The God of Israel" is emphatic, the God who had loved and chosen Israel, and Whom Israel should have served, in contrast with the idol which they had placed in His temple.

(5) **The way toward the north.**—This shows that Ezekiel in his vision was within the court of the priests, as otherwise he could not have looked *toward* the north to see the idol in the north gate. He had already seen this; but now his attention is directed to it particularly. It was not enough that he should see it; it was to be especially pointed out as a part of the reason for the Divine judgments. The expression, "Gate of the altar," may find an additional explanation in the fact mentioned in 2 Kings xvi. 14, that Ahaz removed the altar towards the north, and thus would have placed it very near this gate.

(6) **That I should go far off from my sanctuary.**—In the original this is simply an infinitive, without any subject expressed, "for the removing far off," and may therefore be understood either of the removing of the people or of the Divine abandonment of the sanctuary. The latter sense, however, which is that given in the Authorised Version, is more probable and more in accordance with the whole teaching of the vision. There was a strong feeling among the people that they were safe at Jerusalem; God, Whom they still regarded, notwithstanding their idolatries, as a powerful national God, would certainly protect His temple. It is the office of the prophet to show that the transgressions of the people led, as their natural consequence, to his giving over the city to desolation. The "great abominations" spoken of are the constant refrain of this chapter (verses 9, 13, 15, 17). The people's own acts make necessary the judgments impending over them. Still worse is in store.

(7) **To the door of the court.**—This is clearly a different place from that in which the prophet had hitherto been in his vision, and yet is not so described that its locality can be certainly fixed. He had been inside the inner court near its north gate; in verse 14 he is taken to the north gate of the outer enclosure of the temple precincts. It is probable, therefore, that this was between them. We do not know from the description of Solomon's temple that there were any other than the inner and the outer courts; but as there were others in the temple of Herod built upon the same area, it is altogether likely that there was a further division, and that it was to such a dividing wall, with chambers attached, that the prophet was now brought. Here he finds a hole, or window, too small

hole in the wall. (8) Then said he unto
me, Son of man, dig now in the wall:
and when I had digged in the wall, be-
hold a door. (9) And he said unto me,
Go in, and behold the wicked abomina-
tions that they do here. (10) So I went
in and saw; and behold every form of
creeping things, and abominable beasts,
and all the idols of the house of Israel,
pourtrayed upon the wall round about.
(11) And there stood before them seventy
men of the ancients of the house of
Israel, and in the midst of them stood
Jaazaniah the son of Shaphan, with
every man his censer in his hand; and
a thick cloud of incense went up.
(12) Then said he unto me, Son of man,
hast thou seen what the ancients of the
house of Israel do in the dark, every man
in the chambers of his imagery? for they
say, [a]The LORD seeth us not; the LORD
hath forsaken the earth.

a ch. 9. 9.

---

for entrance, and is directed to enlarge it that he may go in. Having done so, he finds a door which he is told to enter. The object of this part of the vision is to show the extreme secrecy of what he is now to see—a secrecy made necessary by the connection of this idolatry with Egypt, the foe of Chaldæa. Any question in regard to the way the idolaters themselves entered is out of place, as all is only in vision.

(10) **Every form of creeping things, and abominable beasts.**—The description of the idolatrous rites here practised clearly indicates their Egyptian origin. Creature worship was indeed practised among other nations, and the painting of idolatrous objects upon walls is expressly mentioned in chap. xxiii. 14—16, as introduced by the Jews from Chaldæa; yet the combination is so thoroughly Egyptian, and the political relations of the time also point so strongly in the same direction, that the origin seems settled. It was during this period that Jeremiah was obliged to contend strenuously against the desire of a considerable part of the court to enter into an alliance with Egypt against Chaldæa. The party among the Jews who sought an Egyptian alliance, as abundantly appears from Jeremiah, was also the party most unwilling to submit to the Divine commandments. They were the persons who engaged in this creature-worship; and they are here represented as constituting the leaders of the nation. As if this were not enough, "all the idols of the house of Israel," gathered from every quarter, were also portrayed upon the walls.

(11) **Seventy men of the ancients of the house of Israel.**—There may have been no enclosed chamber about the courts of the temple capable of actually containing so large a number; but again we are to remember that as this is in vision and for purposes of instruction, it is not necessary that all the details should be actually possible. The seventy elders were not the sanhedrin, which was not constituted until after the return from Babylon; but the number has probable reference to the seventy chosen to enjoy with Moses the Theophany of Exod. xxiv. 9, 10, and the other seventy selected to share with him in the gifts of the Spirit (Num. xi. 16). In contrast with those selected for especial nearness to God, these seventy are engaged in abominations most abhorrent to Him.

Jaazaniah, the son of Shaphan.—*Son* is perhaps used here, as often in Scripture, in the sense of *grandson.* In this case he may have been the same with "Jaazaniah, the son of Azur," mentioned in xi. 1 as one of the wicked princes of the people, against whom Ezekiel was directed to prophesy. It is hardly probable that two persons of the same character and the same (not very common) name should have been among the leaders of the people at the same time. The mention of his grandfather here would be appropriate, as bringing out the contrast in their characters, and showing the change for the worse that had been going on among the people. Shaphan was an officer of the court of King Josiah, and active in the reformation instituted by him (2 Kings xxii. 3, 14); while his son (Elasah) was one of the messengers by whom Jeremiah sent his prophecies to the Captivity (Jer. xxix. 3); and another son, Gemariah, was a scribe, having a chamber "in the higher court, at the entry of the new gate of the Lord's house," in the fourth year of Jehoiakim (Jer. xxxvi. 10). At the same time his grandson, Michaiah, was sufficiently prominent at court to join in the intercession of the princes against the destruction of Jeremiah's prophecies (*ib.* 11, 25); and a little later, in the general captivity of the ninth year of Zedekiah, another grandson, Gedaliah, had the person of Jeremiah given into his charge (Jer. xxxix. 14; xl. 5), and was made governor over the remnant of the people (Jer. xl. 11). Such being the family connections of Jaazaniah, the corruption which could make him a leader of idolatry is strongly shown.

With every man his censer in his hand.—The burning of incense was the exclusive function of the priesthood (Num. xvi.; 2 Chron. xxvi. 16—18); and it was alike the necessity and the choice of the idolaters of Israel to devolve this office upon those who were not of the Aaronic family. (Comp. 1 Kings xii. 31.) When the seventy elders offered incense to their idols they claimed thereby to be the priests of those idols.

(12) **Do in the dark,** *i.e.,* in secret. Hence the difficulty of access to the place of their worship. The ordinary idolatries of Israel, as of most heathen, consisted in the worship of the true, or of a supposed spiritual Deity, by means of sensible images (comp. Exod. xxxii. 8). This was open and public enough at Jerusalem at this time; but the peculiar sin here portrayed was the actual worship of the creature by means of images and paintings. This, although joined in by the chief people of the nation, was practised secretly, perhaps, not only for the purpose of concealing its Egyptian tendencies from the Chaldæans, but also to throw over it the charm of mystery, as was so common among the heathen.

Every man in the chambers of his imagery.—By "chambers of imagery" (the same word as in Lev. xxvi. 1) is intended chambers painted with images like the one now shown to the prophet. This was not a solitary case; on the contrary, it was but an example of what was done everywhere. The people stifled the voice of conscience then, as in every age, by saying "The LORD seeth us not," comp. Pss. x. 11, xciv. 7, &c. Yet, besides this, they argued, doubtless from the calamities that had already fallen upon their country, "the LORD hath forsaken the earth," or,

(13) He said also unto me, Turn thee
yet again, *and* thou shalt see greater
abominations that they do. (14) Then he
brought me to the door of the gate of
the LORD's house which *was* toward the
north; and, behold, there sat women
weeping for Tammuz. (15) Then said he
unto me, Hast thou seen *this,* O son of
man? turn thee yet again, *and* thou
shalt see greater abominations than
these.

(16) And he brought me into the inner
court of the LORD's house, and, behold,
at the door of the temple of the LORD,
between the porch and the altar, *were*
about five and twenty men, with their
backs toward the temple of the LORD,
and their faces toward the east; and
they worshipped the sun toward the
east. (17) Then he said unto me, Hast
thou seen *this,* O son of man? [1] Is it a
light thing to the house of Judah that
they commit the abominations which
they commit here? for they have filled
the land with violence, and have re-
turned to provoke me to anger: and,
lo, they put the branch to their nose.
(18) Therefore will I also deal in fury:
mine [a] eye shall not spare, neither will I
have pity: and though they [b] cry in mine
ears with a loud voice, *yet* will I not hear
them.

CHAPTER IX.—(1) He cried also in
mine ears with a loud voice, saying,
Cause them that have charge over the

1 Or, *Is there any thing lighter than to commit.*

a ch. 5. 11; & 7. 4.

b Pro. 1. 28; Isa. 1. 15; Jer. 11. 11; Mic. 3. 4.

---

rather, the land; and therefore they must have recourse to other help. But the prophet was to see yet worse things.

(14) **Women weeping for Tammuz.**—The prophet is now taken to the north gate of the outer enclosure of the Temple courts, and there sees a new and exceedingly corrupt form of idolatry. Tammuz is nowhere else mentioned in Scripture, but is identified by ancient tradition (incorporated into the Vulg.) with the Greek Adonis, the beloved of Venus. The name *Adonis* could not well have been used, because in its Hebrew form it means *Lord,* and is frequently used of God. His worship is first heard of in Phœnicia, and was wide-spread throughout Syria and the adjacent countries. As the creature worship before mentioned was undoubtedly connected with political reasons, while aid was being sought from Egypt, so the worship of Adonis may have been affected by the league which Zedekiah attempted to form (Jer. xxvii. 1—11) with the Edomites, Moabites, Ammonites, and Philistines against Nebuchadnezzar. The annual feast of Adonis consisted of a mourning by the women for his death, followed by a rejoicing over his return to life, and was accompanied by great abominations and licentiousness. The myth of Adonis was also closely associated with the worship of nature. This festival did not fall in the "sixth month," but the description is not necessarily of what was actually occurring at the moment; there is brought before the prophet's vision a representation of the wickedness practised at various times in Jerusalem. Women engaged in the service of idolatry near the Temple are mentioned in 2 Kings xxiii. 7. (Comp. Jer. vii. 18.)

Thus far, the prophet has seen in the different courts of the Temple the general image worship of the people, then the creature worship of their elders, and now the corrupt and debasing rites of their women.

(16) **Between the porch and the altar.**—Ezekiel now returns to the court of the priests, and there sees —not *about,* but *as it were* (referring to the nature of the vision)—" twenty-five men." These are probably the high priest and the heads of the twenty-four courses, representing the whole body of the priests, as the elders represented the whole body of the people. They were standing between the altar and the Temple, therefore in the most sacred part of the court, and there, turning their backs upon the Temple of the Lord, worshipped the sun. The adoration of the sun, probably the earliest form of false religion, was the especial worship of Persia, but had been long since practised by the kings and people of Judah (2 Kings xxiii. 5, 11). Thus all classes of the nation are seen to be involved in common sin; and the priests particularly, the especial guardians of true religion, are found practising this sin under circumstances of peculiar insult to God. That the "chief priests" did pollute the sanctuary at this time is expressly asserted in the history at 2 Chron. xxxvi. 14.

(17) **For they have filled the land with violence.**—Corruption in religion here, as always, bore its proper fruit in moral deterioration. A people who go astray from their duty to God are always found to neglect also their duty to man. Israel had before fallen into great and grievous sins. Within the memory of those still living, the good king Josiah, supported by the prophet Jeremiah and many others, had made great effort at reformation, and had purged the Temple of its abominations; hence God says the people "have *returned* to provoke me to anger."

Put the branch to their nose.—This is an obscure expression, on which the learning and ingenuity of commentators have been spent in vain. It is an allusion to some custom well known at the time, but now lost. The simplest explanation seems to be in a reference to the habit of the Parsees (mentioned by Strabo) in their worship to hold twigs of the tamarisk, palm, and the pomegranate before their mouths.

(18) **Will I not hear them.**—The time for prayer was past. They had rejected God, and when His wrath came upon them it was too late to turn to Him. (See Prov. i. 24—28; Matt. vii. 22, 23.) The possibility of sinning beyond the term of the day of grace is one of the most important lessons of this chapter.

IX.

This chapter forms part of the same continuous vision with the preceding one, but while the former is occupied with the exposure of the sin, this latter specifies the consequent punishment.

(1) **He cried also . . . with a loud voice.**—The pronoun refers to the same Being as throughout

city to draw near, even every man *with*
his destroying weapon in his hand.
(2) And, behold, six men came from the
way of the higher gate, [1]which lieth to-
ward the north, and every man [2]a
slaughter weapon in his hand; and one
man among them *was* clothed with
linen, with a writer's inkhorn [3]by his
side: and they went in, and stood be-
side the brazen altar. (3) And the glory
of the God of Israel was gone up from
the cherub, whereupon he was, to the
threshold of the house. And he called
to the man clothed with linen, which
had the writer's inkhorn by his side;
(4) And the LORD said unto him, Go
through the midst of the city, through
the midst of Jerusalem, and [4]set [a]a mark
upon the foreheads of the men that
sigh and that cry for all the abomina-
tions that be done in the midst thereof.
(5) And to the others he said in [5]mine
hearing, Go ye after him through the
city, and smite: let not your eye spare,

1 Heb., *which is turned.*

2 Heb., *a weapon of his breaking in pieces.*

3 Heb., *upon his loins.*

4 Heb., *mark a mark.*

a Ex. 12. 7. Rev. 7. 3.

5 Heb., *mine ears.*

---

the previous chapter. His nature is sufficiently shown by the prophet's address to Him in verse 8: "Ah, Lord God!" The "loud voice" was to give emphasis to what is said; it is the natural expression of the fierceness of the Divine indignation and wrath.

Them that have charge over the city.—Not earthly officers, but those to whom God has especially entrusted the execution of His will concerning Jerusalem. The word is, no doubt, used often enough of human officers, but such sense is necessarily excluded here by the whole circumstances of the vision. Nor does the phrase "every man" at all indicate that they were human beings, the same expression being constantly used of angels (as in Gen. xviii. 1, 2; Josh. v. 13; Judges xiii. 11; Dan. viii. 16, &c.), and the representation here being plainly that of angelic executioners of God's wrath. They appear only in the light of the administrators of vengeance, the description of them being that each had "his destroying weapon in his hand." This is repeated in the following verse.

(2) **One man among them was clothed with linen.**—He was *among* them, but not of them. There were six with weapons, and this one without a weapon formed the seventh, thus making up the mystical number so often used in Scripture. He was "clothed in linen," the ordinary priestly garment, and the special garment of the high priest at the ceremonies on the great Day of Atonement (Lev. xvi.); yet also used by others, and on other occasions, simply as a garment of purity and of distinction (comp. Dan. x. 5), so that there is no need here to suppose a priestly character attached to this one. He carried in his girdle the "inkhorn," *i.e.*, the little case, containing pens, knife, and ink, commonly worn by the Oriental scribe. There is no occasion to understand this person either, on the one hand, as a representation of the Babylonian god Nebo, "the scribe of heaven," nor, on the other, as is done by many commentators, of our Lord. There is nothing mentioned which can give him any special identification. He is simply a necessity of the vision, an angelic messenger, to mark out those whose faithfulness to God amid the surrounding evil exempts them from the common doom (comp. Rev. vii. 3). This party are seen coming "from the way of the higher gate." The courts of the Temple were built in stages, the innermost the highest. This, then, was the gate of the inner court, and was on the north, both as the place where the prophet had been shown the idolatries, and as the quarter from which the Chaldæan destruction was poured out upon the nation. They took their station "beside the brazen altar," as the central point at once of the true worship of Israel and of the present profanation of that worship.

(3) **The glory . . . to the threshold.**—In chap. viii. 4 the prophet had seen the same vision as he has described in chap. i. standing at the entrance of the court of the priests, and there it still remained. The word *cherub* is here used collectively. Now that special glory above the cherubim, which represented the Divine Being Himself, was gone from its place to the threshold of the house, but is returned again in chap. x. 1. At the same time, there is also suggested the idea that the ordinary presence of God between the cherubim in the Holy of Holies within the Temple has left its place, and come out to the door of the house. The two ideas are indeed distinct, and yet by no means incapable of being blended in the imagery of a vision. The significance of the former is that the command for judgment proceeds from the very Temple itself to which the Pharisaic Jews looked as the pledge of their safety; while the other would mean that the Lord had already begun to forsake His Temple. Both thoughts are true, and both are emphasised in the course of the vision.

(4) **Set a mark upon the foreheads.**—The word for mark is literally a *Tau*, the last letter of the Hebrew alphabet. This, in many of the ancient alphabets, and especially in that in use among the Hebrews up to this time, and long retained upon their coins, was in the form of a cross—X or +. Much stress was laid upon this use of the sign of the cross as the mark for the Divine mercy by the older Christian writers, Tertullian, Origen, Cyprian, and Jerome. This marking was done, it is true, in vision, but the symbolism is taken from such passages as Gen. iv. 15; Exod. xii. 7, 13, xxviii. 36; and it is used several times in the Apocalypse (chaps. vii. 3, ix. 4, xiv. 1). Such marks may be necessary for the guidance of the angelic executors of God's commands, and at all events, the symbolism is of value to the human mind. It is with reference to such Scriptural instances of marking, doubtless, that the Church has provided for the signing of the baptized with the sign of the cross. It is to be observed here that the distinction of the marking has reference wholly and only to character. No regard is paid to birth or position; they and they only are marked who mourned for the prevailing sinfulness, and kept themselves apart from it.

(5) **Go ye after him.**—No interval is allowed. Here, as in the corresponding visions in Revelation referred to above, judgment waits only until those whom mercy will spare have been protected. (Comp. the deliverance of Lot, Gen. xix. 22—25.) The destruction was to be utter and complete, and was to begin at the sanctuary, where the gross sin of the people had culminated. This is one of those many important passages in Scripture (comp. Matt. xxv. 41; Luke xxiii. 30; Rev. vi. 16, &c.) in which God reveals Him-

neither have ye pity: (6) slay [1]utterly old
and young, both maids, and little chil-
dren, and women: but come not near
any man upon whom *is* the mark; and
begin at my sanctuary. Then they
began at the ancient men which *were*
before the house. (7) And he said unto
them, Defile the house, and fill the
courts with the slain: go ye forth.
And they went forth, and slew in the
city.
(8) And it came to pass, while they
were slaying them, and I was left, that
I fell upon my face, and cried, and said,
Ah Lord God! wilt thou destroy all the
residue of Israel in thy pouring out of
thy fury upon Jerusalem?
(9) Then said he unto me, The iniquity
of the house of Israel and Judah *is* ex-
ceeding great, and the land is [2]full of
blood, and the city full of [3]perverseness:
for they say, [a]The Lord hath forsaken
the earth, and the Lord seeth not.
(10) And as for me also, mine [b]eye shall
not spare, neither will I have pity, *but*
I will recompense their way upon their
head. (11) And, behold, the man clothed
with linen, which *had* the inkhorn by his
side, [4]reported the matter, saying, I have
done as thou hast commanded me.

CHAPTER X.—(1) Then I looked,
and, behold, in the [c]firmament that was
above the head of the cherubims there
appeared over them as it were a sapphire
stone, as the appearance of the likeness
of a throne. (2) And he spake unto the
man clothed with linen, and said, Go in
between the wheels, *even* under the
cherub, and fill [5]thine hand with coals
of fire from between the cherubims, and
scatter *them* over the city. And he went
in in my sight. (3) Now the cherubims
stood on the right side of the house,
when the man went in; and the cloud
filled the inner court. (4) Then the glory
of the Lord [6]went up from the cherub,
and stood over the threshold of the
house; and the house was filled with
the cloud, and the court was full of the

1 Heb., *to destruction.*
2 Heb., *filled with.*
3 Or, *wresting of judgment.*
a ch. 8. 12.
b ch. 5. 11; & 7. 4; & 8. 18.
4 Heb., *returned the word.*
c ch. 1. 22.
5 Heb., *the hollow of thine hand.*
6 Heb., *was lifted up.*

self as one who will ultimately take vengeance without pity upon those who have rejected and insulted His mercy and long-suffering kindness. The revelation of future wrath is no less clear and distinct than that of love to those who trust in Him.

(7) **Defile the house.**—The utmost possible pollution under the Mosaic economy was the touch of a dead body. (See Num. xix. 11; 1 Kings xiii. 2; 2 Kings xxiii. 16.) It might be thought that the Temple would be spared this defilement; but not only must the execution of justice override all technicalities, as at the execution of Joab (1 Kings ii. 28—31), but in this case the very defilement itself was a part of the judgment, since God was about to forsake His sanctuary, and give over even this to the desolations of the heathen. From the Temple the destroying angels passed out into the city.

(8) **I was left.**—The words imply *left alone.* The prophet had just before seen the courts of the sanctuary thronged with idolaters in the full glory of their heaven-defying sin. Now it is a city of the dead, and he is left standing alone in the midst of the dead. He falls upon his face in consternation, and pleads that "the residue of Israel" may not be utterly destroyed. The sternness of the Divine answer leaves no room for hope of any mitigation of the judgment. No mention is made here of those who were to be saved; they were so few among the mass as to have no effect upon the general impression of the vision. Yet they are not forgotten; and to show that they are not, the man in linen is represented in the next verse (11) as reporting that he had executed the command given him.

X.

This chapter is chiefly occupied with a fresh description of the vision of chap. i., but includes two new points: the giving up of the city to fire (verse 2), and the abandonment of the Temple (verses 18, 19).

(1) **As it were a sapphire stone.**—Comp. chap. i. 26. No mention is here made of a being upon the throne, but it is implied by the "he spake" of the following verse. The word *cherubim* corresponds throughout this chapter to the *living creatures* of chap. i.

(2) **Unto the man clothed with linen.**—Hitherto, in chap. ix., he has been employed only in a work of mercy and protection. It is not without significance that now the same person is made the agent of judgment. As God's love is turned to wrath by man's impenitence, and as His blessings given to man become curses by their abuse, so those employed by Him as the instruments of His loving-kindness become the very executioners of his "fury." The "coals of fire," the symbols of Divine wrath, are represented as "between the cherubim." In every possible way it is signified that the impending doom is not from man's will, however men may be used as its instruments, or from any accident, but from God Himself.

Scatter them over the city.—For its destruction. Perhaps the imagery does not signify anything more than destruction, without especial reference to the means employed; but 2 Kings xxv. 9 and 2 Chron. xxxvi. 19 show that the Temple and city were actually burned by the Chaldæans, as was often done with conquered cities that had resisted obstinately.

(4) **The glory of the Lord went up from the cherub.**—As in verse 2, the singular, *cherub,* instead of the usual plural. Here it is thought to designate, not the four living creatures of the vision, but the cherubim overshadowing the mercy-seat, and to indicate that the manifestation of the Divine presence now left the Holy of Holies, and went to the threshold of the door of the house, preparatory to leaving it altogether. The expression is obscure, since the place of the manifestation of the Divine presence in the most holy place is usually described as "between the cherubim" (Exod. xxv. 22; Num. vii. 89; Pss. lxxx. 1, xcix. 1, &c.). Of

brightness of the LORD's glory. (5) And
the [a]sound of the cherubims' wings
was heard *even* to the outer court, as
the voice of the Almighty God when he
speaketh.
(6) And it came to pass, *that* when he
had commanded the man clothed with
linen, saying, Take fire from between
the wheels, from between the cherubims;
then he went in, and stood beside the
wheels. (7) And *one* cherub [1]stretched
forth his hand from between the cheru-
bims unto the fire that *was* between the
cherubims, and took *thereof*, and put *it*
into the hands of *him that was* clothed
with linen: who took *it*, and went out.
(8) And there appeared in the cherubims
the form of a man's hand under their
wings.
(9) And when I looked, behold the four
wheels by the cherubims, one wheel by
one cherub, and another wheel by ano-
ther cherub: and the appearance of the
wheels *was* as the colour of a [b]beryl
stone. (10) And *as for* their appearances,
they four had one likeness, as if a wheel
had been in the midst of a wheel.
(11) When they went, they went upon
their four sides; they turned not as they
went, but to the place whither the head
looked they followed it; they turned
not as they went. (12) And their whole
[2]body, and their backs, and their hands,
and their wings, and the wheels, *were*
full of eyes round about, *even* the wheels
that they four had. (13) As for the
wheels, [3]it was cried unto them in my
hearing, O wheel. (14) And every one
had four faces: the first face *was* the
face of a cherub, and the second face
was the face of a man, and the third the
face of a lion, and the fourth the face of
an eagle. (15) And the cherubims were
lifted up. This *is* the living creature
that I saw by the river of Chebar.
(16) And when the cherubims went, the
wheels went by them: and when the
cherubims lifted up their wings to
mount up from the earth, the same
wheels also turned not from beside
them. (17) When they stood, *these*
stood; and when they were lifted up,
these lifted up themselves *also*: for the
spirit [4]of the living creature *was* in
them.
(18) Then the glory of the LORD de-
parted from off the threshold of the
house, and stood over the cherubims.
(19) And the cherubims lifted up their
wings, and mounted up from the earth

[a] ch. 1. 24.
[1] Heb., *sent forth.*
[b] ch. 1. 16.
[2] Heb., *flesh.*
[3] Or, *they were called in my hearing, wheel,* or, *galgal.*
[4] Or, *of life.*

---

the main point, however, there can be no doubt—that the Divine presence is represented as in the act of leaving the Temple. "The house was filled with the cloud, and the court was full of the brightness of the Lord's glory" as He departed, in striking contrast with the similar manifestations (Exod. xl. 34, 35; 1 Kings viii. 10, 11), when God accepted the tabernacle and the Temple as the peculiar place of His abode.

(5) **The sound of the cherubims' wings.**—This sound indicates that the cherubim were already in motion, for when they stood they "let down their wings" (chap. i. 24). They were now just on the eve of going away, and the movement was a great one, so that the sound was "heard even to the outer court." Throughout this chapter the *s* in cheru*bims* is quite unnecessary, since cheru*bim* is already the Hebrew plural of cherub.

Verses 6 and 7 are not subsequent in time to verse 5, but are simply a more particular account, given parenthetically, of what had already been briefly mentioned in verse 2.

Verses 8—17 are largely a repetition of the description of the vision in chap. i., but it is here given in parts, parenthetically, in connection with the progress of the narrative. The course of the narrative itself is as follows:—After the man in linen has gone out (verse 7), a command is issued, "O wheel." They were to set themselves in motion. Then (verse 15) they "were lifted up," and (verses 18, 19) "the glory of the Lord departed" from the Temple, and "mounted up from the earth." The repetition of the description of chap. i. is by no means accidental, but serves partly to connect the various particulars with the course of the symbolic narrative, and mainly to emphasize the identity of the glory departing from the Temple with the Divine glory before seen. There are, however, several variations from the former description. Particularly in verse 12 (as in Rev. iv. 6) there is mention of the abundance of eyes, a symbol of vigilance and activity, covering the whole body of the cherubim and the wheels. In verse 14, after saying that "every one had four faces," as in chap. i., the particular faces are described, but with this important variation:—the first is said to be "the face of a cherub," instead of "the face of an ox," as in chap. i.; more exactly it is "the face of *the* cherub," since the Hebrew has the definite article. The reason of this variation and the meaning of "the face of the cherub" are both obscure. In verse 22 it is expressly said that their faces were the same as those seen by the Chebar; and again, in verses 15—20, the whole vision is described as the "living creature" seen by the Chebar. It is plain, therefore, that the variation is only in the description, and not in the thing described. The most natural solution of the difficulty in the text as it stands is that a cherub was ordinarily represented with the face of an ox. But there is no evidence of this, and it is not impossible that a slight error may have been introduced into the text. The Greek version did not contain the verse in the time of St. Jerome, and in its Roman form does not now. It was introduced into the Alexandrian copies from the later version of Theodotion, and Theodoret does not recognise it.

(19) **Mounted up from the earth.**—In verse 3 the cherubim stood by "the right side of the house,"

in my sight: when they went out, the
wheels also *were* beside them, and *every*
one stood at the door of the east gate of
the LORD'S house; and the glory of the
God of Israel *was* over them above.
(20) This *is* the living creature that I
saw under the God of Israel by the
river of Chebar; and I knew that they
were the cherubims. (21) Every one had
four faces apiece, and every one four
wings; and the likeness of the hands of
a man *was* under their wings. (22) And
the likeness of their faces *was* the same
faces which I saw by the river of Chebar,
their appearances and themselves: they
went every one straight forward.

CHAPTER XI. — (1) Moreover the
spirit lifted me up, and brought me
unto the east gate of the LORD'S house,
which looketh eastward: and behold at
the door of the gate five and twenty
men; among whom I saw Jaazaniah the
son of Azur, and Pelatiah the son of
Benaiah, princes of the people. (2) Then
said he unto me, Son of man, these *are*
the men that devise mischief, and give
wicked counsel in this city: (3) which
say, [1]*It is* not [a]near; let us build houses:
this *city is* the caldron, and we *be* the
flesh. (4) Therefore prophesy against
them, prophesy, O son of man.
(5) And the Spirit of the LORD fell
upon me, and said unto me, Speak;
Thus saith the LORD; Thus have ye
said, O house of Israel: for I know the

1 Or, It is *not* for us *to build houses near.*

a 2 Pet. 3, 4.

---

and in verse 18 "the glory of the Lord" left the threshold, and resumed its place above the waiting cherubim; now the whole mount up from the earth, and go "to the east gate of the Lord's house"—that is, to the main entrance of the outermost court. The words "every one" are not in the original, and should be omitted. "They stood," or "it stood," would be better, the vision being regarded as a whole.

XI.

This chapter continues and concludes the vision; yet its scenes are not to be considered as consecutive with those which have gone before. In chap. ix. all who had not the Divine mark upon their foreheads were slain by the destroying angels; in chap. x. the city itself was given up to fire; but here the evil-doers are again seen, and again made the subject of the prophetic denunciation. It is, therefore, rather a looking at the same things from another point of view than an account of them in historical sequence. The prophetic vision shifts as in a dream, without any attempt to be consecutive.

The first part of the chapter (verses 1—12) is occupied with judgment upon the sins of the princes, while the latter part (verses 13—21) foretells the Divine blessing upon the repentant and restored remnant of the exiles. At the close (verses 22—25) the glory of the Lord is seen to depart altogether from the city, and the prophet is restored to Chaldæa to communicate the vision to the captives.

(1) **Brought me unto the east gate of the Lord's house.**—This is the same place, the main outer entrance to the whole Temple enclosure, to which the prophet had seen the cherubim go (chap. x. 19). It is not expressly said where he was brought from; but the last place mentioned was the court of the priests (chap. viii. 16), and so far the vision appears to be consecutive. Standing in that innermost court, he had seen the Divine presence go forth to the outer entrance; and he also is now transported thither.

Here he sees twenty-five men, the same number whom he had seen worshipping the sun in the inner court. They appear, however, to have been priests, while these seem to be secular leaders. Hence they are generally supposed to be a different set of men. It is nevertheless by no means impossible that they may be the same idolatrous priests, who, by prostituting their holy office to idolatry, gained an ascendancy over a sinful people. Otherwise, the number twenty-five may represent the king, with two princes from each of the twelve tribes; or is possibly a number without any other especial significance than as representing a considerable array of the most prominent people of the nation. Two of these are mentioned by name. If the Jaazaniah here is the same with the Jaazaniah of chap. viii. 11, it settles the point that the men here are not to be understood of the priests, since he there represented a different class (see Note on chap. viii. 11). The names are significant: Jaazaniah = Jehovah hears, son of Azur = the helper; Pelatiah = God rescues, son of Benaiah = Jehovah builds. Names of this sort were common enough among the Jews, but they seem here intended to bring out the false hopes with which the people beguiled themselves; and in view of this, the sudden death of Pelatiah (verse 13) was particularly impressive. These princes were active in misleading the people to their destruction.

(3) **It is not near; let us build houses.**—Neither the text nor the marginal reading of the Authorised Version quite accurately represent the original. The expression is literally *not near to build houses;* and it is to be explained by the prophecy and narrative of Jer. xxix. After the 10,000 (among whom was Ezekiel) had been carried captive—and apparently shortly after—Jeremiah had sent word to the captives to build houses and make themselves comfortable, because the captivity would be long (verses 5—10). This greatly offended the captives; and Shemaiah, a false prophet among them, had consequently sent letters to Jerusalem, asking that Jeremiah might be punished for thus prophesying (verses 24—28). The princes of the people now appear in Ezekiel's vision as taking up this prophecy of Jeremiah's and contradicting it: "this need of building houses for a long captivity is not near." In chaps. vii. 2, 3, 12, xii. 23, Ezekiel expressly declares that it is very near. The princes further confirmed the people in their fancied security by comparing the city to a caldron, the strong walls of which should protect the flesh within it, *i.e.*, the people, from the fire of all hostile attack. In the prophecy of chap. xxiv. 6 this figure is taken up, and a very different application given to

things that come into your mind, *every*
one of them. (6) Ye have multiplied
your slain in this city, and ye have
filled the streets thereof with the
slain. (7) Therefore thus saith the
Lord GOD; Your slain whom ye have
laid in the midst of it, they *are* the flesh,
and this *city is* the caldron: but I will
bring you forth out of the midst of it.
(8) Ye have feared the sword; and I will
bring a sword upon you, saith the Lord
GOD. (9) And I will bring you out of
the midst thereof, and deliver you into
the hands of strangers, and will execute
judgments among you. (10) Ye shall fall
by the sword; I will judge you in the
border of Israel; and ye shall know that
I *am* the LORD. (11) This *city* shall not
be your caldron, neither shall ye be the
flesh in the midst thereof; *but* I will
judge you in the border of Israel: (12) and
ye shall know that I *am* the LORD: [1] for
ye have not walked in my statutes, neither executed my judgments, but have
done after the manners of the heathen
that *are* round about you.

(13) And it came to pass, when I prophesied, that Pelatiah the son of Benaiah
died. Then fell I down upon my face,
and cried with a loud voice, and said,
Ah Lord GOD! wilt thou make a full
end of the remnant of Israel?

(14) Again the word of the LORD came
unto me, saying, (15) Son of man, thy
brethren, *even* thy brethren, the men of
thy kindred, and all the house of Israel
wholly, *are* they unto whom the inhabitants of Jerusalem have said, Get you
far from the LORD: unto us is this land
given in possession. (16) Therefore say,
Thus saith the Lord GOD; Although I
have cast them far off among the

1 Or, *which have not walked.*

---

it; it is also turned against them immediately in verse 7. In consequence of this attitude and these sayings of the princes, the prophecy of verses 5—12 is now directed against them.

(6) **Ye have multiplied your slain.**—Crimes of violence, as well as of licentiousness, are always the fruit of defection from God. In this case the apostacy of the people had produced its natural result; and the abundant crimes against life formed a prominent feature of the terrible indictment against the city.

(7) **Your slain . . . they are the flesh.**—They had boasted of the protection of their strong city: it should be a security only to the dead who had fallen by their own violence. The living who vainly trusted in its strength should be brought out of it, and delivered as captives to the stranger. The prophecy here takes up their own simile of verse 3, and shows that it shall not avail them. On the contrary, in verse 11 it is expressly said that the figure, in their sense of it, shall not be true. The use of and repeated recurrence to this singular figure may illustrate the familiarity of the people with language of this kind, and help us to appreciate the figurative character of many of Ezekiel's expressions.

(10) **In the border of Israel.**—The judgment should be cumulative: first, the sword should come upon them (verse 8); then they should be driven out of the city in which they trusted, and delivered into the hands of strangers (verse 9); and then, finally—what was most terrible to a Jew—they were to be arraigned and punished "in the border," *i.e.*, at the extremity or outside of the land of Israel. Historically, it appears from 2 Kings xxv. 20, 21, and Jer. lii. 9—11, that the general of Nebuchadnezzar, after the capture of the city, carried the people of the land to the king at Riblah, just on the northern confines of Palestine. There Nebuchadnezzar pronounced his cruel judgments upon them, slaying the king's sons before his eyes, and executing many others, and then, putting out Zedekiah's eyes, carried him and the rest captive to Babylon. By all this, not in repentance, but through the experiencing of the Divine judgments, they should be at last forced to recognise Jehovah as the Almighty Ruler and Disposer of events. This place of the judgment, and this consequence of it, are emphatically repeated in verses 11, 12.

(13) **Pelatiah . . . died.**—This Pelatiah was one of the "princes of the people" mentioned in verses 1, 2 as "those that devise mischief and give wicked counsel." The prophet's mind is greatly affected by his sudden death, and he earnestly intercedes that in the judgments God will not "make a full end of the remnant."

(14) **Again the word.**—This does not mark the beginning of a separate prophecy, but only the Divine answer to the prophet's intercession. This answer differs entirely from the denunciations that have gone before, because it no longer relates to the people of Jerusalem (for whom intercession was in vain: chap. ix. 9, 10), but turns to the exiles, and foretells God's mercy and blessing upon them.

(15) **Thy brethren** — *i.e.*, those who were with Ezekiel in the Captivity. The expression is made emphatic by repetition, and by the addition, "men of thy kindred." The people remaining in Jerusalem, with arrogant confidence in themselves, and without sympathy for the exiles, had said to them, by words and by deeds, "We are holier than you; we dwell in the chosen city, we have the Temple, the appointed priesthood and sacrifices, and we have in possession the land of the Church of God; you are outcasts." The prophet is taught that these despised exiles, deprived of so many privileges, are yet his true brethren, and that he is to regard these as his true kindred rather than the corrupt priests at Jerusalem. In this word there is an allusion to the office of *Göel*, the next of kin, whose duty it was in every way to assist his impoverished or unfortunate kinsman. Still further, these exiles are called "all the house of Israel wholly;" the others, not these, are cast out, and God will make His people from those who are now undergoing His purifying chastisement. This contrast is carried out in the following verses.

(16) **Therefore say.**—These words, again repeated in verse 17, refer to what the people of Jerusalem had said in verse 15. Their saying these things was a reason, not for what God would do, but for His declaring His merciful purpose beforehand.

heathen, and although I have scattered
them among the countries, yet will I be
to them as a little sanctuary in the
countries where they shall come.
(17) Therefore say, Thus saith the Lord
GOD; I will even gather you from the
people, and assemble you out of the
countries where ye have been scattered,
and I will give you the land of Israel.
(18) And they shall come thither, and they
shall take away all the detestable things
thereof and all the abominations thereof
from thence. (19) And [a]I will give them
one heart, and I will put a new spirit
within you; and I will take the stony
heart out of their flesh, and will give
them an heart of flesh: (20) that they
may walk in my statutes, and keep mine
ordinances, and do them: and they shall
be my people, and I will be their God.
(21) But *as for them* whose heart walketh
after the heart of their detestable things

[a] Jer. 32. 39; ch. 36. 26.

As a little sanctuary.—Rather, *as a sanctuary for a little.* The original word is to be taken as an adverb rather than an adjective, and in itself may refer either to time or to amount: either a sanctuary for a little time, or a sanctuary in some degree. The connection points to the former as the true sense; for a little while, during the term of their captivity, God's presence with them spiritually would be instead of the outward symbolical presence in His Temple. The contrast is striking. God has already said that he would abandon the Temple, and give up Jerusalem to destruction, and cast out its people; but now to the exiles, scattered among the heathen, He would Himself be for a sanctuary.

(17) **I will give you the land of Israel.**—Again in contrast to the people of Jerusalem, who claimed the land as their own exclusive possession. They shall be cast out; the exiles whom they despised shall be gathered again and possess the land. (Comp. Num. xiv. 3, 31, 32, where when the people refused the Divine command to take possession of the land, and feared that their little ones should be a prey, the doom came that they should all themselves perish in the wilderness, but their little ones should inherit the land.)

(18) **They shall take away.** — Chastened and purified by their chastisement, they should return to the land to do away utterly with the abominations which had caused their exile. Historically, this was fully realised in the abomination in which idolatry, the great sin of the people, was ever after held among the Jews. The change of person from *you* to *they*, though so common as not necessarily to call for remark, may yet here possibly indicate that what is foretold was to belong rather to their children than to themselves.

(19, 20) Here follows one of those germinant and ever developing prophetic promises which in fuller and fuller degree have formed from the very first, and still form, the hope of the future. True religion and a service acceptable to God must spring from a subjection of the affections of the heart to His will. Accordingly, the promise to Israel of old was: "The Lord thy God will circumcise thine heart, and the heart of thy seed, to love the Lord thy God with all thine heart, and with all thy soul" (Deut. xxx. 6). This, too, had been the prayer of the devout penitent, "Create in me a clean heart" (Ps. li. 10). But this change is necessarily the most difficult to effect in man, and consequently the promise, though with some degree of accomplishment as the ages roll by, still looks forward to the future. Ezekiel here, and with more fulness in chap. xxxvi. 26, 27, speaks of it as a part of the blessing of the restoration. A marked progress was then made towards it in the hearty abandonment of idolatry, and the better appreciation of religion as a matter of internal heart service; but the prophecy of Jer. xxxi. 33, given about the same time, shows that it looked forward to the Messianic days for a more complete realisation. And certainly under the Christian dispensation a great advance has been made in this respect; but even the closing Book of Revelation still points forward to the future state of existence, when this promise shall attain its full realisation (Rev. xxi. 3). It is remarkable that this closing prophecy of the inspired volume follows exactly the plan here laid out, of adding to this glorious promise the warning to "the fearful and unbelieving." What Ezekiel foretells of the time of the restoration must therefore be considered as not expected then to receive its ultimate and complete fulfilment, but only a fulfilment in a degree, to be ever after more and more realised, until it shall reach its consummation in the heavenly state.

(19) **One heart.**—Unity of purpose among the restored exiles was to be at once a consequence and a condition of their improved moral condition. The opposite evil is spoken of as one of the sins of the people in Isa. liii. 6: "We have turned every one to his own way." Self-will, which leads to division, and submission to God's will are necessarily contradictory terms. Hence the corresponding promise in Jer. xxxii. 39: "I will give them one heart and one way," and the blessed realisation of this, described in the first fervency of the early Church (Acts iv. 32): "The multitude of them that believed were of one heart and of one soul."

Stony heart . . . heart of flesh. — This phraseology is peculiar to Ezekiel, but the same thing is often described in other terms. The figure here seems to be that of a *stony* heart as unnatural, in the higher sense of that word, unfitting, and incongruous; this is to be removed, and in its place is to be substituted "an heart of flesh"—one that can be moved by the Divine appeals, and is suitable to the whole being and condition of the people. (Comp. chap. xxxvi. 26.) The effect of this change will be obedience to the Divine will, and consequently a realisation of the covenant relation in a fellowship with God.

(21) **I will recompense their way.**—In striking contrast to the mercy granted to the repentant, is set forth here, as in Rev. xxi. 8, the Divine wrath upon the impenitent. It has never been promised that all men shall be brought to a true sense of their relations to God, for human responsibility, and consequently power of choice, is not removed; but God's grace is never in vain, and if it does not lead to blessing through its acceptance, must result in greater condemnation through its rejection. (Comp. 2 Cor. ii. 16.)

The heart of their detestable things, is a figurative expression. Idols in themselves are inanimate things, but the heart of the people was so given to the spirit of idolatry and alienation from God, that

and their abominations, I will recom-
pense their way upon their own heads,
saith the Lord God.
(22) Then did the cherubims lift up their
wings, and the wheels beside them; and
the glory of the God of Israel *was* over
them above. (23) And the glory of the
Lord went up from the midst of the
city, and stood upon the mountain which
is on the east side of the city.
(24) Afterwards the spirit took me up,
and brought me in a vision by the Spirit
of God into Chaldea, to them of the cap-
tivity. So the vision that I had seen
went up from me. (25) Then I spake unto
them of the captivity all the things that
the Lord had shewed me.

CHAPTER XII.—(1) The word of the
Lord also came unto me, saying,
(2) Son of man, thou dwellest in the
midst of a rebellious house, which have
eyes to see, and see not; they have ears
to hear, and hear not: for they *are* a
rebellious house. (3) Therefore, thou son
of man, prepare thee [1]stuff for removing,
and remove by day in their sight; and
thou shalt remove from thy place to
another place in their sight: it may be
they will consider, though they *be* a re-
bellious house. (4) Then shalt thou bring
forth thy stuff by day in their sight, as
stuff for removing: and thou shalt go
forth at even in their sight, [2]as they that
go forth into captivity. (5) [3]Dig thou
through the wall in their sight, and carry
out thereby. (6) In their sight shalt thou
bear *it* upon *thy* shoulders, *and* carry *it*
forth in the twilight: thou shalt cover
thy face, that thou see not the ground:
for I have set thee *for* a sign unto the
house of Israel.

1 Or, *instruments.*

2 Heb., *as the goings forth of captivity.*

3 Heb., *Dig for thee.*

---

the abstract, as usual with this prophet, is represented in this concrete, figurative form.

(22) **And the wheels beside them.**—These are the wheels described as with the cherubim, and animated in their movements by one common impulse with them, and, as all along, the Divine glory was above.

(23) **Stood upon the mountain.**—This mountain, on the east of the city, is that which was afterwards known as the Mount of Olives. It is considerably higher than the city, and commands a view over its entire extent. Here the Divine glory rested after taking its departure from the Temple and the city in the vision of the prophet. Here, in the vision of a later prophet (Zech. xiv. 4), the Lord is represented as standing in the day of final judgment. Here, not in vision, the incarnate Son of God proclaimed the second destruction of the obdurate city (Matt. xxiv.; Luke xxi. 20); and from the same mountain He made His visible ascension into heaven (Luke xxiv. 50, 51; Acts i. 11, 12). The vision is now closed, and the prophet is transported in spirit back into Chaldæa, to declare what he had seen to his fellow-captives, and show them the vanity of their trust in the preservation of the guilty city.

XII.

The vision being finished, there follows a series of connected prophecies, extending through chap. xix., just as the vision of chaps. iv., v. was followed by the prophecies of chaps. vi., vii.; and in this case, as in the former, the prophecy includes symbolical action (verses 3—7). In verse 9 the people are represented as inquiring the meaning of this action, and in verse 8 the Divine answer is spoken of as given "in the morning" after the action; it was, therefore, undoubtedly actually performed. The object of this whole series of prophecies is the same as that of the preceding vision: to show the worthlessness of the trust in the preservation of the kingdom of Judah and Jerusalem, and in an early release from the Babylonian yoke. In the present chapter the prophet is required to foreshow the captivity of the king and the people by a symbolical action (verses 3—7); to explain this action (verses 8—16); to set forth by another symbolical action the distress of the people (verses 17—20); and, finally, to meet the objection that these things will either never occur, or at least will be long delayed (verses 21—28).

(2) **A rebellious house.**—Comp. Deut. i. 26; Rom. x. 21. The *seeing not* and *hearing not* is that perverse refusing to see and to hear so often spoken of in Scripture. (See Deut. xxix. 4; Isa. vi. 9; Jer. v. 21; Matt. xiii. 14, 15.) It was because of this disposition that the prophet was to give them a sign to which they could not shut their eyes.

(3) **Prepare thee stuff for removing.**—The same words are translated in Jer. xlvi. 19, "Furnish thyself to go into captivity." *Stuff* includes all that an emigrant would require, clothes, utensils, &c.; and "removing" is the same word as is translated *captivity* in verse 4. The symbolical action was that of one preparing to leave his home to go into captivity. The prophet is to make his preparations during the day, and to carry forth his stuff (verse 7), but not himself to go forth until even (verse 4). The action seems to be that of one who must abandon his home, using the whole day to carry out all he can with the purpose of saving it, and then himself leaving the house when the day is done.

(5) **Dig thou through the wall.**—This is a subsequent action, as shown by verse 7. The wall was probably of adobe, sun-dried brick, the common building material of the country, and there was, therefore, no great difficulty in digging through it; but this way of entering the house indicates something of stealth and secrecy. He was to carry forth his goods openly through his door during the day, and then to re-enter at evening, and secretly to carry forth those things which he would not otherwise be allowed to take away.

(6) **Bear it . . . carry it.**—The pronouns are not in the original, and are better omitted. Otherwise, the "it" might seem to refer to the stuff already carried out during the day. Read, "Thou shalt bear upon thy shoulders, and carry forth in the dark." The word rendered "twilight" is used only here and in verse 12, and in Gen. xv. 17, and means *dark*.

That thou see not the ground.—This covering of the face might primarily be a token of grief; but as

(7) And I did so as I was commanded:
I brought forth my stuff by day, as stuff
for captivity, and in the even I [1]digged
through the wall with mine hand; I
brought *it* forth in the twilight, *and*
I bare *it* upon *my* shoulder in their
sight.
(8) And in the morning came the word
of the LORD unto me, saying, (9) Son of
man, hath not the house of Israel, the
rebellious house, said unto thee, What
doest thou? (10) Say thou unto them, Thus
saith the Lord GOD; This burden *con-*
cerneth the prince in Jerusalem, and all
the house of Israel that *are* among them.
(11) Say, I *am* your sign: like as I have
done, so shall it be done unto them:
[2]they shall remove, *and* go into captivity.
(12) And the prince that *is* among them
shall bear upon *his* shoulder in the twi-
light, and shall go forth: they shall dig
through the wall to carry out thereby:
he shall cover his face, that he see not
the ground with *his* eyes. (13) My [a]net
also will I spread upon him, and he shall
be taken in my snare: and I will bring
him to Babylon *to* the land of the Chal-
deans; yet shall he not see it, though
he shall die there. (14) And I will scatter
toward every wind all that *are* about
him to help him, and all his bands; and
I will draw out the sword after them.
(15) And they shall know that I *am* the
LORD, when I shall scatter them among
the nations, and disperse them in the
countries. (16) But I will leave [3]a few
men of them from the sword, from the
famine, and from the pestilence; that
they may declare all their abominations
among the heathen whither they come;
and they shall know that I *am* the
LORD.
(17) Moreover the word of the LORD
came to me, saying,
(18) Son of man, eat thy bread with
quaking, and drink thy water with
trembling and with carefulness; (19) and
say unto the people of the land, Thus

1 Heb., *digged for me.*

2 Heb., *by removing go into captivity.*

a ch. 17. 20.

3 Heb., *men of number.*

---

the whole action is distinctly prophetic (and is so interpreted; see verses 11—14), so especially was this sign. (See the account of the capture of Zedekiah in 2 Kings xxv. 4—7; Jer. xxxix. 4—7, lii. 7—11.) The king, with his men of war, escaped from the city secretly by night, was pursued and captured, and carried to Riblah, where his eyes were put out, and he was then taken in chains to Babylon.

(8) **In the morning.**—This implies that the foregoing symbolical action was actually performed, since the Divine message comes in answer to the inquiry of the people (verse 9), "What doest thou?"

(10) **All the house of Israel.**—The *burden* (or message of woe) was directed immediately to the king and his princes, but the people were also necessarily involved. Israel is here, as elsewhere, used for the then existing nation, which was considered as representing the whole, although composed chiefly of the tribe of Judah.

(11) **Your sign.**—The change of pronoun is intentional. The prophet's action was to be a sign not only to Zedekiah and the people in Jerusalem, but also to those in captivity, since they rested their hope upon the safety of the holy city.

(12) **They shall dig through the wall.**—This circumstance is not mentioned in the history of Zedekiah's flight; yet it is not necessary to understand it figuratively, since such a breach in the walls at a place unwatched by the enemy might easily be arranged to secure secrecy, and as easily be passed over in the brevity of the historical account. (See Note on verse 6.)

Shall cover his face.—This he would naturally do to avoid recognition; but the words were doubtless meant also as an intimation of what is more plainly hinted in the following verse.

(13) **Yet shall he not see it, though he shall die there.**—The prophet does not explain how this could be; but Jeremiah (chap. lii. 11) makes it plain by recording that Zedekiah's eyes were put out in Riblah, before he was carried to Babylon. Josephus has a curious story (*Antiq.* x. 7, § 2), that Zedekiah was inclined to believe the warnings of Jeremiah that he should be carried captive to Babylon; but when Ezekiel sent this prophecy to Jerusalem, saying that he should not see the land, he conceived the two prophecies to be contradictory, and so disbelieved them both. Zedekiah's death in Babylon is mentioned in Jer. lii. 11.

(14) **I will scatter toward every wind.**—The people of Judah were not carried captive to Babylon only, but many of them were scattered wherever they could find refuge; and, finally, the remnant left in the land by Nebuchadnezzar, after the murder of his governor Gedaliah, escaped into Egypt (Jer. xli—xliii.).

(16) **May declare all their abominations.**—This they were to do, that the false impression that God was unable to protect His people might be removed from the minds of the heathen, and the truth that He was punishing them for their sins be made known. They should do it both by word of mouth (as in Jer. xxii. 8, 9), and also by their conduct (as in chap. xiv. 22, 23). The word "few" is literally, as shown in the margin, *men of number, i.e.*, men who can easily be numbered or counted; and in the very similar expression in the original for "declare," there is a play upon the word, something like our "count" and "recount."

They shall know, may grammatically refer either to the heathen, or to the Israelites in their dispersion; but the latter is so constantly the refrain of these prophecies (see verse 20, *e.g.*), that it is also to be understood here.

(18) **Eat thy bread with quaking.**—This is another symbolical action, the meaning of which is immediately explained. The prophet is to eat and drink as men in the terror and distress of a siege.

(19) **Unto the people of the land,**—*i.e.*, of the land of Chaldæa: Ezekiel's fellow-captives. All these prophecies, though concerning Jerusalem and its people,

saith the Lord GOD of the inhabitants
of Jerusalem, *and* of the land of Israel;
They shall eat their bread with careful-
ness, and drink their water with asto-
nishment, that her land may be desolate
from [1]all that is therein, because of the
violence of all them that dwell therein.
(20) And the cities that are inhabited
shall be laid waste, and the land shall
be desolate; and ye shall know that I
am the LORD.
(21) And the word of the LORD came
unto me, saying,
(22) Son of man, what *is* that proverb
that ye have in the land of Israel, say-
ing, The days are prolonged, and every
vision faileth? (23) Tell them therefore,
Thus saith the Lord GOD; I will make
this proverb to cease, and they shall no
more use it as a proverb in Israel; but
say unto them, The days are at hand,
and the effect of every vision. (24) For
there shall be no more any vain vision
nor flattering divination within the
house of Israel. (25) For I *am* the LORD:
I will speak, and the word that I shall
speak shall come to pass; it shall be no
more prolonged: for in your days, O
rebellious house, will I say the word,
and will perform it, saith the Lord GOD.
(26) Again the word of the LORD came
to me, saying,
(27) Son of man, behold, *they of* the
house of Israel say, The vision that he
seeth *is* [a]for many days *to come*, and he
prophesieth of the times *that are* far off.
(28) Therefore say unto them, Thus saith
the Lord GOD; There shall none of my
words be prolonged any more, but the
word which I have spoken shall be done,
saith the Lord GOD.

CHAPTER XIII.—(1) And the word
of the LORD came unto me, saying,
(2) Son of man, prophesy against the
prophets of Israel that prophesy, and
say thou unto [2]them that prophesy out
of their own [b]hearts, Hear ye the word
of the LORD; (3) Thus saith the Lord
GOD; Woe unto the foolish prophets,
that [3]follow their own spirit, [4]and have
seen nothing! (4) O Israel, thy pro-

1 Heb., *the fulness thereof.*

a 2 Pet. 3. 4.

2 Heb., *them that are prophets out of their own hearts.*

b Jer. 23. 16.

3 Heb., *walk after.*

4 Or, *and things which they have not seen.*

---

were immediately addressed to the exiles, and their teaching was primarily for them. It is not unlikely, however, as St. Jerome says, that all these prophecies of Ezekiel were sent to Jerusalem, and the corresponding utterances of Jeremiah, made in Jerusalem, were sent to Chaldæa.

From all that is therein.—The margin, which is the literal rendering, explains this: "The land shall be stripped of its richness and excellence, of all that makes it desirable."

(21–28) These verses contain two distinct messages from the Lord (verses 21—25 and 26—28), both designed to meet the objection that warning prophecies had been uttered now for a long time, and as they had not come to pass there was no reason to expect their fulfilment, at least until some far distant future. It is always the tendency of sinful man to take this ground while experiencing the long-suffering and forbearance of God (see Eccles. viii. 11; Amos vi. 3; Matt. xxiv. 43; 1 Thess. v. 3); and the scoff, "Where is the promise of His coming?" will still continue to the end of time (2 Pet. iii. 4). In this case, the objection was evidently encouraged by false prophets (verse 24), and accordingly the following chapter is devoted to them.

(22) **In the land of Israel,** is not here simply equivalent to the "in Israel" of verse 23, but refers to a proverb current among those who had not yet been carried into captivity, and who fancied that they should not be.

(23) **The effect of every vision.**—The sense would be made clearer by rendering "the accomplishment" of every vision.

XIII.

A prophecy very similar to this was uttered by Jeremiah (chap. xxiii.), only a few years before, against the false prophets in and around Jerusalem. It is not unlikely that Ezekiel may have read it; as Jeremiah (chap. xxix. 1) certainly sent some of his prophecies to those in the captivity, and it is altogether probable that he knew its substance. He, however, addresses himself here to the false prophets among the captives (see verse 9), and in the latter part of the chapter (verses 17—23) especially to the prophetesses. In both parts their conduct is first described (verses 3—7, 17—19), and then their doom (verses 8—16, 20—23). Such false prophets have always been a chief hindrance to the truth (just as false teaching within the Church now is far more dangerous than any attack from without), and they especially abounded in times of difficulty and danger. Jeremiah speaks repeatedly of their opposition to him in Judæa (chaps. xiv. 13, 14, xxiii. 9, 13, 16, 21, 25, xxvii., xxviii.), and expressly mentions also their activity among the exiles (chap. xxix. 15—22).

(3) **Foolish prophets.**—They were certainly *foolish* who undertook to forge the name of the Omniscient, as it were, to utterances of their own devising. Folly, according to the use of the word in the Old Testament, was not merely an intellectual failing, but was always associated with moral obliquity. (See Ps. xiv. 1, and Proverbs throughout.) The last clause of the verse is better expressed in the margin: these prophets were "seers of that which they have not seen."

(4) **Like the foxes in the deserts.**—The comparison is sufficiently close if it is considered as extending only to these mischievous men living unconcerned among the ruins of their state and country, as the foxes find their home in desolated cities (Lam. v. 18); but many extend the simile to the undermining of the ground by the foxes, as these prophets accelerated the ruin of their people.

phets are like the foxes in the deserts.
(5) Ye have not gone up into the [1]gaps,
neither [2]made up the hedge for the
house of Israel to stand in the battle in
the day of the LORD. (6) They have seen
vanity and lying divination, saying, The
LORD saith: and the LORD hath not sent
them: and they have made *others* to
hope that they would confirm the word.
(7) Have ye not seen a vain vision, and
have ye not spoken a lying divination,
whereas ye say, The LORD saith *it;* albeit
I have not spoken?

(8) Therefore thus saith the Lord GOD;
Because ye have spoken vanity, and seen
lies, therefore, behold, I *am* against you,
saith the Lord GOD. (9) And mine hand
shall be upon the prophets that see
vanity, and that divine lies: they shall
not be in the [3]assembly of my people,
neither shall they be written in the writ-
ing of the house of Israel, neither shall
they enter into the land of Israel; and
ye shall know that I *am* the Lord GOD.

(10) Because, even because they have
seduced my people, saying, [a]Peace; and
there was no peace; and one built up [4]a
wall, and, lo, others daubed it with un-
tempered *morter:* (11) Say unto them
which daub *it* with untempered *morter,*
that it shall fall: there shall be an
overflowing shower; and ye, O great
hailstones, shall fall; and a stormy wind
shall rend *it.* (12) Lo, when the wall is
fallen, shall it not be said unto you,
Where *is* the daubing wherewith ye
have daubed *it?* (13) Therefore thus
saith the Lord GOD; I will even rend *it*
with a stormy wind in my fury; and
there shall be an overflowing shower in
mine anger, and great hailstones in *my*
fury to consume *it.* (14) So will I break
down the wall that ye have daubed with
untempered *morter,* and bring it down to
the ground, so that the foundation
thereof shall be discovered, and it shall
fall, and ye shall be consumed in the
midst thereof: and ye shall know that I
am the LORD. (15) Thus will I accom-
plish my wrath upon the wall, and upon
them that have daubed it with untem-
pered *morter,* and will say unto you, The
wall *is* no *more,* neither they that
daubed it; (16) *to wit,* the prophets of
Israel which prophesy concerning Jeru-
salem, and which see visions of peace for
her, and *there is* no peace, saith the Lord
GOD.

1 Or, *breaches.*
2 Heb., *hedged the hedge.*
3 Or, *secret,* or, *council.*
a Jer. 6. 14.
4 Or, *a slight wall.*

---

(5) **Ye have not gone up into the gaps.**—The change of person is frequent enough in prophecy, and especially common in Ezekiel. It is changed back in verse 6, and changed again in verse 7. The *gaps* refer to the breaches in the wall made by the enemy, which became the rallying point of every brave leader (see chap. xxii. 30), and the following words express essentially the same thought. The word "hedge" should rather be translated *wall*—"neither have ye built up the wall." The false prophets, like the hireling shepherds of John x. 12, were only selfish, and had no care for the flock. The whole language is figurative, the breaches in the material walls representing the moral decay of the people.

(6) **They have made others to hope.**—Omit the word "others," which is not in the original, and translate, "The Lord hath not sent them that they should hope" —*i.e.*, they have no ground to expect that their prophecies will prove true, because they have no warrant for uttering them.

(9) **The assembly of my people.**—The original word bears also the meanings placed in the margin, but the sense here is correctly given in the text. The several clauses are intended to emphasise the utter exclusion of the false prophets from the people of God: they shall not be in the congregation; their names shall not be written in the genealogical registers of Israel; they shall not even enter the land when the purified and repentant people should once more return.

(10) **One built up a wall.**—The original word is used for a partition wall—of course a comparatively slight wall—as noted in the margin; in verse 12, however, the ordinary word for an outer, or a city wall, is used. One of the false prophets would build a wall, set up of his own device—some vision as a defence against the warnings of calamity; and his fellows would join in his deceit by covering this wall "with untempered mortar." The word is not the usual one for plaster, and indeed is used in this sense only in these verses and in chap. xxii. 28. Elsewhere, the word is used in Job vi. 6=*unsavoury*, Lam. ii. 14=*foolish things*, and a closely-related form in Jer. xxiii. 13=*folly* (marg., *an absurd thing*). Here (and also in verses 11, 14, 15) it must mean plaster, but the use of the word elsewhere shows plainly enough what sort of plaster is intended. Calvin understands it of mortar mixed with sand and water only, the lime being left out. It is still a common practice in the East, as it has always been, to cover over their walls with stucco. In this case the other false prophets are represented as joining with the one who built the wall by covering over its weaknesses and defects with a fair-seeming plaster. (Comp. Matt. xxiii. 27; Acts xxiii. 3.) They helped on the delusion by giving it the weight of their influence, and persuading the people to believe a lie.

(11) **Great hailstones.**—Hail is unusual in Palestine, but its destructive effects were well known. The figure of this prophecy may be compared with the parable of Matt. vii. 27.

(12) **Where is the daubing?**—The basis of all their false prophesying being destroyed by the coming judgments, the folly and falsehood of their words would be exposed to the eyes of all. As it is said in verse 14, the wall itself being thrown down to its very foundation, they who have tried to make the people trust in it shall be overwhelmed in its ruin.

(17) Likewise, thou son of man, set thy
face against the daughters of thy people,
which prophesy out of their own heart;
and prophesy thou against them, (18) and
say, Thus saith the Lord GOD; Woe to
the *women* that sew pillows to all [1]arm-
holes, and make kerchiefs upon the head
of every stature to hunt souls! Will ye
hunt the souls of my people, and will ye
save the souls alive *that come* unto you?
(19) And will ye pollute me among my
people for handfuls of barley and for
pieces of bread, to slay the souls that
should not die, and to save the souls
alive that should not live, by your lying
to my people that hear *your* lies?
(20) Wherefore thus saith the Lord
GOD; Behold, I *am* against your pil-
lows, wherewith ye there hunt the souls
[2]to make *them* fly, and I will tear them
from your arms, and will let the souls
go, *even* the souls that ye hunt to make
them fly. (21) Your kerchiefs also will I
tear, and deliver my people out of your
hand, and they shall be no more in your
hand to be hunted; and ye shall know
that I *am* the LORD. (22) Because with
lies ye have made the heart of the
righteous sad, whom I have not made
sad; and strengthened the hands
of the wicked, that he should not
return from his wicked way, [3, 4] by pro-
mising him life: (23) therefore ye shall
see no more vanity, nor divine divina-
tions: for I will deliver my people out
of your hand: and ye shall know that I
am the LORD.

1 Or, *elbows.*

2 Or, *into gardens.*

3 Or, *that I should save his life.*

4 Heb., *by quickening him.*

B.C. cir. 594.

CHAPTER XIV.—(1) Then came cer-
tain of the elders of Israel unto me, and

(17—23) **Likewise, thou son of man, set thy face . . .**—This passage deals with a class of people, the false prophetesses, who are not mentioned elsewhere in the Old Testament. True prophetesses, as in the case of Miriam (Exod. xv. 20), Deborah (Judges iv. 4), and, at this very time, Huldah (2 Kings xxii. 14; 2 Chron. xxxiv. 22), and somewhat later, Noadiah (Neh. vi. 14), are frequently spoken of, and continued to exist in New Testament times, as in the case of Anna (Luke ii. 36). It was naturally to be expected that as false prophets dogged the steps of the true, the same thing would happen with the other sex, and we find express mention of a false prophetess in Rev. ii. 20. Their course, in prophesying "out of their own heart," deceiving the people, was essentially the same as that of the false prophets; but they are described as doing this in ways suited to their sex. Of the general meaning of this description there can be no doubt; but it is difficult to follow it with certainty in the details, because of the occurrence of some words of uncertain meaning, found nowhere else, and of some others in an unusual sense. Without attempting a discussion of each single word, (which would be useless except with a careful examination of the original), the following is given as the most probable translation of verses 18—21; but it is to be remembered that several of the words, like the similar ones in Isa. iii. 16—24, are so uncertain that there is a difference of opinion in regard to their exact meaning:—"Woe to those who fasten charms on every finger-joint, that place kerchiefs on heads of every height to snare souls. Will ye snare the souls of my people, and keep your own souls alive? (19) And will ye profane me with my people for handfuls of barley, and for pieces of bread, to slay souls that should not die, and to make live souls that should not live, by your lying to my people who hearken to a lie? (20) Therefore, thus saith the Lord Jehovah, Behold, I am against your charms, when ye snare the souls like birds, and I will tear them from your arms, and will let the souls go, the souls that ye are snaring like birds. (21) Your kerchiefs also will I tear, and deliver my people out of your hand, and they shall be no more in your hand to be snared; and ye shall know that I am the Lord." (*See Excursus viii.* at the end of this book, on chap. xiii. verses 6, 7, 14.)

(18) **Souls.**—This word is used in the Old Testament in a variety of significations. Here and in the following verses it is nearly equivalent to *persons.*

(19) **Handfuls of barley.**—It was an ancient custom to bring presents to a prophet on consulting him (1 Sam. ix. 7, 8; 1 Kings xiv. 3); but as barley was a cheap grain, and handfuls a very small quantity, these words show the exceedingly small gains for which these false prophetesses were willing to pervert the truth, and lead the people to destruction. God was "polluted" by attaching His name and authority to that which was not true, and would not come to pass, thus "making Him a liar" like themselves. Like all falsehood, their lies tended both ways—to entice the upright to their ruin, and to give false security to the wicked. It is always impossible that a perversion of the truth, especially in regard to the Divine judgments, can be harmless.

Hear your lies.—Or, *hearken to a lie.* The words imply a willingness to listen to the pleasing falsehood, and the state of things is that described by Jer. v. 31. "The prophets prophesy falsely, and the priests bear rule by their means, and my people love to have it so."

(23) **Ye shall see no more vanity.**—As so often the judgment is expressed in the same form with the sin. These false prophetesses had sinned by their lying visions, and they should see them no more, because the event should soon expose their utter falsity to the eyes of all. The result would be the deliverance of God's people, whom they sought to ensnare, and their own conviction, not in penitence, but under judgment, that He is the Lord.

XIV.

This chapter consists of two distinct but closely-connected prophecies, the first of which (verses 1—11) was called out by the coming of the elders to enquire of the prophet, and announces to them that God will not answer, but will destroy idolatrous enquirers; while the second (verses 12—23) shows the falsity of the hope that God will spare the land for the sake of the righteous that may be therein. Both of these are closely connected with the prophecies that have gone

sat before me. (2) And the word of the
LORD came unto me, saying, (3) Son of
man, these men have set up their idols
in their heart, and put the stumbling-
block of their iniquity before their face:
should I be enquired of at all by them?
(4) Therefore speak unto them, and say
unto them, Thus saith the Lord GOD;
Every man of the house of Israel that
setteth up his idols in his heart, and
putteth the stumblingblock of his ini-
quity before his face, and cometh to the
prophet; I the LORD will answer him
that cometh according to the multitude
of his idols; (5) that I may take the
house of Israel in their own heart, be-
cause they are all estranged from me
through their idols.

(6) Therefore say unto the house of
Israel, Thus saith the Lord GOD; Re-
pent, and turn [1]*yourselves* from your
idols; and turn away your faces from
all your abominations. (7) For every one
of the house of Israel, or of the stranger
that sojourneth in Israel, which separ-
ateth himself from me, and setteth up
his idols in his heart, and putteth the
stumblingblock of his iniquity before
his face, and cometh to a prophet to en-
quire of him concerning me; I the LORD
will answer him by myself: (8) and I will
set my face against that man, and will
make him a [a]sign and a proverb, and I
will cut him off from the midst of my
people; and ye shall know that I *am*
the LORD.

1 Or, others.

a Deu. 28. 37; ch. 5. 15.

---

before, and are doubtless placed in their chronological order, as uttered in the second year of Ezekiel's ministry, the sixth or seventh year of his captivity.

(1) **Certain of the elders of Israel.**—There is no distinction intended here between the elders of *Israel* and the elders of *Judah* mentioned in viii. 1, and therefore there is no occasion to suppose a deputation sent to the prophet from Jerusalem. Israel is now becoming the ordinary name of the existing nation, except where it is used with some special mark of distinction. The object of their enquiry is not mentioned, nor is it even expressly said that they made any enquiry; but the message to them implies this, and from what is said to them we may probably gather what was uppermost in their minds. Already told by the previous prophecies that God would not spare Jerusalem for its own sake, and that His long forbearance hitherto was no warrant for its continuance, they still evidently cherished the hope that, however sinful they might be in themselves, their city would yet be delivered for the sake of the holy men who lived therein. With such thoughts in their minds the elders came and sat before the prophet, in whose fearless words they had already learned to have confidence, and awaited what he might have to say to them.

(3) **Have set up their idols in their heart.**—It was not the open idolatry of Judæa which is reproved among these elders of the captivity; that had already passed away, but still their heart was not right. Like Lot's wife, they longed for that which they dared not do. With such a disposition, they were in the greatest danger, putting "the stumbling-block of their iniquity," the temptation to sin, directly before them. And not only so, but they kept themselves in a state of alienation from God, so that it was idle to imagine He would allow Himself to be enquired of by them. The question implies the negative answer which is fully expressed in the following verses.

(4) **Will answer him that cometh.**—The words *that cometh*, not being in the original, should be omitted. The verb *answer* in the original is in the passive, and has a reflexive sense="I will show myself answering," a softer form than the English. The principle that when man persists in going counter to God's known will He will allow him to misunderstand that will, is abundantly established by such instances as that of Balaam (Num. xxii. 20) and of Micaiah (1 Kings xxii. 15). No man can hope to know what God would have him to do unless his own heart is truly submissive to the Divine will. The threat here is, that the man coming to inquire of God with a heart full of idolatry, shall receive no true answer from that Omniscience which he does not respect; but will rather find himself deceived by the illusions of his own heart. This idea is more fully developed in the following verse. (Comp. Isa. xliv. 20.)

(6) **Repent and turn.**—The announcements of the previous verses form the basis for the earnest call to a true repentance. There can be no hope for Israel in any merely outward reformation; they have to do with the Searcher of hearts, and the only repentance acceptable to Him is that which has its seat in the affections of the heart.

(7) **Or of the stranger.**—Under the Mosaic legislation, "the stranger" living among the Israelites was bound to observe a certain outward deference to the law of the land, just as a foreigner in any country now is bound to respect in certain things the law of the country in which he lives. Israel being a theocracy, its fundamental law against idol-worship could not be violated with impunity by those who sought the protection of its government (Lev. xvii. 10; xx. 1, 2, &c.). In this case, however, outward idolatry is not alleged, as the accusations of this verse and verse 4 refer only to the secret idolatry of the heart; and the point insisted upon is not so much the idol-worship in itself, as the hyprocrisy of attempting to join with this the enquiring of the Lord. God declares that He will answer such hypocrisy, in whomsoever it may be found, not by the prophet through whom the enquiry is made, but by Himself interposing to punish the enquirer, and to make him an example to deter others from a like course.

(8) **Will make him a sign.**—The text of the Hebrew is here preferable to its margin, which has been followed by our translators, as well as by the ancient versions. There is a similar threat in Deut. xxviii. 37; and the clause should be rendered, "will make him desolate (or destroy him) for a sign and a proverb." The English almost loses the idea of the wonder which will be occasioned by the severity of God's dealings with the false worshipper.

(9) And if the prophet be deceived
when he hath spoken a thing, I the
LORD [a]have deceived that prophet, and
I will stretch out my hand upon him,
and will destroy him from the midst of
my people Israel. (10) And they shall
bear the punishment of their iniquity:
the punishment of the prophet shall be
even as the punishment of him that
seeketh *unto him;* (11) That the house of
Israel may go no more astray from me,
neither be polluted any more with all
their transgressions; but that they may
be my people, and I may be their God,
saith the Lord GOD.
(12) The word of the LORD came again
to me, saying, (13) Son of man, when the
land sinneth against me by trespassing
grievously, then will I stretch out mine
hand upon it, and will break the [b]staff
of the bread thereof, and will send famine
upon it, and will cut off man and beast
from it: (14) [c]though these three men,
Noah, Daniel, and Job, were in it, they

[a] 1 Kings 22. 23.

[b] Lev. 26. 26; ch. 4. 16; & 5. 16.

[c] Jer. 15. 1.

(9) **And if the prophet be deceived.**—The exact sense of the original is, "If a prophet be persuaded and speak a word, I the LORD have persuaded that prophet." The thought is thus in close connection with what precedes; in verses 3, 4, 7, the Lord has refused to allow an answer through the prophet to the hypocritical enquirer; but if the prophet, by giving the desired answer, allows himself to become a partaker of the sin which God abhors, then God will treat him according to that general method of dealing with sin which is here described. He "persuades" the prophet in the same sense in which He hardened Pharaoh's heart, by making such persuasion the natural consequence of the immutable moral laws which He has ordained. Men are held back from sin only by God's own Holy Spirit drawing them towards Himself. When they set this aside by transgressing God's commands, the inevitable tendency—the tendency under the moral laws God has established—is to further sin. Hence the prophet who allowed himself to be persuaded, contrary to God's command, to answer the hypocritical enquirer at all, would inevitably be persuaded further to answer him according to his desires. God does not *force* men either to receive the truth or to act righteously. If, notwithstanding His remonstrances, their hearts are set upon wrong, He will even give them up and "send them strong delusion that they should believe a lie" (2 Thess. ii. 11). We are too often told in Scripture of this method of the Divine dealing to leave any room for us to misunderstand the principle. The result is a terrible one, but it is quite in keeping with all we can observe of the Divine work in nature. The man that refuses the medicine, must sink under the disease. The principle is clearly exemplified in the case of Ahab (1 Kings xxii. 19—23), where the Lord is represented as sending a lying spirit into the mouths of the prophets, that they might counsel the king to the wrong course he was already determined to take. God is declared to do this because it was the result under His moral laws of the wicked and domineering spirit of the king who had driven away the true prophets and gathered around himself those who were willing to pervert their office and prophesy falsely to gratify his wishes. Of course this is not to suppose that God can ever be the author of sin and deceit; but He has ordained that sin shall punish itself, and when the heart rejects Him, He withdraws His Spirit from it and gives it up to its own delusions. Thus when Saul's heart became alienated from God, and "the Spirit of the Lord departed from" him, the evil spirit, which came instead, is said to be "from the LORD" (1 Sam. xvi. 14). This kind of judgment is necessarily more common in times of great and general declension from the right. Hence false prophets were especially abundant towards the close of the kingdom of Judah, and form a marked characteristic in the New Testament prophecies of "the last days." No more terrible judgment can be imagined than that of thus giving up the sinner to the consequences of his own sin.

Will destroy him from the midst of my people Israel.—This is not the word which is so often used in the penalties of the law, "will cut him off from my people." The latter refers only to excommunication, to exclusion from the privileges of the chosen people; but this means that the untrue prophet shall literally be destroyed, like Balaam (Num. xxxi. 8), among the enemies of God with whom he had cast in his lot.

(11) **May go no more astray.**—Here is given the object of all the previous severity of judgment—that Israel may be brought to a true repentance and be reunited in communion with God.

The prophet is now directed, in a distinct communication, to meet the thought which was evidently in the minds of the people, that Jerusalem would yet be spared for the sake of the righteous dwelling therein, as had been promised to Abraham even in the case of Sodom and Gomorrha (Gen. xviii. 23—32). The course of thought is this: If any land should sin as grievously as Israel had done, and God should send a judgment, it would not be spared, though Noah, Daniel and Job were in it. This is repeated in connection with each one of four successively mentioned judgments; and then the climax is reached, that much less can Jerusalem be spared when all these judgments are combined together. In the end, the justice of the Divine dealings shall be acknowledged.

A few years earlier, Jeremiah (chaps. xiv., xv.) had uttered a very similar prophecy in connection with the denunciation of false prophets (chap. xiv. 13, 15) in which not only he himself is forbidden to intercede for the people (chap. xiv. 11), but it is said (chap. xv. 1) that the presence of Moses and Samuel would be unavailing.

(13) **When the land sinneth.**—The definite article is not in the Hebrew, and should be omitted, as the proposition is a general one. Also the future tenses throughout the verse should be rendered as present, in accordance with this character of a general statement: "When a land sinneth . . . and I stretch out . . . and break the staff . . . and send famine . . . and cut off." The particular judgment of famine was threatened in the warnings of the law (Lev. xxvi. 26; Deut. xxviii. 38—40), and also, in immediate connection with it, all the other woes here mentioned.

(14) **Noah, Daniel, and Job.**—These three are selected, doubtless, not only as examples of eminent

should deliver *but* their own souls by
their righteousness, saith the Lord God.
(15) If I cause noisome beasts to pass
through the land, and they [1] spoil it, so
that it be desolate, that no man may
pass through because of the beasts:
(16) *though* these three men *were* [2] in it,
as I live, saith the Lord God, they shall
deliver neither sons nor daughters; they
only shall be delivered, but the land shall
be desolate.
(17) Or *if* I bring a sword upon that
land, and say, Sword, go through the
land; so that I cut off man and beast
from it: (18) though these three men *were*
in it, *as* I live, saith the Lord God, they
shall deliver neither sons nor daughters,
but they only shall be delivered themselves.
(19) Or *if* I send a pestilence into that
land, and pour out my fury upon it in
blood, to cut off from it man and beast:
(20) though Noah, Daniel, and Job, *were*
in it, *as* I live, saith the Lord God, they
shall deliver neither son nor daughter;
they shall *but* deliver their own souls by
their righteousness.
(21) For thus saith the Lord God;
[3] How much more when I send my four
sore judgments upon Jerusalem, the
sword, and the famine, and the noisome
beast, and the pestilence, to cut off from
it man and beast? (22) Yet, behold,
therein shall be left a remnant that
shall be brought forth, *both* sons and
daughters: behold, they shall come
forth unto you, and ye shall see their
way and their doings: and ye shall be
comforted concerning the evil that I
have brought upon Jerusalem, *even* concerning all that I have brought upon it.
(23) And they shall comfort you, when ye
see their ways and their doings: and ye
shall know that I have not done without
cause all that I have done in it, saith the
Lord God.

1 Or, *bereave.*

2 Heb., *in the midst of it.*

3 Or, *Also when.*

B.C. cir. 594.

CHAPTER XV.—(1) And the word of

holiness themselves, but as men who had been allowed to be the means of saving others. For Noah's sake his whole family had been spared (Gen. vi. 18); Daniel was the means of saving his companions (Dan. ii. 17, 18); and Job's friends had been spared in consequence of his intercession (Job xlii. 7, 8). Moses and Samuel might seem still more remarkable instances of the value of intercessory prayer; but these had already been cited by Jeremiah (chap. xv. 1). The mention of Daniel, a contemporary of Ezekiel, with the ancient patriarchs, Noah and Job, need occasion no surprise. The distance in time between Noah and Job was greater than between Job and Daniel, and it has been well said that there was need of the mention of a contemporary to bring out the thought—were there in Jerusalem the most holy men of either past or present times it would avail nothing. It is also to be remembered that Daniel was separated from Ezekiel by circumstances which created a distance between them corresponding to that which separated him in time from the patriarchs. Ezekiel was a captive among the captives; Daniel had now been for about twelve years in important office at the royal court, and possessed of the very highest rank. There is, therefore, no occasion for the strange supposition that the reference is to some older Daniel, of such eminence as to be spoken of in the way he is here and in chap. xxviii. 3, and yet whose name has otherwise completely faded out from history. But besides all this, there was an especial propriety, and even necessity for the purpose in hand, that Daniel should be mentioned. He was not only in high office, but was the trusted counsellor of Nebuchadnezzar by whom Jerusalem was to be destroyed. He was also a very holy man, and a most patriotic Israelite. The Jews, therefore, might well have thought that his influence would avail to avert the threatened calamity, and by placing his name in the list, their last hope was to be dashed as it could be by nothing else.

(15–20) In these verses the same declaration is repeated, for the sake of emphasis, with each one of three other instruments of punishment, with only such variations of phraseology as are required for rhetorical reasons. The phrase "their own souls" is here also simply equivalent to "themselves." The judgments mentioned are all taken from the warnings in Lev. xxvi., the famine from verse 26, the wild beasts from verse 22, the sword and also the pestilence from verse 25.

(21) **My four sore judgments.**—The teaching of the preceding eight verses is here gathered up into its climax. In the case of any one of the four punishments mentioned in succession, the presence of the holiest of men should be of no avail to avert it; how much more then, when all these are combined in the judgment upon Jerusalem, will it be impossible to stay its doom.

(22) **Ye shall be comforted concerning the evil.**—In this and the following verse it is promised that a remnant shall be brought from Jerusalem; and it is clearly implied that they shall come to Babylonia. There the present exiles shall see them, and thus be comforted. But in what sense comforted? The connection absolutely decides this: "when ye see their ways and their doings, ye shall know that I have not done without cause all that I have done in it." That is, when you see the wickedness of this remnant, you will cease to mourn over the judgment, for you cannot but perceive that it was a righteous act of God. The expression "sons and daughters" is used in verse 22 with reference to the same phrase in verses 16, 18, and 20; and the form "they shall comfort you" in verse 23 is explained by what is said in verse 22, not as meaning "they shall administer comfort," but "they shall be a cause of comfort" by showing you their exceeding wickedness.

XV.

This short chapter contains a single simile and its application, designed to show that Israel, having failed to fulfil the purpose for which they had been chosen,

the LORD came unto me, saying, (2) Son
of man, What is the vine tree more than
any tree, *or than* a branch which is
among the trees of the forest? (3) Shall
wood be taken thereof to do any work?
or will *men* take a pin of it to hang any
vessel thereon? (4) Behold, it is cast
into the fire for fuel; the fire devoureth
both the ends of it, and the midst of it
is burned. [1]Is it meet for *any* work?
(5) Behold, when it was whole, it was
[2]meet for no work: how much less
shall it be meet yet for *any* work, when
the fire hath devoured it, and it is
burned?

(6) Therefore thus saith the Lord GOD;
As the vine tree among the trees of the
forest, which I have given to the fire for
fuel, so will I give the inhabitants of
Jerusalem. (7) And I will set my face
against them; they shall go out from
one fire, and *another* fire shall devour
them; and ye shall know that I *am* the
LORD, when I set my face against them.
(8) And I will make the land desolate,
because they have [3]committed a tres-
pass, saith the Lord GOD.

CHAPTER XVI.—(1) Again the word
of the LORD came unto me, saying,
(2) Son of man, cause Jerusalem to know
her abominations, (3) and say, Thus saith
the Lord GOD unto Jerusalem; Thy
[4]birth and thy nativity *is* of the land of
Canaan; thy father *was* an Amorite,
and thy mother an Hittite. (4) And *as
for* thy nativity, in the day thou wast
born thy navel was not cut, neither wast
thou washed in water [5]to supple *thee;*
thou wast not salted at all, nor swaddled

1 Heb., *Will it prosper?*

2 Heb., *made fit.*

B.C. 594.

3 Heb., *trespassed a trespass.*

4 Heb., *cutting out,* or, *habitation.*

5 Or, *when I looked upon thee.*

---

were worthless, and could have no other end than destruction.

(2) **What is the vine tree?**—The comparison of Israel to a vine or to a vineyard is common in Scripture (Ps. lxxx. 8—13; Isa. v. 1—7; Jer. ii. 21; Hosea x. 1; Matt. xxi. 33—41, &c.), and is very apt; for the vine, bringing forth its appointed fruit, was among the most precious of the earth's productions, but failing this, was utterly worthless for anything but fuel. The fact that Israel did not yield the fruit required is not especially mentioned, being taken for granted here, and abundantly expressed in the connected prophecies. The fruit of righteousness, as our Lord has shown in John xv. 1—8, under the same figure of the vine, is only possible by a steadfast clinging to the Source of righteousness, and this was the point in which the Jews of this time had signally failed.

(5) **How much less shall it be meet?**—The worthlessness of the wood of the vine having been shown in verse 3, and it having been said in verse 4 that it is therefore "cast into the fire," the climax is here reached. According to verse 4, it is burned off at the ends, and then the remnants are pushed also into the fire to be burned, just as one would do with grape branches to save the trouble of cutting them up. This comparison is carried out in verse 7.

(7) **Shall go out from one fire and another fire . . .**—The words *one* and *another* are not in the original and may be omitted, and the articles inserted: "they go from the fire, and the fire devours them." This was exactly the condition of Israel. Partially consumed in the fire of the Divine judgments, they had been again and again overtaken. The "ends" were already gone; now "the midst of it" was to be burned up—the final result, as always, being a recognition of God.

XVI.

In the magnificent allegory which occupies this chapter, the sin and consequent rejection of Israel is set forth in still stronger terms than in anything which has gone before. There are three main parts of the chapter: the sin (verses 3—34), the punishment (verses 35—52), and the final restoration of Israel (verses 53—63). The extreme aggravation of the sin is shown from the fact that Israel had no original claim upon God's favour, nor anything to make her attractive—she was merely an exposed and repulsive foundling (verses 3—5)—when God took pity upon, and saved, and cared for her (verses 6, 7). Then when she had come of age, He entered into covenant with, and greatly blessed her (8—14); but she proved utterly unfaithful to her covenant—an unfaithful wife; wanton beyond all precedent (15—34). Hence her punishment.

(3) **Thy birth and thy nativity is of the land of Canaan.**—In the original the words "births" and "nativities" are in the plural, already indicating what the whole context makes plain, that the reference is not to the natural, but to the spiritual origin of Israel. So our Lord says to the Jews of His time, "Ye are of your father, the devil" (John viii. 44; comp. Matt. iii. 9); and Isaiah addresses his contemporaries as "rulers of Sodom" and "people of Gomorrha" (Isa. i. 10). The word *births,* as indicated by the margin, comes from a verb meaning *to cut* or *dig out,* as stone from the quarry; and there is a play upon this sense in Isa. li. 1. Israel's character, her spiritual nativity, was thoroughly Canaanitish.

An Amorite . . . an Hittite.—These two tribes, especially the former, as the most prominent in Canaan, are frequently put for the whole (Gen. xv. 16; Deut. i. 44, with Num. xiv. 45; Josh. x. 5; 2 Kings xxi. 11, &c.). The dealings of the patriarchs in Canaan were particularly with the Hittites (Gen. xxiii.; xxvi. 34, 35; xxvii. 46; xxviii. 1, 6—8). This once great and powerful nation had almost faded from history; but their monuments and inscriptions are just now beginning to be discovered and deciphered.

(4) **Washed in water to supple thee.**—The various particulars of this and the following verse describe a child cast out into the field immediately upon its birth, unpitied by any one, and in a condition in which it must soon have perished. Neither the text nor the margin seems to have hit upon the sense of the word translated "to supple," the probable meaning of which is "to cleanse." The rubbing of the body of the new-born infant with salt, a custom still prevailing

at all. (5) None eye pitied thee, to do
any of these unto thee, to have compas-
sion upon thee; but thou wast cast out
in the open field, to the lothing of thy
person, in the day that thou wast born.
(6) And when I passed by thee, and
saw thee [1]polluted in thine own blood,
I said unto thee *when thou wast* in thy
blood, Live; yea, I said unto thee *when
thou wast* in thy blood, Live. (7) I have
[2]caused thee to multiply as the bud of
the field, and thou hast increased and
waxen great, and thou art come to [3]ex-
cellent ornaments: *thy* breasts are fash-
ioned, and thine hair is grown, whereas
thou *wast* naked and bare. (8) Now when
I passed by thee, and looked upon thee,
behold, thy time *was* the time of love;
and I spread my skirt over thee, and
covered thy nakedness: yea, I sware
unto thee, and entered into a covenant
with thee, saith the Lord GOD, and thou
becamest mine. (9) Then washed I thee
with water; yea, I throughly washed
away thy [4]blood from thee, and I
anointed thee with oil. (10) I clothed
thee also with broidered work, and shod
thee with badgers' skin, and I girded
thee about with fine linen, and I covered
thee with silk. (11) I decked thee also
with ornaments, and I put bracelets
upon thy hands, and a chain on thy neck.
(12) And I put a jewel on thy forehead,
and earrings in thine ears, and a beau-

1 Or, *trodden under foot.*

2 Heb., *made thee a million.*

3 Heb., *ornament of ornaments.*

4 Heb., *bloods.*

---

in some parts of the east, probably had a symbolical, as well as a supposed physical effect; and is recommended for the latter reason by Galen (*De Sanit.* i. 7). The wrapping the body tightly in swaddling-bands (Comp. Luke ii. 7) is still common, even in Italy. The time here referred to in the life of Israel is that in which it passed from its embryonic state in the family of the patriarchs to a nation in the bondage of Egypt. Despised, oppressed, and enslaved, no other people ever became a nation under such circumstances. Humanly speaking, national life was an impossibility for them.

(6) **Live.**—While they were in this condition, God took pity on them. He delivered them from their oppressors; He raised up a leader for them; He gave them a law and a Church, with its priesthood and its sacraments; He led them into the land of promise, delivered them from their enemies, and constituted them a nation under the most favourable circumstances for their growth and development in all righteousness. The sense is well expressed in our version; but the original does not contain the word *when*, nor words corresponding to the words in italics. The connection shows that "in thy blood" is to be taken with "I said," and not with "live;" it was while Israel was in its unclean and neglected condition that the gracious word "live" was spoken. The Chaldee paraphrast has adopted the other connection, and ingeniously explained, "I revealed myself that I might redeem you, because I saw that you were afflicted in your bondage; and I said unto you, In the blood of circumcision I will pity you, and I said unto you, In the blood of the passover I will redeem you." The word *polluted* is better rendered by the margin, *trodden under foot*, referring to their oppressed condition in Egypt.

(7) **I have caused thee.**—Omit the "have," and modify the tenses throughout the verse. "I caused thee . . . thou didst increase and wax tall . . . and came to beauty . . . were fashioned . . . was grown." In the first clause, "caused thee to multiply," the literal sense takes the place of the figurative; but the rest of the verse describes Israel as a young woman just growing up into the beauty of early womanhood. The phrase "excellent ornaments" is somewhat difficult; but is now generally understood as meaning literally "ornament of cheeks," *i.e.*, beauty. The *whereas* in the last clause may give the impression of a contrast between the state described and the former one of infancy; this is not intended. But the meaning is, that while Israel was thus growing into the full development and beauty of womanhood, she was still "naked and bare."

(8) **Now when I passed by thee.**—Here, as in verse 6, omit the *when*, and render, "and I passed by thee." Two separate visits are spoken of: the one in Israel's infancy in Egypt, when God blessed and multiplied her (verse 6); the other when she had become a nation, and God entered into covenant with her in the Exodus and at Sinai. The verse describes this covenant in terms of the marriage relation, a figure very frequent in Scripture. On the phrase "spread my skirt," comp. Ruth iii. 9, and on "becamest mine," Ruth iv. 10.

(9—14) These verses describe the purifications and preparations for marriage to one of high rank (comp. Esth. ii. 9, 12). The reality corresponding to the figure is, of course, the Divine care over Israel at Sinai, in the wilderness, and in the conquest of Canaan.

(10) **Badgers' skin.**—See Ex. xxv. 5. The thing intended is a fine kind of leather prepared from the skin of some sea animal; but the critics differ as to the particular animal intended, whether the dolphin or the dugong. "Fine linen" was a luxury much valued by the ancients, while "silk" is a word used only here and in verse 13, and its meaning is much questioned. By its etymology it is thought to express fineness of texture; and our translators have followed the rabbinical tradition in understanding it to mean silk.

(11—14) In these verses the Divinely-given prosperity and glory of Israel is set forth under the sustained figure of the ornaments and food of a royal eastern bride. The various particulars mentioned are familiar to all readers of the Scripture histories. The latter part of verse 13 and verse 14 evidently refer to the times of David and Solomon, when the kingdom of Israel extended from the Euphrates to the "river of Egypt," and very many of the surrounding kingdoms were made tributary. Israel then was renowned among the heathen, but its glory was pre-eminently as the nation of Jehovah, "through my comeliness which I had put upon thee."

(12) **A jewel on thy forehead.**—Literally, *a nose-ring on thy nostril*, the custom of the time sanctioning this mode of ornament.

tiful crown upon thine head. (13) Thus
wast thou decked with gold and silver;
and thy raiment *was of* fine linen, and
silk, and broidered work; thou didst
eat fine flour, and honey, and oil: and
thou wast exceeding beautiful, and thou
didst prosper into a kingdom. (14) And
thy renown went forth among the
heathen for thy beauty: for it *was* per-
fect through my comeliness, which I
had put upon thee, saith the Lord
GOD.

(15) But thou didst trust in thine own
beauty, and playedst the harlot because
of thy renown, and pouredst out thy
fornications on every one that passed
by; his it was. (16) And of thy gar-
ments thou didst take, and deckedst thy
high places with divers colours, and
playedst the harlot thereupon: *the like
things* shall not come, neither shall it be
so. (17) Thou hast also taken thy fair
jewels of my gold and of my silver,
which I had given thee, and madest to
thyself images [1] of men, and didst com-
mit whoredom with them, (18) and tookest
thy broidered garments, and coveredst
them: and thou hast set mine oil and
mine incense before them. (19) My meat
also which I gave thee, fine flour, and
oil, and honey, *wherewith* I fed thee,
thou hast even set it before them for [2] a
sweet savour: and *thus* it was, saith the
Lord GOD. (20) Moreover thou hast
taken thy sons and thy daughters, whom
thou hast borne unto me, and these hast
thou sacrificed unto them [3] to be de-
voured. *Is this* of thy whoredoms a
small matter, (21) that thou hast slain
my children, and delivered them to
cause them to pass through *the fire* for
them? (22) And in all thine abomina-
tions and thy whoredoms thou hast not
remembered the days of thy youth, when
thou wast naked and bare, *and* wast
polluted in thy blood.

1 Heb., *of a male.*

2 Heb., *a savour of rest.*

3 Heb., *to devour*

In contrast to God's kindness and abundant blessing, Israel's grievous sin is now described (verses 15—34). It is to be remembered that however this extraordinary sin was the natural fruit of neglected grace, it yet was extraordinary. It is not by mere hyperbole that Israel is represented as worse than others. The grace which does not elevate always reacts by directing to a lower depth. (See Excursus at end of this Book on chap. v. 7).

(15) **Didst trust in thine own beauty.**—Comp. Deut. xxxii. 15; Hos. xiii. 6. There can scarcely be a more striking instance of the working of the hand of Providence in history than the story of the kingdom of Israel during and after the reign of Solomon. Raised as a theocracy to great power and wealth by the Divine blessing, it began to trust in its own beauty. Solomon's policy was to make it a great and powerful empire among the nations of the earth, losing sight of its true character as the kingdom of God. Consequently the very means he took to aggrandise it became the instruments of its fall. His vast Oriental harem, gathered from all surrounding nations, introduced idolatry into the palace, and fostered it throughout the land. His magnificence was sustained by taxation, which gave the pretext for revolt. The doom was pronounced that the kingdom should be divided, and when this was fulfilled at Solomon's death, his empire outside the boundaries of Palestine fell apart like a rope of sand, while within, instead of one compact and united monarchy, were two petty kingdoms often in hostility to one another, and each inviting to its assistance the most powerful neighbouring monarchs, to whose rapacity the whole ultimately fell a prey.

Playedst the harlot . . his it would be.—The political relation of the two parts of Israel just described, placed her at the mercy of every more powerful nation, and gave the impetus to every sort of idolatry which her masters chose to encourage. This apostacy from God, still keeping up the figure of the earlier part of the chapter, is represented as harlotry; and not only so, but as indiscriminate harlotry, for Israel never adopted and clung to any one false God, but worshipped the abominations of every nation which prevailed over her.

(16) **Deckedst thy high places with divers colours.**—The use of colours, and especially of tapestry in colours, in the adornment of places of worship, was universal throughout the religions of antiquity. It formed a striking feature of the adornment of the Tabernacle, and what is censured here is the perversion of this, which should have been for the glory of God, to the honour ot idols. Translate the last clause of the verse, as in apposition with what goes before, "Things which should not come, and that which should not take place."

The three following verses emphasise the apostacy of Israel by taking up various particulars of the symbolical good gifts which God had given her, and showing how she had perverted them to idolatry. It was a chief feature of the charge against her that these gifts were from God, and that she had given them to another—a charge which must for ever remain true of the perversion of the talents God has given to any other than His own service.

(20) **Hast sacrificed unto them,** *i.e., hast sacrificed the children unto the idols.* This was a terrible development of the later idolatries of Israel. At first the custom appears to have been a ceremony of passing young children through the fire to thereby consecrate them to Moloch; but afterwards it became an actual sacrifice of them in the fire to the idol. The Lord speaks of them in verse 20, as "*thy* children whom thou hast borne unto Me;" they were indeed Israel's children, but still children whom God had given to her. Then in verse 21, by a most significant change of the pronoun, He calls them "My children," the sin itself being aggravated by giving to the idol that which belonged to Jehovah. The last clause of the verse would be better translated, *Were thy whoredoms too little?—i.e.,* was

(23) And it came to pass after all thy
wickedness, (woe, woe unto thee! saith
the Lord GOD;) (24) *that* thou hast also
built unto thee an [1] eminent place, and
hast made thee an high place in every
street. (25) Thou hast built thy high
place at every head of the way, and hast
made thy beauty to be abhorred, and
hast opened thy feet to every one that
passed by, and multiplied thy whore-
doms. (26) Thou hast also committed
fornication with the Egyptians thy
neighbours, great of flesh; and hast
increased thy whoredoms, to provoke
me to anger. (27) Behold, therefore, I
have stretched out my hand over thee,
and have diminished thine ordinary *food*,
and delivered thee unto the will of them
that hate thee, the [2] daughters of the
Philistines, which are ashamed of thy
lewd way. (28) Thou hast played the
whore also with the Assyrians, because
thou wast unsatiable; yea, thou hast
played the harlot with them, and yet
couldest not be satisfied. (29) Thou hast
moreover multiplied thy fornication in
the land of Canaan unto Chaldea; and
yet thou wast not satisfied herewith.

(30) How weak is thine heart, saith the
Lord GOD, seeing thou doest all these
things, the work of an imperious whorish
woman; (31) [3] in that thou buildest thine
eminent place in the head of every way,
and makest thine high place in every

1 Or, *brothel house.*

2 Or, *cities.*

3 Or, *In thy daughters is thine, &c.*

---

not apostacy enough without adding thereto this terrible and unnatural crime?

(23) **After all thy wickedness.**—The sin and idolatry hitherto described had been derived by Israel chiefly from the Canaanites, the old inhabitants of the land; but now, in accordance with what was said in verse 15, the prophet goes on to speak of the other abundant idolatries adopted eagerly by the Israelites from foreign nations.

(24) **Built unto thee an eminent place.**—The word means literally, *arches.* Such arched rooms were used in connection with the worship of idols for licentious purposes, and hence the translation of the margin indicates the real object of the structure, whether the word be taken in its literal sense, or spiritually, of unfaithfulness to God. In the following verse the indiscriminateness of Israel's idolatry is expressed in the strongest terms, and then in the following verses the adoption of the idolatries of several nations in particular is specified.

(26) **The Egyptians . . . great of flesh.**—The Egyptians are properly named first, because, even in the golden calf of the wilderness, the Israelites turned with avidity to the worship of Egypt. This tendency seems to have been only suppressed, not extinguished, during the subsequent ages, and remained ever ready to develop itself, as in the calves of Jeroboam (1 Kings xii. 28—30); but it received great accession of strength during the reigns of Solomon and his successors. The Egyptians are called "great of flesh" from the character of their popular worship, which was a thoroughly sensuous nature worship. The connection of Israel with Egypt in the latter part of the monarchy was not only religious, but political, in bold defiance of the reiterated Divine commands. Especially at this time, a great part of the work of Jeremiah was to oppose the tendency of the successive kings of Judah to alliance with Egypt.

(27) **Diminished thine ordinary food.**—This cutting short of the power and prosperity of Israel was a discipline of correction designed to bring her to a consciousness of her sin.

The daughters of the Philistines, *i.e.*, their cities, according to the figurative language of the chapter, and indeed the common figurative language of Scripture. Philistia was but a small power in the south-west corner of Palestine, yet from the time of the Judges down through the whole period of the monarchy, they were the persistent foes of Israel. During the time immediately before Samuel, they held nearly the entire land in subjection, and although subdued by David, they became troublesome again in the times of the later kings (see 2 Chron. xxvi. 7, xxviii. 18), and are often spoken of not only by the earlier prophets, Isaiah and Amos, but also by Jeremiah (chaps. xxv. 20, xlvii. 1, 4), Ezekiel (chap. xxv. 15, 16), and Zechariah (chap. ix. 6).

Ashamed of thy lewd way.—The Philistines, true to their own false gods, despised the Israelites for their unfaithfulness to Jehovah. It is the old but ever new story of the heathen repelled from the truth by the unworthiness of its professed followers.

(28) **With the Assyrians.**—The Assyrians and Egyptians were for many centuries in deadly hostility against each other, and it would seem that Israel could hardly have formed alliances with and adopted the idolatries of both. Nevertheless they had done so, and in addition to their Egyptian idolatries, had gone to the extent, in the time of Ahaz, of displacing the altar in the court of the Temple, and putting in its stead an altar of the gods of Assyria (2 Kings xvi. 10—16).

(29) **In the land of Canaan unto Chaldæa.**—Canaan was originally the name of only that strip of land between the hills and the sea occupied by the Phœnicians, in other words, the lowlands. Thence it became extended over the whole land. It is thought by some writers to revert here to its original meaning, and be equivalent to the low, flat land. The expression will become clearer if translated, "the Canaan land Chaldæa." The word, however, bears also the meaning of traffic, commerce (Isa. xxiii. 8; Hos. xii. 7; Zeph. i. 11), and in this sense is applied to Babylon in chap. xvii. 4, and this is the better meaning here. The idea will then be that Israel, beginning its idolatries in the actual Canaan, had extended them along with her commercial intercourse on every side, until at last she had carried them even to Chaldæa, the great commercial emporium of the time.

(30) **Weak.**—The English word scarcely expresses the force of the original:—languishing with desire. The word *heart* occurs here only in the feminine.

(31) **Eminent place.**—See note on verse 24.

In that thou scornest him.—It was characteristic of both the kingdoms of Israel after the division,

street; and hast not been as an harlot,
in that thou scornest hire; (32) *but as* a
wife that committeth adultery, *which*
taketh strangers instead of her hus-
band! (33) They give gifts to all
whores: but thou givest thy gifts to all
thy lovers, and [1] hirest them, that they
may come unto thee on every side for
thy whoredom. (34) And the contrary is
in thee from *other* women in thy whore-
doms, whereas none followeth thee to
commit whoredoms: and in that thou
givest a reward, and no reward is given
unto thee, therefore thou art contrary.
(35) Wherefore, O harlot, hear the
word of the LORD: (36) Thus saith the
Lord GOD; Because thy filthiness was
poured out, and thy nakedness dis-
covered through thy whoredoms with
thy lovers, and with all the idols of thy
abominations, and by the blood of thy
children, which thou didst give unto
them; (37) behold, therefore I will gather
all thy lovers, with whom thou hast
taken pleasure, and all *them* that thou
hast loved, with all *them* that thou hast
hated; I will even gather them round
about against thee, and will discover
thy nakedness unto them, that they may
see all thy nakedness. (38) And I will
judge thee, [2] as women that break wed-
lock and shed blood are judged; and I
will give thee blood in fury and jealousy.
(39) And I will also give thee into their
hand, and they shall throw down thine
eminent place, and shall break down thy
high places: they shall strip thee also
of thy clothes, and shall take [3] thy fair
jewels, and leave thee naked and bare.
(40) They shall also bring up a company
against thee, and they shall stone thee
with stones, and thrust thee through
with their swords. (41) And they shall
[a] burn thine houses with fire, and
execute judgments upon thee in the
sight of many women: and I will cause
thee to cease from playing the harlot,
and thou also shalt give no hire any
more. (42) So will I make my fury to-
ward thee to rest, and my jealousy shall
depart from thee, and I will be quiet,
and will be no more angry.

[1] Heb., *bribest.*

[2] Heb., *with judgments of.*

[3] Heb., *instruments of thine ornament.*

[a] 2 Kings 25. 9; Jer. 52. 13.

---

that the interference of foreign nations in their affairs was generally sought first by Israel itself and purchased at a heavy price. The people were so situated on the great highway between the rival nations of Egypt and Assyria, that their friendship ought to have been of value to either of them, and to have been sought with great inducements. But Israel, in its weakness and wickedness, more than threw itself away and purchased its own ruin. The particulars mentioned in this verse belong to the past rather than to the present, and all the tenses should be so translated.

(33) **Thou givest thy gifts.**—2 Kings xvi. 8, 9, may be referred to as an instance in illustration. Ahaz "took the silver and gold that was found in the house of the Lord," as well as "the treasures of the king's house," and used it to secure the alliance of the king of Assyria.

The prophet, having up to this point described the sin, now turns to pronounce the punishment upon Israel (verses 35—52). The same allegory is still preserved, and the punishment is depicted in the same figurative language as the sin. This portion of the prophecy may be subdivided into two parts, in the first of which (verses 35—43) the punishment itself is described in terms taken from the legal punishment of the adulteress and murderess; while in the second (verses 44—52) the justice of this doom is vindicated, especially by a comparison with Samaria on the one side, and with Sodom on the other.

(36) **Thy filthiness.** — Literally, *thy brass, i.e.,* money, which, as said in the previous verses, Israel had lavished upon the surrounding nations. Either gold or silver is the more common term for money, and the prophet appears to have here used brass contemptuously. In this verse the people's apostasies are briefly recapitulated, under the names of adultery and child murder, as the basis for what follows.

(37) **Thou hast loved . . . hast hated.**—Not only those with whom Israel had sought alliances, but those who had been her hereditary foes, like the Philistines and Edomites, shared in the spoil of her land. Much of this had been already accomplished (see 2 Kings xvi. 6; 2 Chron. xxviii. 17, 18, &c.). Israel's weakness and wickedness should be fully exposed to all her enemies.

(38) **Women that break wedlock and shed blood.**—Under the Mosaic law the penalty for adultery was death (Lev. xx. 10), and the same penalty also was attached to the devotion of "seed to Moloch" (Lev. xx. 1—5), and to murder (Exod. xxi. 12). The Jewish method of capital punishment on individuals was by stoning (see Lev. xx. 2, and comp. John viii. 5), and of punishing an apostate city was by the sword (Deut. xiii. 15). Hence both modes are mentioned together in verse 40, though somewhat at the expense of the consistency of the allegory. The last clause would be more exactly translated, "I will make thee blood of fury and jealousy," the fury referring to the avenging of murder, and the jealousy to the punishment of adultery, each requiring the life, or blood, of the offender.

(39) **Eminent places.**—See Note on verse 24. The destruction of her idolatries as well as the desolation of Israel herself is foretold.

(41) **Shall burn thine house.**—Comp. Deut. xiii. 16. The figurative and the literal sense here blend together; the house of the unfaithful wife shall be destroyed, and the houses of Jerusalem shall be burned.

(42) **My fury . . . to rest.**—Not in pity but in satiety, as having accomplished the utter desolation of Israel.

(43) Because thou hast not remembered
the days of thy youth, but hast fretted
me in all these *things;* behold, therefore
I also will recompense thy way upon
thine head, saith the Lord God: and
thou shalt not commit this lewdness
above all thine abominations. (44) Be-
hold, every one that useth proverbs shall
use *this* proverb against thee, saying,
As *is* the mother, *so is* her daughter.
(45) Thou *art* thy mother's daughter, that
lotheth her husband and her children;
and thou *art* the sister of thy sisters,
which lotheth their husbands and their
children: your mother *was* an Hittite,
and your father an Amorite. (46) And
thine elder sister *is* Samaria, she and
her daughters that dwell at thy left
hand: and [1] thy younger sister, that
dwelleth at thy right hand, *is* Sodom
and her daughters. (47) Yet hast thou
not walked after their ways, nor done
after their abominations: but, [2] as *if
that were* a very little *thing*, thou wast
corrupted more than they in all thy
ways. (48) *As* I live, saith the Lord God,
Sodom thy sister hath not done, she
nor her daughters, as thou hast done,
thou and thy daughters. (49) Behold,
this was the iniquity of thy sister Sodom,
pride, fulness of bread, and abundance
of idleness was in her and in her
daughters, neither did she strengthen
the hand of the poor and needy. (50) And
they were haughty, and committed
abomination before me: therefore [a] I
took them away as I saw *good.*
(51) Neither hath Samaria committed half
of thy sins; but thou hast multiplied
thine abominations more than they, and
hast justified thy sisters in all thine
abominations which thou hast done.

1 Heb., *lesser than thou.*

2 Or, *that was lothed as a small thing.*

a Gen. 19. 24.

---

(43) **Hast fretted me.**—Better, *hast raged against me.* This form of the verb does not have a transitive sense. (Comp. Gen. xlv. 24; Prov. xxix. 9; and in this particular form, 2 Kings xix. 27, 28; Isa. xxxvii. 28, 29, where the same word is used.)

Thou shalt not commit. — The English here follows the Masoretic punctuation, putting the verb in the second person. Probably it should be read in the first person (which only changes the Masoretic vowels) and translated "that I may not commit wickedness concerning all thine abominations." The word for *wickedness* is the especial word used for one who tolerates sin in another who is under his control (see Lev. xix. 29). God represents that it would be wrong to allow Israel's sin to go unpunished.

(44) **As is the mother.**—The sin of the people had become so notorious as to attract general attention, and lead to the application of this proverb. The nativity of Israel described in verse 3 is here in mind, and the proverb becomes equivalent to saying, these sins belong to every people living in Canaan; once practised by the Amorites and Hittites, they are now continued by the Israelites.

(45) **Which lothed their husbands.** — Israel, like Samaria and Sodom, being spiritually of Amorite and Hittite descent, they are represented as her sisters. A certain difficulty arises from the statement that they, too, "lothed their husbands and their children," and this is only removed by remembering that, notwithstanding their heathenism and long course of idolatry, they are still regarded as having gone astray from primeval revelation, and proved false to the only true God whom they once had known.

(46) **Thine elder sister.** — The words *elder* and *younger* mean, literally, *greater* and *smaller*. They thus come, like the Latin *major* and *minor*, to be used for *older* and *younger;* but still their original and most common meaning, which should be retained here, is greater and smaller. Chronologically, Sodom was not younger than Jerusalem, nor is there evidence that Samaria was older. The terms are to be understood of Samaria as the capital of the far larger northern kingdom, and of Sodom as a single city of no great population. The orientals, in describing geographical positions, considered themselves as facing the east, and hence Samaria (at the north) was on the left, and Sodom on the right. Sodom is spoken of poetically as if still in existence. They were both the spiritual sisters of Judah, just as all alike were daughters of the Amorite and Hittite.

(47) **As if that were a very little thing.**—Better, *thou hast not walked after their ways, nor done after their abominations a little only, but hast done more corruptly than they, &c.* This excess of wickedness is constantly charged upon the Jews (see chap. v. 6, 7). Sodom had indeed sinned grievously in its day, but more than 1,000 years had since passed, in which resistance to Divine admonitions had led on to a still more grievous depth of wickedness; and Samaria had been carried into captivity more than a century before the time of the prophet, and during this period the people, with now and then a few short intervals of reformation, had been tending steadily downwards. This same thought is dwelt upon in the four following verses, in which the sin of Sodom is described, while that of Samaria is passed over as being sufficiently well known.

(49) **Pride, fulness of bread, and abundance of idleness.**—The description strikes at the causes rather than the overt acts of sin, and the unnatural crimes which are always associated in our minds with the name of Sodom are not mentioned. It is noticeable, however, that the distinct sin which is mentioned in this passage is the negative one too common in all ages, "neither did she strengthen the hand of the poor and needy."

(50) **As I saw good.**—The word *good* is not in the original, and should be omitted, and the particle translated *when*: "Therefore I took them away when I saw this." Punishment followed upon the manifestation of their sin. (Comp. Gen. xviii. 21.)

(51) **Hast justified thy sisters.**—The same expression is repeated in the following verse. In both it is evidently used in a comparative sense. By the greatness of Judah's sins even Sodom and Samaria were made to appear innocent in comparison.

(52) Thou also, which hast judged thy
sisters, bear thine own shame for thy
sins that thou hast committed more
abominable than they: they are more
righteous than thou: yea, be thou con-
founded also, and bear thy shame, in
that thou hast justified thy sisters.
(53) When I shall bring again their
captivity, the captivity of Sodom and
her daughters, and the captivity of
Samaria and her daughters, then *will I*
bring again the captivity of thy captives
in the midst of them: (54) that thou
mayest bear thine own shame, and
mayest be confounded in all that thou
hast done, in that thou art a comfort
unto them. (55) When thy sisters,
Sodom and her daughters, shall return
to their former estate, and Samaria and
her daughters shall return to their
former estate, then thou and thy
daughters shall return to your former
estate. (56) For thy sister Sodom was
not [1] mentioned by thy mouth in the day
of thy [2] pride, (57) before thy wickedness
was discovered, as at the time of *thy*
reproach of the daughters of [3] Syria, and
all *that are* round about her, the
daughters of the Philistines, which
[4] despise thee round about. (58) Thou
hast [5] borne thy lewdness and thine
abominations, saith the LORD. (59) For
thus saith the Lord GOD; I will even
deal with thee as thou hast done, which
hast despised the oath in breaking the
covenant. (60) Nevertheless I will re-
member my covenant with thee in the
days of thy youth, and I will establish
unto thee an everlasting covenant.
(61) Then thou shalt remember thy ways,

1 Heb., *for a report*, or, *hearing*.

2 Heb., *prides*, or, *excellencies*.

3 Heb., *Aram*.

4 Or, *spoil*.

5 Heb., *borne them*.

---

(52) **Hast judged thy sisters.**—Judah had approved the judgments upon Sodom and Samaria, as it is always easy for man to approve judgments upon the sins of others; but now this must be brought home to herself for her own greater sins. (Comp. Rom. ii.)

Having described the sin and the punishment, the prophet now goes on in the remainder of the chapter to speak of the restoration of Israel. This is first declared in the strongest terms to be impossible (verses 53—59), and the efforts of many commentators to transform the language into a covert promise of restoration are entirely unsuccessful. After this, indeed, in verses 60—63, the establishment of the Divine covenant with Israel is fully and distinctly promised. Yet there is no contradiction between the two, for the prophet had a right to suppose that the people would remember what had been so plainly declared before: that while the nation as a whole must perish, yet after the purifying chastisements of the Lord He would have mercy upon and bless a remnant who should be saved. The general doom is first announced as irrevocable; then the exception is made for the few.

(53) **Shall bring again their captivity.**—This is not a promise of restoration to Israel; but, on the contrary, is an expression of the utter hopelessness of their punishment in the strongest possible form. The "bringing again of captivity" does not, indeed, necessarily mean a return from exile (into which Sodom had not been carried); but, as explained in verse 55, a return to the former estate, that is, a state of happiness and prosperity. In the case of Sodom this was manifestly impossible; and even in the case of Samaria it would, if accomplished, lack any historical identification. Sodom and her daughters (the surrounding cities) had perished with all their inhabitants many ages ago, leaving no descendants behind. Restoration was, therefore, obviously impossible; and by conditioning the restoration of Jerusalem on an impossible thing, it is meant to be most strongly denied.

(54) **Art a comfort unto them.**—Compare what was said of justifying them in verses 51, 52. The greater sin of Judah became a comfort by throwing their own evil into the shade.

(57) **Thy reproach of the daughters of Syria.**—The pronoun should be omitted, and the phrase read, "the reproach." The time referred to, when Jerusalem was too proud to make mention of Sodom, was in the days of her prosperity. Later her "wickedness was discovered," and her pride humbled by such disasters as fell upon her, especially from the days of Ahaz onward. At that time she was hard pressed both by the Syrians and by the Philistines (2 Kings xv. 37; 2 Chron. xxviii. 18, 19), and impoverished herself to obtain aid from Assyria (2 Kings xvi. 8); and such straits continued to mark her subsequent history. (See 2 Kings xxiv. 2.) In the weakness and disasters towards the close of her kingdom, Judah became an object of contempt to the surrounding nations, "despised" by Syria and Philistia alike. Another view less probably refers "thy reproach" to Judah's exultation at the fall of Syria and the Philistines before the march of the Assyrians.

(59) **In breaking the covenant.**—This was the especial point of the heinousness of the sin of the Jews, and the one which so greatly aggravated their guilt. The sin was necessarily proportioned to the light against which it had been committed. (Comp. John ix. 39, 41; xv. 22, 24.)

(60) **I will remember my covenant.**—The remembrance of God's covenant is made the basis of His mercy to His penitent people (Lev. xxvi. 42—45) from the beginning, and it is often spoken of as an everlasting covenant. In the New Testament (Luke i. 54, 55, 72, 73, &c.) this covenant is regarded as fulfilled in the Christian dispensation. At the same time, the Christian covenant is described as new in Jer. xxxi. 31—34; it was both the continuation and designed fulfilment of the old, and in its superiority and plainer revelation of the Divine will was new. Hence the contrast between *My* covenant here and *Thy* covenant in the following verse. The covenant to be afterwards established shall be "an everlasting covenant."

(61) **Give them unto thee for daughters.**—The humiliation of Jerusalem must be so complete that she will gladly receive these once-despised enemies to the closest family relationship. We are not here to think of Sodom specifically, but (the concrete passing into

and be ashamed, when thou shalt receive
thy sisters, thine elder and thy younger:
and I will give them unto thee for
[a] daughters, but not by thy covenant.
(62) And I will establish my covenant
with thee; and thou shalt know that I
am the LORD: (63) that thou mayest re-
member, and be confounded, and never
open thy mouth any more because of
thy shame, when I am pacified toward
thee for all that thou hast done, saith the
Lord GOD.

CHAPTER XVII.—(1) And the word
of the LORD came unto me, saying,
(2) Son of man, put forth a riddle, and
speak a parable unto the house of Israel;
(3) and say, Thus saith the Lord GOD;
A great eagle with great wings, long-
winged, full of feathers, which had
[1]divers colours, came unto Lebanon,
and took the highest branch of the
cedar: (4) he cropped off the top of his
young twigs, and carried it into a land
of traffic; he set it in a city of mer-
chants. (5) He took also of the seed of
the land, and [2]planted it in a fruitful
field; he placed *it* by great waters, *and*
set it *as* a willow tree. (6) And it grew,
and became a spreading vine of low
stature, whose branches turned toward
him, and the roots thereof were under
him: so it became a vine, and brought
forth branches, and shot forth sprigs.

a Gal. 4. 26.

1 Heb., *embroidering.*

B.C. cir. 594.

2 Heb., *put it in a field of seed.*

---

the general) of that which Sodom represented, the heathen world at large. This shall be received with Jerusalem to the church of God; "but not by thy covenant." The covenant with Israel, however it may have been preceded by a "preaching of the Gospel" to Abraham (Gal. iii. 8), was distinctly a covenant of works, under which neither Jew nor Gentile could attain salvation (see Rom. and Gal. throughout). Not, therefore, by this should the nations of the earth be given to Jerusalem as representing the Church.

(62) **Establish my covenant with thee.**—The old covenant, having failed, is merged in the new and better covenant promised in xi. 19; xviii. 31; and more fully in Jer. xxxi. 31—34. This new covenant, established through a perfect Mediator, can alone perfectly fulfil God's gracious designs for man, although the way for it must necessarily have been prepared by the less perfect covenant of old.

(63) **Pacified toward theo.**—Better, *when I pardon thee.* The original word is the one used technically in the law for the atonement or "covering up" of sins; and the thought is, when God shall forgive the sins of His people, and receive them to communion with Himself.

XVII.

This chapter contains a "riddle" or "parable" (verses 3—10), with its explanation (verses 11—21), closing with a clear Messianic prophecy couched in language taken from the parable (verses 22—24). While it is a distinct communication, it belongs to the same series of prophecies which began with the vision of chaps. viii.—xi., and is continued through chap. xix. The meaning of the parable is made entirely clear by the explanation the first eagle (verses 3—6) is Nebuchadnezzar; "the top of his young twigs" is Jehoiachin, carried to Babylon; the "vine of low stature" is Zedekiah; the second eagle is Pharaoh (verse 7). The historical facts on which the parable is based are recorded in 2 Kings xxiv. 8—20; 2 Chron. xxxvi. 9—13; Jer. xxxvii. and lii. 1—7.

(2) **A riddle . . . a parable.**—What the prophet has to say is called a riddle as well as a parable, because there is something in it recondite and obscure—something which, until it is explained, should excite the minds of the people to guess its meaning.

(3) **A great eagle with great wings.**—In the original "*the* great eagle." This is explained in verse 12 of "the king of Babylon." Nebuchadnezzar is compared to an eagle also in Jer. xlviii. 40; xlix. 22; and Cyrus to a bird of prey in Isa. xlvi. 11. He has great and long wings, because he has already flown victoriously over wide-spread lands; and he is "full of feathers which had divers colours," because he had embraced in his empire a variety of nations differing in languages, manners, and customs.

Came unto Lebanon.—Jerusalem is called Lebanon, as in Jer. xxii. 23, because Lebanon is the home of the cedar, and the royal palace in Jerusalem was so rich in cedar as to be called "the house of the forest of Lebanon" (1 Kings vii. 2).

The highest branch.—This is a word occurring only in Ezekiel (verse 22, and chap. xxxi. 3, 4, 10). It is of uncertain etymology, but is explained in verse 4 as meaning "the top of his young twigs." The English *branch* hardly conveys the exact idea, and it would be better to translate "topshoot."

(4) **Into a land of traffick.**—Literally, *a land of Canaan,* the word being sometimes used for merchant or merchandise, as in Hosea xii. 8 (Engl. 7); Isa. xxiii. 8; Zeph. i. 11. The parallelism of the next clause shows that this is its meaning here. Babylon has already been called Canaan in chap. xvi. 29, probably from its commercial character.

(5) **Of the seed of the land.**—In place of the captive Jehoiachin Nebuchadnezzar did not set over the land an eastern satrap, but appointed a native prince, Zedekiah, the uncle of Jehoiachin. He was "planted," not like the tall cedar on the mountain, but yet like "a willow tree by great waters" where it might flourish in its degree (see verse 14).

(6) **A spreading vine of low stature.**—Had Zedekiah been faithful to his oath and allegiance to Nebuchadnezzar and to his higher allegiance to God, Israel might have been fruitful and prosperous as a dependent kingdom.

Whose branches turned towards him.—Better, *That its branches might turn towards him, and its roots might be under him.* This was Nebuchadnezzar's object—to make of Israel a flourishing kingdom, which should yet be entirely dependent upon himself and helpful to him in his great struggle with the power of Egypt; and hence his especial rage when his politic

(7) There was also another great eagle
with great wings and many feathers:
and, behold, this vine did bend her roots
toward him, and shot forth her branches
toward him, that he might water it by
the furrows of her plantation. (8) It
was planted in a good [1]soil by great
waters, that it might bring forth
branches, and that it might bear fruit,
that it might be a goodly vine.
(9) Say thou, Thus saith the Lord
GOD; Shall it prosper? shall he not
pull up the roots thereof, and cut off
the fruit thereof, that it wither? it shall
wither in all the leaves of her spring,
even without great power or many
people to pluck it up by the roots
thereof. (10) Yea, behold, *being* planted,
shall it prosper? shall it not utterly
wither, when the east wind toucheth it?
it shall wither in the furrows where it
grew.
(11) Moreover the word of the LORD
came unto me, saying, (12) Say now to
the rebellious house, Know ye not what
these *things mean?* tell *them,* Behold,
the king of Babylon is come to Jeru-
salem, and hath taken the king thereof,
and the princes thereof, and led them
with him to Babylon; (13) and hath
taken of the king's seed, and made a
covenant with him, and hath [2]taken an
oath of him: he hath also taken the
mighty of the land: (14) that the king-
dom might be base, that it might not
lift itself up, [3]*but* that by keeping of his
covenant it might stand. (15) But he re-
belled against him in sending his ambas-
sadors into Egypt, that they might give
him horses and much people. Shall he
prosper? shall he escape that doeth such
things? or shall he break the covenant,
and be delivered? (16) *As* I live, saith the
Lord GOD, surely in the place *where* the
king *dwelleth* that made him king, whose
oath he despised, and whose covenant
he brake, *even* with him in the midst of
Babylon he shall die. (17) Neither shall
Pharaoh with *his* mighty army and great
company make for him in the war, by

1 Heb., *field.*

2 Heb., *brought him to an oath.*

3 Heb., *to keep his covenant, to stand to it.*

---

arrangements were frustrated by Zedekiah's treachery and folly.

(7) **Another great eagle.**—This is explained in verse 15 of Pharaoh. He was also powerful, ruling a populous land, but is not described as with the variegated feathers of verse 3, because he did not rule over the same diversity of people with Nebuchadnezzar. Zedekiah, while owing his position to Nebuchadnezzar, treacherously sought the aid of Egypt, as mentioned in verse 15, and more fully in the historical passages referred to in the note at the beginning of this chapter. A chief task of the prophet Jeremiah was to endeavour to dissuade Zedekiah from this Egyptian alliance.

(9) **Of her spring.**—Our translators probably intended by this word, as they evidently did in Ps. lxv. 10, "her springing forth," her growth; but it would be better now to substitute the word *growth.*

Pluck it up by the roots.—The word here is a different one from the "pull up" in the earlier part of the verse, and has rather the sense of "raise up from the roots." The whole clause would be better translated, "not *even* with great power and many people is it to be raised up from its roots again." The meaning is explained in verse 17, that the strength of Pharaoh would be utterly insufficient to restore the people whom God had blighted.

(11) **Moreover the word of the Lord.**—The form of expression leaves it uncertain whether the explanation of the parable was given at the same time with the parable itself, or whether, as is more probable, a little time was suffered to elapse, during which it should be "a riddle" to the people that they might be the more attentive to its meaning when given to them.

(14) **That the kingdom might be base.**—(See the Notes on verse 6.)

(15) **Shall he escape that doeth such things?**—The faithlessness of Zedekiah and his court to his own sworn covenant was an act, in addition to all his other wickedness, especially abominable to God. The sanctity of an oath had always been most strongly insisted upon in Israelitish history. It must be remembered that even when, as in the case of the Gibeonites (Josh. ix.), the oath had been obtained by fraud, and centuries had passed since it was given, God yet sorely punished the land for its violation (2 Sam. xxi. 1, 2); and in this case the king had been more than once Divinely warned through the prophet Jeremiah of the danger of his treachery. As Zedekiah's intrigues with Egypt were just now going on, it was particularly important that they should be exposed, and their result foretold to the captives who were yet trusting in the safety of Jerusalem.

(16) **In the place . . . he shall die.**—The distinct prophecy of the death of Zedekiah at Babylon is here given in a form to bring out in the strongest light the fitness and justice of his punishment. It was to be in the place of the king to whom he owed his crown, and to whom he had given his fealty, yet against whom he had rebelled. The tense here changes to the future, because the events of this and the following verse were yet to be fulfilled.

(17) **By casting up mounts.**—This translation implies that "the casting up mounts and building forts" were to be the act of Pharaoh; but such things are done not by the relieving, but by the besieging army. A better translation would be, "when they cast up mounts," &c.—*i.e.,* at the time of the siege. We learn from Jer. xliv. 30 that the particular Pharaoh here referred to was Hophra, the Apries of the Greeks. In Jer. xxxvii. 5—11, it is said that an Egyptian army did come up and temporarily raise the siege of Jerusalem; but it was of no avail. Pharaoh did him no good—did not "make for him in the war." The Chaldæans speedily returned, drove away the Egyptians, and renewed the siege, finally capturing and burning the city.

casting up mounts, and building forts,
to cut off many persons: (18) seeing he
despised the oath by breaking the cove-
nant, when, lo, he had given his hand,
and hath done all these *things*, he shall
not escape. (19) Therefore thus saith the
Lord God; *As* I live, surely mine oath
that he hath despised, and my covenant
that he hath broken, even it will I re-
compense upon his own head. (20) And I
will [a]spread my net upon him, and he
shall be taken in my snare, and I will
bring him to Babylon, and will plead
with him there for his trespass that he
hath trespassed against me. (21) And all
his fugitives with all his bands shall fall
by the sword, and they that remain shall
be scattered toward all winds: and ye
shall know that I the Lord have
spoken *it*.

a ch. 12. 13; & 32. 3.

(22) Thus saith the Lord God; I will
also take of the highest branch of the
high cedar, and will set *it;* I will crop
off from the top of his young twigs a
tender one, and will plant *it* upon an
high mountain and eminent: (23) in the
mountain of the height of Israel will I
plant it: and it shall bring forth boughs,
and bear fruit, and be a goodly cedar:
and under it shall dwell all fowl of every
wing; in the shadow of the branches
thereof shall they dwell. (24) And all the
trees of the field shall know that I the
Lord have brought down the high tree,
have exalted the low tree, have dried up
the green tree, and have made the dry
tree to flourish: I the Lord have spoken
and have done *it*.

B. C. 594.

CHAPTER XVIII.—(1) The word of

---

(19) **Mine oath . . . my covenant.**—Zedekiah's oath and covenant to Nebuchadnezzar are called the Lord's, because made in the Lord's name, and also because He had commanded them. Rebellion against Nebuchadnezzar was, therefore, under the circumstances, apostasy from the Lord Himself.

With verse 21 the explanation of the parable ends. What follows is a distinct Messianic prophecy, which, although couched in the same figurative language, has nothing corresponding to it either in the parable or in its explanation.

(22) **I will also take.**—In what has passed all has been done according to God's will, but yet through human instrumentality: Israel has been punished, Jehoiachin has been, and Zedekiah is about to be, carried into captivity, as God designed; yet Nebuchadnezzar has done it all for his own purposes. Now God Himself directly interposes, and takes a scion of the same "high cedar," the royal house of David. In accordance with the allegory, this can only be an historical personage, and from the description which follows, this person can only be the Messiah. So it has been understood by nearly all interpreters, Jewish and Christian.

A tender one.—This epithet is used of the Messiah in reference to the lowliness of His immediate human origin and condition. (Comp. Isa. liii. 2.) David applies the same expression to himself (2 Sam. iii. 39), and to Solomon (1 Chron. xxii. 5, xxix. 1), in reference to their want of strength for the work required of them as the heads of Israel. This figure of the Messiah as a scion of the royal tree of David, though naturally growing out of the allegory here, had been used by the prophets long before, as in Isa. xi. 1, and the name "the Branch" had almost become a distinctive title for Him (Isa. iv. 2; Jer. xxiii. 5, &c.).

(23) **In the mountain of the height of Israel,** *i.e.*, Mount Zion, called in the parallel passage (chap. xx. 40) "mine holy mountain." Similar prophecies are also to be found in Isa. ii. 2—4; Micah iv. 1—3; Ps. ii. 6. No point is made more clear in the prophecies of the Christian dispensation than that it is to have its roots in the Jewish, that the "law shall go forth from Zion," and that the new covenant shall yet be a covenant with God's people of old. This mountain is to be understood as the representative of the centre and seat of the kingdom of Israel, and not to be confined too literally to the actual hill of Zion itself.

Be a goodly cedar.—Not like the vine of low stature; this shall grow into a strong and great tree, under whose shadow all the inhabitants of the earth shall find sustenance and protection. A similar figure is used by the contemporary prophet Daniel (chap. iv. 20, 21), and by our Lord Himself in the parable (Matt. xiii. 32). The universality of the blessings of the Christian dispensation, in contrast with the narrowness of the Jewish, is one of its features most frequently dwelt upon both in prophecy and in the New Testament, and shall still enter into the burden of the songs of the redeemed (Rev. v. 9). The last clause of the verse repeats and emphasises the permanence of the connection of the believer with Christ.

(24) **All the trees of the field shall know.**—As the cedar represents the kingdom of Israel, so the other trees represent all other earthly powers who shall ultimately acknowledge the work of the Lord in the redemption of mankind through His Son.

Have brought down the high tree.—Comp. the song of Hannah (1 Sam. ii. 1—10) and that of the Virgin Mary (Luke i. 52—55). In all alike there is the acknowledgment that all power is from God, and that He, in the working out of His purposes, gives and takes away as to Him seems good. Very precious to His Church of old in its desolation and distress must have been the announcement of this truth, and very precious it is still to all who pray "Thy kingdom come."

XVIII.

This chapter connects itself closely with the foregoing series of prophecies. The certainty of the Divine judgments had now been repeatedly and most emphatically foretold, but that this might have the effect of leading the people to true repentance, it was still necessary that the sense of sin should be brought home to them individually. The people were by no means inclined to acknowledge their own personal guilt, but were

the LORD came unto me again, saying,
(2) What mean ye, that ye use this proverb
concerning the land of Israel, saying, The
[a]fathers have eaten sour grapes, and the
children's teeth are set on edge? (3) As
I live, saith the Lord GOD, ye shall not

a Jer. 31. 29.

rather, like sinners of every age, disposed to look upon their sufferings as the consequence of the sins of others who had gone before. This disposition is here met by the most full and emphatic assurance that God deals with each man in view of his own acts—that no one shall be either punished or rewarded for another's guilt or virtue, but only for his own.

The statements here made are exposed to two difficulties:—(1) that it is expressly declared in the second commandment that God does visit the sins of the fathers upon the children (Exod. xx. 5, xxxiv. 7; Deut. v. 9), and that all history shows that this is a law of His moral government of the world; and (2) that it is by no means true that individual suffering and happiness are exactly proportioned in this world to individual character and conduct. On the contrary, from the time of Job to that of our Lord, this was one of those pernicious views of the Jews which the inspired word takes great pains to combat. How, then, are the statements of this chapter to be justified? In regard to the first difficulty, simply by remembering the two-fold relation, the individual and the federal, in which each man stands to his Maker. It is in virtue of the federal relation that, on the one hand, as children of Adam, we are all born into the world with a pre-disposition to sin; and, on the other, are all partakers of the benefits of the redemption wrought out for us by the second Adam. Under the laws of nature it must necessarily come about that the children shall suffer or enjoy in consequence of the uprightness or the sin of their fathers. Yet more important, and prevailing above this federal relation, is the attitude of each individual towards God. By this, through the reconciliation effected by the redemption of Christ, he is brought into communion with God, and becoming one with Christ, is viewed and treated as a member of the body of the only begotten Son. This does not hinder that the laws of nature shall still work out their natural effects—we still must be subject to death, because our first father sinned; but it does bring about that all these natural sufferings become transformed into higher blessings. Even death becomes to us, through Him who has overcome death, but the gateway to a new and higher life. Thus it is true that God does both visit the sins of the fathers upon the children, and at the same time does, through all, punish and reward each single person according to their own individual bearing towards Him.

These considerations have already met the second difficulty. In a sense, and to a certain extent, individual suffering is certainly the consequence of individual sin, for the violation of the laws of nature—in other words, of the will of God—must always be attended with disastrous consequences; but these consequences are often slow in their development, and may fall not upon the individual who has done the wrong, but upon some more or less remote descendant, or even upon some wholly disconnected person, as in the case of David's suffering with his whole people for Saul's treatment of the Gibeonites. From this it results that the ills of life are by no means proportioned to the deserts of those upon whom they fall. But more important than this consideration is the fact that these ills are factors in God's moral government of the world, having in view the development in man of the character which He approves. Hence it comes about that "whom the Lord loveth he chasteneth" (Prov. iii. 11, 12; Heb. xii. 6), and leads them through earthly suffering to heavenly joy. The same events happen to the godly and the wicked. God causeth His sun to shine and His rain to fall alike upon the just and the unjust; but the effect of both dispensations depends upon the character of the person to whom they come. To him who is alienated in heart from God the sunshine becomes no blessing, while the rain of calamity and sorrow only too often results in further alienation and hardening; but on him who accepts both as the dispensations of a loving Father, they produce their intended effect, and he finds that in them, as in all else, God makes all things work together for good to them that love Him.* This, too, is in accordance with natural law, where the effect of any force is often dependent upon the substance on which it is exerted. The dew is drunk in by the already growing vegetation, but does not fall on the dry and thirsty gravel at its side. It was precisely this sort of discipline through which this very people were now passing. They had been chosen and blessed for the faith of Abraham, yet they were suffering for many generations of persistent neglect of and rebellion against God. (See especially Jer. xv. 4; Lam. v. 7; 2 Kings xxiv. 3.) All this belonged to their federal relation; but, at the same time, they stood each one individually before the Lord, to hear or to refuse His word. Such as obeyed His voice would find in these very calamities the ground and the means of repentance, and their sorrows would become transformed into the richest of all possible blessings, while those who continued obdurate would find their present calamity but the shadow of the darker approaching judgment of being utterly cast out from God's presence. This great truth culminated for the Jews in both its parts at the Christian era, when, on the one side, our Lord represents the punishment of the sins of their whole history as coming "upon this generation" (Matt. xxiii. 35, 36); and, on the other, He then remembered His promise to their fathers, and established with those who would receive Him an everlasting covenant.

There was thus an important truth contained in the perverted views of the people, and it was very necessary that the still higher truths of this chapter should be impressed upon them; for only thus could the inferior and more obvious facts be correlated with the justice of God and His purposes of love towards His people.

(2) **What mean ye?**—Almost the same expression occurs in chap. xii. 22. The literal translation would be, *What is it to you who are using this proverb?* and the sense is "*Why* do you, &c.?" *Proverb* shows that it was a common saying, a way in which the people habitually sought to shirk the responsibility for their guilt. The same proverb is quoted in Jer. xxxi. 29, and condemned in the same way. "Concerning the land" should rather be *in the land, i.e.*, among the people, including both those at Jerusalem and in captivity. The teaching of this chapter concerning individual responsibility is, in one form or another, often repeated by Ezekiel. It is set forth in regard to the prophet and people, in chap. iii. 18—21; in regard to those upon whom the mark was set, in chap. ix. 4—6; in regard to those who enquire of the Lord, in chap. xiv.

* See Augustine: *De Civ. Dei*, I. c. 8.

have *occasion* any more to use this pro-
verb in Israel. (4) Behold, all souls are
mine; as the soul of the father, so also
the soul of the son is mine: the soul
that sinneth, it shall die.

(5) But if a man be just, and do that
which is [1]lawful and right, (6) *and* hath
not eaten upon the mountains, neither
hath lifted up his eyes to the idols of
the house of Israel, neither hath [a]defiled
his neighbour's wife, neither hath come
near to [b]a menstruous woman, (7) and
hath not [c] oppressed any, *but* hath re-
stored to the debtor his [d]pledge, hath
spoiled none by violence, hath [e]given his
bread to the hungry, and hath covered
the naked with a garment; (8) he *that*
hath not given forth upon [f]usury, neither
hath taken any increase, *that* hath with-
drawn his hand from iniquity, hath
executed true judgment between man
and man, (9) hath walked in my
statutes, and hath kept my judgments,
to deal truly; he *is* just, he shall surely
live, saith the Lord GOD.

(10) If he beget a son *that is* a [2] robber,
a shedder of blood, and [3] *that* doeth the
like to *any* one of these *things*, (11) and
that doeth not any of those *duties*, but
even hath eaten upon the mountains,
and defiled his neighbour's wife,
(12) hath oppressed the poor and needy,
hath spoiled by violence, hath not
restored the pledge, and hath lifted up

1 Heb., *judgment and justice.*

a Lev. 18. 20.

b Lev. 18. 19; & 20. 18.

c Ex. 22. 21; Lev. 19. 15; & 25. 14.

d Ex. 22. 26; Deut. 24. 12.

e Deut. 15. 7; Isa. 58. 7; Mat. 25. 35.

f Ex. 22. 25; Lev. 25. 36, 37; Deut. 23. 19; Ps. 15. 5.

2 Or, *breaker up of an house.*

3 Or, *that doeth to his brother besides any of these.*

3—9; and generally the teaching of this chapter is repeated in chap. xxxiii. 1—20.

(4) **All souls are mine.**—This is the basis of the subsequent teaching. Since all alike belong to God and are absolutely in His power, He has no occasion to punish one lest another should escape; and again, since all are His, He loves and would save them all, and inflicts punishment only when it is deserved and His grace is rejected. Four cases are now discussed separately: (1) That of the righteous man who honestly seeks to follow the ways of the Lord (verses 5—9); (2) that of his wicked son (verses 10—13); (3) that of the righteous son of the wicked (verses 14—20); (4) that of a change of character in the individual, whether from sin to righteousness or the reverse (verses 21—29). The word "soul" throughout the chapter does not mean exclusively the immortal part of our nature, but, as so often in Scripture, is equivalent to *man*, or *person*, or *self*; and the word "die" is used, as often elsewhere, in the broad sense of *suffer punishment*.

(5) **If a man be just.**—At the opening and close of the statement in regard to the righteous man (verses 5, 9), he is described in general and comprehensive terms; while in the intermediate verses various particulars of an upright life are specified as examples of the whole. These particulars have reference, first, to religious duties (verse 6*a*), then to moral obligations, such as the avoidance of adultery (verse 6*b*), and finally to duties negative and positive towards one's neighbour (verses 7, 8). The whole, including verses 5 and 9, may be considered as a terse summary of the practical duty of man.

(6) **Eaten upon the mountains.**—The various sins here specified are all enumerated again, with others, and charged upon Jerusalem in chap. xxii. 2—12. The particular of eating upon the mountains is mentioned in verse 9, and refers to the feasts in connection with sacrifices to idols which were commonly held in high places. The Lord Himself, indeed, was also worshipped in high places, in express violation of the law (Deut. xii. 17, 18), but the connection here points to the sacrificial idol-feasts (comp. Exod. xxxii. 6; 1 Cor. x. 7). The lifting up of the eyes to the idols is probably meant to express any longing after them short of actual worship (comp. Gen. xix. 26). The other sins mentioned in this verse were expressly forbidden in the law (Exod. xx. 14; Lev. xviii. 19), and were to be punished either with death (Lev. xx. 10; Deut. xxii. 22) or with excommunication (Lev. xx. 18).

(7) **To the debtor his pledge.**—In the simple state of early Hebrew society borrowing was resorted to only by the very poor, and the law abounds in precepts against any oppression or taking advantage in such cases (Exod. xxii. 25—27; Lev. xxv. 14, 17, &c.). Especial provision was made for restoring in a considerate way a pledge for borrowed money (Exod. xxii. 26; Deut. xxiv. 6, 10, &c.).

Given his bread.—In addition to the negative duties mentioned, were also the positive ones of feeding the hungry and clothing the naked; and it is to be remembered that these duties, and general helpfulness to those who need our help, are not left optional in Scripture, but are positively required, both in the Old and the New Testament, and their neglect is sin. (See Deut. xxii. 1—4; Job xxxi. 16—22; Isa. lviii. 5, 7; Matt. xxv. 34—46; James i. 27, ii. 15, 16).

(8) **Given forth upon usury.**—In Scripture usury does not mean excessive interest, as often in modern legislation, but any interest at all. This was strictly forbidden in the law to be taken of any Hebrew, though allowed, without limit as to amount, from foreigners. It had nothing to do with the regulation of commercial transactions, but was simply a law of kindness to a fellow member of the same household of faith in a primitive state of society. The Israelite was to lend freely to his impoverished neighbour to assist him, but without any expectation of gain for himself.

Executed true judgment.—This applies, of course, especially and directly to judicial sentences, but extends also to all cases in which one is brought to intervene in any way in transactions between others. What is required is absolute fairness, truthfulness, and integrity in the constant transactions of man with man.

(10) **That doeth the like to any one of these things.**—The prophet now enters upon the consideration of the second case, that of the son of a righteous father who takes to wicked courses, and it is shown that he shall be dealt with according to his own personal character. It is not necessary that he should be wholly given over to evil or have committed all the sins enumerated, but if he show the alienation of his heart from God by choosing to do any of those things which He has forbidden, he must fall under His righteous condemnation.

**his eyes to the idols, hath committed
abomination, (13) hath given forth upon
usury, and hath taken increase: shall he
then live? he shall not live: he hath
done all these abominations; he shall
surely die; his [1] blood shall be upon
him.**

**(14) Now, lo, *if* he beget a son, that
seeth all his father's sins which he hath
done, and considereth, and doeth not
such like, (15) *that* hath not eaten upon
the mountains, neither hath lifted up
his eyes to the idols of the house of
Israel, hath not defiled his neighbour's
wife, (16) neither hath oppressed any,
[2] hath not withholden the pledge, neither
hath spoiled by violence, *but* hath given
his bread to the hungry, and hath
covered the naked with a garment,
(17) *that* hath taken off his hand from the
poor, *that* hath not received usury nor
increase, hath executed my judgments,
hath walked in my statutes; he shall
not die for the iniquity of his father, he
shall surely live. (18) *As for* his father,
because he cruelly oppressed, spoiled his
brother by violence, and did *that* which
is not good among his people, lo, even
he shall die in his iniquity.**

**(19) Yet say ye, Why? doth not the
son bear the iniquity of the father?
When the son hath done that which is
lawful and right, *and* hath kept all my
statutes, and hath done them, he shall
surely live. (20) The soul that sinneth,
it shall die. [a] The son shall not bear
the iniquity of the father, neither shall
the father bear the iniquity of the son:
the righteousness of the righteous shall
be upon him, and the wickedness of the
wicked shall be upon him. (21) But if
the wicked will turn from all his sins
that he hath committed, and keep all
my statutes, and do that which is lawful
and right, he shall surely live, he shall
not die. (22) All his transgressions that
he hath committed, they shall not be
mentioned unto him: in his righteous-**

1 Heb., *bloods.*

2 Heb., *hath not pledged the pledge,* or, *taken to pledge.*

a Deut. 24. 16; 2 Kin. 14. 6; 2 Chr. 25. 4; Jer. 31. 29.

---

(13) **Hath done all these abominations.**—This expression is collective, while that in verse 10 is partitive. This is not because he who commits one sin is considered as having committed all, but because he who willingly commits any sin thereby puts himself into the class of sinners, of those who do not wish or intend to abide by the Divine will, but choose rather to do their own. Such a man places himself among the enemies of God. (Comp. James ii. 10.)

(14) **Doeth not such like.**—This is the third case—that of the righteous son of a wicked father. The general principle is the same, that each man is to be judged according to his own individual character. The son of the righteous man has advantages, and the son of the wicked has hindrances in the way of righteousness which are not specified here, although elsewhere we are abundantly taught that responsibility is directly proportioned to privilege; but here the object is only to set forth in the clearest way, and apart from any other issues, the single fact of individual responsibility. In each case the particular examples of sin are somewhat varied, to show that they are mentioned only as examples, in order to set forth more clearly the general principle.

(18) **As for his father.**—There is here a recurrence to the second case, to bring out more sharply the contrast between the two, and to emphasise the fact insisted upon, that each individual must be judged according to his own character, without help or prejudice from that of his father.

This third case was especially adapted to the prophet's purpose of refuting the proverb, because here was the father who had "eaten sour grapes," and his son's teeth were not to be set on edge.

(19) **Why? Doth not the son bear?**—It would be clearer to read this as a single question, "Why doth not the son, &c?" It is the question proposed by the people in objection to what has been declared. To them it seemed the law of nature, the necessity of the case, the teaching of history, that the son should bear the iniquity of his father. Their ideas had not risen to the conception of man's individual responsibility to God; to them the individual was still but a part of the nation or the family. They ask, therefore, why this universal law should now be reversed. It was not true that any law was reversed, it was only that the superior prevailed over the inferior law; but, as usual in such cases, the Divine word does not reason with the human objection, but in this and the following verse only reiterates most emphatically the law of individual responsibility.

(21) **If the wicked will turn.**—The prophet now takes up the fourth and last case—that of a change in the individual character. This has necessarily two sub-divisions: (1) that of the wicked repenting and doing righteousness (verses 21—23, and verses 27, 28), and (2) that of the righteous falling into wickedness, (verses 24—26), which latter case is more briefly treated, because the object is to encourage hope in repentance. This case, in both its parts, is first treated in verses 21—24, and then, for the sake of emphasis, repeated in reverse order in verses 26—28.

(22) **Shall not be mentioned unto him.**—A strong way of expressing the completeness of the Divine forgiveness. Here, again, at first sight, there seems to be an inconsistency between the Divine promise and the actual facts of the world. The penitent and forgiven sinner is continually seen to suffer through life from the consequences of his sin, as David's whole reign was overclouded with trouble and sorrow after his great sin in the matter of Bath-sheba and Uriah. But here also it is the natural law continuing to work in subservience to a higher moral law. The natural consequences of any acts are not changed, or are only partially modified, by the subsequent moral state of him who has done them; but that moral state determines whether those consequences, however painful they may be in themselves,

ness that he hath done he shall live.
(23) [a] Have I any pleasure at all that the
wicked should die? saith the Lord GOD:
and not that he should return from his
ways, and live? (24) But when the
righteous turneth away from his
righteousness, and committeth iniquity,
and doeth according to all the abomi-
nations that the wicked *man* doeth, shall
he live? All his righteousness that he
hath done shall not be mentioned: in
his trespass that he hath trespassed, and
in his sin that he hath sinned, in them
shall he die.
(25) Yet ye say, [b] The way of the Lord
is not equal. Hear now, O house of
Israel; Is not my way equal? are not
your ways unequal? (26) When a right-
eous *man* turneth away from his
righteousness, and committeth iniquity,
and dieth in them; for his iniquity that
he hath done shall he die. (27) Again,
when the wicked *man* turneth away from
his wickedness that he hath committed,
and doeth that which is lawful and
right, he shall save his soul alive.

a ch. 33. 11.

b ch. 33. 20.

c Matt. 3. 2.

1 Or, others.

d Jer. 32. 39; ch. 11. 19; & 36. 26.

e ch. 33. 11; 2 Pet. 3. 9.

2 Or, others.

(28) Because he considereth, and turneth
away from all his transgressions that he
hath committed, he shall surely live, he
shall not die.
(29) Yet saith the house of Israel, The
way of the Lord is not equal. O house
of Israel, are not my ways equal? are
not your ways unequal? (30) Therefore
I will judge you, O house of Israel,
every one according to his ways, saith
the Lord GOD. [c] Repent, and turn
[1] *yourselves* from all your transgressions;
so iniquity shall not be your ruin.
(31) Cast away from you all your trans-
gressions, whereby ye have transgressed;
and make you a [d] new heart and a new
spirit: for why will ye die, O house of
Israel? (32) For [e] I have no pleasure in
the death of him that dieth, saith the
Lord GOD: wherefore turn [2] *yourselves*,
and live ye.

CHAPTER XIX.—(1) Moreover take
thou up a lamentation for the princes
of Israel, (2) and say, What *is* thy
mother? A lioness: she lay down among

---

shall or shall not be really for his own highest gain. The absoluteness of the Divine forgiveness is seen by us, under the Christian dispensation, to be a necessary result of the ground on which it rests—the atonement of Christ. If the believer is truly united to Him by faith, he is a new creature (2 Cor. v. 17), and is looked upon no longer as a sinful son of Adam, but, as he is in reality, a member of the beloved and only-begotten Son of God. Hence his forgiveness must be complete, for his sins are atoned for, covered up, hidden from God's sight.

(23) **Have I any pleasure at all?**—This brings out that fundamental truth which underlies the whole teaching of both the Old and New Testaments, and which should have satisfied Israel of the Lord's readiness to receive every penitent sinner. God created man; and when he had fallen, ordered both the old and the new dispensations, and employed methods of infinite love to win him to salvation. He can have no pleasure in the death of the wicked; His delight can only be when man fulfils the design for which he was created, and returns to obedience and communion with God. Yet neither, as is declared in the next verse, can the Almighty suffer that His creature should set at nought His love and despise His salvation.

(25) **The way of the Lord is not equal.**—The word means literally, *weighed out, balanced.* The accusation of the Israelites was still (here and in verse 29) that the Lord was arbitrary and unjust. His statement in reply is that He rewards and punishes according to eternal and immutable principles of right. Every man must reap that which he has sown. (Comp. Rom. ii. 5—10.)

(27) **Shall save his soul alive.**—This does not mean that any man can by his own power save himself, for that question is not here in view at all, but that the consequence of a certain course of conduct will be his salvation, and that the adoption of that course is within the man's own choice.

(30) **Repent, and turn.**—The three last verses of the chapter contain an earnest exhortation to the Israelites, based on the principles of God's dealings with man just now declared, to repent and receive His mercy and blessing. Here, as before, there is no question of human sufficiency; and when the counsel is given (verse 31), "Make you a new heart and a new spirit," it is not meant to say that this can ever be the work of any other than God's Holy Spirit; but that Spirit is ever given to them that ask Him, and the question of salvation is still one which each man must decide for himself before God. The whole point of the chapter is that God's dealing with man is determined by man's own attitude towards Him. He that is alienated in his heart from God, whatever may have been his previous life, God will judge; and he that now seeks to conform his life to God's will, God will receive and forgive.

XIX.

This chapter forms the close of this long series of prophecies, and consists of a lament over the fall of the royal family of Israel and over the utter desolation of the nation itself. It fitly closes the series of warnings, and takes away any lingering hope of escape from the Divine judgments.

(2) **Thy mother.**—Mother stands for the whole national community—the theocracy, as is plain from verse 10. This was represented, since the captivity of the ten tribes, by Judah; and her "princes," of the line of David, were the legitimate kings of the whole nation. The figure of the lion is a common one in

lions, she nourished her whelps among
young lions. (3) And she brought up
one of her whelps: it became a young
lion, and it learned to catch the prey;
it devoured men. (4) The nations also
heard of him; he was taken in their
pit, and they brought him with chains
unto the land of [a] Egypt. (5) Now when
she saw that she had waited, *and* her
hope was lost, then she took another of
her whelps, *and* made him a young lion.
(6) And he went up and down among the
lions, he became a young lion, and
learned to catch the prey, *and* devoured
men. (7) And he knew [1] their desolate
palaces, and he laid waste their cities;
and the land was desolate, and the fulness thereof, by the noise of his roaring.
(8) Then the nations set against him on
every side from the provinces, and spread
their net over him: he was taken in
their pit. (9) And they put him in ward
[2] in chains, and brought him to the king
of Babylon: they brought him into
holds, that his voice should no more be
heard upon the mountains of Israel.
(10) Thy mother *is* like a vine [3] in thy
blood, planted by the waters: she was
fruitful and full of branches by reason
of many waters. (11) And she had
strong rods for the sceptres of them that
bare rule, and her stature was exalted
among the thick branches, and she appeared in her height with the multitude
of her branches. (12) But she was
plucked up in fury, she was cast down
to the ground, and the [b] east wind dried
up her fruit: her strong rods were
broken and withered; the fire consumed
them. (13) And now she *is* planted in

a 2 Kin. 23. 33; Jer. 22. 11.

1 Or, *their widows.*

2 Or, *in hooks.*

3 Or, *in thy quietness,* or, *in thy likeness.*

b Hos. 13. 15.

Scripture (see Gen. xlix. 9; Numb. xxiii. 24, xxiv. 9), and was also familiar in Babylonia.

(3) **It became a young lion.**—There can be no doubt (see verse 4) of the reference of this to Jehoahaz. After the death of Josiah, "the people of the land took Jehoahaz, the son of Josiah . . . and made him king" (2 Kings xxiii. 30). In verse 6 Jehoiachin is also spoken of particularly. These two are mentioned as examples of all the other kings after Josiah. Jehoiakim and Zedekiah are simply passed over, although it may be that the prophet looked upon them as creatures of Pharaoh and Nebuchadnezzar rather than as legitimate kings of Israel. Jehoiakim, moreover, died in Jerusalem, and Zedekiah was at this moment still upon the throne.

It devoured men.—This at once keeps up the figure, and has also its special justification in the evil courses of Jehoahaz (2 Kings xxiii. 32). He is represented as growing up and being like the heathen kings around. See also, in verse 2, Israel as a whole is represented as going aside from her high calling as a theocracy, and making herself "like the nations round about."

(4) **Brought him with chains unto the land of Egypt.**—Jehoahaz was conquered by Pharaoh-necho, deposed, and carried captive (2 Kings xxiii. 33; 2 Chron. xxxvi. 4). "Chains" is literally *nose-rings,* keeping up the figure of the lion. In the first part of the verse also there is allusion to the custom of assembling the neighbourhood to secure a lion or other wild beast.

(5) **Another of her whelps.** — After the three months' reign of Jehoahaz, his brother Jehoiakim was appointed king by Pharaoh (2 Kings xxiii. 34). He was conquered and "bound in fetters" by Nebuchadnezzar, with the intention of carrying him to Babylon (2 Chron. xxxvi. 7): he died, however, in disgrace in Jerusalem (2 Kings xxiv. 6; comp. Jer. xxii. 18, 19), and was succeeded regularly by his son Jehoiachin without foreign interference. His character, as shown in verses 6, 7 (comp. 2 Kings xxiv. 9; 2 Chron. xxxvi. 9), was evil like that of his father.

(7) **Knew their desolate palaces.**—This verse continues to describe the abominations of Jehoiachin's ways. The word "desolate palaces," although defended by some authorities, should be rendered, as in the margin, *widows.* The mention of the king's violation of these is an unavoidable departure from the figure, such as often occurs in Ezekiel.

(8) **The nations.**—As in verse 4, for one nation: in that case Egypt, in this Babylon. The plural is naturally used, as several nations were concerned in the whole history, of which single particulars only are here mentioned.

(9) **Brought him to the king of Babylon.**—2 Kings xxiv. 8—17. Jehoiachin reigned only three months when Jerusalem was conquered by Nebuchadnezzar. He "went out to the king of Babylon," but only because he could not help doing so, and was carried to Babylon and put in prison, where he was still living at the time of this prophecy. It was not till many years later that he was released (Jer. lii. 31, 32).

(10) **A vine in thy blood.**—The figure here changes to the more common one of a vine, yet by no means the "vine of low stature" of chap. xvii. 6; it is rather a *strong and goodly vine.* The phrase "in thy blood" is obscure, and has occasioned much perplexity to the commentators. Some of the ancient versions and some manuscripts have modified the text; but the meaning seems to be, if the text is taken as it stands, "Thy mother is like a vine living in the blood (*i.e.*, in the life) of her children." This would then be a statement amplified in the following, "fruitful and full of branches." The general sense is plain: Israel is described as having been planted a strong and fruitful vine, with every advantage for growth and full development.

(11) **Thick branches** should rather be translated *clouds.* It is a hyperbolical expression in the figure, to express the excellence of the vine of Israel.

(12) **She was plucked up.**—With the captivity of Jehoiachin and a part of the people the desolation had begun. Much still remained to be accomplished, but it was now close at hand; and the prophet speaks of it in the past tense, as if he saw it already fulfilled.

(13) **In a dry and thirsty ground.**—Such was Babylon to Israel in its national relations, and even after the return from the exile the Jews never rose again to much importance among the nations of the

the wilderness, in a dry and thirsty ground. (14) And fire is gone out of a rod of her branches, *which* hath devoured her fruit, so that she hath no strong rod *to be* a sceptre to rule. This *is* a lamentation, and shall be for a lamentation.

CHAPTER XX.—(1) And it came to pass in the seventh year, in the fifth *month*, the tenth *day* of the month, *that* certain of the elders of Israel came to enquire of the LORD, and sat before me. (2) Then came the word of the LORD unto me, saying, (3) Son of man, speak unto the elders of Israel, and say unto them, Thus saith the Lord GOD; Are ye come to enquire of me? *As* I live, saith the Lord GOD, I will not be enquired of by you. (4) Wilt thou [1] [a] judge them, son of man, wilt thou judge *them?* cause them to know the abominations of their fathers: (5) and say unto them, Thus saith the Lord GOD; In the day when I chose Israel, and [2] lifted up mine hand unto the seed of the house of Jacob, and made myself [b] known unto them in the land of Egypt, when I lifted up mine hand unto them, saying, I *am* the LORD your God; (6) in the day *that* I lifted up

[1] Or, *plead for them.*

[a] ch. 22. 2; & 23. 36.

B.C. cir. 593.

[2] Or, *sware:* and so ver. 6, &c.

[b] Ex. 3. 8; & 4. 31.

earth; but meantime they were being disciplined, that at least a few of them might be prepared for the planting among them of that kingdom not of this world, spoken of at the close of chap. xvi., which should fill the whole earth.

(14) **Fire is gone out of a rod of her branches.**—The rods, as shown in verse 11, are the royal sceptres of her kings. It was by the sin and folly of these kings, together with the sins and follies of the whole people, that judgment was drawn down upon them. Many of them did their full share of the evil work; but a "rod" is here spoken of in the singular, with especial reference to the last king, Zedekiah, who finally brought on the utter ruin of both himself and his people.

This is . . . and shall be.—It is a lamentation now in the half accomplished desolation; it shall remain for a lamentation when all shall be fulfilled.

XX.

Here begins a new series of prophecies, extending to the close of chap. xxiii., and immediately called out (verse 1), like chap. xiv., by an inquiry on the part of the elders of Israel. The subject of the inquiry is not given in either case, and can only be inferred from the prophecy itself. This series begins a little more than two years (two years, one month, and five days) after Ezekiel's call to the prophetic office (chap. i. 2), or a little less than a year (exactly eleven months and five days; comp. verse 1 with chap. viii. 1) after the beginning of the former series; and it is just two years and five months (chap. xxiv. 1) before another series begins. The following series is simultaneous in date with the commencement of the final siege of Jerusalem, and this series therefore, in part at least, must have extended over the time of the preparations for the siege, when generals and armies were marching out for the destruction of Jerusalem and the removal of the people. At this near approach of the long-threatened judgments these prophecies take a peculiarly dark and gloomy tone, relieved only by the briefest intimations of distant good. They are for the most part couched in plain language, though falling occasionally, especially in chap. xxiii., more or less into an allegorical form.

Chapter xx. recounts the history of Israel along with the often repeated warnings given, and may be compared with Neh. ix.; Ps. lxxviii., and the speech of St. Stephen in Acts vii. It is also to a large extent a more literal repetition of the allegory of chap. xvi. After the first four introductory verses, the chapter falls into two main portions, the first of which (verses 5—31) is subdivided into five sections, corresponding to as many marked periods in the history of Israel.

(1) **Came to enquire.**—It does not appear that the elders actually proposed their enquiry. It doubtless had relation not to personal affairs, but to the welfare of the nation, and in this prophecy the Lord meets their unspoken question.

(3) **I will not be enquired of by you.**—As in chap. xiv. 3. St. Jerome thus comments on the words: —"To the holy, and to those who ask for right things, the promise is given, 'While they are yet speaking, I will say, Here I am;' but to sinners, such as these elders of Israel were, and as those whose sins the prophet proceeds to describe, no answer is given, but only a fierce rebuke for their sins, to which He adds His oath, 'As I live,' to strengthen His solemn refusal."

(4) **Wilt thou judge them?**—The form of the repeated question is equivalent to an imperative—judge them. Instead of allowing their enquiry and entreaty for the averting of judgment, the prophet is directed to set before them their long series of apostasies and provocations. "Judge" is used in the sense of "bring to trial," "prefer charges."

(5) **When I chose Israel.**—In verses 5—9 the Lord takes up the first, or Egyptian period of the history of Israel. The record of that period, as it has come to us in the Pentateuch, does not contain either any commands against idolatry, or any notice of the rebellion of the people against such command; but both are clearly implied. The very mission of Moses to deliver them rested upon a covenant by which they were to be the peculiar people of Jehovah (Exod. vi. 2—4); the command to go into the wilderness to sacrifice to the Lord implies that this was a duty neglected in Egypt; and their previous habitual idolatries may be certainly inferred from Lev. xvii. 7, while the disposition of their hearts is seen in their prompt relapse into the idolatry of the golden calf in Exod. xxxii. Their whole murmurings and rebellions were but the manifestation of their resistance to having the Lord for their God, and His will for their guide.

Lifted up mine hand—As the form of taking an oath (see verse 23 and chap. xlvii. 14). The reference is to such passages as Gen. xv. 17—21; Exod. vi. 8; Deut. xxxii. 40, &c. The phrase is repeated in verse 6, which is a continuation of verse 5.

(6) **The glory of all lands.**—So Palestine is constantly spoken of, both in the promise and in its fulfil-

mine hand unto them, to bring them
forth of the land of Egypt into a land
that I had espied for them, flowing with
milk and honey, which *is* the glory of
all lands: (7) then said I unto them,
Cast ye away every man the abomi-
nations of his eyes, and defile not your-
selves with the idols of Egypt: I *am*
the LORD your God. (8) But they re-
belled against me, and would not
hearken unto me: they did not every
man cast away the abominations of their
eyes, neither did they forsake the idols
of Egypt: then I said, I will pour out
my fury upon them, to accomplish my
anger against them in the midst of the
land of Egypt. (9) But I wrought for
my name's sake, that it should not be
polluted before the heathen, among
whom they *were*, in whose sight I made
myself known unto them, in bringing
them forth out of the land of Egypt.

(10) Wherefore I [a] caused them to go
forth out of the land of Egypt, and
brought them into the wilderness.
(11) And I gave them my statutes, and
[1] shewed them my judgments, [b] which *if*
a man do, he shall even live in them.
(12) Moreover also I gave them my
[c] sabbaths, to be a sign between me and
them, that they might know that I *am*
the LORD that sanctify them. (13) But
the house of Israel rebelled against me
in the wilderness: they walked not in
my statutes, and they despised my judg-
ments, which *if* a man do, he shall even
live in them; and my sabbaths they
greatly [d] polluted: then I said, I would
pour out my fury upon them in the
[e] wilderness, to consume them. (14) But
I wrought for my name's sake, that it
should not be polluted before the
heathen, in whose sight I brought
them out.

a Ex. 13. 18.

1 Heb., *made them to know.*

b Lev. 18. 5; Rom. 10. 5; Gal. 3. 12.

c Ex. 20. 8; & 31. 13, &c.; & 35. 2, Deut. 5. 12.

d Ex. 16. 27.

e Num. 14. 29; & 26. 65.

---

ment. (Comp. Dan. xi. 16.) However strange this may seem to us now in regard to parts of the land, after centuries of desolation, misrule, and oppression, it is plain from Josh. xxiii. 14, and many other passages, that at the time the Israelites entered upon its possession it fulfilled their utmost expectation.

(8) **The land of Egypt.**—Of this idolatrous rebellion, and of this threat of the Divine anger while they were still in Egypt, as already said, we have no specific record. But they had the same disposition then as they had afterwards; and, even without such a charge, we could infer the probability of their idolatry. It is possible that the prophet may have had in mind such incidents as are related in Num. xiv. 11—20, happening while the Israelites were still in the neighbourhood of Egypt, and when the report of them would speedily have reached Egyptian ears. It is by no means necessary to suppose that in this broad and general review of the teachings of history each incident is kept in its strict chronological place. Yet idolatry in Egypt is distinctly charged upon the Israelites in chap. xvi. 3, 19, and this verse may well refer to God's judgment for this sin suspended and delayed while they were in Egypt lest it should be misunderstood by the heathen.

(9) **For my name's sake.**—This is the express ground of Moses' pleading for the people in the passage just referred to, and again in Exod. xxxii. 12; Deut. ix. 28; and it is repeatedly given, as in Deut. xxxii. 27, 28, as the ground on which the Lord spared His rebellious people. Had they been treated according to their deserts, and destroyed for their sins, the heathen would have said that God was unable to deliver them.

(10) **Brought them into the wilderness.**—Here begins the second period of the history under review—viz., the earlier part of the life in the wilderness (verses 10—17). It includes the exodus, the giving of the law, the setting up of the tabernacle, the establishment of the priesthood, and the march to Kadesh. By all this the nation was constituted most distinctly the people of God, and brought into the closest covenant relation with him.

(11) **He shall even live in them.**—Comp. Deut. xxx. 15—20. It becomes plain, on a careful perusal of this passage, that what was required was not a mere outward, technical, and perfunctory keeping of certain definite precepts, but a living and loving obedience to God's will from the heart. The same fundamental principle of life underlies the Old Testament as the New; yet the former is justly regarded, and frequently spoken of in the New Testament, as a covenant of works, because the people were not yet sufficiently educated spiritually to be able to receive the principle of faith, and were therefore placed under a law of many definite precepts, that by keeping these with glad alacrity they might show their readiness and desire to do the Lord's will. It is in this sense that a man should live by doing the statutes of the law, and not on the ground of his thereby earning for himself salvation. But even thus, they failed miserably under the test.

(12) **I gave them my sabbaths.**—"Not because it is of Moses, but of the fathers" (John vii. 22). The Sabbath, like circumcision, was an institution far older than the period here spoken of, but was now commanded anew, and made the especial pledge of the covenant between God and His people. The verse is a quotation from Exod. xxxi. 13; and every one must have remarked the great stress everywhere laid in the Old Testament upon the observance of the Sabbath, and the prominence given to it among the privileges of the Divine covenant. It is plain that the day is regarded not in its mere outward character, as a day of rest, but as "a sign" of the covenant, and a means of realising it in the study of God's word, and the communion of the soul with Him. It is in these latter aspects also that the weekly day of rest still retains its inestimable value—that men "might know that I am the Lord that sanctify them."

(13) **Rebelled against me.**—See Exod. xxxii. 1—6; Num. xiv. 1—4, xvi., xxv. 1—3; and for the desecration of the Sabbath in particular, Exod. xvi. 27; Num. xv. 32.

I will pour out my fury.—Comp. Exod. xxxii. 10; Num. xv. 12; and on verse 14 comp. Note on verse 9.

(15) Yet also I lifted up my hand unto
them in the wilderness, that I would not
bring them into the land which I had
given *them*, flowing with milk and
honey, which *is* the glory of all lands;
(16) because they despised my judgments,
and walked not in my statutes, but
polluted my sabbaths: for their heart
went after their idols. (17) Nevertheless
mine eye spared them from destroying
them, neither did I make an end of them
in the wilderness. (18) But I said unto
their children in the wilderness, Walk
ye not in the statutes of your fathers,
neither observe their judgments, nor
defile yourselves with their idols: (19) I
am the LORD your God; walk in my
statutes, and keep my judgments, and
do them; (20) and hallow my sabbaths;
and they shall be a sign between me
and you, that ye may know that I *am*
the LORD your God. (21) Notwithstanding
the children rebelled against me:
they walked not in my statutes, neither
kept my judgments to do them, which
if a man do, he shall even live in them;
they polluted my sabbaths: then I said,
I would pour out my fury upon them, to
accomplish my anger against them in
the wilderness. (22) Nevertheless I with-
drew mine hand, and wrought for my
name's sake, that it should not be
polluted in the sight of the heathen, in
whose sight I brought them forth.

(23) I lifted up mine hand unto them
also in the wilderness, that I would
scatter them among the heathen, and
disperse them through the countries;
(24) because they had not executed my
judgments, but had despised my statutes,
and had polluted my sabbaths, and their
eyes were after their fathers' idols.
(25) Wherefore I gave them also statutes
that were not good, and judgments

---

(15) **I would not bring them into the land.**—Num. xiv. 28, 29. In consequence of their rebellion and want of faith, all the men above twenty years old when they came out of Egypt were doomed by the Divine oath to perish in the wilderness. Yet He did not utterly take His mercy from them, but promised that their children should be brought into the land, as is set forth in verse 17.

(18) **Unto their children.**—The prophet comes now to the third part of his historical retrospect (verses 18—26)—the generation which grew up in the free air of the wilderness, and under the influence of the legislation and institutions given at Sinai. At the same time, it would be a mistake to confine what he says exclusively to that generation. In this, as in the other parts of the discourse, he regards Israel as a whole, and while speaking of one period of their history especially, yet treats of national characteristics which may have come to their most marked development only at a later time. This generation was very earnestly warned against the sins of their fathers, and exhorted to obedience to the Divine law. The whole Book of Deuteronomy is the comment on verses 18—20.

(21) **The children rebelled.**—The history of the wanderings in the wilderness, given in Exodus and Numbers, offers abundant illustrations of the truth of this and the following verse.

(23) **I would scatter them among the heathen.**—This threatening was not designed to be fulfilled in that immediate generation, as abundantly appears from Lev. xxvi. 33; Deut. iv. 27, xxvii. 64, and the other passages in which it is given, especially Deut. xxix. and xxx. It was given to that generation as representing the nation, but was only to be carried out when, by a long course of obdurate sin, it should be shown to be imperatively required. The threat had now been already realised in part, and was on the eve of being fully accomplished. It was important that the people should be made to understand that this had been the Divine warning from the beginning, and that in its fulfilment they were only receiving that punishment which had always been designed for such sin as they had committed.

(25) **Statutes that were not good.**—In this verse the general statement is made of which a particular instance is given in the next. The "statutes that were not good, and judgments whereby they should not live," cannot be the same with those described in verse 11 as "judgments which, if a man do, he shall even live in them." They are not, therefore, to be understood (as many of the fathers took them) of any part of the Mosaic law. Neither is it a sufficient explanation to say that God gave them what was intrinsically good, but it became evil to them through their sins; such a view of the law is emphatically discarded in Rom. vii. 13. The statutes of the Mosaic law are not intended here at all, as is plain from the particular instance of the consecration of children to Moloch in the next verse. These evil statutes and judgments were those adopted from the heathen whom they had suffered to dwell among them, and from the surrounding nations. But how can the Lord say that *He* gave these to them? In the same way that it is said in Isa. lxiii. 17, "O Lord, why hast thou made us to err from Thy ways, and hardened our heart from Thy fear?" So also St. Paul says of the heathen (Rom. i. 21—28) that God "gave them up to uncleanness," "unto vile affections," "to a reprobate mind;" and of certain wicked persons (2 Thess. ii. 11, 12) "God shall send them strong delusion, that they should believe a lie: that they all might be damned who believe not the truth." And St. Stephen says of these very Israelites at this very time, "God gave them up to worship the host of heaven" (Acts vii. 42). It is part of that universal moral government of the world, to which Ezekiel so frequently refers, that the effect of disobedience and neglect of grace is to lead the sinner on to greater sin. The Israelites rebelled against the Divine government, and neglected the grace given them; the natural consequence was that they fell under the influence of the heathen. Comp. Note on chap. xiv. 9.

whereby they should not live; (26) and I
polluted them in their own gifts, in that
they caused to pass [a] through *the fire* all
that openeth the womb, that I might
make them desolate, to the end that
they might know that I *am* the LORD.
(27) Therefore, son of man, speak unto
the house of Israel, and say unto them,
Thus saith the Lord GOD; Yet in this
your fathers have blasphemed me, in
that they have [1] committed a trespass
against me. (28) *For* when I had brought
them into the land, *for* the which I
lifted up mine hand to give it to them,
then they saw every high hill, and all
the thick trees, and they offered there
their sacrifices, and there they presented
the provocation of their offering: there
also they made their sweet savour, and
poured out there their drink offerings.
(29) Then [2] I said unto them, What *is* the
high place whereunto ye go? And the
name thereof is called Bamah unto this
day.

(30) Wherefore say unto the house of
Israel, Thus saith the Lord GOD; Are
ye polluted after the manner of your
fathers? and commit ye whoredom
after their abominations? (31) For when
ye offer your gifts, when ye make your
sons to pass through the fire, ye pollute
yourselves with all your idols, even unto
this day: and shall I be enquired of by
you, O house of Israel? *As* I live, saith
the Lord GOD, I will not be enquired of
by you. (32) And that which cometh
into your mind shall not be at all, that
ye say, We will be as the heathen, as the
families of the countries, to serve wood
and stone.
(33) *As* I live, saith the Lord GOD,
surely with a mighty hand, and with a
stretched out arm, and with fury poured
out, will I rule over you: (34) and I will
bring you out from the people, and will
gather you out of the countries wherein
ye are scattered, with a mighty hand,
and with a stretched out arm, and with

a ch. 16. 21.

1 Heb., *trespassed a trespass.*

2 Or, *I told them what the high place* was, or, *Bamah.*

(26) **To pass through the fire.**—The word "fire" here, as in chaps. xvi. 21 and xxiii. 37, is not in the original, but is rightly supplied from verse 31. The custom referred to was probably that of consecrating their seed to Moloch, expressly forbidden in Lev. xx. 1—5. (Comp. also Acts vii. 43.) The causing children to pass through the fire continued a common sin even to the later days of the monarchy (2 Kings xvii. 17, xxi. 6).

(27) **Your fathers have blasphemed me.**—The fourth period of Israelitish history, though actually far the longest, is very briefly passed over (verses 27—29). It includes the whole period of the settlement in Canaan, from the conquest to the prophet's own time, and was marked by the same characteristics as before. The particular way here specified by which they blasphemed was by the erection of idolatrous altars on every high place.

(29) **Is called Bamah.**—Bamah itself means *high place.* Some have fancied that the word is derived from the two words "go" and "where," and therefore that it contains a play upon the question in the first part of the verse; but this etymology must be considered fanciful.

(30) **Are ye polluted?**—This and the two following verses constitute the fifth and concluding portion of this historical review, and relate to the then existing generation. The questions asked answer themselves, and yet in the following verse are answered for the sake of emphasis. They bring home to Ezekiel's own contemporaries the sins which had characterised their race through nearly all the ages of their history, and show the justice of those long-threatened judgments which were now bursting upon them.

(31) **I will not be enquired of by you.**—This takes up the refrain of verse 3, and with the following verse fitly closes this portion of the prophecy which was introduced by the coming of the elders to enquire.

(32) **As the heathen.**—The desire to be "like the nations that are round about," had long been a ruling ambition with the Israelites, as shown in their original desire for a king (1 Sam. viii. 5, 20), and this desire, as shown in the text, had been one chief reason for their tendency to idolatry.

The second part of this prophecy extends from verse 33 to verse 44, where the chapter closes in the Hebrew, and it would have been better if the same division had been observed in the English, as the fresh prophecy of verses 45—49 is more closely connected with the following chapter. The object of this concluding part of the prophecy is to declare the mingled severity and goodness with which God is about to deal with His people to wean them from their sins, and prepare them to receive His abundant blessing.

(33) **With a mighty hand, and with a stretched out arm.**—As the delineations of this whole passage are founded upon the exodus from Egypt (comp. Hos. ii. 14, 15), so this particular expression is the standing form in the Pentateuch for the series of mighty acts by which the Lord effected that deliverance (see Exod. vi. 1, 6; Deut. iv. 34; v. 15; vii. 19, &c.). In Exod. vi. 6 it is connected with "great judgments"; here and in the next verse, on the contrary, with "fury poured out." Then the Almighty power was manifested for deliverance, but now it shall be for discipline; He "will rule over" and purify them with the same resistless energy which He formerly put forth to save them from their enemies.

(34) **Bring you out from the people.**—This and the parallel clause, "gather you out of the countries," cannot refer to the restoration of the people to their land, both because it is an avenging act, "with fury poured out"; and also because its object is said in the next verse to be to bring them into the wilderness. It must therefore refer to the Divine dealings with the

fury poured out. (35) And I will bring
you into the wilderness of the people,
and there will I plead with you face to
face. (36) Like as I pleaded with your
fathers in the wilderness of the land of
Egypt, so will I plead with you, saith
the Lord GOD. (37) And I will cause you
to pass under the rod, and I will bring
you into [1] the bond of the covenant:
(38) And I will purge out from among
you the rebels, and them that transgress
against me: I will bring them forth out
of the country where they sojourn, and
they shall not enter into the land of
Israel: and ye shall know that I *am* the
LORD.

(39) As for you, O house of Israel, thus
saith the Lord GOD; Go ye, serve ye
every one his idols, and hereafter *also*,
if ye will not hearken unto me: but
pollute ye my holy name no more with
your gifts, and with your idols. (40) For
in mine holy mountain, in the mountain
of the height of Israel, saith the Lord
GOD, there shall all the house of Israel,
all of them in the land, serve me: there
will I accept them, and there will I require your offerings, and the [2] firstfruits
of your oblations, with all your holy
things. (41) I will accept you with your
[3] sweet savour, when I bring you out
from the people, and gather you out of

1 Or, *a delivering.*

2 Or, *chief.*

3 Heb., *savour of rest.*

---

people in their dispersion. He will separate them from other people; He will not allow them, as they proposed (verse 32), to "be as the heathen;" but will bring them out and gather them as a distinct race and spiritually separated from them all, to be dealt with as His own peculiar people.

(35) **Into the wilderness of the people.**—As in the past there was a period of probation and discipline in the wilderness, so shall there be in the future. The similarity is insisted upon in verse 36, and the phrase "face to face" is taken from Deut. v. 4, not to show that the Lord will interpose again with the same sensible manifestations, but will plead with them in ways equally adapted, in their more advanced condition, to show them His overruling hand. As this phrase is plainly to be understood according to its sense, and not according to the letter, so it is quite idle to attempt to locate "the wilderness of the people" as any material wilderness, as that of Arabia, or that between Babylonia and Palestine. The phrase must mean that wilderness condition of the people, scattered among the nations, in which the Lord will plead with them as He did with their fathers. This might refer, as some commentators think, to the state of the Jews in our own time, dispersed among all nations; but there is nothing in the connection to indicate so distant a future, and it may quite as well refer to the then approaching condition of the people. Already many thousands of them had been carried captive to Babylon; others (see Jer. x. 12; xliii. 5) had been scattered among all the surrounding nations; the mass of the ten tribes had long before been carried by the king of Assyria to other regions; and the large remnant still left in Judæa, influenced by their own fears, soon afterwards went down to Egypt. In Ezekiel's own life-time, Israel was scattered widely among all the prominent nations of the earth, and thus brought into the "wilderness of the people."

(37) **To pass under the rod.** — A figure taken from the shepherd's way of counting and examining his flock. (Comp. Lev. xxvii. 32; Jer. xxxiii. 13; Micah vii. 14.) By this the people were to be brought "into the land of the covenant," selected and reconstituted God's covenant people.

(38) **I will purge out.**—The discipline of affliction should have the effect of separating the rebellious in heart from the purified remnant, so that they should not return with them to the land of their fathers. A striking instance of the way in which the Divine purposes are fulfilled through the operations of ordinary laws, occurred on the return of the Jews from their exile. After a residence of more than two generations in Babylonia, they had made themselves homes there, and had become prosperous and contented. Jerusalem and Judæa were utterly desolated and environed with their persistent enemies. The journey thither was long, attended with hardships and danger, and at its close lay the toilsome and self-sacrificing work of pioneers. When therefore, the permission was given for the return, only those who were most earnest in their zeal for the home and religion of their fathers were ready to avail themselves of the opportunity. A great sifting of the people thus took place from the very circumstances of the case, and only a comparatively small portion, constituting the better part, returned to rebuild Jerusalem and the Temple.

(39) **Go ye, serve ye every one his idols.**—Comp. Josh. xxiv. 15. If, after the warning given, ye still refuse obedience, then the Lord gives you up to your fate; "go, serve your idols." Such should be the terrible end of the persistently rebellious part of the nation, as with the obdurate sinner of all ages, they will be given up to the punishment—than which nothing can be imagined more fearful—of being allowed to follow to the end the ways of their own choice.

(40) **In mine holy mountain.**—See note on xvii. 23. The former prophecy was distinctly Messianic; in this, taken by itself, there is nothing which might not refer to the restoration from the exile. Yet in view of the parallelism and connection between the two, we can hardly avoid the supposition, that in predicting the restoration the prophetic eye looked beyond to the greater glory of the Christian dispensation, of which that restoration was a type. But, however this may be, it is not necessary to explain any of the expressions in this passage as looking for their direct and immediate fulfilment beyond the restoration under Zerubbabel.

All the house of Israel.—It has already been shown (see notes on ii. 3; iv. 3) that the existing nation is recognised as constituting "Israel," except where special occasion arises for distinguishing between the ten tribes and the two. Here "Israel" is used throughout for the people whom the prophet is directed to address (verse 39), as is further shown by the parallel, "all of them in the land." Though the restored nation was made up chiefly of Judah and Benjamin, there were also among them considerable

the countries wherein ye have been
scattered; and I will be sanctified in
you before the heathen. (42) And ye
shall know that I *am* the LORD, when I
shall bring you into the land of Israel,
into the country *for* the which I lifted
up mine hand to give it to your fathers.
(43) And there shall ye remember your
ways, and all your doings, wherein ye
have been defiled; and ye shall lothe
yourselves in your own sight for all
your evils that ye have committed.
(44) And ye shall know that I *am* the
LORD, when I have wrought with you
for my name's sake, not according to
your wicked ways, nor according to
your corrupt doings, O ye house of
Israel, saith the Lord GOD.

(45) Moreover the word of the LORD
came unto me, saying, (43) Son of man,
set thy face toward the south, and drop
thy word toward the south, and prophesy
against the forest of the south field;
(47) and say to the forest of the south,
Hear the word of the LORD; Thus saith
the Lord GOD; Behold, I will kindle a
fire in thee, and it shall devour every
green tree in thee, and every dry tree:
the flaming flame shall not be quenched,
and all faces from the south to the
north shall be burned therein. (48) And
all flesh shall see that I the LORD have
kindled it: it shall not be quenched.
(49) Then said I, Ah Lord GOD! they say
of me, Doth he not speak parables?

B.C. 593.

CHAPTER XXI.—(1) And the word
of the LORD came unto me, saying,
(2) Son of man, set thy face toward Jeru-
salem, and drop *thy word* toward the
holy places, and prophesy against the
land of Israel, (3) and say to the land of
Israel, Thus saith the LORD; Behold, I
am against thee, and will draw forth my
sword out of his sheath, and will cut
off from thee the righteous and the
wicked. (4) Seeing then that I will cut
off from thee the righteous and the
wicked, therefore shall my sword go
forth out of his sheath against all flesh

---

remnants of the other tribes; and it is declared that the offerings of them all shall be alike acceptable.

(43) **Ye shall lothe yourselves.**—The especial sin above all others for which Israel had been reproved in past ages, and which still formed the burden of Ezekiel's denunciations, was idolatry; from this they were weaned, once for all, at the restoration, and whatever other sins may have been committed by them, into this, as a nation, they have never since relapsed.

With verse 44 this prophecy ends, and here the chapter closes in the Hebrew and in the ancient versions.

(45) **Toward the south.**—The parable of verses 45—48 forms what might be called the text of the discourse in chap. xxi. The word south, here occurring three times, is represented in the Hebrew by three separate words, which mean, by their derivation, respectively, "on the right hand" (the orientals always supposing themselves to face the east when they speak of the points of the compass), "the brilliant" or "mid-day direction," and "the dry land," a common name for the south of Palestine. Judæa is spoken of as "the south," because, although actually nearly west from Babylon, it could only be approached by the Babylonians from the north, on account of the great intervening desert. Hence the prophets always speak of the armies of Babylon as coming from the north (see Note on i. 4; Jer. i. 14, 15, &c.).

The forest of the south field, might be originally a mere poetic description of the land; but the figure is developed in the following verses, to make the forest the nation, and its trees the people which compose it.

(47) **Every green tree in thee, and every dry tree**—*i.e.*, persons of every condition, the condition here having reference probably to their moral state; the approaching desolation should be so complete, that, like other national judgments, it should sweep away all alike. No distinction could be made in favour of those who might be less ripe in evil. Our Lord may have had this expression in mind in Luke xxiii. 31. At the close of the verse, by introducing the words "all faces," the prophet, as he so often does, breaks away from the figure to its interpretation, and shows plainly the meaning of the former.

(49) **Doth he not speak parables?**—Or enigmas—things that we cannot understand. This the prophet did designedly, as he had done in other cases, to awaken the attention of the people to the explanation he was about to give.

XXI.

This chapter consists of three distinct but closely-connected prophecies, which together may be called the prophecy of the sword. The first, verses 2—7, re-states, in comparatively plain language, the enigmatical denunciation of the last verses of chap. xx.; the second, verses 8—17, substantially repeats and emphasises the first; while the third, verses 18—27, goes again over the same ground, with more of circumstance and detail, closing (verses 28—32) with a prophecy against the Ammonites.

(2) **Set thy face . . . drop thy word . . . prophesy.**—These expressions, with the "say to the land" of verse 3, connect this with xx. 46, 47; but there they were followed by figurative terms, while here we have plainly "Jerusalem," "the holy places," and "the land of Israel."

(3, 4) **The righteous and the wicked.**—This explains *the green tree* and *the dry* of xx. 47; and "all flesh" of verses 4, 5, corresponds to "all faces" of the same. These expressions are meant to show the universality of the approaching desolation. The actual separation in God's sight between the righteous and the wicked has already been plainly set forth in ix. 4—6. But still in this, as in all national judgments,

from the south to the north: (5) that all
flesh may know that I the LORD have
drawn forth my sword out of his sheath:
it shall not return any more. (6) Sigh
therefore, thou son of man, with the
breaking of *thy* loins; and with bitter-
ness sigh before their eyes. (7) And it
shall be, when they say unto thee, Where-
fore sighest thou? that thou shalt answer,
For the tidings; because it cometh:
and every heart shall melt, and all hands
shall be feeble, and every spirit shall
faint, and all knees [1] shall be weak *as*
water: behold, it cometh, and shall be
brought to pass, saith the Lord GOD.
(8) Again the word of the LORD came
unto me, saying, (9) Son of man,
prophesy, and say, Thus saith the LORD;
Say, A sword, a sword is sharpened, and
also furbished: (10) it is sharpened to
make a sore slaughter; it is furbished
that it may glitter: should we then
make mirth? [2] it contemneth the rod of
my son, *as* every tree. (11) And he hath
given it to be furbished, that it may be
handled: this sword is sharpened, and
it is furbished, to give it into the hand
of the slayer. (12) Cry and howl, son of
man: for it shall be upon my people, it
shall be upon all the princes of Israel:
[3] terrors by reason of the sword shall be
upon my people: [a] smite therefore upon
thy thigh. (13) [4] Because *it is* a trial, and
what if *the sword* contemn even the rod?
it shall be no *more*, saith the Lord GOD.
(14) Thou therefore, son of man, prophesy,
and smite *thine* [5] hands together, and let
the sword be doubled the third time,
the sword of the slain: it *is* the sword
of the great *men that are* slain, which

1 Heb., *shall go into water.*

2 Or, it is *the rod of my son, it despiseth every tree.*

3 Or, *they are thrust down to the sword with my people.*

a Jer. 31. 19.

4 Or, *When the trial* hath been, *what then? shall they not also belong to the despising rod?*

5 Heb., *hand to hand.*

---

the innocent must of necessity be involved in the same temporal sufferings with the guilty. The general terms of this prophecy are to be limited by what is elsewhere said of the mercy which shall be shown to a remnant.

(5) **It shall not return any more**—*i.e.*, until it has fully accomplished its purpose. Other judgments upon Israel had been arrested in mercy—the sword had been returned to the scabbard while its work was still incomplete. This will go on to the end.

(6) **With the breaking of thy loins.**—The loins were regarded as the seat of strength (Job xl. 16); and the breaking of these, therefore, expresses entire prostration. Comp. Ps. lxvi. 11; lxix. 23; Isa. xxi. 3; Nahum ii. 10. The prophet was to do this "before their eyes," *i.e.*, was in some way to express before them a sense of extreme dejection and prostration, such as should call forth the question and reply of the following verse. With the expression "Every heart shall melt" comp. Luke xxi. 26.

(8-17) This second prophecy is an expansion of the last, verses 8—13 corresponding to 2—5, and verses 14—17 to verses 6, 7. In several of its clauses modern criticism has been able to improve the translation, and make it clearer.

(10) **Make mirth.**—The answer to this question has already been given in verse 6, and is repeated in verse 12.

Contemneth the rod of my son.—This refers to Gen. xlix. 9, 10, in which Jacob addresses Judah as "my son," and foretells that "the sceptre shall not depart from" him until Shiloh come. There is another allusion to the same passage in verse 27. Comp. also chap. xvii. 22, 23. There is, however, serious difficulty as to the construction and meaning of the clause. The ancient versions and many commentators have more or less changed the text without improvement. The original is obscure in its extreme brevity, and allows "the rod of my son" to be either the object (as it is taken in the text) or the subject (as in the margin). The true sense is probably that which makes the clause into an objection offered by the Jew to the prophet's denunciation: "But 'the rod of my son' despiseth every tree;" *i.e.*, the Divine promise of old to Judah is sure, and his sceptre must remain whatever power arises against it. The objection was in a certain sense true, but the objectors had little idea of the means by which its truth should be established, and vainly imagined that it gave a temporal security to the kingdom of Judah, whatever might be its sins. The prophet does not notice the objection further than to go on with his prediction of the approaching desolation.

(11) **The slayer** is here mentioned indefinitely, but in the next and more circumstantial prophecy (verse 19) is declared to be the king of Babylon.

(12) **Smite therefore upon thy thigh.**—A mark of extreme grief, see Jer. xxxi. 19. The connection of verses 11 and 12 with the objection in verse 10 is this: you think there is security for you in the promise to Judah; do not deceive yourselves, but prepare for sorrow and desolation.

(13) **Because it is a trial.**—Here again the original is obscure from its conciseness and abruptness, leading to great variety of interpretation. Neither the text nor the margin of our translation is quite intelligible. The words for "rod" and "contemn" are the same as in verse 10, and must be taken in the same sense. The most satisfactory translation is this: "For it (the sword) has been proved (viz., on others), and what if this contemning rod shall be no more?" *i.e.*, the power of the sword of Babylon has already been proved; and the sceptre of Judah, which despises it, shall be clean swept away. Various other translations, differing in detail, give the same general sense.

(14) **Smite thine hands together.**—A gesture of strong emotion (see verse 17, chap. xxii. 13, and comp. Note on chap. vi. 11; Num. xxiv. 10).

Let the sword be doubled the third time.—The exact translation is here also obscure and difficult, but the meaning is plain that the activity of the sword is to be intensified to the utmost.

The sword of the slain: it is the sword of the great men that are slain.—Literally, *the sword of the overthrown* (plural), *it is the sword of the overthrown* (sing.), *of the great one.* The word translated *slain* does not necessarily mean actually killed, but is used in a moral as well as physical sense; and in

entereth into their privy chambers.
(15) I have set the [1] point of the sword
against all their gates, that *their* heart
may faint, and *their* ruins be multiplied:
ah! *it is* made bright, *it is* [2] wrapped up
for the slaughter. (16) Go thee one way
or other, *either* on the right hand, [3] *or*
on the left, whithersoever thy face *is*
set. (17) I will also smite mine hands
together, and I will cause my fury to
rest: I the LORD have said *it*.
(18) The word of the LORD came unto
me again, saying, (19) Also, thou son of
man, appoint thee two ways, that the
sword of the king of Babylon may come:
both twain shall come forth out of one
land: and choose thou a place, choose
it at the head of the way to the city.
(20) Appoint a way, that the sword may
come to Rabbath of the Ammonites, and
to Judah in Jerusalem the defenced.
(21) For the king of Babylon stood at the
[4] parting of the way, at the head of the
two ways, to use divination: he made

[1] Or, *glittering*, or *fear*.

[2] Or, *sharpened*.

[3] Heb., *set thyself, take the left hand*.

[4] Heb., *mother of the way*.

---

chap. xx. 16, 21, 24, as often, the verb from which this adjective is formed is translated *polluted*. The sword is called "the sword of the overthrown" because it is the means of their overthrow, and "the sword of the great one overthrown," with especial reference to the king.

Which entereth into their privy chambers.—Rather, *which begirts them round about*, so that none can escape.

(15) **The point.**—The Hebrew word occurs only here. The marginal rendering comes nearer its sense, but the exact meaning is the glance or the whirl of the sword. The glancing or the whirling motion of the sword was to be everywhere, "against all their gates."

Their ruins be multiplied.—Literally, *their stumbling blocks be multiplied*. The thought is that in the coming desolation trouble shall be on every side and, in their perplexity, occasions for ill-advised action shall arise all around. "Bright" means "glittering." (Comp. Deut. xxxii. 41; Job xx. 25; Nahum iii. 3.)

It is wrapped.—The margin has *sharpened*, but the exact sense is *drawn*, "drawn out for the slaughter."

(16) **Go thee one way or other.**—An address to the sword, the animation of which is singularly lost in our version; the sword is addressed as a host, to be prepared for instant action in every quarter: "Gather thyself up (close up ranks) right; set thyself, left."

(17) **My fury to rest.**—As in chap. xvi. 42, because it has accomplished its purpose and has nothing more to do. (Comp. chaps. v. 13 and xxiv. 13.)

At verse 18 the third and final prophecy of the chapter begins, and, besides being much more explicit than the others, includes also a new subject (verses 28—32), a prophecy against Ammon. Hitherto it has only been foretold that Judah shall be desolated, now it is added that this shall be effected by the king of Babylon, and that he shall also extend his conquests to the Ammonites.

(19) **Appoint thee two ways.**—Or, *set before thee*. The prophet is directed to represent Nebuchadnezzar as about to go forth with his armies, and hesitating whether he should take first the road to Jerusalem or to the capital of the Ammonites. His choice of the former is determined, as he supposes, by his divinations, but really by the overruling hand of the Lord, who thus shows beforehand what it shall be. The whole is set forth in the vivid and concrete imagery so characteristic of Ezekiel; but it is impossible that the scene in real life was to be thus determined by the prophet's open interference. The whole is a vision, in which life and action is conveyed by this manner of describing the course of future events as actually taking place before the eyes of his hearers. The two ways "come forth out of one land;" their starting-point is the same, Babylon, and they diverge towards different destinations.

Choose thou a place.—Literally, *make a hand* or, as we say, *a finger-post*. The verb here used never means "choose," nor does the noun ever mean "place"; but the verb is often used both in the sense of *to make* and *to engrave*, and "hand" frequently occurs in the sense of a pillar, and occasionally in that of a guide-post. (See 1 Sam. xv. 12; 2 Sam. xviii. 18; Isa. lvi. 5.) The prophet in vision sets up this guide-post to direct the king on his march. The roads to Rabbah and to Jerusalem from Babylon would be the same for many hundred miles. It is impossible, therefore, to suppose that Ezekiel actually stood at their parting.

Head of the way, called more poetically in verse 21 "mother of the way," is the point where the road forks. From this point the road to Jerusalem would lie on the right, that to Rabbah, the capital of the Ammonites, on the left.

(21) **To use divination.**—Various particular forms of divination are mentioned just afterwards. This is a general term to include them all. Divination was always resorted to by the heathen on occasions of important questions. In this case, while Nebuchadnezzar thought in this way to determine his action, it was already fixed for him by a higher Power.

Made his arrows bright.—Rather, *shook his arrows*. This was a mode of divination in use among the ancient Arabs, as well as in Mesopotamia, and something very similar is mentioned by Homer as practised among the ancient Greeks (*Il.*, iii. 316). It continued to be used among the Arabs until the time of Mohammed, who strictly forbade it in the Koran (chaps. iii. 39, v. 4, 94). Several arrows, properly marked, were shaken together in a quiver or other vessel, and one drawn out. The mark upon the one drawn was supposed to indicate the will of the gods. It was thus simply one form of casting lots.

Consulted with images.—The particular images here mentioned were "teraphim," small idols, which are often spoken of in Scripture as used in divination by the Israelites themselves, and common also among the heathen. (See 1 Sam. xv. 23, where the word "idolatry" is in the original "teraphim.") Nothing is known of the way in which these were used in divination.

Looked in the liver.—The inspection of the entrails of sacrificial victims, and especially of the liver, as a means of ascertaining the will of the gods, is familiar to every reader of classical literature. There is evidence that the same custom prevailed also in Babylonia. The king is represented as employing all these different kinds of divination to make sure of the proper path.

his[1] arrows bright, he consulted with
[2] images, he looked in the liver. (22) At
his right hand was the divination for
Jerusalem, to appoint [3] [4] captains, to
open the mouth in the slaughter, to lift
up the voice with shouting, to appoint
battering rams against the gates, to cast
a mount, *and* to build a fort. (23) And
it shall be unto them as a false divi-
nation in their sight, [5] to them that have
sworn oaths: but he will call to re-
membrance the iniquity, that they may
be taken.

(24) Therefore thus saith the Lord GOD;
Because ye have made your iniquity to
be remembered, in that your trans-
gressions are discovered, so that in all
your doings your sins do appear; be-
cause, *I say*, that ye are come to re-
membrance, ye shall be taken with the
hand. (25) And thou, profane wicked
prince of Israel, whose day is come, when
iniquity *shall have* an end, (26) thus saith
the Lord GOD; Remove the diadem, and
take off the crown: this *shall* not *be* the
same: exalt *him that is* low, and abase
him that is high. (27) [6] I will overturn,
overturn, overturn, it: and it shall be
no *more*, until he come whose right it is;
and I will give it *him*.

1 Or, *knives*.

2 Heb., *teraphim*.

3 Or, battering *rams*.

4 Heb., *rams*.

5 Or, *for the oaths made unto them*.

6 Heb., *Perverted, perverted, perverted, will I make it*.

(22) **At his right hand was.**—This is too exactly literal. The sense is, *into his right hand came* the divination which determined his course towards Jerusalem. "Captains" should be as in the margin, *battering-rams* (see chap. iv. 2), for the siege of Jerusalem; the same word is so translated farther on in this verse. The remaining clauses portray the operations of the attack.

(23) **As a false divination in their sight.**—The divination of the Babylonians seemed false to the Jews, primarily, because they were determined not to believe it; yet, doubtless, there was mingled with this a secret consciousness of the worthlessness of the idolatries which they themselves practised, and a consequent readiness to cast them aside when opposed to their wishes.

To them that have sworn oaths.—These words have been very variously interpreted, but the simplest meaning seems the best; the resolution of Nebuchadnezzar to attack Jerusalem seemed impossible to the Jews, because they were his vassals, and under oaths of fidelity to him. They must have been conscious of their own violation of those oaths, and yet have persuaded themselves that their intrigues with Egypt were not known to Nebuchadnezzar, and that therefore he would not attack them.

But he will call to remembrance the iniquity.—The pronoun is here understood by many as referring to the Lord, and "iniquity" as expressing the general sinfulness of the people. It is better to refer the pronoun to Nebuchadnezzar, who will call to remembrance and punish the violation of their oaths to him. It is constantly to be remembered that Zedekiah was placed upon the throne by him under a solemn oath of fidelity to himself (2 Chron. xxxvi. 10, 13; Jer. lii. 3; Ezek. xvii. 15, 18, &c.).

(24) **In all your doings your sins do appear.**—But one particular has just been mentioned, their rebellion and perjury; but this was only the last act of a long course of sin in many ways. These have been spoken of at large in previous chapters, and therefore, when this last sin is exposed, it may well be said that sin is shown in all their doings.

(25) **Profane.**—The prophet now turns from the people as a whole to the individual prince at their head. The word for "profane" is the same as is translated "slain" in verse 14; it would be better rendered here, as there, *overthrown*. What is close at hand is described as accomplished.

When iniquity shall have an end.—Literally, *at the time of the iniquity of the end.* The same expression is repeated in verse 29, and the meaning is plainly, at the time of that final transgression which shall be closed by the immediate manifestation of the Divine judgment. The representation of iniquity as being allowed to run a certain course through the Divine forbearance, and arrested and punished when it has reached its culmination, is a common one in Scripture. (See Gen. xv. 16; Dan. viii. 23; Matt. xxiii. 34—36, &c.)

(26) **Remove the diadem.**—The word translated "diadem" is rendered in every other place in which it occurs (Exod. xxviii. 4, 37 *bis*, 39, xxix. 6 *bis*, xxxix. 28, 31; Lev. viii. 9 *bis*, xvi. 4) *the mitre* of the high priest, and undoubtedly has the same sense here. Not only was the royal but also the high-priestly office to be overthrown in the approaching desolation. Neither of them were ever recovered in their full power after the captivity. The various verbs here, *remove, take off, exalt, abase*, are in the original in the infinitive, and although it is sometimes necessary to translate the infinitive as an imperative, it is better here to keep to its more common sense of indicating an action without reference to the agent which is most readily expressed in English by the passive: "The mitre shall be removed, and the crown taken off . . . the low exalted, and the high abased."

This shall not be the same.—Literally, *this not this*, or, supplying the verb, as is often required, *this shall not be this*—*i.e.*, as the following clauses express, there shall be an utter change and overturning of the whole existing state of things. For the abasement of the high and exaltation of the low, as an expression of the Divine interposition at the introduction of a new order of things, comp. 1 Sam. ii. 6—8; Luke i. 51—53.

(27) **And it shall be no more.**—Literally, *this also shall not be.* After the emphatic repetition of "overturn" at the beginning of the verse, it is now added that the condition which follows the overthrow shall not be permanent; "the foundations" shall be put "out of course," and everything thrown into that condition of flux and change, without permanent settlement, which was so characteristic of the state of Judæa until the coming of Christ.

Until he come whose right it is.—This is generally acknowledged as a reference to Gen. xlix. 10, "until Shiloh come," even by those who reject the interpretation of *Shiloh* as meaning "he to whom it belongs." The promise here made refers plainly both to the priestly and to the royal prerogatives, and a still more distinct foretelling of the union of both in the

(28) And thou, son of man, prophesy
and say, Thus saith the Lord God concerning the Ammonites, and concerning
their reproach; even say thou, The
sword, the sword *is* drawn: for the
slaughter *it is* furbished, to consume
because of the glittering: (29) Whiles
they see vanity unto thee, whiles they
divine a lie unto thee, to bring thee upon
the necks of *them that are* slain, of the
wicked, whose day is come, when their
iniquity *shall have* an end. (30) [1] Shall I
cause *it* to return into his sheath? I will
judge thee in the place where thou wast
created, in the land of thy nativity.
(31) And I will pour out mine indignation
upon thee, I will blow against thee in
the fire of my wrath, and deliver thee
into the hand of [2] brutish men, *and*
skilful to destroy. (32) Thou shalt be for
fuel to the fire; thy blood shall be in
the midst of the land; thou shalt be
no *more* remembered: for I the Lord
have spoken *it*.

CHAPTER XXII.—(1) Moreover the
word of the Lord came unto me, saying,
(2) Now, thou son of man, [a] wilt thou
[3] judge, wilt thou judge the [4] bloody
city? yea, thou shalt [5] shew her all her
abominations. (3) Then say thou, Thus
saith the Lord God, The city sheddeth
blood in the midst of it, that her time
may come, and maketh idols against

1 Or, *cause it to return.*

2 Or, *burning.*

a ch. 20. 4; & 23. 36.

3 Or, *plead for.*

4 Heb., *city of bloods.*

5 Heb., *make her know.*

Messiah may be found in Zech. vi. 12, 13. In Him, and in Him alone, will all this confusion and uncertainty come to an end; for, as Ezekiel's contemporary declared, "His dominion is an everlasting dominion, which shall not pass away, and His kingdom that which shall not be destroyed" (Dan. vii. 14).

(28) **Concerning the Ammonites.**—At the opening of this prophecy (verses 19, 20) the king of Babylon was represented as hesitating whether to attack Jerusalem or Rabbah, and as being led to the determination of attacking the former. This would leave the inference that the Ammonites might escape altogether; and from the destruction of God's peculiar people, along with the immunity of their ancient enemies, the heathen would be likely to draw conclusions inconsistent with the power and majesty of God. Hence this prophecy is added to show that His judgments shall certainly fall on them also, and in this case the ruin foretold is final and hopeless, without the promise given to Israel in verse 27. Another prophecy against Ammon is given in chap. xxv. 1—7. As a matter of history, the Ammonites were conquered, and their country desolated, by Nebuchadnezzar a few years after the destruction of Jerusalem, and they gradually dwindled away until their name and place among the nations finally disappeared.

Their reproach—*i.e.*, their exultation in the desolation of Israel. (See chap. xxv. 3; Zeph. ii. 8.)

(29) **See vanity unto thee.**—"See" is used in the sense of the utterances of the "seer," or prophet. The Ammonites also had false prophets among them.

Thee upon the necks of them that are slain.—Judah is to fall first, then Ammon immediately after, as it were, upon the necks of those already slain. The figure is taken from the battle, in which one warrior falls upon the body of him who fell before him.

When their iniquity shall have an end.—Not through repentance, but because it ceases of necessity with the death of the sinner.

(30) **Shall I cause it to return?**—There is nothing in the original to indicate either a question, or that this is spoken in the first person. It is addressed to the Ammonites, "Return it" (the sword) "into his sheath;" and it means that all resistance will be vain, the coming destruction cannot be averted. And this judgment is to be executed in the Ammonites' own country: they are to be destroyed at home.

(31) **Mine indignation.**—The figure of the sword, which has been kept up through the entire chapter, is here dropped; but the language immediately falls into another figure, already employed in chap. xx. 47, "I will blow against thee in" (rather, *with*) "the fire of my wrath." (Comp. the same expression in chap. xxii. 21.) The image is that of the consuming fire of God's wrath blown by His power against Ammon, as fire is turned by the wind upon a forest to its destruction. (Comp. Isa. liv. 16.) The word "brutish" of the text in the last clause is better than the "burning" of the margin.

(32) **Shalt be no more remembered.**—Ammon should be utterly destroyed, as fuel in the fire; the life-blood of the nation should be poured out, and her name vanish. For her there should be no future, like that promised to Israel in verse 27.

XXII.

This chapter also consists of three short prophecies, less intimately connected with one another than those of chap. xxi. In the first (verses 2—16) the sins of Jerusalem are recounted, with evident reference to chap. xviii.; in the second (verses 17—22) the punishment and purification of Israel is represented under the figure of melting mixed metals in the furnace; while the third returns to the recounting of other sins than those mentioned in the first, showing that the corruption pervades all classes, and closing with the warning of certain punishment. This chapter, like chap xx., is a justification of the Divine judgment.

(2) **Wilt thou judge.**—The same expression as in chap. xx. 4. (See Note there.) The sense of the margin, "plead for," is not appropriate here.

Bloody city.—In verses 2—6 crimes of bloodshed and idolatry are dwelt upon, between which there seems always to have been a close connection. The same words are used in chap. xxiv. 6, 9, and in Nahum iii. 1.

(3) **That her time may come.**—Her time of punishment. That which will be the inevitable consequence of her acts is represented by a very common figure, as if it were her purpose in doing them. She has been so fully warned of the result that continuance in her course seems to involve the design of bringing on that result.

herself to defile herself. (4) Thou art
become guilty in thy blood that thou
hast[a] shed; and hast defiled thyself in
thine idols which thou hast made; and
thou hast caused thy days to draw near,
and art come *even* unto thy years:
therefore have I made thee a reproach
unto the heathen, and a mocking to all
countries. (5) *Those that be* near, and
those that be far from thee, shall mock
thee, *which art* [1] infamous *and* much
vexed.
(6) Behold, the princes of Israel, every
one were in thee to their [2] power to shed
blood. (7) In thee have they set light by
father and mother: in the midst of thee
have they dealt by [3] oppression with the
stranger: in thee have they vexed the
fatherless and the widow. (8) Thou hast
despised mine holy things, and hast
profaned my sabbaths. (9) In thee are
[4] men that carry tales to shed blood:
and in thee they eat upon the moun-
tains: in the midst of thee they commit
lewdness. (10) In thee have they [b] dis-
covered their father's nakedness: in
thee have they humbled her that was
[c] set apart for pollution. (11) And [5] one
hath committed abomination with his
neighbour's [d] wife; and [6] another hath
[7] lewdly defiled his daughter in law;
and another in thee hath humbled his
[e] sister, his father's daughter. (12) In
thee have they taken gifts to shed blood;
thou hast taken usury and increase, and
thou hast greedily gained of thy neigh-
bours by extortion, and hast forgotten
me, saith the Lord God.
(13) Behold, therefore I have [f] smitten
mine hand at thy dishonest gain which
thou hast made, and at thy blood which
hath been in the midst of thee. (14) Can
thine heart endure, or can thine hands
be strong, in the days that I shall deal
with thee? I the Lord have spoken *it*,
and will do *it*. (15) And I will scatter
thee among the heathen, and disperse
thee in the countries, and will consume
thy filthiness out of thee. (16) And thou
[8] shalt take thine inheritance in thyself
in the sight of the heathen, and thou
shalt know that I *am* the Lord.

a 2 Kings 21. 16.
1 Heb., *polluted of name, much in vexation.*
2 Heb., *arm.*
3 Or, *deceit.*
4 Heb., *men of slanders.*
b Lev. 18. 8; & 20. 11.
c Lev. 18. 19.
5 Or, *every one.*
d Lev. 18. 20; Jer. 5. 8.
6 Or, *every one.*
7 Or, *by lewdness.*
e Lev. 18. 9.
f ch. 21. 17.
8 Or, *shalt be profaned.*

---

(4) **Thy days . . . . thy years.**—Viz., of judgment and visitation. The Rabbinical commentators interpret the *days* of the destruction of Jerusalem, and the *years* of the captivity in Babylon.

A mocking to all countries. — This is frequently spoken of in Ezekiel, and is the necessary result in all ages of the contrast between high professions and inconsistent performance. Israel's law stood far above the legislation of any other nation of the period, but the habitual conduct of her people was in utter disregard of that law. The effect was the same as at a later day, when St. Paul said, "The name of God is blasphemed among the Gentiles through you" (Rom. ii. 24), just as the same evils and the same hindrances to the spread of the Gospel now result from the unworthy lives of Christians. But the Jews peculiarly exposed themselves to derision by their claim, as the chosen people of God, to universal and everlasting dominion, contrasted with their present overthrow and desolation; and this desolation was a punishment for the outrageous sins of a people whose whole national existence was based upon a call to peculiar holiness.

(5) **Infamous and much vexed.**—It is better to omit the words in italics, *which art*. The literal meaning of "infamous" is given in the margin; but the "much vexed" refers to the internal confusion, commotions, and social disorders which characterised the decaying state of the kingdom.

(6) **Were in thee to their power.** — The tense is the same with that of the verbs in verse 7, and both should be translated alike; the order of the words should also be changed: "The princes of Israel, every one according to his power, have been in thee to shed blood." The rulers, who should have preserved order and administered justice, were foremost in deeds of violence. (See the instances of Manasseh, 2 Kings xxi. 16, and of Jehoiakim, 2 Kings xxiv. 4.)

(7) **By father and mother.**—Filial respect was one of the most frequently enjoined precepts of the law (see Lev. xix. 32, xx. 9, &c.). So the other sins mentioned in this and the following verses are transgressions of special Divine commands. "Dealt by oppression" is "dealt oppressively" (see Lev. xix. 10; Exod. xxii. 21; Deut. xxiv. 14, &c.); for "the fatherless and widow" (Exod. xxii. 22—24, &c.). The despising of holy things and the profanation of the sabbaths were the constant subject of the warnings of the law; tale-bearers are forbidden in Lev. xix. 16; the "eating upon the mountains" (which means joining in the idol sacrifices) is often reproved by this and the other prophets; and the sins of lewdness enumerated are all specifically forbidden in Lev. xviii. and xx., as well as elsewhere; while the various sins arising from covetousness, mentioned in verse 12, had been constantly denounced both by the law and in the warnings of the prophets. The expression "hast forgotten me" is at once the root of all these sins, and in itself the climax of all.

(13) **Smitten mine hand.**—See Note on chap. vi. 11, and comp. verse 17 and chap. xxii. 13.

(16) **Shalt take thine inheritance.** — Rather, *thou shalt be profaned by thyself.* The same word occurs in chap. vii. 24, and is there rendered "shall be defiled;" it admits of either sense, according to its derivation. The meaning is that through their own misconduct they forfeit the privileges of a holy nation, and become profaned or dishonoured in the sight of the heathen. The first prophecy of this chapter closes with the terrible warning of verses 14—16, showing the extreme suffering necessary for the purification of Israel.

(17) And the word of the LORD came
unto me, saying, (18) Son of man, the
house of Israel is to me become dross:
all they *are* brass, and tin, and iron, and
lead, in the midst of the furnace; they
are *even* the [1] dross of silver. (19) There-
fore, thus saith the Lord GOD; Because
ye are all become dross, behold, there-
fore I will gather you into the midst of
Jerusalem. (20) [2] *As* they gather silver,
and brass, and iron, and lead, and tin,
into the midst of the furnace, to blow
the fire upon it, to melt *it;* so will I
gather *you* in mine anger and in my
fury, and I will leave *you there*, and melt
you. (21) Yea, I will gather you, and
blow upon you in the fire of my wrath,
and ye shall be melted in the midst
thereof. (22) As silver is melted in the
midst of the furnace, so shall ye be
melted in the midst thereof; and ye
shall know that I the LORD have poured
out my fury upon you.
(23) And the word of the LORD came
unto me, saying, (24) Son of man, say
unto her, Thou *art* the land that is not
cleansed, nor rained upon in the day of
indignation. (25) *There is* a conspiracy
of her prophets in the midst thereof, like
a roaring lion ravening the prey; they
[a] have devoured souls; they have taken
the treasure and precious things; they
have made her many widows in the
midst thereof. (26) Her priests have
[3] violated my law, and have profaned
mine holy things: they have put no
difference between the holy and profane,
neither have they shewed *difference* be-
tween the unclean and the clean, and
have hid their eyes from my sabbaths,
and I am profaned among them.
(27) Her [b] princes in the midst thereof *are*
like wolves ravening the prey, to shed
blood, *and* to destroy souls, to get dis-
honest gain. (28) And her prophets have
daubed them with untempered *morter*,
seeing vanity, and divining lies unto
them, saying, Thus saith the Lord GOD,
when the LORD hath not spoken.
(29) The people of the land have used
[4] oppression, and exercised robbery, and
have vexed the poor and needy: yea,

1 Heb., *drosses.*

2 Heb., According *to the gathering.*

a Mat. 23. 14.

3 Heb., *offered violence to.*

b Mic. 3. 11; Zeph. 3. 3.

4 Or, *deceit.*

---

(18) **Become dross.**—The second prophecy (verses 17—22) is occupied with a figure taken from the refining of silver, which is a favourite one with the prophets (see Isa. i. 25; Jer. vi. 29; Zech. xiii. 9; Mal. iii. 3). The peculiar appropriateness of this figure has been often noted in the fact that the completion of the process of refining silver in the furnace was determined by the parting of the floating dross and the reflection of the image of the refiner from its molten surface. This figure, while setting forth the punishment of Israel, shows clearly that this punishment was for the purpose of purification.

(19) **Into the midst of Jerusalem.**—Jerusalem is represented as the refining pot into which the people were to be cast, because this was at once their national centre, and also the centre of the war by which they were carried into captivity.

(20) **I will leave you there.**— Better, *I will cast you in.*

(24) **That is not cleansed.**—The third and last Divine communication of this chapter begins with verse 23, and contains a further enumeration of the sins of Israel, showing that they have been committed by all classes alike, and ending, like the others, with the prophecy of the outpouring of God's wrath. There is much difference of opinion as to the meaning of the clause "that is not cleansed;" the most probable view is that it speaks of the land as neglected and uncared for—the stones not gathered up and the weeds allowed to grow. It has had neither human care, nor has it received the Divine blessing of rain.

(25) **A conspiracy of her prophets.** — The opposition of false prophets to the Divine measures for the reformation of the people is continually spoken of (comp. chap. xiii., Zeph. iii. 4, and many passages in Jeremiah) as among the most serious obstacles to the work of the true prophets: there is also frequent mention of them in history (1 Kings xxii., &c.), as they had been foretold from of old in prophecy (Deut. xviii. 20—22). Nothing, it may be observed, could have afforded more plausible excuse to the people for not obeying the Divine admonitions than an opposing "Thus saith the Lord." The greed of the false prophets and the disastrous effects of their counsel are spoken of here in stronger terms than in any other passage.

(26) **Have violated my law.**—The next class to be spoken of, as the next in influence, were the priests. It was their especial office to observe and to teach the distinction between the holy and the unholy (Lev. x. 10), and to care for the Sabbath. In all they had been unfaithful. (Comp. Micah iii. 11; Zeph. iii. 4.)

(27) **Her princes.**—These are not only the kings, but also the nobles and those in authority at court—in other words, the ruling class. Their injustice and violence is a constant theme for prophetic rebuke.

(28) **With untempered morter.**—See Note on chap. xiii. 10. The prophets are here again spoken of in reference to their powerful influence upon the princes in leading them astray by falsehoods. "Seeing vanity" is an expression for pretended and false visions. (Comp. chap. xiii. 7, 9, 10.)

(29) **The people of the land,**—*i.e.*, the common people, not belonging to any of the above classes. In regard to their general corruption see chap. xviii.

(30) **Make up the hedge,** is only another form of "stand in the gap," added for the sake of emphasis. Both refer to intercession for the people (see Ps. cvi. 23). It is not meant that there was not a single godly man, but not one of such a pure, strong, and commanding character that his intercessions might avert the threatened doom.

they have oppressed the stranger
[1]wrongfully. (30) And I sought for a
man among them, that should make up
the hedge, and stand in the gap before
me for the land, that I should not
destroy it: but I found none. (31) There-
fore have I poured out mine indignation
upon them; I have consumed them with
the fire of my wrath: their own way
have I recompensed upon their heads,
saith the Lord GOD.

CHAPTER XXIII.—(1) The word of
the LORD came again unto me, saying,
(2) Son of man, there were two women,
the daughters of one mother: (3) and
they committed whoredoms in Egypt;
they committed whoredoms in their
youth: there were their breasts pressed,
and there they bruised the teats of their
virginity. (4) And the names of them
were Aholah the elder, and Aholibah her
sister: and they were mine, and they
bare sons and daughters. Thus *were*
their names; Samaria *is* Aholah, and
Jerusalem Aholibah.
(5) And Aholah played the harlot when
she was mine; and she doted on her
lovers, on the Assyrians *her* neighbours,
(6) *which were* clothed with blue, captains
and rulers, all of them desirable young
men, horsemen riding upon horses.
(7) Thus she [2]committed her whoredoms
with them, with all them *that were* [3]the
chosen men of Assyria, and with all on
whom she doted: with all their idols she
defiled herself. (8) Neither left she her
whoredoms *brought* from Egypt: for in
her youth they lay with her, and they
bruised the breasts of her virginity, and
poured their whoredom upon her.
(9) Wherefore I have delivered her into
the hand of her lovers, into the hand of
the [a]Assyrians, upon whom she doted.
(10) These discovered her nakedness: they
took her sons and her daughters, and
slew her with the sword: and she be-
came [4]famous among women; for they
had executed judgment upon her.
(11) And when her sister Aholibah saw
this, [5]she was more corrupt in her inor-
dinate love than she, and in her whore-
doms [6]more than her sister in *her* whore-
doms. (12) She doted upon the [b]Assyrians
her neighbours, captains and rulers clothed
most gorgeously, horsemen riding upon

1 Heb., *without right.*

2 Heb., *bestowed her whoredoms upon them.*

3 Heb., *the choice of the children of Asshur.*

a 2 Kin. 17. 23.

4 Heb., *a name.*

5 Heb., *she corrupted her inordinate love more than, &c.*

6 Heb., *more than the whoredoms of her sister.*

b 2 Kin. 16. 7.

XXIII.

This chapter closes the series of prophecies beginning with chap. xx., and consists of an extended allegory. Its object, quite in connection with chaps. xxi., xxii., is to set forth the sinfulness of Judah. The allegory is much like that of chap. xvi., but differs from it on the one side by omitting the historical features so prominent there, and on the other by using as a basis here a comparison between the northern and southern kingdoms. The allegory is too plain to need any extended comment. It is almost entirely concerned with the southern kingdom, enough only being added in reference to the northern, which had long since passed away, to bring out the comparison.

(3) **In Egypt.**—The idolatries of Israel in Egypt have already been spoken of in the Note to chap. xx. 8. (See also verse 19 below.)

(4) **Samaria is Aholah, and Jerusalem Aholibah.**—Samaria, as the capital, is put for the northern kingdom, and is called Aholah = *her own tabernacle*, because she set up her own worship instead of resorting to the Temple; while the southern kingdom, represented by Jerusalem, is called Aholibah = *my tabernacle is in her*, because she still contained the sanctuary of the Lord. The word "elder" should be translated *greater*, as in chap. xvi. 46. (See Note there.)

(5) **The Assyrians her neighbours.**—Or, *the Assyrians drawing near.* They are described in verse 40 as those who "come from far." The nearness here spoken of is to be understood not locally, but spiritually, of sympathy in idolatry. Of the earlier connection between Israel and Assyria there is little remaining record. In 2 Kings xv. 19, 20, it is said that Pul exacted tribute of Menahem, and the mention seems to imply a still earlier intercourse. According to the Assyrian records, Jehu was tributary to Shalmaneser; Assyria, as representing the great northern power, in contrast to Egypt on the south, is probably used here in a sense broad enough to include also Syria.

(6) **Horsemen.**—The Assyrians, like the Egyptians, made large use of cavalry, as was necessary to a warlike nation; the multiplication of horses had on this account been forbidden to the Israelites (Deut. xvii. 16).

(7) **With all their idols.**—The reality breaks through the figure, and leaves no doubt of the meaning of the allegory.

(10) **She became famous.**—A better word would be *notorious.* The conquest of Samaria and the captivity of the northern tribes had now been accomplished more than 130 years, and had made them a byword among the nations.

(11) **She was more corrupt.**—Enough having been said of Aholah to form the basis for a comparison, the prophet now turns to Aholibah. The idolatries of Judah not only comparatively but actually exceeded those of her sister kingdom. See, *e.g.*, the account of Manasseh's reign (2 Kings xxi. 1—16; 2 Chron. xxxiii. 1—9). In addition to her connection with Assyria, Judah also formed alliances with Chaldæa, and intrigued with Egypt and other nations.

(12) **Her neighbours.**—See Note on verse 5. In both places the warriors of Assyria are described in the most attractive way to carry out the figure; they are also spoken of as very powerful, to explain the political attraction to them. Israel was both fascinated by their splendour and overawed by their power.

horses, all of them desirable young men.
(13) Then I saw that she was defiled, *that*
they *took* both one way, (14) and *that* she
increased her whoredoms: for when she
saw men pourtrayed upon the wall, the
images of the Chaldeans pourtrayed with
vermilion, (15) girded with girdles upon
their loins, exceeding in dyed attire upon
their heads, all of them princes to look
to, after the manner of the Babylonians
of Chaldea, the land of their nativity:
(16) and [1] as soon as she saw them with
her eyes, she doted upon them, and sent
messengers unto them into Chaldea.
(17) And the [2] Babylonians came to her
into the bed of love, and they defiled
her with their whoredom, and she was
polluted with them, and her mind was
[3] alienated from them. (18) So she dis-
covered her whoredoms, and discovered
her nakedness: then my mind was alien-
ated from her, like as my mind was
alienated from her sister. (19) Yet she
multiplied her whoredoms, in calling to
remembrance the days of her youth,
wherein she had played the harlot in
the land of Egypt. (20) For she doted
upon their paramours, whose flesh *is as*
the flesh of asses, and whose issue *is like*
the issue of horses. (21) Thus thou
calledst to remembrance the lewdness
of thy youth, in bruising thy teats by
the Egyptians for the paps of thy
youth.

(22) Therefore, O Aholibah, thus saith
the Lord GOD; Behold, I will raise up
thy lovers against thee, from whom thy
mind is alienated, and I will bring them
against thee on every side; (23) the Baby-
lonians, and all the Chaldeans, Pekod,
and Shoa, and Koa, *and* all the Assy-
rians with them: all of them desirable
young men, captains and rulers, great
lords and renowned, all of them riding
upon horses. (24) And they shall come
against thee with chariots, wagons, and
wheels, and with an assembly of people,
which shall set against thee buckler and
shield and helmet round about: and I
will set judgment before them, and they
shall judge thee according to their judg-
ments. (25) And I will set my jealousy

1 Heb., *at the sight of her eyes.*

2 Heb., *children of Babel.*

3 Heb., *loosed,* or, *disjointed.*

---

(14) **Men pourtrayed upon the wall.**—Such portraitures, with evidence that they were once executed in brilliant colours, are characteristic both of Egypt and Assyria, where stone for sculpture abounded. From the close connection in race and customs between the Assyrians and Babylonians, it cannot be doubted that the same portraitures were also common upon the more perishable brick of the latter, of whom the prophet is now speaking. The monuments fully concur in representing the warriors of Assyria and Babylonia as delighting in extreme gorgeousness of apparel, but it is difficult to render into English with accuracy each particular of their dress. The exiles, whom Ezekiel immediately addressed, were familiar with these pictures, and his way of speaking of them was important in checking any disposition to fall into idolatries by means of them.

(16) **Saw them with her eyes.**—This is to be taken in a sense wide enough to include knowledge obtained in any way, as well as by actual sight. The intercourse between Judæa and Babylon was so close that many of the people had seen the Babylonians personally, while others knew of them through their report.

Sent messengers.—Ahaz "sent messengers" to Assyria (2 Kings xvi. 7), and Hezekiah entertained ambassadors from Babylon (2 Kings xx. 13); but besides these, the whole history of the times implies that there must have been frequent embassies of which no special mention is made. One from Zedekiah is incidentally mentioned by Jeremiah (chap. xxix. 3), of which there is no record in history.

(17) **Her mind was alienated.**—The original implies the disgust of satiety. Josiah had been the devoted friend of Babylon, and perished in his zeal on its behalf. Judah was then made a dependency of Egypt, and turned for aid to Babylon. Then receiving in turn the yoke of Babylon, she became impatient, and sought the aid of Egypt. This vacillating policy is described in verses 17—19, and at either turn was so entirely wanting in sole reliance upon God as to produce the effect of verse 18: "My mind was alienated from her."

(20) **Their paramours.**—The word is masculine, as indicating the abominable sins copied by the Israelites from the heathen, and asses and horses are introduced to show the intensity of lust. (Comp. Jer. v. 8.)

(22) **I will bring them against thee.**—Here, as everywhere, the fitness of the punishment to the sin, the correlation between them, is strongly brought out. Israel had chosen the idolatries of Egypt, Assyria, and Babylon, and these had drawn down upon her the vengeance of Him in whom alone was her refuge; she had sought strength in their political alliance, and they overwhelmed her with desolation.

(23) **Pekod, and Shoa, and Koa.**—These words were taken as proper names by our translators, and are still considered by some as indicating small Chaldæan tribes; but it is better, with the Vulg. and most modern commentators, to understand them as the names of officers, "rulers, lords, and nobles." Shoa is translated "crying" in Isa. xxii. 5, "liberal" in Isa. xxxii. 5, and "rich" in Job xxxiv. 19; while Pekod is rendered "visitation" in the margin of Jer. l. 21.

(24) **With chariots, wagons, and wheels.**—The word translated "chariots" occurs only here, and is thought to mean some weapon of war. It would be better to translate, *with weapons, chariots, and wheels.* The clause "I will set judgment before them," is equivalent to *I will entrust to them the judgment upon thee.*

(25) **Take away thy nose and thine ears.**—The barbarous custom of mutilating prisoners prevailed

against thee, and they shall deal furi-
ously with thee: they shall take away
thy nose and thine ears; and thy rem-
nant shall fall by the sword: they shall
take thy sons and thy daughters; and
thy residue shall be devoured by the fire.
(26) They shall also strip thee out of thy
clothes, and take away thy [1]fair jewels.
(27) Thus will I make thy lewdness to
cease from thee, and thy whoredom
brought from the land of Egypt: so
that thou shalt not lift up thine eyes
unto them, nor remember Egypt any
more.
(28) For thus saith the Lord God; Be-
hold, I will deliver thee into the hand
of them whom thou hatest, into the hand
of them from whom thy mind is alien-
ated: (29) and they shall deal with thee
hatefully, and shall take away all thy
labour, and shall leave thee naked and
bare: and the nakedness of thy whore-
doms shall be discovered, both thy lewd-
ness and thy whoredoms. (30) I will do
these *things* unto thee, because thou hast
gone a whoring after the heathen, *and*
because thou art polluted with their
idols. (31) Thou hast walked in the way
of thy sister; therefore will I give her
cup into thine hand. (32) Thus saith the
Lord God; Thou shalt drink of thy
sister's cup deep and large: thou shalt
be laughed to scorn and had in derision;
it containeth much. (33) Thou shalt be
filled with drunkenness and sorrow,
with the cup of astonishment and deso-
lation, with the cup of thy sister Sa-
maria. (34) Thou shalt even drink it and
suck *it* out, and thou shalt break the
sherds thereof, and pluck off thine own
breasts: for I have spoken *it*, saith the
Lord God. (35) Therefore thus saith the
Lord God; Because thou hast forgotten
me, and cast me behind thy back, there-
fore bear thou also thy lewdness and thy
whoredoms.
(36) The Lord said moreover unto me;
Son of man, wilt thou [a][2]judge Aholah
and Aholibah? yea, declare unto them
their abominations; (37) that they have
committed adultery, and blood *is* in their
hands, and with their idols have they
committed adultery, and have also caused
their sons, whom they bare unto me, to
pass for them through *the fire*, to devour
them. (38) Moreover, this they have done
unto me: they have defiled my sanctuary
in the same day, and have profaned my
sabbaths. (39) For when they had slain
their children to their idols, then they
came the same day into my sanctuary to
profane it; and, lo, [b]thus have they
done in the midst of mine house. (40) And
furthermore, that ye have sent for men
[3]to come from far, unto whom a mes-
senger *was* sent; and, lo, they came: for
whom thou didst wash thyself, paintedst
thy eyes, and deckedst thyself with orna-
ments, (41) and satest upon a [4]stately bed,
and a table prepared before it, [c]where-
upon thou hast set mine incense and
mine oil. (42) And a voice of a multi-
tude being at ease *was* with her: and
with the men [5]of the common sort *were*
brought [6]Sabeans from the wilderness,
which put bracelets upon their hands,

1 Heb., *instruments of thy decking.*
a ch. 20. 4; & 22. 2.
2 Or, *plead for.*
b 2 Kin. 21. 4.
3 Heb., *coming.*
4 Heb., *honourable.*
c Prov. 7. 17.
5 Heb., *of the multitude of men.*
6 Or, *drunkards.*

---

in the East from the earliest times; it is here mentioned with especial reference to the destruction of the attractiveness of the adulteress Aholibah, and the particulars of verse 26 have the same purpose. (Comp. chap. xvi. 39.) In Egypt adultery was punished by cutting off the nose and ears.

(32) **It containeth much.**—The cup of humiliation already drunk by Samaria was large, and filled with pain and sorrow, yet Jerusalem must drink it amid the derision of her neighbours.

(36) **Wilt thou judge?**—Rather, *judge thou*, as in chaps. xx. 4, xxii. 2.

(38) **In the same day.**—This is explained more fully in verse 39. Emphasis is laid upon the fact that they worshipped in the sanctuary of Jehovah in the same day that they offered their children to their idols, because the passing directly from the one to the other showed an utter disregard of the commands of the Lord, and an entire want of appreciation of His character and holiness. The figure in this and the following verses is partly dropped to bring out better the reality.

(40) **Paintedst thine eyes.**—The figure is that of a lewd woman preparing herself for her paramour, and awaiting his arrival. Painting the eyes, or rather the lids and lashes, was an ancient custom, still preserved in the East. (Comp. 2 Kings ix. 30.)

(41) **A stately bed** is rather the couch or divan used for reclining at a feast. "Mine incense and mine oil" (comp. chap. xvi. 18) may be taken simply as the products of the land, the good gifts of God which Israel bestowed upon the heathen; but as both of these were especially used in sacrifices, it is better to connect with this the perversion to the worship of the idols of the heathen of what should have been Jehovah's only.

(42) **A voice of a multitude being at ease was with her.**—The words "voice of a multitude," wherever else they occur (1 Sam. iv. 14; Isa. xiii. 4, xxxiii. 3; Dan. x. 6), mean *a loud tumult*, and even the word here used for "multitude," when alone, always means a boisterous multitude. Translate *The voice of the tumult was stilled thereat: i.e.*, the tumult of the invading army was stilled by the gifts of Israel, a fact of which there is frequent record in the history.

and beautiful crowns upon their heads.
(43) Then said I unto *her that was* old in
adulteries, Will they now commit
[1]whoredoms with her, and she *with*
them? (44) Yet they went in unto her,
as they go in unto a woman that playeth
the harlot: so went they in unto Aholah
and unto Aholibah, the lewd women.
(45) And the righteous men, they shall
[a]judge them after the manner of adul-
teresses, and after the manner of women
that shed blood; because they *are* adul-
teresses, and blood *is* in their hands.
(46) For thus saith the Lord God; I will
bring up a company upon them, and will
give them [2]to be removed and spoiled.
(47) And the company shall stone them
with stones, and [3]dispatch them with
their swords; they shall slay their sons
and their daughters, and burn up their
houses with fire. (48) Thus will I cause
lewdness to cease out of the land, that
all women may be taught not to do after
your lewdness. (49) And they shall re-
compense your lewdness upon you, and
ye shall bear the sins of your idols: and
ye shall know that I *am* the Lord God.

[1] Heb., *her whoredoms.*

[a] ch. 16. 38.

B.C. 590.

[2] Heb., *for a removing and spoil.*

[3] Or, *single them out.*

CHAPTER XXIV.—(1) Again in the
ninth year, in the tenth month, in the
tenth *day* of the month, the word of the
Lord came unto me, saying, (2) Son of
man, write thee the name of the day,
even of this same day: the king of Ba-
bylon set himself against Jerusalem this
same day. (3) And utter a parable unto
the rebellious house, and say unto them,
Thus saith the Lord God; Set on a pot,

The phrase translated "with her" is rendered "thereby" in Gen. xxiv. 14.

Men of the common sort is better rendered in the margin, *the multitude of men;* and "Sabeans" is not a proper name, but, as in the margin, *drunkards.* They are represented as from the wilderness, not as their home, but as the region through which they passed in marching to Judæa. The whole sense of the verse is that the conquerors attacking the land were satisfied with heavy tribute, and having received this, many of the warriors gave themselves up to drunkenness and debauchery, decking out their tributary with meretricious ornaments.

(43) **Will they now commit?**—This should not be made a question, nor should the opening of verse 44 be made adversative. The thought is that, after all means of reclamation had failed, God gave her up to her sins. Translate, *Now shall her whoredom be committed, even this. And they went in, &c.*

(44) **Unto Aholah and unto Aholibah.**—From verses 11—35 the discourse has been altogether of Aholibah, as the one now immediately concerned; but from verses 36—44, in the enumeration of their sins, both are included, though in the greater part of these verses the singular number is used, because Aholibah was most prominent in the prophet's thoughts. In the denunciation of judgment, with which the prophecy closes (verses 45—49), both are again spoken of in the plural, because, although Aholah had long since suffered, it was important to show that common sin involved both in common punishment.

(45) **The righteous men.**—That is, men to whom the judgment of righteousness is committed.

(47) **With stones . . . with swords.**—The figure and the reality are here designedly mixed. Stoning was the legal punishment of adultery, but the actual overthrow of Jerusalem was by the sword.

(48) **To cease.**—By the removal of the sinners. "All women," in accordance with the allegory, means *all nations.* The judgments upon Israel should be then, and for all time, a conspicuous monument of God's righteous severity.

(49) **Bear the sins of your idols**—*i.e.*, the punishment of the sins which you have committed in worshipping your idols.

XXIV.

On the exact day on which Nebuchadnezzar invested Jerusalem the fact was revealed to the prophet in Chaldæa, and he was commanded to declare the fate of the city by a parable (verses 3—14). Afterwards the sudden death of his wife was foretold, and he was forbidden to make any outward sign of mourning, that by this symbolical act he might further instruct the people (verses 15—24). At the close of the chapter he is told that the fall of the city will be announced to him by a fugitive, and after that he shall again prophesy to the people (verses 25—27).

(1) **In the tenth day of the month.**—Jehoiachin's captivity (by which all these prophecies are dated) coincided with Zedekiah's reign. The date here given is therefore the same as in Jer. xxxix. 1, lii. 4; 2 Kings xxv. 1, and was afterwards observed by the Jews as a fast (Zech. viii. 19). It was doubtless the day on which the investment of the city was completed.

(2) **Write thee the name.**—It is evident that especial attention was to be called to the exact date, and a note made of it at the time. The words "has set himself against" would be more accurately rendered *has fallen upon.* The supposition that the reference is to some point on his march from which Nebuchadnezzar advanced to the attack upon Jerusalem, and that tidings of this were brought to the prophet in the ordinary way, is quite inconsistent with the whole verse. It is plain that the prophet means to say, with especial emphasis and distinctness, that he was informed of what was taking place at Jerusalem on the same day in which it happened.

(3) **Utter a parable.**—What follows (verses 3—14) was not a symbolical action, but was simply a parable spoken to the people, although the language is just that which would describe action.

Set on a pot.—Rather, *the cauldron,* the word being the same as in chap. xi. 3, and preceded by the definite article referring to that passage. Urgency is indicated by the repetition of the command "set on." The people in chap. xi. 3 had called their city the cauldron; so let it be, the Divine word now says, and set that city upon the fire of the armies of my judgment, and

set *it* on, and also pour water into it:
(4) Gather the pieces thereof into it, *even*
every good piece, the thigh, and the
shoulder; fill *it* with the choice bones.
(5) Take the choice of the flock, and [1] burn
also the bones under it, *and* make it boil
well, and let them seethe the bones of it
therein.

(6) Wherefore thus saith the Lord God;
Woe to the bloody city, to the pot whose
scum *is* therein, and whose scum is not
gone out of it! bring it out piece by
piece; let no lot fall upon it. (7) For
her blood is in the midst of her; she set
it upon the top of a rock; she poured it
not upon the ground, to cover it with
dust; (8) that it might cause fury to
come up to take vengeance; I have set
her blood upon the top of a rock, that it
should not be covered. (9) Therefore
thus saith the Lord God; [a] Woe to the
bloody city! I will even make the pile
for fire great. (10) Heap on wood, kindle
the fire, consume the flesh, and spice it
well, and let the bones be burned.
(11) Then set it empty upon the coals
thereof, that the brass of it may be hot,
and may burn, and *that* the filthiness of
it may be molten in it, *that* the scum of
it may be consumed. (12) She hath
wearied *herself* with lies, and her great
scum went not forth out of her: her
scum *shall be* in the fire. (13) In thy
filthiness *is* lewdness: because I have
purged thee, and thou wast not purged,
thou shalt not be purged from thy filthi-

1 Or, *heap*.

a Nah. 3. 1; Hab. 2. 12.

---

gather into it for destruction the people who have boasted of it as their security.

(4) **The pieces thereof.**—Literally, *its pieces*, the pieces which pertain to the cauldron, the Jews, whose centre and capital is Jerusalem. This was the natural effect of Nebuchadnezzar's campaign; the people from every side sought refuge in the city. (Comp. Jer. xxxv. 11.) The mention of the "good piece," "the choice bones," and "the choice of the flock" (verse 5), is not for the purpose of designating any particular class, but only to emphasise that all, even the best, are to be included.

(5) **Burn also the bones under it.**—It is uncertain whether this is or is not the exact sense. The word for "burn" means, as is shown in the margin, *heap*, and is a noun. This is taken by many with a verb implied, in the sense of "make a heap of wood to burn the bones." On the other hand, the sense of the text is that given in most of the ancient versions, and it is certain that bones, before the fat is extracted, may be used for fuel. It is better, therefore, to translate quite literally, *heap the bones under it*, leaving the same ambiguity as in the original as to whether the bones are to be burned upon the fuel or themselves used for fuel. In either case, the bones are those which are left after "the good pieces" have been put into the cauldron. No part of the people shall escape; the refuse alike with the choice is doomed to destruction.

(6–14) These verses contain the application of the parable in two distinct parts (verses 6—8 and 9—14), but in such wise that the literal and the figurative continually run together. A new feature, that of the rust on the cauldron, is also introduced. A somewhat similar figure may be found in Isa. iv. 4, but with the difference that Ezekiel, as usual, goes much more into minute details.

(6) **Scum.**—This word, which occurs five times in these verses (6, 11, 12), is found nowhere else. Interpreters are agreed in the correctness of the old Greek version of it, *rust*. The thought is, that not only the inhabitants of the city are wicked, but that this wickedness is so great that the city itself (represented by the cauldron) is, as it were, corroded with rust. It is therefore to be utterly destroyed, "brought out piece by piece" (see 2 Kings xxv. 10); no lot is to fall upon it to make a discrimination, since nothing is to be spared. All previous judgments had been partial; this is to be complete.

(7) **Upon the top of a rock.**—Crimes of violence are continually charged upon Jerusalem (chaps. xxii. 12, 13, xxiii. 37, &c.), but here she is further reproached with such indifference to these crimes that she did not even care to cover them decently. It was required in the law that the blood even of the sacrifices (Lev. iv. 7, xvi. 15, &c.) and of animals slain for food (Deut. xii. 16) should be poured upon the ground, that it might be absorbed and covered out of sight; but Jerusalem had put the blood of her victims upon the hard rock, and not even covered it with dust, thus glorying in her shame. (Comp. Job xvi. 18; Isa. xxvi. 21.)

(8) **I have set.**—Here God Himself is said to do that which has just been charged upon Jerusalem. There is no inconsistency between the statements; Jerusalem gloried in her crimes, and God made those crimes conspicuous as the cause of her punishment.

(10) **Spice it well.**—With verse 9 the second part of the application of the parable begins, and is marked by great energy of description. In this verse the sense of the word translated "spice" is doubtful. If this be its true meaning, the idea must be, Go on thoroughly with the cooking; but the word is always used in connection with the preparation of compound incense or spices, and seems therefore to refer to the thoroughness of the work, and thus to mean, Boil thoroughly. In Job xli. 31 (Heb. 23) its derivative is used as a simile for the raging sea. The process is to be continued until the water in the cauldron is all evaporated, the flesh consumed, and even the bones burned.

(11) **Set it empty upon the coals.**—Keeping up the strong figure of the parable, after all the inhabitants have passed under judgment the city itself is to be purged by fire. It is unnecessary here to think of heat as removing the rust (scum) from the cauldron; the prophet's mind is not upon any physical effect, but upon the methods of purifying defiled metallic vessels under the law (see Num. xxxi. 23). It was a symbolical rather than a material purification, and in the present case involved the actual destruction of the city itself. In verses 11—14, the obduracy of the people is set forth in strong language, together with the completeness of the coming judgment in contrast to the in-

ness any more, till I have caused my
fury to rest upon thee. (14) I the LORD
have spoken *it:* it shall come to pass,
and I will do *it;* I will not go back,
neither will I spare, neither will I repent;
according to thy ways, and according to
thy doings, shall they judge thee, saith
the Lord GOD.

(15) Also the word of the LORD came
unto me, saying, (16) Son of man, behold,
I take away from thee the desire of
thine eyes with a stroke: yet neither
shalt thou mourn nor weep, neither
shall thy tears [1]run down. (17) [2]Forbear
to cry, make no mourning for the dead,
bind the tire of thine head upon thee,
and put on thy shoes upon thy feet, and
cover not *thy* [3]lips, and eat not the bread
of men.

(18) So I spake unto the people in the
morning: and at even my wife died;
and I did in the morning as I was com-
manded. (19) And the people said unto
me, Wilt thou not tell us what these
things are to us, that thou doest *so?*
(20) Then I answered them, The word of
the LORD came unto me, saying,
(21) Speak unto the house of Israel, Thus
saith the Lord GOD; Behold, I will pro-
fane my sanctuary, the excellency of
your strength, the desire of your eyes,
and [4]that which your soul pitieth; and
your sons and your daughters whom ye
have left shall fall by the sword. (22)And
ye shall do as I have done: ye shall not
cover *your* lips, nor eat the bread of
men. (23) And your tires *shall be* upon
your heads, and your shoes upon your
feet: ye shall not mourn nor weep; but
ye shall pine away for your iniquities,
and mourn one toward another. (24) Thus
Ezekiel is unto you a sign: according to
all that he hath done shall ye do: and
when this cometh, ye shall know that I
am the Lord GOD.

(25) Also, thou son of man, *shall it* not
be in the day when I take from them
their strength, the joy of their glory, the
desire of their eyes, and [5]that whereupon
they set their minds, their sons and their

[1] Heb., *go.*

[2] Heb., *Be silent.*

[3] Heb., *upper lip;* and so ver. 22.

[4] Heb., *the pity of your soul.*

[5] Heb., *the lifting up of their soul.*

---

effectiveness of all former efforts for their reformation (verse 13); and, finally, the adaptation of the punishment to the sin (verse 14). The word translated "lies" in verse 12 means *pains* or *labour.* Translate, *The labour is in vain; her rust does not go out of her, even her rust with fire.* In verse 13 "lewdness" would be better rendered *abomination.*

(15) **Also the word.**—What follows is distinctly separated from the utterance of the foregoing parable and its interpretation, yet verse 18 shows that it took place upon the same day. Ezekiel is warned of the sudden death of his wife, who is described as deeply beloved, and yet he is forbidden to make any sign of mourning for her.

(17) **The tire of thine head.**—This might be either the covering for the head usually worn by the people (see verse 23), or the special "mitre of fine linen" (Exod. xxxix. 28) provided for the priests; but as the peculiar priestly garments were worn only when the priests were on duty within the tabernacle (Lev. vi. 10, 11), it is not likely that Ezekiel used them in his captivity. The priests were expressly allowed to mourn for their nearest relations (Lev. xxi. 2, 3), and Ezekiel is therefore here made an exception. Among the ordinary signs of mourning was the covering of the head (2 Sam. xv. 30; Jer. xiv. 3), the sprinkling of dust upon it (chap. xxvii. 30; 1 Sam. iv. 12; 2 Sam. xv. 32), going barefoot (1 Sam. xv. 30; Isa. xx. 2), and covering the lips, or lower part of the face (Micah iii. 7). All these things are now forbidden to the prophet in his sorrow.

Eat not the bread of men—*i.e.,* the bread furnished by other men. It was customary for friends and neighbours to send food to the house of mourning, a custom which seems to be alluded to in Deut. xxvi. 14; Jer. xvi. 7; Hos. ix. 4; and out of this custom the habit of funeral feasts appears to have grown in later times.

(18) **In the morning: and at even.**—What the prophet "spake unto the people in the morning" was what he has recorded (verses 3—14). Shortly after this the warning of verses 15—17 must have come to him, and then his wife died in the evening of the same day. Accordingly, on the following morning the strange conduct which had been commanded him was observed by the people; their curiosity is awakened, and, rightly surmising that there must be some especial significance in the strange doings of their prophet, they come to inquire the meaning of his actions. In reply (verses 20—24), he announces again the destruction of the Temple, and that in the depth of sorrow and trouble at its fall there shall be no outward show of mourning.

(20) **That which your soul pitieth.**—In the margin *the pity of your soul.* The word rather means in this connection *love,* in the sense of the object of love: "that which your soul loves." The expression in the original is a difficult one, and is used by Ezekiel on account of the alliteration with the previous clause: "the *machmad* of your eyes, and the *machmal* of your souls." (Comp. the parallel in verse 25: "That whereupon they set their minds.")

(21) **Profane my sanctuary.**—Not merely by its destruction, but by the manner of its destruction, the Gentiles being allowed to enter its most sacred precincts, and carry off in triumph its sacred vessels and treasures. It was in the confidence that God would protect this that the last hope of the Jews lay; He tells them that He will Himself profane it.

(23) **Ye shall pine away.**—In the tumult, distress, and captivity of the approaching judgment there would be no opportunity for the outward display of grief; but all the more should it press upon them inwardly, and, according to the terrible threatening of Lev. xxvi. 39, they should "pine away in their iniquity" in their enemies' land. In the original the preposition is the same here as in Leviticus, "*in* your iniquity."

daughters, (26) *that* he that escapeth in that day shall come unto thee, to cause *thee* to hear *it* with *thine* ears? (27) In that day shall thy mouth be opened to him which is escaped, and thou shalt speak, and be no more dumb: and thou shalt be a sign unto them; and they shall know that I *am* the LORD.

CHAPTER XXV.—(1) The word of the LORD came again unto me, saying,

---

(27) **Shall thy mouth be opened.**—The close of the chapter (verses 25—27) tells the prophet that he shall be informed of the fall of Jerusalem by an escaped fugitive. After that his mouth shall again be opened to utter his prophecies to the captives. Meantime, for almost two years (comp. chap. xxiv. 1 with chap. xxxiii. 21), from the investment of the city until he heard of its fall, Ezekiel gave no prophecy to the Israelites. He had abundantly foretold the result, and now awaited the issue in silence. He has, however, recorded a considerable number of prophecies against foreign nations (chaps. xxv.—xxxii.).

Here one great division of the prophecies of Ezekiel closes. They have been hitherto occupied almost exclusively with reproofs for sin and with warnings of impending judgment upon his people. The following prophecies, as far as chap. xxxii., are indeed of the same character, but are directed entirely against foreign nations. This collection, as noticed in the Introduction, § 4, is not arranged chronologically like the rest of the book, but on the plan of putting together the prophecies against each nation. Chapter xxix. 17—31 is dated more than sixteen years after the fall of Jerusalem, and chap. xxxii. about two months after the tidings of that event; all the others which are dated are before, but only a little before, the capture of Jerusalem. Most of those undated seem to be in their chronological place, except that the first of them (chap. xxv.) was evidently after the fall of Jerusalem.

After that great judgment was made known to the prophet, there is a marked change in his utterances, and from that time his general tone is far more cheering and consolatory.

XXV.

Prophecies concerning heathen nations, from the time of Balaam down, mark every period of Scripture history. Sometimes, as in the case of Jonah, Obadiah, and Nahum, the utterance of the seer is against a single nation; sometimes, as in the case of Joel, and possibly also in that of Amos, the prophecies against the heathen are merely incidental and subsidiary to those concerning Israel; and sometimes, as in Isaiah, Jeremiah, and Ezekiel, they are collected in a special portion of the book. Balaam, Jonah, and to some extent Daniel, addressed their warnings directly to the nations concerned; but in most of the other instances it seems unlikely that the prophecies were ever communicated to the people to whom they directly related. In all cases they appear to have been given by God for the sake of His Church as well as for that of its enemies; even that of Jonah was given to Nineveh probably but a little time before the conquest of Israel, and must have impressed upon its haughty monarchs some respect for the God whose people they were soon to make captive; while those of Daniel were given to kings who already held the chosen people in captivity, and who were thereby compelled to make some acknowledgment of the reverence due to the God of Israel.

The reasons for the more general prophecies against the heathen must be sought in the special circumstances of each case in which they were uttered. In the present instance these reasons are not far to seek, for both the nations mentioned and the one omitted suggest a common purpose in the prophecy. Those mentioned are seven in number—Ammon, Moab, Edom, Philistia, Tyre, Sidon, and Egypt. All these were so far allies of Judah that they were in common hostility to Babylon; and it appears from Jer. xxvii. 1—3 that an attempt had been made in the reign of Jehoiakim to unite five of them in a league against Babylon, while Egypt was continually looked to by the disobedient Jews for aid against their common enemy. It was, therefore, necessary for Israel to know that there was no help to be found against Babylon in any earthly power; all the enemies of Chaldæa were to fall alike. Moreover, it was important to show by these prophecies that the judgment about to come upon the surrounding heathen was from God, since it is thus made clear that all events are of His ordering, and hence that the punishment of His people also must be from His own hand. This was especially the place for the prophet to speak of these judgments when he had just finished his denunciations of wrath upon Israel, and when these denunciations were about to be fulfilled. Besides these general reasons, there were other special ones in the case of each nation. Egypt had been a broken reed piercing the hand of Judah as often as she leaned upon it; while of Ammon, Moab, Edom, Philistia, and Tyre it is mentioned that they had exulted in the profanation of the Temple and the captivity of the people, and this especially from their hostility to the religion of Israel. It would help Israel to know that, while they were themselves punished for their unfaithfulness to their religion, those who altogether hated and rejected it were to suffer still more severely. It is remarkable that there is no prophecy in Ezekiel against Babylon, as there is in Isaiah, Jeremiah, and others; for Babylon appears throughout this book as the executor of God's judgments upon His people, and the effect of this would have been marred by the mention of her own ultimate punishment. For the present, all her enemies are to be overthrown, and she remains in strength; although she also would be punished for her sins when she should have accomplished the Divine purposes, yet it would have been worse than useless for the thoughts of Israel to be occupied with this now.

The number of *seven* nations against whom prophecies are uttered has been thought by many to be significant. It is made up by separating Zidon from Tyre, for which there were probably special reasons at the time. Zidon had long since lost its importance, and the prophecy against it is very short (chap. xxviii. 21—24); yet its ancient enmity to God was not to be forgotten, as it might appear to be if left without distinct mention.

The prophecy against Edom is greatly expanded in chap. xxxv., and there are other prophecies against foreign nations in chaps. xxxviii. and xxxix.; but these have so much the nature of promises to Israel that they are more appropriately placed where they are than they would have been in this connection. Even here

(2) Son of man, set thy face [a]against the
Ammonites, and prophesy against them;
(3) and say unto the Ammonites, Hear the
word of the Lord GOD; Thus saith the
Lord GOD; Because thou saidst, Aha,
against my sanctuary, when it was pro-
faned; and against the land of Israel,
when it was desolate; and against the
house of Judah, when they went into
captivity; (4) behold, therefore, I will
deliver thee to the [1]men of the east for
a possession, and they shall set their
palaces in thee, and make their dwellings
in thee: they shall eat thy fruit, and
they shall drink thy milk. (5) And I will
make Rabbah a stable for camels, and
the Ammonites a couchingplace for
flocks: and ye shall know that I *am*
the LORD. (6) For thus saith the Lord
GOD; Because thou hast clapped *thine*
[2]hands, and stamped with the [3]feet, and
rejoiced in [4]heart with all thy despite

a Jer. 49. 1, &c.

1 Heb., *children.*

2 Heb., *hand.*

3 Heb., *foot.*

4 Heb., *soul.*

---

the prophecy against Zidon (chap. xxviii. 25, 26) and that of the latest date against Egypt (chap. xxix. 21) end with promises to Israel.

The utterances against the various nations are very unequal in fulness. Those concerning Ammon, Moab, Edom, and Philistia are all included together in a single prophecy, occupying only one chapter (chap. xxv.); Tyre is the subject of four separate prophecies, filling nearly three chapters (chaps. xxvi.—xxviii. 19); Zidon is disposed of in the few following verses; while Egypt has seven distinct prophecies, filling chapters xxix—xxxii. The relative importance of these various nations is represented in this proportion.

The prophecies of Ezekiel concerning these nations had been anticipated by the older prophets, especially Isaiah and Amos, and similar predictions also abound in the contemporary Jeremiah, but with this marked difference: Ezekiel foretells their utter overthrow, while other prophets look forward to a period of restoration and blessing after their punishment. Thus Isaiah (chap. xxiii. 15—18) says that after a period of seventy years Tyre shall again rejoice, and shall ultimately be converted to the Lord; Jeremiah says of the Moabites, "I will bring again the captivity of Moab in the latter day, saith the Lord" (chap. xlviii. 47), and the same thing of the Ammonites (chap. xlix. 6); and of Egypt, that after its temporary subjection to Nebuchadnezzar, "afterward it shall be inhabited as in the days of old" (chap. xlvi. 26); Isaiah also describes the time when "Israel shall be the third with Egypt and Assyria, even a blessing in the midst of the land" (chap. xix. 24, 25). Yet it has generally been recognised that there is no inconsistency in these prophecies. Isaiah foretells a temporary resuscitation of Tyre, at the same time with Judah, in connection with the Medo-Persian conquest of Babylon; but Ezekiel's prophecies look beyond this, to the final destruction of the Tyrian power. On the other hand, these various prophecies speak of an ultimate gathering of a remnant of the descendants of these nations into the Church of God; while Ezekiel speaks of them only as political powers, and foretells that utter desolation of them which has been so strikingly fulfilled in the course of history.

(2) **Set thy face against the Ammonites.**—It has already been mentioned that the utterances against the four contiguous nations of Ammon, Moab, Edom, and Philistia are all contained in one prophecy, and that this prophecy was evidently spoken after the fall of Jerusalem, and, consequently, after the date of chapter xxvi. 1. The Ammonites, descended from Lot's incest with his younger daughter, had been for centuries persistent enemies of Israel. They had joined the Moabites in their oppression of Israel under Eglon (Judg. iii. 13), and in a later attack had been subdued by Jephthah (Judg. xi. 32, 33); they fought with extreme cruelty and insolence against Saul (1 Sam. xi. 2—11); they insulted and warred against David (2 Sam. x. 1—6), and were utterly crushed by him (*ib.*, xii. 31); their idolatries were favoured by Solomon (1 Kings xi. 7); uniting with Moab and Edom, they attacked Judah under Jehoshaphat (2 Chron. xx. 1—25), but utterly failed, and were tributary to his descendant, Uzziah (2 Chron. xxvi. 8); again they fought with Jotham, and were reduced by him to heavy tribute (*ib.*, xxvii. 5); and not long before this time they had occupied the vacant cities of Gad (Jer. xlix. 1). Now they had joined Nebuchadnezzar's army against Judah (2 Kings xxiv. 2). From verse 3 it appears that their hostility arose not only from national jealousy, but from an especial hatred against the Jewish religion (comp. also Ps. lxxxiii. 7). They are the frequent subject of prophetic denunciation (Isa. xi. 14; Jer. xlix. 1—6; Amos i. 13—15; Zeph. ii. 8—11).

(4) **To the men of the east.**—Literally, *sons of the east, i.e.,* the various nomadic tribes inhabiting the Eastern deserts, who occupy the country to this day. They are described as its possessors, not its conquerors; the conquest was effected by Nebuchadnezzar. In chap. xxi. 20—23 he was represented as hesitating whether to attack first Judah or Ammon, and determined to the former by the Divine direction; in this attack some of the Ammonites joined his army, but he nevertheless afterwards carried out his purpose and desolated their country. (See chap. xxi. 28.)

Palaces.—The word properly means an enclosure for folding cattle. The same word is used in connection with tribes of the desert in Gen. xxv. 16; Num. xxxi. 10, and in both is translated *castles,* a singularly inappropriate sense. It afterwards came to mean a dwelling-place of any kind. The Ammonites and Moabites appear to have practically constituted one nation, the latter being, for the most part, the settled, and the former the nomadic portion. After the conquest of Nebuchadnezzar the Ammonites gradually dwindled away, until lost from history. The Ptolemies founded the city Philadelphia on the site of Rabbah, and there are still extensive ruins there belonging to the period of the Roman occupation; but the Ammonites had no part in either of these successive cities. The place is now utterly without inhabitants, and the most recent traveller says, "Lonely desolation in a rich country was the striking characteristic."

(5) **Rabbah** was the only important town belonging to the Ammonites. It has become literally a stable for the camels of the wandering Bedouins. In the parallel clause the "Ammonites" are put for the land which they inhabit.

(6) **Clapped thine hands, and stamped with the feet.**—See chap. vi. 11 and Note there.

against the land of Israel; (7) behold,
therefore I will stretch out mine hand
upon thee, and will deliver thee for [1]a
spoil to the heathen; and I will cut thee
off from the people, and I will cause thee
to perish out of the countries: I will de-
stroy thee; and thou shalt know that I
am the LORD.

(8) Thus saith the Lord GOD; [a]Because
that Moab and Seir do say, Behold, the
house of Judah *is* like unto all the hea-
then; (9) therefore, behold, I will open
the [2]side of Moab from the cities, from
his cities *which are* on his frontiers, the
glory of the country, Beth-jeshimoth,
Baal-meon, and Kiriathaim, (10) unto the
men of the east [3]with the Ammonites,
and will give them in possession, that
the Ammonites may not be remembered
among the nations. (11) And I will exe-
cute judgments upon Moab; and they
shall know that I *am* the LORD.

(12) Thus saith the Lord GOD; Because
that Edom hath dealt against the house
of Judah [4]by taking vengeance, and
hath greatly offended, and revenged
himself upon them; (13) therefore thus
saith the Lord GOD; I will also stretch
out mine hand upon Edom, and will cut
off man and beast from it; and I will
make it desolate from Teman; and [5]they
of Dedan shall fall by the sword. (14)And
I will lay my vengeance upon Edom by
the hand of my people Israel: and they

1 Or, *meat.*

a Jer. 48. 1, &c.

2 Heb., *shoulder of Moab.*

3 Or, *against the children of Ammon.*

4 Heb., *by revenging revengement.*

5 Or, *they shall fall by the sword unto Dedan.*

---

(7) **For a spoil.**—This is the sense of the margin of the Hebrew; its text is represented by our margin, *meat* or *food.* The word in the text occurs only here, but a compound of it is found in Dan. i. 5, xi. 26. The figure seems to be the same as that which speaks of *devouring* the people.

Shalt know that I am the Lord.— This frequent close of the denunciatory prophecies against Israel in the former chapters is here also used at the close of each message in this chapter, and of many of the other prophecies against foreign nations. It refers not to a penitent recognition of the Lord, but to an experience of His wrath so plain that they can no longer refuse to acknowledge His power (see verse 14).

(8) **Moab and Seir.**—The two nations, here mentioned together, are afterwards treated separately—Moab, verses 8—11, and Edom, verses 12—14. Moab, springing from the same source with Ammon, was closely associated with it in its history and fortune, and is denounced in nearly the same prophecies. It was a more settled and stronger people, and also contributed its quota to the armies of Nebuchadnezzar. Additional prophecies in regard to it may be found in Num. xxiv. 17 and Isa. xv., xvi., besides those immediately connected with the prophecies expressly against Ammon already cited. The Moabites, so far as they were separated from the Ammonites, lay immediately to the south of them.

(9) **Open the side of Moab**—*i.e., lay it open to the enemy.* This is to be done "from the cities," on which a special emphasis is placed. The cities named were all on the north of the Arnon, and before the time of Moses had been wrested from the Moabites by the Amorites, from whom in turn they were taken by the Israelites, and long formed a part of their territory. In the decay of the power of Israel they were re-conquered by Moab, and are here spoken of, perhaps in view of their being rightfully a possession of Israel, as appropriately the point from which desolation should go out over the whole of Moab.

The glory of the country.—The territory designated by the mention of these three cities is still considered by the Arabs as the best part of the land, and is called *Belka.* They have a proverb, "Thou canst find no land like Belka." The sites of all the cities which are alluded to here have been probably identified by existing ruins.

(10) **With the Ammonites.**—The division between the verses here seriously obscures the sense. The meaning is that God will throw open Moab, as well as Ammon, to the sons of the east, and will give both nations in possession to them, so that Ammon shall be no more remembered, and judgment shall be executed on Moab. They were to be conquered and desolated by Nebuchadnezzar, but possessed by the Bedouins. The Ammonites and Moabites were nations so closely connected together that nearly all which has been said of the one applies to the other.

(12) **Edom hath dealt against the house of Judah.**—The reason of Edom's hostility to Israel is expressly said to be revenge. Descended from the elder son, they had never looked complacently on the spiritual superiority given to the descendants of the younger. They showed their hostility from the first in refusing, with a show of violence, a passage to the Israelites through their territory (Num. xx. 18—21); and although they were subdued and made tributary under David and Solomon (2 Sam. viii. 14; 1 Kings ix. 26), yet in the decline of the Jewish power they availed themselves of every opportunity for hostility (2 Chron. xxviii. 17, &c.). At this time they not only joined the armies of Nebuchadnezzar, but appear to have urged on the conqueror to greater cruelty, and to have themselves waylaid the fugitives to cut them off (chap. xxxv. 5; Ps. cxxxvii. 7; Amos i. 11; Obad. 11). They also, during the Captivity, took possession of many towns of Judea, including Hebron (Jos., *Antt.*, xii. 8, § 6; *B. J.*, iv. 9, § 7), which were re-conquered in the time of the Maccabees. Other prophecies against Edom may be found in Num. xxiv. 18, 19; Isa. xi. 14; Jer. xlix. 7—12; Joel iii. 19, besides the extended prophecy of Ezekiel in chap. xxxv.

(13) **From Teman; and they of Dedan.**—Teman (a word meaning *south*) was a southern district of Edom (Jer. xlix. 20, 21; Hab. iii. 3), famed for its wisdom (Jer. xlix. 7; Obad. 8, 9). Dedan is frequently mentioned by the prophets, but in such a way that it has not been certainly identified. A better translation would be, *From Teman unto Dedan,* meaning from one end of the country to the other, *they shall fall by the sword.*

(14) **By the hand of my people Israel.**—This points distinctly to the fact that the Divine vengeance on Edom should be accomplished by the hand of the

shall do in Edom according to mine
anger and according to my fury; and
they shall know my vengeance, saith
the Lord GOD.
(15) Thus saith the Lord GOD; Because
the Philistines have dealt by revenge,
and have taken vengeance with a de-
spiteful heart, to destroy *it* [1]for the old
hatred; (16) therefore thus saith the Lord
GOD; Behold, I will stretch out mine
hand upon the Philistines, and I will
cut off the Cherethims, and destroy the
remnant of the [2]sea coast. (17) And I
will execute great [3]vengeance upon them
with furious rebukes; and they shall
know that I *am* the LORD, when I shall
lay my vengeance upon them.

CHAPTER XXVI.—(1) And it came
to pass in the eleventh year, in the first

[1] Or, *with perpetual hatred.*

[2] Or, *haven of the sea.*

B.C. 588.

[3] Heb. *vengeances.*

Israelites, a prophecy which was fulfilled when they were conquered by John Hyrcanus, and compelled to submit to circumcision as a mark of absorption into the Jewish people. Subsequently Herod (who was himself of Idumean origin), as king of the Jews, reigned over them, and their name disappeared from history.

Many commentators would see in this prophecy a further intimation of their ultimate conversion and incorporation into the Church; but this seems quite foreign, not only to the scope of this series of prophecies, but especially to the connection, "I will lay my vengeance upon Edom," and "they shall know my vengeance."

(15) **The Philistines.**—The historical books of the Old Testament are almost a continuous record of the hostility of the Philistines. At times they held the greater part of the land of Israel in subjection, and at times were subdued in their turn. Although belonging to another branch of the Hamitic family, their land was included with that of the Canaanites in the territory to be given to the Israelites (Josh. xiii. 2, 3). It was never, however, occupied by them, although the cities were fortified and garrisoned by some of the kings. The land lay along the coast of the Mediterranean, on the highway between Egypt and Assyria and Chaldæa, and consequently, in the struggles of those nations with each other the Philistines were gradually more and more reduced, until they disappeared entirely. Among the many prophecies against them, the following may be especially referrred to: Isa. xiv. 29—32; Jer. xlvii.; Amos i. 6—8; Zeph. ii. 4—7.

(16) **Cherethims.**—The Cherethim were a portion of the Philistines living on their southern coast (1 Sam. xxx. 14; Zeph. ii. 5); and are sometimes put for the whole nation. The name is supposed by many to be equivalent to *Cretans*, and to indicate the origin of the Philistines from the island of Crete; but the etymology is doubtful. The reason for the introduction of their name here was probably a *paronomasia* in the original, the phrase "I will cut off the Cherethim" reading *I will slay the slayers.*

XXVI.

Tyre was a great and powerful commercial city, made up of two parts: Old Tyre, situated on a plain on the mainland, and New Tyre, built on a rocky island, or rather two islands joined together, lying about half a mile from the shore. Its territory was insignificant, but it was so strong in its wealth, its ships, and its colonies, that it was able to employ mercenaries (chap. xxvii. 10, 11) in numbers, and being strongly fortified, resisted for five years, and with final success, the siege by the whole power of Assyria under Shalmaneser. According to the Assyrian records, however, it was afterwards captured by Assurbanipal. A few years after the fall of Jerusalem it was again besieged by Nebuchadnezzar for thirteen years. There is no express mention in the histories of the time of the result of this siege, although it is implied in the statement of the ancient historians (*Jos. c. Apion*, i. 20; *Antt.* x., 11, § 1) that Nebuchadnezzar made himself master of all Phœnicia. It is also asserted by St. Jerome that he captured Tyre, and he describes the method by which it was accomplished; it is also very unlikely that such a monarch as Nebuchadnezzar would have allowed himself to be baffled after such effort. (On the difficulty suggested by chap. xxix. 18, see the Note there.) In the days of David and Solomon, the king of Tyre was the close friend of Israel; afterwards the two nations became alienated, and the Tyrians sold Hebrew captives to the Greeks and the Edomites (Joel iii. 4—8; Amos i. 9, 10). Tyre was probably greatly offended when Josiah, in the course of his reformation, defiled the images of their god Baal, and destroyed his sacred vessels, both at Jerusalem and in Samaria. It was subject to the Persian Empire, was captured by Alexander, remained a large city under the Romans, was still flourishing in the time of St. Jerome, was great at the era of the Crusades, but soon afterwards was totally destroyed by the Saracens, and has since remained so utterly desolate that its site might not even be observed by the passing traveller. Besides the prophecies against Tyre just mentioned, that of Isa. xxiii. has already been spoken of in the introductory Note to chapter xxv.

Ezekiel's denunciation of Tyre occupies nearly three chapters, and each of these forms a distinct prophecy, the last verses of chap. xxviii. constituting a separate prophecy against the associated Phœnician city of Sidon. The first of these (chap. xxvi.) is occupied with the threat of the destruction of Tyre; the second (chap. xxvii.) is a lamentation over this destruction; while the third (chap. xxviii. 1—19) is divided into two parts (which may indeed be separate prophecies), of which the former (verses 1—10) is a threat specifically against the king of Tyre, and the latter (verses 11—19) is a lamentation over his fall.

Chapter xxvi. consists of four sections, each introduced with "Thus saith the Lord," the whole preceded by the mention of the sin of Tyre in exulting over the fall of Jerusalem (verse 2). The first of these (verses 3—6) describes the ultimate desolation of Tyre by "many nations;" the second (verses 7—14) describes circumstantially its more immediate conquest by Nebuchadnezzar; the third (verses 15—18) the effect upon the islands and coasts, doubtless with especial reference to her colonies and those with whom she was commercially connected; while the fourth (verses 19—21) is an energetic repetition and summary of her doom.

(1) **In the first day of the month.**—The year was that in which Jerusalem fell (2 Kings xxv.

day of the month, *that* the word of the
LORD came unto me, saying,
(2) Son of man, because that Tyrus
hath said against Jerusalem, Aha, she
is broken *that was* the gates of the
people: she is turned unto me: I shall
be replenished, *now* she is laid waste:
(3) therefore thus saith the Lord GOD;
Behold, I *am* against thee, O Tyrus, and
will cause many nations to come up
against thee, as the sea causeth his
waves to come up. (4) And they shall
destroy the walls of Tyrus, and break
down her towers: I will also scrape her
dust from her, and make her like the
top of a rock. (5) It shall be *a place for*
the spreading of nets in the midst of the
sea: for I have spoken *it*, saith the Lord
GOD: and it shall become a spoil to the
nations. (6) And her daughters which
are in the field shall be slain by the
sword; and they shall know that I *am*
the LORD.
(7) For thus saith the Lord GOD; Be-
hold, I will bring upon Tyrus Nebu-
chadrezzar king of Babylon, a king of
kings, from the north, with horses, and
with chariots, and with horsemen, and
companies, and much people. (8) He
shall slay with the sword thy daughters
in the field: and he shall make a fort
against thee, and [1] cast a mount against

1 Or, *pour out the engine of shot.*

2—4, 8, 9), but the month is not given here, and cannot now be ascertained. It is plain from verse 2 that Tyre already felt sure of the issue of the siege; but there is a marked difference between this and the language in chap. xxv. 3, which could only have been used after the capture of the city. This prophecy may therefore well have been given at any time during the eleventh year. Possibly the Alexandrine Septuagint is right in supplying "the first" month; but as this is omitted in the Roman copy, it is more likely to have been a mere conjecture. There is a similar omission in chap. xxxii. 17, but the number is easily supplied there from verse 1. Probably, in both cases the omission is a mere error of the scribes.

(2) **She is broken that was the gates of the people.**—"Gates" is in the plural simply because the word originally means *a leaf* of a door or gate, and hence the two leaves mean *the gate;* accordingly the sense would be better conveyed by using the singular in English. On the other hand, "people," both here and in chap. xxvii. 3, is intentionally in the plural =the nations. By omitting all the words in italics in this verse a better idea is obtained of the exultation of Tyre over the fall of Jerusalem.

This exultation is described as of a purely selfish and commercial character, and shows nothing of the spitefulness and religious animosity of the nations mentioned in the previous chapter. Jerusalem had been made in the days of Solomon the great commercial emporium of the inland trade from Arabia, and even from India, as well as the negotiator of products between Egypt and the Hittites and other northern nations. Doubtless something of this commercial importance still remained to Jerusalem in her decay, of which we have already seen evidence in chap. xvi.; but however this may have been, a considerable city, situated as Jerusalem was, must of necessity have been the centre of many of those transactions between the surrounding nations which Tyre would gladly have monopolised for herself. Hence her exultation: "Jerusalem being destroyed, all that gave her importance among the nations must come to increase my prosperity."

(3) **Many nations.**—The prophet here, at the outset, glances down through the ages of Tyre's future history. He has in mind not merely the conquest by Nebuchadnezzar, of which he will speak more particularly presently (verses 7—11), but all the successive conquests until the proud city should be reduced to utter desolation. Most appropriate to the situation and habits of Tyre is the illustration, "as the sea causeth his waves to come up": God will bring nation after nation to the destruction of Tyre as the sea throws wave after wave against her rock.

(4) **Her dust.**—Comp. verse 12. The dust is that of her ruined walls and palaces and temples. "Scraping" expresses their utter destruction. As an historic fact, the ruins of the ancient city have all been thrown into the sea, and what now remains is of mediæval construction, although the greater part of even the mediæval ruins have been carried away.

(5) **The spreading of nets.**—Such has been the chief use of insular Tyre for ages, and although a miserable village of 3,000 people has sprung up, chiefly within the present century, upon a part of its site, other parts have still no more important use. The Tyre upon the mainland has so utterly disappeared that even its site cannot be exactly identified.

(6) **Daughters which are in the field.**—Comp. verse 8. A poetic way of describing the dependencies of Tyre upon the mainland.

In verses 7—11 the particular and now impending conquest by Nebuchadnezzar is graphically described, and then, with the change to the plural in verse 12, there seems to be again a looking forward to the long vista of successive devastations.

(7) **Nebuchadrezzar.**—So the name is very often written by Jeremiah and a few times by Ezekiel. It is, perhaps, a closer representation of the *Nabu-kudurri-uzur* of the Babylonian cylinders than the form finally adopted by the Hebrews of Nebuchadnezzar.

A king of kings, from the north.—He is called a "king of kings" because of the many countries subject to his sway, whose kings were his vassals; and he is described as "from the north," because, as often before said, it was from this direction that his armies must approach Tyre, although Babylon itself was in actual latitude to the south of Tyre.

(8) **A fort . . . a mount.**—These and the following particulars of the siege indicate the use of the ordinary methods as in the attack of a city on the mainland. The explanation of this is doubtless partly in the fact that Palæotyrus, Old Tyre, upon the mainland, was approached in the ordinary way, and partly that Nebuchadnezzar must have contrived a bridge of boats, or some other method of approaching the island across the shoal and narrow channel (1,200 yards), which at

thee, and lift up the buckler against
thee. (9) And he shall set engines of
war against thy walls, and with his axes
he shall break down thy towers. (10) By
reason of the abundance of his horses
their dust shall cover thee: thy walls
shall shake at the noise of the horsemen,
and of the wheels, and of the chariots,
when he shall enter into thy gates, [1]as
men enter into a city wherein is made a
breach. (11) With the hoofs of his horses
shall he tread down all thy streets: he
shall slay thy people by the sword, and
thy strong garrisons shall go down to
the ground. (12) And they shall make a
spoil of thy riches, and make a prey of
thy merchandise: and they shall break
down thy walls, and destroy [2]thy plea-
sant houses: and they shall lay thy
stones and thy timber and thy dust in
the midst of the water. (13) [a]And I will
cause the noise of thy songs to cease;
and the sound of thy harps shall be no
more heard. (14)And I will make thee
like the top of a rock: thou shalt be *a*
place to spread nets upon; thou shalt
be built no more: for I the LORD have
spoken *it*, saith the Lord GOD.

(15) Thus saith the Lord GOD to Tyrus;
Shall not the isles shake at the sound of
thy fall, when the wounded cry, when
the slaughter is made in the midst of
thee? (16) Then all the princes of the
sea shall come down from their thrones,
and lay away their robes, and put off
their broidered garments: they shall
clothe themselves with [3]trembling; they
shall sit upon the ground, and shall
tremble at *every* moment, and be asto-
nished at thee. (17) And they shall take
up a [b]lamentation for thee, and say to
thee, How art thou destroyed, *that wast*

1 Heb., *according to the enterings of a city broken up.*

2 Heb., *houses of thy desire.*

a Isai. 24. 8; Jer. 7. 34 & 16. 9.

3 Heb., *tremblings.*

b Rev. 18. 9.

---

that time separated it from the mainland. That if he built a mole it was afterwards removed, is plain from the fact that when Alexander built one, 250 years later, sand accumulated upon it, until the island has now become a peninsula, connected with the shore by a beach of considerable width.

The buckler is that sort of roof made with shields used in ancient warfare by besiegers to defend themselves from the missiles of the besieged. Herodotus (chap. ix. 61, 99, 102) mentions its use among the Persians.

(9) **Engines of war.**—This is now generally understood to mean *battering-rams*, although the word is a different one from that used in chaps. iv. 2, xxi. 22. There are two words here which may form one compound word.

Axes in the original is *swords.* It may either be used, the specific for the general, swords for all instruments of war; or it may be a poetic hyperbole, to express the power of the swords of Nebuchadnezzar's army—they shall even break down the towers.

(10) **Shall enter into thy gates.**—The whole description of this verse again implies that Nebuchadnezzar had contrived some way by which his armies, with horsemen and chariots, could march into the city, and the prophet gives a glowing poetic description of the effect of their entrance.

(11) **Thy strong garrisons.** — This is the only instance in the Bible in which this common word is so translated, although a word closely akin to it is rendered *garrison* throughout the Books of Samuel. Both words mean a pillar set up as a monument or memorial. Translate, therefore, *the pillars of thy strength.* It is probable that the pillars intended are those mentioned by Herodotus (Bk. ii. 44) as standing in the Temple of Hercules at Tyre, one of gold and the other of emerald.

(12) **They shall make.**—In verse 12 the nominative changes. It is no longer Nebuchadnezzar who does these things, but "they." This may intimate that the prophet's vision now again passes beyond the immediate future to the long succession of calamities, beginning indeed with Nebuchadnezzar's conquest, with which Tyre was to be visited. The "spoil" and "prey" is to be understood more of what the Tyrians lost than of what the conquerors gained. In the long-continued sieges to which the city was subjected there was great waste of its substance; but their command of the water generally enabled them before the close to send away their moveable wealth, so that the booty of the victor was small. (With the close of the verse comp. verse 4.) The situation of Tyre led naturally to her ruins being thrown into the sea. Robinson saw in one place as many as forty or fifty marble columns beneath the water.

(13) **I will cause.**—Here God speaks of His own direct action, and declares that all these calamities are ordered by Him; and in this and the following verse the prophecy of verses 4, 5, is repeated that Tyre shall be utterly wasted and desolate, and never be rebuilt.

In verses 15—21 the effect of the fall of Tyre upon other maritime people is set forth. It is to be remembered that these people were either her own colonies, or else in close commercial relations with her.

(15) **The isles.**—This word is constantly used in Scripture, not merely for islands, strictly so called, but for any sea-coasts. The main reference here, no doubt, is to the islands and coasts of the Mediterranean; but as Tyrian commerce extended also beyond, the language need not be entirely restricted to these. The tidings of the conquest of Tyre is poetically represented as "the sound of her fall."

(16) **Princes of the sea.**—Or, as we should say, *merchant princes.* (Comp. Isa. xxiii. 8.) Actual sovereigns are not meant, but those raised by commerce to wealth and power. Their astonishment and grief is poetically described under the figure of the customs of Oriental mourning. (Comp. Jonah iii. 6.) "Thrones" should rather be translated *seats*, as in Judges iii. 20; 1 Sam. i. 9, iv. 13, 18.

(17) **Inhabited of seafaring men.**— Rather, *inhabited from the sea.* The word, which is very common, never bears the sense of men. The thought is that the rock of Tyre, built up with dwellings to the water's edge was like a city rising from the sea.

inhabited [1] of seafaring men, the re-
nowned city, which wast strong in the
sea, she and her inhabitants, which
cause their terror *to be* on all that haunt
it! (18) Now shall the isles tremble in
the day of thy fall; yea, the isles that
are in the sea shall be troubled at thy
departure.
(19) For thus saith the Lord God;
When I shall make thee a desolate city,
like the cities that are not inhabited;
when I shall bring up the deep upon
thee, and great waters shall cover thee;
(20) when I shall bring thee down with
them that descend into the pit, with the
people of old time, and shall set thee in
the low parts of the earth, in places
desolate of old, with them that go down
to the pit, that thou be not inhabited;
and I shall set glory in the land of the
living; (21) I will make thee [2] a terror,
and thou *shalt be* no *more:* though thou
be sought for, yet shalt thou never be
found again, saith the Lord God.

CHAPTER XXVII.—(1) The word of
the Lord came again unto me, saying,
(2) Now, thou son of man, take up a la-
mentation for Tyrus; (3) and say unto
Tyrus,
O thou that art situate at the entry of
the sea, *which art* a merchant of the
people for many isles, Thus saith the
Lord God; O Tyrus, thou hast said, I
am [3] of perfect beauty. (4) Thy borders
are in the [4] midst of the seas, thy builders

1 Heb., *of the seas.*
2 Heb., *terrors.*
3 Heb., *perfect of beauty.*
4 Heb., *heart.*

Which cause their terror.—This clause has occasioned much difficulty. The literal translation is, *she and her inhabitants, which gave their fear to all her inhabitants.* "Fear" is here used in the sense of that which causes fear; and the meaning is, that the power of Tyre was so feared that every Tyrian was respected for her sake, just as at a later day every Roman bore about with him something of the majesty of Rome, or, as now, the citizen of a great Power is respected among foreigners for his country's sake. (Comp. chap. xxxii. 24, 26.)

(18) **The isles tremble.**—"Isles" here, as elsewhere, includes coasts. It must be remembered how numerous the colonies of Phœnicia were. They had been established in Cyprus, Rhodes, Malta, Spain, Sicily, Sardinia, the Balearic Islands, and Africa. In some of these there were several colonies, as Utica and Carthage in Africa, Gades (Cadiz), Kalpe (Gibraltar), and Malaka (Malaga) in Spain. All of these looked up to Tyre as their mother-city, and received from her their high priests. Even Carthage, the greatest of them, sent yearly presents to the Tyrian Hercules.

(19) **Bring up the deep upon thee.**—With verse 19 begins the closing section of this prophecy, and in it the other parts are summed up and emphasised. The figurative language by which the overwhelming of Tyre is here described is again appropriate to her natural situation.

(20) **With them that descend into the pit.**—Comp. Isa. xiv. 9—20. Tyre is here represented, as Babylon is there, as joining itself to the dead—a striking figure to indicate its utter and final destruction. This is to be understood of the Tyre that then was, the proud mistress of the sea. The question whether there might or might not ever be other inhabitants on the rock of Tyre is one which does not at all come within the scope of the prophet's vision. The way of speaking of the place of the dead, as in the lower part of the earth, so common in Scripture (comp. Eph. iv. 9), does not by any means prove that the writers thought this to be the actual place of departed spirits, but only that, as it is a necessity of human thought and expression to indicate some locality, this locality, in association with the burial of the body, is most naturally placed "under the earth." In the same way, men, even on opposite sides of the globe, always speak of God as "above them," and their gestures and looks, as well as their words, unavoidably involve the same idea, though they perfectly know that He is omnipresent. (Comp. even the example of our Lord in Mark vi. 41, vii. 34; Luke ix. 16; John xvii. 1.)

Set glory in the land of the living.—The word for "glory" is the same as that used in chap. xx. 6, 15; Dan. viii. 9, xi. 16, 41, in connection with Palestine. The prediction is that when Tyre, who is now rejoicing in the calamity of Judah, shall be past and forgotten, numbered with the dead, then God will establish His people as a living Church to Himself. A ray of Messianic promise shines through the prediction, although, for the time, it might seem nothing more than a foretelling of the restoration from the Captivity.

XXVII.

This chapter has been very well called "The Dirge of Tyre." It is a lamentation over its fall, not because the prophet could wish it to be otherwise, but simply because of the terror and sorrowfulness of the event itself. It is unique among Scripture representations in the fulness of detail with which the greatness of Tyre is described; but this is quite in accordance with the peculiarity of Ezekiel's mind. The description is carried out under the figure of a well-built ship, thoroughly manned and equipped, sailing everywhere, engaged in lucrative commerce; but at last, brought into rough seas and storm, she is wrecked, and sinks. This prolonged figure is generally well sustained, although, after the manner of this prophet, the reality is occasionally allowed to break through for the sake of clearness and emphasis.

The whole lamentation so much explains itself that it will only be necessary to subjoin brief notes on passages that, in our version especially, are not altogether clear.

(3) **At the entry of the sea.**—The word for "entry" in the original is plural, and means the approaches to the sea, or harbours. Tyre had two of these, both remarkably good: the "Egyptian," facing the south, and the "Sidonian," facing the north, the latter having also an outer harbour or roadstead, formed by a ledge off the north-west extremity of the island. The former

have perfected thy beauty. (5) They have
[1]made all thy *ship* boards of fir trees of
Senir: they have taken cedars from
Lebanon to make masts for thee. (6) *Of*
the oaks of Bashan have they made
thine oars; [2][3]the company of the
Ashurites have made thy benches *of*
ivory, *brought* out of the isles of Chittim.
(7) Fine linen with broidered work from
Egypt was that which thou spreadest
forth to be thy sail; [4]blue and purple
from the isles of Elishah was that which
covered thee. (8) The inhabitants of
Zidon and Arvad were thy mariners:
thy wise *men*, O Tyrus, *that* were in
thee, were thy pilots. (9) The ancients
of Gebal and the wise *men* thereof were
in thee thy [5][6]calkers: all the ships of
the sea with their mariners were in thee
to occupy thy merchandise. (10) They of
Persia and of Lud and of Phut were in
thine army, thy men of war: they hanged
the shield and helmet in thee; they set
forth thy comeliness. (11) The men of
Arvad with thine army *were* upon thy
walls round about, and the Gammadims
were in thy towers: they hanged their
shields upon thy walls round about;

1 Heb., *built.*

2 Or, *they have made thy hatches of ivory well trodden.*

3 Heb., *the daughter.*

4 Or, *purple and scarlet.*

5 Or, *stoppers of chinks.*

6 Heb., *strengtheners.*

---

is now completely, and the latter nearly, filled up with sand and ruins.

(5) **Ship boards.**—Planking for the sides of the ship. The word in the original is in the dual, with reference to its two sides. Senir was the Amorite name of Hermon, or Antilebanon, called by the Sidonians Sirion (Deut. iii. 9). Ezekiel wished to use a foreign name, and the latter may at this time have become obsolete. The timber brought thence for the ship's planking, and called *fir*, was the same with that furnished by Hiram to Solomon for the floor of the Temple (1 Kings vi. 15), and may have been either "fir" (spruce?) or cypress. The Scripture names of trees are not always well identified. Both were esteemed among the ancients for ship-building, especially the cypress, on account of its lightness, durability, and freedom from the attacks of worms.

(6) **The company of the Ashurites have made thy benches of ivory.**—The literal rendering of this clause (with two words of doubtful meaning left blank) is, *they made thy . . . of tooth* (*ivory*), *daughter of . . .* The sense will depend upon the filling up of these blanks. For the first there need be no difficulty. The word is used in Exod. xxvi. 16 of the boards of the tabernacle, and here it is undoubtedly used of some planking about the ship; but it is in the singular number. It is hardly likely, therefore, to mean "benches" (*i.e.*, seats for the oarsmen), since there were usually two or three tiers of these on each side of the ship. It is now generally taken collectively of the planking of the deck. If the Hebrew text, as it stands, is quite correct, we must read the other word "daughter of Ashurites," for there is no authority for rendering "daughter" by *company*. It is difficult or impossible to make any intelligible sense of this; but if the two Hebrew words now written separately be joined together, we shall have "in box-wood," the word being the same as in Isa. lx. 13. There will still be a little doubt, as there is so often in Scripture, as to the exact wood intended, whether box-wood or the sherbin-cedar; but the general sense is plain—"they have made thy deck of ivory, *inlaid* in box-wood."

Isles of Chittim.—Chittim is the Old Testament name for Cyprus, and hence "isles of Chittim" (as in Jer. ii. 10) stands for the islands and coasts whose fleets, in coming to the East, made their rendezvous at Cyprus. Thither were brought both the ivory from the African coast and the precious woods from various quarters.

(7) **Fine linen with broidered work.**—To a modern sailor "fine linen" may seem both an extravagant and an insufficient material for a ship's sails, but the State ships of antiquity were often fitted out in this way, and the sails embroidered in colours in place of a pennon. The clause literally is, *Linen with embroidery from Egypt was for thy spreading out* (*sail*), *to be to thee for a sign.*

Isles of Elishah.—In Gen. x. 4, 1 Chron. i. 7, Elishah is mentioned among the sons of Javan, or Ionia. The regions here referred to are the coasts of Asia Minor, where an abundant supply of the *murex* (from which came the famous purple dye) was obtained, when the quantity on the Tyrian coast was insufficient for its manufactures. "That which covered thee" is the awning spread over the ship's deck.

(8) **Arvad.**—The description now turns to the sailors. The Arvadite is mentioned among the family of Canaan in Gen. x. 18, and corresponds to the Greek Aradus. There were two islands of this name: one in the Persian Gulf, the other (the one here intended) a rocky island north of the coast of Tripoli, on which a city was built like Tyre. The Phœnician cities of Zidon and Arvad furnished the oarsmen, but Tyre itself the superior captains and pilots.

(9) **The ancients of Gebal.**—"The ancients" is a thoroughly Semitic expression for the prominent men of a city. Gebal, the ancient Byblos, the modern Gébeil, and the Gu-ba-lu of the Assyrian inscriptions, was a famous Phœnician town just north of Beirût. Its site is still rich in ruins. Its people were famous builders, and according to the margin of 1 Kings v. 18 (so also the Septuagint and Vulgate) were employed by Solomon on the work of the Temple. The representation is that the whole widely-dispersed Phœnician race were tributary to the works of Tyre. At this point the figure of the ship gives place for a time to plain language, the better to set forth the military resources and power of this great city.

(10) **Of Persia and of Lud and of Phut.**—Tyre, like most commercial nations, depended chiefly on mercenaries for the rank and file of its army. Persia, more anciently called Elam, was just now rising into prominence. Its soldiers were probably obtained by the Tyrians from their commerce in the Persian Gulf. Lud is not the one mentioned among the children of Shem (Gen. x. 22), but the Ludim (Lydians) of Hamite family, descended from Mizraim (Gen. x. 13). Phut was also an African tribe (Gen. x. 6). Both are repeatedly mentioned on the Egyptian monuments as furnishing mercenaries to the army.

(11) **The Gammadims were in thy towers.**—No people of this name is known, and it is extremely

they have made thy beauty perfect.
(12) Tarshish *was* thy merchant by reason
of the multitude of all *kind of* riches;
with silver, iron, tin, and lead, they
traded in thy fairs. (13) Javan, Tubal,
and Meshech, they *were* thy merchants:
they traded the persons of men and
vessels of brass in thy [1]market. (14) They
of the house of Togarmah traded in thy
fairs with horses and horsemen and
mules. (15) The men of Dedan *were* thy
merchants; many isles *were* the mer-
chandise of thine hand: they brought
thee *for* a present horns of ivory and
ebony. (16) Syria *was* thy merchant by
reason of the multitude of [2]the wares of
thy making: they occupied in thy fairs
with emeralds, purple, and broidered
work, and fine linen, and coral, and
[3]agate. (17) Judah, and the land of
Israel, they *were* thy merchants: they
traded in thy market wheat of Minnith,
and Pannag, and honey, and oil, and
[4]balm. (18) Damascus *was* thy merchant
in the multitude of the wares of thy
making, for the multitude of all riches;
in the wine of Helbon, and white wool.
(19) Dan also and Javan [5]going to and
fro occupied in thy fairs: bright iron,
cassia, and calamus, were in thy market.
(20) Dedan *was* thy merchant in [6]precious
clothes for chariots. (21) Arabia, and all
the princes of Kedar, [7]they occupied
with thee in lambs, and rams, and goats:

1 Or, *merchandise.*

2 Heb., *thy works.*

3 Heb., *chrysoprase.*

4 Or, *rosin.*

5 Or, *Meuzal.*

6 Heb., *clothes of freedom.*

7 Heb., *they were the merchants of thy hand.*

---

unlikely that the responsible posts upon the watch-towers would have been entrusted to foreigners. The word occurs only here, and is probably not a proper name, but should be translated *brave men.*

(12) **Traded in thy fairs.**—Tarshish, Tartessus in Spain, was famous in antiquity for the metals enumerated, especially silver. The word for "fairs" occurs only in this chapter (verses 14, 16, 19, 22, 33). In the last case it is translated *wares*, as it should be throughout. The idea of the word is "something left with another in place of something else given in exchange," in accordance with the habits of ancient commerce, which consisted chiefly in barter. Translate the clause, *exchanged for thy wares.*

Verses 12—23 give a general survey of the nations with whom the Tyrians were connected in commerce, omitting those already mentioned in the previous section. To avoid monotony, the prophet also constantly alternates in the use of synonymous words.

(13) **Javan, Tubal, and Meshech.** — Javan is strictly Ionia, more generally Greece. Tubal and Meshech are the classic *Tibareni* and *Moschi*, between the Black and Caspian Seas. They were famous for dealing in slaves and in brass, or rather copper, of which their mountains still contain abundant supplies.

(14) **Togarmah.**—A name for the Armenians, a race of Japhetic descent (Gen. x. 3). They dealt from most ancient times in horses and asses.

(15) **Dedan.**—This Dedan is a descendant of Ham through Cush (Gen. x. 7). The tribe was located in Arabia, probably upon the shores of the Persian Gulf (Isa. xxi. 13). The Dedan of verse 20, on the other hand, is a Semitic tribe, spoken of also in chap. xxv. 13; Jer. xlix. 8. The "many isles" of this Dedan were the islands in the Persian Gulf, on the Arabian coast, and they were "merchandise" in the sense of supplying material for the commerce of Tyre. "Brought thee for a present" might seem to imply tribute, but the original rather conveys the idea of return payment. "Horns of ivory" is, literally, *horns of teeth;* the name "horn" being simply a commercial term derived from the shape of the elephant's tusk. "Ebony" is a word used only here. It was brought both from India and Ethiopia, the wood from the latter being preferred.

(16) **Emeralds.**—The precious stone intended here, and in Exod. xxviii. 18, is now generally understood to be the carbuncle. The word for "fine linen" is not that of verse 7, but a Phœnician word, occurring only in the books written in the time of the captivity. It is thought to mean *cotton*, for the woven fabrics of which Babylon was famous. Agate (marg., *chrysoprase*) is probably the ruby, or certainly some stone of brilliancy (Isa. liv. 12).

(17) **Minnith, and Pannag.** — Minnith was in Ammon (Judges xi. 33), rich in wheat (2 Chron. xxvii. 5), and the Tyrians obtained its products through the Israelites. Pannag is unknown; it is even uncertain whether it is a proper name at all, or some sweet confection, as grape syrup.

(18) **Wine of Helbon.**—Helbon is identified with a village of the same name, three and a half hours north of Damascus, rich in ruins, and still devoted to the culture of the vine, from which the costliest wine of the country was made. It was probably the same with the wine of Chalybon, so much prized in Persia.

(19) **Dan also and Javan.**—This is the only instance in this enumeration in which the name of a people is introduced with a conjunction. Besides this structural difficulty, there seems no appropriateness in the name Dan, a tribe of Israel long since carried into captivity. The city Dan was of quite too little prominence to be mentioned here. It is probable, therefore, that what our translators have taken for the conjunction is really a part of the name Vedan, a place in Arabia not elsewhere mentioned, but which some suppose to be Aden. Javan does not here stand for Greece, but for an Arabian place or tribe, which there is reason to think is Yemen.

Going to and fro.—The margin is better, *Menzal*, or rather—the first letter being a preposition—*from Uzal*, the ancient Sanaa, afterwards the capital of Yemen. Yemen was famous for its sword-blades, which may be meant by the bright (literally, *wrought*) iron, and also for its spices brought from India.

(20) **Dedan.**—See note on verse 15. "Precious clothes," literally, *clothes of spreading*, by which saddle-cloths are probably meant.

(21) **Arabia . . . Kedar.**—Arabia is never used in the Old Testament for the whole of the country now called by that name, but only for the desert part of it occupied by nomadic tribes. Kedar is the name of a nomadic pastoral race descended from Ishmael (Gen. xxv. 13; comp. Isa. lx. 7).

in these *were they* thy merchants. (22) The
merchants of Sheba and Raamah, they
were thy merchants: they occupied in
thy fairs with chief of all spices, and
with all precious stones, and gold.
(23) Haran, and Canneh, and Eden, the
merchants of Sheba, Asshur, *and* Chil-
mad, *were* thy merchants. (24) These
were thy merchants in [1]all sorts *of*
things, in blue [2]clothes, and broidered
work, and in chests of rich apparel,
bound with cords, and made of cedar,
among thy merchandise. (25) The ships
of Tarshish did sing of thee in thy
market: and thou wast replenished, and
made very glorious in the midst of the
seas.

(26) Thy rowers have brought thee into
great waters: the east wind hath broken
thee in the [3]midst of the seas. (27) Thy
[a]riches, and thy fairs, thy merchandise,
thy mariners, and thy pilots, thy calkers,
and the occupiers of thy merchandise,
and all thy men of war, that *are* in thee,
[4]and in all thy company which *is* in the
midst of thee, shall fall into the [5]midst
of the seas in the day of thy ruin.
(28) The [6]suburbs shall shake at the
sound of the cry of thy pilots. (29) And
all that handle the oar, the mariners,
and all the pilots of the sea, shall come
down from their ships, they shall stand
upon the land; (30) and shall cause their
voice to be heard against thee, and shall
cry bitterly, and shall cast up dust upon
their heads, they shall wallow themselves
in the ashes: (31) and they shall make
themselves utterly bald for thee, and
gird them with sackcloth, and they shall
weep for thee with bitterness of heart
and bitter wailing. (32) And in their
wailing they shall take up a lamentation
for thee, and lament over thee, *saying*,
What *city is* like Tyrus, like the de-

1 Or, *excellent things.*
2 Heb., *foldings.*
3 Heb., *heart.*
a Rev. 18. 9, &c.
4 Or, *even with all.*
5 Heb., *heart.*
6 Or, *waves.*

(22) **Sheba and Raamah** were both Hamites, descended from Cush (Gen. x. 7). They occupied that part of Arabia in the south-east which lies on the Bay of Oman, in the Persian Gulf, and were famous in antiquity for the products mentioned in the text, and which, with the exception of gold, are still found there.

(23) **Haran, and Canneh, and Eden.**—The description now turns from Arabia to the Tyrian trade with Mesopotamia. Haran, important in the story of Abraham (Gen. xi. 31, 32; xii. 4), the Charræ of the Romans, was in north-western Mesopotamia, at the junction of two great caravan routes, the one along the Tigris, the other along the Euphrates. Canneh, a contraction for the Calneh of Gen. x. 10, was the most important commercial city on the former, and was later known as Ctesiphon. Eden was an unknown town on the Euphrates (2 Kings xix. 12; Isa. xxxvii. 12), and is to be distinguished from the Syrian Eden.

Sheba, Asshur, and Chilmad.—Sheba is still the same Sheba before mentioned; for Pliny (*Hist. Nat.*, xii. 40) says that the Sabœans brought their goods from the spice country to Carrhæ, where they held markets, and went thence to Syria and Phœnicia. They were, therefore, traders between Mesopotamia and Phœnicia. Asshur is here not the country of Assyria, but the commercial city Sura (modern Essurieh), on the banks of the Euphrates, above Thapsacus. Chilmad is supposed to be the Charmande of Xenophon (*Anab.*, i. 5, 10), "a great city beyond the Euphrates, in the neighbourhood of the desert." Others identify it with Kalwada, near Bagdad. It is mentioned only here.

(24) **All sorts of things.**—The margin, *excellent things*, is better. The word means "that which is perfect." In chap. xxiii. 12 it is "most gorgeously," and in chap. xxxviii. 4, as here, "all sorts." In all "excellent" or "excellently" is the true sense. "Clothes"—literally, *foldings*—refers to the purple embroidered cloaks for which Babylonia was famous.

Chests of rich apparel.—Rather, *treasures of twisted yarn*; and for "made of cedar" read *strong.* An extensive trade in yarns was kept up from Babylonia to Tyre, where they were dyed and woven, or sold for weaving.

(25) **Ships of Tarshish** means simply, *ships of the largest size*, such as were fitted for the voyage to Tarshish: as we now say, "East Indiaman." (Comp. 1 Kings xxii. 48; Ps. xlviii. 7.) "Did sing of thee in thy market" is, literally, *thy* ——, *thy trade*, the blank being an uncertain word, supposed by our translators to mean *singers*. Opinion is now divided as to whether the meaning is *bulwarks* or *caravans*; either gives a good sense. "Thy great ships were at once thy defence and the means of thy commerce," or "were thy caravans of the sea, &c." The former is preferable.

(26) **Thy rowers.**—As the chief means of propelling vessels when the art of sailing was imperfectly understood. The figure of the ship is here resumed. "The east wind" is powerful, gusty, and dangerous in the Levant. (Comp. Ps. xlviii. 7: "Thou breakest the ships of Tarshish with an east wind.")

(27) **And in all.**—Better, as in the margin, *with all.* The thought is that all that went to make up the strength and the glory of Tyre perished in one great catastrophe. Many classes are enumerated, and the statement is made general by adding "with all thy company." All are represented as going down together with the ship. (Comp. verse 34.)

(28) **Suburbs.**—This word means *an open place* around a building or city. There was no land around Tyre, and it is here used, therefore, in a general sense—all thy surroundings.

(29) **Shall come down from their ships.**—The colonies and dependencies of Tyre are, in keeping with the figure, the smaller craft which escape to the shore, and there lament the fall of their mistress.

(30) **Against thee.**—Rather, *over thee.* The commercial nations were not inimical to Tyre, but rather caused their wail for her to be heard over the seas where she had been engulphed. The usual signs of mourning are poetically attributed to them (verses 30, 31), and then a dirge is put in their mouths (verses 32—34).

stroyed in the midst of the sea? (33) When
thy wares went forth out of the seas,
thou filledst many people; thou didst
enrich the kings of the earth with the
multitude of thy riches and of thy mer-
chandise. (34) In the time *when* thou
shalt be broken by the seas in the
depths of the waters thy merchandise
and all thy company in the midst of
thee shall fall. (35) All the inhabitants
of the isles shall be astonished at thee,
and their kings shall be sore afraid, they
shall be troubled in *their* countenance.
(36) The merchants among the people
shall hiss at thee; thou shalt be [1]a
terror, and [2]never *shalt be* any more.

CHAPTER XXVIII.—(1) The word of
the LORD came again unto me, saying,
(2) Son of man, say unto the prince of
Tyrus, Thus saith the Lord GOD; Be-
cause thine heart *is* lifted up, and thou
hast said, I *am* a God, I sit *in* the seat
of God, in the [3]midst of the seas; [a]yet
thou *art* a man, and not God, though
thou set thine heart as the heart of
God: (3) behold, thou *art* wiser than
Daniel; there is no secret that they can
hide from thee: (4) with thy wisdom and
with thine understanding thou hast
gotten thee riches, and hast gotten gold
and silver into thy treasures: (5) [4]by thy
great wisdom *and* by thy traffick hast
thou increased thy riches, and thine
heart is lifted up because of thy riches:
(6) therefore thus saith the Lord GOD;
Because thou hast set thine heart as the
heart of God; (7) behold, therefore I will
bring strangers upon thee, the terrible
of the nations: and they shall draw
their swords against the beauty of thy
wisdom, and they shall defile thy bright-

1 Heb., *terrors.*

2 Heb., shalt *not* be *for ever.*

3 Heb., *heart.*

a Isa. 31. 3.

4 Heb., *By the greatness of thy wisdom.*

(36) **Shall hiss at thee.**—In verse 35 the prophet again drops the figure of the ship, and looking forward (as in chap. xxvi. 4—6, 12—14) to the end, speaks of the final and utter overthrow which shall come upon Tyre. The word *hiss* is used, as in Isa. v. 26, vii. 18; Zech. x. 8, &c., in the sense of *calling for.* The prophet tells us that the people who have had commercial connection with Tyre shall call for her in vain; she shall be (not *a terror*, but, as in chap. xxvi. 21) a sudden destruction, and shall not be for ever.

XXVIII.

This chapter consists of two prophecies: the first and larger one against the prince of Tyre (verses 1—19); the second, a very brief one, against Zidon (verses 20—26). The first prophecy consists of two parts, corresponding to chaps. xxvi., xxvii.; in the former of these the pride of the prince is described, and he is warned of his approaching death (verses 1—10), and then follows a lamentation (verses 11—19). It has been thought surprising that so commercial a nation should have been governed by a monarch; but not only is this a fact of Phœnician history, but the name of the prince who sat on the throne at this time, Ithobal II., has been preserved.

The whole prophecy is full of most varied and striking imagery, and there is no other passage in Scripture where there is such detailed and peculiar irony. It brings out most powerfully "the impiety of all ambition, and the vanity of all greatness, which seeks its foundation and support elsewhere than in the power and goodness of the Eternal."

(2) **I am a God.**—The arraignment of the prince occupies verses 2—5, his consequent doom verses 6—10. The point of the charge is inordinate pride, begotten of great prosperity; this prosperity, being attributed to his own powers instead of to its true source, led him to imagine himself almost more than mortal. Similar instances of what may be called "the insanity of prosperity" may be seen in the case of Sennacherib (2 Kings xviii. 33—35); of the then living monarch of Babylon, Nebuchadnezzar, to whom this prophecy might well serve as a warning (Dan. iii. 15, iv. 30; comp. also chaps. vii. 25, xi. 36, 37); of Pharaoh (chap. xxix. 3); of Herod (Acts xii. 21—23); of the one foretold in 2 Thess. ii. 4; to which list might be added the names of some more modern conquerors, and, in their degree, of many who have been eminently successful in other walks of life, and have consequently sacrificed to their own net (Hab. i. 16). It is not to be supposed that the king of Tyre, like some Oriental monarchs and later Roman emperors, actually claimed for himself religious homage; but he had that proud sense of elevation and self-sufficiency which is only translated into words in the expressions of the text.

The seat of God.—This expression is chosen not merely with reference to the great natural beauty and apparently impregnable position of Tyre, but also to the fact that it was called "the holy island," and looked up to by all its colonies as the central sanctuary of their worship. The Temple of Melkarth was said by the priests to have been founded as far back as 2750 B.C., and Arrian speaks of it as the oldest sanctuary in the annals of mankind. (See also Note on verse 6.)

(3) **Wiser than Daniel.**—This is ironically spoken. Daniel was so famed for his wisdom in the great Chaldæan Empire (Dan. i. 20, ii. 48, iv. 18, v. 11, 12, vi. 3, &c.) that the report must have already reached Tyre. He had been twenty years in Nebuchadnezzar's court when Jerusalem fell, and the siege of Tyre was five years later.

(6) **Set thine heart as the heart of God.**—The same expression as in verse 2. (Comp. Obad. 3, "The pride of thine heart hath deceived thee.") The meaning is plain: thou hast entertained thoughts and purposes fitting only to the Supreme.

(7) **Against the beauty of thy wisdom.**—The figure seems incongruous, but it is to be remembered that the expression is only a form of designating Tyre itself. The description of the Chaldæans as "the terrible of the nations" is repeated in chaps. xxx. 11, xxxi. 12 (comp. also chap. xxvi. 7 and Isa. xlvii. 6; Hab. i. 6). The term, however, is by no means necessarily confined to them.

ness. (8) They shall bring thee down to the pit, and thou shalt die the deaths of *them that are* slain in the midst of the seas. (9) Wilt thou yet say before him that slayeth thee, I *am* God? but thou *shalt be* a man, and no God, in the hand of him that [1]slayeth thee. (10) Thou shalt die the deaths of the uncircumcised by the hand of strangers: for I have spoken *it*, saith the Lord God.

(11) Moreover the word of the Lord came unto me, saying, (12) Son of man, take up a lamentation upon the king of Tyrus, and say unto him, Thus saith the Lord God; Thou sealest up the sum, full of wisdom, and perfect in beauty. (13) Thou hast been in Eden the garden of God; every precious stone *was* thy covering, the [2]sardius, topaz, and the diamond, the [3]beryl, the onyx, and the jasper, the sapphire, the [4]emerald, and the carbuncle, and gold: the workmanship of thy tabrets and of thy pipes was prepared in thee in the day that thou wast created. (14) Thou *art* the anointed cherub that covereth; and I have set thee *so*: thou wast upon the holy mountain of God; thou hast walked up and down in the midst of the stones of fire. (15) Thou *wast* perfect in thy ways from the day that thou wast created, till iniquity was found in thee. (16) By the multitude of thy merchandise they have filled the midst of thee with violence, and thou hast sinned: therefore I will cast thee as profane out of the mountain of God: and I will destroy thee, O covering cherub, from the midst of the stones of fire. (17) Thine heart was lifted up because of thy beauty, thou hast corrupted thy wisdom by reason of thy brightness: I will cast thee to the

1 Or, *woundeth.*
2 Or, *ruby.*
3 Or, *chrysolite.*
4 Or, *chrysoprase.*

---

(8) **Deaths.**—The plural accurately represents the rare form of the original, and indicates emphatically a violent death.

(9) **Thou shalt be a man.**—The future, added to the text by the words in italics, should be omitted. The original form is exactly the same as in verse 2, and should be so translated. In both cases the article is better omitted. The contrast between the weakness of man and the power of God is strongly brought out: "yet thou art man, in the hand of him that slayeth thee."

(10) **The uncircumcised.**—To the Jew this term conveyed all, and more than all, the opprobrium which the Greeks and Romans attached to *barbarians.* (Comp. chaps. xxxi. 18; xxxii. 19. 21, 24—28, &c.) It is equivalent to saying "the profane and impious."

Verses 11—19 contain the doom upon the prince of Tyre. He is represented as like the first man, perfect, and placed in Eden, until, upon his fall (verses 15, 16), he is ignominiously driven forth. The passage is strongly ironical.

(12) **Thou sealest up the sum.**—Thou markest it as complete or perfect. (Comp. Dan. ix. 24; Job. ix. 7.) The word for *sum* occurs only here and in chap. xliii. 10, where it refers to the well measured and arranged building of the Temple.

(13) **Every precious stone.**—There is some uncertainty in regard to the names of some of these stones (as sardius may be *carnelian*, and beryl *chrysolite*), but the general fact is an allusion to the profuse use of precious stones as ornaments of their royal apparel by Oriental monarchs. The stones mentioned are the same with those in the breastplate of the high priest (Exod. xxxix. 10), the third row being omitted; this is supplied in the Greek.

Thy pipes.—The word occurs only here, and its most probable sense is *females*, those who played upon the tambourines. All these things did not need to be collected by the king of Tyre, but were ready prepared to his hand at the moment of his accession to the throne, just as everything was made ready for Adam in Eden.

(14) **Thou art the anointed cherub.**—The tense is not expressed in the Hebrew, and it is better to supply the same simple past as is used throughout the passage: *thou wert.* The imagery is taken from the Temple upon Mount Zion: not that the king of Tyre had at this time any special connection with this, but that these terms were natural to the prophet in this ironical description of him. "The cherub that covereth" the mercy-seat is spoken of as anointed, with reference to Exod. xxx. 26, xl. 9.

Upon the holy mountain of God.—The prophet still has his mind upon Mount Zion (comp. Isa. xi. 9, lvi. 7), but yet the words are ironically spoken of Tyre as a venerated sanctuary, rising up from the sea.

Stones of fire.—An obvious explanation of this expression, given by many writers, is that it refers to the brilliant sparkling jewels on the robes in which the king walked. But if this were the case, the expression would be a strange one, and the connection implies a deeper and a religious meaning. It is better, therefore, to understand the imagery as similar to that in Rev. ii. 1, and to suppose the prophet to have had in mind such a passage as Exod. xxiv. 10, where a paved work of sapphire stone appears as beneath the feet of God, while His glory is "like a devouring fire." This would then be one of the ways in which the king of Tyre is ironically represented as assuming to himself God-like attributes.

(15) **Till iniquity was found in thee.**—This and the following verse renew still more clearly the comparison with Adam. The king was altogether prosperous until his sin became manifest; then, when his heart was corrupted by his prosperity (verse 16), he was cast out for ever, like Adam from his paradise.

(16) **Filled the midst of thee.**—The language passes very naturally here from the king himself to the state over which he presided, and with which he was identified, immediately recurring, however, to the king personally. He, as polluted, should be cast out of his imagined mountain of God: he, the cherub covering the mercy-seat, forsooth, shall be destroyed: his fancied

ground, I will lay thee before kings,
that they may behold thee. (18) Thou
hast defiled thy sanctuaries by the
multitude of thine iniquities, by the
iniquity of thy traffick; therefore will I
bring forth a fire from the midst of
thee, it shall devour thee, and I will
bring thee to ashes upon the earth in
the sight of all them that behold thee.
(19) All they that know thee among the
people shall be astonished at thee: thou
shalt be [1]a terror, and never *shalt* thou
be any more.

(20) Again the word of the LORD came
unto me, saying, (21) Son of man, set thy
face against Zidon, and prophesy against
it, (22) and say, Thus saith the Lord
GOD; Behold, I *am* against thee, O
Zidon; and I will be glorified in the
midst of thee: and they shall know that
I *am* the LORD, when I shall have executed
judgments in her, and shall be
sanctified in her. (23) For I will send
into her pestilence, and blood into her
streets; and the wounded shall be
judged in the midst of her by the sword
upon her on every side; and they shall
know that I *am* the LORD. (24) And there
shall be no more a pricking brier unto
the house of Israel, nor *any* grieving
thorn of all *that are* round about them,
that despised them; and they shall know
that I *am* the Lord GOD.

(25) Thus saith the Lord GOD; When
I shall have gathered the house of Israel
from the people among whom they are

[1] Heb., *terrors.*

God-like walking amid the stones of fire shall for ever cease.

(18) **Defiled thy sanctuaries.**—These are not to be understood so much of the actual temples of Tyre as of the ideal "holy mountain of God," in which the prophet has represented the prince of Tyre as "a covering cherub." Yet still, doubtless, even in the former sense, it was true that the Tyrians, like the Gentiles of whom St. Paul speaks in Rom. i. 21, did not act up to the religious light they had, and violating their own consciences and sense of right, defiled even such representation of the true religion as still remained in their idolatrous worship. The main thought, however, is the former one, and it is in accordance with this that the fire is represented as going forth to consume the king. Many of the Hebrew manuscripts have *sanctuary* in the singular.

By the iniquity of thy traffick.—Here, as so often in other cases, the sin is represented as consisting in the abuse of the very blessings which God had given, and this sin as leading directly to its own punishment. No fact is more striking in history, whether of Israel or of the heathen, than that the gifts of God, which should have been to their blessing and His glory, are perverted by the sinfulness of man: first to their own guilt, and then, in consequence, to their ruin.

Verses 20—26 constitute another distinct prophecy, of which verses 20—24 are occupied with the denunciation of judgment upon Zidon, and verses 25, 26 with promises to Israel. There are several obvious reasons, besides that of making up the number of the nations to seven, why at least a word of prophecy should have been directed especially against Zidon, notwithstanding her forming a part of Phœnicia and contributing to the mariners of Tyre (chap. xxvii. 8). In the first place, Zidon (situated about twenty-five miles north of Tyre) was the more ancient city from which Tyre had sprung, and always maintained her independence. Hence she might seem not to be exposed to the judgment of God upon Tyre, unless especially mentioned. Then also Zidon (rather than Tyre) had been peculiarly the source of corrupting idolatrous influences upon Israel. This had begun as early as the times of the Judges (Judges x. 6); it had been continued and increased in the days of Solomon (1 Kings xi. 33); it reached its consummation under the reign of Ahab, who married Jezebel, the daughter of the king of Zidon and high priest of Baal (1 Kings xvi. 31), and who set up the worship of Baal as the state religion of Israel. That this influence was still powerful in Judah also in the days of Ezekiel is plain from the reference to the Thammuz worship in chap. viii. 14.

There is only one mention (Judges x. 12) of the Zidonians as coming into armed conflict with Israel; but they had rejoiced in her fall. As this prophecy closes the circle of the nations who had thus exulted in the destruction of Jerusalem, there is appropriately placed at the end a promise of restoration to Israel when all these judgments upon her enemies shall have been accomplished.

(24) **A pricking brier.**—The language refers back to the threat of Num. xxxiii. 55, of the reality of which Israel had long had such bitter experience. Nothing is said of the special sins of Zidon, and very little of the detail of her overthrow; these were already sufficiently known, or else included in what has been said of Tyre. It is noticeable that no such utter desolation is foretold as in the former case.

(25) **Sanctified in them in the sight of the heathen.**—The course of God's providence is very distinctly marked out in these verses of promise. The judgment upon Judah had already come, in the fall of their holy city and the captivity of the people. This leads them to repentance, and thus God is "sanctified in the sight of the heathen;" His holiness and justice are exhibited to the world. Then comes the promise of the return, and the judgment of the ungodly enemies who have despised Judah (verse 26). This, too, shall be accomplished in its time, and then peace and prosperity shall return to Israel.

The immediate point of this prophecy is the return of the Jews to their own land; yet, as the struggle between them and their enemies has been a struggle between the Church of God and the powers of the world, and as this particular struggle thus in some sort symbolises the greater contest between religion and the world in all ages, so this promise of rest looks forward in some sense to the final victory over all evil.

scattered, and shall be sanctified in them
in the sight of the heathen, then shall
they dwell in their land that I have
given to my servant Jacob. (26) And
they shall dwell [1]safely therein, and
shall build houses, and plant vineyards;
yea, they shall dwell with confidence,
when I have executed judgments upon
all those that [2]despise them round about
them; and they shall know that I *am*
the LORD their God.

CHAPTER XXIX.—(1) In the tenth
year, in the tenth *month*, in the twelfth
day of the month, the word of the LORD
came unto me, saying, (2) Son of man,
set thy face against Pharaoh king of
Egypt, and prophesy against him, and
against all Egypt: (3) speak, and say,
Thus saith the Lord GOD;
Behold, I *am* against thee, Pharaoh
king of Egypt, the great [a]dragon that
lieth in the midst of his rivers, which
hath said, My river *is* mine own, and I
hath made *it* for myself. (4) But I will
put hooks in thy jaws, and I will cause
the fish of thy rivers to stick unto thy
scales, and I will bring thee up out of
the midst of thy rivers, and all the fish
of thy rivers shall stick unto thy scales.
(5) And I will leave thee *thrown* into the
wilderness, thee and all the fish of thy

1 Or, *with confidence.*

2 Or, *spoil.*

B. C. 589.

a Ps. 74. 13, 14; Isa. 27. 1, & 51. 9.

XXIX.

The series of prophecies against Egypt, occupying the four following chapters, and containing seven separate prophecies, were all delivered in regular order, except the short one at the close of this chapter (verses 17—21), which was much later. The prophecy of chap. xxx. 1—19 is indeed undated, but there is no reason to suppose it is out of its chronological place. Chaps. xxix.—xxxi., with the exception just mentioned, were uttered before the fall of Jerusalem, and consequently before the series of prophecies against other foreign nations just considered, the principle of arrangement here being geographical rather than chronological, and the immediate neighbours of Israel being taken up before the more distant Egypt. In the detail this series is arranged substantially on the same plan as that against Tyre: first, a prophecy against Egypt (chaps. xxix., xxx.); then a picture of her greatness and fall (chap. xxxi.); and finally a dirge over her (chap. xxxii.).

At the time when the first of these prophecies was uttered the Jews still looked upon Egypt as the great power opposed to the Chaldæans, and still hoped for aid from this source. Hence the teaching of this prophecy was very necessary for them. And even afterwards it was important for them to understand that they were not to rely on any earthly aid, and especially that Egypt, to which they had been disposed to look during so many generations, could never help them.

The monarch now upon the throne of Egypt was Pharaoh-Hophra, the Apries of the Greeks. On the question of his death and the conquest of Egypt by Nebuchadnezzar, see Excursus at the end of this book. It is certain that the period was one of a temporary revival of Egyptian power amid its general course of decadence. Egypt had been conquered by Assyria, and again and again subdued after its revolts. On the fall of Assyria it had thrown off all foreign yoke, and Hophra himself had made a successful attack upon the Phœnicians, and had attempted to raise the siege of Jerusalem, in which he momentarily succeeded, but was driven off by Nebuchadnezzar. Not many years afterwards Egypt was finally subdued by the Medo-Persian power, which succeeded the Chaldæan at Babylon, and never regained its independence for any length of time. It continued a Persian satrapy until it fell successively under the Greek, the Roman, and the Mameluke sway.

(1) **In the tenth year, in the tenth month.**—This was exactly a year and two days after the investment of Jerusalem by Nebuchadnezzar (chap. xxiv. 1, 2; 2 Kings xxv. 1), and about six months before its fall, or seven before its destruction (2 Kings xxv. 3—8). It must have been, therefore, after the time when the siege was temporarily raised by the approach of the Egyptians under Pharaoh-Hophra (Jer. xxxvii. 5, 11), and when Jeremiah prophesied the failure of that attempt (*ib.* 6—10); and probably was just when the news of that relief reached Chaldæa, and gave fresh hope to the exiles of the deliverance of Jerusalem.

(3) **The great dragon.**—This word is usually translated *dragon* in the English version, but sometimes *whale* (chap. xxxii. 2), and (in a slightly modified form) *serpent* (Exod. vii. 9, 10, 12). It unquestionably means *crocodile*, the characteristic animal of Egypt, in some parts hated and destroyed, in some worshipped as a deity, but in all alike feared, and regarded as the most powerful and destructive creature of their country.

Lieth in the midst of his rivers.—Egypt, a creation of the Nile, and dependent entirely upon it for its productiveness, is personified by the crocodile, its characteristic animal, basking upon the sand-banks of its waters. The expression "his rivers," used of the branches of the Nile near its mouth, is peculiarly appropriate to the Twenty-sixth Dynasty, to which Pharaoh-Hophra belonged, whose capital was Sais, in the midst of the Delta.

My river is mine own.—This is characteristic of the pride of Hophra, who, according to Herodotus, was accustomed to say that "not even a god could dispossess him of power." The whole dynasty to which he belonged, beginning with Psammeticus, improved the river and encouraged commerce with foreign nations, thereby acquiring great wealth.

(4) **Hooks in thy jaws.**—An allusion to the ancient way of taking and destroying the crocodile, otherwise invulnerable to their arms.

Fish of thy rivers shall stick unto thy scales.—As the crocodile, the lord of the Nile, represents the royal power of Egypt, so the fish represent the people dependent upon him. Pharaoh is not to fall alone, but shall drag his people with him into a common ruin.

(5) **Open fields** is synonymous with "wilderness" in the previous clause. The crocodile and the fish together, drawn from the river, are to be thrown upon

rivers: thou shalt fall upon the [1]open
fields; thou shalt not be brought together,
nor gathered: I have given thee
for meat to the beasts of the field and to
the fowls of the heaven. (6) And all the
inhabitants of Egypt shall know that I
am the LORD, because they have been a
[a]staff of reed to the house of Israel.
(7) When they took hold of thee by thy
hand, thou didst break, and rend all
their shoulder: and when they leaned
upon thee, thou brakest, and madest all
their loins to be at a stand. (8) Therefore
thus saith the Lord GOD; Behold,
I will bring a sword upon thee, and cut
off man and beast out of thee. (9) And
the land of Egypt shall be desolate and
waste; and they shall know that I *am*
the LORD: because he hath said, The
river *is* mine, and I have made *it*.
(10) Behold, therefore I *am* against thee,
and against thy rivers, and I will make
the land of Egypt [2]utterly waste *and*
desolate, from the tower of [3]Syene even
unto the border of Ethiopia. (11) No
foot of man shall pass through it, nor
foot of beast shall pass through it,
neither shall it be inhabited forty
years. (12) And I will make the land
of Egypt desolate in the midst of the
countries *that are* desolate, and her
cities among the cities *that are* laid
waste shall be desolate forty years:
and I will scatter the Egyptians among
the nations, and will disperse them
through the countries.
(13) Yet thus saith the Lord GOD; At
the [b]end of forty years will I gather the
Egyptians from the people whither they
were scattered: (14) and I will bring
again the captivity of Egypt, and will
cause them to return *into* the land of
Pathros, into the land of their [4]habitation;
and they shall be there a [5]base

1 Heb., *face of the field.*

a 2 Kin. 18. 21; Isa. 36. 6.

2 Heb., *wastes of waste.*

3 Heb., *Seveneh.*

b Isa. 19. 23; Jer. 46. 26.

4 Or, *birth.*

5 Heb., *low.*

---

the sands of the neighbouring desert, to be devoured by the birds and beasts of prey: thus representing that Pharaoh and his people, uprooted from their power, are to be given over for a spoil to various nations.

(6) **A staff of reed.**—In Isa. xxxvi. 6 the dependence of Judah upon Egypt is described as trust "in the staff of this broken reed;" but notwithstanding all warnings, they still trusted, especially at the time of this prophecy, and proved in their experience the truth of the Divine word. The figure is taken from the reeds, which grew abundantly on the banks of the Nile, and the statement is historically amplified in the following verse, where the reference is to be understood not of any single fact so much as of a continual, often repeated result. There should be a period in the middle of verse 6, the first half forming the conclusion of the previous denunciation, and the second half being closely connected with verses 7—9. Verse 7 is parenthetical.

(7) **All their loins to be at a stand.**—The expression is a difficult one, but the more probable sense is, *all their loins to shake.* The reed breaks under the weight of the man who leans upon it, and pierces his shoulder as he falls, while in his consternation his loins tremble.

(9) **Because he hath said.**—Again, as in verse 6, the division of the verses is very unfortunate. The expression "shall know that I am the Lord," so common in Ezekiel, always closes a train of thought. The new sentence begins with the reason for the judgment upon Egypt—because of its pride.

(10) **From the tower of Syene.**—The word here translated "tower" is a proper name, Migdol, a town, mentioned in Exod. xiv. 2, near Suez. Syene has in the original the affix denoting *towards*, and the translation should therefore be, *from Migdol to Syene, even unto the border of Ethiopia;* in other words, "the whole length of the land." Syene was a town on the extreme southern border of Egypt, represented by the modern Assouan, which is situated near its ruins. There is a like error of translation in chap. xxx. 6.

(11) **Neither shall it be inhabited forty years.**—In verses 9—12 a state of desolation is predicted for Egypt, which, if understood in the literal sense of the words, has certainly never been fulfilled. In verse 9 it is said that it "shall be desolate and waste," and this is repeated with emphasis in verse 10; while in verse 11 it is declared that neither foot of man nor foot of beast shall pass through it. There is also a difficulty in regard to the time of "forty years," mentioned in verses 11, 12, and 13. No such definite period can be made out from history. The two difficulties go together, and the former is explained by the latter. It has already been seen in chap. iv. 6 that the prophet represents the calamity of Judah in the historic terms of their former suffering in the wilderness, without thereby intending either any specific time or any precise repetition of the same troubles they had then experienced. He does the same thing here in regard to Egypt. The people are to pass into a condition like that of the Israelites in the wilderness, in which they were to endure the judgment of God upon their sins. This is expressed, after the manner of Ezekiel, in strong concrete terms, the literal fulfilment of which was neither intended nor expected.

(12) **Scatter the Egyptians among the nations.**—Megasthenes and Berosus state that Nebuchadnezzar, on his conquest of Egypt, sent great numbers of the people captive to Babylon; others doubtless, as in similar cases, took refuge in Ethiopia, Libya, and other neighbouring lands. The kind of desolation foretold for Egypt is the same as that for "desolate" cities and countries that fell under the power of the conqueror: they were to be plundered and reduced to subjection.

(13) **At the end of forty years.**—See Note on verse 11.

(14) **The land of Pathros.**—Comp. Isa. xi. 11. Pathros is Upper Egypt, the Thebaid. In the following clause this is described as "the land of their birth" (*Marg.*). According to ancient testimony and the opinion of many moderns, this was the original seat of Egyptian power. It may, however, be put only as the part for the whole—Pathros for Egypt.

kingdom. (15) It shall be the basest of
the kingdoms; neither shall it exalt
itself any more above the nations: for
I will diminish them, that they shall no
more rule over the nations. (16) And it
shall be no more the confidence of the
house of Israel, which bringeth *their*
iniquity to remembrance, when they
shall look after them: but they shall
know that I *am* the Lord God.

(17) And it came to pass in the seven
and twentieth year, in the first *month*,
in the first *day* of the month, the word
of the LORD came unto me, saying,
(18) Son of man, Nebuchadrezzar king of
Babylon caused his army to serve a
great service against Tyrus: every head
was made bald, and every shoulder *was*
peeled: yet had he no wages, nor his
army, for Tyrus, for the service that he
had served against it: (19) therefore
thus saith the Lord God; Behold, I
will give the land of Egypt unto
Nebuchadrezzar king of Babylon; and
he shall take her multitude, and [1]take
her spoil, and take her prey; and it
shall be the wages for his army. (20) I
have given him the land of Egypt [2]*for*
his labour wherewith he served against
it, because they wrought for me, saith
the Lord God. (21) In that day will I
cause the horn of the house of Israel to

1 Heb., *spoil her spoil, and prey her prey.*

B.C. 572.

2 Or, *for his hire.*

Shall be there a base kingdom.—Egypt should be restored, but not to its former power. Historically this has been eminently true. For a little while Egypt struggled against its oppressors, but its power was already broken, and from the time of its conquest by Cambyses it has never been for any length of time independent. There are few stronger contrasts in any inhabited country than between the ancient glory, dignity, power, and wealth of Egypt, and its later insignificance.

(16) **The confidence of the house of Israel.**—Here the result of this judgment in God's providence concerning His people is brought out: they had hitherto continually transgressed by looking to Egypt for aid; now this temptation should be entirely removed. This trust of Israel in Egypt had continually brought "their iniquity to remembrance when they looked" to them for help, both by its being against the express command of God, and also by its involving treachery and rebellion against Chaldæa.

(17) **In the seven and twentieth year.**—This is the latest date among all Ezekiel's prophecies, and is more than sixteen years after the prophecy of the former part of the chapter. This date corresponds with the thirty-fifth year of Nebuchadnezzar's reign (see 2 Kings xxv. 2, 8), and, from verse 18, was evidently uttered after the close of the siege of Tyre. As that siege lasted thirteen years, it must have been begun at least as early as Nebuchadnezzar's twenty-second year, or within three years after the destruction of Jerusalem. Josephus, however, states (*Antt.* x. 9, § 7) that in the twenty-third year of his reign Nebuchadnezzar made a successful expedition against Cœlosyria, after which he brought the Ammonites and Moabites into subjection, and then conquered Egypt. The two former campaigns are consistent enough with the still progressing siege of Tyre; but hardly the latter. We must, therefore, suppose a considerable interval between these conquests, of which Josephus takes no notice.

The present utterance may have been either simultaneous with or only just before the conquest of Egypt. Its most probable time is during the early part of the campaign against Egypt.

This passage is placed with the other prophecies against Egypt in order to bring them all together, and is assigned to this particular place, after the analogy of chap. xxvi. 7, in order to bring the mention of the agent by whom the conquest is to be effected immediately after the general prophecy of judgment.

(18) **Yet had he no wages.**—The siege of Tyre is here represented as a service to God, for which Nebuchadnezzar had not yet received his reward. This is quite in accordance with the whole Scriptural representation of that monarch, as a man raised up to execute God's judgments. He was himself unconscious of this, and yet did that which had been foretold—a striking instance that "there is a God in history." It has been argued from this verse, and from the fact that there is no especial mention in history of the result of the siege of Tyre, that Nebuchadnezzar failed in its capture; but all that is meant is that he failed to obtain any considerable booty thereby, the Tyrians having abundant warning and opportunity to convey away their valuables by sea. This St. Jerome expressly asserts to have been done by them, and he further describes the method of the capture of the city by the same means afterwards used by Alexander, that of building a mole from the mainland to the island; thus explaining how in the besieging army "every head was made bald, and every shoulder was peeled" by the bearing of burdens for the structure. Berosus expressly testifies that Nebuchadnezzar "conquered all Syria and Phœnicia" (Jos. *c. Ap.*, i. 21); and Josephus also cites Philostratus, Megasthenes, and Diocles as mentioning Nebuchadnezzar's exploits and the siege of Tyre in a way which, while they do not directly mention, yet certainly imply the capture of the city (*ibid.*, and *Antt.* x. 11, § 1). Besides, it is inconceivable that Ezekiel, who long survived that siege, should have left that prophecy on record if the event was otherwise than as he predicted.

(19) **I will give.**—In the original this is in the form of a participle; literally, *I am giving.* This form is often used of the future, but with especial appropriateness of the immediate future. The other tenses, according to the Hebrew usage, take the temporal meaning of the principal verb. This seems probably to have been spoken at the very time of Nebuchadnezzar's campaign and conquest. On the evidence that he did actually conquer Egypt, see *Excursus* at the end of the book. He must have there found abundant booty, as the kings of the Twenty-sixth Dynasty were commercial, and greatly given to the accumulation of wealth.

(21) **In that day.**—The tenses here change to the future, indicating that if the conquest of Egypt had already taken place, its consequences to Israel were to be only gradually developed. These consequences were primarily the conviction of the futility of trust in any

bud forth, and I will give thee the
opening of the mouth in the midst of
them; and they shall know that I *am*
the Lord.

CHAPTER XXX.—(1) The word of
the Lord came again unto me, saying,
(2) Son of man, prophesy and say, Thus
saith the Lord God; Howl ye, Woe
worth the day! (3) For the day *is* near,
even the day of the Lord *is* near, a
cloudy day; it shall be the time of the
heathen. (4) And the sword shall come
upon Egypt, and great [1] pain shall be in
Ethiopia, when the slain shall fall in
Egypt, and they shall take away her
multitude, and her foundations shall be
broken down. (5) Ethiopia, and [2] Libya,
and Lydia, and all the mingled people,
and Chub, and the [3] men of the land
that is in league, shall fall with them
by the sword.
(6) Thus saith the Lord; They also
that uphold Egypt shall fall; and the
pride of her power shall come down:
from the tower of Syene shall they fall
in it by the sword, saith the Lord God.
(7) And they shall be desolate in the
midst of the countries *that are* desolate,
and her cities shall be in the midst of
the cities *that are* wasted. (8) And they
shall know that I *am* the Lord, when I
have set a fire in Egypt, and *when* all
her helpers shall be [4] destroyed. (9) In
that day shall messengers go forth
from me in ships to make the careless

1 Or, *fear*.
2 Heb., *Phut*.
3 Heb., *children*.
4 Heb., *broken*.

earthly aid, and hence a turning to their neglected God, and, as a result of this, the giving up of their long cherished idolatries. The prophet speaks of this as only in germ, but looking on to its further development, under the figure of making a horn to bud forth, that is, to *sprout* or *grow*. (Comp. Ps. cxxxii. 17.) Israel's reviving prosperity should date from the destruction of its trust in earthly aid.

The opening of the mouth.—This is elsewhere (chap. xxiv. 27) promised to the prophet as a consequence of the fall of Jerusalem, of which he had heard (chap. xxxiii. 21, 22) more than fourteen years before. There is no recorded prophecy of Ezekiel's of later date; the expression must therefore be understood of those encouraging and helpful instructions of the prophet, as the people improved under the discipline of the captivity, which it was not seen fitting to put on permanent record.

XXX.

This chapter is made up of two distinct prophecies: verses 1—19, and verses 20—26. The latter is distinctly dated, and comes in regular chronological order between chaps. xxix. 1—16 and xxxi.; but whether the former belongs to this series, or is connected with chap. xxix. 17—21, has been questioned. There are no sufficient data for a positive determination of the point; but the general presumption is that an undated prophecy belongs in the interval between the dates which precede and which follow. With this presumption the mention of the nearness of the event (verse 3) and of the name of Nebuchadnezzar (verse 10) agree, though not in themselves determinative.

This prophecy is divided into four parts, not strongly distinguished, but each marked by the formula, "Thus saith the Lord" (verses 2, 6, 10, 13).

(3) **The time of the heathen.**—The judgment upon Egypt is but an individual instance, and is symbolic of general judgment upon all merely worldly power. Her fall is one step in the general overthrow of whatever exalts and opposes itself to God. Very similar to verses 2, 3 are the prophecies in Isa. xiii. 6, 9; Joel i. 13, 15, ii. 2; Obad. 15; Zeph. i. 7, 14.

(5) **Ethiopia, and Libya, and Lydia.**—Ethiopia and Egypt were closely connected, and during much of their history were often under one government. Ethiopian soldiers served in great numbers in the Egyptian armies. Libya and Lydia are an unfortunate substitution for the original terms, Phut and Lud, which are preserved in chap. xxvii. 10, where see Note. They are there mentioned as furnishing mercenaries to the Tyrian army; and it is known historically that they supplied them to a still greater extent to the Egyptian army.

All the mingled people, and Chub.—There is the same expression, "mingled people," in reference to Egypt, in Jer. xxv. 20. In the connection here it may be understood especially of the foreign mercenaries from various quarters in the Egyptian armies. Chub is a name entirely unknown. Various conjectures have been hazarded, and various changes in the text proposed, but none are supported by sufficient evidence. It evidently denotes some ally of Egypt, possibly Nubia.

Men of the land that is in league.—Literally, *sons of the land of the covenant*. The ancient interpreters, St. Jerome and Theodoret, understood this expression of the Jews who had sought refuge from Nebuchadnezzar in Egypt after the murder of Gedaliah (Jer. xlii., xliii., xliv.), to whom Jeremiah had expressly prophesied that the sword and famine of which they were afraid should overtake them there (Jer. xlii. 16—18). This interpretation is supported by the translation of the Septuagint, made in Egypt, "land of my covenant." The objection made to this view, that Palestine is never called "the land of the covenant," and that this must therefore signify some unknown country in alliance with Egypt at the time, seems rather specious than real. If it happens that this expression is never used of Palestine, yet that was unquestionably the land of the people of the covenant, and a particular expression may very well be used once without occurring again.

(6) **From the tower of Syene.**—From Migdol to Syene. (See Note on chap. xxix. 10.)

(7) **Shall be desolate.**—This verse is almost an exact repetition of chap. xxix. 12.

(9) **Messengers go forth from me in ships.**—Comp. Isa. xviii. 1, 2. This does not mean the army of Nebuchadnezzar, which did not penetrate into Ethiopia, but the flying Egyptians, who ascend the

Ethiopians afraid, and great pain shall
come upon them, as in the day of Egypt:
for, lo, it cometh.
(10) Thus saith the Lord GOD; I will
also make the multitude of Egypt to cease
by the hand of Nebuchadrezzar king of
Babylon. (11) He and his people with
him, the terrible of the nations, shall be
brought to destroy the land: and they
shall draw their swords against Egypt,
and fill the land with the slain. (12) And
I will make the rivers [1] dry, and sell the
land into the hand of the wicked: and
I will make the land waste, and [2] all
that is therein, by the hand of strangers:
I the LORD have spoken *it*. (13) Thus
saith the Lord GOD; I will also [a] destroy
the idols, and I will cause *their* images
to cease out of Noph; and there shall
be no more a prince of the land of
Egypt: and I will put a fear in the
land of Egypt. (14) And I will make
Pathros desolate, and will set fire in
[3] Zoan, and will execute judgments in
No. (15) And I will pour my fury upon
[4] Sin, the strength of Egypt; and I will
cut off the multitude of No. (16) And I
will set fire in Egypt: Sin shall have
great pain, and No shall be rent asunder,
and Noph *shall have* distresses daily.
(17) The young men of [5] Aven and of
[6] Pi-beseth shall fall by the sword: and
these *cities* shall go into captivity.
(18) At Tehaphnehes also the day shall be
[7] darkened, when I shall break there the
yokes of Egypt: and the pomp of her
strength shall cease in her: as for her,
a cloud shall cover her, and her
daughters shall go into captivity.
(19) Thus will I execute judgments in
Egypt: and they shall know that I *am*
the LORD.
(20) And it came to pass in the eleventh
year, in the first *month*, in the seventh

1 Heb., *drought.*
2 Heb., *the fulness thereof.*
a Zech. 13. 2.
3 Or, *Tanis.*
4 Or, *Pelusium.*
5 Or, *Heliopolis.*
6 Or, *Pubastum.*
B.C. 588.
7 Or, *restrained.*

Nile to seek safety in Ethiopia, and alarm it with the tidings of Egypt's fall. The "careless" are the secure Ethiopians. "As in the day of Egypt" is a reference to a past event, and can only mean, as in the day of judgment upon Egypt at the Exodus.

(12) **Make the rivers dry**—*i.e.*, the canals of Egypt, by which the land was irrigated, and on which its fertility depended. It may also include the comparative drying, the lessening of the inundation of the Nile, which occurred from time to time, and was the cause of the various famines in Egypt mentioned in Scripture.

(13) **Noph.**—A contraction of Menoph, Memphis, the capital of Lower Egypt, situated in the region of the Pyramids, the seat of several dynasties, one of the chief centres of Egyptian idolatry, and celebrated for its Temple of Ptah.

There shall be no more a prince is to be understood, in accordance with the rest of the prophecy, not absolutely, but relatively: there shall be no more a native prince possessing the power of former kings.

(14) **Pathros . . . Zoan . . . No.**—For Pathros, see Note on chap. xxix. 14. Zoan (see Num. xiii. 22; Isa. xix. 11) is Tanis, a city of Lower Egypt, on the Tanitic branch of the Nile. No, mentioned again in the next verse, more fully written No-Amon (Nah. iii. 8), is the celebrated Thebes of Upper Egypt, still famous for its ruins at Luxor and Karnac. The mention of these various cities is to make emphatic the universality of the judgment upon the whole land.

(15) **Sin** is Pelusium, so called from the marshes around it, on the easternmost branch of the Nile, only two-and-a-half miles from the sea. It was the frontier city, strongly fortified, and considered rightly as the key of Egypt, and hence called in the text its "strength." It is mentioned again in verse 16. The expression, "distresses daily" (literally, *by day*), applied to Noph (Memphis), is a difficult one; it is understood by many as *perpetually*, but more probably means *distresses in the open day*. Its enemies shall make no covert attack, but come upon it boldly.

(17) **Of Aven and of Pi-beseth.**—Aven is the same as On of Gen. xli. 45, 50, and as Bethshemesh (House of the Sun) of Jer. xliii. 13, the Heliopolis of the Greeks, so called because from the remotest times a chief seat of the worship of the sun. The vowel points are slightly changed from On to make Aven, *nothingness*, often used of idols. Pi-beseth, on the monuments *Pi-Pasht*—so called from the cat-headed goddess there worshipped—is Bubastis, situated on the canal leading from the Pelusiac branch of the Nile towards Suez.

(18) **Tehaphnehes.**—(Jer. ii. 16, xliii. 7—9, xliv. 1, xlvi. 14.) Otherwise called Tahpanhes; the city Daphne, also a frontier town near Pelusium, strongly fortified. It may be especially mentioned, because the Jews who fled from Palestine through fear of Nebuchadnezzar had taken refuge there (Jer. xliii., xliv.).

The day shall be darkened.—This is a common prophetic form of describing coming calamity. (See verse 3, chap. xxxii. 8; Isa. xiii. 10; Joel ii. 10, 31, iii. 15; Amos viii. 9; Matt. xxiv. 29, &c.)

The yokes of Egypt.—Not the yokes placed upon Egypt, but the tyranny which she exercised over others. The fuller expression, "bands of a yoke," occurs in chap. xxxiv. 27, and also in Lev. xxvi. 13, the latter in reference to the deliverance of Israel from the bondage of Egypt. It appears from Jer. xliii. 9, 10 that there was a royal palace at Tahpanhes, and it was foretold by the prophet that Nebuchadnezzar should there set up his pavilion, and thence smite Egypt. It is correspondingly foretold here that the power of Egypt should there be broken, because this and the neighbouring Pelusium were the frontier fortresses and keys of the land.

(20) **The eleventh year.**—This was the year of the fall of Jerusalem, and the present prophecy (verses 20—26) was uttered a little more than three months and a half before its destruction. Very likely this prophecy had its occasion in the temporary raising of the siege of Jerusalem by Pharaoh-Hophra, and Nebuchadnezzar's driving him away, the news of

day of the month, *that* the word of the
LORD came unto me, saying,
(21) Son of man, I have broken the arm
of Pharaoh king of Egypt; and, lo, it
shall not be bound up to be healed, to
put a roller to bind it, to make it strong
to hold the sword. (22) Therefore thus
saith the Lord GOD; Behold, I *am*
against Pharaoh king of Egypt, and
will break his arms, the strong, and
that which was broken; and I will
cause the sword to fall out of his hand.
(23) And I will scatter the Egyptians
among the nations, and will disperse
them through the countries. (24) And I
will strengthen the arms of the king of
Babylon, and put my sword in his hand:
but I will break Pharaoh's arms, and he
shall groan before him with the groan-
ings of a deadly wounded *man*. (25) But
I will strengthen the arms of the king
of Babylon, and the arms of Pharaoh
shall fall down; and they shall know
that I *am* the LORD, when I shall put
my sword into the hand of the king of
Babylon, and he shall stretch it out
upon the land of Egypt. (26) And I will
scatter the Egyptians among the na-
tions, and disperse them among the
countries; and they shall know that I
am the LORD.

CHAPTER XXXI.—(1) And it came
to pass in the eleventh year, in the third
month, in the first *day* of the month, *that*
the word of the LORD came unto me,
saying, (2) Son of man, speak unto Pha-
raoh king of Egypt, and to his multi-
tude;

Whom art thou like in thy greatness?
(3) Behold, the Assyrian *was* a cedar
in Lebanon [1]with fair branches, and
with a shadowing shroud, and of an
high stature; and his top was among
the thick boughs. (4) The waters [2]made
him great, the deep [3]set him up on high
with her rivers running round about his
plants, and sent out her [4]little rivers
unto all the trees of the field. (5) There-
fore his height was exalted above all
the trees of the field, and his boughs
were multiplied, and his branches be-
came long because of the multitude of
waters, [5]when he shot forth. (6) All the
[a]fowls of heaven made their nests in his
boughs, and under his branches did all
the beasts of the field bring forth their
young, and under his shadow dwelt all

1 Heb., *fair of branches.*
2 Or, *nourished.*
3 Or, *brought him up.*
4 Or, *conduits.*
5 Or, *when it sent them forth.*
a Dan. 4. 12.

---

which would have been some months in reaching Chaldæa.

(21) **I have broken.**—This is in the perfect tense, and refers to the breaking of the power of Egypt by the former conquests of Assyria, and perhaps especially to the great battle of Carchemish (about twenty years before), in which Egypt received a blow from which she never recovered. The word "roller" would be better understood now if translated *bandage*.

(22) **The strong, and that which was broken**—*i.e.*, the whole power of Egypt, both in so far as already crippled, and in so far as it still retained strength.

(23) **Will scatter the Egyptians.**—Repeated verbally in verse 26. (See Note on chapter xxix. 12.)

XXXI.

This chapter consists of a single prophecy, uttered a little less than two months after the previous one, and a little less than two months before the destruction of the Temple. It is a further prophecy against Egypt, but so couched in the form of a parable that it all relates to Assyria, except the opening (verses 1 and 2) and close (verse 18), which bring it to bear upon Egypt. The effectiveness of this comparison with Assyria becomes plain when it is remembered that she had conquered and held Egypt in vassalage, and had then herself been conquered and annihilated only thirty-seven years before the date of this prophecy, and that by the same Chaldæan power now foretold as about to execute judgment upon Egypt. Egypt could not hope to resist the conqueror of her conqueror. There is this great difference between the fate of the two empires: Assyria was to be utterly supplanted by Babylonia, and its nationality blotted out, but Egypt, as the prophet had already foretold (chap. xxix. 14, 15), should continue, though as "a base kingdom," stripped of its supremacy.

The form of parable whereby a kingdom is represented as a tree has already appeared in chap. xvii., and is also used in Dan. iv. It seems to be a Chaldæan mode of representation. As is the custom with Ezekiel, he occasionally interrupts the parable by literal utterances, as in verse 11, and partially in verses 14—16.

(2) **His multitude.**—The word means literally *tumult*, and applies to the multitude as influenced by whatever is the occasion of tumult: their wealth, their idols, their sources of pride of every kind.

(3) **A cedar in Lebanon.**—Lebanon is mentioned only because it was the place where the most famous cedars grew in their greatest perfection. Assyria did, indeed, at one time possess Lebanon, but this was never its home or seat of empire. The word "shroud" in the description refers to the thickness of the shade of the branches.

Among the thick boughs.—Rather, *among the clouds*. (See Note on chap. xix. 11. Comp. also verses 10, 14.)

(4) **His plants.**—Should rather be, *his plantation*.

Sent out her little rivers.—The thought is that the various surrounding and subordinate nations were nourished from the great stream of prosperity which swelled the power and wealth of Assyria.

(6) **All the fowls of heaven.**—Comp. chap. xvii. 23; Dan. iv. 21.

great nations. (7) Thus was he fair in
his greatness, in the length of his
branches: for his root was by great
waters. (8) The cedars in the [a]garden
of God could not hide him: the fir
trees were not like his boughs, and
the chesnut trees were not like his
branches; nor any tree in the garden
of God was like unto him in his beauty.
(9) I have made him fair by the multitude of his branches: so that all the
trees of Eden, that *were* in the garden of
God, envied him.

(10) Therefore thus saith the Lord GOD;
Because thou hast lifted up thyself in
height, and he hath shot up his top
among the thick boughs, and his heart
is lifted up in his height; (11) I have
therefore delivered him into the hand of
the mighty one of the heathen; [1]he
shall surely deal with him: I have driven
him out for his wickedness. (12) And
strangers, the terrible of the nations,
have cut him off, and have left him:
upon the mountains and in all the valleys his branches are fallen, and his
boughs are broken by all the rivers of
the land; and all the people of the earth
are gone down from his shadow, and
have left him. (13) Upon his ruin shall
all the fowls of the heaven remain, and
all the beasts of the field shall be upon
his branches: (14) to the end that none
of all the trees by the waters exalt themselves for their height, neither shoot up
their top among the thick boughs, neither their trees [2]stand up in their height,
all that drink water: for they are all
delivered unto death, to the nether parts
of the earth, in the midst of the children
of men, with them that go down to the
pit.

(15) Thus saith the Lord GOD; In the
day when he went down to the grave I
caused a mourning: I covered the deep
for him, and I restrained the floods
thereof, and the great waters were
stayed: and I caused Lebanon [3]to
mourn for him, and all the trees of the
field fainted for him. (16) I made the
nations to shake at the sound of his
fall, when I cast him down to hell with
them that descend into the pit: and all
the trees of Eden, the choice and best of

a Gen. 2. 8.

1 Heb., *in doing he shall do unto him.*

2 Or, *stand upon themselves for their height.*

3 Heb., *to be black.*

---

(8) **The garden of God.**—See verses 9, 16, 18; also chap. xxviii. 13. This is not a representation of Assyria as being in the garden of God, as in the case of Tyre in chap. xxviii. 13, but only a further expression of its greatness by a comparison of the tree representing it with the trees of Paradise. Yet this comparison may have been suggested by the fact that the traditionary site of Eden was within the bounds of the Assyrian Empire. *Fir trees* are generally understood to be cypresses, and *chestnut* to be plane-trees.

(10) **Among the thick boughs.**—*The clouds,* as in verses 3 and 14, and chap. xix. 11. As verses 3—9 have described Assyria's greatness, so verses 10—14 speak of her fall. This was now a past event, yet is in part poetically spoken of in the future (verses 11, 13), making the whole more graphic and effective. The future may also have been used because the object of this parable is not Assyria, but Egypt, whose fall was still to come. At the outset Assyria is directly addressed in the second person in the vividness of the description, but the third person is used afterwards. The ground of the judgment upon Assyria is its pride, on which 2 Kings xviii. 32—35 may be considered a commentary.

(11) **The mighty one of the heathen.** — The Chaldæan monarch. At the time of the fall of Assyria this was Nabupolassar, Nebuchadnezzar's father. In this verse, and partially in the next, the prophet drops his figure to make clear literal statements.

(12) **Gone down.**—Because the cedar is represented as growing upon the height of Lebanon. Yet "the people of the earth" is literal.

(13) **Upon his ruin shall all the fowls.**—There is no inconsistency between this and the previous verse. At the fall all nations and people rush away, to avoid becoming involved in the catastrophe; but as soon as the giant cedar is prostrate, they gather upon its trunk and branches to fatten upon its ruin.

(14) **Stand up in their height.**—The original is more closely followed by the margin, *stand upon themselves for their height,* and the thought is that the trees (princes) shall no longer rely on their own strength and be infatuated by the prosperity which has been given them.

All that drink water is only a poetical expression for the trees. (Comp. verse 16.) In the constant mention of water and rivers throughout this parable there may be a covert allusion to Egypt, made fertile by the irrigation of the Nile.

To the nether parts of the earth.—See Note on chap. xxvi. 20. In the latter part of this verse the figurative is again exchanged for literal language.

(15) **I covered the deep for him.**—Verses 15—17 describe the effect of Assyria's fall. Verse 15 speaks of the mourning of the nations and of the drying up of the streams, or sources of Assyria's prosperity. "The deep" is the same as in verse 4, the flood of waters which fertilised the great cedar; this is covered, as in mourning. "Floods" is the same word as "rivers" in verse 4, and "great waters" as "multitude of waters" in verse 5. "To mourn" is, literally, *to be black,* and the sense is well given in our version, although the original is more appropriate to the figure of Lebanon with its cedars. "The trees of the field" are, of course, the subordinate potentates, who are dismayed, "faint," at Assyria's fall. (Comp. chap. xxvi. 15—18.)

(16) **Hell** is here, as generally, Sheol, or Hades, the world of the departed.

Shall be comforted.—Comp. Isa. xiv. 9, 10, which was probably in Ezekiel's mind.

Lebanon, all that drink water, shall be
comforted in the nether parts of the
earth. (17) They also went down into
hell with him unto *them that be* slain
with the sword; and *they that were* his
arm, *that* dwelt under his shadow in the
midst of the heathen. (18) To whom art
thou thus like in glory and in greatness
among the trees of Eden? yet shalt thou
be brought down with the trees of Eden
unto the nether parts of the earth: thou
shalt lie in the midst of the uncircum-
cised with *them that be* slain by the
sword. This *is* Pharaoh and all his
multitude, saith the Lord GOD.

CHAPTER XXXII.—(1) And it came
to pass in the twelfth year, in the twelfth
month, in the first *day* of the month,
that the word of the LORD came unto
me, saying, (2) Son of man, take up a
lamentation for Pharaoh king of Egypt,
and say unto him,

Thou art like a young lion of the na-
tions, and thou *art* as a [1]whale in the
seas: and thou camest forth with thy
rivers, and troubledst the waters with
thy feet, and fouledst their rivers. (3) Thus
saith the Lord GOD; I will therefore
[a]spread out my net over thee with a
company of many people; and they shall
bring thee up in my net. (4) Then will I
leave thee upon the land, I will cast thee
forth upon the open field, and will cause
all the fowls of the heaven to remain
upon thee, and I will fill the beasts of
the whole earth with thee. (5) And I will
lay thy flesh upon the mountains, and
fill the valleys with thy height. (6) I will
also water with thy blood [2]the land
wherein thou swimmest, *even* to the
mountains; and the rivers shall be full
of thee. (7) And when I shall [3]put thee
out, [b]I will cover the heaven, and make
the stars thereof dark; I will cover the
sun with a cloud, and the moon shall
not give her light. (8) All the [4]bright
lights of heaven will I make [5]dark over
thee, and set darkness upon thy land,
saith the Lord GOD. (9) I will also [6]vex
the hearts of many people, when I shall
bring thy destruction among the nations,
into the countries which thou hast not
known. (10) Yea, I will make many
people amazed at thee, and their kings
shall be horribly afraid for thee, when I
shall brandish my sword before them;
and they shall tremble at *every* moment,
every man for his own life, in the day of
thy fall.

(11) For thus saith the Lord GOD; The
sword of the king of Babylon shall come

1 Or, *dragon.*

a ch. 12. 13, & 17. 20.

2 Or, *the land of thy swimming.*

3 Or, *extinguish.*

B.C. 587.

b Isa. 13. 10; Joel 2. 31, & 3. 15; Mat. 24. 29.

4 Heb., *lights of the light in heaven.*

5 Heb., *them dark.*

6 Heb., *provoke to anger,* or, *grief.*

---

(18) **To whom art thou thus like.**—In this closing verse the whole chapter is brought to a point. Egypt, like Assyria in glory, shall be like her in experience of the judgments of God. On "uncircumcised" comp. Note on chap. xxviii. 10.

XXXII.

This chapter, which consists of two distinct prophecies (verses 1—16, 17—32), with the interval of only a fortnight between them, closes the series at once against Egypt and against foreign nations. The former of these prophecies is a further declaration of the approaching conquest of Egypt by "the king of Babylon," while the latter is a dirge over its fall, like the dirge over Tyre in chap. xxviii.

(1) **In the twelfth year.**—This was one year and between six and seven months after the destruction of Jerusalem, and when, therefore, one great hindrance to Nebuchadnezzar's march upon Egypt had been removed. It is also nearly two months (chap. xxxiii. 21) since Ezekiel had heard of this calamity through a fugitive. It could not have been very long before the arrival of the fugitive Jews in Egypt, after the murder of Gedaliah; yet that it was somewhat earlier is plain from chap. xxxiii. 24. It was about the same time with the similar prophecies of Jeremiah (chaps. xliii., xliv.); but as the date both of the murder and of the flight are unknown (except that the former occurred in the seventh month—Jer. xli. 1—but of what year is not stated), the exact chronological relation of these things must remain uncertain.

(2) **As a whale.**—Rather, *a crocodile.* (See Note on chap. xxix. 3, where the same word is used.) A striking contrast is brought out in this verse which is lost in our translation. "Thou wast compared to a young lion of the nations," *i.e.*, their leader and glory; "but thou wast (really) like a crocodile in the seas," stirring up and fouling the rivers, the sources of their prosperity.

Thou camest forth with.—Better, *thou didst break forth in thy rivers,* referring to the crocodile basking upon the bank, and suddenly plunging into the stream and stirring up its mud.

(3) **Spread out my net over thee.**—The figure (verses 4—6) of drawing the crocodile to land and casting him upon the desert for food to the birds and beasts of prey is the same as in chap. xxix. 4, 5. (Comp. also chap. xxxi. 12, 13.) In verse 6, "the land wherein thou swimmest" is, literally, *the land of thine outflow,* and may be taken either of the land on which his blood is poured out, or, more probably, the land of the inundations of the Nile, now to be watered with blood.

(7) **Make the stars thereof dark.**—This verse follows very closely Isa. xiii. 10, spoken of Babylon. In this and the following verse the judgments of God are described in the common prophetic figure of changes in the heavenly bodies. (See Note on chap. xxx. 18, and references there.)

(9) **Vex the hearts.**—The margin, *provoke to grief,* is better, as being less ambiguous. "Thy destruction"

upon thee. (12) By the swords of the
mighty will I cause thy multitude to
fall, the terrible of the nations, all of
them: and they shall spoil the pomp of
Egypt, and all the multitude thereof
shall be destroyed. (13) I will destroy
also all the beasts thereof from beside
the great waters; neither shall the foot
of man trouble them any more, nor the
hoofs of beasts trouble them. (14) Then
will I make their waters deep, and cause
their rivers to run like oil, saith the Lord
GOD. (15) When I shall make the land
of Egypt desolate, and the country shall
be [1] destitute of that whereof it was full,
when I shall smite all them that dwell
therein, then shall they know that I *am*
the LORD. (16) This *is* the lamentation
wherewith they shall lament her: the
daughters of the nations shall lament
her: they shall lament for her, *even* for
Egypt, and for all her multitude, saith
the Lord GOD.

(17) It came to pass also in the twelfth
year, in the fifteenth *day* of the month,
that the word of the LORD came unto
me, saying,

(18) Son of man, wail for the multi-
tude of Egypt, and cast them down,
even her, and the daughters of the
famous nations, unto the nether parts
of the earth, with them that go down
into the pit. (19) Whom dost thou pass
in beauty? go down, and be thou laid
with the uncircumcised. (20) They shall
fall in the midst of *them that are* slain
by the sword: [2] she is delivered to the
sword: draw her and all her multitudes.
(21) The strong among the mighty shall
speak to him out of the midst of hell
with them that help him: they are gone
down, they lie uncircumcised, slain by
the sword. (22) Asshur *is* there and all
her company: his graves *are* about him:
all of them slain, fallen by the sword:
(23) whose graves are set in the sides of
the pit, and her company is round about
her grave: all of them slain, fallen by
the sword, which caused [3] terror in the
land of the living. (24) There *is* Elam
and all her multitude round about her
grave, all of them slain, fallen by the
sword, which are gone down uncircum-
cised into the nether parts of the earth,

1 Heb., *desolate from the fulness thereof.*

2 Or, *the sword is laid.*

3 Or, *dismaying.*

---

means, *the news of thy destruction.* As is more fully expressed in the following verse, the fall of Egypt should be such a striking instance of Divine judgment as to awaken fear in every nation that should hear of the catastrophe.

(13) **Will destroy also all the beasts thereof from beside the great waters.**—The figurative description of this and the following verses is taken from the vast herds of cattle in Egypt going to the river to drink, and trampling the banks and disturbing the water with their feet (comp. verse 2). These represent the restless activity and stir of Egyptian life, and its constant disturbance of surrounding nations. With its conquest all this ceases, and, restrained within its own boundaries, Egypt shall no longer be a disturber.

(14) **Deep** should rather be rendered *quiet.* When the restless ambition of Egypt should be curbed, there would come about peace and quiet prosperity. This is thought by many to be a glance forward at the Messianic blessing of the future; but it does not necessarily look so far.

(16) **Daughters of the nations** is a common enough expression for the nations themselves, but is peculiarly appropriate in connection with a lamentation, since the formal mourning of the East was always performed by women.

(17) **The fifteenth day of the month.** — The month itself is not mentioned, but since the previous prophecy was in the twelfth, or last month of the year, this must be in the same. There was thus an interval of just fourteen days between them. This dirge, which occupies the rest of the chapter, is to be compared with Isa. xiv., on which it is evidently founded.

(18) **Cast them down.**—The prophet is here, as often elsewhere, told to do that which he prophesies shall be done. This is a forcible way of stating the certain fulfilment of that which is declared by Divine command.

(19) **With the uncircumcised.**—See Note on chap. xxviii. 10. All question as to the use of circumcision among the Egyptians is out of place; the word is simply used as the ordinary phrase for the heathen.

(20) **Draw her.**—Viz., down to her judgment.

(21) **Speak to him.**—The pronoun oscillates between the masculine and the feminine, because the thought is partly of the king and partly of the kingdom. The pronoun is determined by whichever is for the moment uppermost in the prophet's mind. On *Hell,* see Note on chap. xxxi. 16, 17. It occurs also at verse 27.

(22) **Asshur is there.**—In the previous verses we have had a general picture of the fallen nations awaiting to receive Egypt as their companion; in verses 22—30 there follows an enumeration of the most prominent of them, with a few words about each. Some of them were not yet fallen; but in this prophetic view it is their ultimate condition which rises to the prophet's mind. All worldly power that opposes itself to God must go down and share the judgment soon to fall on Egypt.

His graves are about him.—The graves of the people are about those of their monarch. All are fallen together into one common ruin.

(24) **There is Elam.**—Jeremiah had already prophesied against Elam twelve years before (Jer. xlix. 34). Elam is substantially equivalent to Persia, and had been repeatedly conquered by Assyria and Chaldæa. It was a fierce and warlike nation, and its soldiers had long served in Nebuchadnezzar's army. It was by the aid of Persia that he had succeeded in overthrowing Assyria. It was by a subsequent union of the same Power with the Medes that the Babylonian power was

which caused their terror in the land of
the living; yet have they borne their
shame with them that go down to the
pit. (25) They have set her a bed in the
midst of the slain with all her multi-
tude: her graves *are* round about him:
all of them uncircumcised, slain by the
sword: though their terror was caused
in the land of the living, yet have they
borne their shame with them that go
down to the pit: he is put in the midst
of *them that be* slain.
(26) There *is* Meshech, Tubal, and all
her multitude: her graves *are* round
about him: all of them uncircumcised,
slain by the sword, though they caused
their terror in the land of the living.
(27) And they shall not lie with the mighty
that are fallen of the uncircumcised,
which are gone down to hell [1] with their
weapons of war: and they have laid
their swords under their heads, but their
iniquities shall be upon their bones,
though *they were* the terror of the
mighty in the land of the living. (28) Yea,
thou shalt be broken in the midst of
the uncircumcised, and shalt lie with
them that are slain with the sword.
(29) There *is* Edom, her kings, and all
her princes, which with their might are
[2] laid by *them that were* slain by the
sword: they shall lie with the uncir-
cumcised, and with them that go down
to the pit. (30) There *be* the princes of
the north, all of them, and all the Zi-
donians, which are gone down with the
slain; with their terror they are ashamed
of their might; and they lie uncircum-
cised with *them that be* slain by the sword,
and bear their shame with them that go
down to the pit.
(31) Pharaoh shall see them, and shall
be comforted over all his multitude, *even*
Pharaoh and all his army slain by the
sword, saith the Lord GOD. (32) For I
have caused my terror in the land of the
living: and he shall be laid in the midst
of the uncircumcised, with *them that are*
slain with the sword, *even* Pharaoh and
all his multitude, saith the Lord GOD.

CHAPTER XXXIII.—(1) Again the

1 Heb., *with weapons of their war.*

2 Heb., *given,* or, *put.*

---

overthrown. Not until after that union did Persia become a very prominent nation. It continued a great Power until its conquest by Alexander. The prophet is therefore anticipating the events of the future when he represents Elam as already in the pit. But, as before said, his thought looks on to the ultimate result, without making prominent the comparative dates of the future. It is possible, however, so far to separate Elam from Persia as to look upon the former as one of those nations out of whose ruins the latter arose, and in this case Elam was already past. The former interpretation seems preferable.

(26) **There is Meshech, Tubal.**—See Note on chap. xxvii. 13. It is difficult to obtain historical data for the exact time of the fall of these more obscure kingdoms; but at this period of the world these smaller states were being rapidly swallowed up and absorbed by the greater Powers who were contending for the world's empire. Meshech and Tubal, like Persia, do not appear at this time to have yet attained their greatest development.

(27) **And they shall not lie.**—If this be the correct translation, then a distinction is implied between these nations and the others. The others have been honourably buried "with their weapons of war," while these come to a more disgraceful end. It is better, however, to take it as a question (which the Hebrew fully admits): "Shall they not?" &c.

Their iniquities shall be upon their bones—*i.e., they shall die in their iniquity.* As we say in English, their sins shall be upon their heads.

(29) **There is Edom.**—Edom had been long since conquered and almost destroyed by Israel, but had again revived to mock at her calamity (chap. xxv. 12—14). It was soon, like its neighbours, to be swept away by the armies of Nebuchadnezzar.

(30) **The princes of the north.**—The word is not the same as that used for the princes of Edom in verse 29. That refers to the heads of the Edomite tribes, but this is thought to imply enfeoffed or vassal princes. However this may be, from the connection with the Zidonians it is clear that not the far north is intended, but perhaps chieftains of Syria, Damascus, and the like.

The Zidonians.—With the rise of Tyre, Zidon had long since lost its pre-eminence among the Phœnician cities; but it was still an important and an independent city, and was doomed to far greater humiliation in the future.

(31) **Shall be comforted.**—Comp. chap. xxxi. 16.

Here closes the series of prophecies against foreign nations. It is true that there are other prophecies against them in chaps. xxxv., xxxviii., and xxxix.; but these, as already said, have much more of the character of promises to Israel than of simple denunciation of their enemies The greater part of this series was uttered between the investment and the close of the siege of Jerusalem, a time during which the prophet was to be dumb towards the children of his people, and at the close of which his mouth was again to be opened. At this time, therefore, his prophetic gifts were appropriately exercised towards foreigners, and at the close, with the renewal of his instructions to Israel, a fresh charge is given as a sort of fresh induction to his prophetic office (chap. xxxiii. 1—30).

XXXIII.

This chapter consists of two communications (verses 1—20 and 21—33). The first of them is without date, but at least a very probable conjecture may be formed of the time when it was uttered. In verses 21, 22, it

word of the LORD came unto me, saying, (2) Son of man, speak to the children of thy people, and say unto them,

[1]When I bring the sword upon a land, if the people of the land take a man of their coasts, and set him for their watchman: (3) if when he seeth the sword come upon the land, he blow the trumpet, and warn the people; (4) then [2]whosoever heareth the sound of the trumpet, and taketh not warning; if the sword come, and take him away, his blood shall be upon his own head. (5) He heard the sound of the trumpet, and took not warning; his blood shall be upon him. But he that taketh warning shall deliver his soul. (6) But if the watchman see the sword come, and blow not the trumpet, and the people be not warned; if the sword come, and take *any* person from among them, he is taken away in his iniquity; but his blood will I require at the watchman's hand.

(7) [a]So thou, O son of man, I have set thee a watchman unto the house of Israel; therefore thou shalt hear the word at my mouth, and warn them from me. (8) When I say unto the wicked, O wicked *man*, thou shalt surely die; if thou dost not speak to warn the wicked from his way, that wicked *man* shall die in his iniquity; but his blood will I require at thine hand. (9) Nevertheless, if thou warn the wicked of his way to turn from it; if he do not turn from his way, he shall die in his iniquity; but thou hast delivered thy soul.

(10) Therefore, O thou son of man, speak unto the house of Israel; Thus ye speak, saying, If our transgressions and our sins *be* upon us, and we pine away in them, how should we then live? (11) Say unto them, *As* I live, saith the Lord GOD, [b]I have no pleasure in the death of the wicked; but that the wicked turn from his way and live: turn ye, turn ye from your evil ways; for [c]why will ye die, O house of Israel?

(12) Therefore, thou son of man, say unto the children of thy people, The [d]righteousness of the righteous shall not deliver him in the day of his transgression: as for the wickedness of the wicked, he shall not fall thereby in the day that he turneth from his wickedness; neither shall the righteous be able to live for his *righteousness* in the day that he sinneth. (13) When I shall say to the righteous, *that* he shall surely live; if he trust to his own righteousness, and commit iniquity, all his righteousnesses shall not be remembered; but for his iniquity that he hath committed, he shall die for it. (14) Again, when I say unto the wicked, Thou shalt surely die; if he turn from his sin, and do [3]that which is lawful and right; (15) *if* the wicked restore the pledge, give again

1 Heb., *A land when I bring a sword upon her.*
2 Heb., *he that hearing heareth.*
a ch. 3. 17, &c.
b 2 Sam. 14. 14; ch. 18. 32.
c ch. 18. 31.
d ch. 18. 24.
3 Heb., *judgment and justice.*

---

is said that Ezekiel was informed in the morning by a fugitive from Jerusalem of the destruction of the city, and in accordance with the promise of chap. xxiv. 27, his "mouth was opened, and I was no more dumb." But it is added in verse 22 that "the hand of the Lord was upon me in the evening, afore he that was escaped came." It is clear, then, that Ezekiel uttered some prophecy on the evening before that recorded in the latter part of the chapter, while there is none bearing such a date. The prophecy of the earlier part is, however, just such an one as might be expected at that time; for it is a renewal of the charge to him in his work on entering afresh on his prophetic activity towards Israel. There can, therefore, be no reasonable doubt that this is the prophecy of the evening before he received the official tidings of the fall of Jerusalem, and is placed, like all his other prophecies (except those against foreign nations), in its proper chronological order.

The prophecy itself is an amplification of the charge given in chap. iii. 16—21, but also with constant reference to chap. xviii.

(2) **Set him for their watchman.**—The same figure as in chap. iii. 17. Verses 2—9 form the introduction to this renewed commission, and closely correspond to chap. iii. 17—21. Yet these verses have also a distinct retrospective object, and explain to the people why he had hitherto spoken to them so much of judgments and in such warning tones; this had been his duty, both in obedience to God's commands and in regard for their welfare, and it would still be his duty in the future. The passage is too clear to need comment.

(10) **How should we then live?**—Formerly, when the prophet had given them warning of impending judgments, the people had refused to believe; now, however, when those judgments had been realised, they despaired, and cried out, "If all this is in punishment for our sins, how can there yet be any hope for us?"

(11) **I have no pleasure.**—Comp. chap. xviii. 28, 32 Ezekiel meets the despair of the people by the assurance, long before given in another connection, that the Creator and Father of all can have no pleasure in the death of any, and adds an earnest exhortation to repentance that they may be saved. Yet it was very important that there should be no misunderstanding in regard to the basis of acceptance with God, and the prophet therefore, in the following verses (12—20), briefly reiterates the teaching of chap. xviii. in regard to the individual responsibility of every one for himself before God. This teaching has already been explained under chap. xviii.

that he had robbed, walk in the statutes
of life, without committing iniquity;
he shall surely live, he shall not die.
(16) None of his sins that he hath com-
mitted shall be mentioned unto him: he
hath done that which is lawful and right;
he shall surely live.
(17) Yet the children of thy people say,
The way of the Lord is not equal: but
as for them, their way is not equal.
(18) When the righteous turneth from his
righteousness, and committeth iniquity,
he shall even die thereby. (19) But if the
wicked turn from his wickedness, and
do that which is lawful and right, he
shall live thereby.
(20) Yet ye say, [a]The way of the Lord
is not equal. O ye house of Israel,
I will judge you every one after his
ways.
(21) And it came to pass in the twelfth
year of our captivity, in the tenth *month*,
in the fifth *day* of the month, *that* one
that had escaped out of Jerusalem came
unto me, saying, [b]The city is smitten.
(22) Now the hand of the LORD was upon
me in the evening, afore he that was
escaped came; and had opened my
mouth, until he came to me in the
morning; and my mouth was opened,
and I was no more [c]dumb.
(23) Then the word of the LORD came
unto me, saying, (24) Son of man, they
that inhabit those wastes of the land of
Israel speak, saying, Abraham was one,
and he inherited the land: but we *are*
many; the land is given us for inherit-
ance. (25) Wherefore say unto them,
Thus saith the Lord GOD; Ye eat with
the blood, and lift up your eyes toward
your idols, and shed blood: and shall
ye possess the land? (26) Ye stand upon
your sword, ye work abomination, and
ye defile every one his neighbour's wife:

a ch. 18. 25.

b 2 Kin. 25. 4.

c ch. 24. 27.

---

(21) **In the twelfth year.**—Comp. 2 Kings xxv. 8; Jer. lii. 12. It was now a year and five months since the final destruction of Jerusalem and the Temple, and this seems to be a long time to be occupied in carrying the news to Chaldea. The news itself must have reached Babylon long since, but Ezekiel was to receive the tidings, doubtless with full and circumstantial details, from the mouth of a fugitive, and there are reasons why this could not well have occurred earlier. After the capture of the city, the general, Nebuzaradan, took the mass of the people and the abundant spoil to carry them to Babylon (Jer. lii. 15—27). He first took them to Nebuchadnezzar at Riblah, where a few were executed, and some time must have been occupied in settling the affairs of the desolated land. After this, the journey of the captives, carrying along with them the weighty spoil, was a slow one, and perhaps with frequent halts. We know from Ezra vii. 9 that the returning captives, not thus hindered, occupied exactly four months in the journey from Babylon to Jerusalem. It is not surprising, therefore, that it should have been four times as long from the capture of Jerusalem to the arrival of the captives in Chaldea. This prophecy was nearly two months before that recorded in chap. xxxii.

(22) **Was upon me.**—The sentence becomes clearer by translating this in the *pluperf.: The hand of the Lord had been* (*already*) *upon me.*

(23) **Then the word.**—There is no reason to doubt that the following prophecy was uttered immediately after the arrival of the fugitive; but there may have been a short interval. None of the prophecies from this point to the close of chap. xxxix. are dated. Chaps. xl.—xlviii. form one continuous prophecy, which closes the book, and is dated more than twelve years after the present one. We are then to suppose that the prophecies, to chap. xxxix. inclusive, were uttered at intervals during these twelve years, but we have no means of fixing their dates more exactly.

(24) **Inhabit those wastes.**—It is said in 2 Kings xxv. 12, 22; Jer. lii. 16, xl., that the poor of the people were left in the land for vine-dressers and for husbandmen, and that these were joined by fugitive Jews from Moab and Ammon and other places. It is to these that the present part of this prophecy (verses 23—29) is addressed, and it is plain that the murder of Gedaliah, and consequent flight into Egypt, had not yet taken place.

Abraham was one . . . we are many.—The argument used by these people was a simple one: the land was promised to Abraham and his seed in perpetuity. He was but one, and the promise was fulfilled; we, his seed, are many, and it cannot fail us. This disposition to rely upon their descent from Abraham was characteristic of the Jews in all ages (see Matt. iii. 9; John viii. 33—39). The same tendency to trust in the external privileges given them is apt to be found in all ages among those whose hearts are alienated from God. These Jews, to avoid the force of the prophet's reproofs, passed from one subterfuge to another. First it was that God would not abandon His holy city and Temple; then that the judgments were so far in the future that they need cause no present alarm; now, when these warnings had all been fulfilled, they clung to the fact that the land was theirs by promise, forgetting the conditions which had been attached from the first to its enjoyment.

(25) **Ye eat with the blood.**—The people who remained in the land went on as before in their course of sin. The crimes here charged upon them (verses 25, 26) are the same as those all along alleged against them, and Jeremiah gives a sad picture of their open rebellion against the express commands of God (Jer. xlii., xliii.). This particular sin of eating flesh with the blood had been repeatedly forbidden, first to Noah (Gen. ix. 4), and again under the Law (Lev. iii. 17, vii. 26, xvii. 10—14; Deut. xii. 16).

(26) **Ye stand upon your sword.**—Not to engage in war, which cannot here be thought of, but to take part in individual crimes of violence.

(27) **In the forts**—is rather, in the natural fastnesses in which the land abounded.

and shall ye possess the land? (27) Say
thou thus unto them, Thus saith the
Lord God; *As* I live, surely they that
are in the wastes shall fall by the sword,
and him that *is* in the open field will I
give to the beasts [1]to be devoured, and
they that *be* in the forts and in the
caves shall die of the pestilence. (28) For
I will lay the land [2]most desolate, and
the [a]pomp of her strength shall cease;
and the mountains of Israel shall be
desolate, that none shall pass through.
(29) Then shall they know that I *am* the
Lord, when I have laid the land most
desolate because of all their abomina-
tions which they have committed.
(30) Also, thou son of man, the children
of thy people still are talking against
thee by the walls and in the doors of the
houses, and speak one to another, every
one to his brother, saying, Come, I pray
you, and hear what is the word that
cometh forth from the Lord. (31) And
they come unto thee [3]as the people
cometh, and [4]they sit before thee *as* my
people, and they hear thy words, but
they will not do them: for with their
mouth [5]they shew much love, *but* their
heart goeth after their covetousness.
(32) And, lo, thou *art* unto them as [6]a
very lovely song of one that hath a
pleasant voice, and can play well on an
instrument: for they hear thy words,
but they do them not. (33) And when
this cometh to pass, (lo, it will come,)
then shall they know that a prophet
hath been among them.

1 Heb., *to devour him.*

2 Heb., *desolation and desolation.*

a ch. 7. 24, & 24. 21, & 30. 6, 7.

3 Heb., *according to the coming of the people.*

4 Or, *my people sit before thee.*

5 Heb., *they make loves,* or, *jests.*

6 Heb., *a song of loves.*

CHAPTER XXXIV. — (1) And the
word of the Lord came unto me, say-

---

(28) **Most desolate.**—When the people of the northern kingdom had been carried into captivity, the land had been re-populated by colonies brought from various quarters by the king of Assyria, for the ten tribes were not to return; but now the land of Judah was to be left utterly desolate and uninhabited, that it might yet be re-occupied by the returning exiles. The complete dispersion of the people, not to be effected even by war and conquest, was finally accomplished by the flight of the remnant into Egypt (Jer. xliii. 5—7), in consequence of their fears.

(30) **The children of thy people.**—The few remaining verses of this chapter are concerned with those in exile—perhaps not so much those who had been with Ezekiel all along as fresh captives of a worse moral character now just brought from Jerusalem. Yet of them all alike it was still true that they were much more ready to listen with deferential air to the words of the prophet than to take them to their hearts and act upon them in their life. The prophet is here warned (verses 30—33) not to be misled by the apparent compliance of the people, as he had been before strengthened against their opposition (chap. iii. 8, 9); but it must have carried a pang deep into his heart to know how superficial was the effect of those labours to which he had devoted himself with such faithfulness.

Against thee.—Rather, *of thee.* The people are not represented as opposed to Ezekiel, but rather as enjoying his eloquence, and talking about him as they met one another, but without any serious effort to follow his counsels—much like the treatment of a popular preacher by his people at the present day.

By the walls and in the doors.—Better, *within the walls.* The meaning is, both privately and publicly.

(31) **As the people cometh.**—In the original, *according to the coming of a people—i.e.,* in crowds. In the following clause, "as my people," there is an emphasis on the pronoun, as the true people of God. Such was their outward bearing, while their inward disposition was far different.

(33) **When this cometh to pass.**—"This" refers to what the prophet is commissioned to utter. By the fulfilment of his prophecies of judgment they had already been brought to an outward recognition of his authority; it remained that by the fulfilment of the prophecies yet to come their hearts, or at least the hearts of the better part of them, should be bowed in true submission to the Divine will, as made known through him.

XXXIV.

The latter part of the Book of Ezekiel, after the fulfilment of the great judgment in the destruction of Jerusalem, is consolatory in its character, and full of rich promises to the afflicted people of God. But as this necessarily involves denunciations of the oppressors and enemies of the people, it will aid in obtaining a clear view of the whole to make a brief summary of the contents of chaps. xxxiv.—xxxix. in their literal interpretation. Chap. xxxiv. announces that the Lord will deliver His people out of the hands of the selfish and wicked shepherds who have injured and oppressed them, and will Himself feed, protect, and bring blessings to them through His servant David. Chap. xxxv.: Because Edom has always hated Israel, and sought to possess itself of her land in the time of her distress, therefore its own land shall become a perpetual desolation. Chap. xxxvi.: On the other hand, Israel's land shall be restored to prosperity for the Lord's own sake; His people, gathered from the nations, shall be cleansed from their sins, renewed in heart, and greatly multiplied, and their land made like a garden of God. Chap. xxxvii.: The house of Israel, which has become like dry bones, shall be raised to new life, its two divided kingdoms re-united, and their sins forgiven; and God will make them dwell in their land, under the sovereignty of David, with a perpetual covenant of peace with Himself, and He will establish His sanctuary among them for ever. Chaps. xxxviii., xxxix.: Finally, although the Lord will bring their enemies against them with a powerful array, yet He will ultimately destroy these foes, have compassion on Israel, and hide His face from His people no more for ever. The meaning of these prophecies will be more fully discussed in its place.

Chap. xxxiv. consists of three parts: in the first (verses 1—10) the unfaithful shepherds are denounced, and God promises to take His flock out of their hands;

ing, (2) Son of man, prophesy against
the [a]shepherds of Israel, prophesy, and
say unto them, Thus saith the Lord
God unto the shepherds; Woe *be* to the
shepherds of Israel that do feed them-
selves! should not the shepherds feed
the flocks? (3) Ye eat the fat, and ye
clothe you with the wool, ye kill them
that are fed: *but* ye feed not the flock.
(4) The diseased have ye not strength-
ened, neither have ye healed that which
was sick, neither have ye bound up *that*
which was broken, neither have ye
brought again that which was driven
away, neither have ye sought that which
was lost; but with [b]force and with
cruelty have ye ruled them. (5) And
they were scattered, [1]because *there is* no
shepherd: and they became meat to all
the beasts of the field, when they were
scattered. (6) My sheep wandered through
all the mountains, and upon every high
hill: yea, my flock was scattered upon
all the face of the earth, and none did
search or seek *after them.*

(7) Therefore, ye shepherds, hear the
word of the Lord; (8) *As* I live, saith
the Lord God, surely because my flock
became a prey, and my flock became
meat to every beast of the field, because
there was no shepherd, neither did my
shepherds search for my flock, but the
shepherds fed themselves, and fed not
my flock; (9) therefore, O ye shepherds,
hear the word of the Lord; (10) Thus
saith the Lord God; Behold, I *am*
against the shepherds; and I will re-
quire my flock at their hand, and cause
them to cease from feeding the flock;
neither shall the shepherds feed them-
selves any more; for I will deliver my
flock from their mouth, that they may
not be meat for them.

(11) For thus saith the Lord God; Be-
hold, I, *even* I, will both search my sheep,
and seek them out. (12) [2]As a shepherd
seeketh out his flock in the day that he
is among his sheep *that are* scattered;
so will I seek out my sheep, and will de-
liver them out of all places where they
have been scattered in the cloudy and
dark day. (13) And I will bring them
out from the people, and gather them
from the countries, and will bring them

a Jer. 23. 1.

b 1 Pet. 5. 3.

1 Or, *without a shepherd*: and so ver. 8.

2 Heb., *according to the seeking.*

---

in the second (verses 11—22), He declares that He will Himself take charge of the flock, gather it together, feed it in good pastures in Israel, and root out the evil from it; while in the last part (verses 23—31) He promises to appoint David as His shepherd over it, to make with them a covenant of peace, and to bless the land with all fruitfulness, so that they shall recognise Him as their God, and that there shall be communion between them. The whole chapter may be looked upon as an amplification of the short prophecy in Jer. xxiii. 1—8.

(2) **Shepherds of Israel.**—This is a common Scriptural expression for rulers, and the whole context shows that these are the persons here intended. In the passage in Jer. xxiii. they are treated under this name separately from the prophets and priests, and also in Jer. ii. 8 they are distinguished from prophets and priests. The name itself is a peculiarly appropriate one, and seems to have been in use throughout the East, but especially in Israel, from the time when David was taken from the care of the flocks to feed the Lord's people. (Comp. 2 Sam. v. 2; Ps. lxxviii. 70, 71.)

That do feed themselves.—This selfishness is characteristic of the unfaithful shepherd (comp. John x. 1—17), and is enlarged upon in verses 3, 4. The history shows that for a long time it had been eminently true of the rulers, and especially of the kings of Israel.

(5) **They were scattered, because . . . .**—The calamities of the people are attributed to the fault of the rulers, not because the people themselves were free from sin—the contrary has already been abundantly asserted in this book—but because the people's sins were largely due to the evil example, the idolatries, the oppressions, and the disobedience of their rulers.

(6) **My sheep wandered.**—In the pronouns, *my* sheep and *my* flock, God again claims the people for His own. Without proper guides, they have indeed strayed far away from Him, and there has been none to inquire after or seek them out in their lost condition. The two words *search* and *seek* refer, the former to asking or inquiring, the latter to searching after.

In such a state of things, plainly the first act of mercy to the flock must be the removal of the unfaithful shepherds. This is promised (verses 7—10), but, after Ezekiel's manner, with reiterated declaration of the unfaithfulness of the shepherds.

(11) **Behold, I, even I.**—The rich promises of the following verses are all essentially contained in this, that Jehovah Himself will be the Shepherd of His flock. It is the same assurance as that given by the Saviour in John x., and here, as there, must necessarily be understood spiritually. In the following verses many promises are given of an earthly and temporary character, and these were fulfilled partly in the restoration from exile, partly in the glorious deliverance of the Church from its foes under the Maccabees. But these deliverances themselves were but types of the more glorious Messianic deliverance of the future, and necessary means whereby it was secured. The promise of that deliverance could only be brought at all within the comprehension of the people by setting it forth in earthly language, just as even now it is impossible for us to understand the glories of the Church triumphant, except by the aid of the sensible images in which Scripture has portrayed them. Far less was it possible to this people, so much behind us in spiritual education and enlightenment.

(13) **Bring them to their own land.**—It is not to be forgotten that this is a part of the same figurative

to their own land, and feed them upon
the mountains of Israel by the rivers,
and in all the inhabited places of the
country. (14) I will feed them in a good
pasture, and upon the high mountains
of Israel shall their fold be: there shall
they lie in a good fold, and *in* a fat
pasture shall they feed upon the moun-
tains of Israel. (15) I will feed my flock,
and I will cause them to lie down, saith
the Lord God. (16) I will seek that which
was lost, and bring again that which
was driven away, and will bind up *that
which was* broken, and will strengthen
that which was sick: but I will destroy
the fat and the strong; I will feed them
with judgment.
(17) And *as for* you, O my flock, thus
saith the Lord God; Behold, I judge
between [1]cattle and cattle, between the
rams and the [2]he goats. (18) *Seemeth it*
a small thing unto you to have eaten up
the good pasture, but ye must tread
down with your feet the residue of your
pastures? and to have drunk of the deep
waters, but ye must foul the residue
with your feet? (19) And *as for* my flock,
they eat that which ye have trodden
with your feet; and they drink that
which ye have fouled with your feet.
(20) Therefore thus saith the Lord God
unto them; Behold, I, *even* I, will judge
between the fat cattle and between the
lean cattle. (21) Because ye have thrust
with side and with shoulder, and pushed
all the diseased with your horns, till ye
have scattered them abroad; (22) there-
fore will I save my flock, and they shall
no more be a prey; and I will judge be-
tween cattle and cattle. (23) And I will
set up one [a]shepherd over them, and he
shall feed them, *even* my servant David;
he shall feed them, and he shall be their
shepherd. (24) And I the Lord will be
their God, and my servant David a
prince among them; I the Lord have
spoken *it*. (25) And I will make with
them a covenant of peace, and will cause
the evil beasts to cease out of the land:
and they shall dwell safely in the wilder-
ness, and sleep in the woods. (26) And I
will make them and the places round
about my hill a blessing; and I will
cause the shower to come down in his
season; there shall be showers of bless-
ing. (27) And the tree of the field shall

1 Heb., *small cattle of lambs and kids.*

2 Heb., *great he goats.*

a Isa. 40. 11; John 10. 11.

---

language with "the cloudy and dark day" of the preceding verse, and that they must be explained in the same way. God's people have wandered in the gloom, and they shall be gathered back to Him again.

(16) **The fat and the strong.**—While fatness is in general an emblem of prosperity, it is frequently used in Scripture, as here, for that prosperity which begets hardness of heart and forgetfulness of God. (See Deut. xxxii. 15; Acts xxviii. 27, &c.)

With judgment.—This does not mean, as the ambiguous sense of the English word might make it possible to suppose, *with wisdom*, but with righteousness and authority, as is plainly seen from the connection with the following verses.

(17) **Between cattle and cattle.**—In other words, *between one and another of the flock.* They are not all alike to be saved and blessed, but only those who turn in penitence and submission to God, their Shepherd. The same contrast is again expressed in verses 20 and 22. It is not between "the cattle" on the one side, and "the rams and the he-goats" on the other, but between the cattle themselves, and also between the rams and he-goats themselves; all the evil, of whatever class, are to be rejected. Verses 18, 19 are addressed to those who will be rejected.

(18) **Tread down . . . foul the residue.**—The charge against them is that they not only first supplied and took care of themselves, but with careless insolence destroyed what should have been for others.

(23) **Set up one shepherd.**—He is *one* both with reference to the many evil rulers who have gone before (and this implies the perpetuity of His rule), and also with reference to the two kingdoms of Israel, which are hereafter to be for evermore united in the one Church of God. Obviously this prophecy can find its accomplishment in no merely human ruler.

My servant David.—The name of David is here put simply, as in verse 24, chap. xxxvii. 24, 25; Jer. xxx. 9; Hos. iii. 5, instead of the more usual designations of the Messiah as the Son, the Branch, the Offspring of David; but there can be no possible doubt of the meaning, any more than of who is meant by Elijah in Mal. iv. 5, in view of our Lord's own interpretation in Matt. xi. 14, xvii. 11—14. Yet it should be remembered, if any one should incline to understand this whole prophecy literally, that if one part is to be so understood the rest must be taken in the same way; if we are to think that the prophet here foretells the literal restoration of the two kingdoms of Israel to their own land, and their union under one governor, then that governor must be David himself. The absurdity of such a supposition is one important element in showing that the whole is to be understood of a promise of spiritual blessings, and of the gathering of God's people into His Church as one flock under their Almighty Shepherd. (Comp. John x. 14—18.) David, as the head of the theocracy and the ancestor of our Lord after the flesh, constantly appears in the Scriptures as the type of the Messiah, and there can be no reasonable doubt that this prophecy must have been so understood, even at the time when it was uttered.

(26) **Round about my hill.**—"My hill" is Zion. (Comp. the similar figurative language in Isa. xxxi. 4.) The centre of the old theocracy is always spoken of in Scripture as also the centre from which goes forth the new covenant of salvation, and this was historically fulfilled in the coming of Christ and the cradling of His Church in the Jewish Church. The continuity of the

yield her fruit, and the earth shall yield
her increase, and they shall be safe in
their land, and shall know that I *am* the
LORD, when I have broken the bands of
their yoke, and delivered them out of the
hand of those that served themselves of
them. (28) And they shall no more be a
prey to the heathen, neither shall the
beast of the land devour them; but they
shall dwell safely, and none shall make
them afraid. (29) And I will raise up for
them a [a]plant [1]of renown, and they shall
be no more [2]consumed with hunger in
the land, neither bear the shame of the
heathen any more. (30) Thus shall they
know that I the LORD their God *am*
with them, and *that* they, *even* the house
of Israel, *are* my people, saith the Lord
GOD. (31) And ye my [b]flock, the flock of
my pasture, *are* men, *and* I *am* your God,
saith the Lord GOD.

CHAPTER XXXV.—(1) Moreover the
word of the LORD came unto me, saying,
(2) Son of man, set thy face against
mount Seir, and prophesy against it,
(3) and say unto it, Thus saith the Lord
GOD;

Behold, O mount Seir, I *am* against
thee, and I will stretch out mine hand
against thee, and I will make thee [3]most
desolate. (4) I will lay thy cities waste,
and thou shalt be desolate, and thou
shalt know that I *am* the LORD.

(5) Because thou hast had a [4]perpetual
hatred, and hast [5]shed *the blood of* the
children of Israel by the [6]force of the
sword in the time of their calamity, in

a Isa. 11. 1; Jer. 23. 5.
1 Or, *for renown.*
2 Heb., *taken away.*
b John 10. 11.
3 Heb., *desolation and desolation.*
4 Or, *hatred of old.*
5 Heb., *poured out the children.*
6 Heb., *hands.*

Church was preserved quite as fully through the Christian era as through the Babylonian captivity, quite as large a number of the Jews having embraced Christianity as ever returned from the exile in Chaldea.

(29) **Will raise up for them a plant of renown.**—Better, *a plantation for renown.* The same Hebrew word occurs in chaps. xvii. 7, xxxi. 4, and means *plantation.* The thought is that God would provide Israel with such a fair and fruitful land as should make them famous for their blessings. The idea of the word is not that which seems to be implied by our version (with its marginal references to Isa. xi. 1; Jer. xxiii. 5), a plant or a branch, referring to the Messiah; a different word is used here, which occurs, besides the places named, only in Isa. lx. 21, lxi. 3, and Micah i. 6, in all of which it is translated *planting.*

(31) **The flock of my pasture.**—The chapter closes with the strongest and tenderest assurance that the object of its figurative language is to point out the renewed and close communion which is to come about between God and His people. They are to be His flock, and He is to be their God. Yet still, the vast and infinite distance between them is not left out of view, but rather brought prominently forward—they are men; He is God. They were not yet prepared to understand *how* this infinite chasm could be bridged over; only it should be by their shepherd David. We know that He was the Mediator, both God and man, thus uniting both in one.

XXXV.

This and the following chapter are closely connected: in fact, chaps. xxxv.—xxxvi. 15 form one continuous prophecy, while chap. xxxvi. 16—38 is another and distinct one, and the division of the chapters should have been made between them. The prophecy contains a denunciation of Mount Seir as the enemy of Israel (chap. xxxv.), and in contrast with this, a promise of the richest blessings upon the mountains of Israel. Ezekiel had already foretold the desolation of Edom (Mount Seir, chap. xxv. 12—17); but in the present prophecy this becomes a foil to set off the prosperity of Israel, and in fact, under the circumstances, a necessary element of that prosperity. Moreover, as in the last chapter Israel stood as the representative of the Church of God, so here Edom and Israel, while they stand in the foreground as actually existing nations, are yet evidently regarded in the Divine Word as representing, the one the kingdom of God, and the other all hostile powers of the world. This typical and symbolical way of looking at present things becomes increasingly prominent in all the latter part of Ezekiel.

(2) **Mount Seir.**—This poetical designation of the Edomites from the land which they inhabited is common in Scripture (Gen. xxxvi. 8, 9; Deut. ii. 1, 5; 1 Chron. iv. 42, &c.). The land included the whole mountainous region between the Dead Sea and the Elanitic Gulf, or eastern branch of the Red Sea. The earlier denunciation of the Edomites had in view their historical relations to Israel; this, on the other hand, as already said—like Isa. xxxiv., lxiii. 1-6—while still keeping this historical relation in view, regards them also as representative of the world's hostility to the covenant people of God. This appears from the fact that the desolation of Edom, itself but a small province, is put in contrast (verse 14) with the rejoicing of the whole earth, and that in chap. xxxvi. 5 (and generally verses 3—7) Edom is coupled with "the residue of the heathen." For the phrase "set thy face against," see chap. xiii. 17; and on verse 3, comp. chap. vi. 14.

(5) **Perpetual hatred.**—Enmity towards Israel is also imputed to the Ammonites, Moabites, and Philistines in chap. xxv.; but that of Edom was deeper and coëval with its first ancestor (see Gen. xxv. 22, &c., xxvii. 41); its peculiar malignity is noticed by Amos i. 11. (Comp. also Obad. 10—15.)

Shed the blood.—"Blood" is not in the original, and should be omitted. The verb means literally *to pour out,* and the clause should be rendered *hast scattered the children of Israel.* The same expression occurs in Ps. lxiii. 10; Jer. xviii. 21. The time specifically referred to is that of the overthrow of Jerusalem, as both that of their great "calamity" and that when "their iniquity had an end." (On the last phrase, see Note on chap. xxi. 29.) So the world-power generally, while it may fawn upon and corrupt the Church in the day of its prosperity, shows its undisguised hostility in every time of adversity.

the time *that their* iniquity *had* an end:
(6) therefore, *as* I live, saith the Lord
God, I will prepare thee unto blood, and
blood shall pursue thee: sith thou hast
not hated blood, even blood shall pursue
thee. (7) Thus will I make mount Seir
[1]most desolate, and cut off from it him
that passeth out and him that returneth.
(8) And I will fill his mountains with his
slain *men:* in thy hills, and in thy val-
leys, and in all thy rivers, shall they fall
that are slain with the sword. (9) I will
make thee perpetual desolations, and thy
cities shall not return: and ye shall know
that I *am* the Lord.

(10) Because thou hast said, These two
nations and these two countries shall be
mine, and we will [a]possess it; [2]whereas
the Lord was there: (11) therefore, *as* I
live, saith the Lord God, I will even do
according to thine anger, and according
to thine envy which thou hast used out
of thy hatred against them; and I will
make myself known among them, when
I have judged thee. (12) And thou shalt
know that I *am* the Lord, *and that* I
have heard all thy blasphemies which
thou hast spoken against the mountains
of Israel, saying, They are laid desolate,
they are given us [3]to consume. (13) Thus
with your mouth ye have [4]boasted
against me, and have multiplied your
words against me: I have heard *them.*
(14) Thus saith the Lord God; When the
whole earth rejoiceth, I will make thee
desolate. (15) As thou didst rejoice at
the inheritance of the house of Israel,
because it was desolate, so will I do unto
thee: thou shalt be desolate, O mount
Seir, and all Idumea, *even* all of it:
and they shall know that I *am* the
Lord.

CHAPTER XXXVI.—(1) Also, thou
son of man, prophesy unto the [b]moun-
tains of Israel, and say,

Ye mountains of Israel, hear the word
of the Lord: (2) Thus saith the Lord
God; Because the enemy hath said
against you, Aha, even the ancient high

1 Heb., *desolation and desolation.*

a Ps. 83. 4, 12.

2 Or, *though the Lord was there.*

3 Heb., *to devour.*

4 Heb., *magnified.*

b ch. 6. 2.

(6) **I will prepare thee unto blood.**—Rather, *I will make thee blood.* There is here a play upon the name of Edom in the original: I will make thee *dom* (= blood); Edom itself means *red.* The latter part of the verse brings out, as frequently, the congruity of the punishment: violence shall come upon him who has loved ("not hated") violence.

(7) **Him that passeth out.**—The cutting off of the traveller is a striking feature in the doom of Edom, for her nomadic tribes had been the great carriers between India and the East and Egypt, and she had grown rich by this commerce. The fierceness of the few tribes now wandering over the land make even the occasional visit of the curious traveller a matter of difficulty and danger.

(8) **Rivers.**—As elsewhere = river-courses, in which water was found only at times.

(10) **These two countries shall be mine.**—In verses 3—9 the sin charged upon Edom is its hatred of Israel; in verses 10—15, its desire to possess itself of Israel's inheritance. The *two* nations and countries are, of course, the two kingdoms of Israel and Judah.

Whereas the Lord was there.—This fact brings out the real sin. Edom desired Israel's possessions, not as it might have desired those of other nations, but knowing that this was the peculiar inheritance given by God to His people, and which it thought ought to have been given to itself as the elder branch, thus arraying itself in direct opposition to God.

(12) **Blasphemies.** — Rather, *reproaches.* These indeed became, under the circumstances, constructively blasphemies against God; but it is better not to push the meaning further than was intended.

(14) **The whole earth.**—This is taken by some writers—as, indeed, Hebrew usage very well allows—of the whole land, viz., of Israel. It seems better, however, to keep the sense of our version, for the thought is not confined to Edom. When all the earth shall rejoice in the salvation of God, and "the earth shall be full of the knowledge of the Lord," then Edom, the hostile power of the world, shall be desolate.

(15) **Because it was desolate.**—This is spoken of Israel; yet Israel was to preserve a remnant who should return to their land, and ultimately become the centre of the new covenant. So the desolation of Edom, though ultimately perpetual as far as its nationality is concerned, is not inconsistent with the fact foretold by Amos (chap. ix. 12), that a remnant even of Edom should at last be received into the Church.

All Idumea.—It is better to keep the uniform name of Edom. Idumea is essentially the same country, but is a more modern name, and when it came into use the boundaries had somewhat changed.

XXXVI.

The first fifteen verses of this chapter, as already noted, belong to chap. xxxv., and form part of the same prophecy.

(1) **The mountains of Israel.**—The word "mountains" is used for the land and people of Israel, to keep up the connection (by contrast) with the Mount Seir of the previous chapter. The personification is a strong one, by which the mountains represent the people as well as the land.

(2) **The ancient high places.**—This is very nearly the same expression as in Gen. xlix. 26; Deut. xxxiii. 15, where it is translated "everlasting (or lasting) hills," and is probably an allusion to those passages. "The enemy" is a general term, which may refer to Edom; but from the following verses it is more likely that it is used for the heathen at large. When Israel's land had been left desolate, the surrounding nations claimed that God's promise to His people had failed, and that they themselves might now enter upon its secure possession.

places are our's in possession: (3) there-
fore prophesy and say, Thus saith the
Lord God; [1] Because they have made *you*
desolate, and swallowed you up on every
side, that ye might be a possession unto
the residue of the heathen, and [2] ye are
taken up in the lips of talkers, and *are*
an infamy of the people: (4) therefore, ye
mountains of Israel, hear the word of the
Lord God; Thus saith the Lord God
to the mountains, and to the hills, to
the [3] rivers, and to the valleys, to the
desolate wastes, and to the cities that
are forsaken, which became a prey and
derision to the residue of the heathen
that *are* round about; (5) therefore thus
saith the Lord God; Surely in the fire
of my jealousy have I spoken against
the residue of the heathen, and against
all Idumea, which have appointed my
land into their possession with the joy
of all *their* heart, with despiteful minds,
to cast it out for a prey. (6) Prophesy
therefore concerning the land of Israel,
and say unto the mountains, and to the
hills, to the rivers, and to the valleys,
Thus saith the Lord God; Behold, I
have spoken in my jealousy and in my
fury, because ye have borne the shame
of the heathen: (7) therefore thus saith
the Lord God; I have lifted up mine
hand, Surely the heathen that *are* about
you, they shall bear their shame.
(8) But ye, O mountains of Israel, ye
shall shoot forth your branches, and
yield your fruit to my people of Israel;
for they are at hand to come. (9) For, be-
hold, I *am* for you, and I will turn unto
you, and ye shall be tilled and sown:
(10) and I will multiply men upon you,
all the house of Israel, *even* all of it:
and the cities shall be inhabited, and
the wastes shall be builded: (11) and I
will multiply upon you man and beast;
and they shall increase and bring fruit:
and I will settle you after your old es-
tates, and will do better *unto you* than
at your beginnings: and ye shall know
that I *am* the Lord. (12) Yea, I will
cause men to walk upon you, *even* my
people Israel; and they shall possess
thee, and thou shalt be their inheritance,
and thou shalt no more henceforth be-
reave them *of men*.
(13) Thus saith the Lord God; Because
they say unto you, Thou *land* devourest
up men, and hast bereaved thy nations;
(14) therefore thou shalt devour men no
more, neither [4] bereave thy nations any
more, saith the Lord God. (15) Neither

1 Heb., *Because for because.*

2 Or, *ye are made to come upon the lip of the tongue.*

3 Or, *bottoms*, or, *dales.*

4 Or, *cause to fall.*

---

(3) **In the lips of talkers, and are an infamy.**—A phrase equivalent to *a by-word and a reproach.* (Comp. Deut. xxviii. 37; 1 Kings ix. 7, &c.) In the previous clause the words, "have swallowed you up," should rather be "pant for you," the word being taken from the snuffing and panting of wild beasts. It was after this fashion that "the residue of the heathen," all those whom the conquests of Nebuchadnezzar had yet left, panted for the possession of the lands of Israel.

(5) **Idumea** = Edom, as in chap. xxxv. 15, where see Note. For "cast it out," in the last clause of the verse, read, *empty it out.* The idea of casting out a land for a prey is incongruous, and the other sense is admissible.

(7) **Lifted up mine hand.**—As in chap. xx. 6 = "I have sworn."

Shall bear their shame.—Comp. verse 6. The Israelites have been compelled to bear the reproaches of the heathen, but these now return upon themselves.

(8) **Shoot forth your branches.**—The land of Israel, represented by its mountains, is now to put forth its fruit, for the time is at hand when the people will return—a strong and vivid way of setting forth at once the certainty and the nearness of the return.

(11) **Will multiply upon you.**—The promises of abundant blessing of this, with the previous and following verses, certainly received a partial fulfilment at the time following the return from the exile, and in the subsequent Maccabean period; yet one cannot but feel that the language of promise, if taken only in a literal sense, goes far beyond the historic fulfilment, and hence that these earthly blessings are the shadow and type by which is set forth the higher spiritual blessing given to the Church without stint.

Settle you after your old estates.—This does not mean that particular families are to have again each their own former inheritance—though, doubtless, this was true, as far as circumstances allowed, of the comparatively small number of families who returned—but that they shall in general be settled and prosperous, as of old. And even this promise is eclipsed by the next clause: "I will do better unto you than at your beginnings," which can only be considered as fulfilled in the spiritual blessings, far higher and better than anything of earth, of the Messianic kingdom.

(13) **Thou land devourest up men.**—Comp. Num. xiii. 32, a passage probably in the prophet's mind, though he uses it for a different reason. Israel had so often sinned, and so often, in consequence, suffered the Divine punishments, that the heathen, not recognising the true cause, superstitiously attributed the result to something in the land itself.

With the promises of this chapter comp. Isa. liv. 1—8. It is impossible to interpret that passage otherwise than of spiritual blessings; and Ezekiel, as a devout Jew, as well as a prophet, was thoroughly penetrated with the same hopes as are there expressed by the evangelic prophet.

(15) **Cause . . . to fall.**—In the last four verses there is a delicate play upon words which cannot well be expressed in English. Two verbs are used, each of them twice ("bereave" in verse 14 should be *cause*

will I cause *men* to hear in thee the
shame of the heathen any more, neither
shalt thou bear the reproach of the
people any more, neither shalt thou
cause thy nations to fall any more, saith
the Lord God.
(16) Moreover the word of the Lord
came unto me, saying,
(17) Son of man, when the house of
Israel dwelt in their own land, they de-
filed it by their own way and by their
doings: their way was before me as the
uncleanness of a removed woman.
(18) Wherefore I poured my fury upon
them for the blood that they had shed
upon the land, and for their idols *where-
with* they had polluted it: (19) and I
scattered them among the heathen, and
they were dispersed through the
countries: according to their way and
according to their doings I judged them.
(20) And when they entered unto the
heathen, whither they went, they [a] pro-
faned my holy name, when they said to
them, These *are* the people of the Lord,
and are gone forth out of his land.
(21) But I had pity for mine holy name,
which the house of Israel had profaned
among the heathen, whither they went.
(22) Therefore say unto the house of
Israel, Thus saith the Lord God; I do
not *this* for your sakes, O house of
Israel, but for mine holy name's sake,
which ye have profaned among the

[a] Isa. 52. 5; Rom. 2. 24.

---

to fall, as in margin), one of them meaning to *bereave*, the other to *cause to fall*; and these verbs have the same radical letters, but with the first two of them transposed.

In reviewing this whole prophecy (chaps. xxxv.—xxxvi. 15), it is evident that the time had in view by the prophet was one in which Edom still existed as a nation, and was rejoicing in the fall of Israel. It cannot, therefore, look forward to any literal, but still future, accomplishment, since Edom, as a nation, has long since disappeared; and no future people, occupying the same territory or bearing the same name, could possibly sustain the same historic relations to Israel as are here attributed to Edom. Whatever, therefore, is to be literally understood in the prophecy must have been long ago fulfilled. And this was much. Israel was restored to its land, and there greatly multiplied, so that the country became for ages one of the most fertile and prosperous in Asia. At the same time, the sinfulness of the people, as of old, hindered the fulness of blessing that was within their reach. But a small part of them availed themselves of the opportunity to return to their land; and they who did so suffered themselves so to live that when the crowning blessing of the ages was fulfilled in the coming of the Messiah, the mass of the nation rejected and crucified Him. The blessings promised were fulfilled literally as far as the sinfulness of the people allowed; but inasmuch as these prevented anything like the full realisation of the terms of the prophecy, and as no future realisation of these is possible, on account of the total change of conditions and circumstances, it is plain that under these earthly terms the prophet, like his predecessors, Isaiah and the others, sets forth the glories of the spiritual future, and uses earthly blessings as the types of those better ones which are heavenly.

Verses 16—38 constitute a separate prophecy, but one closely connected with that which has gone before. It is here declared that Israel has been scattered among the heathen because they had defiled the land by their sin (verses 16—19); then, that although they had yet further profaned God's name among the heathen, He yet had pity for that name's sake (verses 20—23); and, accordingly, that He will gather and restore Israel, cleansing them from their sins, and giving them a heart to keep His commandments (verses 24—32); and in consequence of this change that He will greatly bless them (verses 35—38). The great point of the prophecy is the moral change foretold in verses 25—27, 31.

(17) **They defiled it.**—In verses 17—20 the sin of Israel in the past is set forth as the reason of their present condition. "The land" is always regarded in Scripture as peculiarly consecrated to God, and defiled by the sin of the people. (Comp. Lev. xviii. 28; Num. xxxv. 34.) The comparison is with a woman who has been set apart for uncleanness (Lev. xv. 19), who until her purification was not allowed to come into the sanctuary.

(20) **When they said to them.**—We are not here to understand that the Israelites profaned God's name among the heathen in the way spoken of in Rom. ii. 24, though this also may have been done; but they profaned it by the very fact of their captivity, the consequence of their former sins. The heathen regarded Jehovah as merely the national God of the Israelites, and seeing them dispersed, in distress, and in captivity, concluded that He was unable to protect them. Hence, for the vindication of His name (verses 21—24) God would restore His people to their land.

(21) **Pity for mine holy name.**—The meaning of this has been already explained in the Note on the previous verse; and in the following verses it is emphasised that God would restore His people, not for their sakes, but for His own.

(22) **Not . . . for your sakes, . . . but for mine holy name's sake.**—Comp. Exod. xxxii; Num. xiv.; Deut. ix. This is the constant burden of God's teaching to His people throughout their history. Hence it is an idle objection to the Scripture narrative that it represents Israel as the favourite of heaven, and is thus just like the human legends of every other ancient nation. In fact, this narrative is unlike any other. It speaks of God as having chosen one nation as the means of accomplishing His purpose for the salvation of the whole world, but continually chastising them for their sins, again and again setting aside the mass of them, and restoring and purifying and blessing a remnant, not for their own sake, but for the accomplishment of His own holy purpose and promise, thus sanctifying His name.

heathen, whither ye went. (23) And I
will sanctify my great name, which was
profaned among the heathen, which ye
have profaned in the midst of them;
and the heathen shall know that I *am*
the LORD, saith the Lord GOD, when I
shall be sanctified in you before [1] their
eyes. (24) For I will take you from
among the heathen, and gather you out
of all countries, and will bring you into
your own land. (25) Then will I sprinkle
clean water upon you, and ye shall be
clean: from all your filthiness, and
from all your idols, will I cleanse you.
(26) A [a] new heart also will I give you,
and a new spirit will I put within you:
and I will take away the stony heart
out of your flesh, and I will give you an
heart of flesh. (27) And I will put my
[b] spirit within you, and cause you to
walk in my statutes, and ye shall keep
my judgments, and do *them.* (28) And
ye shall dwell in the land that I gave to
your fathers; and ye shall be my people,
and I will be your God. (29) I will also
save you from all your uncleannesses:
and I will call for the corn, and will in-
crease it, and lay no famine upon you.
(30) And I will multiply the fruit of the
tree, and the increase of the field, that
ye shall receive no more reproach of
famine among the heathen. (31) Then
shall ye remember your own evil ways,
and your doings that *were* not good, and
shall lothe yourselves in your own sight
for your iniquities and for your abomi-
nations. (32) Not for your sakes do I
this, saith the Lord GOD, be it known
unto you: be ashamed and confounded
for your own ways, O house of Israel.

(33) Thus saith the Lord GOD; In the
day that I shall have cleansed you from
all your iniquities I will also cause *you*
to dwell in the cities, and the wastes
shall be builded. (34) And the desolate
land shall be tilled, whereas it lay deso-
late in the sight of all that passed by.
(35) And they shall say, This land that
was desolate is become like the garden
of [c] Eden; and the waste and desolate
and ruined cities *are become* fenced, *and*
are inhabited. (36) Then the heathen
that are left round about you shall know
that I the LORD build the ruined *places,*
and plant that that was desolate: I [d] the
LORD have spoken *it*, and I will do *it.*

(37) Thus saith the Lord GOD; I will
yet *for* this be enquired of by the house

1 Or, *your.*

a Jer. 32. 39; ch. 11. 19.

b ch. 11. 19.

c ch. 28. 13.

d ch. 17. 24, & 22. 14, & 37. 14.

---

(23) **Before their eyes.**—The Hebrew text as it stands has *your* eyes, as in the margin. Many manuscripts and other authorities have *their*. Either of them admits of an excellent sense; but the reading *your* brings out the important truth that God must first be sanctified in the eyes of the people themselves by their repentance and moral reformation, and then, through them and the consequent blessing upon them, He will be sanctified in the eyes of the heathen also.

(25) **Sprinkle clean water.**—Comp. Heb. ix. 13, x. 22. Ezekiel, the priest, here refers to those manifold purifications of the Law (*e.g.*, Num. viii. 7, xix. 9, 17; Lev. xiv. 5—7, 9, &c.) which were performed by means of water; yet he refers to these as a whole, in their symbolical signification, rather than to any one of them in particular. He speaks primarily of the cleansing from idolatry and such gross outward sins, and he treats of the people collectively; yet this purification, as the following verses show, must necessarily extend much farther, and be applied to them individually. It was the same symbolism which led in later ages to the use of baptism in the admission of proselytes to the Jewish Church, a practice adopted by the forerunner of our Lord in the preparation of the people for His coming. Baptism is also alluded to by our Lord Himself in His conversation with Nicodemus (John iii. 5.) and afterwards established by Him as the initiatory sacrament of the Christian Church. (Comp. Eph. v. 26; Titus iii. 5; Heb. x. 22.)

(26) **A new heart.**—Comp. chap. xi. 18—20, where the same promise is given, although somewhat less fully than here. On the expression "heart of flesh," see Note there on verse 19. With this prophetic preaching of the Gospel comp. Jer. xxxi. 31—34, and particularly the connection of that passage with the temporal promises in its continuation (verses 35—40).

(28) **Ye shall dwell in the land.**—The Israelites were not yet able to seek the spiritual, except as connected with the temporal blessing; and, indeed, the temporal was, in the ordering of Providence, a necessary means to the spiritual. Therefore the promise of earthly restoration must yet be made, and must in due time be literally fulfilled.

(29) **Your uncleannesses.**—In verse 25 they had already been made clean, and in verse 26 a new heart had been given them; why, then, was there yet further need of cleansing? This cannot, therefore, refer to the idolatries from which they had been already purged, but is plain enough if understood of that ordinary sinfulness of man which, being continually renewed, needs continual forgiveness.

(31) **Shall lothe yourselves.**—Comp. Note on chap. xx. 43.

(32) **Not for your sakes.**—See verse 22.

(35) **Like the garden of Eden.**—This may be meant merely to describe the exceeding excellence and prosperity of the land; but, in connection with what has been previously said, it seems rather to point forward to that state in which man shall again be entirely freed from sin, which has been the state for which the Church in all ages has been preparing.

(37) **I will yet for this be enquired of.**—Comp. chaps. xiv. 3, 4, xx. 3. Formerly God refused to be inquired of by a people whose hearts were far from Him; now that He has given them a new heart He is ready to hear them.

of Israel, to do *it* for them; I will in-
crease them with men like a flock.
(38) As the [1]holy flock, as the flock of
Jerusalem in her solemn feasts; so
shall the waste cities be filled with flocks
of men: and they shall know that I *am*
the LORD.

CHAPTER XXXVII.—(1) The hand
of the LORD was upon me, and carried
me out in the spirit of the LORD, and
set me down in the midst of the valley
which *was* full of bones, (2) and caused
me to pass by them round about: and,
behold, *there were* very many in the open
[2]valley; and, lo, *they were* very dry.
(3) And he said unto me, Son of man, can
these bones live? And I answered, O
Lord GOD, thou knowest.
(4) Again he said unto me, Prophesy
upon these bones, and say unto them, O
ye dry bones, hear the word of the LORD.
(5) Thus saith the Lord GOD unto these
bones; Behold, I will cause breath to
enter into you, and ye shall live:
(6) and I will lay sinews upon you, and
will bring up flesh upon you, and cover
you with skin, and put breath in you,
and ye shall live; and ye shall know
that I *am* the LORD.
(7) So I prophesied as I was commanded:
and as I prophesied, there was a noise,
and behold a shaking, and the bones
came together, bone to his bone. (8) And
when I beheld, lo, the sinews and the
flesh came up upon them, and the skin
covered them above: but *there was* no
breath in them.
(9) Then said he unto me, Prophesy
unto the [3]wind, prophesy, son of man,

1 Heb., *flock of holy things.*

B.C. cir. 587.

2 Or, *champaign.*

3 Or, *breath.*

---

(38) **The flock of Jerusalem.**—The comparison is with the vast flocks of sacrificial animals accustomed to be carried to Jerusalem at the great annual feasts. The object is to give a vivid idea of the numbers of the people, but there is an especial appropriateness in the simile from the fact that these flocks were devoted to the Lord.

XXXVII.

This chapter consists of two distinct communications. In the first (verses 1—14) the prophet sees a vision, and is directed in consequence to utter a prophecy; in the second (verses 15—28) he is told to perform a symbolical act, and explain its meaning to the people. There is a close connection between the two, and also between the latter and the two following chapters. In verses 1—10, Ezekiel, in a vision, sees a plain full of bones and is directed to prophecy to them; in consequence of which they come together, are clothed with flesh, and become alive. In verses 11—14, the vision is expressly explained to mean that the children of Israel, in their scattered and apparently hopeless condition, shall yet be brought together again and restored to national life. The vision is not at all concerned with the future resurrection; and yet it may well be thought that the idea of this was familiar to the mind of the people, as otherwise the prophet would hardly have chosen such a simile.

The course of thought in the later prophecy and its connection with what follows will be explained in its place.

(1) **In the midst of the valley.**—The word is the same as in chaps. iii. 22, viii. 4, and having the definite article prefixed, is very probably the same plain, now seen in spirit, in which Ezekiel had seen his former visions.

Which was full of bones.—It is better, with the Hebrew, to put a stop after "plain" (valley), and then read, *this was full of bones.* The bones, as the subsequent verses show, were not heaped together, but thickly strewn upon the face of the plain. After the prophet's mind had so long dwelt upon the desolating campaigns of Nebuchadnezzar, these ghastly reminders of the loss of human life might naturally enter into his thoughts.

(2) **Very dry**—as showing that it was a long time since life had left them, and that the possibility of their living again was far removed.

(3) **Can these bones live?**—The question is put to the prophet in order to emphasise the human impossibility of that which is immediately brought about by the Divine omnipotence. (Comp. Matt. ix. 5, 6.) It was precisely this teaching which the people needed. As they had formerly refused to believe his announcements of impending judgment, so now that this had come, they were utterly incredulous in regard to his declarations of future blessing. It seemed to them impossible, and what they needed to be taught was that "what is impossible with man is possible with God."

Thou knowest.—The prophet sees the natural impossibility, yet perceives that there must be some deeper reason for the question, and therefore replies in these words. It may be, too, that the question thus asked, before its object is suggested, connected itself in his mind with the thought of the literal resurrection of the dead and the difficulties it suggests.

(4) **Prophesy upon these bones.**—"Prophesy" is here used (as frequently) in its original sense of "speak on God's behalf," and does not convey the idea of *prediction.*

(5) **Breath.**—The three words, "breath," "wind," and "spirit," are represented in the Hebrew by the same word, and the context must determine which sense is intended. Similarly in Greek there is the same word for the last two of these. (Comp. John iii. 5—8.)

(8) **No breath in them.**—The restoration of the dry bones to life is described as taking place in two stages, with evident reference to the record of the creation of man in Gen. ii. 7. In the first, they are restored to perfect form, but yet without life; in the second, they receive breath and become "living creatures," as in Gen. i. 20, 21, 24, ii. 7, in all which the same expression is used.

(9) **Upon these slain.**—The word is used designedly. The bones which Ezekiel had seen were those not merely of dead, but of slain men; and in this was

and say to the wind, Thus saith the
Lord God; Come from the four winds,
O breath, and breathe upon these slain,
that they may live. (10) So I prophesied
as he commanded me, and the breath
came into them, and they lived, and
stood up upon their feet, an exceeding
great army.

(11) Then he said unto me, Son of man,
these bones are the whole house of Israel:
behold, they say, Our bones are dried,
and our hope is lost: we are cut off for
our parts. (12) Therefore prophesy and
say unto them, Thus saith the Lord
God; Behold, O my people, I will open
your graves, and cause you to come up
out of your graves, and bring you into
the land of Israel. (13) And ye shall
know that I *am* the Lord, when I have
opened your graves, O my people, and
brought you up out of your graves,
(14) and shall put my spirit in you, and
ye shall live, and I shall place you in
your own land: then shall ye know that
I the Lord have spoken *it*, and performed
it, saith the Lord.

(15) The word of the Lord came again
unto me, saying, (16) Moreover, thou son
of man, take thee one stick, and write
upon it, For Judah, and for the children
of Israel his companions: then take
another stick, and write upon it, For
Joseph, the stick of Ephraim, and *for*
all the house of Israel his companions:
(17) and join them one to another into
one stick; and they shall become one in
thine hand.

(18) And when the children of thy
people shall speak unto thee, saying,
Wilt thou not shew us what thou
meanest by these? (19) Say unto them,
Thus saith the Lord God; Behold, I
will take the stick of Joseph, which *is*
in the hand of Ephraim, and the tribes
of Israel his fellows, and will put them
with him, *even* with the stick of Judah,

---

their likeness to Israel: as desolated, and their nationality for the time destroyed by their enemies.

(11) **Are the whole house of Israel.**—This Divine interpretation of the vision leaves no doubt of its meaning. Whatever other sense might possibly be attached to its language, there can be no uncertainty as to that which the Spirit intended. The last clause of the verse, "cut off for our parts," is obscure in the English, but in the original is simply *for us—i.e.*, "as for us, we are cut off."

(12) **Open your graves.**—In verse 2 it is said that the bones were "in the open valley," literally, *upon the face of the valley*. This was a necessity of the vision, in order that they might be seen; now the people, whom the bones represented, are spoken of as in *graves*, since this was the normal and proper place for the dead.

(14) **Put my spirit in you.**—Here, as throughout this series of prophecies, the moral resurrection of the people and their restoration to their own land are intimately associated together. The former was at once the necessary condition of the latter, and would also be its consequence in a still higher development. Compare a similar association of the spiritual with the literal resurrection in John v. 21—29.

Verses 15—28 constitute another prophecy, which probably was given very soon after the former, since there is a close connection between the two. In the former, under the figure of the revival of the dry bones, God had set forth His power to accomplish the promise He made of the spiritual resurrection of Israel; in the latter. He adds to this the specific declaration of what had been before only implied, that the two long-severed nations of Israel shall be re-united and prosperous under the rule of the future David, while He Himself will dwell among them, and they shall be obedient to Him. These promises prepare the way for the prophecy of the great and final attack of the enemies of the Church (chaps. xxxviii., xxxix.) and their overthrow by the power of God. The promise of this prophecy is first set forth by a symbolic action (verses 15—17), which is then to be explained to the people (verses 18—20), as in the case of the vision (verse 11), and then the promises of blessing follow.

(16) **One stick . . . another stick.**—These are not rods, as in Num. xvii. 6—9, although Ezekiel may have had that event in mind; the word here is an entirely different one, and means simply a piece of wood. The two pieces were, no doubt, so shaped that being firmly held together they would appear as one.

For Judah, and for the children of Israel his companions.—The object is to represent by the two pieces of wood the two kingdoms. It would be insufficient, therefore, to mention Judah only; for with him Benjamin had been always associated, and also considerable fragments of the other tribes, (2 Chron. xi. 16, xv. 9). After the fall of the northern kingdom, individual members of the ten tribes who had not been carried into captivity joined themselves more or less completely to the kingdom of Judah (2 Chron. xxx. 11—18, xxxi. 1).

For Joseph, the stick of Ephraim.—Joseph, as including the two great tribes of Ephraim and Manasseh, is put for the whole of the ten tribes, and Ephraim is specified as being the leading tribe, and this makes necessary the addition, "and all the house of Israel his companions," to show that the whole northern kingdom is included. The word *for*, in italics, should be omitted.

(19) **Which is in the hand of Ephraim.**—Again Joseph is put for the whole ten tribes, and again it is indicated that the control of these was chiefly with Ephraim. The human power, which led to and perpetuated the division, is in contrast with the "mine hand," where all shall be re-united under Divine rule.

Will put them.—Grammatically the plural pronoun "them" refers to the piece of wood, which is in the sin-

and make them one stick, and they
shall be one in mine hand. (20) And the
sticks whereon thou writest shall be in
thine hand before their eyes. (21) And
say unto them, Thus saith the Lord
God;

Behold, I will take the children of
Israel from among the heathen, whither
they be gone, and will gather them on
every side, and bring them into their
own land: (22) and I will make them one
nation in the land upon the mountains
of Israel; and [a]one king shall be king
to them all: and they shall be no more
two nations, neither shall they be divided
into two kingdoms any more at all:
(23) neither shall they defile themselves
any more with their idols, nor with their
detestable things, nor with any of their
transgressions: but I will save them out
of all their dwellingplaces, wherein they
have sinned, and will cleanse them: so
shall they be my people, and I will be
their God.

(24) And [b]David my servant *shall be*
king over them; and they all shall have
one shepherd: they shall also walk in
my judgments, and observe my statutes,
and do them. (25) And they shall dwell
in the land that I have given unto Jacob
my servant, wherein your fathers have
dwelt; and they shall dwell therein,
even they, and their children, and their
children's children for ever: and my
servant David *shall be* their prince for
ever.

(26) Moreover I will make a [c]covenant
of peace with them; it shall be an ever-
lasting covenant with them: and I will
place them, and multiply them, and will set
my [d]sanctuary in the midst of them for
evermore. (27) My tabernacle also shall

a John 10. 16.

b Isa. 40. 11; Jer. 23. 5, & 30. 9; ch. 34. 23.

c Ps. 89. 3; ch. 34. 25.

d 2 Cor. 6. 16.

---

gular; but the construction is according to the sense, the wood representing the ten tribes.

(20) **Before their eyes.**—The symbolical action was not only to be performed before the people, but the united wood was to remain in the prophet's hand, while he unfolded to them the Divine promise. That promise is essentially a repetition of chaps. xxxiv. 11—31 and xxxvi. 22—30.

(21) **Will gather them.**—The restoration of Israel from their captivity among the heathen here, as often elsewhere, is the first step in the fulfilment of the Divine promises. This, however, like the other Divine promises, was fulfilled only to a "remnant," a course which, as St. Paul shows in Rom. ix., had been foreseen and foretold from the first. A fulfilment on a larger scale was perpetually prevented by the sins of the people; God did for them all that their obdurate disobedience would allow Him to do. Yet He did not wholly reject them, but allowed a remnant to keep alive His Church, and become the channel of those richer blessings of the new covenant, in which all who will accept His salvation are united in a holier bond, and led to a land of higher promise than Israel after the flesh could ever know.

(23) **Out of all their dwellingplaces.**—This expression can hardly refer to their places of exile and temporary sojourn among the heathen, since these were not especially the places where they had sinned. Their sins were rather committed in their own land; the "lands of their captivity" were the places where those sins were punished. "Their dwellingplaces" is then to be understood of their own land of Canaan, where they had been led into idolatry and all abominations by the heathen dwelling among them; and the promise is that this land shall be purged, that all evil shall be cast out from it, and the people delivered from the temptations by which they had hitherto been overcome.

(24) **David my servant.**—Here, as in chap. xxxiv. 23, 24, David personally is described as their one king and shepherd. (See the Note there.)

(25) **For ever.**—Strong emphasis is placed upon this declaration by its frequent repetition. In this verse, the occupancy of the land is to be for ever, and the kingship of David is to be for ever; and in verses 26 and 28 the sanctuary is to be "in the midst of them for evermore," and the covenant of peace is to be "an everlasting covenant." Such promises are taken up continually in the New Testament, and explained of the everlasting reign of the King of kings, the Good Shepherd, over His people, and of the Temple of the Holy Ghost in the heart of the believer.

(26) **Multiply them.**—In accordance with what has gone before, comes this promise of the great increase of the spiritual Israel. Even John the Baptist had said, "God is able of these stones to raise up children unto Abraham"; but our Lord more emphatically taught that the true children of Abraham were those who followed Him (John viii. 39, &c.); while His Apostle St. Paul explains repeatedly, and at length, that Abraham was the father of all those who walk in his faith, whether they be of the circumcision or the uncircumcision (Rom. iv. 12, &c.); and again, "that they which are of faith, the same are the children of Abraham" (Gal. iii. 7). Thus was fulfilled the promise that he should be "the father of many nations" (Gen. xvii. 5, interpreted in Rom. iv. 17), and in the same way also was to be fulfilled the present promise of the multiplication of the seed of Israel.

(27) **My tabernacle also.**—Compare the whole promise of this verse with 2 Cor. vi. 16: "Ye are the temple of the living God; as God hath said, I will dwell in them, and walk in them: and I will be their God, and they shall be my people." This promise of "a sanctuary in the midst of them *for evermore*" was in type and shadow set before the eyes of the people with the restoration of the Temple of Zerubbabel; but in its reality began to be fulfilled at the incarnation of the Son of God, of whom it is said by St. John (chap. i. 14) that "He dwelt (literally, *tabernacled*) among us," and is continued by the indwelling of the Holy Spirit in the hearts of believers (1 Cor. iii. 16, vi. 19); while it is to receive its final consummation in that future when the tabernacle of God shall be with men, and "the Lord God Almighty and the Lamb are the temple" of the heavenly Jerusalem (Rev. xxi. 3—22). See Excursus F at end of this book.

be with them: yea, I will be [a]their God,
and they shall be my people. (28) And
the heathen shall know that I the LORD
do sanctify Israel, when my sanctuary
shall be in the midst of them for ever-
more.

CHAPTER XXXVIII.—(1) And the
word of the LORD came unto me, saying,
(2) Son of man, set thy face against [b]Gog,
the land of Magog, [1]the chief prince of
Meshech and Tubal, and prophesy against
him, (3) and say, Thus saith the Lord
GOD; Behold, I *am* against thee, O Gog,
the chief prince of Meshech and Tubal:
(4) and I will turn thee back, and put
[c]hooks into thy jaws, and I will bring
thee forth, and all thine army, horses
and horsemen, all of them clothed with
all sorts *of armour*, *even* a great company
with bucklers and shields, all of them
handling swords: (5) Persia, Ethiopia,
and [2]Libya with them; all of them with
shield and helmet: (6) Gomer, and all his

a ch. 11. 20, & 14. 11.

b Rev. 20. 8.

1 Or, *prince of the chief.*

c ch. 39. 2.

2 Or, *Phut.*

XXXVIII.

Chapters xxxviii. and xxxix. form one continuous prophecy, divided into four main parts by the renewed command to the prophet, "Son of man" (chaps. xxxviii. 1, 14, xxxix. 1, 17), and these again into smaller divisions by the repetition of the form, "Thus saith the Lord" (chaps. xxxviii. 3, 10, 14, 17, xxxix. 1, 5, 8, 10, 13, 17, 20, 25). The whole passage is to be looked upon as one sustained prophetic parable, in which vividness and force are given to the truth the prophet would set forth by the introduction of so many concrete details that one would be tempted to understand them literally, were it not that they carry within themselves the evidence that they were not so intended. The general meaning will be better understood after considering such obscurities as occur in the names mentioned and in the language used, and is therefore deferred to the Excursus G at the end of this book. Meantime, the details of both chapters may be very rapidly examined.

It is to be remembered that this prophecy immediately follows chap. xxxvii., in which God's people are represented as united in one fold, purified from their sins, and dwelling in perpetual covenant with Him, under the care of His "servant David." It is also not to be forgotten that a final conflict is described in Rev. xx. 7—10 between the saints and their enemies, under the names of Gog and Magog, in which those enemies, as here, are destroyed by the immediate Divine interposition.

(2) **Gog, the land of Magog.**—"Magog" is mentioned in Gen. x. 2 (1 Chron. i. 5) in connection with Gomer (the Cimmerians) and Madai (the Medes), as the name of a people descended from Japhet. Early Jewish tradition, adopted by Josephus and St. Jerome, identifies them with the Scythians; and this view has seemed probable to nearly all modern expositors. But the name of Scythians must be understood rather in a geographical than in a strictly ethnological sense, of the tribes living north of the Caucasus. Driven from their original home by the Massagetæ, they had poured down upon Asia Minor and Syria shortly before the time of Ezekiel, and had advanced even as far as Egypt. They took Sardis (B.C. 629), spread themselves in Media (B.C. 624), were bribed off from Egypt by Psammeticus, and were finally driven back (B.C. 596), leaving their name as a terror to the whole eastern world for their fierce skill in war, their cruelty, and rapacity. It was probably the memory of their recent disastrous inroads that led Ezekiel to the selection of their name as the representative of the powers hostile to the Church of God.

The name Gog occurs only in connection with Magog, except in 1 Chron. v. 4, as the name of an otherwise unknown Reubenite. It is also the reading of the Samaritan and Septuagint in Num. xxiv. 7 for Agag. It has generally been supposed that Ezekiel here formed the name from Magog by dropping the first syllable, which was thought to mean simply *place* or *land;* but an Assyrian inscription has been discovered, in which *Ga-a-gi* is mentioned as a chief of the Saka (Scythians), and Mr. Geo. Smith ("Hist. of Assurbanipal") identifies this name with Gog. The text should be read, *Gog, of the land of Magog.*

The chief prince of Meshech and Tubal.—Rather, *the prince of Rosh, Meshech, and Tubal.* Our version has followed St. Jerome in translating *Rosh* "chief," because formerly no people of that name was definitely known; but they are frequently mentioned by Arabic writers as a Scythian tribe dwelling in the Taurus, although the attempt to derive from them the name of *Russian* cannot be considered as sufficiently supported. In Rev. xx. 8, Gog and Magog are both symbolic names of nations. For Meshech and Tubal see Note on chap. xxvii. 13.

(3) **The chief prince.**—As in verse 2, the prince of Rosh.

(4) **I will turn thee back.**—This is the more common meaning of the word; but if this meaning be retained here, it is not to be taken in the sense of turning back from the holy land, but rather, in connection with the figure of the next clause, of turning away the wild beast from his natural inclination to the fulfilment of God's purpose. It is better, however, to take it in the sense in which it is used in Isa. xlvii. 10 (perverted) and Jer. viii. 5 (slidden back; comp. chap. l. 6), "I will lead thee astray." In Rev. xx. 8, this leading astray of the nations is ascribed to Satan, just as in 2 Sam. xxiv. 1, God, and in 1 Chron. xxi. 1, Satan, are said to move David to number the people; in either case God is said to do that which He allows to be done by Satan. For the same Divine gathering of the nations against God's people see Joel iii. 2; Zech. xiv. 2, 3.

Hooks into thy jaws.—See the same figure in chap. xxix. 4.

(5) **Persia, Ethiopia, and Libya.**—Having summoned the nations from the extreme north, the prophet now turns first to the east, and then to the south and west. No neighbouring nations are mentioned at all, but only those living on the confines of the known world are summoned to this symbolic contest. The supposition of a literal alliance of nations so situated is out of the question.

(6) **Gomer . . . Togarmah.**—Again the address turns to the extreme north. Gomer, like Magog, a

bands; the house of Togarmah of the
north quarters, and all his bands: *and*
many people with thee. (7) Be thou pre-
pared, and prepare for thyself, thou, and
all thy company that are assembled unto
thee, and be thou a guard unto them.
(8) After many days thou shalt be visited:
in the latter years thou shalt come into
the land *that is* brought back from the
sword, *and is* gathered out of many
people, against the mountains of Israel,
which have been always waste: but it is
brought forth out of the nations, and
they shall dwell safely all of them.
(9) Thou shalt ascend and come like a
storm, thou shalt be like a cloud to
cover the land, thou, and all thy bands,
and many people with thee.

(10) Thus saith the Lord God; It shall
also come to pass, *that* at the same time
shall things come into thy mind, and
thou shalt [1] think an evil thought: (11) and
thou shalt say, I will go up to the land
of unwalled villages; I will go to them
that are at rest, that dwell [2] safely, all of
them dwelling without walls, and having
neither bars nor gates, (12) [3] to take a spoil,
and to take a prey; to turn thine hand
upon the desolate places *that are now*
inhabited, and upon the people *that are*
gathered out of the nations, which have
gotten cattle and goods, that dwell in
the [4] midst of the land. (13) Sheba, and
Dedan, and the merchants of Tarshish,
with all the young lions thereof, shall
say unto thee, Art thou come to take a
spoil? hast thou gathered thy company
to take a prey? to carry away silver and
gold, to take away cattle and goods, to
take a great spoil? (14) Therefore, son
of man, prophesy and say unto Gog,
Thus saith the Lord God; In that day
when my people of Israel dwelleth safely,
shalt thou not know *it?* (15) And thou
shalt come from thy place out of the
north parts, thou, and many people with
thee, all of them riding upon horses, a
great company, and a mighty army:

1 Or, *conceive a mischievous purpose.*

2 Or, *confidently.*

3 Heb., *to spoil the spoil, and to prey the prey.*

4 Heb., *navel.*

---

people descended from Japheth (Gen. x. 2; 1 Chron. i. 5), is identified with the Cimmerians; and for the house of Togarmah, the Armenians, see Note on xxvii. 14. In the last clause of the verse, *people* should be in the plural. This was to be a general gathering of the strength of the world against the Church of God.

(7) **Be thou a guard unto them.**—Every preparation is to be made on the part of Gog and the nations, and then Gog himself is to be their guard, or to control and guide the assault.

(8) **After many days thou shalt be visited.**—This clause has been variously interpreted. The expression "after many days" is the common one to indicate that what is predicted is yet far in the future, and corresponds to the "latter years" of the next clause. The words "thou shalt be visited" are the usual form of expressing a coming judgment. Various ingenious attempts have been made, with no great success, to give the words a different sense here. The supposed difficulty arises from not observing that the whole course of Gog is here viewed together as a single transaction. It is not merely his ultimate destruction, but the steps which led to it, his hostile attacks upon the Church, which are represented as brought about under God's providence and forming a part of the visitation upon him. It is as if one spoke now of a man's whole career of sin as a Divine visitation upon the sinner in consequence of his neglect of proffered grace, instead of speaking only of his ultimate punishment.

The land.—Rather, *a land.* Judæa had been long desolated, but was now restored. The word *people* here, as in verse 6, is in the plural and marks the gathering back, not from one, but from many quarters.

Always waste.—Literally, *continually waste.* The mountains of Israel had been by no means *always* waste, but during the period of the captivity had been so constantly. Yet the word is commonly used for a relatively long period, for which the time of the captivity seems too short. It may therefore, with the dispersion among "many peoples" of the previous clause, indicate the time of the later and longer continued dispersion of the Jews. In the last clause "shall dwell" is not to be taken as a future, but as a description of the existing condition of the people.

(10) **Think an evil thought.**—In verses 10—14 the motives of Gog in his attack upon Israel are fully exposed. It is to be remembered that in verse 4, and again in verse 16, the leading of this foe against the Church is represented as God's own act; here it is explained that God did this by allowing him to follow out the devices of his own heart.

(11) **The land of unwalled villages.**—Again, omit the definite article before *land,* as in verse 8. The description of a people living in prosperity and security looks quite beyond anything hitherto realised in the history of the Jews, and points to such a state of things as is described in Zech. ii. 4, 5. The description of the attack of Gog and Magog in Rev. xx. 9 corresponds to this.

(12) **In the midst of the land.**—Literally, *in the navel of the earth.* (See Note on chap. v. 5.) The important position of Israel in reference to the other nations of the earth combined with its unsuspecting security and its riches to tempt the cupidity of Gog and his allies,

(13) **Sheba, and Dedan . . . . Tarshish.**—The first two are districts of Arabia, and the last is probably the Tartessus in Spain. These names seem to be added to those of verses 5, 6, to show that all the nations of the world sympathise in this attack upon the Church.

(14) **Shalt thou not know it?**—The second part of this prophecy (verses 14—23), describing the doom of Gog, is introduced (verses 14—16) with a repetition of the peaceful security of Israel, and of God's leading against her this great foe in whose destruction He shall be magnified before all people. The whole

(16) and thou shalt come up against my
people of Israel, as a cloud to cover the
land; it shall be in the latter days, and
I will bring thee against my land, that
the heathen may know me, when I shall
be sanctified in thee, O Gog, before their
eyes.
(17) Thus saith the Lord God; *Art* thou
he of whom I have spoken in old time
[1]by my servants the prophets of Israel,
which prophesied in those days *many*
years that I would bring thee against
them? (18) And it shall come to pass at
the same time when Gog shall come
against the land of Israel, saith the
Lord God, *that* my fury shall come up
in my face. (19) For in my jealousy *and*
in the fire of my wrath have I spoken,
Surely in that day there shall be a great
shaking in the land of Israel; (20) so
that the fishes of the sea, and the fowls
of the heaven, and the beasts of the
field, and all creeping things that creep
upon the earth, and all the men that *are*
upon the face of the earth, shall shake
at my presence, and the mountains shall
be thrown down, and the [2]steep places
shall fall, and every wall shall fall to
the ground. (21) And I will call for a
sword against him throughout all my
mountains, saith the Lord God: every
man's sword shall be against his brother.
(22) And I will plead against him with
pestilence and with blood; and I will
rain upon him, and upon his bands, and
upon the many people that *are* with him,
an overflowing rain, and great hailstones,
fire, and brimstone. (23) Thus will I
[a]magnify myself, and sanctify myself;
and I will be known in the eyes of many
nations, and they shall know that I *am*
the Lord.

CHAPTER XXXIX.—(1) Therefore,
thou son of man, prophesy against Gog,
and say, Thus saith the Lord God; Be-
hold, I *am* against thee, O Gog, the chief
prince of Meshech and Tubal: (2) and I
will turn thee back, and [3]leave but the
sixth part of thee, and will cause thee
to come up from [4]the north parts, and
will bring thee upon the mountains of
Israel: (3) and I will smite thy bow out
of thy left hand, and will cause thine
arrows to fall out of thy right hand.
(4) Thou shalt fall upon the mountains of
Israel, thou, and all thy bands, and the
people that *is* with thee: I will give thee
unto the ravenous birds of every [5]sort,
and *to* the beasts of the field [6]to be de-
voured. (5) Thou shalt fall upon [7]the
open field: for I have spoken *it*, saith
the Lord God. (6) And I will send a fire
on Magog, and among them that dwell

1 Heb., *by the hands.*

2 Or, *towers*, or, *stairs.*

a ch. 36. 23, & 37. 28.

3 Or, *strike thee with six plagues;* or, *draw thee back with an hook of six teeth,* as ch. 38. 4.

4 Heb., *the sides of the north.*

5 Heb., *wing.*

6 Heb., *to devour.*

7 Heb., *the face of the field.*

passage becomes clearer by omitting the question and reading simply, "When Israel dwells securely thou wilt observe it and come," &c.

(16) **Latter days.**—The expression is indefinite but concurs with those in verse 8 in indicating a distant future.

(17) **Of whom I have spoken in old time.**—This is put in that interrogative form which is often used for emphatic assurance. The word *many* before "years" is not in the original, but is correctly inserted to mark the accusative of duration. The statement is then an emphatic one, that God had of old and for a long time foretold by His prophets this attack of Gog. But the name of Gog is not mentioned in any earlier prophecy now extant, nor is it likely that any such, far less that any long series of such prophecies, have been lost. This concurs with many other indications in the prophecy to show that it does not relate to any particular event, but that Gog and his allies represent the enemies of the Church in general, and that the prophet is here depicting the same great and prolonged struggle between evil and good, between the powers of the world and the kingdom of God, which has formed the burden of so much of both earlier and later prophecy.

(20) **The mountains shall be thrown down.**—In verses 19—22 the whole earth, animate and inanimate, is represented as affected by the terrible judgment of the Almighty upon His enemies. Such, as has been already noted, is the common language of prophecy in describing great moral events, and it is especially used in connection with the judgments of the last day.

XXXIX.

This chapter is a continuation of the preceding, and contains the two latter parts of the prophecy (verses 1—16, 17—29). It opens with a brief summary of the earlier part of chap. xxxviii.

(2) **Leave but the sixth part of thee.**—This word occurs only here, and the translation is based on the supposition that it is derived from the word meaning *six*; but even on this supposition the renderings in the margin are as likely to be right as that of the text. This derivation, however, is probably wrong; all the ancient versions give a sense corresponding to xxxviii. 4, 16, and also to the clauses immediately before and after, "I will lead thee along." The greater part of the modern commentators concur in this view.

(4) **Unto the ravenous birds.**—Compare the account of the destruction of Pharaoh in chap. xxix. 4, 5.

(6) **A fire on Magog.**—Magog is the country of Gog (chap. xxxviii. 1), and the Divine judgment is to fall therefore not only upon the army in the land of Israel, but also upon the far-distant country of Gog. In Rev. xx. 9 this fire is represented as coming "down from God out of heaven."

[1]carelessly in the isles: and they shall
know that I *am* the LORD. (7) So will I
make my holy name known in the midst
of my people Israel; and I will not *let*
them pollute my holy name any more:
and the heathen shall know that I *am*
the LORD, the Holy One in Israel. (8) Be-
hold, it is come, and it is done, saith the
Lord GOD; this *is* the day whereof I have
spoken.

(9) And they that dwell in the cities of
Israel shall go forth, and shall set on
fire and burn the weapons, both the
shields and the bucklers, the bows and
the arrows, and the [2]handstaves, and the
spears, and they shall [3]burn them with
fire seven years: (10) so that they shall
take no wood out of the field, neither
cut down *any* out of the forests; for
they shall burn the weapons with fire:
and they shall spoil those that spoiled
them, and rob those that robbed them,
saith the Lord GOD. (11) And it shall
come to pass in that day, *that* I will give
unto Gog a place there of graves in
Israel, the valley of the passengers on
the east of the sea: and it shall stop the
[4]*noses* of the passengers: and there shall
they bury Gog and all his multitude:
and they shall call *it* The valley of
[5]Hamon-gog. (12) And seven months
shall the house of Israel be burying of
them, that they may cleanse the land.
(13) Yea, all the people of the land shall
bury *them*; and it shall be to them a re-
nown the day that I shall be glorified,
saith the Lord GOD. (14) And they shall
sever out [6]men of continual employment,
passing through the land to bury with
the passengers those that remain upon
the face of the earth, to cleanse it: after
the end of seven months shall they
search. (15) And the passengers *that*
pass through the land, when *any* seeth
a man's bone, then shall he [7]set up a
sign by it, till the buriers have buried
it in the valley of Hamon-gog. (16) And
also the name of the city *shall be* [8]Ha-
monah. Thus shall they cleanse the
land.

1 Or, *confidently.*
2 Or, *javelins.*
3 Or, *make a fire of them.*
4 Or, mouths.
5 That is, *The multitude of Gog.*
6 Heb., *men of continuance.*
7 Heb., *build.*
8 That is, *The multitude.*

In the isles.—This common Scriptural expression for the remoter parts of the earth is added here to show the universality of the judgment upon all that is hostile to the kingdom of God.

(9) **Shall burn them with fire seven years.**—The representation of this and the following verse, that the weapons of the army of Gog shall furnish the whole nation of Israel with fuel for seven years, cannot, of course, be understood literally, and seems to have been inserted by the prophet to show that we are to look for the meaning of his prophecy beyond any literal event of earthly warfare.

Verses 11—16 again present the magnitude of the attack upon the Church by describing the burial of the host after it is slain. The language, if it could be supposed it was meant to be literally understood, would be even more extravagant than that of verses 9, 10. The whole nation of Israel is represented as engaged for seven months in burying the bodies (verses 12, 13); after this an indefinite time is to be occupied by one corps of men appointed to search the land for still remaining bones, and by another who are to bury them.

(11) **The valley of the passengers.**—The name cannot be derived from the Scythians, as if they were spoken of "as a cloud passing over and gone," because the same word is used again in this verse, and also in verses 14, 15, evidently in a different sense. It simply denotes some (probably imaginary) thoroughfare, which is to be blocked up by the buried bodies of the slain. No definite locality is assigned to it, except that it is "on the east of the sea," meaning the Dead Sea. It was to be, therefore, on the extreme south-eastern outskirts of the land. This is another of the features of the description which indicate some other than a literal interpretation; for how should such a host, invading the land from the north for purposes of plunder, be found in that locality, and how could such vast numbers of dead bodies be transported thither?

Stop the noses.—The word "noses" is not in the original, and should be omitted. The meaning is simply that the bodies of the host shall so fill up the valley as to stop the way of travellers.

The valley of Hamon-gog.—It is better to translate the word Hamon, as in the margin: *The valley of the multitude of Gog.* So also in verse 15.

(13) **All the people of the land.**—"It would be but a very moderate allowance, on the literal supposition, to say that a million of men would be thus engaged, and that on an average each would consign to the tomb two corpses in one day; which, for the 180 working days of the seven months, would make an aggregate of 360,000,000 of corpses!" (Fairbairn.)

(14) **Men of continual employment.**—The word for "continual" is the same as that translated *always* in chap. xxxviii. 8, where see Note. It implies that this occupation is to be one of long continuance, and the fact that they are to search the land through for the remains shows that the army of Gog is not conceived of as perishing when collected in one place, but when distributed all over the land. This search is only to begin after the close of the burying for seven months already described.

(16) **Shall be Hamonah.**—As a further monument of this great overthrow some city (not more definitely described, but probably yet to be built) shall be called "Multitude."

Thus shall they cleanse the land.—The extremest defilement, according to the Mosaic law, was caused by a dead body or by human bones. From this the land could only be purified by the burial of the last vestige of the host of Gog. In the spiritual contest which this prophecy is designed to set forth under these material figures, this cleansing looks to the puri-

(17) And, thou son of man, thus saith
the Lord God; Speak [1]unto every fea-
thered fowl, and to every beast of the
field, Assemble yourselves, and come;
gather yourselves on every side to my
[2]sacrifice that I do sacrifice for you, *even*
a great sacrifice upon the mountains of
Israel, that ye may eat flesh, and drink
blood. (18) Ye shall eat the flesh of the
mighty, and drink the blood of the
princes of the earth, of rams, of lambs,
and of [3]goats, of bullocks, all of them
fatlings of Bashan. (19) And ye shall eat
fat till ye be full, and drink blood till
ye be drunken, of my sacrifice which
I have sacrificed for you. (20) Thus ye
shall be filled at my table with horses
and chariots, with mighty men, and
with all men of war, saith the Lord
God.

(21) And I will set my glory among the
heathen, and all the heathen shall see
my judgment that I have executed, and
my hand that I have laid upon them.
(22) So the house of Israel shall know that
I *am* the Lord their God from that day
and forward. (23) And the heathen shall
know that the house of Israel went into
captivity for their iniquity: because
they trespassed against me, therefore
hid I my face from them, and gave them
into the hand of their enemies: so fell
they all by the sword. (24) According to
their uncleanness and according to their
transgressions have I done unto them,
and hid my face from them.

(25) Therefore thus saith the Lord God;
Now will I bring again the captivity of
Jacob, and have mercy upon the whole
house of Israel, and will be jealous for
my holy name; (26) after that they have
borne their shame, and all their tres-
passes whereby they have trespassed
against me, when they dwelt safely in
their land, and none made *them* afraid.
(27) When I have brought them again
from the people, and gathered them out
of their enemies' lands, and [a]am sancti-
fied in them in the sight of many nations;
(28) then shall they know that I *am* the
Lord their God, [4]which caused them to
be led into captivity among the heathen:
but I have gathered them unto their own
land, and have left none of them any
more there. (29) Neither will I hide my
face any more from them: for I have
[b]poured out my spirit upon the house of
Israel, saith the Lord God.

1 Heb., *to the fowl of every wing.*

2 Or, *slaughter.*

3 Heb., *great goats.*

a ch. 36. 23.

4 Heb., *by my causing of them, &c.*

b Joel 2. 28: Acts 2. 17.

---

fication of the Church from everything "that defileth and is unclean." (Comp. Eph. v. 26, 27; Rev. xxi. 27.)

With verse 17 the last part of this remarkable prophecy is introduced. Its representations are not to be considered as subsequent to those of the former part of the chapter, but as depicting the same thing under another figure.

(17) **Every feathered fowl.**—Compare verse 4, also chaps. xvii. 23, xxix. 5. The birds and beasts of all kinds represent all nations.

A great sacrifice.—The representation of a destructive judgment upon the Lord's enemies as a sacrifice is found also in Isa. xxxiv. 6; Jer. xlvi. 10. The figure is not to be pushed beyond the single point for which it is used—"to fill out and heighten the description of an immense slaughter."

(18) **Drink the blood of the princes.**—In these verses there is a curious mingling of the figurative and the literal; thus the "princes" are immediately explained by the mention of the various sacrificial animals; and in verse 20 these are again interpreted of "horses and chariots, with mighty men, and with all men of war." And when the figure is so far explained it only leads to a literal sense which must yet be considered as itself but the symbol of something further. (Comp. Rev. xix. 17, 18.)

(21) **My glory among the heathen.**—In this and the following verse the ultimate effect of the Divine judgments in the world is spoken of, and then, in verses 23, 24, this is applied to the present captivity of Israel. But the effect is too far-reaching to be limited to the latter, and the kingdom of God was never so established among the restored exiles, either by external triumphs over their enemies or by its internal development in the hearts of men, that the Divine glory was generally recognised among the heathen. In the time foretold the judgments shall be of such a character that all shall perceive that they are from God. Yet it must not be forgotten that the restoration from the exile was one step, and an important one, in the course of events leading to this end.

(22) **The house of Israel shall know.**—The knowledge here spoken of is evidently practical, and is expressly declared to remain for ever. It can only be considered as realised, and that still but in germ, in the Christian Church.

(23) **For their iniquity.**—In the times foretold God's dealings shall no longer be misunderstood, nor the sufferings of Israel considered as the result of His want of power to protect them. All the world shall so far understand His righteousness, that they shall see the reasonableness and necessity of His punishing even His chosen people for their sins, and purifying them that they may become His indeed.

(25) **Now will I bring again the captivity.**—It was needed for the exiles in their distress that the prophet at the close of this far-reaching prophecy should bring out the first step in the long course of events leading to its fulfilment, because that step was one of especial interest and comfort to them; but even this promise is mingled with predictions which still look on to the then distant future.

(29) **I have poured out.**—Comp. Joel ii. 28, 29; Acts ii. 17. See *Excursus* G at the end of this book.

EZEKIEL, XL.

PRELIMINARY NOTE ON CHAPTERS XL.—XLVIII.

These closing chapters of Ezekiel form one continuous prophecy of a distinctly marked character. They present a vision of the Temple in minute detail, with careful measurements of its parts; various ordinances for the Temple, for the Levites, and the priests, and for the prince; a new and remarkable division of the land; and the vision of the life-giving waters issuing from the sanctuary. The whole passage differs too much from anything in the past to allow for a moment the supposition that it is historical in character; and uttered, as it was, at a time when the Temple lay in ashes, and the land desolate, it is equally clear that it cannot describe the present. It must, therefore, have been prophetic; but this fact alone will not decide whether it looked to a literal fulfilment, or was ideal in its character; although the *à priori* presumption must be in favour of the latter, since all was seen "in the visions of God" (chap. xl. 2)—an expression which Ezekiel always applies to a symbolic representation rather than to an actual image of things. Certainly the Temple was afterwards rebuilt, and the nation re-established in Palestine; but the second Temple was quite unlike the one described by Ezekiel, and no attempt was ever made to carry out his division of the land. The few interpreters who have supposed that he meant to foretell literally the sanctuary and the state of the restoration have been compelled to suppose that the returning exiles found themselves too feeble to carry out their designs, and hence that this prophecy remains as a monument of magnificent purposes which were never accomplished. If this were the correct view, it is inconceivable that there should be no allusion to the language of Ezekiel in the historical books of Ezra and Nehemiah, and in the prophecies of Haggai, which all relate to this period, and describe the return and settlement in the land, and the rebuilding of the Temple, with no reference to this prophecy, nor any trace of a desire to conform their work to its directions. Other objections to this view will be mentioned presently.

At the same time, it is to be remembered that a remnant of the people were restored to their land, and their Temple was rebuilt upon Mount Zion; it is but reasonable to suppose that these events, so often foretold, were present to the prophet's mind, and that he looked out from them upon a more distant future, in the same way that near and typical events often with the other prophets form the basis of their foreshadowing of the future.

The only other way in which this prophecy can be literally understood is by supposing that its fulfilment is still in the future. In general, it is difficult to say that any state of things may not be realised in the future; but in this case there are features of the prophecy, and those not of a secondary or incidental character, but forming a part of its main delineations, which enable us to say unhesitatingly that their literal fulfilment would be in plain contradiction to the Divine revelation. For it is impossible to conceive, in view of the whole relations between the old and the new dispensations, as set forth in Scripture, that animal sacrifices can ever again be restored by Divine command, and find acceptance with God. And it may be added that it is equally impossible to conceive that the Church of the future, progressing in the liberty wherewith Christ has made it free, should ever return again to "the weak and beggarly elements" of Jewish bondage here set forth. But besides these obvious reasons, there are several indications in the detail of the prophecy that show it was never intended to be literally understood. These cannot all be seen without a careful examination of the details, but a few points may be presented which will make the fact sufficiently clear.

In the first place, the connection between the Temple and the city of Jerusalem is so deeply laid in all the sacred literature of the subject, as well as in the thought of every pious Israelite, that a prophecy incidentally separating them, without any distinct statement of the fact, or assignment of a reason for so doing, is scarcely conceivable. Yet in this portion of Ezekiel the Temple is described as at a distance of nearly nine and a half miles from the utmost bound of the city, or about fourteen and a quarter miles from its centre. This holds true, however the tribe portions of the land and the "oblation" be located (see the map in the Notes to chap. xlviii.); for the priests' portion of the "oblation" (chap. xlviii. 10), in the midst of which the sanctuary is placed, is 10,000 reeds, or about nineteen miles broad; to the south of this (xlviii. 15—17) is a strip of land of half the width, in which the city with its "suburbs" is situated. occupying its whole width.

A Temple in any other locality than Mount Moriah would hardly be the Temple of Jewish hope and association; but Ezekiel's Temple, with its precincts, is a mile square, larger than the whole ancient city of Jerusalem. It is hardly possible that the precincts of any actual Temple could be intended to embrace such a variety of hill and valley as the country presents. However this may be, the prophet describes it as situated many miles north of the city, and the city itself as several miles north of the site of Jerusalem. This would place the Temple well on the road to Samaria.

But, still further, the description of the oblation itself is physically impossible. The boundaries of the land are the Jordan on the one side and the Mediterranean on the other (chap. xlvii. 15—21). The "oblation" could not have reached so far south as the mouth of the Jordan; but even at that point the whole breadth of the country is but fifty-five miles. Now measuring forty-seven and one-third miles north (the width of the oblation) a point is reached where the distance between the river and the sea is barely forty miles. It is impossible, therefore, that the oblation itself should be included between them, and the description requires that there should also be room left for the prince's portion at either end.

Again, while the city of the vision is nowhere expressly said to be Jerusalem, it is yet described as the great city of the restored theocracy. It cannot, as already said, be placed geographically upon the site of Jerusalem. Either, then, this city must be understood ideally, or else a multitude of other prophecies, and notably many in Ezekiel which speak of the future of Zion and of Jerusalem, must be so interpreted. There is no good reason why both should not be interpreted figuratively, but it is impossible to understand both literally; for some of these prophecies make statements in regard to the future quite as literal in form as these of Ezekiel, and yet in direct conflict with them. To select a single instance from a prophecy not much noticed: Obadiah, who was probably a contemporary of Ezekiel, foretells (verses 19, 20) that at the restoration "Benjamin shall possess Gilead;" but, according to Ezekiel, Gilead is not in the land of the restoration at all, and Benjamin's territory is to be immediately south of the "oblation." Again, Obadiah says, "The captivity of Jerusalem" (which, in distinction from "the captivity of the host of the children of Israel," must refer to the two tribes) "shall possess the cities of the south;" but, according to Ezekiel, Judah and Benjamin are to adjoin the central "oblation," and on the south four of the other tribes are to have their portion. Such instances might be multiplied if necessary.

The division of the land among the twelve tribes; the entire change in assigning to the priests and to the Levites large landed estates, and to the former as much as to the latter; the enormous size of the Temple precincts and of the city, with the comparatively small allotment of land for its support, are all so singular, and so entirely without historical precedent, that only the clearest evidence would justify the assumption that these things were intended to be literally carried out. No regard is paid to the differing numbers of the various tribes, but an equal strip of land is assigned to each of them; and, the trans-Jordanic territory being excluded and about one-fifth of the whole land set apart as an "oblation," the portion remaining allows to each of the tribes but about two-thirds as much territory as, on the average, they had formerly possessed. The geographical order of the tribes is extremely singular: Judah and Benjamin are, indeed, placed on the two sides of the consecrated land, and the two eldest, Reuben and Simeon, are placed next to them, and Dan is put at the extreme north, where a part of the tribe had formerly lived; but the classification extends no further, and the remaining tribes are arranged neither in order of seniority nor of maternity, nor yet of ancient position. Moreover, nearly the whole territory assigned to Zebulon and Gad is habitable only by nomads, except on the supposition of physical changes in the land.

Another consequence of this division of the land is important: the Levites, being now provided for in the "oblation," no longer have their cities among the tribes. But it had been expressly provided that the "cities of refuge" (which must be distributed through the land in order to fulfil their purpose) should be Levitical cities (Num. xxxv. 9—15). With this change, therefore, the provision for cities of refuge ceases, and a profound alteration is made in the whole Mosaic law in regard to manslaughter and murder.

The ordinances for the sacrifices and feasts, as given in chaps. xlv., xlvi., differ greatly from those of the Mosaic law, as will be pointed out in the commentary. For the variation in the amount of the "meat offering," and of the number and character of the victims on various occasions, it is difficult to assign any other reason than that they were intended as indications that the prophet's scheme was not to be taken literally; it is certain that no attempt was made at the restoration thus to modify the Mosaic ritual, although this could have been done without difficulty if it had been understood that it was intended. The ample provision for the prince, and the regulations for his conduct, were politically wise and useful additions to the Mosaic economy, if literally understood, but which no attempt was ever made to carry out in practice. But in the ordering of the great cycle of feasts and fasts, the modification of the Mosaic system is so profound as quite to change its symbolic value. The "feast of weeks" and the great day of atonement are altogether omitted; and also the "new moons," except that of the first month, which is enhanced in value. The fact that the men who received these teachings from Ezekiel's own lips and had charge of the ordering of the services in the restored Temple,* paid no attention to these changes, is strong evidence that they did not consider them as meant to be literally carried out.

In connection with the omission of the day of atonement, all mention of the high priest is carefully left out. That this is not accidental is shown by the fact that the laws of marriage and of mourning for all the priests are made more strict than in the legislation of Moses (chap. xliv. 22—27), evidently as a sort of compensation for the omitted legislation in regard to the high priest. But the Levitical system without a high priest becomes a different institution in itself, and is also greatly changed in its symbolism.

It may be remarked in passing that the system here set forth is not at all of the nature of an intermediate or transitional ritual between that which we know existed under the monarchy, and that which is set forth in the Levitical law, and therefore affords no basis for the theory that the Levitical system was the outgrowth of the captivity. The absence of the high priest, so prominent both in the law and in the history, is alone a sufficient proof of this; and to this may be added the full regulations for the prince in Ezekiel, of which there is no trace in either the earlier or the subsequent history.

A further difficulty with the literal interpretation may be found in the description of the waters which issued from under the eastern threshold of the Temple (chap. xlvii. 1—12). These waters run to the "east country," and go down "to the sea," which can only be the Dead Sea; but such a course would be physically impossible without changes in the surface of the earth, since the location of the Temple of the vision is on the west of the watershed of the country. They had, moreover, the effect of "healing" the waters of the sea, an effect which could not be produced naturally without providing an outlet from the sea; no supply of fresh water could remove the saltness while this water was all disposed of by evaporation, and Ezekiel (in chap. xlvii. 11) excludes the idea of an outlet. But, above all, the character of the waters themselves is impossible without a perpetual miracle. Setting aside the difficulty of a spring of this magnitude upon the top of "a very high mountain" (chap. xl. 2) in this locality, at the distance of 1,000 cubits from their source, the waters have greatly increased in volume; and so with each successive 1,000 cubits, until at the end of 4,000 cubits (about a mile and a half) they have become a river no longer fordable, or, in other words, comparable to the Jordan. Such an increase, without accessory streams, is clearly not natural. But, beyond all this, the description of the waters themselves clearly marks them as ideal. They are life-giving and healing; trees of perennial foliage and fruit grow upon their banks, the leaves being for "medicine," and the fruit, although for food, never wasting. The reader cannot fail to be reminded of "the pure river of water of life" in Rev. xxii. 1, 2, "on either side" of which was "the tree of life" with "its twelve manner of fruits," and its leaves "for the healing of the nations." The author of the Apocalypse evidently had this passage in mind; and just as he has adopted the description

* This prophecy was given in the twenty-fifth year of the captivity, and was, therefore, forty-five years before the restoration. The elderly men of the restoration must have been of full age to appreciate this prophecy at the time it was uttered, and in the immediately subsequent years of its perusal and discussion. There can be no reasonable doubt, also, that the prophecies of Ezekiel were carried back to Judæa by the returning exiles, and from their very nature they must have been made generally known to those who were in the captivity.

CHAPTER XL.—(1) In the five and
twentieth year of our captivity, in the
beginning of the year, in the tenth *day*
of the month, in the fourteenth year
after that the city was smitten, in the
selfsame day the hand of the LORD was
upon me, and brought me thither. (2) In
the visions of God brought he me into
the land of Israel, and set me upon a
very high mountain, [1] by which *was* as

B.C. 574.

1 Or, *upon which.*

of Gog and Magog as an ideal description, and applied it to the events of the future, so he has treated this as an ideal prophecy, and applied it to the Church triumphant.

It is to be remembered that this whole vision is essentially one, and that it would be unreasonable to give a literal interpretation to one part of it and a figurative to another. All the objections, therefore, which lie against the supposition of the restoration of animal sacrifices hold also against the supposition of the general restoration of the Jewish Temple and polity. This was felt at an early day, and such Christian commentators as Ephrem Syrus, Theodoret, and Jerome adopted throughout a symbolic or typical explanation. The changes in the Mosaic law are indeed great, but still are only of detail, and leave it open to the Apostolic description as a "bondage" to which we cannot suppose the providence of God would ever lead back the Church Christ has redeemed at the cost of the sacrifice of Himself. Either the whole argument of the Epistle to the Hebrews is a mistake, not to speak of those to the Romans and Galatians, nor of our Lord's own discourses (as with the woman of Samaria), or else the Holy Spirit could not have intended a literal realisation in the future of this vision of Ezekiel.

We thus come to regard this prophecy as an ideal one on every ground, not looking for any literal and material fulfilment. If it should be asked, Why then is it given with such a wealth of minute material detail? the answer is obvious, that this is thoroughly characteristic of Ezekiel. The tendency, strongly marked in every part of his book, merely culminates in this closing vision. The two previous chapters, especially, have abounded in concrete and definite details of the attack of a great host upon the land of Israel, while yet these very details have given evidence upon examination that they could not have been meant to be literally understood, and that the whole prophecy was intended to shadow forth the great and final spiritual conflict, prolonged through ages, between the power of the world and the kingdom of God. So here, the prophet, wishing to set forth the glory, the purity, and the beneficent influence of the Church of the future, clothes his description in those terms of the past with which his hearers were familiar. The use of such terms was a necessity in making himself intelligible to his contemporaries, just as to the very close of the inspired volume it is still necessary to set forth the glory and joy of the Church triumphant under the figures of earthly and familiar things, while no one is misled thereby to imagine that the heavenly Jerusalem will be surrounded with a literal wall of jasper, "twelve thousand furlongs" = 1,500 miles (Rev. xxi. 16, 18), or that its twelve gates shall be each of an actual pearl. It is remarkable that in two instances, that of Gog and that of the river of life, the imagery is the same in Ezekiel and in Revelation. At the same time Ezekiel is careful to introduce among his details so many points that were impossible, or, at least, the literal fulfilment of which would have been strangely inconsistent with his main teaching, as to show that his description must be ideal, and that its realisation is to be sought for beneath the types and shadows in which it was clothed. It may be as impossible to find the symbolical meaning of each separate detail as it is to tell the typical meaning of the sockets for the boards of the tabernacle, although the tabernacle as a whole is expressly said to have been a type. This is the case with every vision, and parable, and type, and every form of setting forth truth by imagery; there must necessarily be much which has no independent signification, but is merely subsidiary to the main point. It is characteristic of Ezekiel that these subsidiary details should be elaborated with the utmost minuteness. His purpose was understood by his contemporaries, and by the generation immediately succeeding, so that they never made any attempt to carry out his descriptions in the rebuilding of the Temple and reconstitution of the State. The idea of a literal interpretation of his words was reserved for generations long distant from his time, from the forms of the Church under which he lived, and from the circumstances and habits of expression with which he was familiar, and under the influence of which he wrote.

XL.

(1) **In the five and twentieth year.**—It is the habit of Ezekiel in giving the year to make no mention of the era from which it was reckoned; but in a few important passages (chaps. i. 2, xii. 21, and here) it is described as "of our captivity." This vision was seen "in the beginning of the year." The Jews always reckoned the month Abib, or Nisan, in which the Passover was celebrated, as the beginning of the year, according to the command given in Exod. xii. 1, and the "tenth day" of that month was the day in which the preparations for the Passover began, and hence a most appropriate season for this vision of the Church of the future. Others consider that this was a Jubile year (for which there is no evidence); and since the Jubile began at the great fast of the Atonement, on the tenth day of the seventh month, it is thought that this is the day here intended. At a much later time the Jews sometimes reckoned the years from the Jubile, but there is nothing to show that this custom began so early. In either case the text distinctly says that it was fourteen years after the destruction of Jerusalem; a substantial period had, therefore, elapsed in which this great judgment would have produced its effect upon the minds of the exiles; there was thus now occasion for bringing before them the brighter hopes of the future.

(2) **In the visions of God.**—This expression presupposes that what follows is an ideal description rather than an account of anything that ever had or ever should have a literal existence. The same expression has been used in the same sense in regard to chaps. i.—iii., and again chaps. viii.—xi. It always refers, not to an actual image of existing things, but to a symbolic representation of their substance.

Upon a very high mountain.—Comp. Isa. ii. 2; Mic. iv. 1. This cannot apply literally to the hill of Moriah, surrounded by greater heights, but is frequently used to mark the spiritual importance of the

the frame of a city on the south. (3) And
he brought me thither, and, behold,
there was a man, whose appearance *was*
like the appearance of brass, with a line
of flax in his hand, and a measuring
reed; and he stood in the gate. (4) And
the man said unto me, Son of man, behold
with thine eyes, and hear with thine
ears, and set thine heart upon all that I
shall shew thee; for to the intent that I
might shew *them* unto thee *art* thou
brought hither: declare all that thou
seest to the house of Israel. (5) And behold
a wall on the outside of the house
round about, and in the man's hand a
measuring reed of six cubits *long* by the
cubit and an hand breadth: so he measured
the breadth of the building, one
reed; and the height, one reed.
(6) Then came he unto the gate [1]which
looketh toward the east, and went up
the stairs thereof, and measured the

[1] Heb., *whose face was the way toward the east.*

Temple site. (Comp. chap. xvii. 22, 23; also Rev. xxi. 10.)

By which.—The margin is more accurate, *upon which.* This proposition and the one just before translated *upon* are different in the original, but *upon* is the proper sense of this one, while the former has the meaning of *unto.* The structure which the prophet sees is *upon* the mountain, and is not the city, but in size and with walls, &c., "as the frame of a city;" in fact, it was the greatly enlarged Temple, as the whole following description shows.

On the south.—The prophet, although transported only in vision, has in mind the usual way of entering Palestine from Chaldæa, viz., *at the north.* Hence he sees the Temple "on the south."

(3) **A line of flax . . . a measuring reed.**—The former for the longer, the latter for the shorter measures, a characteristic definiteness in details.

(5) **By the cubit and an hand breadth.**—The sense will be more clearly conveyed by reading, "each being a cubit and a hand-breadth," *i.e.*, each of the six cubits which made up the reed was an ordinary cubit and a hand-breadth more. It is difficult or impossible to fix with precision the length of the cubit of Scripture, more especially as the value of the measure appears to have changed in the course of ages. In 2 Chron. iii. 3 the measurements of Solomon's Temple are given "by cubits after the first [or ancient] measure." It appears, therefore, that the cubit in common use at the time of the compilation of that book (after the return from the captivity) was different from the standard Mosaic cubit. Ezekiel evidently intends to use the latter in his Temple measurements, and therefore adds "an hand breadth" to the common cubit. Different writers vary in their estimate of the length of the measure thus obtained from eighteen to twenty-four inches. By considering it twenty inches we shall have a convenient number for use, and cannot be far wrong. The "reed of six cubits" was therefore about ten feet long.

The breadth of the building—*i.e., the thickness of the wall surrounding the court.* The length of this wall is not given until verse 47. The thickness and height are made equal, evidently for the sake of the symmetry of the measures. (Comp. Rev. xxi. 16.)

Verses 6—16 contain a description of the eastern gate, or rather, gate-building of the Temple, by which one entered from the precincts into the outer court. The other gates were like it, but this is described first, because it had the pre-eminence. It looked straight to the door of the Temple itself; it was by this that the glory of the Lord was afterwards seen to enter His house (chap. xliii. 1); and in consequence this gate was to be kept shut, except for the prince (chap. xliv. 2, 3). The accompanying plan may be a help in understanding the description. Notwithstanding the minuteness of detail in the text, a few points remain undetermined; but the plan represents the main features correctly, and gives the most probable view of the parts that are not entirely settled.

PLAN I.—OUTER GATE.

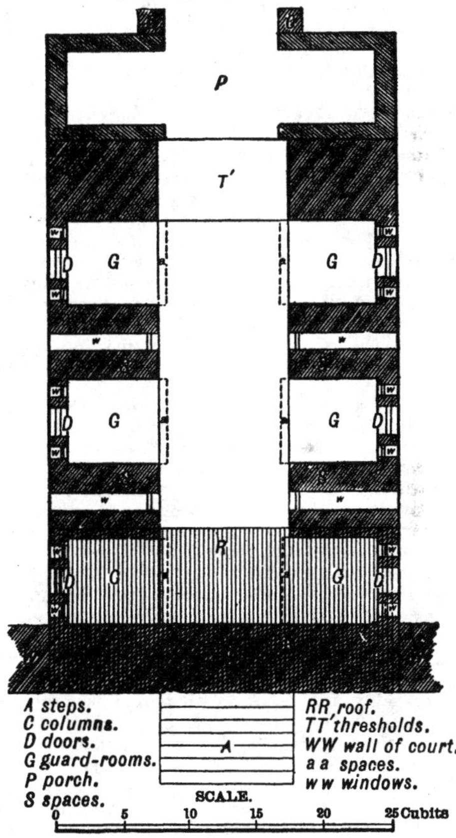

(6) **The stairs.**—These steps to the porch were seven in number (verses 22, 26) for the north and south gates, and therefore probably also for this. They were entirely outside of the threshold, and hence are not reckoned in the dimensions of the gate-building. (See plan, A.)

One reed broad.—That is, from east to west (see plan, T). This was just the thickness of the enclosing

threshold of the gate, *which was* one
reed broad; and the other threshold *of*
the gate, which was one reed broad.
(7) And *every* little chamber *was* one reed
long, and one reed broad; and between
the little chambers *were* five cubits; and
the threshold of the gate by the porch of
the gate within *was* one reed. (8) He
measured also the porch of the gate
within, one reed. (9) Then measured he
the porch of the gate, eight cubits; and
the posts thereof, two cubits; and the
porch of the gate *was* inward. (10) And
the little chambers of the gate eastward
were three on this side, and three on that
side; they three *were* of one measure:
and the posts had one measure on this
side and on that side. (11) And he mea-
sured the breadth of the entry of the
gate, ten cubits;. *and* the length of the
gate, thirteen cubits. (12) The [1]space
also before the little chambers *was* one
cubit *on this side*, and the space *was* one
cubit on that side: and the little cham-
bers *were* six cubits on this side, and six
cubits on that side. (13) He measured
then the gate from the roof of *one* little
chamber to the roof of another: the
breadth *was* five and twenty cubits, door
against door. (14) He made also posts of

[1] Heb., *limit*, or, *bound*.

---

wall, W (verse 5). The text of this verse becomes clearer by omitting the words in italics which are not in the original; also throughout the description it is better to omit the inserted words *was* and *were*, since the various things mentioned are all dependent upon *measured.*

The other threshold.—This is the threshold at the opposite, or inner end of the gate-building (T′). It is mentioned here to bring out the fact that the two were alike, but is spoken of again in its place in verse 7.

(7) **Little chamber.**—Rather, *guard-chamber*, and so throughout this passage. The original word is quite different from that translated "chamber" in verse 17, and is used in 1 Kings xiv. 28; 2 Chron. xii. 11 in the sense of guard-chamber. These rooms were only ten feet square, but there were three of them (verse 10) on each side of the entrance-way. They were for sentries who were to guard against the entrance of any improper person or thing (see plan, G). These guard-rooms were separated by spaces (S) one cubit narrower than themselves, which probably formed a part of the solid wall, and the ward-rooms were therefore in reality large niches in the wall.

(8) **The porch of the gate within.**—The same expression as in the previous verse, and indicates a porch or vestibule to the gateway on the inner or Temple side. Its width from east to west was the same as that of the guard-rooms, added to the thickness of the porch-walls, and was probably equal also to the space occupied by the steps leading to the other end of the gateway (P).

(9) **Eight cubits.**—This is often considered the measurement of the porch from north to south. A more probable suggestion is that this is the same measurement as in verse 8, but is now the external instead of the internal length. In this case the porch must be considered as built independently of the gateway proper, and having short return walls on the east and west of a cubit each. In this way the whole length of the gateway (including the porch and its "posts"), as given in verse 15, exactly agrees with the details. It is accordingly so drawn on the plan.

(10) **The posts.**—This verse gives the further information about the guard-chambers of verse 7, that they were all alike, and also about the "posts" of verse 9, that they were alike (see plan, C). The supposition, therefore, that there was a colonnade inside the gateway is quite uncalled for. Such an arrangement would have seriously obstructed the passage-way, and is hardly supposable in view of the height of the columns mentioned in verse 14.

(11) **The breadth of the entry of the gate.**—This is the measurement of the clear space between the sides of the gate, and, according to the length of the cubit adopted, was $16\frac{1}{2}$ feet.

The length of the gate, thirteen cubits.—This is a difficult expression, and has been variously explained. It is now generally understood of that part of the gateway which was roofed over, including the threshold of six cubits, and the first pair of guard-chambers of six cubits more, together with one cubit of the space or wall between these guard-chambers and the next. The reason for extending it over this last cubit was doubtless that the width was otherwise too great (10 cubits $+ 6 \times 2 = 22$) to span with the roof without support. It was therefore necessary to carry it one cubit further. In the plan the part supposed to be thus roofed is marked by lines (RR). Whether there was a corresponding roofing at the other end of the gateway does not appear, but that some at least of the guard-chambers were roofed is certain from verse 13.

(12) **The space.**—The guard-chambers themselves were just six cubits square (verse 7), but in front of each was a space (*a*) of one cubit projecting into the passage-way. This must have been separated by some sort of railing from the passage-way itself, although there is no mention of this. The object of this space was evidently to allow the guard to command a view of the passage-way, as they could not have done if kept behind the line of its walls.

(13) **From the roof . . . . to the roof.**—This is a measurement across the gateway from north to south. The passage-way was ten cubits, each guard-chamber six, and an allowance of a cubit and a half for the outer wall will exactly make up the sum of "five and twenty cubits" ($10 + 2 \times (6 + 1\frac{1}{2}) = 25$).

Door against door.—The immediate object of this clause is to mark the direction in which the above measurement was taken; but besides this, it shows that there were doors to the guard-rooms. These doors were presumably in the outer wall to allow the watchmen free passage between the court and their posts of duty. There is no mention of an inner wall between these chambers and the passage-way, and it is more probable that there was none. If any existed its thickness must be deducted from that given above for the outer wall.

(14) **He made also posts of threescore cubits.**—The word "made" instead of *measure*

threescore cubits, even unto the post of
the court round about the gate. (15)And
from the face of the gate of the entrance
unto the face of the porch of the inner
gate *were* fifty cubits. (16) And *there were*
[1]narrow windows to the little chambers,
and to their posts within the gate round
about, and likewise to the [2]arches: and
windows *were* round about [3]inward: and
upon *each* post *were* palm trees.

(17) Then brought he me into the out-
ward court, and, lo, *there were* chambers,
and a pavement made for the court
round about: thirty chambers *were*
upon the pavement. (18) And the pave-
ment by the side of the gates over
against the length of the gates *was* the
lower pavement. (19) Then he measured
the breadth from the forefront of the
lower gate unto the forefront of the

1 Heb., *closed.*

2 Or, *galleries*, or, *porches.*

3 Or, *within.*

correctly represents the original, and the change is for the obvious reason that columns of the height mentioned could not be directly measured by the reed. *Made* is therefore used in the sense of *determined* or *fixed*, although we are not told by what method of calculation.

The height of these columns, sixty cubits, though only half that given in 2 Chron. iii. 4 as the height of the porch of Solomon's Temple, is sufficient to remind us of the Egyptian custom of placing obelisks before the doors of their temples. The height is also very great in proportion to the size of the columns, which were but two cubits square (verse 9). Probably the columns were engaged with the wall as far as the height of the porch, as the original word for "posts" seems to indicate, and as the dimensions of the gateway suggest. Thus buttressed the size would be sufficient for stability. It is to be remembered, however, that as in the case of the wheels in i. 16, 17, we are here studying only a vision, not an actual structure.

Even unto the post of the court round about the gate.—This is scarcely intelligible, and even the original is obscure: *lit.*, "And unto the post the court the gate round about;" and the proper translation seems to be, "the court (extended) to the column and (was) round about the gate." The object is to show that the court reached quite to the gate-building and encircled it on three sides, so that the gate structure projected inwards from the line of the wall and terminated in the columns, beyond which, and on each side of the gate, the outer court of the Temple began.

(15) **Fifty cubits.**—The length of the gate-building was just twice its breadth, and was made up as follows: outer threshold, 6 cubits; three guard-rooms, each 6 cubits = 18; two "spaces" between these, each 5 cubits = 10; inner threshold, 6 cubits; porch, 8 cubits; columns, 2 cubits ($6 + 18 + 10 + 6 + 8 + 2 = 50$).

(16) **Narrow windows.**—This is an abbreviated form of the expression used in 1 Kings vi. 4 of the windows in Solomon's Temple. *Narrow* should be *closed*, as in the *margin;* the windows had over them lattice-work which could not be opened. It is difficult to understand the situation of these windows on account of the uncertainty in the meaning of the words translated "their posts" and "the arches." The former, from its use in 1 Kings vi. 31, and also in chap. xli. 3, of the "side posts" of the door into the Holy of Holies, must mean the *jambs* or parts of the wall to which the doors were attached; and the latter indicates some projection of the wall which is most probably to be explained of the "spaces" between the guard-chambers and at the sides of the inner threshold. The meaning of the whole verse will then be, that within the gateway windows were seen on both sides, both at the side of the doors leading from the court to the guard-chambers, and also in the parts of the wall projecting between the guard-chambers. On the plan these are marked (w).

Upon each post were palm trees.—The palm had been largely used in the carving of Solomon's Temple (1 Kings vi. 29, 32, 35).

The prophet is now taken across the outer court, which he describes on the way (verses 17—19), to the north gate (verse 20), and then to the south gate (verse 24).

(17) **Outward court.**—The Temple of Ezekiel has two courts, an outer and an inner; but there is no appropriation of these courts to the special use of any classes. It may be assumed that the inner court, from its size and arrangements, was for the priests engaged in the sacrifices, and the outer for the people generally.

A pavement.—Comp. 2 Chron. vii. 3; Esther i. 6. The word is generally understood to mean a tesselated or mosaic pavement.

Thirty chambers.—The size and location of these chambers is not given. In accordance with the general symmetry of the arrangements, it may be assumed that there were ten on each of the three sides not occupied by the Temple buildings, and that five were on each side of the gate. They are conjecturally indicated on Plan II. (page 124) by DD. They are drawn as if joined together; but this is not certain. Such chambers for the use of officiating priests and Levites, and for the storage of the tithes, are mentioned both in connection with Solomon's Temple and with that of the restoration (see Jer. xxxv. 4, xxxvi. 10; 1 Chron. ix. 26; Neh. x. 38—40).

(18) **Over against the length of the gates.**—The width of the pavement was the same as the projection of the gateways into the court, *i.e.*, 44 cubits (50 cubits, less the thickness of the wall).

Lower pavement.—In contradistinction to the pavement of the inner court, which was upon a higher level.

(19) **An hundred cubits eastward.**—As the prophet is taken through the outer court its width is measured from the eastern gate, which he had already examined, and from the northern gate, to which he is next taken (verse 20). Afterwards (verse 27) the same measurement is made to the southern gate, and these all agree as 100 cubits each. The starting-point of the measurement is clearly defined as "from the forefront of the lower gate," *i.e.*, from the western or innermost extremity of the outer gate-building; but the final point, as given in this verse, "the forefront of the inner court," leaves the question open, whether this was to the wall of the inner court itself, or only to the outer extremity of its gate. This doubt is removed in verses 23 and 27, which expressly say that the measurement was "from gate to gate," *i.e.*, between the nearest points of the gate-buildings.

inner court [1]without, an hundred cubits
eastward and northward.
(20) And the gate of the outward court
[2]that looked toward the north, he mea-
sured the length thereof, and the breadth
thereof. (21) And the little chambers
thereof *were* three on this side and three
on that side; and the posts thereof and
the [3]arches thereof were after the mea-
sure of the first gate: the length thereof
was fifty cubits, and the breadth five
and twenty cubits. (22) And their win-
dows, and their arches, and their palm
trees, *were* after the measure of the gate
that looketh toward the east; and they
went up unto it by seven steps; and the
arches thereof *were* before them. (23) And
the gate of the inner court *was* over
against the gate toward the north, and
toward the east; and he measured from
gate to gate an hundred cubits.
(24) After that he brought me toward
the south, and behold a gate toward
the south: and he measured the posts
thereof and the arches thereof ac-
cording to these measures. (25) And
there were windows in it and in
the arches thereof round about, like
those windows: the length *was* fifty
cubits, and the breadth five and twenty
cubits. (26) And *there were* seven steps to
go up to it, and the arches thereof *were*
before them: and it had palm trees, one
on this side, and another on that side,
upon the posts thereof. (27) And *there*
was a gate in the inner court toward
the south: and he measured from gate
to gate toward the south an hundred
cubits.
(28) And he brought me to the inner
court by the south gate: and he mea-
sured the south gate according to these
measures; (29) and the little chambers
thereof, and the posts thereof, and the
arches thereof, according to these mea-
sures: and *there were* windows in it and
in the arches thereof round about: *it*
was fifty cubits long, and five and twenty
cubits broad. (30) And the arches round
about *were* five and twenty cubits long,
and five cubits [4]broad. (31) And the
arches thereof *were* toward the utter
court; and palm trees *were* upon the
posts thereof: and the going up to it
had eight steps.
(32) And he brought me into the inner

1 Or, *from without.*

2 Heb., *whose face was.*

3 Or, *galleries*, or, *porches.*

4 Heb., *breadth.*

Verses 20—23 describe the north gate, which was exactly like the east, already described. In verse 22 is the first mention of the number of steps leading up to the gates (see also verse 26), and in verse 23 the first mention of the gates of the inner court (see also verse 27).

Verses 24—27 describe the south gate, exactly like the other two and with the same dimensions. The space between the outer and inner gates has now been measured on the east (verse 19), on the north (verse 23), and on the south (verse 27), each being 100 cubits.

(28) **Brought me to the inner court.**—The preposition should be translated *into*, being the same with that in verse 32. The prophet having entered the inner court by the south gate, this is first described (verses 28—31). This and the other gates of this court are essentially the same, and require the same changes of translation as in the case of the outer gates. The same plan will serve for both, remembering that it must be reversed, the porches of one set of gates facing the porches of the other set; of course the steps led to the porches of the inner gates instead of to the opposite end. The few points of difference between them will be noted as they occur.

(30) **The arches round about.**—This word, as already noted under verse 16, should be *projections of the walls*, if it has been correctly pointed by the Masorets; but it is exceedingly difficult to understand what is meant by the dimensions given, twenty-five cubits long and five cubits broad. This statement occurs nowhere else in the description of the gates, and the verse is omitted in the Greek translation, and either considered spurious or else passed over in silence by many commentators. One explanation given is that the twenty-five cubits is the sum-total of all the "projections of the walls" into the interior of the gateway: thus there were two "spaces" (S on the plan), each of five cubits; two thresholds (TT′), each of six cubits; and two walls of the porch, each of one cubit, or in all $(5\times2+6\times2+2)$ twenty-four cubits, the remaining cubit being made up by mouldings at the angles of these several projections. But it is fatal to this explanation that in no other case is any measurement thus made up by adding together the details of parts which do not adjoin. The same explanation requires the breadth of five cubits to be the transverse measurement of these projecting parts, which certainly could not apply to the first threshold, and would require a very awkward or even impossible narrowing of the gateway where the "spaces" are placed. The true solution of the difficulty seems to be in a slight change in the vowels of the Masoretic punctuation, which will transform the word into "porch." That porches were connected with the inner gates also is plain from verse 39, yet they are nowhere mentioned in the description unless here. Being a somewhat independent part of the gate, the measures are taken in a different direction from that of the gate itself. The "length" is the long way of the porch, just as long as the gateway is wide, twenty-five cubits; and the breadth is the measurement between the walls, five cubits, thus allowing a half-cubit for the thickness of each wall, and one cubit less clear space than in the outer gates.

(31) **Utter** = Outer, and so in verse 37; chap. xlii. 1, 3, 7, 14; chap. xliv. 19; chap. xlvi. 20, 21. In old English *utter* and *outer* appear to have been often interchanged.

court toward the east: and he measured
the gate according to these measures.
(33) And the little chambers thereof, and
the posts thereof, and the arches thereof,
were according to these measures: and
there were windows therein and in the
arches thereof round about: *it was* fifty
cubits long, and five and twenty cubits
broad. (34) And the arches thereof *were*
toward the outward court; and palm
trees *were* upon the posts thereof, on this
side, and on that side: and the going up
to it *had* eight steps.

(35) And he brought me to the north
gate, and measured *it* according to these
measures; (36) the little chambers thereof,
the posts thereof, and the arches thereof,
and the windows to it round about: the
length *was* fifty cubits, and the breadth
five and twenty cubits. (37) And the posts
thereof *were* toward the utter court; and
palm trees *were* upon the posts thereof,
on this side, and on that side: and the
going up to it *had* eight steps. (38) And
the chambers and the entries thereof
were by the posts of the gates, where
they washed the burnt offering. (39) And
in the porch of the gate *were* two tables
on this side, and two tables on that side,
to slay thereon the burnt offering and
the sin offering and the trespass offering.
(40) And at the side without, [1]as one goeth
up to the entry of the north gate, *were*
two tables; and on the other side, which
was at the porch of the gate, *were* two
tables. (41) Four tables *were* on this side,
and four tables on that side, by the side
of the gate; eight tables, whereupon
they slew *their sacrifices*. (42) And the
four tables *were* of hewn stone for the
burnt offering, of a cubit and an half
long, and a cubit and an half broad, and
one cubit high: whereupon also they
laid the instruments wherewith they
slew the burnt offering and the sacrifice.
(43) And within *were* [2]hooks, an hand
broad, fastened round about: and upon
the tables *was* the flesh of the offering.

[1] Or, *at the step.*

[2] Or, *end-irons*, or, *the two hearth-stones.*

Eight steps.—All the gates of the inner court (see verses 34, 37) had one more step than those of the outer, the inner court being raised so much more above the outer than the outer was above the precincts. The two sets together made up fifteen steps, the same number as led up in the later Temple from the court of the women to the court of Israel, and on which, according to Jewish tradition, the Levites stood to chant the fifteen Psalms (Ps. cxx.—cxxxiv.) called "Songs of Degrees."

Verses 32—34 describe the east gate, and verses 35—37 the north gate, both exactly like the one already described.

(38) **And the chambers and the entries thereof.**—These words in the original are in the singular, and have no article. The word for *chamber* is an entirely different one from that used in the former part of the chapter (verses 10, 12, 13). The verse should be translated, "And a cell with its door by the posts of the gates; there they washed the burnt offering." All the arrangements for sacrificing are here described in connection with the north gate, although in chap. xlvi. 2 it is said that at certain festivals the prince shall enter by the east gate, and there worship while the priests prepare his offerings. In the law it was required (Lev. i. 11; vi. 25; vii. 2) that all sacrifices should be slain in the court at the north side of the altar. Here the slaying is done at the north gate, but within the outer court. The reason appears to be that in the law each offerer was to slay his own victim, but here (chap. xliv. 11) the sacrifice is to be slain by the Levites, and it was therefore desirable that it should be done in the presence of the offerer and the people, *i.e.*, in the outer court. There was also a further reason in the convenience of disposing of the flesh of the victims. Only the whole burnt offerings and the fat and the kidneys of the others required to be taken to the altar in the inner court; while all the flesh of the sin offerings and the priests' portion of the peace offerings was to be carried to the priests' cooking place (F, Plan II.) to which a walk led from this point. The rest of the flesh of the peace offerings was taken to the people's cooking places (E) in the corners of the outer court.

(39) **In the porch.**—The preposition admits the sense of either *in* or *by*, but as the porch was very small for two tables on either side, and as a thoroughfare would be an inconvenient place for the slaughter of the victims, it is better to take the sense of *by*. The four tables were arranged, two on either side, near the porch.

(40) **At the side without.**—If there could be any doubt that this means *in the outer court*, it would be removed by the explanation "as one goeth up," *lit.*, at this ascent. These tables were of stone (verse 42), and they stood, two on each side, just in advance of the steps, for the purpose (verse 42) of slaying the sacrifices upon them.

(41) **Four tables.**—The eight tables of this verse are evidently meant to be distinguished from those of verses 40 and 42, and make twelve tables in all. They stood four on each side of the gate, somewhat nearer, therefore, than the others to the wall of the inner court. They were used for the same sacrificial purpose, except that the others only are mentioned (verse 42) as places "whereupon they laid" the sacrificial instruments.

(43) **Hooks.**—This is a word of doubtful meaning, found elsewhere only in Ps. lxviii. 13, where it is translated *pots*. It certainly designates something "within" the porch, and therefore could not have been anything attached to the tables which were "without." Our translators, following the ancient Chaldee paraphrast, have probably given the true sense, *hooks*, upon which the flesh of the victims was hung after it had been prepared upon the tables.

(44) And without the inner gate *were* the
chambers of the singers in the inner
court, which *was* at the side of the north
gate; and their prospect *was* toward the
south: one at the side of the east gate
having the prospect toward the north.
(45) And he said unto me, This chamber,
whose prospect *is* toward the south, *is*
for the priests, the keepers of the [1] charge
of the house. (46) And the chamber whose
prospect *is* toward the north *is* for the
priests, the keepers of the charge of the
altar: these *are* the sons of Zadok among
the sons of Levi, which come near to the

[1] Or, *ward*, or, *ordinance*: and so ver. 46.

(44) **Without the inner gate.**—*Without* must here be understood in a different sense from the *without* of verse 40, because this is expressly said to be "in the inner court;" it means, therefore, only *outside the gateway.*

Chambers of the singers.—The description of the chambers in verses 44—46 is not very clear, and has caused very great difference of opinion, and even a disposition to modify the text. But the text as it stands is supported by the ancient versions, Greek, Chaldee, and Syriac, as well as by the Masoretic punctuation. There seem to have been three or more chambers altogether, two at least at the side of the north gate opening to the south, *i.e.*, towards the altar, and one at the east gate opening toward the north. The purpose of the chamber at the east gate is perfectly clear; it was "for the priests, the keepers of the charge of the altar," *i.e.*, for those priests who were on duty at the time in connection with the sacrifices. It is not mentioned on which side of the gate it was placed, nor how large it was, but it is drawn on the plan on the north (Plan II., O). The chambers at the north gate (N), however, are called (verse 44) "chambers of the singers," and yet in verse 45 one of them is said to be for the priests "in charge of the house." The difficulty arises simply from the very common use of the plural in connection with only one of several persons or things, the other being separately specified. To make it entirely clear, we should say, "the chambers, one for the singers, and one for the priests." The *singers* were particular families of the Levites (1 Chron. vi. 31—37; ix. 33; xxv.; 2 Chron. v. 12), and were not of the priestly order.

PLAN II.—THE TEMPLE COURTS.

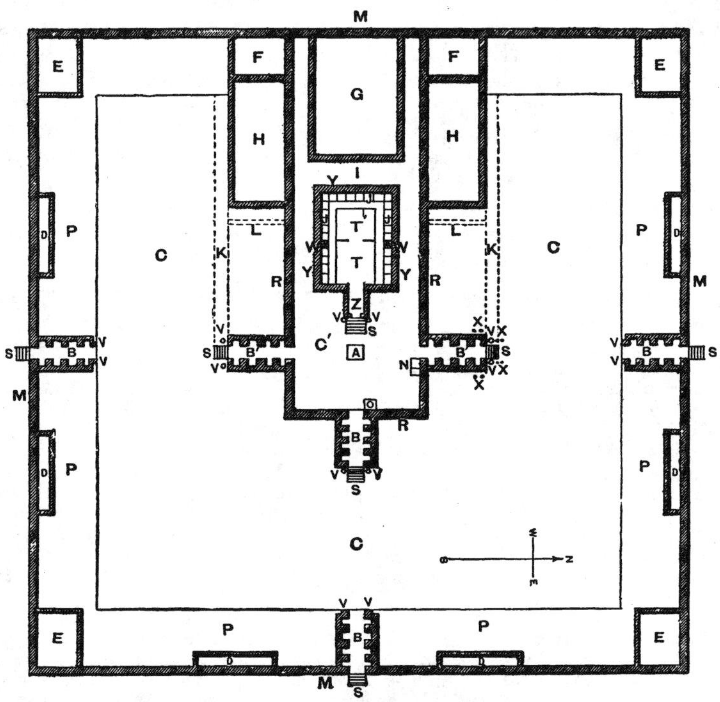

A, Altar.
B B B, Outer gate.
B' B' B', Inner gates.
C C, Outer court.
C', Inner court.
D D, Chambers in outer court.
E E, People's cooking-places.
F F, Priests' " "
G, Building in separate place.
H H, Priests' chambers.
I, Space in separate place.
J, Chambers adjoining Temple.
K K, Walk.
L L, Screen walls.
M M, Wall of outer court.
N, Chambers in inner court for priests and singers.
O, Chamber for officiating priests.
P P, Pavement.
R R, Wall of inner court.
S S, Steps.
T, Temple.
T', Holy of Holies.
V V, Columns.
W W, Winding staircases.
X X, Places for killing sacrifices.
Y Y, Platform around chambers.
Z, Porch of Temple.

The general arrangement appears to have been as follows: the offerer brings his victim into the outer court (C) near to the north gate leading into the inner court; there the Levites slay it (at X) and prepare it for the altar upon the tables provided, and then hang its flesh upon the hooks within the porch of the gate; the priests "in charge of the house" in the chamber near the inner end of the gate (N) now notify the singers in the other chamber and also the priests on duty at the altar in the chamber at the east gate (O), that both may enter upon their functions.

(46) **The sons of Zadok.**—By the law all sons of Aaron were entitled to become priests, but in Ezekiel the offering of sacrifice appears to be confined to the sons of Zadok (comp. xliii. 19; xliv. 15; xlviii. 11). The reason for this is obscure. According to 1 Sam. ii. 30—36 the high-priesthood was to be transferred from the house of Eli, and this was accomplished by Solomon in deposing Abiathar and putting Zadok into his place (1 Kings ii. 26, 27); but there must have been many other priests descended from Ithamar and Eleazar besides the families of Eli and Zadok, and it is hardly possible that all these could have perished in

LORD to minister unto him. (47) So he
measured the court, an hundred cubits
long, and an hundred cubits broad, four-
square; and the altar *that was* before
the house.

(48) And he brought me to the porch
of the house, and measured *each* post
of the porch, five cubits on this side,
and five cubits on that side: and the
breadth of the gate *was* three cubits
on this side, and three cubits on that
side. (49) The length of the porch
was twenty cubits, and the breadth
eleven cubits; and *he brought me* by the
steps whereby they went up to it:
and *there were* pillars by the posts,
one on this side, and another on that
side.

CHAPTER XLI.—(1) Afterward he
brought me to the temple, and measured
the posts, six cubits broad on the one
side, and six cubits broad on the other
side, *which was* the breadth of the taber-
nacle. (2) And the breadth of the [1]door
was ten cubits; and the sides of the
door *were* five cubits on the one side,
and five cubits on the other side: and
he measured the length thereof, forty
cubits: and the breadth, twenty cubits.
(3) Then went he inward, and measured
the post of the door, two cubits; and

1 Or, *entrance.*

---

the slaughter of the eighty-five priests by Saul at Nob (1 Sam. xxii. 17—19). But the body of the priests must have been thereby much reduced, and it is very possible that in the subsequent disorders of the times so few were left who, outside of the family of Zadok, had not fallen into idolatry, that all who were allowed to officiate at the altar came to be called by his name.

(47) **He measured the court.**—This is the inner court (c′), in front of the Temple building itself, and was just 100 cubits square. In this stood the brazen altar (A), the measurements of which are given in xliii. 13—17.

(48) **The porch of the house.**—Verses 48, 49 describe the porch of the Temple itself (z) and may be considered as belonging more properly to the next chapter; still, as this porch projected into the inner court, they are not inappropriate here. The first point to be determined in regard to the construction of this porch is the direction in which its length is measured. The porch in front of Solomon's Temple equalled in length the *interior* breadth of the house (1 Kings vi. 3; 2 Chron. iii. 4), the thickness of the walls and the chambers at the sides projecting beyond the ends of the porch. The same thing is true here, even if the length should be measured from north to south; the exterior front of the house (independently of the side chambers) was thirty-two cubits, each of the side walls being six cubits thick (xli. 5). But writers who adopt this supposition find it necessary to alter the text in order to harmonise the measurements of both verses. It is better to understand the measurements as taken the other way, like those of all the gates of both the outer and inner court. The exterior width of the porch will then be sixteen cubits or just half the exterior width of the house; and the projection into the court will be twenty cubits added to the thickness of the exterior wall and diminished by the thickness of the wall of the house, *i.e.*, $16\frac{1}{2}$ cubits $(20 + 2\frac{1}{2} - 6)$, the exterior being thus almost exactly square.

Each post of the porch.—The front wall, on which the gates were hung, was five cubits on each side, and each leaf of the gate was three cubits, giving sixteen cubits $(5 \times 2 + 3 \times 2)$ for the whole exterior breadth of the porch.

(49) **The breadth eleven cubits.**—This interior measure subtracted from the exterior gives $2\frac{1}{2}$ cubits for each wall—a fair proportion between the thickness of the wall and the size of the porch.

The steps.—The number is not stated, but is given in the Greek as *ten.* It shows that the house itself stood upon a still higher elevation than the inner court.

Pillars by the posts.—On either side of the steps, and near the front wall of the porch, was a pillar corresponding to those in front of the porches of the gates. They answered to the pillars Jachin and Boaz of Solomon's Temple (1 Kings vii. 15—22), and appear to have been placed there for the same general purposes as the obelisks in front of the Egyptian temples.

XLI.

This chapter gives the measurements and describes the ornaments of the Temple itself and its various appurtenances.

(1) **Six cubits broad.**—These *posts,* as in other cases, are the parts of the wall at the sides of the entrance. There is an apparent discrepancy between this and the following verse, where "the sides of the door" are said to be "five cubits," and the latter agrees with the whole width of the house $(5 + 10 + 5 = 20.)$ It is necessary, therefore, to understand the measurement of this verse as taken the other way—as we should say, the side walls of the doors were of the same thickness with the other walls—viz., six cubits. The words *which was* are not in the original, and tend to give a false impression. *Tabernacle* or *tent* is the name by which the sanctuary was known before the erection of the Temple.

(2) **The length thereof, forty cubits.**—These are exactly the dimensions of the Holy Place in Solomon's Temple. The Holy of Holies is not included, being measured by itself in verse 4.

(3) **Went he inward.**—There is here a noticeable change in the usual expression; in all other cases the angel had brought the prophet to the places to be measured, but as he is here entering the Holy of Holies, into which, under the law, Ezekiel might not enter, the angel goes in alone. The prophetic vision was not yet sufficiently clear to speak of the way into the true Holy of Holies as at length opened to all (Heb. ix. 8, 12, x. 19).

The door, six cubits.—*Door* is here used for *doorway,* the clear space between the posts. The "breadth of the door" itself is immediately said to be seven cubits, the door overlapping the posts in a shoulder half a cubit on each side.

the door, six cubits; and the breadth of
the door, seven cubits. (4) So he mea-
sured the length thereof, twenty cubits;
and the breadth, twenty cubits, before
the temple: and he said unto me, This
is the most holy *place*.
(5) After he measured the wall of the
house, six cubits; and the breadth of
every side chamber, four cubits, round
about the house on every side. (6) And
the side chambers *were* three, [1]one over
another, and [2]thirty in order; and they
entered into the wall which *was* of the
house for the side chambers round about,
that they might [3]have hold, but they
had not hold in the wall of the house.
(7) And [4]*there was* an enlarging, and a
winding about still upward to the side
chambers: for the winding about of the
house went still upward round about
the house: therefore the breadth of the
house *was still* upward, and so increased
from the lowest *chamber* to the highest
by the midst. (8) I saw also the height
of the house round about: the founda-
tions of the side chambers *were* a full
reed of six great cubits. (9) The thick-
ness of the wall, which *was* for the side
chamber without, *was* five cubits: and
that which *was* left *was* the place of the

1 Heb., *side chamber over side chamber.*

2 Or, *three and thirty times*, or, *foot.*

3 Heb., *be holden.*

4 Heb., it was *made broader, and went round.*

(4) **Before the temple.**—*Temple* is here, as in verse 1, used of the Holy Place, and *before*, or west of this, was the Holy of Holies, an exact cube, of the same size as in Solomon's Temple. The thickness of the dividing wall between the Holy Place and the Holy of Holies is nowhere mentioned, nor is it taken into account in the measurements. It was merely a division, either a vail, or perhaps a screen of wood, and occupied little room.

(5) **The wall of the house, six cubits.**—The thickness of the wall is the same with that of the wall of the outer court (chap. xl. 5), about ten feet. Great massiveness is characteristic of Oriental architecture, but is carried to excess in this vision, to set forth the firmness and security of the things symbolised.

Every side chamber. — *Every* is not in the original, and is unnecessary. He measured the range of side rooms, the word being used collectively. These (J J) entirely surrounded the house, except on the front or east side where the porch stood.

(6) **Three, one over another, and thirty in order.**—Literally, *three* (and that) *thirty times*—*i.e.*, there were three storeys of chambers one above the other, and this was repeated thirty times, giving thirty chambers in each storey, or ninety in all. These chambers were exactly like those surrounding Solomon's Temple, except that they were one cubit narrower, and the description of them is made clearer by a comparison with 1 Kings vi. 5—10. The Greek version says that there was a space between these chambers and the wall of the house, and several interpreters have followed this explanation; but this is quite inconsistent with the language of the original, and would involve an inner wall for the chambers, of which there is no mention, and for which no space is allowed.

Entered into the wall . . . but they had not hold.—More exactly, *they came upon the wall.* The "house" cannot without violence be understood of anything but the Temple itself. The construction was the same as in Solomon's Temple (1 Kings vi. 6), the wall receding with each storey of the chambers, thus leaving a ledge on which the beams should rest, "that the beams should not be fastened in the walls of the house."

Nothing is said of the distribution of these chambers, but, as will be seen by the plan, a uniform size requires that they should be placed twelve on each side, and six at the end of the Temple.

(7) **And there was an enlarging.**—The description in this verse is difficult to understand, and has called out much variety of opinion. The main facts are clear: that there was an increase in the width of each storey of the side chambers by the distance which the wall receded, as is expressly said in 1 Kings vi. 6; but whether there was a corresponding recession in the thickness of the outer wall of the chambers is not stated. It is also plain that the side chambers surrounded the house; and that the two upper storeys were reached by a winding staircase (W). It is impossible to enter into more detail without a careful discussion of the words in the original, the meaning of some of which is disputed.

(8) **I saw also the height of the house.**—This does not mean the height of the house itself, which is nowhere stated. The words are, literally, *I saw for the house a height* (*i.e.*, an elevation) *round about*, and the meaning of this is explained in what follows. The Temple, as has been already said (chap. xl. 49), was entered by a flight of steps leading up to the porch, and was therefore on a higher level than the court. We are now told that the side chambers had a foundation of six cubits. Whether this "foundation" of the Temple and the side chambers was built of masonry, or, as is more probable, was a sort of basement to contain cisterns and storage rooms, we are not told; but it probably extended, under the name of "the place that was left" (verses 9, 11), five cubits beyond the outer wall of the chambers, forming a platform from which they were entered.

Six great cubits.—Literally, *six cubits to the joint*, or *to the armpit*, for the word has both significations. It is plain that a cubit of a different length, measured to the armpit, cannot be intended, both because no such cubit is known to have been in use at any time, and because Ezekiel in chap. xl. 5 has already fixed the length of the cubit he uses. The sense of *joint* is therefore to be taken, and this applied architecturally can only mean the point at which one part of the building joins another; here, the point where the superstructure meets the foundation, or, as we should say, "six cubits to the water-table."

(9) **That which was left.**—After stating the thickness of the outer wall of the side chambers at five cubits, the prophet speaks of the remaining space left unoccupied by the building. The clause should be translated, "*and so also* (*i.e.*, of the same width) *was that which was left free against the house of side chambers which belonged to the house*," *i.e.*, to the Temple. The same width is assigned to this space in verse 11.

side chambers that *were* within. (10)And
between the chambers *was* the wideness
of twenty cubits round about the house
on every side. (11) And the doors of the
side chambers *were* toward *the place that*
was left, one door toward the north, and
another door toward the south: and the
breadth of the place that was left *was*
five cubits round about.
(12) Now the building that *was* before
the separate place at the end toward the
west *was* seventy cubits broad; and the
wall of the building *was* five cubits thick
round about, and the length thereof
ninety cubits. (13) So he measured the
house, an hundred cubits long; and the
separate place, and the building, with
the walls thereof, an hundred cubits
long; (14) also the breadth of the face of
the house, and of the separate place to-
ward the east, an hundred cubits.
(15) And he measured the length of the
building over against the separate place
which *was* behind it, and the [1]galleries
thereof on the one side and on the other
side, an hundred cubits, with the inner
temple, and the porches of the court;
(16) the door posts, and the narrow win-
dows, and the galleries round about on
their three stories, over against the door,
[2]cieled with wood round about, [3]and
from the ground up to the windows, and
the windows *were* covered; (17) to that
above the door, even unto the inner

1 Or, *several walks, or, walks with pillars.*

2 Heb., *cieling of wood.*

3 Or, *and the ground unto the windows.*

---

(10) **Between the chambers.**—There was a space of twenty cubits (1) between the foundation on which the chambers and the Temple stood and the wall of the court on all three sides on which the chambers extended.

(11) **The doors of the side chambers.**—These doors opened upon the platform, that for the series on the north side to the north, and for the other to the south. There was but one door on each side, so that the series of chambers must have been entered one from another.

We may now sum up the measurements of the Temple with its chambers and surrounding space. The wall, 6 cubits; the chambers, 4; their outer wall, 5; the platform beyond, 5; the space beyond this, 20 $(6 + 4 + 5 + 5 + 20 = 40)$. This was on each side, and therefore is to be doubled, making 80 cubits; to this add the 20 cubits of the inner width of the Temple, and we have exactly the 100 cubits, the width of the inner court. In the same way the length: here the porch is considered as belonging to the court, and with it the front wall of the Temple, the thickness of which is included in the length of the porch. Beginning then at the inside of the outer walls, we have the inner length of Temple, 60 cubits; rear wall, 6; chambers, 4; outer wall, 5; platform, 5; space, 20; in all, 100 cubits, thus making an exact square.

(12) **The separate place.**—This is the space at the west end of the Temple (20 cubits broad) before coming to another building. Nothing is here said of the purposes of this other building; but it is probably "the appointed place" (chap. xliii. 21) for the burning of the sin-offering, and also of any remains of other sacrifices which required to be consumed by fire, and of any other refuse from the Temple. Its total width of 80 cubits (70 cubits + 2 walls of 5 cubits each) leaves a passage-way of 10 cubits on each side; while its length (90 cubits + two walls of 5 cubits each = 100 cubits) just fills the space from "the separate place" to the wall of the court. (See plan II., G.) The sum-total of the exterior measurements is given in verses 13, 14.

(15) **And he measured.**—The rest of the chapter consists of an enumeration of various details, for the most part not before mentioned, and this is introduced by a summary of the measurements already made. This clause is therefore to be understood as equivalent to "So he measured," or, "And he had measured." The dimensions of each of the principal parts is then repeated: the building to the west of the Temple, the Temple itself, and the porches of the court. The only new point introduced is "the galleries thereof." It seems certain that this must refer to the building beyond "the separate place;" but the word for *galleries* occurs only here and in verse 16, and chap. xlii. 3, 5, and its derivation is quite unknown. The translation, *galleries*, is probably correct; and as there was a space of 10 cubits on each side of the building in question, there may very well have been galleries covering and protecting its entrances, although they are not located with sufficient definiteness to be drawn on the plan.

(16) **The door posts.**—This is the same word as in chap. xl. 6, 7, &c., and means *thresholds.* The various particulars mentioned—the thresholds, the windows, and the galleries—are all to be taken in connection with the "he measured" of verse 15, and are details of the three buildings there spoken of, yet they did not all of them necessarily belong to each building.

Narrow windows.—Rather, *closed windows.* (See Note on xl. 16.)

On their three stories.—"Stories" is not in the original, and introduces a wrong idea. He measured the three buildings (verse 15), and various details about their three (constructions) (verse 16).

Over against the door, cieled with wood round about.—This is really a parenthesis, although scarcely intelligible as it stands. Translate, *Opposite the thresholds* (*was*) *a ceiling of wood round about.* The part strictly opposite the threshold was the lintel; but the expression is here broad enough to include also the sides of the doorway. The doorways in the various buildings were all ceiled with wood, and it is afterwards said that this was carved.

And from the ground.—After the parenthesis, the construction dependent upon "he measured" is resumed. As everything else was measured, so also the space between the ground and the windows; then, again, it is mentioned parenthetically that the windows were covered, viz., as in chap. xl. 16, by lattices fastened so as not to be opened.

(17) **To that above the door.**—Better, (*The space*) *over above the door, both to the inner house and without* . . . (*was*) *by measure.* The verse is an

house, and without, and by all the wall
round about within and without, by
[1]measure. (18) And *it was* made with
cherubims and palm trees, so that a
palm tree *was* between a cherub and a
cherub; and *every* cherub had two faces;
(19) so that the face of a man *was* toward
the palm tree on the one side, and the
face of a young lion toward the palm
tree on the other side: *it was* made
through all the house round about.
(20) From the ground unto above the door
were cherubims and palm trees made,
and *on* the wall of the temple. (21) The
[2]posts of the temple *were* squared, *and*
the face of the sanctuary; the appear-
ance *of the one* as the appearance *of the*
other. (22) The altar of wood *was* three
cubits high, and the length thereof two
cubits; and the corners thereof, and the
length thereof, and the walls thereof,
were of wood: and he said unto me, This
is the table that *is* before the LORD.
(23) And the temple and the sanctuary
had two doors. (24) And the doors had
two leaves *apiece*, two turning leaves;
two *leaves* for the one door, and two
leaves for the other *door*. (25) And *there*
were made on them, on the doors of the
temple, cherubims and palm trees, like
as *were* made upon the walls; and *there*
were thick planks upon the face of the
porch without. (26) And *there were*
narrow windows and palm trees on the
one side and on the other side, on the
sides of the porch, and *upon* the side
chambers of the house, and thick planks.

CHAPTER XLII.—(1) Then he brought
me forth into the utter court, the way

1 Heb., *measures*.

2 Heb., *post*.

emphatic repetition of the fact that everything was by measure.

(18) **With cherubims and palm trees.**—Verses 18—21 describe the interior ornamentation of the Temple, which was like that of the Temple of Solomon (1 Kings vi. 29, 30). It may be assumed that here, as there, these figures were carved upon the woodwork. The "s" at the end of "cherubims" is quite unnecessary, "cherubim" itself being plural.

Every cherub had two faces.—In chaps. i. and x. the cherubim are represented each with four faces, but being merely symbolic, not actual creatures, they may be modified at pleasure, and here, in accordance with the exigencies of the carving, they have but two faces.

(20) **Unto above the door.**—The height of the door is nowhere mentioned, and therefore there is nothing to determine how high up the carving was carried; but as it is said that it was also "upon the wall of the Temple," we may assume that the whole interior wall was ceiled with carved wood as in Solomon's Temple.

(21) **The posts of the temple.**—*Posts* is a different word from that hitherto used, and always means the framework in which the doors were hung. *Temple* is, as before, the Holy Place, in distinction from the *sanctuary*, or Holy of Holies. The door-frames of both were square and just alike.

(22) **The altar of wood.**—This is what was known in the tabernacle (Exod. xxx. 1—3) as the altar of incense, and in the Temple as the altar of gold (1 Kings vii. 48), although here its dimensions are enlarged.

The corners thereof.—This doubtless includes the "horns," or projecting pieces at the corners, which were always an important part of the symbolism of the altar. The expression "length" in its repetition is generally thought to mean (by a slight change in the text) "the stand" or "base." *Table* and *altar* are used synonymously, as in Mal. i. 7.

(24) **Two turning leaves.**—The doors both of the Holy Place and of the Holy of Holies are more fully described in 1 Kings vi. 31—35. It is to be understood that each of them was made in two parts, and each part again in two leaves folding back, so that there were in all four leaves in each door.

(25) **Thick planks.**—After stating that the doors just described were ornamented like the walls, the prophet speaks of something that was on the outer front of the porch. What this was, is extremely doubtful, as the word is elsewhere used only in 1 Kings vii. 6, of something in front of Solomon's cloisters or "porch of pillars." Perhaps the best suggestion is that it may have been a moulding of wood. The word in the original is in the singular.

(26) **Windows and palm trees.** — These have already been mentioned in connection with the gateways (chap. xl. 16), and are now further described as in the "side chambers of the temple." The last word, translated "thick planks," is very obscure. If it be the plural of the word used in verse 25, it would mean that the mouldings in front of the porches were also carved with palm trees.

It is to be observed that in these outer parts of the Temple only palm trees were used in the ornamentation, the cherubim being reserved for the Holy Place and the Holy of Holies.

The description of the Temple proper is now finished, and it is noticeable how very little is said of its interior furniture and arrangements. There is no mention at all of that profuse overlaying with gold so characteristic of Solomon's Temple; nothing is said of the candlestick, or the table of show-bread; even the ark itself, that climax of Israel's symbolic worship, is not mentioned. The prophet seems to be looking forward to the time described by his contemporary, Jeremiah, when these outward symbols should be forgotten in the higher spiritual presence of the Lord: "They shall say no more, The ark of the covenant of the LORD; neither shall it come to mind. . . . At that time they shall call Jerusalem the throne of the LORD, and all the nations shall be gathered unto it" (Jer. iii. 16, 17).

XLII.

This chapter describes what is not only new in this vision, but also unknown in either the former or the later Temple. Verses 1—14 are occupied with the account of certain chambers for the priests adjoining

toward the north: and he brought me
into the chamber that *was* over against
the separate place, and which *was* before
the building toward the north. (2) Be-
fore the length of an hundred cubits *was*
the north door, and the breadth *was* fifty
cubits. (3) Over against the twenty *cubits*
which *were* for the inner court, and over
against the pavement which *was* for the
utter court, *was* gallery against gallery
in three *stories.* (4) And before the cham-
bers *was* a walk of ten cubits breadth
inward, a way of one cubit; and their
doors toward the north. (5) Now the
upper chambers *were* shorter: for the
galleries [1]were higher than these, [2]than
the lower, and than the middlemost of
the building. (6) For they *were* in three
stories, but had not pillars as the pillars
of the courts: therefore *the building* was
straitened more than the lowest and the
middlemost from the ground. (7) And
the wall that *was* without over against
the chambers, toward the utter court on

[1] Or, *did eat of these.*

[2] Or, *and the building* consisted *of the lower and the middlemost.*

---

the inner court, but actually within the area of the outer. From verse 14 it is plain that these chambers, although thus situated in the outer court, were considered for ecclesiastical purposes as belonging to the inner. Verses 15—21 describe a very large area enclosing the Temple and its courts as an additional safeguard to its sanctity.

(1) **Utter court.**—*Outer court* (see Note on xl. 31). The "into" of the next clause should be "unto"; so also in chap. xlvi. 19.

Before the building.—The preposition is the same as that translated just before, and also twice in verse 3, "over against." The length of this chamber, or series of chambers, was 100 cubits (verse 2), and as it appears from chap. xlvi. 19 that it did not reach to the western wall, it must have extended the whole remaining length of the building to the west of the separate place, across the separate place itself, and probably also across the chambers at the west end of the Temple (see Plan II., H, H). The chamber on the north is particularly described in verses 1—9, and in verses 10—12 mention is made more briefly of a corresponding one on the south.

(2) **Before the length.**—This verse is still a part of the same sentence, and means, "he brought me before the long side of 100 cubits with the door toward the north, and the breadth 50 cubits." The entrance being on the north was necessarily in the outer court, and the whole description requires that the long way of the building should be east and west. The width therefore of 50 cubits projected into the court just as far as the gateways of the inner court. The measurements of this "chamber" are external, since the prophet did not enter it.

(3) **Over against the twenty.**—See under verse 1. This was the space of twenty cubits (I) to the west of the western Temple chambers.

The pavement.—There is but one pavement mentioned in the outer court, that which ran along the inside of the wall. The chamber in question was opposite to the pavement on the north side, as it was opposite to the separate place, &c., on the south—*i.e.,* its length was parallel to both, or east and west. "Utter" again means *outer.*

Gallery against gallery.—The expression is a difficult one in the original. "Against" is literally, *unto the face of,* or *in front of,* and *stories* is altogether wanting. The meaning seems to be that in each chamber building, on the north and on the south, there was a gallery in the third storey, so placed on the south side of the north building and the north side of the south building that they faced each other.

(4) **A walk of ten cubits breadth inward.**—The meaning of this clause depends upon that of the next, "a way of one cubit." There is every reason to suppose here an error of the text, and that *one cubit* should be *one hundred,* as it reads in the Greek. The change requires only a transposition of the first letters in one word, and a consequent alteration of one letter in the other. Exactly the same transposition has occurred in verse 16, where it is corrected in the margin of the Hebrew, and properly translated "five hundred" instead of "five cubits." One cannot conceive of a walk or an entrance of one cubit (twenty inches) serving any useful purpose. Assuming this change, the meaning will be that a walk (see Plan II., K) of 10 cubits wide and 100 long led to the entrance of the chambers. That this was on the north is plain from its being expressly said that the door was on the north. It may seem surprising that this should have been in the outer court, but a glance at the plan in connection with what is said below will explain the reason of the arrangement. The length of the walk, 100 cubits, just reaches to the steps of the north gate of the inner court. It will be remembered that in chap. xl. 39—43 this was described as the place for killing and preparing the sacrifices. Now, only the fat and kidneys of the sin and trespass and peace offerings were burnt upon the altar; the whole of the former (ordinarily) and the priests' portion of the latter were to be carried to this chamber (verse 13). The walk was therefore placed in the best possible situation.

(5) **For the galleries were higher than these.**—Translate this verse, *And the upper chambers were shortened, because the galleries took off from them* (literally, *eat of them*) *in comparison with the lower and the middle* [*chambers*] *of the building.* The building was in three storeys (verse 6), like the chambers round the Temple, but the gallery is mentioned only in connection with the third (verse 3). As it must have been taken out of the width of the chambers, it made those of the third storey narrower.

(6) **As the pillars of the courts.**—This statement is introduced to show that as there was no external support for the galleries, they must have been taken from the width of the chambers; but it gives incidentally the interesting information that there were pillars in the courts. These could not have been the ornamental pillars at the entrance of the various porches, for the connection implies that they supported something. It is quite likely, therefore, that there were cloisters around the inside of the wall of the courts (on the pavement), as in the later Temple.

(7) **The wall that was without.**—We have two indications of what wall is here meant. In the first place, the word itself is neither of those which have been hitherto used, but one signifying a *fence-*

the forepart of the chambers, the length
thereof *was* fifty cubits. (8) For the length
of the chambers that *were* in the utter
court *was* fifty cubits: and, lo, before
the temple *were* an hundred cubits.
(9) And [1] from under these chambers *was*
[2] the entry on the east side, [3] as one
goeth into them from the utter court.
(10) The chambers *were* in the thickness
of the wall of the court toward the east,
over against the separate place, and over
against the building. (11) And the way
before them *was* like the appearance of
the chambers which *were* toward the
north, as long as they, *and* as broad as
they: and all their goings out *were* both
according to their fashions, and according to their doors. (12) And according to
the doors of the chambers that *were* toward the south *was* a door in the head
of the way, *even* the way directly before
the wall toward the east, as one entereth
into them.

(13) Then said he unto me, The north
chambers *and* the south chambers, which
are before the separate place, they *be* holy
chambers, where the priests that approach unto the LORD shall eat the most
holy things: there shall they lay the
most holy things, and the meat offering,

1 Or, *from the place.*

2 Or, *he that brought me.*

3 Or, *as he came.*

---

wall, and is translated in chaps. xiii. 5, xxii. 30, *hedge*; and in Num. xxii. 24, a vineyard wall. Its length is also said to be fifty cubits (the breadth of the chamber). It must, therefore, have been a screen wall at one end of the chambers, and it could not have been at the western end, as that was otherwise occupied (chap. xlvi. 19, 20). It was then at the eastern end, and was doubtless for the purpose of screening the windows at that end from the outer court while the priests were changing their garments. The word here translated *over against* is not the one used in verses 1, 3, and may equally well be rendered *parallel to.*

(8) **The length of the chambers.**—We should say the breadth, since a longer measurement the other way immediately follows; but the word is used in connection with, and as a reason for, the length of the wall mentioned in verse 7, as if it were said, "The wall was fifty cubits long, because this side of the building was fifty cubits long." To prevent any possible misunderstanding it is immediately added, "Before (literally, *upon the face of*) the Temple an hundred cubits;" *i.e.*, the length east and west was 100 cubits.

(9) **From under these chambers.**—This verse as it stands in our version is scarcely intelligible. Translate: *And from underneath it* (*i.e.*, the wall just spoken of) *these chambers.* The wall screened the lower part of the chambers so that to one looking from the east they appeared to rise out of it. Then a new clause begins: "The entrance was from the east, as one goeth to them from the outer court." It is perfectly clear that this does not refer to any entrance from the inner court, because it expressly says "as one goeth from the outer court." The object of the statement is probably to show that the access to the chambers was from the outer court by means of the walk already described, leading from the east, from the porch of the gate to the inner court.

Verses 10—12 describe briefly another chamber-building at the south of the "separate place," exactly like the one already described at the north. There is only need to notice some required changes in the translation. Thus read verse 10, *On the breadth of the wall of the court going toward the east, over against the separate place and over against the building were the chambers.* The *wall* is here the same word as in verse 7, and means therefore not the wall of a building, but a fence-wall; it is here defined, however, as "the wall of the court," and must be understood of the division wall between the inner and outer courts. Along this, as it stretched to the east, the building was situated. Some writers, by a slight alteration of the text, would change *east* into *south*, so that for "going toward the east" we should read *on the south.* This makes the sense clearer, but is not necessary.

(11) "And a way in front of them like the chambers which were towards the north; as long as these and as broad as these, and [like] all their goings out, and their arrangements, and their doors."

(12) "So were the doors of the chambers which were toward the south, a door at the head of the way, the way over against the corresponding (?) wall, the way as one enters from the east." The word here translated *corresponding* occurs only in this place, and is of doubtful signification; but the word for wall is the same as in verse 7, and there can be no doubt that it refers to the screen-wall to the east of the chambers. The way from the porch of the gate to the inner court was directly "over against" the passage between this wall and the chambers, and in fact joined it at right angles.

This closes the somewhat obscure and difficult description of these chambers, where we do not have, as in the other cases, any similar construction in the ancient Temple to guide the interpreter. It would seem altogether probable that there must have been an additional entrance to these chambers from the space at the side of or behind the Temple, for the convenience of the priests in changing their garments. Perhaps there was such an entrance to the second storey, which must have been about on the same level with the Temple court, but is not mentioned because only the plan of the lower storey is described.

(13) **Shall eat the most holy things.**—In the next clause it is said, "There shall they lay the most holy things," both clauses referring to the priests' portion of the sacrifices. We cannot think of their laying the uncooked flesh of the sacrifice in the same room where they ate (the cooking was done in another room west of this, chap. xlvi. 19, 20); but the great size of this building—166 ft. long and half as broad—allowed of its division into several separate rooms. It is noticeable that there is no mention of the peace offerings, for it was not required in the law that they should be eaten in a holy place. For the others, see Lev. vi. 16, 26; vii. 6. The "meat offering" is the unbloody oblation usually accompanying the animal sacrifices

and the sin offering, and the trespass
offering; for the place *is* holy. (14) When
the priests enter therein, then shall they
not go out of the holy *place* into the
utter court, but there they shall lay
their garments wherein they minister;
for they *are* holy; and shall put on
other garments, and shall approach to
those things which *are* for the people.

(15) Now when he had made an end of
measuring the inner house, he brought
me forth toward the gate whose prospect
is toward the east, and measured it
round about. (16) He measured the east
[1] side with the measuring reed, five hun-
dred reeds, with the measuring reed
round about. (17) He measured the north
side, five hundred reeds, with the mea-
suring reed round about. (18) He mea-
sured the south side, five hundred reeds,
with the measuring reed. (19) He turned
about to the west side, *and* measured
five hundred reeds with the measuring
reed. (20) He measured it by the four
sides: it had a wall round about, five
hundred *reeds* long, and five hundred
broad, to make a separation between the
sanctuary and the profane place.

CHAPTER XLIII.—(1) Afterward he
brought me to the gate, *even* the gate
that looketh toward the east: (2) and,
behold, the glory of the God of Israel
came from the way of the east: and his
voice *was* like a noise of many [a] waters:
and the earth shined with his glory.
(3) And *it was* [b] according to the appear-
ance of the vision which I saw, *even* ac-
cording to the vision that I saw [2] when I
came to destroy the city: and the visions
were like the vision that I saw by the
river Chebar; and I fell upon my face.
(4) And the glory of the LORD came into
the house by the way of the gate whose
prospect *is* toward the east. (5) So the
spirit took me up, and brought me
into the inner court; and, behold, the
glory of the LORD filled the house.

1 Heb., *wind.*

a ch. 1. 24.

b ch. 1. 4, & 8. 4.

2 Or, *when I came to prophesy that the city should be destroyed*: see ch. 9. 2, 5.

---

(14) **There they shall lay their garments.**—It was apparently the requirement of the law that the priests should wear their official garments only when engaged in priestly duties within the tabernacle; this is not expressly stated in general terms, but it is said that they were to wear them when engaged in such duty (Ex. xxviii. 43), and in some particular cases that they were to put them off when they went out of the tabernacle (Lev. vi. 10, 11; xvi. 23). It seems probable, therefore, that Ezekiel here recognises the ancient custom.

(15) **The inner house.**—This expression is here evidently used neither of the Holy of Holies, nor of the whole Temple building exclusively, but of all that had been measured, all that was included within the wall of the outer court. The prophet is led out from this by the eastern gate to measure a much larger space around it. It is not said in what part of this space the Temple with its courts was situated; but, for the reason given in verse 20, it is to be supposed that it was in the centre.

(16) **With the measuring reed.**—According to chap. xl. 5 the reed was six cubits long; 500 reeds therefore, the measure of each side of the square, was 3,000 cubits, or about 5,000 feet = nearly a mile. Of course such a space, quite as large as was ever enclosed by the walls of ancient Jerusalem, would have been impossible upon the hill of Moriah, and various efforts have been made by some of the commentators to reduce the size; but the use of the reed as the unit of measurement is decisive. The objection to the size is without value, as Keil well says, "for the simple reason that in chaps. xlv. and xlviii. there follow still further statements concerning the separation of the sanctuary from the rest of the land, which are in perfect harmony with this, and show most indisputably that the Temple seen by Ezekiel was not to have its seat in the ancient Jerusalem;" nor, it may be added, in any other earthly locality. It is a vision not designed to have a material realisation.

(20) **It had a wall.**—Around this vast enclosure on all sides was a wall, not of the slight character of that in verse 7; but the same word is used as in chap. xl. 5, of the massive wall surrounding the outer court. The object of this enclosure was to protect the sanctity of the Temple and its courts, "to make a separation between the sanctuary and the profane place."

XLIII.

The new Temple had now been shown to the prophet with all its arrangements and measurements; it remained that the structure should be divinely accepted by the manifestation of the glory of the Lord, as in the case of the Tabernacle (Exod. xl. 34, 35), and of the former Temple (1 Kings viii. 10, 11; 2 Chron. v. 13, 14; vii. 1—3). The description of this and the accompanying message occupy verses 1—12. With verse 13 the account of the ordinances of Divine worship to be celebrated in the Temple begins, and is continued to the close of chap. xlvi.

(2) **From the way of the east.**—The prophet had been brought (verse 1) to the east gate, from which he had formerly seen the glory of the Lord depart (chaps. x. 18, 19; xi. 1, 23) on account of the pollution of His house. By the same way the glory of the Lord was now to return to the sanctuary prepared for it.

(3) **When I came to destroy the city.**—That is *to announce its destruction.* (Comp. chap. xxxii. 18; Gen. xlix. 7; Isa. vi. 10; Jer. i. 10.)

Like the vision that I saw.—Comp. chaps. i. 4, &c.; iii. 23; x. 15, 22. The manifestation of Divine glory to the prophet was the same throughout.

(5) **Brought me into the inner court.**—Having seen the Divine glory enter by the eastern gate, the prophet, himself a priest, is brought into the court of the priests, and there sees the glory of the Lord fill the house as of old.

(6) And I heard *him* speaking unto me
out of the house; and the man stood
by me. (7) And he said unto me,
Son of man, the place of my throne, and
the place of the soles of my feet, where
I will dwell in the midst of the children
of Israel for ever, and my holy name,
shall the house of Israel no more defile,
neither they, nor their kings, by their
whoredom, nor by the carcases of their
kings in their high places. (8) In their
setting of their threshold by my thres-
holds, and their post by my posts, [1]and
the wall between me and them, they
have even defiled my holy name by their
abominations that they have committed:
wherefore I have consumed them in mine
anger. (9) Now let them put away their
whoredom, and the carcases of their
kings, far from me, and I will dwell in
the midst of them for ever.
(10) Thou son of man, shew the house
to the house of Israel, that they may be
ashamed of their iniquities: and let
them measure the [2]pattern. (11) And if
they be ashamed of all that they have
done, shew them the form of the house,
and the fashion thereof, and the goings
out thereof, and the comings in there-
of, and all the forms thereof, and all the
ordinances thereof, and all the forms
thereof, and all the laws thereof: and
write *it* in their sight, that they may
keep the whole form thereof, and all
the ordinances thereof, and do them.
(12) This *is* the law of the house; Upon
the top of the mountain the whole limit
thereof round about *shall be* most holy.
Behold, this *is* the law of the house.
(13) And these *are* the measures of the
altar after the cubits: The cubit *is* a
cubit and an hand breadth; even the
[3]bottom *shall be* a cubit, and the breadth
a cubit, and the border thereof by the
[4]edge thereof round about *shall be* a
span: and this *shall be* the higher place

1 Or, *for there was but a wall between me and them.*

2 Or, *sum,* or, *number.*

3 Heb., *bosom.*

4 Heb., *lip.*

---

(6) **I heard him speaking.**—Although the pronoun is not expressed in the original, there can be no question that God Himself spoke directly to the prophet, as in chap. xliv. 2, 5, 9, &c. "The man" is without the article in the Hebrew, which leaves it uncertain whether the same being is meant who had hitherto guided the prophet; but as measurements were also made by this guide (xlvii. 3, 4, 5), he was probably the same.

(7) **The place of the soles of my feet.**—Comp. 1 Chron. xxviii. 2; Ps. cxxxii. 7.

I will dwell . . . for ever.—This should be the peculiar distinction of the Temple seen in the vision. The Tabernacle and Solomon's Temple had both been accepted as the peculiar dwelling-place of God, but both had passed away. So also it would be with the material Temple of the restoration. But in this Temple of the vision God promises that He would dwell for ever.

By the carcases of their kings.—The "shall defile" with which the later clauses of this verse are connected is not an imperative, but a simple future, and is in accordance with the generally ideal character of the vision. The word "carcases" is here a difficult one. Some commentators understand it literally of the burial of some of the kings in the Temple area; but there is no historical proof that any were so buried, the gardens of the royal palace being quite too distant for the language here used, nor is there anywhere any allusion to such defilement. The simplest explanation is that the language is founded upon Lev. xxvi. 30, and means *idols*. Manasseh and others had introduced their idols into the very courts of the Temple (2 Kings xxi. 4—7; see also 2 Kings xvi. 11).

(8) **And the wall between.**—The sense is given in the margin: there was *only* a wall between me and them.

(9) **Now let them.**—This is not an imperative, but a simple future, as in verse 7. The house of Israel will now put away their abominations, and God will dwell in their midst for ever. Carcases = idols, as in verse 7.

(10) **Shew the house.**—This is still in vision; "make known to the people the new Temple and its appointments," that, seeing God's gracious purposes, they may repent of their evil doings.

Let them measure the pattern.—That is, let them carefully consider and follow out the provisions God had made for their worship. (Comp. Heb. viii. 5.) Exactness in the observance of all positive enactments is a necessary result of a desire to serve God.

(11) **If they be ashamed.**—The same thing which had already been declared positively is now expressed contingently, showing that the sanctification of the people and God's dwelling among them were correlative facts; the one could not be without the other. Many expressions of nearly the same meaning are heaped up, as it were, in the latter part of this verse, to emphasise the significance of the arrangements of the new Temple, and to secure for them the thought and consideration of the people.

(12) **Upon the top of the mountain.**—Comp. xl. 2. The command to keep and observe everything is closed, as often in similar cases, by a summary statement of the reason: for the whole surroundings of the dwelling-place of the Most High are holy.

With verse 13 a new part of the vision begins, extending to the close of chap. xlvi., describing the new ordinances of the sanctuary. This is fitly opened with a description of the altar for the sacrifices, the central act of the ancient worship.

(13) **A cubit and an hand breadth.**—The measurement of the altar begins with the statement that the cubit used was of the same length as before (see xl. 5). The description that follows (verses 13—17) will be made clearer by a simple diagram, with references to the parts described. The size of the base of the altar, it will be seen, was 16 cubits square, and its entire height was either 11 or 12 cubits. The

cf the altar. (14) And from the bottom
upon the ground *even* to the lower settle
shall be two cubits, and the breadth one
cubit; and from the lesser settle *even* to
the greater settle *shall be* four cubits,
and the breadth *one* cubit. (15) So [1]the
altar *shall be* four cubits; and from [2]the
altar and upward *shall be* four horns.
(16) And the altar *shall be* twelve *cubits*
long, twelve broad, square in the four
squares thereof. (17) And the settle *shall
be* fourteen *cubits* long and fourteen
broad in the four squares thereof; and
the border about it *shall be* half a cubit;
and the bottom thereof *shall be* a cubit
about; and his stairs shall look toward
the east.

(18) And he said unto me, Son of man,
thus saith the Lord God; These *are* the
ordinances of the altar in the day when
they shall make it, to offer burnt offer-
ings thereon, and to sprinkle blood
thereon. (19) And thou shalt give to the
priests the Levites that be of the seed
of Zadok, which approach unto me, to
minister unto me, saith the Lord God, a
young bullock for a sin offering. (20)And
thou shalt take of the blood thereof, and
put *it* on the four horns of it, and on the
four corners of the settle, and upon the
border round about: thus shalt thou
cleanse and purge it. (21) Thou shalt
take the bullock also of the sin offering,
and he shall burn it in the appointed
place of the house, without the sanc-
tuary. (22) And on the second day thou
shalt offer a kid of the goats without
blemish for a sin offering; and they

1 Heb., *Harel*, that is, *the mountain of God.*

2 Heb., *Ariel*, that is, *the lion of God.*

---

altar in Solomon's Temple was of brass, 20 cubits square, and 10 cubits high (2 Chron. iv. 1), while that in the Tabernacle (of shittim-wood overlaid with brass) had been 5 cubits square, and 3 cubits high (Exod. xxvii. 1). That in Herod's Temple is said to have been 32 cubits square, and 10 cubits high, and was of hewn stone. The dimensions of Ezekiel's altar seem to have been selected for the symmetry of the numbers in the several parts. In height it exceeded any of the others.

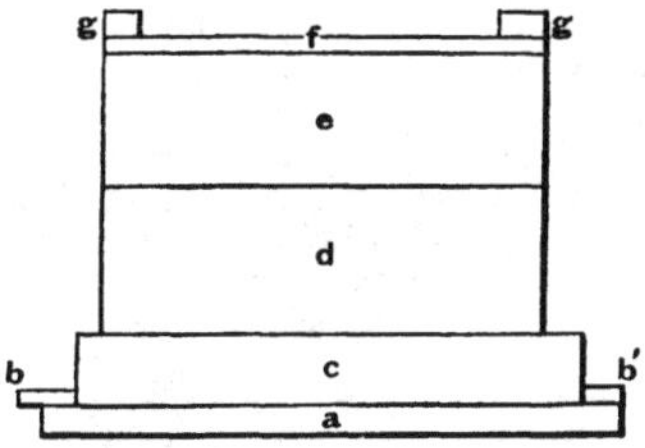

(*a*) Base or "bottom," 1 cubit high, and 1 broad. This was 16 cubits square.
(*bb'*) "The border thereof," a span or ½ cubit. It is uncertain whether this projected, forming a moulding as at *b*, and in this case was under *c*, and so increased the height of the altar; or whether it was as at *b'*, a ledge around *c*. In verse 13 "higher place" should be *base*. The word means, primarily, *arched*, then *a back*, and then *a support*.
(*c*) The "lower settle," 2 cubits high, and 1 broad.
(*d*) The "greater (or higher) settle," 4 cubits high.
(*e*) The "altar" (*Harel*)—literally, *the mountain of God*—4 cubits high, and 12 cubits square.
(*f*) The "altar" (*Ariel*)—literally, *the lion of God*—the hearth of the same size, but the height not given, but probably not more than ½ cubit.
(*gg*) The "horns." The whole height was eleven cubits or more, according to whether the height of *f* is included in that of *e*, and whether *b* passed under *c*, or was merely a ledge.

Verses 18—27 make careful provision for the consecration of the altar just described. This is to be compared with Exod. xl. and Lev. viii., although in that case the consecration of the altar and of the priests were joined together, while here that of the altar alone is described.

(18) **In the day when they shall make it.**—This looks to the future, and implies that the whole structure of the Temple, and its acceptance by the manifestation of the Divine glory, though necessarily represented in the vision as already done, were yet in the future. The phrase, "in the day when they shall make it," is intended only to require the consecration of the altar before it is used. The actual time occupied by the consecration (verses 25, 26) was to be seven days, as in Exod. xxix. 37.

(19) **Thou shalt give.**—Ezekiel is not actually to do this, like Moses, as the appointed consecrator; but, as frequently in prophecy, he is told *to do* that which he foretells is to be done.

Of the seed of Zadok.—See Note on xl. 46. (Comp. also xliv. 15.)

A young bullock.—In the case of the altar of the Tabernacle, the consecration began with anointing with oil (Lev. viii. 11), and this was a prominent feature of the service; but is here wholly omitted. The service began with the offering of a sin offering, which was always, according to the law, to be first offered when several kinds of sacrifice were to occur together. The propriety of this is manifest, since the first act of man's approach to God must always consist of the confession of his sin.

(20) **Take of the blood thereof.**—Comp. Exod. xxix. 12; Lev. viii. 15; Heb. ix. 18, 22. Nothing is here said of the pouring the rest of the blood at the foot of the altar, as required in the law, and nothing of the burning of the fat upon the altar, because the prophet throughout supposes the ritual of the sacrifices to be well known, and only mentions a few particulars to indicate the whole, and also a few others now introduced, peculiar to the new ceremonial.

(21) **Burn it in the appointed place.**—The flesh of the ordinary sin offerings was to be eaten by the priests; but when the victim was a bullock, as in case of a sin offering for the high priest (Lev. iv. 3, 11, 12), or for the whole congregation (*ib.* 13, 20), it was to be burned without the camp. Here it is to be burned "in the appointed place of the house," and yet "without the sanctuary," or Temple building itself; it must, therefore, have been in the building described in xli. 12

(22) **A kid of the goats.**—More exactly, *a buck of the goats*. This was the sin offering prescribed for a ruler (Lev. iv. 22, 23). The expression "as they did with the bullock," implies that the ritual was the same,

shall cleanse the altar, as they did
cleanse *it* with the bullock. (23) When
thou hast made an end of cleansing *it*,
thou shalt offer a young bullock without
blemish, and a ram out of the flock with-
out blemish. (24) And thou shalt offer
them before the LORD, and the priests
shall cast salt upon them, and they shall
offer them up *for* a burnt offering unto
the LORD. (25) Seven days shalt thou
prepare every day a goat *for* a sin offer-
ing: they shall also prepare a young
bullock, and a ram out of the flock,
without blemish. (26) Seven days shall
they purge the altar and purify it; and
they shall [1]consecrate themselves. (27) And
when these days are expired, it shall be,
that upon the eighth day, and *so* forward,
the priests shall make your burnt offer-
ings upon the altar, and your [2]peace
offerings; and I will accept you, saith
the Lord GOD.

[1] Heb., *fill their hands.*

[2] Or, *thank offerings.*

CHAPTER XLIV. — (1) Then he
brought me back the way of the gate of
the outward sanctuary which looketh
toward the east; and it *was* shut.
(2) Then said the LORD unto me; This
gate shall be shut, it shall not be opened,
and no man shall enter in by it; be-
cause the LORD, the God of Israel, hath
entered in by it, therefore it shall be
shut. (3) *It is* for the prince; the prince,
he shall sit in it to eat bread before the
LORD; he shall enter by the way of the
porch of *that* gate, and shall go out by
the way of the same.
(4) Then brought he me the way of the
north gate before the house: and I
looked, and, behold, the glory of the

---

and the flesh burned in the same way. At the consecration of the altar in Exod. xxix. 36, a bullock was required for the sin offering on each of the seven days for the consecration of both the altar and the priests.

(23) **Hast made an end of cleansing it.**—Not an end of the entire service of consecration, but of the sin offering for the day, for verse 25 says distinctly that both a sin offering and a burnt offering were to be offered on each day of the seven. The reason that the burnt offering is not mentioned on the first day is, that the sin offering being changed on the second day, the prophet first describes that for both days, and then goes to the other, which remained the same throughout. Here the burnt offering is a bullock and a ram; in Exod. xxix. two rams.

(24) **Cast salt.**—The word means *throw* or *pour*, indicating a more copious use of salt than the seasoning ordained by the law (Lev. ii. 13).

(26) **Shall consecrate themselves.**—Our version has here followed the Masoretic emendation of the text; the literal translation of the text itself is, *shall fill its hand*, referring to the altar. To "fill the hand" is a synonym for consecration, commonly applied to the priests, who were consecrated by placing in their hands the gifts they were to offer to God. Here it is better to keep to the text as it stands, "filling the hand of the altar" being a strong figurative expression to denote that it shall always be supplied with sacrificial gifts. Nothing is said throughout the passage of the consecration of the priests, the whole family of Aaron having been consecrated once for all by the ceremonies of Lev. viii.

XLIV.

The altar being consecrated, the next thing is to provide for the purity of the worship of which it is the centre. The pollutions of former times had been largely introduced by the princes, and by the Levites and priests; and these classes are therefore treated of in this chapter. Only three verses are here given to the prince, since he is to be spoken of at greater length hereafter, and the rest of the chapter is occupied with directions as to the exclusion of strangers, and the duties of the Levites and priests.

(1) **The gate of the outward sanctuary.**—This is better rendered, *the outer gate of the sanctuary*. The prophet had been in the inner court, or court of the priests, where the altar stood, and is now brought back to the eastern gate of the outer court. He finds it shut, as it was ordinarily to remain; but with the exceptions mentioned in verse 3, and in chap. xlvi.

(2) **Hath entered in by it.**—See chap. xliii. 1, 2. The thought is, that the gate which had been sanctified by such a manifestation of the Divine presence, should not afterwards be used for the ordinary purposes of the entrance of the people.

(3) **The prince.**—The Rabbis understood this to refer to the Messiah, and unquestionably the same person must be meant as by David in chaps. xxxiv. 23, 24; xxxvii. 24. This gives another and a conclusive reason for regarding the sacrificial worship of chap. xlvi. as symbolical.

To eat bread before the Lord.—This is the common scriptural expression for partaking of the sacrifices (see Gen. xxxi. 54; Exod. xviii. 12), and there is no reason for restricting it to the shew-bread and other unbloody offerings. The eating of the latter was an exclusively priestly prerogative, and the "prince" of Ezekiel, though greatly distinguished, is not in any way endued with priestly functions. He is to partake of his sacrificial meals within this highly-honoured gate, while the people eat in the outer court. There has been much discussion as to whether the prince was to go in and out by this gateway, or only, having entered by one of the others, to eat in this. The language here seems sufficiently plain, and if there could be any doubt, it would be removed by chap. xlvi. 1, 2, 8, 10, 12. It appears there that the prince is always to enter and leave by this gate except "in the solemn feasts;" then he is to enter in the midst of the people, by either the north or the south gate, and go out by the opposite one.

(4) **The north gate.**—The prophet is now carried to the north gate, and since this is described as "before the house" and was in full view of it, it must have been the gate of the inner court, the appointed place for the killing of the sacrifices, and therefore especially fitting for the announcement of the ordinances of the priests. There he saw the "glory of the Lord" filling

Lord filled the house of the Lord: and
I fell upon my face. (5) And the Lord
said unto me, Son of man, [1]mark well,
and behold with thine eyes, and hear
with thine ears all that I say unto thee
concerning all the ordinances of the
house of the Lord, and all the laws
thereof; and mark well the entering in
of the house, with every going forth of
the sanctuary. (6) And thou shalt say to
the rebellious, *even* to the house of
Israel, Thus saith the Lord God; O ye
house of Israel, let it suffice you of all
your abominations, (7) in that ye have
brought *into my sanctuary* [2]strangers,
uncircumcised in heart, and uncircum-
cised in flesh, to be in my sanctuary, to
pollute it, *even* my house, when ye offer
my bread, the fat and the blood, and
they have broken my covenant because
of all your abominations. (8) And ye
have not kept the charge of mine holy
things: but ye have set keepers of my
[3]charge in my sanctuary for yourselves.
(9) Thus saith the Lord God; No
stranger, uncircumcised in heart, nor
uncircumcised in flesh, shall enter into
my sanctuary, of any stranger that *is*
among the children of Israel. (10) And
the Levites that are gone away far from
me, when Israel went astray, which went
astray away from me after their idols;
they shall even bear their iniquity.
(11) Yet they shall be ministers in my
sanctuary, *having* charge at the gates of
the house, and ministering to the house:
they shall slay the burnt offering and
the sacrifice for the people, and they
shall stand before them to minister unto
them. (12) Because they ministered unto
them before their idols, and [4]caused the
house of Israel to fall into iniquity;
therefore have I lifted up mine hand
against them, saith the Lord God, and
they shall bear their iniquity. (13) And
they shall not come near unto me, to do
the office of a priest unto me, nor to
come near to any of my holy things, in
the most holy *place*: but they shall bear
their shame, and their abominations
which they have committed. (14) But I
will make them keepers of the charge of
the house, for all the service thereof, and
for all that shall be done therein.

(15) But the priests the Levites, the
sons of Zadok, that kept the charge of
my sanctuary when the children of Israel
went astray from me, they shall come
near to me to minister unto me, and
they shall stand before me to offer unto
me the fat and the blood, saith the Lord
God: (16) they shall enter into my sanc-
tuary, and they shall come near to my
table, to minister unto me, and they shall
keep my charge.

(17) And it shall come to pass, *that* when
they enter in at the gates of the inner
court, they shall be clothed with linen

1 Heb., *set thine heart.*

2 Heb., *children of a stranger.*

3 Or, *ward,* or, *ordinance:* and so ver. 14 & 16.

4 Heb., *were for a stumblingblock of iniquity unto,* &c.

---

the house, and was commanded to give the utmost attention to the laws now to be announced.

(7) **Strangers, uncircumcised in heart.**—The heathen living in Israel, or coming to worship at the Temple, were allowed, and even in some cases required, to offer sacrifices (Lev. xvii. 10, 12; Num. xv. 14, 26, 29). This seems also to have been recognised in Solomon's prayer at the consecration of the Temple (1 Kings viii. 41—43); but the ground on which the Israelites are here censured for the licence given to strangers is, that they allowed those to draw near in worship who were *uncircumcised in heart* as well as in flesh, *i.e.*, ungodly men who had no real purpose to worship God.

(8) **For yourselves.**—Comp. 1 Kings xii. 31.

(9) **Shall enter into my sanctuary.**—To guard against the evils of the past, the command is now given that none of the strangers described shall even enter the sanctuary; but our version gives a wrong impression of this prohibition by rendering, "*nor* uncircumcised in flesh." It should be, as in verse 7, *and.* The command is not that no uncircumcised person should be allowed to enter the sanctuary, for the residence of strangers among the Israelites is expressly provided for in chap. xlvii. 22, 23; but the emphasis here, as before, is upon the "uncircumcised in heart." No godless heathen should be allowed to enter in to profane the Divine worship.

(10) **And the Levites that are gone away.**—The connection between this and the preceding verse is made clearer by translating the first words, "Yea, even;" not only the uncircumcised in heart among the heathen are to be excluded from the sanctuary, but even the Levites who had apostatised are to bear their guilt. *Levites* is here used (see verse 13), as often, emphatically of the Levitical priests. At the great schism of the northern kingdom these had remained true to the worship of Jehovah (2 Chron. xi. 13); but in the subsequent general religious declension many of them, as has appeared from chap. viii., had fallen into idolatry. Such priests are to be allowed, like the priests under the law who had any physical blemish (Lev. xxi. 17—23), to minister in the more menial offices of the priesthood, but not to approach the altar (verses 11—14).

(15) **The sons of Zadok.**—See Note on chap. xl. 46. They are here described as those who continued faithful in the general apostasy, and it is probable that Ezekiel uses the term in this sense. As Zadok had continued faithful in the rebellion of Adonijah, when even the high priest and life-long friend of David went astray (1 Kings i. 7, 8), so all the faithful priests in the time of apostasy were called "sons of Zadok."

(17) **Clothed with linen garments.**—The rest of the chapter is occupied with directions for the clothing

garments; and no wool shall come upon
them, whiles they minister in the gates
of the inner court, and within. (18) They
shall have linen bonnets upon their
heads, and shall have linen breeches
upon their loins; they shall not gird
themselves [1][2] with any thing that causeth
sweat. (19) And when they go forth into
the utter court, *even* into the utter court
to the people, they shall put off their
garments wherein they ministered, and
lay them in the holy chambers, and they
shall put on other garments; and they
shall not sanctify the people with their
garments. (20) Neither shall they shave
their heads, nor suffer their locks to
grow long; they shall only poll their
heads. (21) Neither shall any priest drink
wine, when they enter into the inner
court. (22) Neither shall they take for
their wives a [a]widow, nor her that is
[3]put away: but they shall take maidens
of the seed of the house of Israel, or a
widow [4]that had a priest before. (23) And
they shall teach my people *the difference*
between the holy and profane, and cause
them to discern between the unclean
and the clean. (24) And in controversy
they shall stand in judgment; *and* they
shall judge it according to my judg-
ments: and they shall keep my laws and
my statutes in all mine assemblies; and
they shall hallow my sabbaths. (25) And
they shall come at no [b]dead person to
defile themselves: but for father, or for
mother, or for son, or for daughter, for
brother, or for sister that hath had no
husband, they may defile themselves.
(26) And after he is cleansed, they shall
reckon unto him seven days. (27) And in
the day that he goeth into the sanc-
tuary, unto the inner court, to minister
in the sanctuary, he shall offer his sin
offering, saith the Lord God. (28) And it
shall be unto them for an inheritance:
I [c]*am* their inheritance: and ye shall
give them no possession in Israel: I *am*
their possession. (29) They shall eat the
meat offering, and the sin offering, and
the trespass offering; and every [5]dedi-
cated thing in Israel shall be their's.
(30) And the [6][d]first of all the firstfruits of
all *things*, and every oblation of all, of
every *sort* of your oblations, shall be the
priest's: ye shall also give unto the
priest the first of your dough, that he
may cause the blessing to rest in thine
house. (31) The priests shall not eat of
any thing that is [e]dead of itself, or torn,
whether it be fowl or beast.

1 Or, *in sweating places.*

2 Heb., *in*, or, *with sweat.*

a Lev. 21. 13.

3 Heb., *thrust forth.*

4 Heb., *from a priest.*

b Lev. 21. 1, 11.

c Num. 18. 20; Deut. 10. 9, & 18. 1, 2; Josh. 13. 14, 33.

5 Or, *devoted.*

6 Or, *chief.*

d Ex. 13. 2, & 22. 29, 30; Num. 3. 13, & 18. 12.

e Ex. 22. 31; Lev. 22. 8.

---

and conduct of the priests. The dress (verses 17—19) is the same as that prescribed in Lev. xxviii., only a few special points being mentioned partly for emphasis, and partly as recalling to mind the whole.

(19) **They shall put off their garments.**—The requirement that the priests shall wear their official dress only when engaged in official duty, putting it on when they entered the inner court, and putting it off when they went out, which is only implied in Exodus and Leviticus, is here expressly enjoined. *Utter* here, as elsewhere, means *outer*.

(20) **Their locks to grow long.**—The law forbade the shaving of the head (Lev. xxi. 5), but only condemned letting the hair grow long by implication, providing for it in the exceptional case of the vow of the Nazarite. The prohibition of verse 21 is given in Lev. x. 9.

(22) **A widow that had a priest before.**—In regard both to marriage and to mourning (verses 25—27) the Levitical law made a broad distinction between the ordinary priest and the high priest. The former was only forbidden to marry a divorced woman (Lev. xxi. 7), but was allowed to marry a widow; the latter could marry only a virgin of Israel (*ib.* 14). So also in the law of mourning; the high priest might not be "defiled" nor make any sign of mourning even for his nearest of kin (Lev. xxi. 11—14). Ezekiel does not recognise this distinction, and in fact nowhere mentions the high priest at all; but, instead, gives a general law for all priests, somewhat between the two.

(26) **Reckon unto him seven days.**—In verses 23, 24, the general duties of the priests are prescribed in terms taken from the Mosaic law, and in verses 25—27 special instructions are given about the defilement from a dead body. These are in general an exact repetition of Lev. xxi. 1—4; but, in accordance with the principle mentioned in the last Note, there is added to the ordinary cleansing of seven days (Num. xix. 11—17) another period of seven days, after which Ezekiel requires (verse 27) the priest to offer a sin offering before entering again on his duties.

(28) **I am their inheritance.**—This is a simple repetition of the frequent declarations in the law (Num. xviii. 20; Deut. x. 9; xviii. 2); the priests were to be supported by the tithes given to God, and by their portion of the offerings made to Him. These are here summarily mentioned in verses 28, 29, and may be found more particularly described, as regards the priests' share of the meat, sin, and trespass offerings, in Lev. ii. 3; vi. 25, 29; vii. 6, 7; the devoted field, Lev. xxvii. 21; the first-fruits, Exod. xxiii. 19; xxxiv. 26; Num. xviii. 13; Deut. xviii. 4; and for the special heave offerings, Num. xv. 19—21; xviii. 19. As it was not inconsistent with these provisions that the priests should also have assigned to them cities for residence, with their suburbs for pasturage, so these gifts are not now excluded by the fact that the priests should possess the "oblation" of land (chap. xlv. 1—5), although their portion is thereby greatly increased.

(31) **Dead of itself, or torn.**—Comp. Lev. xxii. 8. The same law was binding upon all the Israelites. (Lev. xvii. 15.) In the wilderness they were required to "cast it to the dogs" (Exod. xxiii. 31); afterwards they might give it to a stranger or sell it to an alien. (Deut. xiv. 21.)

CHAPTER XLV.—(1)Moreover,[1]when
ye shall divide by lot the land for inherit-
ance, ye shall offer an oblation unto the
LORD, [2]an holy portion of the land: the
length *shall be* the length of five and
twenty thousand *reeds*, and the breadth
shall be ten thousand. This *shall be*
holy in all the borders thereof round
about. (2) Of this there shall be for the
sanctuary five hundred *in length*, with
five hundred *in breadth*, square round
about; and fifty cubits round about for
the [3]suburbs thereof. (3) And of this
measure shalt thou measure the length
of five and twenty thousand, and the
breadth of ten thousand: and in it shall
be the sanctuary *and* the most holy *place*.
(4) The holy *portion* of the land shall be
for the priests the ministers of the sanc-
tuary, which shall come near to minister
unto the LORD: and it shall be a place
for their houses, and an holy place for

1 Heb., *when ye cause the land to fall.*

2 Heb., *holiness.*

3 Or, *void places.*

XLV.

This and the first part of the following chapter form a remarkable portion of the book. They first describe the setting apart of a large part of the whole land for the sanctuary, the priests, the prince, and the city, in a way and in a geographical position entirely unknown either in the past or the subsequent history of the people (verses 1—8). The portion assigned to the prince is to prevent violence and exaction on his part; in this connection all unjust measurements are to cease, and standard weights and measures are prescribed (verses 9—12). Then follow directions for the tax or "oblation" to be paid by the people to the prince, that he may be able to furnish the required sacrifices (verses 13—17). The chapter closes with directions concerning the daily sacrifices and the feasts, these feasts being in part unknown to the law; while some feasts that were prominent in the law are entirely omitted, and the ritual of nearly all is greatly changed. The whole is so different from the arrangements of the Mosaic economy, and so foreign to the restoration of that economy on the return from the exile, that it can only be explained of an ideal picture which both prophet and people understood was not to receive a literal realisation.

(1) **When ye shall divide by lot.**—The same expression is used in chaps. xlvii. 22; xlviii. 29, as it had long before been used in Josh. xiii. 6; but that it does not imply anything of chance is plain from the fact that in chap. xlviii. a definite portion of the land is assigned to each of the tribes by name. The idea seems to be the same as is conveyed by our word *allotment*.

An oblation.—Literally *a heave offering*. This portion of the land is thus called from its analogy to the sacrificial gifts which were lifted up or *heaved* before the Lord. As a small portion of these was burned upon the altar and the rest given to the priests, so here, a small part of this territory was to be occupied by the sanctuary and the rest given to the priests and Levites. A fuller description of this oblation is given in chap. xlviii. 8—22; it is here merely mentioned in connection with the support of the priests and the prince.

Five and twenty thousand.—In the original there is no mention of the measure to be used, but the English has rightly supplied *reeds*. This is plain both from the size of the precincts of the Temple, which are made 500 reeds square in chap. xlii. 16—20, and from the special mention of cubits in verse 2 implying that the measure in other cases was different. The length is from east to west, as shown by chap. xlviii. 8. This length of 25,000 reeds or 150,000 cubits is something over forty-seven statute miles. For its location and comparative size see the map under chap. xlviii.

The breadth shall be ten thousand.—The Greek here reads *twenty* thousand, and many would alter the text accordingly, but without any advantage. We know from chap. xlviii. 8, 20, that the whole width of the oblation was 25,000, the same as its length; and this was made up of three portions: the northernmost, 10,000 wide (chap. xlviii. 13), for the Levites; the next, of the same width (chap. xlviii. 10), for the priests, in the midst of which was the sanctuary; and the remainder, half as wide (chap. xlviii. 15), for "a profane place for the city, for dwelling, and for suburbs." Yet while this whole territory is there called the *oblation*, the particular portion for the priests is also called by the same name (chap. xlviii. 9). The word may therefore be used here in the same sense as there, for that part of the oblation which was for the priests: the oblation of the oblation.

(2) **Fifty cubits round about.**—In chap. xlii. 16—20 the space of 500 reeds square is described, which was "for," or belonged to, the sanctuary, to guard it from any profanation; but here we have, still farther, a narrow strip of 50 cubits wide (about 83 feet) of open space outside the wall to prevent the priests' houses being built too close to the sacred precincts. The word *suburbs* is better rendered in the margin, *void* or *open place*. The situation of the sanctuary and its surroundings within the priests' portion is more definitely fixed in chap. xlviii. 10 as "in the midst thereof."

(3) **Of this measure.**—If the Hebrew text of verse 1 be preserved unchanged, we must understand this to refer to the whole oblation of 25,000 reeds broad which was in the prophet's mind, though he does not speak of it until afterwards; this verse will then be a repetition of the latter part of verse 1, for the sake of specifying that the sanctuary was to be within it. The territory here assigned to the priests, more than 47 miles long by nearly 19 broad, with only one square mile deducted for the sanctuary, is enormously larger than the 13 cities assigned for their residence in Josh. xxi. 19, and is also considerably larger than that given (chap. xlviii.) to any of the tribes. It has been suggested that, as Ezekiel makes no mention of the tithes, this large territory may have been given to the priests for their support instead of the tithes; but the law of tithes was a very ancient institution (see Gen. xiv. 20; xxviii. 22), and was important for the good of the people as well as for the support of the priests. It is unlikely that Ezekiel would have introduced so radical a change without any allusion to it. The enlargement of the priests' possessions is quite in proportion to the enlargement of the sanctuary, and both seem designed in this symbolical vision to set forth the prominence of the Divine worship, and its precedence over all other things.

the sanctuary. (5) And the five and
twenty thousand of length, and the ten
thousand of breadth, shall also the Le-
vites, the ministers of the house, have
for themselves, for a possession for
twenty chambers. (6) And ye shall ap-
point the possession of the city five
thousand broad, and five and twenty
thousand long, over against the oblation
of the holy *portion:* it shall be for the
whole house of Israel. (7) And *a portion
shall be* for the prince on the one side
and on the other side of the oblation of
the holy *portion*, and of the possession of
the city, before the oblation of the holy
portion, and before the possession of the
city, from the west side westward, and
from the east side eastward: and the
length *shall be* over against one of the
portions, from the west border unto the
east border. (8) In the land shall be his
possession in Israel: and my princes
shall no more oppress my people; and
the rest of the land shall they give to
the house of Israel according to their
tribes.

(9) Thus saith the Lord GOD; Let it
suffice you, O princes of Israel: remove
violence and spoil, and execute judg-
ment and justice, take away your [1]exac-
tions from my people, saith the Lord
GOD. (10) Ye shall have just [a]balances,
and a just ephah, and a just bath.
(11) The ephah and the bath shall be of
one measure, that the bath may contain
the tenth part of an homer, and the
ephah the tenth part of an homer: the
measure thereof shall be after the

1 Heb., *expulsions.*

a Lev. 19. 35, 36.

---

(5) **For a possession for twenty chambers.**—Adjoining the priests' portion of the oblation, another equal portion is assigned to the Levites. The last clause of the verse, as it stands, admits of no satisfactory explanation. The suggestion that it may refer to twenty out of the thirty chambers in the outer court of the sanctuary (chap. xl. 17) is quite out of place. Even if these were intended for the use of the Levites (which does not appear), it would be strange that they should be abruptly spoken of in the midst of this description of the oblation. A slight change in the text—the transposition of two letters in the first word, and the change of one letter in the second for another much like it—will make the clause read, "for a possession of gates to dwell in," *gates* being used, as in Deut. xii. 18; xiv. 27; xvi. 11 (comp. Exod. xx. 10; Deut. v. 14), for cities. The sense would then be that this portion should be to the Levites what the former portion was to the priests, a place for their dwellings.

(6) **The possession of the city.**—This portion, more particularly described in chap. xlviii. 15—20, is there called "a profane place," though still constituting a part of the oblation. It was the same length and half the width of either of the other portions, and was for the city, and for a common possession of the nation, to supply food for those who "serve the city" "out of all the tribes of Israel" (chap. xlviii. 18, 19). Nothing is anywhere said to identify this city with Jerusalem, and, indeed, it is described as in a different position geographically (see map). Jerusalem, like the ark, appears to have faded from the prophet's sight in this vision of the future Church.

(7) **For the prince.**—The portion here assigned to the prince included all the land between the northern and southern bounding lines of the "oblation" continued to the Jordan on the east, and the Mediterranean on the west, not already included within the "oblation" itself. Two pieces of land are thus given to him, separated from each other by the whole width (47⅓ miles) of the "oblation." (See the map under chap. xlviii.)

From the west side westward.—The prince's position is to adjoin the "oblation" in its entire width of 25,000 reeds, stretching westward from its western side, and eastward from its eastern side.

The length.—Throughout the measurements of the land, *length* is from east to west; *breadth* from north to south. The east and west measurement of the prince's portion was to be "over against"—*i.e.*, parallel to—one of the portions of the tribes.

(8) **My princes shall no more oppress.**—The use of the plural does not imply that more than one prince should reign at a time, nor is it intended to include the family of the prince; but as everything in the future is described in terms of the past, so the royal authority is conceived of as vested in a succession of rulers, although we have been already told that there shall be but one king over them for ever (chaps. xxxiv. 23, 24; xxxvii. 24, 25). The declaration that the "princes shall no more oppress my people" follows naturally on the assignment of this portion. Former kings of Israel had no domain given them, and this had tempted them to acquire private property by violence and extortion. The people had been forewarned of this (1 Sam. viii. 14), had often experienced it in their history, and had heard the rebukes of their prophets on account of it (*e.g.*, Jer. xxii. 13—19).

(9) **Take away your exactions.**—Verses 9—12 are an exhortation to the princes to observe justice in all their dealings. (Comp. Jer. xxii. 3.) "Exaction" is, literally, as in the margin, *expulsion*, or ejection, with allusion to such cases as 1 Kings xxi. 1—16. In the following verses the exhortation to justice is extended to the whole people. (Comp. Lev. xix. 35, 36; Deut. xxv. 13—15.)

(11) **Shall be of one measure.**—The Ephah is first mentioned in Exod. xvi. 36, and appears to be a word of Egyptian origin; it was used for dry measure. The Bath is not met with before 1 Kings vii. 26, and was the largest of the liquid measures in use. The statement that these were of the same capacity, and each equal to the tenth part of the Homer, is important in the comparison of the Hebrew dry and liquid measures, but it is exceedingly difficult to determine their absolute value. If we calculate on the estimates of Josephus, the Homer was 86·696 English gallons; if on those of the Rabbinists, 42·286. Modern estimates differ nearly as much. The *Homer*, which was ten Ephahs, is to be carefully distinguished from the *Omer*, which was the tenth part of an Ephah. The two words are quite different in Hebrew.

homer. (12) And the [a]shekel *shall be*
twenty gerahs: twenty shekels, five
and twenty shekels, fifteen shekels,
shall be your maneh.
(13) This *is* the oblation that ye shall
offer; the sixth part of an ephah of an
homer of wheat, and ye shall give the
sixth part of an ephah of an homer of
barley: (14) concerning the ordinance of
oil, the bath of oil, *ye shall offer* the
tenth part of a bath out of the cor,
which is an homer of ten baths; for ten
baths *are* an homer: (15) and one [1]lamb
out of the flock, out of two hundred, out
of the fat pastures of Israel; for a meat
offering, and for a burnt offering, and
for [2]peace offerings, to make reconciliation for them, saith the Lord GOD.
(16) All the people of the land [3]shall give
this oblation [4]for the prince in Israel.
(17) And it shall be the prince's part *to*
give burnt offerings, and meat offerings,
and drink offerings, in the feasts, and in
the new moons, and in the sabbaths, in
all solemnities of the house of Israel:
he shall prepare the sin offering, and
the meat offering, and the burnt offering, and the [5]peace offerings, to make
reconciliation for the house of Israel.
(18) Thus saith the Lord GOD; In the
first *month*, in the first *day* of the month,
thou shalt take a young bullock without
blemish, and cleanse the sanctuary:
(19) and the priest shall take of the blood
of the sin offering, and put *it* upon the
posts of the house, and upon the four
corners of the settle of the altar, and
upon the posts of the gate of the inner
court. (20) And so thou shalt do the
seventh *day* of the month for every one
that erreth, and for *him that is* simple:
so shall ye reconcile the house.

[a] Ex. 30. 13; Lev. 27. 25; Num. 3. 47.

[1] Or, *kid.*

[2] Or, *thank offerings.*

[3] Heb., *shall be for.*

[4] Or, *with.*

[5] Or, *thank offerings.*

---

(12) **The shekel.**—The first part of this verse is merely a re-statement of the old law (Exod. xxx. 13; Lev. xxvii. 25; Num. iii. 47) that the shekel should be of the value of twenty gerahs, or of the estimated weight of 220 grains; but the latter part of the verse is extremely obscure. The *maneh* is mentioned elsewhere only in 1 Kings x. 17; Ezra ii. 69; Neh. vii. 71, and is translated in our version *pound*. Its actual value is unknown. If the text as it stands is correct, it is possible that in Ezekiel's time three different *manehs* were in use, of the values respectively assigned to them; but of this there is no other evidence.

(13) **The oblation.**—Verses 13—16 provide for a regular tax to be paid to the prince, in order that he may be able to furnish the required offerings at the sanctuary. This, like the oblation of land (verse 1), is described as a "heave offering," and was the sixtieth part of the grain, the hundredth of the oil, and the two-hundredth of the flock, all being from the year's increase.

(14) **The cor.**—This measure is first met with in 1 Kings iv. 22; v. 11; 2 Chron. ii. 10; xxvii. 5, and is here fixed as exactly equal to the "Homer." In the English it is always translated elsewhere *measure*.

(17) **The prince's part.** — The prince, receiving these contributions from the people, was bound to provide the offerings on the various stated occasions of sacrifice. This is an entirely new feature, for the Mosaic law made no provision in regard to the source from which the festal sacrifices were to be obtained. What had been left to free-will offering now becomes established duty.

Shall prepare.—The word means simply *provide*, not prepare in a priestly sense.

(18) **In the first month, in the first day of the month.**—The rest of this and the first fifteen verses of the following chapter are occupied with the ritual of the sacrifices on certain special occasions. In each case the deviations from the Mosaic law are remarkable, as well as the omission of any mention of the Feast of Weeks (Pentecost) and of the Great Day of Atonement. Ezekiel, as a priest, must have been familiar with the law in these matters, and therefore the changes he introduces must have been intentional. Like the changes in the division of the land, they seemed designed to show that this was an ideal vision. No attempt was ever made to follow the arrangements here laid down. The Mosaic law prescribed (in addition to the burnt offerings and meat offerings) a sin offering, which was to be a he-goat (Num. xxviii. 15) for the first of every month; also on the tenth day of the seventh month, on the Great Day of Atonement, two he-goats (one for the "scape-goat") were to be offered. Of all these Ezekiel mentions only the sin offering for the beginning of the first month, and also for the seventh day of the same, of which the Mosaic law knows nothing; but he provides for these bullocks instead of goats. In the ritual of the blood he makes a corresponding change. The law gives no special directions for the sprinkling of the blood of the sin offerings on the first of each month, because they were included in the ordinary rule (Lev. iv. 25, 30, &c.) of sprinkling upon the sides of the altar of burnt offering; only in the case of the sin offering for the high priest or for the whole congregation (when the victim was a bullock) was the blood brought within the Temple itself, and sprinkled seven times before the vail, and applied to the horns of the altar of incense. On the Day of Atonement it was carried into the Holy of Holies, and sprinkled upon and before the mercy-seat. All this is here changed. Some of the blood of these sin offerings (verse 19) is to be put upon the "posts of the house" (see chap. xli. 21), upon the "corners of the settle of the altar," and "upon the posts of the gate of the inner court."

(20) **So shall ye reconcile the house.**—The object of "the sin offering" on the first day of the month is expressly said to be to "cleanse the sanctuary" (verse 18); but here the offering is for "every one that erreth, and for him that is simple," *i.e.*, for all who have sinned thoughtlessly rather than wilfully. Yet it is added, "so shall ye reconcile the house," more literally, make an atonement for the house; and the question has therefore been raised whether this offering on the seventh day was still for the purification of the sanctuary or for the sins of the people. The answer to this question must be sought in the sacrifices of the

(21) In the first *month*, in the fourteenth
day of the month, ye shall have the
passover, a feast of seven days; unleav-
ened bread shall be eaten. (22) And upon
that day shall the prince prepare for
himself and for all the people of the
land a bullock *for* a sin offering. (23) And
seven days of the feast he shall prepare
a burnt offering to the LORD, seven bul-
locks and seven rams without blemish
daily the seven days; and a kid of the
goats daily *for* a sin offering. (24) And
he shall prepare a meat offering of an
ephah for a bullock, and an ephah for a
ram, and an hin of oil for an ephah.
(25) In the seventh *month*, in the fifteenth
day of the month, shall he do the
like in the [a]feast of the seven days,
according to the sin offering, according
to the burnt offering, and according to
the meat offering, and according to
the oil.

[a] Num. 29. 12.

CHAPTER XLVI. — (1) Thus saith
the Lord GOD; The gate of the inner
court that looketh toward the east shall
be shut the six working days; but on
the sabbath it shall be opened, and in
the day of the new moon it shall be
opened. (2) And the prince shall enter
by the way of the porch of *that* gate
without, and shall stand by the post of
the gate, and the priests shall prepare
his burnt offering and his peace offer-
ings, and he shall worship at the
threshold of the gate: then he shall
go forth; but the gate shall not be
shut until the evening. (3) Likewise
the people of the land shall worship at
the door of this gate before the LORD in

Day of Atonement (Lev. xvi.), which these days seem intended to replace. These were very distinctly for the sins of the priests and the people, and at the same time for the tabernacle. The one involved the other, and the holy place required purification because of the sins of "the holy people" among whom it was placed.

(22) **A bullock for a sin offering.**—In verse 21 the Passover is appointed quite in accordance with the Mosaic institution, although there is a peculiarity in the language of the original which has led some writers to infer, unnecessarily, that the feast was to be kept for seven weeks. But the sacrifices are in many respects quite different. Nothing is said of the Paschal lamb itself: but this may be because it was understood as a matter of course. The sin offering by the Mosaic law (Num. xxviii. 17, 22) was to be a he-goat for each day; here, a bullock for the first day, and a he-goat for the other days (verse 23). The burnt offering by the law was to be two bullocks, a ram, and seven yearling lambs for each day; here, seven bullocks and seven rams. The meat offering was to be three-tenths of an ephah of meal, mixed with oil, for each bullock, two-tenths for each ram, and one-tenth for each lamb, or one and a half ephahs in all daily; here, a whole ephah for each victim, making in all fourteen ephahs daily and as many hins of oil (verse 24). The offerings required here therefore are much richer than under the law.

(25) **In the seventh month.**—This corresponds to the Feast of Tabernacles, though the name is not mentioned, doubtless because the custom of living in booths is to be discontinued. The sacrifices at this feast are to be the same as at the Passover, and are to be repeated for each day of the feast. There is in this an entire change from the peculiar ordinances of the Mosaic law (Num. xxix. 12—24), and on the whole a great diminution in the number of sacrifices, with a simplification of the ritual, and an omission of the eighth day, added to the feast by the Mosaic law.

Ezekiel here omits altogether the Feast of Pentecost, the Day of Atonement, and the Day of Trumpets (the first of the seventh month); for these he substitutes a special sin offering for the first and seventh days of the first month, and for the first day of the Paschal feast; he, moreover, largely modifies the ritual of the two feasts which he retains. All this essentially transforms the ideas which form the basis of the cycle of the Mosaic feasts. No attempt was ever made by the Jews of the restoration to carry out the scheme here set forth; and it appears to have been regarded by the prophet's contemporaries and successors as purely ideal.

XLVI.

The first fifteen verses of this chapter belong to chap. xlv. The prince was required to provide and bring the sacrifices for himself and for the people (chap. xlv. 17); therefore, as soon as the yearly festivals have been described, directions are given (verses 1—3) for the conduct of the prince at these sacrifices. He was required to be always present, while attendance on the part of the people was obligatory only at the yearly festivals. The prophet then goes on to provide for the sacrifices for the Sabbaths and new moons, for free-will offerings, and for the daily sacrifices.

(1) **The gate of the inner court.**—It has already been provided (chap. xliv. 1—3) that the outer gate on the east should be kept closed, except for the prince. The same thing is now commanded for the east gate of the inner court also; and, further, the days are specified, the Sabbaths and new moons, on which it shall be used by the prince.

(2) **Stand by the post of the gate.**—The prince shall enter the sanctuary by the east gate of the outer court, pass through that court to the inner gate, and "worship at the threshold of the gate" immediately adjoining the inner court, while the priests make ready his sacrifices. But he is not to enter the inner court, or to assume any priestly functions. Afterwards he is to go forth by the same way (verse 8, and chap. xliv. 3), and the gate stands open until evening, though no one else is to enter thereby.

(3) **Worship at the door.**—The people, in so far as they might be present on the Sabbaths and new moons, are not to worship in the same place with the prince; but in the outer court, at the entrance of the east gate to the inner court.

the sabbaths and in the new moons.
(4) And the burnt offering that the prince
shall offer unto the LORD in the sabbath
day *shall be* six lambs without blemish,
and a ram without blemish. (5) And the
meat offering *shall be* an ephah for a
ram, and the meat offering for the lambs
[1]as he shall be able to give, and an hin
of oil to an ephah. (6) And in the day
of the new moon *it shall be* a young
bullock without blemish, and six lambs,
and a ram: they shall be without
blemish. (7) And he shall prepare a
meat offering, an ephah for a bullock,
and an ephah for a ram, and for the
lambs according as his hand shall attain
unto, and an hin of oil to an ephah.
(8) And when the prince shall enter,
he shall go in by the way of the porch
of *that* gate, and he shall go forth by
the way thereof. (9) But when the people
of the land shall come before the LORD
in the solemn feasts, he that entereth in
by the way of the north gate to worship
shall go out by the way of the south
gate; and he that entereth by the way
of the south gate shall go forth by the
way of the north gate: he shall not re-
turn by the way of the gate whereby he
came in, but shall go forth over against
it. (10) And the prince in the midst of
them, when they go in, shall go in; and
when they go forth, shall go forth.
(11) And in the feasts and in the solem-
nities the meat offering shall be an
ephah to a bullock, and an ephah to a
ram, and to the lambs as he is able to
give, and an hin of oil to an ephah.
(12) Now when the prince shall prepare a
voluntary burnt offering or peace offer-
ings voluntarily unto the LORD, *one* shall
then open him the gate that looketh to-
ward the east, and he shall prepare his
burnt offering and his peace offerings, as
he did on the sabbath day: then he shall
go forth; and after his going forth *one*
shall shut the gate.
(13) Thou shalt daily prepare a burnt
offering unto the LORD *of* a lamb [2]of the
first year without blemish: thou shalt
prepare it [3]every morning. (14) And thou
shalt prepare a meat offering for it every
morning, the sixth part of an ephah, and
the third part of an hin of oil, to temper
with the fine flour; a meat offering con-
tinually by a perpetual ordinance unto
the LORD. (15) Thus shall they prepare
the lamb, and the meat offering, and the
oil, every morning *for* a continual burnt
offering.
(16) Thus saith the Lord GOD; If the
prince give a gift unto any of his sons,

1 Heb., *the gift of his hand.*

2 Heb., *a son of his year.*

3 Heb., *morning by morning.*

---

(4) **Six lambs . . . and a ram.**—The burnt offering for the Sabbath, according to the Mosaic law (Num. xxviii. 9), was two lambs. This is greatly increased here, and the "meat offering" for the ram is also made larger, while that for the lambs (verse 5) is left to the prince's generosity.

(6) **A young bullock . . . and six lambs, and a ram.**—The law required for the new moons, for a burnt offering, two bullocks, seven lambs, and a ram (Num. xxviii. 11), so that this sacrifice is here diminished; it also required a he-goat for a sin offering, of which no mention is here made.

(9) **In the solemn feasts.**—Different arrangements were required for the great or "solemn" feasts, because at these all the males of Israel were commanded to be present, and therefore the numbers were very large. This affects both the people and (verse 10) the prince. The first provision is one for securing order in the vast concourse of people: by whichever (outer) gate any one enters (the north or the south), he shall pass out by the opposite one.

(10) **The prince in the midst of them.**—On occasion of these yearly feasts, it was no longer necessary that the prince should represent the people, they being themselves present. He, therefore, now worships in their midst, entering with them at the north or south gate, and going out by the opposite one.

(11) **And in the solemnities.**—The new rules for the proportion of the meat offering, as laid down in verses 5, 7, chap. xlv. 24, are here repeated for the feast days; and it is added that the same is to hold for all established seasons, a different proportion being prescribed only for the daily sacrifice (verse 14).

(12) **A voluntary burnt offering.**—One case in which the prince might present a sacrifice is yet unprovided for. He might offer, like any of the people, a voluntary sacrifice at any time, either a burnt offering or a peace offering. In this case he is still to enter by the east gate; but the gate, instead of standing open until evening, as on the Sabbaths and new moons, is to be immediately shut as soon as he retires after the completion of the sacrifice.

(13) **Daily prepare a burnt offering.**—Verses 13—15 contain regulations for the daily sacrifice. The victim is the same as under the Mosaic law; but instead of being offered every morning and evening (Num. xxviii. 3—5), it is here provided only for the morning. On the other hand, the accompanying meat offering is increased from the tenth to the sixth of an ephah of flour, and from a fourth to a third of a hin of oil.

The rest of the chapter is occupied with the rights of the prince in regard to the conveyance of his land (verses 16—18), and a short description of the sacrificial kitchens for the priests and the people (verses 19—24).

(16) **If the prince give a gift.**—Verses 15—18 contain provisions in regard to the prince's alienation of his domain. According to chap. xlv. 7, 8, he was to have a portion of land on each side of the "oblation,"

the inheritance thereof shall be his sons';
it *shall be* their possession by inherit-
ance. (17) But if he give a gift of his in-
heritance to one of his servants, then it
shall be his to the year of liberty; after
it shall return to the prince: but his
inheritance shall be his sons' for them.
(18) Moreover the prince shall not take of
the people's inheritance by oppression,
to thrust them out of their possession;
but he shall give his sons inheritance
out of his own possession: that my
people be not scattered every man from
his possession.
(19) After he brought me through the
entry, which *was* at the side of the gate,
into the holy chambers of the priests,
which looked toward the north: and,
behold, there *was* a place on the two
sides westward. (20) Then said he unto
me, This *is* the place where the priests
shall boil the trespass offering and the
sin offering, where they shall bake the
meat offering; that they bear *them* not
out into the utter court, to sanctify the
people.
(21) Then he brought me forth into the
utter court, and caused me to pass by
the four corners of the court; and, be-
hold, [1]in every corner of the court *there*
was a court. (22) In the four corners of
the court *there were* courts [2]joined of
forty *cubits* long and thirty broad: these
four [3]corners *were* of one measure.
(23) And *there was* a row *of building* round
about in them, round about them four,
and *it was* made with boiling places under
the rows round about. (24) Then said he
unto me, These *are* the places of them
that boil, where the ministers of the
house shall boil the sacrifice of the people.

CHAPTER XLVII.—(1) Afterward he
brought me again unto the door of the

1 Heb., *a court in a corner of a court, and a court in a corner of a court.*

2 Or, *made with chimnies.*

3 Heb., *cornered.*

---

which should be sufficiently ample to prevent any attempts on his part at violence and exaction. For the same purpose, it was necessary that this territory should remain inalienably in his family. He might therefore convey any portion of it to his sons in fee simple, for they would naturally inherit it; but a conveyance to any one else came under the Mosaic law (Lev. xxv.), and reverted to him or his heirs in the year of Jubile, here called "the year of liberty."

(18) **Shall not take of the people's inheritance.**—Fresh warning is here given against oppression on the part of the prince, and he is reminded that the territory given inalienably to him and his heirs is to provide for his sons' inheritance.

(19) **At the side of the gate.**—The concluding verses of the chapter are occupied with the arrangements for cooking the sacrificial food of the priests and the people. The latter could partake only of the peace offerings, but the priests, in addition to their portion of these, were required to consume the flesh of the sin and trespass offerings, and the greater part of the "meat offerings." The prophet is first shown the rooms for the priests' cooking. He was taken along the walk (Plan II., K) mentioned in chap. xlii. 4, which led from the steps of the gate of the inner court to the priests' chambers. There he saw "a place on the two sides westward," *i.e.*, two places, one at the west of each building of priests' chambers. Nothing is said of their size, and they may be assumed to have had the same dimensions (40 cubits by 30—verse 22) as those of the people's kitchens. They are marked F on Plan II.

(20) **Shall boil . . . shall bake.**—The flesh of all sacrifices except the Passover was by the law required to be boiled, and the unbloody "meat offering," when not already cooked, was to be baked.

Bear them not out into the utter court.—In one sense the priestly chambers and also these cooking rooms were themselves in the outer court; but as already remarked, these, with the walk that led to them, although within the enclosure of the outer, were considered as appurtenances of, and therefore belonging to, the inner court. The reason given for not bearing the flesh of the sin and trespass offering into the outer court is, lest they should thereby "sanctify the people," and the same reason is given in chap. xliv. 19 for not allowing the priests' garments to come into the outer court. Under the law all those offerings which it was the duty of the priests to consume are called "most holy," and whoever touched them or the sacred vessels of the sanctuary became "holy" in the sense of set apart to God (Lev. vi. 18; also Exod. xxix. 37; xxx. 29). The object of the command is therefore to prevent that ceremonial sanctification of the people which would interfere with their ordinary life.

(21) **The utter court.**—The prophet had just been in those chambers which, although they stood within the area of the outer court, were considered as belonging to the inner. He is now brought into the outer court, properly so called.

In every corner of the court there was a court.—In each of the angles of the outer court a place was set apart for the boiling of the flesh of the peace offerings. These were of considerable size—40 cubits by 30 (verse 22), and appear to have been enclosed by a wall but not covered above. The word translated *joined* is of very uncertain meaning, but its most probable sense is *enclosed.* These courts are marked E on Plan II.

(23) **A row of building.**—Around the walls of these enclosures were fixed tables of masonry with boiling places underneath.

(24) **Ministers of the house.**—Not priests, but Temple servants, who were usually Levites.

XLVII.

The first twelve verses of this chapter constitute what is generally known as "the vision of the living waters;" the latter part of the chapter, verses 13—23, more properly belongs with chap. xlviii., and, with that, gives an account of the boundaries of the land, of its distribution among the tribes, and of the building of the holy city.

house; and, behold, waters issued out
from under the threshold of the house
eastward: for the forefront of the house
stood toward the east, and the waters
came down from under from the right
side of the house, at the south *side* of
the altar. (2) Then brought he me out
of the way of the gate northward, and
led me about the way without unto the
utter gate by the way that looketh east-
ward; and, behold, there ran out waters
on the right side. (3) And when the man
that had the line in his hand went forth
eastward, he measured a thousand cubits,
and he brought me through the waters;
the [1]waters *were* to the ancles. (4) Again
he measured a thousand, and brought
me through the waters; the waters *were*
to the knees. Again he measured a
thousand, and brought me through; the
waters *were* to the loins. (5) Afterward
he measured a thousand; *and it was* a
river that I could not pass over: for the
waters were risen, [2]waters to swim in, a
river that could not be passed over.

(6) And he said unto me, Son of man,
hast thou seen *this?* Then he brought
me, and caused me to return to the
brink of the river. (7) Now when I had
returned, behold, at the [3]bank of the
river *were* very many [a]trees on the one
side and on the other. (8) Then said he
unto me, These waters issue out toward
the east country, and go down into the
[4]desert, and go into the sea: *which being*
brought forth into the sea, the waters

1 Heb., *waters of the ancles.*

2 Heb., *waters of swimming.*

3 Heb., *lip.*

a Rev. 22. 2.

4 Or, *plain.*

The ideal character of this vision of the waters is so plain upon its face that little need be said on this point. The stream is represented as issuing from the summit of "a very high mountain" (chap. xl. 2), and as constantly and rapidly increasing its volume, without the accession of tributaries, so that in a little more than a mile it becomes a river no longer fordable. The trees upon its banks, too, are evidently symbolical, and its effect upon the Dead Sea (as already said in the introductory note to chaps. xl.—xlviii.) is such as could not naturally occur. Such imagery is common in prophecy. Joel (chap. iii. 18) says, "All the rivers of Judah shall flow with waters, and a fountain shall come forth of the house of the LORD, and shall water the valley of Shittim." Zechariah (chap. xiv. 8), "Living waters shall go out from Jerusalem, half of them toward the former sea, and half of them toward the hinder sea;" and finally, the description of the "pure river of water of life" in Rev. xxii. 1—3, is evidently founded upon this passage of Ezekiel. Passages in which water is used as the symbol of the influence of the Spirit are too numerous and familiar to need quotation. (Comp. Isa. xliv. 3; Ezek. xxxvi. 25—27; Zech. xiii. 1, &c.)

Ezekiel, having in the previous chapters described the dwelling of the Lord among His people with characteristic minuteness of detail, now proceeds to set forth the blessings that flow from this presence.

(1) **Door of the house.**—This is the entrance of the Temple itself; the waters come out from under its threshold, just as in Rev. xxii. 1 they proceed "out of the throne of God and of the Lamb." The prophet, who had just been in the outer court (chap. xlvi. 21, &c.), is brought in to the door of the house that he may see the waters.

From the right side of the house.—Although the waters issue directly from the threshold which was in the centre of the east front of the Temple, and their general course was due east, it was necessary that they should be deflected a little at the start to the south in order to pass the porch and the altar, as well as both the inner and outer gateways.

(2) **Out of the way of the gate northward.**—Rather, *out by the way of the north gate.* The east gate, the direct way, was shut (chap. xliv. 2); the prophet was therefore carried round to the outside of it by the way of the north gate. There he saw the waters on the right, or south, side of the gateway.

(3) **Brought me through the waters.**—The point from which the measurement began is not distinctly mentioned, but is to be assumed as from their source, the threshold of the house. The prophet is "brought through the waters" to impress upon him a vivid sense of their size and depth, and this is repeated at each 1,000 cubits until the waters become impassable.

(5) **A river that could not be passed over.**—The whole distance measured is 4,000 cubits, or less than a mile and a half, during which the waters, without external addition, have swollen from a mere streamlet to an impassable river, in direct opposition to the ordinary fact in nature. A large part (1,500 cubits, or half of 3,000 cubits) of this distance must have been within the precincts described in chap, xlii. 16—20, but the prophet takes no notice of this, as the whole is ideal, and the precincts were to set forth one truth, the river another. The point thus far brought out is plainly the increase of the kingdom of God—the same truth illustrated by our Lord in the parable of the mustard seed (Matt. xiii. 31, 32), and often declared by the prophets (see Isa. xi. 9; Hab. ii. 14; Dan. ii. 44; vii. 27; &c.). All history, since the Christian era, has been occupied with the fulfilment of the prophecy.

(6) **To return to the brink.**—The angel, having called the prophet's attention to this marvellous increase, now causes him to return *along* the bank to observe other things. The word *brink* in this verse and *bank* in the next are the same in the original. The prophet does not *return* to the brink, for he had not left it, but is told to pass *along* it.

(7) **Very many trees.**—In the corresponding vision of Rev. xxii. 2 the same thought is symbolised by the "tree of life, which bare twelve manner of fruits."

(8) **Go down into the desert.**—The word for *country* is the same as is used in Josh. xxii. 10, 11, for the borders of the Jordan, and undoubtedly has the same meaning here: the valley of the Jordan, called the *Ghor.* The word *desert* is better translated in the margin, *plain,* and refers to that expansion of the Jordan valley just north of the Dead Sea in which the city of Jericho was situated. So far the course of the

shall be healed. (9) And it shall come to
pass, *that* every thing that liveth, which
moveth, whithersoever the [1]rivers shall
come, shall live: and there shall be a
very great multitude of fish, because
these waters shall come thither: for
they shall be healed; and every thing
shall live whither the river cometh.
(10) And it shall come to pass, *that* the
fishers shall stand upon it from En-gedi
even unto En-eglaim; they shall be a
place to spread forth nets; their fish
shall be according to their kinds, as the
fish of the great sea, exceeding many.
(11) But the miry places thereof and the
marishes thereof [2]shall not be healed;
they shall be given to salt. (12) And by
the river upon the bank thereof, on this
side and on that side, [3]shall grow all
trees for meat, whose leaf shall not fade,
neither shall the fruit thereof be consumed:
it shall bring forth [4]new fruit
according to his months, because their
waters they issued out of the sanctuary:
and the fruit thereof shall be for meat,
and the leaf thereof [5]for [a]medicine.
(13) Thus saith the Lord God; This
shall be the border, whereby ye shall in-

1 Heb., *two rivers.*

2 Or, *and that which shall not be healed.*

3 Heb., *shall come up.*

4 Or, *principal.*

5 Or, *for bruises and sores.*

a Rev. 22. 2.

---

river has been due east; now, without any allusion to the Jordan, it apparently takes its place and flows into the sea. Both the situation and the description show that the Dead Sea is intended. By its entrance "the waters of the sea shall be healed," that is, they shall be so changed that, from being incapable of supporting life, they shall become the home of life in all abundance and variety (verses 9, 10).

(9) **The rivers.**—According to the pointing of the Hebrew text this is *the two rivers,* as is expressed in the margin. This peculiar form has occasioned some perplexity, especially because in the vision of Zechariah (chap. xiv. 8) the waters are represented as divided, half of them flowing to the Dead Sea and half of them to the Mediterranean. It is plain, however, that but one river is intended here, flowing into the Dead Sea. Possibly there is an allusion in the dual form to the Jordan flowing with it into the sea; but this vision throughout pays so little regard to the natural features of the country that it seems more likely that the dual form is simply used to express the greatness of the river, "a double river." By a division of the word and a slight change in the vowels the expression would become "river of the sea," that is, flowing into the sea.

Shall live.—This is to be understood as a pregnant expression; all kinds of life shall spring into being whithersoever the waters come. The same thing is emphatically repeated at the close of the verse, and in the intermediate clause the same thought is expressed by the "very great multitude of fish."

(10) **From En-gedi even unto En-eglaim.**—En-gedi, "the fountain of the goat," is a well-known copious spring about midway on the western coast of the Dead Sea. En-eglaim occurs only here, and has not been certainly identified. St. Jerome speaks of "Engallim" as at the junction of the Jordan with the sea, and near this point there is a fountain now known as *Ain-el-Feshkhah.* Others consider that the dual form of the name indicates "one of the double cities of Moab," thus placing it on the eastern side of the sea, and this seems more probable, since the expression would then be equivalent to "the whole breadth of the sea." Everywhere they shall stretch their nets, and the variety and abundance of the fish shall be as great as in "the great sea," that is, the Mediterranean. This whole verse in regard to the fishermen is a striking illustration of Ezekiel's way of carrying out the most ideal description into detail.

(11) **The marishes thereof shall not be healed.**—The picture of the life-giving waters would be imperfect without this exception to their effects. The Dead Sea at the southern end is very shallow, and beyond there is an extensive tract of very low land. In the season of the flood of the Jordan this is overflowed to a considerable distance, and as the river subsides, is again left bare and encrusted with salt from the evaporation of the water. This allusion, therefore, shows plainly that the prophet did not have in mind a flowing on of the river through the *Arabah,* or valley leading from the Dead to the Red Sea, and that the effect of the life-giving waters should cease where the waters themselves ceased to flow; at the same time, in the thing symbolised, it shows that we are not to expect, as the effect of the Gospel, a perfect and universal obedience to its teachings. Man is still left free to hear or forbear, and the world must be expected always to contain its unhealed miry and marshy places.

(12) **Be consumed.**—Better, *fail.* The fruit is to be eaten, but shall not fail to grow as it is wanted. These trees with their supernatural virtues are represented as produced by the waters because "they issued out of the sanctuary," thus presenting a most effective image of the life-giving power of those spiritual influences which come from God upon men.

It has been objected to the spiritual interpretation of this vision, that under it nothing can be made of the fishermen of verse 10, and that, therefore, the whole is to be considered as a glorification of nature in the future Palestine. But this is to forget that in every figure and parable there are, and must be, details necessary to the figure which have nothing answering to them in the thing signified, and that it is the habit of Ezekiel to carry out such details very far. In this case, the mention of the fishermen greatly heightens the imagery of the life-giving power of the waters; while, if the whole were to be literally understood, they would really have no place, because there would be no such fishermen in the supposed glorified condition of the land.

Verses 13—23, which, as already said, properly belong to chap. xlviii., give the boundaries of the land to be divided among the tribes, together with provision for the inheritance of strangers living among them. The tracing of the boundary itself is introduced by some general statements in verses 13, 14, concerning the distribution.

(13) **According to the twelve tribes of Israel.**—In the ideal land of the restoration, not Judah and Benjamin only, but all the twelve tribes are to have

herit the land according to the twelve
tribes of Israel: Joseph *shall have two*
portions. (14) And ye shall inherit it, one
as well as another: *concerning* the which
I [1a]lifted up mine hand to give it unto
your fathers: and this land shall fall
unto you for inheritance. (15) And this
shall be the border of the land toward
the north side, from the great sea, the
way of Hethlon, as men go to Zedad;
(16) Hamath, Berothah, Sibraim, which *is*
between the border of Damascus and
the border of Hamath; [2]Hazar-hatti-
con, which *is* by the coast of Hauran.
(17) And the border from the sea shall
be Hazar-enan, the border of Damascus,
and the north northward, and the border
of Hamath. And *this is* the north side.

1 Or, *swore.*

a Gen. 12. 7, & 17. 8, & 26. 3, & 28. 13.

2 Or, *the middle village.*

their portions. Yet Levi is otherwise provided for in the "oblation," and therefore Joseph, in accordance with Gen. xlviii. 5, 22, and with the whole history of the nation, is to have two portions. The Hebrew is simply "Joseph portions" in the plural, but that these portions were to be two and no more was a matter of course, not needing to be specified.

(14) **One as well as another.**—This is the ordinary expression for equality. Unlike the former division of the land, the territory is to be arranged in twelve equal portions. This is generally understood to mean that the strips of territory assigned to each tribe shall be of equal width, and such is undoubtedly the prophet's meaning, since the vision throughout makes little account of the natural features of the country. It may be well to notice in passing, however, that the actual area of the territory given to the tribes is thus made very unequal. The country was nearly three times as broad at the south as at the north, and the southern tribes would thus have actually nearly three times as much land as the northern, although they were ideally equal. Were the portions to be made actually equal, the map given under chap. xlviii. would be much changed. Such an arrangement would move the "oblation" farther south and give it ample room between east and west. Its north line would be a little north of Jerusalem, and its south within ten or twelve miles of Beersheba, and the Temple would be situated a few miles north-west of Hebron and still on the western watershed.

(15) **This shall be the border of the land.**—The boundaries are essentially the same as those given in Num. xxxiv. 1—15, only that there the southern boundary is given first to the Israelites coming up from Egypt, while here the northern is first described for the people supposed to be returning from Babylon. There is also more detail given in Numbers, and as the points mentioned here are the same, it is fair to fill out this description from the earlier one. It is remarkable that in both cases the eastern boundary is the Jordan. The inheritance of the tribes on the east of that river having been a modification of the original allotment, and not being taken into consideration at all here, portions are assigned on the west of the river to the two and a half tribes who had lived all through Israel's history on the east.

The way of Hethlon.—The boundary begins at the Mediterranean, but at what precise point cannot be determined; for although it is evident that the lines between the tribes were straight and parallel, yet it does not appear whether they were perpendicular to the Jordan, which would be substantially parallel to the lines of latitude, or perpendicular to the Mediterranean, which would make a small angle with them. *Hethlon* is mentioned only here and in chap. xlviii. 1, and has not been identified. It was probably a place of little importance, as its situation is described "as men go to Zedad." The latter place is mentioned in Num. xxxiv. 8 as one of the points in the original northern border of the land. It is clear from the passage in Numbers that it lay eastward of the "entrance to Hamath," and has been identified by some writers with the modern village of *Sadad*, but this is thirty miles from "the entrance of Hamath," which seems quite too far. Ezekiel may have passed through it when carried captive to Babylon.

(16) **Hamath** is not to be understood of the city of Hamath on the Orontes (which was much too far to the north), but of the boundary of the district of Hamath; this cannot be now precisely fixed, but certainly came as far south as the "entrance of Hamath" (Num. xxxiv. 8), or the defile between the Lebanon and Antilebanon Mountains which leads to Hamath. This defile, however, is many miles in length, and the authorities differ as to whether its southern end or its northern (where the Lebanon and Antilebanon ranges end, and a rolling country several miles broad intervenes between them and the next ranges) should be called "the entrance to Hamath.'

Berothah is also mentioned in 2 Sam. viii. 8, as one of the cities conquered by David from the king of Zobah, and it is evident from this passage that it was between "Hamath" and Damascus; but nothing further is known of its situation.

Sibraim may be the same with Ziphron of Num. xxxiv. 9, and must have been on the confines of the two kingdoms of Hamath and Damascus; but nothing more is known of it, and it is not mentioned elsewhere.

Hazar-hatticon.—That is, as noted in the margin, *the middle Hazar*, to distinguish it from the Hazar-enan mentioned in the next verse. All that is known of it is from this passage, that it was on the border of the district of Hauran. Hauran, here and in verse 18, is used in a wider sense than the classic *Auranitis*, and includes also Gaulanitis (Golan), and Batanœa (Bashan), in fact the whole land between the territories of Damascus and Gilead (verse 18).

(17) **The border from the sea shall be Hazar-enan.**—Comparing this with Num. xxxiv. 9, it is plain that the sense is, "The (north) boundary which started from the sea shall terminate at Hazar-enan, where it meets the boundaries of Damascus." Hazar-enan means "the village of springs," and is mentioned in chap. xlviii. 1, and in Num. xxxiv. 9, 10, as the end of the north and beginning of the east boundary of the land. For "and the border of Hamath," read *even the border—i.e.*, the northern boundary is the (south) boundary of Hamath. While it is impossible to locate precisely this northern boundary, either as given in Numbers or by Ezekiel, it is evident that the two are identical, and that the line stretched from the Mediterranean to the territory of Damascus. The whole width of the country at this point would therefore be somewhat over thirty miles.

(18) And the east side ye shall measure
[1]from Hauran, and from Damascus, and
from Gilead, and from the land of Israel
by Jordan, from the border unto the
east sea. And *this is* the east side.
(19) And the south side southward, from
Tamar *even* to the waters of [2]strife *in*
Kadesh, the [3]river to the great sea.
And *this is* the south side [4]southward.
(20) The west side also *shall be* the great
sea from the border, till a man come
over against Hamath. This *is* the west
side. (21) So shall ye divide this land
unto you according to the tribes of
Israel.
(22) And it shall come to pass, *that* ye
shall divide it by lot for an inheritance
unto you, and to the strangers that
sojourn among you, which shall beget
children among you: and they shall be
unto you as born in the country among
the children of Israel; they shall have
inheritance with you among the tribes
of Israel. (23) And it shall come to pass,
that in what tribe the stranger so-
journeth, there shall ye give *him* his in-
heritance, saith the Lord GOD.

CHAPTER XLVIII.—(1) Now these
are the names of the tribes. From the
north end to the coast of the way of
Hethlon, as one goeth to Hamath,

1 Heb., *from between.*
2 Or, *Meribah.*
3 Or, *valley.*
4 Or, *toward Teman.*

(18) **From Hauran, and from Damascus.**—The eastern boundary is also the same as that given in Num. xxxiv. 10—12, although more particularly described there. In both cases it excludes the territory of the trans-Jordanic tribes, which was not included in Palestine proper, even after its conquest by Moses, and in which the two and a half tribes were allowed to settle with some reluctance (Num. xxxii.). The word "from," occurring four times in this verse, is literally *from between*, as is noted in the margin; it means that the boundary was to run between the territories of Hauran, Damascus, and Gilead on the one side, and that of Israel on the other. The boundary is to be the Jordan; but as this does not extend so far north, it became necessary to mention the territory of Damascus as bounding the land of Israel, and in this connection Hauran and Gilead are also spoken of. The boundary extends, as of old, beyond the mouth of the Jordan to the southern end of the Dead Sea and thence to Kadesh. The extreme length of the land is somewhat uncertain, but must have fallen short of 250 miles.

(19) **From Tamar even to the waters of strife.**—The southern border, as given in Num. xxxiv. 3—5, is identical with that described here, as far as the two can be compared. Tamar has been identified with Kurnub, a ruined village some twenty-five miles west of the southern end of the Dead Sea; but as the old boundary certainly went far to the south of this, and as the next place mentioned is Kadesh, about thirty miles nearly south from the Dead Sea, the Tamar here meant is more probably some place not yet identified. Kadesh, known from the "waters of strife" as *Meribah* (Num. xx. 3—14), is called Kadesh-barnea in Num. xxxiv. 4. It has been identified by Robinson with the *Ain-el-Weibeh*, about thirty miles slightly west of south from the Dead Sea. Its exact situation, however, is somewhat doubtful.

The river to the great sea.—Literally, *riverward to the great sea.* From Kadesh the boundary was to strike across the mountainous desert to what is often called in Scripture "the river of Egypt," and was anciently known as the *Rhinocolura*, now called the *Wady-el-Arish.* It followed this to the Mediterranean. The length of the southern boundary, following the curve of the Rhinocolura, must have been nearly 100 miles, or about eighty-seven miles from east to west.

(20) **Over against Hamath.**—The western boundary, as in Num. xxxiv. 6, is the Mediterranean, and continues to the starting-point, Hamath being here, as in verses 16, 17, the district of Hamath.

(22) **By lot.**—See Note on chap. xlv. 1.

To the strangers.—An entirely new feature is here added to the Mosaic law. According to Lev. xix. 34, strangers were to be treated with kindness, but the entire territory was to be divided among the Israelites, and strangers could therefore acquire no land except in so far as they might purchase a temporary right between the years of Jubilee. Now, however, such of them as "shall beget children among you," thus showing a disposition to permanent residence, are to receive an inheritance along with the tribes and in the portion of that tribe where they may have chosen to fix their residence. This privilege is absolute, without any condition of receiving circumcision.

XLVIII.

The closing chapter of Ezekiel is mainly occupied with the distribution of the land in detail. Beginning at the north, a portion is assigned to each of seven tribes (verses 1—7); then the "oblation" is described, with its parts for the Levites, the priests and Temple, the city and those that serve it, and for the prince (verses 8—22), and lastly portions for the remaining five tribes. The chapter and the book close with an account of the size and the twelve gates of the city, the whole ending with its name, "The Lord is there."

The distribution of the land is entirely different from that made under Joshua, nor is it easy to trace any historical reasons for it, except that the central portion, containing the Temple, the land of the priests and the prince, is flanked by the two tribes of the southern kingdom, Judah and Benjamin. The chapter can best be understood by the aid of a small map, the outline of which is traced from Dr. Wm. Smith's ancient atlas. This might be drawn with the lines between the tribes perpendicular either to the general course of the Jordan, or to the general coast-line of the Mediterranean. The latter would give a little more width for the oblation, but still not enough, and would leave no space at all on the west for the prince. The former arrangement is on the whole preferred. It will be seen that the tribes are not arranged either according to their seniority or their maternity. The territory falling to each tribe was much smaller than of old, partly because of the large space occupied by the "oblation" (fully one-fifth of the whole), and partly because the remainder was to be divided among the whole twelve tribes, instead of among

Hazar-enan, the border of Damascus
northward, to the coast of Hamath; for
these are his sides east *and* west; a *por-
tion for* Dan. (2) And by the border of
Dan, from the east side unto the west
side, a *portion for* Asher. (3) And by the
border of Asher, from the east side even
unto the west side, a *portion for* Naph-
tali. (4) And by the border of Naphtali,
from the east side unto the west side, a
portion for Manasseh. (5) And by the
border of Manasseh, from the east side
unto the west side, a *portion for* Eph-
raim. (6) And by the border of Ephraim,
from the east side even unto the west
side, a *portion for* Reuben. (7) And by
the border of Reuben, from the east
side unto the west side, a *portion for*
Judah.

(8) And by the border of Judah, from
the east side unto the west side, shall be
the offering which ye shall offer of five
and twenty thousand *reeds in* breadth,
and *in* length as one of the *other* parts,
from the east side unto the west side:
and the sanctuary shall be in the midst
of it. (9) The oblation that ye shall offer
unto the LORD *shall be* of five and twenty
thousand in length, and of ten thousand
in breadth. (10) And for them, *even* for
the priests, shall be *this* holy oblation;
toward the north five and twenty thou-
sand *in length*, and toward the west ten
thousand in breadth, and toward the
east ten thousand in breadth, and to-
ward the south five and twenty thousand
in length: and the sanctuary of the
LORD shall be in the midst thereof.
(11) [1] *It shall be* for the priests that are
sanctified of the sons of Zadok; which

1 Or, *The sanctified portion shall be for the priests.*

---

only nine and a half. The portion thus given to each tribe was rather less than two-thirds that assigned, on the average, by Joshua.

(1) **These are his sides east and west.**—*Lit., The east side, the west side, shall be to him,* meaning that the portion of Dan stretches across the country from the eastern to the western boundary. So of them all. The original portion of Dan was at the west of Benjamin, but a part of the tribe having conquered Laish, and settled at the extreme north, Dan is now made the most northern of the tribes. Asher, Naphtali, Manasseh, and Ephraim are so far approximated to their old places as to be north of the sanctuary.

(8) **In length as one of the other parts.**—The oblation, which has been already spoken of in chap. xlv. 1—7 in a different connection, is here (verses 8—22) more exactly described. Its whole width is again stated as 25,000 reeds, and its length from the eastern to the western boundaries of the land "as one of the other parts," no account being taken in this of the varying distance between the Jordan and the Mediterranean. It cannot, however, be so placed as not to exceed that distance.

(9) **The oblation.**—This is the same word as is translated *offering* in verse 8. It is used in this passage in three different senses:—(1) as including the whole strip from the Jordan to the Mediterranean and 25,000 reeds wide; (2) for that part of this set aside for the priests, and for the Levites; (3) for the most sacred part of this, appropriated to the priests and Temple, 25,000 reeds from east to west, and 10,000 from north to south. This last portion, although in the middle, is mentioned first on account of its especial sacredness.

(10) **In the midst thereof.**—The whole connection shows that this is to be understood strictly; the sanctuary was to be not merely within the priests' portion, but in its centre.

(11) **Sons of Zadok.**—See Note on chap. xl. 46.

As the Levites went astray.—That the Levites were far more affected than the priests by the general apostasy, may be reasonably inferred from the fact that at the restoration less than 400 Levites, and as many

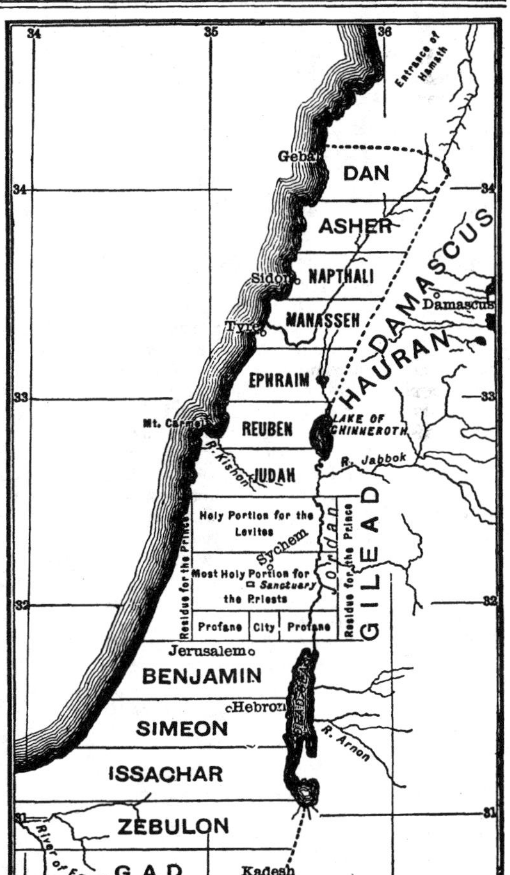

MAP OF PALESTINE,
Showing the Divisions among the Tribes.

have kept my [1]charge, which went not
astray when the children of Israel went
astray, as the Levites went astray.
(12) And *this* oblation of the land that is
offered shall be unto them a thing most
holy by the border of the Levites.
(13) And over against the border of the
priests the Levites *shall have* five and
twenty thousand in length, and ten
thousand in breadth: all the length
shall be five and twenty thousand, and
the breadth ten thousand. (14) And they
shall not sell of it, neither exchange, nor
alienate the firstfruits of the land: for
it is holy unto the LORD.
(15) And the five thousand, that are
left in the breadth over against the five
and twenty thousand, shall be a profane
place for the city, for dwelling, and for
suburbs: and the city shall be in the
midst thereof. (16) And these *shall be*
the measures thereof; the north side
four thousand and five hundred, and the
south side four thousand and five hundred,
and on the east side four thousand
and five hundred, and the west side four
thousand and five hundred. (17) And the
suburbs of the city shall be toward the
north two hundred and fifty, and toward
the south two hundred and fifty, and toward
the east two hundred and fifty, and
toward the west two hundred and fifty.
(18) And the residue in length over
against the oblation of the holy *portion*
shall be ten thousand eastward, and ten
thousand westward: and it shall be over
against the oblation of the holy *portion;*
and the increase thereof shall be for food
unto them that serve the city. (19) And
they that serve the city shall serve it
out of all the tribes of Israel. (20) All
the oblation *shall be* five and twenty
thousand by five and twenty thousand:
ye shall offer the holy oblation four-square,
with the possession of the city.
(21) And the residue *shall be* for the
prince, on the one side and on the other
of the holy oblation, and of the possession
of the city, over against the five and
twenty thousand of the oblation toward
the east border, and westward over
against the five and twenty thousand
toward the west border, over against the
portions for the prince: and it shall be
the holy oblation; and the sanctuary of
the house *shall be* in the midst thereof.
(22) Moreover from the possession of the
Levites, and from the possession of the

[1] Or, *ward*, or, *ordinance.*

Nethinims, returned (Ezra ii. 40—58; Neh. vii. 43—60), while there were 4,289 of the priests.

(14) **Shall not sell of it.**—The Levites' portion (verse 13) was of the same size as that of the priests, instead of their having (as under the law) nearly three times as many cities, and the restriction of Lev. xxv. 34 that they might not even temporarily alienate the fields attached to their cities, is here extended to their whole land on the express ground that it is "first-fruits."

(15) **The five thousand that are left.**—The two strips of territory for the Levites and the priests, each 10,000 reeds wide, being deducted from the whole width of the oblation, leaves a strip of 5,000 wide and 25,000 long which is here apportioned to the city and its suburbs. It is called "profane" in contrast to the "holy" possession of the Levites (verse 14), and the "most holy" of the priests (verse 12), though it was still a part of the oblation.

(16) **The measures.**—The city itself is to be an exact square of 4,500 reeds, and according to verse 17, was to have "suburbs," or rather *an open space* on all sides of 250 reeds. The whole was, therefore, 5,000 reeds—a little less than ten miles—square, the exact width of the space that was left of the oblation, and leaving 10,000 reeds on each side of it.

(18) **Shall be for food.**—This piece of land, only four times the size of the city itself, would seem a very insufficient provision for raising all the food required for the labourers of the city. But here, as everywhere, it is to be remembered that the description is ideal.

(19) **Out of all the tribes of Israel.**—The city itself is no longer, as of old, to belong to any particular tribe, but is to be situated on the common oblation, and its labourers are to be taken alike from all the tribes. Thus the old jealousies are to be extinguished, and in this, as in all other respects, each tribe is to be treated like every other.

(21) **The residue shall be for the prince.**—The length of the oblation from east to west is supposed to leave a strip at either end which is assigned to the prince. This strip is to extend from north to south, the whole width of the oblation. The expression "over against the portions for the prince" is somewhat obscure from its extreme brevity and want of punctuation in our version; it means that the part of the oblation *over against the tribe portions shall be for the prince—i.e.,* he is to have all that is left of the oblation between it and the portions assigned to the tribes. As already said, this was geographically impossible on the estimate of the length of the cubit here adopted. Even if the cubit were reduced to eighteen inches, which is the smallest estimate that can well be made, the side of the oblation would still be $42\frac{6}{10}$ miles long, or more than the distance between the Jordan and the Mediterranean at its northern end. It is quite idle, therefore, to attempt any calculation of the prince's portion. The description is necessarily ideal, and no hint is given in the vision of how much was intended for the prince. If it be suggested that the prophet may have had in mind measures following the uneven surface of the ground and the sinuosities of the roads, it can only be replied that such a supposition at once destroys all possibility of following his measures, and is singularly opposed to the whole symmetry of his description, as well as inconsistent with the equality of the measure on the four sides.

city, *being* in the midst *of that* which is the prince's, between the border of Judah and the border of Benjamin, shall be for the prince.

(23) As for the rest of the tribes, from
the east side unto the west side, Benja-
min *shall have* [1]a *portion.* (24) And by
the border of Benjamin, from the east
side unto the west side, Simeon *shall*
have a *portion.* (25) And by the border of
Simeon, from the east side unto the west
side, Issachar a *portion.* (26) And by the
border of Issachar, from the east side
unto the west side, Zebulun a *portion.*
(27) And by the border of Zebulun, from
the east side unto the west side, Gad a
portion. (28) And by the border of Gad,
at the south side southward, the border
shall be even from Tamar *unto* the waters
of [2]strife *in* Kadesh, *and* to the river to-
ward the great sea.
(29) This *is* the land which ye shall
divide by lot unto the tribes of Israel
for inheritance, and these *are* their por-
tions, saith the Lord GOD.
(30) And these *are* the goings out of the
city on the north side, four thousand and
five hundred measures. (31) And the
gates of the city *shall be* after the names
of the tribes of Israel: three gates north-
ward; one gate of Reuben, one gate of
Judah, one gate of Levi. (32) And at the
east side four thousand and five hundred:
and three gates; and one gate of Joseph,
one gate of Benjamin, one gate of Dan.
(33) And at the south side four thousand
and five hundred measures: and three
gates; one gate of Simeon, one gate of
Issachar, one gate of Zebulun. (34) At
the west side four thousand and five
hundred, *with* their three gates; one
gate of Gad, one gate of Asher, one gate
of Naphtali. (35) *It was* round about
eighteen thousand *measures:*

And the name of the city from *that* day *shall be*, [3]The LORD *is* there.

1 Heb., *one* portion.

2 Heb., *Meribah-kadesh.*

3 Heb., *Jehovah-shammah.*

---

(23) **The rest of the tribes.**—In verses 23—29 the remaining five tribes have their portions assigned on the south of the oblation in precisely the same way as the seven on the north.

(30) **The goings out of the city.**—In verses 30—34 the dimensions of the city are again given for the purpose of introducing the mention of the gates, three on each side, one for each of the tribes of Israel. In this enumeration Levi takes his place as a tribe, and Joseph is therefore reckoned as only one tribe; but the order of their names is neither that of their geographical arrangement nor of their seniority. It will be remembered that the symbolism of the twelve gates enters also into the vision of Rev. xxi. 12, 21.

(35) **Round about eighteen thousand.**—The circuit of the city, not including its "suburbs," or open space, was $4 \times 4{,}500 = 18{,}000$ reeds, or something over thirty-four miles. Josephus reckoned the circuit of Jerusalem in his day at four miles.

Measures.—This word is rightly supplied from verses 30, 33. On the symmetry of the city and its gates and the names of the gates, comp. Rev. xxi. 12, 13, 16.

The Lord is there.—With this name of the city Ezekiel closes his vision and his book. It is a most fitting close; for the object has been to depict, under the figures of the Jewish dispensation, the glories of the Church of the future. The culmination of this glory must ever be that the Lord, according to His promise (John vi. 56), will dwell in the believer, and the believer in Him. Imperfectly as this may be carried out here on earth, the effect of the Gospel is to bring about ever more and more fully its realisation; and the closing book of the volume of Revelation, catching the echoes of Ezekiel's prophecy, looks forward to the Holy City, the New Jerusalem "coming down from God out of heaven," and declares, "Behold, the tabernacle of God is with men, and He will dwell with them, and they shall be His people, and God Himself shall be with them and be their God" (Rev. xxi. 2, 3).

EXCURSUS ON NOTES TO THE BOOK OF THE PROPHET EZEKIEL

EXCURSUS A (at end of chap. iii.): ON THE FIGURATIVE LANGUAGE AND SYMBOLICAL ACTIONS OF EZEKIEL.

At this point, when the prophet has been fully commissioned for his work, and his actual prophecies begin, it may be well to consider their general character, especially as the very next chapter brings us at once into the midst of symbolical action. That much of Ezekiel's language is figurative, and that some of the actions he records were done in vision only, it is impossible to doubt. Thus, for example, in chap. xxiv. 6 the prophet is told to "bring it (the city) out piece by piece," and then to set it upon the coals (verse 11), which of course could only have been done mentally or symbolically, and that it was the former is plain from verse 3. In chap. xxi. 19, the appointing of two ways, from which the king of Babylon was to choose, could not have been literally done; and there are many like passages, in which it is plain that the prophet has merely expressed in concrete figures (thus giving them vividness and force) the ideas he wished to convey. On the other hand, there are passages in which a symbolical use is made of events and acts which are evidently to be taken in a literal sense. Thus in chap. xxiv. 16—24, it would be impossible to understand the sudden death of Ezekiel's wife and the prohibition of mourning for her as otherwise than strictly literal, and yet he is directed to make important symbolical use of them. What has been said of actions applies equally to prophecies. There is in them also the same mingling of the literal and the symbolical, the same intense disposition to embody every thought in some concrete form.

How then, it may be asked, is the literal to be distinguished from the figurative, whether in language or in act? It may not always be possible to do so in regard to every detail; to be absolutely certain whether the binding of chap. iii. 25, for instance, was only a figurative expression or a symbolical act, although, in this case, we believe the former to be the true explanation. But the details of the application are comparatively unimportant; and sometimes there may well be a difference of opinion in regard to them. The literal and the figurative blend together, and pass the one into the other, in the prophet's teaching of these spiritual infants, as children often carry on their tales partly by sensible images and partly by pure imagination. In fact, this is often a necessity in the teaching of things which lie partly above human comprehension, as may be seen, for instance, in our Lord's description of the end of the world, and in many other passages. No serious harm can come of occasionally understanding literally that which was meant figuratively, provided it contains no internal marks of its figurative character. In the chapter which immediately follows there has always been a difference of opinion whether the prophet actually performed the symbolic actions recorded, or whether they were only mentally done, and then related. The latter seems almost the necessary interpretation, for several reasons: the mere lying upon one side for 390 days, so bound that he could not move, if not an impossibility, is extremely unlikely; it is also inconsistent with the command for the preparation of his food during the same time; the amount of food allowed, though sufficient to sustain life, would have led to great emaciation; the preparation of the food itself would have been, in the eyes of the law, abominable; and although this is very effective as a vision, it would have been exceedingly strange as a reality; the tile seems quite insufficient in size for all the uses to which it is put; and, finally, the time of 430 days in all is scarcely possible. From the fifth day of the fourth month in the fifth year (chap. i. 1, 2), to the fifth day of the sixth month of the sixth year (chap. viii. 1), according to the length of either the Jewish or Chaldean year, would have been 420 days only, and at least eight days of this had already passed. There is, then, too little time by eighteen days, and even if we were to suppose that this was the year for an intercalary month (of which there is no evidence), it would yet leave but twelve intervening days for the two important prophecies of chaps. vi. and vii. Still there has been a difference of opinion here, and it is not of much consequence in itself. The important point is to recognise the general habit of the prophet's mind; for there can be no satisfactory interpretation of his writings without a full appreciation of his readiness to clothe his thoughts in concrete forms, whether those forms were sensible realities or only the creations of his own mind.

EXCURSUS B: ON CHAPTER IV. 5, 6.

The explanation of the periods of time here mentioned has occasioned great difficulty and difference of opinion among the commentators. The subject may be best approached by first observing what points are clearly determined in the text itself, and then excluding all interpretations which are inconsistent with these.

In the first place, it is expressly stated in each of these verses that these days represent years. No interpretation, therefore, can be admitted which requires them to be literal days. Secondly, it is plain that the period is one of "bearing their iniquity"; not a period in which they are becoming sinful, but one in which they are suffering the punishment of their sin. Thirdly, it is plain from the whole structure of the symbolism that this period is in some way intimately connected with the siege of Jerusalem. Finally, the two periods of 390 and of forty days are distinct. If the symbolism was carried out in act, they must have been consecutive, and it is still the natural inference that they were so, even if it was only in vision. The two periods together, then, constitute 430 days; yet this is not to be emphasised, since no express mention is made of the whole period.

These points of themselves exclude several of the explanations that have from time to time been put forward. Among these must be mentioned, first, one which has perhaps been more generally adopted than any other of its class, the supposition that the 390 years of Israel's punishment are to be reckoned from some point in the reign of Jeroboam to the destruction of Jerusalem by Nebuchadnezzar. This, however, was far more a period of accumulation of Israel's transgression than of suffering its punishment; neither in this case could the period be fairly considered as extending beyond the end of the kingdom of Israel (which lasted in all but 253 years) unless it was also extended indefinitely. Moreover, expositors who adopt this view are quite unable to give any satisfactory account of Judah's forty years; for the proposal to reckon them from the reformation of Josiah is quite at variance with the character of the period described.

Every attempt to make these periods refer to a future time, stretching on far beyond the date of the prophecy, fails for want of any definite event at the end of either 390, 40, or 430 years.

The periods cannot be understood of events occurring in the course of the siege because, as already said, the numbers are expressly said to stand for years. Moreover, even if they could be taken of literal days, there would be nothing to correspond to them, since from the investment of the city to the flight of Zedekiah was 539 days, and to the destruction of the Temple twenty-eight days more (2 Kings xxv. 1, 3, 8).

Of two other explanations, it is only necessary to say a word: that of Theodoret is based upon the Greek version, which, by a curious mistake, has 190 instead of 390 days, and of course falls to the ground when the true number is considered; the ancient Jews and some early Christians interpreted the passage of a period of 430 years, which they conceived was to be fulfilled from the destruction of Jerusalem and the Temple, in the second year of the Emperor Vespasian, to its expected restoration, which the event has shown to be groundless.

Another ancient interpretation makes of the period of 430 years, the time from the building to the destruction of Solomon's Temple. This is open to the same objections already urged to others, and besides, it makes the total number the prominent thing, while there is no point of division for the 390 and the 40. St. Jerome reckoned the 390 years from the captivity of the northern kingdom to the deliverance of the Jews from danger in the time of Esther, and the 40 years from the destruction of the Temple by Nebuchadnezzar to the decree of Cyrus for the restoration of the Jews; but his chronology is at fault, and the former part of the explanation takes no notice of the main point of the siege of Jerusalem, while the events in the time of Esther cannot be looked upon as the termination of the punishment of the Israelites.

The later Jews make up the two periods by selecting throughout the period of the Judges and the monarchy the various times in which the sins of Israel and of Judah were especially marked, and adding these together; but this is utterly arbitrary and unsatisfactory.

So much space has been given to these different interpretations in order to show that there is no definite term of years, either before or after the date of the prophecy, which the ingenuity of the commentators has been able to discover, satisfying the conditions of the prophecy itself. We are, therefore, left free to accept the interpretation now generally given by the best modern expositors.

This takes for its starting-point the evident allusion of Ezekiel to Num. xiv. 14, "After the number of the days in which ye searched the land, even forty days, each day for a year shall ye bear your iniquities;" and the earlier prophecies declaring that the people in punishment for their sins should be brought again into Egypt, which yet should not be Egypt (Deut. xxviii. 68; Hosea viii. 13; ix. 3; xi. 5), but Assyria or Babylonia, as is expressly defined in some of these prophecies. The meaning is plainly that they should endure sufferings corresponding to the Egyptian bondage, but in another locality. Ezekiel himself elsewhere (xx. 35) speaks of God's dealings with the captives as a pleading with them "in the wilderness." Now if this be once recognised as the basis of Ezekiel's language—the representation of the future in terms of the historic past, which is so common in all prophecy—there need be no difficulty in the mention of the precise numbers. They become mere catch-words to carry the mind to the period he would indicate. The wanderings in the wilderness were always reckoned at 40 years, and the sojourn in Egypt (see Exod. xii. 40) at 430 years. Ezekiel merely follows here his habit of putting everything into vivid and concrete form. Are his people to suffer for their sins as they suffered of old? Judah is to endure the 40 years of wilderness sufferings, and Israel those of the Egyptian bondage; only, if he spoke of the latter as 430 years, it might seem that Israel was to endure the punishment belonging to both Israel and Judah, and therefore he takes from it the period already assigned to Judah, leaving for Israel 390 years. This accounts for his not mentioning the 430 years at all, and could be done the more easily because the actual *bondage* in Egypt was far less than either number. No precise period whatever is intended by the mention of these numbers, but only a vivid comparison of the future woes to the past. Again, whatever might be their present sufferings, they still had hope, and even indulged in defiance, while Jerusalem and the Temple stood. This hope was vain. The holy city and the Temple itself should be destroyed, and then they would know that the hand of the Lord was heavy upon them indeed for the punishment of their sins. The siege of Jerusalem is, therefore, the prominent feature of the prophecy; and there is foretold, as the consequence of this, the eating of "defiled bread among the Gentiles" (verse 13) as in Egypt of old, together with the various forms of want and suffering set forth in the striking symbolism of this chapter.

EXCURSUS C: ON CHAPTER V. 7.

The expression in this verse, and also that in chap. xvi. 47, are explained in the commentary as meaning that the Israelites were not absolutely worse than the heathen, but only relatively, in view of their opportunities and privileges; yet the language in both places, as well as in many other passages of the prophets, seems on its face to be absolute. The question may, therefore, be naturally asked whether it is justifiable to interpret it in a relative sense, and if so, on what grounds? The answer to these questions must be sought in a consideration of the whole character and history of Israel, which will show that what might be only a relatively greater wickedness in them according to a human standard, becomes, under the circumstances, an absolutely greater sin against God.

It certainly is not true that the Israelites as a nation habitually committed sins which were, in themselves considered, of greater enormity than the abominations of the heathen; nor is it to be supposed that they were originally chosen of God because they had a worse disposition than any other people. How, then, did they come to be regarded by Him as worse, and how did they come to have a greater proclivity to evil? The law of the moral government of the world, that responsibility is proportioned to privilege, is much insisted upon in Scripture; and hence the neglect or misuse of privilege leads to a severer condemnation than if the privilege had never been given. This law is in accordance with the fact of universal experience that grace, when resisted, hardens the heart and alienates it further from God. It is only in view of this fact that we can account for the rejection of our Lord by those among whom His mighty works were done. The same fact explains the strong terms in which the prophets continually reproach their people. The Gentiles, with less of grace and of religious privilege, could not fall into the same extreme hardness of heart by their rejection.

But this suggests the still more radical question, Why should the Israelites have been more prone to abuse their greater privileges than the Gentiles to slight those which were far inferior? The reason lies in the very nature of the privileges themselves; for the opposition of the natural heart was far more roused by the one than by the other. The various religions of the heathen were alike in imposing little check on the passions and selfishness and self-will of man; in fact, they often not only encouraged but deified the worst traits of human nature. The law of God, on the contrary, set before men as the object of their worship a Being of absolute purity and holiness, and made the devotion to Him of heart and soul and strength its first and most absolute command. If the privilege of the Israelite was far greater, it yet required of him a harder struggle against the evil of his nature to avail himself of its benefits; and the failure in this, as it led him away from a higher standard of holiness, necessarily precipitated him into a greater depth of sin. Hence arose the striking contrasts in Israel's history between the saintliness of an Elijah, an Isaiah, or a Daniel, and the extreme wickedness of the people whom the prophet was now sent to rebuke. There is nothing therefore strange or abnormal in the history of Israel as compared with that of the Gentiles. The same old story is constantly repeated in the vices of Christian lands, and is seen everywhere in the greater faithfulness to their standards of the devotees of every false or corrupted religion. In passing, one cannot but remark upon that merciful providence of Almighty God by which His revelation has been ever progressive, rising only as men were in some degree prepared by the lower revelation to bear the higher.

Yet, while these results may thus be traced to the working of providential laws, the fault is without excuse, whether in ourselves or in the Israelites of old. Neither they nor we would willingly forego the privilege, and with this the responsibility for its improvement is inseparably joined. God gave then, as He gives now, sufficient grace to those that seek it; and freely pardons the sin of all that strive against its power.

EXCURSUS D: ON CHAPTER XIII. 6, 7, AND 17.

In these verses a broad and crucial distinction is made between the self-imagined vision and that which is sent from the Lord. It may be that in this case the prophets and prophetesses were untrue to their own convictions, and wilfully declared what they knew to be false; or it may be that they simply uttered as God's message that which they had persuaded themselves would be the issue. This point is not entirely clear from the passage, and is of secondary importance. What deserves to be carefully noted is the difference here made between subjective views of truth—that which comes "out of their own heart"—and those objective communications which God gave to His true prophets. This distinction has a most important bearing upon the whole subject of revelation, and establishes clearly the fact that the Scriptures look upon it as something expressly communicated to their writers, and not as a thing which could be the result of their own thought and reflection. He, therefore, who puts "Thus saith the Lord" before that which God has not in some objective way made known to him, must fall under the condemnation pronounced here and elsewhere upon "the prophet which shall presume to speak a word in my name, which I have not commanded him to speak" (Deut. xviii. 20).

EXCURSUS E: ON CHAPTER XXIX. 19.—ON NEBUCHADNEZZAR'S CONQUEST OF EGYPT.

The fact of this conquest having been called in question, it may be well to state very briefly the points of evidence in its favour. It is admitted by all that Pharaoh-Hophra was dethroned, and died a violent death, and was succeeded by Amasis, who was at first little regarded by the people, though he afterwards won their confidence. The account given of this revolution by the Egyptian priests to Herodotus makes no mention of any foreign interference, but represents it as wholly an internal affair, caused by a revolt of the troops of Hophra. He sent Amasis to them to bring them back to their allegiance, but they saluted him as king. This authority is suspicious, since the priests were prone to cover up whatever they considered against the honour of their country; and the two facts of the popularity of Amasis with the troops and his unpopularity with the people are scarcely consistent, since it is said that he spared Hophra for a time, but afterwards, yielding to the wishes of the people, strangled him. Now against this .suspicious and interested story stands the much more probable supposition that Hophra was dethroned and Amasis put into his place by the power of Nebuchadnezzar. Megasthenes and Berosus, according to Josephus, expressly testify that "Nebuchadnezzar conquered a great part of Africa, and having invaded Egypt, took many captives, who were committed to the charge of persons appointed to conduct them after him to Babylon." This conquest, according to the dates already given, must be placed just at the time of the fall of Hophra. Besides this, there is a very full prophecy of the conquest of Egypt by Nebuchadnezzar in Jeremiah (chap. xlvi.), uttered in the first year of his reign (comp. chap. xlvi. 1 with chap. xxv. 1). But Jeremiah was himself afterwards carried into Egypt, and while there uttered other prophecies to the same effect (chaps. xliii., xliv.). It is altogether probable that he was still living there at the time of Nebuchadnezzar's expedition; and, on the lowest grounds, it is inconceivable that he should have allowed these various prophecies to remain on record if they had been proved false by the event. The same thing substantially may be said also of the present prophecy of Ezekiel, and of that in chap. xxx. 10, although the prophet was not, like Jeremiah, living where he could be an eye-witness of the result of the attack. Other prophecies against Egypt (Isa. xviii., xix., xxxi.; Joel iii. 19) are more general, and may not have in view this particular conquest.

Again, Ezekiel represents Egypt as spoiled by Nebuchadnezzar, while both ancient history and the monuments describe the country as rich and prosperous under Amasis. There is really no inconsistency, but entire harmony between these accounts. The great drain upon the resources of Egypt for many generations had been her foreign wars with the powers of Mesopotamia. Relieved of this, and at peace with Nebuchadnezzar, under the government of his vassal, Egypt would soon have recovered her prosperity in wealth and art, while still politically desolated and no longer able to appear as a great power among the nations. From this time through all subsequent history Egypt was a base kingdom, and never again able to dispute, as in former days, the sovereignty of the world.

There is an apparent difficulty about the date of this conquest, alluded to under verse 17. The prophecy of Ezekiel is in the future, and yet was spoken in the thirty-fifth year of Nebuchadnezzar (the twenty-seventh from the accession of Zedekiah). Now, Jerusalem was taken in his nineteenth year (2 Kings xxv. 8), and an interval of sixteen years seems, at first sight, inconsistent with the statement of Josephus. But if that statement be examined, it will be found to be entirely indefinite (see under verse 17), and it is hardly to be supposed that Nebuchadnezzar would have undertaken the conquest of Egypt while still engaged in the siege of Tyre; in fact, verses 18, 19 distinctly imply that the one was subsequent to the other. Now, the siege of Tyre appears to have been begun about two years after the capture of Jerusalem, and lasted thirteen years. It closed then fifteen years after the destruction of Jerusalem, and supposing the campaign against Egypt to have followed immediately, in the next year, we get the exact date of this prophecy. (For the references to Josephus, see *Antiqq.*, Bk. x., cap. ix., § 7; *Cont. Ap.*, Bk. i., § 19, 20.)

EXCURSUS F: ON CHAPTER XXXVII.

So much has been said in the interpretation of this chapter of the high spiritual view which can alone explain these prophecies consistently with themselves, that it may be unnecessary to add anything further; yet as correct views upon this point are absolutely essential to the right understanding of the remaining parts of this book, and as much misapprehension exists in regard to them, it may be well very briefly to mention some of the reasons why it is impossible to understand the language of Ezekiel in regard to the future as referring only to the Israelites after the flesh, and to the land in which they once lived.

Every one who compares the general scope and purpose of the two dispensations must see that they are essentially one, that the end was foreseen from the beginning, and that the earlier was distinctly preparatory for the later. The "Gospel was preached before unto Abraham," and then "the law was added because of transgressions, until the promised seed should come" (Gal. iii. 8, 19); and this preparatory character of the old dispensation, recognised even by Moses (Deut. xviii. 15—18, &c.), was more and more insisted upon by the prophets (*e.g.*, Jer. xxxi. 31—34; Hag. ii. 6—9, &c.). At the same time, they describe the future continually by means of already familiar events in their history (see Isa. xl.—lxvi. throughout, especially chaps. lxii., lxiii.), even going to the extent of promising again the reign of David (Jer. xxx. 9; Ezek. xxxiv. 23, 24; xxxvii. 24, 25; Hos. iii. 5), and the coming in the last days of the prophet Elijah (Mal. iv. 5). These prophecies are repeatedly and expressly interpreted of Christ and His forerunner, while the promised "new covenant" is explained of the Christian dispensation; and the description of the wonders accompanying its introduction (Joel ii. 28—32, &c.) is applied to the circumstances connected with the first promulgation of the Gospel (Acts ii. 16, &c.). Moreover, it was from the first expected that the "seed of Abraham" should embrace far more than his descendants after the flesh, and the promise that he should be "the father of many nations" is shown by St. Paul to mean that all who embraced his faith should be recognised as his children (Rom. iv. 16); while the correlated promise, "To thy seed will I give this land," is extended in the same connection (*ib.* verse 13) to a promise "that he should be the heir of the world." When these facts are joined (1) with our Lord's teaching that the types and shadows of the old economy were fulfilled in Himself; that the time had come when Jerusalem should no longer be the place where the Father should be worshipped (John iv. 21); and (2) with the apostle's declaration that all earthly distinctions between Jew and Greek, or of whatever other kind, are passed away: that "if ye be Christ's, then are ye Abraham's seed" (Gal. iii. 28, 29); and also (3) with the whole argument in the Epistle to the Hebrews that the Aaronic priesthood culminated and was absorbed in the higher priesthood of Christ, and that the whole sacrificial and Temple arrangements of old were typical and temporary, and were superseded by the realities of the Christian dispensation—there seems no longer room for doubt that the Jewish Church and nationality are things of the past, and have been merged for ever in the Church of Christ. At the same time, it is never to be forgotten that the prophets foretold, and history has fulfilled, that "salvation is of the Jews" (John iv. 22), and that the law should "go forth from Sion," and the "new covenant" be made with God's chosen people; for it is abundantly evident that our Lord, after the flesh, was a Jew, and all His immediate followers were Jews. His Church was cradled among them, and it was not until some years after it had entered upon its career for the salvation of the world that its doors were thrown open to the Gentiles.

If, however, it were still urged that, all this being admitted, many prophecies, and notably those of Ezekiel, still seem, over and above these things, to look forward to a future restoration of the Jews to their own land, in a condition of great prosperity and power, it must be replied that the above considerations of the absolute removal in Christ of all distinctions among those who believe in Him are inconsistent with the future revival of these distinctions in His Church; and that even such an explicit prophecy of the restoration of the fallen "tabernacle of David" as is contained in Amos ix. 11, 12 is expressly applied by the apostles (Acts xv. 16) to the union of Gentiles and Jews in the Christian Church.

Besides all this, in predicting the future under the figures of what has gone before, the prophets frequently foretell what would be contradictory if it were to be understood literally. Thus Zechariah (chap. xiv. 16—19) declares that all nations shall come up to Jerusalem to keep the Feast of Tabernacles: an evident physical impossibility. So also there is continual mention of the restoration of animal sacrifices with acceptance to God, which is inconceivable in the light in which those sacrifices are viewed in the New Testament. The offering of the "one sacrifice for sins for ever" (Heb. x. 12) by Him who was the Antitype of all sacrifice necessarily brought to an end the whole typical system.

Finally, it is to be considered that the very representations of the old prophets are sometimes repeated in the New Testament as a means of describing a state of things which no one would dream of interpreting literally. This is particularly noticeable in the present passage. Ezekiel has been describing a spiritual resurrection of the people (comp. John v. 21), and then goes on to foretell an assault by their enemies which shall be frustrated by the power of God (chaps. xxxviii., xxxix.). The same thing is foretold in Rev. xx.: the power of evil is restrained for a time, and there is a resurrection of the believers in Christ, with a period of blessing and prosperity; then the enemies of God (under the very same names of Gog and Magog) are gathered to battle, and destroyed by the power of God; and finally, the Church of the future, the heavenly Jerusalem, is revealed in its power and glory, in much the same way as in this passage of Ezekiel.

It can scarcely be necessary to add that the figurative interpretation of these prophecies does not affect the important question in regard to the purpose of Divine Providence in the continued preservation of the Jews as a distinct people, and the intimations in regard to their future, given in the Epistle to the Romans and elsewhere. Whatever may be the future designed for Israel, the question here is simply, What was the instruction intended to be conveyed in this chapter? And the reasons above given seem sufficiently to indicate the interpretation adopted.

EXCURSUS G: ON CHAPTERS XXXVIII. AND XXXIX.

Various indications of the nature and intent of this prophecy have been already given in commenting upon its verses in detail, but it is desirable to gather up these indications and combine them with others of a more general character.

It is not at all unlikely that the starting-point of the prophecy may have been in some recent events, such as the Scythian invasion already spoken of. It is also plain that a prophecy of such a general character, concerning the struggle of worldliness against the kingdom of God, and its final overthrow, may have had many partial fulfilments of a literal kind, such as in the contest between the Maccabees and Antiochus Epiphanes, because such struggles must always be incidents in the greater and wider contest. It is further evident from the prophecy itself that the restoration of the Jews to their own land, then not far distant, was constantly before the mind of the prophet, and formed in some sort the point of view from which he looked out upon the wider and more spiritual blessings of the distant future. But these things being understood, there are several clear indications that he did not confine his view in this prophecy to any literal event, but intended to set forth under the figure of Gog and his armies all opposition of the world to the kingdom of God, and to foretell, like his contemporary Daniel, the final and complete triumph of the latter in the distant future.

The first thing that strikes one in reading the prophecy is the strange and incongruous association of the nations in this attack. No nations near the land of Israel are mentioned, and few of those who, either before or since, have been known as its foes. On the contrary, the nations selected are all as distant from Palestine and as distant from each other (living on the confines of the known world) as it was possible to mention. The Scythians, the Persians, the Armenians, the Ethiopians and Libyans, the tribes of Arabia, Dedan and Sheba, and the Tarshish probably of Spain, form an alliance which it is impossible to conceive as ever being actually formed among the nations of the earth. Then the object of this confederacy, the spoil of Israel (chaps. xxxviii. 12, 13; xxxix. 10), would have been absurdly incommensurate with the exertion; Palestine, with all it contained, would hardly have been enough to furnish rations for the invaders for a day, far less to tempt them to a march of many hundreds, or even thousands, of miles. Further, the mass of the invaders, as described in chap. xxxix. 12—16, is more than fifty times greater than any army that ever assembled upon earth, and great enough to make it difficult for them to find even camping-ground upon the whole territory of Palestine. This multitude is so evidently ideal, and the circumstantial account of their burial so plainly practically impossible, that it is unnecessary to add anything farther to what has been said in the Notes to this passage. Finally, in the statement (chap. xxxviii. 17) that this prophecy was the same which had been spoken in old time by the prophets of Israel, we have a direct assurance that it was not meant to be literally understood, because no such prophecies are anywhere recorded; but prophecies of what we conceive to be here pictorially represented, the struggle of the world with the kingdom of God and its final utter overthrow, do form the constant burden of prophecy, and constitute one of the striking features of all Revelation.

To this is to be added the fact that, however the passage in Rev. xx. 7—10 may be interpreted, the author of the Apocalypse, by the use of the same names, and a short summary of the same description, has shown that he regarded this vision of Ezekiel as typical, and its fulfilment as in his time still future.

The prophecy, thus interpreted, falls naturally into the place it holds in the collection of Ezekiel's writings. There has been in the last few chapters, especially in chap. xxxvii., an increasing fulness of Messianic promise; then follows, in the closing section of the book, a remarkable setting forth of the perfected worship of God by a purified people under the earthly figure of a greatly changed and purified temple-worship, with a new apportionment of the land, a purified priesthood, and other figures taken from the old dispensation. But these things are not to be attained without trial and struggle; and, therefore, just here is placed this warning of the putting forth of the whole power of the world against the kingdom of God under the symbol of the gathering of the armies of Gog, with the comforting assurance, given everywhere in Revelation, that in the ultimate issue every power which exalts itself against God shall be utterly overthrown, and all things shall be subdued unto Him.

THE BOOK OF DANIEL

INTRODUCTION

TO

THE BOOK OF DANIEL

I. Personal history of Daniel.—Of the personal history of this great seer nothing is known beyond what is recorded of him in the Book of Daniel. Being apparently of royal descent (chap. i. 3), and when still a youth, he was taken to Babylon captive by Nebuchadnezzar in the fourth year of Jehoiakim. As history does not state that he ever revisited his native land, it is highly probable that he continued in the East from the year of his exile till the third year of Cyrus, which is the last date mentioned in the book. Here his position and his well-known character, no doubt, enabled him to render much aid to his fellow-countrymen, whether at home or in exile.

During this long period he had witnessed the marvellous and rapid growth of the Babylonian empire under Nebuchadnezzar. He then watched the gradual decay of this mighty empire after the decease of its founder; he saw the final collapse of it, and witnessed the first beginning of the Persian supremacy, under which, as well as during the short period that a Median viceroy presided over Babylonia, he probably maintained the high position which he had filled during his younger days. The date of his death, like that of his birth, is unknown, but his prophetic activity must have lasted over seventy years. The first of the exiles himself, he lived to see the return of the Jews under Zerubbabel, and to hear of the opposition offered by the Samaritans to the progress of the works at Jerusalem. His fame spread among the exiles who resided in remoter parts of the Babylonian empire, and one of these, the prophet Ezekiel, mentions his wisdom (chap. xxviii. 3), and hints at his intercession (Ezek. xiv. 14) for the lives of certain persons. (See Daniel ii. 24.)

II. Authorship of the Book of Daniel.—The Book of Daniel is anonymous. No title is prefixed to it such as appears in the case of the books of Isaiah or Jeremiah. It begins abruptly with the statement of a historical fact connected with the reign of Jehoiakim. It then proceeds to state certain incidents that occurred in the lives of Daniel and of his three friends; it then gives an account of various visions and revelations which God gave to the seer; and concludes with the solemn words, "Thou shalt rest and stand in thy lot at the end of days" (chap. xii. 13). In no place is it definitely stated that the author of the book was Daniel himself.

A closer inspection of the book, however, brings to light a remarkable feature in it. Throughout the first six chapters Daniel is invariably spoken of in the third person. Throughout the last six chapters, with three exceptions, Daniel invariably speaks of himself in the first person. Hence a conclusion might be drawn that we have traces of two authors, a biographer and an autobiographer, and that the book is a compilation taken from the two sources. But is such a conclusion justifiable?

Apparently not. For throughout the last six chapters Daniel claims to have seen certain visions, and to have received certain revelations; a vision of four beasts (chap. vii.), which represented four kingdoms, three of which the reader has to identify for himself; a vision of two beasts (chap. viii.), which, according to the words of the heavenly messenger, represented the Medo-Persian and the Greek empires; a revelation of a period of seventy weeks (chap. ix.), which were closely connected with the destiny of his people; and, finally, a revelation concerning certain events which were to occur after the dissolution of the Greek empire. Each of these visions and revelations is introduced to the reader respectively by the words, "I saw in my vision," "a vision appeared unto me," "I understood by books," "I lifted up mine eyes and looked." It is obvious, therefore, that the last six chapters claim to have been composed by Daniel.

But we notice a remarkable correspondence between the first six and the last six chapters. Each chapter of the former series is a prelude to the latter series. The whole of the first series is essential to render the latter series intelligible. Again, the writer of each series is equally familiar with Hebrew and Chaldee. The same peculiar phrases and forms of language, some of them being exceedingly rare, may be noticed in each series. It is highly improbable that a work which is written upon so definite a plan, which has, moreover, such complete uniformity of style, should be the work of more than one author. If then the author of the latter part was a man named Daniel, it is reasonable to suppose that the former part was written by the same Daniel. In fact, the change from the third to the first person no more disproves that Daniel was the author of the whole work, than a similar alteration of persons in Jer. xxiv. 1, xxv. 1, proves that Jeremiah wrote the former but not the latter chapter. It may then be assumed that the whole book claims to have been written by Daniel.

III. Date of authorship of the Book of Daniel.—Let it be granted that there was only one author of the book, and this is now almost universally acknowledged, it remains to make an approximation to the period when it was composed. And first we must examine what the author states about himself. He claims to have "continued" (chap. i. 21) from the time of Nebuchadnezzar to the first year of Cyrus, and also (chap. x. i.) to have received a revelation from God in the third year of Cyrus. He thus gives the extreme limits within which his activity continued. He adds that he was appointed by Nebuchadnezzar "to be ruler over the whole province of Babylon" (chap. ii. 48). He was employed at court in the third year of Belshazzar (chap. viii. 27), and on the night when Belshazzar was slain became "third ruler in the kingdom" (chap. v. 29). Some similar position he occupied during the obscure reign of Darius the Mede (chap. vi. 3). From what the author states of himself we gather that he lived chiefly under the Babylonian empire.

The internal evidence of the book bears this out. The author exhibits a very minute acquaintance with Babylon. He is aware of the three classes of magicians (chap. ii. 2), who are known from external sources to have existed in Babylon. He knows the magician's phraseology "dissolving of doubts" (chap. v. 12); their theology, which recognised "gods whose dwelling is not with flesh" (chap. ii. 11); and the sacred character of Babylonian numbers (chap. iii. 1, 19). Besides other smaller points, he is acquainted with Babylonian dress (chap. iii. 21), and Babylonian punishments (chaps. ii. 5, iii. 6). Minute particulars like these, recorded as they are casually and parenthetically, betray an author living in Babylon.

His knowledge of Persia is very slight. He does not even profess to have lived later than Cyrus, and consequently he only knew Persia, as it were, in her infancy. He was only aware of three Persian kings after Cyrus (chap. xi. 2), instead of a series of monarchs whose united reigns extended over nearly two hundred years. He was aware of the existence of Greece, and claims to have received a revelation that the power of Greece would overthrow the Persian empire, and that the Greek empire would only last during the reign of the first king. But he is uninformed of the important stages by which the Persian empire was dissolved and superseded by the Grecian.

Of historical events that occurred after the establishment of the Greek empire he knows still less. It is revealed to him that the Greek empire would finally be divided into four parts, and perhaps also that two of these should materially influence the fortunes of his people; but it is remarkable that there is an absence of anything like minute accuracy in the delineation of many of the most important events of this time. While certain events, such as the wars of Ptolemy Philopator and Antiochus the Great, or the persecutions in the time of Antiochus Epiphanes, may perhaps be pointed out, yet other events of great importance are omitted, such as the Maccabee wars, and others are described in such a way as is not recorded in history, such as the death of Antiochus. (See Notes on chap. xi.)

It appears then that the internal evidence, slight though it is, favours the hypothesis that the author lived in the Babylonian period rather than later. Difficulties have to be encountered under any hypothesis as to the date of the authorship of the book, but those that are involved in the hypothesis of an early date are the least formidable. (See below, § 6.)

Another fact deserves notice. The author, though not claiming the title of prophet, and not anywhere styled as such in the Old Testament, yet claims to have received certain revelations from God. If therefore he was desirous that his book should be received by his contemporaries, he must have lived at a time when the gift of prediction, or the spirit of prophecy, was still extant. But this gift was extinct in the times of Ezra and Nehemiah. It is therefore necessary to place the author of the book of Daniel at an earlier period: it would certainly be inconsistent with the Maccabee times to suppose that so great a seer as Daniel could have then existed, for, according to the trustworthy historian of those times, the people then complained of the entire absence of prophets. (1 Macc. iv. 45, 46, ix. 27, xiv. 41.)

The external evidence bearing upon the date of the book of Daniel is very slight. We know that it existed in the first century of the Christian era, from the evident allusions to it in Matt. xxiv. 15, John v. 28, Matt. xiii. 43. (Comp. Dan. ix. 27, xii. 2, 3.) These references, and the words of our Saviour (Luke xxi. 27, where He refers to Dan. vii. 13), are sufficient for those who believe in His divinity to establish the authority of the book.

To the testimony of the New Testament must be added that of Josephus. He cites largely from the Book of Daniel, and states that the author was favoured by God as one of the greatest of prophets, that his writings were then read, and that it might be inferred that Daniel had converse with God (*Ant.* X. 11, 7). Josephus states still further that Daniel not only foretold the future as other prophets had done, but that he defined the time when the events should occur. (See also *Ant.* X. 8, § 5.)

At least 150 years previous to Josephus, if not earlier, we find references to the book of Daniel as a work already in existence. In three passages of the work already referred to (1 Macc. i. 54, ix. 27, 40) there appears to be a verbal allusion to the Greek version of Dan. ix. 27, xii. 1, xi. 27, while it is hard to read the speech of Mattathias (1 Macc. ii. 49) without seeing references to the language in which Daniel spoke of the coming tribulation; and not only is the example of Daniel mentioned (1 Macc. ii. 60), but also the story of the three holy children is alluded to as one that was well known. It is highly improbable that a book of recent origin should have acquired so great a notoriety. And on the other hand, as there is no other known source of the story of Daniel except the book of Daniel, it is highly probable that if the story was known B.C. 167, the book must have existed also.

Unfortunately we are unable to find any earlier traces of the book. There are hardly any fragments remaining of Hebrew literature which belong to the period intervening between the last book in the Old Testament canon and the book of Maccabees. We are therefore led back to the times of Daniel himself, and then we find a man named Daniel mentioned by Ezekiel, who corresponds (see § 1) with the Daniel who claims to be the author of this book.

It must be remembered that very little is known of Hebrew literature or of Jewish history from the time of Nehemiah down to the Maccabee period. It is therefore impossible to give a series of authorities who bear witness to the existence of the book of Daniel up to the earliest times, and so to give a rigid demonstration of the date of the book. The following facts, however, have been stated above. (1) The Book of Daniel claims to have been written by a man named Daniel. (2) This Daniel was intimately acquainted with Babylon and many customs of Babylon. (3) He was much less acquainted with Persia. (4) He betrays still less knowledge of the Greek empire and of the Seleucidæ. (5) He lived at a time when the spirit of prophecy was extant. (6) The Book of Daniel was known B.C. 167. (7) Previous to the year B.C. 167 there is a blank of nearly 250 years in Jewish literature, but one of the latest Jewish authors, Ezekiel, was acquainted with a man named Daniel, who corresponds with the person who claims to be the author of the Book of Daniel.

IV. Place of the Book of Daniel in the Old Testament Canon.—The Book of Daniel, though placed in the English Version after that of Ezekiel, and reckoned among "four prophets the greater" (*Art.* vi.), yet occupies a very different position in the

Hebrew canon. It is there placed among the Hagiographa, or sacred writings, immediately before the Book of Ezra, and not in the collection of prophetical books. This is to be accounted for by the following reasons. (1) The Hebrew prophet had a special function to fulfil under the Theocracy. He was the authorised teacher of the people. This was his special task, and it was only incidentally that he predicted the future. The prophet was essentially the preacher of righteousness to the generation amidst which he lived, and it was God's will that in every instance simple prediction should be a subordinate function. But the case of Daniel is just the reverse. He appears before us as one that reveals the hidden future, rather than as a preacher. This is apparent by a reference to Dan. iv. 20—27, v. 17—28, where it will be noticed that while predicting the future he inculcates a moral lesson. This great difference between Daniel and a prophet strictly so-called will partly account for the position of the book in the Hebrew canon. But (2) not only is Daniel a prophet in an improper sense, but the style and matter of his predictions are totally different from those of other prophets. The reader of the Book of Daniel may be compared to a person looking down a long gallery hung transversely with curtains, on which are painted different scenes, and as curtain after curtain is drawn aside the scene behind it is unveiled to his view, till at last he sees the picture at the end. In this way the writings of Daniel are apocalyptic rather than predictive. He presents the future in a series of enigmatic pictures rather than in enigmatic language. But it is not only in style that his writings differ from those of the prophets—the subject matter which he reveals is of a different nature also. While the Holy Spirit limits for the most part the prediction of the prophets to the Captivity, and to the Messiah who is to come after the close of the Captivity, Daniel mentions the Captivity and the overthrow of Jerusalem only once, and taking this as his point of view, predicts that before the coming of the Messiah Israel has to undergo another period of tribulation. The first impression produced upon the reader by the words of the prophets is that after the return from the Exile a golden age will ensue. Daniel foretells the golden age, but places it in the remote future, and mentions a further probation of Israel, which must occur before the commencement of that epoch. It may be inferred that the great difference in matter and style between the Book of Daniel and the prophetical books, strictly so called, led the men of the Great Synagogue to "write Daniel" in a different collection from that in which they inserted the twelve prophets.

V. **Object of the Book of Daniel.**—The Book of Daniel has more than one aim. (1) In the first place it is essential to complete the continuity of revelation. At the time of the Exile the Israelite had before him the Law, the Prophets, and the Sacred Books so far as they had been received into the canon. These were sufficient to teach him the will of God, the certainty of the return from the Exile, and the coming of the Messiah. But, as was stated above, it might have been supposed that the Messianic days were to appear immediately after the return from the Exile. The book of Daniel corrects this impression, and prepares Israel for the period that is to intervene between the close of the Captivity and the advent of the Messiah. Those glorious days cannot come till a period has passed far darker than any that has been as yet known. In fact, just as the writings of Isaiah and Jeremiah led the Israelite to expect a captivity, so those of Daniel prompted him to look for a period of persecution after the return from the Exile; but at the same time they comforted him with the assurance that the duration of the persecution would be no greater than what the mercy of God would enable His servants to bear. The examples of the three holy children and of Daniel would encourage them, and the words of Daniel would comfort the Israelite in his martyrdom, as the persecuted Christian derived hope from the Saviour's sentence, "Behold I have told you before" (Matt. xxiv. 25). (2) But, secondly, the Book of Daniel had a very distinct object to fulfil amidst the generation in which it was written. Israel was in captivity. Her last hope at Jerusalem—the temple—was destroyed. Must it not have been a temptation to the sufferer to think that God's promises had proved false? And even though Jeremiah had foretold a return from the Captivity at the end of seventy years: if God's promises to King Solomon had failed, Israel might argue, why should not Jeremiah's prophecy fail as well? Accordingly the Book of Daniel shows by what means the hopes of God's people were sustained. The two great miracles recorded in the Book proved that God was as close to His people in Babylon as He had been at Jerusalem or in the temple. They are led to believe that He is still with them, and that He will deliver them from Babylon as He did of old from Egypt. In this way the object of the Book of Daniel was to support Israel in times of doubt and despair. (3) A further purpose of the Book may be noticed. It will be remembered that there was a considerable amount of missionary zeal among the Hebrew prophets. Not only were there instances when men like Jonah were specially sent to preach righteousness to the Gentiles, but occasionally, in the ordinary course of their ministry, the prophets addressed nations who were outside the covenant. The Book of Daniel exhibits this missionary character. We know that it was a general belief among eastern nations that when a neighbouring tribe was conquered, its gods were conquered as well. Nebuchadnezzar and Belshazzar both held this opinion. They thought that when Jerusalem fell Bel-Merodach had conquered Jehovah. If we may take an inference from some of the Psalms, it appears that the children of the Captivity were taunted about the weakness of their God; the enemy are described as "blaspheming God's name," and asking, in mocking triumph, "Where is now their God?" The Book of Daniel shows us how God made Himself known to the Babylonians, how He asserted His own power, and how in the end the king himself was brought to own the sovereign authority of Jehovah. It may therefore be said that the object of the Book of Daniel is (1) to supply a missing link in the chain of the continuity of revelation; (2) to support Israel amidst the doubts and fears occasioned by the Exile; (3) to reveal to a polytheistic nation the eternal power of the One true God.

VI. **Objections to the authenticity of the Book of Daniel.**—The objections to the early date of the Book of Daniel are weighty and numerous, and require more space for discussion than can here be given. They depend partly on the language, and partly on the history recorded in the book. It is asserted that (1) many names in the Book of Daniel are not of Babylonian origin, while some betray a very late date, showing that the writer must have lived as late as the Macedonian period. The proper names which are stated to be of non-Babylonian origin are Ashpenaz and Hamelsar; while neither Shadrach nor Meshach have as yet been found in Babylonian inscriptions. Nothing, however, as to the date of the Book can be inferred from these words. All that is proved by them amounts to nothing more than that certain exotic words were prevalent in Babylonia during Nebuchadnezzar's reign, just as French and German words occasionally appear among us in an English garb. Further difficulty in identifying these names is caused by the difficulty of transliterating foreign words into Hebrew characters. Again (2) the derivation of the name Belteshazzar (ch. iv. 8), has been stated to be erroneous. It must be remembered, however, that the authority for this statement is the king himself, who, perhaps, did not excel in philology so much as he did in military tactics. Another word, *saknu*, is stated to be used in a wrong sense. Whereas the word really denotes a high civil officer, it is used in ch. ii. 48 to mean an arch magician. On this point, as well as on the presence of Greek words, we must defer our judgment till we have more evidence before us. The principal historical difficulties are with regard to Belshazzar and Darius the Mede. The latter is spoken of as son of Ahasuerus. Now if by Ahasuerus is meant Xerxes, and by Darius the Mede Darius Hystaspis, the author has fallen into a considerable chronological error; but as neither of the two kings has been as yet identified, the inconsistency is only assumed. We know from Esther i. 1 that there was more than one Ahasuerus, and Greek tradition knows of more than one Darius. It is possible that Darius, like Sargon, may some day be brought to light unexpectedly, and then the difficulty about the satraps (ch. vi. 1) may find a solution. The difficulty with regard to Belshazzar is not insuperable. (See *Excursus* C.) We know that Nabonidus had a son named Belshazzar, and that Maruduk-sarra-usur (probably Belshazzar) was the last king of Babylon. When the queen speaks of Nebuchadnezzar as being Belshazzar's father, the words are not to be taken literally. That Daniel lived at a late date has also been inferred from the absence of his name in the list of worthies mentioned in Ecclus. xliv. 1. It is not plain upon what principles exactly the list was drawn up. It is certainly surprising that the names of Ezra, Mordecai, and Esther should be omitted. It appears as if the writer selected the names from the books of the Law and the Prophets, and then mentioned Nehemiah (chap. xlix. 13) as the most noteworthy saint that is recorded in the Hagiographa. Of course Ezra or Daniel would seem more naturally mentioned instead of Nehemiah; but the writer had his own peculiar views, and omitted both names. But objections of this nature are of no value, compared to those which are to be drawn from the language and history contained in the Book of Daniel. In the course of time it is possible that further discoveries will be made, which will make us as well acquainted with the period of the Exile as with the reigns of Ahaz and Hezekiah. Till then, we must suspend a hasty judgment pronouncing this Book to be "obviously" of a later date.

THE BOOK OF DANIEL

CHAPTER I.—(1) In the third year
of the reign of Jehoiakim king of Judah
[a] came Nebuchadnezzar king of Babylon
unto Jerusalem, and besieged it. (2) And
the LORD gave Jehoiakim king of Judah
into his hand, with part of the vessels
of the house of God: which he carried
into the land of Shinar to the house
of his god; and he brought the vessels
into the treasure house of his god.
(3) And the king spake unto Ashpenaz
the master of his eunuchs, that he
should bring *certain* of the children of
Israel, and of the king's seed, and of
the princes; (4) children in whom *was*
no blemish, but well favoured, and
skilful in all wisdom, and cunning in
knowledge, and understanding science,
and such as *had* ability in them to
stand in the king's palace, and whom
they might teach the learning and the
tongue of the Chaldeans. (5) And the
king appointed them a daily provision
of the king's meat, and of [1] the wine
which he drank: so nourishing them
three years, that at the end thereof they
might stand before the king. (6) Now
among these were of the children of

B.C. cir. 607.

a 2 Kin. 24. 1; 2 Chr. 36. 6.

1 Heb., *the wine of his drink.*

---

(1) **In the third year.**—Two questions are involved in this verse. (1) Is it historically true that Jerusalem was taken by Nebuchadnezzar in the third year of Jehoiakim's reign? (2) Does the language of the verse imply that he did so? The second question is rightly answered in the negative. The word *came* means *went,* as Gen. xlv. 17; 2 Kings v. 5, and it is the natural word for a Hebrew to use who wrote from Babylon, and may be translated *marched.* It is therefore implied in this verse that Nebuchadnezzar started from Babylon in the third year of Jehoiakim. The rest of the history is easily supplied from other portions of Scripture. In the fourth year of Jehoiakim he conquered Pharaoh at Carchemish (Jer. xlvi. 2), and then advanced upon Jerusalem. (See marginal reference.) The name Nebuchadnezzar is sometimes more correctly spelt Nebuchadrezzar, but no argument can be based upon the different modes of spelling the name, as the difficulties of transliteration of Babylonian names into Hebrew characters are considerable.

(2) **Part of the vessels.**—Literally, *from one point to another.* He did not take them all at once, but on different occasions. (On Shinar, see Note, Gen. x. 10.)

His god—*i.e.,* Bel-Merodach, who was originally an Accadian deity, the signification of the second part of the name being "he that measures the path of the sun." The planet Jupiter was worshipped under this name. He was the tutelary god of Babylon, and to his honour Nebuchadnezzar dedicated a temple. For a further description of this deity see Baruch vi. 14, 15.

(3) **Ashpenaz . . . his eunuchs**—*i.e.,* the courtiers or attendants upon the king. (See marginal translation of Gen. xxxvii. 36; and compare Jer. xxxix. 3, where a Rab-saris, or chief of the courtiers, is mentioned. See also Isa. xxxix. 7.)

The king's seed.—According to the story of Josephus (*Ant.* X. 10, 1), Daniel and the three holy children were all connected with Zedekiah. The context makes this opinion perfectly admissible.

(4) **Children.**—If the Babylonian customs were similar to the Persian, it is probable that the course of education would commence at an early age. So elaborate a system of science as the Babylonian, whether theological, astronomical, or magical, would naturally require an early training. It is reasonable to suppose that these "children" were quite young. So much may be inferred from Nebuchadnezzar's amazement at what he considered to be Daniel's precocious genius (chap. ii. 26).

To stand, *i.e.,* to act as courtiers or servants. (Comp. 2 Kings v. 25, and below, verse 19.)

Learning . . . Chaldeans.—Many interesting specimens of this may be seen in the volumes of the *Records of the Past,* which are devoted to Assyrian and Babylonian subjects. Many more examples may be seen in the British Museum, and among them the large treatise on magic, which originally consisted of no less than two hundred tablets. It appears, from comparing this with verse 19, that some form of examination was held by the king, before he admitted the courtiers into his immediate service. The language of Chaldæa at this time was Semitic; but there was a sacred language in use besides, which probably belonged to the Turanian family. In both these languages was Daniel educated.

(5) **A daily portion.**—(Comp. Jer. lii. 34.) The meat was solid food, as opposed to the wine and vegetables which formed so important a part of Babylonian diet. The food appears to have been sent from the king's table.

Three years.—The king appears to have had sufficient insight into the extraordinary character of these youths, to enable him to prescribe not only the subjects of their studies, but also the length of their course of instruction. It appears that Nebuchadnezzar was a man of far higher character than many Assyrian and Babylonian kings. We shall see, in the course of the book, that his heart was fitted for the reception of Divine truth, and that in the end he was brought to know the true God.

(6) **Now among these . . .**—Four persons only are mentioned here, because the narrative of the book is only concerned with four. Daniel calls our attention to the fact that the very four whom Providence had

B.C. cir. 607.

Judah, Daniel, Hananiah, Mishael, and Azariah: (7) unto whom the prince of the eunuchs gave names: for he gave unto Daniel *the name* of Belteshazzar; and to Hananiah, of Shadrach; and to Mishael, of Meshach; and to Azariah, of Abed-nego.

(8) But Daniel purposed in his heart that he would not defile himself with the portion of the king's meat, nor with the wine which he drank: therefore he requested of the prince of the eunuchs that he might not defile himself. (9) Now God had brought Daniel into favour and tender love with the prince of the eunuchs. (10) And the prince of the eunuchs said unto Daniel, I fear my lord the king, who hath appointed your meat and your drink: for why should he see your faces [1]worse liking than the children which *are* of your [2]sort? then shall ye make *me* endanger my head to the king.

(11) Then said Daniel to [3]Melzar, whom the prince of the eunuchs had set over Daniel, Hananiah, Mishael, and Azariah, (12) Prove thy servants, I beseech thee, ten days; and let them give us [4]pulse [5]to eat, and water to drink. (13) Then let our countenances be looked upon before thee, and the countenance of the children that eat of the portion of the king's meat: and as thou seest, deal with thy servants. (14) So he consented to them in this matter, and proved them ten days. (15) And at the end of ten days their countenances appeared fairer and fatter in flesh than all the children which did eat the portion of the king's meat. (16) Thus Melzar took away the portion of their meat, and the wine that they should drink; and gave them pulse.

(17) As for these four children, God gave them knowledge and skill in all learning and wisdom: and [6]Daniel had understanding in all visions and dreams.

(18) Now at the end of the days that the king had said he should bring them in, then the prince of the eunuchs brought them in before Nebuchadnezzar. (19) And the king communed with them; and among them all was found none like Daniel, Hananiah, Mishael, and Azariah: therefore stood they before the king. (20) And in all matters of [7]wisdom *and* understanding, that the king enquired of them, he

1 Heb., *sadder*.
2 Or, *term*, or, *continuance*.
3 Or, *the steward*.
4 Heb., *of pulse*.
5 Heb., *that we may eat*, &c.
6 Or, *he made Daniel understand*.
7 Heb., *wisdom of understanding*.

---

endowed with the greatest natural gifts were those by whose constancy and example the king was converted. The names of these four were subsequently changed, with the view of showing that they had become nationalised Chaldee subjects. (Comp. 2 Kings xxiii. 34, xxiv. 17.) The name Belteshazzar must be carefully distinguished from Belshazzar. It is said to mean, *protect his life* (*balatsu-usur*). Daniel appears, if this be the true meaning of the name, to have endeared himself at a very early period to Ashpenaz. (See chap. iv. 18.) Abed-nego is apparently *Servant of Nebo*, the *b* and *g* having been designedly interchanged, on account of Azariah's unwillingness to bear a heathen name. Shadrach and Meshach have not as yet been explained, but probably the clue to their interpretation is to be found in the last syllable, *ach*, which occurs also in Merodach and Arioch.

(8) **Daniel purposed in his heart.**—He was cautious from the first. He feared that he might eat something that had been consecrated to idols. (See 1 Cor. viii.)

(9) **Into favour.**—The close correspondence between Daniel and Joseph has been frequently remarked. Each finds favour with his master, and afterwards with a foreign monarch. The grace of God enables each to overcome the temptations into which his circumstances lead him. The acute natural faculties of each are miraculously increased by God; and, lastly, each is sent into a foreign land to comfort exiled Israel. (See Gen. xxxix. 21; 1 Kings viii. 50; Neh. i. 11; Ps. cvi. 46.) No less striking is the resemblance of Nebuchadnezzar to Pharaoh.

(10) **Of your sort,** *i.e.*, of your contemporaries, those who are of the same age with you.

(11) **Melzar.**—(See *Introduction*, § VI.) Not a proper name (Hamelsar), but a *cellarman*. The appeal of Daniel to the chief chamberlain having proved insufficient, he applies to the man with whom he was on more familiar terms.

(12) **Ten days.**—The number "ten" is treated as a round number here, and in verse 20. (Comp. Gen. xxxi. 41.) By adopting this mode of life, Daniel resumes the simple diet commonly used by his ancestors previously to their entering Canaan (Deut. xii. 15, 16, xxvi. 5, 9). This simplicity of life prevailed till the early times of David (1 Sam. xvii. 17, 18). At the Persian court, in later times, Daniel changed his rule of life (chap. x. 3), the infirmities of age beginning to tell upon his constitution.

(15) **Appeared fairer.**—Thus was God beginning to assert His power among the Babylonians. This change in the appearance of Daniel was the effect of his free grace, not of the meat that came from the king's palace. May it not have been that the young exiles thought of the words of Isaiah (chap. lii. 11), "Depart ye, depart ye, go ye out thence, touch no unclean thing"?

(17) **Learning and wisdom.**—These appear to be contrasted in this verse. The former refers to literature, and implies the knowledge of secular subjects; the latter implies philosophy and theology, and perhaps, also, an acquaintance with the meaning of portents. Abundant instances of the latter may be found in the *Records of the Past* (see vol. v., p. 167).

(18) **At the end of the days,** *i.e.*, the three years specified in verse 5. Before the conclusion of this time, it appears (chap. ii. 1), Daniel was enabled to give a proof of his wisdom. (See chap. ii. 28.)

found them ten times better than all
the magicians *and* astrologers that *were*
in all his realm.
(21) And Daniel continued *even* unto
the first year of king Cyrus.

CHAPTER II.—(1) And in the second
year of the reign of Nebuchadnezzar
Nebuchadnezzar dreamed dreams, where-
with his spirit was troubled, and his
sleep brake from him. (2) Then the
king commanded to call the magicians,
and the astrologers, and the sorcerers,
and the Chaldeans, for to shew the
king his dreams. So they came and
stood before the king. (3) And the king
said unto them, I have dreamed a
dream, and my spirit was troubled to
know the dream.
(4) Then spake the Chaldeans to the
king in Syriack, [a]O king, live for ever:
tell thy servants the dream, and we will
shew the interpretation.
(5) The king answered and said to the
Chaldeans, The thing is gone from me:
if ye will not make known unto me the
dream, with the interpretation thereof, ye
shall be [b][1]cut in pieces, and your houses
shall be made a dunghill. (6) But if ye
shew the dream, and the interpretation
thereof, ye shall receive of me gifts and
[2]rewards and great honour: therefore
shew me the dream, and the interpre-
tation thereof.
(7) They answered again and said, Let
the king tell his servants the dream,
and we will shew the interpretation
of it.

a ch. 3. 9.

B.C. cir. 603.

b ch. 3. 29.

1 Chald., *made pieces.*

2 Or, *fee*, ch. 5. 17.

(21) **Continued.**—(See *Introduction*, § I.) The phrase does not mean that "he prophesied," but that he lived until the time specified; by no means implying that he died in the first year of Cyrus. This year is specified on account of its importance to the Jewish people as the year of their deliverance. We are led to think of Daniel during this period holding high positions in the courts of Nebuchadnezzar, Belshazzar, and Darius, yet so using the things of this world that at the close of his life (chap. x. 11) he became the man greatly beloved by God. (See Pusey: *Daniel the Prophet*, pp. 21—23).

II.

(1) **The second year.**—Nebuchadnezzar was proleptically spoken of as "king of Babylon" in chap. i. 1, for his father did not die till after the battle of Carchemish. On the reign of Nebuchadnezzar, see Notes on 2 Kings xxiv. 1.)

Dreams.—Spoken of in verse 3 as "a dream." The one dream consisted of several parts, and is therefore spoken of in the plural. For the effects of the dream upon the king's mind, comp. Gen. xli. 8.

His sleep brake.—*i.e.*, his sleep finished. A similar use of the word occurs chap. vi. 18; Esther vi. 1. The anxiety which the vision caused him prevented him from sleeping again. And no wonder. The battle of Carchemish, which forced Egypt to retire within her ancient frontiers, had indeed made Nebuchadnezzar master of all the district east of the Euphrates; but there was a growing power northward of him, the Median, which he may have dreaded, though at this time he was on good terms with it, and this may have increased his alarm, and led him to feel some presentiment of evil.

(2) **Magicians.** — Heb. *chartummim*, so called, most probably, from the pencil or stylus with which they wrote. The word is elsewhere used of the Egyptian magicians. (See Schrader, *Keil-Inschriften*, p. 26; *Records of the Past*, vol. i. p. 131.)

Astrologers.—Heb. *ashshaphim*, a name derived from the whisperings or mutterings made by them while employed in their incantations. They are mentioned by Daniel only.

Sorcerers.—Heb. *mekashshaphim*; are spoken of in the Pentateuch both as male and female, (*e.g.* Deut. xviii. 10). They are mentioned by Isaiah (chap. xlvii. 9, 12) as prevalent in the Babylon of his days. Probably the Chaldæans spoken of in this verse did not form a separate class of magicians, but denoted the priests, such as those mentioned *Herod.* i. 181, and was contained in the first class of magicians mentioned in the verse. It appears that Daniel excelled (chap. i. 17) in all classes of magic learning, whether it required a knowledge of "learning, wisdom, or dreams."

(3) **I have dreamed.**—It has been questioned whether the king had really forgotten his dream, or whether he only pretended to have done so in order that he might prove the skill of his wise men. The conduct of the Chaldæans (verse 10) makes the latter hypothesis possible. However, it is more in accordance with what is stated about the anxious condition of the king's mind to assume that he remembered a portion of the dream, but that he had lost the general outline of it.

(4) **In Syriack.**—Probably a fresh title, indicating to the copyist that the Chaldee portion of the book begins here. It has been conjectured that this portion of the book (chap. ii. 4—vii.) is a Chaldee translation of an original Hebrew work, but there is no authority for the conjecture. God is about to reveal facts connected with the Gentile world, and therefore a Gentile language is used as the vehicle of the revelation. (See 1 Tim. ii. 3, 4; Matt. ii. 1, 2).

Live for ever.—For this common form of salutation, comp. chaps. iii. 9, v. 10, &c.

(5) **Is gone from me.**—This difficult word, the etymology of which is very uncertain, appears only here and verse 8. It seems to mean, "The order has been published by me (comp. Esther vii. 7; Isa. xlv. 23), and therefore cannot be recalled."

Cut in pieces.—This was by no means an uncommon form of punishment: (See Smith's *Assurbanipal*, pp. 137, 245.)

(6) **Rewards.**—A word of uncertain meaning. It occurs again chap. v. 17, and probably is correctly rendered.

(7) **Let the king tell.**—The request was reasonable enough, according to the principles of Babylonian sorcery. Nebuchadnezzar's doubts, however, were awakened, and he was not sure of the veracity of his magicians. He speaks with great common sense

(8) The king answered and said, I
know of certainty that ye would [1] gain
the time, because ye see the thing is
gone from me. (9) But if ye will not
make known unto me the dream, *there*
is but one decree for you: for ye have
prepared lying and corrupt words to
speak before me, till the time be
changed: therefore tell me the dream,
and I shall know that ye can shew me
the interpretation thereof.
(10) The Chaldeans answered before the
king, and said, There is not a man upon
the earth that can shew the king's
matter: therefore *there is* no king, lord,
nor ruler, *that* asked such things at any
magician, or astrologer, or Chaldean.
(11) And *it is* a rare thing that the king
requireth, and there is none other that
can shew it before the king, except
the gods, whose dwelling is not with
flesh.
(12) For this cause the king was angry
and very furious, and commanded to
destroy all the wise *men* of Babylon.
(13) And the decree went forth that the
wise *men* should be slain; and they
sought Daniel and his fellows to be
slain.
(14) Then Daniel [2] answered with counsel
and wisdom to Arioch the [3] [4] captain of
the king's guard, which was gone forth
to slay the wise *men* of Babylon: (15) he
answered and said to Arioch the king's
captain, Why *is* the decree *so* hasty
from the king? Then Arioch made the
thing known to Daniel. (16) Then Daniel
went in, and desired of the king that
he would give him time, and that he
would shew the king the interpretation.
(17) Then Daniel went to his house, and
made the thing known to Hananiah,
Mishael, and Azariah, his companions:
(18) that they would desire mercies [5] of the
God of heaven concerning this secret;
[6] that Daniel and his fellows should not
perish with the rest of the wise *men* of
Babylon.

1 Chald., *buy*.
2 Chald., *returned*.
3 Or, *chief marshal*.
4 Chald., *chief of the executioners, or slaughtermen*.
5 Chald., *from before God*.
6 Or, *that they should not destroy Daniel, &c.*

(verse 9), "If you can tell me the dream, I shall be sure that your interpretation is correct."

(8) **Gain time.**—They hoped that by continual postponement they would induce the king to let the matter pass over; or, if not, that they might be able to wheedle the dream out of him,

(9) **There is but one decree.**—He refers to the decree mentioned verse 5, that both the dream and the interpretation must be told. These two things must go together, for they form the subject of one decree.

Ye have prepared . . . be changed—*i.e.*, "you have made an agreement among yourselves to postpone the matter till a more lucky time for explaining the dream shall come." On Eastern notions about fortunate days, comp. Esther iii. 7 and the standard inscription of Nebuchadnezzar towards the end.

(10) **No king.**—A further argument of the wise men, offering a delicate flattery to the king, and, at the same time, assuming as a proof of their wisdom, that *all* possibilities had been already submitted to them. "Because no king," they say, "has left any precedent for such a request, therefore the thing is impossible."

(11) **A rare thing**—*i.e.*, a difficult matter. The difficulty is so great, that the gods whose dwelling is not with flesh are alone able to solve it. Here the reference is to a doctrine of Babylonian theology, according to which every man from his birth onward had a special deity attached to him as his protector. It lived in him, or "dwelt with flesh," as the wise men here remark. The deity, being united to the man, became a partaker of human infirmities. For instance, it was subject to the action of evil spirits, and to the influence of the spirits of sickness to such an extent that it might injure the person whom it was bound to protect. Even these deities, the wise men urge, cannot do what the king requires. Such wisdom belongs only to the gods whose dwelling is apart from man. (See Lenormant, *La Magie*, pp. 181—183.)

(12) This order to massacre the wise men extended apparently only to those who were resident in the city of Babylon, where they had a fixed habitation. Though Daniel had been already trained in their schools, he had not as yet been appointed "a wise man." However, being a student, his death was implied in the general order, which, as appears from verse 13, had already begun to be executed.

(14) **Arioch.**—See Note on Gen. xiv. 1.

(15) **So hasty.**—Literally, *why is this severe decree of the king?* By this question Daniel wished Arioch to understand that after all the matter was not impossible, as the wise men had stated it to be.

(16) **Daniel went in.**—Two characteristics of the prophet strike us, which distinguish the one who trusts in God's help from those who relied entirely upon their secular wisdom. (1) The courage of Daniel, which led him to venture into the king's presence upon a humane errand. (2) His humility, in asking the king to give him time. The wise men regarded the whole matter as an impossibility, and treated it as such, not even asking for any extension of time. But the faith of Daniel inspired him with this courageous humility, and was amply rewarded.

We are not told in so many words that this extension of time was granted, or that Daniel undertook to show more than the interpretation of the dream. A true account of what happened can only be gathered by reading verses 18 and 28 by the side of this verse. It should be remembered that many narratives of scripture are related in a very condensed form, fuller details being added afterwards. (See verse 24, Note.)

(18) **The God of heaven.**—We meet with this title of Almighty God for the first time in Gen. xxiv. 7. After the Captivity, it frequently designates the true God as contrasted with the heathen gods. (See Ezra i. 2, Neh. i. 5, Ps. cxxxvi. 26.) It is used by Daniel in this sense in this verse.

(19) Then was the secret revealed unto
Daniel in a night vision. Then Daniel
blessed the God of heaven. (20) Daniel
answered and said, [a]Blessed be the name
of God for ever and ever: for wisdom
and might are his: (21) and he changeth
the times and the seasons: he removeth
kings, and setteth up kings: he giveth
wisdom unto the wise, and knowledge
to them that know understanding:
(22) he revealeth the deep and secret
things: he knoweth what *is* in the
darkness, and the light dwelleth with
him. (23) I thank thee, and praise thee,
O thou God of my fathers, who hast
given me wisdom and might, and hast
made known unto me now what we
desired of thee: for thou hast *now*
made known unto us the king's matter.
(24) Therefore Daniel went in unto
Arioch, whom the king had ordained to
destroy the wise *men* of Babylon: he
went and said thus unto him; Destroy
not the wise *men* of Babylon: bring me
in before the king, and I will shew unto
the king the interpretation. (25) Then
Arioch brought in Daniel before the
king in haste, and said thus unto him,
[1] I have found a man of the [2] captives of
Judah, that will make known unto the
king the interpretation.
(26) The king answered and said to
Daniel, whose name *was* Belteshazzar,
Art thou able to make known unto me
the dream which I have seen, and the
interpretation thereof?
(27) Daniel answered in the presence of
the king, and said, The secret which
the king hath demanded cannot the
wise *men*, the astrologers, the magicians,
the soothsayers, shew unto the king;
(28) but there is a God in heaven that

a Ps. 113. 2 & 115. 18.

B.C. 603.

1 Chald., *That I have found.*

2 Chald., *children of the captivity of Judah.*

---

(19) **Night vision.**—Not in a dream, but literally in a vision; but that Daniel saw a repetition of the king's dream cannot be inferred from the words. We know from Num. xii. 6 that God was pleased to reveal the truth both by dreams and by visions.

(20) **Blessed be the name.**—Daniel's prayer is for the most part framed upon the model of scriptural language, while on the other hand it appears to have been adapted to their own special needs by later pious servants of God. The Doxology, with which it commences, is founded upon the liturgical formula concluding Ps. xli., the substance of it being repeated by Nehemiah (Neh. ix. 5).

(21) **Changeth times**—*i.e.,* He orders the events which occur at different times and seasons. Daniel refers to the dream which had been recently revealed to him, in which the changes of future times and seasons were depicted in so marvellous a way. "Times" are opposed to "seasons," as circumstances of time may be contrasted with epochs of time. (Comp. chap. vii. 12.)

He removeth.—Comp. 1 Sam. ii. 8.

Wisdom . . .—Comp. Jer. xxxii. 19.

The wise—*i.e.,* wise men generally. Wise men become what they are, not through their own study and natural ability, but by the grace and mercy of God.

(22) **He revealeth.**—Comp. Job xii. 22.

He knoweth.—Comp. Ps. cxxxix. 12.

The light dwelleth.—Perhaps "illumination" rather than "light" expresses the actual meaning. Man himself requires illumination from an external source. This source is God, the "sun of man's soul," in Whom light dwells as if He were a palace, and in "His light do we see light" (Ps. xxxvi. 9).

(23) **Who hast given me.**—The Hebrew perfect represents what has already occurred and still continues. (See Jer. ii. 2.) The wisdom spoken of here does not refer to the dream, but to the same subjects as in chap. i. 7.

God of my fathers.—Comp. 1 Kings xviii. 36, Ps. cv. God dealt gloriously with Israel of old. He continues to be faithful to His promises to Israel by blessing Daniel's education in secular subjects, and finally by the dream. Observe that to Daniel each appears alike supernatural, his proficiency in Chaldean wisdom, and his skill in interpreting dreams.

(24) **Therefore**—*i.e.,* now that he knows the dream and the interpretation. Daniel approached the king through Arioch, for it is probable that the Babylonian custom, like the Persian (Esther v. 1) or Median (Herod. i. 99), did not permit any persons except the principal officers of state to have direct access to the royal presence. We must suppose that in verse 16 (where see Note) Daniel approached the king as he does here, through Arioch, the captain of the guard.

Destroy not.—Observe Daniel's humanity towards his heathen teachers. It was owing to his intercession only that the king's decree was not carried out. (See Ezek. xiv. 14.)

(25) **I have found.**—It is not strictly true that Arioch had diligently searched for any interpreters of the king's dream. However, the circumstances mentioned in verses 16, 24, warrant the language which he uses.

(26) **Whose name was Belteshazzar.**—A parenthetic clause, introduced to remind the reader that by this name only Daniel was known to the king. (Comp. chap. iv. 8.)

Art thou able.—The king does not pretend to be ignorant of the person of Daniel. He had, in fact, only recently (chap. i. 19, 20) examined him in "matters of wisdom and understanding." What surprises him is, that after the wise and experienced had failed to tell him his dream, one so young and a mere novice should succeed.

(27) **The secret . . .**—In this and the next verse Daniel justifies the astonishment of the king, and explains to him that what the wise men had stated was perfectly true. The "gods whose dwelling was with flesh" (see Note on verse 11) could not reveal the secret, but there was a God in heaven who had made it known. Daniel here teaches us what Scripture lays down elsewhere (Gen. xx. 3, xli. 16, 25, 28; Num. xxii. 35), that all power of prediction is to be excluded from heathen gods, and is possessed by wise men only so far as they acquire it through the God of heaven.

(28) **Visions of thy head.**—Called "thoughts," verse 29, which were the natural means through which

revealeth secrets, and [1] maketh known
to the king Nebuchadnezzar what shall
be in the latter days. Thy dream, and
the visions of thy head upon thy bed,
are these; (29) As for thee, O king, thy
thoughts [2] came *into thy mind* upon thy
bed, what should come to pass here-
after: and he that revealeth secrets
maketh known to thee what shall come
to pass. (30) But as for me, this secret
is not revealed to me for *any* wisdom
that I have more than any living, but
for their sakes that shall make known
the interpretation to the king, and that
thou mightest know the thoughts of
thy heart.

(31) Thou, O king, [3] sawest, and behold
a great image. This great image, whose
brightness *was* excellent, stood before
thee; and the form thereof *was* terrible.
(32) This image's head *was* of fine gold,
his breast and his arms of silver, his
belly and his [4] thighs of brass, (33) his
legs of iron, his feet part of iron and
part of clay. (34) Thou sawest till that
a stone was cut out [5] without hands,
which smote the image upon his feet
that were of iron and clay, and brake
them to pieces. (35) Then was the iron,
the clay, the brass, the silver, and the
gold, broken to pieces together, and
became like the chaff of the summer
threshingfloors; and the wind carried
them away, that no place was found for
them: and the stone that smote the
image became a great mountain, and
filled the whole earth. (36) This *is* the
dream; and we will tell the interpre-
tation thereof before the king.

(37) Thou, O king, *art* a king of kings:
for the God of heaven hath given thee
a kingdom, power, and strength, and
glory. (38) And wheresoever the children
of men dwell, the beasts of the field
and the fowls of the heaven hath he
given into thine hand, and hath made
thee ruler over them all. Thou *art* this
head of gold. (39) And after thee shall
arise another kingdom inferior to thee,
and another third kingdom of brass,

1 Chald., *hath made known*.

2 Chald., *come up*.

3 Chald., *wast seeing*.

4 Or, *sides*.

5 Or, *which* was *not in hands*: as ver. 45.

---

the supernatural revelation was communicated. These "came" into his mind without his forcing them upon himself. He was thinking of other things, further conquests, perhaps, and the like, but these thoughts came from a higher source.

(29) **Hereafter**—*i.e.*, in the course of history, not only in the Messianic days.

(30) **For any wisdom**—*i.e.*, by reason of any wisdom of his own, but "for the sake of the king."

(31) **A great image.**—Properly, *one great image*. This is one important feature in the vision. The image, though representing many things, was itself only "one." (See Note on verse 1.) That the image was of human form is evident from the further descriptions of the various parts of the body given in verses 32, 33, 42. The "greatness" of the image implies the magnificence and size of it. As will be shortly seen, throughout the various parts it represented the many complex phases of the one history of the world.

(32) **Breast . . .**—It should be remarked that though many different parts of the body of the image are mentioned, Daniel regards the whole thing as made up of only four parts, each corresponding to one of the four metals. Similarly he shows the history of the world in its relation to God's people, complicated though it may be and varied in its aspect, consists of no more than four principal parts. It will be noticed that by the additional matter mentioned verses 41, 42, certain minor complications of history are intended, which, however, do not interfere with the fourfold division of which the outline is here given.

(34) **Thou sawest.**—Literally, the king *kept on gazing* in wonder at the image.

(35) **Like the chaff.**—This language recalls Ps. i. 4, ii. 9. It is emblematic of Divine judgments, as Isa. xli. 15, 16; Jer. li. 33, &c. Comp. with this the description of the Judgment, chap. vii. 9—14. Observe, however, that the stone did not crush the head, breast, or loins of the body. These became fragments by falling when the feet were broken. (Comp. chap. vii. 12.)

(36) **We**—*i.e.*, Daniel and his three friends, for to their intercession (verses 17, 18) the revelation was due.

(37, 38) Interpretation of the vision. Nebuchadnezzar is the head; or, in other words, he is the first of the four kingdoms which are denoted by the image. His kingdom was the largest that the world had till then known; in fact, a writer cited by Josephus (*Ap.* i. 20), compares him to Hercules. We find a similar allusion to the beasts of the field as Nebuchadnezzar's servants Jer. xxvii. 6, xxviii. 14. The title of "king of kings" is also ascribed to Nebuchadnezzar by Ezekiel (chap. xxvi. 7). We are therefore left in no doubt as to what is meant by the first of the four empires. It is the Babylonian Empire, of which Nebuchadnezzar was in every sense the head, being the actual founder of it, and its mainstay during his long reign of forty-three years.

(39) **Another kingdom.**—These words make it clear that by "the king" in the last verse "kingdom" was meant; or, in other words, Nebuchadnezzar was identified with his kingdom (comp. chap. vii. 5, viii. 3, 20). The second kingdom is the Medo-Persian (as appears more fully below, *Exc.* E). The inferiority is to be found in the divided character of that empire, as compared with the massive solidity of its predecessor. This is signified in the image, partly by the inferiority of the metal, silver instead of gold, and partly by the symbol of division, the *two* breasts opposed to the *one* head. It must not be forgotten that in other respects, such as extent of territory and duration of empire, the Medo-Persian far exceeded the Babylonian kingdom.

Another third.—The metal implies a certain inferiority, but the phrase "shall bear rule over the whole earth" speaks of an empire that extended further than the preceding. This is the Græco-Macedonian Empire (see *Exc.* E, and comp. chap. vii. 6, viii. 5—7).

which shall bear rule over all the earth.
(40) And the fourth kingdom shall be
strong as iron: forasmuch as iron
breaketh in pieces and subdueth all
things: and as iron that breaketh all
these, shall it break in pieces and bruise.
(41) And whereas thou sawest the feet
and toes, part of potters' clay, and part
of iron, the kingdom shall be divided;
but there shall be in it of the strength
of the iron, forasmuch as thou sawest
the iron mixed with miry clay. (42) And
as the toes of the feet *were* part of iron,
and part of clay, *so* the kingdom shall
be partly strong, and partly [1] broken.
(43) And whereas thou sawest iron mixed
with miry clay, they shall mingle them-
selves with the seed of men: but they
shall not cleave [2] one to another, even
as iron is not mixed with clay. (44) And
in [3] the days of these kings shall the
God of heaven set up a kingdom, [a] which
shall never be destroyed: and the [4] king-
dom shall not be left to other people,
but it shall break in pieces and consume
all these kingdoms, and it shall stand
for ever. (45) Forasmuch as thou sawest
that the stone was cut out of the moun-
tain [5] without hands, and that it brake
in pieces the iron, the brass, the clay,
the silver, and the gold; the great God
hath made known to the king what
shall come to pass [6] hereafter: and the
dream *is* certain, and the interpretation
thereof sure.
(46) Then the king Nebuchadnezzar fell
upon his face, and worshipped Daniel,
and commanded that they should offer

1 Or, *brittle.*
2 Chald., *this with this.*
3 Chald., *their days.*
a ch. 4. 3, 34 & 6. 26, & 7. 14, 27; Mic. 4. 7; Luke 1. 33.
4 Chald., *kingdom thereof.*
5 Or, *which* was *not in hand.*
6 Chald., *after this.*

---

(40) **And the fourth.**—It should be observed that the description of this kingdom is much fuller than those of the preceding empires. The same fact will be remarked in the later visions (chap. vii. 7, 8, 19, 20).

Breaketh all things.—Remembering that the comparison is between iron and the fourth empire, this portion of the vision implies that the Roman empire, which is here intended (see *Exc.* E), will crush out all traces that remain of preceding empires, just as iron is capable of breaking gold, silver, or copper. Of the second and third empires, each borrowed something from that which preceded it. The fourth empire introduces a new system, and a new civilisation.

(41) **Shall be divided.**—The meaning seems to be, "notwithstanding that there will be inward divisions in this last empire, as is signified by the divisions, first into two legs, then into two feet, and lastly into ten toes, yet the outward character of it will be the strength of iron."

(42) **So the kingdom.**—This strength, however, is only apparent. There are certain discordant elements in the fourth empire. These are here represented by the iron and clay, which cannot be made to cohere.

(43) **Seed of men.**—The great obscurity of this verse is partially cleared by a reference to Jer. xxxi. 27. Daniel appears to be contrasting what man is endeavouring to accomplish by his own efforts with that which the God of heaven (verse 44) will carry out. Man will form his plans for uniting the discordant parts of this empire, by encouraging marriages between the royal families that rule the various component kingdoms. (Comp. chap. xi. 6, 17, Notes.)

(44) **In the days of these kings.**—Yet no kings have been mentioned hitherto. They must therefore correspond to the toes of the image. (Comp. chap. vii. 24.) It appears therefore that while this fourth kingdom still contrives to exist in some modified form, while its component parts are in a state of war and turmoil, the kingdom of God shall come. (Comp. chap. vii. 25—27.)

God of heaven.—(See verse 18).

(45) **The stone cut out of the mountain.**—The mountain was not mentioned in verse 34. In the language of prophecy, it must mean Mount Zion, which appears in other passages to be closely connected with the Messiah and His Kingdom, *e.g.*, Isa. ii. 2; Ps. l. 2. The stone is set free from this mountain, and as it rolls on in its destructive course, overthrows all the kingdoms of the world, and becomes a mountain which fills the whole earth. The Messiah is elsewhere spoken of under the figure of a stone (Isa. xxviii. 16; Matt. xxi. 42). The phrase "cut without hands" refers to the supernatural agency by which the stone accomplishes its work. The stone is now rolling, as the kingdom of God spreads further and further day by day. The image is still standing, the stone has not yet fallen upon it. When that moment arrives, and not till then, "the kingdoms of the world will become the kingdoms of our Lord and of His Christ" (Rev. xi. 15).

Throughout the vision we must notice one great contrast. There is on the one hand the image, which, of course, was weak, by reason of being formed of such incongruous elements, composed of the most precious metals at the top, while the lower parts ended in "miry clay"—in fact, the image was top-heavy. On the other hand, there is the stone, an emblem of strength and solidity, single, notwithstanding the countless atoms which unite in forming it, growing in strength, as it continues its historic course till it becomes a mountain, the type of all that is solid and indestructible. And one further point of contrast must be noted. While one earthly empire passes into another as insensibly as the head yields to the trunk of the body, and as this passes into arms, legs, hands, and feet, without any discontinuity—that is, as empire after empire passes away, while the history of the world remains continuous—such is not the case with the stone. The work that it does is instantaneous. The moment it falls on the feet of the image the whole collapses, or, in other words, the history of the world comes to an end. Such is the relation in which the kingdom of God stands to the kingdoms of this world. They are all transient, in spite of their apparent strength, and their history will cease, as soon as the "stone shall fall and grind them to powder" (Matt. xxi. 44).

(46) **Worshipped.**—This act is of an entirely different nature from such as are mentioned Gen. xxxiii. 7; 1 Kings i. 16. The Hebrew word employed here is always used (*e.g.*, Isa. xlvi. 6) of paying adoration to an idol. Probably the king imagined that the

an oblation and sweet odours unto him.
(47) The king answered unto Daniel, and
said, Of a truth *it is*, that your God *is*
a God of gods, and a Lord of kings,
and a revealer of secrets, seeing thou
couldest reveal this secret. (48) Then
the king made Daniel a great man, and
gave him many great gifts, and made
him ruler over the whole province of
Babylon, and [a]chief of the governors
over all the wise *men* of Babylon.
(49) Then Daniel requested of the king,
and he set Shadrach, Meshach, and
Abed-nego, over the affairs of the pro-
vince of Babylon: but Daniel *sat* in the
gate of the king.

CHAPTER III.—(1) Nebuchadnezzar
the king made an image of gold, whose
height *was* threescore cubits, *and* the
breadth thereof six cubits: he set it
up in the plain of Dura, in the province
of Babylon.
(2) Then Nebuchadnezzar the king
sent to gather together the princes, the
governors, and the captains, the judges,
the treasurers, the counsellors, the
sheriffs, and all the rulers of the pro-
vinces, to come to the dedication of the
image which Nebuchadnezzar the king
had set up. (3) Then the princes, the
governors, and captains, the judges, the
treasurers, the counsellors, the sheriffs,
and all the rulers of the provinces, were
gathered together unto the dedication
of the image that Nebuchadnezzar the
king had set up; and they stood before
the image that Nebuchadnezzar had
set up.
(4) Then an herald cried [1]aloud, To
you [2]it is commanded, O people, nations,
and languages, (5) *that* at what time ye
hear the sound of the cornet, flute,
harp, sackbut, psaltery, [3] [4]dulcimer, and
all kinds of musick, ye fall down and
worship the golden image that Nebu-
chadnezzar the king hath set up: (6) and
whoso falleth not down and worshippeth

a ch. 4. 9.

1 Chald., *with might.*

2 Chald., *they command.*

3 Or, *singing.*

4 Chald., *symphony.*

---

gods were dwelling in Daniel in a higher sense from that in which they dwelt with his other wise men, and worshipped them on account of the marvellous revelation which they had vouchsafed to him through the means of Daniel.

Oblation.—That is, the unbloody offering customary among the Babylonians; some honour different from the present mentioned in verse 48.

(47) **God of gods.**—He does not acknowledge Jehovah as the true God, but deems Him worthy of a place in the Babylonian Pantheon.

(48) **The Province.**—According to chap. iii. 2, the Babylonian empire consisted of several provinces, each of which had its own ruler or *Shilton.* Daniel became ruler of this one province of Babylon. What the other office was to which he was advanced may possibly be explained when further discoveries have been made. Hitherto it has been inexplicable.

(49) **Over the affairs.**—Compare Neh. ii. 16; Esther iii. 9. These holy children, it appears from this verse, were satraps, under Daniel's supervision.

Gate of the king.—Compare Esther iii. 2, &c. Daniel was of higher rank than his three friends, and was therefore admitted into the inner part of the palace.

III.

An important addition appears in both Greek Versions of Daniel, in accordance with which the event recorded in this chapter took place in the eighteenth year of Nebuchadnezzar. Whence the tradition arose cannot be ascertained. It was certainly unknown to Josephus. It has been supposed that the date was added by the translators, on account of their supposing the erection of the image to be connected with the taking of Jerusalem. However, this is improbable, as the siege itself was not finished till the nineteenth year of Nebuchadnezzar (2 Kings xxv. 8). It has also been conjectured that the statue was one of the king himself, erected in commemoration of some great victories recently won by him. This is not impossible; but, partly from the mention of the sacred numbers, 6, 60, partly from the language of verses 12, 14, 18, 20, it appears more probable that the image was erected in honour of some god. There is no doubt (see *Records of the Past*, vol. v., p. 113) that this king did erect an image of Bel Merodach. Possibly we have in this chapter a parallel account of the dedication of the image.

(1) **An image.**—If this image was made after the manner described (Isa. xliv. 9—20), the body was formed of wood, and the whole, when properly shaped, was covered with thin plates of gold. As the height of the whole is disproportionate to the width, it is probable that the height of the pedestal on which the image stood is included under the sixty cubits.

Plain of Dura.—The older commentators identified this place with various sites, some north, some east of Babylon. Recent discoveries place it nearer to Babylon, in a place still called by a similar name.

(2) **Sent**—*i.e.*, sent heralds, as appears from verse 4. (On the Babylonian officers, see *Exc.* A.)

(4) **People, nations.**—In Biblical language the latter word is used (Gen. xxv. 16) of the tribes of Ishmael, each of which had its own head, or of the Midianites (Num. xxv. 15). The former is applied to Israel in Ps. cxi. 6, where occurs the phrase, "people of Jehovah." The word "languages" is applied (Gen. x 5, 20, &c.) to tribes as represented by their languages. Hence these three expressions denote all nations subject to the empire, of whatever description of language, government, or federation. (Comp. verses 29, and chap. iv. 1, vii. 14.)

(5) **The cornet.**—On the musical instruments, see *Exc.* B.

(6) **Shall be cast . . .**—This punishment was not uncommon among the Babylonians. One instance of it is mentioned by Jeremiah (chap. xxix. 22; see

shall the same hour be cast into the
midst of a burning fiery furnace.
(7) Therefore at that time, when all the
people heard the sound of the cornet,
flute, harp, sackbut, psaltery, and all
kinds of musick, all the people, the
nations, and the languages, fell down
and worshipped the golden image that
Nebuchadnezzar the king had set up.
(8) Wherefore at that time certain
Chaldeans came near, and accused the
Jews. (9) They spake and said to the
king Nebuchadnezzar, O king, live for
ever. (10) Thou, O king, hast made a
decree, that every man that shall hear
the sound of the cornet, flute, harp,
sackbut, psaltery, and dulcimer, and
all kinds of musick, shall fall down
and worship the golden image: (11) and
whoso falleth not down and wor-
shippeth, *that* he should be cast into
the midst of a burning fiery furnace.
(12) There are certain Jews whom thou
hast set over the affairs of the province
of Babylon, Shadrach, Meshach, and
Abed-nego; these men, O king, [1] have
not regarded thee: they serve not thy
gods, nor worship the golden image
which thou hast set up.
(13) Then Nebuchadnezzar in *his* rage
and fury commanded to bring Shadrach,
Meshach, and Abed-nego. Then they
brought these men before the king.
(14) Nebuchadnezzar spake and said unto
them, *Is it* [2] true, O Shadrach, Meshach,
and Abed-nego, do not ye serve my
gods, nor worship the golden image
which I have set up? (15) Now if ye
be ready that at what time ye hear the
sound of the cornet, flute, harp, sack-
but, psaltery, and dulcimer, and all
kinds of musick, ye fall down and wor-
ship the image which I have made;
well: but if ye worship not, ye shall be
cast the same hour into the midst of a
burning fiery furnace; and who *is* that
God that shall deliver you out of my
hands?
(16) Shadrach, Meshach, and Abed-nego,
answered and said to the king, O Nebu-
chadnezzar, we *are* not careful to an-
swer thee in this matter. (17) If it be
so, our God whom we serve is able to
deliver us from the burning fiery fur-

B.C. cir. 580.

1 Chald., *have set no regard upon thee.*

2 Or, *of purpose:* as Ex. xxi. 13.

---

also *Transactions of the Society of Biblical Archæology,* vol. ii., p. 361). The occasion being a national festival, any refusal to worship the national gods would be regarded as high treason. Any foreign subjects would be expected to take part in the ceremony, their gods being supposed to have been conquered, and being regarded as demons. (Comp. 2 Kings xix. 12; 2 Chron. xxviii. 23.)

(8) **Wherefore.**—*i.e.,* because certain Jews were noticed to be absent at the time. It is natural to suppose that the promotion of three men of Jewish extraction would have been viewed with the greatest jealousy by the Babylonian officers, who, no doubt, had been carefully watching their opportunity of revenge. (Comp. chap. v. 11.)

Chaldeans.—Not to be confused with the astrologers mentioned in chap. ii. 5, but Chaldean native subjects, contrasted with the Jewish colonists spoken of at the end of the verse.

(12) **Whom thou hast set.**—The high position of these men is mentioned partly to explain the king's anger on account of their supposed ingratitude, and partly to account for the malice and jealousy of their calumniators. But why was Daniel absent from the ceremony? His behaviour some years later (chap. vi. 10) leaves it beyond question that he would not have taken part in any idolatrous rites. Possibly his position as "chief of the wise men" (chap. ii. 48) made his presence unnecessary. Possibly he was absent on other duties. Two things are certain: (1) the object of the book is not to glorify Daniel; (2) a writer of a fictitious story would have recorded a miracle to deliver Daniel, as well as the three children.

(14) **Is it true?**—Literally, *Is it of design* or *of set purpose that you have done this?*

(15) **Well.**—The word is not in the Chaldee, where an aposiopesis is to be observed, as in Exod. xxxii. 32. Comp. Luke xiii. 9.

Who is that God?—Nebuchadnezzar has so little belief in his own gods that he ranks himself as far above them as above Jehovah. He defies all supernatural powers. Very different is the boast of Sennacherib (Isa. xxxvi. 18—20), who pits his own god Assur against Jehovah.

(16) **O Nebuchadnezzar.**—They mention the king by name, so as to make their address correspond with his (verse 14). His attention would in this way be directed to the strong antithesis between his statement (verse 15) and theirs (verse 17). Great though the distinction was between king and subject in such a country as Babylon, yet that distinction was lost when any collision occurred between duty to Jehovah and obedience to a royal edict.

We are not careful.—More correctly, as translated by Theodotion, *We have no need—i.e.,* it is needless for us to give any reply.

(17) **If it be so.**—The meaning becomes clearer by omitting the word "so." The sentence will then stand as follows: "If our God is able to deliver us . . . then He will do so; but if He does not deliver us, be assured that we will not serve thy gods." The three holy children are quite content to leave the whole matter in the hands of Providence. They know that the law of obedience is the first law of all, and this they are resolved to keep. There is not the slightest ground for supposing that they expected a miraculous deliverance. Their language implies no more than faithful obedience. (See Isa. xliii. 2.)

Is able.—They did not question His power; they did not know whether He would will to exercise the use of it. (Comp. Gen. xix. 22.)

nace, and he will deliver *us* out of thine
hand, O king. (18) But if not, be it
known unto thee, O king, that we will
not serve thy gods, nor worship the
golden image which thou hast set up.
(19) Then was Nebuchadnezzar [1] full of
fury, and the form of his visage was
changed against Shadrach, Meshach,
and Abed-nego: *therefore* he spake, and
commanded that they should heat the
furnace one seven times more than it
was wont to be heated. (20) And he
commanded the [2] most mighty men that
were in his army to bind Shadrach,
Meshach, and Abed-nego, *and* to cast
them into the burning fiery furnace.
(21) Then these men were bound in their
[3] coats, their hosen, and their [4] hats, and
their *other* garments, and were cast into
the midst of the burning fiery furnace.
(22) Therefore because the king's [5] com-
mandment was urgent, and the furnace
exceeding hot, the [6] flame of the fire
slew those men that took up Shadrach,
Meshach, and Abed-nego. (23) And these
three men, Shadrach, Meshach, and
Abed-nego, fell down bound into the
midst of the burning fiery furnace.
(24) Then Nebuchadnezzar the king
was astonied, and rose up in haste,
and spake, and said unto his [7] coun-
sellors, Did not we cast three men
bound into the midst of the fire? They
answered and said unto the king, True,
O king. (25) He answered and said, Lo,
I see four men loose, walking in the
midst of the fire, and [8] they have no
hurt; and the form of the fourth is like
the Son of God.
(26) Then Nebuchadnezzar came near
to the [9] mouth of the burning fiery fur-
nace, *and* spake, and said, Shadrach,
Meshach, and Abed-nego, ye servants
of the most high God, come forth, and
come *hither*. Then Shadrach, Meshach,
and Abed-nego, came forth of the midst
of the fire. (27) And the princes, gover-
nors, and captains, and the king's coun-
sellors, being gathered together, saw
these men, upon whose bodies the fire
had no power, nor was an hair of their
head singed, neither were their coats
changed, nor the smell of fire had
passed on them.
(28) *Then* Nebuchadnezzar spake, and
said, Blessed *be* the God of Shadrach,
Meshach, and Abed-nego, who hath sent
his angel, and delivered his servants
that trusted in him, and have changed
the king's word, and yielded their
bodies, that they might not serve nor
worship any god, except their own God.
(29) Therefore [10] I make a decree, That
every people, nation, and language,

1 Chald., *filled.*
2 Chald., *mighty of strength.*
3 Or, *mantles.*
4 Or, *turbans.*
5 Chald., *word.*
6 Or, *spark.*
7 Or, *governors.*
8 Chald., *there is no hurt in them.*
9 Chald., *door.*
10 Chald., *a decree is made by me.*

---

(19) **One seven times.**—It is doubtful whether "seven" is used here as a round number or not. According to the Babylonian mythology, there were seven demons, named "Maskim," who were the most formidable of the infernal powers. Perhaps the number "seven" has a reference to them, for the religious nature of the punishment favours the view that the over-heating of the furnace was regarded as a religious act.

Than it was wont.—More correctly, *than it was fitting.* The improper heating of the furnace led to the death of the mighty men (verse 22).

(20) **The most mighty men.**—He selected these as being the most likely to be able to bear the unusual heat of the fire. Whether he had any expectation that some attempt at a rescue would be made does not appear. We may gather, however, that the army was present at this horrible tragedy.

(21) **Their coats.**—The dresses spoken of here correspond with what Herodotus tells us (i. 195) of the Babylonian costume. As far as can be determined from the etymology of the words, the "coat" was an under-clothing, which covered the whole body; the "hose" was some species of tunic—something "spread out" over the under-clothing; the "hat" (the only one of the three words of which no Hebrew root exists (see 1 Chron. xv. 27), was a sort of cloak, used probably for State occasions only.

(22) **Urgent.**—The same word is translated *hasty* (chap. ii. 15). The king's command had been uttered while he was in a furious rage, and in consequence of this, the furnace was raised to so high a temperature that the executioners were slain. The death of the executioners forms an evident contrast with the deliverance of those who had been sentenced to die.

(24) **Was astonied.**—He had been watching the proceedings from a distance through the "mouth" (verse 26), which was in the side of the furnace.

(25) **The Son of God.**—These words, let us remember, are uttered by a heathen king, who calls this same Person, in verse 28, "an angel" of the God whom the three children worshipped. Probably Nebuchadnezzar thought that He stood to Jehovah in the same relation that he himself did to Merodach. His conceptions of the power of Jehovah were evidently raised by what he had witnessed, though as yet he does not recognise Him as being more than a chief among gods. He has not risen to that conception of the unity of God which is essential to His absolute supremacy. But still the question has to be answered, What did the king see? The early Patristic interpretation was that it was none other than Christ Himself. We have no means of ascertaining anything further, and must be content with knowing that the same "Angel of God's presence" who was with Israel in the wilderness watched over the people in Babylon.

(28) **Have changed.**—Literally, *have transgressed.*

(29) **Anything amiss.**—The marginal version is to be preferred.

which speak [1]any thing amiss against the God of Shadrach, Meshach, and Abed-nego, shall be [a][2]cut in pieces, and their houses shall be made a dunghill: because there is no other God that can deliver after this sort. (30) Then the king [3]promoted Shadrach, Meshach, and Abed-nego, in the province of Babylon.

CHAPTER IV.—(1) Nebuchadnezzar the king, unto all people, nations, and languages, that dwell in all the earth; Peace be multiplied unto you. (2) [4]I thought it good to shew the signs and wonders that the high God hath wrought toward me. (3) How great *are* his signs! and how mighty *are* his wonders! his kingdom *is* [b]an everlasting kingdom, and his dominion *is* from generation to generation.

(4) I Nebuchadnezzar was at rest in mine house, and flourishing in my palace: (5) I saw a dream which made me afraid, and the thoughts upon my bed and the visions of my head troubled me. (6) Therefore made I a decree to bring in all the wise *men* of Babylon before me, that they might make known unto me the interpretation of the dream. (7) Then came in the magicians, the astrologers, the Chaldeans, and the soothsayers: and I told the dream before them; but they did not make known unto me the interpretation thereof. (8) But at the last Daniel came in before me, whose name *was* Belteshazzar, according to the name of my god, and in whom *is* the spirit of the holy gods: and before him I told the dream, *saying*, (9) O Belteshazzar, [c]master of the magicians, because I know that the spirit of the holy gods *is* in thee, and no secret troubleth thee, tell me the visions of my dream that I have seen, and the interpretation thereof. (10) Thus *were* the visions of mine head in my bed; [5]I saw, and behold a tree in the midst of the earth, and the height thereof *was* great. (11) The tree grew, and was strong, and the height thereof reached unto heaven, and the sight thereof to the end of all the earth: (12) the leaves thereof *were* fair, and the fruit thereof much, and in it *was* meat for all: the beasts of the field had shadow under it, and the fowls of the heaven dwelt in the boughs thereof, and all flesh was fed of it. (13) I saw in the visions of my head upon my bed, and, behold, a watcher and an holy one came

1 Chald., *error.*
a ch. 2. 5.
2 Chald., *made pieces.*
3 Chald., *made to prosper.*
4 Chald., *It was seemly before me.*
b ch. 2. 44.
c ch. 2. 48.
B.C. cir. 570.
5 Chald., *I was seeing.*

---

(30) **Promoted**—*i.e.*, he reinstated them to their former posts, from which they had been temporarily deposed.

IV.

(1) **Peace . . .**—For this mode of address comp. Ezra iv. 17, vii. 12. The date of the matter recorded in this chapter cannot be ascertained, as a blank falls upon the last eighteen years of Nebuchadnezzar's reign. The only facts that occurred during this period, so far as is known, are the terrible form of mania from which the king suffered, by reason of which he was kept under restraint for some time, and the further extension of his dominions after his recovery (verse 34).

All the earth.—By this time the king has become so powerful that he regards himself as universal monarch, so that some time must have elapsed since the events mentioned in the last chapter.

(2) **Signs and wonders.**—Comp. Isa. viii. 18. The appearance of various scriptural phrases in this letter leads us to believe that Daniel must have written it at the king's request.

The high God.—Referring to his language (chap. iii. 26).

(4) **Flourishing.**—A word generally employed to signify the growth of trees. Here, no doubt, it is suggested by the dream which follows, and is for that reason selected by Daniel. It may be observed that the LXX. version here, as in chap. iii. 1, gives the eighteenth year as the date.

My palace.—See Layard's *Nineveh and Babylon*, p. 506.

(8) **At the last.**—On account of his position as the chief of the governors of the wise men, Daniel would not "come in" till last.

Belteshazzar.—See Note on chap. i. 7; Introduction, § vi.

The spirit . . .—He means his own gods, for though he recognised Jehovah to be a "high God," yet he acknowledged Him only as one out of many.

(9) **Troubleth thee.**—Literally, *goadeth thee,* or, *causeth thee this difficulty.*

(10) **A tree.**—For this symbol of majesty, comp. Ezek. xxxi. 3, &c. The dream of Cambyses (Herod. i. 108) was of a similar nature.

(11) **The tree grew.**—It appeared in the vision to grow gradually larger and larger. According to the LXX., "The sun and moon dwelled in it and gave light to the whole earth."

The sight thereof—*i.e.*, the tree could be seen from the most distant parts of the known world.

(12) **The fruit thereof much.**—By this is implied the great quantity of fruit as well as the largeness of it.

(13) **A watcher and a holy one**—*i.e.*, a holy one who is watchful; translated "angel" by the LXX., but simply transliterated into "Eir" by Theodotion. The word is used twice by the king, and once by Daniel (verse 23), but it is to be noticed that the prophet substitutes "the Most High" for the words of the king in verse 17). We must suppose that Nebuchadnezzar dreamed in a language familiar to himself, and that the objects of his dream were things with which his Babylonian education had made him acquainted.

down from heaven; (14) he cried [1] aloud,
and said thus, Hew down the tree, and
cut off his branches, shake off his leaves,
and scatter his fruit: let the beasts get
away from under it, and the fowls from
his branches: (15) nevertheless leave the
stump of his roots in the earth, even
with a band of iron and brass, in the
tender grass of the field; and let it be
wet with the dew of heaven, and *let* his
portion *be* with the beasts in the grass
of the earth: (16) let his heart be
changed from man's, and let a beast's
heart be given unto him; and let seven
times pass over him. (17) This matter *is*
by the decree of the watchers, and the
demand by the word of the holy ones:
to the intent that the living may know
that the most High ruleth in the king-
dom of men, and giveth it to whomso-
ever he will, and setteth up over it the
basest of men. (18) This dream I king
Nebuchadnezzar have seen. Now thou,
O Belteshazzar, declare the interpre-
tation thereof, forasmuch as all the
wise *men* of my kingdom are not able
to make known unto me the interpre-
tation: but thou *art* able; for the spirit
of the holy gods *is* in thee.
(19) Then Daniel, whose name *was*
Belteshazzar, was astonied for one
hour, and his thoughts troubled him.
The king spake, and said, Belteshazzar,
let not the dream, or the interpretation
thereof, trouble thee. Belteshazzar an-
swered and said, My lord, the dream *be*
to them that hate thee, and the inter-
pretation thereof to thine enemies.
(20) The tree that thou sawest, which
grew, and was strong, whose height
reached unto the heaven, and the sight
thereof to all the earth; (21) whose leaves
were fair, and the fruit thereof much,
and in it *was* meat for all; under which
the beasts of the field dwelt, and upon
whose branches the fowls of the heaven
had their habitation: (22) it *is* thou, O
king, that art grown and become strong:

1 Chald., *with might.*

According to his mythology, the god of Nergal was regarded as "manifesting himself in watching," so that he may have dreamed that he witnessed a descent of one of his deities. In this he is corrected by Daniel, being assured that the whole is sent from heaven, that the decree is ordered by the one true God, and that the holy watcher is an angel of God.

(14) **Aloud**—*i.e.*, like a king's herald. (Comp. chap. iii. 4.)

Hew down.—The plural is here used, implying that several persons are employed in carrying out the order.

(15) **The stump.**—The whole tree was not to be destroyed, but just so much was to remain as could produce a new sapling. (Comp. Isa. xi. 1.) As long as the stump remained, it might be hoped that the green branches might shoot forth again. (Comp. verse 36.)

A band.—As the vision continues, the typical language is gradually laid aside, and it begins to appear that by the tree a man is intended. We must not understand by "the band" the chains by which the unfortunate king would be confined, but metaphorically trouble and affliction, as Pss. cvii. 10, cxlix. 8. It has been assumed that during his malady the king wandered about at large. This is highly improbable. That his courtiers did not avail themselves of his sickness to substitute some other king in his place is sufficient proof of their regard for him. It is natural to suppose that he was confined in some court of his palace. The inscriptions of Nebuchadnezzar, and accounts of his reign written by historians, being all composed with the view of glorifying the monarch, naturally suppress all mention of his madness.

(16) Here the metaphor of verse 15 is entirely discontinued, and a man is mentioned.

Seven times.—On the use of the number "seven" see Note on chap. iii. 19. The period intended by "time" is very uncertain: from the use of the word in Judges xvii. 10 it has been inferred that "years" are intended. This is purely conjectural. It is more probable that the word is used to signify some definite period of time, which, as appears from the words "over him," was in some way marked out by the heavenly bodies. The word "time" is used by Daniel in the same sense (chap. vii. 25). (Comp. chap. xii. 7, where, however, a different word is employed.)

(17) **By the decree**—*i.e.*, the message to the king rests on this decree or sentence, and it is ascribed to the "watcher," because to him pertained the execution of the decree.

The demand.—Comp. Isa. xliv. 26. According to the use of the word in Chaldee elsewhere, this can be the only true meaning. The "holy one" makes this request of God, and the carrying out of His decree pertains to the "watcher." "This," says Dr. Pusey, "gives another glimpse into the interest of the holy angels in ourselves. They, too, longed that oppression should cease, and joining in the cry which for ever is going up from the oppressed to the throne of mercy and judgment, prayed for that chastisement which was to relieve the oppressed and convert the oppressor" (*Lectures on Daniel*, p. 525).

Ruleth . . .—*i.e.*, Almighty God disposes of human empires as He pleases. (Comp. chap. v. 21.)

(18) **This dream.**—More correctly translated, *This in a dream I saw*—*i.e.*, it was communicated to me in a vision.

(19) **Hour.**—Literally, *moment*. (Comp. chap. iii. 6.)

To them that hate thee.—A delicate way of expressing his hopes for the best. "May that which is implied in the interpretation overtake thine enemies."

(20) It should be noticed that both in this and in the following verse the description of the tree given in verses 11, 12 is curtailed. It was observed that, on the contrary, there was an expansion of details in the interpretation of the former dream. (See Note on verse 23.)

(22) This gives us to understand that Nebuchadnezzar had arrived at the zenith of his power. The extent of

for thy greatness is grown, and reacheth
unto heaven, and thy dominion to the
end of the earth. (23) And whereas the
king saw a watcher and an holy one
coming down from heaven, and saying,
Hew the tree down, and destroy it; yet
leave the stump of the roots thereof in
the earth, even with a band of iron and
brass, in the tender grass of the field;
and let it be wet with the dew of heaven,
and *let* his portion *be* with the beasts of
the field, till seven times pass over him;
(24) this *is* the interpretation, O king,
and this *is* the decree of the most High,
which is come upon my lord the king:
(25) that they shall [a]drive thee from men,
and thy dwelling shall be with the beasts
of the field, and they shall make thee
to eat grass as oxen, and they shall wet
thee with the dew of heaven, and seven
times shall pass over thee, till thou
know that the most High ruleth in the
kingdom of men, and giveth it to whom-
soever he will. (26) And whereas they
commanded to leave the stump of the tree
roots; thy kingdom shall be sure unto
thee, after that thou shalt have known
that the heavens do rule. (27) Where-
fore, O king, let my counsel be accept-
able unto thee, and break off thy sins
by righteousness, and thine iniquities by
shewing mercy to the poor; if it may
be [1]a lengthening of thy tranquillity.
(28) All this came upon the king Nebu-
chadnezzar. (29) At the end of twelve
months he walked [2]in the palace of the
kingdom of Babylon. (30) The king spake,
and said, Is not this great Babylon, that
I have built for the house of the king-
dom by the might of my power, and for
the honour of my majesty? (31) While
the word *was* in the king's mouth, there
fell a voice from heaven, *saying*, O king
Nebuchadnezzar, to thee it is spoken;

a ch. 5. 21, &c.

1 Or, *an healing of thine error.*

2 Or, *upon.*

---

his dominions may be estimated with tolerable accuracy as follows:—Northwards he possessed Armenia, and a considerable portion of Asia Minor; in the west, Syria, and at one time Egypt; southwards, his power reached the Persian Gulf; while in the east, the Medes and Elamites were subject to him. Possessing, as he did, the Mediterranean and the Persian Gulf, all the treasures of the known world were at his command. In his first vision he was represented as the golden head of the image. In his pride he desired the whole image to be of gold, and himself to be the image—but this was the sin for which he was to suffer.

(23) **Destroy it.**—Observe how, in this verse, these words stand for the whole of the latter part of verse 14.

(24) **Which is come upon.**—See Note on verse 13.

(25) **They shall drive thee.**—The third person plural verb in the active with an impersonal subject frequently stands for the second person singular passive. Thus these words mean "thou shalt be driven." (Comp. Luke xvi. 9.)

(26) **They commanded**—*i.e.*, the watchers. We observe, however, in verse 13 that the command is only ascribed to one of the watchers. This makes it appear that they form a council in which one acts in behalf of all.

Thy kingdom.—To make the sense plain we must supply before this word, "The interpretation of it is," or some sentence to that effect.

Shall be sure.—Literally, *shall arise.* No successor shall be appointed during his life.

Do rule—*i.e.*, the heavens, or One in heaven ruleth the kingdoms of men.

(27) **Break off.**—The metaphor is taken from a refractory beast casting off the yoke. (Comp. Gen. xxvii. 40, where it is foretold that Esau's posterity shall "break off" the yoke of Jacob.) In Chaldee the word is used for the most part in the sense of putting on one side. Daniel therefore counsels the king to rebel against his sins, such as pride, harshness, and cruelty towards his captives, and to put all these sins aside. And how can he do this in a better manner than by practising the contrary virtues?

Righteousness.—In all wars of conquest many acts of injustice are perpetrated. The king is warned here to show justice or to act justly for the future. Similar counsel is given, though in different language (Micah vi. 8). The idea of "alms" and "redeeming" is not conveyed by the Chaldee words, so that the translation "redeem thy sins by alms" is incorrect and unwarrantable.

If it may be—*i.e.*, if Nebuchadnezzar will repent, his prosperity and peace will be prolonged.

(29) **Twelve months**—*i.e.*, counting from the time of the vision. Sufficient time for repentance was mercifully granted to the king.

Palace of the kingdom of Babylon.—He had palaces in other towns. Daniel lays a stress upon the fact that this occurred in the town of Babylon. Nebuchadnezzar, the golden head of the image, was in the very centre of his dominions, in his own proud capital, when this occurred. It is needless, therefore, to assume that this was written by a person who lived a long way off from Babylon.

(30) **Great Babylon.**—The area of Babylon is said to have been 200 square miles. It was surrounded by walls 85 feet in width, 335 feet high. In these were brazen gates leading to various terraces which faced the river Euphrates. Within the walls the city was laid out in smaller towns, separated from each other by parks and plantations and gardens; in fact, it is stated that corn sufficient for the whole population could be grown within the walls. There were also magnificent public buildings. Nebuchadnezzar (*Records of the Past*, vol. v., pp. 113—135) mentions no less than eight temples which he completed, besides the huge temple of Merodach immediately across the Euphrates facing the royal palace. Walking on the flat roof of this palace, and with this grand spectacle before him, the king uttered these words. True, indeed, they were, but they show that during the twelve months which had been allotted to the king for repentance his pride remained unabated; he had not repented as Daniel had counselled him.

The kingdom is departed from thee.
(32) And they shall drive thee from men,
and thy dwelling *shall be* with the beasts
of the field: they shall make thee to eat
grass as oxen, and seven times shall pass
over thee, until thou know that the most
High ruleth in the kingdom of men, and
giveth it to whomsoever he will.
(33) The same hour was the thing fulfilled upon Nebuchadnezzar: and he was
driven from men, and did eat grass as
oxen, and his body was wet with the
dew of heaven, till his hairs were grown
like eagles' *feathers*, and his nails like
birds' *claws*.
(34) And at the end of the days I
Nebuchadnezzar lifted up mine eyes unto
heaven, and mine understanding returned unto me, and I blessed the most
High, and I praised and honoured him
that liveth for ever, whose dominion
is [a] an everlasting dominion, and his
kingdom *is* from generation to generation: (35) and all the inhabitants of the
earth *are* reputed as nothing: and he
doeth according to his will in the army
of heaven, and *among* the inhabitants of
the earth: and none can stay his hand,
or say unto him, [b] What doest thou?
(36) At the same time my reason returned
unto me; and for the glory of my kingdom, mine honour and brightness returned unto me; and my counsellors
and my lords sought unto me; and I
was established in my kingdom, and
excellent majesty was added unto me.
(37) Now I Nebuchadnezzar praise and
extol and honour the King of heaven,
all whose works *are* truth, and his ways
judgment: and those that walk in pride
he is able to abase.

B.C. cir. 569.

a ch. 7. 14; Mic. 4. 7; Luke 1. 33.

B.C. cir. 563.

B.C. cir. 538.

c Job 9. 12; Isa. 45. 9.

CHAPTER V. — (1) Belshazzar the
king made a great feast to a thousand
of his lords, and drank wine before the
thousand. (2) Belshazzar, whiles he tasted

---

(31) **A voice.**—By this he would be reminded of his dream (verse 14), when he heard the watcher "cry aloud."

(32) **They shall drive thee.**—This verse is only slightly abridged from verse 25 by the omission of the clause "they shall wet thee with the dew of heaven."

(33) **The thing fulfilled.**—The malady of Nebuchadnezzar has frequently formed the subject of discussion, and it is now for the most part agreed that it was a form of mania known as *lycanthropy*. The peculiar features of it mentioned in this verse are partially connected with the life which the sufferer's delusion forced him to lead. It appears, however, from the account in Daniel, that he retained his consciousness, as "he lifted up his eyes to heaven" (verse 34) before "his understanding" returned to him. Of this sickness nothing is recorded by Berosus, unless the vague statement "Nebuchadnezzar fell sick and died after a reign of forty-three years" be pressed. It is remarkable to observe that an interval is mentioned in his inscription during which he executed no great public works.

(34) **Lifted up mine eyes.**—A sign of seeking help from heaven, as Ps. cxxiii. 1. By his "understanding" is not meant his consciousness so much as his sense of personality, which had been lost for a time.

Whose dominion . . .—These words, like those in verse 3, recall Ps. cxlv. 13; and the next verse is not unlike Isa. xl. 17, xliii. 13, 21. It is hard to suppose that the king was so thoroughly versed in the Hebrew Scriptures that he should be able to make use of them as doxologies. This gives support to the conjecture that the letter was composed by Daniel and not by the king.

(36) **For the glory.**—He means that the splendour returned, so as to increase the honour and glory of his reign.

(37) **The King of heaven.**—How far the king arrived at a belief in one God is not clear. There may be noticed, however, a progress in his spiritual-character, effected by the grace of God, after each of the interviews which he held with the prophet. At first (chap. ii. 26) his belief was no higher than that which a heathen has in his own superstitions. This develops (chap. ii. 47) into a belief that Daniel's God is "a God of gods, a Lord of kings, and a revealer of secrets." But even at that time he had not arrived at anything like a belief that Jehovah was equal to his own gods. The story of the three holy children shows how little depth there was in his former profession, for in chap. iii. 15 he is represented as setting himself above all gods. After the miracle wrought in their behalf he acknowledges Jehovah to be "the most high God," though he continued to regard Him as only on a level with his own Bel-Merodach. This chapter represents him as recognising "the Most High" to be the cause of his recovery, and as praising the "King of heaven." Holding, as he did, the Babylonian theory of sickness, he must have supposed himself to have been under the influence of some evil spirit; and, with a view to his recovery, his magicians must have treated his disease with charms, amulets, exorcisms, and by placing before him images of his gods. This thanksgiving makes it possible to suppose that he had relinquished much of his belief in his former superstitions, and that he was advancing towards, if not actually in possession of, the truth.

V.

(1) **Belshazzar.**—On this king see *Excursus C.* As he was the son of Nabonidus, a space of about thirty years must have elapsed since the event recorded in the last chapter. The Babylonian empire survived the death of Nebuchadnezzar only twenty-five years.

A thousand.—There is nothing unreasonable in the number of the guests; in fact, the LXX. have doubled the number. (See Esth. i. 3, 4.)

Before the thousand.—The king appears to have had a special table reserved for himself apart from the guests. For this custom comp. Jer. lii. 33.

(2) **Whiles he tasted**—*i.e.*, while he was enjoying the wine. The sacred vessels were brought out of the

the wine, commanded to bring the golden
and silver vessels which his father Nebu-
chadnezzar had [1]taken out of the temple
which *was* in Jerusalem; that the king,
and his princes, his wives, and his con-
cubines, might drink therein. (3) Then
they brought the golden vessels that
were taken out of the temple of the
house of God which *was* at Jerusalem;
and the king, and his princes, his wives,
and his concubines, drank in them.
(4) They drank wine, and praised the
gods of gold, and of silver, of brass, of
iron, of wood, and of stone.

(5) In the same hour came forth fingers
of a man's hand, and wrote over against
the candlestick upon the plaister of the
wall of the king's palace: and the king
saw the part of the hand that wrote.
(6) Then the king's [2]countenance [3]was
changed, and his thoughts troubled him,
so that the [4][5]joints of his loins were
loosed, and his knees smote one against
another. (7) The king cried [6]aloud to
bring in the astrologers, the Chaldeans,
and the soothsayers. *And* the king
spake, and said to the wise *men* of Baby-
lon, Whosoever shall read this writing,
and shew me the interpretation thereof,
shall be clothed with [7]scarlet, and *have*
a chain of gold about his neck, and shall
be the third ruler in the kingdom.
(8) Then came in all the king's wise
men: but they could not read the
writing, nor make known to the king
the interpretation thereof. (9) Then was
king Belshazzar greatly troubled, and
his [8]countenance was changed in him,
and his lords were astonied.

(10) *Now* the queen by reason of the
words of the king and his lords came
into the banquet house: *and* the queen
spake and said, O king, live for ever:
let not thy thoughts trouble thee, nor let
thy countenance be changed: (11) [a]there
is a man in thy kingdom, in whom *is*
the spirit of the holy gods; and in the
days of thy [9]father light and under-
standing and wisdom, like the wisdom of
the gods, was found in him; whom the

1 Chald., *brought forth.*
2 Chald., *brightnesses.*
3 Chald., *changed it.*
4 Or, *girdles.*
5 Chald., *bindings,* or, *knots.*
6 Chald., *with might.*
7 Or, *purple.*
8 Chald., *brightnesses.*
a ch. 2. 48.
9 Or, *grandfather.*

---

temple of Merodach, and profaned in this manner for the purpose of defying Jehovah. But it may be reasonably asked, What led him to think of Jehovah in the midst of the revelry? It may have been that some drunken fancy seized him. It may have been that he had been warned that the prophets of Jehovah had foretold the overthrow of Babylon by Cyrus, whose armies were now in the neighbourhood. Whatever the true explanation may be, there can be no doubt, from Daniel's language (verse 23), and from the way in which Belshazzar's gods are mentioned (verse 4), that the whole act was one of defiance of Jehovah.

(5) **In the same hour**—*i.e.,* suddenly and unexpectedly. (Comp. chap. iii. 6.) Observe that it was only a portion of the hand that the king saw (comp. verse 24), and that we are not told whether the guests saw the hand or not. That the writing was visible to all is plain from verse 8. We remark here, as in other supernatural manifestations recorded in Scripture, that a portion only has been witnessed by many, while the whole has been seen only by one or by a few. (Comp. John xii. 28, 29; Acts ix. 7.)

Candlestick.—This, of course, would make both the hand and the writing more distinctly visible to the king.

Plaister.—This was invariably used in the inner chamber of the Assyrian and Babylonian palaces. (See Layard, *Nineveh and Babylon,* p. 529.)

(6) **The king's countenance was changed.**—The effect of the vision on the king changes his whole expression to that of alarm instead of drunken mirth.

(7) **The astrologers.**—It is worthy of notice that on this occasion the magicians (the *chartummim*) do not appear. We must either suppose that they are included under the general term "Chaldeans," or that the king in his terror forgot to summon them. The "wise men" spoken of (verse 8) were the body over which Daniel was president—a post which it appears from chap. viii. 27, he held at this time. It is needless to discuss why Daniel did not come in at first.

The third ruler.—See *Excursus C.* Those who adopt another view of Belshazzar maintain that a triumvirate existed at this time similar to that in the days of Darius the Mede (chap. vi. 2), and that the king promises to raise to the rank of "*triumvir*" the person who could interpret the vision successfully. It may be noticed that the form of the ordinal "third," both here and in verses 16, 29, is very peculiar, and that in the last two passages it resembles a substantive rather than an adjective.

(8) **Then**—*i.e.,* after the king had addressed the wise men whom he had summoned. But why could not they read an inscription which Daniel deciphered at first sight? It has been conjectured (1) that the character was old Semitic, or one which the wise men did not know; (2) that the language of the inscription was unknown to them; (3) that the words were written in vertical columns, and the wise men endeavoured to read them horizontally. The only true explanation is to be found in the supernatural character of the inscription, and in the inspiration of Daniel. In this way God asserts Himself against the false wisdom of the heathens.

(9) The terror of Belshazzar and his lords is caused by the impression that the inability of the wise men to read the inscription is the portent of some terrible calamity.

(10) **By reason of the words.**—The noise and confusion in the banquet-hall was heard by the queen-mother in her apartments. Her respect for Daniel is evident from her language. The position which she held was one of influence, for it appears that her advice was no sooner offered than it was accepted.

(11) **The spirit.**—Comp. chap. iv. 8, 9.

Thy father.—No blood relationship is necessarily implied by this word. It means no more than "predecessor." (See *Introd.,* sec. VI.)

king Nebuchadnezzar thy [1]father, the
king, *I say*, thy father, made [a]master of
the magicians, astrologers, Chaldeans,
and soothsayers; (12) forasmuch as an
excellent spirit, and knowledge, and
understanding, [2]interpreting of dreams,
and shewing of hard sentences, and
[3]dissolving of [4]doubts, were found in
the same Daniel, whom the king named
Belteshazzar: now let Daniel be called,
and he will shew the interpretation.
(13) Then was Daniel brought in before
the king. *And* the king spake and said
unto Daniel, *Art* thou that Daniel, which
art of the children of the captivity of
Judah, whom the king my [5]father brought
out of Jewry? (14) I have even heard of
thee, that the spirit of the gods *is* in
thee, and *that* light and understanding
and excellent wisdom is found in thee.
(15) And now the wise *men*, the astrologers,
have been brought in before me, that
they should read this writing, and make
known unto me the interpretation there-
of: but they could not shew the inter-
pretation of the thing: (16) and I have
heard of thee, that thou canst [6]make
interpretations, and dissolve doubts:
now if thou canst read the writing, and
make known to me the interpretation
thereof, thou shalt be clothed with
scarlet, and *have* a chain of gold about
thy neck, and shalt be the third ruler in
the kingdom.
(17) Then Daniel answered and said
before the king, Let thy gifts be to
thyself, and give thy [7]rewards to another;
yet I will read the writing unto the king,
and make known to him the interpreta-
tion. (18) O thou king, the most high
God gave Nebuchadnezzar thy father a
kingdom, and majesty, and glory, and
honour: (19) and for the majesty that he
gave him, all people, nations, and lan-
guages, trembled and feared before him:
whom he would he slew; and whom he
would he kept alive; and whom he
would he set up; and whom he would
he put down. (20) But when his heart
was lifted up, and his mind hardened
[8]in pride, he was [9]deposed from his
kingly throne, and they took his glory
from him: (21) and he was [b]driven from
the sons of men; and [10]his heart was
made like the beasts, and his dwelling
was with the wild asses: they fed him
with grass like oxen, and his body was
wet with the dew of heaven; till he
knew that the most high God ruled
in the kingdom of men, and *that* he
appointeth over it whomsoever he will.
(22) And thou his son, O Belshazzar, hast
not humbled thine heart, though thou
knewest all this; (23) but hast lifted up
thyself against the Lord of heaven; and
they have brought the vessels of his
house before thee, and thou, and thy
lords, thy wives, and thy concubines,
have drunk wine in them; and thou
hast praised the gods of silver, and
gold, of brass, iron, wood, and stone,
which see not, nor hear, nor know: and
the God in whose hand thy breath *is*,
and whose *are* all thy ways, hast thou

1 Or, *grandfather*.
a ch. 4. 9.
2 Or, *of an interpreter*, &c.
3 Or, *of a dissolver*.
4 Chald., *knots*.
5 Or, *grandfather*.
6 Chald., *interpret*.
7 Or, *fee*, as ch. 2. 6.
8 Or, *to deal proudly*.
9 Chald., *made to come down*.
b ch. 4. 32.
10 Or, *he made his heart equal*, &c.

---

(12) **Forasmuch as.**—The effect of these words is to combine the two facts mentioned in verse 11, and to make the advice at the end of this verse more forcible. "Because Daniel is a wise man, and has proved his wisdom in the days of Nebuchadnezzar, therefore send for him now."

Dissolving of doubts.—See marginal alternative; and for an illustration comp. *Records of the Past*, vol. iii., p. 141.

(13) **And the king spake.**—The words of the queen-mother, especially her mention of the circumstance that Daniel's name had been changed to Belteshazzar, at once recalls the whole of the circumstances to the king's mind. That Belshazzar knew him by reputation is plain from the description given of him at the end of the verse: "which art of the children of the captivity of Judah."

Art thou that Daniel?—He calls him by his Hebrew name, so as to avoid one which sounded so much like his own. Daniel was now nearly ninety years of age.

(15) **The thing**—*i.e.*, the whole of this miraculous transaction.

(17) **Let thy gifts be to thyself.**—Daniel refused the king's offer of reward at first, but afterwards accepted it. In this way he showed his determination to speak the truth without any respect to fee, gift, or reward. (Comp, the conduct of Elisha, 2 Kings v. 16, viii. 9.)

(18) **The most high God.**—Comp. this and the three following verses with chap. iv. 16, 17, 22—25.

(21) **His dwelling . . .**—This is a fact supplementary to what is stated in chap. iv.

(22) **Though thou knewest.**—The whole history of Nebuchadnezzar was known to Belshazzar. He had not, however, learned the moral lesson conveyed by it. He was therefore doubly guilty in the sight of God, because his blasphemy was wilful.

(23) **Gods of silver . . .**—Comp. Deut. iv. 28. Belshazzar had exceeded those limits of authority over Israel which he had by right of conquest. The Israelites were, indeed, his subjects, but he had no right to blaspheme their God. For similar instances of men exceeding the limits of their authority while acting as ministers of God's chastisement, see Isa. x. 5—18; Jer. li. 20—25; Hosea i. 4, 5.

Not glorified—*i.e.*, dishonoured.

not glorified: (24) then was the part of
the hand sent from him; and this writing
was written.

(25) And this *is* the writing that
was written, MENE, MENE, TEKEL,
UPHARSIN. (26) This *is* the interpreta-
tion of the thing: MENE; God hath
numbered thy kingdom, and finished
it. (27) TEKEL; Thou art weighed in
the balances, and art found wanting.
(28) PERES; Thy kingdom is divided,
and given to the Medes and Persians.

(29) Then commanded Belshazzar, and
they clothed Daniel with scarlet, and
put a chain of gold about his neck, and
made a proclamation concerning him,
that he should be the third ruler in the
kingdom.

(30) In that night was Belshazzar the
king of the Chaldeans slain. (31) And
Darius the Median took the kingdom,
[1]*being* [2]about threescore and two years
old.

CHAPTER VI.—(1) It pleased Darius
to set over the kingdom an hundred and
twenty princes, which should be over
the whole kingdom; (2) and over these
three presidents; of whom Daniel *was*
first: that the princes might give ac-
counts unto them, and the king should
have no damage. (3) Then this Daniel
was preferred above the presidents and
princes, because an excellent spirit *was*
in him; and the king thought to set him
over the whole realm.

(4) Then the presidents and princes
sought to find occasion against Daniel
concerning the kingdom; but they could
find none occasion nor fault; forasmuch
as he *was* faithful, neither was there any
error or fault found in him. (5) Then
said these men, We shall not find any
occasion against this Daniel, except we
find *it* against him concerning the law
of his God. (6) Then these presidents
and princes [3]assembled together to the
king, and said thus unto him, King
Darius, live for ever. (7) All the presi-
dents of the kingdom, the governors,
and the princes, the counsellors, and the
captains, have consulted together to
establish a royal statute, and to make a
firm [4]decree, that whosoever shall ask a

1 Chald., he as the *son of*, &c.

2 Or, *now*.

B.C. cir. 537.

3 Or, *came tumultuously*.

B.C. cir. 538.

B.C. cir. 538.

4 Or, *interdict*.

---

(24) **Then.**—Not only "at that time," but also "because of this." Daniel here expressly designates the writing as something proceeding from God.

(25) **Mene . . .**—It should be remarked that the word *Mene*, which occurs twice in the inscription, is found only once in the interpretation, and that the "Medes" who are mentioned in the interpretation are not spoken of in the inscription. Hence it has been conjectured that the second *Mene* was originally *Madai*, or Media. This, though it appears plausible, has no external support. The word *Mene*, "numbered," is repeated twice for the sake of emphasis. The days of Babylon are numbered; it is God Himself who has numbered them. "Mene" is used in the double sense of "numbering" and "bringing to an end." Similarly, "Tekel" implies both the act of "weighing" and the fact of "being light." The "*u*" in *Upharsin* is the conjunction "and," while *pharsin*, or, rather, *parsin*, is the plural of *peres*, a noun which implies "divisions" and also Persians. It appears from verse 28 that the divided empire of Babylon and the Medo-Persian empire are signified.

(31) **Darius the Median.**—Note the LXX. variation: "And Artaxerxes of the Medes took the kingdom, and Darius, full of days and glorious in old age." (See *Excursus D.*)

Took—*i.e.*, received it from the hands of a conqueror. (Comp. chap. ix. 1, where Darius is said to have been "made king over the realm of the Chaldeans.")

VI.

(1) **Princes.**—See *Excursus A.* The LXX. make the number 127, so as to agree with Esth. i. 1.

(2) **Three presidents.**—See Note on chap. v. 7. If there had been a triumvirate in Babylon, Darius continued the form of government which he found already existing, and retained Daniel in the official post to which he had been promoted by Belshazzar.

(3) **Was preferred.**—Literally, *he outshone* the others. The pronoun "this" is prefixed to Daniel's name so as to point him out as the favoured one already mentioned. (Comp. verses 5, 28.)

(4) **Concerning the kingdom**—*i.e.*, *in his official capacity*. The plan of the conspirators was to place Daniel in such a situation that his civil and religious duties might be forced to clash with each other.

(5) This conspiracy was evidently the result of jealousy on the part of the other officers at the advancement of Daniel.

(6) **Assembled.**—See margin. Such conduct was very unusual in Eastern Courts, where, as a rule, the strictest decorum and order was preserved. This breach of etiquette must have prepared the king to expect some terrible crisis in the State.

(7) **All the presidents.**—Observe the order in which the State officers are mentioned—civil rulers, legal advisers, military governors—and comp. Note on chap. iii. 2. The spokesman represents all these officers to have come to a fixed determination after due deliberation. This was false, as it is plain from verse 24 that all were not involved in the conspiracy. The object of the decree was political, as well as hostile towards Daniel. By consenting to the plan proposed, Darius would acknowledge the Babylonian system of theology, according to which the king was "the living manifestation of all the gods," while, at the same time, his subjects would have an opportunity of doing him religious homage. Probably this prevented the king from perceiving any plot against Daniel. We see from this history the antiquity of *espionage* in political matters.

petition of any God or man for thirty days, save of thee, O king, he shall be cast into the den of lions. (8) Now, O king, establish the decree, and sign the writing, that it be not changed, according to the [a] law of the Medes and Persians, which [1] altereth not. (9) Wherefore king Darius signed the writing and the decree.

(10) Now when Daniel knew that the writing was signed, he went into his house; and his windows being open in his chamber [b] toward Jerusalem, he kneeled upon his knees [c] three times a day, and prayed, and gave thanks before his God, as he did aforetime. (11) Then these men assembled, and found Daniel praying and making supplication before his God. (12) Then they came near, and spake before the king concerning the king's decree; Hast thou not signed a decree, that every man that shall ask *a petition* of any God or man within thirty days, save of thee, O king, shall be cast into the den of lions? The king answered and said, The thing *is* true, according to the law of the Medes and Persians, which altereth not. (13) Then answered they and said before the king, That Daniel, which *is* of the children of the captivity of Judah, regardeth not thee, O king, nor the decree that thou hast signed, but maketh his petition three times a day.

(14) Then the king, when he heard *these* words, was sore displeased with himself, and set *his* heart on Daniel to deliver him: and he laboured till the going down of the sun to deliver him. (15) Then these men assembled unto the king, and said unto the king, Know, O king, that the law of the Medes and Persians *is*, That no decree nor statute which the king establisheth may be changed. (16) Then the king commanded, and they brought Daniel, and cast *him* into the den of lions. *Now* the king spake and said unto Daniel, Thy God whom thou servest continually, he will deliver thee. (17) And a stone was brought, and laid upon the mouth of the den; and the king sealed it with his own signet, and with the signet of his lords; that the purpose might not be changed concerning Daniel.

(18) Then the king went to his palace, and passed the night fasting: neither were [2] instruments of musick brought before him: and his sleep went from him. (19) Then the king arose very early in the morning, and went in haste unto the den of lions. (20) And when he came to the den, he cried with a lamentable voice unto Daniel: *and* the king spake and said to Daniel, O Daniel, servant of the living God, is thy God, whom thou servest continually, able to deliver thee from the lions? (21) Then said Daniel unto the king, O king, live for ever. (22) My God hath sent his angel, and hath shut the lions' mouths, that they have not hurt me: forasmuch as before

a Esth. 2. 1 & 8. 8.

1 Chald., *passeth not.*

b 1 Kin. 8. 48.

c Ps. 55. 17.

2 Or, *table.*

---

(8) **Sign the writing.**—Literally, *record the decree*, so that there might be no possibility of its being recalled. (Comp. Esth. viii. 8.)

(10) **Toward Jerusalem.**—On the custom of praying thus see 1 Kings viii. 33, 35; Pss. v. 7, xxviii. 2; and on prayer at the intervals mentioned here, see Ps. lv. 17. There is nothing ostentatious in Daniel's prayer. He removed the lattices (see Ezek. xl. 16) from his window, that he might see as far as possible in the direction of Jerusalem, and then continued his devotions just as though the king's decree had not been recorded. The prophet must by this time have been close upon ninety years of age, but still his faith is as firm and unwavering as that of his three companions many years before.

(13) **Which is of the children.**—By adding this to the charge of disobedience to the king's commandment, they hoped to incense him still further against the prophet. Here was a foreigner, who had received the highest favours from the Court, setting himself up in antagonism to the laws of the kingdom.

(16) **They brought Daniel.**—According to Eastern custom, the sentence was generally executed on the day when it was pronounced. This explains why the king's efforts to commute the sentence were prolonged till sunset (verse 14). The lions were probably kept here for sporting purposes. The form of the den is unknown, but the etymology suggests a vaulted chamber.

(17) **Sealed it.**—This sealing both by the king and his nobles appears to have been due to the fear that the nobles had (verse 16) of the king's attempting to rescue Daniel. The nobles also would be unable to put Daniel to death in the event of his escaping the fury of the lions.

(18) **Instruments of musick.**—A word of very doubtful meaning. The root whence it is derived means *to rejoice*, but what is signified cannot be exactly ascertained.

(20) **Is thy God . . . able?**—The faith of this king is very weak. In verse 16 he expressed a vague hope that God would protect His servant. That hope seems now to have died out, though afterwards (verse 26) it appears stronger than that of Nebuchadnezzar. (Comp. chap. iv. 37.) The phrase "living God" is remarkable, coming as it does from a heathen king. (See 1 Sam. xvii. 36.)

(22) **His angel.**—Comp. Ps. xxxiv. 7, 10; chap. iii. 28. **Before thee**—*i.e.*, thou knowest full well.

him innocency was found in me; and
also before thee, O king, have I done no
hurt. (23) Then was the king exceeding
glad for him, and commanded that they
should take Daniel up out of the den.
So Daniel was taken up out of the den,
and no manner of hurt was found upon
him, because he believed in his God.
(24) And the king commanded, and they
brought those men which had accused
Daniel, and they cast *them* into the den
of lions, them, their children, and their
wives; and the lions had the mastery of
them, and brake all their bones in pieces
or ever they came at the bottom of the den.
(25) Then king Darius wrote unto all
people, nations, and languages, that
dwell in all the earth; Peace be multi-
plied unto you. (26) I make a decree,
That in every dominion of my kingdom
men tremble and fear before the God of
Daniel: for he *is* the living God, and
stedfast for ever, and his kingdom *that*
which shall not be [a]destroyed, and his
dominion *shall be even* unto the end.
(27) He delivereth and rescueth, and he
worketh signs and wonders in heaven
and in earth, who hath delivered Daniel
from the [1]power of the lions.
(28) So this Daniel prospered in the
reign of Darius, and in the reign of
[b]Cyrus the Persian.

CHAPTER VII.—(1) In the first year
of Belshazzar king of Babylon Daniel
[2]had a dream and visions of his head
upon his bed: then he wrote the dream,
and told the sum of the [3] matters.
(2) Daniel spake and said, I saw in my
vision by night, and, behold, the four
winds of the heaven strove upon the
great sea. (3) And four great beasts came
up from the sea, diverse one from another.
(4) The first *was* like a lion, and had
eagle's wings: I beheld till the wings
thereof were plucked, [4]and it was lifted
up from the earth, and made stand upon
the feet as a man, and a man's heart
was given to it. (5) And behold another
beast, a second, like to a bear, and [5]it

a ch. 2. 44 & 4. 3 & 7. 14, 27; Luke 1. 33.

1 Heb., *hand.*

B.C. cir. 555.

b ch. 1. 21.

2 Chald., *saw.*

3 Or, *words.*

4 Or, *wherewith.*

5 Or, *it raised up one dominion.*

---

(26) **Unto the end.**—The language of this decree is remarkably Scriptural. This is due, no doubt, to the share which Daniel had in the composition of it. By the "end" is meant the end of all the heathen kingdoms which shall arise upon the earth, or, in other words, the setting up of the kingdom of the Messiah.

(28) **So this Daniel.**—The first part of the book, which terminates here, concludes with a notice similar to that in chaps. ii. 48, iii. 30. The history of Daniel and of the three holy children has thus far been traced in its relation to their work amongst the people in the midst of whom they were living as exiles. We have seen the purpose of the miracles which God wrought in behalf of His servants, all tending to exalt Him in the eyes of the Gentiles. The second part of the book, which begins with chap. vii., speaks of the future destinies of the kingdoms of the world in relation to the kingdom of God. The whole of this remaining section presents to us a series of revelations supplementary to that which was recorded in chap. ii.

VII.

(1) The date of this and of the following chapter comes in chronological order after the fourth chapter. As St. Jerome has observed, "*In superioribus ordo sequitur historiæ quid sub Nebuchadonosor et Balthasar, et Dario sive Cyro mirabilium signorum acciderit. In his vero narrantur somnia quæ singulis sint visa temporibus: quorum solus propheta conscius est, et nullam habent apud barbaras nationes signi vel revelationis magnitudinem, sed tantum scribuntur, ut apud posteros eorum quæ visa sunt memoria perseveret.*"

Visions.—From this, and from the phrase "sum of the matters," it appears that Daniel had other visions at this time. By "sum" is meant the principal parts of the vision.

(2) **The great sea.**—In general (*e.g.*, Josh. xv. 47), these words imply the Mediterranean. Such cannot be the meaning here, so that according to verse 17 we are justified in explaining the "sea" to mean the nations of the world, which are compared to the sea (Isa. xxvii. 1; Ps. xlvi. 3). The raging of the winds from the four quarters of the sky points to the various political and social agitations which disturb the world's history, and lead to the changes and revolutions which mark its progress as it tends towards the end.

(3) **Four great beasts.**—The monstrous forms of the beasts are implied, rather than the hugeness of their size. Other instances of beasts being taken as emblems of kingdoms may be found in Isa. xxvii. 1; Ezek. xxix. 3, xxxii. 2. It must be observed that the beasts do not rise up simultaneously, but in succession to each other. In this way, and in the difference of their character, they form a parallel to the subject-matter of the vision recorded in chap. ii.

(4) **The first was like a lion.**—The lion and the eagle are chosen as being emblems of strength and swiftness respectively. They characterise the empire of Nebuchadnezzar, and correspond to the golden head of the Colossus (chap. ii.).

The wings . . . plucked.—The eagle, deprived of its wings, loses its power of swiftness and unrestrained motion.

From the earth.—The beast was raised from being on its four feet into the position of a man, as is indicated by the words "a man's heart." We have not sufficient historical details respecting the last years of Nebuchadnezzar's reign to enable us to point to the reference. It has been suggested by St. Jerome that the words refer to the madness of the king and to his subsequent recovery; but it must be borne in mind that it is the kingdom rather than the king of Babylon which is the subject of the vision.

(5) **And behold another beast.**—We are not told what became of the first beast. (Comp. verse 12.) The word "behold" implies that this was the

raised up itself on one side, and *it had*
three ribs in the mouth of it between
the teeth of it: and they said thus unto
it, Arise, devour much flesh. (6) After
this I beheld, and lo another, like a
leopard, which had upon the back of it
four wings of a fowl; the beast had also
four heads; and dominion was given to
it. (7) After this I saw in the night
visions, and behold a fourth beast, dread-
ful and terrible, and strong exceedingly;
and it had great iron teeth: it devoured
and brake in pieces, and stamped the
residue with the feet of it: and it *was*
diverse from all the beasts that *were*
before it; and it had ten horns. (8) I
considered the horns, and, behold, there
came up among them another little
horn, before whom there were three of
the first horns plucked up by the roots:
and, behold, in this horn *were* eyes like
the eyes of man, and a mouth speaking
great things.
(9) I beheld till the thrones were cast
down, and the Ancient of days did sit,
whose garment *was* white as snow, and
the hair of his head like the pure wool:
his throne *was like* the fiery flame, *and*
his wheels *as* burning fire. (10) A fiery
stream issued and came forth from be-
fore him: [a]thousand thousands minis-
tered unto him, and ten thousand times
ten thousand stood before him: the
judgment was set, and the [b]books were

a Rev. 5. 11.

b Rev. 20. 12.

---

next object which arrested the seer's attention. The second beast corresponds to the silver portion of the Colossus (chap. ii.).

One side.—In explaining this very difficult phrase, it must be remembered that the *two* sides of the bear are parallel in meaning to the two breasts and two arms of the Colossus. It is implied, therefore, that the second kingdom consists of two parts, and the raising up of one side implies that one part of the kingdom would come into greater prominence than the other. Such was the case with the Medo-Persian Empire (comp. chap. viii. 3), in which the Persian element surpassed the Median.

Three ribs.—These cannot signify the people who constitute the second empire, but rather some kingdoms which had already been subdued by it; and by the command, "Arise and devour," the second empire is permitted to make further conquests before its disappearance. The three ribs have been understood from the time of St. Hippolytus to mean three nations: the Babylonians, the Lydians, and the Egyptians.

(6) **A leopard.**—More correctly, *a panther.* On the great vigilance and swiftness of the panther, comp. Jer. v. 6; Hosea xiii. 7; Hab. i. 8. The third beast corresponds to the copper belly and thighs of the image (chap. ii.). It should be noticed that as unity characterises the first beast, and duality the second, so quadruplicity marks the third. It has four wings—wings as of a bird, not of an eagle—by which a degree of swiftness is implied inferior to that of the first beast. It has four heads, indicating four kingdoms, into which the third kingdom should develop itself. (Comp. chap. viii. 8, where the same predominance of the number "four" is to be observed.)

(7) **A fourth beast.**—This is so different from the preceding three, and so terrible in appearance, that Daniel can hardly find words to describe it. The distinguishing feature of it is the power which it possesses of breaking and stamping out all that it meets. In this way it corresponds to "iron that breaketh in pieces, and subdueth all things." (Comp. chap. ii. 40.) The description of the destructive might of this beast is heightened by the mention of "iron teeth" and "brazen claws." It should be noticed that the horns imply strength, while the ten horns correspond to the ten toes of the image.

The residue—*i.e.*, what it did not destroy with its teeth it trampled upon and annihilated with its feet

(8) **I considered.**—Literally, *I kept on looking.* Here, for the first time in the course of the vision, there appears a change taking place in the object itself. While the three beasts had passed away unchanged in any material addition, among the ten horns of the fourth beast there was seen to grow up a "little horn," which destroyed three of the other horns. That a man, and not a kingdom, is intended, though the man may be the representative of a kingdom, appears from the mention of "the eyes of a man," indicating craft and cunning, and "the mouth speaking great things," implying vain-glory and blasphemy.

(9) **I beheld.**—Literally, *I kept on looking,* and suddenly seats were placed, on which the assessors of the Great Judge were to sit. These have been interpreted from Ps. lxxxix. 7 to be the angels, but a truer explanation is to be found in Matt. xix. 28. It should be noticed that those who sat on the thrones are distinguished from the countless multitude mentioned in verse 10.

Ancient of days.—Literally, *a very aged man.* (Comp. Ezek. i. 26—28.) The attribute of age expresses the majesty of the judge. (Comp. Ps. lv. 19; Deut. xxxiii. 27.) It may be remarked that notwithstanding the title "Ancient" is applied to the Deity, "Anou," yet His titles, "generator and father of the gods," are so completely at variance with Old Testament doctrines that it is inconceivable that Daniel should have incorporated in his vision any portions of Babylonian mythology. Similar remarks apply to Silik-moulou-khi, between whom and the Son of man (verse 13) a parallel has been pointed out. The conception of the former is completely different from what is revealed about the latter.

White as snow.—Indicating, like the "pure wool," the purity and justice of the Judge.

Fiery flame.—Fire appears in Scripture sometimes as a metaphor for affliction or punishment (*e.g.*, 1 Cor. iii. 13, &c.), sometimes as a symbol of the chastening and punitive righteousness of God (Ezek. i. 13, 14, 27, 28). Elsewhere it sets forth the fiery indignation which devours the enemies of God (Heb. x. 27; Rev. xix. 11, 12). The figure of speech is here used in each of these senses. The "wheels" represent the omnipresence of Almighty God.

(10) **The books**—*i.e.*, the unerring record of man's thoughts, words, and deeds, which is written in the un-

opened. (11) I beheld then because of
the voice of the great words which the
horn spake: I beheld *even* till the beast
was slain, and his body destroyed, and
given to the burning flame. (12) As con-
cerning the rest of the beasts, they had
their dominion taken away: yet [1]their
lives were prolonged for a season and
time.

(13) I saw in the night visions, and,
behold, *one* like the Son of man came
with the clouds of heaven, and came to
the Ancient of days, and they brought
him near before him. (14) And there was
given him dominion, and glory, and a
kingdom, that all people, nations, and
languages, should serve him: his do-
minion *is* [a]an everlasting dominion, which
shall not pass away, and his kingdom
that which shall not be destroyed.

(15) I Daniel was grieved in my spirit
in the midst of *my* [2]body, and the visions
of my head troubled me. (16) I came
near unto one of them that stood by,
and asked him the truth of all this. So
he told me, and made me know the in-
terpretation of the things. (17) These
great beasts, which are four, *are* four
kings, *which* shall arise out of the earth.
(18) But the saints of the [3]most High
shall take the kingdom, and possess the
kingdom for ever, even for ever and
ever.

(19) Then I would know the truth of
the fourth beast, which was diverse [4]from
all the others, exceeding dreadful, whose
teeth *were of* iron, and his nails *of* brass;
which devoured, brake in pieces, and
stamped the residue with his feet; (20) and
of the ten horns that *were* in his head,
and *of* the other which came up, and
before whom three fell; even *of* that
horn that had eyes, and a mouth that
spake very great things, whose look *was*
more stout than his fellows. (21) I beheld,
and the same horn made war with the
saints, and prevailed against them;
(22) until the Ancient of days came, and
judgment was given to the saints of
the most High; and the time came that
the saints possessed the kingdom.

(23) Thus he said, The fourth beast shall
be the fourth kingdom upon earth, which
shall be diverse from all kingdoms, and
shall devour the whole earth, and shall
tread it down, and break it in pieces.
(24) And the ten horns out of this king-
dom *are* ten kings *that* shall arise: and
another shall rise after them; and he shall
be diverse from the first, and he shall
subdue three kings. (25) And he shall
speak *great* words against the most High,

1 Chald., *a prolonging in life was given them.*

a ch. 2. 44; Mic. 4. 7; Luke 1. 33.

2 Chald., *sheath.*

3 Chald., *high ones,* that is, *things,* or, *places.*

4 Chald., *from all those.*

---

failing memory of God. (Comp. Exod. xxxii. 32; Pss. lvi. 8, lxix. 28; Isa. iv. 3; Mal. iii. 16.)

(11) **Because of . . .**—The blasphemy uttered by the little horn was the cause of the judgment, and being such, it attracted Daniel's attention. We might have expected that the crowning scene of this vision would have been the uprooting of the little horn and the complete destruction of it, but it appears that the blaspheming spirit with which it was inspired issued from the fourth monster, which "was slain and burned."

Burning flame.—Such is the doctrine of final retribution, as revealed to Daniel. (Comp. Isa. lxvi. 24; Rev. xix. 20, xx. 10.)

(12) **The rest of the beasts**—*i.e.,* the three first beasts which Daniel had seen coming out of the sea. He now learns what had befallen them. Their dominions had passed away, and their lives had been prolonged up to that definite point and time which had seemed fit to God, and no further. The period of life allotted to them by God was only a little while. (On "times" and "seasons," see Note on chap. ii. 21.)

(13) **The Son of man.**—Hence our Saviour adopts the title which designates Him as Judge (Matt. xxiv. 27, &c.). The title implies one descended from man; but as this Person is spoken of as being "like" one of human descent, it follows that He was not merely a man. The early Jewish and Christian interpretations that this is the Messiah are confirmed by our Saviour's solemn appropriation of the title to Himself (Matt. xxiv. 30). In this verse the judgment is supposed to have already taken place upon earth, and the Son of man comes in the clouds to claim His kingdom.

(14) **Serve him.**—In Biblical Chaldee this word is only used of rendering Divine service or worship. The "Son of man" is therefore here spoken of as God.

(15) **Midst.**—See margin. The body was regarded as the *sheath* of the soul.

(16) **That stood by**—*i.e.,* one out of the multitudes mentioned (verse 10).

(17) **Four kings.**—Kingdoms are frequently represented by their heads or founders; hence kings and kingdoms are occasionally used synonymously. (Comp. chap. viii. 21.)

(19) **Whose teeth.**—The recapitulation in this verse of what was stated in verse 7 must be noticed. The additional features mentioned here are the brazen claws. (Comp. chaps. ii. 37, iv. 20.)

(21) **Made war.**—This corresponds to "the mouth speaking great things" (verses 8, 20). These events occur while the saints are expecting their deliverance.

(23) **The fourth kingdom.**—The ten are spoken of as existing simultaneously. Of the various attempts to account for them, none have proved satisfactory. (See *Excursus E.*) We must wait in patient humility for the fulfilment of this part of the prophecy, noting that marks by which the little horn may be identified have been graciously revealed to us by God Himself.

(25) **And he shall speak.**—The marks of identification of the little horn are—(1) blasphemy of God; (2)

and shall wear out the saints of the
most High, and think to change times
and laws: and they shall be given into
his hand until a time and times and the
dividing of time. (26) But the judgment
shall sit, and they shall take away his
dominion, to consume and to destroy *it*
unto the end. (27) And the [a]kingdom and
dominion, and the greatness of the king-
dom under the whole heaven, shall be
given to the people of the saints of the
most High, whose kingdom *is* an ever-
lasting kingdom, and all [1]dominions shall
serve and obey him.
(28) Hitherto *is* the end of the matter.
As for me Daniel, my cogitations much
troubled me, and my countenance
changed in me: but I kept the matter
in my heart.

CHAPTER VIII.—(1) In the third
year of the reign of king Belshazzar a
vision appeared unto me, *even unto* me
Daniel, after that which appeared unto
me at the first.
(2) And I saw in a vision; and it came
to pass, when I saw, that I *was* at
Shushan *in* the palace, which *is* in the
province of Elam; and I saw in a vision,
and I was by the river of Ulai. (3) Then I
lifted up mine eyes, and saw, and, behold,
there stood before the river a ram which
had *two* horns: and the *two* horns *were*
high; but one *was* higher than [2]the
other, and the higher came up last. (4) I
saw the ram pushing westward, and
northward, and southward; so that no
beasts might stand before him, neither
was there any that could deliver out of
his hand; but he did according to his
will, and became great.
(5) And as I was considering, behold,
an he goat came from the west on the
face of the whole earth, and [3]touched

a Luke i. 33.

1 Or, *rulers*.

2 Heb., *the second*.

3 Or, *none touched him in the earth*.

B.C. cir. 553.

---

persecution and affliction of the saints; (3) attempts, apparently ineffectual (he will "think to change"), against all institutions, whether of Divine or human authority: in short, a general spirit of lawlessness and unbelief. It appears that the little horn, the Antichrist of the last days, or the beast, will be successful for a time in his blasphemies and persecutions, but in the end he will be destroyed. (See 2 Thess. ii. 8.)

Time and times and the dividing of time.—This is frequently explained to mean three years and a half. Those who adopt this explanation assume that by "times" a dual is implied, which in Chaldee is represented by the plural. They next assume that by "a time" is meant one year, resting their assumption partly on chap. iv. 16, and partly on a comparison of chap. xii. 7 with Rev. xiii. 5, xi. 2, 3. This gives a sum of three years and a half, which is interpreted either literally, or explained to mean half a sabbatical period, or half some divinely-appointed period symbolised by the number "seven." According to the second interpretation, Daniel teaches us that the days of tribulation shall be shortened (Matt. xxiv. 22). But it may be questioned whether "years" are intended in chap. iv. 16. Also the language in chap. xii. 7 is very obscure. A more correct view of the prediction is that the reign of Antichrist will be divided into three periods—the first long, the second longer, the third shortest of all. It also appears that the last is to be the severest time of trial. It may be remarked that in chap. ix. the seventy weeks are divided into three periods, forming a similar series, 7 + 62 + 1 = 70.

(26) **The judgment.**—The language is similar to that in verse 10. The destruction of the beast recorded in verse 11 is here omitted.

Unto the end.—Comp. chap. vi. 26.

(27) Comp. verses 14, 18.

(28) **The matter**—*i.e.*, the vision and the revelation.

In my heart.—Daniel suffers as in verse 15 and chap. x. 8. However, he comforts himself by keeping in his heart the words of the angel spoken in verse 17. (Comp. Luke ii. 19.)

VIII.

(1) The Hebrew language is here resumed. The visions recorded in the remaining portion of the book having no connection with Babylon, the Chaldee dialect is dropped.

Third year.—Most probably, not long before the end of his reign. This vision is supplementary to the one recorded in the preceding chapter, giving various details respecting the second and third empires there omitted, showing also how a "little horn" is to grow out of the third as well as out of the fourth empire.

At the first—*i.e.*, earlier. (Comp. chap. ix. 21.)

(2) **At Shushan**—*i.e.*, Susa. At this time (see *Records of the Past*, vol. i., p. 71, &c.) Susa was, as Daniel describes it, in the province of Elam; at a later period it became the capital of the Persian empire. Daniel was at Susa only in vision, he was not bodily transported thither. The Ulai is the river Eulæus, and is mentioned in connection with Susa in the inscription cited above.

(3) **A ram**—*i.e.*, a single ram. The ram was standing before the river, or eastward of it, and represented the Medo-Persian empire (verse 20). The two horns, like the two breasts and arms of the image, or the two sides of the bear, symbolise the twofold character of this empire. The higher horn denotes the Persians, the dominant race. For other instances of rams and goats representing nations, comp. Isa. xiv. 9; Jer. l. 8; Zech. x. 3.

(4) **I saw the ram pushing.**—The ram pushes in three different directions. This corresponds to the three ribs in the mouth of the bear. The animal does not push towards the east, as it is presumed that he has already made conquests in those quarters.

(5) **An he goat.**—This, according to verse 21, means the Greek empire, the large horn being the first king, or Alexander the Great. It may be remarked that the goat and the ram form the same contrast as the panther and the bear. Matchless activity is contrasted with physical strength and brutal fierceness.

not the ground: and the goat *had* [1]a
notable horn between his eyes. (6) And
he came to the ram that had *two* horns,
which I had seen standing before the
river, and ran unto him in the fury of
his power. (7) And I saw him come close
unto the ram, and he was moved with
choler against him, and smote the ram,
and brake his two horns: and there was
no power in the ram to stand before
him, but he cast him down to the ground,
and stamped upon him: and there was
none that could deliver the ram out of
his hand. (8) Therefore the he goat
waxed very great: and when he was
strong, the great horn was broken; and
for it came up four notable ones [a]toward
the four winds of heaven. (9) And out of
one of them came forth a little horn,
which waxed exceeding great, toward
the south, and toward the east, and to-
ward the [b]pleasant *land*. (10) And it
waxed great, *even* [2]to the host of heaven;
and it cast down *some* of the host and of
the stars to the ground, and stamped
upon them. (11) Yea, he magnified *him-
self* even [3]to the prince of the host, and
[4]by him the daily *sacrifice* was taken
away, and the place of his sanctuary was
cast down. (12) And [5]an host was given
him against the daily *sacrifice* by reason
of transgression, and it cast down the
truth to the ground; and it practised,
and prospered.
(13) Then I heard one saint speaking,
and another saint said unto [6 7]that
certain *saint* which spake, How long
shall be the vision *concerning* the daily
sacrifice, and the transgression [8]of deso-
lation, to give both the sanctuary and
the host to be trodden under foot?
(14) And he said unto me, Unto two
thousand and three hundred [9]days; then
shall the sanctuary be [10]cleansed.

1 Heb., *a horn of sight.*
a ch. 11. 4.
b Ps. 48. 2; Ezek. 20. 6.
2 Or, *against the host.*
3 Or, *against.*
4 Or, *from him.*
5 Or, *the host was given over for the transgression against the daily* sacrifice.
6 Or, *the numberer of secrets*, or, *the wonderful numberer.*
7 Heb., *Palmoni.*
8 Or, *making desolate.*
9 Heb., *evening morning.*
10 Heb., *justified.*

Touched not the ground.—An exact prediction of the early conquests of Alexander, all whose movements were characterised by marvellous rapidity. This is expressed by "the wings of a fowl" (chap. vii. 6).

A notable horn.—See margin. This is explained (verse 21) to be Alexander himself.

(6) **Ran unto him.**—The wonderful rapidity of Alexander's movements, incredible, if it were not so well attested in history, is here pointed out. From the battle of Granicus to that of Arbela only three years elapsed. During this brief period the whole Persian empire fell to pieces.

(8) **Was broken.**—This points to the sudden and unexpected end of Alexander, B.C. 323. The "four horns," which take the place of the "notable horn," may mean either that this empire was dispersed to the four winds of heaven on the death of its founder (comp. chap. vii. 2, xi. 4; Jer. xlix. 36; Zech. ii. 6), or it may hint at the ultimate division of the empire into four parts, Thrace, Macedonia, Syria, Egypt, under Symmachus, Cassander, Seleucus, and Ptolemy respectively.

(9) **Little.**—Literally, *out of littleness*. (Comp. chap. vii. 8.) This is explained more fully in verse 23. The southern campaigns of Antiochus Epiphanes are related 1 Macc. i. 16; for his eastern wars see 1 Macc. iii. 31—37, vi. 1—4.

The pleasant land—*i.e.*, Palestine, which here, as in Isa. xix. 23, 24, is spoken of as a third land, between south and east. The phrase, "pleasant land," or "glorious land," which recurs chap. xi. 16—41, was suggested to Daniel by the language of Jer. iii. 19; Ezek. xx. 6, 15.

(10) **The host of heaven.**—Probably meaning the stars, as Jer. xxxiii. 22, but in a metaphorical sense indicating the people of Israel. (Comp. Exod. vii. 4; Num. xxiv. 17.) The actions of Antiochus, predicted here, are related 1 Macc. i. 24, 30, 37, ii. 38; 2 Macc. ix. 10.

(11) **Prince of the host**—*i.e.*, Jehovah Himself. (Comp. verse 25, chap. xi. 36.)

The daily—*i.e.*, everything permanent in the worship of God, such as sacrifices, &c. (See Note on Lev. vi. 13.) On this conduct of Antiochus see 1 Macc. i. 39, 45, &c., iii. 45.

Place of his sanctuary—*i.e.*, the Temple. (Comp. 1 Kings viii. 13.)

(12) **An host . . .**—The host is apparently the same as that which is mentioned in verse 10, and means some of the Jewish people. It is known that some of them lapsed under the persecutions of Antiochus, and joined in his idolatrous rites. These apostates were given into his hand, and on account of their apostasy the daily sacrifice also was taken away. (Comp. verse 13.)

The truth—*i.e.*, the word of God, as appears from 1 Macc. i. 43—52, 56, 60.

(13) **One saint**—*i.e.*, an angel, who, however, has not been mentioned before. This part of the vision recalls chap. vii. 16. It is implied that the angels were conversing upon the subject of this awful revelation concerning the future of God's people. Only a portion of what they said is here recorded.

The vision.—The inquiry means, "How long shall be the duration of the object of this vision, so far as it has to do with the great apostasy?"

Transgression of desolation. — Comp. chap. ix. 27. Probably these words mean the same as the "abomination that maketh desolate" (chaps. xi. 31, xii. 11; see 1 Macc. i. 59).

(14) **Unto two thousand and three hundred days.**—It is clear from the language that the period here spoken of terminates with the cleansing of the sanctuary, and that it begins with the transgression that led to the awful events that occurred in the time of Antiochus Epiphanes. Judas Maccabeus took Jerusalem in the year B.C. 165, and kept the Feast of Dedication the same year, Antiochus being at the time in Armenia. The period apparently commences with the events mentioned in 2 Macc. iv. 32—39, which occurred about B.C. 171. The dates, however, not being recorded precisely, it is impossible to reckon with certainty whence the starting-point is to be dated. The

(15) And it came to pass, when I, *even*
I Daniel, had seen the vision, and sought
for the meaning, then, behold, there
stood before me as the appearance of
a man. (16) And I heard a man's voice
between *the banks of* Ulai, which called,
and said, [a]Gabriel, make this *man* to
understand the vision. (17) So he came
near where I stood: and when he came,
I was afraid, and fell upon my face: but
he said unto me, Understand, O son of
man: for at the time of the end *shall be*
the vision. (18) Now as he was speaking
with me, I was in a deep sleep on my face
toward the ground: but he touched me,
and [1]set me upright. (19) And he said,
Behold, I will make thee know what
shall be in the last end of the indigna-
tion: for at the time appointed the end
shall be.

(20) The ram which thou sawest having
two horns *are* the kings of Media and
Persia. (21) And the rough goat *is* the
king of Grecia: and the great horn that
is between his eyes *is* the first king.
(22) Now that being broken, whereas four
stood up for it, four kingdoms shall
stand up out of the nation, but not in
his power. (23) And in the latter time of
their kingdom, when the transgressors
[2]are come to the full, a king of fierce
countenance, and understanding dark
sentences, shall stand up. (24) And his
power shall be mighty, but not by his
own power: and he shall destroy won-
derfully, and shall prosper, and practise,
and shall destroy the mighty and the
[3]holy people. (25) And through his policy
also he shall cause craft to prosper in
his hand; and he shall magnify *himself*
in his heart, and by [4]peace shall destroy
many: he shall also stand up against
the Prince of princes; but he shall be
[b]broken without hand. (26) And the vision
of the evening and the morning which
was told *is* true: wherefore shut thou up
the vision; for it *shall be* for many days.

(27) And I Daniel fainted, and was sick
certain days; afterward I rose up, and
did the king's business; and I was

a ch. 9. 21.

1 Heb., *made me stand upon my standing.*

2 Heb., *are accomplished.*

3 Heb., *people of the holy ones.*

4 Or, *prosperity.*

b 2 Mac. 9. 9.

---

phrase "evening morning" (see margin) is used to indicate a complete night and day, and 2,300 complete days of twenty-four hours make a period of six years 140 days. It has been observed that this period falls short of seven years (a week of years) by about two-thirds of a year. If, then, seven years is the number of years symbolical of Divine chastisements, the prophecy implies that the people shall not suffer persecution according to their full deserts, but "for the elect's sake those days shall be shortened." (See Note on chap. vii. 25.)

Be cleansed.—Literally, *be placed in its proper state.*

(15) **Appearance of a man.**—From verse 16 it appears that this was the angel Gabriel. The "man's voice" mentioned in verse 16 proceeded from Him Who alone has authority to command angels. (Comp. chap. xii. 6, 7.)

(16) **Between the . . . Ulai.**—The city, as it would appear, stood between the two branches of the river. The two branches were the Eulæus and the Choaspes.

(17) **The time of the end**—*i.e.*, either at the final period of earthly history, or at the time which lies at the limit of the prophetic horizon. St. Jerome observes that what happened in the times of Antiochus was typical of what shall be fulfilled hereafter in Antichrist.

(18) **A deep sleep.**—On the effects of heavenly visions upon those who beheld them, see Gen. xvi. 13, Exod. xxxiii. 20, &c.

(19) **End of the indignation**—*i.e.*, the revelation of God's wrath at the end of the time of the prophecy.

At the time appointed—*i.e.*, the vision refers to the appointed time in the end.

(20—22) See Notes on verses 3—8.

(22) **Not in his power**—*i.e.*, not like the first king.

(23) **Transgressors . . .**—When transgressors have filled up the measure of their guilt so as to exceed the limits of God's mercy, then this event shall take place. The transgressors are the apostate Jews. Here, as in the other visions, the particulars respecting the most prominent objects of the vision are given more fully in the interpretation than in the early part of the chapter. The king is represented as being "of a fierce countenance," he is shameless, he has no reluctance in pursuing the cruelties which he has designed. He "understands dark sayings," or uses falsehood and dissimulation to carry out his purposes.

(24) **Not by his own power.**—Not might, but cunning, will cause his success. (Comp. 1 Macc. i. 10, &c.) Thus his destructive powers become astonishing.

The mighty.—No special individuals are pointed out, but rulers in general.

(25) **Through his policy.**—This is explained more fully in the next two sentences. Through his craft he succeeds, and becomes able to destroy many unexpectedly, and finally raises up himself against God.

Without hand.—Not by the hand of man (comp. chap. ii. 34), but by the act of God.

(26) The concluding words of the angel are intended to comfort the Jewish Church in the days of her persecution. They teach her that God has foreseen her affliction, that it comes from Him in His love, and that it shall last only for a short while. This promise accounts for the firmness which was exhibited by the saints of the Maccabees, which entitles their faith to a place in the same list of faithful men which contains the names of Abel, Abraham, and Moses (Heb. xi. 34—38).

Shut thou up.—The revelation is to be kept safe, because the time of fulfilment is far off, and then the comforting words will be needed. Comp. Rev. xxii. 10, where the opposite counsel is given, "seal it not, for the time of fulfilment is near."

astonished at the vision, but none under-
stood *it*.

CHAPTER IX.—(1) In the first year
of Darius the son of Ahasuerus, of the
seed of the Medes, [1]which was made
king over the realm of the Chaldeans;
(2) in the first year of his reign I Daniel
understood by books the number of the
years, whereof the word of the LORD
came to [a]Jeremiah the prophet, that he
would accomplish seventy years in the
desolations of Jerusalem. (3) And I set
my face unto the Lord God, to seek
by prayer and supplications, with fast-
ing, and sackcloth, and ashes: (4) and I
prayed unto the LORD my God, and
made my confession, and said,
O [b]Lord, the great and dreadful God,
keeping the covenant and mercy to
them that love him, and to them that
keep his commandments; (5) [c]we have
sinned, and have committed iniquity,
and have done wickedly, and have re-
belled, even by departing from thy
precepts and from thy judgments:
(6) neither have we hearkened unto thy
servants the prophets, which spake in
thy name to our kings, our princes,
and our fathers, and to all the people
of the land. (7) O Lord, righteousness
[2]*belongeth* unto thee, but unto us con-
fusion of faces, as at this day; to the
men of Judah, and to the inhabitants
of Jerusalem, and unto all Israel, *that
are* near, and *that are* far off, through all
the countries whither thou hast driven
them, because of their trespass that
they have trespassed against thee. (8) O
Lord, [d]to us *belongeth* confusion of face,
to our kings, to our princes, and to our
fathers, because we have sinned against
thee. (9) To the Lord our God *belong*
mercies and forgivenesses, though we
have rebelled against him; (10) neither
have we obeyed the voice of the LORD
our God, to walk in his laws, which he
set before us by his servants the pro-
phets. (11) Yea, all Israel have trans-
gressed thy law, even by departing,
that they might not obey thy voice;
therefore the curse is poured upon us,

1 Or, *in which he*, &c.

B.C. cir. 538.

a Jer. 25. 12 & 29. 10.

b Deut. 7. 9; Neh. 1. 5.

c Bar. 1. 17.

2 Or, *thou hast*, &c.

d Bar. 1. 15.

IX.

(1) On Darius the Mede see *Excursus D.*

Was made king.—The phrase corresponds with "took the kingdom" (verse 31), and shows that Darius was not king by his own right, but that he received his authority from another—*i.e.*, Cyrus.

(2) **Understood.**—He gave special attention to Jeremiah's prophecy of the seventy years of the Captivity. Two passages occur in that prophet's writings where the duration of the Captivity is mentioned (Jer. xxv. 11 and xxix. 10), to the former of which Daniel refers (see especially verses 9, 11, 12). It will be observed that there existed at this time a collection of sacred books, consisting of what had been already admitted into the Canon.

Seventy years.—It appears from Haggai i. 2, Zech. i. 12, that considerable uncertainty prevailed as to the time whence the seventy years were to be reckoned. It has been pointed out (Professor Leathes' *Old Testament Prophecy*, p. 179) that three periods of seventy years occur in connection with the Captivity:—(1) from B.C. 606, the date of Jeremiah's prophecy, to B.C. 536, the edict of Cyrus; (2) from B.C. 598, Jehoiachin's captivity, to B.C. 528, the period of Ezra iv. 6; (3) from B.C. 588, the destruction of the Temple, to B.C. 518, the edict of Darius (Ezra vi. 1). In the first year of Cyrus, seventy years had elapsed since the captivity of Daniel, but to him it was a question of melancholy importance whether his computation had begun at the right date.

(3) **I set my face.**—Comp. chap. vi. 11. Probably he prayed, as on that occasion, with his face towards Jerusalem. The prayer of Daniel bears some resemblance to those offered by Ezra and Nehemiah, while that of Baruch resembles it much more closely. (On this see *Excursus F.*)

(4) **The covenant.**—See Exod. xix. 5.

(5) **We have sinned.**—It has been remarked that four stages of sin are pointed out by the prophet, corresponding to the four different words which he uses. "Sin" refers especially to sins of deed, "committing iniquity" to sins of word, "done wickedly" to sins of thought, "rebelled" implies the person against whom the sin has been committed. The whole result of sin under these several aspects is expressed by the words "departing from Thy precepts."

(6) **Neither have we hearkened.**—The aggravation of guilt. All God's warnings have been unheeded by high and low alike, by all to whom they were addressed.

(7) **Righteousness.** — The absolute righteousness of God appears distinct and clear in spite of the chastisement from which the nation suffers. Meanwhile, the humble looks of the devout part of the nation show that it feels the present shame and confusion.

All the countries.—See Isa. xi. 11, 12. In the midst of his sorrow for the past, the mind of the prophet recurs unconsciously to the great promise of future deliverance by "the root of Jesse."

(8) **Confusion of face.**—Repeated from verse 7, so as to bring into stronger contrast the mercy of God (verse 9) with the "righteousness" mentioned in verse 7. St. Jerome well remarks, "*Post sententiam judicantis provocat eum ad clementiam.*" The absolute mercy and forgiveness of God is implied by the article in this verse, just as His absolute righteousness is in verse 7.

(11) **The curse.**—The passages in the books of Leviticus and Deuteronomy, to which Daniel refers, had already been noticed by Isaiah (chap. i.), as having received a partial fulfilment in his times. It remains for Daniel to realise the complete "pouring" out of

and the oath that *is* written in the [a]law
of Moses the servant of God, because
we have sinned against him. (12) And
he hath confirmed his words, which he
spake against us, and against our judges
that judged us, by bringing upon us a
great evil: for under the whole heaven
hath not been done as hath been done
upon Jerusalem. (13)As [b]*it is* written in
the law of Moses, all this evil is come
upon us: yet [1]made we not our prayer
before the LORD our God, that we
might turn from our iniquities, and
understand thy truth. (14) Therefore
hath the LORD watched upon the evil,
and brought it upon us: for the LORD
our God *is* righteous in all his works
which he doeth: for we obeyed not
his voice. (15) And now, O Lord our
God, that hast brought thy people
forth out of the land of Egypt with
a mighty hand, and hast [2]gotten thee
[c]renown, as at this day; we have
sinned, we have done wickedly. (16) O
Lord, according to all thy righteous-
ness, I beseech thee, let thine anger and
thy fury be turned away from thy city
Jerusalem, thy holy mountain: because
for our sins, and for the iniquities of
our fathers, Jerusalem and thy people
are become a reproach to all *that are*
about us. (17) Now therefore, O our
God, hear the prayer of thy servant,
and his supplications, and cause thy
face to shine upon thy sanctuary that
is desolate, for the Lord's sake. (18) O
my God, incline thine ear, and hear;
open thine eyes, and behold our deso-
lations, and the city [3]which is called by
thy name: for we do not [4]present our
supplications before thee for our right-
eousnesses, but for thy great mercies.
(19) O Lord, hear; O Lord, forgive; O
Lord, hearken and do; defer not, for
thine own sake, O my God: for thy city
and thy people are called by thy name.
(20) And whiles I was speaking, and
praying, and confessing my sin and the
sin of my people Israel, and presenting
my supplication before the LORD my
God for the holy mountain of my God;
(21) yea, whiles I *was* speaking in prayer,
even the man [d]Gabriel, whom I had
seen in the vision at the beginning,
being caused to fly [5]swiftly, touched me
about the time of the evening oblation.

a Lev. 26. 14, &c.; Deut. 28. 15, &c., & 29. 20, &c., & 30. 17, 18 & 31. 17, &c., & 32. 19, &c.

b Lev. 26. 14; Deut. 28. 15; Lam. 2. 17.

1 Heb., *intreated we not the face of the*, &c.

2 Heb., *made thee a name.*

c Ex. 14. 18.

3 Heb., *whereupon thy name is called.*

4 Heb., *cause to fall.*

d ch. 8. 16.

5 Heb., *with weariness*, or, *flight.*

---

the curse. It is poured out like a torrent of rain (see Exod. ix. 33); as the fire melts the silver (Ezek. xxii. 20—22), so does the curse cause the nation to melt away.

(12) **Our judges.**—Used in a wide sense to signify kings, princes, and rulers generally. (Comp. Hosea vii. 7.)

(13) **Made we not our prayer.**—The reference is, as in verse 6, to the conduct of the nation from the first. There had been plenty of external show of praying, as appears from Isa. i. and elsewhere, but these prayers were of no effect on account of their formalism. The conditions of acceptable prayer are implied in the closing words of the verse "turning from iniquity, and wisdom in the truth," *i.e.,* in the revelation of God. On the phrase "make prayer," see Exod. xxxii. 11.

(14) **Watched.**—By the use of this word it seems that Daniel is again referring to the prophecies of Jeremiah. (See Jer. i. 12, &c.) He prays that as all the curses foretold by that prophet have been poured upon the nation, so also the release from the Captivity, which was also promised by him, may be accomplished also.

(15) **Thou hast brought.**—The mention of past mercies moves Daniel to pray that future mercies may be granted. His language is founded partly upon Jer. xxxii. 17—23, and partly upon Isa. lxiii. 11—16. The Babylonian exile is frequently compared by Isaiah (*e.g.,* Isa. li. 9, 10) to Egyptian bondage. Daniel reproduces the thought in this verse.

(16) **Righteousness.**—Those acts of Jehovah which evince His righteousness, or His faithfulness to His promises. Mount Zion, the "holy mountain," holds a very important place in prophecy. It is the outward visible sign of the stability of God's promises to David, the "sure mercies of David," as well as the centre of all that is Holy in the kingdom of God. (See Pss. lxviii. 15, 16; cxxxii. 13, 14; Isa. ii. 2—4; and comp. verse 20.)

(17) **Cause thy face to shine.**—See Num. vi. 25. The meaning is "let thy works show the fulfilment of 'thy Word.'"

For the Lord's sake.—Comp. verse 19, "because Thou art the Lord." Never does prayer rise higher, than when the soul humbly appeals to God as the sovereign lord of all, and patiently waits for Him to do as He pleases. (Comp. Ps. xliv. 9—26.)

(20) **Whiles I was speaking.**—The answer to Daniel's prayer. He had not even finished his prayer when the answer came. The angel Gabriel, whom he had seen (chap. viii. 16), comes to him, and reveals to him the mystery of the seventy weeks.

(21) **Being caused to fly swiftly.**—A very difficult expression, occurring only here. The Authorised Version follows the LXX. and Theodotion. The rendering has been defended on the ground that the word translated "swiftly" comes from a root meaning "to fly," and is literally rendered by *flight.* Thus "caused to fly in flight" means "caused to fly swiftly." The marginal version "with weariness" finds supporters, and, if adopted, must be taken to refer to the bodily condition of Daniel (chap. viii. 17—27). The former translation is most in accordance with the context. The "flight" of angels is implied in Isa. vi. 2, and should not be regarded as an idea foreign to the Old Testament.

Touched me.—Literally, *reached me.* (Comp. this use of the word, Jonah iii. 6.) The time of the evening sacrifice is 3 P.M., being the hour of evening prayer. (See Exod. xxix. 39; Num. xxviii. 4.)

(22) And he informed *me*, and talked with
me, and said, O Daniel, I am now come
forth [1] to give thee skill and under-
standing. (23) At the beginning of thy
supplications the [2] commandment came
forth, and I am come to shew *thee;* for
thou *art* [3] greatly beloved: therefore
understand the matter, and consider
the vision.
(24) Seventy weeks are determined upon
thy people and upon thy holy city, [4] to
finish the transgression, and [5] to make
an end of sins, and to make reconciliation
for iniquity, and to bring in everlasting
righteousness, and to seal up the vision
and [6] prophecy, and to anoint the most
Holy. (25) Know therefore and under-
stand, *that* from the going forth of the
commandment to restore and to build
Jerusalem unto the Messiah the Prince

1 Heb., *to make thee skilful of understanding.*

2 Heb., *word.*

3 Heb., a man *of desires.*

4 Or, *to restrain.*

5 Or, *to seal up.*

6 Heb., *prophet.*

---

(22) **He informed me**—*i.e.*, gave me understanding (as verse 2, chap. viii. 16). The angel gave Daniel understanding in the perplexing words of Jeremiah, showing him that what affected his people was a period of seventy weeks that were yet to come, rather than seventy years which were already passed.

(23) **The commandment.**—The marginal version is to be preferred, which points to the revelation which follows verses 24—27. The title "greatly beloved" occurs again (chap. x. 11, 19). It implies that Daniel was worthy of this proof of God's love. St. Jerome compares (2 Sam. xii. 25) Jedidiah.

(24) **Seventy weeks.**—Great difficulty is experienced in discovering what sort of weeks is intended. Verses 25—27 are sufficient to show that ordinary weeks cannot be meant. Possibly, also, the language (chap. x. 2, margin "weeks of days") implies that "weeks of days" are not intended here. On the other hand, it is remarkable that in Lev. xxv. 1—10 the word week should not have been used to signify a period of seven years, if year-weeks are implied in this passage. However, it is generally assumed that we must understand the weeks to consist of years and not of days (see Pusey's *Daniel*, pp. 165, 166), the principle of year-weeks depending upon Num. xiv. 34, Lev. xxvi. 34, Ezek. iv. 6. The word "week" in itself furnishes a clue to the meaning. It implies a "Heptad," and is not necessarily more definite than the "time" mentioned in chap. vii. 25.

Are determined.—The word only occurs in this passage. Theod. translates συνετμήθησαν; LXX., ἐκρίθησαν; Jer. "*abbreviatæ sunt.*" In Chaldee the word means "to cut," and in that sense "to determine."

The object "determined" is twofold: (1) transgression and sin; (2) reconciliation and righteousness.

To finish.—The Hebrew margin gives an alternative rendering, "to restrain," according to which the meaning is "to hold sin back" and to "prevent it from spreading." If this reading is adopted it will be parallel to the second marginal alternative, "to seal up," which also implies that the iniquity can no more increase. Although the alternative readings may be most in accordance with the Babylonian idea of "sealing sins," the presence of the word "to seal" in the last clause of the verse makes it more probable that the marginal readings are due to the conjectures of some early critics, than that they once stood in the text. However, it must be observed that while St. Jerome translates the passage "*ut consummetur prævaricatio, et finem habeat peccatum,*" Theodotion supports the marginal reading "to seal."

To make reconciliation—*i.e.*, atonement. (Comp. Prov. xvi. 6; Isa. vi. 7, xxvii. 9; Ps. lxxviii. 38.) The two former clauses show that during the seventy weeks sin will cease. The prophet now brings out another side of the subject. There will be abundance of forgiveness in store for those who are willing to receive it.

Everlasting righteousness.—A phrase not occurring elsewhere. The prophet seems to be combining the notions of "righteousness" and "eternity," which elsewhere are characteristics of Messianic prophecy. (Isa. xlvi. 13, li. 5—8; Ps. lxxxix. 36; chaps. ii. 44, vii. 18, 27.)

To seal up.—σφραγίσαι, Theod.; συντελεσθῆναι, LXX.; *impleatur*, Jer.; the impression of the translators being that all visions and prophecies were to receive their complete fulfilment in the course of these seventy weeks. It appears, however, to be more agreeable to the context to suppose that the prophet is speaking of the absolute cessation of all prophecy. (Comp. 1 Cor. xiii. 8.)

To anoint the most Holy.—The meaning of the sentence depends upon the interpretation of the words "Most Holy" or "Holy of Holies." In Scripture they are used of (1) the altar (Exod. xxix. 37); (2) the atonement (Exod. xxx. 10); (3) the tabernacle and the sacred furniture (Exod. xxx. 29); (4) the sacred perfume (Exod. xxx. 36); (5) the remnant of the meat offering (Lev. ii. 3, 10); (6) all that touch the offerings made by fire (Lev. vi. 18); (7) the sin offering (Lev. x. 17); (8) the trespass offering (Lev. xiv. 13); (9) the shewbread (Lev. xxiv. 9); (10) things devoted (Lev. xxvii. 28); (11) various offerings (Num. xviii. 9); (12) the temple service and articles connected with it, or perhaps Aaron (1 Chron. xxiii. 13); (13) the limits of the new temple (Ezek. xliii. 12); (14) the sanctuary of the new temple (Ezek. xlv. 3); (15) the territory set apart for the sons of Zadok (Ezek. xlviii. 2). Which of these significations is to be here adopted can only be discovered by the context. Now from the careful manner in which this and the following verse are connected by the words "Know therefore," it appears that the words "most Holy" are parallel to "Messiah the Prince" (verse 25), and that they indicate a person. (See Lev. vi. 18; 1 Chron. xxiii. 13.) This was the opinion of the Syriac translator, who renders the words "Messiah the most Holy," and of the LXX. εὐφρᾶναι ἅγιον ἁγίων, on which it has been remarked that εὐφρᾶναι would have no meaning if applied to a place, and the phrase employed in this version for the sanctuary is invariably τὸ ἅγιον τῶν ἁγίων. Any reference to Zerubbabel's temple, or to the dedication of the temple by Judas Maccabæus, is opposed to the context.

(25) **Know therefore.**—The difficulty of this verse is considerably increased by the principal accent in the Hebrew text being placed after the words "seven weeks." According to the present punctuation, the translation is "Unto an Anointed one a prince shall be seven weeks, and during sixty and two weeks [Jerusalem] shall be built up" . . . This is opposed (1) to ancient translations except the LXX.; (2) to verse 26, which con-

shall be seven weeks, and threescore and two weeks: the street [1]shall be built again, and the [2]wall, even [3]in troublous times. (26) And after threescore and two weeks shall Messiah be cut off, [4]but not for himself: and the people of the prince that shall come shall destroy the city and the sanctuary; and the end thereof *shall be* with a flood, and unto the end of the war [5]desolations are determined. (27) And he shall confirm the covenant with many for one week: and in the midst of the week he shall cause the sacrifice and the oblation to

1 Heb., *shall return and be built.*
2 Or, *breach,* or, *ditch.*
3 Heb., *in strait of times.*
4 Or, *and shall have nothing.*
5 Or, *it shall be cut off by desolations.*

---

nects the sixty-two weeks with the Anointed, and not with the building of the city.

The commandment.—To be explained, as in verse 23, to mean revelation. But to what revelation is the allusion? Is it to the edict of Cyrus (Ezra vi. 14), which Isaiah predicts (Isa. xliv. 28)? Or are we to explain it of what happened in the twentieth year of Artaxerxes? (See *Excursus G.*) It is obvious that there is no reference to Jeremiah's prophecy, for nothing is there stated which can be interpreted to be a command to rebuild Jerusalem.

Messiah the Prince.—Literally, *an Anointed one, a prince,* the two nouns being placed in apposition, and the article omitted before each, the person and the office of the person contemplated being sufficiently definite. He is to be "anointed," that is, King and Priest at once (see 1 Sam. x. 1, xiii. 14, xxv. 30); in fact, He is to possess those attributes which in other passages are ascribed to the Messiah. It is needless to point out that Cyrus, though spoken of (Isa. xlv. 1) as an "anointed of Jehovah," cannot be indicated here. By no calculation can he be said to have come either seven weeks or sixty-nine weeks from the time of the commencement of the Captivity.

The street . . . the wall.—By the street is meant the large square, which, according to Ezra x. 9, was in front of the Temple. With this the "wall" is contrasted, but what is meant cannot be ascertained. According to the etymology, it means "something cut off." The English Version follows the ancient translations.

In troublous times.—The whole history of the rebuilding of Jerusalem tells us one long tale of protracted opposition. Zerubbabel was compelled to undergo the persecution of his adversaries, and to bear their misrepresentations (Ezra iv. 1—6). Attempts to delay the works were made in the reign of Darius (Ezra v. 6). In later times (Ezra iv. 12) complaints were made that the walls were being rebuilt. Probably on this occasion the works that had been executed were destroyed (Neh. i. 3), and it was not until the twentieth year of Artaxerxes that Nehemiah succeeded in completing the walls, and not even then without the most indefatigable labours.

(26) **After threescore and two weeks.**—These words can only mean that in the seventieth week the Anointed one shall be cut off. Observe the care with which the seventy weeks are arranged in a series of the form 7 + 62 + 1. During the period of seven weeks Jerusalem is to be rebuilt. The "troublous times" are not to be restricted to this period, but may apply to the sixty-two weeks which follow. After the end of the sixty-nine weeks Messiah is to be cut off. By "Messiah" we must understand the same person who is spoken of in verse 25. It should also be observed that the word "prince," which is applied to Messiah in verse 25, is here used of another person—some secular prince, who stands in opposition to the Messiah. The Greek versions render "unction" instead of "anointed," whence Jacob of Edessa explains "the cutting off" to mean "the cessation of the unction by which judgment and sovereignty were established." The word "to cut off," however, applies to a person more appropriately than to a thing. It is frequently used of excommunication, *e.g.,* Exod. xxx. 33, 38, Ps. xxxvii. 9, and must not be mistaken for the word "to cut off" (Isa. liii. 8).

But not for himself.—On the marginal rendering comp. John xiv. 30. Literally the words mean, *and He has not,* but what it is that He loses is left indefinite. Taking the sense according to the context, the meaning is either that He has no more a people, or that His office of Messiah amongst His people ceases.

That shall come.—These words imply coming with hostile intent, as chaps. i. 1, xi. 10. Two such princes have been already mentioned (chaps. vii. 23, &c., viii. 23, &c.), the one being Antiochus, the other his great antitype, namely, Antichrist. Are we to identify this "prince" with either of these? Apparently not. Another typical prince is here introduced to our notice, who shall destroy the city and the sanctuary after the "cutting off" or rejection of the Messiah. But it must be noticed that the work of destruction is here attributed to the "people," and not to the "prince."

The end thereof.—It is not clear what end or whose end is signified. According to grammatical rules, the possessive pronoun may either refer to "sanctuary," the last substantive, or to "prince," the chief nominative in the sentence. The use of the word "flood" (chap. xi. 22) (comp. "overflow," chap. xi. 26) makes it, at first sight, more plausible to think of the end of a person than of a thing. (Comp. also Nahum i. 8.) But upon comparing this clause with the following, it appears that by "the end" is meant the whole issue of the invasion. This is stated to be desolation, such as is caused by a deluge.

Unto the end.—That is, until the end of the seventy weeks, desolations are decreed. The words recall Isa. x. 22, 23.

(27) **And he shall confirm.**—The subject of the sentence is ambiguous. Theod. makes it to be "one week." LXX. "the covenant;" others take it to be the Antichristian prince spoken of in the last verse, an opinion which derives some support from chap. vii. 25. According to this interpretation, the covenant refers to the agreement which the prince makes with the large number of persons who become apostates. But (1) the word "covenant" does not apply to any such agreement, but rather to a covenant with God, and (2) in verse 26 it is the people of the prince, and not the prince, which is the subject of the sentence. It is therefore more appropriate to take Messiah as the subject. During the last closing week of the long period mentioned, Messiah, though cut off, shall confirm God's covenant (comp. chap. xi. 22, 28, 30, 32) with many, that is, with those who receive Him.

In the midst of the week.—Or, during half the week (the latter half of the week, according to the LXX.), he will cause to cease all the Mosaic sacrifices (possibly those mentioned in chap. viii. 11), whether

cease, and [1]for the overspreading of
[a]abominations he shall make *it* desolate,
even until the consummation, and that
determined shall be poured upon the
desolate.

CHAPTER X.—(1) In the third year
of Cyrus king of Persia a thing was
revealed unto Daniel, whose name was
called Belteshazzar; and the thing *was*
true, but the time appointed *was* [2]long:
and he understood the thing, and had
understanding of the vision. (2) In those
days I Daniel was mourning three [3]full
weeks. (3) I ate no [4]pleasant bread,
neither came flesh nor wine in my
mouth, neither did I anoint myself at
all, till three whole weeks were fulfilled.

(4) And in the four and twentieth day
of the first month, as I was by the side
of the great river, which *is* [b]Hiddekel;

[1] Or, *with the abominable armies.*
[a] Matt. 24. 15; Mark 13. 14; Luke 21. 20.
[2] Heb., *great.*
B.C. cir. 534.
[3] Heb., *weeks of days.*
[4] Heb., *bread of desires.*
[b] Gen. 2. 14.

---

bloody or unbloody. The verb "cause to cease" is used here as in Jer. xxxvi. 29.

And for the overspreading . . .—The Greek versions agree in translating this as follows, καὶ ἐπὶ τὸ ἱερὸν βδέλυγμα τῶν ἐρημώσεων, which St. Jerome follows, "*et erit in templo abominatio desolationis.* However, it is not possible to obtain any such meaning from our present Hebrew text without omitting the last letter and altering the last vowel of the word translated "abominations." As the text stands it can be literally translated only as follows, "and upon the wing of abominations is a desolator." The desolator, of course, is the person who causes the desolations mentioned in verse 26. But what is meant by the "*wing of abominations?*" The language is without parallel in the Old Testament, unless such passages as Ps. xviii. 10, civ. 3 are adduced, where, however, the plural "wings," and not the singular, is used. If the number is disregarded, the words before us are explained to mean that "the abomination" or idolatry is the power by which the desolator accomplishes his purposes. He comes riding on the wings of abominations, using them for his ministers as God does the winds or the cherubim. As it appears decisive against this interpretation that Daniel has written "wing," and not "wings," it is better to explain the words as referring to the "sanctuary" spoken of in the last verse. The sense is in that case, "and upon the wing—*i.e.*, the pinnacle of the abominations (comp. the use of πτερύγιον, Matt. iv. 5) is a desolator. The Temple is thus called on account of the extent to which it had been desecrated by Israel.

Until the consummation.—These words refer back to verse 26, and mean that these abominations will continue till the desolation which God has decreed shall be poured upon that which is desolated. Though the word "desolate" is active in chaps. viii. 13, xii. 11, it appears in this passage to be used in a passive sense, as also in verse 18. That which is foretold by Daniel is the complete and final destruction of the same city and temple which evoked the prophet's prayer. There is no prophecy that the desolator himself is destined to destruction. Of his doom nothing is here stated. The "prince" appears merely as the instrument pre-ordained by God, by whose people both city and sanctuary are to be destroyed.

X.

This and the two following chapters form the concluding section of the book of Daniel. The vision occurred two years after the departure of the exiles from Babylon, and at a time when those who were rebuilding the city were beginning to experience the "troublous" times spoken of in chap. ix. 25. This section is partly supplemental to chaps. viii., ix., and introduces details with regard to the fourth Empire, certain features of chap. vii. being developed. The date of the vision is the third year of Cyrus, the prophet continuing to be known by the name which he had received more than seventy years previously.

(1) **A thing.**—A revelation, as chap. ix. 25. The contents of the revelation are specified in the perplexing words, "the thing was true, and the time appointed (comp. chap. viii. 12) was long," by which is meant apparently that truth and long tribulation were the subject of their vision. "Time appointed" is translated "warfare" (Isa. xl. 2), and is here used in the same sense, meaning "hardship" or "tribulation." This revelation, however, speaks of the "warfare" which not Israel only, but all God's people must undergo before the coming of the Messiah in His kingdom.

And he understood.—Comp. chap. viii. 27. It appears from chap. xii. 8 that the whole was not understood by him. Certainly the duration of the tribulation was not clearly revealed to the prophet, though he received enigmatic declarations respecting it (chap. xii. 10, &c.).

I . . . was mourning.—It is needless to suppose that Daniel's fast was in consequence of some breaches of the passover ritual, of which his people had been guilty. The Jews were involved in troubles, and had committed sins of faithlessness which justified the prophet in turning to God with fasting and praying. At Jerusalem there were the factious oppositions offered to the newly returned colonists, of which we read in the book of Ezra. They experienced the want of spiritual guides (Ezra ii. 63) in one very important matter; nor need we doubt that the circumstances mentioned in Ezra iv. 1—6 had occasioned many complications. But there was in Israel the sin of faithlessness to God's promises, which grieved the aged seer's heart. The number of those who had obeyed the prophet's command, "Go ye forth from Babylon" (Isa. xlviii. 20), was comparatively insignificant, and those who should have been foremost in leading their fellow-countrymen—namely, the Levites—had preferred the life in Babylon to the trials and hardships of rebuilding their own city (Ezra ii. 40; comp. Ezra viii 15).

(3) **Pleasant bread**—*i.e.*, delicate food. Abstaining from this as well as from the use of oil (comp. 2 Sam. xii. 20; Amos. vi. 6) were the outward signs of Daniel's grief.

(4) **The four and twentieth day.**—After the end of his three weeks' fast the prophet was upon the bank of the Tigris, where he saw the following vision. Hiddekel is the Accadian name of the river. (Comp. Gen. ii. 14.) "Great river" is an epithet usually applied to the river Euphrates, as Gen. xv. 18. Daniel was here in the body, and not only in the spirit, as chap. viii. 2.

(5) Then I lifted up mine eyes, and
looked, and behold [1]a certain man
clothed in linen, whose loins *were* [a]girded
with fine gold of Uphaz: (6) his body
also *was* like the beryl, and his face as
the appearance of lightning, and his
eyes as lamps of fire, and his arms and
his feet like in colour to polished brass,
and the voice of his words like the
voice of a multitude.
(7) And I Daniel alone saw the vision:
for the men that were with me saw not
the vision; but a great quaking fell
upon them, so that they fled to hide
themselves. (8) Therefore I was left
alone, and saw this great vision, and
there remained no strength in me: for
my [2][b]comeliness was turned in me into
corruption, and I retained no strength.
(9) Yet heard I the voice of his words:
and when I heard the voice of his
words, then was I in a deep sleep on
my face, and my face toward the ground.
(10) And, behold, an hand touched me,
which [3]set me upon my knees and *upon*
the palms of my hands. (11) And he
said unto me, O Daniel, [4]a man greatly
beloved, understand the words that I
speak unto thee, and [5]stand upright:
for unto thee am I now sent. And
when he had spoken this word unto me,
I stood trembling. (12) Then said he
unto me, Fear not, Daniel: for from
the first day that thou didst set thine
heart to understand, and to chasten
thyself before thy God, thy words were
heard, and I am come for thy words.
(13) But the prince of the kingdom of
Persia withstood me one and twenty
days: but, lo, Michael, [6]one of the chief

1 Heb., *one man.*
a Rev. 1. 13, 14, 15.
2 Or, *vigour.*
b ch. 7. 28.
3 Heb., *moved.*
4 Heb., *a man of desires.*
5 Heb., *stand upon thy standing.*
6 Or, *the first.*

---

(5) **A certain man.**—The appearance of this person is minutely described, while that of the angels is not mentioned. The dress especially recals to our minds the clothing of the high priest. (See Exod. xxxix. 27—29, and comp. Rev. i. 13.) The person himself is carefully distinguished from Michael (chap. x. 21), and as we may infer from Daniel's silence (comp. chap. ix. 21), he is distinct from Gabriel also. He is the same man who stood before Daniel (chap. viii. 15), and must be regarded as "the Angel of God" (Exod. xxxii. 34), or "God's Presence" (Exod. xxxiii. 14), or "God's Name;" in fact, the One who was the Logos.

Uphaz.—A place only mentioned in this passage and Jer. x. 9. The locality of it is unknown. The additions of the LXX. should be noted.

(6) **Beryl.**—Heb., *Tarshish,* a variety of the topaz.

His feet.—More correctly, *the place where his feet were,* or the lower extremities of his limbs. We are not told in what position the man was when Daniel first saw him. Later on (chap. xii. 6) he is described as being upon or above the waters. In this position he symbolises God as supreme over the nations who are represented by the Tigris.

(7) **I . . . alone saw the vision.**—St. Jerome compares the account of St. Paul (Acts xxii. 9). It may be added that, as upon that occasion (comp. Acts ix. 7), the companions of the prophet heard the voice but saw nothing. The words of the voice (verse 6) are unrecorded.

(8) **This great vision.**—Daniel again distinguishes this from former visions. The glory of the man who appeared to him was far in excess of what he had witnessed previously (chap. viii. 17). The effects of the vision upon him are also mentioned. His "comeliness was turned," or, he grew pale with terror at what he saw, and fainted.

(9) **His words.**—He refers to the unrecorded words of verse 6. (Comp. chap. viii. 17, 18.)

(10) **An hand.** — This hand was that of the person who appeared, but it is spoken of as "felt," not as seen. But though supported by this hand, the prophet is unable to stand upright. He crouches in a terrified posture. It should be noticed that the equivalent of "set" is translated "scatter" (Ps. lix. 11 [12]). It is used in the same sense in the passage before us. (See Amos ix. 9.)

(11) **Greatly beloved.**—See chap. ix. 23, Note. The assuring words thus addressed to the prophet enabled him to stand upright, but his alarm had not as yet subsided.

(12) **From the first day.**—The meaning appears to be that this vision was vouchsafed to him in consequence of his prayer to understand what would befal his people in the future. The prayer was heard from the first day that he offered it, but it had been impossible for him to realise the answer before the present time, for reasons mentioned in the next verse.

(13) **The prince of the kingdom.**—Perhaps no single verse in the whole of the Scriptures speaks more clearly than this upon the invisible powers which rule and influence nations. If we were without a revelation, we should have thought it congruent that God Himself should direct all events in the world without using any intervening means. But revelation points out that as spiritual beings carry out God's purpose in the natural world (Exod. xii. 23; 2 Sam. xxiv. 16) and in the moral world (Luke xv. 10), so also they do in the political world. From this chapter we not only learn that Israel had a spiritual champion (verse 21) to protect her in her national life, and to watch over her interests, but also that the powers opposed to Israel had their princes, or saviours, which were antagonists of those which watched over Israel. The "princes" of the heathen powers are devils, according to 1 Cor. x. 20. The doctrine of the ministry of angels is taught in Pss. xxxiv. 7, xci. 11, xcvi. 5 (LXX.); Isa. xxiv. 21, xlvi. 2; Jer. xlvi. 25, xlix. 3. Further passages in the New Testament bearing upon the question are 1 Cor. viii. 5; Col. i. 16.

Withstood me.—The phrase is identical with "stood over against him" (Josh. v. 13). The verse implies that the spiritual powers attached to Persia were influencing Cyrus in a manner that was prejudicial to the interests of God's people. It must be borne in mind that the vision occurred at the time of the Samaritan intrigues with the Persian Court in opposition to Zerubbabel.

Michael.—Mentioned only in the Book of Daniel and Jude 9, Rev. xii. 7. The title "chief princes,"

princes, came to help me; and I re-
mained there with the kings of Persia.
(14) Now I am come to make thee under-
stand what shall befall thy people in
the latter days: for yet the vision *is* for
many days.
(15) And when he had spoken such
words unto me, I set my face toward
the ground, and I became dumb. (16) And,
behold, *one* like the similitude of the
sons of men touched my lips: then I
opened my mouth, and spake, and said
unto him that stood before me, O my
lord, by the vision my sorrows are
turned upon me, and I have retained no
strength. (17) For how can [1] the servant
of this my lord talk with this my lord?
for as for me, straightway there re-
mained no strength in me, neither is
there breath left in me.
(18) Then there came again and touched
me *one* like the appearance of a man,
and he strengthened me, (19) and said, O
man greatly beloved, fear not: peace *be*
unto thee, be strong, yea, be strong.
And when he had spoken unto me, I
was strengthened, and said, Let my lord
speak; for thou hast strengthened me.
(20) Then said he, Knowest thou where-
fore I come unto thee? and now will I
return to fight with the prince of
Persia: and when I am gone forth, lo,
the prince of Grecia shall come. (21) But
I will shew thee that which is noted in
the scripture of truth: and *there is*
none that [2] holdeth with me in these
things, but Michael your prince.

CHAPTER XI.—(1) Also I in the first
year of Darius the Mede, *even* I, stood
to confirm and to strengthen him. (2) And
now will I shew thee the truth.

1 Or, *this servant of my lord.*

2 Heb., *strengtheneth himself.*

---

rightly explained in the margin, shows that the charge of Israel had been entrusted by God to the highest of the heavenly powers; but the name "first prince" points out that, great though he is, he is inconsiderable when compared with God.

I remained there.—Literally, *I prevailed there*, as Gen. xlix. 4. The person is explaining to Daniel how it had happened that he had received no visible answer to a prayer that had been offered with success three weeks previously. There had been a conflict between the powers of light and darkness, in which the former had gained the victory, which had been decisive. By the kings of Persia are meant all the successors of Cyrus. It may be remarked that from this time onward the Persian kings were, upon the whole, favourable to the interests of Israel.

(14) **The latter days.**—Comp. chaps. ii. 28, viii. 17. The time is here more narrowly defined as "those days," that is, the period when the vision of chap. xi. shall receive its complete fulfilment. The "vision" is identical with "the thing" (chap. x. 1), or "the vision" (verse 16). It must be carefully borne in mind that there is no reference to preceding visions, except so far as the revelation contained in chap. xi. develops certain details of other visions.

(15) **I set my face.**—The conduct of Daniel described in this verse is not to be ascribed to his fear, for that had been already driven away (verse 12), but to his reverence for the majestic person who was before him, and to the gratitude that he felt for the answer to his prayer. (Comp. chap. ix. 3, 4.)

(16) **One like . . .**—Comp. chap. viii. 15. However, there is no reason for supposing that the person is different from the one mentioned in verses 10, 18. By "sorrows" is meant the pain produced by terror.

(17) **For how.**—The whole verse must be regarded as addressed by Daniel to the angel. On the phrase "neither is there any breath in me" comp. 1 Kings xvii. 17. Here we may notice the same fear which possessed Isaiah at the time of his vision (Isa. vi. 5).

(19) **Be strong.**—Comp. 2 Sam. x. 12.

(20) **Then said he.**—The meaning of this verse is obscure. Apparently the person who is speaking refers back to what he had said (verses 12—14); and from the question "Knowest thou?" &c., we are to infer that Daniel was perfectly aware of the reasons which caused him to come, viz., "to make thee understand what shall befal thy people in the latter days." But before he proceeds to make this revelation, he prepares Daniel's mind for a portion of what is about to be revealed, by mentioning the spiritual powers which ruled over Greece. "I shall return to fight," referring to the Providence which watched over Israel during the Persian sovereignty; "but while I am gone forth" (the word being used in a military sense, as in Josh. xiv. 11) "the prince of Javan will come," this word being also used in a hostile sense. The prophet is in this manner prepared for troublous times, which shall occur under the Macedonian supremacy.

(21) **But.**—A further contrast is introduced by the adversative. This may be brought out by paraphrasing the verse as follows: "It is true that the prince of Javan will attack you, but do not despair at the thought of one persecuting empire succeeding another. It is all written in the Scripture of truth:" that is, in the revelations which God had already conveyed, or shortly would convey, to Daniel, and in the book of Providence (Ps. cxxxix. 16). We have here a striking parallel to our Saviour's words, "Lo, I have told you before."

And there is none . . .—A still further ground of encouragement. Michael, who stood up as Israel's champion under the Persian troubles, will prove himself strong against the evil powers which lead Javan.

XI.

(1) **In the first year of Darius.**—These words must be closely connected with the last verse of chap. x. The allusion is, most probably, to the fall of Babylon and the return from the Exile, at which time, as at the Exodus, the angel of the Lord went before His people. There is also a reference to chap. vi. 22.

(2) **The truth.**—Comp. chap. x. 21. This is the commencement of the revelation promised in chap. x. 14; and from this point till the end of the book the difficulties that have to be encountered in attempting an exposition are almost insuperable. It has been cus-

Behold, there shall stand up yet three
kings in Persia; and the fourth shall
be far richer than *they* all: and by his
strength through his riches he shall stir
up all against the realm of Grecia.
(3) And a mighty king shall stand up,
that shall rule with great dominion,
and do according to his will. (4) And
when he shall stand up, his kingdom
shall be broken, and shall be divided
toward the four winds of heaven; and
not to his posterity, nor according to
his dominion which he ruled: for his
kingdom shall be plucked up, even for
others beside those.
(5) And the king of the south shall be
strong, and *one* of his princes; and he
shall be strong above him, and have
dominion; his dominion *shall be* a great
dominion. (6) And in the end of years
they [1] shall join themselves together;
for the king's daughter of the south
shall come to the king of the north to
make [2] an agreement: but she shall not
retain the power of the arm; neither
shall he stand, nor his arm: but she

1 Heb., *shall associate themselves.*

2 Heb., *rights.*

---

tomary from the time of St. Jerome, if not from an earlier epoch, to explain most of what follows as referring to the Ptolemies and Seleucidæ. The difficulties which oppose this interpretation will be pointed out in the notes. It is a question whether, after all, the early interpretation is correct, and, if not, whether this revelation does not still await its complete fulfilment. The mere similarity which exists between certain things predicted here and what actually occurred in the times of the Ptolemies is not sufficient to limit the fulfilment of the prophecy to those times, still less to justify the assumption that the section before us is a history of what occurred from the disruption of the Greek Empire to the death of Antiochus. "History repeats itself;" and just as Antiochus (chap. viii. 23—25) is a type of Antichrist (chap. vii. 21), so the events and political combinations which preceded Antiochus may be regarded as typical of what will occur before the coming of the Messiah and the general resurrection, with a prediction of which (chap. xii. 2, 3) this revelation concludes.

Three kings.—It is hard to say who these were. Cyrus being on the throne already, it is most probable that his three successors are intended—Cambyses, Darius, and Xerxes. Those four kings appear to have been selected whose influence was most prominent in its bearings upon Israel. Xerxes is called the fourth king because the reckoning dates from Cyrus, and the short reign of the Pseudo Smerdis is not taken into account. Not only do the riches of Xerxes point him out as the last king, but also his conduct towards Greece may be correctly described as "stirring up" against himself "the realm of Grecia."

Against . . .—The passage gives better sense if translated, *he shall stir up all, the kingdom of Greece,* that is, amongst those stirred up the kingdom of Greece is most prominent. It should be noticed that at the time of the invasion of Europe by Xerxes, Greece was in no sense "a kingdom." Such language is incompatible with an authorship during the Maccabee period.

(3) **A mighty king.**—No clue is given to show over what nation this king reigns. According to the context he might be either a Greek or a Persian, or he might belong to a kingdom not yet mentioned. Those who explain what follows to refer to the Ptolemies and Seleucidæ identify him with Alexander the Great, and compare with this verse chaps. vii. 6, viii. 5—8, 21, 22. Certainly the self-will spoken of in this verse was characteristic of Alexander (comp. also chap. viii. 4), but there was nothing in the context which makes it necessary to limit the passage to him. Some autocrat may arise "in the latter times" to whom it will apply with greater force than it did to Alexander.

(4) **Broken.**—The shortness of the king's reign is implied; the moment that he has arisen he will come to nothing. As in chap. viii. 8, the great horn was broken, so here the kingdom is broken and dismembered. This has been explained to mean the sudden collapse of the Greek empire after the death of Alexander.

Not to his posterity.—The kingdom disappears without the members of the king's family reaping any benefit from it. It is "plucked up for others besides these"—*i.e.,* to the exclusion of his lawful heirs—and strangers shall possess the fragments of his empire. This is explained of the partition of Alexander's empire among his generals, and of the murder of his two sons, Hercules and Alexander, but the language is too indefinite to make any such identification certain. The revelation directs our attention to a self-willed king, whose large empire is to come to a sudden and unexpected end; the ruins of it are not to benefit his posterity, but apparently two strangers, who are designated king of the north and king of the south respectively.

(5) **The king.**—This king of the south (see verse 8) is suddenly introduced to our notice. The vagueness of the language prevents us from asserting that the reference is to Ptolemy Soter, who assumed the title of king about B.C. 304. Equally obscure is the phrase "one of his princes." Both the Greek versions interpret the passage to mean "that one of the princes of the king of the south shall be stronger than his former master." It is hard to see how Seleucus Nicator can be called a "prince" of Ptolemy Soter. Any attempt at making the pronoun "his" refer to the mighty king mentioned in the last verse is opposed to the context, and to introduce any fresh sentence such as "shall arise" is an unwarrantable assumption. The obscurity of the Hebrew text is well reproduced in the English Version. It should be stated that Ptolemy took Jerusalem B.C. 320, and that these times must have been very critical to the Jews.

(6) **In the end.**—Comp. verses 8, 13, and 2 Chron. xviii. 2. Here again the reference is most obscure. If the "joining themselves together" refers to the marriage of Antiochus II. with Berenice, the daughter of Ptolemy Philadelphus, and if "the agreement" (comp. "upright ones," verse 17) refers to the terms of the marriage, which were that Antiochus should put away his former wife Laodice, and appoint her first-born son successor to the throne, then it must be remarked that history is irreconcilable with the prophecy. Also it appears from chap. x. 14 that this revelation bears upon the future of Israel, and it does

shall be given up, and they that brought
her, and [1]he that begat her, and he
that strengthened her in *these* times.
(7) But out of a branch of her roots
shall *one* stand up in his estate, which
shall come with an army, and shall
enter into the fortress of the king of
the north, and shall deal against them,
and shall prevail: (8) and shall also carry
captives into Egypt their gods, with
their princes, *and* with [2]their precious
vessels of silver and of gold; and he shall
continue *more* years than the king of
the north. (9) So the king of the south
shall come into *his* kingdom, and shall
return into his own land.
(10) But his sons [3]shall be stirred up,
and shall assemble a multitude of great
forces: and *one* shall certainly come,
and overflow, and pass through: then
shall he return, and be stirred up, *even*
to his fortress. (11) And the king of the
south shall be moved with choler, and
shall come forth and fight with him,

B.C. cir. 534.

1 Or, *whom she brought forth.*

2 Heb., *vessels of their desire.*

3 Or, *shall war.*

---

not appear that this marriage affected the Jewish people more than any other marriage. This, and the fact that a period of more than fifty years intervened between the events supposed to be implied in verses 5, 6, make the traditional interpretation very unsatisfactory. The language refers to what is mentioned as one of the characteristics of the last empire (chap. ii. 43), various attempts to consolidate earthly powers by political marriages. These do not characterise the era of the Seleucidæ any more than they do the times of Ahab, or many other periods of history.

Shall not retain.—The Greek versions show the difficulties experienced by the translators, the LXX. apparently following a different text. The meaning appears to be that the marriage will not accomplish its intended purpose. The king of the south, instead of becoming independent of his northern rival, will only become more subjected to him than he was previously. This does not appear to have happened with regard to Ptolemy Philadelphus and Antiochus Theos, the former of whom is generally identified with "*he that begat her*," the latter with "*he that strengthened her*."

(7) As yet there has been no account of any war between the northern and southern king, but it must not be forgotten that Ptolemy Philadelphus and Antiochus Theos were at war for ten years or more. In this and the following verses there is a description of a severe war, in which the southern king is victorious. This is explained of the war between Ptolemy Evergetes and Seleucus Callinicus, which lasted B.C. 246—243, and in which Ptolemy was successful, carrying back with him into Egypt on his return large quantities of spoil and images of gods which he had taken. The coincidence between history and prophecy is far from establishing the truth of the explanation; but the mention of Egypt in verse 8 directs our attention to a country which will hereafter become the scene of the fulfilment of the prophecy.

Out of a branch of her roots.—The same words occur in Isa. xi. 1. The meaning is, "a branch growing from her roots shall stand up in the place of the person last mentioned." It is not easy to say which king is meant, nor is there any agreement among commentators as to what is intended by "her roots." According to one view, "her parents" are intended, so that "the branch" is some one of collateral descent with herself. According to another view the words mean "her family."

With an army.—Literally, *to the army.* Theodotion and the LXX. both translate by *δύναμιν*, which Theodoret explains to be a name for Jerusalem. The person spoken of comes to attack the army, and the fortress has been supposed to be Seleucia. However, the use of the plural "them" in the latter part of the verse makes it more probable that the word "fortress" is used collectively for fortified cities.

(8) **He shall continue.**—Apparently the meaning is (comp. the use of the preposition in verse 31) "He shall stand on the side of [*i.e.*, as an ally of] the northern king several years." Others translate, "He shall abstain from the king of the north some years." In either case the sense is nearly the same. The reference is said to be to the cessation of hostilities between Ptolemy and Seleucus, but there is nothing in these verses which leads us to infer what history states as a fact, that the northern king was completely crippled by a serious defeat, and that his fleet was dispersed by a storm.

(9) **The king of the south.**—According to the Hebrew text, these words are in the genitive case (so Theod. Jer.), though the English Version is supported by the LXX. In this case the meaning is, "The king of the north shall come into the kingdom of the southern king," and then shall return to his own land—*i.e.*, the north—apparently without gaining any advantage.

(10) **His sons.**—The pronoun refers to the subject of verse 9, which is the northern king (though, according to the LXX. and English Version, it must be his rival). There is a marginal alternative in the Hebrew "son." The LXX. supports the text. If the king of the north last mentioned is Seleucus Callinicus, his sons must be Seleucus Ceraunus, a man of no importance, and Antiochus the Great. It is here stated of the sons that they are stirred up; that they collect a vast army, which advances steadily, overflowing like a torrent, while its masses pass through the land; that they shall return and carry on the war up to the frontier of the southern king. Considering the uncertainty of the readings in the Hebrew text, and the ambiguity of the language, this is anything but a definite statement. However, it has been explained to refer to the wars of Antiochus and Ptolemy Philopator, in course of which they took Seleucia, Tyre, and Ptolemais, besieged the Egyptians in Sidon, and actually took possession of Gaza.

One shall certainly come.—Not the king, but the multitude just spoken of. The words "overflow," "pass through" "return," all refer to the ebbing and flowing of the tide of war.

(11) **And the king.**—The ambiguity of this verse is very great. "He" may refer to either king; so that while some commentators see in the words an account of the successes of Ptolemy against Antiochus in the battle of Raphia (B.C. 217)—the "multitude" being the army of Antiochus, which was severely defeated at that place—others infer that the northern king is represented as defeating his rival. Evidently the words "with the king

even with the king of the north: and
he shall set forth a great multitude;
but the multitude shall be given into
his hand. (12) *And* when he hath taken
away the multitude, his heart shall be
lifted up; and he shall cast down *many*
ten thousands: but he shall not be
strengthened *by it.* (13) For the king of
the north shall return, and shall set
forth a multitude greater than the
former, and shall certainly come [1]after
certain years with a great army and
with much riches. (14) And in those
times there shall many stand up against
the king of the south: also [2]the robbers
of thy people shall exalt themselves to
establish the vision; but they shall fall.
(15) So the king of the north shall come,
and cast up a mount, and take [3]the
most fenced cities: and the arms of the
south shall not withstand, neither [4]his
chosen people, neither *shall there be any*
strength to withstand. (16) But he that
cometh against him shall do according
to his own will, and none shall stand
before him: and he shall stand in the

1 Heb., *at the end of times of years.*

2 Heb., *the children of robbers.*

3 Heb., *the city of munitions.*

4 Heb., *the people of his choices.*

---

of the north" are added, as in Exod. ii. 6, for the sake of clearness. This makes it most probable that the first of the two interpretations just given is correct, and that "he" refers to the northern king, "his hand" to the hand of the southern king. This is supported by verse 12, where we read of the conduct of the southern king after his victory.

(12) **And when he.**—It is not clear whether "the multitude" or "the king" is subject of the sentence, or whether the verb "he hath taken away" is to be translated active or passive. The verse might mean, "And the multitude is lifted up—*i.e.*, takes courage—and its heart is exalted," or, "when the multitude takes courage the king's heart is exalted." The English translation is most in accordance with the context, but the second rendering is preferred by many, according to which the king's courage and pride increase as he perceives the mightiness of his troops. The LXX. follow a different reading throughout the verse.

And he shall cast down.—These words describe the victory of the southern king after he has taken the "multitude" of the northern king.

But he shall not be strengthened—*i.e.*, he does not prove so successful as he had hoped. His aim was to gain complete supremacy over his rival, but for reasons which are about to be stated he was unable to gain his object. Those interpreters who see a distinct reference to the wars of Ptolemy and Antiochus point out that though the loss of the Syrians was very great, yet Ptolemy did not follow up his success as he should have done. Instead of striking a decisive blow, he was content with regaining the towns which Antiochus had taken from him.

(13) **Shall return.**—In this and the next two verses the causes are mentioned to which the failure of the southern king was due. He returns some years after his defeat to take revenge, and brings with him a larger army than he had on the previous occasion.

Much riches—*i.e.*, all that is necessary for the maintenance of a large army; literally, *anything acquired.* This has been explained of the invasion of Egypt by Antiochus and Philip of Macedon, some thirteen or fourteen years after the battle of Raphia, when Ptolemy Epiphanes, a mere child, had succeeded his father, Philopator. On the hypothesis that these chapters refer to this period, it is surprising that there should be no allusion to the religious persecutions to which the Jews in Egypt had been subjected by Ptolemy Philopator, who, after his victory at Raphia, attempted to enter the Holy Place, as is mentioned in the Third Book of Maccabees. It should be remembered that the Jews suffered considerably from both parties during the whole of this period; but though the prophecy is supposed to have been written for their comfort and encouragement at this very juncture, yet not a word is said which bears allusion to them.

(14) **In those times.**—It must be noticed that at this verse—the earliest in which there is any reference to Daniel's people and to the vision (chap. x. 1, 7, 8)—we appear to be approaching the great crisis. We appear to be within "a very few days" (see verse 20) of the vile person who corresponds to the little horn of the fourth beast. At this period the king of the south suffers from many hostile opponents, while certain others, more closely connected with the Jews, become prominent for a while, but then fail. The obscurity of the Hebrew text was felt by the LXX., and distinct historical allusions can be found by those only who are determined to find them. These are stated to be some insurrections during the early years of Ptolemy Epiphanes, and a league which some of the Jews made with Antiochus the Great against Ptolemy.

Robbers of thy people.—This difficult expression occurs only in five other passages (Ps. xvii. 4; Isa. xxxv. 9; Jer. vii. 11; Ezek. vii. 22, xviii. 10). The words in this passage can only refer to certain Jews who committed various violent breaches of the Law, and on this occasion revolted against the king of the south.

To establish the vision.—The meaning is, the result of their acts is to bring about the accomplishment of the vision (chap. x. 14). The significant part of the verse is the "falling" of the robbers. It seems to mean that the conduct of these men shall bring them just the reverse of what they had expected.

(15) **The king of the north.**—This prince attacks the fortress of his rival, who is unable to resist him. Here it is supposed that the allusion is to the capture of Sidon by Antiochus the Great. The troops of Ptolemy under Scopas had acquired possession of Jerusalem and of various portions of Syria during the absence of Antiochus. Scopas and the Egyptian troops under him fled to Sidon, where they were forced by famine to surrender to the Syrians (B.C. 198).

The arms of the south.—Comp. verse 31. The phrase means the armed force of the south.

(16) **But he that cometh.**—We now hear of further proceedings of the northern king. He follows up the vision mentioned in the last verse, enters the glorious land (*i.e.*, Palestine), and commits great ravages in it. The king is described in language which reminds us of chap. xi. 3. He acts just as he pleases after his entrance to the southern kingdom. This has been applied to the con-

[1][2]glorious land, which by his hand shall
be consumed. (17)He shall also set his
face to enter with the strength of his
whole kingdom, and [3]upright ones with
him; thus shall he do: and he shall
give him the daughter of women, [4]cor-
rupting her: but she shall not stand *on*
his side, neither be for him. (18) After
this shall he turn his face unto the isles,
and shall take many: but a prince [5]for
his own behalf shall cause [6]the reproach
offered by him to cease; without his
own reproach he shall cause *it* to turn
upon him. (19) Then he shall turn his
face toward the fort of his own land:
but he shall stumble and fall, and not
be found.

(20) Then shall stand up in his estate
[7]a raiser of taxes *in* the glory of the
kingdom: but within few days he shall
be destroyed, neither in [8]anger, nor in
battle.

(21) And in his estate shall stand up a
vile person, to whom they shall not give

1 Or, *goodly land.*
2 Heb., *the land of ornament.*
3 Or, *much uprightness:* or, *equal conditions.*
4 Heb., *to corrupt.*
5 Heb., *for him.*
6 Heb., *his reproach.*
7 Heb., *one that causeth an exacter to pass over.*
8 Heb., *angers.*

---

duct of Antiochus the Great, but history does not speak of any acts of destruction committed by him in Palestine. On the contrary, it is recorded of him that he treated the Jews with kindness. (On the "glorious land," see chap. viii. 9.)

Which by his hand . . .—Literally, *destruction being in his hand.*

(17) **He shall also.**—He has further plans for subduing the dominions of the southern king. He brings together all the forces he can amass, and then attempts by means of a political marriage to establish peace; but this also proves a failure.

Upright ones.—Literally, *all that is right;* hence the words have been explained, "straightforward pleas." If "persons" are intended, it is not impossible that there may be a hint at the Jews taking the part of the northern king in the contest.

Daughter of women—*i.e.*, a woman. (Comp. the phrase "son of man," Ezek. ii. 1.) The rest of the verse is obscure. It seems to mean that the consequence of this marriage was the destruction of the woman mentioned. Or it is possible that "her" refers to the southern kingdom. St. Jerome explains it, "*ut evertat Ptolemœum sive regnum ejus.*" This has been supposed to point to the marriage of Ptolemy Epiphanes with Cleopatra, the daughter of Antiochus the Great. However, the language is very general. (Comp. verse 6.)

But she shall not stand.—These words form an explanatory clause, meaning that the plan will not answer.

(18) **Shall he turn.**—He goes northward, this being the direction indicated by "the isles." This has been explained of the victories gained by Antiochus the Great in Asia Minor. He is stated to have reduced various towns and islands, and finally to have taken Ephesus. He was in this way brought into contact with the Romans, and was defeated by L. Scipio, who is identified with "the prince" mentioned in this verse. The Greek versions exhibit considerable variations.

A prince.—It is doubtful whether this is to be taken as nominative or as accusative. The English Version treats it as nominative, St. Jerome and Theodotion as accusative. In accordance with the latter rendering, the meaning is, "The king of the north will cause to cease the princes who have been his reproach. But the princes shall return him his reproach." The word "prince" is used collectively to mean the rulers of the islands mentioned in the first part of the verse. It is stated that in the first instance the northern king will be successful, but in the end the princes will repay him the reproach which he inflicted upon them, as appears more fully in the next verse.

(19) **The fort.**—The king of the north is forced to take refuge in his fortresses, and here meets with his end. This is explained of the death of Antiochus the Great at Elymais, where he had profaned a temple.

(20) **A raiser of taxes.**—The marginal version is to be preferred, as it gives the meaning of the word "exactor," or "oppressor," which it has in Exod. iii. 7, and in every passage where it occurs, except perhaps Isa. ix. 4. The new king of the north causes the "oppressor" to pass through "the majesty of the kingdom" (a phrase occurring elsewhere only in Ps. cxlv. 12; but comp. 1 Chron. xxix. 25), meaning the "richest parts of his kingdom," and not necessarily Palestine. The effect of this policy was that the king fell a victim to a conspiracy in a few days. According to St. Jerome, the person alluded to was Seleucus Philopator.

With this verse the first part of the prophecy concludes. It is to be observed that thus far (1) notes of time are very scanty; we only meet with indefinite expressions, such as "in the end of years" (verse 6), "certain years" (verse 13), "within few days" (verse 20), and vague terms expressing sequence of time. (2) There is nothing in the text which implies any change of sovereigns, except in verses 7 and 19. It follows from a careful study of these verses that according to their natural and literal sense they speak of only two southern kings and only one northern king. The southern king of whom we read most is apparently the offspring of the daughter of the first southern king, mentioned in verse 5, and it is he who engages in conflict with the first northern king, and with his sons (verse 10). The whole prophecy is eschatological, and refers to two opposing earthly powers which will affect the destiny of God's people in the last times. It relates a series of wars and political intrigues between these two powers, all of which prove futile, and it concludes with the account of the death of the first northern king. Verse 20 is a transition verse, in which another character is introduced, who will mark the approach of the end; while verse 21 introduces the most prominent object of the prophecy—a person who remains before the reader till the end of the chapter, while the southern king gradually disappears (verses 25, 27, 40), and what is apparently his country is mentioned without its sovereign in verse 43.

(21) **A vile person.**—The meaning of the language will be plainer after a reference to Ps. cxix. 141; Jer. xxii. 28. The moral character of the man is especially described. The words that follow explain more fully that he was not worthy of receiving royal majesty. This person is generally identified with Antiochus Epiphanes. The description certainly agrees with him very closely. In fact, just as his predecessors resembled in various points the kings spoken of in verses 1—20, so Antiochus resembles the person here described. The language of St. Jerome about early

the honour of the kingdom: but he
shall come in peaceably, and obtain the
kingdom by flatteries. (22) And with the
arms of a flood shall they be overflown
from before him, and shall be broken;
yea, also the prince of the covenant.
(23) And after the league *made* with him
he shall work deceitfully: for he shall
come up, and shall become strong with
a small people. (24) He shall enter
[1] peaceably even upon the fattest places
of the province; and he shall do *that*
which his fathers have not done, nor
his fathers' fathers; he shall scatter
among them the prey, and spoil, and
riches: *yea,* and he shall [2] forecast his
devices against the strong holds, even
for a time. (25) And he shall stir up his
power and his courage against the king
of the south with a great army; and
the king of the south shall be stirred
up to battle with a very great and
mighty army; but he shall not stand:
for they shall forecast devices against
him. (26) Yea, they that feed of the
portion of his meat shall destroy him,
and his army shall overflow: and many
shall fall down slain. (27) And both these
kings' [3] hearts *shall be* to do mischief,
and they shall speak lies at one table;
but it shall not prosper: for yet the
end *shall be* at the time appointed.
(28) Then shall he return into his land
with great riches; and his heart *shall*

1 Or, *into the peaceable and fat, &c.*

2 Heb., *think his thoughts.*

3 Heb., *their hearts.*

---

interpreters of the Book of Daniel is striking: "*Cumque multa quæ postea lecturi et expositori sumus super Antiochi persona conveniant, typum eum volunt Antichristi habere, et quæ in illo ex parte præceperint, in Antichristo ex toto esse complenda.*"

Peaceably.—Unexpectedly, as LXX. (Comp. chap. viii. 25.) The king is here represented as taking possession of the kingdom by craft, and in the following clause he is said to gain his end by "flatteries," or by intrigues and cunning hypocritical conduct. It does not appear that this was done by Antiochus Epiphanes.

(22) **With the arms.**—More correctly, *and the arms in a flood;* that is, the overwhelming forces of invading armies are swept away by the troops of this terrible king. But besides the enemy, the "prince of the covenant" is to be destroyed also. This expression is most readily explained by observing that it stands in contrast with the hostile armies mentioned in the first clause. It is an expression similar to "men of covenant," "lords of covenant," and means "those who were at peace with him," "prince" being used as a collective noun (see verse 18). This has been supposed to refer to the murder of Onias III. (2 Macc. iv. 1, &c., 33, &c.); but there is no reason for supposing that the high priest was ever called by such a title as "prince of the covenant."

(23) **He shall work.**—Apparently this verse explains more fully the means by which the king succeeds in maintaining his influence. He has already destroyed those who are at peace with him. From the time that he first becomes their confederate, he works deceitfully, coming up with hostile intent, accompanied only by a few people, and in this way throwing off their guard those whom he would destroy.

(24) **Peaceably.**—The subject continues to be the perfidious conduct of the king mentioned in the last two verses. While the inhabitants are expecting nothing of the sort, he enters the richest parts of the province, and while he scatters largesses with profuseness and in apparent friendship, he is really planning attacks against the fortresses of the district, endeavouring to reduce them into his power.

This has been referred to the conduct of Antiochus Epiphanes, mentioned in 1 Macc. iii. 27—30, after the defeat of the Syrian army by Judas Maccabæus. According to another interpretation, the meaning is that he will scatter or disperse the accumulated wealth of the different provinces "among them"—that is, to their hurt. The former explanation appears to be most in accordance with the deceit and craft which the prophecy attributes to the king.

For a time.—That is, the end of the time decreed by God. (Comp. verse 35, chaps. viii. 17, 19, xii. 4, 6.)

(25) **The south.**—Here, for the first time in the second portion of the prophecy, mention is made of the southern king. It is highly probable that the deceit mentioned in the last three verses had this king and his provinces for its object. This and the next two verses are supposed to describe the war of Antiochus with Ptolemy Philometor (see 1 Macc. i. 16—19), or his war with Physcon, on which see Livy, xliv. 19.

His power and his courage—*i.e.,* his military skill as well as his personal energy.

But he shall not stand.—Comp. chap. viii. 4. The subject is the king of the south, who finds the devices of his opponent are more than a match for him. The "devices" are explained in the next two verses.

(26) **They that feed.**—The context points to treachery. The false companions of the southern king betray him to the enemy; he is broken, the hostile army pours in, and many are slain. This has been referred to the second campaign of Antiochus in Egypt; however, history is silent of any treachery against Physcon. St. Jerome remarks: "*Nostri secundum superiorem sensum interpretantur omnia de Antichristo qui nasciturus est de populo Judæorum, et de Babylone venturus, primum superaturus est regem Egypti, qui est unus de tribus cornibus.*"

(27) **Both these kings.**—The two rival kings are here described as living upon terms of outward friendship, while each is inwardly trying to outwit the other. The context is opposed to any reference to the combination of Antiochus and Philometor against Physcon (see Livy, xlv. 11; Polyb. xxix. 8). The object of the paragraph is to show that the southern king was attempting to fight his rival with his own weapons—viz., deceit—but the plots of each king fail.

For yet . . .—*i.e.,* the end of each will come only at the time definitely ordained by God for the consummation of His kingdom (verse 35). Man cannot hasten the events decreed by God's providence. For an interesting commentary, read Isa. xviii. 4—6.

(28) **Then shall he return.**—He returns, apparently bringing abundant spoils with him, and while on the journey sets his heart against the holy covenant.

be against the holy covenant; and he
shall do *exploits*, and return to his own
land.
(29) At the time appointed he shall
return, and come toward the south; but
it shall not be as the former, or as the
latter. (30) For the ships of Chittim
shall come against him: therefore he
shall be grieved, and return, and have
indignation against the holy covenant:
so shall he do; he shall even return,
and have intelligence with them that
forsake the holy covenant. (31) And
arms shall stand on his part, and they
shall pollute the sanctuary of strength,
and shall take away the daily *sacrifice*,
and they shall place the abomination
that [1] maketh desolate. (32) And such as
do wickedly against the covenant shall
he [2] corrupt by flatteries: but the people
that do know their God shall be strong,
and do *exploits*. (33) And they that un-
derstand among the people shall instruct
many: yet they shall fall by the sword,
and by flame, by captivity, and by spoil,
many days. (34) Now when they shall
fall, they shall be holpen with a little
help: but many shall cleave to them

1 Or, *astonisheth.*

2 Or, *cause to dissemble.*

Great riches.—The prophecy points distinctly to Antiochus after his return from Egypt. (See 1 Macc. i. 19—28; 2 Macc. v. 11—17.) This was the occasion of his first attack upon the theocracy. The typical character of Antiochus is drawn in verses 30, &c., with still greater clearness.

He shall do—*i.e.*, prosper in his undertakings against the covenant. (See the passages from the Books of Maccabees referred to in the last Note.)

(29) **At the time appointed**—*i.e.*, in God's own time. According to 1 Macc. i. 29, it was after two years were fully expired since his return to Syria that Antiochus made another attack upon Jerusalem. This attack was made after his return from Egypt.

But it shall not be.—No such success attended him at the latter as at the former invasion.

(30) **Ships of Chittim.**—On Chittim, see Gen. x. 4; comp. Num. xxiv. 24. The LXX. explain this of the Romans, referring to the story in Livy, xlv. 11.

He shall be grieved.—Literally, *he shall lose heart.* Compare the words of Livy, which describe the feelings of Antiochus at the peremptory demands of Popilius: "*Obstupefactus tam violento imperio.*" Theodotion apparently imagined that the Cyprians came as allies to the aid of Antiochus.

Return.—That is, to Palestine, where he will indulge his anger.

Have intelligence—*i.e.*, pay attention to them. These persons are such as those who are mentioned in 1 Macc. i. 11—16, who were anxious to Hellenise all their institutions, not only forsaking the outward sign of the covenant, but actually taking Greek names.

On the manner in which Antiochus treated the apostates, see 2 Macc. iv. 14, &c., and comp. verse 39.

(31) **Arms.**—A further statement of the assistance which the king obtains in his attacks upon all sacred institutions. The word "arms," as in verse 5, means "assistance," especially military assistance, or some other aid, with which is contrasted in the next verse the help given by the apostates.

The sanctuary of strength.—In the Hebrew (see Theodotion) there are two nouns in apposition. Apparently the two words are a name for the Temple, which is so called because it was the spiritual support of God's people, as well as a very powerful fortress. (See Isa. xxv. 4, &c.; Ps. xxxi. 2—4; and compare 1 Macc. i. 44, vi. 7; 2 Macc. vi. 4, which speak of the various deeds of Antiochus upon this occasion.) On the daily sacrifice, and on the abomination of desolation, see the Notes on chap. viii. 13.

(32) **Such as do wickedly.**—In these verses are traced the effects of the apostasy upon the people of God. These persons have been already spoken of in verse 30. They had begun with indifference to true religion, they have now become intolerant of it.

Corrupt.—Literally, *make profane.* On the Hebrew notion of profanity, see Cheyne's *Isaiah*, vol. i., p. 3. These persons have now become as the heathen. (See 1 Macc. ii. 17, 18.)

But the people. . . .—While the large mass of people becomes obedient to the persecutor, there is a party of true believers remaining, who are "strong," or rather, confirm the covenant, and "do," *i.e.*, succeed in their attempt. That such a party existed in the time of Antiochus Epiphanes appears from 1 Macc. i. 62, &c., ii. 3, &c. Similarly in all times of persecution there will be a remnant, though it may be very small, which will remain firm to their covenant with God. (Comp. 1 Kings xix. 18.)

(33) **They that understand.**—This is the name by which those are called who were spoken of in the last verse as "knowing their God." (Comp. chap. xii. 10; Ps. cxi. 10.)

Shall instruct many.—That is, their example shall give instruction to "the many" who yield to the flatteries mentioned in the last verse. They show them whither they are drifting. For illustration, see 1 Macc. ii. 1, &c.; 2 Macc. vi. 18. Others may be found in the history of any religious persecution.

Yet they shall fall.—The prophecy obviously refers to martyrdom, but whether to the sufferings of "those who understand" or of "those who are instructed" is not clear. Probably both are intended, as appears from verse 35. The deaths mentioned in 1 Macc. i. 57, &c., iii. 41, v. 13, may be taken as typical of the sufferings of the Church in the last times.

(34) **Now when they shall fall.**—Referring to those who suffer during this persecution, to whichever class they belong. (See last Note). These will not be entirely without help, but there will be some small assistance given them. It will be small, either compared with their present needs, or contrasted with the great help which will be given them when the tribulation attains its greatest severity. In the Maccabee persecutions help was given to the sufferers by Judas and his brethren (1 Macc. iii. 11, &c., iv. 14, &c.). This prevented the faithful from disappearing entirely.

Many shall cleave. . . .—Dissimulation will cause some to declare themselves upon the side of "those that understand." This is a feature which will

with flatteries. (35) And *some* of them
of understanding shall fall, to try [1] them,
and to purge, and to make *them* white,
even to the time of the end: because *it*
is yet for a time appointed.
(36) And the king shall do according
to his will; and he shall exalt himself,
and magnify himself above every god,
and shall speak marvellous things
against the God of gods, and shall
prosper till the indignation be accomplished:
for that that is determined
shall be done. (37) Neither shall he
regard the God of his fathers, nor the
desire of women, nor regard any god:
for he shall magnify himself above all.
(38) But [2] in his estate shall he honour
the God of [3][4] forces: and a god whom
his fathers knew not shall he honour
with gold, and silver, and with precious
stones, and [5] pleasant things. (39) Thus
shall he do in the [6] most strong holds
with a strange god, whom he shall
acknowledge *and* increase with glory:
and he shall cause them to rule over
many, and shall divide the land for
[7] gain.
(40) And at the time of the end shall
the king of the south push at him: and
the king of the north shall come against
him like a whirlwind, with chariots, and
with horsemen, and with many ships;

1 Or, *by them.*

2 Heb., *as for the almighty God, in his seat he shall honour, yea, he shall honour a god whom, &c.*

3 Or, *munitions.*

4 Heb., *Mauzzim.*

5 Heb., *things desired.*

6 Heb., *fortresses of munitions.*

7 Heb., *a price.*

---

be noticed in religious persecutions; according as one party or the other gains in power, as its prospects brighten, it gains fresh adherents. This held true in the days of Antiochus. (See 1 Macc. vi. 21, &c., ix. 23.)

(35) **Some of them.**—The reason of this persecution is revealed. Whilst in verse 33 it appears that the sufferings of "those that understand" would instruct others, it appears that they would themselves profit by their sufferings. These gradations are mentioned (1) "to try"—*i.e.*, to refine, as a precious metal is refined by fire; (2) "to purge"—*i.e.*, to separate the bad from the good; (3) "to make white"—*i.e.*, to cause them to become completely purified. (Comp. Ps. li. 7; Isa. i. 18). In this way the dissemblers are made known. The patient example of the sufferers is followed by others who are faithful, while the "flatterers" become open apostates.

(36) **The king.**—He raises himself by his thoughts and deeds, not only above the heathen deities, but above the true God. Though there can be no doubt that the northern king is still spoken of, it must be remarked that the features of Antiochus are gradually fading away from the portrait. In no sense can Antiochus be called an Atheist; nor does the language of the writer of 2 Macc. ix. 12, "think of himself as if he were God," correspond with the words of this verse. Antiochus' main object was to Hellenise the Jewish religion, and to force the Greek gods upon the Jews. The character of the northern king, on the contrary, finds a parallel in St. Paul's description of Antichrist (2 Thess. ii. 4).

Marvellous things.—That is, his utterances and blasphemies against the true God will be astounding. (Comp. chap. vii. 8, 11, 20.) This will continue till God's indignation against His people is accomplished.

(37) **Neither shall they.**—A further description is now given of the godlessness of this king, but the people of Israel are no longer mentioned in their relation to him. The northern king appears twice again in Palestine (verses 41, 45), and apparently dies there. He discards his hereditary religion, he has no regard to that natural affection which women look upon as most desirable, but exalts himself over all.

Desire of women.—The language used by Isaiah (chap. xliv. 9), "delectable things," has led some commentators to think that an idol is here intended. It has been stated that the allusion is to the Asiatic goddess of nature, Mylitta, who, again, has been identified with the "queen of heaven" (Jer. vii. 18, where see Notes). The context, however, leads us rather to think of human affection, or some other thing highly prized by women, for the words "neither shall he regard any god" would be unmeaning if a god were designated by "the desire of women." It should be remembered that according to Polybius xxvi. 10, sec. 11, Antiochus exceeded all kings in the sacrifices which he offered at the gates, and in the honours which he paid to the gods.

In his estate—*i.e.*, in the place of the God whom he has rejected, he will worship the "god of forces." There is no reason for taking this to be a proper name, as is done by the Syriac translator and Theodotion. It can only mean "fortresses" (see margin), so that the whole religion of this king is the taking of fortresses. To him war is everything, and to war everything else must give way. To war, as if it were a god, he does honour with all his wealth.

(39) **A strange god.**—By this help he carries out his schemes, and all who acknowledge him are rewarded. (Comp. Rev. xiii. 4, 16, 17.)

Divide the land.—This is evidently done as a reward offered to those who join his ranks. No such conduct of Antiochus is recorded. Bribery, however, was not an unusual mode of persuasion adopted by him. (See 1 Macc. ii. 18, iii. 30.)

(40) **At the time of the end.**—These verses speak of the last expedition of the northern king, and of the disappearance of the king of the south. The portrait of Antiochus, as noticed in the Note on verse 36, was gradually fading away, and now not a line of it remains. No such invasion of Egypt as that mentioned here is mentioned in history. From the time mentioned in verse 30 he appears to have abstained from approaching too closely to the Roman authorities. The story related in 1 Macc. iii. 27—37 states that on hearing of the successes of the Maccabee princes he went into Persia on a plundering expedition, leaving Lysias his representative in Palestine. Lysias was defeated at Bethsur, and the news of the overthrow of his army was brought to Antiochus while he was in Persia. So appalling was the effect upon him of these tidings, that "he fell sick for grief" (1 Macc. vi. 8), and died. It is unnecessary to suppose that the revelation resumes the narrative from verse 29 after a parenthetic passage (verses 30—39), or to assume that we have a general recapitulation of the wars of Antiochus, described in verses 22—39, without distinguishing the different campaigns. (For a good account of Antiochus, see *Judas Maccabæus*, by C. R. Conder, R.E., chap. iii.)

and he shall enter into the countries, and shall overflow and pass over. (41) He shall enter also into the [1,2]glorious land, and many *countries* shall be overthrown: but these shall escape out of his hand, *even* Edom, and Moab, and the chief of the children of Ammon. (42) He shall [3]stretch forth his hand also upon the countries: and the land of Egypt shall not escape. (43) But he shall have power over the treasures of gold and of silver, and over all the precious things of Egypt: and the Libyans and the Ethiopians *shall be* at his steps. (44) But tidings out of the east and out of the north shall trouble him: therefore he shall go forth with great fury to destroy, and utterly to make away many. (45) And he shall plant the tabernacles of his palace between the seas in the [4,5]glorious holy mountain; yet he shall come to his end, and none shall help him.

CHAPTER XII.—(1) And at that time shall Michael stand up, the great prince which standeth for the children of thy people: and there shall be a time of trouble, such as never was since there was a nation *even* to that same time: and at that time thy people shall be delivered, every one that shall be found written in the book. (2) And many of them that sleep in the dust of the earth shall awake, [a]some to everlasting life,

1 Or, *goodly land.*

2 Heb., *land of delight,* or, *ornament.*

3 Heb., *send forth.*

4 Or, *goodly.*

5 Heb., *mountain of delight of holiness.*

a Matt. 25. 46; John 5. 29.

Time of the end.—Comp. chap. viii. 17. The words mean the end of the world, with which (verse 45) the end of this king coincides. The word "push" occurs also in chap. viii. 4, and from the context it may be inferred that the southern king begins the last conflict, in the course of which both kings come to an end.

(41) **The glorious land.**—See verse 16. On the occasion of his hasty march against Egypt, while passing through Palestine, the king takes the shortest route, avoiding the three tribes which had been distinguished by their hostility towards the people of Israel. It is remarkable that these nations (two of which appear as figures of Antichrist, Isa. xxv. 10, lxiii. 1) should escape, while other nations fell before Antichrist. It is also noteworthy that these three tribes are called nations, for after the return from the exile it appears that they ceased to have any distinct national existence. As tribes they had some considerable power, taking the part of Antiochus in the Maccabee wars. (See 1 Macc. iii. 10, v. 1—8.) Judas also fortified Zion against the Idumæans.

The chief of—*i.e.*, the best of them. (Comp. Num. xxiv. 20.)

(42) **He shall stretch forth.**—He seizes various countries through which he passes, and among them Egypt is especially selected for mention, representing, as it does, the most powerful of them. The king has at last attained his object. He has frequently been partially successful in his attempts (see verses 12, 13, 15, 29), but now Egypt is completely overthrown.

(43) **Libyans . . . Ethiopians.**—These nations are specified as allies of Egypt. (See Ezek. xxx. 5; Jer. xlvi. 9.) They are represented as following the steps of the conqueror (comp. Exod. xi. 8), and as submitting themselves to him.

(44) **He shall go forth.**—The end of the northern king. While in Egypt he has bad news brought to him from the north and from the east, which stirs up feelings of revenge. Once again he halts in Palestine, where he comes to an end. That this cannot apply to Antiochus is evident from the following facts—(1) Antiochus was in Persia when the news of the defeat of Lysias reached him; (2) Judæa and Jerusalem cannot in any sense be regarded as either east or north of Persia; (3) Antiochus died in Persia, and not near Jerusalem.

(45) **He shall plant . . .**—For a similar prophecy, comp. Jer. xliii. 10 (where see the Targum). The king is here represented as halting while a palatial tent is being erected for him. The word "palace" is omitted by the LXX., and simply transliterated "Apedno" by St. Jerome and Theodotion, as if it were a proper name.

Between the seas—*i.e.*, between the Mediterranean and the Dead Sea.

The glorious holy mountain.—Literally, *The mountain of the holy ornament*, generally explained to be Mount Zion. (Comp. Ps. xlviii. 2.) This he threatens, as once did the Assyrian (comp. Isa. x. 32—34), but without success.

He shall come to his end.—It is to be remarked that the end of this king is placed in the same locality which is elsewhere predicted by the prophets as the scene of the overthrow of Antichrist (Ezek. xxxix. 4; Joel iii. 2, 12; Zech. xiv. 2).

XII.

(1) **At that time**—*i.e.*, in the times spoken of in chap. xi. 45, previous to the overthrow of the king. During the tribulation which precedes his overthrow, Michael (see chap. x. 13) comes to stand up in aid of the people.

A time of trouble.—This is the tribulation spoken of in Matt. in xxiv. 21, 22, which follows, as it does in the Book of Daniel, the wars, rumours of wars, and uprisings of sundry nations. (See Matt. xxiv. 6, 7.) It should be observed that the mere presence of Michael does not avert the times of trouble. He helps God's people during the time of their trouble. On the mode in which the intensity of the tribulation is described, comp. Jer. xxx. 7.

Written in the book.—Comp. chap. vii. 10; Phil. iv. 3; and see Note on Exod. xxxii. 32.

(2) **Many . . . that sleep in the dust.**—Literally, *Many sleepers in the land of dust.* The word "sleep" is applied to death (Jer. li. 39; comp. 1 Thess. iv. 14); while "dust" is used for the grave (Ps. xxii. 29). Some difficulty is presented by the use of the word "many" where "all" would have been expected. Theodoret explains it from Rom. v. 15, where he observes "many" stands for "all." It is, however, more in accordance with the language to suppose that by the word "many" some contrast is implied, which is apparently between the *many* who sleep in the dust and the comparatively small number of those

and some to shame *and* everlasting con-
tempt. (3) And they that be [1] wise shall
[a] shine as the brightness of the firmament;
and they that turn many to righteousness
as the stars for ever and ever.

(4) But thou, O Daniel, shut up the
words, and seal the book, *even* to the
time of the end: many shall run to and
fro, and knowledge shall be increased.

(5) Then I Daniel looked, and, behold,
there stood other two, the one on this
side of the [2] bank of the river, and the
other on that side of the bank of the
river. (6) And *one* said to the man clothed
in [b] linen, which *was* [3] upon the waters
of the river, How long *shall it be to* the
end of these wonders? (7) And I heard
the man clothed in linen, which *was*
upon the waters of the river, when he
[c] held up his right hand and his left
hand unto heaven, and sware by him
that liveth for ever that *it shall be*
for a time, times, and [4] an half; and
when he shall have accomplished to
scatter the power of the holy people,
all these *things* shall he finished.

(8) And I heard, but I understood not:
then said I, O my Lord, what *shall be*

1 Or, *teachers.*
a Matt. 13. 43.
2 Heb., *lip.*
b ch. 10. 5.
3 Or, *from above.*
c Rev. 10. 5.
4 Or, *part.*

---

who "are alive and remain." (See John v. 28, &c.) It should be noted that this passage not only teaches the doctrine of a general resurrection, which had already been incidentally revealed by Daniel's contemporary, Ezekiel (chap. xxxvii. 1—4), but also the facts of eternal life, and a resurrection of the unjust as well as of the just.

Shame and everlasting contempt.—The latter word occurs only in this passage and Isa. lxvi. 24, where see the Note. For the use of the word "shame," comp. Jer. xxiii. 40.

(3) **They that be wise.**—Comp. Matt. xiii. 43, Notes. "The wise" are the same as "those that understand" who were spoken of in chap. xi. 33, meaning those who by their own righteousness—that is, by their faithfulness to their covenant with God—had set a bright example to the others, as in chap. xi. 35. Such is the consolation held out for the support of those who shall witness the tribulation of the last days. (See Notes on Matt. xxiv. and the parallel passages.)

(4) **Shut up the words.**—The revelation, which commenced in chap. x. 20, now draws towards a close, and the prophet receives a further revelation respecting the time of the end. The revelation continues to be called by the same name, "the words," as in chap. x. 1; and now the prophet is told that the book in which this revelation is written must be placed in a safe and sure place, for the need of it will be felt in "the time of the end," that is, in the time when the fulfilment makes the meaning of the prophecy clear and unambiguous.

Many shall run to and fro.—The verb "to run" is used in Jer. v. 1 of searching after knowledge. In this sense it is used of "the eyes of the Lord" (Zech. iv. 10; comp. Amos viii. 12). In the same sense it is used in this verse. Many will anxiously search in this book for knowledge of the manner of God's dealings with His people, and will derive comfort and understanding therefrom.

(5) **Other two.**—Two heavenly beings are now seen by the prophet. As the absence of the article shows he had not seen them before, St. Jerome supposes them to be the angels of Persia and Greece, but of course it is impossible to identify them.

The river—*i.e.*, the Hiddekel, as in chap. x. 4, though a different word for "river" is used, which is generally employed to designate the Nile. For the reason of the choice of this word, see the next Note.

(6) **And one said.**—The speaker is evidently one of the persons just mentioned, but the LXX. and St. Jerome suppose Daniel to address the man clothed in white linen, who is obviously the same person who has already spoken (chap. x. 5, &c.). The position which he occupies is striking. He appears "*upon*" or (see margin) from above, *i.e.*, hovering over the waters of the Tigris. If, as is frequently the case in the symbolical language of Scripture (see Isa. viii. 6, 7, Ps. xciii. 4), waters or streams are the emblems of nationalities, the Hiddekel will represent the Persian Empire, in the third year of which Daniel had this vision, and the position of the person implies his power to protect his people from all the assaults of the Persians. But at the same time, the remarkable word used for "river" recalls the Nile, and seems to be employed for the purpose of assuring the readers of the book that "He who smote the waters of the Nile" will restrain all earthly powers which war against His people.

How long . . end.—The end is that which has been frequently spoken of (chaps. xi. 40—xii. 3). The question asks, "How long will the end of these wonders continue? The end always appears to be at hand, yet it never comes. How long will this continue?"

(7) **Held up his right hand . . .**—In general, a person when swearing lifted up the right hand only (see Gen. xiv. 22; Deut. xxxii. 40). Both hands are represented here as being raised up, so as to give greater importance to the words. (See Note on Rev. x. 5, and comp. chap. iv. 34.)

A time, times . . .—See Note on chap. vii. 25; and observe that any reference to the period of the persecution under Antiochus is impossible, on account of the difference between the measures of time. (See chap. vii. 14.)

To scatter.—The ancient versions (not the LXX., however) appear to have understood this to mean the dispersion of Israel (see Deut. vii. 6), and seem to have connected the "*end*," of which Daniel speaks, with the cessation of the dispersion of Israel, or, in other words, to have regarded it as a prediction of the re-gathering of Israel, which would immediately precede the coming of Elias. (See the remarks of Theodoret on the passage.) But by the "holy people" are meant, more probably, those who shall suffer in the last days (comp. chap. vii. 25, "the saints"), and the word "scatter" means to break in pieces, as Ps. ii. 9, &c. So that the words imply that the end will not come till "the shattering of the power of the saints" has been accomplished, or till persecution appears to have stamped out all that remains of godliness. This makes the prophecy accord with chap. vii. 25 and the parallel passages in the New Testament.

(8) **I understood not.**—He did not understand the answer given in verse 7. The question did not seem

the end of these *things?* (9) And he said, Go thy way, Daniel: for the words *are* closed up and sealed till the time of the end. (10) Many shall be purified, and made white, and tried; but the wicked shall do wickedly: and none of the wicked shall understand; but the wise shall understand. (11) And from the time *that* the daily *sacrifice* shall be taken away, and [1]the abomination that [2]maketh desolate set up, *there shall be* a thousand two hundred and ninety days. (12) Blessed *is* he that waiteth, and cometh to the thousand three hundred and five and thirty days. (13) But go thou thy way till the end *be:* [3]for thou shalt rest, and stand in thy lot at the end of the days.

1 Heb., *to set up the abomination, &c.*

2 Or, *astonisheth.*

3 Or, *and thou, &c.*

---

to have had any reply. It had been asked how long the end should continue, and the answer had been only the obscure words, "time, times, and an half."

What shall be the end?—Daniel refers to the "wonderful things" mentioned in verse 6, and using a different word for "end," asks which of these wonders is to be the last—*i.e.*, which of them is to come immediately before the end of all things.

(9) **Go thy way.**—That is, be at peace. Observe that the matter is not explained to Daniel any further. He is assured that the end will most certainly come. Compare another gentle rebuke that was addressed to one who wished to see further than was fitting into the future (John xxi. 21, 22).

Closed up and sealed.—To be explained as in verse 4. The book is to be carefully preserved till the end of time.

(10) **Many shall be purified.**—See Notes on Rev. xxii. 11, and comp. chap. xi. 35. The words imply that all shall be fulfilled, the time of persecution shall certainly arise, the righteous will be purified, while the wicked will become apostates. The wise (see chap. xi. 33), and they only, will understand the true meaning and profit of tribulation as it is set forth in this prophecy.

(11) **From the time.**—It appears as if at this verse the prophecy recurs to the more immediate future, and that these words point to the same subject as chap. xi. 31. The language used respecting the "abomination" is almost verbally the same as that in chaps. viii. 3, 11, ix. 27, and prevents us from arriving at any other conclusion. The great and apparently insoluble difficulty is the relation which the 1,290 or the 1,335 days occupy with regard to the 2,300 days, or the time, times, and the dividing of a time. Assuming that these four periods all commence at the same epoch (see Note on chap. viii. 14), the death of Antiochus closes the 1,290 days, and the 1,335 days point to some event which occurred forty-five days, or a month and a half, later. The principal objection to this view is that the exact date of the death of Antiochus is uncertain, and therefore all calculations based upon the precise day of his death must be untrustworthy. It is obvious that neither of the two periods mentioned in this and the following verse can be made to agree with three years and a half without setting the rules of arithmetic at defiance. Also the obscurity which rests over the greater portion of the history of Israel should guard us against assuming that we can explain all the contents of the last three chapters by means of what occurred in those times, and also against assuming our historical facts from Daniel, and then making use of them to illustrate his prophecies.

(12) **Blessed is he.**—Last words to Daniel. He shall rest in the grave, and stand up in his own lot at the end of the days.

(13) **In thy lot.**—The reference is to the partition of Palestine by lot in the times of Joshua. Even so shall one greater than Joshua divide the heavenly Canaan among His saints who follow Daniel in faith, firmness, and consistency. (See Col. i. 12.)

CHRONOLOGICAL TABLES, ILLUSTRATIVE OF THE PROPHECIES OF DANIEL.

B.C.

605. Deportation of Daniel.
604. First Year of Nebuchadnezzar.
598. Submission of Jehoiakim.
597. Deportation of Jehoiachin. Reign of Zedekiah commences.
593. Rebellion of Zedekiah. Date of Ezek. i.—vii.
592. Date of Ezek. viii.—xix.
591. Date of Ezek. xx.—xxiii.
590. War of Cyaxares with Alyattes.
389. Nebuchadnezzar comes to Riblah. Date of Ezek. xxiv.—xxv.
588. Date of Ezek. xxix. 1—16.
587. Fall of Jerusalem. Capture of Zedekiah. Date of Ezek. xxvi.—xxviii., xxx. 20—26, xxxi.
586. Siege of Tyre resumed. Ezek. xxxii.—xxxiv., xxxv. (?), xxxvi.—xxxix. (?)
582. Deportation of Jews, mentioned Jer. lii. 20 (Nebuchadnezzar's 23rd year).

B.C.

577. Probable Capture of Tyre.
573. Date of Ezek. xl.—xlviii.
571. Date of Ezek. xxix. 17—xxx. 20.
562. Death of Nebuchadnezzar. Evil Merodach.
561. Release of Jehoiachin, aged 55.
560. Murder of Evil Merodach. Neriglissar or Nergal-Sharezer.
559. Accession of Cyrus to the Median Empire.
556. Laborosoarchod. Nabonidus.
541. Probable date of Dan. vii. Belshazzar's 1st year (?)
539. Date of Dan. viii. (?) Fall of Babylon, Dan. v. Darius the Mede. Date of Dan. ix.
538. First year of Cyrus according to the Scripture reckoning. Return of the Jews under Zerubbabel.
537. Foundation Stone of the Temple laid.
536. Samaritan Opposition. Date of Dan. x—xii.

GENEALOGICAL TABLE OF THE PTOLEMIES AND SELEUCIDÆ, ILLUSTRATIVE OF THE LAST THREE CHAPTERS OF THE PROPHET DANIEL.

Seleucus Nicator.

Antiochus I. (Soter) B.C. 280.

Ptolemy (Soter). Dan. xi. 5.

Ptolemy Philadelphus, B.C. 285—247. Dan. xi. 6.

Laodice = Antiochus II. (Theos.) = Berenice

Laodice: Deposed for the sake of Berenice. She afterwards murdered Antiochus.

Antiochus II.: B.C. 261—246. Dan. xi. 6.

An infant murdered by Laodice.

Ptolemy Evergetes, B.C. 285—247. Dan. xi. 7. 8

Seleucus Callinicus (died B.C. 226)

Antiochus.

Ptolemy Philopator, B.C. 222—205. Dan. xi. 10—12.

Seleucus Ceraunus, Assassinated B.C. 223.

Antiochus III. (Magnus) B.C. 224. Dan. xi. 10—12, 14.

Antiochus IV. B.C. 175. Epiphanes.

Seleucus Philopator.

Cleopatra = Ptolemy Epiphanes, B.C. 205—181. Dan. xi. 14.

Antiochus V. B.C. 164.

Demetrius.

Ptolemy Philometor, B.C. 181—146. Dan. xi. 25—30.

Ptolemy Evergetes II.

⁂ It must be noticed that only the principal characters are inserted in the above genealogy, and also that the application of them to the passages in Daniel rests upon only one system of interpretation.

EXCURSUS ON NOTES TO DANIEL

EXCURSUS A: THE BABYLONIAN FORM OF GOVERNMENT.

In the Babylonian records hitherto deciphered very few government officials are mentioned. Of military officers we find generals spoken of, and of civil officers, judges. If we bear in mind that the object of the inscriptions was to magnify the king rather than to give an account of the internal social organisation of the country, we shall not find much difficulty in accounting for the silence with which state officials are treated. Enough, however, remains of an ancient inscription some centuries earlier than Daniel (see *Trans. Soc. Bibl. Arch.*, vol. i , p. 31) to show that the government of the country was carried on by "viceroys" and "rulers." None of the names of the state officials mentioned by Daniel are etymologically connected with these, nor, strange to say, have any traces been found in the inscriptions of Nebuchadnezzar of the three state officers mentioned by Jeremiah—Rab-Mag, Rab-Saris, Sar-Sechim.

It remains for us, in the face of this silence, to trace out as far as possible from Daniel's language what was the form of government at Babylon in his days. He mentions :—(1) *Princes*. This is apparently a Persian word, which in Greek takes the form of *satrap*. It occurs again in Dan. vi. 1, &c.; Ezra viii. 36; Esth. iii. 12. As the name implies, these persons were guardians of the subject kingdoms, and representatives of the monarch. They are called "kings" (Isa. x. 8), and with respect to them the monarch is called "king of kings" (Ezek. xxvi. 7). (2) *Governors*, also of Persian derivation, meaning commanders. From the position of the word (Jer. li. 57), between "captains" and "mighty men," it appears that they were military officers. (3) *Captains*, also a Persian word, though occurring as early as 1 Kings x. 15. The position of these officials at Babylon is known from Jer. li. 57, Ezek. xxiii. 6, 23. In Persian times the title is given to the rulers of Palestine (Neh. v. 14), or to the governors of Persian provinces (Esth. iii. 12). They were subordinate to the "princes," their functions being civil rather than military. (4) *Judges*, apparently from a Semitic root, meaning "to decree." The word does not occur elsewhere, but if the etymology is correct it must mean literally "a decider." (5) *Treasurers*, a Persian word connected with the same root as the word "gaza." (6) *Counsellors*, connected with a Persian word meaning "law," which is found in the books of Daniel and Esther. (7) *Sheriffs*, a Semitic word, apparently formed from a root which signifies "to give just sentence." (8) *Rulers*, a Semitic word, the root of which is frequently found in Hebrew, whence also the modern word "Sultan" is derived.

It appears that of the eight classes of officers mentioned by Daniel, seven may be arranged in three groups: (1) provincial rulers; (2) home ministers; (3) legal advisers. The last class, the "rulers," may perhaps comprehend the three classes already mentioned, or else may denote the subordinate rulers in each province.

These groups may be arranged as follows:—(1) Provincial officers, consisting of princes, governors, and captains. It appears as if the officers are arranged in descending order of magnitude; and first is placed the superior officer who administered the affairs of the province. As was observed above, under the Assyrian rule he was called a king, and as Daniel applies to Nebuchadnezzar the title of king of kings (chap. ii. 37), it is probable that the same custom prevailed in Babylon. He seems, therefore, to correspond to the "viceroy" who is mentioned in the ancient inscription cited above. Although the name of this officer was applied in Persian times to the satrap, it appears that under the Babylonian empire the person thus designated held a higher position than the Persian satrap. After the prince comes the governor, who, being a military man, stands to the prince in the same position as the commander of an army does to the governor of a colony. His duties were entirely secular, the only evidence to the contrary being the use of the word "governor" in chap. ii. 48. The last in authority is the captain. He most closely resembles the Persian satrap, as his office appears to be of a civil rather than of a military character. Thus far it appears that the Babylonian government was carried on by viceroys, who were each responsible to the king alone; but each viceroy had civil and military officers subordinate and responsible to himself. (2) The home ministers appear in two classes only, the "judges" and the "treasurers." As stated above, the first of these is only mentioned in this passage, so that apart from the etymology it is impossible to infer what his duties may have been. However, paying regard to this, he seems to have performed all those duties which now fall to the share of the vizier. In home as opposed to foreign affairs, there must always have been some persons with whom lay the final appeal in all civil causes. Such, in all probability, were these judges. The "treasurers," who are associated with the judges, were connected with the fiscal department of the administration. They would be required to examine the correctness of the revenues paid into the treasury by the provincial collectors, and perhaps a later development of their office may be traced in the royal scribe who was sent every year from the capital to inquire into the state of the province, so as to secure the allegiance of the satrap. (3) The legal advisers consist of "counsellors" and "sheriffs." The "counsellor" was evidently the man "learned in the law." In such a case as the decree of Nebuchadnezzar his advice would be necessary to secure due formality in the decree. The "sheriff," in accordance with the supposed derivation of the word, was the officer entrusted with the administration of justice and pronouncing of sentences. According to this view, these two classes of officers represent the theoretical and practical lawyer, the law-maker and the executer of the law, or perhaps the civil and the criminal judge.

EXCURSUS B: THE MUSICAL INSTRUMENTS MENTIONED IN DANIEL III.

THE Babylonians as a nation appear to have been remarkably fond of music. Isaiah (chap. xiv. 11) speaks of the noise of the viols of Babylon as forming part of her pomp, and it may be presumed that the desire of the Babylonians to hear some of the strains of Zion (Ps. cxxxvii. 2, 3) was not uttered in mockery, but from a genuine wish, such as all persons have who really care for music at all, to hear the melodies of foreign countries. Further evidence is afforded by sculptures, which represent various musical instruments and considerable bands of performers.

Whence the Babylonian music was originally derived is not known, though probably we must look to Egypt as the source; but it may be asserted that whatever was not indigenous to Babylonia itself must have come from the same sources whence articles of commerce were acquired. At the time of Daniel, Babylon held commerce in the west with Egypt and Tyre. By means of both these lines of commerce Babylon was brought into contact with Greece, the great mistress of art in the sixth century B.C. And as we find traces among the Greek instruments of the Semitic Nabla and Kinura, it seems, *à priori*, highly probable that some of the Greek instruments should have found their way to Tyre, and to Egypt, and then penetrated to Babylon.

For many years previous to Nebuchadnezzar there had been considerable communication between Greece and the East. We know that 300 years earlier Sargon made Javan or Greece tributary. The statue of this king found at Idalium proves that he conquered the Greek colony of Cyprus. His son Sennacherib, we know, was engaged in war with Greeks in Cilicia. His grandson, Esarhaddon, had Greeks fighting on his side during his Asian campaign. It would be very remarkable if, during the many years throughout which Greece and Assyria were brought into connection, the musical instruments of the one nation should not have become known to the other. And if Assyria acquired Greek musical instruments, what is more probable than that many years before Nebuchadnezzar's time they were known in Babylon?

The connection between Greece and the East did not cease with the fall of the Assyrian empire. In the army of Nebuchadnezzar we find serving as soldier the brother of the poet Alcæus, and a few lines are extant in which this great lyric writer welcomes home his brother from the Babylonian campaign. The historical notices of these times are very scanty, so that it is not easy to demonstrate the extent of Greek commerce in the sixth century B.C., but the facts mentioned above give us strong grounds for supposing that at an early period there was an interchange of musical instruments between the East and the West, and with the instruments would pass their names, which in the course of time would become more or less corrupted as the people who adopted them found it hard or easy to pronounce and transliterate the words.

We should expect therefore, *à priori*, in any list of Babylonian instruments, to find some of the names of Semitic, some of Greek extraction, and some of very doubtful etymology. This is precisely what we find in the book of Daniel. Of the names of the six instruments mentioned, two are undoubtedly of Semitic origin, one if not two are Greek, one is uncertain, while the sixth is perhaps not an instrument at all, though the word is undoubtedly Greek.

The instruments that have Semitic names are the "cornet" and the "flute." They are both of great antiquity. The former is frequently found in the reliefs which represent military scenes, and the mention of it in this chapter is probably to be accounted for by the fact that the army was present.

The instruments which appear to have been derived from Greece are the "harp" and the "psaltery." The former is frequently represented in the reliefs, possessing strings in number from three upwards. The psaltery is of uncertain etymology, but looks like a Greek word. The context requires a word to denote "cymbals," which occur very frequently in the sculptures, and do not readily find an equivalent among the instruments mentioned by David.

What the "sackbut" may have been must be left undecided. It is true that a word *sambuca* occurs in Greek, but it is of foreign extraction.

The "dulcimer," *sûmphonia* in the Chaldee, is probably not the name of a musical instrument, but means a "concerted piece of music." The passages upon which it has been inferred that the *sûmphonia* was an instrument are Polyb. xxvi. 10, § 5, Athen. x. 53 (near the end); neither passage, however, is conclusive.

EXCURSUS C: BELSHAZZAR (chap. v.).

Before any opinion can be pronounced upon the identification of this king with other known kings, the following questions require an answer. In chap. v. 11, Are the words to be taken literally, and explained to mean that Belshazzar was Nebuchadnezzar's own son? In verse 13, Does Belshazzar claim Nebuchadnezzar to be his father? (Comp. verses 18, 22.) And lastly. Is it stated in verse 30 that the Chaldean Empire passed over into the hands of the Medes and Persians? or is it only implied that an insurrection occurred in the town where the events recorded in chap. v. occurred, and that after the murder of Belshazzar a Median prince, called Darius, was made king in his stead?

Scripture affords us very little assistance in answering any of the above questions. The only fact which we know from the Bible about Belshazzar is that he reigned at least three years. This appears from the headings of chaps. vii., viii.

If we adhere to the literal sense of the words (chap. v. 11), it follows that Belshazzar was the son and immediate successor of Nebuchadnezzar. But when we come to examine what is known from other sources about the posterity of Nebuchadnezzar, we find no such name as Belshazzar given to his immediate successor. Evil Merodach came to the throne upon the death of his father (Jer. lii. 31); but the fact that he had a brother named Belshazzar rests on no other authority than the interpretation which Eusebius gave of the story in Daniel. Herodotus knows nothing of Belshazzar or of Nebuchadnezzar. He mentions only two Babylonian princes, both of whom were named Labynetus (probably Nabonidus). One of these was the husband of Nitocris, and erected some of the most stately buildings in Babylon; the other was a son of hers, in whose reign Cyrus took Babylon.

The fragments of Berosus and Abydenus, and the

Canon of Ptolemy, confirm the Scriptural account, according to which Nebuchadnezzar was succeeded by Evil Merodach. They add that after a "lawless and lustful reign," Evil Merodach was murdered in a conspiracy led by Neriglissar. Neriglissar reigned four years, and was succeeded by his son Laborosoarchod, who was soon murdered. Then Nabonidus, one of the conspirators, usurped the throne, which he held for eighteen years, when, upon the assault of Babylon by Cyrus, he was taken prisoner at Borsippa, where he had fled for safety. It seems impossible to identify Belshazzar with any of these. If he was the same as Evil Merodach, then Darius the Mede and Neriglissar must have been the same person, which is impossible. Similar difficulties prevent us from identifying him with Laborosoarchod, so that the ancient fragments do not help us to arrive at any conclusion.

Babylonian inscriptions, however, speak of a certain Bel-sar-usur as the son of Nabonidus. An inscription (*Records of the Past*, vol. v., p. 147) concludes with a prayer of Nabonidus, praying the moon to preserve "his eldest son, the offspring of his body, Bel-sar-usur." Thus the existence of Belshazzar is unquestionable, though no inscription hitherto discovered speaks of him as king. However, the name of the last king of Babylon was Maruduk-sarra-usur, which is not unlike Belshazzar.

Still more recent discoveries have been made, and in the inscription of Cyrus we find that he mentions his taking Babylon without bloodshed, and states that Nabonidus was taken prisoner. He also mentions that the king's son—probably Belshazzar—was at Accad, "with his great men and soldiers," in the same year as the capture of Babylon, and that the men of Accad raised a revolt. Farther on in the inscription, which is much mutilated, a statement is made, "and the king died. From the seventh of the month Adar unto the third day of the month Nisan there was weeping in Accad." Now, according to the last mention made of Nabonidus in this inscription, he was taken bound to Babylon. It is highly probable, therefore, that the king who died at Accad was the "king's son" mentioned in an earlier part of the inscription. May it not be conjectured that this was Belshazzar, and that the scene described in Daniel v. occurred at Accad, and not at Babylon? Further discoveries may throw light upon this point.

Ancient opinions about Belshazzar are various. Ephraim Syrus, the earliest writer on Daniel whose commentary has come down to us complete, states that he was son of Nebuchadnezzar, and wisely refrains from further attempts at identification. St. Jerome, a little later, identifies him with Laborosoarchod, cautioning the reader against supposing that he was son of Nebuchadnezzar. Theodoret, adhering to the literal sense of Daniel, supposes him to have been the younger brother of Evil Merodach. The opinion of St. Jerome is supported by Hävernick, Hengstenberg, and Keil; Kranichfeld, Zöckler, and Zündel believe in the identity of Belshazzar and Evil Merodach; Dr. Pusey, Delitzsch, Schrader, and the two most recent of English commentators, identify him with his father, Nabonidus, or assume that he was appointed co-regent with his father.

EXCURSUS D: DARIUS THE MEDE (chap. v. 31).

It appears from the account given by Daniel that Darius the Mede was the sovereign appointed to rule over Babylonia after the death of Belshazzar. Cyrus, after the capture of Babylon, appointed a man named Gubaru (Gobryas) as his governor at Babylon. Can he and Darius the Mede be the same person? It is impossible to identify Darius with any personage mentioned in profane history, and hitherto no traces of any such name have been found in Babylonian inscriptions belonging to this period. Till time or circumstances shall give further information, we must maintain that a book like Daniel's, which is correct on many minor points, cannot fail to be accurate upon the subject of Darius.

Difficulties were experienced at a very early time in reference to this subject. The LXX., assuming that Ahasuerus (chap. ix. 1) was Xerxes, identified him with Artaxerxes. The opinion of Josephus is that Darius (*Antt.* x. 11, § 4) and his kinsman Cyrus destroyed the supremacy of Babylon; and at the fall of the capital, this Darius, son of Astyages, took Daniel with him to Media, and placed him in an exalted situation. St. Jerome agrees to this relationship between Cyrus and Darius. St. Ephraim is silent; but Theodoret goes further, and identifies Darius with Cyaxares, son of Astyages. In modern times the identity of Darius with Cyaxares II. has been strongly maintained, though without paying sufficient attention to the very slight evidence in favour of the existence of the latter. The identification of Darius with Astyages has an obvious refutation, for in B.C. 536 Astyages would have exceeded the age ascribed to Darius by Daniel (chap. v. 31).

It is evident from history that Cyrus was the immediate conqueror of Babylon, and that no Median Empire came between the Babylonian and the Persian Empires. It is also clear that Daniel regards Darius as one who "received the kingdom" (chap. v. 31), and who "was made king" (chap. ix. 1). If the word Darius means "a maintainer," all that is mentioned in this chapter amounts to no more than the statement that "a Median governor took the kingdom." However, the use of the word (chap. ix. 1) requires the name of a person rather than an office.

EXCURSUS E: THE FOUR KINGDOMS (chaps. ii., vii.).

In the notes upon the parallel, though supplementary, vision contained in chaps. ii. and vii. attention has been directed to each of the four empires which has hitherto governed the world. It has been explained in the notes that these four empires are the Babylonian, the Medo-Persian, the Græco-Macedonian, and the Roman. The fourth empire in each case is succeeded by the kingdom of the Messiah, which in chap. ii. is symbolised by a stone, but in chap. vii. 27 is described more clearly as the "kingdom of the people of the saints of the Most High." This view of the four kingdoms is found in the early part of the second century A.D. maintained by the author of the epistle of Barnabas, who speaks of the ten kingdoms (Barn., *Ep.* iv. 4, 5) foretold by Daniel as then existing, and of the fourth beast as then reigning. The fragments of St. Hippolytus show that the same opinion prevailed in the Church a century later. The longer ecclesiastical commentaries of St. Jerome and Theodoret maintain the same opinion, which has been followed in modern times, with some modifications, by a large number of commentators.

A second view, of great antiquity, is mentioned by Porphyry, who flourished in the third century. His opinion coincided with the interpretation just mentioned up to a certain point. He made the panther, or third beast, represent Alexander the Great; but the fourth beast, according to him, meant the four successors of Alexander. He then enumerated up to the time of Antiochus Epiphanes those kings whom he conceived to have been most remarkable for persecuting God's people in the times of the Ptolemies and Seleucidæ, and ultimately identified the little horn with Antiochus Epiphanes, in whose time he believed the Book of Daniel to have been written. This view has not been without support in recent times.

A third view, which has antiquity to support it, is due in the first instance to St. Ephraim Syrus, according to whose teaching the four kingdoms are the Babylonian, the Median, the Persian, and the Greek. He is careful, however, to point out that the fulfilment which the prophecy received in the times of the Maccabees is only typical of a further fulfilment to be expected in the last days. It exceeds the limit of a note to trace the origin of this opinion in the Syrian Church, and the development of it in modern times. It is sufficient to observe that, like Porphyry's interpretation, it limits the horizon of the prophet chiefly to the Greek period.

This view, which, more or less modified, finds many adherents in the present day, rests upon the identification of the little horn in chap. vii. 8, with the little horn in chap. viii. 9. If Antiochus is the horn of chap. viii., why should he not be hinted at in chap. vii.? and if so, why should not the goat (chap. viii. 5), which is known (chap. viii. 21) to be the kingdom of Greece, be identical with the fourth beast of chap. vii.? It is then argued that the period of persecution hinted at in chap. vii. 25 coincides with that which is mentioned in chap. ix. 27, being half a week, or three days and a half, and that the same measure of time occurs in chap. xii. 7. Is it possible, it is asked, that these similar measures of time represent different events? Again, it is observed that there is no interval mentioned as occurring between the last times and the times of the persecutions mentioned in chaps. vii., viii., and x.—xii., and also that the words in which Antiochus is predicted (chap. viii. 19) are spoken of as the "last end of indignation" and "the end." This is stated to support the view that the predictions of Daniel are limited by the times of Antiochus.

On these grounds the persecution mentioned in chap. vii. 25 is supposed to be that of Antiochus. The Greek Empire is represented by the fourth beast, while the second and third beasts represent the Median and the Persian Empires respectively. But here the question arises, Are there any grounds for believing that Daniel intended to speak of a distinct Median Empire? The passages alleged in support are chaps. v. 28, 31, vi. 8, 12, 15. Daniel states of Darius expressly that he was a Mede and of Median descent (chaps. v. 31, ix. 1, xi. 1), and, on the contrary, that Cyrus was a Persian (chaps. vi. 28, x. 1). Also in chap. vi. 28 the writer appears to be contrasting Darius the Mede with Cyrus the Persian, as if each belonged to a different empire. And though the kings of Media and Persia are distinctly mentioned in chap. viii. 20, it is maintained that the unity of the Medo-Persian Empire is not established thereby, because the two horns, and not the body, of the goat are assumed to be the key of the vision. If the brief duration and slight importance of the so-called Median Empire is objected, it is replied that the importance of it to Israel was very great, for in the first year of it the exile terminated, and at that very time Darius was under the special protection of the Angel of the Lord (chap. xi. 1).

Upon this hypothesis the visions in chaps. ii. and vii. are explained in the following manner:—The materials of which the feet of the image were formed corresponds to the two divisions of the Greek Empire noticed in chap. xi., the iron representing the Ptolemies, the clay the Seleucidæ. The mixture of the iron and clay points to such attempts as are mentioned in chap. xi. 8, 17 to unite certain heterogeneous elements in the political world. The silver breasts and arms are the Median Empire, which was inferior to the Babylonian (chap. ii. 39), which, it is asserted, does not hold true of the Persian Empire. Then comes the Persian Empire, which, as Daniel interpreted the vision (chap. ii. 39), "bare rule over all." Similarly, in chap. vii., those who maintain the interpretation find no difficulty about the first beast; but the second beast is Darius the Mede; the three ribs are the three satrapies mentioned in chap. vi. 2 (St. Ephraim explains them of the Medes, the Babylonians, and the Persians). The command, "Arise, and devour much flesh," means that the empire of Darius had a great future prospect, which he would not realise. Then the panther is Cyrus; the four wings are the Persians, Medes, Babylonians, and Egyptians; the four heads are four Persian kings, Cambyses, Smerdis, Darius Hystaspes, and the last, who is either Xerxes or Darius Codemannus. It remains that the fourth beast is the Greek Empire, the first which was of a totally distinct character from the Asiatic empires which had preceded it. The little horn is Antiochus Epiphanes, and the other ten horns are ten kings, who are not supposed to be reigning simultaneously; three of them, however, were contemporaneous with the little horn. The ten kings are assumed to be—(1) Seleucus Nicator, (2) Antiochus Soter, (3) Antiochus Theos, (4) Seleucus Callinicus, (5) Seleucus Ceraunus, (6) Antiochus the Great, (7) Seleucus Philopator, (8) Heliodorus, (9) Demetrius, (10) Ptolemy Philometor. The last three were deposed by Antiochus Epiphanes, the allusion being to Demetrius (chap. xi. 21) and to Ptolemy Philometor (chap. xi. 22—28). It is then alleged that all the events which are explicitly mentioned in chap. xi. are figuratively expressed by the ten toes of the image and by the ten horns of the fourth beast.

In this interpretation there is much that appears plausible at first sight. It seems to make the whole plan of the book more distinct, and to introduce a symmetry and coherence among the several parts which is wanting to the interpretation given above. But though the truth is simple, everything simple is not true. Grave difficulties will be found, upon closer inspection, to underlie this hypothesis respecting the four kingdoms.

(1) What reason is there for identifying the little horn in chap. vii. 8 with the little horn in chap. viii. 9? In one case it grows up amongst ten, in the other out of four. In one case it destroys three of the other horns, in the other none. Or, to take Daniel's own interpretation, the "kink of a fierce countenance"

(chap. viii. 23) arises while the four horns are still in existence, though "in the latter time of their kingdom." Bearing in mind that the ten toes of the image correspond to the ten horns of the fourth beast, there appears to be strong *primâ facie* evidence for supposing that the horizon of chap. viii. is different from that of chaps. ii., vii., and xi.

(2) Further consideration shows that Antiochus Epiphanes does not correspond with the little horn (chap. vii.), or with the king mentioned (chap. xi. 21, &c.). Antiochus is foretold (chap. viii. 9—12, 23—25) as "becoming great toward the south, and toward the east, and toward the pleasant land, and waxing great even to the host of heaven," &c.; but the person foretold in chap. vii. 8, 20, 25, "has a mouth speaking proud things," &c. In no point do these two awful personages agree, except in blaspheming God and in making war against His people. They differ in many important respects.

(3) The measures of time, again, are different in each vision. Antiochus Epiphanes carries on his destructive work for 2,300 (or 1,150) days, but the Antichrist mentioned in chap. vii. 25 has the saints in his power for a "time, times, and the dividing of time." By no possible calculation can these two measures of time be made identical. Nor can the same measure of time which occurs in chap. xii. 7 be identified either with the 1,290 days, or with the 1,335 days mentioned in chap. xii. 11, 12.

(4) Further, in chap. viii. 9 "the last end of indignation" does not mean the end of all things, any more than it means the end of the captivity. It points to the persecution of Antiochus, when, for the last time in Jewish history, the innocent suffered for the guilt of the apostates. This was a persecution of which the adherence of the Jews to their religion was the cause. Politics provoked later persecutions, but in this they were involved in only a secondary manner. The plain question was, would the Jews suffer their religion to be Hellenised, or would they not? This, again, is alien to the thoughts contained in chap. vii. 21, 25.

(5) Nor is it clear that Daniel knew of a Median as distinct from a Persian Empire. If Darius "received the kingdom," some superior power must have given it to him. If he was "made king," some higher authority must have invested him with the sovereignty. Nor does history give us any reasons for supposing that there was at this time any broad national distinction between the Medes and Persians.

(6) Lastly, the empire of Alexander the Great does not correspond to the fourth empire, which is described in chaps ii., vii. None of the elements of iron appear in it. The leading characteristic of it was not "breaking in pieces and bruising" other empires, but rather assimilation. The policy of it was to Hellenise them, to clothe their ideas in Greek forms, to unite widely separated nations which it had subdued, by treating them courteously, adopting their national customs, and by polishing the whole external with Greek culture.

Great and undoubted though the difficulties are which are contained in the interpretation given above in the Notes, they are not so great as those which are involved by the so-called "modern" interpretation just mentioned.

EXCURSUS F: DANIEL'S PRAYER (chap. ix.).

The resemblance between Daniel's prayer and those recorded in the books of Ezra, Nehemiah, and Baruch will appear more distinctly from the following table:—

Daniel ix.	Ezra ix.	Neh. ix.	Baruch.
4		32	
5	7	33, 34	i. 11.
6	7	32, 33	
7	6, 7	32, 33	i. 15—17
8	6, 7	33	
9		17	
13			ii. 7.
14	15	33	
15		10	ii. 11.
18			ii. 19.
19			ii. 15.

The resemblance is due to the fact that most of the corresponding thoughts are taken from earlier works, such as the Law of Moses, or prophetical writings. It will be observed that this similarity can be traced chiefly in verses 4—9, 13—19. The language, however, is very general, and can be traced for the most part to earlier sources. A short analysis of the prayers of Ezra and Nehemiah shows that the similarity of the prayers is less striking than appears at first sight. Ezra confesses the sins of the congregation from the early period of Israel's history down to his own time; he blesses God for allowing a remnant to escape, he then confesses the special sin of which the nation was guilty at that time, and acknowledges that neither he nor his people are able to stand before God. Not once in the course of his prayer does he ask for forgiveness. Nehemiah, after thanking God for His mercies, using the language of Psalmists, proceeds to bless God for the mercies which He has showered upon his people in spite of their frequent relapses into sin. He frequently contrasts the righteousness of God with the guiltiness of the nation, and, like Ezra, does not pray for forgiveness or to be delivered from bondage. But Daniel's prayer is just the reverse. Not only does he pray for the pardon and deliverance of his people, but he concludes with a petition that he himself may be heard (verses 17, 18). It is therefore unreasonable to suppose that Daniel's prayer should have been founded upon the model of the prayers of Ezra and Nehemiah. Still more improbable is the hypothesis that it was curtailed from the prayer of Baruch. The date of the book of Baruch is almost universally acknowledged to be late, and the prayer contained in it depends as much upon the book of Nehemiah as it does upon Daniel.

EXCURSUS G: THE SEVENTY WEEKS (chap. ix. 24).

It may be questioned in what way this prophecy presents any meaning to those who follow the punctuation of the Hebrew text, and put the principal stop in verse 25 after "seven weeks," instead of after "three score and two weeks." The translation would be as follows, "From the going out . . . until Messiah the prince shall be seven weeks; and during sixty-two weeks the city shall be rebuilt . . . and after sixty-two weeks shall Messiah be cut off" . . . This can only be explained upon the hypothesis that the word "week" is used in an indefinite sense to mean a period. The sense is then as follows:—The period from the command of Cyrus or of Artaxerxes to rebuild Jerusalem, down to the time of Messiah, consisted of seven such weeks; during the sixty-two weeks that followed the kingdom of Messiah is to be established amidst much persecution. During the last week the persecution will be so intense that Messiah may be said to be annihilated by it, His kingdom on earth being destroyed. At the end of the last week the Antichristian prince who organises the persecution is himself exterminated, and destroyed in the final judgment.

According to this view the seventy weeks occupy the whole period that intervenes between the times of Cyrus or Artaxerxes and the last judgment. The principal objection to it is that it gives no explanation of the numbers "seven" and "sixty-two," which seem to have been chosen for some particular purpose. Nor does it furnish any reason for the choice of the word "weeks" instead of "times" or "seasons," either of which words would have equally served the same indefinite purpose.

The traditional interpretation follows the punctuation of Theodotion, which St. Jerome also adopted, and reckons the seventy weeks from B.C. 458, the twentieth year of Artaxerxes. From this date, measuring seven weeks of years—that is, forty-nine years—we are brought to the date B.C. 409. It is predicted that during this period the walls of Jerusalem and the city itself should be rebuilt, though in troublous times. It must be remembered that very little is known of Jewish history during the times after Ezra and Nehemiah. The latest date given in Nehemiah is the thirty-second year of Artaxerxes, or B.C. 446. It is highly probable that the city was not completely restored till nearly forty years later. Reckoning from B.C. 409 sixty-two weeks or 434 years, we are brought to A.D. 25, the year when our Saviour began His ministry. After three and a half years, or in the "midst of a week," he was cut off. The seventy weeks end in A.D. 32, which is said to be the end of the second probation of Israel after rejecting the Messiah. The agreement between the dates furnished by history and prediction is very striking, and the general expectation that there prevailed about the appearance of a Messiah at the time of our Saviour's first advent points to the antiquity as well as to the accuracy of the interpretation. However, the explanation of the latter half of the seven weeks is not satisfactory. We have no chronological account of events which occurred shortly after the Ascension, and there are no facts stated in the New Testament that lead us to suppose that Israel should have three and a half years' probation after the rejection of the Messiah.

The modern explanation adheres in part to the Masoretic text, and regards the sixty-two year-weeks as beginning in B.C. 604. Reckoning onwards 434 years, we are brought to the year B.C. 170, in which Antiochus plundered the Temple and massacred 40,000 Jews. Onias III., the anointed prince, was murdered B.C. 176, just before the close of this period; and from the attack upon the Temple to the death of Antiochus, B.C. 164. was seven years, or one week, in the midst of which, B.C. 167, the offering was abolished, and the idolatrous altar erected in the Temple. The seven weeks are then calculated onwards from B.C. 166, and are stated to mean an indefinite period expressed by a round number, during which Jerusalem was rebuilt after its defilement by Antiochus. This explanation is highly unsatisfactory. It not only inverts the order of the weeks, but arbitrarily uses the word week in a double sense, in a definite and in an indefinite sense at once. There is still a graver objection to assuming that the starting point of the seventy weeks is the year B.C. 604. No command to rebuild Jerusalem had then gone forth.

HOSEA

INTRODUCTION

TO

HOSEA

THE importance of Hosea is testified not only by the foremost position which his prophecy occupies in the LXX. and Masoretic Canon, but by the evident traces of his influence on Isaiah, Jeremiah, and Ezekiel. Moreover, he is probably the only prophet of the kingdom of Israel whose oracles have come down to us in complete and literary form, bearing in their very language traces of the dialect of Northern Palestine.

Respecting the prophet Hosea (Hebrew הוֹשֵׁעַ, salvation, LXX. Ωσηέ, and even Αὐσή), we only know for certain that he was the son of Beeri, and from internal indications we infer that he prophesied in the northern kingdom during the closing years of its existence. This epoch was characterised by moral and social dissolution. The death of Jeroboam II. left Israel a prey to anarchy. A series of short and violent usurpations undermined the prestige of royalty, and the kingdom fell a victim to disorder. While idolatrous sensuality and excess prevailed as it had done from the days of Israel's disruption, robbery and oppression grew to alarming proportions. Bands of priests waylaid pilgrims on the way to local shrines, and the nobles were given up to violence and drunkenness. Meanwhile, the vast overshadowing military power of Assyria was advancing with rapid strides under the energetic rule of Tiglath-pileser. Egypt was unable to present an effectual resistance, and the tide of Assyrian conquest rolled with scarcely a check to the banks of the Jordan.

"The word of the Lord that came unto Hosea, the son of Beeri, in the days of Uzziah, Jotham, Ahaz, and Hezekiah, kings of Judah, and in the days of Jeroboam, the son of Joash, king of Israel." This superscription, or heading to the prophecy, in the first verse, furnishes a rough conception of the period over which Hosea's prophetic activity extended. Without discussing the question whether the superscription, like that of the collected prophecies of Amos and of Isaiah, proceeded from the prophet's own hand or from that of a later editor (as many critics assume), it may be affirmed that no cogent argument has yet been adduced impugning its historic accuracy. Formerly difficulties were felt to exist in the excessive length of active life therein assigned (65 years according to Keil, in his *Introduction to the Old Testament*). But the whole question of Scripture chronology has been profoundly affected by the results of Assyrian discovery, and is a problem still unsolved. (See Geo. Smith, *Assyrian Eponym Canon*, pp. 150 *sqq.*; Kamphausen, *Die Chronologie der hebräischen Könige*; Bleek, *Einleiting in das alte Testament*, 4th ed., pp. 263—66; Schrader, *Keilinschriften*, 2nd ed., pp. 222 *sqq.*, 458 *sqq.*); and the tendency of modern inquiry is to abridge the interval between the reign of Jeroboam II. and that of Hoshea. (See article *Hosea* in *Encyc. Brit.*)

Critics at the present time lay stress on the argument that the internal evidence of the oracles themselves leads to the assumption that the mention of the Judæan kings is due to a later and incorrect interpolation. (1) It is said that the allusions to Gilead are incompatible with a time subsequent to its depopulation by Tiglath-pileser (734 B.C.). But in the first place the extent of the destruction there wrought cannot be ascertained from the mutilated records of his campaign; while, secondly, the very disorders in that region, graphically portrayed by the prophet, may have been aggravated by the disturbing effects wrought by that invasion. This is confirmed by the language of chap. xii. 11, where the prophet refers to the destruction which had been wrought in Gilead, and points to the ruined "stone-heaps" which were once the altars of a false worship in the adjoining district of Gilgal on the west side of the Jordan. (See Notes on chap. vii. 9, 11.) (2) It is urged that these prophecies, if subsequent to the Syro-Ephraimitic war against Judah, would not have passed over it in silence. But the *argumentum e silentio* is perilous, unless adequate motive can be assigned for such allusions *relative to the general scope and purpose of the prophecy*. That purpose was to awaken the slumbering consciousness of Israel (the *northern* kingdom) to a sense of its unfaithfulness to Jehovah. But why should war against so unworthy a representative of David as the effeminate and superstitious Ahaz (Isa. iii. 4) appear in the eyes of the prophet dishonouring to Jehovah, and why should we expect a special reference to the subject in these oracles? If, as some writers argue, the policy of Rezin and Pekah was to compel Ahaz to unite in resisting the encroachments of Assyria (see Cheyne's *Isaiah*, Introduction to chap. vii.), the moral sympathies of Hosea may well have been on the side of his countrymen, and opposed to a monarch whose policy of subservience to Asshur he would emphatically condemn. (Comp. chaps. v. 13, vii. 11, xiv. 3.)

On the other hand, indications are not wanting that the year 726 B.C. circ. may be assumed as the *terminus ad quem* of the prophet's career. This was admitted by Bleek (*Introduction to Old Testament*). The references to Judah in chaps. iv.—xiv. are such as point to the national degradation brought about by the reign of Ahaz (chaps. iv. 6, 13, vi. 11). Moreover, Samaria was not yet destroyed, but there are evidences in the closing chapters that the impending shadows of that terrible catastrophe darkened his soul (chaps. ix. 13, x. 3—8, 14, 15, xiii. 7—11, 15, 16), and added pathos to his last appeal (chap. xiv.).

The writings of Hosea, like most Old Testament oracles, are in a minor key, but are characterised by the prevalence of a tragic discord, which was the ever-recurring grief of a sorrow-stricken heart. For Hosea was doomed by the chastening hand of God to suffer the domestic misery of an unfaithful wife. Soon after his marriage to Gomer, daughter of Diblaim, the infidelities of her past and present conduct became apparent. The children born under these sad auspices received significant names from the prophet, which exhibit how the mind of the seer was working by Divine enlightenment to a clear interpretation of the sorrowful mystery. Did the prophet's marriage become to him ultimately a Divine summons to his sacred office? We do not know, but we are justified in inferring from his language that this marriage was regarded by him as part of a special Divine purpose. The wrongs he had suffered were now understood by him to be a parable of the sins committed by Israel against Jehovah, and of the long history of unfaithfulness to the God of Jacob who had brought His people out of Egypt. In the Commentary it will be seen that we have maintained the view that regards the marriage with Gomer not as mere allegory, but as historic fact. The opinion there adopted is that of Duhm (*Theologie der Propheten*, p. 82), Wellhausen, and Nowack, and has also been followed by Mr. W. R. Smith. In the second part of this collection of prophecies it will be seen that Israel's unfaithfulness to Jehovah, which is the central theme, falls into two clearly marked types.

(1) *Unfaithfulness in political relations.* From 2 Kings xv. 19, 20 we learn that Menahem purchased immunity from the attacks of Pul (Tiglath-pileser II.) by paying a tribute of 1,000 talents of silver. This event may probably be assigned to about 738 B.C., and is confirmed by the mention in Tiglath-pileser's records of Menahem of Samaria in a list of monarchs who paid tribute to Assyria. This may, with considerable likelihood, be assumed to have taken place at a time when a confederacy organised by the powerful and valiant Azariah (Uzziah), king of Judah, was being broken up by the rapid successes achieved by the Assyrian monarch. Menahem thus inaugurated a fatal policy of dependence on Assyria, which was only too faithfully imitated by Ahaz, king of Judah, and opened the way to the complete subjugation of the Western Syro-Palestinian chain of kingdoms and states. This policy was carried to its highest pitch in the reign of king Hoshea. This monarch, as we clearly see from the inscriptions of Tiglath-pileser (G. Smith, *Assyrian Eponym Canon*, pp. 123, 4), obtained his elevation to power by the aid of Assyria, and paid tribute to Assyria as a humble vassal. But Hoshea could not have maintained his position long under such conditions. He had to reckon with a powerful party in Israel who aimed at throwing off the yoke of Assyria by courting an alliance with Egypt, and at length he felt compelled to adopt their views, and play a double part between these two world-powers. But all this policy of subservience to foreign empires was in flagrant violation of the old theocratic principle. To the mind of the prophet it was treacherous abandonment of Israel's God, and with scathing words he denounced the unfaithfulness of Ephraim to Jehovah, the Lord of Hosts, the leader of Israel's armies, and the supreme protector of their soil. Ephraim is compared to a silly dove hovering between Egypt and Assyria (chap. vii. 11, comp. chap. v. 13). "A covenant is made with Assyria and oil is carried to Egypt" (chap. xi. 1). "Strangers have devoured his strength, and he knoweth it not" (chap. vii. 9). It was the aim of these stern denunciations to lead Israel back to faithful dependence on the God of Jacob, that they might "return to Jehovah their God" and confess with penitence: "Asshur shall not save us" (chap. xiv. 1—3).

(2) *Unfaithfulness shown in idolatry.* The worship of the true God had been degraded in the northern kingdom into the calf-worship erected by Jeroboam I. into a state-religion. The step from the calf-worship to the Baal-worship of the Canaanites was an easy one. The latter, indeed, had long exercised its fatal seductions upon the Hebrew race. Jehovah was even called by the name of Baal, as Hebrew proper names, closely analogous to Phœnician, clearly testify; and the God of Israel was thus in reality worshipped in local shrines with all the loathsome accompaniments of licentious excess (see chaps. ii. 13, 16, 17, iv. 12—14, ix. 10, &c.; comp. Introduction to Amos), and hence there resulted a hideous blending of a foreign cultus with a national religion. This idolatry was regarded by Hosea, as it was by Elijah, and afterwards by Isaiah, as treachery to the pure and Holy God of Israel. It was the aim of the prophet to awaken a yearning for the olden time and the old covenant-relations when "by a prophet Jehovah led Israel out of Egypt," so that the nation might be brought to make the solemn vow, "We will say no more to the work of our hands, Ye are our gods" (chaps. xii. 13, xiv. 3).

The latter aspect of Hosea's prophecy is highly important. Some modern critics attempt to represent Amos and Hosea as epoch-making in the sense of introducing entirely new religious conceptions. But this is an unwarrantable inference. The language clearly points in the opposite direction. Hosea recognises what all Israel likewise recognised from the days of Ahab to those of Hezekiah, that an old order and system of worship existed (chaps. viii. 11—14, xii. 9, 10, 13), and to this they were summoned to return. If this common ground did not exist, on what basis could the prophet's appeal to the national conscience rest?

Was this appeal in vain? We are disposed to think that a considerable awakening of Israel's slumbering religious life was the result. The brighter visions of the concluding strophes (chap. xiv.) might seem to indicate, when connected with a phrase in 2 Kings xvii. 2, that even in the worldly heart of king Hoshea a change had been wrought by the exhortations of the prophet. In the kingdom of Judah the policy and utterances of his younger contemporary, Isaiah, were profoundly moulded by the words of Ephraim's great preacher of repentance, and more than a century after the language of Jeremiah shows traces of the same influence.

We have seen that the oracles of Hosea are linked by one dominant conception arising out of his personal history. These writings, like the "Faust" of Goethe, are fragmentary in character, and were composed at intervals extending over a large part of the prophet's lifetime.

An exact chronological arrangement of the prophecies of Hosea is, from the conditions of the case, impossible. They may, however, with some probability, be divided according to their general contents as follows:—

I. Chaps. i—iii. (written in the closing years of the reign of Jeroboam II., as is shown by the references to the "house of Jehu" in chap. i. 4).—Descriptive of the unfaithfulness of Hosea's wife as figurative of Israel's sin.

II. Chaps. iv.—xiv.—A series of discourses (belonging to a later period), in which the key-note of

Israel's fidelity to Jehovah, her Lord, constantly recurs.

Chap. iv.—Moral degradation and idolatrous corruption of people and priests.

Chaps. v., vi. (Tiglath-pileser's invasion).—Demoralisation of nobles and priests in Judah and Ephraim. Their repentance is a hollow one, as is proved by the murders in Gilead.

Chaps. vii., viii. (Hoshea's reign).—The drunkenness of the princes, and the foolish alliances with Assyria or Egypt. Idolatrous corruption of Ephraim and unfaithfulness to Jehovah.

Chaps. ix.—xi.—Divine chastisement and Divine pleading.

Chaps. xii.—xiv.—The teachings of patriarchal history. Last words of rebuke and final hope.

It has been well observed that Hosea is "a man of emotion rather than of logic, a poet rather than a preacher," in this respect standing in contrast with Amos, the prophet of well-ordered argument. Justice is the key-note of the denunciations of Amos; love, outraged love, is the key-note of Hosea's pleading. And with what a wealth of resource the pleading is enforced! "The language of the prophet," says Eichhorn, "resembles a garland of divers flowers; images are woven to images, similes strung to similes, metaphors ranged on metaphors." And the rapidity of transition from one to another, especially when confused by corruption of the text, occasionally renders the path of interpretation perilous and uncertain (*e.g.*, chaps. vi. 9, ix. 12). For further information we would refer the reader to the admirable chapter in W. R. Smith's *Prophets of Israel*, pp. 159—169, and to Prof. Davidson's article on "Hosea" in the *Expositor* (1879). The many points of contact between Hosea and the Pentateuch are clearly indicated in Curtiss' *Levitical Priests*, pp. 175—181.

HOSEA

CHAPTER I.—(1) The word of the
LORD that came unto Hosea, the son of
Beeri, in the days of Uzziah, Jotham,
Ahaz, *and* Hezekiah, kings of Judah,
and in the days of Jeroboam the son of
Joash, king of Israel.
(2) The beginning of the word of the
LORD by Hosea. And the LORD said to
Hosea, Go, take unto thee a wife of
whoredoms and children of whoredoms:
for the land hath committed great
whoredom, *departing* from the LORD.
(3) So he went and took Gomer the
daughter of Diblaim; which conceived,
and bare him a son. (4) And the LORD
said unto him, Call his name Jezreel;
for yet a little *while,* and I will [1] avenge
the blood of Jezreel upon the house of
Jehu, and will cause to cease the king-
dom of the house of Israel. (5) And it
shall come to pass at that day, that I
will break the bow of Israel in the
valley of Jezreel.
(6) And she conceived again, and bare
a daughter. And *God* said unto him,
Call her name [2] Lo-ruhamah: for [3] I
will no more have mercy upon the house
of Israel; [4] but I will utterly take them
away. (7) But I will have mercy upon
the house of Judah, and will save them
by the LORD their God, and will not
save them by bow, nor by sword, nor by
battle, by horses, nor by horsemen.
(8) Now when she had weaned Lo-

B.C. cir. 785.

1 Heb., *visit.*

2 That is, *Not having obtained mercy.*

3 Heb., *I will not add any more to.*

4 Or, *that I should altogether pardon them.*

---

(1) **In the days of Uzziah.**—On the historical questions involved in this verse, see *Introduction.*

(2) **The beginning of the word . . .**—More correctly, *In the beginning when the Lord spoke to Hosea, the Lord said . . .*

Go, take unto thee a wife of whoredoms.—How are we to interpret the prophet's marriage to the licentious Gomer? Is it an historic occurrence, the only too real tragedy of the author's personal experience, employed for the purpose of illustration? (Comp. the domestic incident, Isa. viii. 1—4.) Or is this opening chapter a merely allegorical representation, designed to exhibit in vivid colours the terrible moral condition of Israel? (Comp. the symbolic actions described in Jeremiah xxv. 15—29; Ezek. iv. 4—6; and perhaps Isaiah xx. 1—3.) Able writers have advocated each of these opposed theories; but in our opinion the balance of evidence inclines to the former view, which regards the events as historic. The further question arises, Was Gomer guilty before or after the marriage? The former supposition involves the harshness of conceiving such a marriage as the result of a Divine command; but the latter supposition admits of a satisfactory interpretation. The wickedness which *after* marriage revealed itself to the prophet's agonised heart was transfigured to the inspired seer into an emblem of his nation's wrong to Jehovah. In the light of this great idea, the prophet's past came before him in changed aspect. As he reflected on the marvellous symbolic adaptation of this episode to the terrible spiritual needs of his fellow-countrymen, which he was called by God to supply, the Divine purpose which shaped his sorrowful career became interpreted to his glowing consciousness as a Divine command—"Go, take unto thyself a wife of whoredoms." He had suffered acutely, but the agony was part of God's arrangement, and the very love that was repeatedly outraged proves ultimately to have been suggested by a Divine monition.

Children of whoredoms.—Children of Hosea's marriage. The whole result of his family history was included in this divinely ordered plan.

(3) **Gomer the daughter of Diblaim.**—Gomer means complete, or perfect, but whether in external beauty or in wickedness of character is not easy to determine.

(4) **Jezreel** means "God shall sow." The prophet had already discovered the faithlessness of his spouse, and that his married life was symbolic of his nation's history. Observe the resemblance in sound between Jezreel and Israel, and the historic associations of the former. It was the name of a very fertile plain in the tribe of Issachar, which was many times the scene of terrible struggles (Judg. iv. 13, vi. 33, vii. 1; 1 Sam. xxix. 1). It was also the name of a town associated with the guilt of Ahab and Jezebel in bringing about the murder of Naboth (1 Kings xxi.), and with the final extinction of Ahab's house by Jehu (2 Kings ix. 21, x. 11).

(5) **I will break the bow of Israel in the valley of Jezreel.**—Jehu was to be punished for the assassination of Ahab's descendants. Though the destruction of the house of Ahab was divinely appointed, its value was neutralised by Jehu's tolerance of the calf-worship.

(6) **Lo-ruhamah.**—"Unloved," or, perhaps, "unpitied." The prophet's growing despondency about his country's future is revealed in her name. The rest of the verse is best rendered—*For I will no longer have pity on the house of Israel, that I should indeed forgive them.*

(7) **Will save them . . .**—We may consider this verse to have been literally fulfilled in the destruction of Sennacherib's army. The prophetic outlook antici-

ruhamah, she conceived, and bare a son.
(9) Then said *God*, Call his name [1] Lo-
ammi: for ye *are* not my people, and
I will not be your *God.* (10) Yet the
number of the children of Israel shall
be as the sand of the sea, which cannot
be measured nor numbered; [a] and it
shall come to pass, *that* [2] in the place
where it was said unto them, Ye *are* not
my people, *there* it shall be said unto
them, *Ye are* the sons of the living God.
(11) [b] Then shall the children of Judah
and the children of Israel be gathered
together, and appoint themselves one
head, and they shall come up out of
the land: for great *shall be* the day of
Jezreel.

CHAPTER II.—(1) Say ye unto your
brethren, [3] Ammi; and to your sisters,
[4] Ruhamah. (2) Plead with your mother,
plead: for [c] she *is* not my wife, neither
am I her husband: let her therefore
put away her [d] whoredoms out of her
sight, and her adulteries from between
her breasts; (3) lest I strip her naked, and
set her as in the day that she was [e] born,
and make her as a wilderness, and set
her like a dry land, and slay her with
thirst. (4) And I will not have mercy
upon her children; for they *be* the
children of whoredoms. (5) For their
mother hath played the harlot: she
that conceived them hath done shame-
fully: for she said, I will go after my
lovers, that give *me* my bread and
my water, my wool and my flax,
mine oil and my [5] drink.
(6) Therefore, behold, I will hedge up
thy way with thorns, and [6] make a wall,

1 That is, *Not my people.*
a Rom. 9. 25, 26.
2 Or, *instead of that.*
b Jer. 3. 18; Ezek. 34 & 37.
3 That is, *My people.*
4 That is, *Having obtained mercy.*
c Isa. 50. 1.
d Ezek. 16. 25.
e Ezek. 16. 4.
5 Heb., *drinks.*
6 Heb., *wall a wall.*

---

pates the fact that when Judah is captive and exiled, her restoration by the divine hand would take the form of mercy and forgiveness. (Comp. Ps. lxxvi, Isa. xl. 1, 2.)

(9) Closes the chapter in the Hebrew text. The episode above described is, in some particulars, the model for Ezek. xvi. Gomer's child *Lo 'Ammi* (not my people), is type of utter and final repudiation.

(10) An abrupt transition from dark presage to bright anticipation. The covenant-blessings promised to Abraham shall yet be realised.

(11) **Shall come up out of the land.**—Better, *shall go up out of*, &c., a phrase frequently occurring in Scripture, to denote the marching forth to war. Israel shall then be united. The envy of Israel and Judah shall cease. (Is. xi. 12, 13; Ezek. xxxiv. 24, xxxvii. 24). A world-wide dominion shall be established under the restored theocracy. Under the word "land," no reference is made by the prophet to exile, either in Babylon, Assyria, or Egypt, but Palestine is evidently meant. Then the true Israel, having chosen their true king, shall demonstrate the greatness of the day of Jezreel. The brothers and sisters will then drop the curse involved in their names, and recognise the Divine proprietorship of Jehovah and the abundance of His pity.

II.

(1—23) Gives the explanation of the strange enigma of the first chapter. Hosea's domestic misery and his symbolically named children pass out of sight, and Jehovah is represented as taking up the language of the prophet, and uttering His terrible and yearning cry over Israel, who had been unfaithful to Him, and who, by her idolatries, had forfeited all claim to His covenanted love.

(2) **Plead with your mother . . .**—Contend, or plead in judgment. Let the awakened conscience of the present generation rise up in judgment with the nation as a whole. By "mother" we are to understand the nation Israel, viewed as a collective abstract; and by the "children" (verse 4) the inhabitants who are units in the total aggregate. *Ammi* and *Ruhamah* without the negative prefix, show that this awakening of conscience has given them back their privileges.

Render, *That she may put away her whoredoms from her face: i.e.*, her meretricious guiles, her unblushing idolatry, her voluptuous service of gods that are no God. This strong image was constantly on the lips of the prophets, and had been burned by cruel sorrow into the very heart of Hosea. It acquired portentous meaning in the hideous impurities of the worship of Baal-peor and Ashtoreth, against which the Jehovah worship was a tremendous protest.

(3) **Set her . . .**—Reduce Israel to the destitute exposed condition in which she struggled into being in Egyptian bondage, and endured the wanderings and terrors of the wilderness. Probably we have here an allusion to the custom of female infanticide, which still prevails very widely in the East, as it did in the ancient world, the child being simply abandoned to death on the day that she was born. (Comp. Ezek. xvi. 4.)

(4) **Her children.**—The children are like their mother: not only are they born of doubtful parentage, but are personally defiled. Not only is idolatry enshrined in the national sanctuary and the royal palace, but the people love to have it so. They endorse the degradation of their mother.

(5) **For their mother hath played . . .**—We might render, with Ewald, *yea, their mother hath played . . .* This would more easily account for the change of person ("your" . . . "their"), which is, however, very frequent in Hebrew prophecy. The next "for" introduces a parenthetical clause—"her lovers" —a word used in a bad sense. The aggravation of her shame is that she seeks them, and not they her. She attributes to these idol-gods all those temporal benefits which theocratic history shows to have been Jehovah's gift, and the consequence of loyalty to Him. The modern analogue of this sin of Israel is the use of "Fortune," "Nature," "Destiny," "Impersonal Law," and even "Humanity," as the giver of all good things, as though it were superstitious or heretical to speak of God as the giver.

(6—7) Contains a brief introductory prelude, summarizing the general contents of verses 8—23. Jehovah addresses the adulterous wife: "I will erect impassable barriers that shall pierce and mangle her flesh. The path of evil shall be a path of thorns."

that she shall not find her paths.
(7) And she shall follow after her lovers,
but she shall not overtake them; and
she shall seek them, but shall not find
them: then shall she say, I will go and
return to my first husband; for then
was it better with me than now. (8) For
she did not know that I gave her corn,
and [1] wine, and oil, and multiplied her
silver and gold, [2] *which* they prepared for
Baal. (9) Therefore will I return, and
take away my corn in the time thereof,
and my wine in the season thereof, and
will [3] recover my wool and my flax *given*
to cover her nakedness. (10) And now
will I discover her [4] lewdness in the
sight of her lovers, and none shall
deliver her out of mine hand. (11) I will
also cause all her mirth to cease, her
feast days, her new moons, and her
sabbaths, and all her solemn feasts.
(12) And I will [5] destroy her vines and
her fig trees, whereof she hath said,
These *are* my rewards that my lovers
have given me: and I will make them
a forest, and the beasts of the field shall
eat them. (13) And I will visit upon her
the days of Baalim, wherein she burned
incense to them, and she decked herself
with her earrings and her jewels, and
she went after her lovers, and forgat
me, saith the LORD.
(14) Therefore, behold, I will allure her,
and bring her into the wilderness, and
speak [6] [7] comfortably unto her. (15) And
I will give her her vineyards from
thence, and the valley of Achor for a door
of hope: and she shall sing there, as in

[1] Heb., *new wine.*
[2] Or, wherewith *they made Baal.*
[3] Or, *take away.*
[4] Heb., *folly*, or, *villany.*
[5] Heb., *make desolate.*
[6] Or, *friendly.*
[7] Heb., *to her heart.*

Hedge up . . . and make a wall.—In accordance with most Hebrew texts, the literal rendering is, *wall up her wall.* Here, again, we have a sudden change of person.

She shall . . .—She may anticipate in her exile closer proximity to her idol-lovers, but in respect of national prosperity or religious satisfaction she will make complete mistake.

(8) Translate in the *present* tense: *and she knows not that it is I who gave, &c.* This yearning of Jehovah over the results of his chastisements is a wonderful anticipation of Luke xv.

Corn, and wine . . .—Corn, wine, and oil are here mentioned as the chief indigenous products of Canaan (Gen. xxvii. 28; Deut. xxxiii. 28, &c.). Gold was largely imported from Ophir (probably the west coast of India, where Tamil is spoken: Delitzsch, *Genesis*, pp. 258—9. On the other hand, Fried. Delitzsch, in his work on the *Site of Paradise*, p. 99, holds that Ophir was a coast or island between the north end of the Persian Gulf and the south-west corner of Arabia). Silver was obtained from Tarshish, through Phœnician markets. Observe that Israel at this time abounded in the possession of precious metals. (Comp. Isa. ii. 7; Wilkins, *Phœnicia and Israel*, pp. 111—116.)

Which they . . . Baal.—They have transformed Jehovah's gift into an image of Baal. Baal-worship was anterior to calf-worship (Judges ii., iii., viii.), and was diametrically opposed to Jehovah-worship, as gross Pantheism is to pure and stern Monotheism.

(9) **Therefore will I return, and take . . .**—The Hebrew form of saying, "Therefore I will take *back*." Jehovah resumes all that had been misappropriated. The king of Assyria (Tiglath-pileser, 734 B.C.) was the agency whereby this was to be accomplished. (Comp. Isa. x. 5.) The raiment (wool and flax) was Jehovah's gift to cover her nakedness, *i.e.*, to meet the actual necessities of Israel. This He will tear away, and the idol-gods whom she has courted shall see her prostration, and their own helplessness to deliver or relieve.

(11) **Mirth . . . Cease.**—The mirth is here indicative of the general character of the ceremonial—certainly not in itself a bad sign. David danced before the Lord, and justified the act. No one was to appear with sad countenance before Jehovah, any more than before an earthly potentate. (Comp. Nehem. ii. 2.)

The "feast days" are to be distinguished from the "solemn feasts." The latter term is more generic in Hebrew, while the former denoted the three great festivals of the year (especially the Feast of Tabernacles). These feasts, which Jeroboam I. had instituted, are not spoken of in themselves as sinful.

(12) **Destroy.**—For this read, with margin, *make desolate.* The vine and fig tree are employed as the symbol of possession and peace (1 Kings iv. 25; Isa. xxxvi. 16, &c.). The desolation may be by fire or drought.

Make them a forest.—The LXX. render *make them a testimony*, reading in the Hebrew text *l'ed* instead of *l'ya'ar.* The latter certainly yields a more vivid sense. The rest of the verse in the LXX. is amplified: "And the wild beasts of the field, and the birds of the heaven, and the creeping things of the earth shall devour them." While no candid critic will deny the possibility that such words may have originally stood in the text, it is *à priori* more probable that it is a gloss from verse 18 (verse 20 in LXX.). Even so late as in Hadrian's days wild beasts rushed in upon the blood-stained ruins of Jerusalem.

(13) **The days of Baalim.**—The plural Baalim refers to the worship of the same deity in different places, with distinguishing local characteristics. Thus there was a Baal-Zephon, a Baal-Hermon, a Baal-Gad, &c. (See W. R. Smith, *Old Testament in the Jewish Church*, p. 229.) "The days of Baalim" mean the whole period during which Baal has been worshipped by the faithless Israel.

(14) **Therefore.**—This word does not make God's gentle treatment a consequence of the sin of Israel. Some prefer to render by *nevertheless*, but the Hebrew word *lakhēn* is sometimes used in making strong transitions, linked, it is true, with what precedes, but not as an inference. (Comp. Isa. x. 24.) Grace transforms her suffering into discipline. The exile in Babylon shall be a repetition of the experiences of the wilderness in which she was first espoused to Jehovah. *There will I speak to her heart; i.e.*, comfortingly, lovingly.

(15) **From thence**—*i.e.*, away from thence, meaning, as soon as she has left the wilderness of exile and

the days of her youth, and as in the day
when she came up out of the land of
Egypt. (16) And it shall be at that day,
saith the LORD, *that* thou shalt call me
[1] Ishi; and shalt call me no more [2] Baali.
(17) For I will take away the names of
Baalim out of her mouth, and they shall
no more be remembered by their name.
(18) And in that day will I make a
[a] covenant for them with the beasts of
the field, and with the fowls of heaven,
and *with* the creeping things of the
ground: and I will break the bow and
the sword and the battle out of the
earth, and will make them to lie down
safely. (19) And I will betroth thee
unto me for ever; yea, I will betroth
thee unto me in righteousness, and in
judgment, and in lovingkindness, and in
mercies. (20) I will even betroth thee
unto me in faithfulness: and thou shalt
know the LORD.
(21) And it shall come to pass in that
day, I will hear, saith the LORD, I will
hear the heavens, and they shall hear
the earth; (22) and the earth shall hear
the corn, and the wine, and the oil; and
they shall hear Jezreel. (23) And I will
sow her unto me in the earth; and I
will have mercy upon her that had not
obtained mercy; and I [b] will say to *them
which were* not my people, Thou *art* my
people; and they shall say, *Thou art*
my God.

CHAPTER III.—(1) Then said the
LORD unto me, Go yet, love a woman
beloved of *her* friend, yet an adulteress,
according to the love of the LORD to-
ward the children of Israel, who look to
other gods, and love flagons [3] of wine.
(2) So I bought her to me for fifteen
pieces of silver, and *for* an homer of
barley, and an [4] half homer of barley:

1 That is, *My husband*.
2 That is, *My lord*.
a Job 5. 23.
b Rom. 9. 26; 1 Pet. 2. 10.
3 Heb., *of grapes*.
4 Heb., *lethech*.

discipline. The valley of Achor (or trouble) was associated with the disgrace and punishment which befel Israel on her first entrance into Palestine (Josh. vii. 25, 26), but it would in later days be regarded as the threshold of a blessed life. The sorrowful associations of the past were to be illuminated with happy anticipation.

Sing may suggest a reference to the dances and responsive songs at the village festivals, as well as to the triumphant strains of Exod. xv.

(16) **Baali.**—The husband of the bride was frequently called her "lord" (Isa. liv. 5; Exod. xxi. 22; 2 Sam. xi. 25; and Joel i. 8, in the Heb.). But such a name, as applied to Jehovah, was henceforth to be strictly avoided, on account of its idolatrous associations.

(18) **Make a covenant . . .**—There shall be harmony without corresponding to the moral harmony within. The brute creation shall change from hostility to man. (Comp. verse 12; so also Isa. xi. 6—9.) Wars with foreign foes shall not desolate Israel's borders.

(19, 20) Then Jehovah, turning again to the wife of His youth, says to her, "*I will betroth thee*" (as at the first, when maiden undefiled). Three times is this phrase repeated. "Righteousness" and "judgment" indicate the equitable terms on which God would accept the penitent; and lest this thought should crush her with fear, "lovingkindness" and "tender mercies" follow; and lest this should seem too good, He adds "with faithfulness" (to myself).

I will betroth thee.—It is in the betrothal of humanity to God in Christ's incarnation that the human race, which had so deeply revolted, returns to Him, and knows the Lord.

(21—23) **Will hear.**—More correctly, *I will answer* (the prayer of) *the heavens.* A sublime personification! Heaven pleads with Jehovah, the earth pleads with heaven, and the products of the soil plead with the earth. To all these prayers an answer is vouchsafed. Jehovah answers the heavens with the gifts of dew and rain, wherewith the heavens answer the cravings of the earth, and the earth the cravings of the corn, wine, and oil. And these last, in their turn, answer the wants of Jezreel, a name which, like Achor, is to be invested with brighter meanings. It is to represent a Divine seed—the people whom the Lord hath blessed. (See Stanley, *Lectures on the Jewish Church*, II. Series, Lecture 32 *ad fin.*, where this idea is eloquently set forth.)

(23) St. Paul considers this great prediction to be truly fulfilled when, by the acceptance of the Divine hope of Israel, both Jews and Gentiles shall be called the children of the living God (Rom. ix. 25, 26).

III.

We must assume some interval to have elapsed since the events of Hosea's domestic life, detailed in chap. i. Meanwhile the immoralities of Gomer have continued. She at length abandons the home of her lawful husband, and cohabits with one of her lovers. At this point comes the Divine injunction to the prophet.

(1) **Adulteress.**—The woman described here is the daughter of Diblaim—*beloved of her friend;* better rendered, *loved by another.* This is preferable to the LXX., "a lover of evil," which is based on a different reading of the same original text. Gomer is now the concubine slave of another—possibly in poor and destitute condition. And yet the prophet's love for her is like Jehovah's love for "the children of Israel, even when they are turned to other gods, *and love grape-cakes*"—the luscious sacrificial cakes used in idolatrous worship: a term generally descriptive of the licentious accompaniments of the Ashtoreth worship. (Comp. Jer. vii. 18.)

(2) **Pieces of silver.**—Shekels.

So I bought her.—Gomer was treated as no longer a wife, but requiring to be restored to such a position. The purchase of wives is still a very common practice in the East. (See Henderson's *Commentary*, and Deut. xxi. 14.)

Half homer of barley.—Half a homer is the translation given to the Hebrew word *lethekh,* which occurs only in this passage. This rendering is founded on the interpretation half a cor (cor = homer), which is

(3) And I said unto her, Thou shalt [a]abide
for me many days; thou shalt not play
the harlot, and thou shalt not be for
another man: so *will* I also *be* for
thee.
(4) For the children of Israel shall
abide many days without a king, and
without a prince, and without a sacri-
fice, and without [1]an image, and with-
out an ephod, and *without* teraphim:
(5) Afterward shall the children of Israel
return, and seek the LORD their God,
and [b]David their king; and shall fear
the LORD and his goodness in the [c]latter
days.

B.C. cir. 780.

a Deut. 21. 13.

1 Heb., *a standing*, or, *statue*.

b Jer. 30. 9; Ezek. 34. 23.

c Isa. 2. 2.

d Mic. 6. 2.

2 Heb., *bloods*.

CHAPTER IV.—(1) Hear the word of
the LORD, ye children of Israel: for the
LORD hath a [d]controversy with the
inhabitants of the land, because *there is*
no truth, nor mercy, nor knowledge of
God in the land. (2) By swearing, and
lying, and killing, and stealing, and
committing adultery, they break out,
and [2]blood toucheth blood. (3) There-
fore shall the land mourn, and every one
that dwelleth therein shall languish,
with the beasts of the field, and with
the fowls of heaven; yea, the fishes
of the sea also shall be taken away.
(4) Yet let no man strive, nor reprove

---

given in all the Greek versions except the LXX. The latter read "and a *nébhel* of wine," the *nébhel* being probably a skin bottle of a certain liquid capacity. This pre-supposes a different Hebrew text. From 2 Kings vii. 1 we may infer that an ephah of barley at ordinary times would cost one shekel (comp. Amos viii. 5), and since a homer contains ten ephahs, the price paid by the prophet was thirty shekels altogether. Reckoning a shekel as = two drachms (so LXX.), or 2s. 6d., the price paid by Hosea was about £3 15s. According to Exod. xxi. 32, this was the compensation enacted for a slave gored to death by a bull, and is a hint of the degradation to which Gomer had sunk.

(3) **Shalt abide for me**—*i.e.*, shalt abide in seclusion at my discretion. The "many days" are an indefinite period of amendment, while watchful care was being exercised over her. During this time she is to withdraw herself from her paramour and also from her husband.

Will I also be for thee.—Better, *to thee: i.e.*, I will have no intercourse with thee. So Aben Ezra, Kimchi, and others. That this was only to be a temporary discipline is evident from verses 4 and 6.

(4) The prophet suddenly passes from his personal history to that of Israel, which it symbolised.

Without a king . . .—The isolation of Gomer's position pre-figured that of Israel in the exile. Her bitter experience was a parable of Israel's utter deprivation of all civil and religious privilege. There was to be no king, or prince, or sacred ritual of any kind. Observe that the terms of both cultus are here intermingled, suggesting the idolatrous conceptions of the pure ancient practice which Jeroboam's calf-worship was only too likely to introduce. By "image" we are to understand upright stones, representing Baal or the sun-god. (Comp. chap. x. 1 and Exod. xxiv. 4.) On "ephod," see Judg. xvii. 5, xviii. 14, 17—20; on "teraphim," Gen. xxxi. 19—35; 1 Sam. xix. 13—16; Ezek. xxi. 21; Zech. x. 2. In the last two passages the word is translated "idols," "images," their use as instruments of divination being condemned.

(5) **David their king.**—Meaning the predicted representative of the Davidic dynasty. Thus Rehoboam and his house are spoken of as "David" (1 Kings xii. 16). The phrase "latter days" is used indefinitely of the distant future, the horizon of the seer's gaze. It occurs in Gen. xlix. 1 (Authorised version, "last days"). We can only see the fulfilment of this anticipation in the Messianic reign. (Comp. Ezek. xxxiv. 23, xxxvii. 24.)

IV.

Here commences a new part in the collection of Hosea's prophecies. The entire chapter is one terrible series of accusations, supporting the severe character of the imagery already employed. It is difficult to assign it to any particular period. It may have been composed during the years that immediately succeeded the reign of Jeroboam II. Ewald divides it into four strophes: verses 1—5; 6—10; 11—14; 15—19. The first two expand the former part of the reproach conveyed in verses 1 and 2; verses 11—14 point to the licentiousness of Israel; while in verses 15—19 judgment is pronounced.

(1) **Controversy.**—A judicial suit, in which Jehovah is plaintiff as well as judge (Isa. i. 23, xli. 21). By the "children of Israel" we are to understand the northern kingdom of the ten tribes, as distinguished from Judah.

Mercy.—Better rendered *love*. The Hebrew word *chésed* expresses (1) the love of God for Israel under covenant relationship; (2) the corresponding quality in man exhibited to God or towards his fellow-men. (See Hupfeld on Ps. iv. 4; and Duhm, *Theologie der Propheten*, p. 100.)

(2) **Blood toucheth blood**—*i.e.*, murder is added to murder with ghastly prevalence. References to false swearing and lying are repeated in terrible terms by Amos ii. 6—8 and Micah vii. 2—8; and the form of the charge suggests the Decalogue and pre-existing legislation (Exod. xx. 13—15).

(3) The mourning of the land is the judgment of famine, which follows not only upon the living men, but upon all living things (the LXX. have introduced into the enumeration the creeping things of the earth). Even the fishes of the sea are swept away. There is plague on fish as well as murrain on cattle, and starvation of the birds of heaven.

(4) **Yet let no man strive, nor reprove another.**—Better, *Nevertheless, let no one contend, let no one reprove*, for the voices of wise counsel, the warnings of the prophet, will be silenced. Ephraim will in his obstinate wrong-doing be left alone. The last clause of the verse is rendered by nearly all versions and commentators, *Though thy people are as those who contend with a priest—i.e.*, are as guilty as those who transgress the teaching of the Torah by defying the injunctions of the priest (Deut. xvii. 12, 13; Num. xv. 33). But the *Speaker's Commentary* gives a different rendering, which is better adapted to the denunciations of the priest in the following verses (comp.

another: for thy people *are* as they
that strive with the priest. (5) Therefore
shalt thou fall in the day, and the
prophet also shall fall with thee in the
night, and I will [1] destroy thy mother.
(6) My people are [2] destroyed for lack
of knowledge: because thou hast re-
jected knowledge, I will also reject thee,
that thou shalt be no priest to me: see-
ing thou hast forgotten the law of thy
God, I will also forget thy children.
(7) As they were increased, so they
sinned against me: *therefore* will I
change their glory into shame. (8) They
eat up the sin of my people, and they
[3] set their heart on their iniquity. (9) And
there shall be, [a] like people, like priest:
and I will [4] punish them for their ways,
and [5] reward them their doings. (10) For
they shall eat, and not have enough:
they shall commit whoredom, and shall
not increase: because they have left off
to take heed to the LORD.

(11) Whoredom and wine and new wine
take away the heart. (12) My people ask
counsel at their stocks, and their staff
declareth unto them: for the spirit of
whoredoms hath caused *them* to err, and
they have gone a whoring from under
their God. (13) They sacrifice upon the
tops of the mountains, and burn incense
upon the hills, under oaks and poplars
and elms, because the shadow thereof *is*
good: therefore your daughters shall
commit whoredom, and your spouses
shall commit adultery. (14) [6] I will not
punish your daughters when they com-
mit whoredom, nor your spouses when
they commit adultery: for themselves
are separated with whores, and they
sacrifice with harlots: therefore the
people *that* doth not understand shall
[7] fall.
(15) Though thou, Israel, play the
harlot, *yet* let not Judah offend; and
come not ye unto Gilgal, neither go ye

1 Heb., *cut off.*
2 Heb., *cut off.*
3 Heb., *lift up their soul to their iniquity.*
a Isa. 24. 2.
4 Heb., *visit upon.*
5 Heb., *cause to return.*
6 Or, *Shall I not, &c.*
7 Or, *be punished.*

---

chap. vi. 9). By a slight change in the punctuation of the Hebrew we obtain the interpretation, "And thy people, O priest, are as my adversaries." The position of the vocative in Hebrew, and the absence of the article, are, no doubt, objections to such a construction, but they are not insuperable, and the compensating advantage to exegesis is manifest.

(5) The priest's function is discharged in the day, and the prophet dreams in the night. Both will totter to their fall.

Thy mother—*i.e.*, thy nation.

(6) **For lack of knowledge,** which you, O priest, should have kept alive in their hearts. The knowledge of God is life eternal. (Comp. John xvii. 3.) The Lord's "controversy" repudiates the entire priesthood, as they had rejected the true knowledge of God. They had inclined to calf-worship, had been vacillating respecting Baal, and had connived at moral offences. If, on the other hand, with most commentators, we consider the people themselves as thus addressed, the passage refers to the cessation of the position of priesthood, which every member of the true theocracy ought to have maintained. (Comp. Exod. xix. 6.) The people should no longer be priests to Jehovah.

(7, 8) The increase in numbers and prosperity probably refers to the priesthood, who, as they grew in numbers, became more alienated from the true God. These eat up, or fatten on, the very sins they ought to rebuke. The reference here may be either to the portion of sacrificial offerings which fell to the share of the priests, or (less probably) to the sin-money and trespass-money exacted in place of sin-offerings of 2 Kings xii. 16. (On the general condition of the priesthood at this time, see W. R. Smith, *Prophets of Israel*, pp. 99—101.)

(9, 10) As the people will be punished, so will the priest. The latter will not be saved by wealth or dignity. *And I will visit upon him his ways* (observe here the collective singular in the pronoun), *and cause his doings to return upon him.* The form of the punishment is to be noticed. The eating of the sin of the people shall leave them hungry, and their licentiousness shall leave them childless.

(11) **Heart.**—The whole inner life, consumed by these licentious indulgences.

(12) **Their stocks.**—Blocks of wood fashioned into idols (Heb., *his wood,* the collective singular being maintained).

Their staff.—Cyril regarded this as referring to divinations by means of rods (ῥαβδομαντεία), which were placed upright, and after the repetition of incantations, allowed to fall, the forecast of the future being interpreted from the manner in which they fell. But perhaps the "staff" may refer, like the "stocks," to the idol itself. The Canaanite goddess Asherah was worshipped under this form.

(13) The tops of the hills were continually chosen for idolatrous temples, *i.e.*, "high places."

Poplar—*i.e.*, the white poplar, not the *storax* of the LXX., which is a shrub only a few feet high.

Elms should be "terebinth tree" (*'ēlah*).

(14) Jehovah threatens to visit no punishment on the women for their licentiousness, because they are more sinned against than sinning.

Sacrifice with harlots.—Referring to the sensuality of the religious rites, as represented by the women (*q'dēshôth*) who dedicated themselves to these impurities.

(15) **Israel . . . Judah.**—The prophet warns Judah of Israel's peril, and perhaps hints at the apostacy of some of her kings, as Ahaziah, Joram, and Ahaz. He returns to the symbolic use of the word "whoredom"; and Judah is exhorted not to participate in the idolatries of Gilgal or the calves of Bethel. There are three different places named Gilgal mentioned in Joshua (chaps. iv. 19, xii. 3, and xv. 7), and a fourth seems to be mentioned in Deut. ix. 30; 2 Kings ii. 1. The Gilgal here referred to is the first of these, which Joshua for a considerable time had made his head-quarters. In the days of Samuel it acquired some importance as a place for

up to [a]Beth-aven, nor swear, The LORD
liveth. (16) For Israel slideth back as a
backsliding heifer: now the LORD will
feed them as a lamb in a large place.
(17) Ephraim *is* joined to idols: let him
alone. (18) Their drink [1]is sour: they
have committed whoredom continually:
her [2]rulers *with* shame do love, Give ye.
(19) The wind hath bound her up in her
wings, and they shall be ashamed be-
cause of their sacrifices.

CHAPTER V.—(1) Hear ye this, O
priests; and hearken, ye house of Israel;
and give ye ear, O house of the king;
for judgment *is* toward you, because ye
have been a snare on Mizpah, and a net
spread upon Tabor. (2) And the revolters
are profound to make slaughter, [3]though
I *have been* [4]a rebuker of them all. (3) I
know Ephraim, and Israel is not hid
from me: for now, O Ephraim, thou
committest whoredom, *and* Israel is de-
filed. (4) [5][6]They will not frame their
doings to turn unto their God: for the
spirit of whoredoms *is* in the midst of
them, and they have not known the
LORD.

(5) And the pride of Israel doth testify
to his face: therefore shall Israel and
Ephraim fall in their iniquity; Judah
also shall fall with them. (6) They shall
go with their flocks and with their
herds to seek the LORD; but they shall
not find *him*; he hath withdrawn him-
self from them. (7) They have dealt
treacherously against the LORD: for
they have begotten strange children:
now shall a month devour them with
their portions.

a 1 Kings 12. 29.

1 Heb., *is gone.*

2 Heb., *shields.*

3 Or, *and, &c.*

4 Heb., *a correction.*

5 Heb., *They will not give.*

6 Or, *Their doings will not suffer them.*

---

sacrificial worship and the dispensation of justice. Bethel had a grand history. But Hosea and Amos call it by the altered name *Beth-aven* (house of vanity, or idols), instead of Beth*el* (house of God). The LXX. in Alex. MS. read *Ôn* instead of *Aven* in the Hebrew, Ôn being the name for Heliopolis, the seat of sun-cultus, whence Jeroboam may have derived his calf-worship. (See Smith's *Dict. of the Bible*, Art. "On.") But the Vat. MS. has ἀδικίας, in accordance with the Masoretic tradition (similarly Aquila and Symmachus).

(16) **Slideth back.**—More correctly, *is stubborn as a stubborn cow.*

Will feed them as a lamb in a large place.—An expression of tender commiseration (so Ewald). But most commentators understand it in an unfavourable sense, *i.e.*, will lead them forth into the desolate wilderness, a prey to wild beasts, or into the loneliness that a lamb would feel in a boundless pasture.

(17) **Ephraim . . . idols.**—The prophet calls on Judah to leave Ephraim to himself. The Jewish interpreters Rashi and Kimchi understand this as the appeal of Jehovah to the prophet to leave Israel to her fate, that so perhaps her eyes might be opened to discern her doom.

(18, 19) The Authorised version is here very defective. Translate, *Their carousal hath become degraded; with whoring they whore. Her shields love shame. A blast hath seized her in its wings, so that they are covered with shame for their offerings.* "Shields" mean the princes of the people, as in Ps. xlvii. 9. The fem. "her" in these verses refers to Ephraim, in accordance with the common Hebrew idiom. The change of person to the masculine plural is characteristic of the style of Hebrew prophecy. The storm-wind hath seized upon her with its wings—carried her away like a swarm of locusts or a baffled bird.

V.

The prophet now addresses himself more definitely to the priests and royal house of Israel, at the commencement of the reign of Pekah.

(1) **House of the king** refers to his following on both sides of the Jordan—Mizpah on the east side, in Gilead, and Tabor on the west. They are singled out as being military strongholds, where the princes of the royal house, with the apostate priests, exercised their deadly hold upon the people, waylaying them, as birds and beasts are snared in the mountains of prey. (Comp. chap. vi, 8, 9.)

Judgment is toward you.—More accurately, *is meant for you.*

(2) **Are profound to make slaughter.**—Ewald, followed recently by Nowack, is right in interpreting the Heb. text as meaning, "The apostates have gone deep in iniquity." In the last clause the Authorised version is again incorrect. Render, *But I* (*i.e.*, Jehovah) *am chastisement to them all.* The deceivers and deceived shall alike perish.

(4) The margin, "Their deeds will not suffer (them)," requires the introduction of the word "them," not in the Hebrew. It is favoured by the Jewish commentators, Schmoller, and others, but it is better to render, with the Authorised version, *They frame not their doings*, &c. The knowledge of the only true God is life.

(5) **The pride of Israel** may be either the true object of pride and boasting, viz., Jehovah Himself (comp. Amos viii. 7), or the false object of pride to which they had yielded. The latter interpretation is to be preferred, and is supported by Amos vi. 8. Arrogance led Ephraim, on numerous occasions in earlier sacred history, to resent the supremacy of Judah. This jealousy culminated in the rebellion of Jeroboam I., and characterised their history till the reign of Ahab. Arrogance will be their ruin now; and in this Judah is represented as likewise involved. This last feature is a new note in prophetic utterance. (Comp chap. iv. 15.) We are therefore justified in regarding chap. v. as delivered at a later time than the oracle standing immediately before it.

(6) The vain effort to repent when it is too late. The spirit with which sacrifices of flocks and herds were offered is of more consequence than the multitude of such oblations (Mic. iii. 4; Isa. i. 11; Ps. xl. 6). Ghastly and revolting results follow the substitution of ritual of any kind for the weightier matter of the law.

(7) **Strange children** refers to offspring that followed in the ways of their mother. (Comp. chap. i.)

(8) Blow ye the cornet in Gibeah, *and*
the trumpet in Ramah: cry aloud *at*
Beth-aven, after thee, O Benjamin.
(9) Ephraim shall be desolate in the day of
rebuke: among the tribes of Israel have
I made known that which shall surely be.
(10) The princes of Judah were like them
that remove the bound: *therefore* I will
pour out my wrath upon them like water.
(11) Ephraim *is* oppressed *and* broken
in judgment, because he willingly walked
after the commandment. (12) Therefore
will I *be* unto Ephraim as a moth, and
to the house of Judah as [1]rottenness.
(13) When Ephraim saw his sickness,
and Judah *saw* his wound, then went
Ephraim to the Assyrian, and sent [2]to
king Jareb: yet could he not heal you,
nor cure you of your wound. (14) For I
will be unto Ephraim as a lion, and as a
young lion to the house of Judah: I,
even I, will tear and go away; I will
take away, and none shall rescue *him*.
(15) I will go *and* return to my place,
[3]till they acknowledge their offence,
and seek my face: in their affliction
they will seek me early.

CHAPTER VI.—(1) Come, and let us
return unto the LORD: for he hath torn,
and he will heal us; he hath smitten,
and he will bind us up. (2) [a] After two

1 Or, *a worm.*

2 Or, *to the king of Jareb*: or, *to the king* that *should plead.*

3 Heb., *till they be guilty.*

a 1 Cor. 15. 4.

Some reference is involved to the consequences of intermarriage with heathen. The "month" may be a personification of the period of a month (Henderson), during which takes place the now closely impending (perhaps already commenced) invasion by Tiglath-pileser (2 Kings xv. 29; 2 Chron. xix. 21). This invasion was due in part to Ahaz having sought the aid of Assyria against Pekah and Rezin.

(8) **Cornet . . . trumpet.**—The two kinds of trumpet mentioned here are the *cornet*, made like the bent horn of an animal, and the *long, straight metallic trumpet*, used for sounding an alarm and convoking the congregation (Num. x. 2). Gibeah and Ramah were lofty hills on the northern boundary of Benjamin. From the parallel passage, Isa. x. 29, we conclude that Gibeah lay between Jerusalem and Ramah (the modern *Er Ram*), not far from the road which passes in a northern direction from Jerusalem to Mount Ephraim. A lofty hill, which satisfies these conditions (*Tel el Ful*), has been discovered by Robinson, where there is a prospect over almost the whole tribal region of Benjamin, and with this spot Gibeah is probably to be identified. Hosea does not mention the metropolis, but he reveals the imminent peril of Jerusalem if these high towers, within sight of her defenders, were giving the alarm at the approach of the Assyrian king.

After thee is obscure. Translate, *He* (*the enemy*) *is behind thee, O Benjamin*, the tribe in which the metropolis was situated. This combined disaster for both Israel and Judah is reiterated in a variety of ways. "The tribes of Israel" are in parallelism with "Ephraim."

(10) **The princes of Judah,** such as Ahaz, whose pusillanimity brought untold evil on both Israel and Judah (2 Kings xvi. 10—18).

Like them that remove the bound (landmark).—A practice prohibited in Deut. xix. 14, and included in the curses of Mount Ebal (Deut. xxvii. 17), an indication that this very legislation existed before the time of the prophet. They break down the barrier between right and wrong, between truth and falsehood, between Jehovah and Baalim.

(11) **Broken in judgment.**—The Authorised version is probably right in this rendering, the phrase having reference to rights pertaining to individuals. Interpreters differ as to the rare word *tsav*, translated "commandment." It only occurs in one other place (Isa. xxviii. 10, 13). Ewald regards it as meaning "wooden post," *i.e.*, their idol, but this has no basis in Old Testament usage, though etymologically ingenious. The majority of Jewish and modern commentators take it as meaning the evil ordinance of Jeroboam, who demanded the reverence of his subjects for the calf-symbol of Jehovah. The LXX. had another text (*shav* instead of *tsav*), which they render "vanities," and are followed by the Targum and Syriac version. This is worthy of attention.

Willingly—*i.e.*, "waywardly."

(12) **Rottenness.**—The Authorised version is right in this rendering (the disease *caries*) rather than *worm* (margin). Both images express concealed causes of irreparable destruction which come suddenly to view when *it is too late*.

(13) **To the Assyrian.**—Their adversity leads Ephraim to seek protection from their formidable foe instead of turning to the Lord. (On "Jareb," see *Excursus.*)

(14) **As a lion.**—First the trans-Jordanic tribes, then additional provinces, and lastly the whole population, were carried away as in the teeth of a beast of prey. (Comp. Amos iii. 6.) Assyria is here referred to as represented by Tiglath-pileser. We might also quote from the inscription of Sargon in fulfilment of this prediction: "Samaria I besieged; I captured 27,290 people dwelling in the midst of it; I carried captive" (George Smith, *Assyrian Eponym Canon*, p. 125). A similar fate overtook Jerusalem in 587 B.C., at the hands of Babylonia, in the reign of Nebuchadnezzar (2 Chron. xxxvi. 4—10; 2 Kings xxiv. 10—16, xxv. 1—11).

(15) Tenderness blends with judgment, and insulted love bleeds and hopes. The image of the lion is dropped. Jehovah speaks of "His own place"—Heaven. He will cause all manifestations of His regard for them to cease till "they suffer punishment, and seek my face," and, like the prodigal in the flush of a new morning, will arise and go unto the Father.

VI.

This chapter stands in immediate connection with the close of the preceding. The words of imperfect penitence (verses 1—3) are put by the prophet into the lips of those who are in trouble, and are counting too soon on the boundless compassion of Jehovah. They are not an exhortation to repentance, for they are followed by indignant expostulation.

(2) The haste of the seeming penitents for the fulfilment of their hope. They expect the rapid restoration of the national prosperity, prompted by the abundance

days will he revive us: in the third day
he will raise us up, and we shall live in
his sight. (3) Then shall we know, *if*
we follow on to know the LORD: his
going forth is prepared as the morning;
and he shall come unto us as the rain, as
the latter *and* former rain unto the earth.
(4) O Ephraim, what shall I do unto
thee? O Judah, what shall I do unto
thee? for your [1]goodness *is* as a morn-
ing cloud, and as the early dew it goeth
away. (5) Therefore have I hewed *them*
by the prophets; I have slain them by
the words of my mouth: [2]and thy
judgments *are as* the light *that* goeth
forth. (6) For I desired [a]mercy, and not
sacrifice; and the knowledge of God
more than burnt offerings. (7) But
they [3]like men have transgressed the
covenant: there have they dealt trea-
cherously against me. (8) Gilead *is* a
city of them that work iniquity, *and is*
[4]polluted with blood. (9) And as troops
of robbers wait for a man, *so* the com-
pany of priests murder in the way [5]by
consent: for they commit [6]lewdness.
(10) I have seen an horrible thing in the
house of Israel: there *is* the whoredom
of Ephraim, Israel is defiled. (11) Also,
O Judah, he hath set an harvest for
thee, when I returned the captivity of
my people.

1 Or, *mercy*, or, *kindness*.

2 Or, *that thy judgments might be*, &c.

a 1 Sam. 15. 22; Eccles. 5. 1; Matt. 9. 13 & 12. 7.

3 Or, *like Adam*.

4 Or, *cunning for blood*.

5 Heb., *with one shoulder*, or, *to Shechem*.

6 Or, *enormity*.

---

of the Divine love, and His response to the first touch of penitence (signified in chap. v. 15).

After two days.—A phrase sometimes used for the second day, *i.e.*, to-morrow.

In the third day—*i.e.*, after a short time. This and the above expression are not identical in the designation of time. Some Christian interpreters (Jerome, Luther, Pusey) consider the passage has sole reference to the resurrection of Christ. But with Calvin, Henderson, Schmoller, &c., we consider this to be contradicted by the form of the expression. To bring in the resurrection of Christ with no authority from the New Testament is far-fetched over-refinement, and breaks the consistency of the passage.

(2, 3) Render, *So that we shall live in his presence, and shall know and strive after the knowledge of Jehovah, whose coming forth is sure, like the dawn* (another play on verse 15, "I will return to my place, &c."), *so that he may come as the plentiful* (dashing) *rain for us, as the latter rain* (needed for the ripening corn) *which watereth the earth.*

(4) Here ends the supposed language of the penitents. If it were genuine, and accompanied by a deep sense of sin, it would not be in vain. But the prophet utters the heartrending response and expostulation of Jehovah, who bewails the transitory nature of their repentance.

Your goodness . . .—Better rendered, *Your love* (to me) *is like the morning cloud* (which promises rain, and does not give it; *like the dew* (or, "morning mist;" see Note, chap. xiv. 5), *which early goeth away*, vanishing in the blaze of summer day—your tears leaving you parched and dried as before.

(5) The LXX. render, *Therefore I have mowed down their prophets;* but this would destroy the parallelism, in which "prophets" correspond to "words of my mouth." The sense is, I have slain them by the announcement of deserved doom.

Thy judgments . . .—An error has crept here into the Masoretic text from which the LXX. and other ancient versions are free. The mistake consists in misplacing an initial letter as a final one. Translate, *My judgment shall go forth as the light*, clear, victorious, and beneficent. (Comp. the language of Ps. xxxvii. 6 and Isaiah lxii. 1, 2.)

(6) **Mercy.**—Better rendered, *love.* This passage is richly sustained by our Lord's adoption of its teaching (Matt. ix. 13, xii. 7). Mark xii. 33 shows that according to even Old Testament teaching, the moral ranks above the ceremonial, that ritual is valueless apart from spiritual conformity with Divine will.

(7) Critics differ much as to the interpretation of this verse. The marginal rendering supplies the strongest meaning. God made a covenant with Adam, and promised him the blessings of Paradise on condition of obedience. He broke the condition, transgressed the covenant, and was driven from his Divine home. So Israel had violated all the terms on which the goodly land of conditional promise had been bestowed. For the other references to Adam in the Old Testament see Ps. lxxxii. 7; Job xxxi. 33. (See *Excursus.*)

(8) **Polluted . . .**—More accurately, *betrodden* (or foot-tracked) *with blood.* We infer from Judg. x. 17 that there was a town called Gilead east of the Jordan, distinct altogether from Mizpah (identified by many with the city of refuge Ramoth-Gilead), and this is confirmed by notices in Eusebius and Cyril. Murder in a "city of refuge" adds to the horror. On the murderous propensities of the Gileadites see 2 Kings xv. 25.

(9) Should be rendered, *As a robber lies in wait, so the company of priests murder on the road to Shechem; yea, they execute the plot.* Shechem, charged with historic interest (Genesis to Judges), is also a city of refuge, a Levitical city, on the road to Bethel, where the priests of the calves resided. (Comp. chap. v. 1.)

(10) **House of Israel.**—This phrase means Ephraim and Judah subsequently discriminated. The "horrible thing" refers to polluting idolatry. This peculiar word occurs again in Jeremiah. According to the punctuation of the Hebrew the reciter hesitates before pronouncing the "horrible thing" which grated through his teeth.

(11) **An harvest.**—The harvest is not of joy, but of sorrow and affliction, befalling Judah, like Israel, for her sins: a contrast to the usual accompaniments of the season when the Feast of Tabernacles was celebrated (Deut. xii. 13—16; Lev. xxiii. 40; Ps. cxxvi. 5, 6). In regard of the last clause of the verse, "when I turn the captivity of my people," it is best to unite it with the succeeding chapter. (So Ewald, Reuss, &c.) Some writers (as recently, Nowack) explain the Hebrew word for captivity by a different etymology, and here interpret "destiny," or "fate." The full turning of the captivity cannot be realised till Ephraim and Judah accept the Christ.

CHAPTER VII.—(1) When I would
have healed Israel, then the iniquity
of Ephraim was discovered, and the
[1]wickedness of Samaria: for they com-
mit falsehood; and the thief cometh in,
and the troop of robbers [2]spoileth with-
out. (2) And they [3]consider not in their
hearts *that* I remember all their wicked-
ness: now their own doings have beset
them about; they are before my face.
(3) They make the king glad with their
wickedness, and the princes with their
lies. (4) They *are* all adulterers, as an
oven heated by the baker, [4]*who* ceaseth
[5]from raising after he hath kneaded the
dough, until it be leavened. (5) In the
day of our king the princes have made
him sick [6]with bottles of wine; he
stretched out his hand with scorners.
(6) For they have [7]made ready their
heart like an oven, whiles they lie in
wait: their baker sleepeth all the night;
in the morning it burneth as a flaming
fire. (7) They are all hot as an oven,
and have devoured their judges; all
their kings are fallen: *there is* none
among them that calleth unto me.
(8) Ephraim, he hath mixed himself
among the people; Ephraim is a cake
not turned. (9) Strangers have devoured
his strength, and he knoweth *it* not:
yea, gray hairs are [8]here and there upon
him, yet he knoweth not. (10) And the
[a]pride of Israel testifieth to his face:
and they do not return to the LORD
their God, nor seek him for all this.
(11) Ephraim also is like a silly dove
without heart: they call to Egypt, they

1 Heb., *evils*.
2 Heb., *strippeth*.
3 Heb., *say not to*.
4 Or, *the raiser will cease*.
5 Or, *from waking*.
6 Or, *with heat through wine*.
7 Or, *applied*.
8 Heb., *sprinkled*.
a ch. 5. 5.

VII.

This oracle is probably in the beginning of Hoshea's reign, and deals exclusively with the condition of the northern kingdom.

(1) Translate, *When I heal Israel* (referring to a cessation in the attacks of the menacing foe, or to such a thrill of finer feeling as that which is recorded in 2 Chron. xxviii. 8—15), *then is revealed the iniquity of Ephraim and the wickedness of Samaria, that they commit falsehood.* Samaria here sustains the same relation to Israel that Jerusalem does to Judah, and it is the very source of the corruption of the whole country.

(2) **Have beset them about.**—The wicked deeds of the nation crowded around them as witnesses to reveal their treason against Jehovah.

(3) **Glad.**—The evil awakens no alarm, but rather sympathy and gladness, in the breasts of their kings and rulers, who are ready to follow suit in all deeds of violence.

(4) Render, *ceaseth heating from the kneading of the dough till its leavening.* The baker is unremitting in his exertions to keep up the heat of the oven, the smouldering fire being fed on camel's dung and the like fuel, except when he is obliged to occupy himself with preparing the dough for baking—an apt image of the incessant burning rage of lust and violence.

(5) Following the hint of the LXX. and other versions, the rendering of which is based on a slightly different punctuation of the Hebrew, we prefer to translate, *the day of our king the princes have begun with the glowing* (or *fever*) *of wine*—*i.e.*, the carousal of the princely retinue in celebration of the sovereign's coronation-day (or birthday) commences at an early hour, significant of monstrous excess. (Comp. Acts ii. 15.) There is bitterness in the use of the pronoun "our" before "king." Otherwise we must render, *have made themselves ill with the fever of wine* (the Authorised version is here inaccurate). The last clause is obscure; probably it means "he (*i.e.*, our king) hath made common cause with scorners," and is boon-companion of the dissolute and depraved. (Comp. Exod. xxiii. 1.)

(6) Render, *Yea, they draw nigh together. Like an oven in their heart with their wiles. Their baker sleepeth all the night,* &c. The metaphor of verse 4 is resumed. The baker, having left his dough to become leavened and his fire to smoulder, can afford to sleep. The baker may mean the evil passion which has been raging. Indeed, Wünsche and Schmoller, by a slight change of punctuation, obtain the rendering "their anger," instead of "their baker," which is supported by the Targum and Syriac version. After the murderous plots and carousal, the conspiracy ripens with the day; then will come the outburst of violence.

(8) **Cake not turned.**—Referring to the destructive effect of foreign influences. Ephraim was consumed by the unhallowed fire of Baal-worship, with all its passion and sensualism—a cake burnt on one side to a cinder, and on the other left in a condition utterly unfit for food. So the activity of foreign idolatries and foreign alliances, and the consequent unfaithfulness to Israel's God, are the nation's ruin.

(9) **Have devoured.**—The past tense may refer to the invasions of Tiglath-pileser. Both Egypt and Assyria had come to regard Israel as the earthen pipkin between iron pots. These strangers have devoured his strength—*i.e.*, he has less power to resist aggression, less treasure, less land, smaller population. The signs of senility are upon him. "Grey hairs are his passing bell." He is under sentence of death, and knoweth it not.

(10) See Note on chap. v. 5.

(11) **Silly dove.**—No creature is less able to defend itself than the dove, which flies from the bird of prey to the net of the fowler. In this powerful metaphor we have a political allusion. King Hoshea is called *Ausih* on the Assyrian monuments. Having usurped the throne after the murder of Pekah, he "purchased his recognition as king of Israel by giving a large present to the Assyrian monarch" (730 B.C.). (See Geo. Smith, *Assyria*—S.P.C.K.) But while Hoshea was sending tribute to Assyria he was secretly coquetting with Egypt. The alliance between Egypt and the king of Israel, mentioned in 2 Kings xvii. 4, took place later, after Tiglath-pileser's death, and led to Israel's ruin. On the other hand, many commentators (Ewald, Nowack, &c.) refer the allusions of this verse to the reign of Menahem.

Without heart.—Better, *without understanding.*

go to Assyria. (12) When they shall go,
I will spread my net upon them; I will
bring them down as the fowls of the
heaven; I will chastise them, as their
congregation hath heard. (13) Woe unto
them! for they have fled from me:
[1]destruction unto them! because they
have transgressed against me: though I
have redeemed them, yet they have
spoken lies against me. (14) And they
have not cried unto me with their heart,
when they howled upon their beds: they
assemble themselves for corn and wine,
and they rebel against me. (15) Though
I [2]have bound *and* strengthened their
arms, yet do they imagine mischief
against me. (16) They return, *but* not to
the most High: they are like a deceit-
ful bow: their princes shall fall by the
sword for the [a]rage of their tongue:
this *shall be* their derision in the land of
Egypt.

CHAPTER VIII.—(1) *Set* the trumpet
to [3]thy mouth. *He shall come* as an
eagle against the house of the LORD,
because they have transgressed my
covenant, and trespassed against my
law. (2) Israel shall cry unto me, My
God, we know thee. (3) Israel hath cast
off *the thing that is* good: the enemy
shall pursue him. (4) They have set up
kings, but not by me: they have made
princes, and I knew *it* not: of their
silver and their gold have they made
them idols, that they may be cut off.
(5) Thy calf, O Samaria, hath cast *thee*
off; mine anger is kindled against them:

1 Heb., *spoil.*

B.C. cir. 760.

2 Or, *chastened.*

a Ps. 78. 9.

3 Heb., *the roof of thy mouth.*

---

(12) **When they shall go.**—Best rendered, *Whenever they go,* &c. The ultimate ruin produced by this policy of dependence on foreign states and of double-dealing intrigue was even at this early stage foreseen by the prophet, and portrayed under the simile of Jehovah's net snaring the unwary bird.

As their congregation hath heard.—Should be, *according to the report to their assembly*—*i.e.*, according to what they hear, perhaps from Hosea himself. The threatenings of the Pentateuch (Lev. xxvi. 14—39; Deut. xxviii. 13—68, xxxii. 15—35) find their echoes here.

(13) **Fled.**—The word thus translated is used of the wandering flight of birds, and arises naturally out of the images employed in verses 11 and 12.

(13) **Though I have redeemed.** — Should be, *Though I would fain redeem them:* an impressive picture of all the insults to longsuffering Divine love.

(14) **Cried . . . Howled**—God discriminates between a heart-cry to Him, and a howl of despair, resembling the yell of a wild beast. A howl upon their bed is not a sob of true repentance.

They assemble themselves.—To supplicate Jehovah for fruitful harvests. This rendering is supported by several eminent authorities. Others follow Ewald in translating, "they *excite* themselves" with dervish-like devices and cries. The LXX. render with great force, "they cut themselves." (Comp. 1 Kings xviii. 28; Deut. xiv. 1; Jer. xvi. 6.) This is based on a slightly different reading, contained in some of Kennicott's and De Rossi's MSS., which is not improbably the right one. The charge is that all their simulated penitence is to secure physical comforts, not to show conformity with the Divine will.

(15) **Bound.**—Should be *instructed.* God has imparted skill and power to fight their enemies. (Comp. Ps. cxliv. 1.) So the grace of the Spirit is often slighted by its recipients.

(16) **Like a deceitful bow.**—Religious observance has the appearance of a bow with the arrow on the string, apparently aimed at some object, but the string being slack, the aim is diverted.

The "raving insolence of their tongue" may mean the boasts that were made of the friendship of King *Shebaka* of Egypt, who made Israel his tool. In the land of Egypt they would thus become objects of derision. (Comp. Isaiah's warning to his countrymen, chap. xxx. 1—8.)

VIII.

A continuation of the same indictment along a new line of illustration. Jehovah bids the prophet put the trumpet to his lips and blow a shrill blast, announcing the approach of disaster.

(1) **Eagle.**—The image of swiftness (Jer. iv. 13, xlviii. 40). So Assyria shall come swooping down on Samaria, to which Hosea, though with some irony, gives the name "House of Jehovah," recognising that the calf was meant to be symbolic in some sense of Israel's God. (See, however, Note on chap. ix. 15.)

(2) Should be rendered, *To me they cry, My God, we know Thee, we Israel.*

(3) **Cast off.**—Jehovah's reply to Israel's hollow repentance. The word "cast off" means a scornful loathing of what is putrescent or obscene. "The thing that is good" is the name of God, which is the salvation of Israel (Aben Ezra).

(4) **Set up kings.**—It is possible that the prophet alludes to the history of the northern kingdom as a whole. Though the revolt of the Ten Tribes received Divine sanction (1 Kings xi. 9—11), it was obviously contrary to the Divine and prophetic idea which associated the growth of true religion with the line of David (chap. iii. 5). But it is best to regard the passage as referring to the short reigns of usurpers and to the foul murders which disgraced the annals of the northern kingdom since the death of Jeroboam II. Jehovah repudiates all participation in their anarchy.

Knew it not.—Should be, *knew them not*—viz., the gold and silver splendours wherewith Israel had adorned its apostacy.

(5) **Thy calf . . . hath cast thee off.**—Rather, *is loathsome.* Nothing can exceed the scorn of this outburst. The last clause should be rendered, *How long are ye unable to attain purity?* The attribution of consuming fire to God is not peculiar to the prophet. (Comp. Heb. xii. 29.)

how long *will it be* ere they attain to innocency? (6) For from Israel *was* it also: the workman made it; therefore it *is* not God: but the calf of Samaria shall be broken in pieces. (7) For they have sown the wind, and they shall reap the whirlwind: it hath no [1]stalk: the bud shall yield no meal: if so be it yield, the strangers shall swallow it up.

(8) Israel is swallowed up: now shall they be among the Gentiles as a vessel wherein *is* no pleasure. (9) For they are gone up to Assyria, a wild ass alone by himself: Ephraim hath hired [2]lovers. (10) Yea, though they have hired among the nations, now will I gather them, and they shall [3]sorrow a little for the burden of the king of princes. (11) Because Ephraim hath made many altars to sin, altars shall be unto him to sin. (12) I have written to him the great things of my law, *but* they were counted as a strange thing. (13) [4]They sacrifice flesh *for* the sacrifices of mine offerings, and eat *it*; *but* the LORD accepteth them not; now will he remember their iniquity, and visit their sins: they shall return to Egypt. (14) For Israel hath forgotten his Maker, and buildeth temples; and Judah hath multiplied fenced cities: but I will send a fire upon his cities, and it shall devour the palaces thereof.

1 Or, *standing corn.*

2 Heb., *loves.*

3 Or, *begin.*

4 Or, *In the sacrifices of mine offerings they, &c.*

CHAPTER IX.—(1) Rejoice not, O

(6) It is best to abandon the Masoretic punctuation, and translate, *For it* (*i.e.*, the calf) *is from Israel* (not of Divine origin); *as for it, an artificer made it, and it is no god. Yea, the calf of Samaria shall be shattered to fragments* (literally, *become splinters* or *fine dust*).

(7) **Wind . . . whirlwind.**—The great law of Divine retribution, the punishment for sin being often a greater facility in sinning—indifference to God becoming enmity, forgetfulness of duty or truth becoming violent recoil from both. "Wind" expresses what is empty and fruitless, and the pronoun "it" refers, in accordance with the metaphor, to such unproductive seed.

It hath no stalk.—Not even incipient prosperity, as in the days of Jeroboam II. "The growth shall yield no grain," as we might express the play of words in the Hebrew.

(8) **Vessel wherein is no pleasure**—*i.e.*, worthless (comp. Jer. xlviii. 38; Ps. xxxi. 13; 2 Tim. ii. 20); a vessel devoted to vilest uses, or smashed up as worthless.

(9) **Gone up to Assyria.**—The word thus translated is elsewhere used for "going up" to the sanctuary of the Lord. (See Note on chap. vii. 11.) *Wild ass* is the image of untamed waywardness (Job xxxix. 5, *seq.*) it is described by Wetzstein as inhabiting the steppes, a creature of dirty yellow colour, with long ears and no horns, and a head resembling a gazelle's. Its pace is so swift that no huntsman can overtake it. It is seldom seen alone, but in herds of several hundreds. From Jer. ii. 24 we infer that the animal wanders alone after the object of its lust. Israel, like a solitary wild ass, seeks strange loves, courts strange alliances. On the last clause, see Ezek. xvi. 32—34. Ephraim pays abnormally for her own shame.

(10) There is much difference of opinion as to the interpretation of this verse. Much depends on the reference of the word "them." We prefer to regard it as referring to Ephraim rather than to the nations (*i.e.*, Assyria and Egypt). Render, *I will gather them* (*Israel*) *together, so that in a short time they may delay* (this translation approved by Ewald, Wünsche, and Simson) *to render the tribute burden due to the king of princes* (*i.e.*, the Assyrian monarch). "Gather them together," *i.e.*, in restraint, so that they cannot roam so wildly, seeking help (Ewald). This accords with chaps. ii. 8, 9, iii. 4. Such non-payment of tribute actually occurred a few years later (2 Kings xvii. 4). Others render it: I will gather these nations (of the East) round about her to look scornfully on her ruin, and they shall sorrow a little (used ironically) at the imposition of the king of the princes.

(11) **Many altars.**—Multiplication of altars was condemned in the law (Deut. xii. 5 *seq.*). The narrative in Josh. xxii. shows that unity of altar and sanctuary was essential to the unity of the nation. The last clause should be rendered, *he had altars for sinning.* The worship of God was degraded into the sensuous approaching Baal-worship. In the first clause sin equals transgression, in the last transgression *plus* guilt and peril.

(12, 13) The rendering should be, *though I write for him a multitude of my precepts.* The tense "I write" is imperfect, and represents the continuous process—the prophetic teaching as well as the ancient Mosaic law. In the wild lust for a foreign religion the pure and spiritual Mosaic worship and the religious influence of prophecy had been forgotten. It seemed something "strange;" as Christ's cross and claims have been accounted strange by so-called Christians.

(13) **They sacrifice flesh . . .**—Should be, "They sacrifice the sacrifices of my gifts—flesh, and eat it." Clear reference to the Mosaic institute. Ye shall go back to Egypt, says the prophet, and there learn again the bitter lessons of the past—either the positive return to Egypt or the disastrous hankering after Egyptian alliances.

(14) **Temples.**—The word here used for temple is used sixty times for Jehovah's temple. The building of these temple-palaces was a distinct sin against the unity of the Godhead.

Judah hath multiplied fenced cities.—Referred to by Sennacherib, in the inscription relating to the campaign of 701 B.C.: "Forty-six of his (Hezekiah's) strong cities, fortresses . . . I besieged, I captured." These were erected by Uzziah and Jotham (2 Chron. xxvi. 10, xxvii. 4). With the allusions to Israel's temples (palaces) compare Amos iii. 11, 15.

IX.

It is now harvest and vintage-time—the period of annual vintage festivals, as at Shechem and Shiloh, to which the neighbouring villages gathered. The corn is being reaped, the wine-press is trodden, and the vats are overflowing. But behind this bright picture there

Israel, for joy, as *other* people: for thou
hast gone a whoring from thy God,
thou hast loved a [a]reward [1]upon every
cornfloor. (2) The floor and the [2]wine-
press shall not feed them, and the new
wine shall fail in her. (3) They shall
not dwell in the LORD's land; but
Ephraim shall return to Egypt, and
they shall eat unclean *things* in Assyria.
(4) They shall not offer wine *offerings* to
the LORD, neither shall they be pleasing
unto him: their sacrifices *shall be* unto
them as the bread of mourners; all that
eat thereof shall be polluted: for their
bread for their soul shall not come into
the house of the LORD. (5) What will
ye do in the solemn day, and in the day
of the feast of the LORD? (6) For, lo,
they are gone because of [3]destruction:
Egypt shall gather them up, Memphis
shall bury them: [4][5]the pleasant *places*
for their silver, nettles shall possess
them: thorns *shall be* in their taber-
nacles. (7) The days of visitation are
come, the days of recompence are come;
Israel shall know *it*: the prophet *is* a
fool, [6]the spiritual man *is* mad, for the
multitude of thine iniquity, and the
great hatred. (8) The watchman of
Ephraim *was* with my God: *but* the
prophet *is* a snare of a fowler in all his
ways, *and* hatred [7]in the house of his

a Jer. 44. 17.

1 Or, *in*, &c.

2 Or, *winefat.*

3 Heb., *spoil.*

4 Or, *their silver shall be desired, the nettle,* &c.

5 Heb., *the desire.*

6 Heb., *man of the spirit.*

7 Or, *against.*

---

looms to the prophet's gaze a sombre background. This and the following two chapters, which form a connected whole, contains another outburst of prophetic denunciation of the follies of idolatrous Israel.

(1) **For joy.**—Better, *to exultation.* "The harlot's hire on every corn-floor" expresses in bold imagery the prophet's scorn for the idolatrous corruption of the people. The bounteous yield of the harvest is called the "harlot's hire," which lures Jehovah's faithless bride to worship the false deity from whose hands these gifts were supposed to come. The people's momentary prosperity is attributed to their idols. (See chap. ii. 12; Jer. xliv. 17—19.)

(2) **Winepress.**—Read *wine-vat* (with margin), into which the *tîrôsh*, new wine ("grape-juice"), flowed from the winepress. (Comp. Isa. v. 2.) For "fail in her" read *deceive her*, with LXX. and Vulgate.

(3, 4) Canaan, the land of Jehovah, is holy, Assyria unholy (Amos vii. 17), where there was no temple or sacred ordinances. Since meat was not a divinely sanctioned food, except in connection with a Jehovah festival, it became in the land of exile unclean. This became true in the eyes of Hosea of all eating. "In the family every feast was a Eucharistic sacrifice" (W. R. Smith, *Old Testament in the Jewish Church*, pp. 235 and 237). (Comp. Ezek. iv. 13.)

(4) **Offer**—*i.e.*, pour out as a libation. A better rendering is to be obtained by abandoning the Hebrew accentuation: *And their sacrifices will not be pleasing to Him; it shall be to them as bread of sorrow—i.e.*, funeral food, which defiles for seven days those who partake of it. Another reference to the Mosaic legislation (Deut. xxvi. 14)—*Yea, their bread is for their appetite* (*i.e.*, *only for bodily sustenance*), *it cometh not to Jehovah's house* as a sacred offering.* These verses show that Hosea did not consider the worship of the Northern Kingdom as in itself illegal.

(5) See Note on chap. ii. 11.

(6) Translate, *Behold if they have gone from the desolation* (*i.e.*, Palestine laid waste by the invader), *Egypt shall gather them, Memphis bury them*—Memphis, the vast city and necropolis of Ptah, where Apis and Ibis, kings and men, lay by thousands mummied, the religious shrine of Egyptian faith in the under-world, from which Israel had been emancipated at the Exodus.—*There is a longing for their silver* (*i.e.*, they shall long for the silver left behind concealed in their desolate land.—*The thistle shall possess them, the thorn shall be in their tents.* Hosea prophesies an exile to Egypt after the anticipated invasion. That many exiles took refuge in Egypt in 721 B.C., after the great overthrow of the northern kingdom (as in the case of Judah in the days of Jeremiah), cannot admit of doubt. (Comp. chap. viii. 13 and verse 3 above; see chap. xi. 5, Note.)

(7) The latter part of the verse should be translated *Crazed is the prophet, mad the inspired one, because of the multitude of thy iniquity, while persecution is increased.* The prophet is crazed either in the depraved public opinion that Hosea scornfully describes, or, he is driven mad, distracted, by the persecutions to which he is subjected. The latter is more probable. (Comp. the following verse.) Other commentators, including Maurer and Hitzig (preceded by Jerome and many Jewish as well as Christian expositors) take the words for prophet in this verse as signifying "false prophet," and would connect the clauses thus:—"Israel shall recognise that the prophet (who prophesied good to them) is a fool, the inspired one a madman, because of," &c. But it is doubtful whether the Hebrew for "inspired one" (*îsh harûach*) can bear this unfavourable sense, with the definite article affixed (comp. 1 Kings. xxii. 21, Heb.); so Nowack. The passage is very difficult, and no decisive superiority can be claimed for any rendering yet proposed.

(8) **Prophet.**—Many hold that here (as in the previous verse) this word is used in a bad sense (false prophet), and standing contrasted with "the watchman of Ephraim" (or true prophet, Hosea himself, Jer. vi. 17; Ezek. iii. 17). They would render:—"The watchman of Ephraim is with my God." But the verse is capable of an altogether different, and, on the whole, more satisfactory interpretation: *Ephraim is a lier-in-wait, in conflict with my God. As for the prophet, the fowler's snare is in all his ways.* (Comp. Matt. xxiii. 34, 35.) *There is persecution in the house of his God.* The objection to this rendering lies in this use of the Hebrew *'im* ("in conflict with"). But the word might be read *'am*, "people" (comp. LXX. on 2 Sam. i. 2): "Ephraim, the people of my God, is a lier-in-wait"—a thought full of pathos, and in harmony with the main idea of this prophecy.

* Kuenen (Hibbert Lecture, p. 312) proposes an alteration in the text, whereby the parallelism becomes more harmonious and the construction simpler. He then renders, "They shall pour no libation of wine to Jehovah, and shall not lay out their sacrifices before Him: as food eaten in mourning is their food." This agrees better with chap. iii. 4.

God. (9) They have deeply corrupted
themselves, as in the days of [a]Gibeah:
therefore he will remember their iniquity,
he will visit their sins.
(10) I found Israel like grapes in the
wilderness; I saw your fathers as the
firstripe in the fig tree at her first time:
but they went to [b]Baal-peor, and separa-
ted themselves unto *that* shame; and
their abominations were according as
they loved. (11) *As for* Ephraim, their
glory shall fly away like a bird, from
the birth, and from the womb, and from
the conception. (12) Though they bring
up their children, yet will I bereave
them, *that there shall* not *be* a man *left*:
yea, woe also to them when I depart
from them! (13) Ephraim, as I saw
Tyrus, *is* planted in a pleasant place:
but Ephraim shall bring forth his
children to the murderer. (14) Give
them, O LORD: what wilt thou give?
give them a [1]miscarrying womb and dry
breasts. (15) All their wickedness [c]*is* in
Gilgal: for there I hated them: for the
wickedness of their doings I will drive
them out of mine house, I will love them
no more: all their princes *are* revolters.
(16) Ephraim is smitten, their root is
dried up, they shall bear no fruit: yea,
though they bring forth, yet will I slay
even [2]the beloved *fruit* of their womb.
(17) My God will cast them away, be-
cause they did not hearken unto him:
and they shall be wanderers among the
nations.

CHAPTER X.—(1) Israel *is* [3]an empty
vine, he bringeth forth fruit unto him-
self: according to the multitude of his
fruit he hath increased the altars; ac-
cording to the goodness of his land they

a Judg. 19. 18.

b Num.

1 Heb., *that casteth the fruit.*

c ch. 12. 11.

2 Heb., *the desires.*

3 Or, *a vine emptying the fruit which it giveth.*

---

(9) For the reference to Gibeah, see Judg. xix.

(10) **Grapes in the wilderness.**—Rich dainties to the desert traveller. So had Jehovah regarded His people at the commencement of their national history in the wilderness.

Firstripe.—The early fig that ripens in June, while the rest come to maturity about August (Isa. xxviii. 4; Micah vii. 1; Jer. xxiv. 2).

Baal-peor was the place where Moabitic idolatry was practised. This great disgrace had burned itself into their national traditions and literature (Num xxv.; Deut. iv. 3; Ps. cvi. 28—31).

Shame.—Heb. *bosheth* was a euphemism for Baal. Observe that names ending in "-bosheth" (Ish-bosheth, &c.) are replaced by the older forms in "-baal" in 1 Chron. Render the last clause, *they have become abominations like their love* (*i.e.*, Baal).

(11) **From the birth . . .**—Or rather, *so that there shall be no childbirth, nor pregnancy, nor conception*—an ascending climax. Progeny was the glory of ancient Israel (Gen. xxii. 17; Deut. vii. 13, 14; Ps. cxxvii. 5; Prov. xvii. 6).

(13) The LXX. suggest a doubt as to the validity of our text. They render "Ephraim, even as I saw, gave their children for a prey." The reference to Tyre is very obscure. Some would render the Hebrew word for "meadow" by "resting-place," and interpret, "I look on Ephraim even as I look on Tyre, planted in a sure resting-place." The impregnable fortress of Tyre was a conspicuous object in the days of Hosea. Similarly Samaria was a stronghold which was able to resist prolonged sieges. (Comp. Isaiah's graphic words: Isa. xxviii. 1—4, and Amos vi. 1)—"*Yet* Ephraim shall bring forth sons to the murderer," *i.e.*, in the impending overthrow and massacre, 721 B.C.

(14) Better universal childlessness than that the offspring should be exposed to so terrible a fate. Compare this with our Lord's words: "Blessed are the barren, and the wombs that never bare," &c.

(15) **Gilgal.**—On Gilgal as a seat of idolatrous worship, see chap. iv. 15. "My house" here, and in chap. viii. 1 ("Jehovah's house"), is interpreted by Wünsche and Nowack, with considerable show of reason, to mean the "holy land," Canaan. This interpretation is confirmed by the use of the Assyrian word *Bîtu*, corresponding to the Hebrew *bêth* "house." The term seems to have blended the conception of a people and the territory they occupied. (See Schrader, *Keilinschriften und das alte Testament*, p. 540, where the examples are cited *Bît-Am-ma-na* "Ammon," *Bît-A-di-ni*, "Beth-Eden.") Similarly, Egypt is called in Exod. xx. 2, "the house of slaves." We are reminded by the word "house" of the domestic episode (chaps. i.—iii.): Ephraim, like an adulterous wife, is turned out of house and home (comp. chap. iii. 4), and is no longer Jehovah's people (chap. i. 9).

(16) **They shall bear no fruit.**—Ephraim, whose very name signifies fruitfulness.

(17) **Wanderers.**—Strangely confirmed from Assyrian monuments and the entire subsequent history of the bulk of Israel; and Israel still wanders, not coalescing with any nation, unless they lose their ancient faith by corruption into idolatry, or conversion to Christianity. (See Pusey.)

X.

(1) **Empty** in the English version is wrong, being inconsistent with what follows. (Comp. LXX. and Vulg.) Read *luxuriant*. The metaphors of the vintage (comp. also Gen. xlix. 22, and *Introduction* to chap. ix.) are still prevalent in the mind of the prophet. Wünsche has powerfully illustrated this wild strong growth of Israel as compared with Judah. Joash prevailed over Amaziah, and plundered Jerusalem (2 Kings xiv. 12—14). Jeroboam II. extended his power as far as Hamath (2 Kings xiv. 23—25). The kingdom had resisted the attacks of Syria, and had become insolent as well as idolatrous. The last clause should be rendered, *The more abundant his fruit, the more he increased altars; the fairer his land, the fairer the Baal-pillars.* On "Baal-pillars," see W. R. Smith, *Old Testament in the Jewish Church*, pp. 248, 425. (Comp. ix. 1 and ii. 5.) Misapprehending the cause of their temporal prosperity, and wilfully ignoring Jehovah's forbearance and love, they attributed their mercies to the grace of Baal, and multiplied idolatrous shrines (see Romans ii. 4.)

have made goodly [1]images. (2) [2]Their
heart is divided; now shall they be
found faulty: he shall [3]break down
their altars, he shall spoil their images.
(3) For now they shall say, We have no
king, because we feared not the LORD;
what then should a king do to us?
(4) They have spoken words, swearing
falsely in making a covenant: thus
judgment springeth up as hemlock in
the furrows of the field. (5) The inhabit-
ants of Samaria shall fear because of
the calves of Beth-aven: for the people
thereof shall mourn over it, and [4]the
priests thereof *that* rejoiced on it, for
the glory thereof, because it is departed
from it. (6) It shall be also carried unto
Assyria *for* a present to [a]king Jareb:
Ephraim shall receive shame, and Israel
shall be ashamed of his own counsel.
(7) *As for* Samaria, her king is cut off as
the foam upon [5]the water. (8) The high
places also of Aven, the sin of Israel,
shall be destroyed: the thorn and the
thistle shall come up on their altars;
[b]and they shall say to the mountains,
Cover us; and to the hills, Fall on us.
(9) O Israel, thou hast sinned from the
days of Gibeah: there they stood: the
battle in Gibeah against the children of
iniquity did not overtake them. (10) *It is*
in my desire that I should chastise them;
and the people shall be gathered against
them, [6]when they shall bind themselves
in their two furrows. (11) And Ephraim
is as an heifer *that is* taught, *and* loveth
to tread out *the corn;* but I passed over
upon [7]her fair neck: I will make
Ephraim to ride; Judah shall plow, *and*
Jacob shall break his clods. (12) Sow to
yourselves in righteousness, reap in
mercy; [c]break up your fallow ground:

1 Heb., *statues*, or, *standing images*.
2 Or, *He hath divided their heart.*
3 Heb., *behead.*
B.C. cir. 740.
4 Or, *Chemarim.*
a ch. 5. 13.
5 Heb., *the face of the water.*
b Isa. 2. 19; Luke 23. 30; Rev. 6. 16 & 9. 6.
6 Or, *when I shall bind them for their two transgressions*, or, *in their two habitations.*
7 Heb., *the beauty of her neck.*
c Jer. 4. 3.

---

(2) **Their heart is divided** is the rendering of the LXX., Raschi, Aben-Ezra, and most ancient versions. But modern expositors prefer to translate "Their heart is treacherous (*smooth*)." The rest of the verse should run thus:—*Now shall they suffer punishment. He shall break* (*the horns of*) *their altars; he shall destroy their pillars.*

(3) **To us.**—Better, *as for a king, what will he do for us?* The prophet having witnessed a succession of Israelite kings overthrown, and anarchy as its consequence, predicts yet another time of confusion and helplessness, a full vindication of the threatenings of the prophet Samuel. (Comp. 1 Sam. viii. 19.)

(4) **Judgment**—*i.e.*, Divine judgments shall prevail not as a blessing, but as a curse; not as a precious harvest, but as a poisonous plant (poppy or hemlock) in the ridges of the field.

(5) It is hard to express the sarcastic force and concentrated scoff of the original: "calves," literally, *she calves*, the feminine form to express contempt, the plural in allusion to the scattered worship in numerous shrines throughout Israel (or, perhaps, a *pluralis majestatis* of mockery). The next clause should read thus:—*For it* (pers. pronoun, referring to *the* calf *par excellence* of the chief seat of worship at Bethel, here degraded into Bethaven), *people mourn because of it, and its priests tremble because of it.* (The word for "priests," *kemarim*, means always idolatrous priesthood.

(6) Translate, *Even that* (*i.e.*, the calf) *shall be carried* (in triumphant state) *to Assyria, an offering to King Jareb.* (See chap. v. 13, *Excursus.*)

(7) **Foam . . . Water.**—One of the most striking images in the prophecy. The word *qetseph*, rendered "foam"—*Speaker's Commentary* reads "bubble"—properly signifies "chip", or "fragment." Translate: *Like a chip on the waters' surface.* The king is tossed on the raging seas of political life like a helpless fragment. Such was the instability of the throne of Israel at this period. (Comp. chap. xiii. 11.)

(8) **Aven.**—On Beth-Aven, see Note on chap. iv. 15. The "thorn and thistle" are part of the first curse upon apostate Adam (Gen. iii. 18), and the prophet not only predicts utter ruin for king and calf, temple and shrine, but the future desolation which should conceal all. Meanwhile, the people shall desire death rather than life. The awful words in the latter part of this verse are used by our Lord concerning the terrors of the impenitent in the fall of Jerusalem (Luke xxiii. 30), and twice by St. John (Rev. vi. 16, ix. 6), to denote the extremity of despair.

(9) **O Israel . . . Gibeah.**—Thou didst commence thy obscene transgressions long before the disruption of the kingdom of Rehoboam, even at Gibeah. Gibeah is emblematic of gross and cruel sensuality, in allusion to Judges xix. 20, just as Sodom is used for unnatural vice.

There they stood.—Or rather, *remained* sinning after the same manner. The rest of the verse should be rendered, *Shall there not overtake them in Gibeah* (used mystically) *the war made against the wicked?* (Comp. Judges xx.) But Dr. Pusey and others take it categorically, implying that though the exterminating war against the men of Gibeah did not overtake them, and has not yet, it shall now, and soon. But the former interpretation is to be preferred.

(10) Translate (see Margin; so Jerome), *When I desire, I will chastise them, and peoples shall be gathered against them, when I chastise them for their two iniquities* (*i.e.*, the two calves which had been the source of heresy and treason against Jehovah).

(11) **Heifer.**—Translate, *Ephraim is a trained heifer, which loves to thresh.* Here the idea may be that Ephraim loves the easy and free work of treading out the corn, and so becomes fat and sleek; or the act of treading and threshing may point to the rough treatment which Ephraim has in her pride dealt out to her neighbours and enemies. But the former interpretation is more probable. The verse should continue to read thus:—*And I passed by the fairness of her neck* (to arrest her self-indulgence). *I will harness Ephraim for riding*—*i.e.*, I will cause a rider, Assyria, to take possession of her, and she shall be bound in unwelcome toil to do the bidding of another.

(12) In their despair come some characteristic gleams of hope on the desolation; the eternal law which

for *it is* time to seek the LORD, till he
come and rain righteousness upon you.
(13) Ye have plowed wickedness, ye have
reaped iniquity; ye have eaten the
fruit of lies: because thou didst trust
in thy way, in the multitude of thy
mighty men. (14) Therefore shall a tu-
mult arise among thy people, and all
thy fortresses shall be spoiled, as Shal-
man spoiled [a]Beth-arbel in the day of
battle: the mother was dashed in pieces
upon *her* children. (15) So shall Beth-el
do unto you because of [1]your great
wickedness: in a morning shall the king
of Israel utterly be cut off.

CHAPTER XI.—(1) When Israel *was*
a child, then I loved him, and [b]called
my son out of Egypt. (2) *As* they called
them, so they went from them: they
sacrificed unto Baalim, and burned in-
cense to graven images. (3) I taught
Ephraim also to go, taking them by
their arms; but they knew not that I
healed them. (4) I drew them with
cords of a man, with bands of love: and
I was to them as they that [2]take off the
yoke on their jaws, and I laid meat unto
them.

(5) He shall not return into the land of
Egypt, but the Assyrian shall be his
king, because they refused to return.
(6) And the sword shall abide on his
cities, and shall consume his branches,
and devour *them*, because of their own
counsels. (7) And my people are bent to

a 2 Kin. 18. 34 & 19. 13.

1 Heb., *the evil of your evil.*

b Matt. 2. 15.

2 Heb., *lift up.*

---

makes reaping a consequence of sowing will still apply. The mercy of God will be the harvest of a sowing to the Spirit. (Comp. Gal. vi. 8; Rom. viii. 7—13; and Micah vi. 8.) The very soil of the soul is fallow and unbroken. Break it up, seek Jehovah, and He will come as never before. This momentary rift in the storm-cloud shows the light behind it.

(13) **Thy way.**—By a slight change of the Hebrew word thus rendered it acquires the sense, *thy chariots*, a reading followed by the LXX. and Ewald, Kuinöl, and Nowack. It establishes a good parallelism, and harmonises with prophetic teaching (chap. xiv. 3; Isa. ii. 7). The Masoretic text gives, however, a fine meaning.

(14) Then comes the crash of the thunder-peal. The prophet seems to hear the advance of the invading army, and see the fall of Samaria's fortress.

Shalman.—The references in the margin are not to the same historic event. The allusion is very obscure. Schrader (*Keilinschriften*, 2nd ed., pp. 440—2) suggests two theories: one that it refers to an episode in the campaign of Shalmaneser III. to the "cedar country" (Lebanon), in 775 B.C., or to Damascus in 773. He might then have penetrated into the Transjordanic country, and destroyed Arbela, near Pella (Beth-arbel). The other theory, that we have here a mention of the Moabitish king *Salmanu*, whose name occurs in Tiglath-pileser's inscription, is far-fetched and improbable. On the other hand, Geiger, following the hint of Jerome, identifies Shalman with Zalmunna (Judges viii. 18; comp. Ps. lxxxiii. 11). The kind of barbarity here referred to is illustrated by 2 Kings viii. 12; Ps. cxxxvii. 8, 9.

(15) **King . . . Cut off.**—The close of the kingdom (721 B.C.), already more than once referred to (comp. verse 7), is here prophesied. Translate, *So shall He do to you at Bethel.*

In the morning.—Should be, *in the early morning* Hoshea was utterly cut off, leaving neither root nor branch.

XI.

(1) Comp. chap. ix. 10 and Exod. iv. 22, 23. In this context there cannot be a prophecy of the Christ, for obstinate conduct and rebellion would thus be involved in the prediction. It is true that Matt. ii. 15 quotes the passage in illustration of the fact that the true Son of God was also submitted in His youth to the hard schooling of a cruel exile. The calling out of Egypt of the Messiah gave a new indication of the cyclical character of Hebrew history. The passage helps us to understand what is meant by the formula, "that it might be fulfilled," &c.

(2) **As they** (*i.e.*, the prophets) **called them, so they** (Israel) **went from them.**—Sought to avoid the voice and presence of the men of God.

(3) Read, *Yet it was I who guided Ephraim's steps, taking him by his arms.* There is a beautiful parallel to this in Deut. xxxii. 10, 11.

Knew not . . .—This obtuseness to the source of all mercies—the refusal to recognise the true origin in Divine revelation of those ideas which, though they bless and beautify life, are not recognised as such revelation, but are treated as "the voice of nature," or "development of humanity," or "dictum of human reason"—is one of the commonest and most deadly sins of modern Christendom. The unwillingness to recognise the Divine Hand in "creation," "literature," "history" takes the opposed forms of Pantheism and Pyrrhonism. To each of these the prophet's words apply.

(4) **Cords of a man.**—In contrast with the cords with which unmanageable beasts are held in check. Israel is led with "bands of love," not of compulsion. Render the last clause, *And gently towards them gave I food to eat*, expressing the tenderness, delicacy, and condescension of his personal regard.

(5) It is best, with Ewald, to take the two clauses as interrogative, *Shall he not return into the land of Egypt? And shall not the Assyrian, &c.?* (See Notes on chaps. viii. 13, x. 3—6. Comp. also verse 11.)

Return—*i.e.*, to God.

(6) The rendering of the English version is here incorrect. Render, *Then shall the sword be brandished amid his cities, and utterly destroy his princes.* The word for "princes" is, literally, *bars*, the heroes, leaders, or defenders of the state being aptly called barriers, or bulwarks. Analogous metaphors frequently occur in the Old Testament; such is the interpretation of the Targum.

(7) No imagery is used, as of unfaithful wife, recalcitrant heifer, or furnace-piling baker, but homely literal commonplace. The people were called by sufficient means to the highest worship, but they were bent on the lowest.

backsliding from me: though they called
them to the most High, [1]none at all
would exalt *him*.
(8) How shall I give thee up, Ephraim?
how shall I deliver thee, Israel? how
shall I make thee as [a]Admah? *how* shall
I set thee as Zeboim? mine heart is
turned within me, my repentings are
kindled together. (9) I will not execute
the fierceness of mine anger, I will not
return to destroy Ephraim: for I *am*
God, and not man; the Holy One in the
midst of thee: and I will not enter into
the city. (10) They shall walk after the
LORD: he shall roar like a lion: when he
shall roar, then the children shall tremble
from the west. (11) They shall tremble
as a bird out of Egypt, and as a dove out
of the land of Assyria: and I will place
them in their houses, saith the LORD.

(12) Ephraim compasseth me about with
lies, and the house of Israel with deceit:
but Judah yet ruleth with God, and is
faithful [2]with the saints.

CHAPTER XII.—(1) Ephraim feedeth
on wind, and followeth after the east
wind: he daily increaseth lies and deso-
lation; and they do make a covenant
with the Assyrians, and oil is carried
into Egypt. (2) The LORD hath also a
controversy with Judah, and will [3]punish
Jacob according to his ways; according
to his doings will he recompense him.
(3) He took his brother [b]by the heel in
the womb, and by his strength he [4c]had
power with God: (4) yea, he had power
over the angel, and prevailed: he wept,
and made supplication unto him: he
found him *in* [d]Beth-el, and there he

1 Heb., *together they exulted not.*

a Gen. 19. 24; Amos 4. 11.

2 Or, *with the most holy.*

3 Heb., *visit upon.*

b Gen. 25. 26.

4 Heb., *was a prince,* or, *behaved himself princely.*

c Gen. 32. 24.

d Gen. 35. 9. 10.

---

(8) In the depth of despair the prophet delivers himself of one of the most pathetic passages in Hebrew prophecy. On the darkest cloud gleams the bow of promise. A nation so much beloved as Israel cannot be destroyed by Him who has fostered it so tenderly. As the prophet loved his faithless bride, so Jehovah continued to love His people. The "how?" of this verse expresses the most extreme reluctance. Admah and Zeboim were cities of the plain destroyed with Sodom and Gomorrah, which are often referred to as the type of irremediable catastrophe. (Comp. Isa. i. 9, xiii. 19; Matt. x. 15.)

Mine heart is turned within me.—Better, *against me*—a violent revulsion of feeling. Divine compassion pleads with Divine justice.

(9) This sublime passage is remarkable as drawing illustrations from human emotions, and yet repudiating all human weakness. It suggests a hint of Divine mercy in its greatness, and of Divine justice too, which shows how, both being alike infinite, they can adjust themselves beyond the power of human experience and imagination.

The Holy One in the midst of thee is such a blending of justice and mercy.

I will not enter into the city.—So ancient versions. "Enter"—*i.e.*, as a destroyer. (Comp. verse 6.) But many commentators interpret the Hebrew *b'îr* ("into the city") to mean *in wrath*. This is preferable.

(10) Render, *They shall go up after Jehovah, who roars as a lion; yea, he shall roar so that the children,* &c. Lions accompanied Egyptian monarchs to the battle-field. Read the picturesque description of Rameses II. in his battle with the Kheta, by George Ebers in *Uarda*. "West" means the coast and islands of the Levant.

Tremble—*i.e.*, come with an awe-stricken joy to the voice of the Divine summons.

(11) **Will place them.**—Better, *will cause them to dwell.* The prophetic word looks beyond the restoration of the sixth century B.C. to the gathering together of some from east and west, from all the places where they are hidden in exile under the lion of the tribe of Judah; the broader and grander accomplishment will satisfy and more than fulfil the yearnings of the spiritual Israel.

(12) Should stand as the first verse of chap. xii., just as in the Hebrew text. The rest of the prophecy appears as a distinct composition, a new commencemen, of judgment and incrimination, followed at last by one more utterance of Divine promise.

The rendering of the latter part of the verse in the English version was that of the Jewish scholars who saw here a reference to the reign of Hezekiah, but it is opposed to the mention of the "controversy with Judah" in chap. xii. 3. Accordingly, the rendering adopted by Ewald, Wünsche, Nowack, and others, is more probable:—"And Judah still roves unbridled towards God, and towards the faithful Holy One," Judah's inconstancy being contrasted with the faithfulness of God. The plural form, the Holy Ones, may, like the plural forms, Elohîm, Adonîm, suggest personalities within the substance of deity. The LXX. seem to indicate that we have not the right Hebrew text here.

XII.

(1) **East wind.**—Comp. Isa. xxvii. 8 and Job xxvii. 21. On the latter passage Wetzstein remarks:—"This wind is more frequent in winter and early spring, when, if it continues long, the tender vegetation is parched up, and a year of famine follows. Both man and beast feel sickly while it prevails." Hence, that which is unpleasant and revolting in life is compared by Orientals to the east wind. The idea expressed by the east wind here is the same as in Job xv. 2, combining the notions of destructiveness and emptiness. The covenant with Assyria refers to the events of the reign of Hoshea. Covenants with Assyria, and presents to Egypt were to Hosea curses in disguise. (See Note on chap. vii 11.)

(2) **Jacob** refers to the northern kingdom.

(3, 4) **Had power.**—Should be, *strove.* Prayers and tears were the weapons used in the memorable struggle for pardon, reconciliation, peace in the self-conquest as well as the God-conquest which was achieved. "At Bethel He (Jehovah) found him (Jacob)" not once only, but on repeated occasions

spake with us; (5) even the LORD God
of hosts; the LORD *is* his [a]memorial.
(6) Therefore turn thou to thy God: keep
mercy and judgment, and wait on thy
God continually.

(7) *He is* [1]a merchant, the balances of
deceit *are* in his hand: he loveth to
[2]oppress. (8) And Ephraim said, Yet I
am become rich, I have found me out
substance: [3]*in* all my labours they shall
find none iniquity in me [4]that *were* sin.
(9) And I *that am* the LORD thy God from
the land of Egypt will yet make thee to
dwell in tabernacles, as in the days of
the solemn feast. (10) I have also spoken
by the prophets, and I have multiplied
visions, and used similitudes, [5]by the
ministry of the prophets. (11) *Is there*
iniquity *in* Gilead? surely they are
vanity: they sacrifice bullocks in [b]Gil-
gal; yea, their altars *are* as heaps in
the furrows of the fields.

(12) And Jacob [c]fled into the country
of Syria, and Israel [d]served for a wife,
and for a wife he kept *sheep*. (13) [e]And
by a prophet the LORD brought Israel
out of Egypt, and by a prophet was he
preserved. (14) Ephraim provoked *him*
to anger [6]most bitterly: therefore shall
he leave his [7]blood upon him, and his
reproach shall his Lord return unto
him.

a Ex. 3. 15.
1 Or, *Canaan.*
2 Or, *deceive.*
3 Or, *all my labours suffice me not:* he shall have *punishment of iniquity in whom* is *sin.*
4 Heb., *which.*
5 Heb., *by the hand.*
b ch. 4. 15 & 9. 15.
c Gen. 28. 5.
d Gen. 29. 20, 28.
e Ex. 12. 50, 51 & 13. 3.
6 Heb., *with bitternesses.*
7 Heb., *bloods.*

(Gen. xxviii. 11, xxxv. 1), and in the subsequent history of the children of Israel.

(5) **Lord God of hosts.**—See Cheyne's *Isaiah*, vol. i., pp. 11, 12, and Nowack's commentary on this passage. Probably the hosts were the stars which were conceived of as celestial spirits standing upon or above Jehovah's throne in Micaiah's vision, on the right hand and on the left (1 Kings xxii. 19). These are to be identified, in all probability, with the sons of God (Gen. vi. 2), described in Job i. 6 as presenting themselves in council before Jehovah. In Ps. ciii. 21 they are described as God's ministers; also in Ps. civ. 4, quoted in Heb. i. 7.

His memorial—*i.e.*, his name. (See Notes on Exod. iii. 15, vi. 3.) Jehovah—*i.e.*, the self-existent One who nevertheless came into personal relations with Israel.

(6) **Therefore . . .** —More correctly, *But do thou return to thy God.* There is an implied contrast between the patriarch and his degenerate descendants in the days of Hosea.

(7) **He is a merchant.**—The vivid and fierce light of the prophet's words is obscured in the English version. The rendering "he is a merchant" originates from the fact that Canaan (rendered "merchant") is often used predominantly of Phœnicia, and Canaanites of Phœnicians, the great trading race (Isa. xxiii. 11; Job xl. 30). Translate: *As for Canaan, in his hand are false balances. He loves cheating.* The descendants of Canaan (the son of Ham, the abhorred son of Noah) became in their whole career a curse and a byeword in every religious and ethical sense. The princes of Tyre, the merchandise of Phœnicia, were, perhaps, then in the prophet's mind. (Comp. Ezek. xxvii.)

Moreover, the prophet hints that Ephraim had imbibed Phœnicia's love of gain and habits of unscrupulous trade. The literature of this period contains frequent references to these tendencies in Israel (Amos ii. 6, viii. 5; Micah vi. 10).

(8) Translate, *And Ephraim saith, Surely I have become wealthy; I have gotten me substance* (*i.e.*, by legitimate means, not robbery): *all my earnings bring me not guilt as would be sin* (*i.e.*, requiring expiation). Such a coarse pursuit of wealth, and such glorying in the innocence of the entire process by which it has been obtained, has its parallel in the moral position of the Laodicean Church, rebuked by our Lord (Rev. iii.).

(9) **Tabernacles.**—The prophet here speaks of Israel's moral restoration under the form of a return to "the old ideal of simple agricultural life, in which every good gift is received directly from Jehovah's hand." To the true theocratic spirit the condition here spoken of is one of real blessedness, but to the worldly, grasping Canaan or Ephraim it would come as a threat of expulsion, desolation, and despair. (Comp. chaps. ii. 14, iii. 3.)

(11) Translate, *If Gilead be worthless, surely they have become nought. In Gilgal they sacrificed bullocks; their altars also are like heaps upon the field's furrows,* referring to a past event, the desolating invasion of Gilead by Tiglath-pileser, in 734 B.C. To this military expedition we have undoubted references in the inscriptions of Tiglath-pileser II. But unfortunately they are in a very mutilated condition. From one passage we learn:—"The city Gil [ead] and [A] bel [Maacha] which is on this side the land Beth Omri (Samaria) the distant . . . I joined in its whole extent to the territory of Assyria." The biblical passage, 2 Kings xv. 29, supplements this account by stating that Naphtali and Galilee also fell victims to the victorious arms of the invader. From the verse before us we infer that Gilgal, on the western bank of the Jordan near Jericho (see Note on iv. 15), likewise felt the heavy hand of the conqueror, or perhaps the inhabitants fled in panic and the local shrines became deserted ruins. From this time forth we hear no more of Gilgal as a religious centre. Nowack, however, follows Ewald in regarding the passage as prophetic of a coming calamity. (See *Introduction.*) In the word for "heaps" (*galîm*) there is a play on the name *Gilgal.*

(12) **Jacob . . . Israel.**—Resuming the retrospect over early patriarchal history, begun in verse 4. Notwithstanding the loneliness and humble position of the patriarch, God took care of him, and he won the mighty name of Israel, and gave it to his descendants.

Country.—More accurately, *plain.*

(13) **A prophet.**—Moses is here referred to, and there is, perhaps, a hint that the Lord would yet again save Israel from worse than Egyptian bondage by the words and warnings of a prophet.

(14) But the rift in the clouds closes again, and another severe rebuke follows. "Jacob" and "Israel" give place to the proud tribal name of Ephraim. This portion of the whole house of Israel incurs the charge. Read, *Ephraim hath provoked bitter feeling.* The bloodguiltiness of Moloch sacrifices and other iniquity God will not remove. (Comp. Gen. xxvii. 43, xxviii., xxix., for the foundation of these references.)

CHAPTER XIII.—(1) When Ephraim
spake trembling, he exalted himself in
Israel; but when he offended in Baal,
he died. (2) And now [1]they sin more
and more, and have made them molten
images of their silver, *and* idols accord-
ing to their own understanding, all of
it the work of the craftsmen: they say
of them, Let [2]the men that sacrifice kiss
the calves. (3) Therefore they shall be
as the morning cloud, and as the early
dew that passeth away, as the chaff *that*
is driven with the whirlwind out of the
floor, and as the smoke out of the
chimney.

(4) Yet [a]I *am* the LORD thy God from
the land of Egypt, and thou shalt know
no God but me: for *there is* no saviour
beside me. (5) I did know thee in the
wilderness, in the land of [3]great drought.
(6) According to their pasture, so were
they filled; they were filled, and their
heart was exalted; therefore have they
forgotten me. (7) Therefore I will be
unto them as a lion: as a leopard by
the way will I observe *them:* (8) I will
meet them as a bear *that is* bereaved *of
her whelps,* and will rend the caul of
their heart, and there will I devour them
like a lion: [4]the wild beast shall tear
them.

(9) O Israel, thou hast destroyed thy-
self; but in me [5]*is* thine help. (10) I
will be thy king: where *is any other*
that may save thee in all thy cities?
and thy judges of whom thou saidst,
Give me a king and princes? (11) I gave
thee a [b]king in mine anger, and took
him away in my wrath. (12) The iniquity
of Ephraim *is* bound up; his sin *is* hid.
(13) The sorrows of a travailing woman
shall come upon him: he *is* an unwise

1 Heb., *they add to sin.*

2 Or, *the sacrificers of men.*

B.C. cir. 725.

a Isa. 43. 11; ch. 12. 9.

3 Heb., *droughts.*

4 Heb., *the beast of the field.*

5 Heb., *in thy help.*

b 1 Sam. 8. 5. & 15. 23 & 16. 1.

XIII.

(1) There is a difference of opinion as to the construction and rendering of this verse. We adopt the interpretation, *When Ephraim uttered terror, he rebelled in Israel; then he committed sin through Baal, and died.* This points to the revolt of the Ten Tribes, and the consequent abandonment of the pure traditions of Jehovah worship for those of Baal. This idea and that of the previous verse (chap. xii. 14) may have been brought into prominence by the recent untoward antagonism aroused by the Syro-Ephraimitish war against Judah.

(2) Ewald, following the hint of the LXX. (who had a slightly different text), renders "according to their pattern of idols." (Comp. the language of satire in Ps. cxv.; Isa. xliv. 10—17.)

Men that sacrifice.—More accurately, *sacrificers from among men.* Others would render "sacrificers of men." But the former is quite consistent with Hebrew usage, while the latter compels us to adopt the unwarrantable supposition that human sacrifices formed part of the calf-worship. The calf images were kissed like those of the Madonna in Roman Catholic churches at the present day. The Greek προσκυνέω, "to worship," meant originally to adore by kissing (Curtius, *Greek Etymology,* p. 158).

(3) **Early dew . . .**—Better, *dew that early passeth away, like chaff that flies in a whirlwind from the threshing-floor, and like smoke from the window* (*i.e.,* the lattice beneath the roof through which it vanished).

(4) The LXX. have an addition which was not found by Jerome in any Hebrew copy of his day, and was pronounced by him to be spurious: "I am the Lord thy God, that establisheth the heavens and createth the earth, whose hands have fashioned all the host of heaven; but I did not show them to thee that thou shouldest go after them, and I brought thee up out of the land of Egypt, and thou shalt know," &c.

(6) **According to their pasture.**—Rather, *As they pastured.* (Comp. the language of Deut. viii. 7—18, xxxi. 20, xxxii. 15.) The gifts of Divine love concealing the giver.

(7) **I will be . . .**—More correctly, *have become . . . as a panther in the way do I lie in wait.* The idea of this and the following verses is that of a Divine judgment suspended over Israel, destined soon to fall with overwhelming ruin (721 B.C.). The English version follows the interpretation of the Targum. But the LXX., Vulg., and Syriac versions are based on a slightly different reading of the text contained in some Hebrew MSS. They render, "as a panther on the way to Assyria."

(8) The same imagery is continued to describe the destructive wrath of the Lord. "The caul of the heart" means here the covering of the heart, not the pericardium, but the breast in which the claws of the beast are fastened.

(9) **In me . . . Help.**—The close of this verse is rhetorically abrupt, which is altogether missed in the English version. Render, *but against Me thy help.* We must supply "Thou hast rebelled," the construction being the same as in verse 16. "Thy captivity, O Israel, is from thee; thy redemption is from Me; thy perishing is from thee: thy salvation is from Me" (Pusey).

(10) The rendering should be, *Where, pray, is thy king, that he may save thee?* &c. The original demand for a king who should be a visible token to Israel of protection against their surrounding foes was adverse to the true spirit of the kingdom of God upon earth, and, though granted, proved to the united kingdom, and afterwards to the kingdom of Israel, an age-long curse. Probably the special reference here is to the latter—the erection of the Ten Tribes into a separate monarchy.

(11) **Gave . . . Took.**—The past tenses should be present: "I give . . ." "take away." The whole succession of Israelite kings, who generation after generation had been taken away, some by violent death, would close with Hoshea, who was to disappear as "a fragment on a stormy sea" (chap. x. 7).

(12) **Bound up . . . Hid.**—The binding up and hiding away of Ephraim's sin as in a secret place, for ultimate disclosure, prepares us for the terrible words that follow.

(13) **Travailing woman.**—Ephraim is first addressed as a travailing woman; but the imagery passes

son; for he should not stay [1]long in *the*
place of the breaking forth of children.
(14) I will ransom them from [2]the power
of the grave; I will redeem them from
death: [a]O death, I will be thy plagues;
O grave, I will be thy destruction:
repentance shall be hid from mine
eyes.
(15) Though he be fruitful among *his*
brethren, [b]an east wind shall come, the
wind of the LORD shall come up from
the wilderness, and his spring shall become
dry, and his fountain shall be
dried up: he shall spoil the treasure of
all [3]pleasant vessels. (16) Samaria shall
become desolate; for she hath rebelled
against her God: they shall fall by the
sword: their infants shall be dashed in
pieces, and their women with child shall
be ripped up.

CHAPTER XIV.—(1) O Israel, return
unto the LORD thy God; for thou hast
fallen by thine iniquity. (2) Take with
you words, and turn to the LORD: say
unto him, Take away all iniquity, and
[4]receive *us* graciously: so will we render
the [c]calves of our lips. (3) Asshur shall
not save us; we will not ride upon
horses: neither will we say any more to
the work of our hands, *Ye are* our gods:
for in thee the fatherless findeth mercy.
(4) I will heal their backsliding, I will
love them freely: for mine anger is
turned away from him. (5) I will be as
the dew unto Israel: he shall [5]grow as

1 Heb., *a time.*
2 Heb., *the hand.*
a 1 Cor. 15. 55.
b Ezek. 19. 12.
3 Heb., *vessels of desire.*
4 Or, *give good.*
c Heb., 13. 15.
5 Or, *blossom.*

---

to the condition of the unborn child, which tarries just where it should issue into the light of the world. Lack of seasonable repentance increases the danger at this critical stage of Israel's destiny. The latter part of the verse is missed in the rendering of the English version. Read, *For at the right time he standeth not in the place where children break forth.* But the use of the Hebrew word for "at the right time" (*'ēth*) is doubtful. Perhaps the word should be read *'attah* ("now"), as Buhl, in *Zeitschrift für Kirchliche Wissenschaft,* suggests. (Comp. Ezek. xxvii. 34.)

(14) **O death . . . O grave.**—The rendering should be, *Where is thy plague, O death? Where is thy sting, O Sheol?* as the LXX. have it, and as it is quoted in 1 Cor. xv. 55. The rendering of the English version is, however, supported by the Targum, Symmachus, Jerome, and many modern expositors. But the former interpretation is to be preferred. Many Christian interpreters (Henderson, Pusey, &c.) regard this as the sudden outburst of a gracious promise (as St. Paul takes it). The last clause then signifies that the gift and calling of God are without repentance. There is no room for any further merciful change of purpose. But the objection to this interpretation is that in the same breath the prophet rushes on to the most sweeping condemnation. Accordingly Schmoller, Wünsche, Huxtable (*Speaker's Commentary*), and others understand the passage thus: "Shall I ransom them (doomed and dying in agonised travail) from the hand (or power) of Hades? Shall I redeem them from death? (Alas! no.) Where are thy plagues, O death? (Bring them forth.) Where is thy sting, O Hades? (Strike these reprobate ones.) Relenting is hid from my eyes." It should be remembered that St. Paul quoted from Isaiah, "Death shall be swallowed up in victory," and then, as here, calls in derisive irony upon death and Sheol to do their very worst at the very moment when they are about to be cast into the lake of fire.

(15, 16) **Fruitful.**—Observe the play on Ephraim's name.

Wind of the Lord stands in apposition to *east wind.* Render *a wind of the Lord rising from the wilderness.* The armies of Assyria are referred to.

Become desolate.—Or rather, *suffer punishment.* Thus rolls the thunder of Divine judgment in one last tremendous crash of doom, beyond which scarce anything worse can be thought or said. It is not until the awful silence is reached, after the blast of denunciation, that the prophet hopes that his appeal may not be in vain. In the last chapter, uttered in gentlest mood, he shows a bow of promise painted on the darkness of the storm-cloud.

XIV.

(1) **Thy.**—Tenderness and inextinguishable love are suggested by the use of the pronoun. "Repentance (say the Rabbis) presses right up to the Eternal Throne."

(2) **Say unto him.**—This putting of words into the lips of penitents and others is found in Ps. lxvi. 3; Isa. xlviii. 20; Jer. xxxi. 7. In the latter part of the verse render, *Accept of good, and we will render as calves* (or sacrificial offering) *our lips*—*i.e.,* the words of true repentance which we take with us shall be our offerings in place of calves. (Comp. Ps. li. 17.)

(3) The three crying sins of Israel are here recounted: (1) Expected salvation from Assyria; (2) dependence on the world-power of Egypt, famed for war-horses and chariots; (3) ascription of Divine names and homage to wrought images of the Divine glory. God's paternal love to the orphan, peculiarly applicable to Israel now, cast on a cold and fatherless world.

(4) **Heal . . . Love.**—If the foregoing be the offering of penitent lips, then the majestic reply of Jehovah is full of superlative grace.

(5, 6) **As the Dew.**—For this imagery see Ps. cxxx. 3. Properly it is "a copious mist, shedding small invisible rain, that comes in rich abundance every night in the hot weather, when west or north-west winds blow, and which brings intense refreshment to all organised life" (Neil's *Palestine Explored,* p. 136). The lily, which carpets the fields of Palestine (Matt. vi. 29), has slender roots, which might easily be uptorn, but under God's protection, even these are to strike downward like the roots of the cedars.* Branches are to grow like the banyan-tree, until one tree becomes a forest, and the

* The lily of the Bible is identified by some with the *Lilium chalcedonicum,* or Scarlet Martagon, which grows profusely in the Levant, and is said to abound in Galilee in the months of April and May. Wetzstein, on the other hand, identifies it with a beautiful dark violet lily which grows in the large plain south-east of the Hauran range of mountains, and is called *susân.* The opinion of the Chaldee paraphrast and of Rabbinical writers, that the rose was really meant by the Hebrew, may safely be rejected.

the lily, and [1]cast forth his roots as
Lebanon. (6) His branches [2]shall spread,
and his beauty shall be as the olive tree,
and his smell as Lebanon. (7) They that
dwell under his shadow shall return;
they shall revive *as* the corn, and [3]grow
as the vine: the [4]scent thereof *shall be*
as the wine of Lebanon. (8) Ephraim
shall say, What have I to do any more
with idols? I have heard *him,* and
observed him: I *am* like a green fir tree.
From me is thy fruit found.
(9) Who *is* wise, and he shall understand these *things?* prudent, and he shall know them? for the ways of the LORD *are* right, and the just shall walk in them: but the transgressors shall fall therein.

1 Heb., *strike.*
2 Heb., *shall go.*
3 Or, *blossom.*
4 Or, *memorial.*

---

beauty of the olive in its dancing radiance is to cover all, while the fragrance shall go abroad like the breezes from the forest of Lebanon.

(7) It would be more in accordance with the Hebrew idiom to render, *The dwellers under its shadow shall once more cause the corn to grow.* The word translated "scent" (margin, "memorial") should be *renown.* The form of these promises is derived from the external signs of national prosperity. (Comp. chap. xii. 10.) But corn and wine are throughout the Scriptures the great symbols of spiritual refreshment, and are still the memorials of the supreme love of Him whose body was broken and whose blood was shed for us.

(8) It would be better to adopt the slightly different reading indicated by the rendering of the LXX., and translate, *As for Ephraim, what has he to do with,* &c. Here again, as in chap. xiii. 15, the Hebrew for "thy fruit" contains a play on the name Ephraim. *I* (says Jehovah) *am to thee an evergreen tree of life and protection, and from me is thy fruit found.*

(10) **Who is wise.**—Hosea hands his words over to all students of the ways of God. The exhortation to wisdom is expressed in the form of a question. "Wisdom" and "wise men" take in the later Hebrew literature the place of "prophecy" and "prophets." Wisdom interprets both the word and its fulfilment. Christ's own teaching goes beyond wisdom and prudence (Matt. xi. 28; comp. 1 Cor. i. 20): it was spirit and life (John vi. 63).

EXCURSUS ON NOTES TO HOSEA

EXCURSUS A: ON JAREB (Chap. v. 13).

Schrader, in his "Cuneiform Inscriptions and the Old Testament," has the following note:—"King Combat, or Contention (Jareb), is not a proper name—none such being found in the Assyrian lists. In the prevailing uncertainty respecting Biblical chronology, it is hard to determine what Assyrian monarch is meant by this appellative. If we are to understand Salmanassar III. (781—772) as the king in chap. x. 14, under the name Salman, the allusion here may be to *Assur-dan-ilu* (771—754), who conducted a series of expeditions to the West." But when we turn to Schrader's comment on Hosea x. 14, we find that he abandons the theory that Salman is Salmanassar III. (see *ad. loc.*). On the other hand, Tiglath-pileser, whom Schrader and Sir H. Rawlinson identify with the Pul of Scripture, was a warrior of great prowess, to whom such a designation as "King Combat" from Hosea and his contemporaries would admirably apply. The verse might then be taken to refer to the events of the reign of Menahem (2 Kings xv. 19, see also *Introduction*). But this explanation, probable as it is, is complicated with questions of Biblical chronology. (See *Introduction*).

EXCURSUS B (Chap. vi. 7).

Buhl, in *Zeitschrift für Kirchliche Wissenschaft,* Part v., 1881, throws some light on the enigmatical phrase *k*e*Adam,* by pointing out that *Adam* is employed in many places to express all the other races of mankind as opposed to Israel. Thus, he translates Jer. xxxii. 20, "Thou who didst perform wonders in Israel, as well as in Adam." Similarly Isaiah xliii. 4, on which Delitzsch remarks that those who do not belong to the chosen people, are called *Adam,* because they are regarded as nothing but descendants of Adam. In this passage the emphatic position of the Hebrew pronoun *hemmah* lends significance to the contrasted term *Adam.* The meaning, therefore, is—the Israelites, who should be a chosen race, belong now, through their violation of the covenant, to the heathen: have become, in fact, *Lo'Ammi.* (Comp. chap. i. 9.) The word "there" in the last clause may refer to some local sanctuary, notorious for idolatrous corruption. This is confirmed by the mention of localities in the next verse. We prefer, however, to understand it (with the Targum of Jonathan) as referring to the Holy Land.

JOEL

INTRODUCTION

TO

JOEL

JOEL has a peculiar claim upon the attention of the Christian reader, inasmuch as he foretells the advent of the Comforter, who would hereafter carry on and complete the work of the Saviour. Joel is as emphatically the prophet of the Holy Ghost as Isaiah is emphatically of the Messiah. If, therefore, it is permissible to discover in the twenty-third verse of the second chapter (see Note) a reference to Jesus Christ, as in the third chapter there is described the coming of the Almighty Father to judge the world at the Last Day, the prophet Joel has in his short book an evidence of the doctrine of the most Holy Trinity.

We may claim for him also one of the earliest places among the sixteen prophets (see Note on Acts ii. 17); but Henderson, in his Introduction to the Minor Prophets, considers him chronologically the first of all. There is absolutely nothing known of his personal history, except the name of his father, Pethuel, and his conjectured residence in Jerusalem. The condition of the kingdom of Judah, as indicated in his prophecy, suggests that he flourished in the reign of Joash. Besides, had he lived at a later period than this, in his enumeration of the imminent enemies of his country he would hardly have omitted the names of the Babylonians, Assyrians, and Syrians. Dean Milman, in his *History of the Jews* (vol. i., p. 370), says: "In my judgment the silence about the Assyrian power is conclusive as to this early period assigned to the prophecies of Joel." We therefore assign to him the date of about 870 B.C.

This period of Jewish history saw a great revival of the worship of Jehovah, after the idolatrous movement under Athaliah, the queen-mother, daughter of Ahab and Jezebel, had been suppressed. The protectorate of the kingdom during the minority of Joash was in the hands of the high priest Jehoiada; and he had excited immense enthusiasm in the Temple and its services. And such an enthusiasm as then existed is in a marked manner evident in the prophecy of Joel. In the vivid description of the straits to which the kingdom was reduced by the famine and locusts, the most grievous calamity is the enforced suspension of the Temple sacrifices. "Gird yourselves, and lament, ye priests: howl, ye ministers of the altar: come, lie all night in sackcloth, ye ministers of my God: FOR THE MEAT OFFERING AND THE DRINK OFFERING IS WITHHOLDEN FROM THE HOUSE OF YOUR GOD" (chap. i. 13). While, on the other hand, when there is a glimpse of better days the prophet's joy culminates in the hope that these sacrifices will be restored: "who knoweth if he will return and repent, and leave a blessing behind him; EVEN A MEAT OFFERING AND A DRINK OFFERING UNTO THE LORD YOUR GOD?" (chap. ii. 14). There is further teaching in the words of this inspired prophet of extreme importance at all times, and especially in these latter days—the teaching that God heareth prayer in respect of those events which are due, as it is said, to the laws of nature. We are sometimes met with the argument that it is even an impertinence to endeavour to interfere with such laws by our prayers. But we have a wiser teacher in Joel. When our land is threatened with famine through excessive drought (or through excessive rain) and the natural impulse of our hearts is to offer up prayers and intercessions to Almighty God, we may turn to the striking precedent which God has given us in this prophet, for who knoweth whether (even in *our* emergency) He will turn and repent, and leave a blessing behind Him?

All the commentators who have earnestly considered the nature and the matter of this prophecy have found immense difficulty in the question whether Joel intended literally a plague of locusts to be understood as the calamity which he described, or whether he rather desired to convey under that figure a description of the human enemies of Judah. It is well known that the ravages of locusts were among the punishments of God most highly dreaded by the Jews. Solomon enumerated them among the special causes for prayer to the Lord, in his supplication at the dedication of the Temple. And, as will be found noticed in the Commentary, the Eastern nations without exception dreaded, and dread, an incursion of locusts as one of the greatest scourges of their countries. But although such a plague may, in the first instance, have aroused the prophet's extreme apprehension, and stirred his soul to its lowest depths, still we rise up from the perusal of his words convinced that they refer to some greater anxiety yet to come—some incursion of enemies, who would inflict terrible ravages upon the land, leaving it desolate and bare behind them, after the manner of these locusts.

Under such circumstances as we have suggested, Joel appeared at Jerusalem with the suddenness of an Elijah before Ahab. He came, as it were, out of the darkness of the unknown to declare the wrath of God, as manifest in the visitation on the land. He exercised on the instant the office and authority of a prophet, calling upon the priests to perform their duties in a terrible emergency. He demanded of them a solemn Litany to deprecate the anger of the Lord, and to invoke His compassion on the devastated country. He described the horror of the situation in graphic details. There was an enemy in their midst, countless in number, inexorable, remorseless. Their ravages stared them in the face on every side. The foliage of the country is gone, the trees stand stark and bare, as if fired, all vegetation is destroyed; vines, fig-trees, pomegranates, palms, apple-trees—all are withered, the corn is wasted, the seed is sodden, the very beasts of the field are dying for lack of moisture. The locusts of various kinds are at work, sparing nothing; at the same time, a drought assists their ravages. The locusts found the land a Garden of Eden, they leave it a wilderness. Fields, streets, houses, walls are occupied by this terrible pest. Let the priests therefore stir themselves, proclaim a fast for high and low, that a common supplication may be made for the removal of this plague.

But there lay something still more anxious beneath the visitation, although it far surpassed all previous experience of locusts. It was in a marked manner symbolical of that scourge which David most feared, the scourge of war; so that the national Fast called for by the present overwhelming calamity was quickened by the apprehension of an invasion by foreign enemies. In this apprehension the prophetic description of Joel culminated. The unparalleled visitation of the locusts was an advanced guard of greater terrors to come. So the prophet interpreted it.

Joel then saw the submission of the people, and as its effect the plague averted. Once more plenty smiled upon the land—plenty, which was the gift of God. And the material gift was an earnest of a spiritual gift which was to come to pass "afterward." The Spirit of God was to be poured out, as St. Peter declared it was poured out in the last days, on the Day of Pentecost. Thenceforward Joel was caught up, so to speak, into the regions of apocalyptic vision. He beheld the victory of the people completed in the eternal victory of the last day. The multitudes came together to be judged in the eponymous valley of Jehoshaphat, and the Lord was the judge. After the conflict, after the judgment, there was the vision of peace. The enemies have ceased to exist; the people of the Lord are in the mansions of eternal blessedness, and in their midst is God, blessed for ever.

JOEL

CHAPTER I.—(1) The word of the
Lord that came to Joel the son of
Pethuel.
(2) Hear this, ye old men, and give
ear, all ye inhabitants of the land.
Hath this been in your days, or even
in the days of your fathers? (3) Tell
ye your children of it, and *let* your
children *tell* their children, and their
children another generation. (4) [1]That
which the palmerworm hath left hath
the locust eaten; and that which the
locust hath left hath the cankerworm
eaten; and that which the cankerworm
hath left hath the caterpiller eaten.
(5) Awake, ye drunkards, and weep;
and howl, all ye drinkers of wine, be-
cause of the new wine; for it is cut
off from your mouth. (6) For a nation
is come up upon my land, strong, and
without number, whose teeth *are* the
teeth of a lion, and he hath the cheek
teeth of a great lion. (7) He hath laid
my vine waste, and [2]barked my fig tree:
he hath made it clean bare, and cast
it away; the branches thereof are made
white.
(8) Lament like a virgin girded with
sackcloth for the husband of her youth.
(9) The meat offering and the drink
offering is cut off from the house of the
Lord; the priests, the Lord's ministers,

B.C. cir. 800.

1 Heb., *The residue of the palmerworm.*

2 Heb., laid *my fig tree for a barking.*

(1) **Joel.**—Compounded of Jehovah—El, the composite title of the God of Revelation and of Nature, which is the subject of Psalm xix. It was a favourite name among the Jews, and was borne by an ancestor of Samuel, who gave it to his elder son. There is nothing known of the personal history of Joel the prophet, except the name of his father, Pethuel, or—LXX.—Bethuel.

(2, 3) **Hath this been in your days.**—The introduction points to the startling nature of the portent: it was unexampled; it was a cause of consternation to all who beheld it; it would be recollected as a subject of wondering comment among succeeding generations. The hand of God was evident, recalling the marvellous things he did in the land of Egypt, in the field of Zoan.

(4) **That which the palmerworm hath left.**—The picture is introduced suddenly and graphically. "Behold the desolation!" "Note the cause." The earth is bared by locusts beyond all previous experience. There were different sorts of locusts; as many as ninety have been reckoned. The four names, palmerworm, locust, cankerworm, caterpiller, indicate different swarms of the insect. The first—*Gazam*—points to its voracity; the second—*Arbeh*—its multitude; the third—*Yelek*—its manner of "licking up" the grass like cattle; the fourth—*Chasil*—its destructive effect. The number enumerated, *four*, draws attention to the "four sore judgments" with which Ezekiel was instructed to threaten Jerusalem, and to the four foreign invasions by the Assyrians, Chaldæans, Macedonians, and Romans.

(5) **Awake, ye drunkards**—*i.e.*, awake from such an insensibility as wine causes. The people failed to see the hand of God in the terrible calamity, like an acted parable, of the locusts. Insensate, as the revellers in the halls of Belshazzar, they carried on their feasting even while the enemies were at the city gates.

It is cut off from your mouth.—Either joy and gladness, as given in the LXX., or the means of indulgence have been suddenly taken away.

(6) **A nation.**—It was not uncommon with Hebrew writers to apply the name people or folk to animals, as, "The ants are a people not strong;" "The conies are but a feeble folk" (Prov. xxx. 25, 26); but the word used by Joel is different from that in the Proverbs. He selected a word indicative of *foreign* nations, suggestive of attack, including both the irrational invader and the foreign conqueror. The surpassing strength of the nation is indicated by the extraordinary power of the locust's teeth, compared to that of the lion's jaws. The same comparison is made by St. John (Rev. ix. 8): "Their teeth (the locusts) were as the teeth of lions."

(7) **My vine.**—This expression might well captivate the Jewish ear. God appropriates to Himself this land on which the trouble was, by His providence, to fall, and in wrath remembers mercy. It is "my vine," "my fig-tree," the people of God's own choice, that were afflicted; and the affliction, however fully deserved, was, to speak as a man, painful to the Lord, "who doth not afflict willingly." Yet the devastation was to be complete. God's pleasant vine was doomed, and the fig-tree was to be cut down.

(8) **For the husband of her youth.**—The land is addressed as a virgin betrothed, but not yet married, and forfeiting her marriage by unworthy conduct. Such was the relation of Israel to the Lord: He was faithful, but Israel unfaithful. Now let her mourn the penalty.

(9) **The meat offering and the drink offering**—*i.e.*, all the outward and visible signs of communion with God are cut off. The means are lost through this visitation. There is a total cessation of "the creatures of bread and wine." The immediate significance of this fact is naturally appreciated first by "the priests, the Lord's ministers."

mourn. (10) The field is wasted, the land
mourneth; for the corn is wasted:
the new wine is [1]dried up, the oil lan-
guisheth. (11) Be ye ashamed, O ye hus-
bandmen; howl, O ye vinedressers, for
the wheat and for the barley; because
the harvest of the field is perished.
(12) The vine is dried up, and the
fig tree languisheth; the pomegranate
tree, the palm tree also, and the apple
tree, *even* all the trees of the field, are
withered: because joy is withered away
from the sons of men.
(13) Gird yourselves, and lament, ye
priests: howl, ye ministers of the altar:
come, lie all night in sackcloth, ye
ministers of my God: for the meat
offering and the drink offering is with-
holden from the house of your God.
(14) [a]Sanctify ye a fast, call a [2]solemn
assembly, gather the elders *and* all the
inhabitants of the land *into* the house
of the LORD your God, and cry unto
the LORD, (15) Alas for the day! for [b]the
day of the LORD *is* at hand, and as a
destruction from the Almighty shall it
come. (16) Is not the meat cut off be-
fore our eyes, *yea*, joy and gladness from
the house of our God? (17) The [3]seed
is rotten under their clods, the garners
are laid desolate, the barns are broken
down; for the corn is withered. (18) How
do the beasts groan! the herds of cattle
are perplexed, because they have no
pasture; yea, the flocks of sheep are
made desolate.
(19) O LORD, to thee will I cry: for
the fire hath devoured the [4]pastures
of the wilderness, and the flame hath
burned all the trees of the field. (20) The
beasts of the field cry also unto thee:
for the rivers of waters are dried up,
and the fire hath devoured the pastures
of the wilderness.

CHAPTER II.—(1) Blow ye the
[5]trumpet in Zion, and sound an alarm
in my holy mountain: let all the in-
habitants of the land tremble: for the
day of the LORD cometh, for *it is* nigh

1 Or, *ashamed.*
a ch. 2. 15.
2 Or, *day of restraint.*
b Isa. 13. 6.
3 Heb., *grains.*
4 Or, *habitations.*
5 Or, *cornet.*

---

(10) **The new wine.**—The necessaries and delights of life are all gone: "the wine that maketh glad the heart of man, the oil that makes his face to shine, the bread that strengtheneth man's heart" (Ps. civ. 15).

(12) **The vine is dried up.**—The ravages produced by the locusts and the drought are universal. There seems to be a method in the enumeration of the trees. The vine is the favourite term for the chosen people; the fig-tree has its life prolonged at the intercession of the "dresser of the vineyard," in our Lord's parable (Luke xiii. 8); the tall and stately pomegranate is of such importance as to give its name to the idol Rimmon; yea, and the palm-tree, even that is gone; the apple also, including the lemon, citron, &c.—all joy is vanished.

(13) **Gird yourselves, and lament.**—The priests are exhorted to commence preparations for a national humiliation, beginning with themselves; for the visitation touches them in a vital part: they have no sacrifices to offer to the Lord.

(14) **A solemn assembly.**—The Hebrew word strictly means a festival day, on which the people gathered themselves together, being relieved from work. Here they are summoned for a fast. The word may also be translated, as in the margin, "a day of restraint," its root signifying *to shut, to hold back.*

(15) **Alas.**—The exclamation is repeated three times in the LXX. and Vulg., thus giving occasion to Jeremy Taylor's comment: "When the prophet Joel was describing the formidable accidents in the day of the Lord's judgment, and the fearful sentence of an angry judge, he was not able to express it, but stammered like a child, or an amazed imperfect person, *A. A. A. diei, quia prope est Dies Domini*" ("Christ's Adv. to Judgment," Serm. iii., pt. 3).

Almighty.—*Shaddai.* A title signifying the omnipotence of God, especially with reference, as here, to His power to destroy. The Hebrew preserves the alliteration, Shod Mishaddai, destruction from the destroyer. The Almighty was the general title of God. "I appeared unto Abraham, unto Isaac, and unto Jacob by the name of God ALMIGHTY, but by My name JEHOVAH was I not known unto them." (See Note on Gen. xvii.)

(17) **The corn is withered.**—The results of the terrible drought, coincident with the ravages of the locusts, are now described. The ancient versions present difficulty and variety in the exact rendering of this verse, owing to several words occurring in it being not found elsewhere in Holy Scripture. On the whole the English text seems correct and satisfactory.

(18) **How do the beasts groan.**—All creation is represented as sharing in the dread perplexity; the beasts are involved in it, as also in Nineveh the animals were united in the proclamation of the general fast by the king's decree, when he had heard of the preaching of Jonah.

(19) **The fire hath devoured.**—This may be explained as produced by the scorching heat bringing about spontaneous combustion, or by the efforts of the people to exterminate the locusts by burning the trees, or by the mark, as of fire, left upon all vegetation after the locusts had finished their work of devastation.

(20) **The beasts of the field cry also unto thee.**—The prophet has cried to God; the very beasts echo that cry, "looking up" to Him. As yet, man seems dumb.

II.

(1) **Blow ye the trumpet.**—The preaching of the prophet increases in its intensity. Behind the locusts, exemplified by them, there is a still more terrible visitation. He sees on the horizon a mustering of the nations hostile to his people, bent on destroying them. Let the priests stir up the people for a fast, and for the defence of their land by the trumpet. The locusts have done

at hand; (2) a day of darkness and of
gloominess, a day of clouds and of thick
darkness, as the morning spread upon
the mountains: a great people and a
strong; there hath not been ever the
like, neither shall be any more after
it, *even* to the years [1]of many genera-
tions. (3) A fire devoureth before them;
and behind them a flame burneth: the
land *is* as the garden of Eden before
them, and behind them a desolate wil-
derness; yea, and nothing shall escape
them. (4) The appearance of them *is*
as the appearance of horses; and as
horsemen, so shall they run. (5) Like
the noise of chariots on the tops of
mountains shall they leap, like the noise
of a flame of fire that devoureth the
stubble, as a strong people set in battle
array. (6) Before their face the people
shall be much pained: all faces shall
gather [2]blackness. (7) They shall run
like mighty men; they shall climb the
wall like men of war; and they shall
march every one on his ways, and they
shall not break their ranks: (8) neither
shall one thrust another; they shall
walk every one in his path: and *when*
they fall upon the [3]sword, they shall
not be wounded. (9) They shall run to
and fro in the city; they shall run
upon the wall, they shall climb up upon
the houses; they shall enter in at the
windows like a thief. (10) The earth
shall quake before them; the heavens
shall tremble: [a]the sun and the moon
shall be dark, and the stars shall with-
draw their shining: (11) and the LORD
shall utter his voice before his army:
for his camp *is* very great: for *he is*
strong that executeth his word: for the
[b]day of the LORD *is* great and very
terrible; and who can abide it?

(12) Therefore also now, saith the
LORD, [c]turn ye *even* to me with all
your heart, and with fasting, and with

1 Heb., *of generation and generation.*

2 Heb., *pot.*

3 Or, *dart.*

a Isa. 13. 10; Ezek. 32. 7.

b Jer. 30. 7; Amos 5. 18; Zeph. 1. 15.

c Jer. 4. 1.

---

their symbolical work, they have left their mark on the country. Now the day of Jehovah, the manifestation of His power, is approaching—it is imminent.

(2) **The morning spread upon the mountains.**—The Hebrew word here used for morning is derived from a verb, *Shachar*, which has for one meaning "to be or become black," for the second "to break forth" as light. From this latter signification is derived the word for morning—dawn; from the former comes the word "blackness," which gives the name *Sihor* to the Nile (Isa. xxiii. 3). It seems accordingly more in harmony with the present context to take the sense of the word in its reference to blackness, and to understand it as indicating a thick, dark, rolling cloud settled upon the mountain top. The description following comprehends equally the natural and political locusts.

(3) **Before them . . . behind them.**—As with the locusts, so with the invading hosts of enemies: the country is found a paradise, and left a desert.

(4) **As the appearance of horses.**—So also are locusts described in the Revelation: "And the shapes of the locusts were like unto horses prepared unto battle" (from this likeness the Italians call a locust cavalletta) . . . "and the sound of their wings was as the sound of chariots, of many horses running to battle" (Rev. ix. 7, 9).

(6) **All faces shall gather blackness.**—There are different explanations of this Hebrew phrase, which expresses the result of terror. Some translate it "withdraw their ruddiness," *i.e.*, grow pale; others, "draw into themselves their colour;" others, "contract a livid character." The alternative rendering in the margin, "pot," which is that of the LXX., the Vulg., and of Luther's translation, is obtained from the similarity of the Hebrew words for "ruddiness" and "pot." The comparison is in this case between the faces growing black under the influence of fear, and of pots under the action of fire. The prophet Nahum uses the same expression (chap. ii. 10).

(7—9) **They shall run like mighty men.**—The onward irresistible march of the invaders is graphically described by the illustration of the advance of locusts. They appear on the mountains which environ the city, they mount the walls, they rush through the streets, they enter the houses, they are in possession of Jerusalem. Dr. Thomson (*The Land and the Book*, p. 416) describes the movements of a locust army in the following terms:—"Their number was astounding; the whole face of the mountain was black with them. On they came, like a living deluge. We dug trenches, and kindled fires, and beat and burned to death heaps upon heaps; but the effort was utterly useless. Wave after wave rolled up the mountain-side, and poured over rocks, walls, ditches, hedges—those behind covering up and bridging over the masses already killed."

(10) **The earth shall quake before them.**—Some commentators call this description "a specimen of the highly-wrought hyperbolical features of Hebrew poetry," but it is the presence and judgment, the voice of the Lord in the thunder, which causes this trepidation. The signs in the heavens will be manifested at the judgment day.

(11) **His army.**—"In every stage of their existence these locusts give a most impressive view of the power of God to punish a wicked world" (*The Land and the Book*, p. 417).

(12) **Saith the Lord.**—The word *saith* is here no common word in the Hebrew. It implies an authoritative and most weighty utterance, as in Psalm cx. 1, "The Lord *said* unto my Lord." "The word is used in almost every instance of the immediate utterance of God Himself; more rarely of that of the prophet or inspired organ of the Divine revelations" (Perowne, *Commentary on the Psalms*, vol. ii., p. 300).

Turn ye even to me.—The question, "Who can abide it?" is left unanswered. But the only possible reply is inferred in the touching appeal which the prophet is inspired by Jehovah to make, that His righteous anger may be averted.

weeping, and with mourning: (13) and
rend your heart, and not your garments,
and turn unto the LORD your God:
for he *is* [a] gracious and merciful, slow
to anger, and of great kindness, and
repenteth him of the evil. (14) [b] Who
knoweth *if* he will return and repent,
and leave a blessing behind him; *even*
a meat offering and a drink offering
unto the LORD your God?
(15) Blow the trumpet in Zion, [c] sanc-
tify a fast, call a solemn assembly:
(16) gather the people, sanctify the con-
gregation, assemble the elders, gather
the children, and those that suck the
breasts: let the bridegroom go forth
of his chamber, and the bride out of
her closet. (17) Let the priests, the min-
isters of the LORD, weep between the
porch and the altar, and let them say,
Spare thy people, O LORD, and give
not thine heritage to reproach, that
the heathen should [1] rule over them:
[d] wherefore should they say among the
people, Where *is* their God?

(18) Then will the LORD be jealous
for his land, and pity his people. (19) Yea,
the LORD will answer and say unto his
people, Behold, I will send you corn,
and wine, and oil, and ye shall be
satisfied therewith: and I will no more
make you a reproach among the hea-
then: (20) but I will remove far off from
you the northern *army*, and will drive
him into a land barren and desolate,
with his face toward the east sea, and
his hinder part toward the utmost sea,
and his stink shall come up, and his ill
savour shall come up, because [2] he hath
done great things.
(21) Fear not, O land; be glad and re-
joice: for the LORD will do great things.
(22) Be not afraid, ye beasts of the field:
for the pastures of the wilderness do
spring, for the tree beareth her fruit,
the fig tree and the vine do yield their
strength. (23) Be glad then, ye children
of Zion, and rejoice in the LORD your
God: for he hath given you [3] the former
rain [4] moderately, and he [e] will cause to

a Exod. 34. 6; Ps. 86. 5; Jonah 4. 2.

b Jonah 3. 9.

c ch. 1. 14.

1 Or, *use a byword against them.*

d Ps. 42. 10; & 79. 10; & 115. 2.

2 Heb., *he hath magnified to do.*

3 Or, *a teacher of righteousness.*

4 Heb., *according to righteousness.*

e Lev. 26. 4; Deut. 11. 14.

---

(13) **Repenteth him of the evil**—*i.e.*, in the sense that of His own will He would not the death of a sinner. The judgments of God, like His mercies, are conditional. As the "Lord repented (*i.e.*, grieved) that He had made Saul king over Israel," and revoked the appointment, so now He repenteth Him of the evil which will fall on His people if impenitent. If they will repent, it may be He will do it not.

(14) **Even a meat offering.**—The returning favour of the Lord will enable the daily sacrifices to be restored, which had failed through the visitation (chap. i. 9).

(15, 16) **Sanctify a fast.**—The prophet renews, therefore, his summons to the priests to proclaim a day of humiliation, on which all, without distinction of age or circumstances, are to be required to present themselves before the Lord. There was no room for the plea, "I have married a wife, and therefore I cannot come."

(17) **That the heathen should rule over them.**—All mention of the locusts is dropped. The lesser calamity is swallowed up in the apprehension of the greater.

(19) **I will no more make you.**—The reply of the Lord is directed to remove the fear that by reason of the destruction of the fruits of the land the people would be at the mercy of the invading nations.

(20) **The northern army.**—Literally, *him of the north.* "This is an exception to the usual direction of the flight of locusts" (Stanley, *Jewish Church*), but it may be literally applied to the Assyrian hordes, whom the Jews generally spoke of as dwelling in the north. In Jeremiah i. 13 the symbolical caldron is represented as pouring its contents (the Chaldæan army) southwards from the face of the north. And even though the wind might be conceived as capriciously blowing the locusts from the north, yet the addition of the patronymic syllable to the Hebrew word indicates a *native* of the north, which excludes a reference to locusts. Under the image of the destruction of the locusts, the prophet points to the deliverance from the northern invaders.

The east sea is the Dead Sea; the utmost or hinder sea is the Mediterranean; the desolate land is the southern desert. The northern invader shall be expelled all along the coasts of Palestine. His stink shall come up. In the eighth plague of Egypt, when on the repentance of Pharaoh the locusts were removed, they were cast into the Red Sea, and there remained not one locust in all the coasts of Egypt (Exod. x. 19). In the present instance there is the result stated in the case of the decomposition of the bodies of the locusts left on the land: the air was infected with a horrible pestilence. There are various allusions to this terrible result of their putrefaction in the writers who describe the horrors of a plague of locusts. St. Jerome tells of the awful sufferings inflicted on man and beast through this cause; and St. Augustine (*De Civitate Dei*, iii. 31) relates that eight hundred thousand men perished from this reason in the kingdom of Masinissa alone, besides many more near the coast. Thus Joel declares the complete destruction of the enemies of Israel, who having completed the purpose of vengeance for which they were summoned, and, like the Assyrians under the walls of Jerusalem, having exalted themselves against the Lord, perish miserably under the stroke of His power.

(21) **Fear not, O land . . .**—The sentence of the reversal of judgment has gone forth, and all nature—animate and inanimate, rational and irrational—which had been included in the curse is summoned to rejoice in the blessing vouchsafed by the Lord.

(23) **Ye children of Zion**—*i.e.*, they were called upon to manifest their rejoicings in the place where the trumpet had been sounded for the proclamation of the fast.

The former rain moderately.—St. Paul adduces the gift of the rain as a witness to the people of

come down for you the rain, the former
rain, and the latter rain in the first
month. (24) And the floors shall be full
of wheat, and the fats shall overflow
with wine and oil. (25) And I will re-
store to you the years that the locust
hath eaten, the cankerworm, and the
caterpiller, and the palmerworm, my
great army which I sent among you.
(26) And ye shall eat in plenty, and be
satisfied, and praise the name of the
LORD your God, that hath dealt won-
drously with you: and my people shall
never be ashamed. (27) And ye shall know
that I *am* in the midst of Israel, and
that I *am* the LORD your God, and none
else: and my people shall never be
ashamed.
(28) And it shall come to pass after-
ward, *that* I [a] will pour out my spirit
upon all flesh; and your sons and your
daughters shall prophesy, your old men
shall dream dreams, your young men
shall see visions: (29) and also upon the
servants and upon the handmaids in
those days will I pour out my spirit.
(30) And I will shew wonders in the
heavens and in the earth, blood, and
fire, and pillars of smoke. (31) [b] The
sun shall be turned into darkness, and
the moon into blood, before the great
and the terrible day of the LORD come.
(32) And it shall come to pass, *that* [c] who-
soever shall call on the name of the
LORD shall be delivered: for in mount
Zion and in Jerusalem shall be deliver-
ance, as the LORD hath said, and in the
remnant whom the LORD shall call.

a Isa. 44. 3; Acts 2. 17.

b ch. 3. 15.

c Rom. 10. 13.

CHAPTER III.—(1) For, behold, in
those days, and in that time, when I
shall bring again the captivity of Judah
and Jerusalem, (2) I will also gather
all nations, and will bring them down
into the valley of Jehoshaphat, and will
plead with them there for my people

Lystra of the existence and beneficence of God, who "gave us rain from heaven, filling our hearts with food and gladness." The possibility of the interpretation of "the former rain moderately" out of the Hebrew words by a "teacher of righteousness," as in the Vulg. and in our margin, has led to the connection of this passage with a prophetic intimation of the advent of the Messiah.

In the first month.—Better, *as at first, as before.*

(25) **I will restore to you the years**—*i.e.*, the years which would have been necessary in the ordinary course of nature for the land to recover from the ravages of the "great army."

(27) **I am in the midst of Israel.**—This Divine assurance, similar to that with which the book ends, prepares the way for the spiritual blessings about to be announced.

(28) **I will pour out my spirit upon all flesh.**—Holy Scripture is itself the interpreter of this most weighty promise. St. Peter's quotation and application of it in the Acts is its commentary. "Afterward"—LXX., after these things becomes in the apostle's mouth—"in the last days"—*i.e.*, in the Christian dispensation, when, after the punishment of the Jews by the heathen, their king came—"my Spirit"—St. Peter renders "of my spirit," after the LXX., indicating the gifts and influences of the Holy Ghost—"upon all flesh"—*i.e.*, without distinction of race or person—"they of the circumcision were astonished because that on the Gentiles also was poured out the gift of the Holy Ghost." The outward manifestation of these gifts, as shown on the Day of Pentecost, in accordance with this prediction, was gradually withdrawn from the Church; the reality remains.

(29) **And also** (better, *even*) **upon the servants . . .**—The result of which promise, according to St. Peter's interpretation, is "They shall prophesy." "The promise is to you and to your children, and to all that are afar off, even as many as the Lord our God shall call" (Acts ii. 39).

(30, 31) **The sun . . . and the moon.**—These words, recalling some of the portents in the ancient history of the Jews (especially as instanced in some of the plagues of Egypt) are taken up by our Lord Himself, as ushering in the great day of judgment; and they are echoed again by St. John in the vision of the opening of the sixth seal: "For the great day of His wrath is come, and who shall be able to stand?" (Comp. verse 11 of this chapter.) The sun and moon, &c., may include the luminaries in heaven and the potentates on earth.

(32) **Deliverance.**—Or, perhaps better, *those that escape.* St. Paul quotes from this verse (Rom. x. 13), transferring the reference to the Messianic advent, to prove the universality of the deliverance effected by our Lord, who abolished the difference between Jew and Greek. In His Church, the heavenly Jerusalem, freed from the persecutions and defilements of the world, there is salvation for all who call upon the name of the Lord, their names are inscribed upon the roll as citizens of Zion.

III.

(1) **That time.**—The whole course of the events of the world is shown to lead up by Divine providence to the Great Day of the Lord, when "the crooked shall be made straight, and the rough places plain, and the Lord shall be exalted." Then will be "the times of the restitution of all things;" then will the people of God be brought out of captivity, and vengeance executed upon their enemies. This progress, with its final consummation, is the subject of the concluding lines of Joel's prophecy.

(2) **The valley of Jehoshaphat.**—Some fifty years before Joel prophesied the kingdom of Judah had been menaced by an imposing confederacy of hostile tribes. It was an occasion of great anxiety. A national fast was proclaimed, and after it Jehoshaphat engaged and completely routed the enemy in a valley in the wilderness of Tekoa. (See 2 Chron. xx.) The victory was an occasion of immense exultation, and

and *for* my heritage Israel, whom they have scattered among the nations, and parted my land. (3) And they have cast lots for my people; and have given a boy for an harlot, and sold a girl for wine, that they might drink.

(4) Yea, and what have ye to do with me, O Tyre, and Zidon, and all the coasts of Palestine? will ye render me a recompence? and if ye recompense me, swiftly *and* speedily will I return your recompence upon your own head; (5) because ye have taken my silver and my gold, and have carried into your temples my goodly [1] pleasant things: (6) the children also of Judah and the children of Jerusalem have ye sold unto [2] the Grecians, that ye might remove them far from their border. (7) Behold, I will raise them out of the place whither ye have sold them, and will return your recompence upon your own head: (8) and I will sell your sons and your daughters into the hand of the children of Judah, and they shall sell them to the Sabeans, to a people far off: for the LORD hath spoken *it*.

(9) Proclaim ye this among the Gentiles; [3] Prepare war, wake up the mighty men, let all the men of war draw near; let them come up: (10) [a] beat your plowshares into swords, and your [4] pruninghooks into spears: let the weak say, I *am* strong. (11) Assemble yourselves, and come, all ye heathen, and gather yourselves together round about: thither [5] cause thy mighty ones to come down, O LORD. (12) Let the heathen be wakened, and come up to the valley of Jehoshaphat: for there will I sit to judge all the heathen round about. (13) [b] Put ye in the sickle, for the harvest is ripe: come, get you down; for the press is full, the fats overflow; for their wickedness *is* great. (14) Multitudes, multitudes in the valley of [6] decision: for the day of the LORD *is* near in the valley of decision. (15) The [c] sun and the moon shall be darkened, and the stars shall withdraw their shining. (16) The LORD also shall [d] roar out of Zion, and utter his voice from Jerusalem; and the heavens and the earth shall shake: but the LORD *will be* the

1 Heb., *desirable.*
2 Heb., *the sons of the Grecians.*
3 Heb., *Sanctify.*
a Isa. 2. 4.
4 Or, *scythes.*
5 Or, *the LORD shall bring down.*
b Rev. 14. 15.
6 Or, *concision*, or, *threshing.*
c ch. 2. 31.
d Jer. 25. 30; Amos 1. 2.

---

seems to supply the imagery with which Joel describes the day of the Lord. The name of Jehoshaphat was at some period given to the Kedron Valley, but it is here used rather in its grammatical meaning as the scene of the Divine judgment, the words signifying "the valley where Jehovah judgeth."

(3) **Cast lots . . .**—The nations who oppressed and carried away the Jews treated them as chattels, cast lots for the possession of them as slaves, and purchased a night's revelry or other indulgence with the captives they had taken.

(4) **What have ye to do with me?**—Rather, *What are ye to me?* God, identifying Himself with His people, threatens retaliation upon their enemies for the wrongs they had inflicted upon them. Tyre and Zidon had oppressed the Jews in the time of the judges, and would do so again: the Philistines also were to the last the inveterate enemies of Israel; but in the end, could they measure strength with God?

(5) **My silver.**—Mine, as being the property of my people, not as being dedicated to the service of the Temple. In the time of Jehoram, the Philistines and others had "carried away all the substance that was found in the king's house" (2 Chron. xxi. 17).

(6) **Unto the Grecians.**—Javan, the Hebrew name for Greece, is mentioned in Ezekiel as one of the representatives of the heathen nations who "traded (with Tyre) the persons of men and vessels in her market" (Ezek. xxvii. 13). The Grecian traffic in slaves was enormous.

(8) **I will sell your sons . . . .**—The Philistines came under the power of Uzziah and Hezekiah, who may have sold them to the Sabeans on the Persian Gulf, by whom they would have been passed on to India. The Philistines were also sold in great numbers by the Grecian conquerors in the time of the Maccabees.

(9) **Prepare war . . .**—Literally, *sanctify war.* It was to be taken up deliberately, and after due religious rites, according to the customs of the nations. They are thus challenged, or rather summoned, to a trial of strength with Jehovah at a typical "Armageddon."

(10) **Beat your plowshares . . .**—When the contest was over, and the victory of the Lord achieved, Micah foresaw the reversal of this order: the weapons of offence were once more to resume their peaceful character. "They"—*i.e.*, the nations—"shall beat their swords into plowshares, and their spears into pruning-hooks; nation shall not lift up sword against nation, neither shall they learn war any more" (Micah iv. 3).

(11) **Thy mighty ones**—*i.e.*, *thy*, because Jehovah had summoned them to take arms, as champions against Him in the final conflict.

(13) **Put ye in the sickle.**—In the enthusiasm of his vision the prophet crowds together metaphors to intensify the description of the coming encounter between Jehovah and the enemies of His people. It is represented by the judgment seat, the harvest, and the vintage. The hour of judgment has arrived—Jehovah Himself is judge. The harvest-time, which is the end of the world, has come—let the angel-reapers put in their sickle. In the wine-press the grapes are gathered in—let the labourers hasten to press the juice out with their feet.

(14) **Multitudes.**—The command has gone forth; it is obeyed; and the prophet stands aghast at the vast multitudes assembling in the valley of decision, the place of judgment.

(16) **The Lord also shall roar . . .**—This is the key-note of the prophecy of Amos, who opens his

[1] hope of his people, and the strength
of the children of Israel. (17) So shall
ye know that I *am* the LORD your
God dwelling in Zion, my holy moun-
tain: then shall Jerusalem be [2] holy,
and there shall no [a] strangers pass
through her any more.
(18) And it shall come to pass in that
day, *that* the mountains shall [b] drop
down new wine, and the hills shall
flow with milk, and all the rivers of
Judah shall [3] flow with waters, and a
fountain shall come forth of the house
of the LORD, and shall water the valley
of Shittim. (19) Egypt shall be a deso-
lation, and Edom shall be a desolate
wilderness, for the violence *against* the
children of Judah, because they have
shed innocent blood in their land.
(20) But Judah shall [4] dwell for ever,
and Jerusalem from generation to
generation. (21) For I will cleanse their
blood *that* I have not cleansed: [5] for
the LORD dwelleth in Zion.

1 Heb., *place of repair*, or, *harbour*.

2 Heb., *holiness*.

a Rev. 21. 27.

b Amos 9. 13.

3 Heb., *go*.

4 Or, *abide*.

5 Or, *even I the LORD that dwelleth in Zion*.

---

appeal with these words. The majestic roar of the lion is transferred to express victorious utterance of the Lord's judgment: it is irresistible. As St. Paul wrote, "The Lord Himself shall descend from heaven with a shout, with the voice of the archangel, and with the trump of God" (1 Thess. ii. 16). The temporal success of the Jews in their future conflict with their enemies is blended with the final triumph of the Lord in the judgment day.

(17) **No strangers pass through her.**—Strangers signify the aliens who had hitherto oppressed. They are like the spots and wrinkles which would defile the bride—the Church of God.

(18) **The mountains shall drop down new wine.**—The material prosperity depicted in these verses symbolises the glorious reign of Jehovah when the last enemy has been destroyed, and "God is all in all."

A fountain shall come forth.—The spiritual fertilising power of the knowledge of the Lord is compared to the life-giving influence of a stream of water, which causes luxuriance to the trees on its banks. This imagery is exemplified by Ezekiel, who traces the course of the waters issuing from under the threshold of the house of the Lord (Ezek. xlvii.). (Comp. Zech. xiv. 8; Rev. xxii. 1.)

The valley of Shittim.—Heb., *acacias.* Shittim, in the land of Moab, is symbolical of the barrenness and sterility of land where there is no water; of the dry places of the world, where there are trees lacking moisture: the heathen, to whom God is not known, shall yet become covered with the knowledge of the Lord.

(19) **Egypt shall be a desolation.**—Egypt and Edom always excited feelings of abhorrence in the hearts of the Jews. The memory of the exile in Egypt was always fresh and keen; no retrospect of their past history could leave it out of account. And the national detestation of the false and cruel-hearted Idumæan kinsmen is recalled by Obadiah in his prophecy and touching record; as also in Ps. cxxxvii., as rendered in the Prayer Book, "Remember the children of Edom, O Lord, in the day of Jerusalem, how they said, Down with it, down with it, even to the ground."

(21) **I will cleanse . . .**—The LXX. translate this sentence, "I will avenge their blood, and not leave it unavenged"—*i.e.*, the "innocent blood" mentioned in verse 19; but the promise seems rather to indicate, as in the English Version, the extension of God's pardon to those hitherto unpardoned.

The Lord dwelleth in Zion—*i.e.*, over a raging and swelling world, probably unconscious of Him, the Lord nevertheless reigns in the heavenly Jerusalem, and all His redeemed shall dwell securely under His eternal rule. "And the name of the city from that day shall be Jehovah Shammah, the LORD IS THERE" (Ezek. xlviii. 35).

AMOS

INTRODUCTION

TO

AMOS

THE early life of the prophet Amos was spent at Tekoa, the modern *Tekûa*, an elevated spot between four and five English miles due south of Bethlehem. This spot, according to Robinson (*Biblical Researches*, i. 486), has "a wide prospect. Towards the north-east the land slopes down towards Wady Khureitûn; on the other side the hill is surrounded by a belt of level table land, beyond which are valleys, and then other higher hills. On the south, at some distance, another deep valley runs off south-east towards the Dead Sea. The view in this direction is bounded only by the level mountains of Moab, with frequent bursts of the Dead Sea seen through openings among the rugged and desolate intervening mountains." No fitter scene can be imagined as the home of the prophet, whose far-seeing vision and trumpet voice were to awaken the corrupt and selfish life of the northern kingdom. Amos was by birth not a prophet, but a herdsman, and likewise a dresser of sycamore-fruit. How long he plied his peaceful tasks in his Judæan home, secure against invasion or disturbance under the strong rule of King Uzziah, we do not know. But to him—a layman, and no prophet—there came the Word of the Lord as he meditated among the lonely hills and their wide prospects, urging him to utter God's doom against nations and kingdoms.

Respecting his prophetic work, we know that it was directed almost entirely to the northern kingdom, and was likewise exercised there. It is uncertain whether the striking episode described in chap. vii. 10—17 belonged to the beginning or the end of his ministry. We there read that the prophet boldly presented himself at Bethel, celebrated for its ancient historic associations, its important temple, and as being a place of royal residence. There Amos delivered the striking series of symbolic oracles contained in chaps. vii. and viii. This provoked the hostility of Amaziah, priest of the sanctuary, who endeavoured to obtain from King Jeroboam a sentence of banishment against the prophet, on the ground that he was speaking treason against the throne. To the charges and menaces of Amaziah Amos replied with a sentence of doom against king and priest.

It is extremely difficult to assign a probable date for the entire collection of oracles. We know from the superscription (1) that they were delivered two years before "the earthquake," an event so terrible and marked in its character that it is referred to again by Zechariah (Zech. xiv. 5); (2) that he prophesied during the reigns of Jeroboam and Uzziah. But we do not know the date of the earthquake, nor whether the prophetic ministry of Amos continued after the death of Jeroboam II. It is also doubtful how long a period is covered by the extant collection of oracles, though internal indications favour a short rather than a long interval. To this must be added the uncertainty which now prevails respecting Biblical chronology. (See Introduction to Hosea.) If we adopt Mr. Sharpe's chronology, which seems more free from difficulties than other systems, the death of Jeroboam II. took place in 764. The Assyriologist, Professor Brandes, would put it several years later (Geo. Smith, *Assyr. Eponym Canon*, pp. 14, 15). We might, therefore, place the period of the prophet's activity between 804 (the year of Jeroboam's accession, according to Sharpe) and about 760 B.C. We shall assign reasons for showing that the prophetic career of Amos was probably subsequent to 780 B.C. The fact that the prophet never makes mention of the name of Assyria, though he refers expressly to the destinies of surrounding nations, seems to imply that Assyria was at that period not so disturbing a force in Syro-Palestinian politics as it had been in a former generation, and as it was destined to become during the ministry of the prophet Hosea, when the terrible invasions of Tiglath-Pileser made the names of Asshur and King Combat (Jareb) to be names of dread. Accordingly we prefer to regard the prophetic ministry of Amos as exercised when Syria had begun to recover from the disastrous invasion of Vulnirari III. (see Geo. Smith, *Assyr. Eponym Canon*, p. 115; Schrader, *Cuneiform Inscriptions*, second edition, pp. 212—216, calls him *Ramman-nirari*), *i.e.*, about 780 B.C.*

For the social, moral, and religious condition of the northern kingdom during this period we fortunately possess varied sources of information. Apart from the accounts contained in the historical books, we have the numerous allusions scattered throughout the prophet Hosea, whose discourses belong to a somewhat similar period, and are extremely valuable as illustrating those of Amos.

We thus obtain a tolerably vivid conception of this momentous and tragic century—the last days of Israel's history. The energetic rule and successful wars of Jeroboam II, had extended the bounds of the kingdom. Syria had been compelled to yield up to him a large tract of country extending from Hamath to the Dead Sea. Ammon and Moab had become tributary. But the ease with which these conquests were obtained were due to the dangers which threatened the very existence of the Syrian states from the Assyrian power which had for many centuries been formidable, but was now extending itself westward, under the energetic sway of Vulnirari III. Under that monarch, as we learn from his inscription, Syria received a terrible blow;† and it is extremely probable that the recovery of the Trans-

* Additional confirmation of this view is to be found in the reference of chap. viii. 9 to an eclipse, which probably occurred in 784 B.C. (See Excursus to the passage.)

† "To Syria I went. Mariha, king of Syria, in Damascus, his royal city, I besieged. Fear and terror of Assur his lord overwhelmed him, and my yoke he took. Submission he made; 2,300 talents of silver, 20 talents of gold, 3,000 talents of copper, 5,000 talents of iron, clothing of wool and flax, a couch of ivory, a high table, his goods and his furniture without number in Damascus, his royal city, in his palace, I received." This event is placed by Schrader in 800 B.C., and by G. Smith in 797.

jordanic district by Jeroboam from Syrian domination is to be closely connected with this temp rary overthrow of Syria and the neighbouring kingdoms. (See Note on chap. vi. 14.)

But the external power and foreign conquests of Jeroboam were evidently viewed with mistrust by the prophet; and, though Assyria is never expressly named, it looms in the background of the seer's gaze, as the sword of Jehovah's vengeance, which is one day to make a full end of Israel. (Comp. Isa. x. 5.) The oracles of both Amos and Hosea abound in allusions to the moral and social rottenness of the northern kingdom. Amos dwells upon the splendour of the public buildings and of many private dwellings of the land (chap. iii. 15, v. 11: comp. Hosea viii. 14). Within Samaria's strong fortresses the wealthy nobles indulged in their drunken orgies, stretched upon ivory divans, singing their "lean and flashy songs" in wretched parody of David's minstrelsy, and bidding farewell to all thoughts of coming evil (chap. vi.). He rebukes the empty boasts of power in which these profligate leaders indulged (*ibid.*). He sternly censures the ladies of fashion who encouraged their lords to acts of gross self-indulgence (chap. iv. 1). Meanwhile their luxurious life is purchased at the cost and on the gains of frightful oppression. In the days when Amos lived, the simple agricultural life of earlier times had given place to the changed social conditions produced by growing civilisation and commerce (Hosea xii. 7, 8), by the growth of large towns, and by the extension of art and refinement, of unscrupulous trade, and accumulated wealth (Amos viii. 5; Isa. ii. 7). The poor cultivators of the soil were ground down to abject poverty by the princely landowners. The debts of the peasant, however paltry, could only be redeemed by a personal service, which was slavery (chap. ii. 6, 7). Their lords were also their judges in the courts of justice at the city gates, and extortionate bribes were the appointed means of averting a harsh sentence (chap. v. 11, 12).

But the root of all the social and moral disorder was indicated by Amos and Hosea (especially the latter) to consist in the idolatrous and sensuous corruption into which the people had sunk. Baal and calf-worship had become to the popular intelligence the degraded substitute and symbol of the ancient pure conception of the one true God inculcated in the Mosaic law and worship to which the prophet Hosea endeavoured to restore Israel. The whole of Canaan, from Dan to Beersheba, was studded with local shrines, in which Baal or the calf-symbols were adored. Of the former, probably Beersheba and Gilgal, of the latter, Samaria, Bethel, and Dan were the chief centres. (See chap. viii. 14, Note, also chap. iv 4; Hosea xii. 11.) Moreover, all these sanctuaries possessed an elaborate ritual and calendar of feast-days (Amos v. 21, 22). Both prophets threaten foreign invasion and exile as the penalty for this abandonment of ancient law and observance (Amos v. 26, 27; Hos. ii. 11). There are likewise traces, though obscure, of the worship of the Ammonitish star deity, Moloch, of the star deity *Kevan*, and of the Syrian *Hadad-Rimmon*. But the passages on which this is based are doubtful (chap. iv., 3, v. 26).

That the herdsman of Tekoa was a man of wide and varied culture, in the current acceptation of the times, is clearly evidenced by his writings. In that age the free movements of human intercourse diffused knowledge more widely and equably among all classes of mankind than is possible under present social conditions. The mind of the prophet was especially open to all physical phenomena. The rising of the Nile, the constellations of the sky, the eclipse, and the earthquake stirred his imagination. It is noteworthy that in Amos we have the first clear indication of the enlarging sweep of the prophet's gaze. His eye ranges over the surrounding kingdoms. Israel is no longer thought of exclusively, its destiny is no longer contemplated apart from that of the surrounding empires with which it was closely connected. Jehovah is God of the world, and not of his peculiar people the Hebrew race only. He brought Philistia from Caphtor as well as Israel from Egypt.

This conception of universal Divine sovereignty was certainly not a new one in Israel. But it was made especially prominent by Amos, and is the key-note of his prophecies. It is from this standpoint that the oracles are delivered. While to Hosea, Ephraim's sin, whether in morals or worship, appeared as an outrage to the relationship of loyalty and love to the Divine Lord, it was regarded by Amos as the violation of a supreme rule and a supreme justice.

The prophecies may be divided according to their contents as follows:—

I. Chaps. i.—vi. Prophetic threatenings directed against the nations.

- (i.) Chaps. i. 2—ii. 5. Brief denunciations of surrounding peoples;—against Damascus, Philistia, Tyre, Edom, Ammon, Moab, and closing with Judah.
- (ii.) Chaps. ii. 6—vi. Indictment against Israel. The prevailing idolatry—The oppression of the poor, and the debauched and indolent lives of the nobles.

II. Chaps. vii.—ix. Symbolic visions of the coming doom of Israel interrupted by the episode of the hostility of the priest Amaziah to the Prophet. The series closes with the Messianic anticipations of reunited and restored Israel dwelling in peace under the reign of the house of David.

AMOS

CHAPTER I.—The words of Amos,
who was among the herdmen of Tekoa,
which he saw concerning Israel in the
days of Uzziah king of Judah, and in
the days of Jeroboam the son of Joash
king of Israel, two years before the
[a]earthquake. (2) And he said, The LORD
will [b] roar from Zion, and utter his voice
from Jerusalem; and the habitations of
the shepherds shall mourn, and the top
of Carmel shall wither.
(3) Thus saith the LORD; For three
transgressions of Damascus, [1]and for
four, I will not [2]turn away *the punishment*
thereof; because they have
threshed Gilead with threshing instruments
of iron: (4) but I will send a fire
into the house of Hazael, which shall
devour the palaces of Ben-hadad.
(5) I will break also the bar of Damascus,
and cut off the inhabitant from [3]the
plain of Aven, and him that holdeth the
sceptre from [4]the house of Eden: and
the people of Syria shall go into
captivity unto Kir, saith the LORD.
(6) Thus saith the LORD; For three
transgressions of [c]Gaza, and for four, I
will not turn away *the punishment*
thereof; because they [5]carried away
captive the whole captivity, to deliver
them up to Edom: (7) but I will send a
fire on the wall of Gaza, which shall

B.C. 787

a Zech. 14.5.

b Jer. 25. 30; Joel 3. 16.

1 Or, *yea, for four.*

2 Or, *convert it*, or, *let it be quiet*: and so ver. 6, &c.

3 Or, *Bikathaven.*

4 Or, *Beth-eden.*

c 2 Chron. 28. 18.

5 Or, *carried them away with an entire captivity.*

The *Prologue* to the Prophecies of Amos consists of a series of denunciations of the surrounding peoples. The ground of the awful threatenings is the word of Jehovah made known to the prophet. The reason for the doom predicted on such high authority, is the resistance and cruelty that were offered by these nations to the theocratic people, and, still more, their own moral offences, condemned by universal conscience. The denunciations begin with a judgment upon *Syria*, the age-long enemy of Judah, sometimes confederate with Israel. Then he passes to Philistia, which had been a thorn in the side of Israel and Judah from the days of the Judges till his own. Then he directs his gaze upon Phœnician cities, the emporium of the most extensive commerce in the world. Next he passes in review other three tribes, or nations, more closely related to Israel in blood, language, and proximity, and which, nevertheless, had often manifested an undying hatred of the covenanted people. After this Judah, his own tribe, does not escape. Lastly, the prophet gathers up all his strength to denounce Israel, then at the height of prosperity and splendour.

(1) See Introduction.

(2) **Roar.**—The prolonged thunder-peal, or lion's roar, of the Divine voice, reverberates from the theocratic metropolis of Zion, to the luxuriant slopes of the noble Carmel, which forms the southern promontory of the Bay of Acre. The "pastures of the Shepherds" remind us of Psalm xxiii., and refers us to the prophet's own home in the wilderness of Tekoah. The same expression "head (or 'top') of Carmel" occurs in 1 Kings xviii. 42, and in chap. ix. 3. Compare the modern name *Ras-el-Kerum*. The whole country from south to north is summoned to listen to the Divine voice.

CURSE ON DAMASCUS.

(3) **Three transgressions . . .**—This form of transgression, which occurs eight times in the prologue, is not an arithmetical, but a strongly idiomatic phrase, signifying "multiplied or repeated delinquencies" (*Henderson*).

Turn away . . .—Rather, *will not turn it back*—*i.e.*, the sore judgment I have purposed. (Comp. 2 Kings x. 32, 33.)

(4) **I will send a fire . . .**—Compare Jer. xlix. 27, where this language is repeated at a time when punishment had fallen for a while on Damascus, and she had become, as Isaiah predicted, "a ruinous heap" (Isa. xvii. 1).

(5) **I will break . . .**—The "bar" means the bolt of iron or brass with which the city was defended. But it is possible that it may be used of persons, *i.e.*, princes or leaders (comp. Hosea iv. 18, xi. 6); and this seems confirmed by the parallelism. The plain or valley cleft between Libanus and Antilibanus is still called by the Arabs by a name closely resembling the rendering in the margin, "the valley." It is probable that the word rendered "vanity," (*aven*) is simply a Masoretic reading, and not what Amos intended. It is better to follow the LXX. and read the word *On* (as in Ezek. xxx. 17), the reference being to the Temple of Baalbec, then in ruins, the Syrian Heliopolis. (Comp. Hosea iv. 15.)* The site of Beth-eden (house of Eden) cannot be satisfactorily determined. Kir is the region of the river Cyrus, or, perhaps, the E. of the Upper Euphrates (see ix. 7). (2 Kings xvi. 9, we see fulfilment of this doom.)

CURSE ON PHILISTIA.

(6–8) The marginal reading is more literal, and points to the special bitterness of the proceedings of Philistia, here represented by Gaza as the principal city (comp. 2 Chron. xxi. 16, 17, which implies a veritable sack of Jerusalem). The extreme barbarity from which Judah suffered was that her children were delivered up to the

* On the other hand the Masoretic reading seems to have been suggested (if not confirmed) by Amos v. 5, where LXX. read *aven*.

devour the palaces thereof: (8) and I
will cut off the inhabitant from Ashdod,
and him that holdeth the sceptre from
Ashkelon, and I will turn mine hand
against Ekron: and the remnant of the
Philistines shall perish, saith the Lord
GOD.

(9) Thus saith the LORD; For three
transgressions of Tyrus, and for four, I
will not turn away *the punishment*
thereof; because they delivered up the
whole captivity to Edom, and remem-
bered not [1] the brotherly covenant:
(10) but I will send a fire on the wall of
Tyrus, which shall devour the palaces
thereof.

(11) Thus saith the LORD; For three
transgressions of Edom, and for four,
I will not turn away *the punishment*
thereof; because he did pursue his
brother with the sword, and [2] did cast
off all pity, and his anger did tear per-
petually, and he kept his wrath for
ever: (12) but I will send a fire upon
Teman, which shall devour the palaces
of Bozrah.

(13) Thus saith the LORD; For three
transgressions of the children of
Ammon, and for four, I will not turn
away *the punishment* thereof; because
they have [3] ripped up the women with
child of Gilead, that they might enlarge
their border: (14) but I will kindle
a fire in the wall of Rabbath, and
it shall devour the palaces thereof, with
shouting in the day of battle, with a
tempest in the day of the whirlwind:
(15) and their king shall go into captivity,
he and his princes together, saith the
LORD.

CHAPTER II.—Thus saith the
LORD; For three transgressions of Moab,
and for four, I will not turn away *the
punishment* thereof; because he [a] burned
the bones of the king of Edom into

1 Heb., *the covenant of brethren.*

2 Heb., *corrupted his compassions.*

3 Or, *divided the mountains.*

a 2 Kings 3. 27.

---

implacable enemy Edom. (Comp. the language of Joel iii. 4—6.) This may have occurred in the border warfare, in which defenceless Judæan villages were overpowered, and the inhabitants sold to the Oriental tribes through the medium of the Edomites. The utter fall of Philistian independence is depicted (comp. chap. vi. 2). The cities here mentioned are often referred to in the books of Joshua, Judges, and Samuel, and by the prophet Zephaniah.

CURSE ON TYRUS.

(9) **The brotherly covenant.**—The "*covenant of brethren*" (margin) was the league made between Hiram and David, and afterwards between Hiram and Solomon (2 Sam. v. 11; 1 Kings v. 1, 12). This ancient covenant was forgotten in Phœnicia's mercantile cupidity, and Tyre was tempted to sell Hebrew captives to Greeks and Idumeans. (Comp. Isa. xxiii.; Ezek. xxvi., and the special excursus in the *Speaker's Commentary.*)

CURSE ON EDOM.

(11) **Edom.**—Comp. the prophecy of Obadiah and Isaiah xxxiv. 5. See also *Dict. of the Bible*, art. "Edom." All through their history Edom sided with the enemies of Israel. (Comp. 1 Sam. xiv. 47; 2 Sam. viii. 14; Ps. lx. 9; and 2 Chron. xxi. 8—10.)

Cast off.—It would be better to render *stifled.* In the following clause read "And his indignation rended continually, and his wrath lurked ever on the watch." But another punctuation of the Hebrew original yields a different sense. "As for his wrath, he hath kept it for ever" (almost as E.V.). This corresponds closely with Jer. iii. 5.

(12) **Teman.**—According to Gen. xxxvi. 11, a name for a grandson of Esau. The district and chief town of this name are often referred to in the Prophets (Jer. xlix. 7, 8; Ezek. xxv. 13; Hab. iii. 3; Obad. 8, 9). The wisdom and might of the Temanites were well known, and Eliphaz the Temanite was one of the sage interlocutors of the Book of Job. It was situated, according to Burckhardt and Robinson, south of the Wady Musa.

Bozrah.—Referred to in Jer. xlix. 13, 22; Micah ii. 12; Isa. xxxiv. 6, lxiii. 1. Quite distinct from Bozrah in Moab (Jer. xlviii. 24). The former is situated south of the Dead Sea, identified by Robinson and Burckhardt with the village of *El Buseireh* in Jebal.

CURSE ON AMMON.

(13) **Ammon.**—See art. in Smith's *Dict. of the Bible.* The precise event of atrocious cruelty is not mentioned in the historical books; but the barbarous modes of warfare which prevailed in those days are darkly conveyed in 1 Sam, xi. 2; 2 Kings xv. 16; Hosea xiii. 16, &c., and in Assyrian inscriptions *passim.*

(14) Jeremiah gives a vivid account of the impending doom of Ammon, quoting and expanding this very passage (chap. xlix. 1—3).

(15) **Their king.**—Not as Syrian and Vulg. read the original, *Malcam* or *Milcom, i.e.*, Moloch. E.V. is supported by LXX., Targ., and context of the passage. So far we find the prophet denouncing the sin which trifles with blood, covenants, and ancient agreements, and recognising the responsibilities of race; but closer inspection shows in this, and in chap. ii., that the prophet condemns all violations of those natural laws and rights of which he regards Jehovah as custodian and executor.

II.

CURSE ON MOAB.

(1) Comp. Isa. xv., xvi., xxv. 10—12, and Jer. xlviii. Translate "burned to lime the bones of the king of Edom." The historical reference is obscure. (See 2 Kings iii. 26, 27.) Whether Moab was guilty of desecrating royal tombs, or offering the heir of the king of Edom in sacrifice, cannot be determined. When Moab took revenge upon Edom, the latter was subject to Jehoram.

lime: (2) but I will send a fire upon
Moab, and it shall devour the palaces of
Kirioth: and Moab shall die with tumult,
with shouting, *and* with the sound of the
trumpet: (3) and I will cut off the
judge from the midst thereof, and will
slay all the princes thereof with him,
saith the LORD.

(4) Thus saith the LORD; For three
transgressions of Judah, and for four, I
will not turn away *the punishment*
thereof; because they have despised the
law of the LORD, and have not kept his
commandments, and their lies caused
them to err, after the which their
fathers have walked: (5) but I will send
a fire upon Judah, and it shall devour
the palaces of Jerusalem.

(6) Thus saith the LORD; For three
transgressions of Israel, and for four, I
will not turn away *the punishment*
thereof; because [a] they sold the right-
eous for silver, and the poor for a pair
of shoes; (7) that pant after the dust of
the earth on the head of the poor, and
turn aside the way of the meek: and a
man and his father will go in unto the
same [1] maid, to profane my holy name:
(8) and they lay *themselves* down upon
clothes laid to pledge by every altar,
and they drink the wine of [2] the con-
demned *in* the house of their god.
(9) Yet destroyed I the [b] Amorite before
them, whose height *was* like the height
of the cedars, and he *was* strong as the
oaks; yet I destroyed his fruit from
above, and his roots from beneath.
(10) Also [c] I brought you up from the
land of Egypt, and led you forty years
through the wilderness, to possess the
land of the Amorite. (11) And I raised
up of your sons for prophets, and of

a ch. 8. 6.

1 Or, *young woman.*

2 Or, *such as have fined, or, mulcted.*

b Num. 21. 24; Deut. 2. 31; Josh. 24. 8.

c Ex. 12. 51.

---

(2) **Kirioth.**—This properly signifies a group of towns, but here refers to a single large town in Moab, the modern *Kureiât.* (Comp. Jer. xlviii. 24.)

CURSE ON JUDAH.

Great privileges have met with mad and foolish despite. Exalted to the highest heaven of possibility, Judah has despised the "Law of the Lord," instead of preserving, with sacred reverence, His ordinances and institutions.

Their lies.—*i.e.*, their false deities, which they have treated as divine. "The lies after which the fathers walked deceived the children. The children canonise the errors of their fathers. Human opinion is as dogmatic as revelation" (*Pusey*).

(5) **Judah.**—Such high privilege does not involve immunity from punishment. Judah shall be chastised with the same penalty as Edom, Philistia, Ammon, and Moab.

CURSE ON ISRAEL.

(6) **Transgressions of Israel.**—The storm of Divine threatening which had swept over the whole political horizon gathers, at last, over Israel. The sins and ingratitude of the people are aggravated by a recital of the Divine Mercy. By comparing this verse with chap. viii. 6, it is clear that the Jewish interpreters (followed by Keil) were incorrect in charging this sin upon corrupt judges, who, by *bribery,* would deliver unjust judgments against the righteous. The sin consists in the perverse straining of the law, which allowed an insolvent debtor to sell himself into bondage to redeem a debt (comp. 2 Kings iv. 1; also Lev. xxv. 39). In this case the debtor was a righteous man in sore straits for no fault of his own. Render, *on account of a pair of sandals.* A paltry debt, equivalent, in worth, to a pair of sandals, would not save him from bondage at the hands of an oppressive ruler (see Introduction).

(7) **Dust of the earth on the head of the poor.**—Can only mean, as Ewald and Keil interpret: they long to see the poor reduced to such distress that dust is thrown on their heads in token of grief. The meek are defrauded as being too weak to claim their own. The latter part of the verse points to the sensuality of the popular worship, the word "maid" being really the prostitute (Heb. *k'dêshah*) who was devoted to the lustful ritual of Ashera.* This obscenity is regarded by the prophet as part of a deliberate act of desecration to the name of the Holy One of Israel. Moreover, the relation of "father" and "son" was thereby sullied and degraded. (Comp. Lev. xviii. 8, 15, xx. 11.)

(8) Rapacity and cruelty follow on pride, selfishness, and lust. With this verse compare the provisions of the Mosaic law (Exod. xxii. 25). Render, *And upon garments received in pledge they stretch themselves,* and for "condemned" adopt the marginal translation *mulcted.* The money that had been wrung from those who could not pay, or, who have been sold into slavery, is spent in rioting and feasting. The LXX. read this passage very differently, but the Masoretic text is justified by the translations of the Targum, Aquila, Symmachus, and Jerome.

In the house of their god.—Probably here, as in the previous verse, we are to understand the high places of syncretic, or heathenish, Jehovah worship as referred to. "They drank the wine of the amerced. Where? 'In the house of their God.' What hard-heartedness to the wilfully forgotten poor is compensated by a little church-going!" (*Pusey.*)

(9) **Destroyed I.**—Emphasis belongs to the pronoun "I." The Amorites proper occupied the S.W. coast of the Dead Sea. Their formidable stature and power were attributed occasionally to all the inhabitants of the land. (Josh. xxiv. 18; Jud. vi. 10.) They were absorbed before the time of Amos.

(10) **Forty years.**—The forty years' wandering was a punishment for fickleness and cowardice, but during the incidence of this judgment, of which we have only one or two events recorded in the Book of Numbers, God was disciplining and organising a tribe of restless wanderers into a nation. (Deut. xxxii. 9—13.)

(11, 12) God added to the mercies of His providence, the transcendent blessings of special revelation. The

* Kuenen, *Religion of Israel,* vol. i., pp. 92, 93.

your young men for Nazarites. *Is it*
not even thus, O ye children of Israel?
saith the LORD. (12) But ye gave the
Nazarites wine to drink; and commanded
the prophets, [a] saying, Prophesy not.
(13) Behold, [1] I am pressed under you, as
a cart is pressed *that is* full of
sheaves. (14) Therefore the flight shall
perish from the swift, and the strong
shall not strengthen his force, neither
shall the mighty deliver [2] himself.
(15) Neither shall he stand that handleth
the bow; and *he that is* swift of foot
shall not deliver *himself:* neither shall
he that rideth the horse deliver himself.
(16) And *he that is* [3] courageous among
the mighty shall flee away naked in
that day, saith the LORD.

CHAPTER III.—Hear this word that
the LORD hath spoken against you, O
children of Israel, against the whole
family which I brought up from the
land of Egypt, saying,
(2) You only have I known of all the
families of the earth: therefore I will
[4] punish you for all your iniquities.
(3) Can two walk together, except they
be agreed? (4) Will a lion roar in the
forest, when he hath no prey? will a

a ch. 7. 12.

1 Or, *I will press your place as a cart full of sheaves presseth.*

2 Heb., *his soul,* or, *life.*

3 Heb., *strong of his heart.*

4 Heb., *visit upon.*

---

prophets of Israel were numerous, and renowned, and exposed to frequent persecution, *e.g.*, the cases of Micaiah, Elijah, and others. "The Nazarite vow to abstain from wine, which, in the earliest case, that of Samson, appears a life-long vow, was undoubtedly a religious protest against Canaanite civilisation in favour of the simple life of ancient times." (W. R. Smith, *Prophets of Israel,* p. 84.) The Nazarite was, moreover, a link between the prophet and the priest, upon whom, without hereditary rank or sacerdotal rite, great privileges were bestowed. The assault upon both is highly characteristic of the disloyalty of Israel.

(13) **I am pressed.**—Baur, Pusey, and *Speaker's Commentary* support this rendering of the Heb. *mē'îq*, the corresponding form in the next clause also being taken in the intransitive (*i.e.*, passive sense). But it is unlikely that God, in this passage, should declare Himself "crushed" under the weight of Israel's sin, for in the context it is Israel, and not God, who is described as the victim. Moreover, grammatical usage is against the rendering of *mē'îq* as passive; nor does it favour Ewald's, as well as Keil's, interpretation "press you *down*" Translate (see margin) *Behold, I am pressing down beneath you* (literally, *your place*), *just as the waggon, filled up with sheaves, presses down.* Jehovah, in the awful judgment which He inflicts, is symbolised by the heavily-laden waggon. The expression "beneath you" suggests that the evil is not confined to the present. Israel, the nation weighted with the doom of past iniquities, bequeathes a yet more crushing load to future generations. If the text is sound, this appears the only satisfactory rendering of a difficult passage.

(14) This doom Amos darkly foreshadows to be invasion and military overthrow, with all its attendant calamities.

(15) Is omitted in some of Kennicott's and De Rossi's MSS., but without authority.

III.

Chaps. iii.—vi. form a connected series, standing, however, as a natural sequence upon the previous section (chaps. i., ii.). In the denunciations with which the oracles of Amos open, the last strophe refers to Israel. The same subject is the burden of the following discourses, chaps. iii.—vi., and with searching minuteness the whole of Israel's sin and doom are laid bare by the prophet; the blindness to the warnings of prophecy, the pride and luxury of the powerful, and the misery of the oppressed, as well as the prevailing idolatrous corruption. In chap. iv. 5, the utterance of the prophet assumes the form of a measured strain (as in chap. i.), with an intercalary refrain, which may have been the model for Isaiah's yet more artistic effort (chaps. ix. 7—x, 4, v. 25—30). A solemn dirge over Israel and Judah (chaps. v. and vi.) closes the first part of these prophetic addresses.

(1) **Children of Israel** rather than "house of Israel" is a phrase not so usual in Amos. Hence in many MSS. the latter phrase is substituted. There is, however, significance in the former, as Amos addresses himself to both kingdoms in the phrase "the whole family." Yet the kingdom of the Ten Tribes seems to be chiefly in the mind of the prophet.

(2) **Known.**—The knowledge of God is love. There was special knowledge and intimacy between God and Israel. Upon such knowledge followed advantages and privileges innumerable.

Therefore I will . . .—This may mean, in proportion to your privileges will be your doom—but more probably that this intimacy of knowledge is the ground of gracious chastisement. For nation or man to be allowed to go on in sin without rebuke is the greatest curse that can befall it or him.

(3) **Two.**—Who are the two here represented? Some commentators say, two prophets; Rosenmüller, "God and the prophet." But Grotius, Lowth, Henderson, and Pusey refer it, with more reason, to God and Israel, the expression denoting, not merely God's knowledge of a man, but man's response to God. His practical obedience, his communion of heart and will, are described as "walking with" or "before God." (Gen. v. 22, vi. 9, xvii. 1; Ps. lvi. 13, cxvi. 9.) Will, then, God walk with man, guiding, shielding, strengthening him, if man is not in harmony with Him? This is the first of a series of parabolic apothegms, all of which require a negative answer. (Lev. xxvi. 23, 24.) Each states an event, closely and indissolubly related to another in the bond of cause and effect. All these symbolic utterances point on to the climax in verses 7, 8.

(4) **Lion.**—The questions suggest that the prey is being seized. This is intimated by the lion's roar, the loud roar of the lion in the forest, the growl of the famished young lions in the den. Aben-Ezra thus interprets; but G. Baur thinks that *Caphir* distinguishes a "hunting lion" from the beast that growls in his lair. (Comp. chap. i. 2.) Amos, by his graphic representation of the terrifying threat, signifies that nations, and kingdoms, and this family of Israel, are, at the present moment, trembling in the grasp of the great Avenger.

young lion [1] cry out of his den, if he
have taken nothing? (5) Can a bird
fall in a snare upon the earth, where
no gin *is* for him? shall *one* take up a
snare from the earth, and have taken
nothing at all? (6) Shall a trumpet be
blown in the city, and the people
[2] not be afraid? shall there be evil in
a city, [3] and the LORD hath not done *it?*
(7) Surely the Lord GOD will do nothing,
but he revealeth his secret unto his
servants the prophets. (8) The lion hath
roared, who will not fear? the Lord GOD
hath spoken, who can but prophesy?
(9) Publish in the palaces at Ashdod,
and in the palaces in the land of Egypt,
and say, Assemble yourselves upon the
mountains of Samaria, and behold the
great tumults in the midst thereof, and
the [4] oppressed in the midst thereof.
(10) For they know not to do right, saith
the LORD, who store up violence and
[5] robbery in their palaces. (11) Therefore
thus saith the Lord GOD; An adversary
there shall be even round about the land;
and he shall bring down thy strength
from thee, and thy palaces shall be
spoiled. (12) Thus saith the LORD; As
the shepherd [6] taketh out of the mouth
of the lion two legs, or a piece of an ear;
so shall the children of Israel be taken
out that dwell in Samaria in the corner
of a bed, and [7] in Damascus *in* a couch.
(13) Hear ye, and testify in the house of
Jacob, saith the Lord GOD, the God of
hosts, (14) that in the day that I shall
[8] visit the transgressions of Israel upon
him I will also visit the altars of Beth-el:
and the horns of the altar shall be cut
off, and fall to the ground. (15) And I
will smite the winter house with the
summer house; and the houses of ivory
shall perish, and the great houses shall
have an end, saith the LORD.

1 Heb., *give forth his voice.*
2 Or, *not run together.*
3 Or, *and shall not the LORD do somewhat?*
4 Or, *oppressions.*
5 Or, *spoil.*
6 Heb., *delivereth.*
7 Or, *on the bed's feet.*
8 Or, *punish Israel for.*

---

(5) **Can a bird.**—Better, *Does the snare rise up from the ground, and take nothing at all?*" E.V. "take up" is due to ambiguity of the Hebrew. The idea is that Israel "like a silly dove" is falling into snares. The snare, even now, may be seen springing from the earth. The armies and politics of the nation that will enclose Israel are already in motion.

(6, 7) **Surely the Lord . . .**—In this, and the preceding verse, the future tense should be replaced by a present. Render *doeth nothing,* and in verse 6 *is a trumpet sounded . . . are not afraid . . . is there evil;* for the prophet intends to express a continually-recurring fact. The word translated "evil" is commonly, but not universally, used for moral evil. (See Gen. xix. 19, xliv. 34; Exod. xxxii. 14.) "Evil which is sin the Lord hath not done, evil which is punishment for evil the Lord bringeth." (*Augustine.*) Compare, as illustrations of the truth of verse 7, the revelation of the Divine purpose to Noah with reference to the Deluge, to Abraham with respect to Sodom, to Joseph about the famine in Egypt, and to Moses concerning Pharaoh. The prophets of the Lord have given full warning of the judgment of God upon all sin.

(8) **Roared.**—Comp. the imagery of chap. i. 2, and that of verse 4. The voice of the Lord is so audible, so clearly portending the coming judgment, that universal terror inevitably follows. (Comp. "If these should hold their peace, the stones would cry out."

(9) **In the palaces.**—Rather, *on the palaces, i.e.,* on their roofs in such conspicuous places that the population, high and low, would hear the summons.

Mountains of Samaria.—In the high ground around the city, from which can be observed all that is passing in the metropolis. Foreign people, even Philistines and Egyptians, are gathered to witness the evils of the doomed realm. The marginal rendering "oppressions" should be adopted. This is shown by the parallelism.

(10) **Know not to do right.**—Not merely have lost the perception of what is and what is not right, but are indifferent to such distinctions. They know not and care not; the awful state of utter moral impotence, wherein not only the intellectual consciousness, but the impulses to action, are languid or even paralysed—a dead conscience! Nothing is more condemnatory than this brief sentence. The light within them is darkness.

(11) **An adversary.**—This rendering is to be preferred to "affliction" (Chald., Syr.). It is the subject of the following verb "bring down," Assyria being referred to, though not in express terms. The reading of LXX., "O Tyre, thy land round about thee is desolate," is incoherent, and confounds *Tzăr* with *tzôr.*

Thy strength points mainly to the stronghold of Samaria, which the enemy was to bring down or reduce to ruins, but it may likewise include the chief warriors who were to be led away captive.

(12) **Taketh out . . . taken out.**—Should be (as in margin) *delivereth . . . be delivered.* The agricultural image, used by Amos, is very impressive. The shanks and pieces of the ear, worthless portions, saved from the lion's jaws, represent the remnants of Samaria's population that shall escape.

In Damascus in a couch.—Some would render "in Damascus on that of (*i.e.,* corner of) a couch," Damascus corresponding to Samaria in the parallel clause. But this construction is very questionable, and it would be much simpler and safer to adopt the reading of most Hebrew texts, and render *on a couch's damask* (so Gesenius and Ewald), referring to the silken (?) or white woollen fabric for which Damascus, even in that early age, was famous. The relations between Syria and Israel at this moment were intimate. The meaning is that even the noblest and wealthiest will be regarded, if saved, as worthless salvage.

(13) **Hear ye.**—Addressed to the foreign nations Egypt and Philistia referred to in verse 9.

(15) **Houses.**—It is uncertain whether by "winter and summer houses" are meant two classes of royal abodes, or different chambers of the same house (Judges iii. 20; Jer. xxxvi. 22, are compatible with either).

CHAPTER IV.—Hear this word, ye
kine of Bashan, that *are* in the moun-
tain of Samaria, which oppress the poor,
which crush the needy, which say to
their masters, Bring, and let us drink.
(2) The Lord GOD hath sworn by his
holiness, that, lo, the days shall come
upon you, that he will take you away
with hooks, and your posterity with
fishhooks. (3) And ye shall go out at
the breaches, every *cow at that which is*
before her; and [1] ye shall cast *them* into
the palace, saith the LORD.

(4) Come to Beth-el, and transgress; at
Gilgal multiply transgression; and bring
your sacrifices every morning, *and* your
tithes after [2] three years: (5) and [3] offer
a sacrifice of thanksgiving with leaven,
and proclaim *and* publish the free offer-
ings: for [4] this liketh you, O ye children
of Israel, saith the Lord GOD.

(6) And I also have given you cleanness
of teeth in all your cities, and want of
bread in all your places: yet have ye
not returned unto me, saith the LORD.
(7) And also I have withholden the rain
from you, when *there were* yet three
months to the harvest: and I caused it
to rain upon one city, and caused it not
to rain upon another city: one piece
was rained upon, and the piece where-
upon it rained not withered. (8) So two
or three cities wandered unto one city,
to drink water; but they were not satis-
fied: yet have ye not returned unto me,
saith the LORD. (9) I have smitten you
with blasting and mildew: [5] when your
gardens and your vineyards and your

1 Or, *ye shall cast away the things of the palace.*

2 Heb., *three years of days.*

3 Heb., *offer by burning.*

4 Heb., *so ye love.*

5 Or, *the multitude of your gardens, &c., did the palmer-worm, &c.*

"Ivory houses" mean mansions adorned with ivory. For "great houses" should be read *many houses.*

IV.

A continuation in highly tropical and sarcastic language of the denunciation of the kingdom and nobles of Samaria, which was commenced in the previous chapter.

(1) **Bashan.**—This contained the rich pasture-lands east of the Jordan, between Hermon and the mountains of Gilead, where cattle flourished. The "strong bulls of Bashan" (Ps. xxii. 12) were descriptive of the malignant enemies of the ideal sufferer. The feminine "kine" refers to the luxurious self-indulgent women of fashion in Samaria.

Which say to their masters (*i.e.*, their husbands), **Bring, and let us drink.**—Their very debauch being paid for by the robbery of the poor. Some regard the feminines as sarcastic epithets, merely expressing effeminacy on the part of men. But this is not a probable explanation.

(2) **Fishhooks.**—Descriptive of the suddenness and irresistible character of the seizure, whereby, as a punishment for their wanton selfishness, the nobles were to be carried away as captives from their condition of fancied security. The strangeness of the imagery has led to a variety of interpretations. Döderlein translates "ye shall be driven into thorny districts, and among thorn bushes."

(3) **Every cow . . .**—Render *each one* (ref. to the women, verse 1) *straight before her.* The enemy shall have broken down the city's defences, and the women shall tamely go forth through the breaches into captivity. The next clause is very obscure. It is best to take the verb as passive, *Ye shall be thrown out.* The word that follows is rendered "the palace" by the E.V. with Kimchi and other authorities, under the assumption that the Heb. *harmôn* is another form of the word elsewhere used in Amos *armôn.* But this is mere guess-work, and yields no good sense. It would be better to adopt a slight emendation of our text, and treat the obscure word as a proper name (LXX., Targ., Syr., Vulg.). Many commentators (Michaelis, G. Baur, De Wette) follow the Targ. and Syr. and render "Ye shall be cast out to the mountains of Armenia" (their place of banishment). For further information see Excursus.

(4) **Bethel . . . Gilgal.**—In bitterly ironical words the prophet summons Israel to the calf-worship of Bethel, and to similar rites of bastard Jehovah-worship at Gilgal. These spots were full of sacred associations. The sarcastic force of the passage is lost in E.V. For "three years" read *every three days.* The law only required a tithe every third year (Deut. xxvi. 12); but here the prophet is lashing the people with hyperbolical irony for their excessive generosity to the base priests and spurious sanctuaries.

(5) The margin is more correct, and gives the key to the passage. Render, *and offer by burning your thank-offering of leaven.* Leaven was not allowed in any sacrifice offered by fire. Amos ironically calls upon them to break the Levitical law (Lev. vii. 13, xxiii. 17), as he knew they were in the habit of doing.

(6) **Cleanness of teeth** is, by the poetic parallelism, identified with the want of bread, the former phrase being a graphic representation of one of the ghastly aspects of famine; clean, sharp, prominent teeth projecting from the thin lips. Notwithstanding their chastisement, God says, "Ye have not returned even up to me." Jehovah is here introduced as grieving over the failure of his disciplinary treatment of Israel.

(7, 8) **Three months to the harvest.**—The withdrawal of rain at this period (February and March) is at the present day most calamitous to the crops in Palestine.

Caused it to rain . . .—The tenses should be regarded as expressing repetition of the act, and might be, with advantage, rendered as present *cause it to rain . . . is rained upon,* &c. The inhabitants of the most suffering districts wander, distracted and weary, to a more favoured city, and find no sufficiency. Comp. the graphic description in Jer. xiv. 1—6. Moreover, the specialties of affliction, in particular localities, reveal the purpose of God rather than the operation of universal laws.

(9) **Blasting and mildew.**—Burning up the corn before it is ready to ear, and producing a tawny yellow, instead of golden red, was another judgment. Nothing

fig trees and your olive trees increased,
the palmerworm devoured *them:* yet
have ye not returned unto me, saith the
LORD. (10) I have sent among you the
pestilence [1]after the manner of Egypt:
your young men have I slain with the
sword, [2]and have taken away your
horses; and I have made the stink of
your camps to come up unto your nos-
trils: yet have ye not returned unto me,
saith the LORD. (11) I have overthrown
some of you, as God overthrew [a]Sodom
and Gomorrah, and ye were as a fire-
brand plucked out of the burning: yet
have ye not returned unto me, saith the
LORD.

(12) Therefore thus will I do unto thee,
O Israel: *and* because I will do this unto
thee, prepare to meet thy God, O Israel.
(13) For, lo, he that formeth the moun-
tains, and createth the [3]wind, and
declareth unto man what *is* his thought,
that maketh the morning darkness, and
treadeth upon the high places of the
earth, The LORD, The God of hosts, *is*
his name.

CHAPTER V.—Hear ye this word
which I take up against you, *even* a
lamentation, O house of Israel.
(2) The virgin of Israel is fallen; she
shall no more rise: she is forsaken upon
her land; *there is* none to raise her up.
(3) For thus saith the Lord GOD; the
city that went out *by* a thousand shall
leave an hundred, and that which went
forth *by* an hundred shall leave ten, to
the house of Israel.
(4) For thus saith the LORD unto the
house of Israel, Seek ye me, and ye shall
live. (5) But seek not [b]Beth-el, nor
enter into Gilgal, and pass not to Beer-
sheba: for Gilgal shall surely go into
captivity, and Beth-el shall come to

1 Or, *in the way.*
2 Heb., *with the captivity of your horses.*
a Gen. 19. 24.
3 Or, *spirit.*
b ch. 4. 4.

escapes the Divine visitation. "Your gardens, vineyards, fig-trees, and olive-trees"—which in a well-watered enclosure might escape the general drought—*the locust devours in vast numbers* (so the Heb. should be rendered); comp. Joel i. 4.

(10) **With the captivity of your horses.**—This, the marginal reading, is more exact. Egypt is the birthplace of the plague or black death, and the circumstances augmenting its horror are here terribly portrayed. G. Baur thinks, that since the drought is mentioned after the famine as its true cause, so here the prophet explains the cause of the pestilence, or the way in which it would be brought about, viz., by the hosts of slaughtered warriors scattered over the camp.

(11) **Overthrown.**—Another awful calamity, an earthquake, is referred to, and perhaps a volcanic eruption. Dr. Pusey enumerates a long series of earthquakes, which distressed Palestine, though not the central parts of the country, from the time of Julian to the twelfth century. The allusion to Sodom and Gomorrah gives a hint of the fierce licence and vice which had prevailed in some parts of the Northern kingdon, and called for chastisement.

Some of you.—More accurately *among you.*

Brand plucked . . .—Men would cast such a brand back into the fire. "Behold the goodness and severity of God."

(12) **Thus will I do.**—What is he about to do? It is left in awful uncertainty, but the doom is wrapt up in the boundless possibilities of the Divine judgment involved in the drawing very near of the Lord Himself, to execute what He has said and sworn by His Holiness in verses 2 and 3. All that had previously been done in famine, drought, blighting pestilence, and earthquake, was not final, and had failed in its effect. The summons to meet God in some other unknown form than these is very solemn.

(13) **God of hosts.**—The Lord whom they have to meet is no mere national deity, but the supreme Creator.

Createth the wind.—Not "spirit" (as margin). But the two ideas "wind" and "spirit" were closely associated in Heb. (as in Greek), being designated by the same word *ruach* (in Greek πνεῦμα, comp. John iii. 8). Hence the transition in thought to the next clause is natural. This is curiously rendered in LXX. "and declareth to man his Christ" through a misunderstanding of the original.

V.

Commences with a veritable dirge over the calamity already threatened. The form of the dirge belongs to the second verse only (its poetic expression resembling the lament of David over Saul and Jonathan, 2 Sam. i.), but the spirit of the dirge extends through the entire chapter.

(2) **Forsaken.**—Or rather *dashed to the earth.* "Virgin" is a feminine designation of Israel poetically expressive of grace and beauty. Comp. the epithet "daughter of Zion," nations and cities being represented by a feminine personification. She is not annihilated, but obliterated as a nation.

(3) **Shall leave an hundred.**—*i.e.*, shall have an hundred only as a remnant of the thousand who went forth to war. The great cities were to be decimated in the coming struggle with Assyria.

(4) **Seek . . . live.**—Search after God is rewarded by finding Him, and this is life in the highest sense.

(5) **Seek.**—The same word is used for the searching, or inquiring at idol shrines, which is here fervently condemned. Respecting Beersheba, see Note on chap. viii. 14. On Gilgal there is a play of words in the original, which it is impossible to express accurately in translation.

Bethel shall come to nought.—Render (with Luther) *Bethel* (*house of God*) *shall become Bethaven* (*house of vanity*). The form *Bethaven* here is supported by the LXX., and appears to confirm the Masoretic reading of Hos. iv. 15, x. 5; and Amos i. 5, where other reasons incline critics to read *On* for Aven (see the passages).

nought. (6) Seek the LORD, and ye shall
live; lest he break out like fire in the
house of Joseph, and devour *it*, and *there*
be none to quench *it* in Beth-el.
(7) Ye who turn judgment to worm-
wood, and leave off righteousness in the
earth, (8) *seek him* that maketh the
[a]seven stars and Orion, and turneth the
shadow of death into the morning, and
maketh the day dark with night: that
[b]calleth for the waters of the sea, and
poureth them out upon the face of
the earth: the LORD *is* his name:
(9) that strengtheneth the [1]spoiled
against the strong, so that the spoiled
shall come against the fortress.
(10) They hate him that rebuketh in
the gate, and they abhor him that
speaketh uprightly. (11) Forasmuch
therefore as your treading *is* upon the
poor, and ye take from him burdens of
wheat: [c]ye have built houses of hewn
stone, but ye shall not dwell in them;
ye have planted [2]pleasant vineyards, but
ye shall not drink wine of them.
(12) For I know your manifold transgres-
sions and your mighty sins: they afflict
the just, they take [3]a bribe, and they
turn aside the poor in the gate *from their*
right.
(13) Therefore the prudent shall keep
silence in that time; for it *is* an evil
time. (14) Seek good, and not evil, that
ye may live: and so the LORD, the God
of hosts, shall be with you, as ye have
spoken. (15) [d]Hate the evil, and love the
good, and establish judgment in the
gate: it may be that the LORD God of
hosts will be gracious unto the remnant
of Joseph. (16) Therefore the LORD, the
God of hosts, the Lord, saith thus;
Wailing *shall be* in all streets; and they

a Job 9. 9, & 38. 31.
b ch. 9. 6.
1 Heb., *spoil*.
c Zeph. 1. 13.
2 Heb., *vineyards of desire*.
3 Or, *a ransom*.
d Ps. 34. 14, & 97. 10; Rom. 12. 9.

---

(6) Render, *lest he rush down like fire on the house of Joseph* (*i.e.*, the Northern Kingdom). For "in Bethel" read "*for* Bethel." Let the blending of mercy with judgment be here observed, "Seek Jehovah and live, lest this evil befall you." The curse is still conditional.

(7) Is placed after verse 9 by Ewald, since verses 7 and 8 stand in the Heb. without any connecting-link. The holy thing "judgment" is perverted into the bitter thing "wormwood," that which is execrated.

Leave off.—Or rather, *cast down righteousness to the earth, i.e.*, by false judgments and unjust decrees. Pusey sees here the analogue of the humiliation of the Holy One by wicked hands, when He was crowned with thorns, and fell beneath His cross.

(8) Connected by E.V. with verse 6 through the verb "seek ye," so that it may thus be linked to verse 7. To regard it as a solemn assertion "There is one who maketh, &c.," is not satisfactory. We prefer to render, *As for him who made the Pleiades . . . Jehovah is his name, i.e.*, The God of the Hebrews is the supreme universal Lord (comp. chap. iv. 13). This is profoundly impressive, since the prophets were surrounded by the pompous nature-worship of the East.

The Heb. word for the Pleiades (seven stars) means properly "heap" or "cluster," and that for Orion signifies "stout, strong one." The appearance of the Pleiades indicated the "sweet influences" of spring, that of Orion the winter solstice. Observe that Amos the herdsman, and Job the Arabian Emir, accustomed to the naked sky of the desert, make these special references to astronomical facts. The death-shadow suggests the darkest experiences of human life. Jehovah pours His light upon the deepest gloom of our lot. He, too, can make the day dark with night, covering the noonday sky with funereal pall, as at the Crucifixion. God is also made the perennial source of the rain, that "river of God which is full of water," and which is ever rising at His command from the great sea.

(9) **That strengtheneth.**—The rendering should be *who causeth desolation to gleam upon the strong* (who were priding themselves on their immunity), *so that desolation cometh on the stronghold.*

(10) **Rebuker in the Gate.**—The person so described might be the prophet himself. So also *he that speaketh uprightly.*

(11) **Burdens of wheat.**—*i.e.*, Ye take gifts of sifted corn, as a contribution to your own luxury, and which the poor man was not bound to offer, and only would offer to purchase your good will. Therefore your pomp and luxury shall be of no avail. Such is God's judgment on indifference to the wants and feelings of the poor.

(12) **I know.**—Most of the commentators imply that the "I" is Jehovah, but it is more likely to be the prophet himself. The adjectives "manifold," "mighty," should be rendered as predicates, *That manifold are your transgressions, and mighty your sins, ye afflicters of the just and takers of a bribe, and ye who bow down the poor in the gate.* The idea involved in the word rendered "bribe" is the ransom which the poor and defenceless were obliged to pay to a tyrannical judge, in order to escape a harsh sentence. The "gate" is the place where judgment is passed by the chief men.

(13) **Prudent . . . silence.**—The dumb silence of the prudent is the awful curse which comes upon a people when they are given up to selfishness and rapacity. Thus the doom:—"Ephraim is joined to idols, let him alone."

(14, 15) Break in like a beam of sunshine in the darkness. The fearful doom, already spoken of, is after all conditional. Let a moral change be wrought in them, and even now Jehovah, God of hosts, may deign to be with them. Enlist your passions on the right side. No virtue is safe till it is enthusiastic.

(16) **Therefore.**—Probably a pause occurs here, for once more the words of the prophet assume a more mournful tone. "Therefore" points back to the transgressions condemned in verses 11—13. On the Divine name "Lord of hosts," see note on Hosea xii. 5, and Oehler, *Biblical Theology of the Old Testament*, §§ 194—8. It is a grand phrase to denote the antithesis between "the Portion of Jacob," and all heathen deities.

The "streets" are the open wide squares near the gates, and the "highways" are more properly the narrow alleys of the crowded cities of the East. The

shall say in all the highways, Alas! alas!
and they shall call the husbandman to
mourning, and such as are skilful of
lamentation to wailing. (17) And in
all vineyards *shall be* wailing: for
I will pass through thee, saith the
LORD.
(18) [a] Woe unto you that desire the day
of the LORD! to what end *is it* for you?
the day of the LORD *is* darkness, and not
light. (19) As if a man did flee from a
lion, and a bear met him; or went into
the house, and leaned his hand on the
wall, and a serpent bit him. (20) *Shall*
not the day of the LORD *be* darkness,
and not light? even very dark, and no
brightness in it?
(21) [b] I hate, I despise your feast days,
and I will not [1]smell in your solemn
assemblies. (22) Though ye offer me
burnt offerings and your meat offerings,
I will not accept *them:* neither will I
regard the [2]peace offerings of your fat
beasts. (23) Take thou away from me
the noise of thy songs; for I will not
hear the melody of thy viols. (24) But
let judgment [3]run down as waters, and
righteousness as a mighty stream.
(25) [c] Have ye offered unto me sacrifices
and offerings in the wilderness forty
years, O house of Israel? (26) But ye have
borne [4]the tabernacle of your Moloch
and Chiun your images, the star of
your god, which ye made to yourselves.
(27) Therefore will I cause you to go into
captivity beyond Damascus, saith the
LORD, whose name *is* the God of
hosts.

[a] Isa. 5. 19; Jer. 30. 7; Joel 2. 2; Zeph. 1. 15.

[b] Isa. 1. 11; Jer. 6. 20.

[1] Or, *smell your holy days.*

[2] Or, *thank offerings.*

[3] Heb., *roll.*

[c] Acts 7. 42.

[4] Or, *Siccuth your king.*

---

word for wailing (*mispēd*) denotes properly the beating of the breast, the Oriental symptom of grief. The calling of the husbandman from his agricultural pursuits to lamentation is an indication that the disaster was universal. Those "skilled in wailing" were generally, and are still, women who tear their hair and dress, throw dust over the head, and utter the monotonous wail and piercing cry of distress. The last clause should properly be inverted, *And wailing to such as are skilful of lamentation.* (Eccles. xii. 5; Jer. ix. 17—19.

Pass through thee.—Properly *through the midst of thee.* Whenever Jehovah is said to pass through a land or a city, heavy punishment is intended. (Comp. Exod. xii. 12.) The reference to the "vineyards" adds to the terror of the picture.

(18) **Desire the day of the Lord.**—Expecting that day to bring you deliverance and judgments upon your enemies. It shall bring the reverse! There is a dark side to the pillar of fire.

(19) *Your escape will be impossible.* You will avoid one calamity, only to fall into a worse.

(20) **Darkness.**—In the form of an interrogative, the condemnation contained in verse 18 is emphatically reasserted. The term rendered "very dark" is that used to denote the gross Egyptian darkness that might be felt (Exod. x. 22), the awful gloom, such as fell on Jerusalem at the Crucifixion, which is always accompanied by the sense of confusion, terror, and intolerable suspense. (Comp. the graphic metaphorical language of Isa. v. 30.)

(21, 22) These verses closely resemble the condemnation which Isaiah pronounces (chap. i. 10—15) upon mere ritual, however punctilious, mere profession of orthodoxy, however exacting, which was not accompanied by righteousness and mercy, and was not the expression of inward penitence and purity.

Will not smell in your . . .—A strong expression for "I take no delight in them." That Baal worship, as well as the worship of the true God, was characterised by similar offerings and sacrificial terms is indicated by a Phœnician tablet inscribed with a code of sacrificial dues, discovered at Marseilles. The word rendered peace offering should be translated as in the margin. The word for "*meat* offering" is better interpreted "*meal* offerings," since it consisted of vegetable products used in food, meal, oil, cakes, &c.

(23) **Songs.**—The very sound of their tumultuous songs was a burden to Jehovah. As Christ cleansed the Temple, so would He dispel all this hypocritical and perilous confusion of ideas.

(24) **Mighty stream.**—Or rather *perennial stream.*

(25, 26) Much uncertainty belongs to the interpretation of these verses and their connection in thought. Some commentators would treat verse 25 as a statement, and not a question, the first word being read as a definite article, and not an interrogative prefix in the Hebrew. But the construction of the following words forbids this supposition, and nearly all exegetes follow the LXX., Vulg., Targ., in taking the sentence as interrogative. Is the expected answer negative or affirmative? Heb. usage points to the former. So Ewald and Keil. According to the latter, the words apply to the nation as a whole, or to the great mass of the people, individual exceptions being passed by. The following verse is then taken in an adversative sense, "To me ye have offered no sacrifices, but ye have borne," &c. The opposition is between the Jehovah-worship, which they suspended, and the idol-worship which they carried on. This is a possible interpretation, as Driver (*Heb. Tenses,* § 119a, foot-note) admits. But as that writer shows (l.c.), it is more in consonance with grammatical usage to translate in verse 26 by a future, as Ewald does: "So ye shall carry away the tabernacle," &c., *i.e.,* when driven into exile. To this thought verse 27 forms a natural development: *And I will carry you away captive,* &c. Moreover, in the light of this interpretation the logical connection of verses 21—27 becomes much simpler: "I, Jehovah, abhor the mechanical round of corrupt and hollow ceremonial cloaking wickedness of conduct. Live righteously. Did I exact punctilious discharge of ceremonial in the desert wanderings? [No.] Therefore I shall submit you once more to the discipline of exile wanderings." On the meaning of the difficult clause, *Chiun your images, the star of your god, which ye made for yourselves,* as well as on the rendering of the LXX. and St. Stephen's quotation of the passage, see *Excursus B.* Kuenen is scarcely justified in founding an argument on this passage as to the origin of the Sabbath.

CHAPTER VI.—[a] Woe to them *that*
[1] *are* at ease in Zion, and trust in the
mountain of Samaria, *which are* named
[b] [2] chief of the nations, to whom the
house of Israel came! (2) Pass ye unto
Calneh, and see; and from thence go ye
to Hamath the great: then go down to
Gath of the Philistines: *be they* better
than these kingdoms? or their border
greater than your border? (3) Ye that
[c] put far away the [d] evil day, and cause
the [3] seat of violence to come near;
(4) that lie upon beds of ivory, and
[4] stretch themselves upon their couches,
and eat the lambs out of the flock, and
the calves out of the midst of the stall;
(5) that [5] chant to the sound of the viol,
and invent to themselves instruments of
musick, like David; (6) that drink [6] wine
in bowls, and anoint themselves with
the chief ointments: but they are not
grieved for the [7] affliction of Joseph.
(7) Therefore now shall they go captive
with the first that go captive, and the
banquet of them that stretched them-
selves shall be removed. (8) [e] The Lord
GOD hath sworn by himself, saith the
LORD the God of hosts, I abhor the
excellency of Jacob, and hate his palaces:
therefore will I deliver up the city
with [8] all that is therein. (9) And it
shall come to pass, if there remain ten
men in one house, that they shall die.
(10) And a man's uncle shall take him up,
and he that burneth him, to bring out
the bones out of the house, and shall say
unto him that *is* by the sides of the
house, *Is there* yet *any* with thee? and

a Luke 6. 24.
1 Or, *are secure.*
b Ex. 19. 5.
2 Or, *firstfruits.*
c Ezek. 12. 27.
d ch. 5. 18.
3 Or. *habitation.*
4 Or, *abound with superfluities.*
5 Or, *quaver.*
6 Or, *in bowls of wine.*
7 Heb. *breach.*
e Jer. 51. 14.
8 Heb., *the fulness thereof.*

VI.

The prophet now turns his rebuke, not only to the Northern kingdom, but to the House of Judah, though the burden of the subsequent charges are specially applicable to the former.

(1) **Trust.**—The word for "trust" is a participle, and we should translate as the parallelism indicates: *the confident* (or *complacent*) *dwellers in the mountain of Samaria: i.e.*, the upper luxurious classes, "the chief of the first of nations," meaning the rulers, to whom Israel, the supreme and highly-favoured nation, comes up for judgment and for guidance in all civil affairs. These are now summoned to listen to the rebuke of the Divine Judge.

(2) The meaning is obscure. Kalneh, the Kalno of Isa. x. 9, the Assyrian *Kulunu* (comp. Gen. x. 10), is here probably mentioned first because it is most easterly. It is identified by Kiepert with *Holwân*, but its position is uncertain, though generally regarded as lying in the neighbourhood of the Greek Ctesiphon, on the Tigris. Hamath is the ancient Hittite city in the valley of the Orontes, and it had felt the strong hand of Jeroboam II. (2 Kings xiv. 28). We have no reason for believing that at this period the Assyrian power had destroyed the importance of these places, though the prophet may have regarded that issue as imminent. Hamath the Great (or Rabba; comp. Josh. xi. 8), according to the inscriptions, sustained defeats from Salmanassar II. about 850 B.C. It was finally overthrown by Sargon in 720 B.C., who in his own boastful language "swept over its land like a flood." Gath, the home of Goliath, had probably lost its original importance. Uzziah destroyed it. Were Calno, Hamath, Gath, more important than Zion or Samaria? Then, says the prophet, do not expect in your opulence and self-satisfaction immunity from a worse doom.

(3) **Far away.**—They choose to think that the day of reckoning is far off, and cling yet closer to their habits of defrauding the poor at the seat of judgment. (Comp. Ezek. xii. 21—28.)

(4) **Of ivory**—*i.e.*, inlaid with that material.

(5) **Chant.**—The original Hebrew only occurs in this passage, and is best rendered *prattle*, or *jabber*. The comparison with David is ironical. He made these instruments to please the Lord, these princes to please themselves.

(6) **Bowls.**—The extent of their potations is indicated by the fact that they drink, not from wine-cups, but from large bowls (in which the wine was probably mixed). The same word is used in Exod. xxxviii. 3 to describe the sacrificial basons.

And anoint themselves . . .—Render, *anoint themselves with the choicest of oils, and are not sick at heart for the ruin of Joseph.* Self-indulgence is indifferent to the call of duty or danger.

(7) *Therefore* (as a punishment for this self-indulgence) *they shall go into captivity at the head of the captives, and the shout of the loungers* (rioting in their banquets) *shall cease.* All their loud merriment will come to a sorry end.

(8) **By himself.**—Literally, *by His soul.* Jehovah swears by His life or soul because He could swear by no greater—the eternal "I Am." (Comp. the formula of Divine asseveration: "As I live, saith the Lord," which derives illustration from the custom of swearing by the life of a monarch; Gen. xlii. 15, 16.) With the eternal unchangeable being of the Supreme Monarch stands contrasted "the excellency of Jacob," the false futile glory which Jehovah abhors. In chap. viii. 7 the phrase is used for God Himself; not, however, in either passage God's absolute perfection or objective glory, but the thoughts, sometimes wise, sometimes base, which men have entertained about Him. From the context we infer that the splendid shrine of Samaria, with its unacceptable offerings and calf-worship, is here meant. The reference to the coming destruction of buildings great and small (verse 11) lends colour to this interpretation. (Comp. verse 13.)

(9, 10) **Ten . . . uncle.**—In some large house it might be that ten are left remaining, but even these are devoured by the pestilence which hovers in the track of war. Nine have fallen victims. Fathers and brothers are all gone, and the uncle comes in as the funereal burner, to carry out the corpse to the pyre, and finds in the innermost parts of the house the tenth victim of the fell disease yet alive. A hurried word or two passes between them: "Is there yet another with thee?" and the answer comes, "Not one." Then shall he say "Hush!" The lonely sufferer begins to curse the Lord for His

he shall say, No. Then shall he say,
[a] Hold thy tongue: for [1] we may not make
mention of the name of the LORD.
(11) For, behold, the LORD commandeth,
and he will smite the great house with
[2] breaches, and the little house with
clefts.
(12) Shall horses run upon the rock?
will *one* plow *there* with oxen? for ye
have turned judgment into gall, and
the fruit of righteousness into hemlock:
(13) ye which rejoice in a thing of nought,
which say, Have we not taken to us
horns by our own strength? (14) But,
behold, I will raise up against you a
nation, O house of Israel, saith the LORD
the God of hosts; and they shall afflict
you from the entering in of Hemath
unto the [3] river of the wilderness.

CHAPTER VII.—Thus hath the
Lord GOD shewed unto me; and, behold,
he formed [4] grasshoppers in the begin-
ning of the shooting up of the latter
growth; and, lo, *it was* the latter
growth after the king's mowings.
(2) And it came to pass, *that* when they
had made an end of eating the grass of
the land, then I said, O Lord GOD,
forgive, I beseech thee: [5] by whom shall
Jacob arise? for he *is* small. (3) The
LORD repented for this: it shall not be,
saith the LORD.
(4) Thus hath the Lord GOD shewed

a ch. 5. 13.

1 Or, *they will not*, or, *have not*.

2 Or, *droppings*.

3 Or, *valley*.

4 Or, *green worms*.

5 Or, *who of (or, for) Jacob shall stand?*

---

judgments, or it may be he begins to call upon the Name of the Lord when it is too late, when, as a finishing touch of darkest gloom and despair, he is interrupted by a warning not to stir up Jehovah's wrath in this day of His visitation by even mentioning His name. This and one other passage (1 Sam. xxxi. 12) imply that under special circumstances the Hebrews burned their dead. In this case pestilence made cremation a necessity. The references in 2 Chron. xvi. 14, xxi. 19; Jer. xxxiv. 5, are to honorific burning of spices in memory of the dead.

(11) **Breaches.**—For this read *ruins.* (See end of Note on verse 8.) The overthrow of all classes of the population is here referred to.

(12) The questions require a negative answer, and show that the conduct of Israel is as inconsistent and senseless as the supposition involved in the interrogation: that horses should climb steep cliffs, or oxen plough in the rocky gorge. The conception of oppression, luxury, and pride being the forerunners of prosperity and peace is anomalous. The idea is, that that which should have insured the stability of the state, the embodiment of its conscience, had been turned into narcotic poison—the self-satisfaction of personal greed. *Rôsh*, the Hebrew for "gall," is a poisonous kind of plant with bitter taste, and resembling, according to Jerome, stalks of grass, and propagating itself with such rapidity that it is difficult to exterminate it. (Comp. Hosea x. 4. *Speaker's Commentary* suggests "poppy-head.") In chap. v. 7 the word expressed here by "hemlock" is rendered "worm-wood," as in Jer. ix. 15, xxiii. 15; Deut. xxix. 18, &c., a rendering which should have been retained here. Gall and worm-wood are constantly associated in Old Testament prophecy in this metaphorical sense.

(13) **A thing of nought** refers to the calf-worship, the idol that Israel is glorying and trusting in, the idolatrous travesty of the Eternal that they call "the excellency of Jacob." (Comp. verse 8, and chap. viii. 7.)

Taken to us horns—*i.e.*, instruments of resistance and aggression, the horn being symbolic of strength (Jer. xlviii. 25; Pss. lxxv. 10, lxxxix. 17, xcii. 10; 1 Sam. ii. 10). The sacred historian takes quite a different view of the success of Jeroboam II. (2 Kings xiv. 26, 27). These boasters reckoned the success of arms as due to their own ingenuity or "power." (Comp. the language put into the mouth of Pharaoh by Ezekiel xxix. 3: "My river is my own: I made it for myself.")

(14) **From . . . unto.**—The entire limits of the kingdom of Israel after the victories of Jeroboam II. were, according to 2 Kings xiv. 25, identical with the region which is here threatened with invasion, *i.e.*, extending from the mouth of the Orontes valley (comp. Num. xxxiv. 8; Josh. xiii. 5) to the *Wady el Ahsa*, the southern boundary of Moab. (Comp. Isa. xv. 7, where the Hebrew name appears under a slightly different form, implying "torrent of the poplars.")

VII.

Here commences the third portion of the prophecy. It is of a different class from that which has preceded, and may have formed the main heads of public discourses, the parabolic ministry of the prophet in the earlier stages of his career. These fiats of destruction, contained in the visions and dreams of coming doom, had been arrested by the intercession of the prophet himself. But the time was approaching when prayer would be of no avail, and the desolation of the kingdom would be complete.

(1) Each of the visions is introduced with closely resembling words. For "grasshopper," read *locusts.* The phrase "king's mowings" suggests that the king claimed tyrannically the first-fruits of the hay harvest, which was ordinarily followed by the early "rain upon the mown grass." (Comp. 1 Kings xviii. 5.)

(2) **The grass of the land.**—The same word is used in the original in Gen. i. 11, signifying herbs and vegetables. Amos saw the first wave of disaster in the destruction of the food of the people, and he interceded for respite and forgiveness. The cry takes the form, *Who is Jacob that he should stand?* (E.V., "by whom," is incorrect) *for he is small.*

(3) **The Lord repented.**—The judgment is withheld. On the anthropomorphism of Jehovah repenting, comp. Gen. vi. 5 and other passages.

(4) **Fire.**—The poetical description of a yet more terrible calamity. God announces His intention of judging, *i.e.*, punishing by fire (the word in E.V., "contend," is to be understood in this sense). For "a portion" read *the portion.* The image is that of a prairie fire, that should eat up the later grass spared by the locusts. The consuming of the "great deep" is a strong hyper-

unto me: and, behold, the Lord GOD
called to contend by fire, and it devoured
the great deep, and did eat up a part.
(5) Then said I, O Lord GOD, cease, I
beseech thee: by whom shall Jacob
arise? for he *is* small. (6) The LORD
repented for this: This also shall not be,
saith the Lord GOD.

(7) Thus he shewed me: and, behold,
the Lord stood upon a wall *made* by a
plumbline, with a plumbline in his hand.
(8) And the LORD said unto me, Amos,
what seest thou? And I said, A plumb-
line. Then said the Lord, Behold, I
will set a plumbline in the midst of my
people Israel: I will not again pass by
them any more: (9) and the high places
of Isaac shall be desolate, and the sanc-
tuaries of Israel shall be laid waste;
and I will rise against the house of
Jeroboam with the sword.

(10) Then Amaziah the priest of
Beth-el sent to Jeroboam king of Israel,
saying, Amos hath conspired against
thee in the midst of the house of Israel:
the land is not able to bear all his
words. (11) For thus Amos saith, Jero-
boam shall die by the sword, and Israel
shall surely be led away captive out of
their own land. (12) Also Amaziah said
unto Amos, O thou seer, go, flee thee
away into the land of Judah, and there
eat bread, and prophesy there: (13) but
prophesy not again any more at Beth-el:
for it *is* the king's [1] chapel, and it *is* the
[2] king's court.

(14) Then answered Amos, and said to
Amaziah, I *was* no prophet, neither *was*
I a prophet's son; but I *was* an herdman,
and a gatherer of [3] sycomore fruit:
(15) and the LORD took me [4] as I followed
the flock, and the LORD said unto me,
Go, prophesy unto my people Israel.
(16) Now therefore hear thou the word of
the LORD: Thou sayest, Prophesy not
against Israel, [a] and drop not *thy word*

1 Or, *sanctuary.*

2 Heb., *house of the kingdom.*

3 Or, *wild figs.*

4 Heb., *from behind.*

a Ezek. 21. 2.

---

bole, and can scarcely refer to the "heathen world," as Keil maintains. The meaning rather appears to be that not only the solitary remnant of pasture, but the deepest springs of moisture, will be scorched up in the blaze. The same word for "deep" (*tehôm*) is used in Gen. i. 2, vii, 11, viii. 2. (Comp. the Assyrian *tihamtu.*)

(5, 6) Instead of "forgive," the prophet now only ventures to say "cease," a cry for arrest of judgment. Yet the same plea for pity is urged as before. Jeroboam II. and his house are spared for awhile. But another awful vision comes to the prophet.

(7) **Wall made by a plumbline**—*i.e.*, a perpendicular wall, the stability of the kingdom being represented by the closely-fitting well-jointed stones of a lofty wall. Right in the heart of this strong-built city, the Lord Himself marks the extent of the desolation, the plumb-line being used in dismantling buildings, as well as erecting them (2 Kings xxi. 13; Isa. xxxiv. 11).

(8) **Pass by them.**—In the sense of sparing. There will come a time when prayer will be of no avail. All intercessions, however passionate or eager, will be too late. The door of mercy is shut.

(9) **High places of Isaac.**—The name Isaac is here spelt somewhat differently in the Hebrew from the form we have in Genesis. The LXX. misunderstand the word, and render "altars of *laughter*," in accordance with the etymological sense of the proper name. The residents in the neighbourhood of Beersheba may have boasted of the favour or honour belonging to them, as occupying the home of Isaac and the birthplace of Jacob.

Will rise against.—This dreadful doom fell on the house of Jeroboam, and was the prelude of the final destruction of the nations by Shalmaneser IV., in 721 (2 Kings xv. 10).

(10) There follows a brief historical interlude of much interest. It shows that the effect of the preaching of the Judæan prophet had been felt in the sanctuary at Bethel and the palaces at Samaria. The chief priest of the Temple, with the characteristic exaggeration of fear and anger, accuses Amos of treason against the house of Jeroboam.

(11) **Die by the sword.**—So far as the words of the prophecy are concerned, it was not accurate to say that Amos had threatened Jeroboam with the sword.

(12, 13) Jeroboam treated the charge made by Amaziah with indifference, or perhaps with awe: at least, with silence. And so the priest of Bethel takes upon himself to dismiss the prophet from the kingdom. The word for "seer" is here *chozeh*, one who has visions, a word not used in a contemptuous sense here or in the Old Testament generally. The expression "there eat bread and prophecy" is a *hendiadys* for "there live on your profession as a prophet," not here. To this Amos replies that that was not his profession (verse 14). Bethel is spoken of as the "holy place," or sanctuary, and also as the "royal residence" (E.V., "king's court"). Men blinded by prejudice, and bewildered by the light of our Lord's holy presence, besought him to depart from them. The awful peril of imploring God's messenger to withdraw is frequently referred to in Scripture. (Comp. Luke x. 10—12.)

(14) **I was . . .**—An interesting biographical touch. Prophecy, like other occupations, tended to form a hereditary guild, but Amos was not by birth a prophet. The word for "gatherer" is rendered in the LXX. and Vulg. "nipper," or "pincher." There was a custom mentioned in Theophrastus, *Hist. Plant.*, iv. 2, Pliny, *Hist. Nat.*, xiii. 14, of pinching or scratching the mulberry-fig in order to make it ripen. But it is very doubtful whether this is the meaning of the Hebrew word here, which is nowhere else employed.

(15) **Followed the flock.**—There is no hint of any lack of education or refinement (see Introduction) through the exclusion of any special aid derived from the training of earlier prophets. In this case God's inward call had been more than sufficient.

(16) **Drop not.**—A word used in the Song of Moses for "distil," expressing persuasive and flowing discourse. (Deut. xxxii. 2; Ezek. xxi. 2, 7; Micah ii. 6, 11).

against the house of Isaac. (17) There-
fore thus saith the LORD; Thy wife
shall be an harlot in the city, and thy
sons and thy daughters shall fall by the
sword, and thy land shall be divided by
line; and thou shalt die in a polluted
land: and Israel shall surely go into
captivity forth of his land.

CHAPTER VIII.—Thus hath the
Lord GOD shewed unto me: and behold
a basket of summer fruit. (2) And he
said, Amos, what seest thou? And I
said, A basket of summer fruit. Then
said the LORD unto me, The end is
come upon my people of Israel; I will
not again pass by them any more.
(3) And the songs of the temple [1] shall be
howlings in that day, saith the Lord
GOD: *there shall be* many dead bodies in
every place; they shall cast *them* forth
[2] with silence.

(4) Hear this, O ye that swallow up the
needy, even to make the poor of the
land to fail, (5) saying, When will the
[3] new moon be gone, that we may sell
corn? and the sabbath, that we may
[4] set forth wheat, making the ephah
small, and the shekel great, and [5] falsi-
fying the balances by deceit? (6) That
we may buy the poor for [a] silver, and the
needy for a pair of shoes; *yea*, and sell
the refuse of the wheat? (7) The LORD
hath sworn by the excellency of Jacob,
Surely I will never forget any of their
works. (8) Shall not the land tremble
for this, and every one mourn that
dwelleth therein? and it shall rise up
wholly as a flood; and it shall be cast
out and drowned, as *by* the flood of
Egypt. (9) And it shall come to pass in
that day, saith the Lord GOD, that I
will cause the sun to go down at noon,
and I will darken the earth in the clear

1 Heb., *shall howl.*
2 Heb., *be silent.*
3 Or, *month.*
4 Heb., *open.*
5 Heb., *perverting the balances of deceit.*
a ch. 2. 6.

(17) **Harlot.**—This doom on Amaziah's wife is to be regarded as the hideous consequence of war. She shall be ravished. By the polluted land we are to understand Assyria, or the land of exile; for food eaten in any other land than Canaan, the land of Jehovah, was regarded as unclean (see W. R. Smith, *O.T. in Jewish Church*, pp. 235—8). We hear no more of Amaziah, nor do we know how or where he met his doom.

VIII.

(1, 2) The visions are resumed as though the priest at Bethel had trembled at the presence of Amos, and had ceased to persecute him. There is a remarkable play of words, *qaits* being the Hebrew for "summer fruit," and *qêts* for "end." It is harvest time, the end of the agricultural year. Israel is ripe for his final doom, that shall sweep down like a scythe. For "pass by" see on chap. vii. 8.

(3) **Temple.**—The word thus rendered (*hêchal*) also signifies "palace," and this is probably the meaning in this passage. The "songs" have been already spoken of in chap. vi. 5. The construction of the following clauses in the original is somewhat doubtful. Some commentators would break up the sentence into abrupt ejaculations. Thus Keil:—"corpses in multitude; in every place he hath cast them forth: Hush!" For "he hath cast," some would read (with 2 Heb. MSS.) the imperative, "cast them forth." But it would be better, and more in consonance with the style of Amos, to connect the clauses together thus: *There shall be many corpses in every place that one hath cast away in hushed silence.* The words describe the reign of death and doom, with none to bury or make lamentation—a full end.

(4) **Ye that swallow up . . .**—Better, *ye that pant* (or *are greedy*) *for the very ashes on their heads.*

Make . . . to fail.—Literally, *make . . . to cease: i.e.,* destroy.

(5) **When . . . gone.**—They desired that the festivals of the New Moon and Sabbath should be over, when they might not only return to their secular employments, but pursue their search for ill-gotten gains—a proof that these festivals were observed in the northern nation, even if they were disliked.

Set forth wheat.—The original signifies the opening of the sacks, or granaries, where the wheat was stored. The greedy mercantile class is referred to. The *ephah*, which was a dry measure (= three English pecks), was "made small," so that a smaller quantity might be sold. The shekel was the weight against which the precious metal was weighed. If this were fraudulently augmented, more of the gold or silver than was due was demanded for the impoverished ephah.

Falsifying the balances . . .—More accurately, *falsifying the deceitful balances*, so that the very symbol of justice became the implement of committing injustice. This is frequently condemned in the Law and Prophets (Lev. xix. 35, 36; Deut. xxv. 15; Prov. xi. 1; Micah vi. 11).

(6) On this perverse straining of the Law, comp. chap. ii. 6. Their money-making propensity was carried to such unscrupulous lengths, that they even sold the refuse of corn, little better than mere chaff.

(7) **Excellency of Jacob.**—In the previous use of this remarkable expression (chap. vi. 8) Jehovah is said to abhor it, but here He swears by it. The "excellency" which He abhorred was the miserable substitute which they had made for His great Name. Here He gives it the value which, in itself, it ought to possess.

(8) **Shall not the land . . .?**—The rendering should be, *The whole of it rises as the Nile, surges and subsides* (or *sinks*) *as the Egyptian Nile.* The solid land shall rise up in earthquake, like the Nile that ascends twenty feet in the time of its inundation, and then subsides.

(9) **Darken the earth.**—The darkening of the sun at noon-day gives an image of confusion and terror (comp. chap. v. 20). The eclipse of the sun that is here alluded to (see *Excursus* C), like the earthquake in the preceding verse, is employed as a powerful image of national calamity, the extinction of the royal house, and perhaps the final overthrow of Israel. (Comp. Jer. xv. 9; Ezek. xxxii. 7—10.)

day: (10) and I will turn your feasts into
mourning, and all your songs into lamentation; and I will bring up sackcloth upon all loins, and baldness upon every head; and I will make it as the mourning of an only *son*, and the end thereof as a bitter day.

(11) Behold, the days come, saith the Lord God, that I will send a famine in the land, not a famine of bread, nor a thirst for water, but of hearing the words of the Lord: (12) and they shall
wander from sea to sea, and from the north even to the east, they shall run to and fro to seek the word of the Lord, and shall not find *it*. (13) In that day
shall the fair virgins and young men faint for thirst. (14) They that swear by
the sin of Samaria, and say, Thy god, O Dan, liveth; and, The manner of Beer-sheba liveth; even they shall fall, and never rise up again.

CHAPTER IX.—I saw the Lord standing upon the altar: and he said, Smite the [1] lintel of the door, that the posts may shake: and [2] cut them in the head, all of them; and I will slay the last of them with the sword: he that fleeth of them shall not flee away, and he that escapeth of them shall not be delivered. (2) [a] Though they dig into hell, thence shall mine hand take them; though they climb up to heaven, thence will I bring them down: (3) and
though they hide themselves in the top of Carmel, I will search and take them out thence; and though they be hid from

1 Or, *chapiter*, or, *knop*.

2 Or, *wound them*.

a Ps. 139. 8, &c.

(10, 11) The imagery is very vivid. The prophet threatens a famine of the word of Jehovah, and a parching thirst for the Water of Life, now no longer attainable. Such terrible destitution often supervenes on the neglect of the Word of God, the power to discern the ever-present Word being exhausted. Then comes the withdrawal of revelation, the silence of seers. One of the awful dooms of unbelief in the next world will be this famine, this hopeless thirst and fathomless suspense.

(12) **They shall wander from sea to sea . . .**—Stagger and reel from east to west to find one seer who knows the mind of the Lord: they shall not find one. The reference to the east here has an instructive parallel in Isa. ii. 6, where the house of Jacob is denounced as being "full of the east." Probably Delitzsch is right in interpreting the east there to mean Arabia as inclusive of the whole tract from the Sinaitic peninsula to the banks of the Euphrates. The north would mean Phœnicia and Aram. From these districts the distracted superstitious Hebrew sought vain help in idolatrous forms of divination.

(13) **Faint.**—That fair virgins and strong brave youths should faint by reason of their raging thirst suggests that the less vigorous would suffer even more keenly. It is sad when old men stumble into the darkness of unbelief amid the shining of the noon-day sun, seeing that they can remember the brightness of their morning, but there is always hope that their child-like spirit may return to them, and that at the evening time it may be light; but if fair virgins and strong youths are covered with the inward veil, what will become of them in their westering days? and where will the elders be if they have had no youth?

(14) **Thy God, O Dan, liveth.**—Translate, *By the life of thy God, O Dan, and by the life of the way of Beersheba.* On such forms of oath, see Note on chap. vi. 8. The "way of Beersheba" was the ritual practised at Beersheba, another mode of designating the deity himself (probably Baal).* So LXX. Similarly the "sin of Samaria" means the golden calf that was worshipped there (Hosea viii. 5). The supposition of Hitzig and Duhm (followed by W. R. Smith) that it refers to the Asherah worship (2 Kings xiii. 6) is not so probable.

IX.

(1) The last vision is transferred to the shrine at Bethel, the seat of the calf-worship. The prophet sees Jehovah Himself standing in pomp by the altar of burnt offering, and by His side the angel of His presence, to whom now, as on many other occasions, the mission of destruction has been entrusted. To him the words of Jehovah are addressed (so Aben Ezra, Kimchi). It is doubtful what is meant by the Hebrew *Caphtôr* (mistranslated "lintel of the door"). It may mean the wreathed capital of the columns, as in Zeph. ii. 14. So Hitzig and Keil. The word *sippîm* (mistranslated "posts") properly signifies "thresholds," but is here understood by the first-mentioned commentator to mean the cornice supported by the columns. This is confirmed by the LXX. on Isa. vi. 4 (see Delitzsch *ad loc*). But as there is no mention of the temple building, but only of the altar of burnt offering, it is much safer to adhere to the ordinary and well-established significations of these terms. We should accordingly follow Ewald in taking *Caphtôr* as referring to the *ornamented horns of the altar*. Similarly, in Exod. xxv. 31, xxxvii. 17, it signifies the richly decorated extremities of the golden *candelabra*. The scene is wonderfully vivid. Round the colossal altar of burnt offering a crowd of eager devotees is gathered. Jehovah gives the word of command to His angel, and with a blow that shakes the very threshold the ornamented altar horns are shivered to fragments, which are hurled down upon the panic-stricken multitude below.

And cut . . .—Rather, *and dash them in pieces upon the head of all of them.*

(2) **Dig.**—For this expression *break* should be substituted. "Hell," or rather, *Hades* (*Sheôl*), the dark abode of the gathered dead, is contrasted with "heaven," the abode of light. Escape from the universal Lord is impossible.

(3) **Serpent.**—On this expression, *i.e.*, the "water-serpent," comp. Isa. xxvii. 1.

* From chap. v. 5 we infer that Beersheba, lying far south on the borders of Judah (twenty-five geographical miles south of Hebron), was a famous religious centre, so that inhabitants of the northern kingdom were in the habit of "crossing the frontier" in order to pay their vows, or enquire at this high place.

my sight in the bottom of the sea, thence
will I command the serpent, and he
shall bite them. (4) And though they go
into captivity before their enemies,
thence will I command the sword, and
it shall slay them: and [a]I will set mine
eyes upon them for evil, and not for
good. (5) And the Lord GOD of hosts *is*
he that toucheth the land, and it shall
melt, and all that dwell therein shall
mourn: and it shall rise up wholly like
a flood; and shall be drowned, as *by*
the flood of Egypt. (6) *It is* he that
buildeth his [1,2b]stories in the heaven, and
hath founded his [3]troop in the earth; he
that [c]calleth for the waters of the sea,
and poureth them out upon the face of
the earth: The LORD *is* his name.
(7) *Are* ye not as children of the Ethio-
pians unto me, O children of Israel?
saith the LORD. Have not I brought up
Israel out of the land of Egypt? and
the [d]Philistines from Caphtor, and the
Syrians from Kir? (8) Behold, the eyes
of the Lord GOD *are* upon the sinful
kingdom, and I will destroy it from off
the face of the earth; saving that I will
not utterly destroy the house of Jacob,
saith the LORD. (9) For, lo, I will com-
mand, and I will [4]sift the house of
Israel among all nations, like as *corn* is
sifted in a sieve, yet shall not the least
[5]grain fall upon the earth. (10) All the
sinners of my people shall die by the
sword, which say, The evil shall not
overtake nor prevent us.
(11) In that day will I raise up the
[e]tabernacle of David that is fallen, and
[6]close up the breaches thereof; and I
will raise up his ruins, and I will build
it as in the days of old: (12) that they
may possess the remnant of Edom, and
of all the heathen, [7]which are called by
my name, saith the LORD that doeth
this. (13) Behold, the days come, saith
the LORD, that the plowman shall over-
take the reaper, and the treader of
grapes him that [8]soweth seed; and the
mountains shall drop [9f]sweet wine, and
all the hills shall melt. (14) And I will
bring again the captivity of my people
of Israel, and they shall build the waste

a Jer. 44. 11.
1 Or, *spheres.*
2 Heb., *ascensions.*
b Ps. 104. 3.
3 Or, *bundle.*
c ch. 5. 8.
d Jer. 47. 4.
4 Heb., *cause to move.*
5 Heb., *stone.*
e Acts 15. 16.
6 Heb., *hedge*, or, *wall.*
7 Heb., *upon whom my name is called.*
8 Heb., *draweth forth.*
9 Or, *new wine.*
f Joel 3. 18.

(5, 6) Accumulate in grand imagery the majesty, power, and irresistible resources of the Lord, who has at length become their enemy. The very world itself melts, as Sinai did, at His touch.

The word "is" should be omitted in the rendering. The predicate "Jehovah (the Lord) is His name" (verse 6) stands at the end of a series of attributive clauses.

Like a flood . . .—The sentence should run thus: *The whole of it rises like the Nile, and subsides* (or *sinks*) *like the Egyptian Nile.* The future tenses should be replaced by presents. (Comp. chap. viii. 8.)

Stories—*i.e.*, upper rooms (comp. Ps. civ. 3). The word for "troop" is rightly rendered "arch," or "vault," from a root signifying to bind or compact together, the sky being regarded as a "firmament," or solid extension, which rested on the earth as a foundation.

(7) **Ethiopians.**—Israel had presumed on the special favour of Jehovah. The prophet asks them whether, after all, they are better or safer than the Ethiopians, whom they despised. He who led Israel from Egypt also brought the Philistines from Caphtor, and the Syrians from *Kir*. Caphtor is mentioned in the table of races, Gen. x. 14 (where the clause referring to the Philistines should probably be placed at the end of the verse). The LXX. followed by the Targums and Peshito interpret Caphtor as Cappadocia, probably from resemblance in form. R. S. Poole, art. "Caphtor," in the *Dictionary of the Bible*, compares the Egyptian *Kebtu* or Koptos, and places the Caphtorim in Upper Egypt, while Ebers holds that they had their settlements in the Nile delta. But the identification of Caphtor with Crete is most probable. So Rosenmüller, Ewald, Dillmann, &c. On *Kir*, probably E. of the Euphrates, see Note on chap. i. 5.

(8) **Sinful nation.**—The kingdom of the ten tribes which had so utterly revolted from the true centre and spiritual ideas of the worship of Jehovah.

(9, 10) **Sift.**—Literally, *shake to and fro.* That which is not chaff shall be preserved and dispersed as seed. The race shall live, though the kingdom be destroyed. This peculiar judgment is threatened in Lev. xxvi. 33; Deut. xxviii. 64. (Comp. Hosea ix. 17.) The prediction is very remarkable, as pointing to the indestructible vitality of the race, and its wide diffusion among all nations.

Prevent us.—Better, *assail us.*

(11, 12) These verses present some difficulties, as the quotation of the passage in Acts xv. 15—17 is a free reproduction by St. James of the rendering of the LXX. The apostle uses it to show that there was a prophetic promise that after the dispersion of Israel the power and throne of David should be so re-established that it might be a rallying-place of the rest of the nations, "that the residue of men should seek after the Lord" (LXX. "me"). The clause which is quoted shows that the LXX. made their translation from a different Hebrew text from ours, and probably an inferior one. The word for "men" (*ādām*) was read in place of *Edom* in the Masoretic text. The rendering "seek" can also be accounted for by a slight modification of the Hebrew characters. The remarks of Dr. Stanley Leathes (*Old Testament Prophecy*, p. 70) upon this passage are worthy of attention:—"The Greek text, which the apostle did not make, but found, lent itself even more forcibly than the Hebrew to the peculiar circumstances of the time . . . That he was not speaking critically we are willing to admit, but are we sure that he was bound to do so? At all events, our criticism will best display itself in judging his words according to his standard, and not according to one which, it is plain, he did not follow."

(13) **Shall overtake the reaper.**—So rapidly will the harvest follow the ploughing. These closing

cities, and inhabit *them;* and they shall plant vineyards, and drink the wine thereof; they shall also make gardens, and eat the fruit of them. (15) And I will plant them upon their land, and they shall no more be pulled up out of their land which I have given them, saith the LORD thy God.

---

verses foreshadow the glories of the restored kingdom of David (comp. Hosea iii. 5), wherein we see the germ of the great Messianic prophecies of Isaiah.

EXCURSUS ON NOTES TO AMOS

EXCURSUS A (Chap. iv. 3).

The rendering of the LXX., "to the mountain Remman (or Romman)," has suggested to Ewald the interpretation, *And shall cast Rimmona to the mountain, i.e.,* in their flight (comp. Isa. ii. 18—21), Rimmona being the idol-goddess of love, corresponding to the masculine deity Rimmon (2 Kings v. 18). In this ingenious, though somewhat far-fetched, interpretation of a difficult passage, it will be observed that Ewald takes the Hebrew verb as an active, and not a passive. In this he is supported by most MSS.

But the credit of suggesting the most plausible explanation belongs to Hitzig, who, in his commentary, proposes to read Hadad-Rimmon, and translates, *Ye shall be cast away to Hadad-Rimmon.* On Zech. xii. 11, there is a long note by Steiner supporting the supposition that Hadad-Rimmon was a modified designation of the sun-god, and was likewise the counterpart of the Greek Adonis, over whose wounding and death there was an annual lamentation, in which the women took part, and gave way to all kinds of excess. Hadad-Rimmon was, therefore, the name of the deity and the locality of his worship (comp. *Ashtaroth Karnaim* and other examples), now called *Rummâne,* four miles south of *Ledshûn* (Megiddo). To this spot the women were to be carried off for purposes of prostitution. (Comp. the threat pronounced by the prophet, chap. vii. 17.)

EXCURSUS B (Chap. v. 26).

Three obscure points render this verse one of the most difficult in the Old Testament.

1. As to *tense.* The interpretation to which preference has been given in the commentary on the text—the time being regarded as future—has been decided on grounds of grammatical usage only. But certainly the larger number of commentators have rendered the verb as a *past* tense, "But ye bore the tabernacle," &c., the time referred to being that of the desert wanderings. This view is upheld by Hitzig, Kuenen, Keil, Henderson, and also by R. S. Poole. It is also supported by the LXX.

2. The word *Sikkûth,* rendered tabernacle, or tent, in the E.V. and by the LXX., is derived from a root signifying both to interweave and to cover—an etymology which confirms the above rendering. Ewald's conjecture that it signifies "stake," inferred from the Aramaic *Sekkitho,* is to be rejected. The conception of Moloch being carried in a tent may be illustrated from the Egyptian monuments of Rameses XII. Birch (*Egypt,* S. P. C. K., p. 149), refers to a tablet found in the south-west corner of Karnak: "The picture of the tablet represents Rameses holding a censer, and worshipping the ark of the god [Khons], which, partly covered with curtains, is placed in a boat . . . Figures of priests, a sphinx, and standards are in the boat, while twelve priests carry it on their shoulders."

3. Both Moloch and Chiun were evidently star-deities. R. S. Poole endeavours to connect Chiun with Semitic deities worshipped in Egypt (see art. "Remphan," Smith's *Dict. of the Bible*). The name Chiun appears as *Remphan* in the quotation of this passage in Stephen's speech (Acts vii. 43). And both Remphan and Chiun were held by Mr. Poole to be the corresponding male and female deities of Asiatic type, *Renpu* and *Ken.* But the form Remphan can be clearly shown to have arisen from textual corruption, originating, perhaps, in some false analogy. In the New Testament passage the best MSS. read *Rephan,* and this reading has been adopted in our Revised Version, and occurs in nearly the same form in the LXX., from which Stephen was freely quoting. In the LXX. the original order of the clauses has suffered transposition, and it is certainly safer to adhere to the Hebrew text (as in chap. ix. 11, 12).

Rêphan arose from the Hebrew text by the change of a single character. Instances of such interchange are not infrequent in the Old Testament. Yet the form *Rephan,* though corrupt, is invaluable, as indicating the true reading of the Hebrew word. The word for Chiun was read by the Masoretes as *Kiyyûn* (according to Ewald, "pedestal" [?]). But the LXX. indicate, and much confirmatory testimony establishes the fact, that the word is to be read *Kêvan,* and that Kêvan, like the Ammonitish Moloch, represented the *star-deity*

Saturn. Thus *Kaivono* is the form of the word in the Peshito. This view is supported by Aben Ezra and Kimchi, who cite Kivan as the name for the star Saturn in the Persian and Arabic. This star (see quotations in Henderson's *Commentary*) was held to exert malignant influence. Schrader (*Cuneiform Inscriptions and the Old Testament*, p. 443) compares the name *Ka-ai-vanu*, the Assyrian name for that planet.

EXCURSUS C (Chap. viii. 9).

That an eclipse is here referred to, and employed as a figure to express the overwhelming calamities which were to darken Israel, can hardly admit of doubt, when we compare the similar figurative use of the earthquake in the preceding verse. But to what eclipse does the prophet refer? Mr. J. W. Bosanquet has attempted to identify it with a very special one, mentioned in the Assyrian annals:—"In the eponymy of Bursagale, prefect of Gozan, the city of Asshur revolted, and in the month Sivan the sun was eclipsed." This has been calculated by Hind to have occurred on June 15, 763 B.C. (So Rawlinson, Schrader, G. Smith, &c., as against Oppert's view, which is untenable.) If this eclipse was in the mind of the prophet, it is a fact of considerable importance in chronology. On the whole, however, it is more probable that the prophet was thinking of an earlier eclipse, which took place in 784 B.C., Feb. 9. It was a total eclipse, the time of totality being about 1 p.m. at Jerusalem, thus exactly corresponding with the phraseology of this verse. So remarkable a phenomenon would naturally stamp itself for many years upon the mind of the people, and this vivid impression the prophet summons to his aid in foreshadowing the calamities of the last time.

OBADIAH

INTRODUCTION

TO

OBADIAH

NOTHING whatever is known of the author of the shortest of all the prophetical books except his name. *Obadiah*, or, in its older and longer form, *Obadiahu*, means *servant of Jehovah*, and seems to have been as common among the Hebrews as Abdallah, a name of kindred formation and meaning, is to-day among the Arabs, for as many as twelve Scriptural persons bear it. The LXX. represent the name by Ἀβδίας or Ὀβδίας, the Vulgate by *Abdias*, *Obdias*, or *Obedia*. The prophet has been variously identified with Ahab's famous officer (1 Kings xviii. 3), with the Obadiah, Prince of Judah, whom Jehoshaphat sent with Zechariah, Micaiah, and others to teach in the cities of his kingdom (2 Chron. xvii. 7); with the son of Merari, a Levite, noted for his skill in music (2 Chron. xxxiv. 12); with the son of the Shunamite restored to life by Elisha; with the third of the captains sent by Ahaziah to capture Elijah. There is not a shadow of foundation for any one of these guesses, and the patristic tradition assigning him to the tribe of Ephraim, and fixing his abode at Bethachamar (or Bethacaram), in Shechemite territory, is as mythical as his grave pointed out in later times at Sebaste, by the side of those of Elisha and John the Baptist.

The only external guidance of any kind towards fixing even approximately the date of this prophecy is its place in the canon. An attempt at chronological order evidently directed the arrangement of the minor prophets. The discussion of the internal evidence for date and authorship offers a complicated problem, which will be better reserved for an Excursus. With this question must be reserved that of the immediate circumstances arising out of the relations of Israel and Edom, to which the book primarily refers, since it is so closely bound up with it; but the general purport of the prophecy is independent of these.

The long feud between the brother tribes of the Beni-Israel and the descendants of Esau, which began at the birth of the twin ancestors, and continued with varied fortunes down to the extinction of both as distinct nationalities, forms the subject of Obadiah's vision. It is remarkable how large and complete a view we should have into the relations of the two tribes, even if this were the only extant record of them. Not only the close ancestral relationship and the bitterness of the rivalries that had so early divided Edom and Israel, but even the very nature of the desultory and protracted warfare that they waged, the tactics of the wild but wily sons of the desert, the caution with which they moved, the attitude of watchful neutrality they assumed when it suited them, and the skill with which they seized on the moment of Israel's weakness, come clearly into view. We seem even to see the very gestures of the fierce hillmen, and to hear their words of scorn and derision (verses 12, 13). Their cunning diplomacy, overreaching itself, as is so generally the case (verse 7), and their treachery, the more formidable because of the sagacity for which the tribes of Western Arabia were renowned (verses 14, 8, 9), as well as the unrelenting spirit in which they pursued their object, and the rapacity which followed their victories, are all touched most vividly, though in single words. We are taken also into the mountain home of these warriors, and see them in their rock-hewn dwellings, perched like vultures on their inaccessible cliffs, vaunting their security, their wisdom, and their might (verses 3, 4).

But this graphic picture of the most virulent of all Israel's foes is not presented in the mere spirit of an enemy and a rival. There was a higher purpose controlling the vision of Obadiah, and in this we see the true motive and power of prophecy, that far-stretching, lasting light, by which men behold more than the petty scene around them, a light which spreads over centuries of thought and over the life of nations. He speaks, indeed, exultingly of the destined overthrow of an enemy so bitter; but even in his exultation there is a tone of regret and sadness (see verse 5, Note), equally suggestive, whether it be a touch of the far-off sense of brotherhood with Esau, or a hint of the Divine pity for the sinful and fallen, afterwards to shine forth in the Gospel. Compared with other oracles against Edom, this one bearing Obadiah's name is singularly free from the spirit of unrestrained revenge (compare Obadiah with Isaiah xxxiv. 5, seq., lxii. 1—6; Ps. cxxxvii. 7—9). This undercurrent of regretful tenderness has led some commentators to conjecture that the author was himself an Idumæan, but we need no such conjecture. Occupied with larger interests than those of the immediate present, with his prospect widened beyond the horizon of Edom or Israel, though he addressed himself to the children of Jacob and Esau, and pronounced their doom, and consoled the nation they had injured with the promise of deliverance and restoration, the seer was able to rise above mere exultation in present triumph to the thought of the far grander course of events, in which the present fortunes of his own people and their enemies formed only an episode. It is not on Edom only that the Divine justice will assert itself, not for the salvation of Israel alone that the Divine mercy will be displayed. The "Day of the Lord" is seen to be near upon all the heathen, and in the magnificent utterance which concludes the short prophecy, "the kingdom shall be Jehovah's," we catch the promise of a large and far-off Divine event, and recognise the higher purpose by which the Hebrew prophets were gifted to look through the present into the future, from the needs of Israel to those of a world not yet born.

This promise of a widespread dominion has made the Book of Obadiah a favourite study with the Jews. "They read in his words the certainty, not merely of restoration to their own land, and the extension of their dominion over Idumæa and Philistia (see verse 19), but of the downfall of Christianity, and the conquest by themselves of France and Spain. Naturally we ask for the explanation of so extraordinary an interpretation, and we find that it is a settled principle with the Rabbins that Edom is Rome, and the Edomites all Christians whatsoever. For reasons which will scarcely bear the test of criticism, they believe that Janus, the first King of Latium, was Esau's grandson, and that the Latins were not Trojans, but Idumæans. To the same stock they refer all the early Christians, as if the apostles and first disciples were not Jews, but Edomites; and affirm that when Constantine made the Roman Empire embrace Christianity, it became Idumæan" (*Bible Educator*, iv. 107). Accepting this as an established principle, the Jews very easily arrive at the startling conclusions mentioned in the Notes (verses 20—21).

The book divides naturally into three parts: 1, The general announcement of the pride which has prepared for Edom the retributive justice of God (verses 1—9); 2, Enumeration of the practices of Edom against the brother tribe, and repetition of the doom about to fall (verses 10—16); 3, The forecast of future salvation and glory for Zion, in which, though there is no mention of the Messiah, there breathes the same hope which no earthly grandeur could ever have satisfied, and which waits even yet for its entire fulfilment (verses 17—21).

It is to be remarked that Obadiah uses many words or forms of word peculiar to himself, so that even this short writing gives him an individuality. The style is vigorous, and there is one image (verse 4) of almost startling boldness, but the parallelism is too defective to allow the work to be classed with the poetical books. As a defect in style, the preponderance of interrogations may be noticed.

OBADIAH

CHAPTER I. — (1) The vision of Obadiah.

Thus saith the Lord GOD concerning Edom;

[a] We have heard a rumour from the LORD, and an ambassador is sent among the heathen, Arise ye, and let us rise up against her in battle. (2) Behold, I have made thee small among the heathen: thou art greatly despised. (3) The pride of thine heart hath deceived thee, thou that dwellest in the

B.C. cir. 587.

a Jer. 49, 14.

1—9.—THE DIVINE HOSTILITY AGAINST EDOM PROCLAIMED.

(1) **The vision of Obadiah.**—Properly, *vision of Obadiah*, without the article. There are three recognised headings to prophetical books—*word*, *burden* (*i.e.*, oracle), and *vision*—and all are used without the article, and in a general way, for the contents of the books, without any intention to distinguish between different kinds or modes of prophecy. Thus Nahum combines *burden* and *vision*: "*Burden* of Nineveh. Book of *vision* of Nahum the Elkoshite." Amos speaks of the "*words* which he *saw*;" Isaiah (xiii. 1) of the "*burden* which he did *see*;" and Obadiah, after the word *vision*, instantly proceeds, "Thus *saith*," &c. The word *vision* (Heb., *chazôn*, from the same verb as "seer"), appears, from 1 Sam. iii. 1, ix. 9, to have acquired this general sense at a very early time. It is not necessary from the use of the word to suppose that the future was unfolded to Obadiah "in the form of sights spread out before his mind, . . . a succession of pictures which he may have seen" (Pusey). *Vision* here = *revelation*, however supplied. The question of authorship is discussed in the Excursus.

Thus saith the Lord God concerning Edom.—After these words we should expect the words of the message, not the statement that a message had come. Among the attempts at explanation, the two most plausible are: (1) The two-fold heading is due to a later hand than Obadiah, who only prefixed the first part, "vision," &c., to his work; (2) These words are merely a mode of stating generally that the seer of the vision was divinely inspired. The view taken of the authorship and composition must decide between these two. If an earlier oracle is incorporated in the book, it is more natural to conclude that the second part of the double title, which in a slightly different form occurs also in Jer. xlix. 7, was introduced in order to bring the prophecy into closer similarity to the circle of oracles against foreign nations which is contained in Jeremiah.

Arise ye . . .—Now at length we have the Divine message. Long ago, in the mysterious oracle of Dumah (Isa. xxi. 11), the foreboding of a pending chastisement of Seir found a voice, and now, as in consequence of a signal from heaven, or as if brought by an angel, goes forth the summons to the nations to begin the movement against Edom. The cup of iniquity was full. There is a suggestiveness even in the vagueness of the summons. The nations, without distinction of good or bad, must become the instruments of the Divine chastisement of overweening pride. Edom becomes the type of wickedness that has reached a head, and against which all the sounder elements of the world unite with God. For the full picture, here suggested only in a word, see Isa. xiii. 1—17, and comp. Joel. ii. 11; Jer. li. 11.

(2—9) Edom's pride and consequent humiliation. A general statement of the reason of the Divine wrath against Edom. Particular offences will be enumerated presently (verses 10—14).

(2) **Small among the heathen.**—In comparison with the giant empires of Egypt and Assyria, a mere speck on the map. Edom proper is not to be confounded with the later kingdom of Idumæa, which extended over the wilderness of Et Tih, and even to within the southern borders of Palestine. The original Mount Seir (Gen. xxxii. 3), or, as our prophet calls it, Mount Esau, was a narrow tract of country on the east of Wady Arabah, extending from Elath to the brook Zered (probably the *Wady-el-Ahsy*; see Deut. ii. 8, 13, 14), about 100 miles in length, and nowhere more than twenty miles broad. One of the larger English counties would cover as much territory. In the corresponding passages (Jer. xlix. 15) our version has the future instead of the past, where also, instead of "greatly despised," is the reading, "despised among men." The past is better. The contrast between the size of the nation and its overbearing pride, created by the consciousness of the natural strength of its position, is lost if we give the verse a future sense.

(3) **Clefts of the rock.**—The word *chagâvîm*, clefts, is of doubtful derivation. It only occurs in the corresponding passage to this (Jer. xlix. 16) and in Cant. ii. 14, and always with *selah*—rock. But whether its etymological meaning be *refuges* or *fissures* does not matter, since the actual thing signified is still to be seen. The cliffs at Petra (Selah, or with the article, ha-Selah), the capital of Edom, and in its neighbourhood, are honeycombed with caves, natural or artificial, which from the earliest times to the present day have served as tombs for the dead, and temporary dwellings or shelters for the living. We read in Deut. ii. 12 that the "Horims"—*i.e.*, troglodytes, or *dwellers in caves*—were the original inhabitants of the land. "The whole southern country of the Edomites," says St. Jerome, "from Eleutheropolis to Petra and Selah (which are the possessions of Esau), had minute dwellings (*habitatiunculas*) in caves; and on account of the oppressive heat of the sun, as being a southern province, had underground cottages." All more recent travellers confirm this. Robinson (ii. 529) speaks of "an innumerable multitude

clefts of the rock, whose habitation *is* high; that saith in his heart, Who shall bring me down to the ground?
(4) [a] Though thou exalt *thyself* as the

[a] Jer. 49. 16.

of excavations along the whole coast of perpendicular rocks adjacent to the main area, and in all the lateral valleys and chasms." But those at present existing are but a remnant of the vast number which must at one time have afforded shelter to the densely populated valleys. "What remains are the mere *débris* of what the precipices once presented to view . . . The conduits, cisterns, flights of steps scattered over the rocks and among the precipices, indicate a larger number of rock-dwellings than remain now, very great as that number is" (Miss Martineau, *Eastern Life*, iii. 2). "Wherever your eyes turn along the excavated sides of the rocks, you see steps often leading to nothing, or something which has crumbled away, often with their first steps worn away, so that they are now inaccessible" (Stanley, *Sinai and Palestine*, p. 91). So Miss Martineau speaks of "short and odd staircases twisted hither and thither among the rocks." So, too, E. H. Palmer, Esq., in the Quarterly Statement of the Palestine Exploration Fund, January, 1871: "There are many tombs and dwellings which are now inaccessible, but traces of staircases cut in the rock, and now broken away, may be seen everywhere." . . . "At the northern turn in the Wady, as you leave the western acclivities, are three large tombs, with perfect fronts. The first and largest of these . . . was at the time of our entry occupied by several families of the fellahin. Every tomb has its owner, who dwells there with his wives and family during the cold and wet weather." He goes on to speak of one tomb which was said to hold fifteen families.

Whose habitation is high . . .—Literally, *loftiness of his habitation.* The red sandstone rocks are described as rising "perpendicularly to the height of one, two, or three hundred feet" (Stanley, *Sinai and Palestine*, p. 89). The writer of the article "Selah" in Kitto's *Biblical Cyclopædia* says of the caves, "Some of them are apparently not less than from two hundred to three or four hundred feet above the level of the valley." When we think of the power of the conception which could frame a range of mountain rocks into a city, with ravines for streets and caverns for houses, we can understand the prophet's words, "the pride of thine heart hath deceived thee." Nor was it wonderful that the children of Esau should deem themselves invincible in their mountain fastnesses.

Who shall bring me down to the ground?—From this *eagle's-nest* (verse 4) Edom might well utter proud defiance against even the strongest foes. All travellers describe Petra as almost impregnable. It is not even visible from the heights in the neighbourhood. "The whole space, rocks and valleys, embedded in the mountains which girt it in, lay invisible even from the summit of Mount Hor." "Petra itself is entirely shut out by the intervening rocks. The great feature of the mountains of Edom is the mass of red bald-headed sandstone rocks, intersected not by valleys, but by deep seams. In the heart of these rocks, itself invisible, lies Petra." And it was as strongly guarded by nature as it was securely hidden. "Two known approaches only, from east and west, enter into it," and these are mere ravines. The most famous of them, the defile from the east, the one which "in ancient times was the chief—the only usual—approach to Petra," is named the *Sík*, or *cleft.* "The rocks are almost precipitous, or, rather, they would be if they did not, like their brethren in all this region, overlap, and crumble, and crack, as if they would crash over you. The gorge is about a mile and a half long, and the opening of the cliffs at the top is throughout almost as narrow as the narrowest part of the defile of Pfeffers, which in dimensions and form it more nearly resembles than any other of my acquaintance" (Stanley, *Sinai and Palestine*, p. 89). The other approach, though not so picturesque and striking to the traveller, would have been equally difficult for an attacking army. Miss Martineau describes it as leading amid "wild fantastic mountains," "rocks in towering masses," "over steep and slippery passes," or "winding in recesses below." She continues: "A little further on we stopped in a hollow of the hills; our path, our very narrow path, lay over these whitish hills: now up, now down, and then, and then again, we were slipping and jerking down slopes of gaudy rock. For nearly an hour longer we were descending the pass; down we went, and still down; at length we came upon the platform above the bed of the torrent, near which stands the only edifice in Petra" (quoted from *Eastern Life*, ii. 319, by Pusey). Such approaches might, it is obvious, be held by a very small force against a great superiority of numbers. The width of the *sík* "is not more than just sufficient for the passage of two horsemen abreast," and "a few hundred men might defend the entrance against a large army" (Burckhardt, *Travels in Syria and the Holy Land*, p. 432). Demetrius "the Besieger," at the head of 8,000 men (the 4,000 infantry selected for their swiftness of foot from the whole army), made repeated assaults on the place, but "those within had an easy victory, from its commanding height" (Pusey, from *Diod. Sic.* xix. 96). Little need of art to strengthen such natural defences, yet Mr. Palmer noticed "a fort at the top of the left-hand ravine, occupying a most commanding position, as it overlooks the entire valley, and defends the only part not protected by some difficult mountain pass" (Quarterly Statement, Palestine Exploration Fund, January, 1871). And Dr. Pusey finely remarks: "But even the entrance gained, what gain besides, unless the people and its wealth were betrayed by a surprise? Striking as the rock-girt Petra was, a gem in its mountain setting, far more marvellous was it when, as in the prophet's time, the rock itself was Petra. Inside the defile, an invader would be outside the city yet. He might himself become the besieged rather than the besieger. In which of these eyries along all these ravines were the eagles to be found? From which of these lairs might not Edom's lion-sons burst out upon them? Multitudes gave the invaders no advantage in scaling those mountains' sides, where, observed themselves by an unseen enemy, they would at last have to fight man to man. What a bivouac were it in that narrow spot, themselves encircled by an enemy everywhere, anywhere, and visibly nowhere, among those thousand caves, each larger cave, maybe, an ambuscade! In man's sight Edom's boast was well founded; but what before God?" With the Edomites' vaunt Pusey aptly compares that of the Bactrian, Oxyartes, who, trusting to the strength of another Petra, defied Alexander the Great, bidding him get wings for his soldiers before attacking his stronghold. (Arrian, *Exped. Alex.* iv. 18.)

(4) **Though thou exalt thyself as the eagle.**—"Had, then, the ancient builders of these rock-works wings like the eagles, with which they raised themselves

eagle, and though thou set thy nest
among the stars, thence will I bring
thee down, saith the LORD. (5) If
[a] thieves came to thee, if robbers by
night, (how art thou cut off!) would
they not have stolen till they had
enough? if the grapegatherers came to
thee, would they not leave [1] *some* grapes?
(6) How are *the things* of Esau searched
out! *how* are his hidden things sought
up! (7) All the men of thy confederacy
have brought thee *even* to the border:
[2] the men that were at peace with thee
have deceived thee, *and* prevailed against
thee; [3] *they that eat* thy bread have laid
a wound under thee: *there is* none

a Jer. 49. 9.

1 Or, *gleanings?*

2 Heb., *the men of thy peace.*

3 Heb., the men *of thy bread.*

---

to those perpendicular precipices?" "Who now, even with the feet of the chamois, could climb after them?" (V. Schubert, ii. 429; quoted by Pusey). (Comp. also Miss Martineau, *Eastern Life*, ii. 320, iii. 20.)

This is one of the passages which identifies the *nesher*, always translated "eagle" in the Authorised Version, with the griffon-vulture. "While the eagles and other birds are content with lower elevations, and sometimes even with trees, the griffon alone selects the stupendous gorges of Arabia Petræa and of the defiles of Palestine, and there in great communities rears its young, where the most intrepid climber can only with ropes and other appliances reach its nest" (Tristram, *Nat. Hist. of the Bible*, p. 175; comp. Job xxxix. 27, 28).

And though thou set thy nest among the stars. . .—The image of the eagle nesting among the stars is among the most forcible even in Hebrew poetry. Shakespeare approaches it in "eagle-winged pride of sky-aspiring and ambitious thoughts" (*Richard II.*, i. 3).

Thence will I bring thee down, saith the Lord.—In the original, more striking, "it is Jehovah's declaration." This sentence against pride, not only national, but individual too, is indeed the Divine declaration, uttered in warning voice from one end of Scripture to the other. The doom pronounced against Edom is but one special instance of the universal truth told so powerfully by Isaiah at the end of chap. ii.: "The lofty looks of man shall be humbled, and the haughtiness of men shall be bowed down, and the Lord alone shall be exalted in that day. For the day of the Lord of hosts shall be upon every one that is proud and lofty, and upon every one that is lifted up; and he shall be brought low." And it was the more than once repeated declaration of the Son of God: "He that exalteth himself shall be abased, and he that humbleth himself shall be exalted."

(5–9) The completeness of the overthrow awaiting Edom. It is no mere inroad of a marauding tribe. Something would escape the *robber*, though he might go away quite satisfied with his plunder; and even a raid in vintage time, for the purpose of doing all the mischief possible to the country, would leave here and there a scattered bunch, gleanings for the inhabitants when the spoilers had retired, but now everything is doomed to destruction. Edom is completely robbed and ransacked. Notice how the sad, almost pathetic, conviction of this breaks out—as if rather from a friend (*see* Introduction) than an enemy—in the parenthetical "how art thou cut off!" in the very middle of the sentence. Every one must perceive, the prophet seems to say, a higher hand at work here.

(5) **Some grapes.**—*Gleanings*, as in margin. (Comp. Isa. xvii. 6, xxiv. 13.)

(6) **How are the things of Esau searched out!**—Literally, *How are they searched out Esau!* Where Esau is either taken collectively = Edom as a nation, or we must supply, as in the Authorised Version, "the things of," or, as Ewald, "they of." For *search*, comp. Zeph. i. 12.

His hidden things.—Heb., *matspunîm*, from *tsapan* = to hide, but whether *hidden treasures* or *hiding places* cannot be determined, as the word only occurs here.

(7–9) Overtaken by this terrible calamity, and deserted by her allies, Edom will turn in vain for counsel to her senators and wise men, and for support to her heroes and mighty men, for these will not only share in the general ruin, but are marked out for an overthrow as signal as their renown.

(7) **All the men of thy confederacy. . . .**—This desertion by allies is doubtless put prominently forward as the due retribution on Edom for his treachery and cruelty to his natural ally, his brother Jacob. The members of the confederacy are not specified. In Jer. xxvii. 3 we find Edom associated with Moab, Ammon, Tyre, and Sidon, in the warning to submit to Nebuchadnezzar. The two former would be the natural allies of Edom, and in Ezek. xxv. 8 Seir is joined with Moab as reproaching Israel. From Ps. lx. 8, we may add to these Philistia (comp. also verse 19). The expression "have brought thee to the border" is variously understood. The most natural explanation is that the fugitives from the ruin of Edom, flying into the territory of neighbouring and allied tribes for help, are basely driven back to their own frontier, and left to their fate.

The men that were at peace with thee.—As in margin, *the men of thy peace*, an expressive Hebrew idiom occurring in Jer. xx. 10, xxxviii. 22, and in Ps. xli. 9, where it is translated "mine own familiar friend."

Great difference of opinion exists as to the connection of this and the following clause, and as it stands the text presents considerable difficulty. By dropping the italicised words in our version, and omitting the semicolon, we get, "The men of thy peace have deceived thee, prevailed against thee and thy bread, have laid a wound under thee." There are two verbal difficulties —(1) "wound," Heb., *mazôr*, which occurs in Hosea v. 13 in the sense of a festering wound or abscess, but which the older translators here render *ambush*, or snare; ἔνεδρα (LXX.); *insidiæ* (Vulg.). Ewald and Hitzig, among moderns, prefer *net*, and defend it etymologically. This certainly gives good sense, and if *zûr*, of which it is a derivative, can have the sense of *binding*, may be correct. Our translators in Jer. xxx. 13, and Aquila and Symmachus in this passage, evidently give it that force (see also Lee's *Heb. Lex., sub voce*). To *squeeze* or *crush*, however, seems the true meaning of *zûr*: as in Judges vi. 38, of Gideon's fleece; Job. xxxix. 15, of the eggs of the ostrich. The preposition *tachath* = under, also offers a difficulty; "*Laid a wound under thee*" suggests no intelligible meaning. But on the authority (though possibly somewhat doubtful) of 2

understanding [1] in him. (8) [a] Shall I not
in that day, saith the LORD, even de-
stroy the wise *men* out of Edom, and
understanding out of the mount of
Esau? (9) And thy mighty *men*, O
Teman, shall be dismayed, to the end
that every one of the mount of Esau
may be cut off by slaughter.

(10) For *thy* [b] violence against thy
brother Jacob shame shall cover thee,
and thou shalt be cut off for ever.
(11) In the day that thou stoodest on the
other side, in the day that the strangers
[2] carried away captive his forces, and
foreigners entered into his gates, and
cast lots upon Jerusalem, even thou

[1] Or, *of it.*

[a] Isa. 29. 14; Jer. 49. 7.

[b] Gen. 27. 41; Ezek. 35. 5; Amos 1. 11.

[2] Or, *carried away his substance.*

Sam. iii. 12, where the word is translated "on behalf of," but where the context requires "without his knowledge," and on the analogy of all other languages, we may (with Vatablus, Drusius, Luther, and L. de Dieu; see Keil) translate the word *deceitfully*, or *without thy knowledge*, a rendering in accordance with the parallelism. But the syntax of the passage still remains unexplained. What is the construction of *lachmeka*= of thy bread? From Ps. xli. 9, "The man of my peace which did eat of my bread," we are led to the conjecture that it forms part of a familiar, perhaps proverbial, expression for one bound by the closest ties of fellowship and hospitality, and we must, therefore, either supply a participle, *these eating*, as in the Psalm, or understand a second *anshêy*=men of. It is true there is no other instance of the phrase "men of thy bread," but it is a conceivable Hebrew idiom. Keeping the parallelism we now get an intelligible rendering of the passage.

> "Unto the border they sent thee, all the men of thy confederacy.
> Deceived thee, ruined thee,
> Men of thy peace, men of thy bread;
> (They) gave thee a wound in secret.
> No understanding (is) in him."

For the arrangement of the second clause, which is put for *deceived thee the men of thy peace, ruined thee the men of thy bread*, see Cant. i. 5, and Note there. In the last clause the margin reads *of it: i.e.*, of the injury just mentioned, instead of *in him*. But it is better to take it as an abrupt declaration in the prophet's manner (comp. "how art thou cut off!" in verse 5) of the utter bewilderment that had come or was coming on Edom, unable either by counsel or force to withstand his foes.

(8) **Shall I not . . .**—Literally, *Surely in that day—it is Jehovah's saying—I will make sages disappear from Edom, and understanding from Esau's mountain.*

The tradition of a peculiar sagacity in Edom, and especially in Teman (see Jer. xlix. 7), lingered long. Job's sage friend Eliphaz was a Temanite. In Baruch iii. 22, 23 we read: "It (wisdom) hath not been heard of in Chanaan, neither hath it been seen in Theman. The Agarenes that seek wisdom upon earth, the merchants of Meran and of Theman, the authors (margin, *expounders*) of fables and searchers out of understanding, none of these have known the way of wisdom, or remember her paths." Jeremiah's words show even more strikingly how high the reputation had been: "Is wisdom no more in Teman? is counsel perished from the prudent? is their wisdom vanished?" "The men of the world think that they hold their wisdom and all God's natural gifts independently of the giver. God, by the events of His natural providence, as here by His word, shows, through some withdrawal of their wisdom, that it is His, not theirs. Men wonder at the sudden failure, the flaw in the well-arranged plan, the one over-confident act which ruins the whole scheme, the over-shrewdness which betrays itself, or the unaccountable oversight." So the utter want of perception and foresight in Edom seems unaccountable, till we think of the Divine purpose and end in it all. The wise were destroyed, and the mighty men dismayed, "to the end that every one of the mount of Esau may be cut off by slaughter." It is the prophetic statement of the truth of the old heathen proverb: "Whom God wishes to destroy He first dements."

(9) For **Teman,** see Job ii. 11.

10—16.—THE DIVINE SENTENCE JUSTIFIED BY EDOM'S GUILT.

This justification takes the form of a warning against a repetition of the crimes which have already called forth the sentence of Divine wrath against Edom. Various acts of hostility and treachery towards Israel are specified by the prophet, in a manner to lead to the feeling that though his tone is prohibitory, he is recalling instances of past malignity on Edom's part, as types of what might be found in the future.

(10) **For thy violence . . .**—Literally, *for injury of thy brother Jacob*, &c.; the genitive of the object, as in Joel iii. 19. The crime was the more heinous because against the brother tribe. Probably the birth-name, Jacob, of the twin brother of Esau is used purposely to bring out the full wickedness of the descendants of Esau. In spite of all provocations, Israel long maintained the duty of a friendly feeling for the kindred race—maintained it as a religious duty (Deut. ii. 5, xxiii. 7). On the other hand, Edom from the first assumed a jealous and hostile attitude (Num. xx. 14, *seqq.*), never imitating the generous disposition of their great ancestor (Gen. xxxiii. 4).

Shame shall cover thee.—Comp. Micah vii. 10; Jer. iii. 25.

(11) **In the day . . .**—Literally, *In the day of thy standing over against*, as if to particularise some one occasion; but instead of proceeding to state it, the prophet recalls other events of the same time, and sums up Edom's offence in the charge, "thou, too, as one of them," acting the part of an enemy instead of that of a friend, though probably in the base character of a neutral (comp. "My lovers and my friends stand *aloof* from my sore," Ps. xxxviii. 11), ready to take the winning side.

Forces.—It is difficult to choose between this and the marginal reading, *substance. Shâvah* is usually "to take prisoner," but there are many instances of its use in the sense of carrying off booty (1 Chron. v. 21; 2 Chron. xxi. 17, where see marg., and xiv. 14). And *chayil*, whose root-meaning is strength, while often meaning *forces*, has eleven times the meaning *riches* (Isa. viii. 4, &c.), and eight times *substance* (Job v. 5, &c.).

The three clauses in this verse form a climax:—(1) The plunder of the open country; (2) entry into the

wast as one of them. (12) But [1] thou
shouldest not have looked on the day of
thy brother in the day that he became
a stranger; neither shouldest thou have
rejoiced over the children of Judah in
the day of their destruction; neither
shouldest thou have [2] spoken proudly in
the day of distress. (13) Thou shouldest
not have entered into the gate of my
people in the day of their calamity;
yea, thou shouldest not have looked on
their affliction in the day of their
calamity, nor have laid *hands* on their
[3] substance in the day of their calamity;
(14) neither shouldest thou have stood in
the crossway, to cut off those of his
that did escape; neither shouldest thou
have [4] delivered up those of his that did
remain in the day of distress. (15) For
the day of the LORD *is* near upon all
the heathen: [a] as thou hast done, it
shall be done unto thee: thy reward
shall return upon thine own head.
(16) For as ye have drunk upon my holy
mountain, *so* shall all the heathen drink
continually, yea, they shall drink, and

1 Or, *do not behold, &c.*

2 Heb., *magnified thy mouth.*

3 Or, *forces.*

4 Or, *shut up.*

B.C. cir. 585.

a Ezek. 35. 15.

---

gates of the cities; (3) casting lots for the spoil in the very capital itself. It is natural to regard this latter event as identical with that in Joel iii. 3, the final destruction of Jerusalem and dispersion of its inhabitants into captivity. But for the question of the event intended and its connection with the date of the prophecy, see Excursus.

(12) **Thou shouldest not . . .**—Here, and in verses 13 and 14, correctly as in marg., *Do not, &c. Al* with the apoc. pres. or fut. must be prohibitory. Calasio's Concordance supplies 207 instances (see Pusey's note). But the warning against these particular offences undoubtedly springs from the reminiscence of such conduct in former times. The passage is neither definitely historical nor definitely prophetic. What has happened in the past becomes a type of what will happen in the future. For *look* (*raah*), with the sense of *disdain* or *scorn*, comp. Cant. i. 6; Job xl. 11, xli. 34 (Heb. 26). The word is repeated with the same sense in verse 13. Pusey remarks: "Malicious gazing on human calamity, forgetful of man's common origin and common liability to ill, is the worst form of human hate. It was one of the contumelies of the Cross."

In the day that he became a stranger.—Literally, *in the day of his strangeness.* The form *nokher* is only found here, and in Job xxxi. 3 (*nekher*) with different pointing, where it is translated "strange punishment." The adjective *nokhri*, also, has always the sense of *strange*, though the root-verb seems to have the signification *to recognise.* From *to recognise an apparent stranger* to *treat as a stranger* (which the derived conjugations, that alone are used, sometimes mean) is a natural transition. Perhaps here, "unheard-of calamity."

Spoken proudly.—Literally, as in marg., *made thy mouth great* (comp. Ps. xxxv. 21; Isa. lvii. 4). The mention of *grimaces* adds to the graphic character of the picture. Again we are reminded of the wanton and savage insolence around the Cross.

(13) **The day of their calamity.**—Thrice repeated, to bring into prominence the malignity of Edom's conduct. The same expression used by Ezekiel (chap. xxxv. 5), in the same connection, probably with reference to the same occasion.

Calamity.—Heb., *êyd.* Variously derived and explained, either as *load of trouble* or *dark gloomy time.*

(14) **Crossway.**—Heb., *perek* = separated (English, *fork*). It only occurs here and in Nahum iii. 1, where it is translated *robbery*—*i.e.*, that which is torn or divided. Or it may mean *at the division of the prey*, but "crossway" is better.

Delivered.—Margin, *shut up*—*i e.*, either made prisoners of them, or cut them off at the cross-roads from any chance of escape.

For the open violence assumed by the Edomites when they saw their chance was come, comp. Ps. cxxxvii. 7; Joel iii. 19; Amos i. 11; Ezek. xxxv.

(15) **The day of the Lord.**—Whether this phrase first makes its appearance in written prophecy in Joel or Obadiah depends, of course, on the question of the relative date of the two. But probably it had become a recognised prophetic expression long before it was committed to writing. The primary meaning is not the day of judgment, but the day on which Jehovah reveals His majesty and omnipotence in a glorious manner, to overthrow all ungodly powers and to complete His kingdom. As the misfortunes of Israel increased, and the hostility of surrounding nations gathered to a successful head, it was natural that the idea of retribution upon them for their violence to the chosen race should usurp the prominent place in prophecy. The "day of Jehovah" became the day of Jehovah's *wrath* (Zeph. i. 18) and Jehovah's *vengeance* (Isa. xxxiv. 8). The fading of the temporal hopes implied in the expression naturally led to its higher religious use; and the various phrases for the same idea —"the day," "the great day," "the day of judgment," "the last day"—passed first into Jewish, and afterwards into Christian, eschatology, taking with them all the prophetic imagery which painted the expectancy of Israel: imagery of the splendour of victory and triumph on the one side, of terrible overthrow and slaughter on the other, but rich as well with its infinite spiritual suggestiveness.

As thou hast done . . .—For this stern announcement of the *lex talionis* on the offending nation, comp. (in addition to the reference in marg.) Joel iii. 7; Ps. cxxxvii. 8.

(16) **As ye have drunk . . .**—For the figure, so common in prophecy and so expressive, comp. Jer. xxv. 27, 28; Ps. lxxv. 8; Isa. li. 17; Rev. xviii. 3—6. But who are addressed, the people of Jerusalem or the Edomites? The question is perplexed. If we keep the tropical sense of *drink* in both clauses, which is the most natural way, understanding by it the cup of suffering, since it is said to have been drunk on Mount Zion, it must have been drained by Israelites, as Ewald and others take the passage. On the other hand, it seems awkward to make the prophet turn from addressing Edom to Judah, not else addressed in his prophecy. If taken in a literal sense, the drinking on Mount Zion would, of course, refer to the carousing and revelry which always followed heathen victory, and sometimes

they shall [1] swallow down, and they
shall be as though they had not been.
(17) But upon mount Zion shall be
[2] deliverance, and [3] there shall be holi-
ness; and the house of Jacob shall
possess their possessions. (18) And the
house of Jacob shall be a fire, and the
house of Joseph a flame, and the house
of Esau for stubble, and they shall
kindle in them, and devour them; and
there shall not be *any* remaining of the
house of Esau; for the LORD hath
spoken *it*. (19) And *they of* the south
shall possess the mount of Esau; and
they of the plain the Philistines: and
they shall possess the fields of Ephraim,
and the fields of Samaria: and Ben-
jamin *shall possess* Gilead. (20) And the
captivity of this host of the children of
Israel *shall possess* that of the Canaan-
ites, *even* unto Zarephath; and the
captivity of Jerusalem, [4] which *is* in

1 Or, *sup up*.

2 Or, *they that escape*.

3 Or, *it shall be holy*.

4 Or, *shall possess that which is in Sepharad*.

with terrible aggravation (Joel iii. 3). Taking the passage in this sense, we must understand the prophet to take Edom as a type of all heathen in their attitude towards Israel, so that what he says of one nation applies to all. But it is quite possible that our text embodies an old oracular saying addressed to Israel. This is Ewald's view.

Swallow down.—Margin, *sup up*. The substantive *loa'* signifies a throat. (Comp. Job vi. 3: "Therefore my words are swallowed up.")

Shall be as though they had not been.—For the expression, comp. Job x. 19. Here, *totally insensible from the effects of the draught*, therefore *dead, destroyed*.

The word *continually* offers some difficulty. Ewald translates *immediately*, but this is not the natural sense of *tamîd*, which seems rather to express that *continuous* display of the Divine purpose and judgment in the overthrow overtaking successively the proud monarchies of the heathen. "God employs each nation in turn to give that cup to the other. So Edom drank it at the hand of Babylon, and Babylon from the Medes, and the Medes and Persians from the Macedonians, and the Macedonians from the Romans, and they from the barbarians."

17—21.—ESTABLISHMENT OF THE KINGDOM OF JEHOVAH ON MOUNT ZION.

(17) **Deliverance.**—Better, as in margin, *the fugitives of Israel who have survived the recent calamity*. This is clear from Isa. x. 20, where *pheléytah* is in parallelism with *shear*=remnant, as well as Joel ii. 32; Heb. iii. 5, where it is parallel to *serîdim*, also remnant. (Comp. also Judges xxi. 17; 2 Chron. xx. 24.) While the judgment is falling upon all the heathen nations, Mount Zion will be an asylum for all the Israelites who had fled for safety, and been scattered and dispersed.

Holiness.—See margin. Zion was once more to become a sanctuary, and those who inhabited it holy. (Comp. Isa. vi. 13.)

Their possessions.—Whose—their own that had been lost, or those of the nations? The Vulgate, following the LXX., read "those who had possessed them," indicating subjugation of the heathen tribes. But the parallelism is undoubtedly in favour of the other view—the remnant of Israel would be saved, and regain their old possessions. Having stated this, the prophet goes on to describe what would happen to Edom and its possessions.

(18) Though, in the preceding verse, "house of Jacob" would seem to embrace all the restored Israel, without any reference to the distinction of the two kingdoms, in this verse, being opposed to "house of Joseph," it requires to be taken as synonymous with Judah; as in Isa. xlvi. 3: "Hearken unto me, O house of Jacob, and all the remnant of the house of Israel." (Comp. Pss. lxxvii. 15, lxxx. 1, lxxxi. 4, 5.)

For the expressive imagery, comp. Nahum i. 10; Isa. xxvii. 4, x. 17.

Any remaining.—Heb., *sarîd*, a fugitive. The LXX. must have had a different text, as they read here πυροφόρος, *i.e.*, *wheat-bearer*, apparently (as the various reading shows) a mistake for πυρφόρος, *fire-bearer*.

(19) After the destruction of the heathen the new kingdom of Zion will be restored, at least as far as the ancient territories which are at present held by the Idumæans, to the north and west of the original Edom, are concerned. Three divisions are enumerated of the house of Jacob (*i.e.*, Judah; see Note, verse 18), and separate mention made of Benjamin.

They of the south.—Those at present occupying the *south*—Heb., *negev*—*i.e.*, the *dry parched* country forming the southern portion of the tribe of Judah (Josh. xv. 21), are to inhabit Mount Esau: *i.e.*, are to extend their territory to its extreme south-eastern limit; they of the Shephelah, *i.e.*, the western lowland on the Mediterranean, are to seize on the neighbouring Philistia, at present Idumæan; while they at present confined to the hill-country in the north and centre of Judah are to spread themselves over Ephraim and Samaria. Our present Hebrew text leaves the subject of this latter clause uncertain, as it is in the Authorised Version "they." But the LXX., τὸ ὄρος, indicates that *hahor* = the mountain, has dropped out, a conjecture which is abundantly borne out by the geographical arrangement of the localities in the passage. Benjamin, for which no room is left on the west of Jordan, is to push across it into Gilead instead. This prophetic vision recalls Gen. xxviii. 14.

(20) But there are still others of the restored Israel, besides those comprised within the ancient territory of Judah. The prophetic survey proceeds northwards, and we get a general idea from this verse that there were exiles, who had found refuge on the north-western and northern boundaries of ancient Palestine, who would settle themselves partly on the sea-coast of Tyre and Sidon, partly in the south country, whose inhabitants had pushed downwards into Edom. But while this is plainly its general drift, the text is full of difficulties.

It is difficult to attach an intelligible meaning to "the captivity (*i.e.*, exiles, *galuth*; comp. Isa. xx. 4, xlv. 13) of this host of (literally, *to*) the sons of Israel."

The prophet seems to allude to some body of exiles, including himself, who had escaped from the army. But there is a difference of opinion among grammarians as to the identification of *chēl* with *chayil* = host. Ewald takes it to be a dialectic variety of *chol* = sand, generally of the sea-coast; and so here "the banished ones of *this* coast," where the prophet was at the time.

Sepharad, shall possess the cities of the
South. 21) And [a] saviours shall come up on
mount Zion to judge the mount of Esau;
and the [b] kingdom shall be the LORD's.

a 1 Tim. 4. 16; Jam. 5. 20.
b Luke 1. 33.

The rendering *chël*=trench, or fortification, which some adopt, is out of the question. The LXX. have τῆς μετοικεσίας ἡ ἀρχὴ, but whether ἀρχὴ = *power*, or *beginning*, with allusion to the first dispersion of exiles, cannot be determined. Another difficulty arises with respect to the words *that of the Canaanites—asher Khenaanîm* (literally, *which Canaanites*). To make it an object, as in our version, the particle *eth* is wanted, and Ewald, instead of *asher*, reads *eth-ari=the cities of.* That some change has taken place in the text appears from the LXX., who have γῆ, *the land* (Heb., *erets*). Keil, keeping the present reading, renders, "And the captives of this army of the sons of Israel (will take possession) of what Canaanites there are as far as Zarephath . . ." Pusey: "And the captivity of this host of the children of Israel which are among the Canaanites as far as Zarephath," making it joint subject with "the captives of Jerusalem" to "shall possess the cities of the south," which is in accordance with the construction of the LXX. and the Syriac. But the absence of the preposition *be* before *Khenaanim* seems to make this rendering impossible. The Hebrew as it stands can only mean "which are Canaanites." The choice lies between Ewald's emendation of the text and Keil's interpretation. The Jews understand by Zarephath the country of *France.*

The last clause is better in the text than in the margin: "The exiles from Jerusalem who are in Sepharad shall take possession of the cities of the south." The only difficulty is in the name Sepharad, a place never mentioned elsewhere, and which has not yet been satisfactorily identified. The various conjectures have been—

1. That of the LXX., ἕως 'Εφραθὰ followed by the Arabic translation, probably from reading *Sepharath.* Jerome, in his Commentary on Obadiah, appears to have understood this reading as pointing to the Hebrew *Phrath,* since he translates, *Transmigratio Jerusalem usque Euphratem.*

2. The reading of the Vulg., *quæ in Bosphoro est,* was derived by Jerome from a Jewish instructor, who treated the particle in *Bisparad* as part of the name, and rejected the final *d* altogether.

3. The Targum Jonathan, the Peshito-Syriac, and from them the modern Jews, interpret Sepharad as Spain (Ispamia or Ispania); hence *Sephardim,* a name for the Spanish Jews.

4. Sipphara in Mesopotamia. But this is more probably identified with *Sepharvaim.*

5. Sardis, from a supposed connection with ÇPaRaD, or Çparda, mentioned in the great arrow-headed inscription of Nakshi Rustam, in a list of names of tribes between Cappadocia and Ionia, which De Sacy identified with *Sepharad,* and Lassen with *Sardis.*

6. Sparta. Some relations there were between the Jews after the captivity and the Lacedæmonians (see 1 Macc. xii. 2, *seqq.*, xiv. 16, *seqq.*, xv. 23). Possibly there was a colony of the exiles in Sparta.

7. Ewald conjectures *Sepharam* instead of *Sepharad,* and finds the place in Shefa Amar, a well-known place a few miles south-east of Acco. The general drift of the passage seems to require some place not far distant from, and in the direction of, Zarephath. The only serious objection to this conjecture is the fact that Shefa Amar was within the boundaries of Palestine, and therefore those who had taken refuge there would not strictly be exiles. But it is distinctly stated that these were "of Jerusalem," and they might well be called refugees, since they had had to go so far north to find an asylum.

(21) **Saviours.**—Comp. Judges iii. 9, 15; Neh. ix. 27. The Jewish interpreters understood by "saviours" men like the judges of old, Gideon, Barak, &c., who will chastise the Christians and subdue them. The Mount of Esau is of course, according to this interpretation, Rome.

And the kingdom shall be the Lord's.—See the reference in margin to Zechariah, who gives this anticipation of the pure form of the theocracy in its wider extent. But here, too, the prophetic look over the world seems to extend far beyond Judah and the fortunes of the Jewish race, and as the vision widens Zion and Edom both retire from sight; both are comprehended in the one Divine kingdom, and God is all in all. For the bearing of this conclusion to the prophecy on its date, see Excursus.

EXCURSUS ON NOTES TO OBADIAH

ON THE DATE AND AUTHORSHIP OF THE BOOK.

OBADIAH has been placed as early as the beginning of the ninth century, antecedent to the prophet Joel, and by one commentator at least—Eichorn—has been brought down as late as the first century before Christ. The data for determining the problem are:—

1. The identification of the siege and capture of Jerusalem, mentioned in verse 11, with some one known historical event.

2. The recurrence, in an altered order and form, of certain verses of this prophecy in Jer. xlix.

3. A comparison of Obadiah with other oracles concerning Edom.

1. There is no question that verse 11 records a conquest of Jerusalem, which had already taken place. It is true that in verses 13, 14 the margin, "do not behold," is the correct translation, and not "thou shouldest not" of the Authorised Version. But the tone of this warning makes it evident that the particular practices referred to are enumerated as being such as had been employed by Edom before, such as were customary whenever occasion offered. Verse 11—"In the day of thy standing over against, in the day of taking away strangers his forces (or substance), and foreigners entered his gates, and over Jerusalem cast lots, thou too as one of them"—is too general and indefinite to enable us to identify it with certainty with any one of the seven captures of Jerusalem mentioned in the Old Testament. But some of these we can eliminate. The capture by the Egyptian King Shishak in the reign of Rehoboam is excluded by the fact that at that time Edom was subject to Judah. Obadiah cannot be referring to the civil war between Joash and Amaziah, because he expressly calls the enemy that captured Jerusalem foreigners.

There remain—(1) The capture by the Philistines and Arabians in the reign of Jehoram (related in 2 Chron. xxi. 16, 17); (2) by the Chaldæans in the reign of Jehoiakim (2 Kings xxiv. 1, *seqq.*; 2 Chron. xxxvi. 6, 7); (3) the second capture by Nebuchadnezzar when Jehoiachin was taken prisoner (2 Kings xxiv. 10, *seqq.*; 2 Chron. xxxvi. 10); and (4) the final and decisive siege, which ended in the destruction of the city and general captivity.

There is much to favour the view that our prophet refers to the first of these. We know that Edom revolted from Judah during Jehoram's reign, and though that monarch was able partially to recover his authority, it was never completely recovered. The Arabians mentioned as allied with the Philistines in a raid on his territories may have included the Petræan Arabs. From the account in Chronicles we learn that these marauders burst into the land, forced their way into Jerusalem, plundered the royal palace, and carried away the children and wives of the king, so that only the youngest son was left behind. If, as seems probable from the remarkable coincidence of language between this passage and Obadiah 10—17, Joel iii. 3, 5, 6, they refer to the same events, numbers of the people also were made prisoners, and sold as slaves. On the other hand, the state of things indicated in Obadiah seems to demand a captivity on a much larger scale than even this. The concluding part of the chapter seems to refer to a catastrophe far more wide in its extent than the expedition in Jehoram's reign. The re-settlement of the captives in their old possessions, and overflow of them into the conquered territory of Edom, points to a previous dispersion on a grand scale.

Altogether, it must be left as impossible to decide from this datum to which of the captures of Jerusalem the prophet refers. That he had some comparatively recent event in his mind is clear, not only from the general tone of the language, but also from the probable inference, from verse 20, that he was himself among the captives. (See Note.) At the same time, from verses 11—13 we see that he wrote with the fear of a repetition of Edom's well-known practices in his mind. On the whole, from this doubtful historical reference alone, we incline to the opinion that our prophet's is a voice raised during the early years of the exile, when the memory of Edom's unbrotherly alliance with the Chaldæans was still strong and bitter, although the sight of them enjoying the fruits of their conduct in the lands of Judah had not destroyed prophetic hope, nor weakened the belief, which older oracles had pronounced, of a swift and terrible vengeance on this hated people.

2. If the relation between Jeremiah and Obadiah could be satisfactorily ascertained, the question of the date of the latter would be settled. The forty-ninth chapter of Jeremiah contains an oracle about Edom, in which the earlier part of Obadiah's prophecy is embodied. Out of the sixteen verses of which it is composed, four are identical in language with verses from Obadiah (Jer. xlix. 9, 14, 15, 16 correspond with Obad. verses 5, 1, 2, 3). A fifth embodies the substance of a verse (comp. Jer. xlix. 10 with Obad. 6). In two other verses respectively of the two prophets the same thought appears (Jer. xlix. 7 and Obad. 8); while the image in chap. xlix. 12 is that of Obad. 16. Add to this that the title which Jeremiah prefixes to his oracle —"concerning Edom, thus saith the Lord of hosts"—appears in a slightly changed form in Obadiah, after the proper heading—"vision of Obadiah"—in such a way as to confuse the construction (see Note). Now, of these two passages Obadiah's has undoubtedly the appearance of being the original in form. It is almost inconceivable that a copyist should have culled here and there a sentence from a longer work, and woven them into a connected and harmonious whole like Obad. 1—6. It was also so much in Jeremiah's manner to incorporate and use, for his own immediate purpose, oracles about foreign nations which he found in older works (comp. Jer. xlviii. *passim*, with Isa. xiv., xv., xvi.; Jer. xlix. 1—6 with Amos i. 13, 15; Jer. l. with Isa. xii., &c.) that we should suspect him to be the borrower in this instance. The passage in Obadiah, moreover, reads as the more ancient of the two. It is the more concise and abrupt, is rugged in comparison, and less polished, as we should expect in an older copy, has

an irregular grammatical form where Jeremiah substitutes a regular (*shalluach*, Jer. xlix. 14, for Obadiah's *shullach*, verse 1), does not attempt an easy flow of verse or careful parallelism, and preserves an image which is among the boldest of even Hebrew poetry, and which is omitted in Jeremiah, though the omission makes the construction faulty, "Though thou exalt as the eagle, *and among stars set thy nest*, thence will I bring thee down, saith the Lord." Jeremiah omits the italicised words, and so loses the direct antecedent to "thence."

These considerations lead to the conclusion that Obadiah did not copy from Jeremiah. The first part of the prophecy bearing his name must have been in existence before the date of Jeremiah's forty-ninth chapter; but it does not follow that the whole, as it now exists, had been written at that time. A later hand may have incorporated the earlier vision of Obadiah with fresh matter of his own; and there are indications that such was the case, besides the fact that the verses identical with those of Jeremiah are confined to the first portion of the book, viz., verses 1—9. There is a correspondence between the latter parts and Joel—not so close as that of the first part and Jeremiah, not extending to whole verses, but confined to phrases and expressions—but still a correspondence so close and striking, especially considering the very small limits in which the similarities occur, as to warrant the conclusion of a dependence of one writer on the other. The originality of Joel will hardly be disputed. We are therefore brought to infer that the writer who left the Book of Obadiah in its present shape took the ancient oracle against Edom, of which Jeremiah also availed himself, for the first half of his work, and in what he added was indebted greatly to Joel. This hypothesis accepted brings the composition of the work as we have it within the exile period, but leaves it quite uncertain to what date in that period to assign it. The concluding words of the prophecy are an echo of Zech. xiv. 9 (see Note), or at least belong to the same period.

But the question remains whether Obadiah was the name of this later editor, or whether it was the name of the older seer whose oracle he incorporated. The inscription leads to the second of these two conclusions. There is no reason to doubt that the first title, "vision of Obadiah," belongs to the older part; the second heading, "Thus saith," &c., which as it stands does not harmonise with the first, may have been inserted by some copyist to bring this oracle into similarity with the circle of oracles against foreign nations in Jeremiah, where the recognised introduction is of this form.

3. The time to which we have assigned our prophecy brings it within the circle of well-known prophecies about Edom: viz., Ezek. xxv. 12—14, xxxv. 1—15; Isa. xxxiv., lxiii. 1—6; Ps. cxxxvii. 7—9; Lam. iv. 21, 22; Ezek. xxxii. 29, xxxvi. 5.

It has been noticed that the tone of Obadiah is not so fierce and vindictive as these. It is, however, quite in accordance with their general feeling. We should like to know more of this writer, who, commissioned with only one short message against one of Israel's foes, delivered it with such incisive force, yet such moderation and self-restraint. We only know that, like him whose words he adapted to his own use, he too deserves the name "servant of Jehovah."

JONAH

INTRODUCTION

TO

JONAH

THE Book of Jonah occupies a position unique in the Bible. Classed among the prophetical books, it has no single point in common with them. Its one prediction of the overthrow of Nineveh differs entirely from the judgments announced by Nahum against the same power, by Isaiah and others against Moab, or Philistia, or Babylon. In these, according to the true prophetic spirit, ruin is connected immediately with sin as an inevitable consequence. We have pictures of moral corruption, and of the social and political convulsions that must necessarily, in the course of God's providence, follow. In Jonah's one utterance we have simply a prediction of a coming overthrow, with a date precisely stated in a manner quite foreign to the ordinary prophetic style. In the body of prophecy, therefore, the book has no proper standing. As a narrative in one of the historical books, the story of Jonah's mission would have been in place. Indeed, it appears as if it were a fragment from a series of narratives of prophetic acts, similar to those incorporated in the Books of Kings about Elijah and Elisha.

This displacement from its true position is no doubt due to the opinion of the collectors of the canon as to the authorship of the book. They assumed that Jonah himself wrote it. This assumption is nowhere made in the narrative itself, though the use of the third person must not be taken as conclusive against it.

That the prophet is identical with the Jonah of 2 Kings xiv. 25, the statement of his parentage, "son of Amittai," leaves no doubt. A native of Gath-hepher, of the tribe of Zebulun, Jonah the son of Amittai prophesied at the commencement of the reign of Jeroboam II., *i.e.*, in the latter part of the ninth century B.C. His prophecies, we gather from the same passage, had reference to the victories of Jeroboam. Beyond this we know nothing of him till he abruptly bursts on us as the prophet commissioned to announce the destruction of Nineveh. A passing allusion in the Book of Tobit (chap. xiv. 4), which refers to the prediction as still waiting fulfilment, and evidently knows nothing of its sequel; and the well-known references in the New Testament (Matt. xii. 40, xvi. 4; Luke xi. 30), exhaust all that Scripture has to tell us about Jonah and his mission. Tradition, fastening on the meaning of the name Amittai (*'ĕmet*, "truth") identified him with the son of the widow of Sarepta, because, on receiving him back alive, she knew that the prophet's word was "truth." A tomb at Gath-hepher, mentioned by Jerome, was also assigned to Jonah by tradition.

The most various opinions have prevailed as to the nature of the book. It has been accepted as literal history, it has been described as pure fiction. Some have called it a parable, others an allegory, others a poetical myth,* others a dream; others again, while recognising an historical basis, hold that the narrative has been enlarged and embellished to suit the purposes of the unknown author. It is not within the scope of this Commentary to discuss these various modes of treatment,† and happily the lessons of the book are entirely independent of the views as to its character. Whether history or parable, it conveys in the most striking way some of the profoundest truths of religion, truths which, if to be discovered at all elsewhere in the Old Testament, are certainly nowhere else pronounced with such firmness and power. The story of the threefold deliverance—of the vessel when relieved of its burden of guilt—of the prophet, in whom, however reluctant, the Divine purpose had found its fitting instrument—of the doomed city, saved, in spite of its doom, by repentance—this story does not lose its impressiveness even if read as the work of imagination trying to explain the mysterious dealings of God. Many minds, not sceptical of a basis of miracle, yet find a difficulty in the concentration of so much of the marvellous round one figure and one brief incident. But the figure is none the less striking, the character none the less instructive, if it is the creation of fiction; and the incident, even if unhistorical, carries a wealth of profound spiritual truth. The tradition mentioned above connecting Jonah with Sarepta, however fanciful, is singularly appropriate, since in the book bearing the prophet's name we come upon a clear anticipation of so much of the teaching of Him who commended the faith of the Sidonian woman, and rebuked the exclusiveness of the disciples. That the heathen world might look to the great God for blessings which the favoured race was rejecting or despising, that others beside Israelites had a claim on the justice and mercy of Jehovah, that repentance and prayer could be effectual outside the Mosaic system—these lessons, which even Christ's dis-

* Two classical myths have been by various critics brought into connection with the story of Jonah, that of Hesione, who was chained to a rock as food for a sea-monster, and was delivered by Hercules, and that of Andromeda saved by Perseus from a similar fate. The latter is locally connected with Joppa. A Babylonian myth, in which the name *Oannes*, supposed to be cognate with *Jonah*, occurs, has also been adduced.

† The references of our Lord to Jonah no more attest its literal truth, than his allusion to the Psalms as David's settles the authorship of the whole of the Psalter. It would be strange if He who chose the parabolic method to convey the highest truths of His Kingdom, should have hesitated to enforce them by reference to writings of the same kind, even supposing we are not right in judging of His knowledge on points of literary criticism as limited. The argument of Keil and others, that Jonah could not have been adduced as a type of Christ unless his history is actual fact, is only valid when we have restricted the meaning of the word *type* to suit the argument. And the New Testament does not represent Jonah as a *type*, but as a *sign*.

ciples were slow to learn, are the prominent lessons of this book. Others less obvious are touched on in the notes. The power and universality of their application have been well brought out by Dean Stanley, who thus sums them up. "In the popular traditions of East and West, Jonáh's name alone has survived the lesser prophets of the Jewish Church. It still lives, not only in many a Mussulman tomb along the coasts and hills of Syria, but in the thoughts and devotions of Christendom. The marvellous escape from the deep, through a single passing allusion in the Gospel history, was made an emblem of the deliverance of Christ Himself from the jaws of death and the grave. The great Christian doctrine of the boundless power of human repentance received its chief illustration from the repentance of the Ninevites at the preaching of Jonah. There is hardly a figure from the Old Testament which the early Christians in the Catacombs so often took as their consolation in persecution, as the deliverance of Jonah on the sea-shore, and his naked form stretched out in the burning sun beneath the sheltering gourd. But these all conspire, with the story itself, in proclaiming that still wider lesson of which I have spoken. It is the rare protest of theology against the excess of theology; it is the faithful delineation, through all its various states, of the dark, sinister, selfish side of even great religious teachers. It is the grand Biblical appeal to the common instincts of humanity, and to the universal love of God, against the narrow dogmatism of sectarian polemics. There has never been 'a generation' which has not needed the majestic revelation of sternness and charity, each bestowed where most deserved, and where least expected, in the 'sign of the prophet Jonah'" (Stanley, *J. C.* ii. 356, 357).

If the question of the nature of the narrative may be set aside as of secondary importance, that of authorship and date must be given up from want of sufficient data. The linguistic argument may be used as strongly for the North Palestinian origin of the author, as for his late date. He was evidently familiar, beyond most scriptural writers, with the manners and language of the maritime cities of Phœnicia, and apparently knew more of the appearance of Nineveh and its customs than mere hearsay was likely to give. The repentance of the city, and its consequent salvation from a threatened overthrow, have, as yet, found no confirmation from profane history.* The other references to Nineveh in the Bible are apparently inconsistent with them. Prophets later than Jonah, Isaiah, Nahum, Zephaniah, continue to denounce the idolatries of the Assyrians, and predict their punishment. They give no hint of any previous sudden conversion. The only allusion to Jonah in writings anterior to Christianity (Tobit, see above) is ignorant, as we have seen, of any repentance, a fact which makes the existence of the book of Jonah before the probable composition of the book of Tobit, about B.C. 180, extremely doubtful.

The various theories and counter theories that have been built upon this slender evidence, leave the book with the description that has happily been given of it, "this book of unknown authorship, of unknown date, of disputed meaning, but of surpassing interest."

The division into chapters, in the Authorised Version, gives the best arrangement of the contents of the book. Its language is prose, but with sparks of poetic feeling showing in words and expressions, as well as in the hymn (chap. ii.), which, though modelled on, and in a great degree dependent, both in thought and style, on the Psalter, is yet evidently the work of an original mind.

* Unless we may connect the occurrence with the incursion of the Scyths mentioned by Herodotus (I. 103) which appear to have interfered with the prosecution of the siege of Nineveh by Cyaxares, and saved it for some twenty or twenty-five years. This historical fact may have been used by the author, like the name of Jonah himself, as a basis on which to found his story.

JONAH

CHAPTER I.—Now the word of the
LORD came unto [1] Jonah the son of
Amittai, saying, (2) Arise, go to Nineveh,
that [a] great city, and cry against it; for
their wickedness is come up before me.
(3) But Jonah rose up to flee unto Tar-
shish from the presence of the LORD,
and went down to Joppa; and he found
a ship going to Tarshish: so he paid the
fare thereof, and went down into it, to
go with them unto Tarshish from the
presence of the LORD.
(4) But the LORD [2] sent out a great
wind into the sea, and there was a
mighty tempest in the sea, so that the
ship [3] was like to be broken. (5) Then
the mariners were afraid, and cried
every man unto his god, and cast forth

B.C. cir. 862.

1 Called, Matt. 12. 39, *Jonas.*

a Gen. 10. 11, 12; ch. 3. 3.

2 Heb., *cast forth.*

3 Heb., *thought to be broken.*

JONAH'S DISOBEDIENCE AND PUNISHMENT.

(1) **Now . . .**—More strictly, *And;* but the English quite adequately represents the Hebrew style of beginning a narrative, whether it formed a book by itself, or merely continued an historical account. (See the opening of Exodus, Leviticus, and other historical books; Ezek. i. 1; and comp. 1 Kings xvii. 1, &c.)

Jonah the son of Amittai.—See Introduction.

(2) **Nineveh, that great city.**—The size of Nineveh is throughout the book brought into prominent notice. (See chaps. iii. 2, 3, iv. 11.) The traditions preserved in Greek and Roman writers dwell on the same feature; and modern researches among the huge mounds scattered along the left bank of the Tigris more than confirm the impression produced on the ancient world by the city, or rather group of cities, buried beneath them. (Comp. Gen. x. 11.)

Cry.—A common word for a proclamation by a herald or a prophet. (Comp. Isa. xl. 6, &c.) The English word, in the sense of "proclaim," lingers in the term "public crier."

For their wickedness is come up before me.—"Every iniquity has its own voice at the hidden judgment seat of God" (S. Gregory, *Mor.* v. 20; quoted by Pusey). But, as Pusey remarks, the Hebrew implies especially evil-doing against others, that *violence* which in chap. iii. 8 is recognised by the Ninevites themselves as their characteristic sin.

(3) **But Jonah rose up to flee.**—The motive of the prophet's flight is given by himself (chap. iv. 2). He foresaw the repentance of the city, and the mercy which would be displayed towards it, and was either jealous of his prophetic reputation, or had a patriotic dislike of becoming a messenger of good to a heathen foe so formidable to his own country.

Tarshish.—This can hardly be any other than *Tartessus,* an ancient Phœnician colony on the river Guadalquivir, in the south-west of Spain. (See Gen. x. 4; 1 Chron. i. 7.)

A profound moral lesson lies in the choice of this refuge by Jonah. A man who tries to escape from a clearly-recognised duty—especially if he can at the time supply conscience with a plausible excuse—is in danger of falling all the lower, in proportion as his position was high. Jonah, commanded to go to Nineveh, in the far north-east, instantly tries to flee to the then farthermost west. Often between the saintly height and an abyss of sin there is no middle resting-point. The man with the highest ideal, when unfaithful to it, is apt to sink lower than the ordinary mortal.

From the presence of the Lord.—Rather, *from before the face of Jehovah.* The words may imply (1) the belief in a possibility of hiding from the sight of God (as in Gen. iii. 8), a belief which, as we gather from the insistance on its opposite in Ps. cxxxix., lingered late in the popular conception; (2) a renunciation of the prophetic office. (Comp. Deut. x. 8; 1 Kings xvii. 1); (3) Flight from the Holy Land, where the Divine presence was understood to be especially manifested. Commentators have generally rejected the first of these as implying ignorance unworthy of a prophet; but, on embarking, Jonah went below, as if still more securely to hide, and used the same expression to the mariners, who would certainly take it in its literal and popular sense.

Joppa.—Heb., *Yāpho;* now *Jaffa,* the port of Jerusalem. (See Josh. xix. 46; 2 Chron. ii. 16.)

He found a ship.—Probably a Phœnician vessel trading between Egypt and Spain, and accustomed to touch at Joppa.

(4) **Sent out.**—The Hebrew word (see margin, and comp. verses 5, 12, 15, where the same word is rendered "cast forth") expresses the sudden burst of the storm. A squall struck the ship. The coast was well known to sailors as dangerous. (See Josephus, *Ant.* xv. 9, § 6, *B. J.* iii. 9, § 3.)

So that the ship was like to be broken.—See margin for the literal expression, which is that of a sailor to whom the ship is a living thing, with feelings, hopes, and fears. For the word *break,* of shipwreck (comp. *naufragium*), see 1 Kings xxii. 48.

(5) **And cried every man unto his god.**—If Phœnicians, the sailors would have their favourite deities in the national Pantheon; but they may have been a motley crew composed of various nationalities. For the panic comp. Ps. cvii. 23—30, and Shakspeare's *Tempest,*

"All lost! to prayers! to prayers, all lost!"

Wares.—The Hebrew word is of general import for furniture of any kind, and so including all the movables in the ship. The cargo would probably, as in the case

the wares that *were* in the ship into the
sea, to lighten *it* of them. But Jonah
was gone down into the sides of the
ship; and he lay, and was fast asleep.
(6) So the shipmaster came to him, and
said unto him, What meanest thou, O
sleeper? arise, call upon thy God, if so
be that God will think upon us, that we
perish not. (7) And they said every one
to his fellow, Come, and let us cast lots,
that we may know for whose cause this
evil *is* upon us. So they cast lots, and
the lot fell upon Jonah. (8) Then said
they unto him, Tell us, we pray thee,
for whose cause this evil *is* upon us;
What *is* thine occupation? and whence
comest thou? what *is* thy country? and
of what people *art* thou? (9) And he
said unto them, I *am* an Hebrew; and
I fear the LORD, the God of heaven,
which hath made the sea and the dry
land. (10) Then were the men [1] exceed-
ingly afraid, and said unto him, Why
hast thou done this? For the men knew
that he fled from the presence of the
LORD, because he had told them.
(11) Then said they unto him, What
shall we do unto thee, that the sea [2] may

1 Heb., *with great fear.*

2 Heb., *may be silent from us?*

---

of St. Paul's shipwreck, be reserved till the last extremity.

To lighten it of them.—This gives the sense, though the Hebrew idiom appears to mean, *to give themselves relief.* (Comp. Exod. xviii. 22, "So shall it be easier for thyself;" 1 Kings xii. 10, "Make thou it lighter unto us.")

Sides.—Rather, *recesses.* The word is used of the inner part of the Temple (1 Kings vi. 16), of a cave (1 Sam. xxiv. 3), of a dwelling-house (Ps. cxxviii. 3).

Ship.—The Hebrew is different from the word used earlier in the verse, and is peculiar to this passage. Its derivation from a root meaning "to cover with boards," indicates a *decked* vessel. Jonah had gone below into the cabin, the natural course for a man flying from a disagreeable duty. To stand on deck and watch the slow receding shore would have been mental torture.

And was fast asleep.—The fatigue of the hasty flight to the sea-shore accounts for this deep slumber. The same expression is used of Sisera (Judges iv. 21). Besides, when a resolution is once irrevocably (as we think) taken, conscience ceases to disturb with its wakeful warning, and the restlessness of remorse has not yet arrived. There is a brief time during which "the exile from himself can flee."

(6) **The shipmaster . . .**—Literally, *the chief of those who work at the rope.* Jewish nautical terms are infrequent and therefore obscure. The word *mariners*, in verse 5, correctly renders a term which seems, from its use in Ezek. xxvii. 8, 27, 29, as well as from its derivation (from *salt;* comp. the term "old salts"), to denote seafaring men generally. "Those who work the ropes" may be either "steersmen" or "topmen" as contrasted with rowers.

What meanest . . .—Literally, *What to thee sleeping? i.e.,* How canst thou sleep so soundly? The motive of the question was no doubt partly the need of sympathy, as in the case of the disciples (Mark iv. 38), partly a belief in the efficacy of the prophet's prayer. This belief seems to have sprung not solely from superstitious fear lest any deity should be overlooked, but from a vague sense that the God of Israel was pre-eminently great and good. The term used is *ha Elohîm,* "the God."

(7) **Come, and let us cast lots.**—We are to suppose that Jonah, coming on deck in compliance with the captain's request, adds his prayers to those of the crew. Finding all unavailing, the sailors propose recourse to the ancient custom of casting lots to discover the guilty person against whom the deities are so enraged. Classical authors as well as the Bible (comp. Josh. vii. 14, *seq.*; 1 Sam. xiv. 36—46) afford many illustrations of the belief that the presence of an impious man would involve all who shared his company in indiscriminate ruin. Naturally the feeling expressed itself most strongly at sea.

> "Who drags Eleusis' rite to day,
> That man shall never share my home
> Or join my voyage; roofs give way,
> And boats are wrecked; true men and thieves
> Neglected Justice oft confounds."
> HOR.: *Od.* iii. 2, 26—30. (Conington's trans.)

Comp. the story told by Cicero of Diagoras (*de Nat. Deor.* iii. 3). Æsch. *Sept. cont. Theb.* 601—604. Soph. *Ant.* 372.

(8) **For whose cause . . .**—The Hebrew idiom is peculiar, *on account of which to whom;* but in this verse, when addressed by the sailors to the prophet, it is expressed in a more elegant form than when used to each other in the preceding verse, one among many touches marking the artistic perfection of this narrative. It is true some MSS. omit this repetition of the question, and it is therefore by some commentators treated as a gloss. But the repetition is quite natural. The sailors seeing the lot fall on one whose appearance was so little suspicious, are anxious to have it confirmed by his confession. Not less natural is the rapid and excited leap from question to question. (Comp. Virg. *Æn.* viii. 112, 113.)

(9) **And he said . . .**—"The emergency recalls Jonah to his true self. All the better part of his character now comes out. His conduct throughout the remainder of the chapter is dignified and manly, worthy of a servant and prophet of Jehovah" (Perowne).

I am a Hebrew.—The original order is more striking, *A Hebrew I.* The LXX. read, "a servant of the Lord."

Which hath made . . .—These words mark the great change that has already come upon the prophet. He feels now how futile it was to try to hide or fly from the Creator of all the universe. But he speaks also for the sake of the crew, who, though recognising the existence of Jehovah as the tribal God of Israel, had never realised His relation to themselves as Creator of the world in which they lived, and of the sea on which they sailed. The storm preached the omnipotence of God.

(10) **Why hast.**—Rather, *What is this that thou hast done?* The question expresses horror, not curiosity.

For the men knew that.—Jonah's answer in verse 9 is evidently intended only as an abbreviation of what he actually replied.

(11) **What shall we.**—The prophet would of course know how to appease the God he had displeased.

be calm unto us? for the sea [1] [2] wrought,
and was tempestuous. (12) And he said
unto them, Take me up, and cast me
forth into the sea; so shall the sea be
calm unto you: for I know that for my
sake this great tempest *is* upon you.
(13) Nevertheless the men [3] rowed hard
to bring *it* to the land; but they could
not: for the sea wrought, and was tem-
pestuous against them. (14) Wherefore
they cried unto the LORD, and said, We
beseech thee, O LORD, we beseech thee,
let us not perish for this man's life, and
lay not upon us innocent blood: for
thou, O LORD, hast done as it pleased
thee. (15) So they took up Jonah, and
cast him forth into the sea: and the sea
[4] ceased from her raging. (16) Then the
men feared the LORD exceedingly, and
[5] offered a sacrifice unto the LORD, and
made vows.
(17) Now the LORD had prepared a
great fish to swallow up Jonah. And
[a] Jonah was in the [6] belly of the fish
three days and three nights.

1 Or, *grew more and more tempestuous.*
2 Heb., *went.*
3 Heb., *digged.*
4 Heb., *stood.*
5 Heb., *sacrificed a sacrifice unto the* LORD, *and vowed vows.*
a Matt. 12. 40, & 16. 4; Luke 11. 30.
6 Heb., *bowels.*
b Ps. 120. 1.
7 Or, *out of mine affliction.*
8 Or, *the grave.*

CHAPTER II.—Then Jonah prayed
unto the LORD his God out of the fish's
belly, (2) and said,
I [b] cried [7] by reason of mine affliction
unto the LORD, and he heard me; out
of the belly of [8] hell cried I, *and* thou

May be calm unto us.—See margin. The word rendered *calm* occurs (Ps. cvii. 30) of a *lull* after a storm, and in Prov. xxvi. 20 metaphorically, of *peace* after strife.

Wrought, and was tempestuous.—Literally, *was going, and being agitated;* an idiom rightly explained in the margin. (Comp. a similar idiom Gen. viii. 3.)

(12) **Cast me forth into the sea.**—There was no need of prophetic inspiration to enable Jonah to pass this sentence upon himself. He is too manly not to prefer to perish without involving others in his ruin.

(13) **Rowed hard.**—This is a sufficient rendering of the Hebrew verb, though it misses the metaphor. In every other instance of its use the word refers to the violence employed in breaking through a wall or enclosure. (See Ezek. viii. 8, xii. 5, 7; Job xxiv. 16; Amos ix. 2; and compare the use of the derivative noun in Exod. xxii. 2; Jer. ii. 34.) The figure of forcing the ship through the great wave wall is very striking. The Latin *infindere sulcos* and our *ploughing the main* are kindred metaphors.

It is a fine trait in these sailors that they will not obey the prophet's request to throw him overboard till all efforts to save the ship have been tried.

(14) **Wherefore they cried unto the Lord.**—There is presented here, as throughout the book, a strong contrast between the readiness of the heathen to receive religious impressions, and the stubbornness and obstinacy of Israel.

For this man's life . . .—*i.e.,* for taking it. The *law of retaliation* was as familiar to them as to the Hebrews (Deut. xix. 21). (Comp. 2 Sam. xiv. 7.)

For thou.—The original is more impressive: *For Thou, Jehovah, as it hath pleased Thee, Thou hast done.* The storm, the lot, the request of the prophet himself, all showed that the sailors were but instruments in carrying out the Divine purpose.

(15) **Raging.**—Comp. *maris ira,* Ovid. *Met.* i. 330; *iratum mare,* Hor. *Epod.* ii. 57.

> "At whose burden
> The angered ocean foams."
> SHAKSPEARE: *Ant. and Cleop.*

(16) **Offered.**—There may have been some live-stock on board suitable for sacrifice; but the offering could only be completed on landing, wherefore they *made vows.*

(17) **Now the Lord.**—In the Hebrew, chap. ii. commences with this verse.

Had prepared.—The pluperfect is misleading. Render *appointed,* and comp. chap. iv. 6, 7, 8, where the same word is used of the *gourd,* the *worm,* and the *east wind.* The Authorised version renders the word accurately in Job vii. 3; Dan. i. 5—10. Previous special *preparation* is not implied, still less *creation* for the particular purpose. God employs existing agents to do His bidding.

A great fish.—The Hebrew *dag* is derived from the prolific character of fish, and *a great fish* might stand for any one of the sea monsters. The notion that it was a *whale* rests on the LXX. and Matt. xii. 40. But κῆτος was a term for any large fish, such as dolphins, sharks, &c. (See Hom. *Od.* xii. 97.) And unless we have previously determined the question, whether the Book of Jonah is intended by the sacred writer to be a literal history, or an apologue founded on a history or a parable pure and simple, *tota hæc de pisce Jonæ disquisitio,* as an old commentator observes, *vana videtur atque inutilis.* The explanations given by commentators divide themselves into those of a strictly præternatural kind, as that a fish was created for the occasion; or into the natural or semi-natural, as that it was a ship, or an inn bearing the sign of the whale; or that it was a white shark. (For the last hypothesis see all that can be collected in Dr. Pusey's commentary on Jonah.) In early Christian paintings the monster appears as a huge dragon.

Three days and three nights.—See Matt. xii. 40, *New Testament Commentary.*

II.

JONAH'S PRAYER AND DELIVERANCE.

(1) **Then Jonah prayed.**—This introduction, to what is in reality a psalm of thanksgiving, has its parallel in Hannah's song (1 Sam. ii. 1—10), which is introduced in the same way. Comp. also the Note appended by the psalm collector at the end of Ps. lxxii., "The *prayers* of David the son of Jesse are ended."

(2) **By reason of mine affliction.**—See margin. There is a close correspondence between this opening and that of Ps. cxx. Comp. also Ps. xviii. 6.

Out of the belly of hell.—This remarkable expression—a forcible figure for imminent death—has its nearest parallel in Isa. v. 14, where *sheôl* (see Ps. vi. 5) is represented as opening a huge mouth to swallow the princes of the world and their pomp. The *under-world* represents the Hebrew word *sheôl* more

heardest my voice. (3) For thou hadst
cast me into the deep, in the [1] midst of
the seas; and the floods compassed me
about: all thy billows and thy waves
passed over me. (4) Then I said, I am
cast out of thy sight; yet I will look
again toward thy holy temple. (5) The
[a] waters compassed me about, *even* to
the soul: the depth closed me round
about, the weeds were wrapped about
my head. (6) I went down to the
[2] bottoms of the mountains; the earth
with her bars *was* about me for ever:
yet hast thou brought up my life from
[3] corruption, O LORD my God. (7) When
my soul fainted within me I remembered
the LORD: and my prayer came in unto
thee, into thine holy temple. (8) They
that observe lying vanities forsake their
own mercy. (9) But I will sacrifice unto
thee with the voice of [b] thanksgiving;
I will pay *that* that I have vowed.
[c] Salvation *is* of the LORD.

(10) And the LORD spake unto the
fish, and it vomited out Jonah upon the
dry *land*.

CHAPTER III.—And the word of
the LORD came unto Jonah the second
time, saying, (2) Arise, go unto Nineveh,
that great city, and preach unto it the
preaching that I bid thee. (3) So Jonah
arose, and went unto Nineveh, according
to the word of the LORD.

1 Heb., *heart.*

a Ps. 69. 1.

2 Heb., *cuttings off.*

3 Or, *the pit.*

b Ps. 50. 14, 23. & 116. 17; Hos. 14. 2; Heb. 13. 15.

c Ps. 3. 8.

---

nearly than *hell* or the *grave* (margin). (Comp. Pss. xviii. 5, xxx. 3.)

And thou heardest . . .—The conjunction is unnecessarily introduced. The sudden change of person, a frequent figure in Hebrew poetry, is more striking without the connecting word.

(3) **Hadst cast.**—Rather, *didst cast.* (See Psalm lxxxviii. 6.)

Floods.—Literally, *river,* used here of the ocean currents. (Comp. Ps. xxiv. 2.)

All thy billows and thy waves.—More exactly, *all thy breakers and billows.* (See Ps. xlii. 7, where the same expression is used figuratively for great danger and distress.)

(4) **I am cast out of thy sight.**—"Jonah had wilfully withdrawn from standing in God's presence. Now God had taken him at his word, and, as it seemed, cast him out of it. David had said in his haste, "I am cut off" (Ps. xxxi. 22), Jonah substitutes the stronger word, "I am cast forth," driven forth, expelled like the mire and dirt which the waves drive along, or like the waves themselves in their restless motion, or the heathen (the word is the same) whom God had driven out before Israel, or as Adam from Paradise" (Pusey).

Yet I will look again.—The Hebrew is very impressive, and reads like one of those exile hopes so common in the Psalms: "Yet I have one thing left, to turn towards Thy holy Temple and pray." (For the attitude see Note on Ps. xxviii. 2.)

(5) **The waters.**—See reference in margin.

The weeds were wrapped about my head.—This graphic touch is quite original. The figure of overwhelming waters is a common one in Hebrew song to represent some crushing sorrow, but nowhere is the picture so vivid as here. At the same time the entire absence of any reference to the fish, which would, indeed, be altogether out of place in this picture of a drowning man entangled in seaweed, should be noticed. That on which the prophet lays stress is not on the mode of his escape, but his escape itself.

(6) **Bottoms of the mountains.**—Literally, *ends* or *cuttings off,* as in margin. So the Vulg. *extrema montium.* Mountains were in the Hebrew conception the pillars of the world (see Job ix. 6, xxvi. 11), having their foundations firmly planted in the sea. These "hidden bases of the hills" were therefore the verge of the earth itself, and one lost among them would be close on the under-world of death.

The earth with her bars . . .—Literally, *the earth her bars behind me for ever; i.e.,* the earth's gates were closed upon me for ever, there was no possibility of return. The metaphor of a gateway to *sheôl* is common (Isa. xxxviii. 10, &c.), but the earth is nowhere else said to be so guarded. Ewald therefore proposes to read *sheôl* here. But it is quite as natural to imagine a guarded passage out of the land of the living as into the land of the dead.

Corruption.—Rather, *pit.* (See Note, Ps. xvi. 10.)

(7) **Fainted.**—Literally, *covered itself.* Comp. chap. iv. 8. (See Pss. lxi. 2, cxlii. 3, cxliii. 4, where the same Hebrew word is rendered *overwhelmed.* Comp. Ps. cvii. 5.) Here, apparently, we are to think of the blinding mist of death slowly stealing over sight and sense.

Into thine holy temple.—See verse 4, and comp. Ps. xviii. 6.

(8) **They that observe lying vanities.**—See Note, Ps. xxxi. 6.

Forsake their own mercy—*i.e.,* forfeit their own share of the covenant grace. In Ps. xxxvii. 28 it is said that Jehovah does not forsake his *chasîdîm;* they, however, by forsaking Jehovah (Himself called Israel's *mercy,* Ps. cxliv. 2, margin) and His law (Ps. lxxxix. 30) can forfeit their *chesed* or covenant privilege.

(9) **But I will.**—The prophet, however, is not among such. He has sinned, but is still a member of the covenant people, and by sacrifice can be formally restored to that favour which repentance has regained.

Salvation is of the Lord.—Or, *Deliverance is Jehovah's.* (Comp. Ps. iii. 8.)

III.

THE PROPHET FULFILS HIS COMMISSION. ITS RESULT.

(2) **Preach.**—In chap. i. 2 the word is rendered "cry."

(3) **Now Nineveh was . . .**—The past tense here certainly seems to imply that at the time in which the author wrote the city was no longer in existence, but the force of a Hebrew tense is not to be estimated by the analogy of modern languages.

Now Nineveh was an [1]exceeding
great city of three days' journey.
(4) And Jonah began to enter into the
city a day's journey, and he cried, and
said, Yet forty days, and Nineveh shall
be overthrown.
(5) So the people of Nineveh [a]believed
God, and proclaimed a fast, and put on
sackcloth, from the greatest of them
even to the least of them. (6) For word
came unto the king of Nineveh, and he
arose from his throne, and he laid his
robe from him, and covered *him* with
sackcloth, and sat in ashes. (7) And he
caused *it* to be proclaimed and [2]pub-
lished through Nineveh by the decree of
the king and his [3]nobles, saying, Let nei-
ther man nor beast, herd nor flock, taste

1 Heb., *of God.*

d Matt. 12. 41; Luke 11. 32.

2 Heb., *said.*

3 Heb., *great men.*

An exceeding great city.—Literally, *A city great to God;* an expression equivalent to *a divinely great city,* and taken, as Ewald thinks, from the language of the people, like the Arabic "to Allah," in the saying "to Allah (*i.e., divine*) is he that composed this." In the Hebrew poetic and prophetic writings a finer form is found, *e.g.,* "mountains of God," "cedars of God" (Pss. xxxvi. 6, lxxx. 10), "trees of Jehovah" (Ps. civ. 16), but in Gen. x. 9 a precisely similar proverbial use shows itself, also belonging to the Mesopotamian region, "Nimrod, a mighty hunter before the Lord."

Of three days' journey.—Hitzig takes this as giving the diameter of the city, but most commentators refer it to the circumference. The circuit of the walls was the most obvious measurement to give of an ancient city. Herodotus variously reckons a day's journey at about eighteen or twenty-three miles (v. 53, iv. 101), and the circuit of the irregular quadrangle composed of the mounds of Koujunjik, Nimrud, Karamless, and Khorsabad, now generally allowed to represent ancient Nineveh, is about sixty miles. This agrees sufficiently with the obviously vague and general statement of the text.

(4) **And Jonah began to enter into the city a day's journey.**—This is apparently equivalent to *And Jonah entered the city, and walked for a day through it.* To enter on a minute inquiry as to whether his course was straight or circuitous seems trivial. The writer has no thought of furnishing data for ascertaining the exact dimensions of Nineveh, but only of producing a general sense of its vast size.

Yet forty days.—The conciseness of the original, "Yet forty days, and Nineveh overthrown," forcibly expresses "the one deep cry of woe" which the prophet was commissioned to utter. "This simple message of Jonah bears an analogy to what we find elsewhere in Holy Scripture. The great preacher of repentance, St. John the Baptist, repeated doubtless oftentimes that one cry, "Repent ye, for the kingdom of heaven is at hand." Our Lord vouchsafed to begin His own office with those self-same words. And probably, among the civilised but savage inhabitants of Nineveh that one cry was more impressive than any other would have been, Simplicity is always impressive. They were four words which God caused to be written on the wall amid Belshazzar's impious revelry: *Mene, mene, tekel, upharsin.* We all remember the touching history of Jesus, son of Anan, an unlettered rustic, who, "four years before the war, when Jerusalem was in complete peace and affluence," burst in on the people at the Feast of Tabernacles with the oft-repeated cry, "A voice from the east, a voice from the west, a voice from the four winds, a voice on Jerusalem and the Temple, a voice on the bridegrooms and the brides, a voice on the whole people;" how he went about through all the lanes of the city, repeating, day and night, this one cry, and when scourged till his bones were laid bare, echoed every lash with "Woe, woe, to Jerusalem!" and continued as his daily dirge and his one response to daily good or ill treatment, "Woe, woe, to Jerusalem!" (Pusey.) Instead of "forty days" the LXX. read "three."

(5) **Believed God.**—Or, *believed in God.* Notice again an implied contrast to the dulness of the Jews, who were "slow to believe" the prophetic warnings addressed to themselves.

Proclaimed a fast.—Apparently on a spontaneous resolution of the people themselves. (See Note to verse 6.) The fast would no doubt be for one day, according to the Jewish and the general Oriental custom.

(6) **For word came.**—Rather, *And the matter reached.* The Authorised Version treats the royal edict that follows as the same with the *proclamation* in verse 5. This is possible, but it is more probable that the writer intended to describe the effect produced on each district of the vast city in succession, and on all grades of people. The piercing cry uttered from street to street, from square to square, reaches at last the king on his throne of state.

And he laid . . .—Stripping off the state mantle (the Hebrew word implies *amplitude.* See 1 Kings xix. 13.) It is interesting to find it used of the "Babylonish garment," found in Achan's tent. See Josh. vii. 21), the monarch assumes a mourning dress. To form a conception of the change involved, the descriptions of Assyrian royal magnificence should be studied in Layard, or their representations in the Assyrian courts of the Crystal Palace. For the usual signs of Oriental mourning, comp. Gen. xxxvii. 34; 2 Sam. iii. 31; Job. ii. 8; Ps. xxxv. 13; Ezek. xxvi. 16, &c.

(7) **And he caused . . .**—The fact that the word rendered "decree" in this verse was a technical name for the edicts of Assyrian and Babylonian kings (see Dan. iii. 10, 29) would alone vouch for the accurate acquaintance of the author with the customs he describes. But the very form of the royal edict is here preserved. The verse should probably run: *And he caused to be proclaimed, and be published in Nineveh "According to the decree of the king and his magnates be it proclaimed that,"* &c. The word "saying" is apparently formal like our "thus saith," &c.

And his nobles.—For this association of the great men with the autocrat, comp. Dan. vi. 17. Traces of the custom can also be discovered in Assyrian inscriptions, *e.g.,* "I am Assurbanipal king of nations, king of Assyria, Nabu-damiq and Umbadara the great men," &c. (G. Smith, *Assyrian Discoveries,* p. 413). Ewald thinks the formal "saying" in the edict marks the omission of the names, which in the original would be given.

Beast.—The Hebrew word is general, and might include all the domestic animals, but from the addition

any thing: let them not feed, nor drink
water: (8) but let man and beast be
covered with sackcloth, and cry mightily
unto God: yea, let them turn every one
from his evil way, and from the violence
that *is* in their hands. (9) [a] Who can
tell *if* God will turn and repent, and
turn away from his fierce anger, that
we perish not?

(10) And God saw their works, that they
turned from their evil way; and God re-
pented of the evil, that he had said that
he would do unto them; and he did *it* not.

CHAPTER IV.—But it displeased
Jonah exceedingly, and he was very
angry. (2) And he prayed unto the
LORD, and said, I pray thee, O LORD,
was not this my saying, when I was yet
in my country? Therefore I [b] fled before
unto Tarshish: for I knew that thou *art*
a [c] gracious God, and merciful, slow to
anger, and of great kindness, and
repentest thee of the evil. (3) Therefore
now, O LORD, take, I beseech thee, my
life from me; for *it is* better for me to
die than to live.

(4) Then said the LORD, [1] Doest thou
well to be angry?

(5) So Jonah went out of the city, and

a Joel 2. 14.

b ch. 1. 3.

c Ex. 34. 6; Ps. 86. 5; Joel 2. 13.

1 Or, *Art thou greatly angry?*

---

of "herd nor flock" we must doubtless here confine it to the *horses* and *mules*, &c., which even, according to our ideas, might have their usual gay housings changed to those suited to a time of mourning. "Men think it strange that the horses at Nineveh were covered with sackcloth, and forget how, at the funerals of the rich, black horses are chosen, and are clothed with black velvet" (Pusey). Herodotus (ix. 24) and Plutarch (Alexander), have both preserved instances in which horses and mules were associated with human beings in the signs of public mourning. The instinct which underlies the custom is a true one. Not only are the destinies of the animals which minister to man's wants often identical with his own; but there is a bond of sympathy between them naturally; and one remarkable feature of this book is the prominence given to this truth. (See chap. iv. 11.)

Let them not feed. . . .—Poetically, the beasts are said by Virgil to fast at the death of Daphnis (*Eclog.*, v. 24—28), and in Joel i. 20 their mute appeal against suffering is represented as audible to God. In the horror of the impending ruin of Nineveh, superstition exaggerated the true feeling underlying such representations, and to the belief in the sympathy of the lower animals with man was added the hope that their sufferings would help to appease the wrath of God.

Let them turn.—Notice the insistance on a moral change, and the implied contrast, again showing itself, with the formality of Judaism. Even in this repentance the edict does not stop to distinguish beast from man, but includes all, as all were involved in the threatened destruction.

Violence.—This is the characteristic of Assyrian manners most frequently noticed in the prophets. (See Nahum ii. 11, 12, iii. 1; Isa. x. 13, 14.) The cuneiform inscriptions abundantly illustrate this point. Take this for example from an inscription of Tiglath Pileser II.: "Tiglath Pileser, the great king, the powerful king, king of nations, &c., the powerful warrior who in the service of Assur his lord the whole of his haters has trampled on like clay, swept like a flood, and reduced to shadows" (G. Smith, *Assyrian Discoveries*, p. 254).

In their hands.—Comp. Ps. vii. 3.

Who can tell . . . ?—This sudden recognition of *one* God by a king of Nineveh appears far more striking if contrasted with the long lists of deities usually mentioned in the Assyrian inscriptions, *e.g.*, "By command of Assur, Sin, Shamas, Vul, Bel, Nebo, Ishtar of Nineveh, Sarrat-Kitmuri, Ishtar of Arbela, Ninip, Nergal, and Nusku, into Minni I entered and marched victoriously" (from the *Cylinder of Assurbanipal*, Smith, p. 333).

(10) **And God repented.**—See Note, Gen. vi. 6.

And he did it not.—As we are entirely ignorant of the nature of the threatened destruction, so are we also of the mode in which it was averted. Possibly some inscription throwing light on the book of Jonah may yet be discovered.

IV.

JONAH'S DISCONTENT AND CORRECTION.

(1) **But it displeased Jonah.**—The Hebrew (*it was evil to*) is stronger. The prophet was vexed and irritated.

He was very angry.—Literally, *it* (anger) *burnt to him.* David's feeling at the death of Uzziah (2 Sam. vi. 8; 1 Chron. xiii. 11) is described in the same terms. Selfish jealousy for his own reputation, jealousy for the honour of the prophetic office, a mistaken patriotism disappointed that the great enemy of his country should go unpunished, Jewish exclusiveness which could not endure to see the Divine clemency extended to the heathen, have each been adduced as the motive of Jonah's anger. Possibly something of all these blended in his mind.

(3) **Take, I beseech thee.**—We naturally refer to the history of Elijah for a similar weariness and disgust of life. (Comp. also the case of Moses, Num. xi. 15). It should be noticed, as a contrast of Hebrew with heathen feeling, that none of these men in their loathing of life contemplated the possibility of suicide.

(4) **Doest thou well? . . .**—This rendering may be supported by Deut. v. 28; Jer. i. 12, and agrees better with the context than the marginal translation, which follows the LXX., and is undoubtedly a very likely rendering of the Hebrew idiom if taken by itself. Jonah apparently gave his own interpretation to the question, one that suited his mood, "Is thine anger just?" Such a question might imply that the doom of the city was only deferred, and that he had been too hasty in giving up the fulfilment of his prediction. Accordingly he went outside the walls, and sat down to watch what the issue would be. On the other hand, the rendering "Art thou so very angry?" suits best the reply in verse 9, "I am very angry, even to death." Probably the Hebrew word, like the French *bien*, kept both its original and derived meaning, and must be rendered *well* or *very*, according to the context.

(5) **So Jonah went out.**—The explanation given in the preceding note avoids the necessity of giving the

sat on the east side of the city,
and there made him a booth, and sat
under it in the shadow, till he might see
what would become of the city. (6) And
the LORD God prepared a [1][2] gourd, and
made *it* to come up over Jonah, that it
might be a shadow over his head, to
deliver him from his grief. So Jonah
[3] was exceeding glad of the gourd. (7) But
God prepared a worm when the morning
rose the next day, and it smote the
gourd that it withered. (8) And it came
to pass, when the sun did arise, that
God prepared a [4] vehement east wind;
and the sun beat upon the head of
Jonah, that he fainted, and wished in
himself to die, and said, *It is* better for
me to die than to live.

(9) And God said to Jonah, [5] Doest
thou well to be angry for the gourd?
And he said, [6] I do well to be angry, *even*
unto death.

(10) Then said the LORD, Thou hast
[7] had pity on the gourd, for the which
thou hast not laboured, neither madest
it grow; which [8] came up in a night,
and perished in a night: (11) and should
not I spare Nineveh, that great city,
wherein are more than sixscore thousand
persons that cannot discern between
their right hand and their left hand;
and *also* much cattle?

1 Or, *palmcrist.*
2 Heb., *Kikajon.*
3 Heb., *rejoiced with great joy.*
4 Or, *silent.*
5 Or, *Art thou greatly angry?*
6 Or, *I am greatly angry.*
7 Or, *spared.*
8 Heb., *was the son of the night.*

---

verb in this clause a pluperfect force, which else would be necessary to account for the prophet's continued expectation of the destruction of Nineveh after his irritation at the Divine clemency towards it.

Booth—*i.e.*, of boughs, like those used at the Feast of Tabernacles. (See next Note.)

(6) **Prepared.**—See Note, chap. i. 17.

A gourd.—So the LXX. render the Hebrew *qiqaion*, which, since the time of Jerome, has been usually identified with the Arabic *el keroa*, the castor-oil tree (*Ricinus communis*, or *Palma Christi*; see margin). It is a large shrub, having large palmate leaves, with serrated lobes, and spikes of blossoms which produce the seed, whence the well-known medicinal oil is extracted, in small rough husks. The strongest argument in favour of this view is the proposed derivation of the Hebrew name from the Egyptian *kiki*, and the rabbinical name for castor-oil, *kiki-oil.** In spite of this etymological argument, Dr. Tristram says: "Practical reasons cause me to lean strongly to the rendering of our English version, gourd, *i.e.*, the bottle gourd (*Cucurbita pepo*). In Palestine the vernacular names are almost identical in sound, "kurah" being the gourd, "khurwah" the castor-oil tree. But the gourd is very commonly employed in Palestine for the purpose of shading arbours. Its rapid growth and large leaves render it admirably adapted for training on trellis-work . . . But the plant withers as rapidly as it shoots, and after a storm or any injury to its stem, its fruit may be seen hanging from the leafless tendrils, which so lately concealed it, a type of melancholy desolation" (*Nat. Hist. of the Bible*, p. 449).

Made it to come up.—Rather, *it came up.*

Deliver.—In the original there is a play of words on this word and *shadow.*

(7) **A worm.**—Possibly to be taken collectively, as in Isa. xiv. 11, for a swarm of caterpillars.

(8) **Vehement east wind.**—The derivation from a root meaning *silent* (see margin) points to what travellers describe as the "quiet kind of sirocco," which is often more overpowering than the more boisterous kind. (See Thomson, *The Land and the Book*, pp. 536, 537.) Ewald, however, derives differently, and makes it a *rough, scrapy, stingy* wind.

Fainted.—See chap. ii. 7. Here the effect of *sunstroke*, in Amos viii. 13 of *thirst.*

Wished in himself to die.—Literally, *wished his soul to die.* (Comp. 1 Kings xix. 4.)

It is better.—The italics are unnecessary, and weaken the passage, *Better my death than my life.* Physical suffering was now added to the prophet's chagrin, and, as usual, added to the moral depression. It seemed much worse that the logical consistency of Jonah's teaching should go for nothing now that he was so uncomfortable.

(9) **Doest thou well . . .?**—See Note to verse 4. Jonah was really hurt at the loss of his shade, not sorry for the destruction of the gourd. But it is very true to nature that the moment a worthier excuse is suggested, he accepts it, without perceiving that by so doing he prepared the way for his own condemnation. The lesson is to all who would sacrifice the cause of humanity to some professional or theological difficulty.

(10) **Which came up.**—The original is one of those forcible idioms impossible to reproduce, *which son of a night was, and son of a night perished.*

(11) **More than . . .**—This number of infants, 120,000, according to the usual reckoning, gives a population of 600,000.

And also much cattle.—This, which at first reads like an anti-climax, is really, perhaps, the most striking thing in the whole of this marvellous book. Already the idea that a sympathy could exist between Jonah and the gourd has seemed to anticipate by thousands of years the feeling of modern poetry expressed in the lines,

> "To me the meanest flower that blows can give
> Thoughts that too often lie too deep for tears;"

and now the final touch, laying especial emphasis on the thought that even the cattle are an interest and care to God, seems at once to leap to the truth which even our own age has been slow to learn.

> "He prayeth best who loveth best,
> All creatures great and small,
> For the dear God who loveth us
> He made and loveth all."

* A Semitic origin for the word is rendered probable by its discovery under the form, *quqanitu*, on a small tablet which the Babylonian king *Marduk-bal-iddin* (Merodach-baladan) ordered to be set in a garden. (See letters of Dr. F. Delitzsch, to the *Athenæum* of May 26th and June 9th, 1883.)

MICAH

INTRODUCTION

TO

MICAH

THE Book of the Prophet Micah is presented as the sixth in order of the minor prophets in the Hebrew, Vulgate, and our own canon, but in the LXX. it follows Hosea and Amos as the third.

It would be deeply interesting to construct a life of Micah, for he was so full of vivid personality that it could not fail to be remarkable; but the materials are almost wholly wanting. We conclude that his birthplace was Moresheth, in the maritime plain of the kingdom of Judah, and we conjecture that this was in the neighbourhood of Eleutheropolis. St. Jerome, indeed, mentions that he visited a village in those parts "which formerly contained the sepulchre of Micah, where is now a church."

His name itself* was no uncommon one, as is at once suggested by his adding to it the title of "the Morasthite," indicating his native town; although it seems hardly probable that he assumed it, as some have thought, for the purpose of distinguishing himself from Micaiah the son of Imlah, who lived a century before him. He was evidently a man of profound affection for his nation and fatherland, and from his native town he would doubtless pay anxious visits to Jerusalem to warn the rulers and people of the metropolis, deeply steeped as they were in the grossest wickedness, of the judgment ready to fall upon them if they did not repent. One of these occasions became historic, and was quoted in the time of Jehoiakim, when the priests and prophets were clamouring for the death of Jeremiah, who had ventured to emulate the heroic patriotism of Micah (see Note, chap. iii. 12), and the precedent probably saved that prophet's life. Micah's prophecies extended over the reigns of Jotham and Ahaz into that of Hezekiah; but he would appear to have died a few years after the last-mentioned monarch's accession.

The Prophet Micah foresaw the Assyrian invasion, and described with the vividness of an eye-witness the approach of the enemy destroying city after city, drawing nigh even unto Jerusalem itself. As to the rival capital, Samaria, "it shall be made as an heap of the field, and as plantings of a vineyard: I will pour down the stones thereof into the valley, and I will discover the foundations thereof."

But the message of the prophet was to the people of Judah, for if they, unwarned by the denunciations of the aroused anger of Jehovah, and unmoved by the exhibition of His judgments, continued in their evil course, they would be swept into captivity, carried away to a city the very name of which must have excited ridicule in the minds of his hearers. (See chap. iv. 10.)

This, however, Micah foresaw and foretold, and the scope of his prophecy became thereupon extended. He beheld the execution of the decree, nay, even further than that, its reversal at the appointed time. The Jews shall return to their own land, and once more dwell under the protection of Jehovah. But the vision grew, its horizon was more and more extended, and the prophet uttered predictions which every Jew interpreted as referring to the advent of their Messiah and His triumphant reign. He declared the very town in which He should be born, emphasising the fact, and anticipating the objections which would naturally rise to the mind of the Jews from the insignificance of Bethlehem for such high dignity. The end of Micah's prophecy is Messiah's eternal reign, in accordance with the truth of Jehovah "sworn unto our fathers from the days of old."

No student of the Books of Isaiah and Micah can fail to be struck with a similarity of style in the writings of the two prophets. There is the same power of graphic description; there is the similar identification of themselves with their subject; there are like alternate heights and depths of joy and trouble. But Micah is more terse. He gives the telling touches which, in Isaiah's utterances, expand into long bursts of sustained eloquence. The similarity in the style of Isaiah and Micah is strikingly attested by the passage Isa. ii. 2,3,4, and Micah iv. 1, 2, 3, common to the two writers, but which is eagerly claimed as original in behalf of both. (See Note at the place.)

As far as the individuality of Micah is discovered in his prophecy, he is conspicuous even among prophets for the boldness, the thoroughness of his denunciations, and for the rapidity of his contrasts The thunder-cloud of blackness descending upon sin again and again darkens with the suddenness of a storm his bright visions of glory; and on the other hand, there is always visible through the heaviest clouds the rainbow of hope from the sunshine of God's mercy. The light and the darkness are in constant juxtaposition. The period of Micah's life was cast in very troublous times. The reign of Ahab had impressed itself ineffaceably upon the character of Israel, and had left terrible marks upon that of Judah. Idolatry had been introduced into the Temple itself; statues of the accursed Baal were found even there. The abominations of the heathen in their most repulsive form prevailed; Jewish children were burnt in the fire to propitiate the idol Moloch. All society was disorganised; it was corrupt at the core. The desire of every citizen was to outwit his fellow. No judicial decision was to be obtained except through bribery; every contract was sullied with dishonesty.

In such a time Micah stood forth, and proclaimed the fall and destruction of Samaria, which came to pass in the fourth year of Hezekiah; and he drew attention to the danger which menaced the cities of

* Micaiah is found in many variations until it reaches the shortened form of Micah. There is Micaiah, a great man in Josiah's reign (2 Kings xxii. 12), called Micah (2 Chron. xxxiv. 20). Micaiah is a name given to the wife of Rehoboam (2 Chron. xiii. 12), which may be a mistake for Maachah; and Michaiah son of Gemariah (Jer. xxxvi. 11); and others.

Judah, even the Holy City itself. But his predictions were not satisfied by the Assyrian invasion. Their fulfilment has to be looked for in the terrible descent upon Judæa by the King of Babylon, a city in Micah's time too insignificant to attract any notice from Jewish politicians. And then, further than this, the prophecies of Micah reached to a far more distant horizon. His words spoke to Jewish ears of a Messiah to come, and they were treasured up as indicating the very place of His birth. The nearer and the more remote events immediately covered by his predictions were significant of the whole future of the people of God. There was the terrible wickedness which was to eat more and more deeply into the heart of society; there was the time of mourning for the good, of rejoicing for the evil; and there was the hour of signal punishment committed to the enemies of God against His faithless people; while these enemies, having become insolent and defiant, were to be eventually defeated. And then at the last there was the triumph of the faithful children of God, the Lord Himself passing on at the head of the remnant of Israel.

MICAH

CHAPTER I.—(1) The word of the
LORD that came to Micah the Morasthite
in the days of Jotham, Ahaz, *and* Heze-
kiah, kings of Judah, which he saw
concerning Samaria and Jerusalem.
(2) [1] Hear, all ye people; [a] hearken, O
earth, and [2] all that therein is: and let
the Lord GOD be witness against you,
the Lord from his holy temple. (3) For,
behold, [b] the LORD cometh forth out of
his [c] place, and will come down, and
tread upon the [d] high places of the
earth. (4) And [e] the mountains shall be
molten under him, and the valleys shall
be cleft, as wax before the fire, *and* as
the waters *that are* poured down [3] a
steep place.
(5) For the transgression of Jacob *is*
all this, and for the sins of the house
of Israel. What *is* the transgression of
Jacob? *is it* not Samaria? and what
are the high places of Judah? *are they*
not Jerusalem? (6) Therefore I will
make Samaria as an heap of the field,
and as plantings of a vineyard: and I
will pour down the stones thereof into
the valley, and I will discover the foun-
dations thereof. (7) And all the graven
images thereof shall be beaten to pieces,
and all the hires thereof shall be burned
with the fire, and all the idols thereof
will I lay desolate: for she gathered *it*
of the hire of an harlot, and they shall
return to the hire of an harlot.
(8) Therefore I will wail and howl, I
will go stripped and naked: I will make
a wailing like the dragons, and mourn-
ing as the [4] owls. (9) For [5] her wound *is*

B.C. cir. 750.

1 Heb., *Hear, ye people, all of them.*

a Deut. 32. 1; Isa. 1. 2.

2 Heb., *the fulness thereof.*

b Isa. 26. 21.

c Ps. 115. 3.

d Deut. 32. 13, & 33. 29.

e Ps. 97. 5.

3 Heb., *a descent.*

4 Heb., *daughters of the owl.*

5 Or, she is *grievously sick of her wounds.*

---

(1) **Micah the Morasthite.**—Unlike Joel, who identifies himself by his father's name, Micah introduces his personality with reference to his native village, Moresheth-gath, which was situated in the lowland district of Judah. The name—a shortened form of Micaiah, meaning "Who is like Jehovah"—was not an uncommon one among the Jews, but it was chiefly famous in times prior to the prophet, through Micaiah, the son of Imlah, who, about 150 years previously, had withstood Ahab and his false prophets.

Samaria and Jerusalem.—The younger capital is placed first because it was the first to fall through the greater sinfulness of the northern kingdom. The chief cities are mentioned as representatives of the wickedness of the respective nations.

(2) **Hear, all ye people.**—The three-fold repetition of the appeal, "Hear ye," seems to mark three divisions in the book: 1. "Hear, all ye people" (chap. i. 2); 2. "Hear, I pray you, O heads of Jacob" (chap. iii. 1); 3. Hear ye now what the Lord saith" (chap. vi. 1).

From his holy temple—*i.e.,* from heaven; for "the Lord is in His holy temple, the Lord's throne is in heaven" (Ps. xi. 4).

Micaiah, the son of Imlah, ended his appeal to Ahab and Jehoshaphat with the words with which Micah opens his prophecy, "Hearken, O people, every one of you" (1 Kings xxii. 28).

(4) **The mountains shall be molten.**—The manifestations of the presence of God are taken from the description of the giving of the Law, when "the hills melted like wax at the presence of the Lord, at the presence of the Lord of the whole earth" (Ps. xcvii. 5). Dean Stanley refers the imagery to the memorable earthquake mentioned in Amos i. 1:—"Mountains and valleys are cleft asunder, and melt as in a furnace; the earth heaving like the rising waters of the Nile; the sea bursting over the land; the ground shaking and sliding as, with a succession of shocks, its solid framework reels to and fro like a drunkard" (*Jewish Church,* Lect. 37).

(5) **The transgression of Jacob . . . the sins of the house of Israel.**—The corruption of the country came from the capital cities. Samaria, on her hill, set an example of idolatry, drunkenness, and all the evils of a most profligate society; and even Jerusalem, the city "set on an hill," gave a home in the Temple of Jehovah to heathen deities.

(6) **Samaria as an heap of the field.**—Samaria was to be reduced to what it had been before the days of Ahab; the palatial city of the kings of the northern kingdom should return to the normal condition of a vineyard, which it had before Shemer sold it to Omri. The fruitfulness of its vines suggests one cause of its ruin. "Woe to the crown of pride, to the drunkards of Ephraim, whose glorious beauty is a fading flower, which are on the head of the fat valleys of them that are overcome with wine" (Isa. xxviii. 1).

(7) **And all the hires thereof.**—The falling away of Israel from her loyalty to God is compared generally by the prophets to a wife deserting her husband; and these "hires" are the offerings made to the shrines of the idols to which the Israelites forsaking Jehovah had transferred their worship. All these treasures shall be destroyed; the Assyrians shall carry them off for the adornment of their temples.

(8) **Dragons . . . owls.**—Literally, *jackals and ostriches.* They are selected by reason of the dismal howls and screeches they make during the night.

(9) **Her wound is incurable.**—The state of Samaria is incurable: she is doomed: the destroyer is

incurable; for it is come unto Judah;
he is come unto the gate of my people,
even to Jerusalem.
(10) [a] Declare ye *it* not at Gath, weep
ye not at all: in the house of [1] Aphrah
[b] roll thyself in the dust. (11) Pass ye
away, [2] thou [3] inhabitant of Saphir,
having thy [c] shame naked: the inhabi-
tant of [4] Zaanan came not forth in the
mourning of [5] Beth-ezel; he shall receive
of you his standing. (12) For the inhabi-
tant of Maroth [6] waited carefully for
good: but evil came down from the
LORD unto the gate of Jerusalem.
(13) O thou inhabitant of Lachish, bind
the chariot to the swift beast: she *is*
the beginning of the sin to the daughter
of Zion: for the transgressions of Israel
were found in thee. (14) Therefore shalt
thou give presents [7] to Moresheth-gath:
the houses of [8] Achzib *shall be* a lie to
the kings of Israel. (15) Yet will I bring
an heir unto thee, O inhabitant of
Mareshah: [9] he shall come unto Adullam
the glory of Israel. (16) Make thee [d] bald,
and poll thee for thy delicate children;
enlarge thy baldness as the eagle; for
they are gone into captivity from thee.

CHAPTER II.—(1) Woe to them that
devise iniquity, and work evil upon their
beds! when the morning is light, they

a 2 Sam. 1. 20
1 That is, *Dust.*
b Jer. 6. 26.
2 Or, *thou that dwellest fairly.*
3 Heb., *inhabitress.*
c Isa. 47. 2, 3.
4 Or, *the country of flocks.*
5 Or, *a place near.*
6 Or, *was grieved.*
7 Or, *for.*
8 That is, *A lie.*

B.C. cir. 730.

9 Or, *the glory of Israel shall come, &c.*
d Isa. 22. 12.

---

approaching—nay, he comes near, even to Jerusalem. The outlying towns are described as shuddering at the invader's advance, but Jerusalem itself is spared.

(10) **Declare ye it not at Gath.**—The prophet lets his lament flow after the strain of David's elegy, "Tell it not in Gath, publish it not in the streets of Askelon." In this passage the parallelism seems to require the name of a town where the English Version has "at all." But the Hebrew word thus represented may, by the addition of a letter which has dropped out of the text, be rendered "in Accho," or Ptolemais, now called Acca. The LXX. translation, Οἱ ἐν Γὲθ μὴ μεγαλύνεσθε, καὶ οἱ Ενακείμ μὴ (=οἱ ἐν 'Ακεὶ μή), accords with this reading. The parallelism is thus maintained, and the thought is completed: "Mention not the trouble in our enemies' cities; bewail it in our own."

(11) **Saphir . . . Zaanan.**—The sites of these cities, like that of Aphrah, are a matter of conjecture. They were probably south-west of Jerusalem, the prophet following the march of the invading army.

The inhabitant of Zaanan came not forth—*i.e.*, they remained in their city through fear of the enemy.

In the mourning of Beth-ezel.—Rather, *the wailing of Beth-ezel shall take from you his standing*—*i.e.*, no support will be found in the inhabitants of Beth-ezel.

(12) **Waited carefully.**—There are various ways of arriving at the interpretation of the words, but the result is the same. The people of Maroth were in distress; they were grieved at the spoiling of their property; they longed for good, but evil was the Lord's decree against Jerusalem.

(13) **Bind the chariot to the swift beast**—*i.e.*, make haste to escape with thy goods. Lachish was the most important of the cities enumerated. It was fortified by Rehoboam, and was sought as a refuge by Amaziah from the conspiracy formed against him in Jerusalem. After the capture of the Holy City by Nebuchadnezzar, Lachish alone remained, with Azekah, of the defenced cities of Judah. It appears, from its position as a border city, to have been the channel for introducing into the kingdom of Judah the idolatry set up by Jeroboam in Israel.

(14) **Give presents**—*i.e.*, thou shalt cease to give to Moresheth-gath the protection due from a husband to a wife: thou shalt give her a bill of divorce. The Hebrew word means either the presents sent *with* a daughter or the dismissal sent *to* a wife.

Achzib.—A town on the sea-coast between Accho and Tyre. Its name means false, deceptive; it is used of a river drying up, and disappointing the traveller. In like manner Achzib shall fulfil the import of its name, and prove a lie, a broken reed, to the kings of Israel. (See also Jer. xv. 18, where the prophet asks God, "Wilt Thou be altogether unto me as a liar [Heb., *Achzab*], as waters that fail?")

(15) **Yet will I bring an heir.**—Rather, *the possessor*, one who shall take it by force—*i.e.*, Sennacherib.

Mareshah was a city in the plain of Judah, near the prophet's native place, Moresheth-gath. It was fortified by Rehoboam, and became the scene of Asa's victory over the immense host of Zerah the Ethiopian. Dr. Robinson is of opinion that after its destruction the town of Eleutheropolis was built out of its materials.

Adullam the glory of Israel.—Adullam, in the neighbourhood of Mareshah, was situated at the base of the hills, and gave its name to the famous cave in which David took refuge. Joshua mentions a king of Adullam in the list of those conquered by the Israelites. This, now the last refuge of the glory of Israel, shall be seized by the invader.

(16) **Make thee bald.**—Joel appeals to the land of Judah to go into deep mourning by reason of the loss of her children, slain in war or carried into captivity. The shaving of the head as a token of grief was common amongst Eastern nations, and is distinct from the idolatrous custom of cutting the hair in a peculiar shape denounced by Jeremiah (chap. ix. 26, margin), and forbidden by the Jewish Law (Lev. xix. 27, 28).

As the eagle.—The Hebrew name for eagle includes the different kinds of vultures. Entire baldness is a marked feature of the vulture.

The terms in which Joel speaks of the entire desolation of the cities of Judah must refer to a more complete calamity than that inflicted by Sennacherib; they rather suit the period of the Babylonian captivity.

II.

(1) **Woe to them that devise.**—The prophet proceeds to denounce the sins for which the country was to receive condign punishment at the hands of God. There is a gradation in the terms employed: they mark the deliberate character of the acts: there were no extenuating circumstances. In the night they *formed* the plan, they *thought it out* upon their beds, and *carried it out* into execution in the morning. So also the gradually increasing intercourse with the wicked is

practise it, because it is in the power of
their hand. (2) And they covet [a] fields,
and take *them* by violence; and houses,
and take *them* away: so they [1] oppress
a man and his house, even a man and
his heritage.

(3) Therefore thus saith the LORD;
Behold, against this family do I devise
an evil, from which ye shall not re-
move your necks; neither shall ye go
haughtily: for this time *is* evil. (4) In
that day shall *one* take up a parable
against you, and lament [2] with a doleful
lamentation, *and* say, We be utterly
spoiled: he hath changed the portion
of my people: how hath he removed *it*
from me! [3] turning away he hath divided
our fields. (5) Therefore thou shalt have
none that shall [b] cast a cord by lot in the
congregation of the LORD.

(6) [4] [5] [c] Prophesy ye not, *say they to
them that* prophesy: they shall not pro-
phesy to them, *that* they shall not take
shame. (7) O *thou that art* named the
house of Jacob, is the spirit of the
LORD [6] straitened? *are* these his doings?
do not my words do good to him that
walketh [7] uprightly? (8) Even [8] of late my
people is risen up as an enemy: ye pull off
the robe [9] with the garment from them
that pass by securely as men averse from
war. (9) The [10] women of my people have
ye cast out from their pleasant houses;
from their children have ye taken away
my glory for ever. (10) Arise ye, and
depart; for this *is* not *your* rest: because
it is polluted, it shall destroy *you*, even
with a sore destruction. (11) If a man
[11] walking in the spirit and falsehood do
lie, *saying*, I will prophesy unto thee of
wine and of strong drink; he shall even
be the prophet of this people.

(12) I will surely assemble, O Jacob,
all of thee; I will surely gather the
remnant of Israel; I will put them
together as the sheep of Bozrah, as the
flock in the midst of their fold: they
shall make great noise by reason of *the
multitude of* men. (13) The breaker is
come up before them: they have broken

a Isa. 5. 8.

1 Or, *defraud.*

2 Heb., *with a lamentation of lamentations.*

3 Or, *instead of restoring.*

b Deut. 32. 8, 9.

4 Or, *Prophesy not as they prophesy.*

5 Heb., *Drop*, &c.

c Isa. 30. 10.

6 Or, *shortened.*

7 Heb., *upright.*

8 Heb., *yesterday.*

9 Heb., *over against a garment.*

10 Or, *wives.*

11 Or, *walk with the wind, and lie falsely.*

---

described, as reaching its culmination, in the first Psalm: *Walking* with the ungodly leads to *standing* among sinners, and at last *sitting* habitually in the seat of the scornful.

(2) **And they covet fields.**—The act of Ahab and Jezebel in coveting and acquiring Naboth's vineyard by violence and murder was no isolated incident. The desire to accumulate property in land, in contravention of the Mosaic Law, was denounced by Micah's contemporary, Isaiah: "Woe unto them that join house to house. that lay field to field, till there be no place, that they may be placed alone in the midst of the earth" (Isa. v. 8).

(3) **I devise an evil.**—As they devise evil against their brethren, so am I devising an evil against them: they shall bow their necks under a hostile yoke.

(4) **Shall one take up a parable against you** —*i.e.*, the enemies shall repeat in mockery the doleful lamentations with which you bewail your pitiable state.

Turning away he hath divided.—Rather, *to an apostate—i.e.*, an idolator—*he hath divided our fields.* The land they were taking from others God would give into the hands of an idolatrous king.

(5) **Thou shalt have none . . .**—*i.e.*, thou shalt have no part or inheritance in the congregation of the Lord—apparently referring to the ancient division of the land by lot.

(6) **Prophesy ye not.**—The construction of this verse is very confused, but the intention of it is fairly clear. It contains the address of the oppressors to the true prophets, and their reply. The oppressors desire the prophets to cease prophesying; nevertheless, the prophecies shall be continued, but without benefit to those who will not put away their shame.

(7) **Is the spirit of the Lord straitened?**—In this verse the prophet expostulates with the people who are the people of the Lord, the house of Jacob, in name only. The Spirit of the Lord, who changeth not, is still the same towards them. They brought their sufferings on themselves; those who put away their shame, and walk uprightly, shall receive benefit from the prophet's words.

(8) **Ye pull off the robe.**—Micah dwells upon the continued rapacity of the people. They robbed the quiet inoffensive traveller of both outer and inner garment; they took away both "cloke" and "coat." (Comp. Matt. v. 40; Luke vi. 29.)

(9) **The women of my people.**—They spared not even the widows and fatherless, the objects of God's tender care.

(10) **This is not your rest.**—The Lord, requiting them for their cruelty to the poor and defenceless, declares that their own time of trouble was imminent. They should be thrust forth from the land which they polluted. It was no place of rest for them. "There is no peace, saith my God, to the wicked."

(11) **If a man walking in the spirit and falsehood**—*i.e.*, in a lying spirit, speaking smooth and pleasant things, such as the people loved to hear, after the fashion of Zedekiah, the son of Chenaanah—he will be a fit prophet for this people. So also Jeremiah spake: "The prophets prophesy falsely . . . . and my people love to have it so; and what will ye do in the end thereof?" (chap. v. 31).

(12, 13) **I will surely assemble . . .**—With a characteristic abruptness Micah turns from the height of sin and punishment to the height of the deliverance—from Ebal to Gerizim. Israel and the remnant shall be gathered together as a goodly flock in the luxuriant pastures of Idumæan Bozrah. The Breaker shall go before them as their Saviour and Deliverer, yea, even Jehovah at their head. The return from captivity symbolised the eventual restoration of the people of God into His everlasting kingdom.

(13) **The breaker.**—"This Breaker is, by the confession of the Jews, the title of the Messias. . . . The

up, and have passed through the gate,
and are gone out by it: and their king
shall pass before them, and the LORD
on the head of them.

CHAPTER III.—(1) And I said, Hear,
I pray you, O heads of Jacob, and ye
princes of the house of Israel; *Is it* not
for you to know judgment? (2) Who
hate the good, and love the evil; who
pluck off their skin from off them, and
their flesh from off their bones; (3) who
also eat the flesh of my people, and flay
their skin from off them; and they
break their bones, and chop them in
pieces, as for the pot, and as flesh within
the caldron. (4) Then shall they cry
unto the LORD, but he will not hear
them: he will even hide his face from
them at that time, as they have behaved
themselves ill in their doings.
(5) Thus saith the LORD concerning
the prophets that make my people err,
that [a] bite with their teeth, and cry,
Peace; and he that putteth not into
their mouths, they even prepare war
against him. (6) Therefore night *shall*
be unto you, [1] that ye shall not have a
vision; and it shall be dark unto you,
[2] that ye shall not divine; and the sun
shall go down over the prophets, and
the day shall be dark over them.
(7) Then shall the seers be ashamed, and
the diviners confounded: yea, they shall
all cover their [3] lips; for *there is* no
answer of God. (8) But truly I am full
of power by the spirit of the LORD, and
of judgment, and of might, to declare
unto Jacob his transgression, and to
Israel his sin.

(9) Hear this, I pray you, ye heads of
the house of Jacob, and princes of the
house of Israel, that abhor judgment,
and pervert all equity. (10) They build
up Zion with [b] [4] blood, and Jerusalem
with iniquity. (11) The heads thereof
judge for reward, and the priests thereof
teach for hire, and the prophets thereof
divine for money: yet will they lean
upon the LORD, [5] and say, *Is* not the

a ch. 2. 11.

1 Heb., *from a vision.*

B.C. 710.

2 Heb., *from divining.*

3 Heb., *upper lip.*

b Ezek. 22. 27; Zeph. 3. 3.

4 Heb., *bloods.*

5 Heb., *saying.*

---

same appeareth by that saying of Moses Haddershan in Bereshith Rabba: 'The plantation from above is Messias; as it is written, the Breaker is come up before them'" (*Pearson, On the Creed*, Art. 6, note).

III.

(1) **Hear, I pray you.**—In the second division of his prophecy Micah protests against the evil influences exercised upon the people in high places. The princes, the prophets, and the priests, to whom their interests were confided, were guilty of wrong, oppression, and robbery.

Ye princes.—Rather, *judges, magistrates;* but a different word is used from that which was given to the chiefs in the old days "when the judges ruled."

(2, 3) **Who hate the good.**—The judges, instead of fulfilling the obligations of their office, whereby they should be "for the people to God-ward," perpetrated the most flagrant cruelty upon them. Micah compares it to the process of preparing food, in which every part of the animal, even to the bones, is utilised. So the judges robbed the people until there was nothing left to them.

(4) **Then shall they cry.**—"Then"—*i.e.*, in the day of retribution—"then shall they call upon me, saith the Lord, but I will not hear: they shall seek me early, but they shall not find me; and that because they hated knowledge, and received not the fear of the Lord, but abhorred my counsel and despised my correction. Then shall it be too late to knock when the door shall be shut, and too late to cry for mercy when it is the time of justice" (Commination Service). So also Isaiah declared (Isa. i. 15): "When ye spread forth your hands, I will hide mine eyes from you; yea, when ye make many prayers, I will not hear: your hands are full of blood."

(5) **That bite with their teeth.**—The concluding statement that the false prophets declare war against those who do not put into their mouth indicates the meaning of the former expression, namely, "they say peace to those who feed and bribe them." The Hebrew word, *nashak,* which is rendered "bite," is strictly applied to serpents, to "an adder in the path," and is therefore especially appropriate to the false and lying nature of the prophets.

(7) **They shall all cover their lips.**—As the lepers, who were cut off from all communication with men, so also these false prophets, being cut off from all communion with God, were to "put a covering upon the upper lip." It was also a sign of mourning for one dead, and Ezekiel was commanded to awaken the astonishment of the people by omitting to cover his upper lip when his wife died.

(8) **I am full of power.**—Micah reverts to his denunciation of sin in high places with the fearlessness of his namesake. He contrasts himself with the prophets of the "lying spirit," and declares his own commission from the Spirit of the Lord, and the ample equipment with which he was endowed.

(10) **They build up Zion with blood**—*i.e.*, they acquire money for the erection of splendid buildings by spoliation and robbery, not stopping short of murder. So also Habakkuk (chap. ii. 12) denounces the king of Babylon for the bloody wars with which he obtained wealth for the enlargement of the city.

(11) **For reward.**—Every function is carried out by judges, priests, and prophets through bribery, and yet they claim and count upon the protection of Jehovah. They rely for safety upon the presence of the sacred buildings; they cry, "The Temple of the Lord, the Temple of the Lord, the Temple of the Lord are these!" "Is not the Lord among us?" Isaiah contrasts in scathing terms the profession of holiness with the vicious life as seen in Jerusalem, and likens the city, with its rulers, to Sodom (chap. i. 10—15).

LORD among us? none evil can come
upon us. (12) Therefore shall Zion for
your sake be [a] plowed *as* a field, and
Jerusalem shall become heaps, and the
mountain of the house as the high
places of the forest.

CHAPTER IV.—(1) But [b] in the last
days it shall come to pass, *that* the
mountain of the house of the LORD
shall be established in the top of the
mountains, and it shall be exalted above
the hills; and people shall flow unto it.
(2) And many nations shall come, and say,
Come, and let us go up to the mountain
of the LORD, and to the house of the
God of Jacob; and he will teach us of
his ways, and we will walk in his paths:
for the law shall go forth of Zion, and
the word of the LORD from Jerusalem.
(3) And he shall judge among many
people, and rebuke strong nations afar
off; and they shall beat their swords
into [c] plowshares, and their spears into
[1] pruninghooks: nation shall not lift up
a sword against nation, neither shall
they learn war any more. (4) But they
shall sit every man under his vine and
under his fig tree; and none shall make
them afraid: for the mouth of the LORD
of hosts hath spoken *it*. (5) For all
people will walk every one in the name
of his god, and we will walk in the name
of the LORD our God for ever and ever.
(6) In that day, saith the LORD, will I
assemble her that halteth, and I will

a Jer. 26. 18.

b Isa. 2. 2, &c.

c Isa. 2. 4; Joel 3. 10.

1 Or, *scythes.*

---

(12) **Therefore shall Zion . . .**—Micah declared this sentence of Divine judgment with an intrepidity that was long remembered by the Jews. More than a century later the elders of the land, speaking in justification of the course taken by Jeremiah, used as a precedent the example of Micah. They spake to all the assembly of the people, saying, "Micah the Morasthite prophesied in the days of Hezekiah, king of Judah, saying, 'Thus saith the Lord of hosts, Zion shall be plowed like a field, and Jerusalem shall become heaps, and the mountain of the house as the high places of a forest.' Did Hezekiah, king of Judah, and all Judah put him at all to death? Did he not fear the Lord, and besought the Lord, and the Lord repented Him of the evil which He had pronounced against them?" (Jer. xxvi. 17—19).

Shall become heaps.—So also, in after-days, the doom of Jerusalem was pronounced by our Lord: "The days will come when there shall not be left one stone upon another that shall not be thrown down."

IV.

(1) **But in the last days.**—There is again a sudden transition. As the third chapter commenced with a startling denunciation, following immediately upon the predicted blessings of the restored kingdom, so upon that chapter, closed in deepest gloom, there now rises a vision of glorious light. The first three verses are almost identical with the second chapter of Isaiah, verses 2 to 4; and it has been almost an open question which of the two prophets is the original author of them, or whether indeed they both adopted the words from an older prophecy current at the time. Dr. Pusey takes very decided ground, saying, "It is now owned, well-nigh on all hands, that the great prophecy, three verses of which Isaiah prefixed to his second chapter, was originally delivered by Micah. . . . No one now thinks Micah adopted that great prophecy from Isaiah" (*Minor Prophets*, p. 289). This last statement, however, is far too sweeping; all that can be correctly said is that the preponderance of opinion is in favour of Micah being regarded as the original writer.

In the top of the mountains—*i.e.*, the mountain of the Lord's house shall be spiritually elevated above all else, visible and invisible, and it shall be established for ever.

(2) **Many nations shall come.**—This prepares the way to the more definitive prophecies, that there shall be a common consent among the nations journeying forth to the house of the Lord: asking the way thither in this world—finding the house itself in the eternal world. Even to this day the hearts of Jews and Christians alike yearn towards Jerusalem—a physical representative of the love which turns spontaneously to the Messiah.

(3) The name of the Messiah is the Prince of Peace; and we still look into the dim future out of a present life, rife with wars and rumours of wars, for the full realisation of His reign of peace. And we are sure that the time will come, for "the mouth of the Lord hath spoken it."

They shall beat their swords . . .—See Note on Joel iii. 10.

(4) **They shall sit . . .**—This was a proverbial expression for the feeling of security brought about by a peace which no foreign power was strong enough to disturb. It describes the state of the Israelites under Solomon—"Judah and Israel dwelt safely, every man under his vine and under his fig tree, from Dan even unto Beersheba, all the days of Solomon." The vine and the fig-tree are the representative trees of Palestine.

(5) **For all people will walk.**—The comparatively near future to Micah, and the still distant future to us, are blended in the prophet's vision: just as in the prophecies of our Lord the destruction of Jerusalem is described in terms which have their final accomplishment in the day of judgment. Micah's description of the universal rule of Messiah is primarily applicable to the antecedent prosperity, after the return of the Jews from the captivity. The zeal of the Jews for Jehovah was stirred up after witnessing the example of "the children of this world" in Babylon. The devotion of the Babylonian princes to their god is strikingly evident in the diaries of Nebuchadnezzar and other prophets, as lately brought to light in *The Records of the Past*. That zealous Society for a national return to the strictness of the Law of Moses at first distinguished and honoured by the name of Pharisees took its rise after the return from the captivity.

(6, 7) **Her that halted.**—Like flocks wearied with heat and journeyings. The promise immediately refers

gather her that is driven out, and her
that I have afflicted; (7) and I will make
her that [a] halted a remnant, and her
that was cast far off a strong nation:
and the LORD [b] shall reign over them in
mount Zion from henceforth, even for
ever.

(8) And thou, O tower of the flock, the
strong hold of the daughter of Zion,
unto thee shall it come, even the first
dominion; the kingdom shall come to
the daughter of Jerusalem. (9) Now
why dost thou cry out aloud? *is there*
no king in thee? is thy counsellor
perished? for pangs have taken thee
as a woman in travail. (10) Be in pain,
and labour to bring forth, O daughter
of Zion, like a woman in travail: for
now shalt thou go forth out of the city,
and thou shalt dwell in the field, and
thou shalt go *even* to Babylon; there
shalt thou be delivered; there the LORD
shall redeem thee from the hand of
thine enemies.

(11) Now also many nations are gathered
against thee, that say, Let her be defiled,
and let our eye look upon Zion. (12) But
they know not the thoughts of the LORD,
neither understand they his counsel:
for he shall gather them as the
sheaves into the floor. (13) Arise and
thresh, O daughter of Zion: for I will
make thine horn iron, and I will make
thy hoofs brass: and thou shalt beat in
pieces many people: and I will conse-
crate their gain unto the LORD, and
their substance unto the Lord of the
whole earth.

CHAPTER V.—(1) Now gather thy-
self in troops, O daughter of troops:
he hath laid siege against us: they shall
smite the judge of Israel with a rod
upon the cheek.

(2) But thou, [c] Beth-lehem Ephratah,
though thou be little among the
thousands of Judah, *yet* out of thee
shall he come forth unto me *that is* to
be ruler in Israel; whose goings forth
have been from of old, from [1] everlasting.

[a] Zeph. 3. 19.

[b] Dan. 7. 14; Luke 1. 33.

[c] Matt. 2. 6; John 7. 42.

[1] Heb., *the days of eternity.*

to the return when God would re-establish the Jews, and eventually come Himself to the restored Temple. And, further, His own promise sanctions the words of Micah as to the abiding character of His rule, that legacy which He left to the Church—"Lo, I am with you alway, even unto the end of the world."

(8) **O tower of the flock.**—Israel having been compared to a flock, Jerusalem is called its tower, or protection; and in Messiah the ancient dominion shall return to the Holy City. This is a more satisfactory interpretation than that which makes the tower of the flock *Migdol-Edah* (Gen. xxxv. 21), a place near Bethlehem.

(9) **Now why dost thou cry out aloud?**—The prophet places again, side by side with his vision of returned glory, the circumstances of misery which will intervene. The king and the counsellors of Jerusalem will be powerless to help in the moment of emergency.

(10) **Thou shalt go even to Babylon.**—This prediction has naturally caused difficulty to thoes who doubt the power of prophets to prophesy: for Babylon was not at all considered in the days of Micah, when Assyria was in the ascendant. It was a century after Micah's time before Babylon recovered its ancient dignity. The fact, however, remains that Micah wrote, "Thou shalt go to Babel;" and there is the other fact, that the people of Judah (not Israel) did go. Micah also declared, "THERE shalt thou be delivered:" and in the time of Cyrus the Jews were delivered there. The repetition, "There . . . there," is emphatic.

(11) **Let her be defiled.**—The seventy-fourth Psalm records the calamity foreseen by the prophet: "They have cast fire into Thy sanctuary, they have defiled (*by casting down*) the dwelling-place of Thy Name to the ground."

Look upon—*i.e.*, contemplate her destruction with pleasure.

(12) **They know not the thoughts of the Lord.**—As a commentary upon this passage, we may compare the message of God with reference to the haughty thoughts of Sennacherib. Then the Lord declared that the Assyrian king was but His instrument in all he had done; so that when he presumed to arrogate to himself the glory of his victories, the Lord revoked his commission: "I will put my hook in thy nose, and my bridle in thy lips, and I will turn thee back by the way by which thou camest." And so it came to pass.

(13) **Arise and thresh.**—Micah, having likened Israel to the sheaves safely gathered, pursues the metaphor by calling upon the daughter of Zion to thresh her enemies after the manner of oxen treading out the corn; and under the symbolism of the horn—the weapon of strength—he promises that God will strengthen her for the work.

I will consecrate.—The better reading is that of the LXX., Vulg., and some ancient versions, which give the second person, *Thou shalt consecrate their gain unto the Lord.* The termination, indicating the first person in our Hebrew Version, may be a form of the old second person feminine, of which there are other examples.

V.

(1) **O daughter of troops.**—This verse coheres better with the former chapter, to which it is attached in the Hebrew Version. Micah again interpolates a prediction of trouble and dismay between the sentences describing triumph and glory. The sentence of smiting the judge has its historical fulfilment in the indignities which happened to King Zedekiah.

(2) **But thou, Beth-lehem Ephratah.**—This is a passage of immense significance, through the interpretation given to it by the chief priests and scribes in the Gospel of St. Matthew. Beth-lehem Ephratah: the two names, modern and ancient, are united, each of them having reference to the fertility of the country.

(3) Therefore will he give them up, until the time *that* she which travaileth hath brought forth: then the remnant of his brethren shall return unto the children of Israel. (4) And he shall stand and [1] feed in the strength of the LORD, in the majesty of the name of the LORD his God; and they shall abide: for now shall he be great unto the ends of the earth.

(5) And this *man* shall be the peace, when the Assyrian shall come into our land: and when he shall tread in our palaces, then shall we raise against him seven shepherds, and eight [2] principal men. (6) And they shall [3] waste the land of Assyria with the sword, and the land of Nimrod [4] in the entrances thereof: thus shall he deliver *us* from the Assyrian, when he cometh into our land, and when he treadeth within our borders.

(7) And the remnant of Jacob shall be in the midst of many people as a dew from the LORD, as the showers upon the grass, that tarrieth not for man, nor waiteth for the sons of men. (8) And the remnant of Jacob shall be among the Gentiles in the midst of many people as a lion among the beasts of the forest, as a young lion among the flocks of [5] sheep: who, if he go through, both treadeth down, and teareth in pieces, and none can deliver. (9) Thine hand shall be lifted up upon thine adversaries, and all thine enemies shall be cut off.

(10) And it shall come to pass in that day, saith the LORD, that I will cut off thy horses out of the midst of thee,

1 Or, *rule.*
2 Heb., *princes of men.*
3 Heb., *eat up.*
4 Or, *with her own naked swords.*
5 Or, *goats.*

In the Gospel the scribes quote, evidently from memory, the passage from Micah, in reply to Herod's question; and their first variation is in the title of the town—"Thou, Beth-lehem (not Ephratah, but), land of Judah." So also the people protested against Jesus on the ground of His being from Galilee, for, "Hath not the Scripture said that Christ cometh of the seed of David, and out of the town of Bethlehem, where David was?" (John vii. 42.)

Though thou be little.—Strictly, *art little* among the thousands, or chiliads: a word analogous to our "hundreds;" a division of the tribes. In St. Matthew the word is paraphrased by princes, as representing the chiliads.

Yet out of thee.—St. Matthew—"for out of thee," the illative conjunction—helps to show that the quotation is really a paraphrase, conveying the ultimate intention of the prophet's words, which contrasts the smallness of the chiliad with the greatness of its destiny.

Whose goings forth have been from of old.—The nativity of the governor of Israel is evidently contrasted with an eternal nativity, the depth of which mystery passes the comprehension of human intellect: it must be spiritually discerned. The Creed of the Church expresses the article of faith as "Begotten of His Father before all worlds." He came forth unto Me to be Ruler in Israel, whose goings forth have been of old, from everlasting, from the days of antiquity.

(3) **Therefore will he give them up.**—There is a suggestion here of a parable, setting forth the smallness of Bethlehem, which gave birth to the mighty Ruler that was to come from it. So the nation was to be brought very low before the nativity of the Virgin-born.

(4) **He shall stand and feed**—*i.e.*, He shall stand with the majesty of an assured sovereignty, uniting the dignity of king with the tenderness of a shepherd's care—a thought which, underlying the notion of a Jewish monarch (see Ps. lxxviii. 70—73), becomes a distinguishing attribute of the King Messiah (Isa. xl. 2; see also Note on Ezek. xxxiv. 2).

His God.—The Messiah was to be subordinate to the Father in heaven—"My Father is greater than I"—and they—*i.e.*, His subjects—shall abide. It is impossible to conceive this prophecy as satisfied by any event short of that which is the foundation of the Christian faith.

(5) **And this man shall be the peace**—*i.e.*, He shall Himself be Peace (after the same idiomatic expression David speaks of himself, "For my love they are my adversaries, but *I* am *Prayer*"—Ps. cix. 4). This sentence is connected with the former instead of the following passage, with which the Authorised Version joins it.

When the Assyrian shall come into our land.—This may refer to the imminent apprehension of the invasion of Sennacherib, but the actual event does not correspond to it. It may look forward to the time when the enemies of Israel attacked the Jews in the Maccabean period, and the shepherds, seven or eight—*i.e.*, an indefinite number—successfully resisted the attacks upon the flock. The intention of the passage may be spiritually interpreted as pointing to the eight principal, strictly anointed men, who, as Christian pastors, receive their commission from the Messiah.

(6) **They shall waste.**—Literally, *feed upon, consume, depasture.* The Land of Nimrod represents the opposing world-power.

(7) **As a dew from the Lord.**—The Jews should, on their return from captivity, pour down their influence upon the nations, as God-sent showers upon the grass. So, through the dispersion of Jewish Christians, on the death of St. Stephen, the Lord caused the knowledge of the truth with which the Jews were cloud-charged to descend upon many people: "He shall come down like rain upon the mown grass; as showers that water the earth" (Ps. lxxii. 6).

(8) **As a lion among the beasts of the forest.**—There is righteous wrath as well as all-embracing mercy with God. Christ, whose graciousness is likened to the dew, and His gentleness to the lamb, is at the same time the Lion of the tribe of Judah. At the opening of the "sixth seal" the kings of the earth and great men are represented as in extreme terror at "the wrath of the Lamb" (Rev. vi. 16).

(10) **It shall come to pass in that day.**—The prophet now passes on to the purification of the Church

and I will destroy thy chariots: (11) and
I will cut off the cities of thy land, and
throw down all thy strong holds: (12) and
I will cut off witchcrafts out of thine
hand; and thou shalt have no *more*
soothsayers: (13) thy graven images also
will I cut off, and thy [1] standing images
out of the midst of thee; and thou
shalt no more worship the work of thine
hands. (14) And I will pluck up thy
groves out of the midst of thee: so will
I destroy thy [2] cities. (15) And I will
execute vengeance in anger and fury
upon the heathen, such as they have
not heard.

CHAPTER VI.—(1) Hear ye now what
the LORD saith; Arise, contend thou
[3] before the [a] mountains, and let the
hills hear thy voice. (2) Hear ye, O
mountains, the LORD's controversy, and
ye strong foundations of the earth: for
the LORD hath a controversy with his
people, and he will plead with Israel.
(3) O my people, what have I done
unto thee? and wherein have I wearied
thee? testify against me. (4) For I
brought thee up out of the land of
[b] Egypt, and redeemed thee out of the
house of servants; and I sent before
thee Moses, Aaron, and Miriam.
(5) O my people, remember now what
[c] Balak king of Moab consulted, and what
Balaam the son of Beor answered him
from [d] Shittim unto Gilgal; that ye
may know the righteousness of the
LORD.
(6) Wherewith shall I come before the
LORD, *and* bow myself before the high
God? shall I come before him with
burnt offerings, with calves [4] of a year
old? (7) Will the LORD be pleased with
thousands of rams, *or* with ten thousands
of rivers of oil? shall I give my first-

1 Or, *statues*.
2 Or, *enemies*.
3 Or, *with*.
a Isa. 1. 2.
b Ex. 12. 51, & 14. 30.
c Num. 22. 5, & 23. 7.
d Num. 25. 1; Josh. 5. 10.
4 Heb., *sons of a year?*

---

from the defilements mentioned by Isaiah (chap. ii. 3—10), with reference to the ultimate holiness which shall be established "in that day."

I will cut off thy horses.—The possession of horses was imperatively forbidden to the Jewish king (Deut. xvii. 16), and Isaiah describes the land as at this time "full of horses, neither is there any end of their chariots." As symbolising the power of man, these horses shall be cut off, and the reliance of the Church shall be on God alone. "Some trust in chariots, and some in horses, but we will remember the name of the Lord our God" (Ps. xx. 7).

(11) **I will cut off the cities.**—Fenced cities and the other paraphernalia of war will be unnecessary in the Messiah's kingdom: "they shall not learn war any more" (chap. iv. 3).

(14) **I will pluck up thy groves**—*i.e.*, either the statues, pillars, or trees connected with the worship of Baal and Astarte. Some such statue was placed by Manasseh even in the house of the Lord, from which it was brought out and burnt by Josiah (2 Kings xxiii. 6).

Thy cities—*i.e.*, the pollutions, tumults, &c., of which the cities were the strongholds.

(15) **Such as they have not heard.**—Rather, *which have not been obedient*—*i.e.*, which had not availed themselves of the opportunities of learning the true religion.

VI.

(1) **Hear ye now what the Lord saith.**—The third portion of Micah's prophecy opens with a solemn appeal to Nature to hear the Lord pleading with His people. A similar summons is found in Deut. xxxii. 1: "Give ear, O ye heavens, and hear, O earth, the words of my mouth."

(4) **For I brought thee up.**—There seems a pause intended; but Israel, abashed, remains silent. So the Lord continues to plead: "Thou dost not testify against me? No; for I showed thee the greatest mercies: I redeemed thee out of Egypt, the house of bondage." Moses, Aaron, and Miriam are mentioned as the three great members of the family to whom it was committed to carry out the Divine decree.

(5) **What Balaam the son of Beor answered.**—This incident is adduced in the "pleading" as a signal instance of the controlling power of God, exercised in an unmistakable manner in behalf of the Israelites. Balaam was constrained to bless when he had the highest conceivable motive to curse the Israelites. He apologised for this involuntary action on his part to Balak. There is no more conclusive instance extant of the will of man controlled to do the exact opposite of his intended action in the history of mankind. It is better to put a stop after "answered him." The next sentence records an independent instance of the interposition of God in behalf of Israel. "Remember also the incidents which happened from Shittim to Gilgal." Shittim was the name of a valley in the plains of Moab (Joel iii. 18), from which place Joshua sent two spies to view Jericho immediately before the passage of the Jordan to Gilgal was effected, under the circumstances mentioned in the fourth chapter of Joshua.

Righteousness.—The word rather means here *liberality, beneficence.*

(6) **Wherewith shall I come . . .?**—This has been taken by some commentators as Balak's question to Balaam, who gives his reply in verse 8. Dean Stanley writes, after his picturesque manner, of "the short dialogue preserved, not by the Mosaic historian, but by the Prophet Micah, which at once exhibits the agony of the king and the lofty conceptions of the great Seer" (*Jewish Church*, Lect. 8). But it is rather in harmony with the context to understand it as the alarmed and conscience-stricken reply of the Jewish people impersonated in some earnest speaker to the pleading brought before them by the prophet in the Lord's name.

(7) **The fruit of my body.**—Will God require the sacrifice of such a precious possession, as Isaac was to Abraham, to atone for my wrong-doing? There

born *for* my transgression, the fruit of
my [1] body *for* the sin of my soul?
(8) He hath [a] shewed thee, O man,
what *is* good; and what doth the LORD
require of thee, but to do justly, and to
love mercy, and to [2] walk humbly with
thy God?
(9) The LORD's voice crieth unto the
city, and [3] *the man of* wisdom shall see
thy name: hear ye the rod, and who
hath appointed it.
(10) [4] Are there yet the treasures of
wickedness in the house of the wicked,
and the [5] scant measure *that is* abomi-
nable? (11) [6] Shall I count *them* pure
with the wicked balances, and with the
bag of deceitful weights? (12) For the
rich men thereof are full of violence,
and the inhabitants thereof have spoken
lies, and their tongue *is* deceitful in
their mouth. (13) Therefore also will I
make *thee* sick in smiting thee, in
making *thee* desolate because of thy
sins. (14) Thou shalt eat, but not be
satisfied; and thy casting down *shall be*
in the midst of thee; and thou shalt
take hold, but shalt not deliver; and
that which thou deliverest will I give
up to the sword. (15) Thou shalt [b] sow,
but thou shalt not reap; thou shalt
tread the olives, but thou shalt not
anoint thee with oil; and sweet wine,
but shalt not drink wine. (16) For [7] the
statutes of [c] Omri are kept, and all the
works of the house of [d] Ahab, and ye
walk in their counsels; that I should
make thee a [8] desolation, and the in-
habitants thereof an hissing: therefore
ye shall bear the reproach of my people.

CHAPTER VII.—(1) Woe is me! for
I am as [9] when they have gathered the
summer fruits, as the grapegleanings of
the vintage: *there is* no cluster to eat:
my soul desired the first-ripe fruit.
(2) The [e] [10] good *man* is perished out of
the earth: and *there is* none upright
among men: they all lie in wait for
blood; they hunt every man his brother
with a net. (3) That they may do evil

1 Heb., *belly*.
a Deut. 10. 12.
2 Heb., *humble thyself to walk*.
3 Or, *thy name shall see that which is*.
4 Or, Is there *yet unto every man an house of the wicked*, &c.
5 Heb., *measure of leanness*.
6 Or, *Shall I be pure with*, &c.
b Deut. 28. 38; Hag. 1. 6.
7 Or, *he doth much keep the*, &c.
c 1 Kings 16. 25, 26.
d 1 Kings 16. 30, &c.
8 Or, *astonishment*.
9 Heb., *the gatherings of summer*.
e Ps. 12. 1; Isa. 57. 1.
10 Or, *godly*, or, *merciful*.

---

may possibly be an allusion to human sacrifices, such as Ahaz offered to Molech, or to the act of Mesha, King of Moab, who "took his eldest son, that should have reigned in his stead, and offered him up for a burnt offering upon the wall."

(8) **To do justly . . .**—God "setteth more by mercy than by sacrifice." So also in Ecclesiastes: "Let us hear the conclusion of the whole matter. Fear God and keep His commandments, for this is the whole of man."

(9) **Unto the city**—*i.e.*, Jerusalem, the metropolis of the wealth and sinfulness of Judah.

The man of wisdom shall see thy name—*i.e.*, will regard it. The sentence may be thrown in parenthetically, as in the warning, "Whoso readeth, let him understand." And he will perceive the hand of God in the visitations for sin.

(10) **The scant measure.**—Literally, *the hateful ephah of leanness*—*i.e.*, less than it should be. The Jews were much addicted to the falsification of weights and measures. They made "the ephah small, and the shekel great, falsifying the balances by deceit" (Amos viii. 5).

(11) **Shall I count them pure?**—Rather, *Can I be innocent with the deceitful balances?* The enactments about weights were very stringently expressed in the Law, both affirmatively and negatively: *e.g.*, in Lev. xix. 35, 36, "Ye shall do no unrighteousness in judgment, in meteyard, in weight, or in measure. Just balances, just weights, a just ephah, and a just hin, shall ye have." And, "thou shalt not have in thy house divers weights," . . . and "divers measures, a great and small" (Deut. xxv. 13, 14).

(12) **The rich men thereof**—*i.e.*, of the city. The sins of spoliation and fraud were practised by men who had not even the pitiable excuse of poverty and distress.

(14) **Thy casting down.**—The Hebrew word is found only in this passage. It comes from an unused root, meaning to be void, empty. Hence it may be translated *hunger*.

Thou shalt take hold.—Thou shalt collect thy property for flight, to save it from the enemy; but in vain: it shall be captured.

(15) **Thou shalt tread the olives**—*i.e.*, as wheat upon the threshing-floor. Oil was regarded as indispensable for personal comfort. In Jotham's parable of the trees in council about the choice of a king, the olive-tree was regarded first in estimation, before even the vine and fig-tree.

(16) **The statutes of Omri.**—The people of Judah, instead of keeping the commandments of the Lord diligently, adopted the statutes of the house of Omri, the founder of the idolatrous dynasty of Ahab. They reproduced the sins of the northern kingdom, and their conduct was aggravated by the advantages vouchsafed to them. The greatness of their reproach should therefore be in proportion to the greatness of the glory which properly belonged to them as the people of God.

VII.

(1) **Woe is me!**—Micah gives here a fearful picture of the demoralised state of society in Judah which had called down the vengeance of God. As the early fig gathered in June is eagerly sought for by the traveller, so the prophet sought anxiously for a good man; but his experience was that of the Psalmist: "The godly man ceaseth; the faithful fail from among the children of men."

(2) **With a net.**—The net, which in the Hebrew term comes from a verb meaning to shut up, was used both by the fisherman and the fowler. "They lay wait for one another, as hunters for wild beasts."

(3) **That they may do evil with both hands earnestly.**—Literally, *well*. Dr. Benisch, in his Old Testament newly translated under the supervision of the Rev. the Chief Rabbi of the United Congregations

with both hands earnestly, the prince
asketh, and the judge *asketh* for a re-
ward; and the great *man*, he uttereth
[1] his mischievous desire: so they wrap
it up. (4) The best of them *is* as a brier:
the most upright *is sharper* than a thorn
hedge: the day of thy watchmen *and*
thy visitation cometh; now shall be
their perplexity. (5) Trust ye not in a
friend, put ye not confidence in a guide:
keep the doors of thy mouth from her
that lieth in thy bosom. (6) For [a] the son
dishonoureth the father, the daughter
riseth up against her mother, the daughter
in law against her mother in law; a man's
enemies *are* the men of his own house.
(7) Therefore I will look unto the
LORD; I will wait for the God of my
salvation: my God will hear me. (8) Re-
joice not against me, O mine enemy:
when I fall, I shall arise; when I sit in
darkness, the LORD *shall be* a light unto
me. (9) I will bear the indignation of
the LORD, because I have sinned against
him, until he plead my cause, and exe-
cute judgment for me: he will bring
me forth to the light, *and* I shall behold
his righteousness. (10) [2] Then *she that is*
mine enemy shall see *it*, and shame
shall cover her which said unto me,
[b] Where is the LORD thy God? mine
eyes shall behold her: now [3] shall she be
trodden down as the mire of the streets.
(11) *In* the day that thy [c] walls are to
be built, *in* that day shall the decree be
far removed. (12) *In* that day *also* he
shall come even to thee from Assyria,
[4] and *from* the fortified cities, and from
the fortress even to the river, and from sea
to sea, and *from* mountain to mountain.
(13) [5] Notwithstanding the land shall be
desolate because of them that dwell
therein, for the fruit of their doings.
(14) [6] Feed thy people with thy rod,

1 Heb., *the mischief of his soul.*

a Matt. 10. 21, 35, 36; Luke 21. 16.

2 Or, *And thou wilt see her that is mine enemy, and cover her with shame.*

b Ps. 79. 10, & 115. 2; Joel 2. 17.

3 Heb., *she shall be for a treading down.*

c Amos 9. 11, &c.

4 Or, *even to.*

5 Or, *After that it hath been.*

6 Or, *Rule.*

---

of the British Empire (1852), avoids the oxymoron of doing "evil" "well" by translating the passage, "concerning the evil which their hands should amend," which satisfactorily harmonises with the rest of the passage.

So they wrap it up.—Literally, *twist it, and pervert the course of justice.*

(4) **The day of thy watchmen**—*i.e.*, the time which thy prophets have foreseen, about which they have continually warned thee. "Also I set watchmen over you, saying, Hearken to the sound of the trumpet. But they said, We will not hearken" (Jer. vi. 17).

(5, 6) **Trust ye not . . .**—All is now distrust and suspicion. The households are divided each against itself, and the relationships which should mean mutual confidence and support have become the occasion of the most bitter hostility. Our Lord adopts these words to express the strife and division which, He foresaw, would defile Christianity. (Comp. Matt. x. 35; Mark xiii. 12; Luke xii. 53.)

(7) **Therefore I will look unto the Lord.**—Because of all this gloom which has settled upon the earth, I, for my part, will lift up mine eyes to the everlasting hills, whereon rests the light of Jehovah's presence.

(8) **O mine enemy.**—The Hebrew word is strictly a female enemy (see verse 10), and is used of enemies collectively. The cities of Babylon and Edom are probably intended. They are mentioned together in Psalm cxxxvii.: "Remember, O Lord, the children of Edom." . . . "O Babylon, that art to be destroyed." The fall of those cities should be final, but Jerusalem would rise again.

(9) **I will bear.**—Micah places himself and his people with confidence in the hands of God. So, too, did David speak when his sin was brought home to him by God: "I am in a great strait; let us fall now into the hand of the Lord: for His mercies are great; and let me not fall into the hand of man" (2 Sam. xxiv. 14). "This is the temper of all penitents when stricken by God, or under chastisement from Him."

(10) **Now shall she be trodden down.**—The enemy that had taunted the Jews with the powerlessness of Jehovah should be trodden down when the Jews were delivered. Such was the experience of Sennacherib, who inquired contemptuously whether the Lord could deliver Jerusalem out of his hand.

(11) **In that day shall the decree be far removed.**—The "decree" was something "definite," as an appointed law or statute, and this should be far removed. Some interpret this prophecy to mean the removal of the law of separation between Jews and Gentiles; others explain it as predicting that the decree of God concerned not the Jews only, but distant nations who should press into the kingdom of God. And this explanation coincides with the effect of the decree, which was to bring to Jerusalem people from "the ends of the world."

(12) **In that day also he shall come.**—Rather translate, *In that day shall they* (*impersonal*) *come even to thee from Assyria and* (*from*) *the cities of Matzor* (i.e., *Egypt*), *and from Matzor even to the river* (*Euphrates*), *and from sea to sea, and* (*from*) *mountain to mountain.* The prophet beholds people coming from all parts of the earth to Jerusalem. Isaiah foresaw the like future, and spoke of Assyria, Egypt, and Israel being assembled together, "whom the Lord of Hosts shall bless, saying, Blessed be Egypt, my people, and Assyria, the work of my hands, and Israel, mine inheritance" (Isa. xix. 25). The Christian reader can hardly refrain from discerning on the horizon of Micah's vision that marvellous assembly of the representatives of the nations in Jerusalem on the Day of Pentecost.

(13) **Notwithstanding the land shall be desolate.**—There is still bitterness in the cup. In the midst of the triumphant expectation of the glory to come, there rises up the vision of the desolation of the land in the near future, by reason of the sins of the people.

(14) **Feed thy people with thy rod.**—Or, *with thy shepherd's crook.* The prophet lifts up his prayer

the flock of thine heritage, which dwell solitarily *in* the wood, in the midst of Carmel: let them feed *in* Bashan and Gilead, as in the days of old.

(15) According to the days of thy coming out of the land of Egypt will I shew unto him marvellous *things*. (16) The nations shall see and be confounded at all their might: they shall lay *their* hand upon *their* mouth, their ears shall be deaf. (17) They shall lick the [a] dust like a serpent, they shall move out of their holes like [1] worms of the earth: they shall be afraid of the LORD our God, and shall fear because of thee.

(18) Who *is* a God like unto thee, that [b] pardoneth iniquity, and passeth by the transgression of the remnant of his heritage? he retaineth not his anger for ever, because he delighteth *in* mercy. (19) He will turn again, he will have compassion upon us; he will subdue our iniquities; and thou wilt cast all their sins into the depths of the sea. (20) Thou wilt perform the truth to Jacob, *and* the mercy to Abraham, which thou hast sworn unto our fathers from the days of old.

a Ps. 72. 9.

1 Or, *creeping things*.

b Exod. 34. 6, 7.

---

for the people, either dwelling "alone" among the idolaters of Babylon—among them, but not of them—or living a nation, mysteriously apart from other nations, returned from Babylon, and settled on the fruitful mountain range of Carmel, or in the rich pasture land on the east of Jordan. The extraordinary fertility of this "Land of Promise" has been recently brought into prominence, and its future prosperity predicted in glowing colours by Mr. Oliphant, in *The Land of Gilead*.

(15) **According to the days of thy coming out.**—The promise of Jehovah, in reply to the prophet's supplication, graciously recalls His interposition in the land of Egypt. This interposition shall be repeated.

(17) **They shall lick the dust like a serpent.**—The doom of the determined enemies of the Lord and His people recalls that of Satan, the great enemy, as personified by the serpent. "Dust shalt thou eat all the days of thy life" (Gen. iii. 14).

(18) **Who is a God like unto thee?**—Micah, with an allusion to the significance of his own name, concludes his book with a burst of enthusiastic homage to the God of gods. The gracious character here ascribed to Jehovah is unparalleled in the Bible in human utterances; it is the response of the prophet to the glorious words spoken by Jehovah of Himself (Exod. xxxiv. 6, 7). The promise there made to Moses is here extended by the inspiration of the prophet to the Gentiles. The "remnant" refers to the returned from the captivity.

(20) **Thou wilt perform.**—The closing words in the prophecy of Micah are gloriously taken up some centuries later by Zechariah: "As He spake by the mouth of His holy prophets, which have been since the world began: that we should be saved from our enemies, and from the hand of all that hate us, to perform the mercy promised to our fathers, and to remember His holy covenant, the oath which He sware to our father Abraham, that He would grant unto us, that we being delivered out of the hand of our enemies, might serve Him without fear, in holiness and righteousness before Him, all the days of our life" (Luke i. 54, 55).

NAHUM

INTRODUCTION

TO

NAHUM

I. The Author.—This composition gives us absolutely no information about its author beyond the fact that he styled himself "Nahum the Elkoshite." As it is not known where "Elkosh" is, and it is not impossible that "Nahum," "comforter," is a *nom de plume*, the personality of this prophet is as shadowy as those of Obadiah and Malachi. His date can only be conjectured from his allusions to political events (*vide infra*). If "Nahum" be regarded as a pseudonym, the book will be one of *comfort* to Israel, in that it treats of the overthrow of the notoriously oppressive Assyrian power. Apostolic titles such as "Peter" and "Barnabas" supply an analogue, and some have supposed that "Malachi," "my messenger," is also a title adopted for a special prophetic mission. The symbolical names in Isa. viii. 3, 4; Hosea i. 3, 7, may also be instanced. But the addition of the second designation, "the Elkoshite," tells against the theory that "Nahum" is an assumed appellation. It is natural to interpret the whole title on the analogy of "Elijah the Tishbite," making Nahum the real name of the man, Elkosh that of his abode or birthplace.

Elkosh remains to be discovered. Jerome's guide identified it with *Elcesi*, "a little village in Galilee, small, indeed, and scarcely indicating by its ruins the traces of ancient buildings" (Jerome, *Comm. on Nah.* I., 1). Eusebius mentions Ἐλκεσέ as a Palestinian town "whence was Nahum the Elkesæan," but does not say in what part it lay. Cyril of Alexandria merely says it was somewhere in the country of the Jews. On the other hand, certain modern writers have moved Elkosh altogether away from Jewish territory, and identified it with Alcush, a village within two days' journey of Mosul, where the grave of the prophet is exhibited. This site is favoured chiefly because it brings Nahum close to the scene of the catastrophe which he so graphically describes. It appeared impossible that Nahum could see in a vision the future fall of Nineveh. Date and locality were therefore shifted till the seer of Israel became a historian living in Assyria. The choice of this village Alcush is scarcely creditable to the critical acumen of this school of expositors. There is absolutely nothing to identify Nahum with the place save the pretended tomb, and this has no more claim to genuineness than the tombs of Jephthah, Jonah, and Obadiah in neighbouring localities. "The house containing the tomb," writes Mr. Layard, "is a modern building." Not till the sixteenth century was the place even mentioned in connection with the prophet Nahum. The legend doubtless rests on no more substantial basis than a similarity of sound. It may be added that there is every reason to regard the name Elkosh as of Hebrew derivation (see Fürst, *Lexic.*). The place doubtless lay within the borders of the Holy Land, but it is impossible to determine its situation more precisely.

II. Occasion of Writing.—The object of this composition is sufficiently shown us in the opening words of chap. i.: "The burden of [or sentence against] Nineveh." Nahum treats of the downfall of the Assyrian empire, consequent on the capture of its metropolis, Nineveh. In chap. i. the prophet's attention appears to be fixed mainly on the last Assyrian invasion of Judæa—that which resulted in the destruction of Sennacherib's host recorded in 2 Kings xix. This catastrophe had doubtless already taken place. It is used by the seer as an earnest of a yet more momentous future. Sennacherib's disaster was the first act in a tragedy of which the *dénoûment* lay yet in the womb of time, discernible only to God and God's inspired prophets. The "vision" of Nahum reveals this unknown issue in chapters ii. and iii. Nineveh, the Assyrian metropolis, the centre of oppression, the "bloody city," is to fall before besiegers; her population to be led away captive, her site to remain "empty, void, and waste." We attribute Nahum's knowledge of this catastrophe, which obviously identifies itself with the destruction of Nineveh by the Medes and Babylonians (B.C. 625), to Divine inspiration. The event is certainly future. It is not past not even immediately impending. To prove even the possibility of its happening, the prophet is forced to instance the sack of another mighty city, "populous No" (chap. iii. 8—11). The writer, moreover, claims to be giving an account of a "vision" (chap. i. 1). Were he limited to the events of the past or the present, the claim would be an impertinence, the whole composition robbed of its significance. None will refuse to see predictive inspiration here, save those who start on the assumption that this form of Divine communication is impossible, and that all such prophets as Nahum are mere historians.

For those who are not hampered by this theological prejudice, Nahum's date will be in the period preceding the catastrophe; but it can only be fixed approximately. He writes to foretell the fall of Nineveh; therefore, before B.C. 625. His prophecy is quoted by Zephaniah, therefore it was probably uttered some years before B.C. 630 (see Zephaniah, *Introduction, II.*). He writes, instancing the sack of Thebes; therefore, we believe, not before B.C. 670, perhaps not before B.C. 665 * (see chap. iii. 8—10, Notes). His composition may be assigned to any year between B.C. 665 and B.C. 635.

The great historical event anticipated by Nahum's vision must now be noticed. The Assyrians had been the leading power in Upper Asia for upwards of five hundred years. The original abode of this great tribe appears to have been the flat alluvial plain towards the mouths of the Tigris and Euphrates. From this

* Another terminus in the backward direction is the death of Sennacherib, to which Nahum refers in chap. i. 14 (see Note). This event occurred in B.C. 680.

region Assyrian hordes are found migrating northwards as early as B.C. 1600. The colonists were probably subjugated for awhile by the Babylonians, but before B.C. 1550 had established a monarchy of their own. This gradually rose to equal rank with that of Babylon. Tiglathi-Nin (B.C. 1270) styles himself the "conqueror of Babylonia." It is certain, however, that the rival empire was not effectually weakened till the time of Sargon (B.C. 721), and it appears that nearly every Assyrian monarch engaged in expeditions against Babylonia. The Assyrian empire was at its zenith under Sennacherib (B.C. 704), who records successful campaigns against Babylonia, Susiana, Egypt, Syria, Judæa, and Cilicia, and who is even more eminent as a builder and patron of art than as a conqueror. It would perhaps have been in stricter accordance with the ground-plan of Nahum's prophecy if the decline of the Assyrian power had begun from the time when Sennacherib's army was annihilated before Jerusalem. Josephus states that this was the case. Esar-Haddon's reign, however, was scarcely, if at all, less glorious than that of Sennacherib; and Asshur-bani-pal is described as "a warrior more enterprising and more powerful than any of his predecessors" (*Five Great Monarchies*, ii. 493). The crash came in the time of this king's unwarlike successor, Asshur-emid-ilin, called by the Greek historians, Saracus. Somewhere about the thirteenth year of this reign, the Medes rose in arms, and invaded Assyria. They were repulsed with the loss of their leader and of many soldiers. Their next king, Cyaxares, was interrupted in his preparations for another attack by an invasion of Scythian hordes, who inflicted great damage, both on Media and Assyria. He succeeded in expelling these intruders, and again marched against Nineveh. He was joined by the Susianians and by a faithless Assyrian dependent, Nabo-polassar, king of Babylon. The siege, according to Ctesias, lasted three years. It may well be believed that a city 22½ miles in circumference (Xenophon, *Anab.* iii. 4), with walls 100 feet high, wide enough to admit three chariots abreast, with towers, moreover, 1,200 in number, and each 200 feet high (Diod. Sic. ii. 3), would defy the operations of troops who had hitherto had little experience in siege-work. An important victory was, however, gained at a time when the Assyrian host was celebrating its triumph in revelry. Saracus now resigned the chief command to his brother-in-law, Salæmenes, who experienced another disastrous defeat. The city, however, continued uninjured apparently, until the spring of the third year. Then, according to Ctesias (Diod. Sic. ii. 27), a new power appeared on the side of the besiegers. Heavy rains had fallen and increased the volume of the river. An inundation ensued, which carried away a considerable part of the fortifications (see chap. ii. 6, Note, and comp. chap. i. 8). Saracus saw in the catastrophe the fulfilment of an oracle. He set fire to his citadel, and perished with his concubines and eunuchs in the flames. The enemy entered unopposed, "through the broken part of the wall," and carried off an immense booty to Babylon and Ecbatana.

Ctesias is often untrustworthy and inaccurate; but it is quite credible that his account of the fall of Nineveh is substantially correct. "His account," to borrow the words of Dr. Pusey, "as it is in exact conformity with the obvious meaning of the prophecy of Nahum, so it solves a real difficulty, how Nineveh, so defended, could have fallen." Another remarkable coincidence between the prophecy of Nahum and the historical fact has been noticed by the same commentator. The usual sequel to the capture and sack of a city was not its destruction, but its repeopling. The captors of Nineveh proceeded to destroy it with fire, and it remained uninhabited. The fragments disinterred by excavations at the palaces of Kouyunjik, Khorsabad, and Nimroud bear the marks of this conflagration (comp. chap. ii. 13, iii. 13, 15). Nineveh remained as Nahum had predicted, "a desolation," "empty and void, and waste" (chap. i. 8, ii. 10). Xenophon saw its walls, and went away with a story that "the Medes inhabited it formerly" (*Anab.* iii. 12). Alexander marched by, "not knowing that a world-empire like that which he gave his life to found was buried under his feet" (Pusey). In the second century A.D. Lucian writes, "Nineveh has perished, and there is no trace left where it once was." (Comp. chap. iii. 7, *seq.*, and Zeph. ii. 13, *seq.*)

III. **Contents.**—The chief divisions of Nahum's composition appear to be these:—(*a*) chap. i. 2—8, Jehovah's very character is a guarantee that He will right the oppressed faithful, and annihilate their enemies; (*b*) chap. i. 9—15, the bootless expedition of Sennacherib is portrayed, chiefly with reference to the relief his overthrow afforded Israel, and his own miserable end; (*c*) chap. ii. 1—end, the siege of Nineveh and its issue—viz., the extinction of the ravening oppressor; (*d*) iii. 1—end, a more extended statement of the cause of this catastrophe, and the utter ruin thereby effected.

IV. **Character and style.**—Nahum's composition is descriptive rather than hortatory. Chap. i. 2—8 includes all the ethical or theological teaching of this prophet, and even here picturesque portraiture predominates. The rest of the book presents a series of historical scenes; all of which may be regarded as illustrating the great religious principles laid down in the opening verses. These scenes reveal in their portraiture the master-hand of a true poet. In poetic ability, indeed, Nahum ranks high among the prophets. His chief excellence consists in word-painting of forcible terseness. Chaps. ii. 11—13, iii. 16, 17 are the only places where a figure is expanded. The usual tendency is to compress each thought into the smallest possible compass. The description of the siege in chap. ii. 3—10 is a very model of this kind of sententious eloquence. In his diction Nahum is markedly original. He abounds in peculiarities of expression. These may perhaps be connected with a provincial idiom, but they cannot be attributed to any foreign source. Here and there a resemblance to Joel, Isaiah, and the Psalms perhaps argues indebtedness to earlier authors. He is himself often imitated by Jeremiah. (Comp. chap. i. 13, Jer. xxx. 8; chap. iii. 5, Jer. xiii. 22; chap. iii. 13, Jer. l. 37, li. 30; chap. iii. 19, Jer. x. 19, and see Jer. li. *passim.*) It has been said that Nahum should be read as a supplement to the Book of Jonah. The mission of both prophets concerned Nineveh. The one composition describes the remission of Divine punishment on this offending city, and the other its execution, Nahum i. 3 being a kind of connecting-link between the two phases of God's character—His longsuffering and His justice. In point of style and diction, however, no two prophetic books are more unlike. The nature of Nahum's subject precludes any but the most meagre allusion to his own country, and we learn nothing with regard to the Jewish politics of the time. Save by way of type—the destruction of the oppressive world-power figuring the victory of the Church over the world—there is nothing in the book that bears on the Christian dispensation.

NAHUM

CHAPTER I. — (1) The burden of
Nineveh. The book of the vision of
Nahum the Elkoshite.
(2) [1]God *is* [a]jealous, and the LORD re-
vengeth; the LORD revengeth, and [2]*is*
furious; the LORD will take vengeance
on his adversaries, and he reserveth
wrath for his enemies. (3) The LORD [b]*is*
slow to anger, and great in power, and
will not at all acquit *the wicked*: the
LORD *hath* his way in the whirlwind and
in the storm, and the clouds *are* the dust
of his feet. (4) He rebuketh the sea, and
maketh it dry, and drieth up all the
rivers: Bashan languisheth, and Carmel,
and the flower of Lebanon languisheth.
(5) The mountains quake at him, and
the hills melt, and the earth is burned
at his presence, yea, the world, and all
that dwell therein. (6) Who can stand
before his indignation? and who can
[3]abide in the fierceness of his anger?
his fury is poured out like fire, and the
rocks are thrown down by him.
(7) The LORD *is* good, a [4]strong hold in
the day of trouble; and he knoweth
them that trust in him. (8) But with an
overrunning flood he will make an utter
end of the place thereof, and darkness
shall pursue his enemies.
(9) What do ye imagine against the
LORD? he will make an utter end:
affliction shall not rise up the second
time. (10) For while *they be* folden to-
gether *as* thorns, and while they are
drunken *as* drunkards, they shall be

B.C. cir. 713.

1 Or, *The LORD is a jealous God, and a revenger*, &c.

a Ex. 20. 5.

2 Heb., *that hath fury*.

b Ex. 34. 6, 7.

3 Heb., *stand up*.

4 Or, *strength*.

---

(1) **The burden of Nineveh**—*i.e.*, the *sentence* against Nineveh (see Isa. xiii. 1, Note). On the names Nahum and Elkoshite see Introduction.

(2—8) God's character a pledge that the oppressor of His servants shall be destroyed.

(2) **God . . . furious.**—Better, *A jealous and vengeful God is Jehovah, an avenger is Jehovah, aye, wrathful.* This verse lays the groundwork for the declaration of God's sentence against the offending city. There are, of course, several passages in the Law which attribute the same character to Jehovah, *e.g.*, Exod. xx. 5; Deut. iv. 24. Nahum's model, however, is a passage of opposite purport, the well-known proclamation of Jehovah's attribute of mercy (Exod. xxxiv. 6, 7). To that passage the present is a kind of counterpoise, *Ēl kannô v'nôkêm* here being the pendant to *Ēl rachoom v'channoon* there.

(3) **And great in power.**—Better, *but great in power.* Jehovah's forbearance is not attributable to weakness. To vindicate His power, Nahum, after the manner of other Hebrew poets and prophets, reverts to the wonders of the Exodus (verses 4, 5). The pillars of cloud and fire in the desert march; the quaking cliffs of Sinai; the Red Sea and Jordan divided at His word; Canaan succumbing at every point, upwards to mighty Lebanon in the north, and across from Eastern Bashan to Western Carmel—these are the testimonies to Jehovah's might. (Comp. Hab. iii. 6—10.)

(5) **Is burned.**—Better, *heaves.*

(8) **But.**—Better, *and.* Jehovah protects His afflicted servants, and therefore He exterminates their oppressor.

Overrunning flood.—On the propriety of this figure see chap. ii. 6, Note.

The place thereof—*i.e.*, that of Nineveh. The verse ends, "*and he shall drive his enemies into darkness.*"

(9—15) The first revelation of God's judgment, by the awful overthrow of Sennacherib's invading army in the reign of Hezekiah.

(9) **Affliction**—*i.e.*, Nineveh's affliction of Israel, the same Hebrew word being used in verse 7 to denote Israel's "trouble" or "affliction" proceeding from Nineveh. (See also verse 12.) Nineveh shall not afflict Israel a second time. Applying the whole passage to the destruction of Sennacherib's host, we necessarily prefer this to the other possible interpretation—God will not have occasion to send affliction on Nineveh a second time, *i.e.*, this visitation will be so exhaustive that there will be no need to repeat it. For the judgment on Sennacherib was *not* God's final visitation.

(10) **For while.**—Better, *For they shall be even as bundles of thorn fagots, and even while steeped in their drink they shall be burnt up like stubble fully dry.* Dry thorn cuttings were commonly used as fuel. (See Pss. lviii. 9, cxviii. 12; Eccl. vii. 6.) The verse compares the victims of Jehovah's wrath, first, to a compact bundle of thorn fagots; secondly, to a material equally combustible, the dry straw and stubble of the threshing-floor. With regard to the words "while steeped in their drink," it may be remarked that in the final siege of Nineveh a great defeat of its forces was effected by a surprise while the king and his captains were sunk in revelry (Diod. Sic. ii. 26). Benhadad, king of Syria, and Belshazzar, king of Babylon, were overcome under similar circumstances (1 Kings i. 16; Dan. v. 1—30). Feasting and revelry may have gone on in Sennacherib's camp at the moment when the sudden visitation of the

devoured as stubble fully dry. (11) There
is *one* come out of thee, that imagineth
evil against the LORD, [1] a wicked coun-
sellor.
(12) Thus saith the LORD; [2] Though
they be quiet, and likewise many, yet
thus shall they be [3] cut down, when he
shall pass through. Though I have
afflicted thee, I will afflict thee no more.
(13) For now will I break his yoke from
off thee, and will burst thy bonds in
sunder. (14) And the LORD hath given a
commandment concerning thee, *that* no
more of thy name be sown: out of the
house of thy gods will I cut off the
graven image and the molten image:
I will make thy grave; for thou art
vile.
(15) Behold upon the [a] mountains the
feet of him that bringeth good tidings,
that publisheth peace! O Judah, [4] keep
thy solemn feasts, perform thy vows:
for [5] the wicked shall no more pass
through thee; he is utterly cut off.

CHAPTER II.—(1) [6] He that dasheth
in pieces is come up before thy face:
keep the munition, watch the way, make
thy loins strong, fortify *thy* power
mightily. (2) [b] For the LORD hath turned
away [7] the excellency of Jacob, as the
excellency of Israel: for the emptiers

1 Heb., *a counsellor of Belial.*
2 Or, *If they would have been at peace, so should they have been many, and so should they have been shorn, and he should have passed away.*
3 Heb., *shorn.*
a Isa. 52. 7; Rom. 10. 15.
4 Heb., *feast.*
5 Heb., *Belial.*
6 Or, *The disperser,* or, *hammer.*
b Isa. 10. 12.
7 Or, *the pride of Jacob as the pride of Israel.*

"angel of the Lord" was impending; but on this point we have no information. The introduction of this detail adds to the metaphor a certain grim humour. Soaked in wine though the enemy be, he shall surely burn like driest fuel in the day of Jehovah's fiery wrath. The opening clause of the verse is beset with difficulties, both grammatical and lexical. Kleinert renders "For in thorns they shall be entangled," &c.; Ewald and Hitzig, "For even though they be compact as a wickerwork of thorns," &c.

(11) **Come out of thee.**—Another possible rendering is, *He has retired from thee* [*i.e., Jerusalem*], *who imagineth* . . . We prefer the rendering of the Authorised Version, and regard the verse as addressed to Nineveh. The reference in the verses following is sufficiently plain for us to identify this enemy of God with Sennacherib. (Comp. the language used by his envoy Rabshakeh in 2 Kings xviii., xix.)

(12) **Thus saith the Lord.**—Better, *Thus saith Jehovah, Though they be of unimpaired strength and ever so numerous, yet just in that state shall they be cut down, and he* [viz., the evil counsellor of verse 11] *shall pass away. Though I have afflicted thee* [Jerusalem], *I will afflict thee no more.* Destruction comes upon the Assyrian army in the very hour of prosperity, while unscathed and complete in numbers (2 Kings xix. 32, 33). *Pass away:* so in Ps. xlviii. (a composition generally thought to refer to this very catastrophe), "For lo, the kings were assembled: they *passed away* together."

(13) **Now will I break.**—Similarly Isaiah, "I will break the Assyrian in my land, and upon my mountain tread him under foot: then shall his yoke depart from off them, and his burden depart from off their shoulders" (Isa. xiv. 25; comp. Jer. xxx. 8).

(14) **And the Lord hath given.**—Sudden changes of person are a common feature in Hebrew poetry. The denunciation of the Assyrian here passes from the third to the second person. Sennacherib is told that the royal line of Nineveh is to be suddenly exterminated—a prediction accomplished when his great-grandson Saracus, the last king of Nineveh, destroyed himself in despair. He is also told that the Assyrian idols are destined to destruction, and that their very temple is to witness his own death; the prophet's expression being, *I will make it thy grave: for thou art found worthless* (lit. "light in the balance"—comp. Dan. v. 27). "And it came to pass as he was worshipping in the house of Nisroch his god that Adrammelech and Sharezer his sons smote him with the sword" (Isa. xxxvii. 38). The allusion to Sennacherib's death in the temple of Nisroch appears to us unassailable. That it was admitted in the earliest times is shown by the accentuation and the translation given by the Targum. Keil's explanation that the "Assyrian power personified" is addressed, and that "I am preparing thy grave" is the true rendering, simply emasculates this vigorous passage. If, as is probable, Sennacherib's death had already occurred, it would be strange indeed that Nahum should make no mention of this memorable instance of Divine retribution, while at the same time using words so capable of bearing the allusion.

(15) **Behold upon the mountains.**—It is not plain why this verse has been made the first of chap. iii. in the Hebrew. It is evidently the finale of the proclamation against the Assyrian invader, and rightly stands in the LXX. as the last verse of chap. ii. It portrays the announcement of Sennacherib's fate to the towns and villages of Judah. "From mountain-top to mountain-top by beacon fires they spread the glad tidings. Suddenly the deliverance comes, sudden its announcement. *Behold*, Judah, before hindered by armies from going up to Jerusalem, its cities taken, may now again *keep the feasts* there, and *pay the vows* which in trouble she promised; *for the wicked one*, the ungodly Sennacherib, *is utterly cut off; he shall no more pass through thee* (Pusey). The opening clause necessarily reminds one of the description of deliverance in Isa. lii. 7. The one author probably borrows the language of the other; but which passage we regard as the original must depend on the view taken of the Book of Isaiah.

II.

The siege and sack of Nineveh described. From the destruction of Sennacherib's host in 699 B.C., and his death in the temple of Nisroch in 680, the prophet suddenly passes to the extermination of the Assyrian Empire, cir. 625. Here then, strictly speaking, is the beginning of Nahum's "vision," chap. i. 9—15 being limited to the great blow sustained by Assyria in the preceding generation.

(1) **Keep the munition.**—Better, *guard the fortress.* These four sententious directions to Nineveh are, of course, ironical, like Elijah's instructions to the priests of Baal in 1 Kings xviii. 27. "He that dasheth in pieces" may perhaps be identified with Cyaxares.

(2) Better, *For Jehovah restores the glory of Jacob, so that it is as the glory of* [ancient] *Israel, though the*

have emptied them out, and marred
their vine branches. (3) The shield of
his mighty men is made red, the valiant
men *are* [1] in scarlet: the chariots *shall*
be with [2] flaming torches in the day of
his preparation, and the fir trees shall
be terribly shaken. (4) The chariots
shall rage in the streets, they shall justle
one against another in the broad ways:
[3] they shall seem like torches, they shall
run like the lightnings. (5) He shall re-
count his [4] worthies: they shall stumble
in their walk; they shall make haste to
the wall thereof, and the [5] defence shall
be prepared. (6) The gates of the rivers
shall be opened, and the palace shall be

1 Or, *dyed scarlet.*
2 Or, *fiery torches.*
3 Heb., *their show.*
4 Or, *gallants.*
5 Heb., *covering,* or, *coverer.*

---

plunderers plundered them and marred their vine shoots. The sacred nation is Jehovah's vine, destined to send out its tendrils all over the earth. But Jehovah has allowed its hedge to be broken down. "All they that go by do pluck her . . ." (Ps. lxxx. 12, 13). In the punishment of one notoriously oppressive world-power the prophet sees a pledge that the branch of Jehovah shall be again "beautiful and glorious" (Isa. iv. 2). The construction in the first part of the verse is perplexing. It appears best to attach a special emphasis to the names "Jacob" and "Israel" in connection with their original signification. "Jacob" is the birth-name—the nation regarded apart from its religious privileges, the homeless exile, the down-trodden "worm" (Isa. xli. 14), the younger son among nations. But "Israel" is the chosen of God; he who "had power over the angel and prevailed"; the "beloved son, called out of Egypt." The name given by Jehovah is henceforth to have its full significance, as in the days of old. "Jacob," the name which is so often used after the deportation of the ten tribes, is again to be indicated as "Israel," the favoured people of God. Some commentators render, "For Jehovah restores alike the glory of Jacob and the glory of Israel," &c., making "Jacob" the designation of the southern, "Israel" that of the northern kingdom. But the term "Jacob" nowhere else has this distinctive force.

(3) **His mighty men.**—That is, those of the besieger of verse 1.

Made red.—That is, with blood; not with reference to the bright red copper, which was the material of the shield, for the word usually means "dyed red."

In scarlet.—Red was the favourite colour, not only of the Medes, from whom Xenophon says the Persians obtained their purple tunics, but also of the Babylonians; compare the description in Ezek. xxiii. 14, 15, and Layard's *Nineveh*, p. 347. Both Medes and Babylonians were engaged in the present siege. The rest of the verse runs, *the chariots are* [equipped] *with flashing steel in the day of his preparation, and the cypress lances are brandished.* The "flashing steel" may refer to ornaments of this material attached to the chariot, or, as we incline to think, to scythes or sharp instruments fastened to the wheels. Some form of this weapon may well have been in use long before the present date. Xenophon relates that Cyrus was the first to introduce the scythe-chariot: Ctesias, however, speaks of it as of much earlier origin. The older Hebrew commentators render this word *p'lâdôth,* "torches," as in the Authorised Version. With this rendering, the swiftly-moving war-chariots are likened to flashing torches, as they are in the next verse.

Verses 4 and 5 describe the state of the city while sustaining this siege. There is a slight contrast between this portraiture and that of verse 3, which has been made the most of by Kleinert. "Without, God arranges His hosts; within is the disorder of wild terror: without, a steady approach against the city; within, a frantic rushing hither and thither: without, a joyful splendour; within, a deadly paleness, like torch-light." The last part of verse 4 is thus made a description of the aspect of the Ninevites, not their chariots. This appears to us a fanciful interpretation. In its behalf, the description of a panic in Isa. xiii. 8 has been adduced: "They shall be amazed one at another; their faces shall be as *flames.*" But it is obviously better to restrict the reference throughout to the chariots of the besieged city, darting hither and thither in wild undisciplined attempts to resist the invader's onset.

(5) **And the defence shall be prepared.**—Better, *but* [there] *the storming-shed has been prepared.* Here the surprise and disorder of Nineveh is more plainly portrayed. The Assyrian king bethinks him of his stoutest warriors, but they *stumble in their paths* in nervous perplexity. Men hie to the city wall, but against it the besiegers have already erected their storming-shed—a proceeding which ought to have been prevented by the discharge of stones and other missiles from the walls. The storming-shed protected the battering-rams. Of the representations of these preserved in the monuments of Nineveh, Professor Rawlinson thus writes: "All of them were covered with a framework, which was of osier wood, felt, or skins, for the better protection of those who worked the implement. . . . Some appear to have been stationary, others provided with wheels. . . . Again, sometimes combined with the ram and its framework was a movable tower containing soldiers, who at once fought the enemy on a level, and protected the engine from their attacks" (*Ancient Monarchies*, i. 470).

(6) **The gates of the rivers.**—This verse is one of great importance. The account of Ctesias, preserved by Diodorus Siculus, tells us that for over two years the immense thickness of the walls of Nineveh baffled the engineering skill of the besiegers; but that "in the third year it happened that by reason of a continual discharge of great storms, the Euphrates (*sic*) being swollen, both inundated a part of the city and overthrew the wall to the extent of twenty stadia." The king saw in this the fulfilment of an oracle, which had declared that the city should fall when "the river became an enemy to the city." Determined not to fall into the hands of his foes, he shut himself up with all his treasures in the royal citadel, which he then set on fire. We believe that this account, though inaccurate in detail, may be regarded as based on a substratum of historical fact. So gigantic were the fortifications of Nineveh, that of those on the east, where the city was most open to attack, Mr. Layard writes: "The remains still existing . . . almost confirm the statements of Diodorus Siculus that the walls were a hundred feet high, and that three chariots could drive upon them abreast" (*Nineveh and Babylon*, p. 660). Against ramparts such as these the most elaborate testudo of ancient times may well have been comparatively

[1] dissolved. (7) And [2] Huzzab shall be
[3] led away captive, she shall be brought
up, and her maids shall lead *her* as with
the voice of doves, tabering upon their
breasts. (8) But Nineveh *is* [4] of old like
a pool of water: yet they shall flee away.
Stand, stand, *shall they cry;* but none
shall [5] look back. (9) Take ye the spoil
of silver, take the spoil of gold: [6] for
there is none end of the store *and* glory
out of all the [7] pleasant furniture. (10) She
is empty, and void, and waste: and the
[a] heart melteth, and the knees smite
together, and much pain *is* in all loins,
and the faces of them all gather black-
ness.
(11) Where *is* the dwelling of the lions,
and the feedingplace of the young lions,
where the lion, *even* the old lion, walked,
and the lion's whelp, and none made
them afraid? (12) The lion did tear in
pieces enough for his whelps, and
strangled for his lionesses, and filled his
holes with prey, and his dens with ravin.
(13) Behold, I *am* against thee, saith the
LORD of hosts, and I will burn her
chariots in the smoke, and the sword
shall devour thy young lions: and I will
cut off thy prey from the earth, and the
voice of thy messengers shall no more
be heard.

CHAPTER III.—(1) Woe to the [8][b] bloody
city! it *is* all full of lies *and* robbery;
the prey departeth not; (2) the noise
of a whip, and the noise of the rattling

1 Or, *molten.*

2 Or, *that which was established,* or, *there was a stand made.*

3 Or, *discovered.*

4 Or, *from the days that she hath been.*

5 Or, *cause them to turn.*

6 Or, *and their infinite store, &c.*

7 Heb., *vessels of desire.*

a Isa. 13. 7, 8.

8 Heb., *city of bloods.*

b Ezek. 24. 9; Hab. 2. 12.

---

powerless. On the other hand, the force of a swollen river has often proved suddenly fatal to the strongest modern masonry. It would be specially destructive where, as in the case of Nineveh, the walls inundated were of sun-dried brick or "clay-bat." Thus the fate of the city may well have been precipitated in accordance with the terse prediction of this verse. The "gates of the rivers" (*i.e.*, the dams which fenced the Khausser, which ran through Nineveh, and the Tigris, which was outside it) are forced open by the swelling torrents, and lo, the fate of the city is sealed! ramparts against which the battering-ram might have plied in vain are sapped at the very foundation; palace walls are undermined, and literally "dissolve;" the besieger hastens to avail himself of the disaster, and (in the single word of verse 7) *it-is-decided.* It is unnecessary to identify the "palace" which thus succumbs. Neither is it a reasonable objection that the palaces of Khorsabad and Kouyunjik, lying near the Khausser, bear the marks of fire, not water. If Nahum must have in mind some particular palace, it may be fairly argued that water is not such a demonstrative agency as the sister element; and that nothing would so effectively conceal the damage done by the inundation as the subsequent conflagrations effected by the victorious besieger. The verb *nâmôg,* "dissolved," we thus take in its literal signification of the dissolution of a solid substance by the action of water; not as Dr. Pusey, figuratively, of the "dissolution of the empire itself."

(7) **And Huzzab shall be led away captive . . .**—Better, *And it is decided. She is laid bare. She is removed away. And her maidens moan, as with the cry of doves, smiting on their breasts.*

It is decided, or *established—c'est un fait accompli.* The Authorised Version apparently follows those Rabbinic commentators who treat the Hebrew expression *hutstsab* as the name of an Assyrian queen, or as a symbolical designation of Nineveh. The word is best regarded as a verb-form cognate to the expression rendered by the Authorised Version "of certainty," "certain," "true," in Dan. ii. 48, iii. 24, vii. 16. *Laid bare,* the common figure of the virgin city put to shame by capture (comp. Isa. xlvii. 1—5). The "maidens" who "moan as with the cry of doves" (comp. Isa. xxxviii. 14; lix. 11; Ezek. vii. 16) are probably Nineveh's dependent cities. These are represented as standing gazing on the awful catastrophe, groaning aloud and beating the breast (comp. Luke xxiii. 48) in a horror of despair.

(8) We prefer to adopt the slight change of reading favoured by the LXX. (*mêymeyhâ* for *mîmêy hî*), and to render, *And Nineveh, like a pool of water are her waters, and they* [her inhabitants] *are fleeing away.* The waters which formerly flowed in river-courses and dykes are now one vast expanse of inundation. A panic thereupon seizes the inhabitants. If the present text be maintained, the rendering of the Authorised Version will stand. We may then suppose the heterogeneous population of Nineveh to be compared to "countless drops, full, untroubled, with no ebb or flow, fenced in from the days that she hath been, yet even therefore stagnant and corrupted; not 'a fountain of living waters'" (Pusey). But this appears to us a far-fetched comparison.

The pregnant terseness of the last part of the verse will give the English reader a good idea of Nahum's style and the difficulties therewith connected.

(9) **And glory.**—Better, *there is abundance of all precious vessels.*

(10) **And the faces of them all gather blackness.**—Better, perhaps, *and all faces withdraw their brightness.* (See Note on Joel ii. 6, where the same expression occurs.)

(11—13) The figure of the lion appears so frequently on the Assyrian monuments that we may perhaps suppose it to have been a national scutcheon. The metaphor of the ravening beast is well illustrated by the Assyrian records, wherein the most frequent theme is the levying of gold, silver, brass, oxen, &c., from tributary cities. The "messengers" of verse 13 are royal heralds and delegates, subordinate agents in this business of extortion.

III.

The catastrophe enlarged upon in respect to its provoking cause, and its fearful results.

(1) **Woe to the bloody city!**—Better, *O bloody city! She is altogether deceit, filled with crime: she ceases not from plunder.*

(2) **The noise of . . .**—Better, *Hark to the whip, and hark to the rattling of the wheel, and the*

of the wheels, and of the pransing horses,
and of the jumping chariots. (3) The
horseman lifteth up both [1]the bright
sword and the glittering spear: and
there is a multitude of slain, and a great
number of carcases; and *there is* none
end of *their* corpses; they stumble upon
their corpses: (4) because of the multi-
tude of the whoredoms of the well-
favoured harlot, the mistress of witch-
crafts, that selleth nations through her
whoredoms, and families through her
witchcrafts. (5) Behold, I *am* against
thee, saith the LORD of hosts; and [a]I
will discover thy skirts upon thy face,
and I will shew the nations thy naked-
ness, and the kingdoms thy shame.
(6) And I will cast abominable filth upon
thee, and make thee vile, and will set
thee as a gazingstock. (7) And it shall
come to pass, *that* all they that look
upon thee shall flee from thee, and say,
Nineveh is laid waste: who will bemoan
her? whence shall I seek comforters for
thee?

(8) Art thou better than [2][3]populous
No, that was situate among the rivers,
that had the waters round about it,
whose rampart *was* the sea, *and* her wall
was from the sea? (9) Ethiopia and
Egypt *were* her strength, and *it was* in-
finite; Put and Lubim were [4]thy helpers.
(10) Yet *was* she carried away, she went
into captivity: her young children also
were dashed in pieces at the top of all
the streets: and they cast lots for her
honourable men, and all her great men
were bound in chains.

(11) Thou also shalt be [b]drunken: thou
shalt be hid, thou also shalt seek
strength because of the enemy. (12) All
thy strong holds *shall be like* fig trees

1 Heb., *the flame of the sword, and the lightning of the spear.*

a Isa. 47. 3; Ezek. 16. 37.

2 Or, *nourishing.*

3 Heb., *No Amon.*

4 Heb., *in thy help.*

b Jer. 25. 17.

---

horse galloping, and the chariot bounding. The entry of the victorious besiegers is here described.

(3) **The horseman lifteth up.**—Better, *There is the rearing horseman and the flaming sword, and the glittering lance, and a multitude of wounded, and a mass of corpses . . .*

(4—6) **Because of the multitude.**—In the idolatry and superstition of Nineveh the prophet finds the cause of her destruction. Perversion of religious instinct is frequently denounced under the same figure in Scripture. Here, however, a more literal interpretation is possible, since there is reason to believe the religious rites of Assyria were characterised, like those of Babylon, by gross sensuality. According to Herod. i. 199, the Babylonian worship of Beltis or Mylitta was connected with a system of female prostitution, which was deemed "most shameful" even by the heathen historian. Compare also the Apocryphal Book of Baruch vi. 43. The same deity was worshipped in Assyria. Professor Rawlinson writes: "It would seem to follow almost as a matter of course that the worship of the same identical goddess in the adjoining country included a similar usage. It may be to this practice that the prophet Nahum alludes when he denounces Nineveh as a 'well-favoured harlot,' the multitude of whose harlotries was notorious" (*Five Great Monarchies*, ii. 41).

(7) **Shall flee from thee.**—As in the case of the destruction of Korah, men flee from the stricken city lest they share her punishment. Nor is she an object of compassion whose cruelties have been as extensive as her empire. Hers is the fate of the fallen tyrant—left to

——————"vainly groan,
With pangs unfelt before, unpitied and alone."

(8) **Populous No.**—Better, *No Amon.* Thebes, the capital of Upper Egypt, was known to the Hebrews as "No Amon" (perhaps, "house of the god Amon;" similarly the Greeks called it Διόσπολις). Assyria herself had reduced the power of Thebes. (1) Sargon, the father of Sennacherib, had defeated Shebah, the Egyptian Tar-dan, at Rapikh, cir. B.C. 716. (2) Esar-haddon, Sennacherib's son, had routed the forces of Tirhakah, subjugated the whole of the Nile valley, and taken the city where Tirhakah held his court, probably Thebes, cir. B.C. 670. (3) Asshur-bani-pal invaded Egypt in the year of his accession, B.C. 668, and reinstated certain rulers of his father's appointment, whom Tirhakah had driven out. In B.C. 665, another revolt brought this king again into Egypt. On this occasion Thebes was certainly sacked, and a large booty, including "gold, silver, precious stones, dyed garments, captives (male and female), tame animals brought up in the palace, obelisks, &c., was carried off, and conveyed to Nineveh" (*Five Great Monarchies*, ii. 203). The present passage may refer either to this event or to Esar-haddon's previous capture of Thebes. The fall of the city was certainly a thing of the past when Nahum wrote. The allusion, therefore, helps us to assign the date of the composition (see Introduction). To mere human reasoning the downfall of Thebes testified to the power of Assyria, its conqueror. But to the inspired vision of Nahum, the ruin of the one world-power is an earnest of the ruin of the other. Both had been full of luxury and oppression, both were hated of mankind and opposed to God. If No-Amon has fallen, the city of the hundred gates, the metropolis of the Pharaohs, the conqueror whose countless captives reared the pyramids, why shall Nineveh stand? If Nineveh is protected by rivers—the Tigris and the Khausser—had not Thebes a rampart in the Nile, that "sea" of waters (comp. Isa. xix. 5), and its numerous canals? If Nineveh relies on subordinate or friendly states—Mesopotamia, Babylonia, Syria—had not Thebes all the resources of Africa—Ethiopia in the south, the Egypts in the north, her Libyan allies, Put and the Lubim, in the north-west? Yet what was the fate of No Amon? Her youth carried off in the slave-gangs of Assyria; her infants dashed to pieces at the street-corner (2 Kings viii. 12), as unprofitable to the captor; her senators reserved to grace a triumph, and assigned to the Assyrian generals by lot (Obad. 11).

(11, 12) **Thou also shalt be drunken.**—Nineveh also shall be *drunken* with the cup of God's wrath (see Hab. ii. 16), yea, *hid* from recollection, so that men shall ask, "Where is Nineveh?" (Comp. chap. ii. 11.). She,

with the firstripe figs: if they be shaken,
they shall even fall into the mouth of
the eater. (13) Behold, thy people in the
midst of thee *are* women: the gates of
thy land shall be set wide open unto thine
enemies: the fire shall devour thy bars.
(14) Draw thee waters for the siege,
fortify thy strong holds: go into clay,
and tread the morter, make strong
the brickkiln. (15) There shall the fire
devour thee; the sword shall cut thee
off, it shall eat thee up like the canker-
worm: make thyself many as the can-
kerworm, make thyself many as the
locusts. (16) Thou hast multiplied thy
merchants above the stars of heaven:
the cankerworm [1] spoileth, and fleeth
away. (17) Thy crowned *are* as the
locusts, and thy captains as the great
grasshoppers, which camp in the hedges
in the cold day, *but* when the sun ariseth
they flee away, and their place is not
known where they *are*. (18) Thy shep-
herds slumber, O king of Assyria: thy
[2] nobles shall dwell *in the dust*: thy
people is scattered upon the mountains,
and no man gathereth *them*. (19) *There*
is no [3] healing of thy bruise; thy wound
is grievous: all that hear the bruit of
thee shall clap the hands over thee: for
upon whom hath not thy wickedness
passed continually?

1 Or, *spreadeth himself.*

2 Or, *valiant ones.*

3 Heb., *wrinkling.*

---

too, shall vainly *seek a fortress* (Authorised Version, "strength") to give her shelter, all her own strongholds having fallen as easily as the ripe fruit from the fig-tree.

(13) **Thy people . . . are women,** not in their notoriously effeminate and luxurious habits (see Layard, p. 360), but with reference to their panic-stricken condition at the time of the catastrophe. They are fearful as women (comp. Jer. l. 37, li. 30), because they find avenues laid open to the enemy, and the remaining defences consuming in the flames.

(14) **Draw thee waters.**—In this desperate plight Nineveh is scoffingly advised to protract her resistance. The outer walls are broken down; let her hold out in the citadel. Nay, let her begin anew her preparations for defence. Let her lay in water and provision, and build new buttresses of brick. What shall it avail her? In the midst of her preparations, fire and sword shall again surprise her. The account of this last struggle for existence is minute. Nahum goes back to the repair of the brick-kiln, just as Isaiah, in his description of idol-worship, goes back to the smith working with the tongs, and the carpenter measuring with his rule (Isa. xliv. 12, *seq.*). In both cases the irony gains force by a minute and elaborate description of operations destined to be futile.

(15, 16) The diversion of metaphor here is somewhat repugnant to modern taste. The sword, like the locust, shall devour Nineveh. Yet Nineveh is immediately afterwards compared in its numbers, destructive influence, and sudden disappearance to the locust. It is a transition like St. Paul's "going off at a word." The comparison of the locust suggests the thought that Nineveh herself has been a locust-pest to the world, and the direction of the metaphor is thereupon suddenly changed. A paraphrase will best bring out the meaning. (15) "Hostile swords devour thee, as a locust swarm devours. Vainly clusters together thy dense population, itself another locust-swarm. (16) Yea, as the stars of heaven for number have been thy merchants, as a pest of locusts which plunders one day and is gone the next."

(16) **Spoileth.**—Better, *spreads itself out*: swarms out to spoil.

(17) **Thy crowned.**—The subordinate kings who represent the Assyrian empire in her tributary provinces.

Captains.—*Taphs'rím*, an Assyrian term denoting some high military office. The sudden disappearance of the Assyrian locust-pest is here enlarged upon. A sudden outburst of sunshine will sometimes induce a swarm of locusts to take flight; cold, on the other hand, makes these insects settle, and soon deprives them of the power of flying. Dr. Pusey well observes, "The heathen conqueror rehearsed his victory, 'I came, I saw, conquered.' The prophet goes further, as the issue of all human conquest, 'I disappeared.'" The insect designations, rendered in Authorised Version, "cankerworm," "locust," "great grasshopper," all represent varieties of the locust species.

(18) **Shepherds**—*i.e.*, chief officers, as in Micah v. 2 and *passim*. Their sheep are "scattered upon the mountains and none attempts to gather them." So Micaiah announces to Ahab, "I saw all Israel scattered upon the hills as sheep that have not a shepherd" (1 Kings xxii. 17).

Thy nobles shall dwell.—Better, *thy mighty men are lying still.*

(19) **Clap the hands over thee.**—All that hear the "bruit" or report of the fall of Nineveh clap their hands with joy (Ps. xlvii. 1), for where has not her oppressive rule been felt? The verse is addressed to the king (second person masculine) as the representative of the empire, perhaps also in view of his terrible end. The cruelty of the Ninevite *régime* is illustrated, as Kleinert remarks, in the sculptures, "by the rows of the impaled, the prisoners through whose lips rings were fastened, whose eyes were put out, who were flayed alive. Consequently it would be a joy to all nations to hear the voice of the messengers of the tyrant no more (chap. ii. 14), but to hear that of the messengers of his destruction."

HABAKKUK

INTRODUCTION

TO

HABAKKUK

I. **The Author.**—Habakkuk's own words lead to the inference that he prophesied shortly before the battle of Carchemish, B.C. 605, and therefore in the reign of Jehoiakim (*v. infra*). But we are told nothing concerning his tribe, birthplace, or personal history. The earliest legend bearing on these points is in the apocryphal book, "Bel and the Dragon." It is there recorded (verses 33 *seq.*), that the prophet Habakkuk was commissioned by an angel to feed Daniel in the den of lions, and that for this purpose he was miraculously transported from Judæa to Babylon. The story, worthless in itself, nevertheless indirectly confirms the theory of "date," which we have accepted below. Its existence indicates that the Jewish tradition connected Habakkuk's ministry with the period of Babylonish captivity—with the reign of Jehoiakim, rather than with those of Manasseh, Amon, or Josiah. Another point of interest in the legend is the superscription in Cod. Chisianus of the LXX. (from Origen's Tetraplar, and the Syro-Hexaplar), claiming Habakkuk himself as the author of "Bel and the Dragon." This superscription runs, "From the prophecy of Habakkuk, the son of Joshua, of the tribe of Levi." The reference to the prophet's tribe has attracted special attention, in view of the prescription in chap. iii. 19: "To the chief musician upon *my* stringed instruments." It has been inferred, from the use of the possessive pronoun, that Habakkuk was capacitated for taking a Levite's part in the Temple services. This inference, however, is devoid of substantial basis. It is possible that the term *n'gînôthay* is a dual form, not the plural with the possessive affix—a "double-stringed instrument," not "my stringed instruments." And whatever the meaning of the term, King Hezekiah prescribes the same liturgical use at the end of his psalm in Isa. xxxviii. (Heb. *n'naggên n'gînôthay*, Authorised Version, "We will sing my songs to the stringed instruments.") But Hezekiah was not a Levite. Why must Habakkuk have been one? In fact, the passage (chap. iii. 19) proves nothing whatever with regard to the prophet's tribe. The superscription to "Bel and the Dragon" must be judged on its own merits; and it merely shows that a Jewish tradition of early date made "Joshua" the name of Habakkuk's father, and Levi his tribe.

Later and less respectable traditions appear in the Rabbinic writings. Such is the legend that Habakkuk was the watchman set by Isaiah to observe the destruction of Babylon, a legend based on a combination of Isa. xxi. 16 and chap. ii. 1. Such, too, is the tradition repeated by Abarbanel, that the prophet was that son of a Shunammite woman whom Elisha restored to life (2 Kings iv.). Etymology has here, as in other cases, become the parent of an absurd myth. The name Habakkuk is connected by derivation with the verb *châbak*, "to embrace." In 2 Kings iv. 16 occur the words "thou shalt embrace (*châbak*) a son." This is the sole foundation of the tradition. In this connection we remark that there is no reason to give the name "Habakkuk" any symbolical meaning whatever. It was probably the name which the prophet bore from childhood, not an official or ministerial designation.

II. **Occasion of Writing.**—Habakkuk is summoned to announce Jehovah's intention of punishing the iniquities which prevail among his compatriots. The instruments who are to effect this Divine chastisement are the armies of Chaldæa, or Babylonia (chap. i. 6). Their invasion shall effect a catastrophe of strange and incredible extent: men "shall not believe it, though it be told them" (chap. i. 5). The prophet warns his compatriots that this chastisement shall come "in your days"—*i.e.*, ere the present generation has passed away (chap. i. 5). Most commentators have recognised that the denunciation is to be explained by the events which followed the great battle at Carchemish on the Euphrates, B.C. 605. This battle suddenly brought the chosen nation under the heel of the Babylonian conqueror, Nebuchadnezzar. Jewish sympathy had been on the losing side—that of the Egyptian Pharaoh-Necho, for the Jewish king Jehoiakim was the nominee of Egypt, and Jeremiah had vainly tried to detach his countrymen from the cause of the southern empire. It was only natural that Nebuchadnezzar's victory was followed by an invasion of Judæa. Jehoiakim apparently came to terms with the conqueror, and was suffered to retain his throne as a tributary of Babylon. Three years later he was ill-advised enough to renounce this allegiance. Nebuchadnezzar punished his insubordinate dependent by the agency of other vassals, the Syrians, Moabites, and Ammonites. Judah was ravaged, and a period of great misery ensued. Jehoiakim fell, perhaps by the hands of his own subjects. His son and successor, Jehoiachin, seems to have continued his unwise policy of resistance. Within fourteen weeks of his accession, Nebuchadnezzar himself came up and besieged Jerusalem. The king surrendered himself and his family, and his deposition immediately followed. Nebuchadnezzar now sacked Jerusalem. "And he carried out thence all the treasures of the house of the Lord, and the treasures of the king's house . . . and he carried away all Jerusalem, and all the princes, and all the mighty men of valour, even ten thousand captives, and all the craftsmen and smiths: none remained save the poorest sort of the people of the land" (2 Kings xxiv. 13, 14). It is, we believe, to this crowning disaster that Habakkuk's sentence points—"Behold ye . . . . and wonder marvellously, for I will work a work in your days which ye will not believe, though it be told you" (chap. i. 5).

We have now to consider how far the prophetic sentence is separated in point of time from its completion. Those commentators who repudiate or minimise the preternatural element in the prophetic Scriptures have insisted that Habakkuk's composition must have followed, not preceded, the battle of Carchemish. Critics of the opposite school have, on the contrary, laboured to prove that Habakkuk wrote when no Chaldæan invasion was expected, placing the prophet's date even as far back as the reign of Manasseh (B.C. 698—643). In this behalf it is argued that chap. i. 5 implies that the prophet's readers were altogether unacquainted with the Chaldæans, and would be amazed at the announcement of their approach. Thus Dr. Pusey writes:—"In that he speaks of that invasion as a thing incredible to those to whom he was speaking, he must have prophesied before Babylon became independent by the overthrow of Nineveh, B.C. 625. For when Babylon had displaced Nineveh, and divided the Empire of the East with Media and Egypt, it was not a thing incredible." This argument is, however, of no real value. It is perfectly allowable to interpret chap. i. 5 as we have done above, by the *sequel* of Nebuchadnezzar's invasion. Such a catastrophe as overtook Jerusalem in the reign of Jehoiachin may well have appeared incredible, even after the battle of Carchemish.

Cœteris paribus, the phraseology of chap. i. 6, "Lo, I raise up the Chaldæans," would lead us to infer that the great battle had not yet been fought, nor the Chaldæan king installed as suzerain of Judæa. And this inference has certainly nothing opposed to it but the presumption of modern critics that predictive inspiration has no place in the Hebrew Scriptures, and that the utterances of the prophets are mere *vaticinia post eventum*. On the other hand, common sense suggests that the detailed account of Chaldæan manners and morals given in chap. ii. is based on personal experience. Both writer and readers would seem to be acquainted with the Babylonians—their wild appearance, their vast success, their overweening ambition, their peculiar vices. (See chap. i. 7, 8; ii. 5 *seq.*) To admit such an acquaintance as this is not necessarily to disparage Habakkuk's power of prediction. No experience of such a kind could have justified an expectation of the astounding catastrophe foretold in chap. i. 5 *seq.* Before Judæa could be invaded by the Babylonians, Egypt, the suzerain of Jehoiakim, had to be defeated. And who could have foreseen the actual issue of the battle by the Euphrates? As Dr. Pusey argues, human foresight would rather have predicted another Egyptian triumph at Carchemish. The balance of probability certainly inclined on the side of those "prophets, diviners, dreamers, enchanters, and sorcerers" who told the Jews, "Ye shall not serve the king of Babylon" (Jer. xxvii. 9). It is plain, therefore, that we may place Habakkuk's date, for the sake of chap. ii., in a period when the Babylonian invasion was imminent, and the character of the eastern empire well known in Judæa, and yet in no way impugn his predictive powers, or his Divine legation. His claim to be a "seer" remains unshaken, albeit he only sees into a future not far distant.

It is important to recognise this distinction, because (apart from the details in chap. ii.) the internal evidence seems to point to no earlier reign than Jehoiakim's—*i.e.*, to a date not more than five years anterior to the battle of Carchemish. This will be gathered from the following analysis:—

(*a*) The prophecy can hardly have been uttered more than thirty years before the catastrophe predicted, for chap. i. 5 asserts that it shall occur "in the days" of the present generation. This inference precludes our assigning the prophecy to the reign of *Manasseh*, which came to an end about thirty-eight years before the battle of Carchemish.

(*b*) The successors of Manasseh were Amon (B.C. 643—641) and Josiah (B.C. 641—610). The years B.C. 643—623 (from the accession of Amon to Josiah's Reformation) may be regarded as forming one distinct period, a period of fearful religious decadence. To such an extent did false worship spread during these years, that the female devotees of the *a'shêrâh* (Authorised Version, "grove") set up their obscene rites in the house of the Lord itself. (See 2 Kings xxiii. 4—7.) Josiah, in B.C. 623, had to purge the temple of the *a'shêrâh*, and of vessels made for Baal. Even by those who retained the knowledge of God, Moloch was often put on an equal footing with Jehovah (Zeph. i. 5). Now had Habakkuk written in this period, surely he would, like Zephaniah, have included this fearful prevalence of idolatry among the national sins which called for God's chastisement (chap. i. 1—4). At any rate, he could hardly with consistency ignore these sins at home, and yet denounce Chaldæan idol-worship abroad (chap. ii. 18, 19). Still less appropriate would be an appeal to Jehovah's presence "in His holy Temple" (chap. ii. 20). Nor would such a season be suitable for the composition of a hymn expressly designed for public liturgical performance; see chap. iii. 1, 19.

(*c*) Neither can we find a suitable place for Habakkuk's ministry in the latter part of Josiah's reign (B.C. 623—610). The sweeping reformation of this king's eighteenth year is not likely to have left behind it social disorders such as Habakkuk complains of in chapter i. A king who could put away "workers with familiar spirits, and wizards, and the images and the idols, and all the abominations that were spied in the land of Israel," would surely not have spared the class-oppression and judicial maladministration described in chap. i. 2—4. Prophecies there certainly were at this time of a Divine chastisement on Jerusalem for the sins of the former generation (comp. 2 Kings xxiii. 27 with 2 Chron. xxxiv. 23 *seq.*). But we know of no denunciation of iniquities still existent. Nor is there any reason to believe that the disorders of the preceding period survived Josiah's Reformation.

(*d*) This brings us to 610, the year of the accession of Jehoahaz and Jehoiakim. The former reigned oppressively three months, and was deposed by Pharaoh-Necho in favour of his brother, Eliakim, whose name was changed to Jehoiakim. Bad as both these kings were, they do not appear to have undone Josiah's work of ecclesiastical reform. The worship of Jehovah continued. A hymn for public performance in the Temple would not now be an anomaly as in the reign of Amon. On the other hand, oppression and maladministration prevailed, such as Habakkuk deplores. Jehoiakim's "eyes and heart were only for covetousness, and for to shed innocent blood, and for oppression and violence to do it" (Jer. xxii. 17). Under such a ruler the state of society would necessarily be such as is depicted in chap. i. 1—4. The minute account of the Chaldæans (chap. ii.) is also suitable enough in this reign. In the reign of Josiah, the Jews were probably less perfectly acquainted with Babylonian habits.

The only plausible argument against this theory of date is one that is easily disposed of. It has been argued from a comparison of chap. ii. 20, Zeph. i. 7, that Habakkuk is quoted by Zephaniah, and the latter we know wrote in Josiah's reign. The similarity of diction in these two passages is certainly remarkable. It is perhaps sufficient to prove that one prophet quoted the other, for the phrase "hush at the presence of" (*has mipp'nêy*) does not occur elsewhere. But there is not a particle of proof that Habakkuk did not borrow the phrase from Zephaniah, rather than Zephaniah from Habakkuk. The former explanation is quite as admissible as the latter, although Zephaniah is, as a rule, more dependent on earlier sources than Habakkuk. A close resemblance may be detected also between Hab. i. 8 and Jer. iv. 13. Here, however, there is no reason to think that there is any citation, and the question of date is not affected. We conclude, on the grounds specified above, that Habakkuk's prophecy dates from the reign of Jehoiakim, not more than five years at most before the battle of Carchemish—how much nearer that great event it is impossible to say.

III. **Contents.**—The book of Habakkuk falls into four main divisions (*a*) chap. i. 1—11; (*b*) chap. i. 12 to ii. 20; (*c*) chap. iii. 1—15; (*d*) chap. iii. 16—19. The contents of these divisions may be thus analysed:—

(*a*) While the prophet deplores the anarchy, oppression, and social disorder which prevail among his countrymen (chap. i. 1—4), Jehovah announces that the Chaldæans are commissioned to execute a chastisement of fearful severity (chap. i. 5). The appearance, character, and operations of these invaders are described (chap. i. 6—11).

(*b*) Habakkuk expostulates with God. The sins of his countrymen are surpassed by the cruelty and godless arrogance of the Chaldæans. Is the sacred people to be exterminated by such a race as this? (chap. i. 12—17). After patient waiting, he receives Jehovah's answer. The judgment is yet to be developed. Final triumph is not for the proud godless invader, but for him who waits on Jehovah in faith (chap. ii. 1—4). The sins of the Chaldæans are denounced—viz., drunkenness, greed, cruelty, insatiable ambition, and degraded idolatry. Justice demands their punishment. Jehovah is in His holy temple; let the world await His sentence in silence (chap. ii. 5—20).

(*c*) In a poem of great power and beauty (chap. iii. 1—15), Habakkuk describes the Divine interposition. God shall reveal Himself as He did in the time of the Exodus and the Judges. The nations shall tremble as they see the works of His creation—mountains, rivers, seas, yea, sun and moon in their courses—all acknowledging His awful presence.

(*d*) The prophet reverts to the earlier revelation, and describes his own emotion at the prospect of the impending invasion. But in the midst of the anticipated calamities—war, devastation, and famine—he will cling confidently and cheerfully to Jehovah the all-powerful (chap. iii. 16—19).

IV. **Character and style.**—The historical importance of Habakkuk's composition will be gathered from what has been said under the preceding headings. Nahum concluded the Divine sentences against Assyria; Habakkuk is summoned to denounce the new world-power, whose metropolis is Babylon. Of predictive power we had a remarkable instance in Nahum: the same gift is claimed by Habakkuk, and illustrated scarcely less strikingly. For the Christian, however, the permanent value of this composition lies, not merely in this obvious stamp of inspiration, but in its underlying tone of deep personal faith. It is this that has made certain texts of Habakkuk so familiar to us. The passage, chap. ii. 4 is memorable as pressed into service in those Pauline Epistles which were written to guard the infant Church against Judaism. It received a new and somewhat fatal significance during the religious struggles of the sixteenth century. But for the sincere disciple of Christ it still retains that appropriate application which is given it in Heb. x. 37. "Yet a little while, and He that is to come will come, and will not tarry. The just shall live by faith"—what more suggestive motto for the Church oppressed by the powers of this world, or for the individual believer, beset by the dark hour of perplexity and doubt? Scarcely less familiar is that grand expression of confidence, amid troubles, with which the Book of Habakkuk closes—chap. iii. 17—19. Persevering, patient faith; this is the principle which characterises the whole composition of the prophet Habakkuk, and which still endears it to the Christian. For him its value lies mainly in its practical teaching—

> "To learn from self to cease,
> Leave all things to a Father's will,
> And taste before Him lying still,
> E'en in affliction, peace."

With respect to Habakkuk's manner of writing, it may be said that he shows himself master of two styles, very different in appearance. In the first two chapters, he writes tersely—not so tersely as Nahum—more so than Zephaniah. This part of the book is of an homiletic character, and is sententious, rather than picturesque. Much of it is in a dialogue form. The prophet complains or expostulates: Jehovah answering, denounces or consoles. Chapter iii., on the other hand, introduces a vision of Divine interposition, framed as a lyrical poem. The style necessarily changes with the subject Terseness gives place to florid eloquence, sententious denunciation to an exuberance of ornate description. Here Habakkuk is seen at his best. He is not strictly an original poet, for much of the diction is based on earlier compositions. To Deut. xxxii., Judges v., Ps. lxviii. he owes the same kind of debt that Lucretius owes to Euripides and Empedocles. The result of the adaptation is a piece almost unrivalled for sublimity and vigour. This transition, from rhetorical prose to poetry, might be illustrated from the works of numerous authors, both ancient and modern. The theories that Habakkuk wrote chap. iii. at a later period, or that it was written by some other hand, only deserve notice as examples of hypercritical eccentricity.

HABAKKUK

CHAPTER 1.—(1) The burden which
Habakkuk the prophet did see.
(2) O Lord, how long shall I cry, and
thou wilt not hear! *even* cry out unto
thee *of* violence, and thou wilt not save!
(3) Why dost thou show me iniquity, and
cause *me* to behold grievance? for spoil-
ing and violence *are* before me: and
there are *that* raise up strife and conten-
tion. (4) Therefore the law is slacked,
and judgment doth never go forth: for
the [a]wicked doth compass about the
righteous; therefore [1]wrong judgment
proceedeth.
(5) [b]Behold ye among the heathen, and
regard, and wonder marvellously: for *I*
will work a work in your days, *which* ye
will not believe, though it be told *you*.
(6) For, lo, I raise up the Chaldeans, *that*
bitter and hasty nation, which shall
march through the [2]breadth of the land,
to possess the dwellingplaces *that are*

B.C. cir. 626.

a Job 21. 7; Jer. 12. 1

1 Or, *wrested*.

b Acts 13

2 Heb., *breadths*.

(1—4) Habakkuk complains of the apparent triumph of wickedness among his countrymen.

(1) **The prophet.**—This title (*han-nâbî*) is applied only to Habakkuk, Haggai, and Zechariah. In the later historical books it is used to designate the members of those prophetical colleges which were founded by Samuel, and kept up, at all events, till the time of Elisha. It is uncertain whether in these three minor prophets it has a similar force, or merely, as in the Pentateuch, indicates a chosen minister whom God inspires to reveal His will. On the term *burden*, or *sentence*, see Isa. xiii. 1.

(2) **Even cry out.**—The latter half of the verse is best rendered "*Even cry unto thee 'Violence!' and thou wilt not save.*" The single word "violence!" (*châmâs*) occurs elsewhere, as an appeal for assistance, used as we use the cry "murder!" "fire!" &c., among ourselves. (See Jer. xx. 8, Job xix. 7.)

(3) **Why dost thou shew me iniquity? . . .**—Better, *Why dost thou show me distress and look upon grievance; oppression and violence are before me; and there is strife, and contention exalts itself.*" The question, "Why dost thou . . . *look upon* grievance?" is illustrated by verse 13, "Thou art of purer eyes than to behold evil." *Grievance*, or "trouble wilfully caused." Heb. *âmâl*, associated again with *âven*, a term of similar import, in Ps. x. 7; lv. 11.

(4) **The law**—the Mosaic *tôrâh*—which ought to be a bond of security and social welfare is "slacked" or "*paralyzed*;" and is, therefore, unable to do its work. "Judgment" (*mishpât, i.e.*, "redress of evils") "doth never go forth," for the wicked have hemmed the righteous in; and, therefore, there are no judicial sentences, save such as favour the wicked.

(5—11) Jehovah's answer to Habakkuk's complaint. These disorders are to be punished by an invasion of Chaldæans. The appearance, character, and operations of these invaders are described.

(5) **Among the heathen.**—These words are emphatic. They imply—Jehovah will no longer manifest Himself among His chosen people, but among the Gentiles. Let them look abroad, and they shall see Him using the Chaldæans as His instrument for their own chastisement. They are to "wonder;" not at God's choice of an agent, but at the consequences of the visitation, which resulted in the sack of the Temple, and the deportation of 10,000 captives; a work which the Jews might well not have credited, though it were told them. The words "among the heathen" (*bag-gôyim*) were, probably, misread by the LXX. translators *bôg'dîm*. Hence the translation, καταφρονηταί, "ye despisers." In Acts xiii. 41 St. Paul is represented as citing the verse in its LXX. form, as a warning to his Jewish hearers at Antioch. This citation, of course, gives no authority whatever to the variant. Nor is it certain that St. Paul did not actually quote the Hebrew form of the verse, which would seem more appropriate to the circumstances than the other. (Comp. Acts xiii. 42, 46 *seq.*). That St. Luke should substitute the Greek variant is intelligible enough.

(6) **I raise up the Chaldeans**—*i.e.*, I am bringing up the Chaldæan or Babylonian armies into Judæa. The phrase implies that the Chaldæans were not yet in Judæa, but there is no occasion to find an allusion to the recent rise of the Chaldæan nation. We notice this point because an ethnological theory (now generally abandoned) has regarded the Chaldæans of the prophetic period as raised to national existence only a little time before the date of Habakkuk. It was supposed that they were a race distinct from the Chaldæans of earlier Scripture; being, in fact, an association of northern hordes who had but recently penetrated the lower Mesopotamian valley. Hab. i. 6 and Isa. xxiii. 13 were therefore interpreted as illustrating the fact that these new nationalities "were on a sudden 'raised up,' elevated from their low estate of Assyrian colonists, to be the conquering people which they became under Nebuchadnezzar." The confutation of this theory may be found in Rawlinson's *Ancient Monarchies*, i. 57, 59. It appears that Babylon was peopled at this time, not, as was formerly supposed, with hordes of Armenians, Arabs, Kurds, and Sclaves, but with a mixed population, in which the old Chaldæan and Assyrian elements preponderated. The Chaldæans of the seventh century B.C. were, in fact, as legitimate descendants of the people of Nimrod's empire as we are of the Saxons. Certainly, the rapidity with which Babylon rose from the position of an Assyrian colony to that of ruler of Asia was marvellous. But the work which is to make the Jews wonder is not God's choice of an agent, but that agent's proceeding; not the elevation of one Gentile

not theirs. (7) They *are* terrible and
dreadful: [1]their judgment and their
dignity shall proceed of themselves.
(8) Their horses also are swifter than the
leopards, and are more [2]fierce than the
[a]evening wolves: and their horsemen
shall spread themselves, and their horse-
men shall come from far; they shall fly
as the eagle *that* hasteth to eat. (9) They
shall come all for violence: [3 4]their
faces shall sup up *as* the east wind,
and they shall gather the captivity as
the sand. (10) And they shall scoff at
the kings, and the princes shall be a
scorn unto them: they shall deride
every strong hold; for they shall heap
dust, and take it. (11) Then shall *his*
mind change, and he shall pass over, and
offend, *imputing* this his power unto his
god.
(12) *Art* thou not from everlasting, O
LORD my God, mine Holy One? we shall
not die. O LORD, thou hast ordained
them for judgment; and, O [5]mighty

1 Or, *from them shall proceed the judgment of these, and the captivity of these.*

2 Heb., *sharp.*

a Zeph. 3. 3.

3 Or, *the supping up of their faces, &c.,* or, *their faces shall look toward the east.*

4 Heb., *the opposition of their faces toward the east.*

5 Heb., *rock*

---

power in the place of another, but the attack which that new power is to make upon the sacred city.

Bitter and hasty.—Better, *fierce and impetuous.* The association of these two epithets, *mar* and *nimhâr*, is the more forcible, because of their similarity in sound. With respect to the whole passage 6—11, Kleinert well remarks, "The present passage is the *locus classicus* for the characteristics of this warlike people, just as Isa. v. 26 *seq.* is for the characteristics of the Assyrians."

(7) **Their judgment . . .**—Their "judgment" means their claim to adjudge the affairs of mankind. It proceeds from "themselves," as irresponsible, recognising no Supreme Being as the source of justice.

Their dignity, in like manner, proceeds from "themselves," because self-sustained, unsanctioned by the King of kings and Lord of lords.

(8) **Are more fierce.**—Better, *are sharper.* This is the literal meaning of the verb. The ideas intended are those of activity and ferocity, both prompted by hunger. The evening wolf coming out of his lair to find prey is elsewhere an illustration of ravenous greediness. (See Zeph. iii. 3 and Ps. lix. 7). In Jer. v. 6 God's punishment is likened to "a wolf of the evening," "a lion out of the forest." Jer. iv. 13 "his chariots shall be as a whirlwind; his horses are swifter than eagles," is similar to chap. i. 8, but it is not necessary to regard it either as its original or its echo. Both passages are to some extent based on 2 Sam. i. 23.

(9) **Their faces shall sup up as the east wind.**—Literally, if we could accept this interpretation, *the eagerness of their faces is eastward.* The passage, however, is beset with philological difficulties. If the word *kâdîmâh* could be translated "east wind," the invading Chaldæan host would be compared to a blast from the east, passing over the land, and leaving it scorched and blighted. The captives ("captivity," Authorised Version) whom the invader carries off would then be likened to the cloud of dust, sand, &c., which accompanies this withering blast. This gives a good sense. Unfortunately, however, according to all analogy, *kâdîmâh* must mean either "eastwards" or "forwards." The meaning of *m'gammath* (used here only) is probably either "crowd" or "eager desire." Two plausible renderings are thus presented for our choice—"There is a crowd of their faces pressing forwards;" "Their faces turn eagerly forwards." For other interpretations, we must refer the Hebrew student to the critical commentaries.

(10) **Kings and princes** are deposed or enthroned at the invader's pleasure. Thus Nebuchadnezzar set Jehoiakim as a tributary sovereign on the throne of Jerusalem and three years later deposed his son and successor Jehoiachin and made Zedekiah king.

For they shall heap dust, and take it.—This means that they shall besiege and carry all strongholds by means of the mounds of earth commonly used in sieges. These mounds were employed either to place the besieger on a level with the besieged, and so facilitate the operations of siege engines, or to form an inclined plane, up which the besieger might march his men, and so take the place by escalade. We find they were used by the Egyptians (Ezek. xvii. 17) and the Assyrians (2 Kings xix. 32), as well as by the Babylonians (Jer. vi. 6, and *passim*). They are mentioned as employed by the Spartan king Archidamus in the celebrated siege of Platæa in B.C. 429 (Thucydides, lib. ii.). In the present passage the term "dust" is used to indicate these mounds of earth, as expressing the contemptuous ease with which the invader effects his capture of strongholds.

(11) **Then shall his mind change . . . .**—Better, *Then he sweeps by like a wind and passes. But he is guilty, making this his strength his god.* By an abrupt transition the latter half of the verse diverts our attention from the human view of the world-conqueror to his appearance in God's sight. Men only see an irresistible force sweeping over the face of the earth like a whirlwind; here to-day, and to-morrow nothing but devastation and ruin to testify to its visit. And men are dazzled by this mighty display of power. But, even as Daniel at Belshazzar's feast, Habakkuk pronounces the oppressor's doom in the very hour of triumph. The description of the irresistible invader drops into the sudden depths of anti-climax, "But he is (counted) *guilty.*" His guilt consists just in what men deem so glorious, in his self-reliant irresponsible pursuit of grandeur. The brute force of armaments is the supreme deity of the Chaldæan. His sword and spear are, as it were, his idols. (Comp. verse 16.) God, in whose hands his breath is, and whose are all his ways, has he not glorified. (Comp. Dan. v. 23.) Therefore that God shall bring on him ruin and ignominy, and the very nations which have marvelled at his prowess shall taunt and contemn him (chap. ii. 6). Here, then, is the key-note of so much of the second canto (chap. i. 12 to ii. *fin.*) as relates to the downfall of the invader.

(12—17) Though sore perplexed, Habakkuk feels sure that the God whom this swaggering conqueror has insulted will at last vindicate Himself.

(12) **We shall not die**—*i.e.,* God's people may suffer, but shall not be obliterated, shall not be "given over unto death." The rest of the verse runs literally, *Jehovah, for judgment hast Thou appointed him, and O Rock, for chastisement hast Thou founded him.* "Him," means, of course, the Chaldæan invader, whom

God, thou hast [1]established them for
correction. (13) *Thou art* of purer eyes
than to behold evil, and canst not look
on [2]iniquity: wherefore lookest thou
upon them that deal treacherously, *and*
holdest thy tongue when the wicked de-
voureth *the man that is* more righteous
than he? (14) And makest men as the
fishes of the sea, as the [3]creeping things,
that have no ruler over them? (15) They
take up all of them with the angle, they
catch them in their net, and gather them
in their [4]drag: therefore they rejoice
and are glad. (16) Therefore they sacri-
fice unto their net, and burn incense
unto their drag; because by them their
portion *is* fat, and their meat [5][6]plenteous.
(17) Shall they therefore empty their net,
and not spare continually to slay the
nations?

CHAPTER II.—(1) I will [a]stand upon
my watch, and set me upon the [7]tower,
and will watch to see what he will say
[8]unto me, and what I shall answer
[9][0]when I am reproved. (2) And the LORD
answered me, and said, Write the vision,
and make *it* plain upon tables, that he
may run that readeth it. (3) For the
vision *is* yet for an appointed time, but
at the end it shall speak, and not lie:
though it tarry, wait for it; because it
will [b]surely come, it will not tarry.
(4) Behold, his soul *which* is lifted up

1 Heb., *founded.*
2 Or, *grievance.*
3 Or, *moving.*
4 Or, *flue net.*
5 Or, *dainty.*
6 Heb., *fat.*
a Isa. 21. 8.
7 Heb., *fenced place.*
8 Or, *in me.*
9 Or, *when I am argued with.*
0 Heb., *upon my reproof,* or, *arguing.*
b Heb. 10. 37.

Habakkuk regards as raised up only to be God's instrument of correction. The term "*Rock*" has been paraphrased in the Authorised Version. Used absolutely, it occurs as a Divine title in Deut. xxxii. 4. Generally it is qualified in some way, as "*my* rock," "*our* rock," "rock *of salvation*," &c.

(13) The prophet's confidence is tempered, however, with anxious fear. Why does not God show plainly that He authorises this visitation? The triumph of this godless invader appears to impugn God's majesty.

(16) The prophet has already stated that the Chaldæan deifies his own military prowess. Of this statement the present verse is an expansion. Weapons of war may have been literally worshipped by the Babylonians. Similarly, the Sarmatians offered yearly sacrifices to a sword, as the emblem of their god of war (Clem. Alex. *Protrept.* 64). The Romans also sacrificed to their eagles. But probably the language is metaphorical, and we need not seek a closer illustration than that of Dr. Pusey,—"So the *Times* said at the beginning of the late war, 'The French almost worshipped the mitrailleuse as a goddess.' 'They idolised, it would say, their invention, as if it could do what God alone could.'"

(17) **Shall they therefore empty their net . . .**—Literally, *Shall he therefore empty his net? i.e.,* Shall this voracious Chaldæan plunderer be allowed to consume his prey, and cast in his emptied net again and again?

II.

Habakkuk's doubts are solved by the Divine response. Judgment on Babylon's numerous sins is indeed preparing: meantime, let the righteous wait on God in faith.

(1) **The Tower.**—The practice of ascending a high place to secure an extensive view suggests the figure here. (See 2 Kings ix. 17; 2 Sam. xviii. 24.) In a yet bolder metaphor Isaiah represents himself as appointing a watchman, who brings reports from his tower. We need not suppose that Habakkuk literally betook himself to a solitary height to wait for a revelation. Balaam, the heathen soothsayer, did so (Num. xxiii. 3), but his conduct throws no light on the customs of the Jewish prophets.

What he will say unto me.—Better, *what He will say in me, and what answer I shall make to my complaint: i.e.,* of what solution of the perplexities I am deploring, Jehovah shall make me the mouthpiece.

(2) **On tables.**—Better, *on the tables.* The definite article probably indicates certain well-known tables on which the prophets were wont to inscribe their utterances for public edification. These tables may have been hung up in the Temple (Calvin) or market-place (Luther and Ewald).

That he may run that readeth it—*i.e.,* the prophecy is to be inscribed plainly and legibly, so that the reader may "run his eye" quickly through it.

(3) **For the vision is yet for an appointed time . . .**—Better, *For the vision is to have its appointed day, and it pants for the end, and it shall not disappoint, i.e.,* it pants for the day of completion, which shall do it justice. It longs to fulfil its destiny.

It will not tarry.—This translation is unfortunate. The prophet has just said that it *will* tarry. Nevertheless, he adds, men are to wait for it, because "it will surely come, and *shall not be behindhand,*" *scil,* on its appointed day. This and verse 4 are welded into the Apostle's exhortation in Heb. x. 37. The citation is not from the Hebrew, but is an adaptation of the equally familiar LXX. variant, ὅτι ἐρχόμενος ἥξει καὶ οὐ μὴ χρονίσῃ· ἐὰν ὑποστείληται οὐκ εὐδοκεῖ ἡ ψυχή μου ἐν αὐτῷ.

(4) **Behold his soul . . . .**—Better, *Behold his soul within him is puffed up, it is not upright.* The soul of the Chaldæan invader is inflated with pride, self-dependence ousting from his mind all thoughts of God. It is therefore unsound and distorted. Habakkuk leaves the inference "and therefore it shall die" to be imagined, and hastens to the antithesis, "*But the righteous man shall live by his faith.*" The word *live* is emphatic. The reward promised to patient waiting on God is *life*—deliverance from destruction. How far the promise extends, and whether it includes that aspiration after future life which is plainly expressed by many Hebrew poets and prophets, we cannot determine. The student must be cautioned against such renderings as "he that is righteous-by-faith shall live," or, "he that is justified-by-faith shall live," which have been suggested by the Pauline quotations Rom. i. 17, Gal. iii. 11. If the adjective could be taken in this close collocation with the substantive, "he that is consistent in-his-confidence shall live" would be the only possible

is not upright in him: but the [a]just shall
live by his faith. (5) [1]Yea also, because
he transgresseth by wine, *he is* a proud
man, neither keepeth at home, who en-
largeth his desire as hell, and *is* as death,
and cannot be satisfied, but gathereth
unto him all nations, and heapeth unto
him all people:

(6) Shall not all these take up a parable
against him, and a taunting proverb
against him, and say, [2]Woe to him that
increaseth *that which is* not his! how
long? and to him that ladeth himself
with thick clay! (7) Shall they not rise
up suddenly that shall bite thee, and
awake that shall vex thee, and thou shalt
be for booties unto them? (8) Because
thou hast spoiled many nations, all the
remnant of the people shall spoil thee;
because of men's [3]blood, and *for* the
violence of the land, of the city, and of
all that dwell therein.

(9) Woe to him that [b] [4]coveteth an evil
covetousness to his house, that he may
set his nest on high, that he may be de-
livered from the [5]power of evil! (10) Thou
hast consulted shame to thy house by
cutting off many people, and hast sinned
against thy soul. (11) For the stone shall
cry out of the wall, and the [6]beam out of
the timber shall [7]answer it.

(12) Woe to him that buildeth a town
with [c] [8]blood, and stablisheth a city by
iniquity! (13) Behold, *is it* not of the
LORD of hosts that the people shall
labour in the very fire, and the people

a John 3. 36; Rom. 1. 17; Gal. 3. 11; Heb. 10. 38.

1 Or, *How much more.*

2 Or, *Ho, he.*

3 Heb., *bloods.*

b Jer. 22. 13.

4 Or, *gaineth an evil gain.*

5 Heb., *palm of the hand.*

6 Or, *piece*, or, *fastening.*

7 Or, *witness against it.*

c Ezek. 24. 9; Nah. 3. 1.

8 Heb., *bloods.*

---

rendering. Thus whatever force we assign to St. Paul's citation, here, at least, the words have no doctrinal significance. Their ethical importance is, however, undeniable. (See Introduction iv.)

(5) **Yea, also . . .**—Better, *Add, too, that wine is treacherous* (and that) *he is a braggart and cannot be quiet, whose appetite is large as* (that of) *Hades.* The rest of the verse illustrates this last-named characteristic—restless, rapacious ambition. Two more charges are thus added to the gravamen of verse 4. Not only are the Chaldæans arrogant, but drunkards, and insatiably covetous. The former charge is expressed in a kind of proverb, "(It is a known fact that) wine is treacherous." Perhaps the aphorisms of Prov. xx. 1 are in Habakkuk's mind: "Wine is a mocker, strong drink is noisy." The other charge, that of rapacity, also recalls the Book of Proverbs, where the insatiable appetite of death and Hades is twice described. (See Prov. xxvii. 20; xxx. 16.) The charge of drunkenness is illustrated in Rawlinson, *Ancient Monarchies*, vol. ii., 504—507.

(6—20) The destruction of the Chaldæans has hitherto been only implied. It is now plainly foretold in a denunciatory song, put into the mouths of the invader's victims. In this song there are five strophes, of three verses each, 6—8; 9—11; 12—14; 15—17; 18—20.

(6—8) Woe on the reckless rapacity which has spared neither life nor property.

(6) **How long?**—*i.e.*, how long shall this continual annexation be witnessed?

That ladeth himself with thick clay.—Better, *That accumulates to himself usury.* So the Targum. The rendering "thick clay" originates in a false etymology of the word *abtét*, which the student will find in Rashi's *Commentary*. For the true derivation see Fürst's Lexicon.

(7) **Bite.**—This verb *nâshac* also means "to oppress with usury," and this is its force here. *Thy* turn shall come, and men shall exact usury from thee. Similarly, the verb translated "vex" is, literally, *to shake violently*, in allusion to a creditor's forcible seizure of his debtor. (Comp. Matt. xviii. 28.) The prediction of Habakkuk in these verses was fulfilled by the rise of the Medo-Persian power, and the capture of Babylon by the forces of Cyrus, cir. B.C. 538.

(8) **Violence of.**—Scil., *violence wreaked on*, both here and in verse 17.

(9—11) Woe on the aggrandisement of the new dynasty by force and cunning.

(9) **Woe to him that coveteth . . .**—Better, *Woe to him who accumulates wicked gain for his house, who sets his nest on high to save himself from the hand of evil*—*i.e.*, who gathers spoil from the nations, and stows it away in an impregnable treasure-house. The expression *sets his nest on high* finds more than sufficient illustration in the exaggerated accounts of Babylon given by Herodotus and Ctesias. The former gives 337½ feet, the latter 300 feet, as the height of its walls. The height of the towers was, according to Ctesias, 420 feet. There were 250 of these towers, irregularly disposed, to guard the weaker parts of the wall. The space included by these colossal outworks was, according to Herodotus, about 200 square miles.

The language of this verse recalls Jeremiah's rebuke of Jehoiakim (Jer. xxii. 13 *seq.*). There, however, the sentence is on individual sin, here it is on that of a nation personified.

(10) **And hast sinned . . .**—Literally, *and sinning in thy soul.* All the time the Babylonian oppressor was plundering these peoples he was involving his soul in guilt. (Comp. chap. i. 11.)

(11) **The stone shall cry out.**—Every stone in those giant walls reared by the enforced labour of captives cries aloud to accuse the Babylonian. Every spar out of the woodwork attests the charge.

(12—14) Woe on the extension of Babylon by oppression and enforced labour.

(13) **In the very fire . . . for very vanity.** The preposition is the same in both clauses, and means "for an equivalent in." The sense is sufficiently conveyed if we render "*labour only for the fire . . . weary themselves all for nothing.*" The same expressions occur in Jeremiah's denunciation of Babylon (chap. li. 58). Both prophets predict that Jehovah shall render all this compulsory service fruitless. Jeremiah adds the explanatory clauses, "the broad walls of

shall weary themselves [1]for very vanity?
(14) For the earth shall be filled [2]with the
[a]knowledge of the glory of the LORD, as
the waters cover the sea.
(15) Woe unto him that giveth his neigh-
bour drink, that puttest thy bottle to
him, and makest *him* drunken also, that
thou mayest look on their nakedness!
(16) Thou art filled [3]with shame for glory:
[b]drink thou also, and let thy foreskin be
uncovered: the cup of the LORD's right
hand shall be turned unto thee, and
shameful spewing *shall be* on thy glory.
(17) For the violence of Lebanon shall
cover thee, and the spoil of beasts, *which*
made them afraid, because of men's
blood, and for the violence of the land,
of the city, and of all that dwell therein.
(18) What profiteth the graven image
that the maker thereof hath graven it;
the molten image, and a [c]teacher of lies,
that [4]the maker of his work trusteth
therein, to make dumb idols? (19) Woe
unto him that saith to the wood, Awake;
to the dumb stone, Arise, it shall teach!
Behold, it *is* laid over with gold and
silver, and *there is* no breath at all in the
midst of it. (20) But [d]the LORD *is* in his
holy temple: [5]let all the earth keep
silence before him.

CHAPTER III. — (1) A prayer of
Habakkuk the prophet [6]upon Shigionoth.
(2) O LORD, I have heard [7]thy speech,
and was afraid: O LORD, [8]revive thy
work in the midst of the years, in the
midst of the years make known; in
wrath remember mercy.

1 Or, *in vain?*
2 Or, *by knowing the glory of the LORD.*
a Isa. 11. 9.
3 Or, *more with shame than with glory.*
b Jer. 25. 26.
c Jer. 10. 8, 14; Zech. 10. 2.
4 Heb., *the fashioner of his fashion.*
d Ps. 11. 4.
5 Heb., *be silent all the earth before him.*
6 Or, *according to variable songs, or, tunes, called in Hebrew, Shigioneth.*
7 Heb., *thy report, or, thy hearing.*
8 Or, *preserve alive.*

Babylon shall be utterly broken, and her high gates shall be burned with fire."

(14) **With the knowledge.**—Better, *as concerns the knowledge.* See the same promise in Isa. xi. 9. It is here introduced in contrast to the short-lived glory of Babylon. The enslaved nations raised the Babylonian palaces only for the fire to destroy them. But Jehovah's glory shall be made known all the world over, and shall not be effaced.

(15—17) Woe on the cruel invader who has made the world drink of the cup of wrath.

(15, 16) **Woe unto him.**—It is possible that wanton outrages committed by the debauched Babylonian soldiery in the hour of triumph are here meant. And this is in accordance with the mention of drunkenness as their special sin in verse 5. But we much prefer to treat the language as figurative. The invader has made his neighbours drink the cup of his cruel anger till they have reached the depths of shameful degradation. He, too, shall drink "of the cup of the fierceness of the wrath of Almighty God" (Rev. xvi. 19; see also Ps. lxxvi, 8, Jer. xxv. 26, Lam. iv. 21); and then foul shame, as of a man stupefied with drink, shall take the place of glory and dignity.

Puttest thy bottle.—It is possible to render, *pourest out thy wrath,* and this makes the metaphor less obscure.

(17) **For the violence of Lebanon . . . .**—Better, *For the violence done to Lebanon shall overwhelm thee, and the destruction of the beasts which it frightened away.* The rest of the verse is a refrain taken from the first woe, that of verse 8. The "destruction of beasts" points, we think, to a raid on the cattle feeding on the sides of Lebanon. But more than this is probably included in the phrase *the violence done to Lebanon.* Habakkuk probably foresees how the invader will cut down the cedar forests in Lebanon to adorn the palaces of Babylon. (Comp. Isa. xiv. 7, 8.) All these outrages shall in due time be avenged on himself. Some commentators, however, explain the expression as a bold synecdoche, Lebanon representing the Holy Land (of which it was the beauty), or even the Temple, both of which Nebuchadnezzar laid waste.

(18—20) Woe on him who neglects Jehovah to worship dumb idols of his own making.

(18) **A teacher of lies.**—Not the false prophet, but the idol itself, as pointing out false ways in opposition to God, the teacher of truth.

That the maker . . .—Better, *that he who frames his image trusts in it, so as to make dumb idols. Dumb nothings* is, perhaps, the literal translation of *e'lîlîm ill'mîm,* and the words are chosen for their similarity of sound.

(20) **But the Lord.**—And while all this false worship prevails, the true World-ruler abides, and His presence is in His temple at Jerusalem. To Him the prophet's eyes are now turned. He ceases his denunciations of the invader, and finds solace in the glorious anticipations of the lyrical ode (chap. iii. 1—15) which follows.

III.

(1—15) A hymn describing a future self-manifestation of Jehovah on Israel's behalf, accompanied by the signs and wonders of the early history. It is impossible to give the English reader an idea of the rhythmical structure of this beautiful composition. We will only observe that it is independent of the arrangement in verses, and that the poem (except in verses 7, 8, 13, *fin.*) consists of lines each containing exactly three words.

(1) **Upon Shigionoth.**—This term points, not to the contents of the composition, but either to its metrical structure or its musical setting. See on the Inscription of Psalm vii. Inasmuch as this ode is throughout an account of the deliverance anticipated by prayerful faith, it is called not a Psalm, *mizmôr,* but a Prayer, *t'phillâh.*

(2) **Thy speech.**—Better, *thy report,* as in margin. The tone is that of Ps. xliv. 1, "We have heard with our ears O God! our fathers have told us . . ." Jehovah's doings at the *beginning* of the years are well known; the prophet seeks that they may be manifested again, now in the *midst* of the years. The petition "in wrath remember mercy," is explained by chap. i. 5 *et seq.* It implies—though Thy visitation be well deserved, yet mercifully limit its duration, as on former occasions.

(3) God came from [1]Teman, and the
Holy One from mount Paran. Selah.
His glory covered the heavens, and the
earth was full of his praise. (4) And *his*
brightness was as the light; he had
[2]horns *coming* out of his hand: and there
was the hiding of his power. (5) Before
him went the pestilence, and [3]burning
coals went forth at his feet. (6) He stood,
and measured the earth: he beheld, and
drove asunder the nations; and the
everlasting mountains were scattered,
the perpetual hills did bow: his ways
are everlasting. (7) I saw the tents of
[4]Cushan [5]in affliction: *and* the curtains
of the land of Midian did tremble.
(8) Was the LORD displeased against the
rivers? *was* thine anger against the
rivers? *was* thy wrath against the sea,
that thou didst ride upon thine horses
and [6]thy chariots of salvation? (9) Thy
bow was made quite naked, *according* to
the oaths of the tribes, *even thy* word.
Selah. [7]Thou didst cleave the earth
with rivers. (10) The mountains saw
thee, *and* they trembled: the overflow-

1 Or, *the south.*
2 Or, *bright beams out of his side.*
3 Or, *burning diseases.*
4 Or, *Ethiopia.*
5 Or, *under affliction,* or, *vanity.*
6 Or, *thy chariots were salvation?*
7 Or, *Thou didst cleave the rivers of the earth.*

(3—15) Habakkuk describes the "Theophany" or self-manifestation of Jehovah, which is to introduce the desired deliverance. The Authorised Version has unfortunately rendered all the verbs in this section in the *past* tense, thus obscuring the sense of the poem. They all refer to a scene really future, but brought by the grasp of faith into the immediate *present.* In the Hebrew some of these verbs are in the future tense, others in the past used with the force of a present, the "prophetic perfect" as it is sometimes termed. Such a use of the Hebrew preterite is common in Biblical poetry, notably in the Book of Psalms. It is almost impossible to reproduce in English the slight distinction between these tenses. While, however, his eyes are thus fixed on a future deliverance, the basis of all Habakkuk's anticipations is God's doings in time past; the chief features in the portraiture are, in fact, borrowed from the Books of Exodus and Judges.

(3) **God came.**—Render "*God shall come from Teman, and the Holy One from Mount Paran. Selah. His glory covers the heavens, and the earth is full of His praise.*" Jehovah reveals Himself from the south: *i.e.,* from Mount Sinai, as in Deut. xxxii., Judges v., Ps. lxviii. The southern country is here designated as "Teman," *i.e.,* Edom to the S.E., and "Paran," the mountainous region to the S.W., between Edom and Egypt.

(4) **And his brightness was as the light. . . .**—Better, *And a brightness shall there be, like sunlight, and rays are at His side; and there* [*i.e.,* in this radiance] *is the tabernacle of His power.*

(5) **Before him went the pestilence. . . .**—Better, *Before Him shall go the plague, and burning pestilence shall go forth where He sets His feet.* Kleinert remarks that it was with these angels of death that Jehovah revealed Himself in the south, and destroyed the armies of Sennacherib (2 Kings xix. 35).

(6) **He stood, and measured the earth . . .**—Better, *He has taken His stand and measured the earth, He has looked and made the heathen tremble; and the primeval mountains are broken up, the ancient hills sink down; His goings are as of old; i.e.,* His proceedings are the same as of old time, when He brought up Israel from Egypt. God measures or parcels out the earth; and the usurping invader is put to confusion. The mountains are convulsed, as was Sinai of old. (Comp. Judges v. 5, Ps. lxviii. 8.)

(7) **"I saw."**—Better, *I see.* **Did tremble.**—Better, *are trembling.* Probably the imagery is still borrowed from the Exodus story, the nations instanced being the borderers on the Red Sea—viz., Cushan (Cush, or Ethiopia) on the west, and Midian on the east side. A plausible theory, however, as old as the Targum, connects this verse with later episodes in Israel's history. "Cushan" is identified with that Mesopotamian oppressor, "Cushan-rishathaim," whom the judge Othniel overcame. (Judges iii. 8—10). And "Midian" is interpreted by Judges vi., which records how Gideon delivered Israel from Midianite oppression. Both names thus become typical instances of tyranny subdued by Jehovah's intervention. We prefer the other interpretation, because the prophet's eye is still fixed apparently on the earlier history (see verse 8, *et seq.*), and a reference here to the time of the Judges would mar the climactic symmetry of the composition. "Cushan," however, is never used elsewhere for "Cush," though the LXX. understood it in this meaning. "Curtains" in the second hemistich is merely a variation on "tents" in the first. (Comp. Song of Sol. i. 5.)

(8) **Was the Lord displeased?**—Better, *Is it with the rivers Jehovah is wroth? Is Thine anger against the rivers? Is Thy wrath against the sea?—that Thou* (thus) *ridest upon Thy horses, that Thy chariots* (thus appear) *for deliverance?*

Of salvation.—Better, *for salvation,* or *for deliverance.* The allusion is obviously to Israel's miraculous passage through the Red Sea and the Jordan. The "horses" and "chariots" which are here the symbols of Divine might, come in the more fittingly in view of Exod. xiv. (see verses 14 *seq.*), where Pharaoh, pursued with "horses and chariots," only to find Jehovah Himself arrayed against him.

(9) **Thy bow was made quite naked.**—Better, *Thy bow shall be bared, even the chastisements sworn by Thy word. Selah. With rivers shalt thou cleave the earth.* God's chastisements, which are compared in Ps. xxi. 12 to arrows fitted to the string, are here represented as a bow taken out of the case, and so "made naked," or "bared." The word *matteh,* "rod," "stem" (hence, also, "tribe"), used to denote an instrument of chastisement in Micah vi. 9, Isa. xxx. 32, here apparently means the *punishment,* or *chastisement,* of heathen iniquities, which God has sworn (see Deut. xxxii. 40, 41) to execute. On the term *Selah* see Ps. iii. 4 note. *With rivers shalt thou cleave the earth, i.e.,* the rocks shall send forth new watercourses at Jehovah's bidding, so that "rivers run in the dry places." (See Exod. xvii. 6; Num. xx. 11.)

(10—18) All the verbs in these verses are misrendered as regards tense. (See note on 3—15.)

(10) **The mountains saw thee.**—The earthquake at Sinai and the dividing of the Red Sea, the waters of

ing of the water passed by: the deep
uttered his voice, *and* lifted up his hands
on high. (11) The sun *and* moon [a] stood
still in their habitation: [1] at the light
of thine [b] arrows they went, *and* at the
shining of thy glittering spear. (12) Thou
didst march through the land in indig-
nation, thou didst thresh the heathen in
anger. (13) Thou wentest forth for the
salvation of thy people, *even* for salvation
with thine anointed; thou woundedst the
head out of the house of the wicked, [2] by
discovering the foundation unto the neck.
Selah. (14) Thou didst strike through
with his staves the head of his villages:
they [3] came out as a whirlwind to scatter
me: their rejoicing *was* as to devour the
poor secretly. (15) Thou didst walk
through the sea with thine horses,
through the [4] heap of great waters.

(16) When I heard, my belly trembled;
my lips quivered at the voice: rottenness
entered into my bones, and I trembled
in myself, that I might rest in the day
of trouble: when he cometh up unto the
people, he will [5] invade them with his
troops.
(17) Although the fig tree shall not
blossom, neither *shall* fruit *be* in the
vines; the labour of the olive shall [6] fail,
and the fields shall yield no meat; the
flock shall be cut off from the fold, and
there shall be no herd in the stalls:
(18) yet I will rejoice in the LORD, I will
joy in the God of my salvation. (19) The
LORD God *is* my strength, and he will
make my feet like [c] hinds' *feet*, and he will
make me to walk upon mine high places.

To the chief singer on my [7] stringed instruments.

a Josh. 10. 12.

1 Or, *thine arrows walked in the light, &c.*

b Josh. 10. 11.

2 Heb., *making naked.*

3 Heb., *were tempestuous.*

4 Or, *mud.*

5 Or, *cut them in pieces.*

6 Heb., *lie.*

c 2 Sam. 22. 34; Ps. 18. 33.

7 Heb., *neginoth.*

---

which were lifted up "as a wall on the right hand and on the left" of Israel, lie at the basis of this description. This imagery, however, of sweeping floods and quaking mountains is usual in poetical accounts of Divine interposition.

(11) **The sun and moon stand still in their habitation**—*scil.*, where they were at the beginning of the judgment. Here, of course, Habakkuk has in mind Josh. x. 12, 13. The rest of the verse is best rendered, *at the light of Thine arrows which go abroad, at the bright glancing of Thy spear.* Apparently, the conception is that the surpassing brightness of the theophany shames the heavenly bodies, which accordingly cease to pursue their journey.

(12) **Thou didst march.**—Here the verbs are in the future, and are to be rendered accordingly.

(13) **Thou wentest.**—Here the verbs, though past, are best rendered by the English present.

Even for salvation . . .—Better, *even for the salvation of Thine anointed—scil.*, Thy chosen people, as also, perhaps, in Ps. cv. 15. The rendering of the Authorised Version has the support of Aquila and the Quinta. It is a possible rendering, but few impartial Hebraists will deny that the other is preferable. In the last half of the verse two figures are blended—those of a house and a human body. Literally, it runs, *Thou crushest the head of the house of the wicked* (comp. Ps. cx. 6), *laying bare the foundation even to the neck.* The obvious meaning is that the house or race of the Chaldæans is to be destroyed, "root and branch."

(14) **Thou dost strike through with his staves . . .**—Better, *Thou dost pierce with his* (*scil.*, thine anointed people's) *spears the head of his* (the enemy's) *princes, when they sweep by to scatter me abroad, when they exult as if to devour the afflicted secretly.* The first clause is very obscure. *Matteh* means not only "spear," but also "rod," "stem," "tribe" (see on verse 9); and the word which we translate "princes" may also, perhaps, mean "villages." (See on Judg. v. 7.) It is also uncertain to whom the possessive pronouns attached to these substantives refer. In the last clause we are reminded of several passages in the Psalms, notably, x. 9; xiv. 4; xvii. 12.

(15) **Thou didst walk.**—Better, *Thou walkest.* "Heap" is probably the correct translation of *chômer* here, as in Exod. viii. 10. With this glance at the miraculous passage of the Red Sea (see verse 8) this prophetic poem comes to a sudden termination. The new paragraph begins with verse 16, not, as is indicated in the Authorised Version, with verse 17.

(16—19) Habakkuk now reverts abruptly to the Divine sentence of chapter i. 5 *et seq.*, and describes with what emotion he meditates on the coming disasters, and on his own inability to prevent them. His anxiety is, however, swept aside by a joyful and overpowering confidence in God. These verses are a kind of appendix to the preceding poem.

(16) **That I might rest . . .**—Better, *that I should be resting quiet in the day of trouble, when he cometh up against the people who is to oppress them.*

(17) **Although.**—Better, *For.* The conjunction connects this verse with what precedes, and explains Habakkuk's affliction more fully. With the sword shall come famine, invasion as usual producing desolation.

(18) **Yet**—*i.e.*, in spite of all the afflictions predicted in verse 17. We are reminded of St. Paul's expression of confidence in Rom. viii. 37.

(19) **The Lord God.**—This is an adaptation from Psalm xviii. 33. The "hinds' feet" indicate the strength and elasticity of the prophet's confidence; the "high places" are, as Kleinert observes, "the heights of salvation which stand at the end of the way of tribulation, and which only the righteous man can climb by the confidence of faith."

To the chief singer—*i.e.*, to the precentor, or presiding singer. The rubric may be interpreted either "To the precentor. (To be performed) on my stringed instruments," or, "To him who presides over my stringed instruments." The fact that the same direction occurs with the words in the same order in six Psalms perhaps favours the latter rendering in all cases. The preposition *al* would, however, in this case be appropriate rather than *b'*. On the terms used, see Ps. iv. 1 It has been inferred from the use of the possessive pronoun, "*my* stringed instruments," that Habakkuk was a Levite, and therefore himself entitled to accompany the Temple music. But see Introduction, § i.

INTRODUCTION

TO

ZEPHANIAH

I. **The Author.**—Zephaniah traces his pedigree back through four generations to Hezekiah (Authorised Version *Hizkiah*). Many of the modern commentators have followed Jerome and Aben Ezra in identifying this ancestor with the king of Judah of that name. It favours this view that Zephaniah traces his pedigree back as far as Hezekiah and no farther. The emphasis thus attached to the name argues that it was that of a well-known individual. It is no objection that his royal title is not actually mentioned. Just in the same way Zechariah names as his grandfather the well-known Iddo, without the addition "the priest" (Zech. i. 1). Neither is it material that between Hezekiah and Josiah (in whose reign Zephaniah prophesied), there are only two kings—Manasseh and Amon—to set off against Zephaniah's three ancestors. The fact that Manasseh's reign was unusually long—extending over no less a period than fifty-five years—fully accounts for the disparity. It is quite possible therefore that Zephaniah in chap. i. 1 lays claim to descent from the royal family of Judah. Of the prophet's life nothing is known. The name "Zephaniah" means *Jehovah hides* or *protects* (from root *tsâphan*), not as Jerome explains it, *watchman of Jehovah* (from root *tsâphâh*). But the etymology has no bearing on the present composition, for there is no reason to regard the name as a ministerial title.

II. **Occasion of writing.**—According to chap. i. 1, Zephaniah prophesied in the reign of Josiah. This reign lasted from B.C. 641 to B.C. 610. For the purpose of our present investigation it may conveniently be divided into three periods. (*a.*) That preceding the abolition of idolatry, 641—630. (*b.*) The reformation period. This culminated, in 624–3, in a restoration of the Temple, a renewal of the covenant, and the celebration of the great Passover. (*c.*) The period following this reformation, 623—610. To which of these three periods does the prophecy of Zephaniah belong? *Primâ facie* we feel inclined to connect it with the first period. The prophecy was provoked by the general prevalence of idolatry (chap. i. 4—6), oppression and corruption (chap. iii. 1—7). It is only natural to suppose that it was composed before Josiah was old enough to begin his reformation: *i.e.*, between the years 641—630. The arguments alleged in favour of a later date are insufficient to invalidate this conclusion. These arguments may be tabulated thus:—(1.) The expression "I will cut off the *remnant* of Baal" (chap. i. 4) has been treated as implying that some steps had already been taken to abolish Baal-worship: *i.e.*, that Zephaniah wrote after the inauguration of Josiah's reforms. This interpretation is, of course, possible. But it certainly is not absolutely necessary. (See note on chap. i. 4.) (2.) The guilt of the "king's sons" is denounced (chap. i. 8). But Jehoiakim, the eldest son of Josiah, was not more than six years old at the close of the first period, and only twelve at the close of the second. The denunciation is therefore supposed to prove that Zephaniah wrote about the middle of the third period, when the characters of the two elder princes, Jehoiakim and Jehoahaz, would be sufficiently formed to indicate their irreligious propensities. This argument appears at first sight convincing. But its force disappears entirely when we recollect that this expression need not refer to Josiah's sons at all. Other princes of the blood royal may be meant, sons of Amon or grandsons of Manasseh. (See chap. i. 8, note.) (3.) Phrases from the law, and more particularly from the Book of Deuteronomy, are of frequent occurrence in this prophecy. (Comp. chaps. i. 13, 15, 17; ii. 5, 7, 11; iii. 5, 19, 20.) It is argued that the explanation of these numerous citations lies in Hilkiah's discovery of "the book of the law" in 624 or 623, and its subsequent public recital. (See 2 Kings xxii. 8, xxiii. 2.) But this inference has little force save for those who unwarrantably connect these events with the *composition* of the Book of Deuteronomy. That a discovery of an ancient copy of the law caused a sensation in Jerusalem, and aided Josiah's work of religious reform, appears to us sufficiently natural. It need not commit us to the conclusions that before the year in question the law was quite forgotten or the Book of Deuteronomy non-existent. Those who have jumped at the latter conclusion cannot fairly account for the apparent indebtedness of earlier prophets—*e.g.*, Hosea and Amos —to the Book of Deuteronomy.

That Jerusalem is distinctly represented as in a state of religious and moral decadence sufficiently shows, we think, that the book of Zephaniah preceded the memorable year of iconoclasm B.C. 630. In accordance with this theory of date is the prophet's allusion to the future fate of Nineveh in chap. ii. 13—15. We do not claim this passage as an original prediction, for it is obviously based on an earlier prophecy—that of Nahum. But we infer from the use of the future tense that what Nahum had predicted had not yet been fulfilled: *i.e.*, that Zephaniah wrote, at all events, before the capture of Nineveh in 625. The allusion harmonises with the other argument, which impels us to place Zephaniah's composition in the period 641—630.

Zephaniah's mission was one of mingled reproof and consolation. In the foreground of the prophetic portraiture stands the Chaldean invasion, with its fearful consequences—the sack of Jerusalem and deportation of God's chosen people. This disastrous epoch is obviously "the day of wrath" so vividly depicted in chap. i. Zephaniah, however, does not specify the nation which God has appointed as His instrument of chastisement. This identification is reserved for Habakkuk, writing somewhat later (Hab. i. 6). Far back in the perspective of the picture is that glorious vision of extended religious privileges, which is elsewhere connected with the Messianic Promise, and which certainly finds its historical counterpart only in the advent of the Saviour. Between the foreground and this bright horizon we have a delineation of those political catastrophes in which Jéhovah whelms Israel's enemies—the overthrow of the Philistine strongholds and extinction of the Philistine race; the utter desolation of the lands of Moab and Ammon; carnage and bloodshed in Ethiopia; last, because most important, that overthrow of Nineveh which had been already foretold by Nahum, and which in point of time preceded the Chaldean invasion.

Against Jerusalem, therefore, Zephaniah invokes a "day of wrath," which is to purge her of her idolatry and lawlessness. To the remnant of faithful worshippers on the other hand he promises that the period of affliction shall pave the way for the glorification of God's people and the extension of His kingdom to the Gentiles. In effecting this purpose, God shall bring low the powers of this world (chap. iii. 8). The nations which have afflicted His people in time past shall be effaced (chap. ii. 4—15). Judah's captivity shall be turned, Jerusalem shall become the honoured source of religious enlightenment to the lands which once put her to shame (chap. iii. 19, 20).

An extensive vista is thus opened to our view. Unlike some of his predecessors, Zephaniah does not fix his attention on one historical episode. His prophetic gaze ranges from the sack of Jerusalem, not fifty years after the date of his composition, to the extension of God's kingdom, effected 600 years later. Historically there is no connected course of events discernible. Continuity is brought into the prophecy only by regarding Nebuchadnezzar's invasion, the captivity and the restoration, and the fluctuating fortunes of the surrounding nations as all subsidiary to one divine purpose —that of bringing Israel through suffering to glory. The details of this prophecy are thus incapable of a comprehensive treatment. Their relation to the actual course of history must be treated of in the commentary rather than in the general introduction.

Those who have taken a different view of Zephaniah's prophecy have usually endeavoured to focus the prophet's gaze on some one historical episode in which lie the germs of all the political changes foretold. Two such episodes have found special favour. (1.) The Scythian invasion of Northern Asia, which we have mentioned in our *Introduction* to Nahum (II.) (2.) The upgrowth of the Babylonian empire. We close this section with an examination of these two theories of "occasion."

(1.) The Scythian invasion has been favoured by those who assume that the prophets had no inspired power of prediction. It is supposed that a Scythian incursion into Media and Assyria, which took place about the time of Zephaniah, was extended southwards, menacing Jerusalem itself, and inflicting desolation on the nationalities mentioned in chap. ii. This catastrophe is made the basis of Zephaniah's composition, which thus falls from the level of prophecy to that of a political *brochure*. The entire groundwork of this theory may be included in a few lines.

Herodotus describes (most inaccurately) an irruption of the Scythians into Media, about this time. He says that they established an empire in Upper Asia, to which he ascribes a duration of twenty-eight years (!). (see Herod. i. 103—106). Herodotus also mentions the march of an isolated Scythian force in the direction of Egypt. Psammetichus, the Egyptian king, arrested this incursion "in Palestine-Syria . . . by gifts and entreaties." The only mischief recorded is the plundering of a temple of Venus in Ascalon by "some few" of the Scythians "who were left behind" (Herod. i. 105). This is literally the only record of any Scythian incursions in the south. How far this innocuous march through Philistia illustrates the prophet's account of a depopulation of Jerusalem, a permanent desolation of Philistia, Moab, and Ammon, and a destruction of the Ethiopians, we leave to the judgment of the intelligent student.

(2.) The theory which concentrates the prophet's attention exclusively on the period of the Chaldean ascendancy appears at first sight more plausible. The overthrow of Nineveh, the execution of the Divine sentence on Jerusalem, and the captivity of the tribe of Judah (chap. ii. 13—15, i. 7—18, ii. 7), may all be associated with this subject. So, too, may the promises of Jerusalem's glorification (chap. iii. 14, *et seq.*), since the completion of the punishment, and the return from Babylon, are regarded elsewhere in Scripture as a kind of proem to the reign of Messiah. But it appears impossible to refer the judgments on Philistia, Moab, and Ammon (chap. ii. 4—9) to Chaldean agencies. There is no evidence that Nebuchadnezzar's invasion brought siege and destruction to the four Philistine cities. Moab and Ammon actually aided Nebuchadnezzar in punishing Jerusalem. It is true these two tribes were themselves chastised five years later for the murder of the Chaldean governor, Gedaliah, but no permanent desolation was effected, such as is described in chap. ii. 9. Nor is it certain that the Ethiopians suffered at the hands of the new world-power. This theory, therefore, must be considered as untenable as the other. The Chaldean invasion has an important place in the prophecy. But Zephaniah's political forecasts cannot be associated exclusively with the rise and progress of the Chaldean empire.

III. Division of Contents.—Only one distinct break occurs in this composition—that between chapters ii. and iii. Transitions of a less marked kind divide the book into six distinct sections, varying considerably in length. (*a*) The prophet's exordium announces a far-searching judgment on Judah and Jerusalem, and sets forth the reason of its infliction—viz., the prevalence of idolatry and religious apostacy (chap. i. 1—6). (*b*) The judgment is then described in reference to the various classes on whom it shall light (chap. i. 7—13), and its terribly destructive character (chap. i. 14—18). (*c*) The exhortation to repent in time (chap. ii. 1—3). (*d*) As an encouragement to those who "seek the Lord" the oppressive nationalities are depicted as succumbing on all sides to the might of Jehovah, whose worship is established in all the coasts of the heathen (chap. ii. 4—15). (*e*) Reverting to his own country, the prophet denounces Jerusalem as full of corruption, and as hopelessly obdurate (chap. iii. 1—7). (*f*) From this immediate present he passes again to the final issue: God's wrathful visitations shall result in the extension of His kingdom to the Gentiles (chap. iii. 8—10), and the promotion of the purified remnant of Israel to a position of great honour (chap. iii. 10—20).

IV. Character and Style.—The theological character of Zephaniah's composition is somewhat remarkable. None of the minor prophets takes such a comprehensive view of the Divine administration of human fortunes. In some prophets we have a revelation of Jehovah's retributive judgments on heathen powers;

in others, we meet with the announcement of the purifying judgments which are to visit the sacred nation. Here, however, both these themes are combined as phases in one orderly dispensation. A wide extension of Jehovah's kingdom is the final issue of this dispensation. The nations are to worship the one true God, and Jerusalem is to be honoured of all men as the fountain-head of religious knowledge. It is a result which is predicted in other prophetical passages, and usually it is associated with the reign of Messiah. Here, however, the Messianic promise is not once mentioned. But for this notable omission, Zephaniah's composition might be regarded as a very epitome of all prophetic theology. Next to this comprehensiveness of view, the most striking trait in the book is the importance attached to worship as an indication of the spiritual condition. The crying sin of Jerusalem is her neglect or perversion of the duty of worship (chap. i. 4—6). The result of the chastisement of the Gentile tribes is to be the extension of pure worship (chap. ii. 11, iii. 9), so that from the remotest lands the *minchâh*, or bloodless sacrifice, is offered to Jehovah (chap. iii. 10). The restoration of Israel is represented as re-establishing those sacred festivals which formed so important a part of the national worship (chap. iii. 18). Other noticeable traits are the representation of Israel's spiritual ascendancy, by the figure of an extended territory—see chap. ii. 7, 9; the remarkable deprecation of the sin of spiritual pride in chap. iii. 11; the association of affliction and sanctification in chap. iii. 12; the conception of the Gentiles worshipping Jehovah, not only at Jerusalem, but also at home—"every one from his place" (chap. ii. 11).

The literary style of Zephaniah is apparently deteriorated by the extensive range of his theme. It lacks the precision and sententious vigour which characterise those prophets whose attention is riveted on issues immediately impending. The whole composition is deficient, we feel, as regards symmetry and orderly sequence. One of the most striking sections in the book, the sentence against the foreign nationalities (chap. ii. 4—15), seems to come in half parenthetically, so that we are reminded of that Pauline trait which has been styled "going off at a word." Similarly, at chap. iii. 8, the writer passes, without regard to continuity, from Jerusalem's iniquities to her restoration from captivity. This lack of arrangement extends to minor details. The language is impassioned, but it has not that eloquence which is imparted by sustained rhythm. It is diffuse, but that artistic parallelism which in the higher types of Hebrew poetry makes diffuseness and even tautology palatable, is altogether absent. The diction suggests a memory laden with older Scriptural passages, rather than any creative capacity. The works on which the prophet is more especially dependent are the Pentateuch, and the prophecies of Micah and Isaiah. Peculiarities of construction, such as are common in more original writers, are of rare occurrence in Zephaniah; the book is therefore easy to read. We feel that it is semi-historical, rather than poetical. Unlike more vigorous compositions, such as Nahum's and Habakkuk's, it loses little in an English translation.

ZEPHANIAH

CHAPTER I.—(1) The word of the
LORD which came unto Zephaniah the
son of Cushi, the son of Gedaliah, the
son of Amariah, the son of Hizkiah, in
the days of Josiah the son of Amon,
king of Judah.
(2) [1] I will utterly consume all *things*
from off [2] the land, saith the LORD.
(3) I will consume man and beast; I will
consume the fowls of the heaven, and
the fishes of the sea, and the [3] stumbling-
blocks with the wicked; and I will cut
off man from off the land, saith the
LORD.
(4) I will also stretch out mine hand
upon Judah, and upon all the inhabi-
tants of Jerusalem; and I will cut off
the remnant of Baal from this place,
and the name of the Chemarims with
the priests; (5) and them that worship
the host of heaven upon the housetops;
and them that worship *and* that swear
[4] by the LORD, and that swear by Mal-
cham; (6) and them that are turned back
from the LORD; and *those* that have
not sought the LORD, nor enquired for
him.
(7) Hold thy peace at the presence of
the Lord GOD: for the day of the LORD
is at hand: for the LORD hath pre-
pared a sacrifice, he hath [5] bid his
guests.

B.C. cir. 630.

1 Heb., *By taking away I will make an end.*

2 Heb., *the face of the land.*

3 Or, *idols.*

4 Or, *to the* LORD.

5 Heb., *sanctified* or, *prepared.*

(1—6) Judgment on Judah and Jerusalem is impending on account of a religious apostacy of manifold forms and degrees. The wide range of this judgment.

(1) **Hizkiah.**—Or, *Hezekiah;* possibly the king of that name (see Introd. I.).

(2, 3) In this extensive denunciation there is clearly a reminiscence of Gen. vii. 23. The "fishes of the sea," however, are substituted for the "creeping things." The prophecy in Manasseh's reign (2 Kings xxi. 13) should be compared.

(3) **The stumblingblocks with the wicked.**—*i.e.*, the enticements to sin together with the sinners. The word *macshêlâh* is used in Isa. iii. 6 in the sense of "a ruin." Here, however, such a signification would not be apposite. It is exactly the πάντα τὰ σκάνδαλα of Matt. xiii. 41, a passage wherein we may perhaps see a reminiscence of the text before us.

(4) **The remnant of Baal.**—*i.e.*, Baal worship shall be completely and utterly abolished. Not even a remnant of it shall be left. The term "remnant" need not imply, as Kleinert argues, that a large part of the Baal-worship had been already overthrown, by Josiah's reformation.

The Chemarims.—In 2 Kings xxiii. 5, this is the designation of the "idolatrous priests whom the kings of Judah had ordained to burn incense in the high places." The term is used again in Hos. x. 5. Even the very name of these intruders is to be abolished.

The priests.—Are probably a certain section of the Jewish priesthood who had winked at this establishment of false worship.

(5) The worship "on the housetops" is mentioned elsewhere as the cult of a certain class of apostates (see Jer. xix. 13, xxxii. 29) who ascended roofs and other high places to adore the hosts of heaven. We find it mentioned as part of Josiah's reformatory procedure that he removed "the altars that were on the top of the upper chamber of Ahaz" (2 Kings xxiii. 12). The last half of the verse should be rendered, *And the worshippers who swear to Jehovah, and who swear* (also) *by Malcham*—*i.e.*, those who divide their allegiance between the true God and the false. In the title given to the latter we may perhaps see a combination of "their king" (Hebrew, *malcâm*) and the name Moloch, or Molech. The name Malcham, however, occurs elsewhere as the name of an Ammonite deity, probably identical with Moloch. (See Jer. xlix. 1—3, Notes.) In 1 Kings xi. 5, moreover, we have a deity "Milcham," who is identified two verses later with Molech, "the abomination of the children of Ammon." The allusion to the adoration of the "host of heaven upon the housetops" gains additional force if this deity is identical with the planet Saturn, as some have supposed. (See Gesenius, *sub voce*).

(6) Schmieder observes that the enumeration of verses 4—6 extends from gross external to refined internal apostasy. "The Lord will destroy (1) the idols of Baal; (2) their priests; (3) those who openly worship them on housetops; (4) the secret worshippers; (5) those who, without worshipping idols, have apostatised in their hearts; (6) those who are indifferent to religion."

(7—13) The judgment, in reference to its objects.

(7) **Hold thy peace. . .**—Literally, *Hush at the presence of* the Lord God. This peculiar phrase is repeated in Hab. ii. 20.

A sacrifice.—The word includes the idea of the feast in which it was customary to consume the remains of the sacrifice. (See Ps. xxii. 26, 29.) Hence the clause "He has bid his guests;" or, more literally, *He has consecrated* [set apart for himself] *his invited ones.* (Comp. Isa. xiii. 3.) God's guests are here those foreign nations whom He has selected to be His ministers of chastisement. They are invited, as it were, to banquet upon God's apostate people. The figure is probably borrowed from Isa. xxxiv. 6.

(8) And it shall come to pass in the day
of the LORD's sacrifice, that I will
[1] punish the princes, and the king's
children, and all such as are clothed
with strange apparel. (9) In the same
day also will I punish all those that
leap on the threshold, which fill their
masters' houses with violence and deceit.
(10) And it shall come to pass in that
day, saith the LORD, *that there shall be*
the noise of a cry from the fish gate,
and an howling from the second, and a
great crashing from the hills. (11) Howl,
ye inhabitants of Maktesh, for all the
merchant people are cut down; all they
that bear silver are cut off. (12) And it
shall come to pass at that time, *that* I
will search Jerusalem with candles,
and punish the men that are [2] settled
on their lees: that say in their heart,
The LORD will not do good, neither will
he do evil. (13) Therefore their goods
shall become a booty, and their houses
a desolation: they shall also build houses,
but [a] not inhabit *them;* and they shall
plant vineyards, but not drink the wine
thereof.

(14) The great day of the LORD *is* near,
it is near, and hasteth greatly, *even* the
voice of the day of the LORD: the
mighty man shall cry there bitterly.
(15) That day *is* a day of [b] wrath, a day
of trouble and distress, a day of waste-
ness and desolation, a day of darkness
and gloominess, a day of clouds and
thick darkness, (16) a day of the trumpet
and alarm against the fenced cities,
and against the high towers. (17) And
I will bring distress upon men, that
they shall walk like blind men, because

1 Heb., *visit upon.*

2 Heb., *curded,* or, *thickened.*

a Deut. 28. 30, 39; Amos 5. 11.

b Jer. 30. 7; Joel 2. 11; Amos 5. 18.

---

(8) **The king's children.**—The misfortunes which were to befall Josiah's children, Jehoahaz and Jehoiakim (see 2 Kings xxiii., xxiv.), are perhaps in the prophet's eye. But if we are correct in our view of the date of writing (see Introd. II.) these princes must have been as yet mere children, and could hardly have provoked the prophet's curse by any extraordinary display of wickedness. It therefore appears better to suppose that the king's brothers or uncles are meant. (Comp. the phrase in 2 Kings xi. 2; 2 Chron. xxii. 11.)

Clothed with strange apparel.—Zephaniah means those who have imitated the luxurious dress of foreign nations: *e.g.*, perhaps the gorgeous apparel of Assyria and Babylonia (Ezek. xxiii. 12—15). This desire for strange clothing is specially noticed as a mark of apostasy, because the national dress, with its blue riband at the fringe, was appointed that the Jews might "look upon it, and remember all the commandments of the Lord, and do them" (Num. xv. 38, 39).

(9) **Their masters' houses.**—Better, *their lord's house,* meaning the temple of their idol-deity. Probably the true interpretation of this obscure verse is that the idolaters had adopted a usage prevalent in the Philistine temples of Dagon—that of leaping over the threshold on entering the idol's temple. (See 1 Sam. v. 5.) When they entered it they filled it with "violence and deceit" by bringing thither offerings acquired by fraud and oppression. Another interpretation makes the verse relate exclusively to plunder and unjust acquisition of goods. "Leaping the threshold" is then expounded as "a sudden rushing into houses to steal the property of strangers," and the offenders are identified as "servants of the king, who thought they could best serve their master by extorting treasures from their dependants by violence and fraud" (Ewald). It does not seem likely that such malpractices would have been tolerated among the retainers of the pious Josiah; it is possible, however, to suppose that he had not yet acquired sufficient authority to check them.

(10) **The fish gate.**—See Note on 2 Chron. xxxiii. 14; Neh. iii. 3.

The second.—The word "city" is to be supplied. The new or lower city is meant. The same expression occurs in 2 Kings xxii. 14; Neh. xi. 9.

From the hills.—The "hills" are probably, Mount Zion and Mount Moriah, the sites of the old Davidic city and the Temple. Thus all parts of the city are to be included in this destruction.

(11) **Maktesh.**—Better, *the mortar,* a term indicating probably some part of the city lying in a hollow: perhaps that part which was in the valley of Tyropœon. This quarter is described by Josephus as "full of houses" (*B.J.* V. iv. § 1). Hence some detect in the name "mortar" an allusion to the noisy din of the commerce here conducted. The name occurs here only. Some suppose that it is a term coined by Zephaniah, to signify how everything in Jerusalem should be bruised to pieces as in a mortar.

Merchant people.—Literally, *people of Canaan,* a phrase used elsewhere for traders and merchants, and therefore not to be restricted to its original signification here.

All they that bear silver.—Literally, *all they that are laden with silver.* Another mode of designating this commercial class.

(12) **The men that are settled on their lees.**—The figure is taken from wine which has become harsh from being allowed to stand too long on the lees. The persons intended are selfish sybarites, whose souls have stagnated in undisturbed prosperity, and whose inexperience of affliction has led them to deny the agency of God in the world: men like the rich fool in the parable of Luke xii. 16—20.

(13) Part of the curse on apostasy in Deut. xxviii. is, "Thou shalt build an house, and thou shalt not dwell therein: thou shalt plant a vineyard, and shalt not gather the grapes thereof."

(14–18) The judgment, in reference to its destructive character.

(14) **Even the voice of the day.**—Better, *Hark to the day!* What is heard is the cry of the baffled warrior, unable either to fight or flee.

(15) **Clouds and thick darkness.**—As when Jehovah revealed Himself on Mount Sinai: see Deut. iv. 11.

(16) **Alarm.**—Better, *war cry.*

(17) **Walk like blind men.**—*i.e.,* groping about

they have sinned against the LORD:
and their blood shall be poured out as
dust, and their flesh as the dung.
(18) [a]Neither their silver nor their gold
shall be able to deliver them in the day
of the LORD's wrath; but the whole
land shall be [b]devoured by the fire of
his jealousy: for he shall make even a
speedy riddance of all them that dwell
in the land.

CHAPTER II.—(1) Gather yourselves
together, yea, gather together, O nation
[1]not desired; (2) before the decree bring
forth, *before* the day pass as the chaff,
before the fierce anger of the LORD
come upon you, before the day of the
LORD's anger come upon you. (3) Seek
ye the LORD, all ye meek of the earth,
which have wrought his judgment; seek
righteousness, seek meekness: it may
be ye shall be hid in the day of the
LORD's anger.

(4) For Gaza shall be forsaken, and
Ashkelon a desolation: they shall drive
out Ashdod at the noon day, and Ekron
shall be rooted up. (5) Woe unto the
inhabitants of the sea coast, the nation
of the Cherethites! the word of the
LORD *is* against you; O Canaan, the
land of the Philistines, I will even de-
stroy thee, that there shall be no in-

[a] Prov. 11. 4; Ezek. 7. 19.

[b] ch. 3. 8.

[1] Or, *not desirous.*

---

in fancied insecurity. The metaphor is taken from Deut. xxviii. 29. Their blood shall be poured out as recklessly as dust, and their flesh cast aside like the vilest refuse. Compare the sentence on Jehoiakim (Jer. xxii. 19): "He shall be buried with the burial of an ass," &c.

(18) **He shall make even a speedy riddance.**—Literally, *He shall effect a destruction, yea, a terrible one.* Comp. Isa. x. 23, from which passage this phraseology is probably borrowed.

II.

(1—3) An exhortation to seek God before His day of vengeance is revealed.

(1) **Gather yourselves together.**—This rendering has little to recommend it. Two translations of the obscure verb here used are possible: *Sift yourselves, yea sift—i.e.,* winnow out the sins which have roused Jehovah's anger; or *Bend yourselves, yea bend.* We prefer the latter. The contumacious nation is exhorted to *bend* in submission to Jehovah before His judgment is revealed.

O nation not desired.—Better, *O nation that art not abashed—scil.* by God's threats: the shameless defiant nation; so the LXX., ἔθνος ἀπαιδευτόν.

(2) **Before the decree bring forth.**—*i.e.,* before God's decree or ordinance, against which they have offended, brings forth the curse foretold in chap. i. There is no occasion to identify the "decree" with the Book of the Law brought to light at the time of Josiah's Reformation (see Introd. II.).

Before the day pass as the chaff.—Better, perhaps, parenthetically, *for the day is passing by like chaff.* The time for repentance is speeding by like chaff whirled before the wind.

(3) **Wrought his judgment.**—Or, rather, *executed His sentence*—acted in compliance with His revealed will by refraining from the sins above specified.

(4—15) Jehovah's chastisement of foreign powers. These Divine visitations are introduced somewhat abruptly. The connection is perhaps that they are intended to lead God's people to repent, and put their faith in Him who orders the destinies of all mankind. Also, as being inflicted on hostile peoples, they are in Israel's favour, and ought therefore to elicit gratitude. But more especially are they all steps towards the establishment of Jehovah's supremacy, and the inclusion of the Gentiles in His kingdom upon earth. (Comp. chaps. ii. 11, iii. 9, *et seq.*) This part of the Divine sentence is presented in three strophes of four verses each—viz., the chastisement of Philistia (verses 4—7); of Moab and Ammon (verses 8—11); of Ethiopia and Assyria (verses 12—15).

(4—7) The sentence against the great Philistine strongholds.

(4) In the words "Gaza (*Azzâh*) shall be forsaken (*âzab*)" and "Ekron shall be rooted up (*âkar*)" there is a paronomasia, or play on the words, similar to that in Micah i. 10, *et seq.*

At the noon day.—*i.e.,* this city shall be so weak and defenceless that there will be no need to surprise it at night: it shall be "spoiled at noon day" (Jer. xv. 8).

It is noticeable that it is these four of the five Philistine cities which are denounced by Amos (chap. i. 6—8) and Jeremiah (chap. xxv. 20). See also Zech. ix. 5. Gaza was captured by Alexander the Great in B.C. 332, after a two months' siege, and re-peopled. It was destroyed by Antiochus in B.C. 198, for its fidelity to the cause of Ptolemy. It was razed to the ground by Alexander Jannæus, but was rebuilt, and appears to have been a place of importance in the time of Antipater. It was assigned by the Romans to the kingdom of Herod, and after his death to the province of Syria. The modern Gaza is described as "a place of very considerable size, larger than Jerusalem." Of the ancient Ashkelon little is known, but the town in later times rose to a position of considerable importance. Antipater is said to have conciliated both "the Gazites and Ascalonites by many and large presents" (Jos., *Ant.* XIV. i. § 3. Its inhabitants joined with those of Gaza in the perpetration of some horrible atrocities in A.D. 361. The Ascalonites are described as the "hostes immanissimi" of the Crusaders. Ashdod, the Greek Azotus, was destroyed by the Maccabees, and not restored till the Roman conquest, when Gabinius rebuilt it, B.C. 55. It was allotted to Salome after Herod's death. Ekron is scarcely mentioned in post-Biblical history. The prophecy appears only to indicate broadly that the Philistines as a nation should be obliterated, and the remnant of Judah be exalted. This effacement of the Philistine race had probably occurred before the Christian era. The last mention of the Philistines as a nation is in 1 Macc. iii. 5.

(5) **The Cherethites.**—Perhaps Cretans. See on 1 Sam. xxx. 14; Ezek. xxv. 16, where the same term is applied to the Philistines.

habitant. (6) And the sea coast shall be
dwellings *and* cottages for shepherds,
and folds for flocks. (7) And the
coast shall be for the remnant of the
house of Judah; they shall feed there-
upon: in the houses of Ashkelon shall
they lie down in the evening: [1] for the
LORD their God shall visit them, and
turn away their captivity. (8) I have
heard the reproach of Moab, and the
revilings of the children of Ammon,
whereby they have reproached my people,
and magnified *themselves* against their
border. (9) Therefore *as* I live, saith
the LORD of hosts, the God of Israel,
Surely Moab shall be as Sodom, and the
children of Ammon as Gomorrah, *even*
the breeding of nettles, and saltpits,
and a perpetual desolation: the residue
of my people shall spoil them, and the
remnant of my people shall possess
them. (10) This shall they have for their
pride, because they have reproached
and magnified *themselves* against the
people of the LORD of hosts.
(11) The LORD *will be* terrible unto
them: for he will [2] famish all the gods
of the earth; and *men* shall worship
him, every one from his place, *even* all
the isles of the heathen. (12) Ye Ethio-
pians also, ye *shall be* slain by my sword.
(13) And he will stretch out his hand
against the north, and destroy Assyria;
and will make Nineveh a desolation,
and dry like a wilderness. (14) And
flocks shall lie down in the midst of
her, all the beasts of the nations: both
the [3] [a] cormorant and the bittern shall

1 Or, *when*, &c.

2 Heb., *make lean.*

3 Or, *pelican.*

a Isa. 34. 11.

Canaan originally means "low-lying ground." It here indicates the low maritime plain inhabited by the Philistines.

(6) **Dwellings and cottages for shepherds.**—Better, *places for shepherds' pastures.* In *c'rôth* (best taken as plural of *car*, "a pasture") there is a paronomasia on *c'rêthîm* of verse 5. The term "sea coast" (literally, *line of the sea*) here, as in verse 5, designates maritime Philistia. This tract of country is represented as ravaged and depopulated, so as to be serviceable only as a mere sheep-walk. Afterwards (verse 7) the restored exiles of Judah make it their pasture-ground. That this predominance of the Jewish over the Philistine race actually took place is manifest. The allusion to the captivity of Judah and its termination is remarkable. "Who save He in whose hand are human wills could now foresee that Judah should, like the ten tribes, rebel, be carried captive, and yet, though like and worse than Israel in its sin, should, unlike Israel, be restored" (Pusey). In the opening words of verse 7 there is perhaps another paronomasia, for *chebel* ("sea coast" in verse 6), may also mean "an apportioned inheritance;" and the words here may be rendered, "and it shall be for an inheritance for the remnant of the house of Judah."

(7) **Visit them.**—For their relief, not their punishment. This is plain from the context; but such a use of the verb is rare.

(8—11) The sentence against Moab and Ammon, the descendants of Lot and the enemies of God's people, even in the post-exilic period, comp. Nehem. ii. 19, iv. 1, 3, 7.)

(8) **Reproach.**—*i.e.*, abusive speech, or offensive design expressed in words. Balak's appeal to Balaam, "Come, curse me this people," at once suggests itself. We may instance also the conspiracy described in Ps. lxxxiii. as illustrating this combination of Moab and Ammon for hostile purposes.

(9) **The breeding of nettles.**—Better, *an inheritance of nettles.* The propriety of illustrating the fate of Moab and Ammon by that of the cities of the plain is the greater in that Lot, the ancestor of these nationalities, was an inhabitant of Sodom, and narrowly escaped sharing its destruction. Ravages in Moab and Ammon were effected by Nebuchadnezzar in B.C. 582, probably in revenge for the murder of Gedaliah, the ruler of his appointment (Jos., *Ant.* X. ix. § 7). But the allusion here is to some later and more permanent work of destruction. The national existence of both Moab and Ammon appears to have ceased long before the Christian era. Josephus' assertion (*Ant.* I. xi. § 5.) that in his own time the Moabites were "a very great nation," is simply unintelligible. The extraordinary number of ruined towns in Moab has been noticed by every modern explorer.

(11) **Famish.**—Literally as in margin "make lean:" to "cause to disappear."

Every one from his place.—It is difficult to accept Keil's theory of a pregnant construction, "each one coming from his place:" *scil.* to Jerusalem. This passage, therefore, is one of the very few which foretell that the worship of Jehovah shall find centres outside the Holy Land. The usual prediction, on the other hand, represents the converted nations as "flowing" to Jerusalem.

Isles.—Better, *sea coasts.*

(12) Ethiopia is to suffer by the sword in the execution of God's purpose of magnifying His people. The conjunction of Ethiopia and Assyria is probably suggested by the earlier passage in Nahum iii. 8, *et seq.* In addition to its earlier vicissitudes at the hands of Assyrian invaders, Ethiopia perhaps suffered as an ally of Egypt after the battle of Carchemish. It was probably invaded by Nebuchadnezzar; see on Ezek. xxx. 4. With the Median ascendancy came a fresh series of calamities. Cambyses, the successor of Cyrus, reduced the country to a condition of vassalage, B.C. 525; and in the time of Xerxes the Ethiopians had to furnish a contingent against the Greeks.

(13—15) The sentence against Assyria in the north. This was fulfilled as early as B.C. 625, when Nineveh was taken and destroyed by the Medes and Babylonians. It will be remembered that this catastrophe is the theme of Nahum's prophecy. Its effects are here described in language similar to that of Nahum iii., which Zephaniah doubtless has in mind.

(14) **Both the cormorant. . . .**—Better, *Both*

lodge in the [1]upper lintels of it; *their*
voice shall sing in the windows; deso-
lation *shall be* in the thresholds: [2]for he
shall uncover the cedar work. (15) This
is the rejoicing city that dwelt care-
lessly, that said in her heart, [a]I *am*,
and *there is* none beside me: how is she
become a desolation, a place for beasts
to lie down in! every one that passeth
by her shall hiss, *and* wag his hand.

CHAPTER III.—(1) Woe to [3][4]her
that is filthy and polluted, to the oppress-
ing city! (2) She obeyed not the voice;
she received not [5]correction; she trusted
not in the LORD; she drew not near to
her God. (3) [b]Her princes within her
are roaring lions; her judges *are* evening
wolves; they gnaw not the bones till
the morrow. (4) Her [c]prophets *are* light
and treacherous persons: her priests
have polluted the sanctuary, they have
done [d]violence to the law.
(5) The just LORD *is* in the midst
thereof; he will not do iniquity: [6]every
morning doth he bring his judgment to
light, he faileth not; but the unjust
knoweth no shame. (6) I have cut off
the nations: their [7]towers are desolate;
I made their streets waste, that none
passeth by: their cities are destroyed,
so that there is no man, that there is
none inhabitant.
(7) I said, Surely thou wilt fear me,
thou wilt receive instruction; so their
dwelling should not be cut off, how-
soever I punished them: but they
rose early, *and* corrupted all their
doings. (8) Therefore wait ye upon me,
saith the LORD, until the day that I
rise up to the prey: for my determina-
tion *is* to gather the nations, that I
may assemble the kingdoms, to pour
upon them mine indignation, *even* all
my fierce anger: for all the earth
shall be devoured with the fire of my
[e]jealousy.
(9) For then will I turn to the people
a pure [8]language, that they may all
call upon the name of the LORD, to

1 Or, *knops*, or, *chapiters*.
2 Or, *when he hath uncovered*.
a Isa. 47. 8.
3 Or, *gluttonous*.
4 Heb., *craw*.
5 Or, *instruction*.
b Ezek. 22. 27; Mic. 3. 11.
c Jer. 23. 11; Hos. 9. 7.
d Ezek. 22. 26.
6 Heb., *morning by morning*.
7 Or, *corners*.
e ch. 1. 18.
8 Heb., *lip*.

---

the pelican and the hedgehog shall lodge on her pillar-capitals, these lying strewn upon the ground.

Their voice.—Better, *The voice* [of the bird] *shall sing in the windows*. "In the midst of the desolation, the muteness of the hedgehog, and the pensive loneliness of the solitary pelican, the musing spectator is startled by the glad strain of some song bird, unconscious that it is sitting in the windows of those at whose name the world grew pale" (Pusey). This description of desolation extends even to the cedar panelling of the roofless walls, which is to be laid open to wind and rain.

(15) The earlier part of this verse is doubtless based on Isa. xlvii. 8, "Hear now this, thou that art given to pleasures, that dwellest carelessly, that sayest in thine heart, I am and none else beside me." (See also Isa. xxiii. 7, and compare the language in Rev. xviii. 7.) The remainder of the verse reminds us of Jer. l. 23; Nahum iii. 19.

III.

(1–4) The prophet denounces the corruption and moral obduracy which characterise all classes in Jerusalem. This denunciation comes in with startling abruptness. The prophet does not even name the object of his reproof. The literal rendering is, *Woe, rebellious and polluted, thou oppressive city!*

(2) **Obeyed not the voice.**—Better, *hearkened not to the voice—i.e.*, of Jehovah, when He addresses her, as in chap. ii. 1—3. She trusts not in Jehovah, but in her own wealth (chap. i. 12); she draws not nigh to her God, but to Baal and Moloch (chap. i. 4—6).

(3) **Till the morrow.**—Better, *on the morrow*. The meaning is just the opposite to that given in the Authorised Version. They are so greedy that they devour their prey instantly, leaving *no* portion of it for the morrow.

(4) **Light and treacherous persons.**—Better, *braggarts and men of treachery*.

(5–7) In contradistinction to this universal corruption, Jehovah daily exemplifies the law of righteousness, yet sinners are not moved to repentance (verse 5). He sets forth the great judgments He has executed on other sinful nations, but the warning is not heeded (verses 6, 7).

(6) **The nations.**—Those that were destroyed by the agency of Israel on invading the Promised Land; those also which were cut off by the Assyrians and the other great powers whom God used as His instruments (Isa. xxxvii. 26).

(7) **I said, Surely thou wilt fear me . . .**—Better, *I said, Wouldest thou only fear me? wouldest thou receive correction? then should her dwelling-place not be destroyed, according to all that I have appointed for them; but they only speeded their infamous doings*. Our Saviour's lamentation over Jerusalem in Matt. xxiii. 37 naturally suggests itself.

All that I have appointed—i.e., in the way of punishment.

(8–10) This is an enlargement of the consolation addressed to the "meek of the earth" in chap. ii. 3, and of the prediction of chap. ii. 11. The great day of the Lord, which shall overthrow all that opposes itself to His sovereignty, shall also introduce an extension of religious knowledge to the nations.

(9) **To the people.**—Better, *To the peoples*, or *nations*.

A pure language.—The discord of Babel shall, as it were, give place to unity of language, when the worship of "gods many" shall yield to the pure service of Jehovah, whom men shall "with one mind and one mouth glorify."

serve him with one [1] consent. (10) From
beyond the rivers of Ethiopia my sup-
pliants, *even* the daughter of my dis-
persed, shall bring mine offering.
(11) In that day shalt thou not be
ashamed for all thy doings, wherein
thou hast transgressed against me: for
then I will take away out of the midst
of thee them that rejoice in thy pride,
and thou shalt no more be haughty
[2] because of my holy mountain. (12) I
will also leave in the midst of thee an
afflicted and poor people, and they shall
trust in the name of the LORD. (13) The
remnant of Israel shall not do iniquity,
nor speak lies; neither shall a deceitful
tongue be found in their mouth: for
they shall feed and lie down, and none
shall make *them* afraid.
(14) Sing, O [a] daughter of Zion; shout,
O Israel; be glad and rejoice with all
the heart, O daughter of Jerusalem.
(15) The LORD hath taken away thy
judgments, he hath cast out thine
enemy: the king of Israel, *even* the
LORD, *is* in the midst of thee: thou
shalt not see evil any more. (16) In that
day it shall be said to Jerusalem, Fear
thou not: *and to* Zion, Let not thine
hands be [3] slack. (17) The LORD thy God
in the midst of thee *is* mighty; he will
save, he will rejoice over thee with joy;
[4] he will rest in his love, he will joy over
thee with singing. (18) I will gather
them that are sorrowful for the solemn
assembly, *who* are of thee, *to whom* [5] the
reproach of it *was* a burden. (19) Behold,
at that time I will undo all that afflict
thee: and I will save her that [b] halteth,
and gather her that was driven out;
and [6] I will get them praise and fame in
every land [7] where they have been put to
shame. (20) At that time will I bring
you *again*, even in the time that I
gather you: for I will make you a name
and a praise among all people of the
earth, when I turn back your captivity
before your eyes, saith the LORD.

1 Heb., *shoulder*.

2 Heb., *in my holy*.

a Isa. 12. 6. & 54. 1.

3 Or, *faint*.

4 Heb., *he will be silent*.

5 Heb., *the burden upon it was reproach*.

b Mic. 4. 7.

6 Heb., *I will set them for a praise*.

7 Heb., *of their shame*.

---

(10) **The daughter of my dispersed.**—*i.e.*, dropping the Hebrew idiom, "my dispersed people." Even from the southern limit of the known world shall the new Church draw adherents. The "dispersed people" are not Jewish exiles, but the Gentile tribes of the dispersion (of Gen. xi. 8) which have been hitherto alienated from their Creator by ignorance and vice. Similarly, Caiaphas prophesies that Christ should not only die for the Jewish nation, but that "He should gather together in one" the children of God that "were scattered abroad" (John xi. 51, 52).

Bring mine offering.—The *minchâh* or bloodless oblation. The phrase here merely represents homage rendered to Jehovah as paramount. So in Mal. i. 11 it is foretold that "in every place incense shall be offered unto my name, and a pure *minchâh*." In Isa. lxvi. 20, on the other hand, the Gentiles are represented as bringing the dispersed Jews back to Jerusalem "as a *minchâh* to Jehovah." De Wette and others (wrongly, as we believe), give this passage the same force, rendering, "From beyond the rivers of Ethiopia shall men bring my suppliants, even my dispersed people, as my offering."

(11—13) Jerusalem shall then have no occasion to blush for obdurate iniquity (verse 5), for she shall be inhabited by a remnant who have learnt meekness and righteousness in the school of adversity.

(11) **No more be haughty . . .**—His very privileges—the adoption and the Shechinah, and the covenants, and the giving of the law, and the Temple service—had hitherto been used by the Jew as a pretext for obduracy. "We have Abraham for our father," "The temple of the Lord are these:" such was their response to the preaching of repentance. The reinstated nation shall be purged of this spiritual pride.

(12) **Afflicted.**—*ânî*, a condition which is likely to make them also "meek," *ânâv*, instead of "haughty."

(14—20) The blessedness of Jerusalem when she has been thus brought through suffering to glory.

(15) **Taken away thy judgments.**—*i.e.*, removed what He had "appointed concerning them" (verse 7) in the way of punishments.

The king of Israel.—The recognition of Jehovah as *king* is elsewhere a prominent feature in the portraiture of the extended dispensation. Thus we have, "Say among the heathen that Jehovah is king" (Ps. xcvi. 10). "Jehovah is king" (Pss. xciii. 1, xcvii. 1, xcix. 1). "The kingdom shall be Jehovah's" (Obad. verse 21).

(16) Compare Isa. xxxv. 3, 4, lxii. 11, *et seq.*

(17) **He will rest . . .**—Better, *He will keep silence in His love; He will exult over thee with a shout of joy.* Unutterable yearnings and outbursts of jubilant affection are both the expressions of sexual love. By a bold anthropomorphism, both are attributed to the Heavenly Bridegroom, as He gazes on "a glorious Church . . . holy, and without blemish."

(18) The festival of the accomplishment of salvation is represented under the figure of the joyous Feast of Tabernacles, as in Zech. xiv. 16. None shall be impeded from attending on this joyous occasion, for the oppressors shall be overthrown (verses 19, 20).

To whom the reproach of it was a burden.—Or, *on whom reproach was a burden*—*i.e.*, on whom their exile, and consequent inability to attend at Jerusalem, had brought derision. On the construction, the Hebrew student may consult Hitzig or Kleinert.

(19) **I will undo.**—Better, *I will deal with*, as in Ezek. xxiii. 25. The clauses following are based on Micah iv. 6; Deut. xxvi. 19.

(20) See Deut. xxx. 3, *et seq.*

INTRODUCTION

TO

HAGGAI

I. The Author.—Haggai is in point of time the first of the prophets of the Post-Captivity period. Of his tribe and parentage nothing is recorded in Scripture. It is not even known whether he was born before or during the exile, nor whether his birth took place in Judæa or in Babylon. Ewald infers from the comparison adduced in chap. ii. 3 that the prophet had himself seen the first Temple. In this case he must have been advanced in years at the time of his delivering these prophecies. The passage, however, does not at all necessitate this inference. On the other hand, a worthless Patristic tradition records that Haggai was born at Babylon, and delivered his prophecies in youth, that he survived the completion of the Temple (B.C. 516), and was interred with honour close to the burial-place of the priests. (See Pseudo-Dorotheus, in *Chron. Pasch.* 151 *d.*) The Jewish legend makes Haggai a member of the Great Synagogue of one hundred and twenty elders established by Ezra. To this is attached an absurd account of his surviving till the visit of Alexander the Great to Jerusalem.

All that we certainly know of the personal history of the prophet is gathered from chaps. i. 1, ii. 1, 10, 20, compared with Ezra v. 1, vi. 14. (See below, on *Occasion of Writing.*) The LXX. prefixes the names of Haggai and Zechariah to Pss. cxxxviii., cxlvi.—cxlviii.; the Peshito Syriac to Pss. cxxvi., cxxvii., cxlvi.—cxlviii. Ps. cxlvi. is the first of a group of Psalms known among the Jews as the "five Hallelujahs," and probably composed for the services of the second Temple. Pseudo-Epiphanius records that Haggai was the first to chant the Hallelujah in this Temple. This he apparently regards as the explanation of the LXX. inscription, since he adds the comment, "Wherefore we say Hallelujah, which is the hymn of Haggai and Zechariah" (*de Vitis Proph.*). The name Haggai is certainly connected with the substantive *Chag*, "a feast." It is uncertain whether it means "My feasts" or "feasts of Jehovah;" or is to be regarded as an adjectival form, "festive."

II. **The Occasion of Writing.**—Haggai began to prophesy in the second year of Darius Hystaspis, *i.e.*, in B.C. 520. (Comp. chap. i. 1 and Ezra v. 1.) The object of his mission was to rouse the restored exiles from a condition of religious torpor, and induce them to complete the restoration of the Temple. To understand the circumstances under which Haggai began this work we must cast a glance backward at the history of the preceding fifteen years. The favourable edict of the first year of Cyrus (B.C. 536) had brought up to Judæa a congregation of some 42,360 freemen, besides 7,337 male and female slaves. In the seventh month of this year these restored exiles had set up an altar to Jehovah, and had observed the Feast of Tabernacles according to the ancient ordinance. The next year witnessed the foundation of the second House. We read that the joy appropriate to this occasion was damped by the regrets of the aged men who had seen the Temple of Solomon in its magnificence (Ezra iii. 12). This form of discouragement is found operating again, after Haggai had persuaded his countrymen to resume the work of building. (See chap. ii. 3.) A more direct obstacle to the business of restoration was the antagonistic attitude of the Samaritans. The semi-idolatrous character of the Samaritan religion had induced Zerubbabel and Joshua to decline the co-operation of their brethren of the north. Irritated at this slight, Rehum and Shimshai incited the heterogeneous tribes who had settled in Samaria, and "weakened the hands of the people of Judah, and troubled them in building." In order to obtain legal sanction for their proceedings, these adversaries secured the assistance of certain counsellors at the Persian court. This was in the reign of "Ahasuerus" (Cambyses), the successor of Cyrus. Their intrigue, however, did not come to a head till the accession of "Artaxerxes" (the usurper Pseudo-Smerdis, B.C. 522 or 521). In reply to a Samaritan petition alleging that Jerusalem had always been "a rebellious city, and hurtful unto kings and provinces," Artaxerxes issued an edict forbidding the rebuilding of the city. The prohibition made no mention of the Temple. It was easy, however, for Rehum and Shimshai to extend its scope, and stop the "work of the house of God" "by force and power" (Ezra iv. 23, 24).

It does not appear that the Jews themselves cared to have it otherwise. The usurper's reign lasted less than a year, and the accession of Darius Hystaspis (B.C. 521) might well have been regarded as an opportunity for obtaining an abrogation of the adverse decree. But the duties of religion were now regarded with indifference. The wealthy citizens availed themselves of the change of dynasty to commence building private mansions not void of pretension to magnificence (chap. i. 4, 9). But the dwelling-place of the Most High lay neglected. The work had progressed but slowly during the thirteen years preceding the accession of Artaxerxes. For at least a year and a half it was entirely suspended. It was at the close of this period that Haggai and Zechariah came forward and "prophesied unto the Jews that were in Judah and Jerusalem in the name of the God of Israel" (Ezra v. 1). The mission of both prophets dates from the middle of the year B.C. 520, the second year of Darius. Haggai's earliest utterances occurred in the sixth and seventh months of that year (chap. i—ii. 9). Zechariah next takes up the strain with an exhortation to repentance, dating from the eighth month (Zech. i. 1—6). Haggai delivers his final address on the twenty-fourth day of the ninth month. Exactly two months later begins Zechariah's series of visions (Zech. i. 7 *seq.*).

Haggai's first utterance was exclusively one of rebuke, its theme being his countrymen's neglect of the Lord's house. The effects of this utterance appear to have manifested themselves almost immediately. Zerubbabel the governor and Joshua the high priest, "with all the remnant of the people," turned a willing ear to his exhortation, and the prophet was able to change the accents of reproof for those of comforting assurance (chap. i. 13). Before the end of the month which witnessed the opening of Haggai's mission, the work of building had been resumed. The prophet was now able to extend his consolatory assurances, the prompt obedience of his hearers being rewarded by a twofold promise :—(*a*) the curse that had hitherto rested on all agricultural pursuits was to be removed; henceforth the labours of their hands should be blessed (chap. ii. 15—19); (*b*) the Temple they were rearing was to be connected with a great diffusion of religious knowledge. The old paths of this world's course were to be broken up; earthly powers were to be brought low; the Gentiles were to glorify Jehovah with worship and precious offerings; the royal line of Judah, now represented by Zerubbabel, was to be exhibited as the object of Jehovah's choice (chap. ii. 6—9, 21—23).

The Christian reader hardly needs to be informed when and how this latter promise was realised. Its connection with the New Dispensation is obvious and undeniable. The Saviour derived His man's nature from the royal line of David, and Zerubbabel's name is accordingly included in the pedigrees handed down by St. Matthew and St. Luke. The effect of His Dispensation has been indeed a "shaking of nations," a subjugation of the "kingdoms of the heathen." To the Jewish system and its Temple, His Advent imparted a glory hitherto unknown. It may be said, indeed, that the very presence in the Temple of "God manifest in the flesh" sufficiently illustrates the promise of chap. ii. 9: "There Christ, the Son of God, was as a child offered to God; there He sat in the midst of the doctors; there He taught and revealed things hidden from the foundation of the world." Such a presence was indeed a glory greater than that of the Shechinah.

To press the details of Haggai's prediction more closely than this appears impossible, and unnecessary. The transference of the glory of the Temple to the Messianic Church does not come under treatment. Nor can it be supposed that the second Temple was regarded by the prophet as in any way a type or a material counterpart of the Messianic Church. The commentators have forced ideas of this kind into chap. ii. 9, but they are quite foreign to the prophet's subject. The Hebrew term for the "House" of God does not admit of that variety of meaning which belongs to the Greek ἐκκλησία. It must be interpreted strictly of the material building, and the idea of an ecclesiastical organisation must be carefully excluded. Misinterpretations of another kind may be noticed in connection with the passages chap. ii. 6, 21, 22. Excess of literalism has introduced in these passages actual phenomena of nature such as Christ declared should precede the completion of His Dispensation; or, finding the interpretation in præ-Christian times, the commentators instance actual revolutions, and overturnings of particular dynasties, those of Persia, Syria, and Greece. But the verses in question really admit only of an ethical interpretation. They are to be expounded in accordance with the language of Old Testament prophecy elsewhere. The details are such as belong to the Hebrew idea of the Theophany of Messianic times, and therefore recur repeatedly in the Prophets and Psalms. It may be doubted whether they had any literal force in the conception of the poets. Certainly their historical counterpart must be found in the moral, not in the material sphere. The "House," finally, though the material Temple, is not necessarily the Temple of Zerubbabel. The substantial identity of God's Holy Place in all periods is assumed. The present building is represented as identical with Solomon's as well as with the Temple which is to be filled with glory. Thus the question whether Herod's was not a third Temple rather than a development of the second, need not come into consideration. In this connection we notice that the right rendering in chap. ii. 9 is "the latter glory of this house," &c., not "the glory of this latter house."

We have pointed out the leading features in this portraiture of Messianic times. It is proper to observe that, like many other Old Testament prophecies, it appears defective if subjected to minute analysis. We feel that the Temple fills in the prophetic delineation a far larger space than in the historical fact. It seems as if Haggai conceived of the religious influences of the Messianic age as all radiating from a material Temple Yet the Temple at Jerusalem passed away shortly after the Saviour's Advent, and had neither successor nor counterpart in the New Dispensation. It is an inconsistency which admits of large illustration, the conversion of the Gentiles being represented repeatedly by the prophets as if an accession to Judaism. The nations "flow to the mountain of the House of the Lord" (Micah iv. 1, 2; Isa. ii. 2); they receive a new birth at Jerusalem (Ps. lxxxvii.); they even go up to Jerusalem to keep the Feast of Tabernacles (Zech. xiv. 16). Such are the figures under which the extension of God's kingdom is almost always (see Zeph. iii. 10, note) represented. Instead of "beginning from Jerusalem" (Luke xxiv. 47) it leads men to Jerusalem. Instead of a Christian dispensation superseding a Jewish, the Jews invite the Gentiles into their own body. It is possible that, in some cases, the full significance of such prophetic language is yet to be revealed to the Church of Christ by the course of history. In Haggai's case, however, we believe we need not look beyond the event of the Saviour's first Advent. Obscurity will appear natural if we bear in mind that the facts which have been revealed to us in material historical shape were only presented to the vision of the Hebrew prophet "as in a glass darkly."

III. Division of Contents.—The Book of Haggai presents five distinct utterances, all included within the brief period of four months :—(*a*) In the first, Haggai rebukes his compatriots for their neglect of God's House. Their religious apathy is treated as the cause of the prevalent dearth (chap. i. 1—11). (*b*) Rulers and people showing signs of repentance, the prophet utters a comforting assurance—"I am with you, saith the LORD." The work of building is now actively resumed (chap. i. 12—15). (*c*) In view of a tendency to contrast the humble proportions of the new building with the grandeur of Solomon's Temple, Haggai promises that Jehovah's House shall hereafter have a glory to which the whole universe shall bear witness (chap. ii. 1—9). (*d*) Haggai's fourth address reverts to the prevalent dearth, and shows that the labours of men's hands have hitherto been cursed, because defiled by the sin of religious apathy. Though no signs of better times are visible, the prophet is empowered to utter the assurance, "From this day will I bless" (chap. ii. 10—19). (*e*) The prophet's final utterance attaches the promise of chap. ii. 1—9 to the line of Zerubbabel When the powers of this world are overthrown, this line shall be selected by Jehovah for special honour (chap. ii. 20—23).

IV. Character and Style.—In the prophecy of Zephaniah the extension of Jehovah's kingdom was treated as the climax to which all political changes and catastrophes should tend. Haggai, with the same bright hope before him, treats it almost exclusively in its relation to the restored Temple. Between the two prophets there intervenes the whole period of Chaldæan ascendency. The final warnings of Habakkuk and Jeremiah—the battle of Carchemish—Nebuchadnezzar's invasion—the sack of Jerusalem—the exile—the restoration—these are the steps which lead us upward from the level of the prophet of the Judgment to that of the prophet of the Temple's glories. The "day of wrath" is past. In fulfilment of Zephaniah's prediction the captivity of Judah has been turned; and in the midst of Jerusalem there survives a people "afflicted and poor" (Zeph. ii. 7, iii. 12). It is natural that the first prophecy of the new period should bear on internal reform, and that the restoration of the national religion should occupy the place hitherto filled by great political crises.

The character of the composition necessarily changes with the change of theme. Haggai's discourses are concentrated primarily on one particular phase of religious duty. They embrace details of a commonplace character, and of short-lived interest. High aspiration is not wanting, but it is almost exclusively associated with a theme which, at first sight, appears prosaic. In Haggai's utterances, in fact, the functions of a reformer and practical homilist are combined with those of the prophet. They necessarily lie open to the charge of being deficient in poetical ability. It must be admitted, moreover, that the style of the preacher is not such as recommends itself to a critical taste. Repetitions impair the vigour, anomalous constructions the smoothness of his discourses. His frequent use of interrogation and answer robs them of all rhythmical beauty. He is wont, as has been said, to "utter the main thought with concise and nervous brevity," but it is only after "a large and verbose introduction." Figures and tropes are altogether wanting, except in the predictions of chap. ii. 6, 7, 22. He is the most matter-of-fact of all the prophets. These defects are the more conspicuous in that his utterances are linked together by historical passages of the plainest prose. This composite character may nevertheless serve to explain the literary deficiencies of the book. We have here, it must be remembered, not a continuous outburst of prophetic inspiration, but five inspired utterances welded into one historical book. We do not know that this book proceeded from the pen of Haggai. On the contrary, it is at least as probable that this framework in which the prophet's discourses have been preserved is the work of some contemporary chronicler. In this case it would be natural that something of the eloquence and impressiveness of the preacher should be lost in the annalist's reproduction. It is even possible to suppose that the discourses of Haggai, as they now stand, are only a *résumé* or summary of what the prophet actually uttered.

HAGGAI

CHAPTER I.—(1) In the second year of Darius the king, in the sixth month, in the first day of the month, came the word of the LORD [1]by Haggai the prophet unto Zerubbabel the son of Shealtiel, [2]governor of Judah, and to Joshua the son of Josedech, the high priest, saying,

(2) Thus speaketh the LORD of hosts, saying, This people say, The time is not come, the time that the LORD's house should be built.

(3) Then came the word of the LORD by Haggai the prophet, saying,

(4) *Is it* time for you, O ye, to dwell in your cieled houses, and this house *lie* waste? (5) Now therefore thus saith the LORD of hosts; [3]Consider your ways. (6) Ye have [a]sown much, and bring in little; ye eat, but ye have not enough; ye drink, but ye are not filled with drink; ye clothe you, but there is none warm; and he that earneth wages earneth wages *to put it* into a bag [4]with holes. Thus saith the LORD of hosts; Consider your ways. (8) Go up to the mountain, and bring wood, and build the house; and I will take pleasure in

B.C. cir. 520.

1 Heb., *by the hand of Haggai.*

2 Or, *captain.*

3 Heb., *Set your heart on your ways.*

a Deut. 28. 38; Mic. 6. 14, 15.

4 Heb., *pierced through.*

(1–11) *The First Utterance.*—The neglect of God's House denounced, and declared to be the cause of the prevalent dearth.

(1) **Darius the king.**—*Scil.*, Darius I., son of Hystaspes, who became king of Persia in B.C. 521. The fact that there were still men living who had seen the First Temple (ii. 3), which fell in B.C. 586, sufficiently disproves the absurd theory that Darius Nothus is meant, who did not accede to the throne until B.C. 423–4. Prophecy is now dated by the years of a foreign ruler, for Zerubbabel, though a lineal descendant of David, was only a *pechâh*, or viceroy of Persian appointment, not a king in his own right.

The sixth month.—That named Elul, corresponding nearly with our September.

In the first day—*i.e.*, on the festival of the new moon, a holy day which had always been marked not only by suspension of labour, but by special services in the Temple (Ezek. xlvi. 3; Isa. lxvi. 23). It was thus an appropriate occasion for Haggai to commence a series of exhortations so intimately connected with the Temple. Besides, it appears to have been an ancient custom that the people should resort to the prophets for religious instruction on new moons and Sabbaths. (See 2 Kings iv. 23.)

Came the word . . .—Literally, *there was a word of the Lord by the hand of Haggai*, &c. This expression, which occurs repeatedly in this book, indicates that Jehovah was the direct source of these announcements, and Haggai only their vehicle.

The prophet.—See Hab. i. 1, Note.

Son of Shealtiel.—Strictly speaking, Zerubbabel was the son of Pedaiah, who contracted a Levirate marriage with the widow of his brother Shealtiel. (See Notes on 1 Chron. iii. 17; Jer. xxii. 30, Luke iii. 27.)

Governor.—*Satrap*, or *viceroy*, a term applied in the Old Testament to the provincial prefects of the Assyrian and Babylonian and Persian empires. (See Note on 1 Kings x. 15.) Joshua, the high priest, is a prominent character in the prophecy of Zechariah. Haggai addresses Zerubbabel as the civil, Joshua as the ecclesiastical head of the restored exiles.

(2) **The time is not come.**—Better (unless we alter the received text), *It is not yet time to come*—*i.e.*, it is not yet time to assemble and commence preparations for building. It is not stated on what grounds the people based this assumption; but probably they palliated their indifference to religion by a pretended dread of Persian hostility. Darius, however, unlike his predecessor Artaxerxes, gave the enemies of the Jews no countenance when a report was actually made to him on the subject. (See Ezra v. and vi.)

(4) **Is it time for you . . .**—Literally, *Is it time for you to dwell in your houses, and those ceiled?*—*i.e.*, probably with cedar and other costly woods. A crushing retort. If the adverse decree of Artaxerxes, which disallowed the building of Jerusalem (Ezra iv. 21), had not hindered them from erecting magnificent residences for themselves, how could it reasonably excuse an utter neglect of God's House?

(5) **Consider your ways.**—A common expression in this prophet. The results of their conduct are set forth in verse 6: they are left to infer from these what its nature has been.

(6) **Ye have sown much . . .**—Literally, *Ye have been sowing much and bringing in little; eating, and it was not to satisfaction; drinking, and it was not to fulness; clothing yourselves, and it was not for any one's being warm*, &c. This description of course merely implies that, notwithstanding all their labours, there was not much to eat, drink, or put on. Compare the use of the phrase "ye shall eat and not be satisfied," in Lev. xxvi. 26.

To put it into a bag with holes.—The last clause expresses in a bold metaphor the general prevalence of poverty. Scarcity necessitated high prices, so that money "ran away" as fast as it was earned.

(8) **The mountain.**—No *one* mountain is thought of. The term implies the high lands generally, as growing the most suitable timber for building purposes.

it, and I will be glorified, saith the
LORD. (9) Ye looked for much, and, lo,
it came to little; and when ye brought
it home, I did [1]blow upon it. Why?
saith the LORD of hosts. Because of
mine house that *is* waste, and ye run
every man unto his own house. (10) There-
fore [a]the heaven over you is stayed from
dew, and the earth is stayed *from* her
fruit. (11) And I called for a drought
upon the land, and upon the mountains,
and upon the corn, and upon the new
wine, and upon the oil, and upon *that*
which the ground bringeth forth, and
upon men, and upon cattle, and upon
all the labour of the hands.

(12) Then Zerubbabel the son of Sheal-
tiel, and Joshua the son of Josedech,
the high priest, with all the remnant of
the people, obeyed the voice of the LORD
their God, and the words of Haggai the
prophet, as the LORD their God had
sent him, and the people did fear before
the LORD.

(13) Then spake Haggai the LORD's
messenger in the LORD's message unto
the people, saying, I *am* with you, saith
the LORD.

(14) And the LORD stirred up the
spirit of Zerubbabel the son of Sheal-
tiel, governor of Judah, and the spirit
of Joshua the son of Josedech, the
high priest, and the spirit of all the
remnant of the people; and they came
and did work in the house of the LORD
of hosts, their God, (15) in the four and
twentieth day of the sixth month, in the
second year of Darius the king.

CHAPTER II.—(1) In the seventh
month, in the one and twentieth *day* of
the month, came the word of the LORD
[2]by the prophet Haggai, saying, (2) Speak
now to Zerubbabel the son of Shealtiel,
governor of Judah, and to Joshua the
son of Josedech, the high priest, and to
the residue of the people, saying,

(3) Who *is* left among you that saw
this house in her first glory? and how
do ye see it now? *is it* not in your eyes
in comparison of it as nothing? (4) Yet
now be strong, O Zerubbabel, saith the
LORD; and be strong, O Joshua, son of
Josedech, the high priest; and be strong,
all ye people of the land, saith the
LORD, and work: for I *am* with you,
saith the LORD of hosts: (5) *according to*
the word that I covenanted with you

1 Or, *blow it away.*

a Deut. 28. 23.

2 Heb., *by the hand of.*

---

(9) **Ye looked for much.**—Literally, *There has been a turning about for much.*

I did blow upon it—*scil.,* for the purpose of dispersing it. Even the little that was brought into the garner was decimated by God's continued disfavour.

(10) **Over you.**—Better, *on your account.—Scil.,* because of the neglect of God's House, mentioned in verse 9.

(11) **And I called for a drought upon.**—Better, *And I invoked a desolation upon.* Similarly in 2 Kings viii. 1, Elisha announces to the Shunammite. "The Lord hath called a famine, and it shall also come upon the land seven years."

(12–15) *The Second Utterance.*—The people turn a willing ear to Haggai's exhortation, and the prophet is now charged to inform them of the return of God's favour, in the gracious utterance, "I am with you, saith the Lord."

(12) **With all the remnant of.**—The word may mean either "the remnant" restored from Babylon, or merely "the remainder" of the people. Similarly in verse 14, ii. 2.

(13) **In the Lord's message.**—Or, *on the Lord's mission.*

(15) It must be supposed that the intervening three weeks had been spent in collecting timber in the upland region, as was ordered in verse 8, and resuming the "work of the house of God."

II.

(1–9) *The Third Utterance.*—This utterance treats of the glory which, in a later time, is to attach itself to the sacred spot whereon the returned exiles are labouring. It was intended more especially as a message of consolation to those who remembered Solomon's magnificent structure, and who now gazed sadly on the humble proportions of its successor.

(1) **In the one and twentieth day.**—Here, again, the day selected is significant. The twenty-first day of the seventh month (Tisri) was the seventh and last day of the Feast of Tabernacles. This was the festival of harvest thanksgiving, and its occurrence had always been marked by observances of a peculiarly joyous character. Moreover, the sacrifices on this occasion were very numerous—the number prescribed by the Talmud for the first day exceeding that of any other day in the year. Thus the scanty harvest and the small beginnings of the Lord's House would both be brought into prominence. It would be but natural if feelings of despondency were excited among those who were old enough to remember the Temple of Solomon, with its costly accessories and elaborate ceremonial, and the festive rites wherewith the "joy in harvest" had expressed itself in a more prosperous time. There is no ground, however, for supposing that the prophet was himself one of these aged persons.

(2) **The residue.**—See chap. i. 12, Note.

(3) **Is it not . . .**—Better, *is not such a* (Temple) *as this like nothing in your eyes?*

(5) **According to the word.**—Better, *with the word.* The clause is connected with the closing words of verse 4. Jehovah is present with them, and so is His Promise made by solemn covenant in the days of old.

when ye came out of Egypt, so my
spirit remaineth among you: fear ye
not.
(6) For thus saith the LORD of hosts;
[a]Yet once, it *is* a little while, and I will
shake the heavens, and the earth, and
the sea, and the dry *land;* (7) and I will
shake all nations, and the desire of all
nations shall come: and I will fill this
house with glory, saith the LORD of
hosts. (8) The silver *is* mine, and the
gold *is* mine, saith the LORD of hosts.
(9) The glory of this latter house shall
be greater than of the former, saith the
LORD of hosts: and in this place will I
give peace, saith the LORD of hosts.
(10) In the four and twentieth *day* of
the ninth *month*, in the second year of
Darius, came the word of the LORD by
Haggai the prophet, saying, (11) Thus
saith the LORD of hosts; Ask now the
priests *concerning* the law, saying, (12) If

a Heb. 12. 26.

So my spirit.—Better, *and my spirit.* Besides such promises of God's abiding favour as Exod. xxix. 45, 46, they have among them the abiding presence of His Holy Spirit. Having these, let them not be afraid. The evidence of the Divine Presence was the mission of inspired prophets, such as Haggai and Zechariah, and the Targum and the Rabbis are perhaps right in referring the words "and my spirit" exclusively to the "spirit of *prophecy.*" It may be noticed that the later Jews held that the Holy Spirit left the Church after the deaths of Zechariah and Malachi.

(6) **Yet once, it is a little while.**—The construction is very difficult. The best rendering appears to be *Yet one season more* (supplying *êth* before *achath*), *it is but a little while, and,* &c. The meaning of these clauses is then that given by Keil—viz., "that the period between the present and the predicted great change of the world will be but one period—*i.e.,* one uniform epoch—and that this epoch will be a brief one." The LXX. (followed in Heb. xii. 27) omits the words "it is a little while" altogether, and so is enabled to render "I will yet shake *once*" (*i.e.,* one single time, and one only), a rendering which, if we retain those words, is apparently impossible. The fact is, the original passage here, as in other cases, must be treated without deference to its meaning when interwoven in New Testament argument. There is yet to be an interval of time, of limited duration, and then shall come a new era, when the glory of God's presence shall be manifested more fully and extensively. Notwithstanding its intimate connection with the Jewish Temple (verses 7, 9), this new dispensation may well be regarded as that of the Messiah, for Malachi in like manner connects His self-manifestation with the Temple. (Comp. Mal. iii. 1, and see our Introduction, § 2.) Without pretending to find a fulfilment of all details, we may regard the prophet's anticipations as sufficiently realised when the Saviour's Advent introduced a dispensation which surpassed in glory (see 2 Cor. iii. 7—11) that of Moses, and which extended its promises to the Gentiles. When Haggai speaks here and in verse 22 of commotions of nature ushering in this new revelation, he speaks according to the usage of the Hebrew poets, by whom Divine interposition is frequently depicted in colouring borrowed from the incidents of the Exodus period. (See Hab. iii.; Ps. xviii. 7—15, xciii., xcvii.) If the words are to be pressed, their fulfilment at Christ's coming must be searched for rather in the moral than the physical sphere, in changes effected in the human heart (comp. Luke iii. 5) rather than on the face of nature.

(7) **And the desire of all nations shall come.**—Better, *and the precious things of all the nations shall come—scil.,* shall be brought as offerings. (Comp. Zeph. iii. 10; Zech. xiv. 16.) So apparently the LXX., *ἥξει τὰ ἐκλεκτα πάντων τῶν ἐθνων.* The rendering of the Authorised Version, which is based on Jerome's *et venit desideratus cunctis gentibus,* is grammatically impossible with the present text, for the verb "come" is plural, not singular. Its retention in some of the modern commentaries is mainly attributable to a natural unwillingness to give up a direct Messianic prophecy. Apart, however, from the grammatical difficulty, it must be remarked that the Messiah was not longed for by all nations, and that if He had been there would be no point in mentioning the fact in the present connection. On the other hand, the prediction of Gentile offerings to the Temple is most appropriate. It is the answer to those who sorrowed when they contrasted the mean appearance of this present house with the glories of that built by Solomon (verse 3). It also explains the otherwise meaningless utterance in verse 8. Another possible rendering is that adopted by Fürst, and (at one time) by Ewald, "And the pick of the nations shall come," *scil.,* with offerings to the Temple. The significance of the utterance is the same with either translation—*scil.,* that by agencies not specified the Gentile world is to be converted and induced to offer worship and homage to Jehovah.

(8) **Silver . . . gold.**—It is unnatural to suppose that this is said in the sense of Ps. l. 10, as implying "I have no need of silver or gold." Clearly what is meant is that the treasures of earth are at God's disposal, and that He will incite the Gentiles to offer their silver and gold in His Temple. A rigid application of this prediction is impossible. (See Introduction, § 2.)

(9) **The glory . . .**—Better, *The latter glory of this house shall be greater than the former.* The new sanctuary is regarded as identical with that reared by Solomon. It shall have a claim to celebrity unrivalled even in the palmiest days of olden time, when Jehovah shall turn the attention of all nations to His sacred place, as predicted in verses 6 and 7.

Between this third utterance and the fourth (verses 10—19) intervenes Zechariah's exhortation to repentance (Zech. i. 2—6) uttered in the eighth month.

(10–19) *The Fourth Utterance.*—The recent season of scarcity is again accounted for and immediate blessings are announced. This address dates about two months later than its predecessor—viz., from the ninth month—*scil.,* Chisleu (November—December), when the early rain would be looked for to water the newly-sown crops. At such a time, especially after the scarcity of the preceding season, there would naturally be great anxiety about agricultural prospects.

(12) **Holy flesh.**—The flesh of the sacrifice hallowed the person who touched it (Lev. vi. 27), but this sancti-

one bear holy flesh in the skirt of his
garment, and with his skirt do touch
bread, or pottage, or wine, or oil, or
any meat, shall it be holy? And the
priests answered and said, No. (13) Then
said Haggai, If *one that is* unclean by a
dead body touch any of these, shall it
be unclean? And the priests answered
and said, It shall be unclean.

(14) Then answered Haggai, and said,
So *is* this people, and so *is* this na-
tion before me, saith the LORD; and
so *is* every work of their hands; and
that which they offer there *is* unclean.
(15) And now, I pray you, consider from
this day and upward, from before a
stone was laid upon a stone in the
temple of the LORD: (16) since those *days*
were, when *one* came to an heap of
twenty *measures*, there were *but* ten:
when *one* came to the pressfat for to
draw out fifty *vessels* out of the press,
there were *but* twenty. (17) I smote you
[a]with blasting and with mildew and
with hail in all the labours of your
hands; yet ye *turned* not to me, saith
the LORD. (18) Consider now from this
day and upward, from the four and
twentieth day of the ninth *month*, *even*
from the day that the foundation of
the LORD's temple was laid, consider *it*.
(19) Is the seed yet in the barn? yea, as
yet the vine, and the fig tree, and the
pomegranate, and the olive tree, hath
not brought forth: from this day will I
bless *you*.

a Amos 4. 9.

---

fication was not conveyed to anything he might afterwards touch. On the other hand (verse 13), he who was defiled by such a pollution as contact with a dead body, *conveyed defilement* even to the tabernacle. (See Num. xix. 13: "Whosoever toucheth the dead body of any man that is dead, and purifieth not himself, defileth the tabernacle of the Lord.") Even so, according to Haggai, the guilt of impiety incurred by the Jews in neglecting the Temple had tainted the labour of their hands, and caused famine. And what merit they might claim for restoring the altar-worship and keeping the prescribed feasts (Ezra iii. 2—6) was not conveyed further. It was cancelled by their neglect of an equally important duty. This latter point, however, is not brought out, but is left to be supplied by the prophet's hearers.

(13) **Unclean.**—The defilement incurred by contact with a dead body was one of the deepest. (See Num. xix. 11—16.) On the force of the term *tmê nephesh*, compare the passages Lev. xxi. 11, xxii. 4; Num. vi. 6.

(14) **That which they offer there**—*i.e.*, probably, "on yon altar," but the expression is singular. In Ezra iii. 3 we read, "And they set the altar upon his bases . . . . and they offered burnt offerings thereon unto the Lord, even burnt offerings morning and evening."

(15) **From this day and upward**—*i.e.*, backward.

Before a stone was laid . . .—Alluding to the recent resumption of building, not to the laying of the foundations fifteen years previously.

(16) **Since those days were.**—Better, *from the time when things were so*, or, *since such things were*—*i.e.*, throughout that whole period of neglect up to the date when they resumed the work of restoration. Throughout that period the harvests had grievously disappointed expectation. A heap of sheaves which ought to have contained "twenty"—the measure is not specified—yielded only "ten;" and a quantity of grapes which should have yielded fifty *poorahs*, only produced twenty. The word *poorah* elsewhere means a "wine press;" here, apparently, it is the bucket or vessel which was used to draw up the wine. The last clause of the verse must therefore be rendered "When one came to the pressfat to draw out fifty *poorahs*, there were but twenty."

(17) **I smote you with blasting and with mildew . . .**—This is a reminiscence of Amos iv. 9, "I have smitten you with blasting and mildew . . . yet have not ye returned unto me, saith the Lord." "Blasting" and "mildew" are two diseases on corn enumerated by Moses (Deut. xxviii. 22) among the curses on disobedience. The "hail" is added by Haggai, perhaps as particularly destructive to the vines. On the peculiar phrase, *êyn ethcem êlay*, which here takes the place of the *lô shabtem âday* of Amos, see Ewald, *Grammar*, § 262 *b*.

(18) **Even from the day.**—Better, *even to the day*. The rendering of the Authorised Version makes the passage quite unintelligible, for in no sense can the twenty-fourth day of the ninth month coincide with the day "that the foundation of the Lord's Temple was laid." The Temple had been founded fifteen years before, in the second month of the second year of Cyrus (Ezra iii. 10). The work of building had been carried on intermittently till within two years of the present time. It had then been entirely suspended, and had only been actively taken in hand after Haggai's address in the sixth month of this year. The force of the passage is sufficiently plain if we render as above. "In order to make the blessings to be announced in verse 19 appear in strong contrast to the distress pictured in verses 16, 17, the prophet repeats the injunction of verse 15, but with a larger range of retrospect. The whole period back to the time when the foundation of the Temple was laid in the reign of Cyrus was more or less one of distress on account of the unfaithfulness of the people; for between that time and the present all the efforts that had been made to complete the work were spasmodic and feeble" (McCurdy). The rendering "even to the day" is quite allowable, though the construction is certainly rare.

(19) **Is the seed yet in the barn?**—*i.e.*, There is no grain as yet in the barn, the harvest having been blighted in the last season. The term rendered in the Authorised Version "seed" does not imply grain for sowing, but grain for provision. The fruit harvest was as defective as that of cereals, having been cut off by the hail. (See verse 17.) The prospect was thus one of deepest gloom. But human helplessness is God's opportunity. He pledges His word even at this crisis by the mouth of Haggai, "From this day I will bless."

(20) And again the word of the LORD
came unto Haggai in the four and
twentieth *day* of the month, saying,
(21) Speak to Zerubbabel, governor of
Judah, saying,
I will shake the heavens and the
earth; (22) and I will overthrow the
throne of kingdoms, and I will destroy
the strength of the kingdoms of the
heathen; and I will overthrow the
chariots, and those that ride in them;
and the horses and their riders shall
come down, every one by the sword
of his brother. (23) In that day, saith
the LORD of hosts, will I take thee,
O Zerubbabel, my servant, the son of
Shealtiel, saith the LORD, and will
make thee as a signet: for I have
chosen thee, saith the LORD of
hosts.

(20—23) *The Fifth Utterance.*—The promise of verses 6—9 is enlarged. The heathen powers shall be consumed one of another, but the line of Zerubbabel shall stand secure, and be a witness to Jehovah's faithfulness. Here, as in verses 6—9, the only satisfactory interpretation is that Haggai was charged with a prediction—purposely vague and indistinct in character—of the extension of God's kingdom by the Christian dispensation. "Zerubbabel," the descendant of David, includes in himself Him who was according to the flesh his lineal descendant. Just in the same way in older prophecy "David" is himself identified with that Messiah in whom the glories of the Davidic house were to culminate. (See Ps. lxxxix. 19, and comp. Jennings and Lowe, *Commentary*, Introd. to Ps. lxxxix.) It appears as unnecessary to find a literal fulfilment of the prediction of the overthrow of the world-powers, "every one by the sword of his brother," as of the utterance (repeated from verse 6), "I will shake the heavens and the earth." It is true that the empires of Babylon, Persia, Syria, and Greece each in its turn declined and passed away. But in the Roman Empire the world-power was as strongly represented as ever, when Christ came on earth. It was to succumb later on to moral, not to material force. Nothing, in fact, can be extracted from these passages beyond a dim presage of the heathen kingdoms being pervaded by the moral influence of the Christian Church.

(23) **Signet.**—On the figure of the signet-ring applied to one on whom confidence and affection are bestowed, see Song of Solomon viii. 6; Jer. xxii. 24.

INTRODUCTION

TO

ZECHARIAH

CHAPTERS I.—VIII.

I. **The Prophet.**—He describes himself as "Zechariah, the son of Berechiah, the son of Iddo," which can only mean—(LXX., Jerome, and Cyril are in error)—that he was the grandson of the latter. But in Ezra v. 1, vi. 14, he is called "the son of Iddo." Similarly, Laban, the *grandson* of Nahor, is called his *son* (Gen. xxix. 5); and Jehu is in 2 Kings ix. 14 called "the son of Jehoshaphat, the son of Nimshi," while in verse 20 he is styled simply "the son of Nimshi." The supposition, therefore, that the words "son of Berechiah" (Zech. i. 1) are an interpolation borrowed from Isa. viii. 2, where "Zechariah, the son of Jeberechiah," is mentioned, is superfluous. The conjecture, too, that the Book of Zechariah is made up of the writings of three distinct prophets—Zechariah son of Iddo, Zechariah son of Jeberechiah, and Uriah, fellow-witness of the latter (Isa. viii. 2)—though ingenious, is but based on the erroneous idea that Zech. ix.—xiv. cannot be of post-exilian authorship. In Ezra v. 1, 2, Zechariah is mentioned as prophesying, in conjunction with Haggai, during the time of Jeshua, the son of Josedech (the high priest). A certain Iddo is reckoned as among the heads of priests (and Levites) who came up with Zerubbabel (Neh. xii. 1—4); and again, a Zechariah is spoken of as the lineal representative of Iddo, and one of the heads of the priestly houses in the days of Joiakim, the successor of Jeshua (Neh. xii. 12—16). It may be not unreasonably assumed that this is Zechariah the Prophet, and that this Iddo is his grandfather. From these materials we may fairly deduce that (1) Zechariah was a young man when he entered upon his office; (2) that his father died early, and was, perhaps, never head of his house, which would account for his being passed over by Ezra; (3) that Zechariah, like Jeremiah and Ezekiel, was a priest as well as a prophet. The first of these deductions is sufficient to dispose of the fables of Epiphanius, Dorotheus, and Hesychius (see Köhler, *Einleitung*; Wright, *Introduction*), that Zechariah was an old man at the time of the return from the captivity, and that he had already foretold to Shealtiel the birth of Zerubbabel, and to Cyrus his victory over Crœsus, &c. The second of these fables is also contradicted by the fact that Zerubbabel was not the actual son of Shealtiel, but of his brother Pedaiah (1 Chron. iii. 19). Shealtiel seems to have died without male issue, and Pedaiah to have taken his deceased brother's wife in accordance with Deut. xxv. 5—10. Zerubbabel, or Sheshbazzar, seems to have been the son of this Levirate marriage.

The name *Zechariah* is compounded of the stem *zâchôr*, "to remember," and *Yâh*, the first half of the Holy Name (see Notes on Exod. xv. 2, xvii. 16; Ps. lxviii.), and probably means "Yah remembers." Some, however, take it as meaning "who remembers Yah." (Comp. Μνησίθεος and Τιμόθεος.) Jerome explains it as Μνήμη Κυρίου, *memoria Domini;* Hesychius as Μνήμη Ὑψίστου, "Memory of the Highest," or Νικητὴς λεόντος, "Lion-conqueror;" Marck as "hero of Yah." The last two are impossible. The name has probably no reference whatever to the contents of the prophecies.

II. **Occasion of the Prophecies.**—The genuineness of chaps. i.—viii. has never been called in question, and they are undoubtedly to be referred to the time of the re-building of the Temple (see *Introduction to Haggai*). The date and authorship of chaps. ix.—xiv. must be discussed separately.

III. **Contents of Chapters i.—viii.**—These chapters consist of three distinct prophetic utterances: viz., (1) chap. i. 1—6; (2) chaps. i. 7—vi. 15; (3) chaps. vii. and viii.

(1) Chap. i. 1—6.—A declaration of the prophet's mission, and an earnest exhortation to the people to turn unto the Lord, that He might turn unto them, together with a warning not to fall into that error of neglect of God's word which had proved so fatal to their fathers.

(2) Chap. i. 7—vi. 15.—A series of seven visions, with two appendices, chaps. ii. 6—13, vi. 9—15. Some commentators have maintained that these visions were not, even subjectively, seen by the prophet; but that he deliberately sets forth his experience under the similitude of dreams, as Bunyan does in the *Pilgrim's Progress*. But it seems to us, from the prophet's words, to be imperative to regard these visions as subjectively, though perhaps not objectively, visible to him, just as one would naturally so regard the visions of Amos (chaps. vii.—ix.).

First Vision (chap. i. 7—17).—*The horsemen among the myrtles.* This vision was intended to convey to the prophet the truth that, though as yet there may be little sign of God's "overthrowing the kingdoms" (Haggai ii. 22), yet He, with His all-watchful eye, was scanning the horizon, and preparing to fulfil His word.

Second Vision (chap. i. 18—21).—*The four horses and four workmen* indicate that God would continue to remove the hostility of the Persians, even as He had already broken the power of the Assyrians, Egyptians, and Babylonians.

Third Vision (chap. ii. 1—5).—*The man with the measuring line.* The enlargement and perfect security of the people of God. An appendix (chap. ii. 6—13) prophetic of the ingathering of the nations in the days of BRANCH, the Messiah.

Fourth Vision (chap. iii.)—*Joshua, the high priest, arraigned before the angel of the Lord.* The forgiveness of the sins of the priesthood, and of the people, whose representative he was.

Fifth Vision (chap. iv.).—*The candlestick with the two olive-trees.* The diffusion of God's grace by means of His two channels—the priesthood and civil power. It contains a promise (verse 9) that Zerubbabel's hands should finish the building of the Temple.

Sixth Vision (chap. v. 1—11.)—*The flying roll, and the woman in the ephah,* denoting the curse on sinners, and the banishment of sin.

Seventh Vision (chap. vi. 1—8).—*The four chariots.* God's judgments on the nations. An appendix (chap. vi. 9—15), the crowning of Joshua, which foreshadows the two-fold office of BRANCH, as king and priest. A probable *lacuna* in the text.

(3) Chaps. vii., viii.—The inquiry concerning the fasts. The prophet's rebuke of the people for their formalism. The answer to their inquiry, in the form of a promise that their fasts should be turned into feasts.

CHAPTERS IX.—XIV.

Mede (who died in 1638) was the first to doubt the genuineness of this second part of the book. He was led to do so on observing that in Matt. xxvii. 9, a passage, which is certainly a quotation from Zech. xi. 12, 13, is ascribed to Jeremiah. On further investigation, he conceived that he found internal evidence in support of his theory: that these chapters were of an earlier date than the age of Zechariah. Since that time the question has been continually discussed by scholars of many nations, with such inconsistent results that chapters ix.—xiv. have been ascribed to various times, ranging between 772 B.C. (Hitzig) and 330 (Böttcher).

We need not here attach any weight to the supposed external authority of St. Matthew in the matter. (See the *New Testament Commentary, in loc.*) But the question of internal evidence—first, with regard to style, secondly, with respect to historical standpoint—demands careful investigation. At the same time the reader will do well to bear in mind Pusey's weighty remark: "It is obvious that there must be some mistake either in the tests applied, or in their application, which admits of a variation of at least 450 years."

Seeing that the preponderance of authority appeared to be subversive of the view that the latter chapters were of as late a date as the age of Zechariah, we came to the special study of the subject with a certain inclination to accept the hypothesis that this portion is of pre-exilian origin. But we have since felt compelled to abandon this theory. We now proceed to put before the reader the process of reasoning which has led us to our present conclusions. We shall print the arguments of the impugners of the integrity of the book in *italics*, and give our answer to each objection.

I. Arguments against the genuineness of chaps. ix.—xiv.: (A) from style, (B) from the historical standpoint.

A. DIFFERENCE OF STYLE BETWEEN ZECH. i.—viii. AND ix.—xiv.

1. Zech. i. 7—vi. 8 *consists almost entirely of visions, while in* chaps. ix.—xiv. *there are none.*

Ans. When the prophet saw visions, he related them; when he did not see any, he could not do so. There is no reason in the nature of things why God should not at one time reveal His will to a prophet in visions, and at another by other means. Thus, as a fact, Amos has only visions in the second part, and none in the first; and so, too, Isaiah and Ezekiel related visions when they saw them, but at other times they delivered their oracles in a different manner. Moreover, chaps. vii. and viii. do not consist of visions, and the genuineness of these chapters has not been called in question.

2. *The angel-interpreter and Satan disappear from* chaps. ix.—xiv.

Ans. And so they do from chaps. vii. and viii., simply because they were actors, the one in the whole series of visions, and the other in one portion of it.

3. *The seven eyes, as a symbol of God's Providence, disappear from* chaps. ix.—xiv.

Ans. True; but a writer is not compelled to use continually a certain symbol, because he happens to have done so on a former occasion. Moreover, a very similar expression, "for now have I seen it with mine eyes," is actually used in chap. ix. 8. (Comp. chap. ix. 5.)

4. *Exact dates are given many times in the former chapters, but none in the latter.*

Ans. Similarly, we find dates prefixed to other visions, such as Isa. vi. 1; Ezek. i. 1—3, viii. 1, 2, xl. 1, 2; and dates are frequently found in the prophets, where answers are recorded as given by Divine command to inquiries addressed to them.

5. In chaps. i.—viii. *introductory formulas constantly occur, which are not found in the concluding six chapters.*

Ans. So, too, Hosea uses introductory formulas in the first five chapters of his book, which are wanting in the last nine chapters; and yet no doubt is entertained of the integrity of that book.

6 α. *The style of* chaps. i.—viii. *is utterly different to that of* chaps. ix.—xiv.

Ans. So is that of Hos. i.—iii. different to that of chaps. iv.—xiv; and the style of Ezek. iv., v. is totally different to that of chaps. vi., vii., or of chaps. xxvii., xxviii.

β. *The style of the first eight chapters is prosaic, feeble, poor, while that of the remaining six is poetic, weighty, concise, glowing* (Rosenmüller).

Böttcher, on the other hand, says: "*In comparison with the lifeless language of these chapters* (ix.—xiv.), *as to which we cannot at all understand how any can have removed them into so early pre-exile times, the Psalms attributed to the time of the Maccabees are amazingly fresh.*"

Ans. When critics so disagree as to the respective merits of the styles of the two sections, it seems hardly worth while to consider the argument. We will merely remark that neither sweeping statement is correct. When the prophet is describing a vision, or giving an answer to questions propounded, he naturally writes in the language best suited to his purpose, viz., prose. But when he comes to speak of the distant future, he naturally rises to a loftier style of diction; and this is the case even in the earlier chapters, when occasion requires: *e.g.*, chaps. ii. 10—17, vi. 12, 13. (See further, under *The Integrity of the whole Book*, 7.) Further, the argument from style must be, indeed, very strong to enable us to affirm that this chapter is by one author, and that by another. And even when the evidence appears most forcible to the propounder of the theory, facts may come to light which will prove it to be utterly fallacious. Thus an acute German has found reasons why the Laws of Plato should not be Plato's, and yet Jowett (*Translations of Plato's Dialogues*, vol. iv. 1) has shown them to be undoubtedly genuine by four sets of facts: (1) from twenty citations of them by Aristotle, who must have been intimate with Plato for some seventeen years; (2) by the allusion of Isocrates, writing two or three years after the composition of the Laws:

(3) by the references of the comic poet Alexis, a younger contemporary of Plato; (4) by the unanimous voice of later antiquity.

B. THE HISTORICAL STANDPOINT.—Those who impugn the integrity of the Book of Zechariah on historical grounds may be divided into two classes. (1) Those who ascribe chaps. ix.—xiv. to one author, and (2) those who attribute chaps. ix.—xi. to one author, and chaps. xii.—xiv. to another; or who imagine that they discover the traces of three different pens in chaps. ix.—xiv. We will discuss the integrity of chaps. ix.—xiv. further on. At present we will content ourselves with disposing of the difference with regard to historical standpoint which has been urged in the two sections i.—viii. and ix.—xiv. *generally*. The *particular* passages in which such a difference has been urged we shall discuss in our Notes on those passages, viz., ix. 1—8, ix. 9—17, x. 2, x. 3—12, xi. 1—3, xi. 14, xii. 1—9, xii. 11, xiv. 5, xiv. 1—21.

1 *a*. *In* chaps. ix.—xiv. *the historical standpoint is entirely changed. In* chaps. i.—viii. *the prophet is continually mentioning the rebuilding of the Temple, and the re-inhabiting of Jerusalem; but in* chaps ix.—xiv. *he is occupied with quite different matters.*

Ans. This is true, for the latter chapters were (we have good reason for supposing) written many years after the former, when the rebuilding of the Temple was a *fait accompli*, and when those abuses of the Temple-service, which so vexed the righteous spirit of Malachi, had not yet crept in. It would not, we suppose, be imagined strange if a Parisian, writing in 1871, spoke much of the siege of Paris, while, when writing in 1881, he said nothing whatever about that event, but was engrossed with the affairs of Tunis, and the possibility of eventual collision with other Powers. The case of Zechariah is still stronger, for not ten, but probably some *forty* years, intervened between the delivery of the prophecies of chaps. i.—viii., and those of chaps. ix.—xiv.

β. *In the former chapters he mentions his contemporaries, such as Joshua and Zerubbabel, but not so in the latter portion.*

Ans. In the former chapters he was *chiefly* occupied in contemporary events; in the latter he speaks of a more distant future, which none of his contemporaries would live to see. This difference of subject-matter accounts, also, for the occurrence of such expressions as "in that day," "the people round about," in the latter chapters, which are not found in the former.

2. Chap. ix. 1—8 *is so like to* Amos i. and ii. 1—6, &c., *that it seems impossible that two prophecies so similar should have been uttered at periods so wide apart.*

Ans. There is this much of resemblance between the two passages: viz., that in both Damascus, Tyre, Gaza, Ashdod, Ashkelon, and Ekron are threatened. But here the similarity ceases, and the great dissimilarity becomes apparent. (*α*) In *Amos*, Edom, Ammon, and Moab are included, but not so in *Zechariah*. And this is most natural, for, while in the time of Uzziah these were still powerful nations, on the return from the captivity they were so weak, that when in the time of Nehemiah "Sanballat and Tobiah, and the Arabians and the Ammonites and the Ashdodites" all conspire to hinder the Jews from rebuilding the Wall of Jerusalem, it was found sufficient to repel them that half of the returned exiles should stand to arms, while the other half went on with the work of building. (*β*) Amos expressly states that Aram-Damascus should be carried away to Kir, while there is no such intimation in Zech. ix. (*γ*) The *style* of the two passages is *not* similar. That of Amos i.—ii. 6 is of a marked character, but we find no echo of that style in Zech. ix. 1—8. (*δ*) In Amos ii. 4—6, Judah and Israel are threatened equally with the other nations, and looked on equally with the other people there mentioned as separate governments. But in Zech. ix. 8 God's "house" is promised special protection (see further in our Notes), and in verse 13 "Judah" and "Ephraim" are used as parallel terms.

Thus we see that the arguments in favour of the *pre*-exilian authorship of these chapters, whether urged on the score of style or of historical reference, fall to the ground. On the other hand, there is, we will show, strong internal testimony to the truth of the opposite opinion.

II. Internal Evidence in Favour of the Post-exilian Origin of chaps. ix.—xiv.—1. The writer of chaps. ix.—xiv. shows such a familiarity with the writings of the later prophets as appears to some reconcilable only with the supposition that he wrote at a date posterior to them: *e.g., the Deutero-Isaiah.*[1] Compare

Zech. ix. 12 (*a*) with Isa. xlii. 7, xlix. 9, lxi. 1.	Zech. xii. 2 with Isa. li. 22, 23.
— ix. 12 (*b*) with Isa. lxi. 7.	— xiii. 9 „ — xlviii. 10.
— x. 10 „ — xlix. 19, 20.	— — 16 „ — lx. 6—9, lxvi. 23.
— xi. 15, 16 — lvi. 11.	— — 17 „ — lx. 12.
— xii. 1 with Isa. li. 13.	

Zephaniah. Compare Zech. ix. 5, 6 with Zeph. ii. 4, 5.

Jeremiah. Compare

Zech. ix. 12 with Jer. xvi. 18.	Zech. xi. 6 with Jer. xxvi. 29-33.
— xi. 3 „ — xxv. 34-36.	— xiii. 9 „ — xxx. 22.
— —— „ — xii. 5, xlix. 19, l. 44.	(Comp. also with these Zech. viii. 8, and Hos. ii. 23.)
(The only passages in which "The pride of Jordan" occurs.)	Zech. xiv. 7 with Jer. xxx. 7, 8.
	— — 10 „ Jer. xxxi. 38-40
Zech. xi. 5 with Jer. ii. 3, l. 7.	— — 20, 21 „ — xxxi. 40-

Obadiah. Compare

Zech. xii. 6 with Obad. ver. 18.	Zech. xiv. 9 with Obad. ver. 9.

Ezekiel. Compare

Zech. ix. 2—4 with Ezek. xxviii. 1—23.	Zech. xiii. 8, 9 with Ezek. v. 2, 12, xi. 20.
— x. 2 with Ezek. xxxiv. 5, 8.	— xiv. 2 (xii. 2—9), xxxviii. 14—18.
— x. 3 „ — xxxiv. 12, 17, 20, 22, 31.	— xiv. 4 with Ezek. xxxviii. 19, 20.
— xi. „ — xxxiv. especially vers. 4, 5, 16 with vers. 3, 4, and ver. 9 with ver. 16.	— — 8 „ — xlvii. 1.
	— — 13 „ — xxxviii. 21.
Zech. xi. 7, 14 with Ezek. xxxvii. 16—22.	— — 14 „ — xxxix. 10.
— xii. 10 „ — xxxix. 29.	— — 21 „ — xliv. 9.
— xiii. 1, 2 „ — xxxvi. 25, xxxvii. 23.	

Haggai. Compare
Zech. xiv. 13 with Haggai ii. 21, 22.

Similarly Zechariah, in chaps. i.—viii., exhibits the same familiarity with the *later* prophetic books which we have shown to be a characteristic of chaps. ix.—xiv. Compare, for example:

Chap. ii. 6 with Isa. xlviii. 20, or with Isa. lii. 11 and Jer. li. 6, 9.
Chap. ii. 9, 11, and chap. iv. 9, with Ezek. vi. 7, 10, xxxix. 10, &c.
Chaps. iii. 8, vi. 12, with Jer. xxiii. 5, xxxiii. 15 (Isa. iv. 2).
Chap. vi. 15 with Jer. xvii. 24.
Chap. vii. 5—10 with Isa. lviii. 3—7.
Chap. vii. 9 with Ezek. xviii. 8 and Jer. vii. 5—7, xxii. 3.
Chap. vii. 12 „ Ezek. xi. 19.
Chap. vii. 13 „ Jer. xi. 11.
Chap. vii. 14 „ Jer. xvi. 13, &c.
Chap. viii. 3 „ Jer. xxxi. 23.
Chap. viii. 4 „ Isa. lxv. 20.
Chap. viii. 6 „ Jer. xxxii. 17, 27.
Chap. viii. 7 „ Isa. xliii. 6.
Chap. viii. 8 „ Isa. xlviii. 1.

[1] See *Introduction* to Isaiah. Should the so-called Deutero-Isaiah (chaps. xl.—end) be eventually shown to be by the same author as Isa. i.—xxxix., our argument would not be injured, since the references to the other prophets mentioned afterwards are in themselves sufficient. Further, most critics who regard Zech. ix.—xiv. as *pre*-exilian, consider Isa. xl.—end as contemporaneous with the *later* prophets.

This argument seemed so convincing to De Wette that, after having in the first three editions of his *Introduction* declared for two authors, he felt compelled to change his mind, and in his fourth edition admitted the post-exilian origin of chaps. ix.—xiv., and even the possibility of their having been written by Zechariah. We are not, however, prepared to regard this argument as conclusive. We own the difficulty that there is in computing the exact weight due to the argument derived from the consideration of parallel passages, and concur with Cheyne's pertinent remarks on the subject (*The Prophecies of Isaiah*, vol. ii., p. 210): "The argument from parallel passages is sometimes much overrated. How prone we are to fancy an imitation where there is none, has been strikingly shown by Munro's parallel between the plays of Shakspeare and Seneca (*Journal of Philology*, vol. vi., Camb. 1876, pp. 70—72); and even when an imitation on one side or the other must be supposed, how difficult it is to choose between the alternatives! A recent revolution of opinion among patristic students may be a warning to us not to be too premature in deciding such questions. It has been the custom to argue from the occurrence of almost identical sentences in the *Octavius* of Minucius Felix and the *Apologeticum* of Tertullian, that Minucius must have written later than the beginning of the third century, on the ground that a brilliant genius like Tertullian's cannot have been such a servile imitator as the hypothesis of the priority of Minucius would imply. But Adolf Ebert seems to have definitely proved that Tertullian not only made use of Minucius, but did not even understand his author rightly."

2. In no way can they be so consistently interpreted as by supposing them to have been written after the captivity (as will be seen in our Notes). This is especially the case with regard to the mention of the "sons of Greece" (chap. ix. 13), which can refer to no event of which we have cognizance before the time of Alexander or of the Maccabees; and with regard to the prophecies contained in chaps. xii.—xiv., they would be simply untrue if uttered in reference to the destruction of Jerusalem by Nebuchadnezzar.

We conclude, therefore, that the last six chapters are, equally with the first eight, of post-exilian origin.

We come next to the question of—

III. The Integrity of chapters ix.—xiv.—The theory, which Bunsen has called one of the triumphs of modern criticism, that chaps. ix.—xi. and chaps. xii.—xiv. are the work of two different prophets: viz., chaps. ix.—xi. that of a contemporary of Isaiah, perhaps Zechariah son of Jeberechiah (Isa. viii. 2), and chaps. xii.—xiv., possibly that of Urijah son of Shemaiah (Jer. xxvi. 20—23), falls to the ground with the establishment of the post-exilian origin of the whole section. Archbishop Newcome, who originated this theory, concluded that chaps. ix.—xi. were written much earlier than the time of Jeremiah, and before the captivity of the tribes; but was not so positive as his followers with regard to the pre-exilian authorship of chaps. xii.—xiv., though he thinks the mention of idols (xiii. 2) to be in favour of that supposition. We must therefore discuss a little more fully what have been termed *the grounds for separating* chaps. xii.— xiv. *from* chaps. ix.—xi.

(1) Chap. xi. *has a distinct introductory formula.* But since this formula is the same as that of chap. ix. 1, and that a formula which recurs only in Mal. i. 1, this argument tends rather in the other direction.

(2) *The former chapters speak of Israel and Judah, but the latter do not mention "Israel."* On the contrary, chap. xii. 1 states that the whole of the following prophecy is concerning "Israel."

(3) *In the former, Syrians, Phœnicians, Philistines, and Greeks are mentioned, but Assyrians and Egyptians described as the most powerful. These chapters belong therefore to early times.* We have shown in our Notes that the manner in which the Greeks are here described as enemies of Israel fixes the date of these chapters to the post-exilian period. Egypt and Assyria are spoken of (x. 10) as the nations who had carried off the people, and whence they were to be brought back, while in ver. 11 the stereotyped language of former prophets is evidently used in a figurative sense.

(4) *The anticipations of the two prophets are different. The first trembles for Ephraim, but for Judah he has no fear.* On the contrary, Ephraim and Judah are included equally in the promised protection.

(5) *The second prophet does not mention the northern kingdom, but is full of alarm for Judah, and sees the enemy laying siege to Jerusalem.* "Ephraim" does not denote "the northern kingdom" in chaps. ix.—xi. (see Notes). If Jerusalem was to be besieged at any time after its rebuilding, there is no reason why the same prophet who spoke before in general terms of wars, should not afterwards speak more particularly of a siege. In prophesying concerning a siege of Jerusalem it is only natural that Judah, in which tribe it partly stood, should be especially mentioned. Moreover, as we remarked above, the section is expressly addressed to all "Israel."

(6) *Difference of style:* "And it shall come to pass" *does not occur in* chaps. ix.—xi.; "in that day," *which occurs so often in* chaps. xii.—xiv., *occurs only once in* chaps. ix.—xi., and "saith the Lord" *occurs only twice in* chaps. ix.—xi. *There are also favourite expressions in* chaps. xii.—xiv., such as "all peoples," "all nations round about," "family of Egypt," &c. This is true, but chaps. xii.—xiv. are admitted by all to be a separate section, delivered probably on a different occasion to the former section, and pointing on the whole to a much further distant future. These facts are quite sufficient to account for such very slight differences of style.

IV. The Integrity of the whole Book.—We now proceed to adduce some arguments to prove that there is sufficient correspondence between chaps. i.—viii. and ix.—xiv. to justify us, in default of any positive evidence to the contrary, in regarding the whole book as the work of one prophet.

1. Both portions exhibit, as we have shown, an extensive acquaintance with the writings of the *later* prophets.

2. They both exhibit also an extensive acquaintance with the *earlier* books: thus, in chap. i. 4—6, chap. vii. 12, reference is made to "the former prophets" generally:—

Chap. ii. 12 (E.V. 8) recalls the thought, though not the phraseology, of Ps. xvii. 8.
Chaps. iii. 8, vi. 12, allude to Isa. iv. 2, as well as to Jer. xxiii. 5, and xxxiii. 15.
Chap. iii. 10 is from Mic. iv. 4.
Chap. vi. 13 evidently refers to Ps. cx. 4.
Chap. viii. 8 recalls Hos. ii. 21 (E.V. 19).
Chap. viii. 20—22 in substance may be compared with Mic. iv. 1, 2, Isa. ii. 2, 3.

And in the second part:—

Chap. ix. 1—8 bears some resemblance to Amos i. 3, ii. 6.
Chap. ix. 10 (first half) is borrowed from Mic. v. 10, and (second half) from Ps. lxxii. 8.
Chap. xiii. 2 is a quotation from Hos. ii. 17 or Mic. v. 12, 13 (comp. Isa. ii. 18, 20); and ver. 9, from Hos. ii. 20 (E.V. 23).

Comp. also chap. ix. 16 with Isa. xi. 12.
Chap. x. 12 with Mic. iv. 5.
Chap. x. 10–12 with Isa. xi. 15, xiv. 25, x. 24—27, xxx. 31, &c.
Chap. xii. 8 with Joel iv. 10.
Chap. xii. 10 „ Joel iii. 1, 2.
Chap. xiv. 3 „ Isa. xxxiv. 1–4.
Chap. xiv. 6, 7 „ Amos v. 18, 20, Joel iv. (E.V. iii.) 15, Isa. xxx. 26.
Chap. xiv. 8 „ Isa. xi. 9, ii. 3, Mic. iv. 2.
Chap. xiv. 11 „ Amos ix. 13—15.
Chap. xiv. 20 „ Isa. xxiii. 18.
Chap. xiv. 21 „ Isa. iv. 3, xxxv. 8, Joel iv. (E.V. iii.) 17, &c.

But we cannot lay much stress on this argument, since prophets, belonging as they did in most cases to a school, were in all probability acquainted with the works of their predecessors.

3. In both portions the whole people are similarly styled "the house of Israel, and the house of Judah" (chap. viii. 13); or, "house of Judah, and house of Joseph" (chap. x. 6); or "Judah, Israel, and Jerusalem" (chap. i. 19); or "Judah and Ephraim" (chap. ix. 13); or "Judah and Israel" (chap. xi. 14). And in both portions (see the above reference), as was done by Jer. (chaps. xxiii. 6, l. 20) and Ezek. (chap. xxxvii. 16—19), a future is promised to the re-united Israel-Judah.

4. In both parts (chaps. ii. 9, 11, and xi. 11) we have the prototype of our Lord's saying (John xiv. 29): "And now I have told you before it come to pass, that when it is come to pass ye might believe" (John xiii. 19, xvi. 4). In both (chaps. viii. 10, xi. 6) internal discord is directly attributed to God's Providence. In both (chaps. viii. 12, x. 1) the prophet promises God's gifts of the produce of the earth. In both (chaps. ii. 10, ix. 9) he bids Jerusalem burst out for joy. The only king of Israel mentioned in either portion is the Messiah (chaps. vi. 12, 13, ix. 9).

5. Both portions are written in pure Hebrew, free from Aramaisms. Both (chaps. vii. 14, ix. 8) contain the expression "passes to and fro," in the sense of "all inhabitants," which elsewhere occurs only in Ezek. xxxv. 7. (But we must be careful not to lay too much stress on this latter argument, since, if more Biblical Hebrew were extant, the expression would probably occur often.)

6. In both parts alike may be observed the habit of dwelling on the same thought or word—*e.g.*, in chaps. ii. 14, 15, vi. 10, vi. 12, 13, viii. 4, 5, viii. 23, xi. 7, xiv. 10, 11, xiv. 4, xiv. 5. In both the whole and its parts are, for emphasis, mentioned together—*e.g.*, in chaps. v. 4, x. 4, and x. 11, we have "every family apart," and then in verses 12, 13 the specification. And as an outcome of this fulness of diction we find, in each, instances of one fundamental idea expanded into the unusual number of *five* parallel clauses, *e.g.*:—

Chap. vi. 13—
"And shall build the temple of the Lord;"
"And *He* shall bear Majesty;"
"And *He* shall sit and rule upon His throne;"
"And shall be a priest upon His throne;"
"And a counsel of peace shall be between these twain."

Chap. ix. 5—
"Ashkelon shall see it, and shall fear;"
"Gaza, and shall tremble exceedingly;"
"And Ekron, and disappointed is her expectation;"
"And perished is a king from Gaza;"
"And Ashkelon shall not be inhabited."

Chap. ix. 7—
"And I will take away his blood from his mouth;"
"And his abominations from between his teeth;"
"And he too shall be left to our God;"
"And he shall be as a governor in Judah;"
"And Ekron as a Jebusite."

7. So far from looking upon the difference between the contents of the first eight and of the last six chapters as a sign of difference of authorship, we consider that the high-flown poetic language and imagery and deep prophetic insight of the latter chapters are just such as might have been expected, in his later years, from one who, in his youth, saw and related the mysterious series of visions contained in the former portion. For, as with other gifts of the Spirit, so with the gift of prophecy: we may well suppose that God gives to a man in accordance with that which he hath, and not according to that which he hath not. When, therefore, the seer, who even in his youth was found worthy of such mysterious revelations, had spent many years in communion with God, and meditation on the promises revealed by "the former prophets"—the deep things of God—it seems only in accordance with our experience of the workings of Divine Providence that he should, in after life, become the recipient of the stupendous revelations contained in the concluding chapters.

Thus the *internal* evidence of the two portions has been shown to be on the whole in favour of the integrity of the Book of Zechariah. It remains only to state that there is no *external evidence* (except that which originally led to a doubt on the subject) to the contrary. (1) In the Jewish Canon Zechariah is the eleventh in the book called "the twelve." The books of the Hebrew Scriptures have usually in MSS.* no headings; but after each of the prophets, whether major or minor, three lines are usually, according to rule,† left empty, and then the next prophet is written. Thus between Haggai and Zechariah three lines ought to be left, just as between Jeremiah and Ezekiel. But between Zech. viii. and ix.‡ there is but an "open section" (*pārāshāh pᵉthūchāh*), like that between chaps. vii. and viii., denoting merely that the matter which follows is not so closely connected with what precedes, as would have been denoted by there being only a "closed section" (*pārāshāh sᵉthūmāh*) left between: as, for instance, between Zech. ix. 8, 9. Thus the very manner in which the book is written, when the laws on the subject are observed, points—from a negative, if not from a positive, point of view—to there being no doubt in the opinion of the Synagogue as to its integrity. (2) Neither in Rabbinical or Patristic writings, nor in the ancient versions, is there any trace known to us of a doubt having, in early times, been entertained on the subject. On the contrary, chap. xi. 1 is distinctly ascribed to "Zechariah son of Iddo" (Talmud Babli, *Yoma* 39a). While, on the other hand, Rabbi Akivah, in a remarkable piece of exegesis (Talmud Babli, *Maccoth* 24b), identifies *Zechariah the son of Jeberechiah* with *the author of* Zech. viii. 4, although he is perfectly aware that Zechariah prophesied during the time of the Second Temple. At the same time it must be observed that the so-called "external evidence of the Jewish Canon" has, by previous writers, been much too strongly stated; for it must not be forgotten that

* In the Cambridge MS. of the twelfth and thirteenth centuries, marked Add. 465, a scribe of the latter half of the fourteenth century has supplied running titles to the various books, according to the *Jewish* divisions. At the end of this MS. there is, for the purpose, as is expressly stated, of ready reference in controversy with Christians, a table of the *Christian* divisions of the books, in a hand not later than the early part of the fourteenth century; and a later scribe still has adopted the ordinary Christian divisions, and added them to the MS. throughout.

† Tūr and Shūlchān 'Ārūc, *Yōreh Dēʿāh*, § 283.

‡ These remarks will apply equally to the case of Isa. xxxix. and xl.

the fact that a passage occurs in a book ascribed to a certain prophet is not looked on by the Jews as absolute proof that it was pronounced by him (Talmud Babli, *Baba Bathra* 14[b]). Thus Rabbi Simon, of the third and fourth centuries (*Vayyikrā Rabbah*, xv. 2), ascribes Isa. viii. 19, 20, to Beeri (father of Amos), and says these verses were not written in a separate book, because there was not enough to constitute one. Again, in *Maccoth* 24[b] the verse Mic. iii. 12 is ascribed, without remark, to Urijah the priest, the co-witness with Zechariah son of Jeberechiah (Isa. viii. 2). Whatever people may think of the critical value of these rabbinical statements, they are most significant as pointing to an acknowledged tradition of the Synagogue with regard to the manner of putting together the canonical books. If, therefore, it should be thought that Zech. xi. 1—3, and xiii. 7—9 have no apparent connection with the context in the places in which they stand, it would be quite admissible to suppose them to be fragments, say of Ezekiel and Jeremiah respectively, which had not been included in those books, and which were now inserted in the prophecies of Zechariah to prevent their becoming lost. With regard to the Minor Prophets in particular, Rabbi Shelomoh Yitzchaki (or *Rashi*, the great Jewish traditionalist of the eleventh century) says, in his commentary on Talmud Babli, *Baba Bathra* 15[a]: "As for the Twelve, since their prophecies were short, the prophets did not themselves write each his own book. But, when Haggai, Zechariah, and Malachi came, and said that the spirit of prophecy was on the point of ceasing (for they were the last of the prophets), they arose and wrote down their own prophecies, and combined therewith short prophecies, and made them into one large book, in order that they should not be lost on account of their brevity." By which he means that they took the nine other "Minor Prophets," as we call them, and combined them with their own prophecies into one book. His words leave room also for the theory which we have propounded above, that *small fragments* of prophecies, which had not yet been embodied in the prophetic writings, may have been included in the "Minor Prophets." Such is the tradition. It need not be taken as implying that Haggai, Zechariah, and Malachi were actual contemporaries (indeed it appears probable —see *Introduction to Malachi*—that Malachi prophesied some fifty years after the time of Zechariah's latest productions), but merely that the prophets of the post-exilian period formed their own prophecies and the smaller works of earlier prophets into one book. This tradition is in itself probable, and in so far as concerns the late redaction of even the *older* books of "the Twelve," is corroborated by the following minute piece of internal evidence. The *Massóreth* tells us that with the exception of the passage Song of Songs iv. 4 (on the date of which see *Introduction*), the name *David* is written *fully* (*i.e.*, with a *yod* between the *v* and the *d*) only in three passages of Kings, one of Ezekiel, and throughout the Minor Prophets (viz., in Hosea, Amos, and Zechariah, in which only it occurs). Thus the spelling of the name *David*, even in the early books, Hosea and Amos, agrees with the tradition that they were edited, so to speak, at a late date.

The voice of antiquity is thus unanimous in accepting the last six chapters, without question, as the work of Zechariah, the contemporary of Haggai, equally with the first eight.

In conclusion: seeing that external evidence has nothing to say against the integrity of the book, and that internal evidence (from style and contents) is rather in favour of it than otherwise, we conclude that the whole book called "Zechariah" is probably by Zechariah, grandson of Iddo.

V. Probable Date of Zechariah ix.—xiv.—Prophets, we hold, are by Divine inspiration enabled to foretell events. Therefore it is not necessary to suppose that these chapters were written *after* the events to which we suppose them to refer. But, on the other hand, prophets (except with regard to the Messianic times, which were *ever present in anticipation*) cannot be supposed to speak of things which are not more or less pointed to by "the signs of the times" (Matt. xvi. 3). If they did so, they could not expect to command an audience; for why should people be expected to listen to what could have no interest for them? Accordingly, in fixing the date of these prophecies, we have two guides: it must not be so late that Zechariah could not be still alive, nor so early that the Jews could have as yet had no occasion to fear the Greeks. Supposing Zechariah to have been about twenty-one years of age in the second year of Darius (520), he would have been little over fifty soon after the battle of Marathon (490), nor much over sixty when the Persians sustained their great naval defeat at Salamis (480). It will be easily perceived how, on hearing of the victories of the Greeks over their Persian protectors, the Jews would begin to tremble lest the Greeks, confounding them with the Phœnicians—whose fleets had been requisitioned by the Persians for the subjugation of the rebellious Ionians—should wreak their vengeance on the Holy Land as well as the seaboard. At this time, then—about 489 or 479 B.C.—it seems to us probable that Zechariah was commissioned to encourage his nation with promises of God's continued protection, and with hopes for the time to come.

VI. Contents of Zechariah ix. — xiv. —

ix., x. Doom of adjacent nations. The struggles, but eventual triumph and security, of Israel. The coming of the King (chap. ix. 9, *sqq.*).

xi. [xiii. 7—9 (?)]. The storm threatens the shepherds. Rejection of the Good Shepherd. Doom of the foolish shepherd.

xii. 1—9. Struggles of Israel with the nations.

xiii. 1—4. Zeal against prophets in general.

xii. 10—14. Mourning over Him whom they pierced.

xiii. 5, 6. General disclaiming of prophetic powers.

[xiii. 7—9 (?)].

xiv. "The last things," as seen in the light of the old dispensation.

ZECHARIAH

CHAPTER I.—(1) In the eighth
month, in the second year of Darius,
came the word of the LORD unto
Zechariah, the son of Berechiah, the
son of Iddo the prophet, saying,
(2) The LORD hath been [1] sore dis-
pleased with your fathers. (3) There-
fore say thou unto them, Thus saith the
LORD of hosts; [a] Turn ye unto me, saith
the LORD of hosts, and I will turn unto
you, saith the LORD of hosts. (4) Be ye
not as your fathers, unto whom the
former prophets have cried, saying, Thus
saith the LORD of hosts; [b] Turn ye now
from your evil ways, and *from* your evil
doings: but they did not hear, nor
hearken unto me, saith the LORD.
(5) Your fathers, where *are* they? and
the prophets, do they live for ever?
(6) But my words and my statutes, which
I commanded my servants the prophets,
did they not [2] take hold of your fathers?
and they returned and said, [c] Like as the
LORD of hosts thought to do unto us,
according to our ways, and according
to our doings, so hath he dealt with us.

B.C. cir. 520.

1 Heb., *with displeasure.*

a Mal. 3. 7.

b Isa. 31. 6; Jer. 3. 12 & 18. 11; Ez. 18. 30; Hos. 14. 1.

2 Or, *overtake.*

c Lam. 1. 18.

(1–6) On the four-and-twentieth day of the sixth month of the second year (B.C. 520) of Darius Hystaspis, the re-building of the Temple had been resumed (Haggai i. 15); and in the seventh month, on the twenty-first of that month, the prophet Haggai had foretold "the latter glory of this house shall be greater than its former" (Haggai ii. 9); and now, but a few weeks later, Zechariah receives his mission. He is commanded to exhort the people to avoid such punishments as fell on their fathers, and to make themselves worthy of the glory which should be revealed, by turning unto the Lord with sincere repentance.

(1) **The prophet** is (in spite of the accents), no doubt, to be referred to Zechariah. (See further in my *Hebrew Student Commentary.*) LXX., πρὸς Ζαχαρίαν τὸν τοῦ Βαραχίου υἱὸν Ἀδδὼ τὸν προφήτην, in which υἱὸν appears to be a corruption of υἱοῦ, caused by the common Greek collocation τὸν τοῦ . . . υἱόν.

(2) **Your fathers.**—This verse contains the word of the Lord addressed directly to and through the prophet, who is included among those addressed in the pronoun "*your* fathers." It gives the ground on which the exhortation to repentance is founded.

(3) **Unto them**—*i.e.*, to the prophet's contemporaries, whose fathers are spoken of in the preceding verse.

Turn ye . . . and I will turn.—These words need not imply any special backsliding on the part of the people since the commencement of the re-building of the Temple, when the Lord had declared that He was "with them" (Haggai i. 13, ii. 4); but, rather, that the more sincerely they turned unto Him, the more gloriously would His merciful intentions be revealed to them, and fulfilled in them. Still, it may be seen from Haggai ii. 14—17, how great need they had of repentance. "Zechariah comes forth like John the Baptist, and begins his preaching with a call to repentance, and warns the people by the history of their fathers that no spiritual privileges will profit them without holiness, but rather will aggravate their guilt, and increase their condemnation if they disobey God" (Wordsworth). Observe in this and the next verse the emphatic threefold "saith the Lord of hosts."

(4) **The former prophets**—viz., those who prophesied when Jerusalem was inhabited and in prosperity (chap. vii. 7), before the captivity. LXX., οἱ προφῆται ἔμπροσθεν, [to whom] the prophets before [enjoined], which is inaccurate. Οἱ προφῆται οἱ ἔμπροσθεν, "the prophets of former times," would have been correct.

(5) **Fathers . . . prophets.**—To show the evil result of the obstinate disobedience of their fathers, the prophet asks, "Your fathers, where are they?"—*i.e.*, they are perished through their iniquity. To this the people answer, "But the prophets, do they live [*or* did they go on living] for ever?"—*i.e.*, the prophets, who did not sin, they are dead too; so what is your argument worth?

(6) **My words.**—True, says the prophet, both your fathers and the former prophets are dead; "but" for all that, the words of the prophets were actually fulfilled in your fathers, as they themselves confessed. This is the interpretation of these verses given by Răv (second to third century A.D.) in Talmud Babli, *Synhédrin,* 105*a*. Another view of the passage is that it is equivalent to "The light of prophecy is dying out; while ye have the light, walk as children of the light." But such an interpretation destroys the prophet's argument.

My statutes.—Better, *my decrees,* as in Zeph. ii. 2. LXX. introduce "receive ye," after "my decrees." After "I command," they introduce "by my spirit," probably from chap. vii. 12.

Take hold of.—Better, as marg., *overtake.* LXX., οἳ κατελάβοσαν may be a corruption of οὐ κατελάβοσαν (Comp. Lam. i. 12.)

Returned.—Better, *turned: i.e.,* repented. The same word is used in verse 3. LXX., wrongly, καὶ ἀπεκρίθησαν, "answered."

Like as the Lord of hosts thought to do . . .—So Jeremiah confessed in Lam. ii. 17. Zechariah had no doubt those words of Jeremiah in his mind at the time.

(7) Upon the four and twentieth day of
the eleventh month, which *is* the month
Sebat, in the second year of Darius,
came the word of the LORD unto
Zechariah, the son of Berechiah, the
son of Iddo the prophet, saying,

(8) I saw by night, and behold a man
riding upon a red horse, and he stood
among the myrtle trees that *were* in the
bottom; and behind him *were there* red
horses, [1]speckled, and white. (9) Then
said I, O my lord, what *are* these? And

[1] Or, *bay.*

A SERIES OF SEVEN VISIONS.

Chaps. i. 7—vi. 15. Between the commencement of Zechariah's prophetic labours and the incidents recorded in Zech. i. 7—vi. 15, the Prophet Haggai received the revelation contained in Haggai ii. 10—23. On the four-and-twentieth day of the eleventh month, just five months after the re-building of the Temple was resumed, Zechariah sees a succession of seven visions in one night, followed by a symbolic action (chap. vi. 9—15).

(7) **Sebat.**—The eleventh month. The names of the months, which occur in Zechariah, Esther, and Nehemiah, are of Assyrio-Babylonian origin; they are in use among the Jews to this day.

Came the word of the Lord . . . saying.—This expression is fitly used here of the nocturnal visions, because the substance of them was a Divine revelation, and because the means by which the signification of them was conveyed to the prophet was that of the angel's speaking to him the word of the Lord.

FIRST VISION.—THE HORSEMAN AMONG THE MYRTLES.

(8) **I saw.**—Not in a dream, but apparently, from chap. iv. 1, awake, in an ecstatic vision.

By night.—Better, *on this night.* LXX., τὴν νύκτα. It was during the night of the twenty-fourth of Sebat that the prophet saw this series of visions. The expression does not mean that in his vision it appeared to be night.

Red horse, and . . . the bottom.—Better, *bay horse, and he was standing among the myrtles that were in a certain hollow.* The construction of the Hebrew shows beyond controversy that "the man that stood among the myrtles" and "the angel of the Lord" (verse 11) are identical. On the appellation, "the angel of the Lord," see Note on Gen. xvi. 7. Angels, when they assume the human form, are often called "men"—*e.g.*, in Gen. xviii. 2. There can be no doubt but that "horses" means horses with riders. Commentators endeavour to attach special significance to the expression, "the myrtles which were in the hollow." Some see in "the myrtles" a symbol of the pious; others of the theocracy, or of the land of Judah, and take "the hollow" as a figurative representation of Babylon, or of the deep degradation into which the land and people of God had fallen at that time. Similarly with respect to the colour of the horses: some suppose that the colours either denote the lands and nations to which the riders had been sent, or the three imperial kingdoms, Babylonian, Medo-Persian, and Græco-Macedonian (Kliefoth), or as connected with the various missions which the rider had to perform. The following are specimens of such interpretation—(1) that of Keil: The riders on *red* horses are to cause war and bloodshed; those on *pale-grey* (*seruqqîm*) to cause hunger, famine, and pestilence; those on *white* go to conquest. But this explanation takes no account of the single horseman on the red (bay) horse. Moreover victory implies bloodshed, as much as does war, so that there is no practical distinction made between the *red* and the *white* horses. (2) Ewald deprives "the man standing among the myrtles" of his horse, then he renders the colours of the horses *bright-red, brown, grey,* and supplies *dark-red,* from his interpretation of chap. vi. 3. Having thus arranged the colours to his fancy, he compares this vision with that of the chariots in chap. vi., and sees in the colours the mission of the riders to the four quarters of heaven. The *red* denotes the east; the *brown* (the black of chap. vi.) the north; the *grey,* the west; the *dark-red,* the south. (3) Vitringa interprets the three colours as follows: *red,* times of war; *varicoloured,* times of varying distress and prosperity; *white,* times of complete prosperity, which were sent on the Jewish people. (4) That of Kliefoth, mentioned above. (5) Rabbi Mosheh Alshekh, the cabbalist, interprets *red* of the company of Gabriel which inclines to Strict Justice; *seruqqîm* of that of Raphael (who is the angel of *healing* after smiting, that is Justice tempered with Mercy); *white* of that of Michael who inclines to Free Grace. But all these suppositions are purely conjectural, utterly unsuitable, and perfectly unnecessary. In a vision or a parable we must not expect to find something in the interpretation to correspond with each detail of the figurative representation: the setting must not be confounded with the gem. So, in this case, we are of opinion that the fact that the horsemen were standing among the myrtles in a certain hollow is mentioned merely as a natural incident; for where would a body of scouts so naturally come to a halt, especially in the East, where shade and herbage are scarce, and where travellers always strive to escape as much as possible the observation of hostile tribes, as under the cool and protecting shadow of a grove of myrtles growing in a hollow place? LXX., for "among the myrtles which were in a certain hollow," ἀναμέσον τῶν ὀρέων τῶν κατασκιῶν, misreading seemingly the word for "myrtles," and taking the word for "hollow" as from a similar root meaning "to be shady."

Red.—Better, *bay.* (Comp. chap. vi. 2.)

Speckled, or, *starling grey,* is, perhaps, the meaning of the Hebrew word *seruqqîm,* which occurs only once again—viz., in Isa. xvi. 8, and there in the sense of *vine-tendrils;* nothing certain is known of it as an adjective of colour. The meanings given by the Authorised Version and ourself are merely conjectural, and derived (unsatisfactorily) from a comparison of this passage with verse 3 and Rev. vi. 3. We are almost inclined to suggest that the word is a corruption of *shechorîm,* "black" (see chap. vi.). The colours seem to be mentioned as those most commonly found among horses, in order to give a more realistic form to the vision, or perhaps, rather, because the prophet actually so saw them. The writer of Revelation has (Rev. vi.) adopted the colours mentioned in Zech. vi., and himself given to them a special significance in his own writings. But to interpret Zechariah in this case by the light of the Book of Revelation, as some commentators have done, would be most uncritical. The colours in LXX. of this chapter are πυρροὶ, ψαροὶ καὶ ποικίλοι, λευκοί. In chap. vi. they are πυρροί, μέλανες, λευκοί, ποικίλοι ψαροί. In Rev. vi. the colours are λευκός, πυρρός, μέλας, χλωρός.

(9) **O my lord.**—This is addressed to "the angel that talked with me," or, perhaps, *in me,* according as

the angel that talked with me said unto
me, I will shew thee what these *be.*
(10) And the man that stood among the
myrtle trees answered and said, These
are they whom the LORD hath sent to
walk to and fro through the earth.
(11) And they answered the angel of the
LORD that stood among the myrtle trees,
and said, We have walked to and fro
through the earth, and, behold, all the
earth sitteth still, and is at rest.
(12) Then the angel of the LORD
answered and said, O LORD of hosts,
how long wilt thou not have mercy on
Jerusalem and on the cities of Judah,
against which thou hast had indigna-
tion these threescore and ten years?
(13) And the LORD answered the angel
that talked with me *with* good words
and comfortable words.
(14) So the angel that communed with
me said unto me, Cry thou, saying, Thus
saith the LORD of hosts; I am [a]jealous
for Jerusalem and for Zion with a great
jealousy. (15) And I am very sore dis-
pleased with the heathen *that are* at
ease: for I was but a little displeased,
and they helped forward the affliction.
(16) Therefore thus saith the LORD; I am
returned to Jerusalem with mercies:
my house shall be built in it, saith the
LORD of hosts, and a line shall be
stretched forth upon Jerusalem. (17) Cry
yet, saying, Thus saith the LORD of
hosts; My cities through [1]prosperity
shall yet be spread abroad; and the

a ch. 8. 2.

1 Heb., *good.*

---

we regard him as discharging the office of the Virgil of Dante, or the Daimon of Socrates (but, see Lawes' *History of Philosophy*). LXX., ὁ λαλῶν ἐν ἐμοί. This is the angel-interpreter, whose office it was to interpret the visions (chaps. i. 18, ii. 3, iv. 1, 4, 5, v. 5—10, vi. 4), and who is often referred to simply as "he."

I will shew thee.—viz., by the word of "the man who stood among the myrtles."

(10) **Answered.**—The question which Zechariah had put to the angel-interpreter.

The earth—*i.e.*, the world, "all the earth" (verse 11), not merely "the land of Israel," as is often the meaning of the word (*e.g.*, chap. xiii. 8).

(11) **And they answered** need not necessarily imply that any question had been asked. Like the New Testament ἀπεκρίθησαν, it often implies merely "began to speak."

The angel of the Lord.—That is, *the man riding upon a bay horse.* (See Note on verse 8.) Just two months before this, Haggai had prophesied (chap. ii. 20—23) that God would shake the heavens and the earth, and overthrow the throne of kingdoms, &c. The horsemen had been sent forth to act, as it were, as scouts, and to bring back an account of the state of the world, that at the intercession of the angel of the Lord comforting words might be announced to Zechariah, and by him to the people. They reported the world to be still, and at rest: *i.e.*, dwelling in self-confident security. The overthrow of the kingdoms foretold by Haggai had not yet begun, and so, although the building of the Temple was, by the decree of Darius (Ezra v. and vi.), being carried on, Judah was still insecure as long as the heathen nations flourished.

(12) Consequently, the angel of the Lord intercedes for Jerusalem and the cities of Judah.

These threescore and ten years.—This is an old English expression. The Hebrew has one word—*seventy*—which is often used as a round number. From the taking of Jerusalem by Nebuchadnezzar (B.C. 605—6) to the date of the decree of Cyrus for the return of the Jews (B.C. 538) is sixty-eight years. These are the seventy years of captivity foretold by Jeremiah (chaps. xxv. 11, xxix. 10). But eighteen years had now elapsed since that decree of Cyrus. Consequently the angelic intercessor, in saying "how long . . . these seventy years," can hardly have referred to the seventy years spoken of by Jeremiah, since the actual number of years was now eighty-eight. Therefore it is most probable that the reference is to the period of sixty-eight years between the second taking of Jerusalem by Nebuchadnezzar, when Zedekiah was removed in chains to Babylon (B.C. 588), and the year of this prophecy (B.C. 520).

(13) **Angel.**—The Lord does not reply directly to the intercessor, but addresses the angel-interpreter, who at once, in the words of verses 14—17, delivers the message of comfort to the prophet.

(14) **That communed with me.**—The Hebrew words are the same as those rendered elsewhere, "that spake with me."

I am jealous.—The verb is in the perfect, like "I am returned" (verse 16), and denotes that the Lord *had already* shown His jealous love for Israel in bringing them out of captivity, and that He *would continue to do so* in completing the restoration of Jerusalem. "The hour of darkest desolation to the Church, and of haughtiest triumph to her enemies, is often the very hour when God begins His work of judgment on the one, and returning mercy on the other" (Moore).

(15) **But a little.**—(Comp. 2 Kings. xx. 18.) Or, *for a little while.* (Comp. Job xxiv. 24.)

Helped forward the affliction.—Better, *helped for evil*—*i.e.*, they not only acted as God's instruments to chastise Israel, but even wished to annihilate them. (Comp. Isa. xlvii. 6: "I was wroth with my people . . . thou [Babylon] didst shew them no mercy.") LXX., for "*that are* at ease," τὰ συνεπιτιθέμενα, "which combine to set upon [Israel]," and for "helped," συνεπέθεντο "combined to set upon."

(16) **A line.**—To measure, and mark out its confines. (Comp. chap. ii. 1, 2.)

(17) **Be spread abroad**—*i.e.*, be filled to overflowing; LXX. inserts "And the angel that spake in me said to me." (Comp. chap. ii. 4.) The same verb and conjugation is used in chap. xiii. 7 of "being scattered," in a bad sense, and such is the ordinary use of the verb. But in another conjugation this verb is used in Gen. x. 18 of "being spread," not in a bad sense.

"Then let the world forbear their rage,
The Church renounce her fear;
Israel must live through every age,
And be the Almighty's care."

Lord shall yet comfort Zion, and shall
yet choose Jerusalem.
(18) Then lifted I up mine eyes, and
saw, and behold four horns. (19) And I
said unto the angel that talked with
me, What *be* these? And he answered
me, These *are* the horns which have
scattered Judah, Israel, and Jerusalem.
(20) And the Lord shewed me four
carpenters. (21) Then said I, What come
these to do? And he spake, saying,
These *are* the horns which have scattered
Judah, so that no man did lift up his
head: but these are come to fray them,
to cast out the horns of the Gentiles,
which lifted up *their* horn over the land
of Judah to scatter it.

CHAPTER II.—(1) I lifted up mine
eyes again, and looked, and behold a
man with a measuring line in his hand.
(2) Then said I, Whither goest thou?
And he said unto me, To measure Jeru-
salem, to see what *is* the breadth there-
of, and what *is* the length thereof.
(3) And, behold, the angel that talked
with me went forth, and another angel
went out to meet him, (4) and said unto
him, Run, speak to this young man,
saying, Jerusalem shall be inhabited *as*

Second Vision.—The Four Horns and the Four Smiths (Verses 18—21).

(18) **Horns.**—The horn is a symbol of power and hostility. The "four horns" denote the heathen nations which had oppressed them.

(19) **Scattered.**—This word need not necessarily refer to dispersing into captivity, but may simply mean "endeavoured to destroy the national unity," or "disintegrated." Compare the Roman motto, "*Divide et impera.*"

Judah, Israel, and Jerusalem.—The expression "Israel and Jerusalem" is a closer definition of *Judah*, as in Mal. ii. 11. (For undoubted instances of the name *Israel* being used in reference to *Judah* after the separation of the kingdoms, see 2 Chron. xii. 1., xv. 17, *seqq.*)

(20) **Carpenters.**—Better, *workmen*, for the Hebrew word does not mean "carpenters," unless followed by the word meaning "wood."

(21) Many commentators suppose that this vision refers to the future as well as the past, and that in it the objects are combined together so as to form one complete picture, without any regard to the time of their appearing in historical reality. And so they take the "four horns" to symbolise the four empires—the Assyrian, the Babylonian, the Medo-Persian, and the Græco-Macedonian. But such is not the case, as is clearly shown by this verse. It is true that the word "scattered" might, if standing alone, be taken as discharging the duties of historic and, at the same time, of prophetic perfect. But since in the dependent clause we have, "so that no man *did lift up* his head"—in the perfect—the word "have scattered" can refer only to the actual past. We must, therefore, reject all reference to the four monarchies which we have enumerated, because the Græco-Macedonian had not yet come into existence. If, then, the "four horns" do symbolise four monarchies, they can only be the Assyrian, Egyptian, Babylonian, and Medo-Persian. Some commentators have gone so far as to identify the *four workmen* with Nebuchadnezzar, Cyrus, Cambyses, and Alexander the Great. (Comp. and contrast Hag. ii. 22.) But it seems more probable that here (as in verse 8) we must not draw too close a comparison between the symbol and the thing symbolised, and should understand the "four workmen" as merely figuring the destruction of these nations for the good of the Jewish nation, without the manner of its accomplishment being accurately defined. We may remark, in passing, that some commentators do not take the vision as referring to four distinct nations, but suppose the number four to be used in reference to *all* the powers hostile to Judah, from *whatever quarter* they may have come. The vision, a natural consequent of the preceding, is one of comfort, its object being to assure the people that as the former nations which had been hostile to Israel and Judah had been destroyed, so the present Medo-Persian monarchy, which also had at times oppressed them, should have the horn of its hostility utterly cast out, and should protect them and encourage the re-building of Jerusalem.

II.

Third Vision.—The Man with the Measuring Line.

(1—5) This vision is a prophetic realisation of the fulfilment of the promise (chap. i. 16): "A line shall be stretched forth upon Jerusalem."

(1) **A man** does not seem to mean "an angel," as in chap. i. 8, for he has no message to deliver or mission to perform; but he is to be considered rather as a mere figure in the vision, performing an action for which, indeed, he is implicitly rebuked.

(2) **What is . . .**—Since there is no verb "is" or "will be" expressed in the original, it has been disputed whether the reference is to the actual or to the future condition of Jerusalem. But, we have little hesitation in saying that the whole vision is prophetic of the state of Jerusalem from its restoration to the time when God's protection should be eventually removed from it. To this latter event, however, no reference is as yet made.

(3) **Went forth.**—Literally, *goes forth*, from the prophet's side, in the direction of the man who went to measure. LXX., εἱστήκει.

Went out.—Literally, *comes forth*: viz., from the invisible—*i.e.*, appears, reveals himself. The same word in Hebrew means to *come* and to *go* forth, according to circumstances. (Comp. chap. v. 5, 6.)

(4) **And said unto him.**—Some commentators suppose that it is the angel-interpreter who here speaks; but if this were the case, an "other angel" would be a superfluous figure in the vision, for the angel-interpreter might have addressed "this young man" directly. Accordingly, we agree with the Authorised Version in taking this "other angel" as the speaker.

This young man is by some supposed to be Zechariah: but it gives a much more definite turn to the meaning of the vision to understand the ex-

towns without walls for the multitude
of men and cattle therein : (5) for I, saith
the LORD, will be unto her a wall of fire
round about, and will be the glory in
the midst of her.
(6) Ho, ho, *come forth*, and flee from
the land of the north, saith the LORD :
for I have spread you abroad as the four
winds of the heaven, saith the LORD.
(7) Deliver thyself, O Zion, that dwellest

B.C. 519.

a Deut. 32. 10; Ps. 17. 8.

b Isa. 12. 6 & 54. 1.

with the daughter of Babylon. (8) For
thus saith the LORD of hosts; After the
glory hath he sent me unto the nations
which spoiled you: for he that [a] toucheth
you toucheth the apple of his eye.
(9) For, behold, I will shake mine hand
upon them, and they shall be a spoil to
their servants: and ye shall know that
the LORD of hosts hath sent me.
(10) [b] Sing and rejoice, O daughter of

pression as referring to "the man with the measuring line."

Towns without walls—*i.e.*, unfortified towns. A similar expression in the Hebrew is contrasted with "fortified cities" in 1 Sam. vi. 18. The "other angel," for the instruction of Zechariah, directs the angel-interpreter to inform the man who was measuring that there could be no object in taking an exact measure of Jerusalem, since "for the multitude of men and cattle" it would soon exceed its original limits. It would be an unnecessary forcing of the words to suppose with some commentators that the measurer is called a "young man" on account of his simplicity and ignorance. That this prophecy was fulfilled in the grandeur and extent of Jerusalem may be seen by a reference to the descriptions of it, after its restoration, by Aristéas (Ed. Schmidt), Hecatæus, &c. Josephus (*Bell, Jud.* v. 4, 92) says that in the time of Herod Agrippa Jerusalem had, "by reason of the multitude" of its inhabitants, gradually "extended beyond its original limits," so that another hill had to be taken in, which was fortified, and called "Bezethá."

(5) **A wall of fire.**—This verse is not intended to discountenance the building of walls to Jerusalem, a thing which was actually done under Nehemiah (B.C. 445), but is simply a solemn promise of God's protection. Many indeed were the troubles which fell on the city in the times which intervened between the days of Zechariah and those of our Lord; but still, abundant proof was given that God had not forgotten His promise to shield it. Such troubles, as at other periods of the history of the Jews, were but chastisements, and even those not in proportion to their transgressions. (For the figurative use of the expression "wall," see 1 Sam. xxv. 16.)

(6—13) This address to Zion may be taken as the words of the prophet himself, or of the angel who had been speaking before. In any case, it was intended to be communicated to the people by the prophet, whose mind had been prepared by the foregoing vision for the reception of such a revelation.

(6) **The land of the north**—*i.e.*, Babylonia, as in Jer. i. 14, vi. 22, x. 22.

For I have spread you abroad.—This conjugation of this verb occurs *nine* times in all in the Hebrew Scriptures. *Seven* times it is used of "stretching forth the hands;" once (Ps. lxviii. 15) it means "to scatter." If we assign to it this latter meaning here, the tense must be taken as the actual past, and the reference must be to the dispersions which had already taken place. "The Book of Esther (i. 1, iii. 8, 12—14, viii. 5—9) shows that, sixty years after this, the Jews were dispersed over the one hundred and twenty-seven provinces of the Persian empire, *from* India (the Punjaub) *to Ethiopia*, whether they were purposely placed by the policy of the conquerors in detached groups, as the ten tribes were *in the cities of the Medes* (2 Kings xvii. 6), or whether, when more trusted, they migrated of their own accord. "God, in calling them to return, reminded them of the greatness of their dispersion. He had dispersed them abroad as the four winds of heaven; He, the same, recalled them" (Pusey). Or, if we take the verb in a good sense, the tense must be regarded as the prophetic perfect, meaning, "for it is my fixed intention to spread you abroad." According to this interpretation they are encouraged to flee from Babylon by being warned of the judgments which were to come upon her (verses 8, 9), and because God was determined so to bless them, that they should spread out to all quarters of the globe.

As the four winds of the heaven.—The rendering of some, "for I will scatter you to the four winds," as referring to a new dispersion of Israel, which loomed darkly in the future, rests on a linguistic error. LXX. deliberately paraphrases, ἐκ τῶν τεσσάρων ἀνέμων τοῦ οὐρανοῦ συνάξω ὑμας, "*from* the four winds of heaven I will gather you."

(7) **Daughter of Babylon** means *inhabitants of Babylon*, as (verse 10) "daughter of Zion" means *inhabitants of Zion*. (With the whole passage comp. Isa. xlviii. 20; Jer. li. 6, 9, 45.) LXX. for "O Zion," εἰς Σιῶν—comp. a somewhat similar mistake in Ezek. xxi. 15 (verse 10, LXX.).

(8) **After the glory**—*i.e.*, in search of glory—viz., to display God's glory upon the heathen in judgment and mercy, by first breaking their power (verse 9), and afterwards attaching them to His service (verse 11). (Comp. chap. xiv.: when the prophet gives the *substance* of the Lord's words, as in this verse and verse 9, the first person singular refers to the prophet; but when, as in verse 9, he gives the *actual* words of God, "I" means, of course, the Lord Himself.)

(9) The troubles which overtook Babylon shortly after this time are sufficiently borne witness to by the inscription executed by Darius in the fifth year of his reign (Sir W. Rawlinson) on the great rock of Behistun, near the western frontier of Media. Thereon are recorded two great insurrections in Babylonia, and that Babylon itself was twice taken, once by Darius in person, and again by his general, Intaphres (*Records of the Past*, Vol. I., pp. 118—125). On the latter occasion, "says Darius the king, I made a decree that Arakha and his principal followers should be put to death in Babylon."

(10—13) The prophecy contained in these verses is admitted by most Jewish as well as Christian commentators to be of a Messianic character; but opinion is not so unanimous with regard to the nature of its fulfilment. Now, in considering such passages as this, we must bear in mind that the prophets were but men—inspired men, it is true—but still, men with the un-

Zion: for, lo, I come, and I [a]will dwell
in the midst of thee, saith the LORD.
(11) And many nations shall be joined to
the LORD in that day, and shall be my
people: and I will dwell in the midst of
thee, and thou shalt know that the
LORD of hosts hath sent me unto thee.
(12) And the LORD shall inherit Judah
his portion in the holy land, and shall
choose Jerusalem again. (13) Be silent,
O all flesh, before the LORD: for he is
raised up out of [1]his holy habitation.

CHAPTER III.—(1) And he shewed
me Joshua the high priest standing be-
fore the angel of the LORD, and [2]Satan

a Lev. 26. 12; Ez. 37. 27; 2 Cor. 6. 16.

1 Heb., *the habitation of his holiness.*

2 That is, *an adversary.*

---

restrained use of their natural faculties preserved to them. When they received a prophetic inspiration, some grand idea of God's purpose was impressed on their minds, while they were left to work out the details according to the bent of their human imaginations, and in accordance, more or less, with the views current in their times. If we adopt this reasonable view of the nature of prophecy, we shall not be surprised to find that in the fulfilment, while all that is essential to the grand idea of God's purpose, as revealed to and by the prophet, actually comes to pass, the historical details which surround its accomplishment are not often such as the prophet himself seems to have expected. (See Notes on verses 11, 12, chap. xiv. 16—19.) Even the Apostles themselves were—at any rate, for a time—in error with regard to the time and manner of Christ's second advent. Upon the supposition, then, that Zechariah had no certain knowledge of the time, and was in error with regard to the actual manner, of the fulfilment of God's purpose, of the essential points of which he had, however, a grand and faithful prophetic perception, we shall have no difficulty in interpreting this passage, and others like it, of the coming of Christ in the flesh, and the establishment of the Christian Church.

(10) **I will dwell in the midst of thee.**—These words (comp. chap. viii. 3) were, no doubt, meant by the prophet to refer, in the first place, to God's indwelling in the second Temple (see Note on Hag. ii. 9), although the visible manifestation of His presence (the *Shekinah*) was not again given. This prophecy received a glorious fulfilment, little dreamt of by the prophet, in the great event chronicled in John i. 14.

(11) **Many nations.**—Comp. chap. viii. 20—22. This prophecy, which is clothed in Old Testament imagery, was spiritually fulfilled by the gathering-in of the Gentiles to the Church of Christ.

And . . . . shall be joined.—LXX., *καὶ καταφεύξονται*, "and shall flee for refuge," as in Jer. l. 5 (chap. xxvii. 5, LXX.).

My people.—Heb., *to me for a people.* LXX., *αὐτῳ εἰς λαόν*, "to *Him* for a people." Instead of "And I will dwell," LXX., *καὶ κατασκηνώσουσιν*, "and *they* shall dwell."

And thou . . . unto thee.—The pronouns are in the feminine, and refer to the "daughter of Zion" (verse 10).

Sent me.—The person changes (comp. verse 8). These words seem to imply an expectation of a near fulfilment of the prophecy, such as would prove to the people the truth of the prophet's (or angel's) mission. (Comp. chaps. iv. 9, vi. 15.) But when the promise was fulfilled in Christ, it was just "the city" that *failed* to perceive its fulfilment (Luke xix. 44).

(12) **The holy land.**—This is the only passage in which this term is used. This promise has not been literally fulfilled, for, so far from God's then inheriting "Judah or the Holy Land," and choosing "again Jerusalem," the coming of Christ was but the beginning of the rejection of His people, and the destruction of Jerusalem. But such discrepancies between promise and fulfilment (see Note on verses 10—13) do not cast any suspicion on the prophet's trustworthiness, or in the least invalidate our Christian interpretation of the passage; they simply afford an illustration of the fact that the prophets, as well as others, saw only "through a mirror in enigma" (1 Cor. xiii. 12), and that the truth was never revealed to any one prophet in its entirety, but to all the prophets "in many portions, and in diverse manners" (Heb. i.). We may believe, on the authority of St. Paul, that God hath not cast off His own people, and that a time will come when all Israel shall be saved.

(13) **Be silent.**—Better, *Hush!* (Comp. Hab. ii. 20.)

Raised.—Better, *roused.* The figure is that of a lion roused up from its lair. (Comp. the still bolder metaphor of Ps. lxxviii. 65.) LXX. misread the word for "habitation," which they render correctly elsewhere, and give *ἐκ νεφελῶν ἁγίων αὐτοῦ*, "from His holy clouds."

III.

FOURTH VISION.—JOSHUA BEFORE THE ANGEL OF THE LORD.

(1—7) The accusation against Joshua was not that of neglecting the building of the Temple (for the re-building had been resumed five months before), nor was it that he had allowed his sons to marry foreign wives (for that took place some sixty years later), but, rather, as high priest he was the representative of the priestly nation, and so was looked on as laden, not only with his own, but also with the sins of the whole people. Moreover, the priesthood itself had fallen under the severest condemnation. "Her priests have violated my law, and have profaned my holy things" (Ezek. xxii. 26).

(1) **And he.**—Probably, the angel-interpreter.

Joshua.—The various forms of this name, that of the Saviour of the world, are well worth noticing. The oldest form of the word is that used here, *Yᵉhoshua'*, which was contracted into *Yoshua'* (Mishnah, *passim*), also into *Yeshua'* (Ezra ii. 2), and then into *Yeshu.* This last was represented in Greek by Ιησου, and with the nominative ending *ς* became Ἰησοῦς. In the Talmudim the name takes also the forms *Īsā* and *Īsī*, and in Arabic *'Īsā.*

Standing before.—There is a great variety of opinion among commentators with respect to the capacity in which Joshua is represented as standing before the angel of the Lord. Theodoret, among early expositors, and Hengstenberg, among moderns, maintain that Joshua is seen in the sanctuary engaged in the work of his priestly office *before* the angel of the Lord. Against this view may be urged that, however high may be the dignity of the angel of the Lord, it is hardly in accordance with the spirit of the Old Testament to represent the high priest as ministering before him, as if before God. Observe, too, how in chap. i. 12, 13, the

standing at his right hand [1]to resist him. (2) And the LORD said unto Satan, [a]The LORD rebuke thee, O Satan; even the LORD that hath chosen Jerusalem rebuke thee: *is* not this a brand plucked out of the fire?

(3) Now Joshua was clothed with filthy garments, and stood before the angel. (4) And he answered and spake unto those that stood before him, saying, Take away the filthy garments from him. And unto him he said, Behold, I have caused thine iniquity to pass from thee, and I will clothe thee with change of raiment. (5) And I said, Let them set a fair mitre upon his head. So they set a fair mitre upon his head, and clothed him with garments. And the angel of the LORD stood by.

(6) And the angel of the LORD protested unto Joshua, saying, (7) Thus saith the LORD of hosts;

If thou wilt walk in my ways, and if thou wilt keep my [2] charge, then thou shalt also judge my house, and shalt also keep my courts, and I will give thee

1 Heb., *to be his adversary.*

a Jude 9.

2 Or, *ordinance.*

---

personality of the angel of the Lord is distinct from that of the Lord Himself. Ewald imagines that at this time the high priest was actually accused, or was dreading an accusation, at the Persian court, and that a defamation and persecution of this kind may be discerned as underlying this vision. But there is no historical trace of any such *personal* accusation, nor could Joshua be looked upon as the people's *representative* before the *Persian Court,* since Zerubbabel was their *civil* representative. Koehler regards Joshua as standing before the judgment-seat of the angel, while Satan stands at his right hand (Ps. cix. 6) to accuse him. But, while this interpretation is in the main correct, it must be remembered that no formal judicial process is described in the vision, nor is there any mention of a judgment-seat. Wright's explanation seems to us the best: "The high priest was probably seen in the vision, busied about some part of his priestly duties. While thus engaged, he discovered that he was actually standing as a criminal before the angel, and while the great Adversary accused him, the truth of that accusation was but too clearly seen by the filthy garments with which he then perceived that he was attired."

Satan.—Literally, *the adversary,* who is, not Sanballat and his companion (Qimchi), but ὁ διάβολος, *the* adversary of mankind. A belief in a personal devil was current among the Jews from, at any rate, the time of the composition of the Book of Job to Talmudic times. (See Job i., ii.; 1 Chron. xxi. 1; Talmud Babli, *Baba Bathra,* 26 *b,* &c.)

At his right hand.—The position of the adversay, or complainant, as represented in the original passage (Ps. cix. 6).

(2) **The Lord rebuke thee.**—See Note on Jude 19. Satan is justly rebuked; "for who shall lay anything to the charge of God's chosen?"

The fire.—Of penal suffering in the captivity in Babylon. (Comp. Amos iv. 11) As with the guilt, so with the pardon and promise. in both, Joshua was the representative of the people.

(3) **Filthy garments.**—Such as would render him unfit to appear before God as priest. They are a symbol of the guilt and defilement of sin. (Isa. lxiv. 5.)

And stood before.—See Note on verse 1.

(4) **Those that stood before him** is an expression meaning courtiers and counsellors (1 Kings xiii. 6—8); and here, probably, means angels of inferior grade to the "angel of the Lord."

Thine iniquity—*i.e.,* of thee, and of the people whose representative thou art.

And I will clothe thee.—Better, *and I clothe thee.* The tense is "the aorist of immediate past." (Comp. Gr. ἐδεξάμην, "I welcome.") LXX. change the mood and person, and render καὶ ἐνδύσατε αὐτὸν ποδήρη, "and clothe ye him with a long garment."

Change of raiment.—The word means simply different garments to the filthy ones in which he was clothed before: *clean* ones, in fact. (See next verse.) The figure seems to be borrowed from Isa. lxi. 10: "He hath clothed me with garments of salvation, He hath clothed me with a robe of righteousness." That it does not mean "festal garments" is shown by the ordinary word for "garments" being used in verse 5.

(5) **Fair**—*i.e.,* clean. (Comp. the words of the Rubric, "a fair white linen cloth.") The prophet seems to have felt constrained to make the request contained in this verse from an idea that the changing of Joshua's raiment might be only a sign of the removal of the high priest's own guilt.

Mitre, or *turban,* it was upon which was fastened the golden plate inscribed with "Holiness to the Lord" (comp. chap. xiv. 20), by virtue of which the shortcomings of the sanctuary were atoned (Exod. xxviii. 38). That the prophet was justified in making the request is shown by the fact that it was granted, and that even before the "garments" were put on.

Stood by.—Better, *kept standing* (where he was).

(6—10) The angel of the Lord now proclaims to Joshua a fourfold promise: (1) the confirmation of his official authority, and the elevation of his own spiritual nature; (2) the mission of the Saviour; (3) God's providential care for the House, which was being rebuilt; (4) the peace and prosperity of the nation.

(7) **Walk in my ways** refers to personal holiness.

Keep my charge.—To the due discharge of his official duties.

Then thou.—The word "thou" is emphatic, and helps to mark the apodosis.

My house.—On this passage Wright remarks: "The words 'my house' seem to have been chosen to correspond with 'my courts' in the parallel clause. Though the two ideas are closely related, they are not identical in meaning. The expression 'my house' is probably to be understood in a metaphorical sense for *my people* (comp. Num. xii. 7; Hosea viii. 1, ix. 15, οἶκος Θεοῦ; Heb. iii. 6; 1 Tim. iii. 15), because the word *judge* takes an accusative after it of the person, and not of the thing, with the exception of an accusative of cognate meaning, as 'to judge judgment' (Jer. v. 28, xxx. 13, xxi. 12). The word 'house' may possibly have been chosen in preference to that of 'people' to avoid giving offence, as the people were then under Persian rule (Schegg). If the word 'house' be understood metaphorically, the sense is that the

[1]places to walk among these that stand
by. (8) Hear now, O Joshua the high
priest, thou, and thy fellows that sit
before thee: for they *are* [2]men wondered
at: for, behold, I will bring forth my
servant the [a]BRANCH. (9) For behold
the stone that I have laid before Joshua;
upon one stone *shall be* seven eyes:
behold, I will engrave the graving thereof, saith the LORD of hosts, and I
will remove the iniquity of that land in
one day.

1 Heb., *walks.*

2 Heb., *men of wonder.*

a Isa. 11. 1; Jer. 23. 5 & 33. 15; ch. 6. 12; Luke 1. 78.

---

high priest was to direct the people in all things respecting the law of God, and especially to judge those who ministered in the sanctuary (Hitzig, Pressel, &c.). Others think that the Temple then in course of construction is referred to (Hengstenberg, Keil, Kliefoth, Pusey). In the latter case the meaning is not very different, namely, that the high priest was to rule and direct the services of the sanctuary and Holy of holies, and to keep away every kind of idolatry and ungodliness from its outer courts (Hengstenberg)." Thus Joshua is confirmed in his office of high priest, which had been called in question by the accusation of Satan (*has-Sātān*).

Places to walk—*i.e.*, as in margin, "walks," meaning *paths.* LXX., ἀναστρεφομένους ἐν μέσῳ, "living among" vocalising the word differently. Ewald understands the word as meaning "leaders," but if that were its signification it would be followed by "from among," instead of "among."

Among these that stand by.—The angels of the heavenly court. Etymologically, *assistants*; but in legal phraseology, *assessors.* The whole scene is drawn on the model of an Oriental *Darbár.* He is promised free spiritual access to God among the holy angels. Observe the introverted parallelism of this verse—"wilt *walk,*" "wilt *keep*;" then "shalt *keep,*" "places to *walk.*" "A gratuitous justification furnishes no excuse for inaction and sin, but leads to more entire obedience . . . Fidelity in God's service shall be gloriously rewarded." (Moore.)

(8) **For they**—*i.e.*, thou and they. For this change of person, comp. Zeph. ii. 12, which runs literally, "Also *ye* Cushim slain by my sword (are) they."

Wondered at.—Literally, as in margin, *of sign*—*i.e.*, men to whom signs are given, and for whom miracles are wrought; or, according to others, persons accustomed to interpret the enigmatical sayings of prophets. LXX., ἄνδρες τερατοσκόποι.

For, behold.—Better, simply, *Behold.* (Comp. ὅτι of New Testament.)

I will bring.—Literally, *I* (am) *bringing*, a somewhat indefinite tense, the exact meaning of which can be decided only by the context. (Comp. Haggai ii. 6.) Thus in Isa. vii. 14 the context (verse 16) shows that what the prophet looked on as a fulfilment could not be far off; in Ezek. xxiv. 17 this tense is shown by the next verse to be the imminent future; while in Zech. xii. 2 a similar form of construction seems to refer to a distant future.

My servant. . . .—Better, *my servant Branch*, after Ezek. xxxiv. 23: "my servant David."

Branch.—Hebrew, *Tsĕmach*; occurs in Isa. iv. 2, "Branch of the Lord." (Comp. the expressions in Isa. xi. 1, liii. 2.) These passages (especially Isa. iv. 2) Jeremiah had, doubtless, in mind when he uttered the prophecies of chaps. xxiii. 5, xxxiii. 15, in which he speaks of "A righteous Branch" and a "Branch of Righteousness," as springing from the house of David, to be a Saviour to deliver Israel from the captivity. (See the whole context in both places, especially chaps. xxiii. 7, 8, xxxiii. 12—14.) From these passages Zechariah adopts "Branch" as the proper name of the Saviour. He may have expected that this promised Saviour would be found in Sheshbatstsar (*i.e.*, Zerubbabel), "the Prince of Judah" (Ezra i. 8), who should build the House (Haggai ii. 23; Zech. iv. 9). In Haggai ii. 23, Zerubbabel is expressly called "my servant;" but the expression is also a recognised title of the Messiah in the passage of Ezekiel referred to above, and in Isa. liii. 12—"a righteous one—my servant"—and elsewhere. (This last passage is, probably, the foundation of the expression in Acts iv. 27, τὸν ἅγιον παῖδά σου Ἰησοῦν.) A glimpse of Messianic times is here, indeed, revealed to the prophet, but the clearness of his view is obscured by the medium through which he views them. (See Notes on chaps. ii. 10—13, vi. 11—15.) From "Branch," LXX., ἀνατολήν, "day-spring;" Syriac, "sunrise," since *Tsemcho* in Syriac denotes "shining of the sun." (Comp. LXX. of Isa. iv. 2, ἐπιλάμψει ὁ Θεός.)

(9) **The stone.**—If this were the meaning of the original, the words "upon one stone" ought to have been *upon that stone.* But "the stone" means *the stones*, the singular noun being used as a noun of multitude, as it is in Gen. xi. 3; Exod. xxxix. 10. *The stones* are the material stones with which the House was to be built; the laying them before Joshua is used as figuring the whole command to build the House.

Upon one stone.—Better, *upon one particular stone* (for this use of the numeral "one," comp. Note on chap. xiv. 7), *i.e.*, either the foundation-stone laid in the time of Cyrus, or the stone on which the Ark had formerly stood (Jewish tradition), or the head-stone, or chief corner-stone; or, possibly, *upon each stone* (for this construction comp. Ezek. i. 6, x. 14, and my *Hebrew Student's Commentary* on Zechariah, p. 37)—viz., upon the whole scheme and process of re-building.

Seven eyes.—Ewald supposes the "seven eyes" to have been engraved on the stone, and thinks that they represent the "seven spirits" (Rev. i. 4). But it seems more probable that they represent the all-embracing, and here special, providence of God (chap. iv. 10). The expression "to put the eyes upon" is used in Jer. xxxix. 12, xl. 4, in the sense "to protect," "take care of." The completion of this material building was an important era in the train of events, which, under Divine providence, was preparing the way for the coming of the Messiah. (See a further development of the meaning of "building" in chap. vi. 12, 13.)

Engrave the graving thereof.—As the graving of the figures, &c., puts the finishing touch to precious stones (Exod. xxviii. 36), so the expression is here used to denote putting the final stroke to the work of re-building. It is impossible to take "And I will remove," &c., as the sentence engraved on the stone, as many have done; for such an inscription could not possibly commence with *vāv conversive* and the perfect. Job xix. 25, "Yet I know, my Vindicator liveth," is in no sense a parallel case (see Delitzsch *in loc.*). LXX., ἰδοὺ ἐγὼ ὀρύσσω βόθρον, "lo! I am digging a trench," misreading the word "graving."

In one day.—The day when the Temple should be

(10) In that day, saith the LORD of
hosts, shall ye call every man his neigh-
bour under the vine and under the fig
tree.

CHAPTER IV.— (1) And the angel
that talked with me came again, and
waked me, as a man that is wakened
out of his sleep, (2) and said unto me,
What seest thou? And I said, I have
looked, and behold a candlestick all *of*
gold, [1] with a bowl upon the top of it,
and his seven lamps thereon, and [2] seven
pipes to the seven lamps, which *are*
upon the top thereof: (3) and two olive
trees by it, one upon the right *side* of
the bowl, and the other upon the left
side thereof.

(4) So I answered and spake to the
angel that talked with me, saying, What
are these, my lord? (5) Then the angel
that talked with me answered and said
unto me, Knowest thou not what these
be? And I said, No, my lord. (6) Then
he answered and spake unto me, saying,
This *is* the word of the LORD unto
Zerubbabel, saying, Not by [3] might, nor
by power, but by my spirit, saith the
LORD of hosts. (7) Who *art* thou, O
great mountain? before Zerubbabel

1 Heb., *with her bowl.*

2 Or, *seven several pipes to the lamps, &c.*

3 Or, *army.*

---

completed and consecrated. The successful completion of this great work would be a sign and seal of the forgiveness of the past "iniquity of the land." "In one day" cannot refer to "the day of Golgotha" (Hengstenberg), for how could verse 10 be applied to that day? How could chaps. xii. 10, *sqq.*, and iii. 9, 10, be possibly referred to the same event? For "and I will remove," LXX., καὶ ψηλαφήσω, confounding the verb, which means "to remove," with a somewhat similar verb, meaning "to grope after."

(10) The wording of this verse is a reminiscence of 1 Kings iv. 25, Micah iv. 4, &c. It is an announcement of the approaching fulfilment of the promise of Jeremiah xxxiii. 16: "In those days shall Judah be saved, and Jerusalem shall dwell safely: and this is the name wherewith she (Jerusalem) shall be called, The Lord our righteousness." (Comp. "Jehovah, my standard," as the name of an altar, in Exod. xvii. 15.) Such prophecies were partially fulfilled in the restoration of the Jews after the captivity; but perhaps their complete fulfilment is to be expected in the future, when "all Israel shall be saved" (Rom. xi. 26).

IV.

FOURTH VISION.—THE GOLDEN CANDLESTICK.

(1) **Came again, and waked.**—Better, possibly, *again waked me,* the construction being similar to that of chap. v. 1. But it is not impossible that the angel had gone forth, as before (chap. ii. 3), to receive some fresh instruction from a higher angel, or from God, and that now he came back again. From this verse it would appear that between some of the visions the prophet fell into a state of lethargy, and that the angel roused him; or it may be that all the visions are seen in a dream, and that he only seemed in his dream to be woke up. (See Note on chap. i. 8.)

(2) This visionary candlestick differed in four points from the original of the Tabernacle and Solomon's Temple—viz., in having "a bowl," "pipes," and "olive trees" each side of it, and "two golden spouts."

With a bowl upon the top of it.—This is better than the marg., *her bowl—i.e.,* its bowl—because this was one (*a*) of the points of difference between the visionary candlestick and its original. But the "seven lamps," on the other hand, were in agreement with the original; therefore the prophet says, "and his seven," *i.e.,* its seven lamps, viz., the seven lamps proper to it. So, again, when he comes to the next point of difference, (*b*) the pipes, he does not say "*his* pipes," nor does he (verse 3) say (*c*) "*his* two olive-trees."

Seven pipes.—Better, *seven pipes apiece.* There were, then, forty-nine pipes, but as the candlestick is only visionary, we need not trouble ourselves about the difficulties of its construction. The number *seven* in the original candlestick was, perhaps, mystical, in which case the forty-nine pipes in the vision would be so too. At any rate, it would seem that a great number of pipes is mentioned to indicate the unlimited nature of the supply of oil: "My strength is sufficient for thee." The distributive use of the numerals in this passage has been much disputed, but we have, we think, satisfactorily established it in our *Hebrew Student's Commentary, in loc.* The only other admissible interpretation is that of Koehler—viz., that the number is "seven and seven," not "fourteen," because one group of seven lamps was for supplying the lamps from the reservoir, and the other group of seven to connect the seven lamps. The English version follows LXX., Syriac, and Vulg., in omitting the first word "seven." Hitzig cancels the numeral before "its lamps," and renders "and its lamps upon it were seven, and there were seven pipes to the lamps," &c. But all such emendations are arbitrary and unnecessary. Pressel thinks that "seven" is repeated on account of its importance, as corresponding to "the seven eyes of the Lord;" he renders "seven was the number of its lamps above the same—seven—and seven the number of its pipes."

(4) **These** does not refer merely to the olive-trees, though in verses 11 and 12 they are shown to be the salient point in the vision, but to everything described in verses 2 and 3.

(6) **This . . . word.**—The vision is called "the word," as being a symbolical prophecy. (Comp. chap. i. 7.) As the golden candlestick was placed in the holy place of the Tabernacle (and the Temple) "before the LORD, as an everlasting statute for their generations *on behalf* of the children of Israel" (Exod. xxvii. 21), so did the congregation on whose behalf (or as a symbol of which) was the candlestick, require a sanctuary *in which* to let their light shine before the Lord, and *from which* it might shine before men. This sanctuary Zerubbabel had founded, and his hands were to complete (verse 9); but not by any merit or strength of his own or of Israel, but simply by the Spirit of the Lord of Hosts, which would revive "the dry bones" of the house of Israel, "that they should live, and be placed in their own land" (Ezek. xxxvii. 11—14).

(7) **O great mountain?**—This is figurative of the colossal difficulties put in the way of the completion

thou shalt become a plain: and he shall
bring forth the headstone *thereof with*
shoutings, *crying*, Grace, grace unto it.
(8) Moreover the word of the LORD
came unto me, saying,
(9) The hands of Zerubbabel have laid
the foundation of this house; his hands
shall also finish it; and thou shalt know
that the LORD of hosts hath sent me
unto you. (10) For who hath despised
the day of small things? [1]for they shall
rejoice, and shall see the [2]plummet in
the hand of Zerubbabel *with* those seven;
[a]they *are* the eyes of the LORD, which
run to and fro through the whole earth.

[1] Or, *sith the seven eyes of the LORD shall rejoice.*

[2] Heb., *stone of tin.*

[a] ch. 3. 9.

[3] Heb., *by the hand.*

[4] Or, *empty out of themselves* oil into *the gold.*

[5] Heb., *the gold.*

[6] Heb., *sons of oil.*

(11) Then answered I, and said unto
him, What *are* these two olive trees
upon the right side of the candlestick
and upon the left *side* thereof? (12) And
I answered again, and said unto him,
What *be these* two olive branches which
[3]through the two golden pipes [4]empty
[5]the golden *oil* out of themselves?
(13) And he answered me and said,
Knowest thou not what these *be?* And
I said, No, my lord. (14) Then said he,
These *are* the two [6]anointed ones, that
stand by the Lord of the whole earth.

CHAPTER V.—(1) Then I turned, and

of the building of the Temple by the neighbouring powers. (Comp. Matt. xxi. 21.)

Thou shalt become a plain.—This certainly gives the true meaning of the original, which, however, is singularly graphic, and consists of but one word—literally, *to a plain: i.e.*, thou shalt become. LXX. mistake the word for an Aramaic infinitive, and render τοῦ κατορθῶσαι, "that thou shouldest bring it to a successful issue." In the preceding vision, Joshua, as the high priest—in this, Zerubbabel, as the Prince of Judah—is the representative of the nation; in verse 14 the two are referred to simultaneously.

Grace, grace unto it—*i.e.*, unto the head stone which, as being the crowning stone of the building, is used to represent the whole Temple. The words are a prayer, which takes the form of a shout of triumph (like *Hosanna!*), and mean, May God's grace or favour rest on the house for ever!

(8) **Me.**—The word of the Lord now comes directly to the prophet, as, possibly, in chap. ii. 6—13.

(9) **Thou . . . unto you.**—Such a change in number is common in Hebrew, especially when addressing a nation, which at one time is looked on as a corporate unity, at another as a collection of individuals. Or "thou" may have been addressed to Zerubbabel, and "you" to the people, when the prophet delivered his oracle to them.

(10) **For who hath . . small things?**—*i.e., Surely no one*, who intended to do great things, *ever despised the day of small things.* The interrogative sentence is practically a prohibition: "Let none despise the day of small things."

For they shall rejoice . . . whole earth.—Better, *Then these seven shall with joy behold the plummet line in the hand of Zerubbabel; the eyes of the Lord—they sweep through the whole earth—i.e.*, if ye despise not this day of small things, when ye see but the foundation of the Temple laid, the providential care of the Lord (comp. chap. iii. 9) shall rejoice to see Zerubbabel taking the last perpendicular of the completed work; but if ye doubt the possibility of this, know that God's providence extends over the whole earth, and that, therefore, He can make all things and all nations work together for the good of His chosen, Israel.

(11) **Then answered I . . .**—The prophet is not yet quite satisfied as to the meaning of the vision; he desires to know why there are two olive-trees. For as yet only Zerubbabel has been mentioned, and he could hardly be represented by *two* olive-trees.

(12) **Olive branches.**—Better, *bunches of olives.* Two important points in the vision are here incidentally introduced for the first time: viz., the bunch of fruits on each olive-tree, and the "two golden pipes," or rather, *spouts.*

Which through . . . themselves.—Better, *Which are resting in the two golden spouts, which pour out from themselves the gold*[*en oil*]. The meaning appears to be that on each side of the golden bowl at the top of the candlestick was a golden spout turned upwards, into which the two clusters of olives poured their oil spontaneously, and from which the oil flowed into the bowl, and thence through the forty-nine pipes to the seven lamps. "The gold" stands for pure bright oil. Though the word which we render "resting in" (LXX., ἐν ταῖς χερσὶ, "in the hands") might mean "through"—*i.e.*, "by means of"—the rendering of the English version is inadmissible, because the definite article (equivalent here to the relative) is prefixed to the participle, "empty," or "pour out." LXX., τῶν ἐπιχεόντων καὶ ἀπαναγόντων τας ἐπαρυστρίδας τὰς χρυσᾶς, "which pour into, and lead up into the golden funnels," taking the words "from themselves" as an active participle, and understanding "the gold" as "golden funnels," and not "golden oil," as we do.

(14) **Two anointed ones.**—Literally, as margin, *two sons of oil:* viz., Joshua, the high priest, and Zerubbabel, the Prince of Judah, "who stand by the Lord of the whole earth" as His appointed instruments, and through whom He causes His Spirit to flow to His congregation. Thus, as by the preceding vision it was signified that the *religious* head of the nation was accepted by God and purified, so in this vision the *civil* head receives the assurance of God's assistance in his work. The anointed priest and the anointed prince are mentioned together in the last verse to show that it is by their joint efforts that the prosperity of the nation is to be brought about. It shows too that "in religious development, outward or inward, the efficient cause always lies behind what is seen. God uses human instruments, and rarely, if ever, operates independently of them, but when they effect their aim, the power comes from above" (*Chambers*).

V.

SIXTH VISION.—THE FLYING SCROLL, THE WOMAN IN THE EPHAH, AND THE TWO WOMEN WITH STORKS' WINGS.

This is to be regarded as essentially one vision in three dissolving views (verses 1—4, 5—8, 9—11).

lifted up mine eyes, and looked, and be-
hold a flying roll. (2) And he said
unto me, What seest thou? And I
answered, I see a flying roll; the length
thereof *is* twenty cubits, and the breadth
thereof ten cubits. (3) Then said he
unto me, This *is* the curse that goeth
forth over the face of the whole earth:
for [1]every one that stealeth shall be cut
off *as* on this side according to it; and
every one that sweareth shall be cut off
as on that side according to it. (4) I will
bring it forth, saith the LORD of hosts,
and it shall enter into the house of the
thief, and into the house of him that
sweareth falsely by my name: and it
shall remain in the midst of his house,
and shall consume it with the timber
thereof and the stones thereof.

(5) Then the angel that talked with me
went forth, and said unto me, Lift up
now thine eyes, and see what *is* this
that goeth forth. (6) And I said, What
is it? And he said, This *is* an ephah
that goeth forth. He said moreover,
This *is* their resemblance through all
the earth. (7) And, behold, there was
lifted up a [2]talent of lead: and this *is* a
woman that sitteth in the midst of the
ephah. (8) And he said, This *is* wicked-
ness. And he cast it into the midst of
the ephah; and he cast the weight of
lead upon the mouth thereof.

(9) Then lifted I up mine eyes, and
looked, and, behold, there came out two
women, and the wind *was* in their wings;
for they had wings like the wings of a
stork: and they lifted up the ephah

[1] Or, *every one of this people that stealeth holdeth himself guiltless, as it doth.*

[2] Or, *weighty piece.*

---

(1) **Then I turned . . . eyes.**—Better, *And I again lifted up my eyes.* (Comp. chap. iv. 1.)

Flying roll.—A scroll floating in the air. The form of the vision seems to be suggested by Ezek. ii. 9, 10. LXX., omitting the final *ah* of the word for "scroll," render δρέπανον, "sickle."

(2) **He.**—The angel-interpreter. (Comp. verse 5.)

The length . . . and the breadth . . . —These were the dimensions of the holy place of the Mosaic Tabernacle, also of the porch of Solomon's Temple. If, then, we are to consider the measurement of the scroll as symbolical, we may regard it as indicating that the measure of the sanctuary is the measure of sin: that is, the sinner must not say, "I am not worse than my neighbour," but should measure his conduct by the standard: "Become ye holy, for I am holy" (Lev. xi. 44; comp. Matt. v. 48).

(3) **The whole earth.**—Better, *the whole land:* viz., of Israel.

For every one . . . on this side . . . on that side according to it—*i.e., according to the curse written on this side and on that side of the scroll.* But the Hebrew will hardly bear this interpretation. Koehler proposes to render, instead of "on this side" and "on that side," "from hence" in both cases—viz., from the land. (Comp. Exod. xi. 1). But the contrast, which is evidently implied here, precludes this interpretation. We prefer to render, *For every one that stealeth, on the one hand, shall, in accordance therewith, be certainly destroyed; and every one that sweareth* [falsely], *on the other hand, shall, in accordance therewith, be certainly destroyed.* Thieves are mentioned as a specimen of sinners against the second table of the Decalogue: viz., as false to man; and false swearers as sinners against the first table: viz., as false to God.

(4) **It.**—The curse, as borne on the scroll.

Bring forth.—As it were, from His treasure-house, where all pre-ordained events are stored up (Deut. xxxii. 34, 35).

And shall consume it.—In Herodotus (Book vi. 86) there is an interesting parallel to this verse. A Milesian had deposited with Glaucus a sum of money on trust. When the sons of the depositor came to claim it, Glaucus consulted the oracle of Delphi whether he might perjure himself and keep the money. The priestess told him that it was best for the present to do as he desired, for that death was the common lot of the honest and the dishonest. "Yet," added she, "Oath hath a son, nameless, handless, footless, but swift he pursues, until he seize and destroy the whole race and house."

(5) **Angel . . . went forth.**—The first scene of the vision disappears, and with it, apparently, the angel-interpreter, who now "went forth," *i.e.*, appeared again (see Note on chap. ii. 3); so, too, "that goeth forth" means, that emerges from the region of the invisible into that of the visible.

(6) **What is it?**—*i.e., What does it symbolise?* For, of course, he could see that it was an ephah.

This is an ephah . . . all the earth.—Better, *This, the ephah that cometh forth, this, continued he, is their resemblance throughout the whole lands: i.e.*, this is a symbol of the sinners mentioned above. (For "resemblance" the LXX., by the change of one letter, read *iniquity.*) The nature of the comparison is seen by some to be as follows. As in an ephah the separate grains are all collected together, so will the individual sinners over the whole length and breadth of the land be brought into one confused heap. (Comp. Matt. xiii. 30.) It is not mentioned till later that they are to be carried away.

(7, 8) **Talent.**—Better, *disc.* The construction of these verses is rather difficult. They should be taken as the words of the angel-interpreter, and be rendered: *And behold* (*i.e.*, and you may see) *a leaden disc being lifted up, and this* [which you now see on the removal of the disc] *is a woman sitting in the ephah; this, continued he, is wickedness.* Observe the climax: first, representatives of the two classes of sinners are spoken of; then they are heaped into an undistinguishable mass, and afterwards they are spoken of as *one* woman, who impersonates wickedness.

Cast it.—Better, *her*, the woman.

(9) **Behold . . .**—Here commences the third scene of the vision. We need not enter into the minute details of the verse, as they are, probably, introduced merely to give greater distinctness to the picture. (Comp. Note on chap. i. 8.) The wings of the woman seem, however, to be represented as filled with the

between the earth and the heaven.
(10) Then said I to the angel that talked
with me, Whither do these bear the
ephah? (11) And he said unto me, To
build it an house in the land of Shinar:
and it shall be established, and set
there upon her own base.

CHAPTER VI.—(1) And I turned,
and lifted up mine eyes, and looked,
and, behold, there came four chariots
out from between two mountains; and
the mountains *were* mountains of brass.
(2) In the first chariot *were* red horses;
and in the second chariot black horses;
(3) and in the third chariot white horses;
and in the fourth chariot grisled and
[1]bay horses. (4) Then I answered and
said unto the angel that talked with
me, What *are* these, my lord?
(5) And the angel answered and said
unto me, These *are* the four [2]spirits of
the heavens, which go forth from stand-
ing before the Lord of all the earth.
(6) The black horses which *are* therein
go forth into the north country; and
the white go forth after them; and the
grisled go forth toward the south
country. (7) And the bay went forth,
and sought to go that they might walk
to and fro through the earth: and he
said, Get you hence, walk to and fro
through the earth. So they walked to
and fro through the earth.
(8) Then cried he upon me, and spake
unto me, saying, Behold, these that go

1 Or, *strong.*

2 Or, *winds.*

---

wind to enable them to carry their burden with greater ease and velocity through the air. The prophet, perhaps, borrowed his imagery from some of the grotesque figures he had seen in Babylon.

(11) **Land of Shinar.**—Where mankind had first organised a rebellion against God (Gen. xii. 2); it was also the land of the Captivity of the Jews (Babylonia).

This vision is a circumstantial symbolisation of the promise given in chap. iii. 9: "I will remove the iniquity of the land in one day." While it is a promise of the remission of the punishment of their iniquity (for in Hebrew, "iniquity" often means *punishment*), it serves also as an exhortation to the returned exiles to leave in Babylon the iniquity which had been the cause of their being transported thither.

VI.

SEVENTH VISION.—THE FOUR CHARIOTS.

(1) **And I turned . . . eyes.**—Better, *And again I lifted up my eyes* (chaps. iv. 1, v. 1, viii. 3).

There came.—Better, *coming forth.* The prototypes of these two mountains were, no doubt, the Mount of Olives (chap. xiv. 4) and Mount Zion, between which lies the Valley of Jehoshaphat, where the *Lord judges* (such is the meaning of the name) the nations (Joel iii. 2, *sqq.*). But the mountains themselves were visionary, and are represented as of brass, to denote, according to some, the immovable firmness of the place where the Lord dwells, and where He has founded His kingdom.

(2) **Red.**—Better, *bay,* as in chap. i. 8. "Red" is applicable to cows, but "bay" to horses.

(3) For **grisled and bay,** read only the first word, *grey,* as in chap. i. 8. It is necessary (with the Syriac Version) to make this conjectural emendation, because (as the Hebrew text now stands), in this verse the "grisled and bay horses" are spoken of as identical, while in verses 6, 7 they are distinguished from one another; and, moreover, the "red horses" are not mentioned again. LXX., ποικίλοι ψαροί.

(5) **Spirits.**—Better, *winds.*

Which go forth.—Better, *going forth.* "Winds," out of which He makes His messages (Ps. civ. 4), are most appropriately used here, as symbolical of the working of God's Spirit. (Comp. Jer. xlix. 36; Dan. vii. 21; John iii. 8.) Here the words of the angel-interpreter pass imperceptibly into the prophet's own description of the scene.

From standing is correct; but LXX. have παραστῆναι, "to stand by."

(6) **The black . . . therein go.**—Better, *that in which are the black horses went;* literally, [*were*] *going.* It would seem that *two* chariots go into the "north country," because there were there *two* powers to be overcome: viz., the remnant of the old Asshur-Babylonian and the Medo-Persian.

The south country is Egypt. After the battle of Marathon (B.C. 490), Egypt revolted from Darius, but it was re-conquered by Xerxes (B.C. 485). From that time onward it was continually in a state of revolt, till finally it was subdued to the Persian power by Ochos (B.C. 340). It was afterwards wrested from the hands of Persia by Alexander (B.C. 332).

(7) **Bay.**—Better, *powerful*; but in the Hebrew the word which the English Version renders "red" must be substituted here, and rendered *bay.* Then the destinations of all the four coloured horses—*bay, black, white,* and *grey*—will be accounted for.

Get you hence.—Simply, *Go ye.*

(8) **Cried he upon me,** means *summoned me.* (Comp. "Who *calls on* Hamlet?" — Shakespeare, *Hamlet,* act v., scenes 2, 3.)

Have quieted my spirit.—"Spirit" being used, as in Judge viii. 3, in the sense of "wrath." (For the phrase "to quiet wrath," comp. Ezek. v. 12, xvi. 42, xxiv. 13. This is better than the interpretation, *Have made my spirit to rest, i.e.,* caused my spirit of judgment (Isa. iv. 4) to fall upon. (Comp. lvi. 1.) Many commentators have, without any warrant, drawn their interpretation of the colours of the horses in this vision from the Book of Revelation. According to them, "red" means war, "black" famine, "white" victory, "grisled" various chastisements. They identify the "grisled" with the "bay" of the English Version, or rather *powerful ones* (as they render the word in verses 3, 7), and say that the last mission was not received by the so-called "red horses," but by the "*powerful* ones" (English Version, "bay,") as the "grisled" are also called in verse 3, to indicate that the *manifold* judgments symbolised by the grisled horses will pass over the whole earth *in all their force.* But

toward the north country have quieted
my spirit in the north country.
(9) And the word of the LORD came unto
me, saying, (10) Take of *them of* the captivity, *even* of Heldai, of Tobijah, and of Jedaiah, which are come from Babylon, and come thou the same day, and go into the house of Josiah the son of Zephaniah;
(11) then take silver and
gold, and make crowns, and set *them*
upon the head of Joshua the son of
Josedech, the high priest; (12) and speak
unto him, saying, Thus speaketh the
LORD of hosts, saying,

Behold the man whose name *is* The [a]BRANCH; and he shall [1]grow up out of his place, and he shall build the temple of the LORD:
(13) even he shall
build the temple of the LORD; and he
shall bear the glory, and shall sit and

a ch. 3. 8.

1 Or, *branch up from under him.*

---

it is better to consider that the horses are represented as of different colours merely in order to give greater distinctness to the vision. (Comp. chaps. i. 8, v. 9.) For the commentators fail to discover any ethical or historical reason for famine and victory being especially sent to the north, or why (according to the unamended Hebrew text) the "red" (English Version), *i.e.*, "bay horses," should not have been sent out at all. According to the amended text, "the bay horses" seek, and obtain, permission to go through all the earth, signifying possibly that Israel's Protector would defend His people, not only against their ancient enemies, but also against any who should rise up against them from any quarter whatever. The difficulty with the colours of the horses is supposed by Hitzig to have arisen from the carelessness of the writer; but we agree rather with Maurer, who attributes it to a blunder of an early copyist.

THE SYMBOLICAL CROWNING OF JOSHUA.

(10) **Of them of the captivity.**—Even those who had returned from the Captivity were so called (Ezra iv. 1, vi. 19). These were probably, however, Jews who intended to remain in the land of their exile, but who were come on a visit to Jerusalem, bringing offerings of silver and gold, to show their sympathy with their brethren who were carrying on the work of the rebuilding of the Temple.

Heldai is called "Helem" in verse 14, and **Josiah** seems to be called "Hen." It is very common for a person to be called by several different names in the Bible; thus Hobab, Jethro, Reuel, &c., are some of the names of Moses' father-in-law. LXX. interpret the proper names as follows:—*Heldai* as "rulers," *Tobijah* as "their useful men," *Jedaiah* as "those who understood them."

The same day.—Literally, *on that day:* viz., on the same day on which thou takest, &c.

(11) **Then take.**—Better, *yea take:* viz., from the three mentioned above.

Crowns.—Better, a *composite crown*, since the word is construed with a *singular* verb in verse 14, and though plural in form it seems to be used of a single crown or fillet in Job xxxi. 36. Zechariah is commanded to go to the house of Josiah son of Zephaniah, who was entertaining certain Jews, who seem to have come from Babylon with gifts and offerings for the House of the Lord. From these men he was to take gold and silver, and to cause to be made thereof a composite diadem, with which he was to crown Joshua the high-priest. We cannot, of course, venture with Ewald to insert the words "and upon the head of Zerubbabel" after the words "upon the head of Joshua"; and to insert the name "Joshua" in the clause "and will be a priest upon his throne." Even if such an arbitrary alteration of the text were admissible, it would be most inappropriate. No crown was placed on Zerubbabel, for such an act would have been a seeming restoration of the kingdom, when it was not to be restored. God had foretold that none of the race of Jehoiakim should prosper, "sitting on the throne of David, and ruling any more in Judah" (Jer. xxii. 30). Moreover, the crown had been definitely taken away in the time of Zedekiah, "until he come whose right is" (Ezek. xxi. 27 [32]): viz., the "king who should reign in righteousness" (Is. xxxii. 1), "and prosper," a *Branch* of righteousness (Jer. xxiii. 5).

But there was placed **upon the head of Joshua, the high priest,** this "royal" (2 Sam. xii. 30) crown—for the high priest did not properly wear a crown, and this word is never used for "mitre"—that in his person might be symbolised the twofold office of the Messiah, who, like Melchizedek, was to be a priest and king (Ps. cx.). That the high priests during a succeeding period were practically the rulers of the nation is not sufficient to account for the terms of this prophecy, especially for the emphatic personalty of the royal priest mentioned in the next verses.

(12) **The man.**—Better, *a man*, as in Isa. xxxii. 2.

Branch.—See Note on chap. iii. 8.

Shall build.—This verb is often used in a figurative sense: *e.g.*, of a family (Gen. xvi. 2). Since Zerubbabel is not even mentioned in this passage, Zechariah's hearers could not possibly have thought that this symbolical action was merely a repetition of the promise of chap. iv. 9, but must have perceived that the building of the Temple here spoken of referred to something of a higher nature than the material building then in progress.

(13) **Even he . . . and he.**—The pronoun is most emphatic in both cases. It implies that "He" shall be the true builder, "He" the true ruler.

And he shall be a priest upon his throne.—This is the only natural translation of the words. The word "priest" cannot be here taken as "prince" (as in 2 Sam. viii. 8), for the expression "high priest" (verse 11) sufficiently limits its meaning. Nor can "throne" mean merely "seat" (as in 1 Sam. iv. 13), because the *regal* dignity of "Branch" must have been generally recognised from Jer. xxiii. 5, &c. LXX., *καὶ ἔσται ἱερεὺς ἐκ δεξιῶν αὐτοῦ, καὶ βουλὴ εἰρηνικὴ ἔσται ἀνὰ μέσον ἀμφοτέρων.* "And there shall be a priest at his right hand, and a peaceful council shall be between them twain."

Counsel of peace—*i.e.*, a counsel productive of peace. "Peace" denotes the perfection of all highest blessings, temporal and spiritual.

Shall be between them both.—The interpretations of this verse are various—we will note the chief of them. Hitzig holds that the Messiah and an ideal priest are referred to in the clause "counsel of peace shall be between them both." But we cannot

rule upon his throne; and he shall be a
priest upon his throne: and the counsel
of peace shall be between them both.
(14) And the crowns shall be to Helem,
and to Tobijah, and to Jedaiah, and to
Hen the son of Zephaniah, for a me-
morial in the temple of the LORD.
(15) And they *that are* far off shall come
and build in the temple of the LORD,
and ye shall know that the LORD of
hosts hath sent me unto you. And *this*
shall come to pass, if ye will diligently
obey the voice of the LORD your God.

B.C. 518.

1 Heb., *to intreat the face of the* LORD.

CHAPTER VII. — (1) And it came to
pass in the fourth year of king Darius,
that the word of the LORD came unto
Zechariah in the fourth *day* of the ninth
month, *even* in Chisleu; (2) when they
had sent unto the house of God Sherezer
and Regem-melech, and their men, [1]to
pray before the LORD, (3) *and* to speak
unto the priests which *were* in the house
of the LORD of hosts, and to the pro-
phets, saying, Should I weep in the fifth
month, separating myself, as I have done
these so many years?

---

see how the thought of some ideal priest and king, who would coincide in some unity of purpose, could have occurred to the minds of the prophet's hearers. There would be, moreover, no special reason for speaking of unity as existing between a king and a priest; for, as a matter of history, the priests and kings were seldom at variance, though the prophets and kings were frequently so. Rosenmuller considers that the *offices* of priest and king are alluded to. But a "counsel of peace" could not be spoken of as existing between two abstracts. Keil takes the words as referring to the two *characters* of ruler and priest combined in the person of the Messiah. But in this case the clause would be superfluous. Why should there *not* be unity between two such characters combined in one such person? Koehler thinks that the reference is to the two offices of the Messiah, and that the prophecy speaks of a plan devised by the Messiah in His double character, whereby peace and salvation should be secured to His people. But this is in accord with the modes of thought of neither Old nor New Testament. Such an idea would have been incomprehensible to the prophet's hearers; and in the New Testament any such unity of design for the salvation of mankind is spoken of as existing between the Father and the Messiah (not between two of the offices of the latter), *e.g.*, John vi. 38, x. 15—18, iii. 16, 17; Col. i. 19, 20). The expression "between them both" can only mean between two *persons*, not between the two abstract ideas of royalty and priesthood. Nor can it mean between the king and the priest, for only one person is mentioned, who is himself a priest on a royal throne. The only two persons mentioned are "Branch" (the Prince of Peace: Isa. ix. 6) and the Lord Himself. It can, then, only mean between them. We must admit that the passage would have been easier of interpretation had it run, "between him and the Lord." But when we, in the light of later revelation, consider the Divine nature of "Branch," we can understand the fitness of the expression "between them both," though to the prophet's original hearers it must have sounded enigmatical.

(14) **The crowns.**—Better, *the crown.* (See Note on verse 11.) The verb is in the singular.

For a memorial—viz., of their piety.

(15) **And they that are far off.**—Hardly the Jews of the Dispersion only, but non-Jews also. (Comp. Haggai ii. 7; Zech. ii. 11.)

And build in—*i.e.*, work at building, as in Ps. cxxviii. 1. With regard to the fulfilment, see Notes on the passages cited.

And this shall come to pass.—Better, *And it shall come to pass, if our God.* This must not be looked on as an abrupt aposiopesis, for the hearers could never have filled up the gap for themselves. Nor is the rendering of the English Version (although it has the support of Rashi and Kimchi) admissible. It only remains, therefore, to suppose that the remainder of the passage has been lost, though there is no tradition to that effect, as is the case in several instances.

VII.

THE INQUIRY CONCERNING THE CONTINUED OBSERVANCE OF THE FASTS.

(1) **Fourth year . . .** This was in B.C. 518, the second year after the commencement of the re-building of the Temple, and about two years before its completion.

(2) **When they had sent . . . before the Lord.**—Better, *Then* [the people of] *Bethel* [such as] *Sherezer and Regemmelech, and his men, sent to entreat the Lord.* "Bethel" stands for the inhabitants of Bethel, many of the former inhabitants of which had returned (Ezra ii. 28); similarly "Jerusalem" often means "the inhabitants of Jerusalem." The verb "then there sent" seems to denote an event subsequent to the revelation spoken of in verse 1. (Comp. 1 Kings xiv. 5, where the prophet Ahijah receives warning of the coming of the wife of Jeroboam. Though the literal meaning of "Bethel" is *house of God,* no instance can be adduced of the words being used to denote the Temple (as it is taken by the English Version). Some (with LXX.) translate "to Bethel;" but this rendering is unsuitable, for we have no reason to suppose that "the priests belonging to the house of the Lord" dwelt specially at Bethel. Others, again, render the words, "when Bethel sent Sherezer, and Regem-melech, and their people." *Sherezer*, or rather *Sarezer*, is mentioned as a name of one of the sons of Sennacherib, Isa. xxxvii. 38, and Nergal-Sarezer occurs Jer. xxxix. 3. The name is Assyrian, [*Nirgal*]-*sar-uśur*, "May [Nergal] protect the king" (Schrader).

(3) **In.**—Better, *belonging to.* LXX., wrongly, ἐν τῷ οἴκῳ.

In the fifth month.—On the tenth of the fifth month (*Ab*), Nebuzar-adan burnt the Temple and Jerusalem with fire (Jer. lii. 12, 13), but in 2 Kings xxv. 8—10, the *seventh* day of the fifth month is given as the date; perhaps it was in flames for three days. Now that the re-building was well in progress, they naturally desired to know whether the fast which had been kept in commemoration of the past calamity should be still held.

Separating myself—viz., from meat and drink. LXX., for "shall I weep, separating myself?" give

(4) Then came the word of the LORD
of hosts unto me, saying, (5) Speak unto
all the people of the land, and to the
priests, saying, When ye [a]fasted and
mourned in the fifth and seventh *month*,
even those seventy years, did ye at all
fast unto me, *even* to me? (6) And when
ye did eat, and when ye did drink, [1]did
not ye eat *for yourselves*, and drink *for*
yourselves? (7) [2]*Should* ye not *hear* the
words which the LORD hath cried [3]by
the former prophets, when Jerusalem
was inhabited and in prosperity, and
the cities thereof round about her,
when *men* inhabited the south and the
plain?
(8) And the word of the LORD came
unto Zechariah, saying, (9) Thus speaketh
the LORD of hosts, saying,
[4]Execute true judgment, and shew
mercy and compassions every man to
his brother: (10) and [b]oppress not the
widow, nor the fatherless, the stranger,
nor the poor; and let none of you
imagine evil against his brother in your
heart. (11) But they refused to hearken,
and [5]pulled away the shoulder, and
[6]stopped their ears, that they should
not hear. (12) Yea, they made their
hearts *as* an adamant stone, lest they
should hear the law, and the words
which the LORD of hosts hath sent in
his spirit [7]by the former prophets:
therefore came a great wrath from the
LORD of hosts. (13) Therefore it is come
to pass, *that* as he cried, and they would
not hear; so [c]they cried, and I would
not hear, saith the LORD of hosts:
(14) but I scattered them with a whirl-
wind among all the nations whom they
knew not. Thus the land was desolate
after them, that no man passed through
nor returned: for they laid the [8]pleasant
land desolate.

a Isa. 58. 5.

1 Or, be *not ye they that*, &c.

2 Or, Are *not these the words.*

3 Heb., *by the hand of*, &c.

4 Heb., *Judge judgment of truth.*

b Ex. 22. 21; Isa. 1. 23; Jer. 5. 28.

5 Heb., *they gave a backsliding shoulder.*

6 Heb., *made heavy.*

7 Heb., *by the hand of.*

c Prov. 1. 28; Isa. 1. 15; Jer. 11. 11 & 14. 12.

8 Heb., *land of desire.*

εἰσελήλυθεν ὧδε . . . τὸ ἁγίασμα, reading the same consonants, but different vowels (see my *Student's Commentary*). Consequently, instead of "as I have done," LXX. give *καθότι ἐποίησεν.*

vii. 4—viii. 23. The prophet's answer is contained in four sections (chaps. vii. 4—7, 8—14, viii. 1—17, 18—23), each of which is introduced by the words, "The word of the Lord of Hosts came," &c., as a testimony that he spake not of himself.

(4—7) The people (as in Isa. lviii. 3—8) are rebuked for the hypocritical, or merely formal, nature of their fasts. The prophet does not, even further on, give any direct answer to their inquiry. He seems to have wished to show them that fasting or not fasting was a matter of only secondary consideration. Their fasts were undertaken on account of their sufferings; their sufferings were caused by their sins. So, then, their sins were the origin of their fasts. Let them remove sin from their midst, then fasting would be unnecessary. "All stated fasts tend to degenerate into superstition, unless there is a strong counteracting agency. The original reference to God is lost in the mere outward act. . . . Selfishness is the bane of all true piety, as godliness is its essence" (Moore).

(5) **All the people.**—The question, though asked but by a few, was of interest to all the people; or the people of Bethel may have been the representatives of all the people; at all events the reply is given to the whole nation (chap. vii. 5). Though the mission came in the *ninth* month, no question was asked about the fast of the *tenth* month, but only about that of the *fifth* month. The reason of this appears to be, that the fast in *Ab* being in connection with their mourning for the destruction of the Temple, it was natural that, now the rebuilding of it had progressed so far, they should inquire whether that particular fast should be kept. The prophet, in his first reply, mentions also the fast of the 3rd of the *seventh* month (*Tishri*), which was kept in memory of the assassination of Gedaliah, which took place soon after the destruction of the Temple. The seventy years to which he refers are those between the seventh month B.C. 587 (the date of the assassination of Gedaliah) and the ninth month B.C. 518 (the date of the Bethel mission).

(7) **Should ye not hear the words which . . .**—Better, *are not these the very words which . . .* Haggai ii. 5, and Zech. viii. 17, afford exactly parallel constructions. There is no need to supply any verb, such as "should ye not hear?" "should ye not do?" or "do ye not know?" LXX., rightly, *οὐχ οὗτοι οἱ λόγοι;*

The south.—District belonging to Judah (Josh. xv. 21).

And the plain.—To the west of Judah (*Ibid.*, verse 33).

(8—14) The prophet implies that true fasting is to loose the bands of wickedness and leave off oppression. But Israel had adopted quite the opposite course, and therefore God, in accordance with Deut. iv. 27, had scattered them among the nations.

(10) **And let none of you imagine evil against his brother in your heart.**—Better, *and imagine not evil against one another in your heart.* The LXX., (*καὶ κακίαν ἕκαστος τοῦ ἀδελφοῦ αὐτοῦ μὴ μνησικακείτω*), and Auth. Version are here grammatically incorrect, the pronoun being not here (as it is in chap. viii. 17) the nominative but objective case, as is shown by the collocation.

(11) **Pulled away the shoulder.**—Better, *offered a stubborn shoulder* (Neh. ix. 29), as an ox that refuses to receive the yoke.

(12) **Adamant stone** means a very hard stone; "diamond" is the modern form of the word. "Adamant," *adhámas*, meaning in Greek *unconquerable*, was originally applied to "steel" (*Hesiod*). LXX. explain the metaphor, "made the heart disobedient."

(13) **Therefore it is come to pass.**—LXX., wrongly, *καὶ ἔσται*, the consequence of which mistake is that the following verbs are also put incorrectly in the

CHAPTER VIII.—(1) Again the word
of the LORD of hosts came *to me*, saying,
(2) Thus saith the LORD of hosts; [a] I was
jealous for Zion with great jealousy, and
I was jealous for her with great fury.
(3) Thus saith the LORD; I am re-
turned unto Zion, and will dwell in the
midst of Jerusalem: and Jerusalem
shall be called a city of truth; and the
mountain of the LORD of hosts the holy
mountain.
(4) Thus saith the LORD of hosts;
There shall yet old men and old women
dwell in the streets of Jerusalem, and
every man with his staff in his hand
[1] for very age. (5) And the streets of
the city shall be full of boys and girls
playing in the streets thereof.
(6) Thus saith the LORD of hosts; If
it be [2] marvellous in the eyes of the
remnant of this people in these days,
should it also be marvellous in mine
eyes? saith the LORD of hosts.
(7) Thus saith the LORD of hosts; Be-
hold, I will save my people from the
east country, and from [3] the west coun-
try; (8) and I will bring them, and they
shall dwell in the midst of Jerusalem:
and they shall be my people, and I will
be their God, in truth and in righteous-
ness.
(9) Thus saith the LORD of hosts; Let
your hands be strong, ye that hear in
these days these words by the mouth of
the prophets, which *were* in the day *that*
the foundation of the house of the LORD
of hosts was laid, that the temple might
be built. (10) For before these days
[4] there was no [b] hire for man, nor any
hire for beast; neither *was there any*
peace to him that went out or came in
because of the affliction: for I set all
men every one against his neighbour.
(11) But now I *will* not *be* unto the
residue of this people as in the former
days, saith the LORD of hosts. (12) For

a ch. 1. 14.

1 Heb., *for multitude of days.*

2 Or, *hard*, or, *difficult.*

3 Heb., *the country of the going down of the sun.*

4 Or, *the hire of man became nothing*, &c.

b Hag. 1. 6.

---

future. (For the phraseology comp. Micah iii. 4; Jer. xi. 11, xiv. 12.)

VIII.

The third section of the prophet's answer is divided into seven separate sayings (verses 2; 3; 4, 5; 6; 7, 8; 9—13; 14—17), and the fourth into three (verses 19, 20—22, and 23), each of which commences with "Thus saith the Lord of Hosts:" as much as to say, Do not imagine that these are merely the words of man; they are an express revelation from God.

(2) **I was.**—Better, *I am* in both cases. Here God declares His determination to give expression to His burning love for Zion.

(3) Comp. chap. ii. 10—13.

Of truth—*i.e.*, where truth and fidelity towards God have their home (comp. Isa. i. 21), "the faithful city." (For the other two titles, see Isa. ii. 2, 3; Jer. xxxi. 23.) Zion shall return to her former condition of faithfulness, and consequent favour with God. (Comp. verse 8.)

(4—5) This promise may well be regarded as having been fulfilled to the letter in the days of Simon the Maccabee (1 Macc. xiv. 4—15), when "the ancient men sat in all the streets . . . and the young men put on glorious and warlike apparel," and "every man sat under his vine and his fig-tree, and there was none to fray them."

(6) **If it be marvellous in the eyes of the remnant of this people in these days.**—Better, *though it was marvellous in the eyes of the remnant of this people in those days, was it, therefore* [or *will it, therefore, be*] *marvellous in mine eyes?* (Comp. "With men this is impossible; but with God all things are possible"—Matt. xix. 26.)

(7) **From the east . . . and from the west.**—There were Jews in exile in the west as well as in the east (Joel iii. 6); and, indeed, a very general dispersion may be almost implied from Isa. xliii. 5—6.

(8) See Notes on chap. x. 8—12.

(9) **Prophets.**—It would almost seem that there were other prophets who spoke at the time besides Haggai and Zechariah.

That the temple might be built.—These words seem to be used in reference to the resumption of the building (Haggai i. 15), when the people set themselves to work with a will, as contrasted with the first laying of the foundation in the second year of Cyrus, king of Persia, B.C. 537 (Ezra iii. 10, compared with chap. i. 1), which could hardly be said to have been done "that the temple might be built," since the work of building was then suspended for about sixteen years. There is no reason to suppose that LXX. read a different preposition before the infinitive "to be built," since the Hebrew preposition "to," or rather "with reference to," often denotes "with reference to the time when," *i.e.*, "from the time that." (Comp. chap. i. 1.)

(10) **Before . . . there was no hire for man,** or cattle, because the land was so unproductive (Haggai i. 6, 9—11, i. 16, 17); but "from the day that the foundation of the Lord's temple was laid . . . from this day will I bless *you*" (Haggai ii. 18, 19). LXX., ὁ μισθὸς . . . οὐκ ἔσται εἰς ὄνησιν, "the hire . . . would not be profitable," reading the Hebrew verb, "was not," as an Aramaic future, "will not be profitable."

The affliction.—Better, *the enemy.* Not only were they oppressed by their neighbouring adversaries, but also during the time previous to their energetic resumption of the work of re-building, there took place the expedition of Cambyses against Egypt, when the march of the Persian hosts southwards through Palestine must have caused much distress to the Jews in their narrow circumstances.

(12) **For the seed . . . prosperous.**—Comp. the Syriac, "for the seed shall be peace." Better, as in margin, *For the seed of peace*—viz., "the vine," which is so called because it can flourish only in times of peace: so that to sit under the vine and under the fig-

the seed *shall be* [1]prosperous; the vine
shall give her fruit, and the ground
shall give her increase, and the heavens
shall give their dew; and I will cause
the remnant of this people to possess all
these *things.* (13) And it shall come to
pass, *that* as ye were a curse among the
heathen, O house of Judah, and house
of Israel; so will I save you, and ye
shall be a blessing: fear not, *but* let
your hands be strong.
(14) For thus saith the LORD of hosts;
As I thought to punish you, when your
fathers provoked me to wrath, saith the
LORD of hosts, and I repented not:
(15) so again have I thought in these
days to do well unto Jerusalem
and to the house of Judah: fear ye
not.
(16) These *are* the things that ye shall
do; [a]Speak ye every man the truth to
his neighbour; [2]execute the judgment
of truth and peace in your gates: (17) and
let none of you imagine evil in your
hearts against his neighbour; and love
no false oath: for all these *are things*
that I hate, saith the LORD.

(18) And the word of the LORD of hosts
came unto me, saying,
(19) Thus saith the LORD of hosts; The
fast of the fourth *month,* and the fast of
the fifth, and the fast of the seventh,
and the fast of the tenth, shall be to the
house of Judah joy and gladness, and
cheerful [3]feasts; therefore love the truth
and peace.
(20) Thus saith the LORD of hosts; *It
shall* yet *come to pass,* that there shall
come people, and the inhabitants of
many cities: (21) and the inhabitants of
one *city* shall go to another, saying,
[b]Let us go [4][5]speedily,[6]to pray before the
LORD, and to seek the LORD of hosts: I
will go also. (22) Yea, many people and
strong nations shall come to seek the
LORD of hosts in Jerusalem, and to pray
before the LORD.
(23) Thus saith the LORD of hosts; In
those days *it shall come to pass,* that ten
men shall take hold out of all languages
of the nations, even shall take hold of
the skirt of him that is a Jew, saying,
We will go with you: for we have heard
that God *is* with you.

1 Heb., *of peace.*
a Eph. 4. 25.
2 Heb., *judge truth, and the judgment of peace.*
3 Or, *solemn,* or, *set times.*
b Isa. 2. 3; Mic. 4. 1, 2.
4 Or, *continually.*
5 Heb., *going.*
6 Heb., *to intreat the face of the* LORD.

---

tree is a common figure to denote the enjoyment of peace and prosperity. For the word "seed" applied to the vine, comp. Jer. ii. 21.

Comp. 1 Macc. xiv. 8: "Then did they till their ground in peace, and the earth gave her increase, and the trees of the field their fruit."

(13) Comp. Isa. xlvi. 9 with Jer. xxiv. 9. The contents of this verse is the converse of that of Josh. xxiii. 15.

(14—17) As the Captivity had been brought about by God's decree, so, too, the Restoration. The people, therefore, need not fear, if only they do that which is righteous in His sight.

(16) **Judgment of truth and peace**—*i.e.,* in accordance with the true facts of the case, and such judgment as would tend to peace between man and man. (Comp. chap. vii. 9; and contrast Mal. ii. 8, 9.)

(18—23) This fourth section gives at last all that the prophet deigns to answer concerning the fast of the fifth month (chap. vii. 3), and also concerning the other fasts. On the 9th or 17th of "the fourth" month (*Tammuz*) Jerusalem was taken by Nebuchadnezzar, in the eleventh year of Zedekiah (Jer. xxxix. 2, lii. 6, 7). On the tenth of "the tenth" month (*Tebeth*) siege was laid to Jerusalem by Nebuchadnezzar, in the ninth year of Zedekiah (2 Kings xxv. 1; Jer. lii. 4). As, on account of their sins, their feasts had been changed into fasts, and their days of rejoicing into mourning (Amos viii. 10), so now the prophet promises that if only they will keep the required conditions their fasts should be transformed into feasts. No express command is given with respect to the abolition of the fasts; but according to Jewish tradition (*T. B. Rosh Hashshanah,* 18 *b*), when the nation was in peace and prosperity the fasts were held in abeyance; when it was in trouble again the fasts were resumed. Since the destruction of the Temple by Titus, the Jews have kept the following fasts: the seventeenth of Tammuz, the ninth of Ab, the third of Tishri, and the tenth of Tebeth, on account of various calamities which took place on those days.

(19) **"The fast of the fourth [month]."**—LXX., after the analogy of Gen. i. 31, renders "the fourth fast," and so also with the others.

(20—23) The language of the promises contained in these verses is evidently borrowed from Micah iv. 2; Isa. ii. 2, 3. (Comp. Isa. xlv. 14—17.) According to the figurative language of the Old Testament, the nations are represented as coming up to Jerusalem with the object, doubtless, of keeping there the festivals. (Comp. chaps. ii. 10—13, xiv. 16—19.) But we must not look for a *literal* fulfilment of such prophecies. The one before us seems to be virtually fulfilled, in the fact that through Jesus Christ (who was a Jew according to the flesh) the knowledge of the true God has been spread among most nations of the world. Still, in view of Rom. xi., we are not without warrant in looking forward to a more glorious and perfect fulfilment of such prophecies as this in the unknown future.

(21) **And the inhabitants of one city shall go to another.**—LXX., καὶ συνελεύσονται κατοικοῦντες πέντε πόλεις εἰς μίαν πόλιν, "and the inhabitants of five cities shall come together to one city," borrowing the word "five" possibly from Isa. xix. 18, "In that day there shall be *five* cities . . . . *one* shall be called . . . "

(23) **Ten.**—This number is used indefinitely, to express a large number (comp. Gen. xxxi. 7); the number "seven" is used in a like sense in Isa. iv. 1.

B.C. cir. 487.

CHAPTER IX.—(1) The burden of
the word of the LORD in the land of
Hadrach, and Damascus *shall be* the rest
thereof: when the eyes of man, as of all
the tribes of Israel, *shall be* toward the
LORD. (2) And Hamath also shall border
thereby; Tyrus, and Zidon, though it
be very [a]wise. (3) And Tyrus did build
herself a strong hold, and heaped up
silver as the dust, and fine gold as the
mire of the streets. (4) Behold, the Lord
will cast her out, and he will smite her
power in the sea; and she shall be devoured with fire.
(5) Ashkelon shall see
it, and fear; Gaza also *shall see it*, and
be very sorrowful, and Ekron; for her
expectation shall be ashamed; and the
king shall perish from Gaza, and Ashkelon shall not be inhabited.
(6) And a
bastard shall dwell in Ashdod, and I will
cut off the pride of the Philistines.
(7) And I will take away his [1] blood out
of his mouth, and his abominations
from between his teeth: but he that

a Ezek. 28. 3, &c.

1 Heb., *bloods.*

IX.

On the date and genuineness of chaps. ix.—xiv., see *Introduction.* It has been urged as an argument for the earlier date of Zech. ix. 1—8, that *this oracle speaks of several cities and kingdoms as independent, which had lost their independence before the period of the return from exile. Thus Damascus lost its independence when Tiglath-pileser overthrew Syria in the beginning of the reign of Ahaz, and Hamath was subdued to the Assyrians in the time of Hezekiah.* But since the reference to Tyre and Sidon is admitted by the objectors to afford no clear indication of the early date of the prophecy, we may reply simply that Jeremiah prophesied against Damascus and Hamath even after Nebuchadnezzar had overrun their territories (Jer. xlix. 23—37), and Jeremiah (xxv. 20) and Ezekiel (xxv. 15—17) denounced judgments on the Philistines, so that it is not strange that a post-exilian prophet should speak in general terms of the disasters which would overtake these nations when the Medo-Persian empire should be overthrown by the Greeks. Moreover, in our note on verse 2, we point out that the prophecies contained in chaps. ix. and x. received an accurate fulfilment in the invasion of Palestine by Alexander the Great (B.C. 333). As early as B.C. 499, when Sardis was burnt by the Ionians, an eventual struggle between "the sons of Greece" and "the sons of Zion" must have been foreseen. But these prophecies may have been delivered, even by Zechariah himself, at a still later date than this. (See *Introduction.*)

(1) **In the land.**—Better, *on the land.*

Hadrach.—Until lately this word has been an insuperable difficulty to commentators, but now it is known, from various Assyrian inscriptions, that Hadrach (Ha-ta-ri-ka) was the name of a town or district in the neighbourhood of Damascus and Hamath. (*Records of the Past,* Vol. V.)

The rest[ing place] **thereof.**—viz., of the prophecy: *i.e.,* the judgments of God should begin at that city. LXX., *θυσία αὐτοῦ,* "his sacrifice," reading different vowels.

When the eyes . . . the Lord.—Various renderings of these words have been proposed, but the best is, *for to the Lord* [will] *the eye of man* [be directed], *and* [that of] *all the tribes of Israel: i.e.,* when God's judgments are fulfilled against these districts, the eyes of all will be turned towards Him in wonder. LXX., διότι Κύριος ἐφορᾷ ἀνθρώπους, καὶ πάσας φυλὰς τοῦ Ἰσραήλ, taking "to" as possessive, and "man" as the objective genitive, "For to the Lord is an eye on man."

Instead of **Adam,** "man," some propose to read *Aram,* "Syria," the letters *d* and *r* being easily interchanged in the *Asshurith* (square Hebrew), and many other Oriental characters.

(2) **And Hamath . . . thereby.**—Better, *And even upon Hamath,* [which] *borders on it:* viz., on Damascus.

Thus far concerning Syria; now he speaks of Phœnicia. The terms of the denunciation of Syria are so general, that if they stood alone we should be at a loss to fix the era of their fulfilment. But the case is different with Tyre (verses 2—4); for, though Tyre was besieged by Shalmanezer, and perhaps even taken by Nebuchadnezzar, it was certainly never "devoured with fire" until (B.C. 333) Alexander, "having slain all save those who fled to the temples, ordered the houses to be set on fire" (*Q. Curtius*). At the same time, though he attacked Phœnicia with the main body of his army, he sent a detachment under Parmenio to operate against Syria. To this date, then, we consider this prophecy to refer. (On the mention of these nations in particular, and the argument founded on the supposed similarity of Zech. i. 1—8, and Amos i.—ii. 6, see *Introduction,* B. 2.)

(5) **See it, and fear.**—Well might Philistia fear and tremble on hearing of the destruction of Tyre. Ashkelon and Ekron, it is true, are not mentioned in connection with this march of Alexander, but they must necessarily have been occupied by his troops. But Gaza was certainly taken, after a siege of five months; and special mention is made by Hegesias (a contemporary of Alexander) of the "king" of Gaza being brought alive to Alexander after the capture of that city.

Not be inhabited.—Or, *not remain.*

(6) **A bastard.**—*i.e.,* a mixed race. It was a special point in Alexander's policy to break up nationalities, and to fuse different peoples.

(7) **Blood . . . abominations.**—viz., their *idolatrous sacrifices.*

Jebusite.—Some take this word to mean Jerusalem (comp. Josh. xv. 8, and especially xviii. 28). Others suppose it to be a designation of the remnant of the Canaanitish tribes, who were, like the Gibeonites, retained for servile duties about the Temple. But since the "Jebusite" seems to be parallel with the word *alluph,* "governor" or "prince," rather than contrasted with it, it seems more probable that it refers to the Jebusite *people,* who "dwelt with the children of Judah in Jerusalem," as equals, and not as a conquered race (Josh. xv. 63). But for the fact that the place *Eleph* is distinctly mentioned (*ibid.*) as being in Benjamin, not Judah, one would be inclined to read the word *alluph* (which occurs in the singular in this passage only without the ו distinctly written) as *Eleph,* and to

remaineth, even he, *shall be* for our God,
and he shall be as a governor in Judah,
and Ekron as a Jebusite. (8) And I will
encamp about mine house because of
the army, because of him that passeth
by, and because of him that returneth:
and no oppressor shall pass through
them any more: for now have I seen
with mine eyes.

(9) [a]Rejoice greatly, O daughter of
Zion; shout, O daughter of Jerusalem:
behold, thy King cometh unto thee: he
is just, and [1]having salvation; lowly,
and riding upon an ass, and upon a colt
the foal of an ass. (10) And I will cut off
the chariot from Ephraim, and the horse
from Jerusalem, and the battle bow shall
be cut off: and he shall speak peace unto

a Isa. 62. 11; Matt. 21. 5; John 12. 15.

1 Or, *saving himself.*

understand *Jebusi* as meaning Jerusalem. Perhaps *Eleph* was on the borders of Benjamin and Judah, and so may have sometimes been spoken of as belonging to Judah. Nothing is known of any great conversion of Philistines to Judaism at this time; nay, indeed, in later times we still hear of them as hostile to the Jews (1 Macc. iii. 41, x. 83); but after this last reference they disappear from history as a separate nation, probably because they were no longer distinguishable from the Jews or the Greek settlers of those regions.

(8) Amid all these dangers, Israel is promised, under Divine protection, a certain immunity.

Because of the army.—This is the meaning of the word as pointed in the Hebrew text, but some, altering the vocalisation, would render it "as a garrison;" and others, as LXX., "a column."

Him that passeth . . . returneth.—Pusey refers these words directly to "Alexander, who *passed by* with his army on the way to Egypt, and *returned*, having founded Alexandria," but this appears to us to be too special an application of an expression which occurs in a general sense in chap. vii. 14; Exod. xxxii. 27; Ezek. xxxv. 7. The promise, however, was undoubtedly fulfilled when Alexander entered Jerusalem, prostrated himself before the high priest, and treated the Jews with peculiar favour.

Oppressor.—The same word that is used in chap. x. 4. (Comp. Isa. iii. 12, lx. 17.)

Have I seen.—Compare Exod. iii. 7. In the estimation of the man of little faith, God only *sees* when He actively interferes.

(9—17) The advent of the king. It has been urged as an objection against the post-exilic authorship of this passage that "Ephraim" and "Jerusalem" are mentioned, as though Israel were still separated from Judah. But, on the contrary, Ephraim and Jerusalem are here strictly parallel terms, as are also "Judah" and "Ephraim" (ver. 13), where both are represented as equally opposed to the sons of Javan. The nation was now one (Ezek. xxxvii. 22) and known by the names of "Israel" (xii. 1; Mal. i. 1, 5), "all the tribes of Israel" (ix. 1), also the "house of Judah" (x. 3, 6), "house of Joseph" and "Ephraim" (x. 6, 7). For, now that the "dead bones of the *whole house of Israel*" were revived (Ezek. xxxvii. 11), and "my servant David" was about to be "King over them" (ver. 24), the prophecy of Ezekiel (ver. 16—22) was fulfilled, and the staves (*tribes, shibhᵉte*) of Joseph and of Judah had become one in God's hand. Hence the interchangeable terms. This passage is now generally admitted to be Messianic. But the prophecy was not to be immediately fulfilled. The nation had yet severe sufferings to endure and triumphs to achieve, viz. in those struggles with the "sons of Greece" which render the Maccabean period (B.C. 167—130) one of the most noble pages in Jewish history. Those who still remained in the land of their exile are exhorted to come forth (comp. ii. 7—13), confident in the help of the Lord of Hosts, who would wield the reunited Judah and Ephraim (comp. Isa. xi. 13) as His weapons of war (comp. Jer. li. 20); He Himself will appear as their champion, with the rolling of the thunder as His war-trumpet, the forked lightning as His arrows, "the wild storm blowing from the southern desert, the resistless fury of His might." And then, when they had fought the good fight, and not before, God promises "the flock His people" the blessings of peace (ver. 16, 17).

(9) **Having salvation.**—Better, *saved.* (Comp. the whole tenor of Ps. ii. and Eph. i. 19—23; also Acts ii. 23, 24; Phil. ii. 8; Heb. v. 9.)

Lowly.—Better, *afflicted.* (Comp. Isa. liii. 4.)

Of an ass.—Literally, *of she asses.* (For this use of plural comp. Gen. xxxvii. 31; Judges xiv. 5.) Riding on an ass did not in later, as in earlier times (Judges v. 9, &c.), denote high rank, neither can it be proved that it is here intended to symbolise either peace or humility. But it does indicate an absence of pomp and worldly display. This prophecy was literally fulfilled by our Lord's entry into Jerusalem on Palm Sunday (Matt. xii. 15—20). We have no hesitation in saying that He deliberately, in view of this prophecy, performed that act, not merely in order to fulfil the prophecy, but rather as a symbolical act, by which He intended to correct the false notions concerning the mission of the Messiah entertained by His friends, as well as by His enemies. But our Lord's consciousness that He was fulfilling prophecy, or even His deliberate intention of doing so, does not detract from the value of the act as a fulfilment of the prophecy. For, though it is true that any Jew might have fulfilled that part of the prophecy which consists in riding into the city on an ass, who would have done so amid the acclamations of the multitude, and so have been acknowledged as the expected king, except One, who, by the whole of His previous life, had already won the hearts of the multitude—though that "many-headed monster thing" did change its cry on the following Friday? Any one could have ridden in on an ass, but could *any one* have founded an almost universal religion?

The wording of this verse is borrowed from Micah v. 9—13 rather than from Micah iv. 3; Isa. ii. 4, and seems to indicate that when their King should come, the nation would be enjoying a certain political independence, but that their military power would have come to an end.

(10) **Speak peace.**—Not only to His own people (Isa. lii. 7), but also to the heathen by setting up His spiritual kingdom among them. (Comp. chap. vi. 13.) With the latter part of this verse comp. Ps. lxxii. 8.

The river.—Namely, the Euphrates (Micah vii. 12; Isa. vii. 20).

the heathen: and his dominion *shall be*
[a] from sea *even* to sea, and from the
river *even* to the ends of the earth.
(11) As for thee also, [1] by the blood of
thy covenant I have sent forth thy
[b] prisoners out of the pit wherein *is* no
water. (12) Turn you to the strong hold,
ye prisoners of hope: even to day do I
declare *that* I will render double unto
thee; (13) when I have bent Judah for
me, filled the bow with Ephraim, and
raised up thy sons, O Zion, against thy
sons, O Greece, and made thee as the
sword of a mighty man. (14) And the
LORD shall be seen over them, and his
arrow shall go forth as the lightning:
and the Lord GOD shall blow the
trumpet, and shall go with whirlwinds
of the south. (15) The LORD of hosts
shall defend them; and they shall de-
vour, and [2] subdue with sling stones;
and they shall drink, *and* make a noise
as through wine; and they [3] shall be
filled like bowls, *and* as the corners of
the altar. (16) And the LORD their God
shall save them in that day as the flock
of his people: for *they shall be as* the
stones of a crown, lifted up as an ensign
upon his land. (17) For how great *is* his
goodness, and how great *is* his beauty!
corn shall make the young men [4] cheer-
ful, and new wine the maids.

CHAPTER X.—(1) Ask ye of the
LORD rain in the time of the latter rain;
so the LORD shall make [5] bright clouds,
and give them showers of rain, to every
one grass in the field. (2) For the
[c] [6] idols have spoken vanity, and the di-
viners have seen a lie, and have told

[a] Ps. 72. 8.
1 Or, *whose covenant is by blood.*
[b] Isa. 61. 1.
2 Or, *subdue the stones of the sling.*
3 Or, *shall fill both the bowls, &c.*
4 Or, *grow,* or, *speak.*
5 Or, *lightnings.*
[c] Jer. 10. 8; Hab. 2. 18.
6 Heb., *teraphims.*

---

(11) **Thee**—*i.e.,* Zion.

By the blood of thy covenant.—Comp. Exod. xxiv. 3—8.

By means *in consideration of.*

The pit.—*i.e.,* Babylon.

(12) **Strong hold.**—Better, *steepness* of their own land. Those who still remained in Babylon are exhorted to come forth. Somewhat similarly, in Zech. viii. 8 (which is on all sides admitted to be written after the return from the captivity) we read: "And I will bring them, and they shall dwell in the midst of Jerusalem; and they shall be my people, and I will be their God, in truth and in righteousness." They are "prisoners of hope," being prisoners still in Babylon, and "of hope," because, if they chose to accept them, they are the subjects of glorious hopes and promises.

Double.—Recompense for all these sufferings (Isa. lxi. 7).

(13) **When.**—Better, *for;* and read the verbs in the future, the tense used being the "prophetic perfect." These verses are prophetic of the military prowess of Israel, through the aid of the Lord God, and were signally fulfilled in the triumphs of the Maccabees over the Grecian rulers of Syria (B.C. 167—130), even though the prophet may not have had any distinct notion of such distant events.

With Ephraim.—As though with an arrow. (Ephraim, see Note on verse 10, and on xii. 1.)

(14) **Shall be seen over them.**—Perhaps better, *on their behalf shall He manifest Himself.*

Of the south.—Whence the most violent storms frequently came from over the desert. (Comp. Ps. xxi. 1.)

(15) **Subdue with sling stones.**—Better, *trample on sling stones* in their valorous onslaught on the enemy. For the figures "devour" and "drink," comp. Num. xxiii. 24; Micah v. 8; Ezek. xiv. 20, xxxix. 16, 17.

Be filled.—With the blood of their enemies, like the bowls in which the priests caught the blood of the victims, and then sprinkled it on the corners of the altar.

(16) **Flock.**—Observe here the first introduction of the word and idea of "flock," which plays such a prominent part in the next three (four?) chapters.

(17) **Goodness.**—Better, *goodliness* (Hos. x. 11).

His means Israel's. (Comp. Num. xxiv. 5.)

Make . . . cheerful.—Better, *make to grow numerously.* For the idea, comp. Ps. lxxii. 16, and see also chap. viii. 5; and for the fulfilment, the reference there to Maccabees.

X.

This chapter is immediately connected with what precedes. The people are now directed to pray for that rain which alone could produce the fertility touched on in the concluding verses of chap. ix. It is probable, since the prophet mentions only the *latter* rain, that he was prophesying between the time of the former rains (*Marcheshvan* and *Cislev*), and of the latter rains (*Nisan*).

(1) **Bright clouds.**—Better, *lightnings,* which precede the longed-for rain. (Comp. Jer. x. 13; Ps. cxxxv. 7.)

Grass. . . .—Comp. Deut. xi. 15.

(2) **Idols.**—Better, as in margin, *teraphim.* (See on Judges xvii. 5.) Against the post-exilian origin of this passage, and of xiii. 2, it has been objected that *idols and false prophets harmonise only with a time prior to the exile.* It is true that after the captivity idolatry was not the sin to which the people were especially inclined, as they were in former times. Still, even if the prophet was not speaking of sins of the past, rather than those of his own day, it must be remembered that the marriage with heathen women, which is so often spoken of after the captivity, must have been, as was the case with Solomon, a continual source of danger in that respect. Moreover, idolatry, soothsaying, &c., were actually practised up to the time of the destruction of Jerusalem by Titus. Thus we read of false prophets who opposed Nehemiah (Neh vi. 10—14), and of "sorcerers" in Mal. iii. 5, and so, too, of false prophets in Acts v. 36, 37, xiii. 6, &c., and at the destruction of Jerusalem (Josephus, *Bel. Jud.* vi. 5, §§ 2, 3). And in the wars of the Maccabees we read (2 Macc. xii. 40), "under the coats of every one that was slain they found *things consecrated to the idols of the Jannites,* which is forbidden the Jews by their law."

And have told false dreams.—Better, *and dreams tell that which is vain.* The prophet had,

false dreams; they comfort in vain: therefore they went their way as a flock, they [1]were troubled, because *there was* no shepherd.

(3) Mine anger was kindled against the shepherds, and I [2]punished the goats: for the LORD of hosts hath visited his flock the house of Judah, and hath made them as his goodly horse in the battle.
(4) Out of him came forth the corner, out of him the nail, out of him the battle bow, out of him every oppressor together.

(5) And they shall be as mighty *men*, which tread down *their enemies* in the mire of the streets in the battle: and they shall fight, because the LORD *is* with them, and [3]the riders on horses shall be confounded. (6) And I will strengthen the house of Judah, and I will save the house of Joseph, and I will bring them again to place them; for I have mercy upon them: and they shall be as though I had not cast them off: for I *am* the LORD their God, and will hear them. (7) And *they of* Ephraim shall be like a mighty *man*, and their heart shall rejoice as through wine: yea, their children shall see *it*, and be glad; their heart shall rejoice in the LORD.

(8) I will hiss for them, and gather them; for I have redeemed them: and they shall increase as they have in-

1 Or, *answered that*, &c.

2 Heb., *visited upon.*

3 Or, *they shall make the riders on horses ashamed.*

---

doubtless, in mind the words of Jer. xiv. 22: "Are there any among the vanities of the Gentiles that can cause rain? or can the heavens give showers? Art not thou He, O Lord our God? therefore, we wait upon thee; for thou hast made all these things." Zechariah refers here chiefly to those sins which had in former times caused their captivity. But such passages as Ezra. ix.; Neh. xiii. 23, vi. 10, 12, 14, show that even after the restoration the people were in danger of falling into idolatry, and of being deceived by false prophets. (Comp. also Zech. xiii. 2, and Note on Mal. iii. 5.)

Went their way.—Better, *migrated*—viz., into captivity.

Troubled.—Or, *humbled.*

No shepherd.—*i.e.*, none to guide and lead them aright. This is the interpretation which the context seems to require, and is in accordance with the use of the expression in Ezek. xxxiv. 5, 8, as it is also our Lord's application of the idea (Matt. ix. 36; Mark vi. 34); but some take "shepherd" here to mean *native king.* The paraphrase of the LXX., "because they had no healer" (meaning probably "because the True Shepherd of Israel had ceased to guide and protect them") might possibly be defended.

(3) **Was kindled.**—Better, *is kindled.* (Comp. Note on chap. viii. 2.)

Shepherds.—This term is used of native rulers and guides (Jer. ii. 8, xvii. 16, xxiii. 1—4; Ezek. xxxiv. 2, &c.), and also of foreign rulers and oppressors (Jer. vi. 3, 4, xxv. 34—38, xlix. 19).

I punished.—Better, *I will punish.*

The [he] **goats** are, probably, to be identified with "the shepherds" (as seems to be the case in Ezek. xxxiv.), and both to be referred to foreign rulers and leaders, since the latter part of the verse seems to denote that the whole people (see verses 6, 7, and comp. chap. ix. 13) is to be changed from a timid flock into a nation of warriors.

(4) **Out of him.**—Literally, *from him.* It is much disputed whether "him" means *the Lord of Hosts* or *Judah.* It appears to us best to take it as referring to "Judah"—*i.e.*, to the whole Jewish nation.

Came forth.—Better, *shall proceed.* (Comp. Jer. xxx. 19, 21.)

Corner, or *corner-stone,* denotes a chieftain, on whom the whole national fabric is put together (1 Sam. xiv. 38; Isa. xix. 13).

Nail.—Also a chieftain, as him on which everything hangs, or depends (Isa. xxii. 23); or the figure may be taken from the tent-peg which holds firm the ropes which support the tent.

Oppressor.—Either in the sense of *ruler,* as being one who keeps people to their work, or else it means *oppressor* of the heathen, and is so used in contrast with the heathen "oppressor" of chap. ix. 8.

Together, or *altogether,* is added by way of emphasis. The meaning of the passage is that when the Lord of Hosts visits His flock, He will cause to arise from them such rulers and leaders as may be necessary to enable them to successfully resist their enemies.

(5—7) The preceding idea is now further dwelt on, and Ephraim not merely implicitly, but explicitly (as in chap. ix. 13—16) included in the promise as one with Judah (Ezek. xxxvii. 16, 17, 22). For a fulfilment of the promises contained in this passage, see 1 Macc. iii. 39, iv, 7, 31, vi. 30, 35, ix. 4, 11, x. 73, 77, xv. 13, &c.

THE FURTHER REDEMPTION OF ISRAEL (verses 8—12).

(8) A yet further redemption of Israel was to take place before the consummation of these victorious promises. Some critics have considered this passage as conclusive against the assumption of a post-exilic origin of these latter chapters. But chap. viii. 8 speaks in similar terms: "And I will bring them, and they shall dwell in the midst of Jerusalem;" and yet the genuineness of that passage has never been called in question. The fact is that the restoration under Zerubbabel was most incomplete: only some 42,360 returned from exile under him. There was a further return of exiles under Ezra, in 458 B.C., some twenty years posterior to the probable date of the prophecies contained in these last chapters, and numbers, no doubt, returned at various other times.

I have redeemed.—The decree had gone forth, and had been already, in part, executed.

As they have increased.—viz., in times past (*e.g.*, Exod. i. 8). Jeremiah communicates a similar promise (chap. xxx. 19, 20).

creased. (9) And I will sow them among
the people: and they shall remember
me in far countries; and they shall live
with their children, and turn again.
(10) I will bring them again also out of
the land of Egypt, and gather them out
of Assyria; and I will bring them into
the land of Gilead and Lebanon; and
place shall not be found for them.
(11) And he shall pass through the sea
with affliction, and shall smite the waves
in the sea, and all the deeps of the river
shall dry up: and the pride of Assyria
shall be brought down, and the sceptre
of Egypt shall depart away. (12) And I
will strengthen them in the LORD; and
they shall walk up and down in his
name, saith the LORD.

CHAPTER XI.—(1) Open thy doors,
O Lebanon, that the fire may devour
thy cedars. (2) Howl, fir tree; for the
cedar is fallen; because the [1] mighty
are spoiled: howl, O ye oaks of Bashan;
for [2] the forest of the vintage is come
down. (3) *There is* a voice of the howling
of the shepherds; for their glory is
spoiled: a voice of the roaring of
young lions; for the pride of Jordan
is spoiled.
(4) Thus saith the LORD my God; Feed
the flock of the slaughter; (5) whose

1 Or, *gallants.*

2 Or, *the defenced forest.*

---

(9) **Sow** is never used in a bad sense, *i.e.*, "to scatter," but rather means to *spread* and *multiply* (Hos. ii. 25; Jer. xxxi. 27). There is, therefore, no word here of a new dispersion of the people, but rather of an increasing and in-gathering.

Shall live with.—Comp. Ezek. xxxvii. 14.—*i.e.*, survive with. They will "turn again," because they "remember" God in the land of their captivity, and feel a yearning for the place where He hath set His name again.

(10, 11) These verses are evidently worded after the analogy of Isa. xi. 11—16. Compare especially the mention of Egypt and Assyria, the reference to the dividing of the Red Sea, and the unity of Ephraim and Judah, as spoken of by Isaiah (verse 13), and by our prophet in the foregoing passage.

Egypt is, no doubt, mentioned here as the typical oppressor of Israel (Hos. viii. 13, ix. 3), as the exodus is the typical deliverance (Isa. xi. 16).

Assyria may be mentioned (and not Babylon or Persia), because it was thither that the ten tribes (Ephraim) were carried away; or "out of Egypt and Assyria" may be looked upon as a stereotyped expression for deliverance; or, again, "Assyria" may actually denote Persia, as in post-captivity times the king of Persia in Babylon is often called the king of Assyria (*e.g.*, Ezra vi. 22; 2 Kings xxiii. 29; Judith i. 7, ii. 1; Herod. i. 178—188). The second interpretation seems to us the best, in view of the figurative reference to the passage of the Red Sea in verse 11.

Gilead and Lebanon represent the old territory of the ten tribes on the other side and on this side of Jordan.

(11) **He.**—That is, God.

The sea with affliction.—Better, *the sea* [where is] *affliction*, or *straitness;* unless, with Ewald, we read "sea of affliction." On the construction in the Hebrew, see my *Student's Commentary*, pp. 95, 44.

XI.

(1—3) Here, as in chap. ix. 1—8, we have intimation of an invasion of the land of Israel from the north, only, whereas in the former case Philistia, as well as Syria and Phœnicia, was to be the sufferer, here it is "the pride of Jordan that is to be spoiled." Some have considered the first three verses of this chapter to be a distinct prophecy by themselves. To this supposition no valid objection can be made. But the terms of the prophecy are so vague that it is impossible to decide with any degree of satisfaction to what particular invasion it refers. It might be descriptive of any invasion which took place from the north, whether Assyrian, Babylonian, Greek, or Roman. Others take these verses as introductory to the prophecy that follows, and consider them to be descriptive either of a storm breaking over the country (comp. Ps. xxix. and, with some, Isa. ii. 10—22) from the north, or else of some terrible visitation which would come upon the land, similar to the invasions which had taken place in the days of old. In any case, these verses have so little necessary connection with what follows, that it will make little difference to our interpretation of the remainder of the chapter which of the above theories we adopt. (Compare for similar expressions, Isa. xxxvii. 24, xiv. 8; Jer. xxv. 34—36.)

(4—17) The great difficulty of this passage, which is metaphorical and symbolical throughout, consists in the fact that hardly any clue to the interpretation is given to us. Thus commentators are quite unable to agree as to whether the shepherds spoken of are heathen or native rulers. And on this point the whole nature of the interpretation turns. Guided by the language of verses 6 and 10, we conclude that the shepherds represent foreign oppressors. Our prophet seems to have had Ezek. xxxvii. 16—22 in his mind when he, probably in a vision, performed the symbolical acts of the two shepherds; but he had also Ezek. xxxiv. in view. In feeding the flock, he actually, though, no doubt, unconsciously, represents not only God, who Himself would feed the flock (Ezek. xxxiv. 11, 12, 15, 16), but also that ideal shepherd, "my servant David," whom He would set up as "one shepherd over them" (Ezek. xxxiv. 23, 24). At the same time, he retains his old imagery of chap. x. 3, and speaks of the foreign oppressors as shepherds. The prophet's historical starting-point seems to be the same here as in chaps. ix. and x., though his goal is more distant.

(4) **Of the slaughter**—*i.e.*, which is being slaughtered. (Comp. verse 5.)

(5) **And hold . . . not guilty.**—Comp. Jer. l. 7.

Own is a gloss of the English version.

possessors slay them, and hold them-
selves not guilty: and they that sell
them say, Blessed *be* the LORD; for I
am rich: and their own shepherds pity
them not. (6) For I will no more pity
the inhabitants of the land, saith the
LORD: but, lo, I will [1]deliver the men
every one into his neighbour's hand,
and into the hand of his king: and they
shall smite the land, and out of their
hand I will not deliver *them.*
(7) And I will feed the flock of slaughter,
[2]*even* you, O poor of the flock. And I
took unto me two staves; the one I
called Beauty, and the other I called
[3]Bands; and I fed the flock. (8) Three
shepherds also I cut off in one month;
And my soul [4]lothed them, and their
soul also abhorred me. (9) Then said I,
I will not feed you: [a]that that dieth,
let it die; and that that is to be cut off,
let it be cut off; and let the rest eat
every one the flesh [5]of another. (10) And
I took my staff, *even* Beauty, and cut it
asunder, that I might break my cove-
nant which I had made with all the
people. (11) And it was broken in that
day: and [6]so the poor of the flock that
waited upon me knew that it *was* the
word of the LORD.
(12) And I said unto them, [7]If ye think
good, give *me* my price; and if not, for-
bear. So they [b]weighed for my price
thirty *pieces* of silver. (13) And the

1 Heb., *make to be found.*
2 Or, *verily the poor.*
3 Or, *Binders.*
4 Heb., *was straitened for them.*
a Jer. 15. 2.
5 Heb., *of his fellow,* or, *neighbour.*
6 Or, *the poor of the flock, &c., certainly knew.*
7 Heb., *If it be good in your eyes.*
b Matt. 26. 15.

---

(6) **Of the land.**—Better, *of the world.*

The men.—Better, *mankind.* God would punish the nations for their cruelty to His people (comp. chap. i. 15). He would cause the world to be smitten or broken up with wars and civil tumults.

(7) **Will feed.**—Correctly, *fed.* The prophet, acting as God's representative, performs a symbolical action, figuring thereby God's treatment of His people.

Beauty.—Or, rather, *favour.*

Bands.—Or, as in margin, *binders.* The first staff denotes the return of God's favour to His people; the second (comp. Ezek. xxxvii. 16—22) the binding together of Judah and Ephraim in "brotherhood," which latter took place, for the first time since the separation, on the return from Babylon. When He took His flock into favour once more, "He made with them a covenant of peace . . . so that they should no more be a prey to the heathen." (See Ezek. xxxiv. 25—28.)

(8) The effect of the prophet's (*i.e.,* God's) feeding the flock is that He "cut off three shepherds in one month." As in Ezekiel and Daniel (Ezek. iv. 4—6; Dan. ix. 24—47, &c.), the space of time mentioned here seems to be symbolical; and taking a day for a year, one month will mean about thirty years. Some take "one month" to mean "a short time." This interpretation will also agree with our view of the case. Some, again, take each day to represent seven years—so that thirty days would be two hundred and ten years—and explain the three shepherds as the Babylonian, Medo-Persian, and Macedonian Empires, which lasted two hundred and fifteen years, from the captivity to Babylon up to the death of Alexander the Great. But no instance can be cited in which a prophetic day is equivalent to seven years. "The three shepherds" may be, then (according to the view which we have adopted with regard to the expression "one month"), the Syro-Grecian kings (B.C. 172—141)—Antiochus Epiphanes (who died miserably in Persia), Antiochus Eupator (put to death by Demetrius I.), and Demetrius I. (overthrown by Alexander Balus). As specimens of attempts to find for the passage an historical reference, taking the expression "one month" literally, the following may be cited:—Cyril considers that kings, priests, and prophets are meant; and Pusey, "priests, judges, and lawyers," who, having "delivered to the cross the Saviour, were all taken away in one month, Nisan, A.D. 33." But the rejection of the good shepherd is spoken of by the prophet as posterior to the cutting off of the shepherds. Maurer would interpret the three shepherds of Zechariah (son of Jeroboam II.), his murderer, Shallum, who reigned but a month, and of a *third unknown usurper,* whose downfall speedily took place. But Shallum was certainly murdered by Menahem (2 Kings xv. 10—14), and there is no room for a third unknown usurper. Hitzig would avoid the difficulty by rendering "I removed the three shepherds *which were* in one month" (in support of which construction he refers, and rightly, to such passages as Exod. xxxiv. 31; Isa. xxiii. 17; Ezek. xxvi. 20), and takes them to be the kings Zechariah, Shallum, and Menahem, who in about the space of one month sat upon the throne of Israel. But the difficulty is really not so obviated. Shallum reigned actually "a month of days" (2 Kings xv. 13), and the events referred to occupied much longer.

Them.—The sheep, not the shepherds. In spite of what He did for them, they abhorred Him. Though, at first sight, it would seem more natural to refer the pronoun to "the shepherds," we are precluded from so doing by the consideration that the fact that God loathed the shepherds, and they abhorred Him—shepherds whom He had cut off for the good of His flock—would be no reason for His refusing any more to feed the flock (verse 9); whereas the flock's disregard of all His loving-kindness towards them would afford good cause for His so doing.

(9) Comp. Jer. xv. 1, 2; Isa. ix. 20.

(10) The people rejected Him; therefore He broke His staff "Favour," and so annulled the covenant He had made with the nations in behalf of His people. This was fulfilled at the close of the glorious Maccabean period, when the nation became corrupted, and as a consequence was harassed by the nations on every side. This verse is the converse of Ezek. xxxiv. 25—28.

People.—Better, *nations.* (Comp. chap. xii. 6.)

(12) **My price.**—The shepherd demands a requital for his toil, as a test of the gratitude of the sheep.

And if not, forbear.—Comp. Ezek. iii. 27, &c. God does not force our will, which is free. He places life and death before us; by His grace alone we can choose Him, but we *can* refuse His grace and Himself.

Thirty pieces of silver.—The price set on a foreign slave (Exod. xxi. 32).

(13) This verse proves, if proof be needed, that the prophet, in his action, represents the Lord.

LORD said unto me, Cast it unto the
[a] potter: a goodly price that I was prised
at of them. And I took the thirty
pieces of silver, and cast them to the
potter in the house of the LORD. (14) Then
I cut asunder mine other staff, *even*
[1] Bands, that I might break the brother-
hood between Judah and Israel.
(15) And the LORD said unto me, Take
unto thee yet the instruments of a
foolish shepherd. (16) For, lo, I will
raise up a shepherd in the land, *which*
shall not visit those that be [2] cut off,
neither shall seek the young one, nor
heal that that is broken, nor [3] feed that
that standeth still: but he shall eat the
flesh of the fat, and tear their claws in
pieces. (17) [b] Woe to the idol shepherd
that leaveth the flock! the sword *shall
be* upon his arm, and upon his right
eye: his arm shall be clean dried up,
and his right eye shall be utterly dark-
ened.

a Matt. 27. 9.

1 Or, *Binders.*

2 Or, *hidden.*

3 Or, *bear.*

b Jer. 23. 1; Ezek. 34. 2; John 10. 12.

CHAPTER XII.—(1) The burden of
the word of the LORD for Israel, saith
the LORD, which stretcheth forth the
heavens, and layeth the foundation of
the earth, and formeth the spirit of man
within him.

Potter.—The price was so contemptible that it is flung to the meanest of craftsmen. It seems probable that "to the potter with it!" was a proverbial expression, used of throwing away anything that was utterly worthless. The LXX., by the change of one letter, read for "potter," the "treasury."

A goodly price . . . of them.—Better, *O, the magnificence of the price that I was apprised at of them!* That is to say, "What a price!" ironically. The prophet—in imagination, no doubt—goes into the Temple, and there before God and Israel, in the place where the covenant had been so often ratified by sacrifice, he meets "a potter" (the article is indefinite), and there flings to him the "goodly price," and so pronounces the divorce between God and the congregation of Israel. The prophet, in his symbolical act, represented God (Ezek. xxxiv. 5), but at the same time he might well (or must) have represented God's vice-gerent, "my servant David," or, in other words, the Messiah. (See Notes on chaps. iii. 8, vi. 12, 13.) Thus, though this prophecy received, no doubt, numerous fulfilments in the oft-recurring ingratitude of Israel, yet we can well, with St. Matthew, see its most remarkable and complete fulfilment in Him who was in every sense "the Good Shepherd," and in whose rejection the ingratitude of the chosen nation culminated. The citation in the New Testament is a free paraphrase of the original, made, probably, from memory, and agrees in all the main points with the original. The introduction of the word "field" (Matt. xxvii. 10) was made, probably inadvertently, by an unconscious act of a mind which wished to find an excellent parallel between the prophecy and its fulfilment; but the price, thirty pieces of silver, does not seem to have been a mere coincidence. May not the "chief priests" have viciously proposed to Judas this price of a slave (the same that Hosea paid for the adulterous woman, half in money, and half in kind, chap. ii. 1, 2)? and may not the wretched Judas have maliciously accepted this very sum from the same motives which the prophet supposes to have actuated the people to whom he prophesies? Such a fulfilment would be a fulfilment indeed; while a mere chance coincidence between the sum mentioned in one case and that mentioned in another, apart from any agreement in the latter with the spirit of the former, would, in our estimation, amount to no fulfilment at all.

(14) **That I might break the brotherhood.**—This was the result of their rejection of the Good Shepherd, and of their consequent rejection by Him. It began with the civil discords which followed the victorious days of the Maccabees, and reached its worst in the horrible scenes which took place during the siege of Jerusalem by the Romans.

(15) **Instruments of a foolish shepherd.**—It is needless to inquire in what respects, if any, these instruments differed from those of a wise shepherd. The words merely imply that the prophet, having represented the one character, should now personate the other.

Foolish is almost equivalent to "wicked" in Bible language, whether this word be used, or that of Ps. liii. 2.

(16) **The young one.**—Better, *the scattered.* The foolish shepherd we understand to mean all the misrulers of Israel from the time of the decline of the glories of the Maccabean period to the day when they themselves declared "We have no king but Cæsar." With the latter part of the verse comp. Dan. vii. 7, 19, 23, and contrast it with Ezek. xxxiv. 16.

(17) **Idol shepherd.**—Better, *useless shepherd.* Though the wicked useless shepherd is allowed for a time to ill-treat and neglect the flock, in the end the judgment of God will fall upon him. (Comp. Dan. vii. 26; and for the date of the prophecies of Daniel, see *Introduction* to that book.) Ewald has maintained that the passage chap. xiii. 7—9 is out of place where it now stands, and that it ought to be transferred to the end of this chapter. There is apparently some truth in this supposition. In particular, the expression "Awake, O sword, against my shepherd" (chap. xiii 7) seems to follow naturally after chap. xi. 17. The expression "my fellow" (chap. xiii. 7) would certainly be rather a strong one to be used of a "foolish shepherd;" but still, all shepherds of the people, whether good or bad, are looked upon as God's ministers and representatives, so that we cannot regard the use of this expression as fatal to Ewald's theory. The reader is recommended to turn to chap. xiii. 7—9 (and Notes), and to read that passage in close connection with chap. xi. 15—17, and to judge for himself.

XII.

(1—9) The opening of this chapter is similar to that of chap. ix., and marks the beginning of the second half of these latter prophecies. This prophecy, as far as verse 9, seems to recur to the same events as were foretold in chaps. ix., x.: viz., the successful contests of the Maccabean period.

(1) **Israel.**—Comp. Mal. i. 5, &c., and "all the

(2) Behold, I will make Jerusalem a
cup of [1]trembling unto all the people
round about, [2] when they shall be in the
siege both against Judah *and* against
Jerusalem.
(3) And in that day will I make Jeru-
salem a burdensome stone for all people:
all that burden themselves with it shall
be cut in pieces, though all the people
of the earth be gathered together
against it.
(4) In that day, saith the LORD, I will
smite every horse with astonishment,
and his rider with madness: and I will
open mine eyes upon the house of Judah,
and will smite every horse of the people
with blindness. (5) And the governors
of Judah shall say in their heart, [3]The
inhabitants of Jerusalem *shall be* my
strength in the LORD of hosts their
God.
(6) In that day will I make the go-
vernors of Judah like an hearth of fire
among the wood, and like a torch of fire
in a sheaf; and they shall devour all
the people round about, on the right
hand and on the left: and Jerusalem
shall be inhabited again in her own
place, *even* in Jerusalem. (7) The LORD
also shall save the tents of Judah first,
that the glory of the house of David and
the glory of the inhabitants of Jeru-
salem do not magnify *themselves* against
Judah.
(8) In that day shall the LORD defend
the inhabitants of Jerusalem; and he
that is [4][5]feeble among them at that day
shall be as David; and the house of
David *shall be* as God, as the angel of
the LORD before them. (9) And it shall
come to pass in that day, *that* I will
seek to destroy all the nations that come
against Jerusalem.
(10) And I will pour upon the house
of David, and upon the inhabitants of
Jerusalem, the spirit of grace and of

1 Or, *slumber*, or, *poison*.

2 Or, *and also against Judah shall he be which shall be in siege against Jerusalem*.

3 Or, There is *strength to me and to the inhabitants*, &c.

4 Or, *abject*.

5 Heb., *fallen*.

tribes of Israel" (Zech. ix. 1). Elsewhere, in Zech. ix.—xi. (except in chap. xi. 14), the terms used are Ephraim (chaps. ix. 10, 13, x. 7) and Joseph (chap. x. 6), as well as Judah (chaps. ix. 8, 13, x. 3, 6; comp. Ezek. xxxvii. 15—28). These and similar terms were interchangeable after the captivity, and refer, with a few exceptions, to the nation of the Jews in general. With this verse comp. Isa. xlii. 5; Amos iv. 13.

(2) The first part of this verse seems to imply that all who should attack Jerusalem would do so to their injury. The second part should perhaps be translated, *And also over Judah shall be* (the trembling, or reeling) *in the siege against Jerusalem: i.e.*, Judah should suffer as well as Jerusalem, though, as is promised before and after, they should both come out victorious. This rendering seems, on the whole, the best. The rendering of the E.V. cannot be supported; while that of the margin requires too much to be supplied. Some would refer back to the opening words of the chapter, and render: "and also concerning Judah (is this burden of the word of the Lord)." The explanation of Ewald, "And also upon Judah shall it be [incumbent to be occupied] in the siege against Jerusalem," is grammatically correct, as he shows from the expression (1 Chron. ix. 33) "upon them [it was incumbent to be occupied] in the work." And, if we could understand by it that Judah was to be co-operating *with* (not *against*) Jerusalem in the siege (see verse 5), this translation would have much to recommend it.

(3) **A burdensome stone.**—In lifting which the builders might lacerate themselves: meaning that those who should endeavour to build Jerusalem into the fabric of their own dominion should injure themselves in the attempt. But some (as Jerome) suppose the figure to be borrowed from some such athletic sport as "lifting the weight;" while others take the expression in a more general sense, as referring merely to a weight which is too heavy to be borne.

(4) **Horse**—viz., of the enemy. (Comp. Deut. xxviii. 28 with chap. xxx. 7.)

Open mine eyes.—Comp. 1 Kings viii. 29.

(5) For **shall be,** read *are.* The strength of the fortress of Jerusalem should be the saving of Judah, but that strength would depend on the protection of "the Lord of Hosts, their God."

(6) Comp. Obad., verse 18.

People.—Better, *nations.* (Comp. chap. xi. 10.)

(7) **First.**—There is another reading, supported by the LXX. and a few MSS., *as in former times.* This variant does not materially alter the sense, for in any case the deliverance of Judah is made to take precedence (in importance, if not in time) of that of Jerusalem. "Judah" seems here to denote the rest of the people, in contradistinction to the inhabitants of Jerusalem and the princes of the house of David. The Maccabees were deliverers raised up from the people—viz., Levi (see Macc. ii. 1)—not from the royal house.

(8) **In that day** an almost supernatural power will be given to Jerusalem through God's favour, so that the weakest (comp. Ps. cv. 37) inhabitant will be a hero like David (see 1 Sam. viii. 18), and the house of David will be "as God," or rather, *as supernatural beings*, even "as the angel of the Lord before them." (Comp. Exod. xxiii. 20, *et seq.;* Josh. v. 13, *et seq.*) The first part of this promise was signally fulfilled in the fact that the *aged* Mattathias was the initiator of that glorious struggle for liberty, which was afterwards carried on by his sons (the Maccabees).

(9) **Seek.**—This word is only twice used of God, here and in Exod. iv. 24, where "He sought to slay Moses": *i.e.*, He expressed His determination to do so, but for certain reasons did not carry it out. So in this case He would have utterly destroyed the nations: that is, have given the Jews *complete* victory over them, but for Israel's sin. (Comp. the case of the Canaanites, Josh. xxiii. 5, 12, 13.)

(10—14) These are verses of almost unprecedented difficulty. If the words "and they shall look on me whom they pierced" stood alone, they might possibly

supplications: and they shall [a]look upon
me whom they have pierced, and they
shall mourn for him, as one mourneth
for *his* only *son*, and shall be in bitter-
ness for him, as one that is in bitterness
for *his* firstborn.
(11) In that day shall there be a great
mourning in Jerusalem, [c]as the mourn-
ing of Hadadrimmon in the valley of
Megiddon. (12) And the land shall
mourn, [1]every family apart; the family
of the house of David apart, and their
wives apart; the family of the house of
Nathan apart, and their wives apart;
(13) the family of the house of Levi apart,
and their wives apart; the family of
Shimei apart, and their wives apart;
(14) all the families that remain, every
family apart, and their wives apart.

a John 19. 34, 37; Rev. 1. 7.
b Acts 2. 37.
c 2 Chr. 35. 24.
1 Heb., *families, families.*
2 Heb., *separation for uncleanness.*
d Ezek. 30. 13.

CHAPTER XIII.—(1) In that day
there shall be a fountain opened to the
house of David and to the inhabitants
of Jerusalem for sin and for [2]unclean-
ness.
(2) And it shall come to pass in that
day, saith the LORD of hosts, *that* I will
[d]cut off the names of the idols out of
the land, and they shall no more be
remembered: and also I will cause the
prophets and the unclean spirit to pass
out of the land. (3) And it shall come

---

be taken in a figurative sense, as denoting that they shall look to the Lord whom they had so grievously contemned (see Notes on John xix. 37). Such is the view of the passage taken by Calvin, Rosenmüller, Gesenius, &c., and apparently by the LXX.; but this figurative sense of the word cannot be supported by usage; it always means "to thrust through" (see my *Hebrew Student's Commentary on Zechariah*, pp. 111, 112). Moreover, the words which follow, "and they shall mourn for him," can only mean, according to the said interpretation, that they shall mourn over the slain Jehovah—a notion grotesque, if not blasphemous. We might, indeed, get somewhat over this difficulty by rendering the words *and they shall mourn over it*—viz., the matter; but such an explanation would be forced, and greatly destroy the effect of the following words, "as for his only son and for his firstborn." Neither can we, reading *on Him* for "on me," understand the words "and they shall look on him whom they pierced" as referring to some unknown martyr, or to the Messiah directly, since such a reference would be so abrupt as to have presented no meaning to the prophet's original hearers. We are compelled, therefore, to propound a theory, which we believe to be new, and which will obviate most of the difficulties of the passage. We consider these verses to be misplaced, and propose to place them after chap. xiii. 3, and will comment further on them there.

(11) **Hadadrimmon,** says Jerome, "is a city near Jezreel, now called Maximianopolis, in the field of Mageddon, where the good king Josiah was (mortally) wounded in battle with Pharaoh-necho." (Comp. 2 Chron. xxxv. 22—25). Assyriologists seem to be of opinion that the name should be pronounced *Hadar-Ramman.*

It has been urged as an objection to the post-exilic origin of this prophecy that the expression "*as the mourning of Hadad-rimmon in the valley of Megiddon" is a note of time, which should fix the date of this prophecy to a time shortly after the death of Josiah.* We reply that this mourning over Josiah was a typical instance, and became "an ordinance for Israel" (2 Chron. xxxv. 25), and so was naturally cited with reference to a similar occasion. Moreover, the fact that a place in the tribe of Issachar was, in the prophet's time, known by an Assyrian name seems to us a proof, in itself almost conclusive, that the date of this prophecy is post-exilian.

(12) **Nathan.**—Not the prophet, but the son of David (2 Sam. v. 14).

(13) **Shimei.**—Not the Benjamite tribe (2 Sam. xvi. 5), but of the family of Gershon, son of Levi (Num. iii. 17). Thus, of the two tribes, he mentions one leading family and one subordinate branch, and then (verse 1) embraces all together, and mentions even "their wives apart," to show how general, and yet particular, the mourning should be.

XIII.

(1—3) Some critics consider that chaps. xii., xiii. 1—6, *and* xiv. *were composed in the time of Jehoiakim* (*cir.* 600), *or that* chap. xiv. *was written a little later, when the confidence of victory expressed in the earlier chapters was considerably lessened on account of the more threatening position of political affairs.* To this we can only reply that, if so, the prophet was a false prophet, and proclaimed "Peace, peace, when there was no peace;" and we, at least, are not inclined to undertake the responsibility of making such a statement concerning the author of these chapters. We suggest that these verses should be placed between chap. xii. 9 and 10.

(1) The meaning of this verse seems to be that the people would keep the law with more heartfelt earnestness, and consequently acceptably. There seems to be a reference to Num. viii. 7, xix. 9, *et seq.*

(2) **Unclean spirit.**—This is the only passage in the Old Testament in which we find the expression "unclean spirit," which is of such frequent occurrence in the New. (See on chap. x. 2.)

(3) The reaction from superstition would be scepticism. The people would no longer believe in prophecy at all, and the very parents of a prophet would slay him as an impostor, even though not legally convicted of falsehood (Deut. xviii. 19—22).

But God would have pity of their "zeal not according to knowledge," and "pour out . . . the Spirit . . . so that they should look on Him whom they pierced," &c. The word "pierced" is the same as is better rendered in chap. xiii. 3 by "*thrust through.*" The Hebrew has "shall look upon *me*," but by the addition of the small letter, it would mean "upon *him*," which suits better the succeeding clauses, and has the support of *Aquila, Theodotion,* and *Symmachus,* and is defended by Kennicott, Ewald, Geiger, Bunsen, &c. (and is so quoted in John xix.

to pass, *that* when any shall yet pro-
phesy, then his father and his mother
that begat him shall say unto him, Thou
shalt not live; for thou speakest lies in
the name of the LORD: and his father
and his mother that begat him shall
thrust him through when he prophesieth.
(4) And it shall come to pass in that
day, *that* the prophets shall be ashamed
every one of his vision, when he hath
prophesied; neither shall they wear [1]a
rough garment[2]to deceive: (5) but he shall
say, I *am* no prophet, I *am* an husband-
man; for man taught me to keep cattle
from my youth. (6) And *one* shall say unto
him, What *are* these wounds in thine
hands? Then he shall answer, *Those* with
which I was wounded *in* the house of my
friends.
(7) Awake, O sword, against my shep-
herd, and against the man *that is* my
fellow, saith the LORD of hosts: [a] smite
the shepherd, and the sheep shall be
scattered: and I will turn mine hand
upon the little ones. (8) And it shall
come to pass, *that* in all the land, saith

1 Heb., *a garment of hair.*
2 Heb., *to lie.*
a Matt. 26. 31, Mark 14. 27.

---

87). We, accordingly, adopt this rendering. If our conjecture concerning the original position of chap. xii. 10 in the text be correct, the whole passage will run as follows (chap. x. iii. 1): "In that day shall be a fountain opened, for the house of David and for the inhabitants of Jerusalem, for [removal of] sin and of uncleanness.—(2) And it shall be in that day ('tis the utterance of Jehovah of Hosts) I will cut off the names of the idols from the land, and they shall not be remembered any more; and the [false] prophets and the unclean spirit will I cause to pass away from the land. (3) And it shall be, when a man shall prophesy, then they shall say to him, his father and his mother, they that bare him, "Thou shalt not live, because thou hast spoken lies in the name of Jehovah;" and *they shall thrust him through*, his father and his mother, they that bare him, on account of his prophesying. (Chap. xii. 10) Then will I pour out upon the house of David, and upon the inhabitants of Jerusalem, the spirit of grace and supplication, and they *shall look on him, even him whom they thrust through*, and they shall mourn over him, as the mourning for an only son, and they shall make bitter mourning over him, as one mourneth bitterly for a firstborn. In that day . . . (14) . . . and their wives apart."

When scepticism should have reached such a pitch that parents would without hesitation slay their son if he should pretend to prophetic powers, then God would smite the people with prickings of the heart, and they would look on such a case with the utmost remorse, and make great lamentation for the victim. As with chap. xi. 12 (see Notes), so this prophecy must not be regarded as being fulfilled in one single event only. But, certainly, in the case of Christ it received its most signal fulfilment. *There* was One, professing more than prophetic powers, rejected by His people, and especially by His own relatives—slain, thrust through, and then deeply lamented (Luke xxiii. 48; Acts ii. 37—41).

(4) Now he reverts to those who are *really* false prophets.

(5) **Taught . . . cattle.**—Better, *acquired*, or *bought me.* He pretends to be a purchased slave, kept hard at work, and therefore as having no time for professing inspiration. His meaning is very different from that of Amos. vii. 14.

(6) **In.**—Better, *between*—*i.e.*, on the hands and up the arms. His interrogator accuses him of having cut himself in idolatrous worship (1 Kings xviii. 28). The meaning of the latter part of the verse depends on the interpretation put on "my friends," or "my lovers." Some suppose these to be his false gods, and that he confesses with shame that he had so cut himself in idolatrous worship; but the passive verb is against this explanation. Others, better, suppose him to reply that they are the stripes he has received in loving chastisement in the house of his parents or relatives. In any case, he is anxious to disavow any pretence to prophecy.—Throughout these passages "that day" extends over a considerable period, the limits of which are hidden even from the prophet himself.

(7—9) It has been objected that "*The mention of the 'house of David'* (chaps. xii. 7, xiii. 1) *is inconsistent with the supposition of the authorship of Zechariah.*" The answer is obvious, viz., that the *house* of David had not ceased with the captivity; on the contrary, Zerubbabel was its representative on the return. There is, too (not to mention cases more generally known), a family living to this day at Aleppo, the members of which, on account of its claim to be descended from the "house of David," are, in accordance with Gen. xlix. 10, always allowed to take precedence of all others in exercising the functions of *dayyānīm*, "judges"; the famous Abarbanel also laid claim to be a descendant of David. Moreover, the thought expressed by the prophet in chap. xii. 7, that the glory of the house of David, and that of the inhabitants of Jerusalem, should not magnify itself over Judah, is one which could never have entered into the conceptions of a prophet writing before the exile.

(7) **My shepherd.**—Unless we are to consider that these verses ought to be transferred to the end of chap. xi. (see Notes there), we must take this expression as a title of honour.

Fellow.—This word, except here, occurs only in Leviticus. It means either neighbour, fellow, or, according to others, neighbourly relationship, fellowship. Perhaps the "foolish shepherd" (chap. xi. 15) could hardly be called by the Lord "the man of my fellowship." If so, this argument is conclusive for the retention of this passage in its present position. Other arguments in the same direction are that the mention of the "third part" (verse 8) is very similar to the mention of "half of the city" (chap. xiv. 2), and that the use of *hāāretz* in the sense of "the land" (verse 8) is parallel with chap. xiv. 9, rather than with chap. xi. 6; but it must not be forgotten that, as far as the word itself is concerned, it may in all these passages mean "the land," or in all "the earth." It is only possible to decide on its meaning according to one's own view of the context.

Wicked men are the Lord's sword (Ps. xvii. 13);

the LORD, two parts therein shall be cut
off *and* die; but the third shall be left
therein. (9) And I will bring the third
part through the fire, and will [a] refine
them as silver is refined, and will try
them as gold is tried: they shall call
on my name, and I will hear them: I
will say, It *is* my people: and they shall
say, The LORD *is* my God.

[a] 1 Pet. 1. 6, 7.

CHAPTER XIV.—(1) Behold, the day
of the LORD cometh, and thy spoil shall

through them was to be executed His determinate counsel (Acts ii. 23). The smiting of the shepherd was on account of the sin of the flock. The shepherd, then, must be understood to be He whom they are before represented as having insulted and rejected (chap. xi. 12). Part of this verse is quoted by our Lord (Matt. xxvi. 31).

I will turn mine hand—viz., in merciful chastisement. (Comp. Isa. i. 25.)

The little ones.—The word occurs only here in this form. It means perhaps the humble and patient, and so denotes those who are called afterwards "the third part" (verse 9).

(8) **The land.**—viz., of Israel. (Comp. chap. xiv. 9.)

(9) **The third part.**—Amidst all the calamities which should overtake the land, a remnant should be saved and purified. In the light of the Gospel we may (if we retain them in their present context) understand these words as fulfilled in those who embraced Christianity; but the prophet, from the Old Testament stand-point, speaks vaguely, and after the analogy of the past captivity (Isa. vi. 13).

XIV.

THE DAY OF THE LORD.

The eleventh book of the minor prophets is acknowledged on all sides to be the most difficult of all the prophets. Jews (Talmudists, cabbalists, and literalists) and Christians (fathers, orthodox divines, and rationalists) are all loud in their complaints with regard to the difficulties of interpreting this book. But, difficult as are all the preceding chapters, this chapter surpasses them all in obscurity. It is a chapter which seems to defy all historical explanation. We show in our Notes that the mention of "the earthquake in the days of Hezekiah, king of Judah," gives no secure trace of the date of the delivery of this prophecy; and before proceeding, we may observe that Ewald's idea, that verse 14 indicates that Judah is to take up arms against Jerusalem, is entirely erroneous. We may also dismiss as hardly worthy of notice literal interpretations of verses 4, 8, 16, &c. But even when we have dismissed these preliminary difficulties, which come upon us from without, we have done but little to clear the way for a lucid interpretation of this chapter. (1) If we suppose the writer to have prophesied *before* the captivity of Judah, we are met by the following difficulties. Other prophets, who uttered their oracles before the taking of Jerusalem by Nebuchadnezzar, always—while, with our prophet, they foretold the salvation of a part of the nation (see verse 2)—spoke clearly of a deportation of the people, and a subsequent return, but of neither of these does our prophet say anything. He says nothing of deportation, and verses 10 and 11 are the only ones that could, even by an immense stretch of imagination, be interpreted to refer to a return from captivity. Nor, again, can verses 8, 9 be fairly interpreted of the state of things at any period of Jewish history, either before the captivity or after the return. Witness the whole of the prophecy of Malachi to the contrary. (2) If we, on the other hand, suppose the prophet to be speaking of some catastrophes which were to take place *after* the return from the captivity, to what historical events could he have referred? An extract from Josephus, given in our Note on verse 2, shows that if the destruction of Jerusalem by Titus was the subject of his prophecy, he was woefully deceived in his anticipations. But we cannot, from *a priori* considerations, suppose that he did literally refer to so distant an event. For though we hold that a prophet might foretell distant events, when there were already indications on the political horizon of coming storms—so that Zechariah, in his latter days, might well have foretold the victories of the Maccabees over the Greeks—and though a prophet might, through being imbued with the traditions of his order, foretell, hundreds of years before the event, circumstances in connection with the advent of the Messiah, we cannot imagine that a prophet could, when the *Greeks* were only just becoming of importance in the East, foresee, and in any way consciously foretell, the destruction of Jerusalem by the *Romans*. Compelled, then, by the lack of any historical fulfilment, and guided by the highly figurative language of the whole chapter, we decide to interpret it entirely in a figurative and Messianic sense. The prophet, amid the corruptions of his age, perceives that it is only by passing through the furnace of affliction that his nation can become sufficiently purified to be fit recipients of the spiritual blessings which the whole prophetic school, in one stream of unbroken continuity, had foretold should be the portion of Israel in the days of the Messiah. He foresaw the glorious Messianic "day"—he rejoiced to see that day; "he saw it, and was glad." But what he sees, he sees from the Old Testament point of view. The greatest affliction that had as yet visited the nation was the destruction of Jerusalem by Nebuchadnezzar (comp. Josephus, *Bel. Jud.* x), and accordingly, after the analogy of this catastrophe, the prophet draws the picture of the troubles which should precede the advent of the Messiah. It is true that there is here no definite reference to the Messiah, the spirit in which this chapter is conceived being that of the Psalms of the Theophany (xcvi.—xcix.). God is here, as there, to appear *in person* to fight the battles of His people. But none the less, on that account, are those Psalms and this prophecy Messianic. The two ideas, viz., that of the reign of God Himself, and that of the reign of His anointed, run in parallel, and sometimes even in converging lines, but they never actually meet in the Old Testament. It remained for the Gospel revelation to show how the reign of Jehovah and that of the ideal David were to be combined in one Person. The prophet, in this chapter, by faith and inspiration, foresees, with no degree of uncertainty, that the day *will* come when Jehovah shall be One, and His name One; but the manner was not revealed until "these last days" to the Christian Church, while the complete fulfilment of this prophecy, and the full consummation of that day, will not take place until (1 Cor xv. 28) God shall be all in all, and (Rev. xi.

be divided in the midst of thee. (2) For
I will gather all nations against Jeru-
salem to battle; and the city shall be
taken, and the houses rifled, and the
women ravished; and half of the city
shall go forth into captivity, and the
residue of the people shall not be cut
off from the city. (3) Then shall the
LORD go forth, and fight against those
nations, as when he fought in the day
of battle. (4) And his feet shall stand
in that day upon the mount of Olives,
which *is* before Jerusalem on the east,
and the mount of Olives shall cleave in
the midst thereof toward the east and
toward the west, *and there shall be* a
very great valley; and half of the
mountain shall remove toward the north,
and half of it toward the south. (5) And
ye shall flee *to* the valley of [1]the moun-
tains; [2]for the valley of the mountains
shall reach unto Azal: yea, ye shall
flee, like as ye fled from before the
[a]earthquake in the days of Uzziah king
of Judah: and the LORD my God shall
come, *and* all the saints with thee.
(6) And it shall come to pass in that
day, *that* the light shall not be [3]clear,

[1] Or, *my mountains.*

B.C. cir. 787.

[2] Or, *when he shall touch the valley of the mountains to the place he separated.*

[a] Amos 1. 1.

[3] Heb., *precious.*

15) the kingdoms of this world shall have become the kingdom of the Lord and of His Christ.

(1) **The day of the Lord cometh.**—Better, *A day cometh for the Lord*—viz., on which He will signally manifest His glory. (Comp. Ps. ii. 12, &c.) The second half of the verse gives with, as it were, one stroke of the pen the most vivid description of the first feature of this "day," viz., judgment upon Jerusalem.

(2) This verse is but a further description of the event depicted in the second half of the preceding verse.

And the residue of the people shall not be cut off from the city.—This was the case (with regard to Judah) in the Chaldæan conquest (2 Kings xxv. 22). Whether or no this can be interpreted of the taking of Jerusalem by Titus, we leave our readers to decide, after placing before them the following words of Josephus (*Bel. Jud.* vi. 9, § 2):—"And now, since his soldiers were already quite tired of killing men, yet there appeared to be a vast multitude still remaining alive, Cæsar gave orders that they should kill none but those that were in arms and opposed them, but should take the rest alive. But, together with those whom they had orders to slay, they slew the aged and the infirm; but for those that were in their flourishing age, and who might be useful to them, they drove them together into the Temple, and shut them up within the walls of the court of the women, over which Cæsar set one of his freedmen, as also Fronto, one of his friends, which last was to determine every one's fate according to his merits. So this Fronto slew all those that had been seditious and robbers, who were impeached one by another; but of the young men he chose out the tallest and most beautiful, and reserved them for the triumph; *and as for the rest of the multitude that were above seventeen years old, he put them in bonds, and sent them to the Egyptian mines.* Titus also sent a great number into the provinces, as a present to them, that they might be destroyed upon their theatres by the sword and by wild beasts; *but those that were under seventeen years of age were sold for slaves.*" We simply ask, what room is there for a remnant?

(3) **Then shall the Lord go forth.**—In the hour of Israel's direst need the Lord will appear as their champion, as of old. (Comp. Josh. x. 14—42, xxiii. 3; Judg. iv. 15; 1 Sam. vii. 10; and especially 2 Chron. xx. 15.)

(4) **And his feet . . .**—The language is, of course, figurative.

Shall cleave.—Earthquake is commonly represented as an accompaniment of the Lord's appearing (Exod. xix. 18; Isa. xxix. 6; Ezek. xxxviii. 19, 20). The Mount of Olives shall be cleft eastward to westward, and its two halves will be removed northward and southward respectively, so that a valley will be formed between them.

(5) **And ye shall flee to.**—The Hebrew will not bear the rendering of Luther, "and ye shall flee *before.*" The Oriental Jews, Targ., LXX., &c., by a different vocalisation, read, "And the valley of my mountains shall be stopped;" but this reading is inappropriate. "My mountains," the Mount of Olives, which is divided in twain by the advent of the Lord, he calls "my mountains" (Marg.). It seems that they would flee thither for fear of being overwhelmed in the destruction of Jerusalem, "for the valley of the mountains" will afford a ready place of refuge, for it "shall reach unto Azal." Some suppose Azal to be a place near Jerusalem (some placing it to the west of the Temple-Mount, others to the east of the Mount of Olives), but others take the word as a preposition, and render it "very nigh." In any case, they flee to the valley because of its convenient proximity.

The earthquake in the days of Uzziah is not mentioned in the sacred history, but it was an event that left such an impression on the popular mind that it became an era from which to date (Amos i. 1). "Similarly in Crete recent events are dated by such eras as in the year before the great earthquake." (Blakesley's *Herodotus* i. 263.) Thus the mention of this earthquake does not "*fix the date of the prophecy to the days of Uzziah,*" as some commentators have affirmed. The second person, "ye fled," need not be taken as referring directly to the persons addressed; but, considering the fact of the continuity of the national existence, may be understood as denoting the same nation at an earlier period, as in Josh. xxiv. 5. Moreover, if we cared to dwell on the fact of the addition of the words "king of Judah" to the name of Uzziah, it might be taken to imply that the prophecy was delivered so long after the time of Uzziah that it was necessary for the prophet to remind his hearers who this Uzziah was.

Saints.—Better, *angels.* (Comp. Deut. xxxiii. 2; Ps. lxxxix. 5 [6].)

With thee.—The change into the second person denotes the prophet's own joyful waiting for his God's advent. Some versions and MSS. read "with him."

(6) **That the light shall not be clear, nor**

nor [1]dark: (7) but [2]it shall be [a]one day
which shall be known to the LORD, not
day, nor night: but it shall come to pass,
that at [b]evening time it shall be light.
(8) And it shall be in that day, *that* living
waters shall go out from Jerusalem;
half of them toward the [3]former sea,
and half of them toward the hinder sea:
in summer and in winter shall it be.
(9) And the LORD shall be king over all
the earth: in that day shall there be
one LORD, and his name one. (10) All
the land shall be [4]turned as a plain from
Geba to Rimmon south of Jerusalem:
and it shall be lifted up, and [5]inhabited
in her place, from Benjamin's gate unto
the place of the first gate, unto the
corner gate, and *from* the tower of
Hananeel unto the king's winepresses.
(11) And *men* shall dwell in it, and there
shall be no more utter destruction;
but Jerusalem [6]shall be safely in-
habited.
(12) And this shall be the plague where-
with the LORD will smite all the people
that have fought against Jerusalem;
Their flesh shall consume away while
they stand upon their feet, and their
eyes shall consume away in their holes,
and their tongue shall consume away in
their mouth. (13) And it shall come to
pass in that day, *that* a great tumult
from the LORD shall be among them;
and they shall lay hold every one on the
hand of his neighbour, and his hand
shall rise up against the hand of his
neighbour. (14) And [7]Judah also shall
fight [8]at Jerusalem; and the wealth of

1 Heb., *thickness.*
2 Or, *the day shall be one.*
a Rev. 22. 5.
b Isa. 60. 19; Rev. 21. 23.
c Ezek. 47. 1; Joel 3. 18; Rev. 22. 1.
3 Or, *eastern.*
4 Or, *compassed.*
5 Or, *shall abide.*
6 Or, *shall abide.*
7 Or, *thou also,* O *Judah, shalt.*
8 Or, *against.*

Dark.—Better, *there shall not be light; the glorious ones* (*i.e.*, the heavenly bodies) *shall fail* (literally, *become coagulated*).

(7) **One day.**—*i.e.*, an extraordinary, unique day. (Comp. Ezek. vii. 5.) "An evil, an only (literally, *one*) evil, behold, is come." (Also Jer. xxx. 7.)

Not day, nor night.—But a kind of murky gloom, such as accompanies a sand-storm in the deserts of the East.

It shall be.—Better, *there shall be.* As the darkest hour precedes the dawn, so the climax of man's direst need is the precursor of the day-spring of God's saving power. And so now, when "at evening time" they shall be expecting the gross darkness of night to set in, suddenly they shall be flooded with the light of God's salvation. This second half of verse 7 is to verses 6 and 7A what verse 3 is to verses 1 and 2. In each case the brightness of the Theophany dispels the darkness of despair.

(8) **Living waters.** — The symbol of Divine knowledge and spiritual vitality (Joel iii. 18; Ezek. xlvii.).

Former.—Or *front, i.e.,* eastern (marg.)—meaning the Dead Sea.

Hinder.—*i.e.,* western, meaning the Mediterranean. These boundaries denote the whole of the Holy Land.

In summer and in winter.—The stream shall be perennial, not drying up in summer, as the Eastern wadis do.

(9) **All the earth.**—In accordance with the context, we can only understand this in the sense of "all the land" (chap. xiii. 8). But though this is undoubtedly the meaning of the prophet, there is no reason why his words may not have a wider application than he himself ever contemplated.

Shall there be one Lord.—Better, *Jehovah shall be One: i.e.,* "God shall be all in all."

And his name one.—*i.e.,* and He alone shall be worshipped as God.

(10) **The land . . . from Geba to Rimmon south of Jerusalem.**—*i.e.,* Judah, from north to south, as in 2 Kings xxiii. 8 it is said, "from Geba to Beersheba." Geba, modern "Jeba," is about three hours north of Jerusalem. Rimmon, south of Jerusalem, not Rimmon in Galilee, which was north of Nazareth (Josh. xix. 13), nor the rock of Rimmon, *north* of Jerusalem (Judges xx. 45), but Rimmon, modern *Umm er Rummanin,* four hours to north of Beersheba.

Shall be turned as a plain.—Better, *as the plain,* called in Hebrew the *Hā Arābāh,* and now in Arabic *Al Ghor.* It extends with some interruptions from the slopes of Hermon to the Elamitic gulf of the Red Sea.

And it.—viz., Jerusalem. The idea of the lifting up of Jerusalem is suggested by its geographical position, situated, as it is, in a nest of mountains (Ps. cxxv. 2). The language is, of course, figurative, and denotes the religious prominence of Jerusalem. The very name of Jerusalem at the present time, *Al Kuds,* "the holy place," is so far a testimony to the truth of the prophecy, in that the nations, by adopting this appellation (Jerusalem *ha Kedoshah*) from the Jews, acknowledge the holy city to have been the fountain-head of religious knowledge.

In her place.—Comp. chap. xii. 6.

Benjamin's gate was doubtless in the northern wall.

The place of the first gate was, perhaps, at the north-eastern corner, and "the corner gate" at the north-western corner (2 Kings xiv. 13; Jer. xxxi. 38). Thus this description denotes the whole breadth of the city, from east to west.

The tower of Hananeel (Jer. xxxi. 38; Neh. iii. 1, xii. 39) was at the north corner of the city; and "the king's wine-presses," no doubt, in the king's gardens, at the south end of the city (Neh. iii. 15); thus these latter are the northern and southern boundaries.

(11) **Utter destruction.**—Better, *ban.* (Comp. Mal. iv. 6; Rev. xxii. 3.)

(12, 13) In the description of the plague, and confusion, and rout with which the hostile nations are to be smitten, the prophet had in mind several historical events: *e.g.,* Exod. ix. 14; Ps. xxxvii. 36; 1 Sam. v. 9, xiv. 20; Isa. xxii. 5.

(14) **Judah.**—Then, taking courage from the panic which had struck their adversaries, the whole people of Judah—not merely those who had escaped out of the city, but also those outside the walls—fight once more

all the heathen round about shall be
gathered together, gold, and silver, and
apparel, in great abundance. (15) And
so shall be the plague of the horse, of
the mule, of the camel, and of the ass,
and of all the beasts that shall be in
these tents, as this plague.
(16) And it shall come to pass, *that*
every one that is left of all the nations
which came against Jerusalem shall
even go up from year to year to wor-
ship the King, the LORD of hosts, and
to keep the feast of tabernacles. (17) And
it shall be, *that* whoso will not come up
of *all* the families of the earth unto
Jerusalem to worship the King, the
LORD of hosts, even upon them shall be
no rain. (18) And if the family of Egypt
go not up, and come not, [1]that *have* no
rain; there shall be the plague, where-
with the LORD will smite the heathen
that come not up to keep the feast of
tabernacles. (19) This shall be the
[2]punishment of Egypt, and the punish-
ment of all nations that come not up to
keep the feast of tabernacles.
(20) In that day shall there be upon
the [3]bells of the horses, HOLINESS
UNTO THE LORD; and the pots in
the LORD's house shall be like the bowls
before the altar. (21) Yea, every pot in
Jerusalem and in Judah shall be holi-
ness unto the LORD of hosts: and all
they that sacrifice shall come and take
of them, and seethe therein: and in
that day there shall be no more the
[a]Canaanite in the house of the LORD of
hosts.

1 Heb., *upon whom there is not.*

2 Or, *sin.*

3 Or, *bridles.*

a Isa. 35. 8; Joel 3. 17; Rev. 21. 27 & 22. 15.

"at Jerusalem," or in its very streets, "against the terror-driven, plague-stricken, God-confounded foe" (*Wright*).

And the wealth. . . .—Oriental armies always march with quantities of gold, silver, and other valuables. (Comp. 2 Chron. xx. 25; and for an instance in India, year of the Hejra 964, see Al Badaoni's *Reign of Akbar*, Transl. pp. 9, 10.)

(15) The war-horse (see Note on chap. ix. 9) and beasts of burden (see Note on chap. ix. 9) are to be included in the destruction, even as were the cattle of Achan (Josh. vii. 24).

(16) **Go up . . . to worship.**—The judgment on the nation is to be remedial. The result of it is to be that they will earnestly embrace the worship of the one only true God. "The Feast of Tabernacles" (lasting from the 15th to the 22nd of Tishri) is called *par excellence* "*The* Feast." The chief object in its observance is, from a material point of view, the thanksgiving for the ingathering of the harvest and vintage. On the 21st (called *Hosha'na Rabba*) the Jews always pray that the coming year may not be one of drought. It is most appropriate, then, that the prophet should represent the nations of the earth as joining the Jews in keeping their festival, which is that on which the Lord is especially praised as the beneficent God of nature. This prophecy is, of course, not to be taken literally. The prophet is merely foretelling in Old Testament language the future ingathering of the nations. Our Lord refers to the gathering of people into the kingdom of heaven as a harvesting (John iv. 35).

(17) **No rain.**—Though the worship of the Lord is to become universal, apostacy is not regarded as impossible. The punishment for such deflexion is spoken of in such figurative language as suits the symbolic description of the nations' conversion.

(18) **That have no rain.**—This is an impossible rendering of the original. We must read these words in connection with those which follow, and either take the clause as interrogative, and render, *then will not* (*nonne?*) *the plague fall upon them wherewith, &c.*," or we must, with LXX. and six Hebrew MSS., omit the negative, and render, *then shall fall on them the plague wherewith, &c.* Lange (quoted by Wright) has observed rightly that if the family of Egypt were to be punished by the deficiency of water, the Abyssinians, even though they attended the feast at Jerusalem, would have to suffer at the same time, as Egypt can only suffer from scarcity of water in connection with all the lands in the south of that country. The fact, then, that the withholding of rain is described as the particular punishment of the nations that will not go up to the feast is sufficient proof that the prophecy is not to be taken in its literal sense.

(19–21) We cannot see, as many commentators affirm, that these concluding verses clearly indicate a passing away of everything that is distinctly Levitical. They only state that in that day there will be a general elevation of everything in sanctity. Even "the bells upon the horses" will, like the plate of gold on the mitre of the high priest, have inscribed on them "HOLINESS TO THE LORD" (Exod. xxviii. 36, &c.). The pots of the sanctuary in which the "peace offerings" were cooked will be raised to the grade of sanctity of the bowls in which the blood was caught; and ordinary pots will be raised to the grade of sanctuary pots. Neither can we see in this passage a promise of the restoration of the Mosaic ritual, for the whole chapter is composed in most unmistakably figurative language.

(20) **Canaanite,** in reference to the early days of Israel's existence, denotes *alien, unbeliever.* The word implies just what "Jew," would in the present day to an illiberal German or Russian, or *Cáfir,* or *Frangi* (Frank) to an orthodox Moslem.

INTRODUCTION

TO

MALACHI

I. The Prophet and his Name.—Absolutely nothing is known historically of the life of the prophet Malachi. Josephus, though he speaks of Haggai and Zechariah, does not mention Malachi. By some the word *Malachi*, which might be taken to mean "my messenger," has been regarded as the prophet's official title, not as his personal name. Thus, the Chaldee paraphrase* (the *Targum*) takes the word as a mere appellative, and identifies the prophet with *Ezra the Scribe;* but, as Kimchi well remarks, Ezra is nowhere called a "prophet," but "the scribe." Again, Talmudic testimony is uncertain on the question. Thus, in Talmud Babli, *Megillah*, 15a: after other suggestions an old tradition is adduced to the effect that "Rabbi Yehoshua ben Korcha (first and second century after Christ) says, Malachi is the same as Ezra; but the (other) sages say, Malachi was his name." Haggai, Zechariah, and Malachi are also mentioned in the Talmud together (without any doubt being expressed as to Malachi being a personal name) as the last of the prophets (*e.g.*, Talmud Babli, *Synhedrin*, 11*a*), and as members of the Great Synagogue—*i.e.*, the School of Sages, which existed from the time of Ezra to that of Simon the Just. The testimony of the LXX. is equally uncertain, for while in Mal. i. 1 the word is translated "his angel" (either by way of paraphrase or reading *Malacho*, not *Malachi*), we find, on the other hand, the prophet in the title of the book called Μαλαχίας, just as Zachary (Zechariah) is called Ζαχαρίας. The passage in the Apocrypha (2 Esdr. i. 39, 40), "Unto whom I will give for leaders Abraham, Isaac, Jacob, Oscas, Amos, and Micheas, Joel, Abdias, and Jonas, Nahum and Abacoe, Soponias, Aggeus, Zachary, and Malachy, which is called also an angel of the Lord," is also equivocal. Several of the fathers speak of his name as merely official, an opinion upheld by Vitringa and many modern critics, while Pseudo- Dorotheus, Epiphanius, and others (Köhler *Mal.* pp. 10, 11), state that he was a Levite of Zebulun, and born at *Sophá*, or *Sofirá*. Thus tradition helps us but little, and we are, accordingly, reduced to *a priori* arguments to decide whether *Malachi* was a personal name or no.

(1) Jerome's argument is worthy of notice: he says most reasonably that "if names are to be interpreted, and history framed from them . . . . then Hosea, who is called Saviour, and Joel, whose name means 'Lord God,' and other prophets, will not be men, but rather angels, or the Lord and Saviour, according to the meaning of their name." (2) While it is true that *Malachi* might be a mere official title, meaning *angelic*, or *my messenger*, it is equally true that personal names in *î* (for *iyyah, yahu, yah*, or *î'êl*, meaning "of Yah" and "of God") are of by no means unfrequent occurrence in the Bible. Thus in 2 Kings xviii. 2 we find *Abi* for *Abiyyah* (2 Chron. xxix. 1), *Palti* (1 Sam. xxv. 44) for *Paltiel* (2 Sam. iii. 15), *Zabdi* (Josh. vii. 1) compared with *Zebadyah* (Ezr. viii. 8), *Zabadyahu* (1 Chron. xxvi. 2), and *Zabdiel* (Neh. xi. 14), besides *Gamri, Zichri*, and many other. (3) The use of the word *Malachi* in the sense of "my messenger" (Mal. iii. 1) is no argument against Malachi being the prophet's personal name; on the contrary, his application there of the word *Malach* ("angel") to the Messiah's forerunner, and in chap. ii. 8 to the priesthood—a word which elsewhere, except in Hag. i. 13, Is. xlii. 19, is never used of any but a supernatural being—may be taken as showing that the prophet was fond of making use of a word which carried with it a covert reference to his own name. (4) That no one else in the Old Testament is called Malachi is no valid objection, for neither is there more than one person called Amos (Amos in Isa. i. 1 is quite a different name), Jonah, Habakkuk, &c. (5) Nor is there any force in the argument that the name stands alone in verse 1 without any further personal definition, for that is also the case with Obadiah. (6) If Malachi be a mere official title, the case is an unique one, for in every other instance the prophets have given their real names (if any) in the heading of their books. (7) The case of the names Agar (Prov. xxx. 1) and Lemuel (Prov. xxxi. 1) is not parallel, for even if it were proved that these latter are not historical names, no conclusion bearing upon a prophetic writing could be drawn from a collection of *proverbs*. "A collection of proverbs is a poetical work, whose ethical or religious truth is not dependent upon the person of the poet. The prophet, on the contrary, has to guarantee (to his contemporaries) the divinity of his mission, and the truth of his prophecy by his own name or his own personality."—(*Keil.*) We conclude, therefore, in default of any positive evidence to the contrary, that it is only reasonable to suppose that *Malachi* is the personal name of the prophet, and that it is an apocopated form of Malachiyyah, Malachyahu, Malachyah, or of Malachi'el, meaning "Messenger of Yah," or "of God."

II. Date of the Prophecy.—All are agreed that Malachi prophesied after the captivity, and there is not much difficulty in determining from internal evidence the probable period of his labours. We find that he makes no reference to the re-building of the Temple or of Jerusalem. The Temple seems to have been for

* I have shown (*Fragment of Psachim*, p. 66, Note Hh. 1) that the Targumin of the prophets were in existence in substantially the same form in which we now have them in the time of Rab-Yoseph (270—333 A.D.).

some time completed, and its services so long restored, that the zeal of both priests and people had cooled down, and given place to the most profane slovenliness in the Temple service, and a mere formal observance (chap. iii. 14), or rather a deceitful evasion of the Law (chap. i. 14). The priests admitted to the Temple sacrifices what they should have rejected (chap. i. 7—12), and demonstrated by their whole conduct that they looked on their duties as a wearisome burden (chap. i. 13). They had ceased to give the people true instruction in the Law (chap. ii. 8), and showed partiality in their administration of justice (chap. ii. 9). The people had intermarried freely with the heathen, and heartlessly divorced their Israelitish wives, so that the altar of the Lord was covered with tears and weeping and crying out (chap. ii. 11—16). They neglected to pay the tithes and other dues, and as a punishment were visited with dearth and famine (chap. iii. 8—12). They had begun to cherish the most sceptical views, and openly to scoff at the notion of God's exercising a beneficent providence over them (chaps. ii. 17, iii. 15), though there was still a remnant among them of those who feared the Lord, and that thought upon His name (chap. iii. 16).

Now, the state of the country soon after Ezra came up from Babylon (458—457 B.C.) seems to agree in some respects with the description of it which we have drawn from the materials contained in the prophecies of Malachi. Thus we read that when Nehemiah came up a few years later the people were put to such straits through famine that they came to him with the complaint, "We have mortgaged our lands, vineyards, and houses, that we might buy corn because of the dearth" (Ezra v. 3). Moreover, Ezra on his arrival found that both the people and the priests had "not separated themselves from the people of the lands, for they had taken of their daughters for themselves, and for their sons" (chap. ix. 1, 2). In the space of less than three months he compelled every one of those who had contracted such marriages to divorce his heathen wife, and send her back to her own people, and so "they made an end of all the men that had taken strange wives by the first day of the first month" (chap. x. 17*). On the other hand, of his having to reform any abuses in connection with the Temple service we hear nothing. It should also be mentioned that in Ezra's time, or, at all events, immediately after his arrival, as well as in the time of Darius (Ezra vi. 9, 10), all things that were necessary for the Temple services were provided out of the royal revenues (Ezra vii.), so that the rebukes of the prophet with regard to the niggardly manner in which the people presented the offerings would be out of place, if the prophecy had reference to this period. Nor would the vivid picture which the prophet draws of the state of the "desolate places" of Edom (chap. i. 3—5), have been of much comfort to Israel, if at the time of his speaking their own "city, the place of their fathers' sepulchres, was still lying waste, and the gates thereof consumed with fire," as was the case at this time (Neh. i. 3, ii. 3). We must, accordingly, look for some later events as the occasion of the prophet's ministry.

In 445-4 B.C. Nehemiah obtained leave from Artaxerxes Longimanus to go up to Jerusalem (Neh. ii. 6), and in 433-2 he returned to the Persian Court. During this period of twelve years he acted as governor in the land of Judah (chap. v. 14). In the almost incredibly short space of fifty-two days he rebuilt the walls of Jerusalem, in spite of the opposition of the neighbouring peoples (chap. vi. 15). He worked most important reforms, condemning usury and slavery (chap. v. 1—14); proclaimed a fast, and made the people confess their sins, and enter into a covenant to keep the ordinances of the Law, and abstain from heathen marriages; to observe the Sabbath, and keep the Sabbatical year; to contribute every man the third of a shekel for the services of the Temple, and to pay the legal tithes and offerings (chap. x. 29—39). But when he went back to Persia all the abuses which he had abolished, quickly crept in again, so that on his return, which was before the death of Artaxerxes (424 B.C.), he had to go over the old ground again. The Jews had married wives of Ashdod, of Ammon, and of Moab, and their children spake half in the speech of Ashdod, and could not speak in the Jew's language (Neh. xiii. 23, 24; comp. Mal. iii. 10—16). The portions of the Levites had not been given them (Neh. xiii. 10; comp. Mal. iii. 6—10).

Now, we can hardly suppose that Malachi prophesied during Nehemiah's temporary absence, and that his words had so little effect that when Nehemiah returned he found things as bad as ever. Nor could he have prophesied prior to or during Nehemiah's first reform, or he would not in all probability have been utterly silent with regard to the re-building of Jerusalem and its walls. It only remains, therefore, that we should regard him as Nehemiah's coadjutor in his second reformation. He was, in fact, to Nehemiah what Haggai and Zechariah were to Zerubbabel, Jeremiah to Josiah, and Isaiah to Hezekiah—the prophet of God, co-operating with the civil authority in bringing about the moral reformation of the people. He prophesied, therefore, in all probability some time between 430 and 425 B.C.,* namely, during the first part of the first Peloponnesian War, and was a contemporary of the great Greek tragic poets Sophocles (496-405) and Euripides (480-406), and of the historians Herodotus (484-424), and Thucydides (471-396).

III. **Contents.**—The prophecy is one of continual rebuke from beginning to end. In the form in which we have it, it is certainly to be looked on as one single address. Probably it is but a systematically arranged epitome of the various oral addresses of the prophet.

It may be divided into six sections, all more or less intimately connected with one another.

Chap. i. 1—5. God's love for Israel. Israel's ingratitude.

Chaps. i. 6—ii. 9. Rebuke of the priests. Prophecy of the spiritual worship of God among the heathen. Decree against the priests.

Chap. ii. 10—16. Rebuke of the people for marrying heathen women, and divorcing their Israelitish wives.

* There are two remarkable instances of coincidence of expression between Ezra and Malachi: viz., Ezra ix. 4, Mal. iii. 16; and Ezra ix. 14, 15, Mal. iii. 6.

* Two objections might be made to this conclusion—(1) There is no mention of any dearth at this time, such as is implied in Mal. iii. 10, 11. To this we answer that since the whole history of this period is contained in twenty-five verses (Neh. xiii. 7—31), written in the prolix style of Nehemiah, which does not admit of the compression of many facts into a small space, we cannot be surprised at the omission of any mention of such scarcity. (2) It is said that Malachi and Nehemiah could not be contemporaries, because whereas Malachi upbraids the people with offering to God such poor things as they would not dare to offer to their governor (chap. i. 8), Nehemiah, when governor, "required not the portion of the governor" (Neh. v. 18),—*i.e.*, the allowance granted him by the Persian Government as an impost on the people. To this it may be replied (*a*), Malachi speaks of free-will offerings, not imposts; (*b*) Nehemiah says he did not *require* (demand), not that he would not *accept* under any circumstances; (*c*) there is no evidence that he was governor on his return.

Chaps. ii. 17—iii. 5. Rebuke of sceptics, and prophecy of the sudden coming of the Lord to His Temple.
Chap. iii. 6—12. Rebuke of the people for withholding tithes and offerings.
Chaps. iii. 13—iv. 6. Rebuke of formalists and sceptics. The different destiny of the righteous and of the wicked. The rising of the Sun of Righteousness. Exhortation to remember the Law of Moses. The coming of Elijah.

IV. **Style of Diction.**—Malachi writes in the purest style of the Renaissance. From the very nature of his utterances high-flown poetic imagery is, for the most part, excluded; but when for the moment he removes his gaze from the dark present to look back on the glorious past, or to foretel the events of the still more glorious future, he rises to a high standard of poetic diction. (See chaps. ii. 5, 6, iii. 1—5, iv. 1—6.) His method of administering the most scathing rebuke by means of *preferring an accusation* (in which he shows the deepest insight into the inmost thoughts of the nation), *then supposing an objection on their part* (which exhibits in the most telling manner the moral degradation of the people, and their indifference to their spiritual condition), *and lastly, by confuting their objection* in trenchant terms, is artistic, and at the same time forcible to a degree. (See chaps. i. 2—5, ii. 14 [15?]—17, iii. 7—13.) We cannot, with Lowth, perceive here any decadence in the power of the spirit of prophecy. Prophecy did not cease because its power was exhausted, but because its mission was now fulfilled until the time of its fulfilment should draw near. We will conclude with the words of Nägelsbach, which others before us have thought worthy of citation: "Malachi is like a late evening which closes a long day, but he is at the same time the morning twilight, which bears in its womb a glorious day."

MALACHI

CHAPTER I.—(1) The burden of the
word of the LORD to Israel [1]by Malachi.
(2) I have loved you, saith the LORD.
Yet ye say, Wherein hast thou loved
us? *Was* not Esau Jacob's brother?
saith the LORD: yet I [a]loved Jacob,
(3) and I hated Esau, and laid his moun-
tains and his heritage waste for the
dragons of the wilderness. (4) Whereas
Edom saith, We are impoverished, but
we will return and build the desolate
places; thus saith the LORD of hosts,
They shall build, but I will throw down;
and they shall call them, The border of
wickedness, and, The people against
whom the LORD hath indignation
for ever. (5) And your eyes shall
see, and ye shall say, The LORD
will be magnified [2,3]from the border
of Israel.

B.C. cir. 397.

1 Heb., *by the hand of Malachi.*

a Rom. 9. 13.

2 Or, *upon.*

3 Heb., *from upon.*

1—5. These verses are introductory to the whole prophecy. God had shown His love to Israel; Israel ought to have made a proper return, but, on the contrary, Israel had abused God's loving-kindness.

(1) **The burden.**—See Notes on Isa. xiii. 1; Jer. xxiii. 33—40; Zech. ix. 1, xii. 1.

Malachi.—See *Introduction.*

(2) **I have loved**—*i.e.,* shown abundant proof of my love. The prophet goes on to show how God has shown so great proofs of His love.

Was not Esau Jacob's brother?—And would not one suppose from that fact they would have similar privileges? But not so.

I loved Jacob, (3) and I hated Esau . . .—The ethical reason for God's love of Jacob and hatred of Esau is not touched upon here, nor is it necessary to the argument. It is God's *love* for Israel that the prophet wishes to dwell on, and he mentions the hatred towards Esau merely for the sake of a strong contrast. The nations, Israel and Edom, are here referred to, not the individuals, Jacob and Esau. This passage receives a graphic illustration from the words of Ps. cxxxvii. 7, composed after the return from the captivity: "*Remember, O Lord, the children of Edom in the day of Jerusalem; who said, Raze it, raze it, even to the foundation thereof.*" (On St. Paul's application of the words of Malachi, see Notes on Rom. ix. 13.)

Laid his mountains . . . waste . . .—It is a somewhat disputed point to what historical fact this refers. But, on the whole, we may reasonably infer from Jer. xlix. 7, 17—21, compared with Jer. xxv. 9, 21, that the subjugation of the Edomites by Nebuchadnezzar is here referred to.

Dragons.—Better, *jackals.* The LXX. and Gesenius render the word "habitations," by comparison with a similarly sounding Arabic word.

(4) **Whereas . . . saith.**—Better, *If Edom say.*

We are impoverished.—Better, *we are broken to pieces.* Edom's ineffectual attempts to restore itself will be looked on as proofs of God's wrath against the nation on account of its wickedness, and will acquire for it the titles "border of wickedness," "the people against whom the Lord hath indignation for ever." "Border" means "confines," "territory;" Latin, *fines.*

Keith, *Evidence of Prophecy*, pp. 309, 310, in reference to the literal fulfilment of this prophecy, writes as follows:—"In recording the invasion of Demetrius, about three hundred years before the Christian era, into the land of Edom, Diodorus describes the country as a desert, and the inhabitants as living without houses; nor does he mention any city in that region but Petra alone. Yet the names of some of the cities of Arabia Petræa, enumerated by Josephus, as existing at the time when the Romans invaded Palestine—the names of eighteen cities of Palestina Tertia, of which Petra was the capital, and the metropolitan see, in the times of the Lower Empire—and the towns laid down in D'Anville's map, together with the subsisting ruins of towns in Edom, specified by Burckhardt, and also by Laborde, give proof that Edom, after having been impoverished, did return, and build the desolate places, even as 'the ruined towns and places,' still visible and named, show that though the desolate places were *built again* according to the prophecy, they have, as likewise foretold, been *thrown down*, and are 'ruined places' lying in utter desolation."

(5) **And your eyes shall see.**—Comp. such expressions as Pss. xxxvii. 34, lii. 6, xci. 8. As with the individual, so with a nation: to stand in safety and be a witness to the destruction of the enemy is looked on as a sign of God's favour.

The Lord will be magnified . . . Israel.—Some render, *let the Lord be magnified*, as in Pss. xxxv. 27, xl. 16; others, *the Lord is great: i.e.,* has exerted His greatness. The latter seems the more appropriate rendering here.

From the border.—Some say, *beyond the border.* This translation is not in accordance with the usage of the expression, which means simply "over" or "above." (Comp. Jer. iv. 6.) The meaning seems to be this: The Lord, whose protecting presence hovers specially over the border of Israel, is now great, in that He has

(6) A son honoureth *his* father, and a
servant his master: if then I *be* a
father, where *is* mine honour? and if I
be a master, where *is* my fear? saith the
LORD of hosts unto you, O priests, that
despise my name. And ye say, Where-
in have we despised thy name? (7) [1] Ye
offer polluted bread upon mine altar;
and ye say, Wherein have we polluted
thee? In that ye say, The table of the
LORD *is* contemptible. (8) And if ye
offer the blind [2] for sacrifice, *is it* not
evil? and if ye offer the lame and sick,
is it not evil? offer it now unto thy
governor; will he be pleased with thee,
or accept thy person? saith the LORD
of hosts. (9) And now, I pray you, be-
seech [3] God that he will be gracious unto

1 Or, *Bring unto, &c.*
2 Heb., *to sacrifice.*
3 Heb., *the face of God.*

---

restored Israel, but hath destroyed the nationality of the wicked descendants of the godless Esau. "Border of Israel" is purposely used in contrast to "border of wickedness."

Chaps. i. 6, ii. 9.—The priesthood rebuked. A close connection subsists between the different parts of this section; it ought therefore to be read as one continuous paragraph. The sub-divisions of it are chaps. i. 6—14, ii. 1—9.

(6—14) The prophet's rebuke for the dishonouring of God's name is addressed to the priests as the responsible persons, but applies to the whole nation.

(6) **A father.**—God is distinctly called the Father of Israel in Deut. xxxii. 6, 18. (Comp. Exod. iv. 22: "My son, my firstborn, is Israel.")

A master.—Comp. Isa. i. 3.

Mine honour—*i.e., the respect due to me.*

My fear—*i.e., your dread of me.* Fear is two-fold: servile, whereby punishment, not fault, is dreaded; filial, whereby fault is feared. The fear and love required by God of his children, are that reverence which loveth to serve Him, and that love which dreadeth to offend Him.

(7) **Ye offer.**—Literally, *offering.*

Bread.—This is not the shewbread, which was not offered upon the altar. The word rendered "bread" means in Arabic "flesh;" in Hebrew, "food generally." This word is applied (Lev. iii. 11, 16) to the fat portions of the peace offerings, which were burned, and is there translated "food." (See references there.) In Lev. xxi. 6, 8, 17, 21, 22, xxii. 25, it is used of the sacrifices generally, but is there inconsistently translated "bread."

Polluted.—The Hebrew word does not occur in this sense in the Pentateuch, but we have it in Dan. i. 8 in the reflexive conjugation: "to allow himself to be defiled" with food, and in the active ("polluted thee") in this verse. The context shows that the words "polluted bread" means "food unfit to be offered." "Polluted me" is the same as "profaned [my name]" (verse 12); for in the Hebrew Scriptures "God" and "God's name" are often equivalent expressions (Comp. chap. ii. 5). Keil takes the words, which he wrongly translates, "*ye that offer polluted bread,*" as parallel to the words "despisers of my name," and to a certain degree explanatory of them; while he finds the actual answer to the questions, "Wherein have we despised?" "Wherein have we polluted?" is given in the words, "In that ye say," &c. He renders the passage thus:—

Saith the Lord of hosts unto you,
"Ye priests, who despise my name!"
And yet say, "Wherein have we despised thy name?"
"Ye who offer on mine altar polluted food."
And yet say, "Wherein have we polluted thee?"
(*Ans.*) [Ye have despised my name and polluted me], in that ye say, "The table of the Lord is contemptible."

The error of this rendering consists in supposing that "offering polluted food," which is anathrous, can be parallel to "Ye priests who despise my name," which is defined by the definite article. In truth, the English Version is perfectly correct. We will repeat it with only the slightest possible verbal alterations, and with such parenthetical explanations as are required to make it quite intelligible:—Saith the Lord of hosts unto you, "O priests, that *despise* my name!"

[This is the commencement of a prophetic rebuke to the priests; but they, in accordance with the prophet's graphic style of writing, are supposed to catch him up at the first clause of his utterance.]

"But" [despisers of God's name!] say ye, "wherein have we *despised* thy name?"

(*Ans.*) "Offering [as ye do] *polluted* food upon mine altar."

"But," say ye, "wherein have we *polluted* thee?"

(*Ans.*) "When, now, ye offer the blind for sacrifice, is it not evil?" &c.

Say—*i.e., show by your conduct that such is your feeling.* "This was their inward thought . . . he puts these thoughts into abrupt, bold, hard words, which might startle them for their hideousness, as if he would say, this is what your acts mean. He exhibits the worm and the decay which lay under the whited exterior."—*Pusey.*

Table—*i.e., altar,* as in Ezek. xli. 22: "The altar . . . this is the table that is before the Lord." (Comp. Ezek. xlix. 16.)

(8) **If.**—Better, *when.*

Blind . . . lame . . . sick.—This was contrary to Lev. xxii. 22, &c. And now, to show them the heinous nature of their offence against the majesty of God, the prophet asks them whether they could offer such unsound animals to their civil ruler with any chance of acceptance.

Governor.—The word in the Hebrew is probably of foreign origin, but it occurs as early as to refer to the governors of Judah in the time of Solomon (1 Kings x. 15). On the date of the book of Kings see Introduction to that book.

(9) This verse is severely ironical. The word "God" is expressly used, rather than "the Lord," as a contrast to the human "governor" mentioned above. The meaning is: "You know you dare not treat thus contemptuously your human governor, what hope then is there of such disrespectful conduct finding favour with God—the Judge of all the earth?"

That he will be gracious.—These words refer, perhaps, to the wording of the sacerdotal benediction (Num. vi. 24).

Unto us.—The prophet includes himself with the

us: this hath been [1]by your means:
will he regard your persons? saith the
LORD of hosts.
(10) Who *is there* even among you that
would shut the doors *for nought?* neither
do ye kindle *fire* on mine altar for
nought. I have no pleasure in you,
saith the LORD of hosts, neither will I
accept an [a]offering at your hand. (11) For
from the rising of the sun even unto the
going down of the same my name *shall be*
great among the Gentiles; and in every
place incense *shall be* offered unto my
name, and a pure offering: for my name
shall be great among the heathen, saith
the LORD of hosts.
(12) But ye have profaned it, in that
ye say, The table of the LORD *is* pol-

1 Heb., *from your hand.*

a Isa. 1. 11; Jer. 6. 20; Amos 5. 21.

---

people, as Moses did (Exod. xxxiv. 9): "And pardon *our* iniquity and *our* sin;" and as, in fact, God Himself included Moses (Exod. xvi. 28): "And the Lord said unto Moses, How long refuse *ye* to keep my commandments?"

This hath been by your means.—Better, *by your means hath this been.* "By *your* means" is emphatic by position. The meaning is: "By means of *you* (priests), who ought to have directed the people aright, has this disgraceful conduct been occasioned." Or, perhaps, in view of ver. 8, and the wording of ver. 10, we should render the words thus: "From *your* hands is this [despicable offering]!" *This* being used contemptuously like Lat. *istud.* In either case the clause is parenthetical, so that "will he regard" must be taken in close connection with the preceding, "beseech God that he will be gracious unto us."

Will he regard your persons?—Better, *will he, on your account, show favour to any one?* That is, can ye be deemed worthy intercessors, when these are the actions ye perform? The question is, of course, a practical negation. (Comp. Zech. iv. 10.)

(10) The prophet is now supposed by many commentators to say that the Temple might as well be closed, as far as concerns any pleasure the Lord takes in their offerings.

Who is there even among you . . . doors . . . altar for nought.—Those that take the above-mentioned view of the passage would render, *O that there were one among even you who would shut the doors, that ye might not light mine altar to no purpose.* "To no purpose," like δωρεάν (Gal. ii. 21). The rebuke contained in this verse is, according to this interpretation, very similar to that of Isa. i. 11—15. But the word "even," which can only refer to "you" (Keil thinks differently), seems to us almost fatal to this interpretation. For we could only explain its use in the forced sense of: "Would that some one, among even you (who ought to be the promoters of God's service), would (since His service has now become a mockery) shut, &c." We are therefore inclined to retain the simple rendering of our venerable English Version. In that case, "even among you" (perhaps better, *among even you*) would mean: "even among you whose duty it is, and chief pleasure it ought to be, to minister unto Me," which, in that context, so far from being forced, would be most natural.

For nought.—Comp. the attitude of the priests in 1 Sam. ii. 13—16.

(11) This verse contains no verb, and, as far as the rules of grammar are concerned, its participles may be rendered either by presents or futures. If we take the words as referring to the present, we are met by the insurmountable difficulty that in no sense, at the time of Malachi, could the Lord's Name be said to be great over all the earth, or pure sacrifices to be offered to Him in every place. Nor can we, with many commentators, suppose that heathen rites are here referred to as being offered ignorantly, through idols, to the one true God. (Comp. Pope's universal prayer:—

"Father of all, in every age,
In every clime adored,
By saint, by savage, and by sage,
Jehovah, Jove, or Lord!")

For there is no hint given of any such meaning being intended; and, moreover, such a sentiment would be quite foreign to the Old Testament, which always represents heathen rites as being an utter abomination, and always speaks of the adhesion of the Gentiles to the worship of the true God as a thing of the future. We are compelled, therefore, to take the words as a prophetic announcement of the future rejection of Israel and calling of the Gentiles.

In every place.—In contradistinction to the *one* place (Deut. xii. 5—7). (Comp. our Lord's words to the woman of Samaria: John iv. 21—24.)

Incense shall be offered . . .—This is a possible rendering of the words; but this Hebrew word is not elsewhere used for "incense," and may more naturally be rendered *shall be burnt,* as the passive participle of the verb used in Lev. i. 9. Dr. Pusey's footnote on this passage is well worth reading, as, indeed, his *footnotes* usually are. We prefer, therefore, to take the words thus: "an oblation shall be burnt to my name, even a pure offering." In any case, unless we are to expect some future establishment of a universal offering of material sacrifices, we must understand both expressions in a spiritual sense, which is, in truth, the only reasonable way of interpreting such passages. (See Notes on Zech. ii. 6—13, iii. 8—10, vi. 9—15, and especially xiv. 16—21.) If, therefore, any Christians would claim this verse as a support for their custom of offering incense in churches, they must conform also with Zech. xiv. 16—21, and go up every year to Jerusalem to keep the Feast of Tabernacles. The word "offering," as in the preceding verse (comp. 1 Sam. ii. 17; Isa. i. 13), denotes sacrificial gifts in general, not the flour offerings as distinguished from the flesh offerings. The word "pure" is emphatic, not as signifying the bloodless sacrifice of the Mass (Council of Trent), as distinguished from the bloody sacrifices, but as the converse of "polluted" (verse 7). The above remarks we have made in no controversial spirit, but simply in the interests of truth; and lest any should suppose us to imply that the above interpretation was *originated* by the Council of Trent, we refer the reader to Dr. Pusey's Commentary, in which he shows, by quotations from SS. Justin, Irenæus, Hippolytus, Cyprian, Cyril of Jerusalem, Chrysostom, and Augustine, as also from Tertullian, Eusebius, and Theodoret, that it is *quod semper, quod ab omnibus, quod ubique.* Those, therefore, who prefer so-called *authority* to the results of calm criticism are bound to disagree with us.

(12) **But ye have.**—Better, *but ye profane it*—viz.,

luted; and the fruit thereof, *even* his
meat, *is* contemptible. (13) Ye said also,
Behold, what a weariness *is it!* [1] and ye
have snuffed at it, saith the LORD of
hosts; and ye brought *that which was*
torn, and the lame, and the sick; thus
ye brought an offering: should I accept
this of your hand? saith the LORD.
(14) But cursed *be* the deceiver, [2] which
hath in his flock a male, and voweth,
and sacrificeth unto the Lord a corrupt
thing: for I *am* a great King, saith the
LORD of hosts, and my name *is* dreadful
among the heathen.

1 Or, *whereas ye might have blown it away.*

2 Or, *in whose flock is.*

a Lev. 26. 14; Deut. 28. 15.

3 Or, *reprove.*

4 Heb., *scatter.*

5 Or, *it shall take you away to it.*

CHAPTER II.—(1) And now, O ye
priests, this commandment *is* for you.
(2) [a] If ye will not hear, and if ye will not
lay *it* to heart, to give glory unto my
name, saith the LORD of hosts, I will
even send a curse upon you, and I will
curse your blessings: yea, I have cursed
them already, because ye do not lay *it*
to heart. (3) Behold, I will [3] corrupt
your seed, and [4] spread dung upon your
faces, *even* the dung of your solemn
feasts; and [5] *one* shall take you away
with it. (4) And ye shall know that I
have sent this commandment unto you,

"my name" (verse 11). The word "it" is said by Jewish tradition to be an euphemism for "me." The present contemptuous conduct of God's priests is contrasted with the prophesied reverence of heathen nations.

Fruit . . . meat, denote the same as "bread" of verse 7. They show that they think it contemptible by not taking the trouble to offer such things as are prescribed by the Law.

(13) **Said.**—Better, *say.*

And ye have snuffed at it.—Better, *and ye puff at it*—that is, treat it with contempt, "pooh-pooh it," as we say. The service of the Temple, which they ought to have regarded as their highest privilege and pleasure, they look on as burdensome and contemptible. For "brought," read *bring.*

Torn.—The word *Gâzûl* elsewhere means "stolen" (Deut. xxviii. 31), or "robbed"—*i.e.*, "spoiled" (Deut. xxviii. 29). It is perhaps not impossible that it may here be a later word for *trêphâh*, "torn" (comp. the cogn. Arabic *ajzal*, "galled on the back"), but it is not so used in post-Biblical Jewish writings. On the contrary, Rabbinic tradition uses our word when expressly mentioning *that which is stolen* as unfit to be offered as a burnt offering—*e.g.*, the Sifrā, (*Vayyikrā*, Perek 6, Parashta 5, *ed.* Weis 7*b*), commenting on the words of Lev. i. 10, says: "'From the flock,' and 'from the sheep,' and 'from the goats:' These words are limitations—viz., to exclude the sick (comp. also Mal. i. 8), and the aged, and that which has been dedicated in thought to an idol, and that which is defiled with its own filth; 'its offering' [English Version, *his offering*, comp. Note on Zech. iv. 2], to exclude *that which is stolen.*" (See also Talmud Babli, *Baba Kamma* 66*b*.) The English Version has the same in view in its rendering of Isa. lxi. 8, where it has the authority of Talmud Babli, *Sukkah* 30*a*, and of Jerome and Luther. Perhaps the reason why people were inclined to offer a stolen animal may be, that it might very likely have a mark on it, which would render it impossible for the thief to offer it for sale, and so realise money on it, for fear of detection; so then he makes a virtue of a necessity, and brings as an offering to God that which he could not otherwise dispose of.

(14) Some consider that two cases are mentioned in this verse. (1) One who acts deceitfully (by offering a *female* as a *burnt offering*, which is contrary to the Law, while there is in his flock a *male*); (2) and one who makes *a vow* (to offer a *sacrifice of peace offerings*, for which either a male or a female was allowable, provided it were without a blemish: Lev. xxii. 23), and then offers an animal that has a blemish. But it is better to understand but one case to be mentioned—viz., that of a man who *vows*, and while he has a *male* in his flock offers a *female with a blemish.* A female without blemish would be admissible as a *vow offering*, but a male without blemish would be the most valuable, because it could be offered as a burnt offering, whereas a female could not; while a female with a blemish would be the very worst, and actually illegal. A man is not bound to make a vow, but if he make one his offering should be of the very best, just as he would not dare to offer to a king or to his ruler (verse 6) anything but the best. How cursed, then, must he be who, while he possesses the best, deliberately makes a vow to God, and then offers Him the very worst.

II.

(1–9) The decree against the priests.

(1) **Commandment.**—Better, *decree.* (Comp. the use of the verb from which this substantive is derived in Nah. i. 14; Pss. vii. 6, xlii. 8.)

(2) **Hear . . . lay to heart**—viz., the warning of chap. i. 6—13.

Your blessings.—Some take this as meaning the priests' tithes, atonement money, and their portions of the sacrifices, in accordance with a common usage of the word in the sense of "gift"—*e.g.*, Gen. xxxiii. 11. Others refer the words to the blessing which the priests pronounce on the people (Num. vi. 23—27).

(3) **I will corrupt your seed.**—Better, *I will destroy for you the seed*—viz., of the crops. It must be remembered that because the people neglected to pay the tithes, the Levites were obliged to go and till the fields (Neh. xiii. 10). The LXX. for "seed" reads "corn."

Dung of your solemn feasts.—Or rather, *of your festival sacrifices.* (Comp. Exod. xxiii. 18; Ps. cxviii. 27.) The dung of the sacrificial animals was to be carried to an unclean place outside the camp, and burnt there. The priests, because they had profaned God's Name by offering unfit animals in sacrifice, were to be treated in the most ignominious manner.

And one shall take you away with it—*i.e.*, according to a Hebrew idiom, *and ye shall be carried away to it* (comp. Isa. viii. 4):—ye shall be treated like it.

(4) **Commandment.**—Or rather, *decree*, as in verse 1.

That my covenant might be.—Better, *to be my*

that my covenant might be with Levi,
saith the LORD of hosts. (5) My cove-
nant was with him of life and peace;
and I gave them to him *for* the fear
wherewith he feared me, and was afraid
before my name. (6) The law of truth
was in his mouth, and iniquity was not
found in his lips: he walked with me in
peace and equity, and did turn many
away from iniquity. (7) For the priest's
lips should keep knowledge, and they
should seek the law at his mouth: for
he *is* the messenger of the LORD of
hosts. (8) But ye are departed out of the
way; ye have caused many to [1]stumble
at the law; ye have corrupted the cove-
nant of Levi, saith the LORD of hosts.
(9) Therefore have I also made you con-
temptible and base before all the people,
according as ye have not kept my ways,
but [2][3]have been partial in the law.
(10) [a]Have we not all one father? hath
not one God created us? why do we
deal treacherously every man against
his brother, by profaning the covenant
of our fathers? (11) Judah hath dealt
treacherously, and an abomination is
committed in Israel and in Jerusalem;
for Judah hath profaned the holiness of
the LORD which he [4]loved, and hath
married the daughter of a strange god.
(12) The LORD will cut off the man that
doeth this, [5]the master and the scholar,
out of the tabernacles of Jacob, and

1 Or, *fall in the law.*

2 Or, *lifted up the face against.*

3 Heb., *accepted faces.*

a Eph. 4. 6.

4 Or, *ought to love.*

5 Or, *him that waketh, and him that answereth.*

---

covenant—*i.e.*, so that this new decree, which I have been compelled to make against the house of Levi, may be my covenant with him instead of the old one, of which the prophet goes on to speak.

Levi denotes throughout the tribe of Levi, and especially the priests, the sons of Aaron. (See Note on chap. iii. 3.)

(5) **Of life and peace.**—Better, *life and peace*—*i.e.*, by it life and peace were guaranteed to him.

Life in its highest sense.

Peace as the sum total of blessing: the "fruit of the Spirit is love, joy, *peace*." (Gal. v. 22; comp. Note on Zech. vi. 13.)

Them—viz., life and peace.

For the fear . . . me.—Better, *As fear*—(*i.e.*, as a motive for the fear of God), *and he did fear me.* Or, perhaps, a still better interpretation is that which represents God and Levi as each having performed his part of the covenant—God in bestowing "life and peace," Levi in rendering "fear." According to this view, the words should be translated, *My covenant was with him*—viz., *life and peace—and I gave them to him; fear, and he feared me, and trembled before My Name.*

(6) **The law of truth**—*i.e.*, right instruction in the Law, and judgment in accordance with the Law, the reverse of which is "iniquity," or rather, *perversion.*

Walked with me—*i.e.*, had their conversation in heaven. (Phil. iii. 20; comp. Zech. iii. 7; and Gen. v. 24, of Enoch.)

In peace.—See on the preceding verse.

Equity—*i.e.*, integrity of life.

And did turn . . . . iniquity.—Of this, says Pusey, "What a history of zeal for the glory of God and of the conversion of sinners in those of whom the world knows nothing, of whose working, but for the three words in the closing book of the Old Testament, we should have known nothing."

(7) Comp. Deut. xxxiii. 10.

Keep.—Not as in a repository, but rather, *observe* (Zech. iii. 7)—*i.e.*, speak in accordance with the *knowledge* of God, as revealed in the Law.

Messenger.—Literally, *angel.* (See Note on chap. iii. 1.)

(8) **But ye.**—Priests of the present day have done in every respect the reverse.

Caused many to stumble at the law.—Or rather, *in the Law*; and ye have given them false instruction in the Law, and allowed those things which were forbidden, and so *ye have corrupted the covenant of the* (tribe of) *Levi*: ye have turned the Law, which ought to have been a light to their feet and a lamp to their path, into a stumbling-block.

(9) **Therefore.**—I am no longer bound by the covenant I made with the tribe of Levi, and, instead of "life and peace," I give you contempt, &c.

In the law—*i.e.*, in the administration of justice. The authority of the priests, Levites, and of the judges of the day, in all matters ceremonial and civil, is expressly inculcated by Deut. xvii. 8—13. It was in accordance with this passage that our Lord said (Matt. xxiii. 2): "The scribes and Pharisees sit in Moses' seat; all, therefore, whatsoever they bid you observe, that observe and do," &c.

(10—17) The prophet now rebukes the two great sins of the nation at this time: (1) marriage with idolatresses; (2) divorce of the first (Israelitish) wife. He introduces this rebuke by a general statement, similar to that of chap. i. 2.

(10) **One father**—*i.e.*, not Adam, Abraham, or Jacob (as various commentators have held), but God Himself (chap. i. 6; Deut. xxxii. 6, 18), who is the spiritual Father of the nation, and in whom they are all brothers and sisters; so that when an Israelite married a heathen woman, or divorced an Israelitish wife, it was an offence against God, a "profaning the covenant of the fathers," and a violation of the fraternal relation. Moreover, "one God created" them for His glory (Isa. xliii. 7), for the special purpose of being a witness to His unity. The admission of idolatresses into their families would be fatal to this object.

(11) For the same collocation of "Judah, Israel, and Jerusalem," comp. Zech. i. 19.

The holiness of the Lord.—That is, their own "holy nation" (Deut. vii. 6, xiv. 2; comp. Jer. ii. 3).

Daughter of a strange god—*i.e.*, one who worships a strange god, and such they were forbidden to marry (Exod. xxiv. 16; Deut. vii. 3; comp. 1 Kings xi. 2).

(12) **The man.**—Better, *to the man.*

The master and the scholar.—This is the Talmudic interpretation of the Hebrew expression, which occurs only in this passage, but it is unsuitable (besides

him that offereth an offering unto the
LORD of hosts. (13) And this have ye
done again, covering the altar of the
LORD with tears, with weeping, and
with crying out, insomuch that he re-
gardeth not the offering any more, or
receiveth *it* with good will at your
hand.
(14) Yet ye say, Wherefore? Because
the LORD hath been witness between
thee and the wife of thy youth, against
whom thou hast dealt treacherously:
yet *is* she thy companion, and the wife
of thy covenant. (15) And did not he
make one? Yet had he the [1] residue of
the spirit. And wherefore one? That
he might seek [2] a godly seed. There-
fore take heed to your spirit, and let
none deal [3] treacherously against the
wife of his youth. (16) For the LORD,
the God of Israel, saith [4] that he hateth
[5] putting away: for *one* covereth violence

1 Or, *excellency*.
2 Heb., *a seed of God*.
3 Or, *unfaithfully*.
4 Or, *if he hate her put her away*.
5 Heb., *to put away*.

---

being philologically precarious), for the passage refers to the whole nation rather than to those who were their appointed scholars and teachers. It is better to render it, "*watchman and answerer*: *i.e.*, the watchman who cried in the city, "Who comes there?" and him who answers, "Friend," which is an exhaustive expression for all living persons, and so, in this context, "all posterity." This is the interpretation of Gesenius, who quotes in support of it an Arabic expression from the life of Tímúr-lang (Timur the lame, *Tamerlane*):—"When he left the city, there was not a *crier or an answerer* in it"—*i.e.*, there was not a person left alive. "Neither root nor branch" is another exhaustive term used by our prophet (chap. iv. 19). The Chaldee paraphrase gives the sense of the words in "son and son's son."

And him that offereth an offering . . .—Some refer this to the case in which the offender is a priest (Neh. xiii. 28); others understand it as "any one who might offer a sacrifice for him in expiation of his sin." But since the highest privilege of the Jew was to bring offerings to the Sanctuary, the words may be merely a repetition of the former expression in different terms, and mean "a descendant enjoying religious privileges." The intermarriage with heathens referred to here is that mentioned in Neh. xiii. 23—28, not the earlier case recorded in Ezra ix., x.

(13) The prophet now rebukes the people for their frivolous divorces of their first wives, which was a natural result of their marriage with heathen women.

And this . . . again.—Or perhaps, *And this a second thing ye do*—viz., infidelity to the wife of their youth (verse 14). But the rendering of the English Version is in accordance with the Hebrew accentuation. That rendering is not improbably the right one. It would mean: "And this you do again (Neh. xiii.), even after Ezra has reformed the abuse, and you have solemnly undertaken not to act so again" (Neh. ix. 10).

Covering the altar . . . with tears . . . and with crying out—*i.e.*, with the plaints of the Israelitish women who were divorced against their will.

Insomuch that.—Or rather, *so that*.

(14) Again with supercilious surprise they ask, "Wherefore?"

Witness.—Comp. Gen. xxxi. 49, 50: "The LORD *watch between me and thee*, when we are absent one from another. If thou shalt afflict my daughters, or if thou shalt take other wives beside my daughters, no man is with us; see, *God is witness* betwixt me and thee." If people would seriously consider the meaning of this verse of Genesis, they would not be so fond of putting MIZPAH on their rings, for it denotes a strong suspicion as to the fidelity of the other party.

(15, 16) These are two very difficult verses, which should perhaps, be rendered as follows:—

For did He not make [man and his wife, Gen. ii. 24] *one? and has he* [the husband] *any superiority of spirit* [that he should divorce at will]? *And what is this* [pair which is become] *one?* [Answer.] *It seeketh a godly seed. Therefore take heed to yourselves* [literally, *your spirit*], *and with respect to the wife of thy youth—Let none be faithless.*

(16) *For* [I] *hate divorce* [of the first wife], *saith the God of Israel, and he* [the divorcer of his first wife] *covers his garment with injury, saith the LORD of Hosts; therefore take ye heed to your spirit, and do not be faithless.* According to our interpretation, the whole of these two verses must be taken as the words of the prophet. *Any superiority.*—We take Heb. *sh'ār*, "remnant" in the sense of *yithrōn*, "superabundance," "superiority." *Any superiority of spirit*—*i.e.*, any such essential superiority as to justify him in treating his wife as a mere slave, and divorcing her against her will. This passage coincides more nearly with the spirit of Matt. xix. 3 *seqq.* than with that of Deut. xxiv. 1—4. *To yourselves*, or *to your spirit*. The expressions are equivalent. (Comp. Jer. xvii. 21; Deut. iv. 15; Josh. xxiii. 11.) *Let none be . . .*—Observe the change of person, so common in Hebrew. (Comp. Isa. i. 29.) *His garment.*—Some take this to be an Oriental expression for "his wife." (Comp. Al Koran, ii.:—"Wives are your attire, and you are theirs.") Or *garment* may be taken as the external symbol of the inner state of the man. (Comp. Zech. iii. 4; Is. lxiv. 5; Prov. xxx. 9, &c.) *Injury.*—Heb., *châmâs*. This word is especially used of ill-treatment of a wife. (Comp. Gen. xvi. 5.) Keil takes the first verse as follows: *No man who had ever a remnant of reason* [or a sense of right and wrong] *has done* [*sc.*, what ye are doing, *viz.*, faithlessly putting away the wife of his youth. To this the people are supposed to object.] *But what did the one* [Abraham] *do?* [To this the prophet answers] *He was seeking a seed of God* [viz., the child of promise: *i.e.*, he dismissed Hagar, because God promised to give him the desired posterity, not in Ishmael through the maid Hagar, but through Sarah in Isaac, so that in doing this he was simply acting in obedience to the word of God (Gen. xxi. 12).] Others vary the translation slightly, and render, *And has no one done this who has a remnant of spirit in him?* [This being supposed to be the objection on the part of the people. To this the prophet answers.] *Wherefore did he so act? He was seeking a godly seed.* Moore takes the verse quite differently, and refers it to the saying of verse 10. His words are, "The prophet at the outset had argued the return of the Jewish people . . . therefore these marriages that violated their oneness were

with his garment, saith the LORD of
hosts: therefore take heed to your spirit,
that ye deal not treacherously.
(17) Ye have wearied the LORD with
your words. Yet ye say, Wherein have
we wearied *him?* When ye say, Every
one that doeth evil *is* good in the sight
of the LORD, and he delighteth in
them; or, Where *is* the God of judg-
ment?

CHAPTER III.—(1) Behold, [a]I will
send my messenger, and he shall pre-
pare the way before me: and the Lord,
whom ye seek, shall suddenly come to
his temple, even the messenger of the
covenant, whom ye delight in: behold,
he shall come, saith the LORD of hosts.
(2) But who may abide the day of his
coming? and who shall stand when he
appeareth? for he *is* like a refiner's fire,
and like fullers' sope: (3) and he shall
sit *as* a refiner and purifier of silver:
and he shall purify the sons of Levi,
and purge them as gold and silver, that
they may offer unto the LORD an offer-
ing in righteousness. (4) Then shall the
offering of Judah and Jerusalem be
pleasant unto the LORD, as in the days
of old, and as in [1]former years. (5) And
I will come near to you to judgment;
and I will be a swift witness against
the sorcerers, and against the adulterers,
and against false swearers, and against

[a] Matt. 11. 10; Mark 1. 2; Luke 1. 76 & 7. 27.

[1] Or, *ancient.*

---

wrong . . . He asks again . . . *Did not* [God] *make* [us] *one?* Did He not separate us from other nations into an isolated unity? Yet this was not done because the blessing was too narrow to be spread over other nations . . . *for the residue of the spirit was with Him.* There remained an inexhaustible fulness of spiritual blessing that might be given to other nations. *Why* [then did He choose] *but one? He was seeking a seed of God* [a nation which He should train up to be the repository of His covenant, the stock of His Messiah]." Many other interpretations have been proposed, but these are the only ones which are at all admissible.

REBUKE OF INFIDELITY. THE ADVENT OF THE LORD FORETOLD (chaps. ii. 17—iii. 24).

(17) A new section of the prophecy begins with this verse. The prophet now directs his reproofs against the people for their discontent and their want of faith in the promises of God, because the expected manifestation of God's glory did not take place immediately. Because the doers of evil seem to flourish, the people say that God takes delight in them, "or" *i.e., if this be not the case,* "Where is the God of judgment?" that He does not interpose to punish them. (Comp. Ps. lxxiii., &c.)

III.

(1) **I will send.**—Or, *I send.* It is the participle used as the prophetic present. (Comp. Note on chap. i. 11.)

My messenger.—Heb., *Malachi, my angel,* or *my messenger,* with a play on the name of the prophet. In chap. ii. 7, he calls the priest the *angel* or *messenger* of the LORD. There can be little doubt that he is influenced in his choice of the term by his own personal name (see *Introd.*). This "messenger," by the distinct reference to Isa. xl. 3, contained in the words, "and he shall prepare," &c., is evidently the same as he whom [the deutero-] Isaiah prophetically heard crying, "In the wilderness, prepare ye the way of the LORD, make straight in the desert a highway for our God." Moreover, from the nature of his mission, he is proved to be identical with the "Elijah" of chap. iv. 3. These words had their first, if not their perfect fulfilment in John the Baptist (Matt. xvii. 12).

The Lord.—This word "Lord" occurs eight times with the definite article, but always, except here, with the name of God following it: viz., Exod. xxiii. 17, followed by "Jehovah;" Exod. xxxiv. 23, by "Jehovah, the God of Israel;" in Isa. i. 24, iii. 1, x. 33, xix. 4, by "Jehovah Zebaoth;" and in Isa. x. 16, by "the Lord of Zebaoth." And here, as elsewhere, it must mean God Himself, because He is said to come "to *his* temple," and because He is said to be He "whom ye seek:" *i.e.,* "the God of judgment" (chap. ii. 17).

Even—*i.e.,* "namely," for so the Hebrew conjunction "and" is frequently used: *e.g.,* Exod. xxv. 12; 1 Sam. xxviii. 3.

The messenger (or angel) **of the covenant.**—This expression occurs only in this passage. Identified as He is here with "the Lord," He can be no other than the Son of God, who was manifested in the flesh as the Messiah. In the word "covenant" there is, perhaps, some reference to the "new covenant" (Jer. xxxi. 31), but the meaning of the word must not be limited to this.

Delight in.—Rather, *desire.*

(2) This coming of the Lord to His temple acts as a crucial test (comp. Luke ii. 35); the people ought, therefore, seriously to have considered how far they were prepared for that advent before they desired it so eagerly and impatiently.

(3) **Sons of Levi.**—Meaning especially the priests, the sons of Aaron, son of Amram, son of Kohath, son of Levi (Exod. vi. 16—20); for judgment must begin at the house of God. (Comp. Jer. xxv. 29; Ezek. ix. 6; 1 Pet. iv. 17.)

In righteousness refers rather to the moral character of the offerer than to the nature of the sacrifices, as being such as were prescribed by the Law. This and the following verse do not, of course, imply that there are to be material sacrifices in Messianic times. The prophet speaks in such language as was suitable to the age in which he lived. (See Note on chap. i. 11.)

(4) **Days of old . . . former years.**—Perhaps, if we must define the period, from the time of Moses to the first year of the reign of Solomon. But we cannot be certain on this point. It seems to be one of the characteristics of Malachi to be somewhat of a *laudator temporis acti.* (Comp. chap. ii. 5—7.)

(5) All these crimes were explicitly forbidden by the Law. Sorcery (Exod. xxii. 18), adultery (Exod. xx.

those that [1]oppress the hireling in *his*
wages, the widow, and the fatherless,
and that turn aside the stranger *from*
his right, and fear not me, saith the
LORD of hosts. (6) For I *am* the LORD,
I change not; therefore ye sons of
Jacob are not consumed.
(7) Even from the days of your fathers
ye are gone away from mine ordinances,
and have not kept *them.* [a]Return unto
me, and I will return unto you, saith
the LORD of hosts. But ye said, Where-
in shall we return? (8) Will a man rob
God? Yet ye have robbed me. But ye
say, Wherein have we robbed thee? In
tithes and offerings. (9) Ye *are* cursed
with a curse: for ye have robbed me,
even this whole nation. (10) Bring ye all
the tithes into the storehouse, that
there may be meat in mine house, and
prove me now herewith, saith the LORD
of hosts, if I will not open you the
[b]windows of heaven, and [2]pour you out
a blessing, that *there shall* not *be room*
enough *to receive it.* (11) And I will re-
buke the devourer for your sakes, and
he shall not [3]destroy the fruits of your
ground; neither shall your vine cast
her fruit before the time in the field,
saith the LORD of hosts. (12) And all
nations shall call you blessed: for ye
shall be a delightsome land, saith the
LORD of hosts.
(13) Your words have been [c]stout
against me, saith the LORD. Yet ye
say, What have we spoken *so much*
against thee? (14) Ye have said, It *is*
vain to serve God: and what profit *is it*
that we have kept [4]his ordinance, and
that we have walked [5]mournfully before
the LORD of hosts? (15) And now we
call the proud happy; yea, they that

1 Or, *defraud.*
a Zech. 1. 3.
b Gen. 7. 11.
2 Heb., *empty out.*
3 Heb., *corrupt.*
c Job 21. 14.
4 Heb., *his observation.*
5 Heb., *in black.*

14; Lev. xx. 10; Deut. xxii. 22), false-swearing (Lev. xix. 12), defrauding, or withholding of wages (Lev. xix. 13; Deut. xxiv. 14, 15), oppressing the widow and orphan (Exod. xxii. 22—24), doing injustice to a stranger (Deut. xxiv. 17, xxvii. 19). (Comp. also Zech. vii. 9, 10, viii. 16, 17.)

(6) **For I am the Lord, I change not.**—Better, *For I Jehovah change not.* Because it is the Eternal's unchangeable will that the sons of Jacob, His chosen people, should not perish as a nation, He will purify them by the eradication of the wicked among them, that the remnant (the superior part; see Note on chap. ii. 15) may return to their allegiance. (Comp. Rom. xi.) Ewald renders the words: *For I, the LORD, have not changed: but ye sons of Jacob, have ye not altered?* But the last verb does not mean "to alter;" and, moreover, the former translation is exactly in accordance with the wording of the prayer in Ezra ix. 14, 15.

(7) **Even from . . . fathers.**—Throughout the whole course of their history they had been a stiff-necked people (Exod. xxxii. 9, &c.); and now, when exhorted to repent, they ask in feigned innocence:—

Wherein shall we return? . . . Return unto me . . . unto you.—Comp. Zech. i. 3.

(8) **Robbed me.**—Because the tithes are said to be offered to Jehovah, and then He gives them to the Levites in place of an inheritance (Num. xviii. 24).

In tithes and offerings.—See Notes on Exod. xxiii. 19; Lev. xxvii. 30—33; Num. xviii. 12, 21—24; Deut. xviii. 4; Lev. iii. 1—17, vii. 11—21, 28—36.

(9) Comp. chaps. ii. 2, and iii. 11.

(10) The emphasis is on the word "all."

Storehouse.—From the time of Hezekiah (2 Chron. xxxi. 11) there were at the Sanctuary special storehouses built for this purpose; so, too, in the second Temple (Neh. x. 38, 39, xii. 44, xiii. 12, 13).

Meat—*i.e.*, food for the priests and Levites.

Open you . . .—According to the promise of Deut. xi. 13—15, &c. For a practical commentary on this verse, see 2 Chron. xxxi. 10. "And Azariah, the chief priest of the house of Zadok, answered Hezekiah and said, Since the people began to bring the offerings into the house of the Lord, we have had enough to eat, and have left plenty; *for the Lord hath blessed his people;* and that which is left is this great store."

That.—Better, *until.*

There shall not be room enough . . .—This rendering gives the correct meaning of the words. (Compare an expression of similar import in Zech. x. 10.) We cannot agree with the rendering of Gesenius, "until my abundance be exhausted," as equivalent to "for ever."

(11) **For your sakes.**—The same word as in chap. ii. 3: here in a good sense, there in a bad.

The devourer—*i.e.*, the locust, &c.

Rebuke.—Better, *corrupt.* The same word is used as in chap. ii. 3, but in a different construction. (With this verse comp. Hag. i. 6—11.)

(12) Comp. Zech. vii. 14, viii. 13—23; also Isa. lxii. 4; Dan. xi. 16.

(13) **Your words . . . against me.**—Better, *your words put a constraint on me:* viz., to prove myself to you to be "the God of judgment."

Spoken.—Or rather, *conversed together.* (Comp. verse 16.) They seem to have been in the habit of conversing together, and comparing the promises of God towards them with the then state of affairs. God had promised that they should be a proverb among the nations for blessedness; but, say they, seeing that things are as they are, "we [feel more inclined to] call the proud happy [or blessed]." (See further in Note on verse 15.)

(14) **Mournfully**—*i.e.*, with all outward signs of fasting. (Comp. Matt. vi. 16.) The fasting referred to is not that of the Day of Atonement, but of voluntary fasts. We see here, in already a somewhat developed form, that disposition to attribute merit to observances of outward forms of religion for their own sake, without regard to the secret attitude of the heart, which reached such a pitch among the majority of the Jews in the time of our Lord, and especially among the Pharisees.

(15) **And now** means *and so, consequently.* In this verse the prophet gives the words of the murmurers. (See Note on verse 13.) The statements of verse 13 show that they were of a very different

work wickedness [1] are set up; yea, *they*
that [a] tempt God are even delivered.
(16) Then they that feared the LORD
spake often one to another: and the
LORD hearkened, and heard *it*, and a
book of remembrance was written before
him for them that feared the LORD, and
that thought upon his name. (17) And
they shall be mine, saith the LORD of
hosts, in that day when I make up my
[2] jewels; and I will spare them, as a
man spareth his own son that serveth
him. (18) Then shall ye return, and dis-
cern between the righteous and the
wicked, between him that serveth God
and him that serveth him not.

CHAPTER IV.—(1) For, behold, the
day cometh, that shall burn as an oven;
and all the proud, yea, and all that do
wickedly, shall be stubble: and the day
that cometh shall burn them up, saith
the LORD of hosts, that it shall leave
them neither root nor branch. (2) But
unto you that fear my name shall the
[b] Sun of righteousness arise with healing
in his wings; and ye shall go forth, and
grow up as calves of the stall. (3) And
ye shall tread down the wicked; for
they shall be ashes under the soles of
your feet in the day that I shall do *this*,
saith the LORD of hosts.
(4) Remember ye the [c] law of Moses my
servant, which I commanded unto him
in Horeb for all Israel, *with* the statutes
and judgments.

1 Heb., *are built.*

a Ps. 95. 9.

2 Or, *special treasure.*

b Luke 1. 78.

c Ex. 20. 3.

---

character from such faithful servants of Jehovah as were at times sorely tempted against their will to waver in their faith. We may observe here the seeds of sceptical Sadduceism, as in verse 14 of hypocritical Phariseism. (Comp. Pss. xxxvii., lxxiii., and the Books of Job and Eccl.)

Proud . . . they that work wickedness—*i.e.*, the heathen, who do not profess to serve Jehovah. (Comp. Isa. xiii. 11.)

Proud is a common Biblical expression for *presumptuous sinners;* the same word is also used for *presumptuous sins* (Ps. xix. 13).

Tempt.—The same word is used which in verse 10 is translated "prove." The difference in the two cases consists in the different nature of the actions. In verse 10 the Jews are exhorted to obey the Law faithfully, and prove whether God would not (*i.e.*, experience that God certainly would) perform His part in the covenant. In verse 15 the heathen, by their pride and wickedness, tempt God to judgment.

(16) **Then.**—As a consequence of the unbelieving conversation of the wicked. What "they that feared the Lord" said is not recorded; but it is implied, by His approval of them, that they strengthened one another in their faith and reliance on the goodness and faithfulness of the Lord, in spite of the present appearance of things. As the godless in Israel conversed together, so did the godly; but the converse of the one was the very reverse of the converse of the other. In Ezra ix. 4 we read of such a consultation among those "that trembled at the word of the God of Israel." (Comp. the expression in chap. ii. 5.)

Book of remembrance.—In which men's actions are said figuratively to be recorded (Ps. lvi. 8; Dan. vii. 10, &c.). Compare the custom of the Persian kings (Esther vi. 1).

For them—*i.e., for their future reward.*

Thought upon—*i.e., valued, esteemed.*

(17) **And they shall be . . . my jewels.**—Better, *And they shall be to me, saith the Lord of hosts, a special possession, on the day that I am about to make.* "Special possession" (Exod. xix. 5).

Day . . . make.—The same expression occurs in chap. iv. 3. (Comp. Ps. cxviii. 24.)

(18) **Then shall ye . . . between.**—Better, *Then shall ye again perceive the difference between.* For the construction, comp. Zech. iv. 1. As in former cases God had made this difference manifest, so He would again. Compare, for instance, the difference between the case of the Egyptians and of the Israelites in the matter of the miraculous darkness (Exod. x. 23).

IV.

(1) The day already foretold in chap. iii. 2 shall be as a fire burning fiercely as a furnace, and "the wicked"—not only the heathen, but the murmurers themselves, so far from being accounted happy (chap. iii. 15)—shall be as "stubble." (Comp. Isa. v. 24; Zeph. i. 18; Obad. 18, &c.)

(2) As the rising sun diffuses light and heat, so that all that is healthy in nature revives and lifts up its head, while plants that have no depth of root are scorched up and wither away, so the advent of the reign of righteousness, which will reward the good and the wicked, each according to his deserts, will dissipate all darkness of doubt, and heal all the wounds which the apparent injustice of the conduct of affairs has inflicted on the hearts of the righteous.

Wings.—Figurative for *rays.* The fathers and early commentators have understood Christ by the Sun of Righteousness, and they are so far right that it is the period of His advent that is referred to; but there can be no *personal* reference to Him in the expression, since "sun" is feminine in Hebrew; and the literal rendering of the word translated "in his wings" is "in *her* wings."

Grow up.—Better, *prance*, or *sport.*

(3) **Tread down.**—Comp. Isa. xxvi. 5, 6.

That I shall do this.—Better, *which I am about to make.* (Comp. chap. iii. 17.)

CONCLUDING ADMONITION.

(4–6) As the prophetical books began (Josh. i. 2, 8) with "*Moses my servant* is dead . . . this book of the *Law* shall not be removed from thy mouth, &c.," so they close with the admonition, "Remember ye the *Law of Moses my servant.*" (Comp. Deut. iv. 1, viii. 14.) The path of duty is the path of safety and of light. (Comp. John vii. 17.) "Mysteries belong to the Lord our God, but those things which are revealed are for us and for our children *for ever*, in order to

(5) Behold, I will send you [a] Elijah
the prophet before the coming of
the great and dreadful day of the
LORD: (6) and he shall turn the heart
of the fathers to the children, and the heart of the children to their fathers, lest I come and smite the earth with a curse.

a Matt. 11. 14; Mark 9. 11; Luke 1. 17.

---

perform all the words of this Law" (Deut. xxix. 29; comp. also Eccles. xii. 13). The best preparation for the reception of the New Covenant, when God would "put His law in their inward parts, and write it on their heart" (Jer. xxxi. 32), must needs be the hearty observance of the spirit of the Old.

(5) **Elijah.**—There is no more reason to suppose that this refers actually to "Elijah" the prophet, and that he is to appear upon earth, than to imagine from Hos. iii. 5; Ezek. xxiv. 23, xxxvii. 24; Jer. xxx. 9; that David himself is to come again in the flesh. When John the Baptist answered the question of the deputies of the Sanhedrim, "Art thou Elias?" by "I am not," he simply gave a negative reply to their question, which was formulated on their misapprehension. On the other hand, that John the Baptist is the "messenger" of chap. iii. 1 and the "Elijah" of this verse is shown conclusively (as far as Christians are concerned) by Luke i. 16, 17 before his birth, by Matt. iii. 1—12, Mark i. 2—8, Luke iii. 2—18, at the commencement of his ministry. Moreover, our Lord Himself assured the people that John was this "messenger" and "Elijah" (Matt. xi. 10, *seq.*; Luke vii. 27, *seq.*), and His disciples that he had appeared, and not been recognised (Matt. xvii. 11, *seq.*; Mark ix. 1, *seq.*). Finally, it is a significant fact that these two greatest of Old Testament prophets, Moses and Elias, who are mentioned together in this last prophetic exhortation, are the two who appeared with Christ on the Mount of Transfiguration, when all that which is contained in the Law and the prophets was about to be fulfilled.

(6) **And he shall turn . . . to their fathers.**—This does not refer to the settlement of family disputes, such as might have arisen from marriage with foreign wives. "The fathers are rather the ancestors of the Israelitish nation, the patriarchs, and generally the pious forefathers . . . The sons, or children, are the degenerate descendants of Malachi's own time and the succeeding ages."—*Keil.* "The hearts of the godly fathers and ungodly sons are estranged from one another. The bond of union—viz., the common love of God—is wanting. The fathers are ashamed of their children, and the children of their fathers."—*Hengstenberg.* (Comp. particularly Isa. xxix. 22—24, and the paraphrastic citation of Mal. iv. 6 in Luke i. 17.)

Curse.—Better, *ban.* (Comp. Zech. xiv. 11.) As with the conclusion of Isaiah, Lamentations, and Ecclesiastes, so here the Jew read in the synagogue the last verse but one over again after the last verse, to avoid concluding with words of ill omen, thus: "Behold I send you Elijah the prophet before the coming of the great and dreadful day of JEHOVAH."